APPROACHING DEMOCRACY

APPROACHING DEMOCRACY

FIFTH EDITION

Larry Berman
University of California, Davis

Bruce Allen Murphy
Lafayette College

PEARSON

Prentice Hall

UPPER SADDLE RIVER, NEW JERSEY 07458

Library of Congress Cataloging-in-Publication Data

Berman, Larry.
   Approaching democracy/Larry Berman, Bruce Allen Murphy.—5th ed.
     p. cm.
Includes bibliographical references and index.
   ISBN 0-13-174401-1
    1. United States—Politics and government. 2. Democracy—United States.
I. Murphy, Bruce Allen. II. Title.
   JK274.B524 2006
   320.473—dc22   2006008908

Editorial Director: Charlyce Jones Owen
Executive Editor: Dickson Musslewhite
Editorial Assistant: Jennifer Murphy
Director of Marketing: Brandy Dawson
Senior Marketing Manager: Emily Cleary
Director of Manufacturing and Production: Barbara Kittle
Senior Managing Editor: Lisa Iarkowski
Developmental Editor: Elaine Silverstein
Production Liaison: Joe Scordato
Project Manager: Karen Ettinger, Techbooks, Inc.
Copy Editor: Karen Keady
Prepress and Manufacturing Manager: Nick Sklitsis
Prepress and Manufacturing Buyer: Ben Smith
Creative Design Director: Leslie Osher
Art Director: Amy Rosen
Interior Design: Techbooks, T-9, Running River Design
Cover Design: Running River Design
Director, Image Resource Center: Melinda Reo
Manager, Rights and Permissions: Zina Arabia
Manager, Visual Research: Beth Brenzel
Manager, Cover Visual Research & Permissions: Karen Sanatar
Image Permission Coordinator: Annette Linder
Photo Researcher: Teri Stratford
Cover Image: Jeff Greenberg/Omni Photos Communications, Inc.

This book was set in 10/12 New Baskerville by Techbooks
and was printed and bound by Cadmus Communications.
The cover was printed by Phoenix Color Corp.

Credits and acknowledgments borrowed from other sources and reproduced, with permission, in this
textbook appear on appropriate page within text, or on pages 627–644.

Pearson Education LTD.   Pearson Education, Canada, Ltd.
Pearson Education Australia PTY, Limited   Pearson Educación de Mexico, S.A. de C.V.
Pearson Education Singapore, Pte. Ltd   Pearson Education—Japan
Pearson Education North Asia Ltd   Pearson Education Malaysia, Pte. Ltd

10 9 8 7 6 5 4 3 2 1
ISBN 0-13-174401-1

TO NICOLE AND CAROL

CONTENTS

ix

PART II / Institutions of American Democracy

4 CONGRESS   126

5 THE PRESIDENCY   174

6 THE JUDICIARY   206

7 THE BUREAUCRACY   248

PART III / Processes of American Democracy

8 PUBLIC OPINION   280

9 POLITICAL PARTIES   310

10 PARTICIPATION, VOTING, AND ELECTIONS   350

11 INTEREST GROUPS   382

12 THE MEDIA   420

PART IV / Liberties and Rights in American Democracy

PART V / Policy Making in American Democracy

BOXED FEATURES

Approaching Democracy Around the Globe

U.S.A. Yesterday and Today

PREFACE

Welcome to the fifth edition of *Approaching Democracy*, our ever-evolving exploration of the American experiment in self-governing. A great deal has happened in American politics since we published the first edition a decade ago. We have tried to remain as up-to-date as possible with respect to current events around the globe while retaining our original theme. Although an introductory course in American government is not solely a course on current events, students are always interested in what is going on around them. Throughout the text, we use examples that are at the forefront of the news so that students have background information to draw from and hopefully some of you will be empowered to become more engaged in political discussion and civic life.

Our title and framework came from Vaclav Havel, a former dissident Czechoslovakian playwright once imprisoned by his country's communist government and later elected its president. Addressing a joint session of the U.S. Congress on February 21, 1990, Havel noted that with the collapse of the Soviet Union, millions of people from Eastern Europe were involved in a historically irreversible process, beginning their quest for freedom and democracy. And it was the United States of America that provided the model, the map to democracy and independence, for these newly freed peoples. But Havel put his own spin on the notion of American democracy: "As long as people are people, democracy, in the full sense of the word, will always be no more than an ideal. In this sense, you, too, are merely approaching democracy. But you have one great advantage: You have been approaching democracy uninterruptedly for more than two hundred years, and your journey toward the horizon has never been disrupted by a totalitarian system."[1]

In spite of its astonishing diversity and the consequent potential for hostility and violence, the United States has spent over two centuries moving towards, and sometimes away from, the democratic ideal. The process of approaching democracy is a continual one, and the debate about how to achieve democratic aspirations drives politics in America as well as in far away countries like Iraq. No matter how controversial the lead-up to war in Iraq, the stirring image of Iraqi citizens voting for the very first time and jubilantly waving their blue stained fingers illustrates that approaching the aspirations of democracy remains a universal goal. Still, those very Iraqi elections were only the first step in constructing a stable civil society and providing for a constitution that will allow political institutions to evolve with legitimacy and a chance for sustaining civil society.

American representative democracy remains very much a work in progress, but our approach to democracy serves as a template for people everywhere. The chapters in this textbook sort out the ideals, study the institutions, processes and policies, and analyze the challenges and paradoxes of our system. For example, since the terrible attacks of September 11, 2001, political discussion has raged over how to protect this country and still remain true to the ideals of the democracy as expressed by the Declaration of Independence, The Constitution, and the Bill of Rights. The enormous challenges facing our country in the war on terrorism have

---

[1]Congressional Record-House, February 21, 1990, p. H392–95.

involved two controversial programs, the Patriot Act and the government's domestic surveillance program. Both involve protecting the American people, but both raise fundamental challenges for balancing security and liberty. Our goal is not to end discussion on these topics; rather, we hope students will develop an interest in continuing the dialogue on America's approach to the democratic ideal.

In many respects, the first edition of this book published in 1986 was written with an eye toward measuring whether the emerging democracies from the breakup of the Soviet Union would remain democratic. Four editions and a decade later we are interested in the nature of America's own democracy, as the government continues its policies for fighting a war on terrorism, reshapes a Supreme Court, considers major campaign finance and lobbying reforms and public opinion debates the presence of American troops in Iraq. We believe that our theme "approaching democracy" provides you with a conceptual lens for evaluating the performance of the American political system and for discussing whether this nation will remain a model for emulation. We think it will, but we also believe that the subject needs continuous dialogue, as illustrated by the debate on immigration reform.

ORGANIZATION

Part I presents the foundations of American government. Our theme is introduced in Chapter 1, in which we identify goals and elements useful in evaluating America's approach to democracy. We introduce a few widely accepted "elements of democracy" that serve as markers to identify progress toward the democratic ideals we identified earlier.

Part II explores the institutions of American democracy. It describes the various governmental arenas—the judiciary, Congress, executive branch, and bureaucracy—where the struggle over democratic ideals plays out.

Part III focuses on the processes of American government and democracy. Through the avenues of public opinion, political parties, elections, interest groups, and the media, citizens can reach and direct their government to achieve their desired goals.

Part IV provides a detailed analysis of various issues of civil rights and liberties. They include the most fundamental rights of Americans, such as freedom of speech and religion, and are considered by many to be the foundation of our democracy.

Part V addresses the policy-making process and its consequences. How well national policy makers respond to the challenges of policy making—and how democratic the policies are—remain crucial questions as American government continues the process of approaching democracy.

CHANGES IN THE FIFTH EDITION

As we noted earlier, this fifth edition contains much new material. Here are a few examples of new and updated material: You will find updates on the USA Patriot Act battle; discussion on the Harriet Miers and Samuel Alito Supreme Court nominations; an analysis of the Roberts Court of the new role of Justice Anthony Kennedy as the new swing justice on the Court; the new cyber-lobbying technique for judicial confirmations; the Jack Abramoff–Tom Delay lobbying scandal; analysis of the battle over the Senate's "nuclear option" seeking elimination of filibusters in judicial nominations; federalism battles over California's allowance of the medical use of marijuana and Oregon's "Death With Dignity" law; the battles over gay marriage and civil union laws; campaign finance and lobbying reform; legal battles over religion (creationism, Ten Commandments, monuments, and "intelligent design") in public schools and public life; the effect of the evangelical religious movement on American politics; the "Red State-Blue State" partisan electoral environment; and the continuing battles over affirmative action programs. There is also new and updated material on the Department of Homeland Security and the war on terrorism; the role of bloggers in rewriting the rules of journalism; a five-year assessment of the Bush presidency; an assessment of the Rehnquist Court; a discussion of Operation Enduring Freedom and Operation Iraqi Freedom; an analysis of the Iraqi elections and constitution-drafting process; an analysis of the federal response to Hurricane Katrina; and the most recent 2006 Freedom House maps and opinion surveys.

THE TEACHING AND LEARNING CLASSROOM EDITION

Approaching Democracy, fifth edition, includes a new visual and pedagogical approach to engage students as they journey through their learning experience about American politics. This new edition is designed to stimulate thinking, discussion, analysis, and critical evaluation as well as provide support for learning. The new pedagogical organization of the text is featured in the new *Student Tool Kit* on pages xxix–xxxiv. Throughout the text and in the resources that support it we strive to help prepare students to be motivated, engaged participants in the processes and politics that define our government.

In addition, extensive teaching and learning resources accompany the text to support instructors in the classroom and students as they learn. Review and self-testing resources, unique applications that reinforce the connections of the text's content to everyday life events and issues, and extensive assignment, presentation, and assessment tools will make both the instructor's and student's experiences with *Approaching Democracy* a true and effective journey of discovery and learning.

Resources for Instructors

Instructor's Resource Manual with Test Item File The *Instructor's Resource Manual* contains a summary, review of concepts, lecture suggestions and topic outlines, and additional resource materials—including a guide to media resources—for each chapter in the book. An electronic version is also included on the *Faculty Resource CD-ROM*. Thoroughly reviewed and revised to ensure the highest level of quality and accuracy, the test item file offers more than 1,800 multiple-choice, true/false, and essay questions with page references to the text. ISBN: 0-13-174945-5

Faculty Resource CD-ROM This instructor resource allows flexibility in preparing lectures and assignments. It includes a database of resources including the instructor's manual, test item file, PowerPoint™ presentations, maps, charts and graphs both supplemental to and from the text, and primary source documents, all organized by chapter. ISBN: 0-13-179166-4

Prentice Hall Test Generator A computerized version of the test item file, this program allows full editing of questions and the addition of instructor-generated test items. Other special features include random generation, scrambling question order, and test preview before printing. Available in Windows and Macintosh formats. ISBN: 0-13-229234-3

Transparencies This set of full-color transparency acetates reproduces maps, charts, and figures from the text as well as from additional sources to enhance classroom presentation. ISBN: 0-13-179167-2

ABC News™/Prentice Hall Video Library: American Government—Instructor's Library

Prentice Hall and ABC News™ have assembled a 4-DVD set of more than seven hours of quality ABC News™ programming for classroom use. Through award-winning ABC News™ programs such as *Nightline* and *Primetime*, ABC News™ offers a resource for feature- and documentary-style videos related to the topics in the text. The video set also includes a booklet that provides a brief summary of each video and discussion questions to help students critically evaluate how these real-life events and issues connect to the topics discussed in the American government course. For more information, contact your local Prentice Hall representative. ISBN: 0-13-198665-1

Prentice Hall Custom Video: How a Bill Becomes a Law   This 25-minute video chronicles an environmental law in Massachusetts—from its start as one citizen's concern to its passage in Washington, D.C. Students see the step-by-step process of how a bill becomes a law through narrative and graphics. For more information, contact your local Prentice Hall representative. ISBN: 0-13-032676-3

Films for the Humanities and Social Sciences   With a qualifying order of textbooks from Prentice Hall, you may select from a high-quality library of political science videos from Films for the Humanities and Social Sciences. Contact your local Prentice Hall sales representative for a complete listing and qualifying information.

Choices: An American Government Custom Reader   Exercise real freedom of expression by creating an American government reader that truly reflects your teaching style, your course goals, your perspective! *Choices: An American Government Custom Reader* delivers quality scholarship, pedagogy, and exceptional source materials. You choose the readings and the sequence. You can even add your own work or other favorite materials to create a reader that fits your course precisely. The price of your reader is determined by its length. Your students pay for what they need—no more. More than 250 articles, documents, book excerpts, and speeches—representing classic pieces as well as current articles and covering more than 20 topical areas—are available. Visit the *Choices* Web site at www.choicesreader.com and learn about updates.

Resources for Students

Practice Tests   This comprehensive study aid provides a chapter outline, study notes, a glossary, and practice exams designed to reinforce information in the text and help students develop a greater understanding of American government and politics. ISBN: 0-13-223047-X

The Companion Website™ with Gradetracker   www.prenhall.com/berman Students can now take full advantage of the World Wide Web to enrich their study of American government through the *Approaching Democracy Companion Website™*. The site features interactive practice tests, chapter objectives, and overviews. In addition, it provides access to *The New York Times* online for articles relevant to the study of politics and other Web destinations that provide additional insight into connections between politics and world events. Instructors now have the option of setting up a course to manage student progress through the site's new gradebook feature. Or, they can simply make the site available for students' independent use. *Student Access Code:* ISBN: 0-13-243961-1

Now with MakeItReal!   The new *Companion Website™* helps reinforce the connection of politics to real life with the integration of *MakeItReal,* a unique collection of activities, simulations, and primary sources. **Activities** engage students to think about the relevancy of important issues—voting, social policy, rights and liberties, national security, etc.—to their own lives as well as to the nation as a whole. Moreover, most of these activities suggest a variety of forms of civic participation. Real-life **simulations** invite students to use real data—electoral results and maps,

Census 2000 data—to analyze key topics and issues. The simulations were developed to help students make informed decisions and experience politics as an insider would. **Primary sources** introduce students to key documents and information discussed in the text. The site includes **ABC News™ videos** that highlight issues relevant to politics. These resources correlate to content in the margins throughout the text. For information on student and instructor access to this new enhanced *Companion Website*™ *with Gradetracker,* contact your local Prentice Hall representative.

ABC News™/Prentice Hall Video Library: American Government—Student Library

Bound into every new copy of the text is a 2-DVD set containing more than three hours of award-winning ABC News™ programs. This unique resource offers feature- and documentary-style videos on news events and issues that relate to the topics covered in the text. Included at the end of the text is a guide that provides a brief summary of each video as well as discussion questions to help students critically evaluate these events and issues as they relate to politics. The videos correlate to key topics in the margins throughout the text.

Onesearch: Evaluating Online Sources with Research Navigator™ This brief guide focuses on developing the critical thinking skills necessary to evaluate and effectively use online sources. It also provides an access code and instruction on using *Research Navigator*™, a powerful research tool that provides access to exclusive databases of reliable source material. Each guide includes an access code for the Research Navigator Web site. Contact your local Prentice Hall sales representative for more details.

Research Navigator™ This exciting new Internet resource helps students make the most of their research time. From finding the right articles and journals to citing sources, drafting and writing effective papers, and completing research assignments, *Research Navigator*™ simplifies and streamlines the entire process. Contact your local Prentice Hall sales representative for more details or take a tour on the Web at www.researchnavigator.com.

ACKNOWLEDGMENTS

The fifth edition of Approaching Democracy is a new T*eaching and Learning Classroom Edition.* The idea and force behind the TLC edition came from Vice President and Editorial Director Charlyce Jones Owen. It is impossible to adequately express what her involvement has meant to each of us. Charlyce was there at the very beginning, over a decade ago, committed to the theme of Approaching Democracy and she has to this day remained steadfast in endorsing the theme as a teaching tool. There have been times during brainstorming sessions when we wanted to add Charlyce's name as contributing author. We value her professionalism, collegiality, and friendship. No authors can ever ask for more than Charlyce has given us.

We've been with Prentice Hall long enough to know that their team is made up of many talented and committed people. It is a pleasure to acknowledge them here: Rob DeGeorge, for his work on the supplements; Emily Cleary, for devising the marketing plan; Jennifer Murphy, Editorial Assistant, for maintaining the flow in both communication and packages; and Joe Scordato, Production Liaison, for watching over all the details.

Our thanks also go to the book's talented production team. We are especially grateful to Karen Ettinger, our project manager, for her professionalism and grace under pressure in supervising the entire effort, to Karen Keady for her skilled copyediting, to the Techbooks production staff for creating the fine page layout and rendering art, and to Candice Carta-Myers and Amy Rosen for creating the new design for the book. Our appreciation also goes to our photo researcher, Teri Stratford, for helping us to visually tell the story of "approaching democracy." Without the diligent efforts of all of these people, revising this book would not have been possible. We are also very grateful to James Corey, who added the annotations to the Constitution and to Professor Robert C. Ayer PhD, United States Coast Guard for providing a detailed reading of the fourth edition and for his contributions in the fifth edition.

We also wish to thank the many reviewers of the five editions of *Approaching Democracy* for their valuable suggestions.

William Bianco, Pennsylvania State University
Robert Bradley, Illinois State University
Rebecca Britton, California State University, Chico
Mark A. Cichock, University of Texas at Arlington
Thomas P. Dolan, Columbus State University
Stacy B. Gordon, University of Nevada, Reno
Randy Hagerty, Truman State University
Henneth G. Hartman, Longview Community College
Rebekah Herrick, Oklahoma State University
Richard Himelfarb, Hofstra University
Robert Jacobs, Central Washington University
E. Terrence Jones, University of Missouri, St. Louis
Joseph Jozwiak, Texas A&M–Corpus Christi
Diana Owen, Georgetown University
Kelly D. Patterson, Brigham Young University
Daniel C. Reed, University of Georgia
Dan Shea, Allegheny College
Robert L. Silvey, John Jay College/CUNY
Carolyn Taylor, Rogers State University
Shirley Anne Warshaw, Gettysburg College
John R. Wood, Rose State College

Larry Berman would like to thank his students at UC Davis for their many ideas for revising the book. He is also most appreciative of his former graduate students who are teaching American Government using the book and always providing feedback. He especially thanks Professors Linda Valenty, Monte Freidig, Drew Froelinger, and Stephen Routh in this regard. Berman also thanks Mary Byrne at the UC Washington Center for helping him organize the first set of revisions and for keeping track of the flow of UPS packages and copying of chapters. He is especially indebted to Karen Akerson for the new author's photo that appears in this edition.

Bruce Allen Murphy wishes once again to thank the undergraduate students in his Government 101 course at Lafayette College for their many suggestions for revising the textbook, as well as for providing the opportunity to test out his theories of American politics in front of them. Thanks go also to the incomparable Kirby Library research librarian, Mercedes Sharpless, and the wonderful interlibrary loan and reference staff at Skillman Library, all of who deserve heartfelt thanks for providing countless answers to desperate and seemingly impenetrable late night questions. Once more, my colleague John Kincaid was good enough to offer another extremely thorough and comprehensive critique of the Federalism chapter. My daughter Emily Patricia Wright Murphy was extremely helpful in assisting in the research for some of the images used in this volume. And Lafayette students John Stephenson, Josie Dykstra, and Melissa Mazer were very helpful in performing many research assistance tasks. Sincere thanks go to Fred Morgan Kirby and his family for their generous support of the chair that he now holds. Finally, thanks go to his colleagues at Lafayette College, most especially Government and Law Department Head John McCartney, for continuing to make this work environment so pleasurable and productive.

Since no two scholars can master all of the fields in the political science discipline, we express gratitude to all of our colleagues for the many academic contributions upon which we drew for the writing of this book. We would both like to express appreciation for the generations of students at the University of California and Lafayette College for the continuing flow of unique questions and ideas that spurred us in the writing of this and other editions of the book. We would also like to thank those colleagues in the discipline who have provided us with suggestions for improving the volume after teaching with the first four editions, thus improving this new revision.

Finally, but most importantly, we would both like to recognize our families. Bruce Allen Murphy thanks his wife Carol Lynn Wright, and his children, Emily and Geoffrey, for their never-ending love, support, and encouragement throughout each of this book's revision processes. Larry Berman joins Murphy in the affections to family, adding only what he expressed in previous editions: Scott and Lindsay are reminders that our theme "approaching democracy" has meaning; Nicole is living proof that life only gets better.

Larry Berman
Bruce Allen Murphy

ABOUT THE AUTHORS

Photo by Karen Akerson

Larry Berman is Professor at the University of California, Davis. His research and publications focus on the presidency, foreign policy and Vietnam. He has written three books on the war, most recently *No Peace, No Honor: Nixon, Kissinger and Betrayal in Vietnam.* There is also a Vietnamese language edition, *Khong Hoa Binh, Chang Danh Du: Nixon, Kissinger, Va Su Phan Boi O Viet Nam.* His work has been featured on C-Span's *Book TV,* the History Channel's *Secrets of War,* Bill Moyers PBS series, "The Public Mind;" David McCullough's American Experience series, and "Vietnam: A Television History."

Larry Berman has received fellowships from the Guggenheim Foundation, the American Council of Learned Societies, the National Science Foundation, and research grants from several presidential libraries. He has received the Outstanding Mentor of Women in Political Science Award from the Women's Caucus for Political Science. He is a co-recipient of the Richard E. Neustadt Award, given annually for the best book published during the year in the field of the American Presidency. He received the Bernath Lecture Prize, given annually by the Society for Historians of American Foreign Relations to a scholar whose work has most contributed to our understanding of foreign relations. Berman has been a Fellow at the Woodrow Wilson International Center for Scholars in Washington, D.C. and scholar in residence at the Rockefeller Foundation's Center in Bellagio, Italy.

His class on the American presidency is cited in Lisa Birnbach's *New and Improved College Guide* as one of the most recommended classes for undergraduates at UC Davis. From September 1999–September 2005, Berman served as the founding director of the University of California Washington Center, an experiential learning program offering internships, research opportunities and academic instruction to UC students. He received his B.A. magna cum laude from The American University in Washington, D.C., and his Ph.D. from Princeton University in 1977.

In his spare time Larry enjoys fishing the lakes in the Sierras, camping, wilderness hiking and dreaming about the day when the Sacramento Kings finally win it all.

Photo by Craig M. Lampa

Bruce Allen Murphy is the Fred Morgan Kirby Professor of Civil Rights in the Department of Government and Law at Lafayette College. He is a nationally recognized judicial biographer and scholar on the American Supreme Court, civil rights and liberties, judicial behavior, and judicial biography.

Murphy is the author of many publications, including his newest judicial biography *Wild Bill: The Legend and Life of William O. Douglas, America's Most Controversial Supreme Court Justice*, which has been selected by the Book-of-the-Month and History book clubs. He also wrote *Fortas: The Rise and Ruin of a Supreme Court Justice*, which was nominated for both the Pulitzer Prize and the National Book Award. His bestselling *The Brandeis-Frankfurter Connection: The Secret Political Activities of Two Supreme Court Justices*, which received the American Bar Association's Certificate of Merit, was listed among *The New York Times'* Best Books for 1983 and was serialized by *The Washington Post*. In addition, he edited *Portraits of American Politics: A Reader*.

Murphy has received numerous teaching awards for his courses in American politics, civil rights and liberties, and Constitutional law. He has been a finalist in the Council for the Advancement and Support of Education's national Professor of the Year competition and was cited as a Best Professor in Lisa Birnbach's *New and Improved College Guide*. He is listed in both *Who's Who in America* and *Who's Who in the World*.

SUPPLEMENTAL TEXTS AND READINGS FOR AMERICAN GOVERNMENT

E ach of the following books features specialized topical coverage that will allow you to tailor your American government course to suit the focus and needs of your particular course. Featuring contemporary issues or timely readings, any of the following books is available at a special discount when bundled with *Approaching Democracy*. Please visit our online catalog at www.prenhall.com and contact your local Prentice Hall representative for additional details.

Government's Greatest Achievements: From Civil Rights to Homeland Security
Paul C. Light
ISBN: 0-13-110192-7

21 Debated: Issues in American Politics, 2nd ed.
Gregory Scott/Loren Gatch
ISBN: 0-13-184178-5

Issues in American Political Life: Money, Violence, and Biology, 5th ed.
Robert Thobaben/Donna Schlagheck/Charles Funderburk
ISBN: 0-13-193062-1

Strategies for Active Citizenship
Kateri M. Drexler/Gwen Garcelon
ISBN: 0-13-117295-6

The Political Science Student Writer's Manual, 4th ed.
Gregory M. Scott/Stephen M. Garrison
ISBN: 0-13-040447-0

REAL POLITICS IN AMERICA SERIES

This series is another resource for contemporary instructional material. To bridge the gap between research and relevancy, we have launched a new series of supplemental books with the help of series editor Paul Herrnson of the University of Maryland. More descriptive than quantitative, more case study than data study, these books cut across all topics to bring students relevant details in current political science research. From exploring the growing phenomenon of direct democracy to who runs for the state legislature, these books show students that real political science is meaningful and exciting. Available at a discount when bundled with *Approaching Democracy*. Contact your local Prentice Hall representative or access www.prenhall.com for a complete listing of titles in the series.

NEW!

From Inspiration to Legislation: How a Bill Becomes a Law
Amy E. Black
ISBN: 0-13-110754-2

Presidential Campaign Quality: Incentives and Reform
Bruce Buchanan
ISBN: 0-13-184140-8

Clicker Politics: Essays on the California Recall
Shaun Bowler/Bruce E. Cain
ISBN: 0-13-193336-1

Congress and the Politics of Foreign Policy
Colton C. Campbell/Nicol C. Rae/John F. Stack, Jr.
ISBN: 0-13-042154-5

War Stories from Capitol Hill
Colton C. Campbell/Paul S. Herrnson
ISBN: 0-13-028088-7

Transforming the American Polity: The Presidency of George W. Bush and the War on Terrorism
Richard Conley
ISBN: 0-13-189342-4

Women's PACs: Abortion and Elections
Christine L. Day/Charles D. Hadley
ISBN: 0-13-117448-7

Reforming the Republic: Democratic Institutions for the New America
Todd Donovan/Shaun Bowler
ISBN: 0-13-099455-3

No Holds Barred: Negativity in U.S. Senate Campaigns
Patrick J. Kenney/Kim Fridkin Kahn
ISBN: 0-13-097760-8

NEW!

Smoking and Politics: Bureaucracy Centered Policymaking, 6th ed.
A. Lee Fritschler/Catherine E. Rudder
ISBN: 0-13-179104-4

Stealing the Initiative: How State Government Responds to Direct Democracy
Elisabeth R. Gerber/Arthur Lupia/Mathew D. McCubbins/D. Rodderick Kiewiet
ISBN: 0-13-028407-6

The Medium and the Message: Television Advertising and American Elections
Kenneth M. Goldstein/Patricia Strach
ISBN: 0-13-177774-2

Cities and Privatization: Prospects for the New Century
Jeffrey D. Greene
ISBN: 0-13-029442-X

Playing Hardball: Campaigning for the U.S. Congress
Paul S. Herrnson
ISBN: 0-13-027133-0

NEW!

Electing Congress: New Rules for an Old Game
David Magleby/J. Quin Monson/Kelly Patterson
ISBN: 0-13-243867-4

Congress and the Internet
James A. Thurber/Colton C. Campbell
ISBN: 0-13-099617-3

$\mathcal{S}$tudent Tool Kit

Approaching Democracy is organized around a compelling theme and text and special features that will help facilitate reading and learning.

STUDY AIDS
Chapter Outlines

Each chapter opens with a **Chapter Outline** that serves as a study map to the chapter. Expanded pedagogical support helps students orient themselves to the chapter content.

★ **CHAPTER 5** ★

THE PRESIDENCY

CHAPTER OUTLINE

APPROACHING DEMOCRACY
The Presidency of George W. Bush

INTRODUCTION: The Presidency and Democracy
The Constitutional Design
Functional Roles of the President
Two Views of Executive Power
Expanding Presidential Power: Moving Beyond the Constitution
The Institutionalized Presidency

175

Table 5.3 ▪ The Presidential Job Description

Types of Activity	The Three Subpresidencies		
	Foreign Policy and National Security	Macroeconomics	Domestic Policy and Programs
Crisis management	Wartime leadership; missile crisis, 1962; Gulf War, 1991	Coping with recessions, 1982, 1992	Confronting coal strikes of 1978; LA riots, 1992; LA earthquake, 1992
Symbolic and morale-building leadership	Presidential state visit to Middle East or to China	Boosting confidence in the dollar	Visiting disaster victims and building morale among government workers
Priority setting and program design	Balancing pro-Israel policies with need for Arab oil	Choosing means of dealing with inflation, unemployment	Designing a new welfare program health insurance
Recruitment leadership (advisers, administrators, judges, ambassadors, etc.)	Selection of secretary of defense, UN ambassador	Selection of secretary of treasury, Federal Reserve Board governors	Nomination of federal judges
Legislative and political coalition building	Selling Panama or SALT treaties to Senate for approval	Lobbying for energy-legislation package	Winning public support for transportation deregulation
Program implementation and evaluation	Encouraging negotiations between Israel and Egypt	Implementing tax cuts or fuel rationing	Improving quality health care, welfare retraining programs
Oversight of government routines and establishment of an early-warning system for future problem areas	Overseeing U.S. bases abroad; ensuring that foreign-aid programs work effectively	Overseeing the IRS or the Small Business Administration	Overseeing National Science Foundation or Environmental Protection Agency

Source: From *The Paradoxes of the American Presidency* by Thomas E. Cronin and Michael A. Genovese. Copyright © 1998 by Oxford University Press, Inc. Used by permission of Oxford University Press, Inc.

roles of the presidency? Let us examine two reactions to this system: presidents who accept the restraints and live within them, and presidents who chafe at the restraints and invent ways to surpass or abolish them.

TWO VIEWS OF EXECUTIVE POWER

The Constitution is silent on how much actual power a president should possess. Article II begins with the ambiguous sentence, "The executive Power shall be vested in a President of the United States of America." What did the framers mean? Did "the executive Power" refer to a mere designation of office, or did it imply a broad and sweeping mandate to rule? Scholars and politicians alike have long debated the question without agreement. History has left it up to each president to determine the scope of executive powers, given a president's personality, philosophy, and the political circumstances of the time.

This executive power "wild card" has allowed many a president to outreach the Constitution's narrow prescriptions when conditions call for extraordinary action— or when the president thinks such action is necessary. Activist presidents find ways to justify sweeping policy innovations even if the Constitution has no specific language for those policies.

Franklin Roosevelt exemplified this approach in his March 4, 1933, inaugural address. With the Great Depression holding the country at the brink of economic

Questions for Reflection

How realistic are the expectations for the president to fulfill all these roles?

How would you amend the position to assure that democracy is best served?

Questions for Reflection

Questions addressing each chapter's main subtopics encourage careful consideration of important themes and developments in politics. The questions are included in the margins next to each subtopic to prompt students to think about what they should know after reading the section. These also serve as a resource for reviewing section content.

in establishing only a
...ral court system.
...f authority, of the fed-
...nd the lower federal
...nose arising under the
involving disputes be-
...assadors, the Supreme
...court to hear the case.
...tes as a party, admiralty
...re different states, and
...ppellate jurisdiction, or
...federal or state court.
...me Court's powers, the
...nd weakest of the three
... representative govern-
...no explicitly political or
...ent in *The Federalist*, no.
...the political rights of the
...either the sword or the
...E nor WILL, but merely

...the organization and ju-
...Congress established a
...or trial courts, appellate
...e fully the jurisdiction of
...ower to review state court

...had no cases to decide.
..."intolerable" lack of pres-
...ne—as governor of New
...803 with the decision in

original jurisdiction The authority
of a court to be the first to hear a case.

appellate jurisdiction The authority of a court to hear a case on appeal
after it has been argued in and decided
by a lower federal or state court.

Marbury v. Madison The 1803
case in which Chief Justice John Marshall
established the power of judicial review.

judicial review The power of the
Supreme Court established in *Marbury
v. Madison* to overturn acts of the president, Congress, and the states if those
acts violate the Constitution. This power
makes the Supreme Court the final interpreter of the Constitution.

 MakeItReal

Primary Source: *Federalist #78:
The Judiciary Department
Federalist #79: The Judiciary
Continued*

Primary Source: **The Federal Judiciary Act of 1789**

Primary Source: *Marbury v. Madison*

Marginal Key Terms/Glossary

Important terms are defined in the margin and listed at the end of each chapter with appropriate page numbers. All **key terms** in the text are defined in a glossary at the end of the book.

New! Quick Reviews

The **Quick Reviews,** placed at key locations in the margins of each chapter, provide brief summaries of concepts, events, or topics and serve as a mini-review resource.

Summary

The **summary** is organized according to the main chapter topics and serves as an overview of chapter content.

...dicial Power

...ing president John Adams
... of a lame duck Congress
...pointments in the Senate,
...s from his own party by is-
...fice. When the incoming
...sions, the appointment of
...f Columbia, Marbury sued
... *Madison* decision.
...federal officials to carry out
...mmission—a power given to
...Marshall (1801–35), himself
...n. After conceding that the
...yond the issue to review the
...ower to review the constitu-
...Marshall brilliantly used this
...ause courts interpret law, and
...n interpret the Constitution.
... the Supreme Court's power
...ates if those acts violate the
... to say what the Constitution
...rt and placed it on an equal

Quick Review

Marbury v. Madison

- Appointment of William Marbury as justice of the peace for the District of Columbia was denied by the incoming Jefferson administration.

- Marbury sued for his post, arguing that since courts interpret law, and the Constitution is a form of law, then the Supreme Court can interpret the Constitution.

- Chief Justice John Marshall established the power of judicial review, the power of the Supreme Court to overturn acts of the president.

- Landmark case helped to define the powers of the court.

and the 1973 *Roe v. Wade* abortion decision, it remains to be seen whether the Court, faced with today's cultural issues and wartime posture of the terrorism crisis, back off of issues that they would otherwise like to resolve now. Whatever happens, judiciary actions in America's democracy will continue to have powerful implications for both government and individual rights.

Summary

1. The federal courts decide all legal disputes arising under the Constitution, U.S. law, and treaties. In cases involving disputes between states or involving foreign ambassadors, the Supreme Court has original jurisdiction. For all other federal cases, it has appellate jurisdiction.

2. In the 1803 case of *Marbury v. Madison*, Chief Justice Marshall argued that the Supreme Court has the power to interpret the Constitution. This power, known as judicial review, enables the Court to overturn actions of the executive and legislative branches and to reinterpret the Constitution to fit new situations. The power of statutory construction enables the Court to interpret a federal or state law.

3. The power to appoint justices to the Supreme Court is shared by the president and Congress. The justices are appointed for life and can be impeached only for "High Crimes and Misdemeanors." The president can influence the Court by appointing justices who support a particular philosophy. Congress can change the number of justices or pass a law to reverse a Court decision.

4. Most cases enter the judicial system through a trial court consisting of a single judge and, at times, a jury. The proceedings of the trial court are reviewed by an appellate court consisting of a panel of judges but no jury. Criminal cases involve violations of state or federal criminal law; civil cases involve private disputes. Most criminal cases are resolved by plea bargains, in which ... state agrees to reduce the charges or sentence in re-

which hear cases from thirte...
ually in three-judge panels. Di...
constitutional courts, but the...
cludes legislative courts, cour...

6. Candidates for the Suprem...
senators, governors, the ca...
friends, and federal judges,...
the FBI and the American Ba...
nees to the Court are membe...
and share the president's po...

7. The confirmation process be...
Senate Judiciary Committee,...
dation prior to a vote by the...
dures can constitute major...
rejection of nearly one in five...

8. In nominations to district co...
torial courtesy gives senator...
power. Often, however, ca...
senators in the president's...
have attempted to make the...
resentative of the population...

9. The solicitor general decides...
peal from the lower courts,...
represents the United States...
Appellate cases come to the...
writs of certiorari. If at least...
case, it is placed on the d...
Court has decided fewer case...
of appeals reaching it has ine...

10. When the Court accepts a ...
submit briefs, or written le...
...ments befo...

Review Questions and Suggested Readings

New! **Review questions** help students reconsider and test their understanding of each chapter's main topics. A list of **suggested readings** highlights books that encourage further study and exploration.

hold a conference to discuss and vote on the case, and one of the justices voting with the majority is assigned to draft the opinion, or written version of the decision. The opinion must be approved by at least five justices. A justice who agrees with the majority decision but differs on the reasoning may write a concurring opinion. When a justice disagrees with the Court's ruling, he or she may write a dissenting opinion.

11. Interpretation of a law or a portion of the Constitution as closely as possible to the literal meaning of the words is known as *strict construction*. When the wording is vague, justices may attempt to determine the original

intent of the framers. Justices may consider the effect a ruling would have on public policy. Some justices believe in judicial restraint—deferring to the other branches of government whenever possible—others are judicial activists, believing that judges have a duty to further certain causes.

12. Decisions of the Supreme Court become the law of the land. However, compliance with a decision is influenced by the extent to which the president supports it. It may also be circumvented by Congress, which can pass a new law or propose a constitutional amendment restating its original intentions.

Review Questions

1. Why has the Supreme Court been the institution that has extended existing rights and even created new ones?

2. In what ways and when has the Supreme Court protected us against tyranny of the majority?

3. Why did the founding fathers view the judiciary as the "least dangerous" branch of government?

4. What factors limit the Supreme Court's actions? What factors enhance their independence?

5. What is the role of the law clerks on the "cert pool"? How have they affected the docket? How have they affected the independence of the court? Does this represent an approach to democracy? Why or why not?

6. What factors influence the court's docket in a given year? How have these factors changed over time?

7. Describe the political and legal roles of the "Tenth Justice" or Solicitor General. In what ways has this individual been influential?

Key Terms

original jurisdiction
appellate jurisdiction
Marbury v. Madison
judicial review
statutory construction
trial court
appellate court
criminal cases
plea bargains
civil cases
class action suit

constitutional courts
U.S. district courts
U.S. courts of appeals
en banc
legislative courts
senatorial courtesy
docket
writ of certiorari
rule of four
solicitor general
amicus curiae briefs

briefs
opinion
majority opinion
plurality opinion
concurring opinion
dissenting opinion
stare decisis
precedents
judicial restraint
judicial activism

Suggested Readings

ABRAHAM, HENRY J. *Justices, Presidents and Senators: A History of the U.S. Supreme Court Appointments from Washington to Clinton*. Lanham, Md.: Rowman and Littlefield, 1999. A complete history of presidential appointments to the Supreme Court and the decision making that resulted.

BLACKMUN, HARRY. *The Harry Blackmun Papers at the Library of Congress*, Manuscript Division, Library of Congress, Washington D.C.: www.loc.gov/rr/mss/blackmun/. The most Revealing Primary Source Examination of the Justice and the Recent Courts Available.

BREYER, STEPHEN. *Active Liberty, Interpreting, Out D...* Knopf, 2005. A Thoughtful and ...
Theory of ...

SPECIAL FEATURES

Approaching Democracy Case Study

Each chapter opens with a **Case Study** that integrates the text's theme and lays the groundwork for the material that follows. Special care has been taken to select case studies that serve as anchors for the material covered in each chapter. Topics such as the life and politics of Cesar Chavez, the creation of a Department of Homeland Security, President George W. Bush's leadership in building an international coalition aimed at defeating terrorist networks, and renewal of the USA Patriot Act help students examine political events within the context of approaching democracy and in connection with real events and issues.

New! U.S.A. Yesterday and Today

This special feature examines the theme of approaching democracy from a historical perspective. Here students study points in the development of the American political system in which a choice had to be made. Internet news and the mainstream media, the bureaucratic errors contributing to tragedies in our space shuttle program, and the life of Rosa Parks are a few examples of this feature.

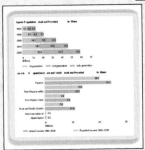

Approaching Democracy Around the Globe

Studying the systems of government in other parts of the world provides the opportunity to highlight and better understand and appreciate the unique and sometimes similar aspects of our own systems. This feature compares aspects of the American political system such as The Constitution and judicial independence with those of other countries. Examples include "A Party Girl Leads China's Online Revolution," "President Bush's Stalwart Ally Gloria Macapagal Arroyo of the Philippines," "Social Security Systems Around the World," and the historic vote of the Iraqi people.

New! Visualizing Democracy

Located at the end of each part, the new *Visualizing Democracy* pictorial essay links the section thematically. An introductory narrative outlines a provocative topic that illustrates the content of the part. A series of supporting images gives a visual overview of democracy in action and an engaging examination of each topic.

fect how Supreme Court decisions are implemented. Even local law enforcement has considerable impact. Decisions limiting the power of the police to search for evidence are implemented only if police and prosecutors choose to observe them and state judges decide to enforce them. Although the vast majority of decisions are implemented without question, a handful of highly controversial ones are not, illustrating the problems the Court faces when issuing decisions. More than four decades after the *Brown* desegregation ruling, many American school systems remain segregated. And three decades after the decision striking down prayer in public schools, students in many public schools still participate in some form of devotional service. Although *Roe* v. *Wade* legalized abortion, state legislatures around the country have placed a wide variety of restrictions on that right.

Public Opinion and the Supreme Court

Finally, supportive public opinion plays an important part in implementation. Although the Supreme Court is an unelected body and need not consult public opinion polls when making its rulings, the views of the American people do play a role in its decision making. Should the Court fail to capture the public's conscience with persuasive reasoning, the decision might never be fully implemented. The sharp public division over the abortion decision in *Roe* v. *Wade*, for example, has affected its level of acceptance.

Research has revealed the Court's general willingness to adhere to majority public sentiment in nearly 60 percent of its decisions.[69] In addition, the Court often signals an accounting for public opinion by counterbalancing bold, innovative decisions with later, more conservative judgments to encourage acceptance. The Court is aware that if it strays too far ahead of public opinion, it risks losing support

↑ Supporters of the Presidential candidates, George Bush and Al Gore, hold their own "oral argument" outside the United States Supreme Court Building while the disputed Florida voting case is being argued inside.

Table 5.1 ■ Presidential Vetoes, 1789–2006

	Regular Vetoes	Pocket Vetoes	Total Vetoes	Vetoes Overridden
Washington	2	–	2	–
Madison	5	2	7	–
Monroe	1	–	1	–
Jackson	5	7	12	–
Tyler	6	3	9	1
Polk	2	1	3	–
Pierce	9	–	9	5
Buchanan	4	3	7	–
Lincoln	2	4	6	–
A. Johnson	21	8	29	15
Grant	45	49	94	4
Hayes	12	1	13	1
Arthur	4	8	12	1
Cleveland	304	109	413	2
Harrison	19	25	44	1
Cleveland	43	127	170	5
McKinley	6	36	42	–
T. Roosevelt	42	40	82	1
Taft	30	9	39	1
Wilson				

---

even its most vocal critic, Chief Justice Rehnquist, voting with the majority and writing the opinion. In overturning Section 3501, Justice Rehnquist argued as the Court did in the *City of Boerne* free exercise of religion case that, "*Miranda*, being a constitutional decision of this Court, may not be in effect overruled by an act of Congress." Rehnquist further explained that the *Miranda* warnings should continue because they "have become part of our national culture" and have "become embedded in routine police practice." Because the warnings caused no measurable difficulties for prosecutors, the Court saw no reason to overturn the case.[131] Just why the Chief Justice wrote the majority opinion in this way is unclear, but although *Miranda* still exists as a legal precedent, studies have found that police continually search for ways to avoid having suspects "lawyer up" in their questioning.[132]

Although the Fourth, Fifth, and Sixth Amendments protect most basic rights of accused persons, the full nature and precise limits of those rights are subject to judicial interpretation. This tension between public safety and the rights of the accused that makes defendants' civil liberties a source of continuing debate also applies to the rights of accused terrorists. In July 2005, U.S. District Court judge Audrey B. Collins of Los Angeles struck down the Patriot Act ban on providing "expert advice" or "training" to foreign terrorist organizations as being unconstitutionally vague. In this case, Judge Collins ruled in favor of groups seeking to aid Sri Lankans displaced by the December 2004 tsunami but fearing prosecution if the Justice Department declared them terrorist organizations. This decision, and future decisions dealing with the nature of the Fifth Amendment's protections against certain types of questioning of terrorist suspects, will help to refine the meaning of this clause.[133]

MakeItReal

ABC News Video: *American Justice*

The Eighth Amendment

Debate over whether the death penalty violates the Eighth Amendment's "Cruel and Unusual Punishment" clause has existed since the Supreme Court ruled in 1976 in the case of *Furman v. Georgia* that this form of punishment cannot be implemented in an "arbitrary and capricious manner." As of January 2006, 1,004 prisoners had been put to death and 3,383 people sat on death row, a disproportionate number of them minorities. However, the standards for determining who will live and who will die vary widely around the nation. In July 2000, President Bill Clinton postponed the first federal execution in nearly forty years when a federal study

ABC NEWS/PRENTICE HALL VIDEO LIBRARY

Crime & Punishment

VISUALS
Photographs

Visual images embedded throughout the text provide as much insight into our government as the written word. The striking images that open each chapter set the tone and context for the topics discussed in the chapter. The photographs provide insight into the events and people that have shaped, influenced, and experienced the evolution of our political systems. Captions provide valuable information that connect the visuals to the content. When studying an image in the text, consider questions such as "Who are these people?" "How were they feeling?" "What event motivated this photograph or painting?" and "What can be learned about the event it represents?" Such analysis allows fuller understanding of the people who illustrate the political journey.

Charts, Graphs, and Tables

The illustrations in the text provide data and summaries of important topics.

COMPANION WEBSITE™ AND VIDEO CORRELATIONS

The *Companion Website*™ that accompanies the text and the **ABC News**™ **Video Library** bound into the text provide supplementary material that connects the topics covered in the text with current events and issues. The activities, primary sources, video segments, and simulations included in these two resources are correlated in the text margins with the appropriate topics so that students can easily find and use these related resources.

MEDIA RESOURCES

Companion Website™

This unique Website lets students test their understanding of text content online, engage in stimulating activities and simulations, or watch videos that bring politics to life.

NEW! ABC News™/Prentice Hall Video Library

The two DVDs bound into the text provide four hours of quality ABC News™ programming on topics related to government and politics. At the end of the text, a student guide to the videos includes a description of the video content and review questions to stimulate critical thinking.

Research Navigator™

This Internet resource helps students make the most of their research time. From finding the right articles and journals to citing sources, drafting and writing effective papers, and completing research assignments, *Research Navigator*™ simplifies and streamlines the entire process.

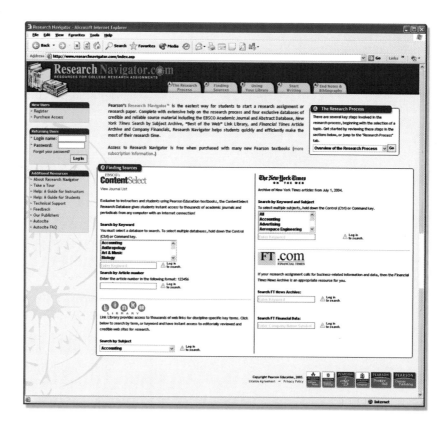

APPROACHING
DEMOCRACY

★ CHAPTER 1 ★

APPROACHING DEMOCRACY

CHAPTER OUTLINE

APPROACHING DEMOCRACY
Sí Se Puede–"It Can Be Done"

INTRODUCTION: Democracy as an Evolutionary Process

- Forming a Picture of Democracy
- The Roots of Democracy
- The Ideals of Democracy
- The Elements of Democracy

Approaching Democracy

Sí Se Puede—"It Can Be Done"

Martin Luther King Jr., Mahatma Gandhi, and Cesar Chavez personified nonviolent protest. Cesar Chavez was the single most important Latino leader in U.S. history. Chavez not only built the United Farm Workers Union (UFW), he also convinced millions of Americans to support the universal struggle for dignity. His main message was about reclaiming dignity for people who had been marginalized by society. This appeal, which went beyond the traditional bread-and-butter issues of unionism, found sympathy in groups everywhere.[1] Through tireless travel across the farms and fields of the West, Chavez politicized migrant Mexican Americans and their communities to stand up for their rights as American workers. In 1965, Chavez led his organization to join the AFL-CIO strike against the grape and wine producers of Delano, California. Chavez maintained the boycott for the next ten years. His activities would help spawn the Latino civil rights movement. In the process of fighting the grape growers, Chavez forged a powerful coalition of unions, church groups, nonprofit organizations, students, minorities, and consumers to extend protective labor legislation to farm workers. Jerry Brown, then Democratic governor in California and sympa-thetic to Chavez's cause, helped pass the Agriculture Labor Relations Act in 1975, enabling UFW members to sign contracts with their employers for the first time.[2]

Most of us associate democracy with expansion of the range of freedoms citizens enjoy. Although democracies do expand certain freedoms, they do not always protect basic human rights, political rights, and civil liberties. People have sometimes been denied their rights to obtain an education, to choose where to live, or to decide which occupations to pursue, simply because of their race, ethnicity, religion, gender, or sexual orientation. American democracy has been remarkably open, over the long run, to expanding rights and liberties for all its citizens—even if those rights and liberties have been achieved only with struggle, sacrifice, and occasional failure.

The struggle never ends. Working on behalf of Mexican Americans, Chavez became a full-time organizer, creating voter registration drives and campaigns against racial discrimination. Demonstrating his resolve through the Ghandian spirit of nonviolence, he conducted several hunger strikes while subsisting on UFW pay of $5,000 a year. When he died of heart failure in 1993, thousands attended his funeral. He received the Presidential Medal of Freedom posthumously in 1994, the highest civilian honor bestowed in the United States.

★ The late Cesar Chavez championed the cause of largely Hispanic migrant workers. Several states have initiated drives for a holiday honoring him.

	Population	Percent distribution
Hispanic	40,424,528	14%
Native born	22,381,207	7.7%
Foreign born	18,043,321	6.2%
Non-Hispanic white	194,876,871	68%
Non-Hispanic black	34,919,473	12%
Non-Hispanic Asian	12,342,486	4%
Non-Hispanic other	5,717,108	2%
Total population	288,280,465	100%

FIGURE 1.1
A U.S. Snapshot: Population by Race and Ethnicity, 2004
Source: Pew Hispanic Center tabulations from the Annual Social and Economic Supplement, Current Population Survey, March 2004.

Considered the "Dr. Martin Luther King" of the Hispanic civil rights movement and the most visible political icon in the Latino community, Chavez also attracted the attention of other Americans who wanted to improve American democracy. In the twelve years following Chavez's death, a surge in the number of Hispanic voters in Arizona, California, Texas, and Florida created a powerful political force. California passed a state holiday in Chavez's name, reflecting the new political voice of Latino voters and revealing the profound political impact of demographic changes in the makeup of the American electorate. The University of California has renamed its administrative holiday in honor of Cesar Chavez. As Hispanics have gained more political power they have altered the American electorate in a way that captures the essence of what we mean by "approaching democracy." The U.S. Hispanic population increased 17 percent between 2000 and 2005 and is now 41.3 million. Projections are that Hispanics will account for 46 percent of all U.S. population growth over the next twenty years.[3] In May 2005 Antonio Villaraigosa was the first Hispanic mayor elected in Los Angeles in 133 years (see Figures 1.1 and 1.2).[4]

★ Labor rights leader Cesar Chavez (third from right) and Coretta Scott King (fourth from right) hold posters as they lead a lettuce boycott march in New York City.

QUESTION FOR REFLECTION

Can you think of groups of underrepresented workers today and what actions might they take to increase their rights?

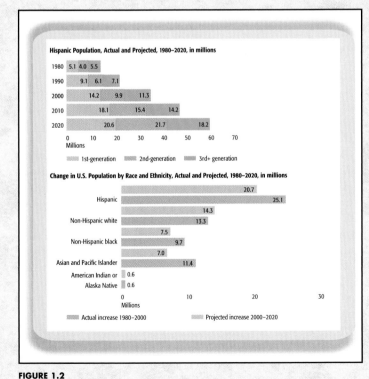

FIGURE 1.2

Source: U.S. Census Bureau for 1980 to 2000; Pew Hispanic Center and Urban Institute for projections for 2010 and 2020.

Introduction
DEMOCRACY AS AN EVOLUTIONARY PROCESS

Question for Reflection

Do you think that the Iraqi experiment in self-government will succeed with respect to achieving legitimacy and stability?

MakeItReal

Simulation: Map of Freedom, Parts I and II

emocracy in America has evolved over time—and continues to evolve. To illustrate, consider how many of your classmates have the power to vote and participate in politics. Virtually all of you do. How many of your classmates are free white males over the age of twenty-one who also own land? This small handful of people in your class would have been the only voters in the nation's earliest elections. When you realize the incredible openness of American politics today, you can appreciate the changes in American history and understand why the United States stands as a beacon throughout the world for those seeking freedom and democratic government.

One of the most eloquent statements on the evolutionary nature of American democracy was made by Vaclav Havel, a former dissident Czechoslovakian playwright once imprisoned by that country's Communist government and later, following the end of Communism there, elected Czechoslovakia's president. Addressing a joint session of the U.S. Congress on February 21, 1990, Havel noted that with the collapse of the Soviet Union, millions of people from Eastern Europe were involved in a "historically irreversible process," beginning their quest for freedom and democracy. And the United States of America represented the model, "the way to democracy and independence," for these newly freed peoples.

But Havel put his own spin on the notion of American democracy as a model:

> As long as people are people, democracy, in the full sense of the word, will always be no more than an ideal. In this sense, you too are merely approaching democracy. But you have one great advantage: you have been approaching democracy uninterruptedly for more than 200 years, and your journey toward the horizon has never been disrupted by a totalitarian system.[5]

This image of an America "approaching democracy" inspired the theme for our textbook, and an excerpt of Havel's address is reprinted in the Appendix. Like Havel, we believe that the United States continues to approach democracy and that we constitute the world's great experiment in republican self-government as well as serving as a beacon for freedom and opportunity. Recall the joy on the faces of the men and women of Afghanistan when Taliban rule came to an end—but then came the hard work in constructing a government with democratic forms. In December 2005, Afghanistan inaugurated its first popularly elected parliament in more than three decades. "This is an important step toward democracy," said President Hamid Karzai of the 249-seat body in which one-third of the delegates are women.[6] Also in December, 70 percent of eligible Iraqi voters went to the polls to elect their 275-member assembly, the first Parliament of the constitutional government.[7]

We live in an era of democratic aspiration. President George W. Bush, in his 2002 State of the Union address, stated, "No people on earth yearn to be oppressed or aspire to servitude or eagerly await the midnight knock of the secret police. If anyone doubts this, let them look to Afghanistan, where the Islamic street greeted the fall of tyranny with the song of celebration."[8] The number of

▲ The Statue of Liberty has frequently been called the "Goddess of Democracy." This NYC Thanksgiving parade carried the Statue's likeness in a "Tribute to America."

◀ A brave Chinese man faces down a column of tanks intent on reaching the democratic student protesters in Tiananmen Square. Eventually, the man was pulled away by bystanders, saving his life, but allowing the tanks to roll toward the protesters.

democracies worldwide is rising, and the appeal of freedom resonates from the Middle East to countries in the former Soviet Union; from Lebanon to Ukraine[9] (see Figures 1.3 and 1.4). These universal ideals of freedom from government oppression influenced the hundreds of thousands of Chinese students who demonstrated in Tiananmen Square during the spring of 1989, with hopes of re-forming their totalitarian government. These so-called dissidents identified their movement as "pro-democracy." They carried a statue similar to the Statue of Liberty through the square, calling it the "Goddess of Democracy," and proclaimed their inalienable rights to life, liberty, and the pursuit of happiness. Their demonstrations revealed something other than the desire to achieve democratic ideals; they also showed the difficulty of doing so under a repressive system. The student movement was crushed by the state, though for many in China the dream of democracy endures. In Iraq, the joy of freedom from Saddam Hussein's tyranny has been followed by the challenge of constructing civil society and a constitution (see Figure 1.5).

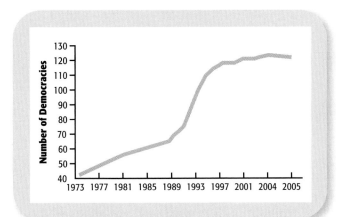

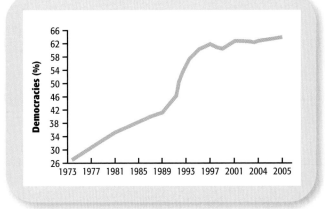

Figure 1.3   Tracking Democracy

Source: Reprinted by permission of The Freedom House, updated by authors.

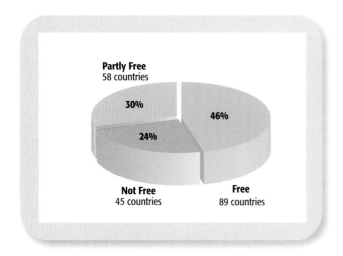

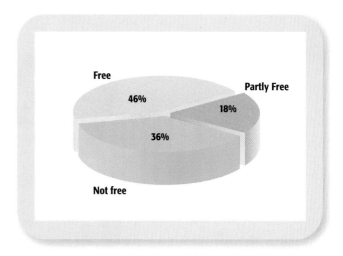

Figure 1.4a Status of Freedom in the World 2006

Source: Reprinted by permission of The Freedom House, updated by authors.

Figure 1.4b World Population by Free, Partly Free, Not Free

Forming a Picture of Democracy

One of the most astute observers of the American experiment in self-government was Alexis de Tocqueville. In 1835, Tocqueville published a book of observations, *Democracy in America,* based on his journey throughout this new nation. "In America I sought more than America," he wrote. "I sought there the image of democracy itself, with its inclinations, its character, its prejudice, its passions, in order to learn what we have to fear or to hope from its progress." This eminent French writer wanted to do more than describe one nation. "America was only the frame," Tocqueville later told the English philosopher John Stuart Mill. "My picture was Democracy."[10]

We wish to portray democracy as a system by showing how it works in the world's oldest democratic state. The United States has been moving toward democracy for more than two hundred years. In spite of its astonishing diversity and the consequent potential for hostility and violence, the United States has approached closer to the democratic ideal than nearly any other country, certainly closer than any other country of comparable heterogeneity and size. But the process of approaching democracy is a continual one. Indeed, even models of democracy such as Sweden engage in a "democratic audit" aimed at taking stock

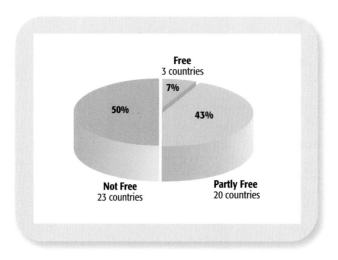

Figure 1.5 Freedom in Muslim Majority Countries 2006

of democratic gains. As Vaclav Havel made clear, the work of democracy is never finished. Understanding that evolutionary process in America begins with a discussion of the term *democracy* itself.

Webster's Dictionary defines **democracy** as "a government by the people, either directly or through elected representatives; rule by the ruled." Basically, democracies place key political powers in the hands of the people. At a minimum, citizens in a democracy choose their leaders freely from among competing groups and individuals. In highly developed democracies, the rights of the people extend well beyond this simple act of choosing leaders. Voters in advanced democracies are free to propose a wide array of public policy options and to join groups that promote those options. Voters may even directly determine through **referenda** (proposed policy measures submitted for direct popular vote) which policy options will become law. This pattern contrasts sharply with that of an **authoritarian regime**, in which government stands apart from the people, oppressing citizens by depriving them of their basic freedom to speak, associate, write, and participate in political life without fear of punishment. The difference between living under a political system that promotes freedom and living under one that enslaves its citizens is clear. Less clear is how to design a system that will foster liberty and freedom even when one disagrees with the government setting the rules.

Although political power in a democracy rests in the hands of the people, not all democracies are alike. Let us look at two types: direct and indirect democracy.

▲ With the Taliban rule over, Afghan women uncovered their faces with no fear of punishment.

Direct and Indirect Democracy

Some democratic systems give their citizens direct political control, others allow only indirect power. **Direct democracy** assumes that people can govern themselves. The people as a whole make policy decisions rather than acting through elected representatives. In an **indirect democracy**, voters designate a relatively small number of people to *represent* their interests; those representatives then meet in a legislative body and make decisions on behalf of the entire citizenry.

Direct Democracy   Think of the political system of Athens and similar Greek city-states of ancient times as an elite-based, direct democracy. Even though most people in Athens were not considered citizens, the few eligible to participate in political life met regularly, debated policy, and voted directly on the issues of the day. They needed no intermediaries and made all political decisions themselves. In contrast, the later Roman republic was an indirect, representative democracy, closer to the structures we recognize in the United States.

The closest American approximation of direct democracy is the New England **town meeting**, a form of governance dating back to the early 1700s. In these meetings, town business is traditionally transacted by consent of a majority of eligible citizens, all of whom have an equal opportunity to express their views and vote at an annual gathering. When it came into being, this method of direct participation represented a startling change from the undemocratic dictates of the English monarchy and the authoritarian traditions of European politics in general. The town meeting system proved durable, even today representing the primary form of government in more than 80 percent of New England townships.

The town meeting instituted two indispensable features of effective democracy—equality and majority rule. **Equality** in this case means that all participants have equal access to the decision-making process, equal opportunity to

democracy A system of government in which the people rule, either directly or through elected representatives.

referenda Proposed policy measures submitted for direct popular vote

authoritarian regime An oppressive system of government in which citizens are deprived of their basic freedom to speak, write, associate, and participate in political life without fear of punishment.

direct democracy A type of government in which people govern themselves, vote on policies and laws, and live by majority rule.

indirect democracy A type of government in which voters designate a relatively small number of people to represent their interests; those people, or representatives, then meet in a legislative body and make decisions on behalf of the entire citizenry.

town meeting A form of governance dating back to the 1700s in which town business is transacted by the consent of a majority of eligible citizens, all of whom have an equal opportunity to express their views and cast their votes at an annual meeting.

equality A state in which all participants have equal access to the decision-making process, equal opportunity to influence the decisions made, and equal responsibility for those decisions.

Approaching Democracy Around the Globe

Freedom in the World 2006

Freedom House's annual survey of Freedom in the World 2006 (see Figure 1.6) showed striking improvement in major countries from Ukraine to Indonesia and notable increases in political rights and civil liberties in the Arab Middle East as well as gains in several Muslim countries in Asia and in sub-Saharan Africa. The number of countries rated "not free" declined from forty-nine in 2004 to forty-five in 2005, "the lowest number of not-free societies identified by the survey in more than a decade." The map below "Freedom in the World 2006" shows that by the end of 2005, eighty-nine free countries offered "broad scope for open political competition, a climate of respect for civil liberties, significant independent civic life, and independent media. This represents 46 percent of the world's 192 countries and 2.969 billion people—45.97 percent of the global population." According to Thomas O. Melia, acting executive director of Freedom House, "The modest but heartening advances in the Arab Middle East result from activism by citizen groups and reforms by governments in about equal measures. This emerging trend reminds us that men and women in this region share the universal desire to live in free societies. . . . As we welcome the stirrings of change in the Middle East it is equally important that we focus on the follow-through in other regions and appreciate the importance of the continuing consolidation of democracy in Indonesia, Ukraine, and other nations."

The global picture thus suggests that the past year was one of the most successful for freedom since Freedom House began measuring world freedom in 1972. "These global findings are encouraging," said Arch Puddington, director of research. "Among other things, the past year has been notable for terrorist violence, ethnic cleansing, civil conflict, catastrophic natural disasters, and geopolitical polarization. That freedom could thrive in this environment is impressive." Among the study's other findings: The number of electoral democracies increased by three, from 119 to 122. This represents 64 percent of the world's countries—the highest number in the survey's thirty-three–year history. Of the four countries that registered an outright decline in status, the most significant was the Philippines. The decision to downgrade this country from "free" to "partly free" drew on credible allegations of massive electoral fraud, corruption, and the government's intimidation of elements in the political opposition (which we discuss in Chapter 5). "The period since September 11, 2001, has witnessed steady progress in majority Muslim countries in regions beyond the Middle East. The steady record of progress observed represents a powerful argument against the proposition that Islam is incompatible with democracy or is an impediment to the spread of freedom. Indeed, there has been a striking improvement in the level of freedom in majority Muslim countries over the past ten years."

Source: Global Survey 2006: Middle East Progress Amid Global Gains in Freedom, December 19, 2005, http://www.freedomhouse.org/template.cfm?page=70&release=317.

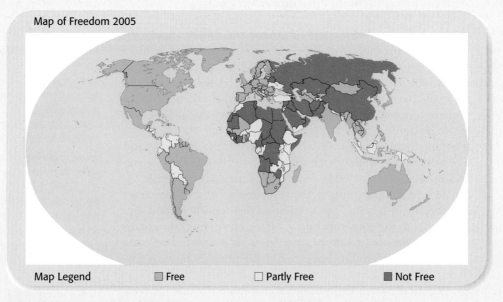

Figure 1.6   Map of Freedom 2005
Source: Reprinted by permission of The Freedom House.

influence the decisions made, and equal responsibility for those decisions. For this reason, the central premise of the Declaration of Independence is that "all men are created equal." Under **majority rule**, when more than half of the voters agree on an issue, the entire group accepts the decision, even those in the minority who voted against it. Acceptance of this key procedural norm allows the government to operate. If minorities were to flout the law as determined by the majority, the result would be anarchy or even civil war. But democracy is about the minority's struggle for their right to be equal and their perspective to be recognized.

Note that minorities accept majority rule for the same reason that majorities accept minority rights. Those in the minority hope to become the majority some day, and when they do, they will want that day's minority to obey the laws they pass. At a minimum, then, obedience to any majority-approved law represents a crude calculation of future self-interest. But for many in a democracy, this constant shifting between majority and minority positions broadens one's perspective. It produces an understanding of, even empathy for, the positions of people in the opposite political camp. The result is a degree of tolerance for different political points of view, an openness to others' opinions that lies at the heart of the democratic ideal.

Direct democracy (as in New England town meetings) works well for small, homogeneous groups of people. Once a population grows and diversifies, however, direct democracy can become cumbersome, even impossible to operate. One form of direct democracy—statewide balloting—is still used in states such as California. Voters there express their views on policy matters (through referenda) or on changes in the state constitution or to state statutes (through initiatives). However, approximately 295 million people live in America; assembling them all to discuss and make collective decisions would be impossible. With large numbers of people and a varied population, an indirect form of democracy makes more sense.

Indirect Democracy As the country grew in size and population, democracy became less pure and direct. The town meeting gave way to *representative town meetings,* a form of indirect democracy in which voters designate a few people to attend town meetings and vote on issues for the entire community. But even this system was ineffective. Myriad decisions cropped up, and towns would come to a standstill if they had to call daily or weekly town meetings. The business of government was too complex and demanding even for this approach. To expedite matters, towns voted for "selectmen," who would conduct routine town business in the periods between full town meetings.

This new system of **representative democracy** allowed larger and more diverse groups of people to govern themselves. Under this system, voters select representatives to make the decisions of government for them. In theory, citizens still retain the ultimate decision-making power, since periodic elections allow them to eject representatives who fail to carry out their wishes. Still, government day-to-day and the workaday flow of policy decisions no longer rest directly in the people's hands. Immediate power to run the government now resides with elected officials, delegates of the people. The resulting system is related to but still different from the framework of direct citizen rule.

Given the choice between direct versus representative democracy, the framers of the Constitution chose the latter, fearing that direct rule by the people—pure democracy—would mean mob rule. As John Adams once wrote: "Remember, democracy never lasts long. It soon wastes, exhausts, and murders itself. There never was a democracy yet that did not commit suicide."[11] Seeking to keep their new democratic system from committing suicide, the framers decided to create a **republic**, a governing structure that places political decision makers at least one step away from the citizens they govern. For instance, citizens grouped into several hundred districts elect members of the U.S. House of Representatives. Each district elects one individual to represent its wishes and interests in an assembly at the nation's capital.

Quick Review

Direct Democracy
- Ancient Athens and a few other Greek city-states had direct democracy.
- The framers of the U.S. *Constitution* feared that direct rule by the people—pure democracy—would mean rule by the mob.
- Our current system contains elements of both representative and direct democracy.

MakeItReal

Great Speeches: William Jennings Bryan, *The Ideal Republic*

majority rule A decision-making process in which, when more than half of the voters agree on an issue, the entire group accepts the decision, even those in the minority who voted against it.

representative democracy A system of government in which the voters select representatives to make decisions for them.

republic A system of government that allows indirect representation of the popular will.

To further dilute the political influence of the American people, the framers placed other units of government even farther from their direct control. The Senate would be chosen by state legislators. The people would not vote directly for president, but for members of an electoral college who would then name the president. The Supreme Court would be even further removed from the people's will—chosen for life tenure by the indirectly elected president and confirmed by the indirectly elected Senate. Thus, the highest court in the land would be three times removed from the popular will.

Although the framers clearly opted for an indirect and representative form of democratic governance, over the years the system they devised moved much closer to the Athenian ideal of direct democracy. Still, we must marvel at how well the original structures, set up more than two hundred years ago, have held up. Everywhere in the country today, we see representative democracy at work: in local, state, and national governments. Something in the original scheme seems to have met with the ideals and goals of the American democratic spirit: equality, freedom for all, a representative democracy based on majority rule and minority rights, a system of open participation.

The Roots of Democracy

Precisely why American democracy has endured and advanced is one of the most interesting and complex questions of our time. To begin to answer this question, it helps to understand the origins of democracy and how it took root in America. Democracy did not begin in America. A movement with a long history, its seeds were first sown in the fertile soil of the ancient Greek city-state of Athens. The term *democracy* is derived from the Greek words *demos* and *kratia*, meaning literally "rule by the people." In Athenian democracy, roughly five centuries before Christ, people were expected to participate actively in political life. To facilitate this participation, Athens organized government around the assembly (*ekklesia*). This body, composed of native-born adult male property owners, met forty times a year to discuss the pressing issues of the day. Plato and Aristotle tell us that Athenian democracy involved such characteristics as citizen participation, rule of law, and free and open political discussion. It thus provided the world's first model of what **politics** in a democratic political system might look like.

Athenian democracy was far from perfect, however. It had two conditions; one is virtually impossible, the other undesirable, in modern democracies. First, this city-state was small, comprising no more than fifty thousand people, with perhaps six thousand of them eligible to participate in the political process. Thus, democracy in Athens emphasized face-to-face political discussion and decision making. Most modern states contain millions of citizens, placing an Athenian town-meeting style of government out of the question. Second, Greek democracy was highly exclusive. Women, slaves, and immigrants formed the majority of residents but were barred from participating in the *ekklesia*. Modern democracies guarantee equal political rights to nearly every adult citizen, thus ensuring a boisterous political life and a much more complex set of institutions.[12]

What is the American conception of democracy? Some of its ideals clearly derive from the Athenian model. One example can be found in Thomas Jefferson's famous phrase from the Declaration of Independence, that America is a government whose "just powers" are derived "from the consent of the governed." Also borrowed from Athens is the idea of freely conducted debates and, following those debates, elections, using majority rule to determine actual public policy.

Despite the Athenian model's influence, however, when our early leaders met to draft the United States Constitution, they clearly hoped to avoid some of its weaker elements. James Madison, for instance, spoke out strongly against the kind of pure democracy represented by Athens, calling it inherently unstable and prone to self-destruct:

politics Greek *politika*; the art or science of government; the art or science concerned with guiding or influencing government; the art or science concerned with winning and holding control over a governmental policy.

Such democracies have ever been spectacles of turbulence and contention; have ever been found incompatible with personal security or the rights of property; and have in general been as short in their lives as they have been violent in their deaths.[13]

It is true that Athenian democracy was short-lived. Its death has often been attributed to a series of citizen decisions that led to disastrous consequences, even though those decisions were made in a perfectly democratic manner. In America, the framers wished to avoid a system in which the immediate desires of average citizens had an instant impact on the policies of the state. The democratic model they chose was less inclusive but ultimately more durable than the Athenian ideal of direct decision making.

THE IDEALS OF DEMOCRACY

America's commitment to democracy rests on a profound belief in an idealistic set of core values: freedom, equality, order, stability, majority rule, protection of minority rights, and participation. If the United States could uphold these values at all times, it might be regarded as the perfect democratic system. It doesn't, however, even today, and it fell short of these ideals even more frequently in the past. Still, these worthy ideals, and the country's long and continuing efforts to move toward them, led Vaclav Havel to see America as "approaching democracy."

Freedom and Equality

Two key values that American democracy claims to safeguard often lead in contradictory directions. Frequently, the more freedom citizens have, the less equality they are likely to achieve, and vice versa. Each of these admirable ideals, when applied to real-world circumstances, can produce contradictory results, depending on how one interprets their meaning. The dilemmas that arise when pursuing these two goals, both individually and together, are many.

To begin, take that quintessential American value, **freedom**. This value suggests that no individual should be within the power or under the control of another. We often take freedom to mean that we should have *freedom from* government interference in our lives. But the notion of freedom means different things to different people. As the noted historian Isaiah Berlin has argued, freedom can be understood in two ways, either negative or positive. Negative freedom implies freedom from government intervention. People have a right to certain liberties, such as freedom of speech, and government cannot violate or interfere with that right. For this reason, the First Amendment begins with the famous words "Congress shall make no law" and goes on to list several key citizen rights that government cannot restrict—notably, the rights to speak, write, assemble, and worship freely.[14]

Contrast that approach with positive freedom, or *freedom to*, such as the freedom to exercise certain rights guaranteed to all U.S. citizens under the Constitution. Examples include the right to vote, the right to legal counsel, and the right to equal protection under the law.

Note how these two views of freedom lead to different roles for government. To ensure negative freedom (freedom *from* restrictions), government is expected to do nothing, to keep its hands off. Negative freedom is, as Supreme Court Justice William O. Douglas put it, the "right to be left alone." For instance, a person can say and write practically anything about any political official, and government agencies in a democracy are supposed to do nothing.

Conversely, to secure rights involving freedom *to*, government is often expected, and even required, to take positive action to protect citizens and ensure that those rights can be exercised. In the 1960s, for instance, the federal government had to intervene with a heavy hand in the South to ensure that African-Americans could

freedom A value that suggests that no individual should be within the power or under the control of another.

exercise a basic democratic freedom: the right to vote. Thus, some elements of freedom require a weak or even nonexistent government, while others require a strong and interventionist one.

Similar contradictions arise in attempting to maximize the key democratic value of equality. This ideal suggests that all citizens, regardless of circumstance, should be treated the same way by government. What equal treatment means in practice, however, is not always easy to say. Does it mean equality of opportunity or equality of result? **Equality of opportunity** reflects the idea that people should have equal rights and opportunities to develop their talents. This idea implies that all people should have the chance to begin at the same starting point. But what if life's circumstances make that impossible, placing people from different situations at different starting points, some much farther behind than others? For example, the person born into a poor family in which no one has ever graduated from high school will be less prepared for college than the son or daughter of generations of college professors. Even more dramatic is the difference in life opportunities available to the children of poor black families, compared with the children of wealthy white families. Equalizing opportunities for all Americans would clearly take an enormous effort, which is why Cesar Chavez organized the farm workers into the United Farm Workers of America.[15]

The difficulty of achieving equal opportunity for all has led some people to advocate another kind of equality: **equality of result**, the idea that all forms of inequality, including economic disparities, should be eradicated. Policies aimed at maximizing this goal deemphasize helping people compete and support redistributing benefits after the competition has taken place. Equality of result would produce a redistribution of goods, services, and income—taking from those who have more and giving to those who have less. These two forms of equality—equality of opportunity and equality of result—are often in conflict and represent different notions of what a democratic society would look like.

Besides these internal contradictions, freedom and equality conflict in several ways. For instance, if you value freedom *from* government intervention, then equality of any kind will be an extremely difficult goal to achieve. If government stays out of all citizen affairs, some people will become extremely wealthy, others will fall through the cracks, and economic inequalities will multiply. On the other hand, if you value equality of *result*, then you will have to restrict some people's freedoms—the freedom to earn and retain an unlimited amount of money, for example.

Order and Stability

The values of freedom and equality, central to a democracy, often stand in tension with the state's power to control its citizens. Every society, to be successful, must maintain **order** and provide social **stability**, so that citizens can go about their business in a secure and predictable manner. Governments make use of laws, regulations, courts, the police, and the military to prevent societal chaos. This need for order does, however, place limits on individual freedom, and it frequently violates certain notions of equality.

Think, for example, about one of the more obvious controls that government places on us to prevent social disorder: the need for a state-approved driver's license before we are allowed to operate a motor vehicle. Americans who wish to drive a car cannot simply get into a car and start driving. They must first fill out many forms, pay a government agency, pass a written examination created by government officials, and then prove to other government officials through a driving test that they actually know how to drive a car. Each of these steps has valid reasons, springing from the desire to make society orderly and safe, but government policies that derive from these goals do have the effect of limiting (modestly, of course) the values of both freedom and equality.

MakeItReal

Census 2000: People and Families in Poverty

equality of opportunity The idea that "people should have equal rights and opportunities to develop their talents," that all people should begin at the same starting point in a race.

equality of result The idea that all forms of inequality, including economic disparities, should be completely eradicated; this may mean giving certain people a starting advantage so that everyone has fair chances to succeed.

order A condition in which the structures of a given society and the relationships thereby defined among individuals and classes comprising it are maintained and preserved by the rule of law and police power of the state.

stability The degree to which an entity is resistant to sudden change or overthrow.

The limit on personal freedom is obvious; we can't do what we want (drive a car) without satisfying certain government requirements. The limit on equality is perhaps less severe but is still there; not everyone is allowed to drive a car (those under a certain age, those who fail the various tests, those whose eyesight is weak, those who have violated certain laws, etc). The constant tension between individual rights and state power creates a great deal of controversy in a democracy and gives rise to numerous policy disputes, many of which we examine in this text.

Questions for Reflection

Can you identify an issue regarding which today you are in the minority but hope one day to be in the majority?

What are you doing to help your cause?

Majority Rule and Protection of Minority Rights

Just as democracies must balance freedom and equality with order and stability, so must they also strike a balance between majority rule (*majoritarianism*) and protection of minority rights. Whenever disagreement arises in a democracy, each party to the dispute seeks to persuade more than half of the populace in its favor. To accomplish this end, supporters of each position must agree among themselves on the desired goal; they must achieve some kind of internal *consensus*. In successful democracies, political scientist E. E. Schattschneider argued, consensus develops out of debate and persuasion, campaigning and voting, rather than being imposed by dictate. The minority becomes the majority, in other words, only through open procedures that encourage popular input and rational argument, not through some small group's authoritarian decision to impose its policy preferences on everyone else.[16]

Furthermore, in a democracy, policy questions are rarely settled "once and for all." Those in the minority are constantly trying to influence the majority to change its mind. Free to express their views without fear of harm, those who hold the minority opinion will speak out persuasively, hoping to see their ideas become the majority perspective. Hence, majorities in a vibrant democracy can never feel secure for long. They must always defend themselves from continuing minority arguments; they must always imagine that the minority will one day claim the majority position.

To make matters more complicated still, note that few people ever find themselves in the majority on all issues. One may hold the majority viewpoint on prayer in public schools and on nuclear power but find oneself in the minority on the minimum wage issue. Democracy is never static; it is an elusive, dynamic, and constantly shifting process.

Knowing that majority status must inevitably be temporary, members of any majority must be careful. They must be reasonable in their demands and programs, seeking not to antagonize the minority excessively, since they would have to expect retribution when leaders of an oppressed minority become part of next week's or next year's majority. The knowledge that one might become the minority any day has a profound effect, leading the current majority in a democratic system to treat minorities fairly.

The idea of **minority rights** springs from this perspective. We give rights to the minority because when we end up in the minority, as inevitably we must, we want to enjoy those rights ourselves rather than endure the repression that is the usual fate of minorities in nondemocratic systems. Thomas Jefferson understood this idea well. When in the minority, his Democratic-Republican party had been victimized by the Alien and Sedition Acts, passed by the majority Federalist party in 1798 in part to restrain the Democratic-Republicans' views. When Jefferson himself entered the majority as president in 1801, he stressed the importance of majority restraint, referring in his first inaugural address to the "sacred principle that though the will of the majority is in all cases to prevail, that will to be rightful must be reasonable."[17]

When those in the minority band together into groups based on particular interests and seek to influence policy by allying with other groups, we have a system of **pluralism**. Continual competition among groups in a democracy ensures that power moves around in shifting alliances of interests. One year, the religious and education groups might unite on the question of government assistance to

minority rights Rights given to those in the minority; based on the idea that tyranny of the majority is a danger to human rights.

pluralism A system that occurs when those in the minority form groups based on particular interests and seek to influence policy by allying with other groups.

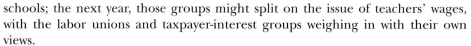

Quick Review

Ideals of Democracy

- Government must protect citizens and ensure that rights can be exercised.
- All citizens, regardless of circumstance, should be treated the same way by government.
- Maintain order and provide social stability.
- Provide a balance between the rule of the majority and the protection of minority rights.
- Provide citizens with ample opportunities to participate in and influence government activities.

universal suffrage The requirement that everyone must have the right to vote.

▲ Supporters of the Equal Rights Amendment chained themselves to the White House fence to demonstrate their support for the ERA.

schools; the next year, those groups might split on the issue of teachers' wages, with the labor unions and taxpayer-interest groups weighing in with their own views.

In a system of democratic pluralism, maintaining a cohesive majority becomes more and more difficult. Coalitions constantly shift, and new majorities appear on every issue. In these circumstances the ephemeral majorities of the day are bound to respect minority rights and pay close attention to unpopular opinions. The large number of groups and the strong likelihood that everyone will frequently be in the minority diminishes the chance that one dominant oppressive group will form. The framers of our Constitution worried a good deal about "the tyranny of the majority," but in a modern, complex democracy this problem seems relatively minor. Indeed, the excessive power of minorities, including special-interest groups, seems more of a worry to many observers today—an issue we examine carefully in later chapters.

Participation

Democracy, rule by the governed, gives *all* citizens an opportunity to influence government activities. That opportunity is best expressed by **universal suffrage**, the right of adults to vote. Democracy also requires that this vote be meaningful; that is, voters must have real choices at the polls, and their choices must be reflected in governmental policies. Beyond voting, democracies must provide citizens with ample opportunities to participate in and influence the direction of their government. Such participation may involve serving in the government, lobbying for governmental action, or simply reading and talking about government actions.

Participation is a central democratic ideal, and the United States has approached it over the years by continually expanding opportunities for Americans to participate in and influence their government. Only a minority of people—free, white, landowning males over the age of twenty-one—could exercise full citizenship rights in 1787. The expansion of citizenship rights toward inclusiveness has continued for two centuries, facilitated in particular by the amendment structure of the Constitution. The Thirteenth and Fifteenth Amendments eliminated slavery and involuntary servitude and gave the freed African Americans the right to vote (though years passed before state laws were changed to ensure this goal); the Seventeenth Amendment conferred the right to vote for senators directly; the Nineteenth Amendment gave women the right to vote; the Twenty-third Amendment gave residents of the District of Columbia presidential electoral college votes; the Twenty-fourth Amendment ended the practice of charging people a "poll tax" before they could vote; and the Twenty-sixth Amendment lowered the minimum voting age from twenty-one to eighteen. Today, the opportunity exists for nearly every adult American to participate in the political life of American society.

THE ELEMENTS OF DEMOCRACY

Following the struggle for democracy in Poland, Adam Michnik, an early leader in the Solidarity movement, noted that "dictatorship has been defeated and freedom has been won, yet the victory of freedom has not yet meant the triumph of democracy. Democracy is something more than freedom. Democracy is freedom institutionalized."[18] Throughout this text, we examine characteristics of American democracy that have helped to "institutionalize freedom." Free elections, competitive political

▲ In March 2005, Moe Hamzeh stands over a crowd of hundreds of thousands of Lebanese gathered in Martyr's Square in Beirut, Lebanon, to mark the one month anniversary of the death of the former prime minister, Rafic Hariri, and to demand the truth about the bombing that killed him. The masses also represent citizens for and against the withdrawal of Syrian troops from Lebanon.

parties, a free press, interest groups, an independent judiciary, civilian control of the military, and a commitment among citizens to the rule of law and a set of democratic ideals are indispensable in preserving democracy. The institutions and traditions of the American system have allowed it to develop toward democracy, a democracy that has not yet "committed suicide," as John Adams feared it would.

How closely have we approached the ideals of true democracy? Scholars constantly try to define and categorize democracy using one or another set of objective indicators. Although healthy debate continues about the nature of these indicators, we have chosen to stress five widely accepted elements of democracy. These institutional elements will serve as markers to identify progress toward the democratic ideals discussed earlier. Only political systems that meet or at least approach those ideals can be considered democratic. Using the following elements, you can measure the strength and robustness of American democracy or any democracy.

A System for Popular Participation   The United States provides numerous opportunities for citizen involvement in politics. In the course of two centuries, increasing numbers of people have gained the opportunity to participate in public life. Elections most clearly allow people to influence government. All adult citizens now can participate in regularly scheduled **elections**, where at least two opposing groups have a chance to win. By voting in elections, citizens can convey their desires to government and can expect government to act with those desires in mind. More than 116 million voted in the 2004 presidential election, with President George W. Bush winning a clear national election in both the electoral college as well as the popular vote.

Voting itself would not be sufficient to influence government, however, if voters could not make meaningful choices at the polling booth. The institution of free, competing **political parties** enables this element of choice to be exercised. Stable political parties exist and, once elected to office, seek to impose their will on policy makers. Parties allow like-minded voters to join together and magnify their individual voices into a focus for government action.

Quick Review

Elements of Democracy

- Popular participation.
- Preserve freedom and equality for all.
- Independent judiciary, free of political influence.
- Civilian control of the military and the police.
- Democratic ideals among all levels of society.

   MakeItReal

Civic Participation: Political Parties

elections The central institution of democratic representative governments in which the authority of the government derives from the consent of the governed. The principal mechanism for translating that consent into governmental authority is the holding of free and fair elections.

political parties Organizations that exist to allow like-minded members of the population to group together and magnify their individual voices into a focus promoting individual candidates and government action.

▲ Newly inaugurated Ukrainian President Viktor Yushchenko frees a white dove decorated with an orange campaign ribbon after his speech at a rally in central Kiev in January 2005. The rally followed another speech in which Yushchenko told supporters that he aims to secure a place for Ukraine in a united Europe.

Important as they are, political parties are never the only outlet for citizen participation in a developed democracy. Citizens must be free to join a wide array of groups that promote particular interests. That situation has long been true in the United States, where a vigorous civil society allows public and private **interest groups** to thrive. These groups allow citizens to meet, organize, plan strategy, and lobby government for action. They even allow people to protest government policies without fear that government will punish them.

interest groups Formal organizations of people who share a common outlook or social circumstance and who band together in the hope of influencing government policy.

right to privacy The right to have the government stay out of the personal lives of its citizens.

free press Media characterized by the open reporting of information without government censorship.

independent judiciary A system in which judges are insulated from the political bodies and public opinion in order to preserve their ability to act as the final arbiter over those groups in interpreting the Constitution and the laws.

judicial review The power of the Supreme Court established in *Marbury v. Madison* to overturn acts of the president, Congress, and the states if those acts violate the Constitution. This power makes the Supreme Court the final interpreter of the Constitution.

A Commitment to Preserve Freedom and Equality for All   For democracy to flourish, the government must work to safeguard democratic ideals for all its citizens. That goal implies several kinds of action. First, it means that government stays out of the personal lives of its citizens, who have an inherent **right to privacy**. Furthermore, citizens must have access to a vigorous **free press** and other means of open exchange of information. Debate must be encouraged and fueled by freedom of speech and thought, not to mention freedom of information.

In a secure democracy, people must be free to think for themselves, inform themselves about governmental policies, and exchange information. A totalitarian government, using the state to maintain total authority over all citizens, suppresses open communication so as to maintain an iron grip over the minds of its populace.

An Independent Judiciary   Central to functioning democracies are the rule of law and the protection of civil liberties. Only an **independent judiciary**, free of political influence, can safeguard citizen rights, protecting both majority and minorities at the same time. Like other federal courts, the U.S. Supreme Court possesses a unique power: **Judicial review** makes it the final interpreter of the Constitution. The day after the 2000 Supreme Court ruling that Florida would have to cease its recount of contested ballots, Al Gore, the vice president of the United States and winner of the popular vote, conceded the election to Governor George W. Bush. We will study this election later, but for now just think about what this peaceful transition says about the values that constitute our system of laws.

The federal judiciary has often protected individual freedoms through the power to strike down government actions. Independent state courts have also acted to preserve individuals rights. Courts have used their authority to make a powerful statement about equality and the rule of law: *All are equal under the law,* and no one, not even the president of the United States, is above it.

Civilian Control of the Military and the Police   In dictatorships, political parties come and go, but the group that controls the military and the police is the real power. This kind of arbitrary military power does not happen in the United States or in any advanced democracy. Thanks in part to the example of George Washington, who resigned from the military after the Revolution, the American military is controlled by the civilian government. Military leaders take no policy actions other than those directed by civilian political leaders; the commander in chief is the president. Furthermore, the military does not intervene in civilian political affairs. Since 1800, when the defeated John Adams turned over power to Thomas Jefferson, every losing political party has simply turned control over to its winning competitors. Never have civilian leaders, rejected by the voters, called on the military or police to keep them in office. Never have the military or police intervened to keep in office a candidate or party that has come up short at the polls. Both occurrences are common in countries where democratic institutions are weak.

This tradition of civilian control of the military allowed President Harry Truman to fire General Douglas MacArthur for insubordination during the Korean War. Moreover, Americans did not have to worry that the same George Bush who commanded the American armed forces in the Persian Gulf War of 1991 would, following his electoral defeat in November 1992, use his powers as commander in chief to call off the election and surround the White House with an army. Or that Vice President Gore would do the same during the uncertain period following the November 2000 election. Indeed, these hypothetical examples, common enough in many nations, seem outrageously unlikely in the American setting. Yet we must understand why they are so unlikely. They seem farfetched precisely because Americans believe deeply in the norm of civilian control over the military and the police, a norm vital to the democratic process. After all, how democratic could a society be if the people's decisions could be arbitrarily set aside by the whims of a powerful few?

A Cultural Commitment to Democratic Ideals among All Levels of Society
Democracy doesn't just happen. People in general and leaders in particular must believe in it, understand how it works, and abide by its norms. All levels of society must agree on a set of common governmental ideals. In the United States, those ideals include reverence for the Constitution, the pursuit of freedom and equality, the value of minority rights, and the rule of law. This commitment to the rule of law is indispensable for maintaining stability. It produces a remarkable result, one found only in a democratic society. Americans unhappy with their government complain but almost never take up arms. That is why Timothy McVeigh and the 1995 bombing of the Oklahoma City federal building or Unabomber Ted Kaczynski are considered aberrations of the values by which Americans have chosen to live. Americans tend to organize and wait for the next election and then vote the ruling party out of power.

U.S.A. Yesterday and Today

The Back of the Bus

Imagine what it would be like to wait for public transportation, pay your fare, and be required to sit in a special section or forced to give up your seat to someone of the racial majority. Well, that is the way it was in Montgomery, Alabama, in 1955. The white majority in the city had constructed a complicated system for riding the bus, all in accord with the 1896 Supreme Court decision *Plessy* v. *Ferguson,* which held that state facilities could be "separate" for white and black citizens as long as they were "equal" in quality. White citizens always rode in front; if there were no whites on the bus, those seats were left vacant. Black citizens sat or stood in the back of the bus. The middle of the bus was not assigned to either race. If there was no demand from the white customers, black customers could ride there. But if a black rider was seated in the middle and a white rider demanded the seat, the black rider was required by Alabama law to move to the back of the bus.

On December 1, 1955, Rosa Parks, a forty-two-year-old African-American seamstress, sat in the middle of the bus, but as the bus filled up, a white patron demanded her seat. Three other black riders vacated their seats, but Parks refused to move. The driver told Parks that she had to move to the back. When she did not move, he had her arrested.

Parks later explained: "I simply decided that I would not get up. I was tired, but I was usually tired at the end of the day, and I was not feeling well, but then there had been many days when I had not felt well. I had felt for a long time, that if I was ever told to get up so a white person could sit, that I would refuse to do so."

Parks had decided that Alabama's bus segregation law was unfair, but the courts offered her no justice. Although the U.S. Constitution guarantees citizens a trial by a jury of their peers before an impartial judge, such was not the case for blacks in the South in 1955. The state judges were all local white lawyers who, like the white majority, supported the "separate but equal" doctrine. They implemented the laws and regulations of the white

▲ Mrs. Rosa Parks is fingerprinted in Montgomery, Alabama, in February 1956 for refusing to give up her seat to a white passenger and move to the back of the bus.

Summary

1. Throughout the world democracy has become increasingly prevalent. The United States is often viewed as a model of the democratic process. However, the formal institutions of a democracy do not by themselves guarantee the protection of individual liberties.

2. The term *democracy* means government by the people, either directly or through elected representatives. Citizens in a democracy choose their leaders freely from among competing groups and individuals. In highly developed democracies, voters are free to propose public policy options and join groups that promote those options. In contrast, an authoritarian government deprives citizens of the freedom to participate in political life.

3. In a direct democracy, the people as a whole make policy decisions. In an indirect democracy, voters designate a few people to represent their interests, to meet in a legislative body and make decisions on behalf of the entire citizenry. Such a system of representative democracy makes it possible for a larger and more diverse group of people to govern themselves.

4. Freedom and equality are core values of American democracy, but they often pull in contradictory directions. The more freedom citizens have, the less equality they are likely to achieve, and vice versa. Each of these ideals can require that government take no action. Conversely, they can each require governmental intervention to protect individual freedom or guarantee equal treatment. The desire for order and stability places limits on freedom and equality.

state legislatures and the white city councils. Through unfair election laws, blacks were almost entirely excluded from voting. Thus, they had little say in who passed or administered the laws they had to live under. Since juries were chosen from the voting rolls, jurors were almost all white. No wonder that Parks was quickly convicted of violating the Alabama transportation laws and sentenced to pay a $14 fine. As a result of this case, Parks lost her job and eventually had to leave the South.

Rosa Parks lost in the courts, but civil rights activists were determined that she and others like her would not lose in the court of public opinion. These activists decided to use this incident to seek change and justice for African Americans. They asked the twenty-six-year-old son of a Baptist minister, Martin Luther King Jr., with his compelling voice and hypnotizing command of the spoken word, to speak at a mass meeting of the newly formed protest group known as the Montgomery Improvement Association. Turnout was impressive.

Speaking from a few notes hastily scribbled on a piece of paper, King observed, "We are here in a general sense because first and foremost—we are American citizens—and we are determined to apply our citizenship—to the fullness of its means. But we are here in a specific sense—because of the bus situation in Montgomery." As he spoke about the injustices suffered by African Americans, the crowd was visibly moved. Finally, King boomed out: "And you know, my friends, there comes a time when people get tired of being trampled over by the iron feet of oppression."

After boycotting for more than a year, the bus segregation policy was overturned by a panel of federal judges who found it unconstitutional. The U.S. Supreme Court in 1956 affirmed this ruling without opinion. Rosa Parks' willingness to stand up for human justice won her the title of "Mother of the Civil Rights Movement."

Today, it is hard to believe that anyone would be required by law to sit in the back of a public bus. Rosa Parks, recipient of the Congressional Gold Medal, is known as a woman who changed a nation. She remained a committed activist, working to stop apartheid in South Africa during the 1980s and creating a career center for black youth in Detroit. Among her tributes are the NAACP's highest honor, the Spingarn Medal, and the Presidential Medal of Freedom, the highest honor that the U.S. government can give a civilian. When she died in October 2005, her remains lay in honor in the Capitol Rotunda for public viewing. Rosa Parks is the first woman, and second African American, to be honored in this way. "I would not be standing here today, nor standing where I stand every day, had she not chosen to sit down," said talk show host Oprah Winfrey. Bishop Adam Jefferson Richardson of the African Methodist Episcopal Church called Parks a "woman of quiet strength" who was "noble without pretense, regal in her simplicity, courageous without being bombastic." Eleanor Holmes Norton, the District of Columbia's congressional representative, said Parks's refusal to give up her seat "was the functional equivalent of a nonviolent shot heard 'round the world." Senator Sam Brownback, a Kansas Republican, observed that "she saw the inherent evil in segregation and she had the courage to fight it in its common place, a seat on a bus."

Sources: Based on Taylor Branch, *Parting the Waters: America in the King Years, 1954–63* (New York: Simon & Schuster, 1988), pp. 124–42; David J. Garrow, *Bearing the Cross: Martin Luther King, Jr., and the Southern Christian Leadership Conference* (New York: Morrow, 1986), pp. 11–47; Ken Thomas, "Those Inspired by Rosa Parks Honor Her Memory in Capital. Tens of Thousands Pass by Her Casket in the Rotunda," *New York Times,* November 1, 2005, p. A1.

---

5. A democracy must strike a balance between the rule of the majority and the rights of the minority. In successful democracies, people reach consensus through debate, persuasion, campaigning, and voting. In a pluralist system those in the minority band together based on particular interests and seek to influence policy by allying with other groups.

6. In a democracy, all citizens must have an opportunity to influence government activities. Influence is achieved through universal suffrage and other opportunities for political participation, such as serving in the government or lobbying for governmental action.

7. A republic places political decision makers at least one step away from the citizens it governs. Thus, in the

United States voters originally chose electors and state legislators, who in turn chose the president and U.S. senators, who then chose the justices of the Supreme Court. Over the years, this system has been modified to move closer to direct democracy.

8. The basic elements of American democracy include a system for popular participation consisting of regularly scheduled elections; free, competing political parties; and public and private interest groups. Another basic element is the commitment to preserve freedom and equality, which implies a right to privacy, a free press, and freedom of speech. Additional elements are an independent judiciary (including the power of judicial review), civilian control of the military and the police, and a cultural commitment to democratic ideals.

Democracy is a process whereby conflict is resolved and consensus achieved between a ruling majority and a minority that has a right to be heard but also accepts the legitimacy of majority rule. The United States has been approaching democracy for more than two hundred years and continues to do so today.

Review Questions

1. Why did the framers of the American Constitution create a republic in which the people were often removed from direct participation in the electoral system? Why might the framers have wished to dilute the will of the people?

2. Explain the basic democratic ideals. Why are there possible trade-offs among these values?

3. Why not create a direct democracy at the national level? What are the logistical barriers to such a system? Would Americans in general support a system in which all citizens were allowed to vote on national policy? Why or why not?

Key Terms

authoritarian regime 9	independent judiciary 18	politics 12
democracy 9	indirect democracy 9	referenda 9
direct democracy 9	interest groups 18	representative democracy 11
elections 17	judicial review 18	republic 11
equality 9	majority rule 11	right to privacy 18
equality of opportunity 14	minority rights 15	stability 14
equality of result 14	order 14	town meeting 9
freedom 13	pluralism 15	universal suffrage 16
free press 18	political parties 17	

Suggested Readings

CRONIN, THOMAS E. *Direct Democracy: The Politics of Initiative, Referendum, and Recall.* Cambridge, Mass.: Harvard University Press, 1989. An informative account of how ballot measures affect democratic politics. Cronin examines the strengths and weaknesses of these measures.

DAHL, ROBERT A. *Democracy and Its Critics.* New Haven, Conn.: Yale University Press, 1989. One of the most prominent political theorists of our era on the assumptions of democratic theory. The book provides a justification for democracy as a political ideal by tracing modern democracy's evolution from the early nineteenth century to the present.

INKELES, ALEX, ed. *On Measuring Democracy.* New Brunswick, N.J.: Transaction, 1991. Articles by social scientists revealing that political democracy is not only conceptually but also empirically distinct from various social and economic patterns and outcomes.

MURCHLAND, BERNARD. *Voices of Democracy.* Chicago, Ill.: University of Notre Dame Press, 2001. This book builds on conversations between the author and many leading political scientists of our time on the subject of democracy.

RAVITCH, DIANE, and ABIGAIL THERNSTROM, eds. *The Democracy Reader.* New York: HarperCollins, 1992. The enduring issues of democracy in a collection of documents, essays, poems, declarations, and speeches.

SCHUDSON, MICHAEL. *The Good Citizen: A History of American Civic Life.* New York: Free Press, 1998. A history of citizenship in the United States of America, in which the new citizens of America must be "monitors of political danger rather than walking encyclopedias of governmental news."

SHARANSKY, NATON. *The Case For Democracy: The Power of Freedom To Overcome Tyranny and Terror.* New York: Public Affairs Press, 2004. This book was a White House favorite. Written by a Soviet dissident turned Israeli cabinet minister, the book addresses the future of Israeli-Palestinian relations.

TISMANEDNU, VLADIMIR. *Reinventing Politics: Eastern Europe from Stalin to Havel.* New York: Free Press, 1992. A well-balanced account of the factors leading to the revolutions of 1989 and the evolution of democratic institutions in Eastern Europe.

WILENTZ, SEAN. *The Rise of American Democracy.* New York: Norton, 2004. A valuable account of the rise of democracy during the first half of the nineteenth century and antebellum politics.

WOLIN, SHELDON S. *Tocqueville Between Two Worlds: The Making of a Political and Theoretical Life.* Princeton, N.J.: Princeton University Press, 2001. The book connects Tocqueville's political and theoretical lives and also provides commentary on the course of Western political life over the past two hundred years.

CHAPTER 2

THE FOUNDING AND THE CONSTITUTION

CHAPTER OUTLINE

$\mathcal{A}$pproaching $\mathcal{D}$emocracy

The Senate Almost "Goes Nuclear"

Not since the Roosevelt Court-Packing Plan of 1937 had the nation seen the kind of political attack on the federal judiciary that occurred in 2005. In 1937, the stated plan was to increase the size of the Supreme Court to a maximum of fifteen members to improve its efficiency while the actual goal was to change its decision-making direction. In 2005, the plan was to make a broad attack on all "liberal activist" members of the federal judiciary. The goal was to change the Senate rules in a way that would appear to guarantee an "up or down vote" on all presidential appointments to the courts. But in reality the change would allow a Senate majority to guarantee or deny confirmation of any presidential appointment to the judiciary. In the end, the Court battle of 2005 was more than just an attack on the federal judiciary: It was a plan to fundamentally change Senate rules, the role of the minority party in government, the nature of future Court appointees, and, eventually, the power of the presidency.

The roots of this epic battle had been more than a decade in the making. Once the Republicans took control of the House of Representatives in 1994, then majority whip Tom Delay of Texas and others began to attack the activist nature of the federal judiciary. While these attacks contin-

ued, each time the presidency was about to change parties, members of the Senate judiciary committee from both parties held up presidential judiciary nominations hoping that their party would get a chance to fill those vacancies. Republicans held up dozens of Clinton appointees in 2000, thus enabling President Bush to fill those seats. Bush, however, became concerned when minority Democrats used a previously little-known bureaucratic procedure called a "hold" to prevent some of his appointees from receiving a final vote by the full Senate. By 2005, after the Senate had confirmed 205 of Bush's nominees, he resubmitted 10 previously rejected nominees over objections by Democrats who claimed that these nominees were too "extreme" in their conservatism. Effectively, this would mean that, according to Senate rules, these votes would never be taken unless sixty votes could be found to end debate, in a move called a "cloture vote." Thus, a minority of forty-one senators, well inside the number of Democrats then serving in the Senate, could prevent a vote on any nominee.

When the Democrats promised to filibuster these nominees, literally preventing their confirmation vote by "talking the nomination to death," Republicans took note of their 55–44 majority (one senator is an independent). Acting on a plan suggested by Alaska Senator Mike Gravel, they proposed a parliamentary procedure known as the "nuclear option." Under this rule, the Senate president, in this case Vice President Dick Cheney, would rule filibusters for court appointments out of order, as not being a constitutional exercise of the Senate's "advise and consent" power. All that would be required to affirm this decision would be a majority vote of the Senate. The result would mean that a simple majority of fifty-one votes could confirm court nominees.

★ Sen. John McCain (R.-AR) left, is pleased as Sen. John Warner (R.-VA), and Sen. Robert Byrd (D.-WA), along with eleven other members of the Senate "Gang of 14" announce on May 23, 2005 their bipartisan agreement averting the "nuclear option" that would have eliminated the use of filibusters for judicial confirmation votes.

Though the Democrats appeared to be powerless to stop this maneuver, they warned that if the Senate used it they would retaliate by using parliamentary procedures to "slow the Senate down to a crawl," preventing any other work from being accomplished. Thus, the plan was deemed to be "nuclear" because it would fundamentally change the way the Senate operated.

As the vote on the ten nominees approached, with no agreement reached to avoid it, a group of moderate and maverick senators from both parties, led by Republican John McCain (AZ) and Democrat Joe Lieberman (CT) began to seek a compromise. The Republicans did not want to give up their nuclear option, but they did want up or down votes on all presidential nominees to the judiciary. The Democrats did not want to give up their right to filibuster against the most "ideologically extreme" nominees or to vote individually for all ten of the stalled nominations. Meanwhile, powerful interest groups on both sides girded for battle, anticipating a proxy war for expected upcoming Supreme Court confirmation battles.

Eventually, two of the most senior senators—John Warner, age 78 (R.-VA), and Robert Byrd, age 87 (D.-WV)—took over the negotiations. Hour after hour they talked, eventually taking out a copy of *The Federalist Papers* to read about James Madison's view of the role of the Senate, and thus the filibuster, in the "advise and consent" process. By now, fourteen senators, many of them first-termers, were involved in the negotiations. On the eve of the vote, Senator Byrd pleaded on the Senate floor, "I implore senators to step back, step back, step back, step back from the precipice. Don't forget that the worm turns." In other words, majorities sometimes turn into minorities, and the Republicans might be glad of the right to filibuster someday. Eventually the Senate voted against use of the nuclear option and allowed a final vote on three of the ten stalled nominees. The Democrats also agreed not to use a filibuster against future nominees, except in the most "extreme circumstances."

The final vote on the nuclear option was averted, and many considered this a victory. Senator Byrd, who had claimed, "We have kept the Republic" by this vote, said, "We have lifted ourselves above politics and we have signed this document in the interest of the United States Senate—in the interest of freedom of speech, freedom of debate, and freedom to dissent in the United States Senate." Senator Susan Collins (R.-ME) added, "You're going to hear over and over again the words 'good faith,' 'mutual respect,' and 'trust' because those words characterized our negotiations. Hour after hour, day after day, we kept working toward a goal that we all believed in."

★ Stephen Weinstein, 19, an engineering student at Princeton University, stages a symbolic mock filibuster near the Capitol on Wednesday, May 11, 2005, protesting the involvement of fellow Princeton graduate, and now Republican Senate Majority Leader, Bill Frist (R.-TN) in seeking to impose the "nuclear option" banning judicial confirmation filibusters.

But others were not so sure. What would happen when the first contested nominee was sent up and Republicans did not agree that this person was "extreme"? What would happen when the Democrats tried to filibuster and the Republicans raised the nuclear option again? As with all of these battles, the approach to democracy is never a clear and straight one.[1]

QUESTIONS FOR REFLECTION

Consider the confirmations of John Roberts and Samuel Alito. Under what conditions should a party consider filibustering a Supreme Court nomination?

And if that occurs, under what conditions should the other party consider going nuclear and forcing a vote on elimination of the filibuster option for judicial nominations?

Introduction
THE ROAD TO DEMOCRACY

Democracy took root early in America. Because of the tremendous distance from the British empire and the rough-and-tumble character of frontier existence, early colonial settlers were forced to devise their own form of self-government. Drawing on a shared commitment to individual security and the rule of law, the frontier governments provided models on which the constitutional structure of American government was eventually built. To trace the development of American democracy from the early settlements to an independent United States, this chapter explores the ideas that inspired the American Revolution, including the impact of European political thinking on the founding and the struggle for independence from England.

To understand democracy in America, it helps to understand where the idea of democracy began. Although the colonists began their fight for independence in 1775, the idea of democracy that inspired them originated much earlier. As we discussed in Chapter 1, democracy in America resulted from the logical progression of an idea over time. Democracy first emerged in the Greek city-state of Athens. The Athenians devised a political system called *demokratia*, meaning "rule of the people." In fact, the framers of the U.S. Constitution looked to the Roman **republic** (rather than to Greece, because Athens appeared to be ruled by mobs) as a model of democracy. In *The Federalist*, no. 55, James Madison argued that, "had every Athenian citizen been a Socrates, every Athenian assembly would still have been a mob." Later, you will see how this fear of democracy led the founders to create a system of government that limited direct popular participation.

Characteristics of the British government also strongly influenced America's political arrangement. Britain's Magna Carta, formulated in 1215, limited the exercise of power by the monarch; the notion of limited government accompanied the early colonists to North America. Its impact is visible on the Mayflower Compact, the Declaration of Independence, and the Articles of Confederation.[2]

THE SEEDS OF AMERICAN DEMOCRACY

Although the colonists drew extensively on the historic forms of democracy, America's political system was as much homegrown as it was imported. The actions and experiences of the early settlers established a foundation for the emergence of a peculiarly American form of democracy, one still developing. In this section we examine early attempts to establish a society under law in the early days of the American colonies. During this period, the first and most enduring seeds of democracy were sown, germinating in the fertile soil of a rugged frontier existence far from the British homeland.

Early Colonial Governments

Most of the New England colonies (including Plymouth, the Providence Plantations, the Connecticut River towns, and New Haven) based their first governments on the idea of a **compact**, a type of agreement that legally binds two or more parties to enforceable rules. Compacts developed directly from Puritan religious theory. Pilgrims, such as those who settled Plymouth Colony, believed that just as they had entered into a covenant with God to found a church and secure their own salvation, so, too, they could forge a covenant or compact among themselves to protect those "natural" liberties provided by God.[3]

republic A system of government that allows indirect representation of the popular will.

compact A type of agreement that legally binds two or more parties to enforceable rules.

Other colonies were created by charters granted to trading companies to exploit the resources of the New World. In 1629, King Charles I chartered the Massachusetts Bay Company, a private business venture. The charter allowed for a governing council that would include a governor, a deputy governor, and eighteen assistants, as well as a General Court composed of the "freemen" of the company, those with property and wealth. In the Cambridge Agreement of 1629, the stockholders in the venture transferred all governing authority from the trading company in England to the Massachusetts Bay Company in the colonies. Thus, Massachusetts Bay became de facto independent of the authority of any British corporation, and the new council became the exclusive government. The stockholders voted John Winthrop, a lawyer, to be their first governor.

Not all of the colonies were based on a compact or evolved from an English trading company. Maryland, New York, New Jersey, Pennsylvania, Delaware, the Carolinas, and Georgia developed from *royal grants*. In these cases, the king discharged Crown debts by issuing a warrant granting land and full governing rights to a lord or baron. The grant recipient became sole proprietor of the land, enjoying virtually absolute authority over its jurisdiction. Any settlement established there became known as a *proprietary colony*, and the original proprietor determined the nature of the colony's local government. Thus, in 1632 Lord Baltimore was granted territory in Maryland, and in 1664 the Duke of York was granted the territory of New York.

Given that the proprietors of these territories enjoyed the power and authority of kings, the proprietary colonies made an unlikely but important contribution to emerging American democracy by importing England's parliamentary system, with its bicameral houses of Lords and Commons, its committee system, and its procedures. A **bicameral legislature** is a representative lawmaking body consisting of two chambers or two houses. In the United States, the Senate and the House of Representatives are the two legislative chambers.

The bicameral colonial legislatures had an upper house, whose members were appointed by the Crown (or by the proprietor on recommendation of the royal governor), and a lower house, whose members were elected based on the traditional English suffrage requirement of a "forty-shilling freehold," meaning that to vote one had to own at least forty shillings' worth of land. Thus, only men who owned land or other property were viewed as sufficiently responsible to vote. Women were not allowed to vote. Many of the colonies prohibited certain religious groups such as Catholics and Jews from voting, and the southern colonies barred "Negroes and mulattoes" from voting, as well as Native Americans and indentured servants.

The colonial legislatures claimed the right to control local legislation, taxes, and expenditures, as well as to fix the qualifications for and judge the eligibility of house members. They also desired freedom of debate, immunity from unrest, and the right to choose their own assembly speakers. To the colonists, these were their rights as English citizens living under British domain in America. However, the British Parliament claimed these rights for itself as the only representative body of a sovereign nation, viewing the colonies as subordinate entities with no inherent **sovereignty**, or independent authority. In Britain's eyes, the colonial legislatures were entitled only to the privileges the king or Parliament chose to give them. This fundamental clash between colonial legislatures and the power of the British Parliament and Crown eventually erupted into the war that separated the fledgling colonies from the British Empire forever.

Every colony had a governor, the principal executive authority acting as the representative of the Crown. The Crown traditionally appointed colonial governors, although Rhode Island and Connecticut chose their own. The governors wielded an absolute veto, had the power of appointment, and commanded the colony's military forces. They also had the power to call the colonial assembly into session and dismiss it, to create courts, and to name and remove judges. The origins of the modern American presidency can, in part, be found here. The governors were

bicameral legislature A legislative system consisting of two houses or chambers.

sovereignty The independence and self-government of a political entity.

Quick Review

Social Contract Theory

- Provides the philosophical foundation for the obligations that individuals and states have toward each other.
- The state is empowered to enforce appropriate punishment if a citizen violates the social contract.
- Citizens have a right to revolt and even to form another government if the state violates the social contract.
- Provided a philosophical foundation for the Declaration of Independence.

assisted by a council whose members they nominated for life. Almost all judicial authority rested in this council.

But confrontations between the colonial assemblies and the governor occurred frequently. Because the colonial governor was the symbol of royal authority within the colonies and represented Britain's interests, such tension was inevitable, particularly since the colonists developed an extreme suspicion of executive power. In addition, the colonists saw advantages to spreading governmental responsibilities among separate compartments of government rather than concentrating power in the hands of one potentially despotic ruler. In this respect, the thinking of the French philosopher Charles de Montesquieu (1689–1755) was influential. Montesquieu viewed the separation of powers as the best way to counteract tendencies toward despotism. He believed that freedom could be best preserved in a system of checks and balances through which the powers of government are balanced against and checked by one another. Montesquieu's writings, particularly *The Spirit of Laws* (1748), eventually helped the framers of the Constitution formalize a three-part government divided into executive, legislative, and judicial functions.

Social Contract Theorists

Democracy developed and flourished in America because of the new settlers' experience with self-government as well as the emergence of influential new theories of governing. Just as religious leaders of the day derived a notion of social compact from the natural order of life under God, a group of European philosophers known as **social contract theorists** reasoned that individuals existed in a state of nature before the creation of a society or an organized government. Social contracts provide the philosophical foundation for the obligations individuals and states have toward each other. If a citizen violates the social contract, the state is legally empowered to enforce appropriate punishment in the name of the people. If the state breaks the social contract, the citizens have a right to revolt against its excessive authority and even to form another government in its stead. This theory provided a philosophical foundation for the Declaration of Independence.

Thomas Hobbes (1588–1679) was the first of the major social contract theorists. In *Leviathan* (1651), Hobbes described human life under the early state of nature as "nasty, brutish, and short." People needed the authority of the state as protection from one another. Hobbes described people's relationships with each other as "war of all against all . . . a general inclination of all mankind, a perpetual and restless desire of power after power, that ceaseth only in death." In Hobbes's view, life without authority lacks security or liberty; he reasoned that human beings require a Leviathan, or authoritarian leader, to produce harmony and safety.

Hobbes also proposed a comprehensive theory of government. Since life in the state of nature was so threatening, individuals surrendered freedom in return for a government that provided protection and order in the form of a supreme authority, the *sovereign*, to whom all were subject. This embrace of absolute power in the form of a sovereign has led many to dismiss Hobbes as a legitimate founding thinker of modern democratic thought. Yet Hobbes clearly stated that even the authority of the sovereign must be carefully codified into a body of laws, and that those laws must be applied to all with absolute equality. This notion of equality under the law, even in the harsh frontier world of the colonial era, was Hobbes's most significant contribution to social contract theory.

The most influential social contract theorist, though, was John Locke (1632–1704). Locke published extensively on many subjects, but his most significant political works are his *Two Treatises on Government*, published in 1690. Here, Locke rejected the notion of a Hobbesian Leviathan or even a divine right to rule. In the *Second Treatise*, Locke explained his theory of a social contract among citizens to create government and protect property, and for the right to revolt against an unjust government. Locke believed that governments exist to preserve the rights already

social contract theorists A group of European philosophers who reasoned that the most effective way to create the best government was to understand human nature in a state prior to government.

present in society under nature: specifically, the protection of life, the enjoyment of personal liberty, and the possession and pursuit of private property. For Locke, these rights were inalienable, emanating from God's natural law. To deny any individual life, liberty, or property was to take away something granted by God, either through birth, social status, or individual effort and ability.

Above all, and in support of the growing merchant class in England, Locke insisted that government was necessary to protect property, which represented all that was noble in the human embodiment of God, the talents and energy that are the tools of divine will on Earth. Because Locke recognized property as a result of individual ability and energy, he also accepted inequality in the distribution of that property. However, as with Hobbes, Locke believed that all individuals must be equally subject to the laws constituting the social contract between all citizens under government.

Along with the principle of an inalienable right to life, liberty, and property, Locke asserted the importance of limited government based on popular consent. By **limited government**, Locke meant that powers of government should be clearly defined and bounded, so that governmental authority could not intrude in the lives of private citizens. Unlike Hobbes, Locke saw no need for an absolute sovereign but argued instead for a strong legislature. His model was, of course, the British Parliament, whereas Hobbes's sovereign bore more resemblance to the British Crown. But, like Hobbes, Locke insisted that whenever government acts against the interests of the people, the people have a right to react. Because the government has thus broken its part of the social contract, the people may revolt against the leader to create a new government that acts more in line with their interests. Locke's limited government is strong enough to provide protection for all citizens and their property but not so strong that it infringes on individual liberty.

Locke's *Second Treatise on Civil Government* was such a clear statement of citizens' rights that much of the Declaration of Independence draws from his rationale to justify severing ties with a tyrannical king. Locke's idea of limited government is also embedded in the Constitution. The separation of governing powers and the numerous guarantees of individual liberties found in the Bill of Rights are derived from the Lockean notion of limited government based on popular consent.

In Britain, where both Hobbes (for most of his life) and Locke lived, the theory of the social contract was just a theory. In the seventeenth century, however, each American colonial territory in part experimented in the practical application of that theory. In a land that indeed often rendered life "nasty, brutish, and short," with little direct governmental authority in their lives, the colonists did live somewhat in the "state of nature." And, just as both Hobbes and Locke theorized they must, the colonists entered into binding contracts, established laws and ruling bodies, and formed governments. The Mayflower Compact, the Fundamental Orders of Connecticut, and even the rather Hobbesian regimes established in the proprietary colonies all required citizens who would willingly enter into a legally ordered arrangement of power—a society under the rule of law.

FIRST MOVES TOWARD A UNION

By 1753, the Board of Trade in London requested that the colonies "enter into articles of union and confederation with each other for the mutual defense of His Majesty's subjects and interests in North America, as well in time of peace as war." The goal was to protect the economic interests of the empire.

French expansionism in the American backwoods led to increasing conflict and to the French and Indian War (1754–1763), which spread to Europe two years later as the Seven Years' War. Following the outbreak of fighting on the frontier, Britain advised the northern colonies to sign a treaty with the Iroquois, and called a meeting in Albany for this purpose. On May 9, 1754, the *Pennsylvania Gazette* published a lead article and cartoon authored by Ben Franklin to illustrate the perils of disunity.

Question for Reflection

Does social contract theory support the "nuclear option" limitation on the use of filibusters for senate judicial confirmation votes that the Senate Republicans considered proposing?

MakeItReal

Primary Source: The Albany Plan

limited government A type of government in which the powers of the government are clearly defined and bounded, so that governmental authority cannot intrude in the lives of private citizens.

▲ Benjamin Franklin's 1754 "Join or Die" woodcut was originally designed to symbolize the need for the colonies to unite for their common defense against the French. The symbol became popular again during the revolutionary period, when the colonies confronted the British.

Quick Review

Taxation by the British

- The Sugar Act of 1764 extended taxes on foreign refined sugar and various other goods imported into the colonies.
- The Stamp Act of 1765 required revenue stamps on all printed matter and legal documents.
- The Townshend Revenue Acts of 1767 imposed taxes on glass, lead, tea, and paper imported into the colonies.

confederation A league of sovereign states that delegates powers on selected issues to a central government.

At the Albany meeting, Franklin proposed a plan of union calling for a self-governing confederation for the colonies. A **confederation** is a league of sovereign states that delegates powers on selected issues to a central government. The plan proposed a forty-eight-member Grand Legislative Council in which all colonies would be represented; its responsibilities would include raising an army and navy, making war, and regulating trade and taxation. The plan also called for a chief executive, to be called president-general of the United Colonies, appointed by the Crown.

The delegates unanimously endorsed Franklin's so-called Albany Plan, but individual colonial assemblies soon rejected it because it appeared to give too much power to the Crown. The British Crown in turn rejected it, claiming it gave the colonists too much power. Franklin later wrote, "If the foregoing plan, or something like it, had been adopted and carried into execution, the subsequent separation of the colonies from the mother country might not so soon have happened."[4] Some twenty years later, Franklin's design would resurface in an early draft of the Articles of Confederation.

REBELLION: CAUSES AND CONSEQUENCES

With the end of the French and Indian War in 1763, France's claim to power and territory in North America came to an end and Britain took control of the interior of the North American continent to the Mississippi River. But Britain was deeply in debt from financing the war. To alleviate this debt, it turned to the colonies with a program of direct taxation. Prior to 1763, the British were interested in the colonies primarily as new markets and sources of raw materials. Now, undertaking a new policy of imperialism, Britain sought more efficient political and military control in the New World. To this end, several units of British soldiers were dispatched to protect the colonial frontier, at great annual expense to the Crown.

To generate revenues sufficient to defray the expense of British occupation and control, the "first lord of the Treasurey," George Grenville, was elected to raise taxes, first on the already burdened British and then on the American colonists, whose taxes had been relatively modest to this point. Such direct taxation of the colonists without their consent and without representation in Parliament had grave consequences. Resistance to British control and to what the colonists perceived as unjust taxation led to revolution and then to independence.

▶ On July 9, 1776, after the Declaration of Independence was read to assembled troops in Bowling Green, New York, the soldiers, joined by New York patriots, pulled down a gilt equestrian statue of King George III. The statue had been the laughingstock of New York because its sculptor, Wilton of London, failed to put stirrups on the horse that the king is riding. The statue was then melted down and used to make bullets.

The Sugar and Stamp Acts

The British viewed taxation as part of the sovereign's inherent authority and sought to extend its influence and extract revenue from the colonists through a series of acts, most notably the Sugar Act of 1764 and the Stamp Act of 1765. The **Sugar Act** extended taxes on molasses and raw sugar to include foreign refined sugar and various other goods imported into the colonies. The preamble of the Sugar Act stated that the tax was to be used for "defraying the expenses of defending and securing the colonies." This was how the British saw it. The colonists, however, viewed the act as a revenue measure imposed on them by the sovereign, without their consent, that would cut into their profits.

On February 13, 1765, Lord Grenville proposed before Parliament another measure to raise money from the colonies—this time to pay the cost of stationing British troops in America. The **Stamp Act** quickly passed in Parliament in March; it required that revenue stamps be placed on all printed matter and legal documents, including newspapers, almanacs, bonds, leases, college diplomas, bills of sale, liquor licenses, insurance policies, playing cards, and dice. The tax would be felt in every aspect of commercial life in the colonies, its influence extending well beyond that of the sugar tax by affecting more people directly. The act was scheduled to go into effect on November 1, 1765.

Most colonists opposed the Stamp Act, and public protest against it raged throughout the spring and summer of 1765. The American colonists reasoned that because they had no representative in Parliament, Parliament had no right to tax them. To counter the colonists' demand of "no taxation without representation," Parliament offered the idea of "virtual representation," explaining that members of Parliament represent the interests of the whole empire, whether the whole of Ireland or the American colonies. In addition, many new and old boroughs and cities in England did not yet have representation in Parliament. Thus, no practical difference existed between Charleston, South Carolina, and Manchester, England: Neither had a representative in Parliament, but each was nevertheless represented by virtue of Parliament's concern for all British subjects.

The colonists' experiences with their town meetings and colonial assemblies led them to reject the idea of virtual representation. "A mere cobweb, spread to catch the unwary, and entangle the weak," argued Maryland legislator Daniel Dulany. If Manchester was not represented in Parliament, "it ought to be," said Boston attorney James Otis. Ideas about compacts, natural rights, and social contracts informed colonial reaction. The colonists, by virtue of written constitutions and documents, expected the rights of freeborn Englishmen, arguing that a legislature should be "an actual representation of all classes of the people by persons of each class" to be a "true picture of the people." And although they accepted the supremacy of Parliament, they embraced the doctrine of limited government, saying Parliament had no claim to a power that would violate the natural rights and laws to which all free people hold claim.

The colonists had some support in Parliament. Edmund Burke argued, "The British Empire must be governed on a plan of freedom, for it will be governed by no other." In the House of Commons William Pitt argued, "Taxation is no part of the governing or legislating power;" the idea of virtual representation is one of "the most contemptible ideas that ever entered the head of man."[5]

In March 1766, Parliament repealed the Stamp Act. At the same time, however, it passed the Declaratory Act, granting the king and Parliament complete legislative authority to make laws binding to the colonies "in all cases whatsoever."

The Townshend Revenue Acts

In 1767, Parliament sought to impose yet another series of taxes on glass, lead, tea, and paper imported into the colonies. The preamble of the **Townshend Revenue Acts** stated that these acts were intended for "the support of civil government, in

Sugar Act A British act of 1764 that levied a three-penny-per-gallon tax on molasses and other goods imported into the colonies.

Stamp Act A British act of 1765 that required that revenue stamps be placed on all printed matter and legal documents, making it felt in every aspect of commercial life in the colonies.

Townshend Revenue Acts A series of taxes imposed by the British Parliament in 1767 on glass, lead, tea, and paper imported into the colonies.

Boston Massacre A 1770 incident in which British soldiers fired a volley of shots into a crowd of hecklers who had been throwing snowballs at the red-coats; five colonists were killed.

such provinces as it shall be found necessary." Revenues would also be used to pay salaries for governors and other officers, thereby diluting the strength of colonial assemblies, which until then had controlled governors' salaries.

Few colonists protested Parliament's authority to regulate trade among the colonies of its empire, but most believed that only the colonial assemblies had the authority to directly tax the colonies. The Townshend Acts provoked numerous boy-cotts and mob actions as well as the fourteen "Letters of a Farmer in Pennsylvania," an eloquent and moderate interpretation of the colonial position written by John Dickinson. "The cause of Liberty is a cause of too much dignity to be sullied by tur-bulence and tumult," Dickenson cautioned. Appearing in the *Pennsylvania Chronicle*, the letters challenged British authority. "For who are a free people? Not those over whom government is reasonably and equitably exercised, but those who live under a government so constitutionally checked and controlled, that proper provision is made against its being otherwise exercised."

The Boston Massacre

Meanwhile, customs commissioners had found it increasingly difficult to collect tax duties and asked Parliament to send troops. The redcoats arrived in Boston in October 1768, where their presence further incited anger. The cause of revolution was soon to have its first martyrs. On March 5, 1770, British soldiers fired a volley of shots into a crowd of hecklers. Five colonists were killed, including Crispus Attucks, son of a black father and Indian mother. The first colonists had now lost their lives protesting taxa-tion without representation. The **Boston Massacre** aroused intense public protest. Within a month, all the Townshend duties were repealed except the tax on tea. The massacre also alerted the colonists to a dramatic truth—organized local resistance revealed the impotence of imperial power in the colonies.

▶ Paul Revere's dramatic engraving of the Boston Massacre depicts the initial bloody conflict between British troops (redcoats) and Boston labor-ers. Months after the shooting, prints of the massacre could be found all over the colony. Revere added the words "Butcher's Hall" over the Customs House, which helped incite those who called the incident a massacre.

Committees of Correspondence

The colonists' ability to publicize Parliamentary encroachment on their rights helped fuel revolutionary fervor. In 1772, Samuel Adams emerged as a major agitator for colonial independence by forming the Boston Committee of Correspondence, which published a statement of rights and grievances warning colonists that Britain could disband colonial legislatures and take away individual rights. Similar committees quickly sprang up throughout Massachusetts and the other colonies. **Committees of Correspondence** thus became the first institutionalized mechanism for communication among the colonies, greatly advancing their cooperation. One loyalist (a person loyal to Britain) called the committees (no doubt a tribute to their effectiveness) "the foulest, subtlest, and most venomous serpent ever issued from the egg of sedition."

The Boston Tea Party

The British East India Company had fallen on hard times. Before the Townshend Acts, the company had been the chief supplier of tea to the colonists. In an effort to avoid paying the Townshend duty, colonists started smuggling in tea from the Netherlands, thus cutting deeply into the East India Company's profits. With 17 million pounds of tea in its warehouses, the company asked Parliament for help. Parliament allowed the company to sell tea to the colonies at a price below market value. The Tea Act, passed in May 1773, retained the hated and symbolic duty on tea.

The colonists were in an uproar, realizing that colonial tea merchants would be undercut. Even worse, no one knew which commodity might be next. Colonial women, among the principal consumers of tea, led a boycott against it. An organization of colonial women known as the Daughters of Liberty committed itself to agitation against British policies, proclaiming that "rather than Freedom, we'll part with our Tea." Parliament's actions also provoked a famous incident, the **Boston Tea Party**. At midnight on December 16, 1773, colonists disguised as Native Americans dumped 342 chests of tea into Boston Harbor.

To punish Massachusetts for the tea party and send a message to the other colonies, the king and his ministers legislated the Coercive Acts. The colonists dubbed this series of punitive measures, passed by Parliament in the spring of 1774, the **Intolerable Acts**. In addition to closing Boston Harbor until the tea was paid for and requiring the quartering of British soldiers in private homes, the acts created the position of military governor. General Thomas Gage, commander in chief of British forces in North America, was named to the post. Gage's consent was necessary for convening most town meetings, making him all but a dictator. In addition, he could use **writs of assistance**, a general search warrant issued for British customs officials to search colonists' houses to enforce the taxes on goods, to also search every part of a house for evidence of a crime, whether real or perceived.

Rather than forcing the colonists to submit to the will of King George III, the Intolerable Acts helped to unify the colonies against the Crown. Massachusetts's plight inspired other colonies to defend its cause. A young member of Virginia's Committee of Correspondence, Thomas Jefferson, proposed setting aside June 1, the date of the closing of Boston Harbor, as a day of fasting and prayer in Virginia, hundreds of miles to the south. With this first instance of one colony's empathy for another's plight, a new nation was beginning to emerge. On learning of Jefferson's proposal, the Virginia royal governor immediately dissolved the assembly, whose members went down the road to the Raleigh Tavern and drew up a resolution calling for a congress with representation from all the colonies.[6]

Committees of Correspondence Formed in Boston in 1772, the first institutionalized mechanism for communication within and between the colonies and foreign countries.

Boston Tea Party A 1773 act of civil disobedience in which colonists dressed as Native Americans dumped 342 chests of tea into Boston Harbor to protest increased taxes.

Intolerable Acts A series of punitive measures passed by the British Parliament in the spring of 1774 as a response to the Boston Tea Party.

writs of assistance A general search warrant issued for British customs officials to search colonists' houses to enforce the taxes on goods that enabled them as well to search every part of a house for evidence of a crime, whether real or perceived.

Question for Reflection

At what point is it acceptable under social contract theory for the people to refuse to observe the laws of their government and even consider breaking away from that government?

REVOLUTION AND THE STIRRINGS OF A NEW GOVERNMENT

In the wake of the Boston Tea Party, the colonists' differences with the Crown moved far beyond the taxation issue. While the tax policies of Lord Grenville had served to ignite the first intense clash between Britain and America, the heavy-handed response of the Intolerable Acts revealed the real basis of the schism between Crown and colonies. The British wanted order and obedience; the colonists wanted greater liberty. "Although Liberty was not the only goal for Americans in the 1770s and 1780s," writes political scientist James MacGregor Burns, "they believed also in Independence, Order, Equality, the Pursuit of Happiness—none had the evocative power and sweep of Liberty, or Freedom—two terms for the same thing. To preserve liberty was the supreme end of government."[7] In Boston, this sentiment had taken the form of standing up to the hated British troops stationed there and dumping tea into the harbor. At the First Continental Congress, the signs of both revolution and American democracy were visible. In a speech before the Virginia Convention on March 23, 1775, Patrick Henry cried out, "Is life so dear, or peace so sweet, as to be purchased at the price of chains and slavery? Forbid it, Almighty God! I know not what course others may take; but as for me, give me liberty, or give me death!"

The First Continental Congress

On September 5, 1774, fifty-six elected delegates from provincial congresses or conventions of all the colonies except Georgia met in the **First Continental Congress** at Philadelphia's Carpenters Hall. They initially sought to reestablish more cordial relations with the British Crown while insisting on the restoration of their rights as English citizens. The delegates included Samuel Adams and John Adams of Massachusetts, John Jay of New York, John Dickinson of Pennsylvania, and Patrick Henry and George Washington of Virginia. Before leaving for Philadelphia, Washington wrote to a friend expressing the intensity of feelings common to those attending the Congress: "The crisis is arrived when we must assert our rights, or submit to every imposition, that can be heaped upon us, till custom and use shall make us as tame and abject [as] slaves, as the blacks we rule over with such arbitrary sway."[8]

The First Continental Congress issued the Declaration of American Rights, claiming in the name of the colonies exclusive legislative power over taxation and "all the rights, liberties, and communities of free and natural-born subjects within the realm of England." The Congress also rejected a plan of union introduced by George Galloway of Pennsylvania that closely resembled Franklin's Albany Plan of twenty years earlier. It did endorse the plan delivered from Suffolk County, Massachusetts by silversmith Paul Revere. These Suffolk Resolves declared the Intolerable Acts null and void, supported arming Massachusetts to defend itself against Britain, and urged economic sanctions on Britain. The delegates agreed to meet again in May 1775 if Britain did not restore the rights it had taken away. Most delegates still hoped to avoid war with Britain; few were ready to publicly declare a war for American independence.[9]

The Shot Heard 'Round the World

Following the Boston Tea Party, Parliament had declared Massachusetts to be in open rebellion, giving British troops the right to shoot rebels on sight. General Gage, determined to put down this rebellion on the night of April 18, 1775, marched west to Concord, near Boston, to destroy ammunition and gunpowder being stored by the local militia. Paul Revere and others rode furiously through the night to give warning. Although Revere was captured, William Dawes was able to alert the colonists. Just after dawn, when the British reached Lexington, they were met by seventy minutemen—as the local militia were called because they were to be ready to take up arms at a minute's

First Continental Congress The meeting of fifty-six elected members (from provincial congresses or irregular conventions) held in Philadelphia's Carpenter's Hall in 1774. It resulted in a resolution to oppose acts of the British Parliament and a plan of association for the colonies.

notice. Gage ordered the militia to disperse. A stray shot was fired, the British opened fire, and eight Americans were killed. The British continued their march on to Concord where they clashed with minutemen at Concord's North Bridge. At Concord the British met with the first American resistance, in Longfellow's words, "the shot heard 'round the world." By day's end, 250 British troops and 90 Americans were dead or wounded. The colonies were now at war with the powerful British Empire, and the American War of Independence was under way.

The Second Continental Congress

Three weeks after the clashes at Lexington and Concord, the **Second Continental Congress** convened on May 10, 1775, with all thirteen colonies represented. The Congress would decide whether or not to break from England and declare independence. The brief but dramatic skirmishes at Lexington and Concord were still fresh in the minds of the delegates. In the absence of any other legislative body, without any legal authority to speak of, and in the midst of growing hostility toward the British, the Congress had little choice but to assume the role of a revolutionary government. It took control of the militia gathered around Boston and named George Washington general and commander in chief of this ragtag army. Then, on June 17, came the first major confrontation between the colonials and British forces—the Battle of Bunker Hill. The delegates, still hoping for a reconciliation, sent the "Olive Branch Petition" to King George III. But the king refused to receive it, and Parliament rejected it as well. The course toward American independence was now fixed.

Common Sense

At the same time, Thomas Paine's pamphlet of January 1776, *Common Sense* (published anonymously to avoid charges of treason) helped crystallize the idea of revolution for the colonists. Paine, who would later serve with General Washington during the war, moved beyond merely stating the colonists' claims against Parliament to questioning the very institution of monarchy. He also concluded that the colonies needed to separate from England immediately. Paine wrote:

> A government of our own is our natural right; and when a man seriously reflects on the precariousness of human affairs, he will become convinced, that it is infinitely wiser and safer to form a constitution of our own in a cool, deliberate manner, while we have it in our power, than to trust such an interesting event to time and chance. . . .
> Ye that tell us of harmony and reconciliation, can ye restore to us the time that is passed? Can ye give to prostitution its former innocence? Neither can ye reconcile Britain and America. The last cord now is broken.

In addition, *Common Sense* enumerated the advantages of republican government over monarchy and argued that an American republic would be a laboratory for a political experiment in which citizens would enjoy full representation and equality of rights. *Common Sense* profoundly influenced thinking in the colonies. As George Washington observed, "*Common Sense* is working a powerful change in the minds of men." More than 150,000 copies of the pamphlet were sold within three months of its first printing. Virtually every colonist had access to it, and the demand for independence escalated rapidly.

The Declaration of Independence

On June 7, 1776, a resolution for independence was introduced by Richard Henry Lee, a Virginia delegate to the Continental Congress:

> Resolved, that these United Colonies are, and of right ought to be, free and independent States, and that they are absolved from all allegiance to the British Crown, and that all connection between them and the State of Great Britain is, and ought to be, totally dissolved.

MakeItReal

Primary Source: The Declaration of Independence (See also Appendix, pages 609–610.)

Second Continental Congress
A meeting convened on May 10, 1775, with all thirteen colonies represented. The Congress met to decide whether or not to sever bonds with England and declare independence.

Common Sense Thomas Paine's pamphlet of January 1776, which helped crystallize the idea of revolution for the colonists.

"O.K., the third of July is out. How about the fourth?"

No longer was the reestablishment of their "rights as Englishmen" sufficient for the colonial leaders attending the Congress; it was to be independence or nothing. Lee's resolution for independence was considered and finally passed when the Congress reconvened on July 2. Writing to his wife, Abigail, John Adams predicted that July 2 would be "the most memorable epoch in the history of America." In the meantime, a committee had already formed to draft a formal proclamation declaring independence. This committee included John Adams, Ben Franklin, and Thomas Jefferson. Jefferson, thirty-three, of Virginia, drafted the final document on which the Congress voted. On July 4, after three days of vigorous debate, the Declaration of Independence was approved and signed. According to legend, John Hancock, the first to sign, wrote his name so large because "I want John Bull to be able to read my signature without spectacles."

The **Declaration of Independence** renounced allegiance to the British Crown, justified the Revolution, and provided a philosophical basis for limited government based on popular consent. Clearly echoing social contract theorist John Locke, the Declaration proclaimed that the colonists were "created equal" and were endowed, by God, with inalienable rights to life, liberty, and the pursuit of happiness. The Declaration also proclaimed that government was instituted to secure these rights and derived its just powers from the consent of the governed. When governments become destructive of these ends, the people have the right to reconstitute it. The Declaration listed the colonists' many grievances against King George III and concluded that he had become "a Tyrant" who was "unfit to be the ruler of a free People." Thus, the colonies "are, and of right ought to be Free and Independent States."

By instituting government based on popular consent, in which power is exercised by representatives chosen by and responsive to the populace, the eighteenth-century revolutionaries sought "to become republican." Political power would come from the people, not a supreme authority such as a king. The ultimate success of a government would depend on the civic virtue of its citizenry. The key assumption was that "if the population consisted of sturdy, independent property owners imbued with civic virtue, then the republic could survive."[10] As James Madison later wrote, "No other form would be reconcilable with the genius of the people of America; with the fundamental principles of the revolution; or with the honorable determination, which animates every votary of freedom, to rest all our political experiments on the capacity of mankind for self-government."

However, the delegates' support of freedom and the social contract, and their opposition to tyranny, did not extend everywhere. Jefferson's initial draft complained that King George had "waged cruel war against human nature itself, violating its most sacred rights of life & liberty in the persons of a distant people, who never offended him, captivating and carrying them into slavery in another hemisphere, or to incur miserable death in their transportation thither, this piratical warfare, the opprobrium of *infidel* powers, is the warfare of the *Christian* king of Great Britain, determined to keep open a market where MEN should be bought & sold . . ." In short, Jefferson, a slave owner himself, was complaining about the practice of slavery in the colonies and seemingly arguing that slaves should be equal as well. But the southern delegates did not agree, and by forcing the convention to strike this clause from the draft to ensure a unanimous call against the King, the Congress left this controversial issue to be resolved by civil war more than three-quarters of a century later.

Also absent from inclusion in the document was a discussion of the rights of women, a fact not missed by Abigail Adams, the wife of John Adams. No women attended the Continental Congress, nor were any involved in the drafting of the Declaration of Independence, but they did play an essential role in campaigns to boycott British goods in protest against the taxes imposed by Parliament. They were also active behind the scenes during the Revolution; women plowed fields, managed shops, and melted down pots to make shot. Yet they played virtually no part in political affairs; women could not vote, nor could they hold elective office.

Declaration of Independence
The formal proclamation declaring independence for the thirteen colonies of England in North America, approved and signed on July 4, 1776.

The only route open to politically inclined women was to persuade their husbands to act on their behalf in Congress and the state assemblies. Abigail Adams did just that in writing to her husband, John, who was then drafting the Declaration of Independence at the Continental Congress. "I desire you would remember the Ladies," she wrote, "and be more generous and favourable to them than your ancestors." Although she conceded that women were "beings placed by providence under [male] protection," she issued a challenge, if only half seriously: "If particuliar care and attention is not paid to the Ladies we are determined to foment a Rebellion, and will not hold ourselves bound by any laws in which we have no voice, or Representation. That your Sex are Naturally Tyrannical is a Truth so thoroughly established as to admit of no dispute, but such of you as wish to be happy willingly give up the harsh title of Master for the more tender and endearing one of Friend."

John was amused by his wife's remarks on behalf of "another Tribe more numerous and powerfull than all the rest. . . . After stirring up Tories, Landjobbers, Trimmers, Bigots, Canadians, Indians, Negroes, Hanoverians, Hessians, Irish Catholicks, Scotch Renegadoes, at last [the members of the Congress] have stimulated the ladies to demand new Priviledges and threaten to rebell." But he was quick to point out that such a rebellion would lead nowhere: "Depend upon it, We know better than to repeal our Masculine systems" and submit to "the Despotism of the Peticoat." Though Abigail appears to have been teasing her husband, we may see in her correspondence a glimmer of what would ultimately emerge as modern feminism.[11]

By signing the Declaration, these revolutionaries were risking "our Lives, our Fortunes and our sacred Honor." The Declaration itself was an act of treason against the Crown, punishable by death. After he put his signature to the document, Ben Franklin is alleged to have remarked, "We must, indeed, all hang together, or most assuredly we shall hang separately."

THE FIRST NEW GOVERNMENT: A CONFEDERATION OF STATES

Even before the War of Independence was won, Americans faced the challenge of devising a new government. To do this, they drew from their experiences with compacts, social contract theory, separation of governmental powers, and natural rights. Between 1776 and 1780, all states adopted new constitutions except Rhode Island and Connecticut, which simply struck from their original governing charters any mention of colonial obligation to the Crown. Seven of the state constitutions contained a separate bill of rights guaranteeing citizens certain natural rights and protection from their government. The Virginia Bill of Rights, for example, provided for the right of revolution, freedom of the press, religious liberty, separation of powers, free elections, prohibition against taxation without consent, and fair legal procedures such as the right to trial by jury and moderate bail.

None of these state constitutions contained any provision for a central governmental authority that would help define the thirteen states as a nation. Thus, a few days after the Declaration of Independence was signed, a committee was called to draft a plan to bring the colonies together as a confederation. Fighting a war for independence necessitated a central direction, a plan for union.

The Articles of Confederation (1781–1789)

On July 12, 1777, after six drafts, the **Articles of Confederation** were presented to the Continental Congress. Following several months of debate, on November 15, 1777, the plan was adopted by the Congress and submitted to the individual states for ratification. The Articles formally took effect on March 1, 1781, after being ratified by all of the states.

Articles of Confederation The first constitutional framework of the new United States of America. Approved in 1777 by the Second Continental Congress, it was later replaced by the current Constitution.

The colonists were not about to jeopardize the power and freedom they had won, so the Articles sought to limit the powers of the government. The confederation they created was a loosely knit alliance of thirteen independent states agreeing to cooperate in certain instances. The central government was extremely weak. All of the national power—executive, legislative, and judicial—was housed in a single house of Congress in which each state had one vote. Fearing a new king, the writers of the Articles did not create a separate executive branch.

Under the Articles, the states reigned supreme in a "league of friendship." They retained almost total sovereignty over their affairs. Congress held strictly limited powers. It could not tax, though it could coin its own money. It could declare war but not raise an army. Thus, after the Revolution was won, Congress could not act when the British refused to decamp from their forts on the Great Lakes in 1783; it was powerless when the Spanish closed off the Mississippi River and the port of New Orleans to United States trade and when both Spain and Britain began arming Native Americans in the hope that they would attack frontier settlements. Their Congress had no power over interstate or international commerce and no power to make treaties with foreign governments. Instead, each state could make its own foreign policy. Congress could not even make laws; it was limited to passing resolutions or regulations. It took the agreement of nine states to pass any legislation and a unanimous vote of all thirteen to amend the Articles. Unable to raise funds, the Congress had to borrow vast sums of money from France and Holland to pay for the war with Britain. Unable to defend itself without voluntary support of state militias and powerless to legislate, the new central government was simply too weak to govern effectively.

The problems of the confederation of states seemed to grow, ranging from financial and commercial difficulties to civil disorder. The inevitable political chaos made the new United States appear not so much a nation as an organization of thirteen little kingdoms, each directed by a state legislature. The irony here, of course, is that the Articles did exactly what they were devised to do. Independent state legislatures often acted against each other, even levying duties on trade that crossed state lines. James Madison summed up the problem: "Experience had proved a tendency in our governments to throw all power into the Legislative vortex. The Executives of the State are in general little more than Cyphers: the legislatures omnipotent. If no effectual check be devised for restraining the instability and encroachments of the latter, a revolution of some kind or other would be inevitable."[12] With the "omnipotent" state legislatures operating to the advantage of their individual interests, certain states flourished economically. Agricultural exports doubled, and the national debt was so low that states were paying back principal as well as interest. The states were cooperating in their trade policies to keep out British goods and were working together to raise money for capital improvements. The central government, however, proved incapable of handling crises.

This was clearly demonstrated in the crisis known as Shays's Rebellion. In 1786, Daniel Shays, a Revolutionary War veteran and a farmer in western Massachusetts, along with other farmers in the region, fought a second revolution, this time for economic independence, striking fear into the hearts of the nation's political leaders. Economic conditions in the new nation had deteriorated, particularly for farmers, who lacked markets and could not pay off their debts. They often were forced to pay exorbitant interest rates, and those who could not pay faced prison or indentured servitude. Making matters worse, the farmers lacked government representation for their interests because the Massachusetts state legislature was dominated by merchants from the eastern part of the state (most farmers were from the western part).

To protest this situation, the farmers succeeded in shutting down several local courts, some by setting them ablaze. They also demanded that the Massachusetts legislature print cheap paper money—as Rhode Island had done—that would be acceptable to creditors. The legislature refused and instead legislated new taxes. When these protests and a series of anti-tax petitions failed to improve their economic situation, the farmers rebelled. Shays led a force of 2,500 men against the state militia. Ironically, members of the militia included men who had fought with Shays at Bunker Hill. After a series of confrontations, the Shaysites were finally repelled by General Benjamin Lincoln, a hero of the Revolution. The populist rebellion horrified most of the new nation's political leaders, who were also of the wealthy, propertied class. By threatening the institutions created to protect property (the banks and courts), the Shaysites appeared to threaten liberty and replace it with anarchy. The revolt was put down, but it became clear that Shays's Rebellion served an important purpose. It helped strengthen the position of those advocating stronger centralized government.[13]

THE NEED FOR A MORE PERFECT UNION

After six years of confederation, it became clear that a stronger, more centralized government was needed. Shays's Rebellion led the colonists to fear anarchy and desire order. Even George Washington recognized that the Articles were founded on a too trusting view of human nature. The states seemed incapable of ensuring order, let alone promoting the common good.

Even as Shays's Rebellion gained momentum, delegates from five states, largely at the instigation of James Madison, met at Annapolis, Maryland. When the dozen men failed to solve the problems of interstate economic competition and promote interstate commerce, Madison and Alexander Hamilton, who emerged as leaders, clearly saw that the solution would require more than mere commercial agreements. So, they persuaded the delegates to invite all of the states to send delegates to a convention in Philadelphia in May 1787.

After five states agreed to send delegates, on February 21, 1787, the Confederation Congress endorsed the meeting "for the sole and express purpose of revising the Articles of Confederation." But most delegates knew that mere revision of the Articles would not be enough. The complex mix of economic, political, and other problems plaguing the confederation required more than a loose arrangement of individual states struggling to sink or swim on their own, it needed a centralized authority for the common protection and prosperity of all.

The Convention met in the East Room of the State House, the same room in which the Second Continental Congress had met in May 1775 and the Declaration of Independence had been signed in 1776. It opened on May 14 but could do nothing for lack of a quorum, and delegates continued straggling in until well into the

◄ The American Revolution was fought on the twin principles of liberty and equality, but slavery became the practice of the land. Several leaders of the Revolution owned slaves. Shown here, a slave auction in Virginia, where human beings of all ages were sold to the highest bidder.

Table 2.1 ▪ The Founding: Key Events

1620 Mayflower Compact signed. Plymouth Colony founded.

1630 Massachusetts Bay Colony founded.

1760 King George III assumes the throne of England.

1764 Sugar Act passed by Parliament.

1765 Stamp Act passed by Parliament. Delegates to Stamp Act Congress draft declaration of rights and liberties.

1766 Stamp Act repealed. Declaratory Act issued.

1767 Townshend Acts passed.

1770 Boston Massacre. Townshend Acts limited to tea.

1772 First Committee of Correspondence formed by Samuel Adams.

1773 Boston Tea Party.

1774 Coercive Acts against Massachusetts passed. First Continental Congress convened.

1775 Skirmish at Lexington and Concord officially begins the War of Independence. Second Continental Congress convened.

1776 *Common Sense* published. Declaration of Independence signed.

1781 Articles of Confederation adopted.

1783 Peace of Paris. Great Britain formally recognizes the independence of the United States.

1786 Shays's Rebellion.

summer. Four months later, they accomplished what is frequently described as "the Miracle at Philadelphia." Table 2.1 summarizes the key events that produced this "miracle."

THE CONSTITUTIONAL CONVENTION

The unique nature of the American Constitution and its success, both in forging a nation fragmented under the Articles of Confederation and in guiding that nation for centuries to come, can be explained in many ways. Part of the answer lies in the democratic political theory of the time, theory applied to the problems facing the government. However, theory does not govern a nation. People do. So the framing of the Constitution in 1787 is better understood by examining the circumstances under which various theories were advanced in debate and the people who debated and who made the compromises that led to success.

The Task

The problems of governing under the Articles of Confederation made it clear that a stronger central government was needed. But the mission of the Constitutional Convention was not quite so clear. Several states had already authorized their delegates "to render the constitution of government adequate to the exigencies of the Union." Some of the delegates came to the Convention with an understanding that the Articles needed to be scrapped altogether, and they were prepared to propose a new form of government from the outset.[14] Their success in doing so would be decided by whichever of the fifty-five men attending the Convention happened to be present during those debates. But it was not a preordained success, as William Grayson, representative from Virginia in the Confederation Congress, wrote: "What will be the result of their meeting I cannot with any certainty determine, but I hardly think much good can come of it: the people of America don't appear to me to be ripe for any great innovations."[15]

The Participants

While many have come to see the participants of the Constitutional Convention as legends, the delegates are better understood as skilled and ambitious politicians. The result came about not from a singular theoretical vision of a government but from a series of brilliant political compromises and fortuitous events.

The delegates came from a narrow band of American society, the elite aristocracy. This fact should not be surprising: Less than 5 percent of the total population (150,000 of 3.9 million people)—free, white males over the age of twenty-one, who owned land—could vote. Many rich men were present. More than half were lawyers, another quarter were large plantation owners, eight were judges, and the rest were doctors, merchants, bankers, clergymen, and soldiers. All of the delegates owned property, and several owned slaves. Although it was a young group, with more than three-fourths under the age of fifty, what distinguished this group was its experience in politics. There were several former members of the Continental Congress, forty-two members of the Confederation Congress, and seven former governors.

Their efforts at drafting earlier political documents gave these experienced states-men an understanding of the issues and the need for compromise. Six delegates had signed the Declaration of Independence; nine more, including George Mason of Virginia, Alexander Hamilton of New York, and John Rutledge of South Carolina, had drafted their state's constitutions. Both Roger Sherman of Connecticut and John Dickinson of Delaware had played a major role in drafting the Articles of Confederation, and three other members—Elbridge Gerry of Massachusetts, and Gouverneur Morris and Robert Morris of Pennsylvania—had been among its signers.

Although elite and experienced, the delegates were far from representative of the general population. Only two delegates were farmers, even though 85 percent of the citizens lived on small farms. No members of the working class, no artisans, business-men, or tradesmen appear among the delegates. African Americans, Native Americans, and women were nowhere to be found in the meeting either. More than 600,000,

◄ Second Street in Philadelphia as the framers saw it. In the center of this view in the late 1700s is Christ Church, where the drafters of the Constitution went to pray for divine guidance in the successful conclusion of their Convention.

▲ James Madison (1751–1836), a political scientist and prolific note-taker at the Constitutional Convention, was very influential in the framing of the Constitution, which applied his theories of government.

or just under 18 percent of the total population, was African American, about 520,000 of whom were slaves living in the South, while most of the rest were poor, working-class laborers in the northern cities.[16] Native Americans did not participate because, viewed as foreigners, they were specifically excluded from the Constitution, except in the "interstate commerce" power of Article I, Section 8, where they were lumped with the foreign nations as possible trading partners. Few Catholics or Jews were among the political elite from which the delegates were drawn.[17] For all practical purposes, women in American society had no political rights. Since they did not have the vote, participation in politics, much less the Convention, was inconceivable. Thus, no woman attended a state ratifying convention or voted for a state convention delegate. Despite this lack of diversity at the Convention, however, the framers crafted a constitution capable of including women and other groups over time.

The Major Players

The proponents of a strong national government (called *nationalists*) were led by James Madison, who would later be called "the Father of the Constitution." A short, thin, painfully shy, thirty-six-year-old bachelor from Virginia, Madison was one of the best political theorists of his day. He spent months preparing for the Convention, studying and developing a new plan for a strong, central national government to counteract the problems of the Articles of Confederation.

Opposing Madison were the states' rights proponents (called *antinationalists*), led by New Jersey's William Paterson. The son of a shopkeeper and a lawyer by trade, Paterson believed that as a representative of the state of New Jersey, his actions should consider the needs of small states. He argued that the power and position of individual states had to be protected from the proposed central government. Joining Paterson was his old friend Luther Martin. The most prominent lawyer in his native Maryland, Martin saw states as sovereign entities deserving greater protection than people, but his characteristic heavy drinking—his nickname was "Lawyer Brandy Bottle"—diminished his persuasiveness at the Convention.

The wide gulf between the nationalists and the antinationalists made Roger Sherman of Connecticut a major player in the discussions. The third oldest delegate to the convention at age sixty-six, Sherman had spent nearly all of his life in public service. As the only man to have signed all of the new nation's formative documents, Sherman was a cautious, careful politician who bargained for the common ground that would secure a negotiated compromise.

Plans for a New Government

Governor Edmund Randolph of Virginia opened the formal debate on May 29, 1787, with a four-hour speech containing fifteen resolves, or resolutions, for a "strong consolidated union" rather than a federal one with continued state power. When the delegates agreed the next day to debate these resolves, the Convention was no longer a debate about improving the Articles of Confederation; it was about creating an entirely new form of government.

Once it was decided that the Articles of Confederation would be replaced, two central questions guided debate:

1. How powerful would the new national government be?
2. How powerful would the states be?

Of five plans submitted to the delegates for consideration, debate centered on two of them: the Virginia Plan and the New Jersey Plan. The differences between these two proposals show clearly the divisions among large-state and small-state advocates.

The Virginia Plan   The **Virginia Plan**, presented by Governor Randolph, was so named because he and its author, James Madison, came from Virginia. Delegates from the bigger states favored this proposal. It was based on the following

Virginia Plan A plan presented to the Constitutional Convention; favored by the delegates from the bigger states.

propositions designed to remedy the perceived defects in the Articles of Confederation:

1. It called for three branches of government: a **legislative branch** that makes laws, an **executive branch** that executes the laws, and a **judiciary** that interprets the laws. Madison feared the negative effects of power and so proposed a system of **checks and balances**. For every power in government, an equal and opposite power in a separate branch would restrain its force. This idea presumed another feature of the new government, the **separation of powers**, meaning that the powers of government are divided among the three branches, thus preventing the accumulation of too much power in any one branch.

2. Operating from a belief that the ultimate power to govern resides in the people, Randolph proposed a system of **proportional representation**, meaning that the size of each state's delegation in both houses of Congress would be based on the size of its population, rather than the one-state, one-vote rule in the Articles of Confederation. The size of Virginia's population (691,737) would give it more than ten times as many members in Congress as Delaware (population 59,096).

3. Congress would have a bicameral legislature, consisting of two houses, both apportioned on the basis of population. A state would send members to the lower house, elected directly by the people. The lower house would elect the upper house from nominees provided by the state legislatures.

4. The executive, whose size was yet to be determined, would be elected for a maximum of one term by Congress.

5. The judiciary, which would consist of one or more supreme courts and other national courts, would be staffed by life-tenured judges.

6. There would also be a **council of revision**, a combined body of judges and members of the executive branch, having a limited veto over national legislation and an absolute veto over state legislation.

7. The legislature would have the power to override state laws.

It is not hard to see the impact of the Virginia Plan. It centered power in the national government, giving it authority over the states. And by placing much of the governing and appointment powers in a legislature chosen by proportional representation, states with the largest population would dominate that branch. Since Congress had established the executive branch, the big states would dominate there as well, thus giving them control over the central government.

The New Jersey Plan   Representatives of small states found the Madisonian notion of proportional representation unacceptable because it allowed populous states to force their will on smaller states. "New Jersey will never confederate on the plan," William Paterson said. "She would be swallowed up. . . . Myself or my state will never submit to tyranny or despotism." This reaction infuriated Pennsylvania's James Wilson, who asked, "Does it require 150 [voters of my state] to balance 50 [of yours]?"[18] The small-state delegates countered with a series of resolutions advanced by Paterson called the **New Jersey Plan**. This plan was designed to refine and strengthen the Articles of Confederation rather than to replace it, and in so doing, it protected the interests of the smaller, less populous states. The New Jersey Plan proposed the following:

1. The power of the national government would be centered in a **unicameral** (one-house) **legislature**, and, to minimize the impact of population, each state would have one vote.

2. A multiperson executive board would be elected by the legislature for one term only, and authorized to enforce national laws even in the face of opposition from the states. The executive could be removed by a majority of state governors.

3. A supreme court, appointed by the executive board, would deal with impeachment of national officers, foreign policy questions, and tax and trade problems.

4. The power to tax imports would be taken away from the states and given to the national government.

legislative branch The branch of government that makes laws.

executive branch The branch of the government that executes laws.

judiciary The branch of government that interprets laws.

checks and balances Systems that ensure that every power in government has an equal and opposite power in a separate branch to restrain that force.

separation of powers State in which the powers of the government are divided among the three branches: executive, legislative, and judicial.

proportional representation A system of representation popular in Europe whereby the number of seats in the legislature is based on the proportion of the vote received in the election.

council of revision A combined body of judges and members of the executive branch having a limited veto over national legislation and an absolute veto over state legislation.

New Jersey Plan A plan presented to the Constitutional Convention of 1787 designed to create a unicameral legislature with equal representation for all states. Its goal was to protect the interests of the smaller, less populous states.

unicameral legislature A legislative system consisting of one chamber.

Table 2.2 ■ Differences Between the Virginia and New Jersey Plans

Issue	Virginia Plan	New Jersey Plan
Source of legislative power	Derived from the people and based on popular representation	Derived from the states and based on equal votes for each state
Legislative structure	Bicameral	Unicameral
Executive	Size undetermined, elected and removable by Congress	More than one person, removable by state majority
Judiciary	Life-tenured, able to veto state legislation in council of revision	No power over states
State laws	Legislature can override	Government can compel obedience to national laws
Ratification	By the people	By the states

5. The legislature would be empowered to tax state governments based on population and collect the money by force if an unspecified number of states agreed.

6. All congressional acts would become "the supreme law of the respective states," and the executive board could use force to "compel an obedience to such acts" if necessary.

Although this plan increased the power of the central government, it clearly left a great deal more power in the hands of the states. In this way, the New Jersey Plan was much closer to what the delegates were originally sent to do at the Convention. And with each state having an equal voice in many government actions, the small states would continue to play a prominent role. In spite of the state-centered philosophy of this plan, its provision making congressional acts "supreme law" and compelling obedience to national acts (not found in the Virginia Plan) became an early version of what is known as the **supremacy clause** of the Constitution. This clause holds that in any conflict between federal laws and treaties and state laws, the will of the national government always prevails. Just as when the government moved against the Communist threat in the 1940s and 1950s, a good part of the effort was left to the national government. If a dispute were to arise now between the national and state governments in dealing with terrorism, the national government's policy would prevail. Provisions like this one, along with granting the central government the power to tax, made possible compromise with strong-central-government advocates of the Virginia Plan.

Whether the New Jersey Plan could have successfully governed America, or whether, as some think, it was a proposal designed specifically to thwart the notion of proportional representation at the convention, remains a matter of debate.[19] Table 2.2 provides a quick overview of the differences between the Virginia and New Jersey Plans.

Swayed by an impassioned speech by James Madison, the delegates chose the Virginia Plan over the New Jersey Plan by a vote of 7 to 3. The representatives of the small states then turned their attention to achieving influence for their states in the new government. Only by securing a compromise on the proportional representation aspects of the Virginia Plan, they reasoned, would their states have any voice in the government. Thus, it was over this issue that the Convention's success would turn.

Debate and Compromise: The Turning Point of the Convention

By the middle of June, the Convention had split into two opposing groups: the "big states" composed of Massachusetts, Pennsylvania, Virginia, New York, the Carolinas, and Georgia (the southern states sided with the big states, believing that given their large size, proportional representation would eventually be in their interest),

supremacy clause A clause in Article IV of the Constitution holding that in any conflict between federal laws and treaties and state laws, the will of the national government always prevails.

against the rest of the "small states," whose only hope for influence lay in the equal representation scheme.

In the early debates, the small states failed repeatedly to pass the New Jersey Plan, partly because Maryland's Luther Martin had alienated his colleagues by giving a virulent, two-day speech against proportional representation. Martin's effort backfired when the delegates quickly approved proportional representation for the legislature. However, when the delegates also voted to establish a bicameral legislative branch to provide some sort of balance of power, the issue now became how the upper house of Congress, known as the Senate, would be apportioned.

During this debate, Georgia delegate Abraham Baldwin later recalled, "The convention was more than once upon the point of dissolving without agreeing upon any system."[20] At this turning point in the debate, selfless action by Baldwin and several other delegates narrowly averted complete failure of the Convention. The large-state delegates sought proportional representation in both the Senate and in the House of Representatives, as the lower house was called, giving them total control over the Congress, while the small-state delegates pressed for the old Articles of Confederation system of equality of votes in the legislature. Because of their numbers, the large states expected to win the issue by a narrow margin.

But well-timed absences and changes of heart by Baldwin and other delegates during key votes ended the big states' chances for dominance in the Senate and in the process saved the Convention. When the vote was taken on the question of Senate representation, Maryland's Daniel of St. Thomas Jenifer, who otherwise had an exemplary record of attendance for the Convention, deliberately stayed away, keeping Maryland allied with the small states. Then, the three Georgia delegates conspired to switch their state's vote from the big-state position to the small-state position. Two of them suddenly left the Convention, and the third delegate, Abraham Baldwin, voted for the small-state position. Thus, proportional representation in the Senate failed.

With compromise now possible, a committee consisting of one member from each state formed to prepare suggestions for resolving the question of representation in the Senate. When the committee selection finished, it turned out that every member favored the small states' position, so the result was preordained. The plan proved acceptable to the small states but capable of passage by the large states as well.

This plan has become known as the **Great Compromise** (also called the Connecticut Compromise), based on a plan advanced by Roger Sherman of Connecticut. This compromise upheld the large-state position for the House of membership based on proportional representation and balanced that decision by upholding the small-state position of equal representation in the Senate, where each state, regardless of size, would have two votes. Since all legislation would have to pass through *both* houses, neither large nor small states could dominate. The compromise also stated that *money bills*, or measures that raise revenue, must begin in the House, to keep the power to tax with the people. This arrangement would prevent an alliance of small states in the Senate voting in programs for which the large states must pay.

The composition and purpose of the two houses of Congress would be markedly different. Members of the House of Representatives would be chosen based on a state's population: one representative for every 40,000 people, as determined by periodic census (at the request of George Washington this number was changed to 30,000 on the last day of the Convention). The House was constructed to be closest to the people and to reflect their desires. The Senate, with its equal representation and indirect method of selection by state legislatures, was intended as a more deliberative council of the political and economic elite. This body would serve as an advisory council to the president and would eventually be entrusted with reviewing presidential executive branch and judicial appointments as well as ratifying treaties.

Delegates voted in favor of the Connecticut Compromise by the narrowest of margins—5 to 4—with one state delegation tied. The compromise effectively ended the debate between the large and small states by giving each a balanced stake in the legislature of the new centralized national government.

Great Compromise (also called the Connecticut Compromise) A plan presented at the Constitutional Convention that upheld the large-state position for the House, its membership based on proportional representation, balanced by the small-state posture of equal representation in the Senate, where each state would have two votes.

three-fifths compromise A compromise that stated that the apportionment of representatives by state should be determined "by adding to the whole number of free persons . . . three-fifths of all other persons" (Article I, Section 2), meaning that it would take five slaves to equal three free people when counting the population for representation and taxation purposes.

The Constitution was on its way to being realized, but two vexing questions remained: one dealing with the issue of slavery and the other with the nature of the new executive.

The Issue of Slavery

Although the word *slavery* was never mentioned in the Constitution, it was much on the minds of the framers. Since the 1600s, Africans had been brought over to the New World and sold as slaves. Southern plantations needed slave labor to operate. Although some delegates wanted to abolish slavery, citing the inalienable human rights of freedom and equality, they understood that such a call would lose much southern support and doom the Convention to failure. Instead, slavery was discussed indirectly through the question of how to distribute the sixty-five seats in the First Congress. Since membership in the Congress was based on population, how to count the slaves, who constituted almost 18 percent of the population, became a point of contention. If the slaves were not included in the count, southern states would have only 41 percent of the House seats; including all of the slaves would give them 50 percent of the seats.

After much debate, the Convention delegates arrived at the **three-fifths compromise**, which stated that the apportionment of taxes and representatives by state should be determined "by adding to the whole Number of free Persons . . . three-fifths of all other Persons" (Article I, Section 2). The phrase "all other persons" was a euphemism for slaves, which meant that five slaves would equal three free people when counting the population for representation and taxation purposes. The stated rationale for this partial counting of slaves was that they produced less wealth than free citizens, but Convention delegates recognized the political compromise.

This compromise represented a victory of political expediency over morality. Because slaves could not vote, their numbers were simply being used to add to the South's political power. Some have argued that even though the compromise kept the Constitutional Convention on track, it was immoral because it denigrated blacks by suggesting that they were only three-fifths as valuable and productive as whites. Others, though, have pointed out that while it did increase southern influence in the Congress and thus the presidential electoral count, this unique political compromise actually weakened the power of the southern states while ensuring the

Constitution's passage. As a result of the compromise, the slave states ended up with only 47 percent of the seats in Congress, thus keeping them in the minority and making it possible to outvote them on slavery issues.[21] As part of the compromise, Congress was barred from legislating on the international slave trade for twenty years, thus allowing slaves to be imported until at least 1808 (Article I, Section 9). Finally, a provision added with little discussion allowed the return of fugitive slaves to their masters (Article IV, Section 2).

In leaving it to later generations to address the practice of slavery and end it, were the framers condoning slavery? Were they hypocrites for protecting slavery while discussing the high principles of freedom and equality? One response is that while they were hypocritical, their thinking reflected the vast majority of public opinion at the time; most people were indifferent to slavery. However, we must also realize, just as Thomas Jefferson discovered when he was forced to strike his criticism of slavery from the draft of the Declaration of Independence, that a successful outcome for the Constitutional Convention would have been impossible without compromise on the slavery issue. Had the southern states walked out, as they surely would have had slavery been banned, the nation would have been doomed to continue operating under the defective Articles of Confederation or perhaps to falter entirely.

The Nature of the Presidency

One of the most original contributions made by the framers of the American Constitution was their blueprint for the presidency, including the means for filling the job. (The presidency is described more fully in Chapter 5.)

The framers were ambivalent about the nature of the position they were creating, fearing that it would lead to a new monarchy in democratic clothing. This fear was reflected in the weak executive branches proposed in the Virginia and New Jersey Plans, which consisted of boards subservient to the legislature. To correct this approach, Charles Pinckney of South Carolina called for the creation of a "vigorous executive," because, in his words, "our government is despised because of the loss of public order." However, Edmund Randolph of Virginia, who instead favored a board of executives, expressed his fear that Pinckney's call for a single executive represented the "foetus of monarchy," or the beginnings of the reinstatement of a British Crown in America.[22]

Quick Review

Slavery and the Constitution

- The topic of slavery was related to the question of how to distribute the sixty-five House seats in the First Congress.
- Membership in the House was based on population.
- Without slaves in the count, southern states would have only 41 percent of the House seats.
- Including slaves (18 percent of the population), southern states would have 50 percent of the House seats.
- The three-fifths compromise stated it would take five slaves to equal three free people when counting the population for representation and taxation purposes.

◄ Few at the Constitutional Convention in Philadelphia in 1787 doubted that its leader, George Washington, would one day lead the nation as President.

U.S.A. Yesterday and Today

One Country—Two Levels of Citizenship?

What do more than 12.8 million people in the United States have in common with the following people: Supreme Court Justice Felix Frankfurter, former ABC News announcer Peter Jennings, former Secretaries of State Madeleine Albright and Henry Kissinger, retired Chairman of the Joint Chiefs of Staff General John Shalikashvili, Senator Mel Martinez (R.-FL), and California Governor Arnold Schwarzenegger? All of these people are naturalized American citizens who make contributions to the United States, but cannot realize the American dream of becoming president of the United States. All of these U.S. citizens are ineligible to become president of the United States because of the provision of Article II, Section 1, Clause 5 of the Constitution that states that American presidents can be only "natural born" citizens. This nativist provision was instituted partly out of fear that a foreign-born aristocrat, autocrat, or even spy might grab America's infant democracy and return it to a foreign-monarchical rule. But the provision might also be termed the "Hamilton Clause," because it was included partly out of personal animosity by certain founders to the English-born Constitution framer Alexander Hamilton, a noted advocate of strong presidential power.

In the early 1990s, there were 6.5 million naturalized U.S. citizens, but the number more than doubled in just over a decade as large numbers of the resident immigrants decided to apply for citizenship. Most of these immigrants are concentrated in states such as California, New York, Texas, Florida, Illinois, and New Jersey. Although granting citizenship confers almost all the rights and privileges of being an American citizen, running for the American presidency remains, according to the Constitution, out of reach.

Since the 1870s, more than two dozen proposals to eliminate this restriction have failed. Does the reason for the "native born" requirement for president still exist? Republicans such as Senator Orrin Hatch of Utah and Congressman Dana Rohrabacher of California are asking this question. Both have proposed a constitutional amendment to allow naturalized citizens to run for president, likely because of the popularity of Austrian-born Governor Schwarzenegger and the open presidential seat in 2008. A separate bipartisan bill proposes this change but also calls for a thirty-five–year citizenship requirement for the candidate. But the larger question is whether we should continue to have two levels of citizenship, one for native-born citizens and the other for naturalized citizens. One argument is that certain government positions are so important that they should be limited to natural-born citizens. On the other side, the argument is that the fourteen years of residence also required to run for president prepares them for the position.

The issue in this post–September 11 attack era goes far beyond naturalized citizens possibly running for president, however. For example, the 2001 Patriot Act and other anti-terrorism legislation impose many additional restrictions on naturalized citizens. For example, thousands of people living in New York's Chinatown have had trouble banking, even trying to deposit their paychecks, because of the Patriot Act, which in an attempt to prevent terrorist money-laundering imposes stringent identification requirements on foreign-born persons. In addition, the Immigration and Naturalization Service maintains computer records on naturalized citizens, lawful permanent residents, refugees, persons granted asylum, and alien immigrants.

The question of this dual citizenship class is sure to be raised, although it may not be resolved in time for Governor Schwarzenegger's own political ambitions. There are over 34 million immigrants residing in this country, 70 percent of whom are eligible to become naturalized, and both political parties look to these potential citizens to expand their voting base. If you were president, that is, if you are lucky enough to be eligible to run for president, how would you decide this issue?

Source: John Yinger, "No American Should be Second-Class Citizens," Maxwell School, Syracuse University, Statement for the House Committee on the Judiciary, Subcommittee on the Constitution, July 24, 2000, http://faculty.maxwell.syr.edu/jyinger/Citizenship/testimony.htm; 2004 Migration Policy Institute www.migrationinformation.org, *A Report to Congress in Accordance with Section 326 (b) of the Uniting and Strengthening America by Providing Appropriate Tools Required to Intercept and Obstruct Terrorism Act of 2001 (USA Patriot Act),* submitted by the Department of the Treasury, October 21, 2002, http://www.treas.gov/press/releases/reports/sec326breport.final.pdf; Martin Kasindorf, "Should the Constitution be Amended for Arnold?" *USA Today,* December 3–5, 2004, p. 1.

It was James Wilson of Pennsylvania, fearing an all-powerful legislature similar to those in some states under the Articles of Confederation, who proposed a plan creating a national executive much like the powerful governor of New York—a one-person executive with substantial powers, such as a veto over legislation. This plan was not debated by the delegates but was instead submitted to the Committee on Detail, which was charged with creating a coherent document out of the resolutions passed by the Convention. Since Wilson and three other strong national government advocates sat on this five-person committee, the matter was settled in his favor. The powerful single executive envisioned by that committee was adopted by the Convention three months later.

Although the delegates agreed on a one-person executive, they disagreed over the term of office for the new president and how to select that powerful person. Some delegates proposed a three-year term with reelections possible, while others sought a single term of seven years. Originally, the Convention narrowly voted for a single seven-year term. This was eventually revised to a four-year term, with reelection possible. Nothing was said about the number of terms a president could serve.

The vital question of how to select the right person for president led to yet another compromise in the form of the **electoral college system**. In an attempt to ensure selection of statesmen like George Washington, the anticipated first president, the framers took selection away from the voters. Instead, the states would decide how to choose "electors" in numbers equal to the total number of their senators and representatives. The electors would vote for two people, at least one of whom could not be from their own state. The highest overall vote-getter would become president, and the runner-up, vice president. The intent was that the best-known and most-qualified candidate would appear somewhere on the ballots of the most electors from around the country. A tie vote would be sent to the House of Representatives for selection, with each state delegation having one vote.

Such a system struck a compromise between the large and small states. The president would not be chosen by direct popular vote or by the legislature because those methods would have favored the large states. Still, the large states would have the advantage of proportional representation. On the other hand, if the matter went to the House through lack of a majority vote in the electoral college, as the delegates fully expected, the one-state, one-vote system would favor the small states. (More will be said about the electoral college in Chapter 10.) This idea mandated that a presidential candidate would need a spread of support from large and small states around the country. In the 2004 presidential election, for instance, had John Kerry gained the support of Ohio, he would have won the presidency instead of George Bush.

After nearly four months of debate, on September 17, 1787, the new Constitution was drafted. The eldest delegate, eighty-two-year-old Benjamin Franklin, moved that the draft be approved, saying, "I consent to this constitution because I expect no better, and because I am not sure that it is not the best." To encourage even those who disagreed with the results to sign it, those who affixed their names became "witnesses" to the document. Even so, several of the delegates refused to sign, and only thirty-nine names were penned. Perhaps the best blessing on the whole enterprise was Franklin's, when the weeping old man told his fellow delegates that he had long puzzled over the half-sun design on the back of the Convention president's chair. Was the design of a rising or setting sun, he often wondered. "Now at length I have the happiness to know that it is a rising and not a setting sun," he told the delegates.[23] With that, George Washington penned in his journal: "The business being closed, the members adjourned to the City Tavern, dined together and took a cordial leave of each other."[24] But, as they would soon discover, the battle had just begun.

electoral college system Votes in the national presidential elections are actually indirect votes for a slate of presidential electors pledged to each party's candidate. Each state has one elector for each of its representatives and senators. The winning slate of electors casts their votes in their state's capital after the public election. In the United States, election of the president and vice president is dependent upon receiving a majority (270) of the votes cast in the electoral college.

 **MakeItReal**

Simulation: What If You Were a
Founding Father?
Primary Source: The Constitution
of the United States (See also the
annotated *Constitution*, pages
72–87.)

THE MIRACLE: RESULTS OF THE CONVENTION

The purpose of the Constitution is laid out in the eloquent preamble:

> We the People of the United States, in Order to form a more perfect Union,
> establish Justice, insure domestic Tranquility, provide for the common defense,
> promote the general Welfare, and secure the Blessings of Liberty to ourselves
> and our Posterity, do ordain and establish this Constitution for the United States
> of America.

This one sentence outlined the goals of the framers' exercise in democracy. America
was now one people rather than thirteen individual states. This nation had certain
hopes—for justice, tranquility, and liberty. Its sovereign power rested in a new constitution that would guide a new national government, a union more perfect than
the one that existed under the Articles of Confederation.

The new constitution was unlike any seen before. It created a republican government, granting indirect power to the voting public, whose desires would be served
by a representative government. Until that time, such a system seemed possible only
for small countries such as Greece or Switzerland.

A Republican Form of Government

At the end of the Convention, a woman asked Ben Franklin what kind of government the delegates had created—a republic or a monarchy? "A republic, Madam,"
responded Franklin, "if you can keep it."[25]

Believing that the people are more interested in their own welfare than the
good of the whole, and realizing that the size of the new nation prevented implementing a pure democracy, the framers created a republican form of government with built-in checks and balances. Instead of governing themselves, the
people elected representatives to protect their interests. These representatives
could, however, vote against the desires of their constituents if it was for the good
of the whole nation. One of the main constitutional changes in the American system of government over the years has been a shift from the purely republican system of government created by the framers to a system that is much more
democratic and inclusive of more people. Six times in our history, the Constitution has been amended to extend the voting base in federal elections, thus giving
more people a direct voice in their government. These changes were the Fifteenth Amendment, which extended the vote to the newly freed slaves; the Seventeenth Amendment, which permitted direct popular election of the Senate;
the Nineteenth Amendment, which extended the right to vote to women; the
Twenty-third Amendment, which gave District of Columbia voters electoral college representation to vote for president; the Twenty-fourth Amendment, which
abolished the poll tax that required people to pay to vote; and the Twenty-sixth
Amendment, which extended the vote to citizens over the age of eighteen. Finally, fewer representatives now act as independent "trustees," choosing instead
to serve as "delegates" instructed by the voters through public opinion polls, mail
counts, and the media (see Chapter 4). In these ways, the American republic has
indeed approached democracy.

Does moving closer to a system of pure democracy place the republican system
designed by the framers to protect liberty in danger? Not at all. The Constitution's
mechanisms for limiting power provide an adequate check on the actions of the
leaders and the demands of the people. A judiciary more powerful than the framers
could ever have imagined, using the Constitution and its amendments to preserve
liberty, also keeps the republic strong. In the end, just how far the country actually
goes toward direct democracy depends on how much confidence the people have
in the motives and wisdom of their leaders.

THE GOVERNMENTAL POWERS

You can better understand the results of the framers' efforts by taking two different approaches to studying the Constitution and the distribution of power: a horizontal view and a vertical view.

Horizontal Powers

Governmental powers are apportioned horizontally among the branches of the national government—the executive, legislative, and judicial branches—according to the system of *separation of powers* (see Figure 2.1). Each major branch of government received a separate set of powers so that no one branch could become too powerful. The first three articles of the Constitution are concerned solely with the powers, responsibilities, and selection processes for each separate branch and include specific prohibitions against a person becoming a member of two branches at the same time.

But James Madison understood that separating the powers among three distinct branches would be insufficient unless each branch had the power to "check" the other, preventing encroachment into its own sphere. A system of *checks and balances* was incorporated into the structure, giving each branch the power to approve, disapprove, or alter what the other branches do. "Ambition must be made to counteract ambition," Madison counseled in *The Federalist*, no. 51, on checks and balances (printed in its entirety in the Appendix). "If men were angels," he explained, "no government would be necessary. If angels were to govern men, neither external nor internal controls on government would be necessary. In framing a government which is to be administered by men over men, the great difficulty lies in this: You must first enable the government to control the governed; and in the next place oblige it to control itself."[26] With the checking powers outlined in Figure 2.1, no one branch can take control and run the government.

Although the president nominates ambassadors, cabinet officials, and justices, the Senate can reject those choices by refusing to give the majority vote required for its "advice and consent." Congress passes laws, but the president can then veto them. Congress can react by overriding a presidential veto with a two-thirds vote of both houses. Theoretically, the president can then refuse to execute the new law, but the president is kept in check by the fact that Congress has an impeachment power if "treason, bribery, or High Crimes or Misdemeanors" are committed. The judiciary has the power to interpret laws or use the power of **judicial review** to judge the constitutionality of, and thereby check the actions of, the other branches (a power not in the Constitution but established by the Court itself in 1803). We saw this in the Supreme Court's ruling against Abraham Lincoln's suspension of the **writ of habeas corpus** as well as its changing the legal standard for restricting First Amendment rights in reaction to Woodrow Wilson's actions during the First World War. Meanwhile, the judiciary itself is checked by the president's prerogative of nominating justices (with the advice and consent of the Senate) and Congress's power to create lower federal courts, alter its jurisdiction, attempt to re-pass laws overturned by the federal courts, or change the Supreme Court's appellate jurisdiction. This power emerged once again in 2005 when Congress began considering a law to overturn the Supreme Court's 2004 decision that eliminated mandatory minimum judicial sentences.

Government functions often require creation of independent agencies or actors to accomplish tasks that bridge the "separation of powers" issue by mixing the functions of the three branches. Some examples of these agencies include the Securities and Exchange Commission, which regulates the activities of Wall Street; the Federal Reserve Board, which regulates the monetary and banking system; and the independent counsel agency created as a result of the Nixon Watergate case but allowed to expire in 1999. Another example is the National Commission on Terrorist

judicial review The power of the Supreme Court established in *Marbury v. Madison* to overturn acts of the president, Congress, and the states if those acts violate the Constitution. This power makes the Supreme Court the final interpreter of the Constitution.

writ of habeas corpus Latin term meaning literally 'to produce the body' this is a judicial order enabling jailed prisoners to come into the court, or return to the court after being convicted and sentenced, in order to determine the legality of their detention. By Constitutional rules it can only be suspended in times of crisis by Congress.

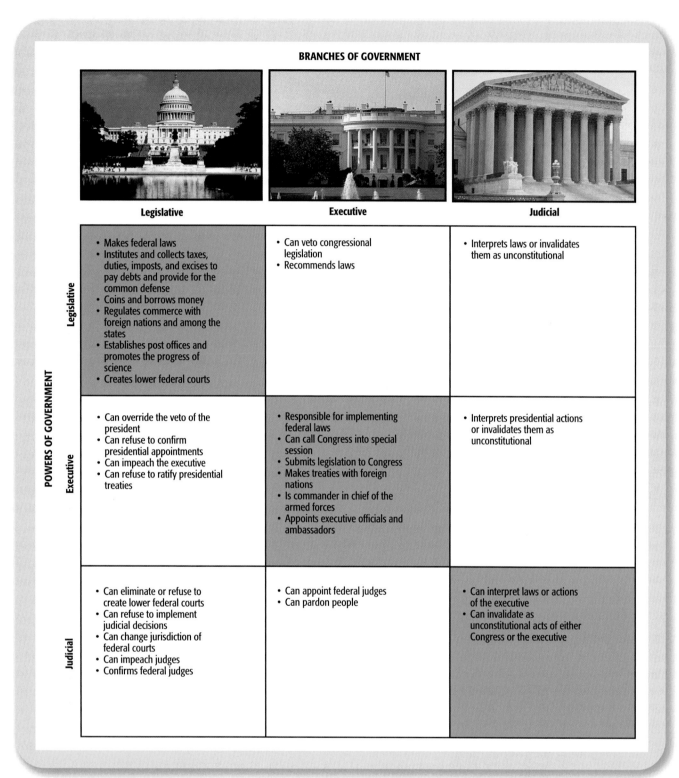

BRANCHES OF GOVERNMENT

	Legislative	**Executive**	**Judicial**
Legislative	• Makes federal laws • Institutes and collects taxes, duties, imposts, and excises to pay debts and provide for the common defense • Coins and borrows money • Regulates commerce with foreign nations and among the states • Establishes post offices and promotes the progress of science • Creates lower federal courts	• Can veto congressional legislation • Recommends laws	• Interprets laws or invalidates them as unconstitutional
Executive	• Can override the veto of the president • Can refuse to confirm presidential appointments • Can impeach the executive • Can refuse to ratify presidential treaties	• Responsible for implementing federal laws • Can call Congress into special session • Submits legislation to Congress • Makes treaties with foreign nations • Is commander in chief of the armed forces • Appoints executive officials and ambassadors	• Interprets presidential actions or invalidates them as unconstitutional
Judicial	• Can eliminate or refuse to create lower federal courts • Can refuse to implement judicial decisions • Can change jurisdiction of federal courts • Can impeach judges • Confirms federal judges	• Can appoint federal judges • Can pardon people	• Can interpret laws or actions of the executive • Can invalidate as unconstitutional acts of either Congress or the executive

POWERS OF GOVERNMENT

Figure 2.1   Constitutional Powers

The blue portions of this figure display the powers allotted to each of the branches and show the separation of powers. The remainder of the diagram indicates the powers that each of the branches holds as a check on the other branches. While each of the branches has primary responsibility in the executive, legislative, or judicial realms, each also shares powers with the other two branches.

Attacks Upon the United States, known as the "9/11 Commission" created in late 2002 to investigate the World Trade Center/Pentagon attacks on September 11, 2001. This commission's mid-2004 hearings and its resulting best-selling report offered a riveting description of the intelligence failings enabling the attacks to succeed and a series of recommendations for laws designed to tighten up the nation's defense against terrorism.

One such agency that became the subject of great debate was the National Energy Policy Development Group in 2004, a task force headed up by Vice President Dick Cheney and charged with "fact-finding" for information on the nation's energy policy. The Sierra Club, a liberal environmental lobbying group, and Judicial Watch, a conservative legal lobbying group, sued to force the government, under the Federal Advisory Committee Act, to disclose the names of this task force. Suspicions emerged that task force members might be working members of the energy industry because of Vice President Cheney's former association with the Halliburton firm, an oil company, and President Bush's previous association with executives from the failed Enron company, another energy firm. Showing how these situations raise unusual separation-of-powers issues, following the appeals court's postponement of the decision until after the 2004 election—an action appealed to the Supreme Court—it was discovered that Justice Antonin Scalia had gone duck hunting with Vice President Cheney earlier that year. The Sierra Club appealed this ruling and petitioned to ask Justice Scalia to remove himself from the case, arguing that it was an "appearance of impropriety." He refused, writing that his ability to judge the case had not been compromised because, among other reasons, he "never hunted in the same blind with the vice-president." After the case was sent back to the lower court for a re-examination, in May 2005 a unanimous appeals court backed Cheney and ruled that the names of the task force members could remain secret. The Bush Administration used the information gathered by the task force in the 2005 proposal of its new energy policy.[27]

Because the framers deliberately allowed for elasticity in each branch's powers, the resulting government was destined to become one in which powers overlap. As Justice Robert Jackson described it: "While the Constitution diffuses power the better to secure liberty, it also contemplates that practice will integrate the dispersed powers into a workable government."[28] The result over the years has not been a strict separation of powers but, as political scientist Richard Neustadt has said, a "government of separated institutions sharing powers." By this, he means that each institution frequently exercises the powers of the others: Judges can make laws, Congress can interpret laws, and presidents can do both.[29]

Vertical Powers

Vertical powers refer to the relationship between the centralized national government and the individual state governments. This distribution of power is known as **federalism**. We cover the subject of federalism more extensively in the next chapter.

During the framing, the delegates tried to create the right balance of power between the national government and the state governments. Having seen that the confederation of states did not work, they wanted to give the national government sufficient authority to govern while leaving the state governments enough power to accomplish what they needed at the local level. The framers created a national government of **delegated powers**, meaning powers expressly granted or enumerated and limited in nature, while leaving the state governments with general **reserved powers**, or the remainder of the authority not specifically delegated to the national government. For example, to avoid the problem of erratic state-by-state foreign policy under the Articles of Confederation, that power was delegated to the national government. However, state governments that wish to seek business investments with foreign government may do so using the power to improve the economic welfare of their citizens, reserved for states. Additionally, the federal government has no power to regulate relations among its citizens, as in marriage laws, or power to

Question for Reflection

If you were on the Supreme Court, how far would you let a president go in withholding information from Congress in forming policy that deals with the war on terrorism, and how would that differ from your answer in other policy areas?

MakeItReal

Civic Participation: State Governments

federalism The relationship between the centralized national government and the individual state governments.

delegated powers Powers expressly granted or enumerated in the Constitution and limited in nature.

reserved powers Powers not assigned by the Constitution to the national government but left to the states or to the people, according to the Tenth Amendment.

create a criminal code. These **police powers**, or the power to regulate the health, morals, public safety, and welfare of citizens, were left to the states.

By viewing the Constitution from a vertical perspective, other features become apparent. For instance, to remedy lack of central economic control under the Articles of Confederation, Congress has the power over commerce *among* the states, while the states individually govern commerce *within* their own boundaries. To handle a rebellion, such as Shays's Rebellion, the president was made commander in chief, and Congress received power both to raise and support an army and to send it into battle. States, however, retained their own powers over a police force to keep order at home. The most important element of the vertical power is the so-called *supremacy clause* (Article VI), which states that in any controversy between the states and federal laws, Constitution, or treaties, *federal dictates will always prevail.* Acceptance of this provision ensured that sovereign states would never again be the dominating power they were under the Articles of Confederation.

The success of this reordering of governmental priorities between the national and state governments depends on one's point of view. Many of these powers have been interpreted to expand the national power to such a degree that individual states today have much less power than many of the framers ever intended. Some praise the uniformity and comprehensive nature of such a government, while others express concerns about the burgeoning size and remoteness of the national government and the need for policy innovation by the individual state governments. As you will learn in Chapter 3, this debate continues to this day with the issue of **devolution**, or returning governmental programs and powers to the states to reduce the size and authority of the national government. Gains from limiting national government, however, may lead to variation in the nature of rights and protections from state to state, as in the early twentieth century and before.

The Articles of the Constitution

The Constitution is divided into seven articles, each with a unique purpose. The first three apportion power among the three branches of national government; two others (Articles IV and VI) apportion power between national and state governments; the remaining two articles (Articles V and VII) lay out procedures for amending and ratifying the Constitution. Gaps were deliberately left in each of these articles, and the language was given a certain elasticity to allow the Constitution to expand and evolve as the nation needed.

Article I　Article I sets forth the powers of the legislative branch. For the framers, this was the most important article (and therefore first) because it sought to expand the powers of the old Confederation Congress while still preventing the omnipotent power of the state legislatures under the Articles of Confederation. This intent is clear from the limiting nature of the first words of the article: "All legislative Powers herein granted shall be vested in a Congress of the United States." The article then contains a long list of specific and narrowly drawn powers. Those include the powers to declare war, borrow and coin money, regulate interstate commerce, and raise and support an army. But the list is not as restrictive as it seems at first; the article also mandates that Congress can "make all Laws which shall be necessary and proper for carrying into Execution the foregoing Powers." As we will see in the next chapter, this **necessary and proper clause**, with its vague grant of power, has allowed a broad interpretation of Congress's powers under the Constitution. Such built-in flexibility makes the Constitution just as viable today as it was in 1787.

From the vertical perspective, Article I, Section 9, denies Congress the power to place a tax or duty on articles exported from any state. Moreover, under Section 10 states are denied the power to execute treaties, coin money, impair the obligation of contracts, and lay any imposts or duties on imports or exports without the consent of Congress.

 **MakeItReal**

Primary Source: The Articles of Confederation

police powers The powers to regulate health, morals, public safety, and welfare, which are reserved to the states.

devolution Reducing the size and authority of the federal government by returning programs to the states.

necessary and proper clause A clause in Article I, Section 8, Clause 18, of the Constitution stating that Congress can "make all Laws which shall be necessary and proper for carrying into Execution the foregoing Powers."

Article II   Article II outlines the powers of the executive. At first glance, it seems to limit the president's power to granting pardons, making treaties, receiving foreign ambassadors, nominating certain officials, and being the "commander in chief" of the army and navy. But, as with the legislative branch, the executive was granted an elastic clause in the ambiguous first sentence of the article: "The executive Power shall be vested in a President of the United States of America." As you will see in Chapter 5 on the presidency, broad interpretation of the words *executive power* provides a president with considerable power. For example, should the life of a Supreme Court justice or a member of Congress be threatened, it is within the "inherent powers" of the president to provide protection using a U.S. marshal. Or, should a member of the president's administration refuse to testify about executive branch actions before Congress, a president can claim "executive privilege," arguing that one of the president's subordinates must keep previous advice secret. The Bush administration record here has been a bit mixed. A Senate request for the memos drafted by Court of Appeals nominee Miguel Estrada while he worked in the solicitor general's office, to determine the depth of his legal conservatism, was denied, thus costing him Senate confirmation. On the other hand, under heavy pressure, then–national security adviser Condoleeza Rice testified before the commission investigating the September 11, 2001 attack, and the president and vice-president testified together in a private session, although all three had previously invoked executive privilege. Executive power allows presidents to decide to "make war" by sending troops to foreign countries, even in the absence of a formal declaration of war by Congress, or create policies like the USA Patriot Act and the military tribunal policy of 2001, which granted sweeping new powers to a government at war.

This article also empowers the president to make judicial appointments and to "return" (*veto*) bills passed by both houses of Congress. Thus the president can check the powers of the other two branches. Article II has additional elasticity built into it in Section 3, which states: "[The President] shall take Care that the Laws be faithfully executed." A president who disagrees with congressional legislation can "faithfully" execute the law by reinterpreting it or by devising a new law. For instance, if Congress appropriates too much money for a program, the president can "take Care" by *impounding*, that is, either delaying or refusing to spend, the full appropriation. Thomas Jefferson did this in 1803, when he withheld money for gunboats on the Mississippi. However, when Richard Nixon tried to expand this power, using it not to save money but to derail programs with which he disagreed, both Congress and the Supreme Court overturned his action.

Article III   Article III outlines the powers of the judicial branch. As we will see in more detail in Chapter 6, the framers provided the most vague grant of powers to the judiciary because they could not agree on the role of this branch. This article establishes a Supreme Court only and grants Congress the power to "ordain and establish" inferior federal courts and to change the Supreme Court appellate jurisdiction. One unique example of Congress's effect on federal court jurisdiction came on March 21, 2005, when a private bill was passed to grant the parents of Theresa Marie Schiavo of Florida standing in the federal district court of Florida to raise once again the issue of whether to reconnect the feeding and hydration tubes for their comatose daughter over her husband's objections. This appeal had already been twice denied by the Supreme Court. As a result, the case was heard once again by the federal and state courts, but was again denied.[30]

Federal judges serve for life as long as they maintain good behavior and are removable only by impeachment. In 2005, a debate continued to grow regarding term limits for federal judges, fueled by Chief Justice William Rehnquist's five-month absence during his unsuccessful battle with thyroid cancer. They have the power to decide "Cases, in Law and Equity" arising under the Constitution and also to interpret federal laws and federal treaties.

© 1999 Akron Beacon Journal By
permission of Chip Bok and Creators
Syndicate, Inc.

Articles IV–VII   Article IV establishes guidelines for interstate relations, absent in
the Articles of Confederation, under which a state could disregard the laws of other
states; it could also treat its own citizens one way and citizens of other states another
way. This article establishes uniformity by guaranteeing that "full Faith and Credit"
must be granted by all states to the "public Acts, Records, and Judicial Proceedings of
every other State." In addition, citizens of all states must receive the same "Privileges
and Immunities" of citizens of "the several States." Divorces in one state must be
recognized by all, and a decision to avoid repaying a state-financed college loan or
even a parking fine by crossing state boundaries is ill advised. Those obligations are in
force in all states of the union, as individuals who try to avoid paying child support or
contest legal custody of children by moving out of state are discovering.

An interesting debate over the effect of interstate recognition of laws arises from the
gay marriage issue that so influenced the 2004 presidential election. By mid-2005,
eighteen states had constitutionally banned gay marriage, with another twenty-four
states banning the practice by law. This represented an increase of five states voting
against gay marriages since the 2003 ruling by the Supreme Judicial Court of Massachusetts, which made gay marriages constitutional. This ruling, which became official on May 17, 2004, now faces a possible ballot question in 2008 as voters are asked to
decide whether or not to ban gay marriages. Government actions on this issue have
been mixed. In 2005, Connecticut became the third state (after Vermont and Hawaii)
to pass a civil union law that extends to same-sex couples many or all of the legal rights
of marriage to gays without allowing formal marriage itself.[31] On the other hand, Ohio
and California have denied legal protection to same-sex couples married in other
states, and in 1996 Congress passed the Defense of Marriage Act (DOMA), withdrawing federal recognition of same-sex marriages. These differences in state rights raised
the issue under Article IV, Clause 1 of the Constitution of whether all other states are
bound under the "full faith and credit" provision to confer equal legal and political
rights and benefits to same-sex couples living within their states who had been married
or legally joined elsewhere. With so many differences in state laws, it is only a matter of
time before this issue comes before the U.S. Supreme Court. At that time, the justices
must decide how to weigh the constitutional issues with the political trends.

Article V outlines the procedure for amending the Constitution. The framers understood that changes might be necessary to correct imperfections in their original
work or to update it for future use, as, for example, with the debate over the Equal

Rights Amendment in the 1970s and the Gay Marriage Ban Amendment proposed by President Bush in 2004 and subsequently considered by Congress.

Article VI deals with federal–state relations and the financial obligations of the new government. This article contains the supremacy clause, affirming the predominance of the national government, and also ensures that all prior debts against the United States are valid under the new Constitution. Moreover, it states that all national officers must swear an oath of office supporting the Constitution and cannot be subjected to a religious test.

Article VII explains the process for ratifying the Constitution.

Approaching Democracy Around the Globe

A Tale of Two Constitutions

In 2005, while the peoples of Iraq and Europe simultaneously considered the creation of new Constitutions, an "outsider," President George Bush, found himself in a curiously influential founding father role. But rather than take his guidance from Madison's *Notes of the Constitutional Convention*, Bush seemed to follow former New York senator Daniel Patrick Moynihan's political axiom: "Forgive and remember."

For Iraq, the process began in March 2004. After the war and downfall of Saddam Hussein, twenty-five American-backed local leaders signed on to a provisional constitution, called the Transitional Administrative Law, that did not include the Sunni Arabs, Iraq's third-largest ethnic group. Under the provisions of the law, the occupying American forces turned over sovereignty to the Iraqis. Much like the American Constitution, the plan included a republican and federalist form of government, using the separation of powers and giving control of the armed forces to the civilian government. Islam was the official religion of the country, but freedom of religion, thought, and speech, as well as equal rights and free elections, were guaranteed under this relatively short and basic document.

Later in the year the process of drafting the final constitution appeared to stall, as the Sunnis decided to boycott the January 2005 elections, giving them little presence in the 275-member National Assembly. In April 2005, President Bush urged that the Iraqis have a "timely write" of their constitution and sent Secretary of State Condoleeza Rice and Deputy Secretary of State Robert B. Zoellick to Baghdad to convince the leaders to include more Sunnis in the drafting process. But when the leaders determined that an entire new document must be drafted by the August 15 deadline—in their opinion the provisional one was "an American document"—the challenges of drafting a constitution continued.

Meanwhile, in June 2004, the fifteen members of the European Union announced a 448-page constitutional treaty that sought to "respect the national identities of its member-states" while coordinating their security, foreign policy, economic policy, monetary system (the euro), and creating a European government with a president, ruling council, and parliament. All that lay between this draft and its implementation was the unanimous agreement of EU members. Nine nations quickly ratified the treaty, but only one, Spain, put the issue to its people in a national referendum. When the decision was made to expand the EU to twenty-five members, including Eastern European nations and possibly later Turkey, without first consulting the people of the member states, the arrangement seemed shakier.

By February 2005, President Bush, slated to speak to the European leaders, considered expressing his support of the draft EU constitution. However, to do so would endanger reelection prospects for British Prime Minister Tony Blair, who had backed the Iraqi invasion, and benefit French president Jacques Chirac, who had criticized Bush's decision to go to war and led other nations to withhold their support. Another consideration was the fact that a stronger Europe would compete with the United States economically. As a result, Bush toned down his remarks, merely supporting Europe's "democratic unity."

Partly due to this tepid endorsement, and the strategic error by European leaders in not taking this matter to the people earlier, in late May 2005 the French people voted overwhelmingly against ratification of the treaty. Just three days later, the Dutch rejected the treaty by a 62–38 percent majority, endangering the entire EU constitutional drafting process.

One Parisian student, Sebastien Dreuillet, said: "They made Europe happen too fast." To which Laurent Fabius, a French Socialist leader, added, "I'm European, but I want a strong, unified Europe. The constitution didn't do that." But they might have added that President Bush got his chance for political payback against President Chirac and the EU, and took it.

Source: Robert Fisk, "Iraq Constitution Sealed At Last," *London Independent,* March 9, 2004; Craig Whitlock, "Circumspect E.U. Turns to Dutch on Constitution," *Washington Post,* May 31, 2005; and David Wastell and Justin Stares, "How British and American Conservatives United to Stop Bush Endorsing the EU Constitution," *London Telegraph,* February 27, 2005.

Federalists Those in favor of the Constitution, many of whom were nationalists at the Convention.

Antifederalists Strong states' rights advocates who organized in opposition to the ratification of the U.S. Constitution prior to its adoption.

RATIFICATION: THE BATTLE FOR THE CONSTITUTION

Drafting the Constitution was just the first step toward creating a new government. The vote for or against the new document was now in the hands of the various state conventions. According to Article VII, nine of the thirteen states had to ratify the Constitution for it to take effect. Realistically, though, everyone understood that unless the most populous states ratified—Pennsylvania, Massachusetts, New York, and Virginia—the Constitution would never succeed.

Ratifying the Constitution involved hardball politics. This reality is often surprising to those who believe that creating the Constitution was a nonpartisan and academic process of debating the philosophical issues concerning a new government. A close look at this political crisis is instructive both for seeing how the nation was formed and understanding why arguments over constitutional issues continue to rage today.

As in every good political fight, the side best organized at the beginning had the advantage. Those in favor of the Constitution, many of whom were nationalists at the Convention, took the lead by calling themselves the **Federalists**. Thus, they stole the semantic high ground by taking the name of supporters of the federal form of government under the Articles of Confederation. The true supporters of the federal form of government, the states' rights advocates, had to call themselves the **Antifederalists**. This group included most but not all of the Convention's antinationalists.

The Federalist Papers

The debate over the Constitution raged in newspapers and hand-distributed pamphlets, the only sources of communication in that period. Federalists Alexander Hamilton, James Madison, and John Jay wrote eighty-five essays in New York newspapers under the pen name of *Publius* (a Latin term meaning "public man"), seeking to influence the New York state convention in favor of ratification. All these articles were intended to answer the arguments of the states' rights advocates that the new central government would be too powerful and too inclined to expand further, and thus likely to destroy liberty. Hamilton, Madison, and Jay argued instead that without this new Constitution, the states would break apart and the nation would fail. With it, they reasoned, the government would act in the national interest while preserving liberty. Later collected as *The Federalist Papers: A Commentary on the Constitution of the United States,* these pieces offer us what historian Henry Steele Commager calls "a handbook on how the Constitution should operate." Although these essays had little effect on the ratification debate, generations of judges, politicians, and scholars have considered them, together with Madison's notes of the Convention, to indicate "the intent of the framers" in creating the Constitution. (See, for example, *The Federalist,* nos. 10 and 51, in the Appendix.) For this reason, many scholars consider *The Federalist Papers* the most important work of political theory in U.S. history.

In opposition, the Antifederalists made their case in scores of articles such as those by Robert Yates, the *Letters of Brutus*; Luther Martin, *Genuine Information;* and Mercy Otis Warren, *Observations on the New Constitution . . . by a Columbian Patriot.* These critics understood that the central government needed more power than it had under the Articles of Confederation, but they feared that the structure established in the Convention would supersede the state governments, rendering them obsolete. By placing too much power in the hands of a government so far removed from the people, they argued, the new government would likely expand its power and rule by force rather than by the consent of the governed. They sought ways to establish a better balance between the power of the central government and the states by placing further checks on the newly established central government.

Quick Review

The Federalists

- Believed *the people,* not *the states,* created the Constitution.
- Sought a centralized government that would unite the entire nation.
- Argued that the powers of the central government should be expandable to meet the needs of the people.
- Realized that some problems spill over state boundaries and need to be resolved by a neutral, national arbiter.

The Antifederalists

- Argued that the Constitution was created by the states.
- Insisted that the states should remain independent and distinct.
- Sought individual state governments that would be closer to the people.
- Believed government could tailor solutions to problems to fit each state.
- Believed states were the best protectors of personal liberty.

Federalists versus Antifederalists

The Federalists and Antifederalists differed on the most fundamental theoretical level. The Federalists, led by Hamilton and Madison, believed that *the people* had created the Constitution, and not *the states*, and they argued that a strong central government best represented the sovereignty of the people. The Federalists sought energy and leadership from a centralized government that would unite the entire nation, thus safeguarding the interests of the people. They also argued for expandable powers of central government to meet the needs of the people and to enable the government to respond to any emergencies that arise.

The Antifederalists argued that the Constitution was created by the states, meaning that the national government's power was carved out of the states' power. Accordingly, they insisted that the states should remain independent and distinct, rather than be led by a supreme national government. The Antifederalists sought to preserve the liberty and rights of the minorities by bolstering individual state governments that would be closer to the people.

In addition to these theoretical differences between Federalist and Antifederalist views, the two groups differed over who would have the authority for solving practical, real-world problems. The Federalists, supporters of a strong central government, realized that some problems spill over state boundaries and need to be resolved by a neutral, national arbiter. These problems include fishing rights in interstate waterways, the coinage of money, and interstate roadways. Federalists believed that a single solution to these problems would be more sensible and cost-effective than having each state devise and pay for its own program. They reasoned that the states would place their economies at a competitive disadvantage by attempting to resolve problems by themselves. While the Federalists were thinking of interstate commerce, such problems as organized crime and pollution control, not to mention control of the Internet, interstate sales of wines, and control over medical uses of marijuana would arise later to prove them correct about the need for a centralized source of authority.

Not surprisingly, the Antifederalists disagreed with the Federalists. To them, the government closest to the people, and thus most accountable to them, could best be trusted to tailor solutions to problems to fit each state. In addition, states appeared the best protectors of personal liberty, as the fear existed that the new central government would be just as oppressive toward individual rights as King George III had been.

Out of these two opposing groups, two political parties would emerge. George Washington's Federalist party, supporting a strong nationalist government, was an outgrowth of the Federalist position. This party evolved, first, into the Whig party and then the Republican Party. The Antifederalists emerged in the Democratic-Republican Party of Thomas Jefferson, which supported states' rights and later became the Democratic Party.

It is clear from their arguments that the Federalists and Antifederalists were motivated by different fears. In one of the most famous of *The Federalist Papers*, no. 10, James Madison tried to explain how the new democratic government would overcome political differences "sown in the nature of man." The nation, he argued, is divided into **factions**, "a number of citizens, whether amounting to a majority or a minority of the whole, who are united and actuated by some common impulse or passion or . . . interest."[32] These groups of people, much like interest groups today, were united largely along the lines of property classifications—for example, farmers versus the manufacturing class—and would seek to have the government protect their own interests to the exclusion of all others. Madison then sought to explain, in this article and later in *The Federalist*, no. 51, how the new government was designed to prevent an "interested and overbearing majority" of the citizens taking away the liberty of those in the minority. Lacking a way to eliminate the divisive *causes* of factions (there will always be rich versus poor and city dwellers versus farming interests), Madison

MakeItReal

Civic Participation: Political Parties

Question for Reflection

Would the current labels of Republican and Democrat still fit their earlier descriptions?

---

factions According to James Madison in *The Federalist,* no. 10: "A number of citizens, whether amounting to a majority or a minority of the whole, who are united and actuated by some common impulse or passion or . . . interests."

explained how the new system of representative government was designed to control the harmful *effects* of factions. The key was to increase the size of the political unit, or "extend the sphere" from the smaller states, in which minorities could easily be outnumbered and oppressed, to the larger central government, with a greater "number of electors" and thus "tak[ing] in a greater variety of parties and interests." As a result, they had a better chance for political protection.

In *The Federalist*, no. 51, Madison expanded his argument to show how the separation of powers would protect liberty by allowing each of the parts of the government to "be the means of keeping each other in their proper places." The two-year term of the popularly elected House of Representatives, the six-year term of the Senate (elected by state legislatures), and the four-year term of the president (elected by the electoral college), ensured that each branch of government would represent different groups. The common people's voice in the House would turn over quickly and be restrained by the long-term elite, aristocratic view of the Senate and the national perspective of the president. Moreover, the powers of each branch would check the others. When combined with the system of federalism, in which national and state governments checked each other, it was hoped that no single majority faction could dominate American politics because every group would have effective representation somewhere. Those in a minority in one branch of the national government or in one state might find a representative in another branch of government or in another state.

At the other end of the spectrum, the Antifederalists argued that the central government could not be trusted; they feared that the Constitution had traded English tyranny for tyranny by the central government at home. Worried that the central government would overrun the states and the rights of those in the minority, they asked what guarantees the Constitution contained to protect and preserve the rights of all Americans.

As far apart as these two groups were at the time of the drafting of the Constitution, some means must be found to secure agreement between them if the new document was to be ratified. The answer was the addition of a protective list of rights to the new constitution.

Ratification by Way of Compromise: A Bill of Rights

Though the Convention delegates had repeatedly refused to include in the new Constitution a long list of rights to be protected, the issue did not end with its signing. The Antifederalists in various states insisted during the ratification debate that a list of amendments be included, guaranteeing that the new central government could not restrict certain rights. The Federalists argued that a constitutional guarantee of rights was unnecessary since citizens were already adequately protected by the Constitution or by the constitutions of the individual states.

The debate over adding amendments to the Constitution presented an interesting philosophical dilemma. Many believed that if the new government did not in fact already protect these rights, it should not have been created in the first place. If it did in fact protect them, why was it necessary to repeat those rights in a series of amendments? In the end, philosophy gave way to politics. Following the tradition of the Magna Carta, compacts, social contracts, and state bills of rights, it was agreed that the people would see their rights guaranteed in writing in the Constitution. In fact, the expectation of such amendments helped sell the Constitution.

Politics the Old-Fashioned Way: A Look at the Battle for Ratification

You might be surprised by the tactics used once the ratification debates moved from being a secret discussion among aristocratic political elites into the public arena. The debates were hardly genteel. Initially, ratification seemed inevitable. After all, the Federalists had the dual advantages of an existing document that defined the terms of the debate and disorganized opposition movement. Within eight months after the Constitution had been signed, eight states had ratified the document. However, the battles in two of them—Pennsylvania and Massachusetts—indicated just how difficult it would be to secure the critical ninth state, not to mention the two large-state holdouts—Virginia and New York.

The lengths that proponents of the Constitution were willing to go to achieve success were made clear in Pennsylvania. Ben Franklin forced the State Assembly, which was about to adjourn, to appoint a ratifying convention even before enough copies of the Constitution arrived for everyone to read. Seeking to derail this effort, the Antifederalists hid, thinking they might deny Franklin a voting quorum. The sergeant at arms was directed to take the necessary action to make a vote possible. A mob of angry Federalists volunteered to help him, roaming the streets of Philadelphia looking for any missing assemblymen they could find. They eventually found two assemblymen hiding in their rooms over a local tavern and, after dragging them through the streets of Philadelphia, threw them into the assembly hall while a mob of Constitution supporters blocked their escape. Not surprisingly, these two men cast their votes against a ratifying convention, but the measure passed by a vote of 44 to 2.

Protests against such strong-arm tactics were ignored. Federalist mobs used similar tactics to ensure that the final ratifying vote favored the Constitution by a 2 to 1 margin. The damage to the Federalists' prestige in Philadelphia was so great that James Wilson, a leading Federalist, was nearly beaten to death by a mob of angry Antifederalists weeks later.

In Massachusetts, clever political strategy rather than strong-arm tactics turned the tide. Three hundred and fifty delegates, many of them from the less populous western part of the state where the Antifederalists dominated, met in Boston on January 8, 1788. The opponents of the Constitution held a slight numerical advantage. Governor John Hancock, a Federalist but also a cagey politician, was so unsure of how the vote would go that he decided to stay away, complaining of the gout. To convince Hancock to join them, the Federalists dangled the possibility that if Virginia failed to ratify the Constitution, it would leave George Washington outside the new nation; then Hancock would be the most likely prospect for the presidency. With that, Hancock's gout miraculously abated, and he was carried to the convention as a hero, with his legs wrapped in flannel. There he proposed a series of amendments protecting such local concerns as taxation and merchants' rights. These amendments, an early version of what would later become the Bill of Rights, changed the terms of the debate. Now those who supported the Constitution could vote for it, and those who opposed it could vote for the document as amended. On February 6, 1788, Massachusetts ratified the Constitution by only nineteen votes (187 to 168). Hancock's amendment strategy was later used by other states to smooth the way to ratification.

By June 2, 1788, with only one state needed to ratify the Constitution and put it into effect, the eyes of the nation turned to Virginia, where some found the notion of "the people" running a democratic government preposterous. Patrick Henry, leader of the Antifederalists, argued that even the first three words of the document were wrong: "Who authorized them to speak the language of *We the people,* instead of, *We the states?* States are the characteristics and the soul of a confederation."[33] But James Madison, thoroughly convinced of the need for a national government, saw no danger to the states, saying that the national government's "delegated powers" would keep it within limits. This sentiment could not persuade George Mason, who had refused to sign the Constitution: "Where is the barrier drawn between the government, and the rights of the citizens?"[34]

The key to success was Edmund Randolph, the politically ambitious thirty-four-year-old governor of Virginia, who had proposed the Virginia Plan in the Convention and then, unhappy with the outcome of the debates, refused to sign the final version of the Constitution. He switched to Madison's side in the ratification debate, arguing that he would "assent to the lopping [of his right arm] before I assent to the dissolution of the union." Randolph urged the acceptance of subsequent amendments

Bill of Rights The first ten amendments to the Constitution, added in 1781.

to the document just as Hancock had done in Massachusetts. Randolph's argument proved decisive. On June 25, 1788, by a narrow margin of ten votes, the Constitution was ratified in Virginia. New Hampshire had moved more quickly, becoming the ninth state to ratify, but, although tenth, Virginia's size made its action important in securing the success of the new government.

A week after Virginia's vote, New York State ratified the Constitution by a razor-thin 30–27 margin. North Carolina waited until after the Bill of Rights had been sent to the states for ratification before adding its assent in November 1789. And Rhode Island continued to take its time, waiting until May 29, 1790, to ratify the Constitution by a narrow 34–32 vote.

This highly political debate over the Constitution was proof that the new system would work because democracy had worked. The American people had freely and without war debated and chosen their new form of government. They had put aside their individual needs and local interests for the common good. As Benjamin Rush, a Philadelphia physician who signed the Declaration of Independence and lived to see the Constitution ratified, said, "'Tis done, we have become a nation."[35]

Adoption of the Bill of Rights

When the First Congress convened in 1789, Representative Roger Sherman of Connecticut, the only man to sign all three of this nation's founding documents, was then serving as a member of a select committee appointed by the House of Representatives to sift through more than two hundred amendments proposed in state debates to compose a possible Bill of Rights consisting of 11 amendments.[36] The Committee never mentioned this draft, instead choosing to send seventeen amendments to Congress for its consideration, with twelve being passed and sent to the states for ratification. Ten were ratified in 1791, becoming known as the **Bill of Rights**. As you can see from Table 2.3, the first eight amendments drafted by the First Congress guaranteed a variety of rights against government control and pro-

---

Table 2.3 ▪ The First Ten Amendments to the Constitution (The Bill of Rights)

Safeguards of Personal and Political Freedoms

1. Freedom of speech, press, and religion, and right to assemble peaceably and to petition government to redress grievances
2. Right to keep and bear arms

Outmoded Protection Against British Occupation

3. Protection against quartering troops in private homes

Safeguards in the Judicial Process and Against Arbitrary Government Action

4. Protection against "unreasonable" searches and seizures by the government
5. Guarantees of a grand jury for capital crimes, against double jeopardy, against being forced to testify against oneself, against being deprived of life or property without "due process of law," and against the taking of property without just compensation
6. Guarantees of rights in criminal trials including right to speedy and public trial, to be informed of the nature of the charges, to confront witnesses, to compel witnesses to appear in one's defense, and to the assistance of counsel
7. Guarantee of right of trial by a jury of one's peers
8. Guarantees against excessive bail and the imposition of cruel and unusual punishment

Description of Unenumerated Rights and Reserved Powers

9. Assurance that rights not listed for protection against the power of the central government in the Constitution are still retained by the people
10. Assurance that the powers not delegated to the central government are reserved by the states, or to the people

vided procedural safeguards in criminal trials and against arbitrary governmental action. The Ninth and Tenth Amendments were intended to describe the new constitutional structure, assuring that the people or the states would retain rights not listed in the Constitution, or powers not delegated to the national government. The amendments placed limits on government power by prohibiting the *national* government from intruding on fundamental rights and liberties. However, the rights of the people against *state* intrusion would be left to the individual state constitutions and legislatures. As we will see in Chapter 13, though, over time America would further approach democracy as the Supreme Court applied all but a few of the provisions of the Bill of Rights to the states as well.

UPDATING THE CONSTITUTION

The framers viewed the Constitution as a lasting document, one that would endure long after the debates and ratification. They did not believe, as Thomas Jefferson and George Washington did, that a new constitution should be written every generation, or twenty years, or so. To create a lasting document, the framers drafted a constitution that included an amendment process to allow for adjustments to their handiwork. In addition, the Supreme Court would play a role, along with the pressures of social and political change, to alter a flexible and responsive constitution. This way, the Constitution could be kept timely and current. But the Constitution is not easy to alter, no matter how strong, compelling, or passionate the need.

Updating the Constitution through the Amendment Process

The framers deliberately made the amendment process difficult, thus placing the Constitution beyond the temporary passions of the people, but they did not require unanimity, which had already failed in the Articles of Confederation. Clearly, the amendment process was to be used for only the most serious issues.

The framers established a two-stage amendment process, resembling the one used to approve the Constitution. First, there must be a **proposal** for a change that the states must then **ratify**. The framers wanted to ensure that each new amendment would be considered carefully. Thus, they required a powerful consensus of political and social support for amendments, known as a **supermajority**. This means that each stage of the process must be approved by more than the simple majority of 50 percent plus one.

The proposal stage for a Constitutional Amendment requires either a two-thirds vote of both houses of Congress or an application from two-thirds of the states for a constitutional convention. Ratification is accomplished by a vote of three-quarters of the state legislatures or a three-quarters vote of specially created state ratifying conventions. While the framers reserved this extraordinary voting requirement for other important tasks, such as overriding a presidential veto and ratifying a treaty, here alone the supermajority must be mustered twice on the same issue. This difference was the basis for the recent Senate nuclear option debate. Republicans were seeking to change the 60 percent supermajority vote required to end a Senate filibuster into a simple majority vote. Interestingly, had this scenario played out, had the vote been tied in the Senate, it could have been accomplished by a simple majority vote (with Vice President Cheney able to cast a tie-breaking vote if necessary). The amendment process is illustrated in Figure 2.2.

No formal time limit was placed on ratifying amendments, but a limit can be included in the body of the amendment, as it was in the ERA, and Congress can extend the limit if it wishes. Although the Supreme Court has been reluctant to rule on the constitutionality of such time limits, in 1921 it did rule that the seven-year limit placed in the Eighteenth Amendment was "reasonable."[37]

Quick Review

Amending the Constitution

- By two-thirds vote in both houses of Congress.
- By legislatures in three-fourths of the states.
- By request of two-thirds of state legislatures for a constitutional convention.
- By ratifying conventions in three-fourths of the states.

 MakeItReal

Primary Source: Amendments to the Constitution

proposal The first stage of the constitutional amendment process, in which a change is proposed.

ratify An act of approval of proposed constitutional amendments by the states; the second step of the amendment process.

supermajority A majority vote required for constitutional amendments; consists of more than a simple majority of 50 percent plus one.

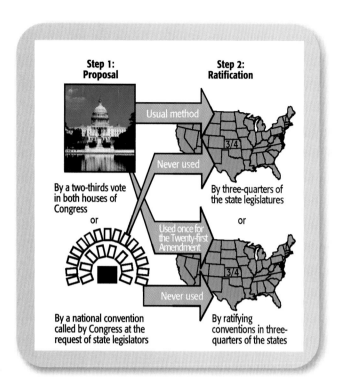

Figure 2.2 Procedures for Amending the Constitution
Although the framers provided four ways to amend the Constitution, only one method is usually used: proposal of an amendment by two-thirds of each house of Congress and ratification by three-quarters of the state legislatures. The sole exception was the Twenty-First Amendment repealing Prohibition. Ratification of this amendment took place in special state conventions.

Although proposed several times, to date no amendment has been approved by constitutional convention. All have been proposed in Congress, and all except the Twenty-first Amendment repealing Prohibition have been ratified using state legislatures. Since there has been only one Constitutional Convention, a variety of interesting questions remain about the prospects for another such event. How would the delegates be selected? How would the votes be apportioned among the fifty states? Must all social groups be represented, and how? And even if a convention is called to consider a specific proposal, might a runaway convention lead to reconsideration of the entire Constitution, as happened to the Articles of Confederation in 1787? The answers to these questions are unknown, and with one runaway convention in our past, few are willing to risk having another. In 1911, thirty-one states called for a convention to consider direct election of the Senate. A fearful Congress quickly proposed such an amendment in 1912 that, after 1913 ratification by the states, became the Seventeenth Amendment.

If you look at the ratified amendments you will see how remarkably few changes have been made in the Constitution, with all of them grouped around four purposes: to expand rights and equality, to correct flaws in or revise the original constitutional plan for government, to make public policy, and to overturn Supreme Court decisions. The amendments and their effects are outlined in Table 2.4.

At times, the amendment proposal process can be used in an attempt to reverse Supreme Court decisions. For example, after the Supreme Court struck down state and federal laws designed to outlaw burning the American flag, an amendment to accomplish the same thing was unsuccessfully proposed. In 1997, when the Supreme Court refused to allow states to impose term limits on candidates for congressional office, and Congress failed to pass a federal term limits law, the idea that this goal could be accomplished by constitutional amendment was considered.

Over the years, special interest groups and political parties have sought to amend the Constitution so as to shape the morality of the nation or further their political agenda. In 1917, the temperance (anti-liquor) movement succeeded in getting the Eighteenth Amendment passed to ban drinking and secured its ratification two years later, only to have it repealed by the Twenty-first Amendment in 1933, thanks

Table 2.4 ▪ The Constitutional Amendments

Number	Proposed	Ratified	Subject	Purpose
11	1794	1795	To sue a state in federal court, individuals need state consent	Overruled a Supreme Court decision
12	1803	1804	Requires separate electoral college votes for president and vice president	Corrected a government plan flaw
13	1865	1865	Prohibits slavery	Expanded rights
14	1866	1868	Gives citizenship to freed slaves, guarantees them due process and equal protection of the laws, and protects their privileges and immunities	Expanded rights
15	1869	1870	Grants freed slaves the right to vote	Expanded voting rights
16	1909	1913	Grants Congress power to collect income tax	Overruled a Supreme Court decision
17	1912	1913	Provides for direct election of the Senate (formerly elected by state legislatures)	Expanded voting rights
18	1917	1919	Prohibited the manufacture, sale, and transportation of intoxicating liquor	Public policy
19	1919	1920	Grants women the right to vote	Expanded voting rights
20	1932	1933	Changes presidential inauguration date from March 4 to January 20, and opening date of Congress to January 3	Revised a government plan
21	1933	1933	Repeals the Eighteenth Amendment	Public policy
22	1947	1951	Limits the president to two terms in office	Revised a government plan
23	1960	1961	Grants citizens of Washington, D.C., status in electoral college to vote for president	Expanded voting rights
24	1962	1964	Prohibits charging a poll tax to vote	Expanded voting rights
25	1965	1967	Provides for succession of president or vice president in the event of death, removal from office, incapacity, or resignation	Revised a government plan
26	1971	1971	Grants the right to vote to eighteen- to twenty-year olds	Expanded voting rights
27	1789	1992	Prohibits a pay raise voted by Congress from going into effect until the following session	Public policy

to a ratification by state constitutional conventions—the only time in American history an amendment passed in that way. In recent years, cultural interest groups have sought to use the amendment process to ban gay marriages and abortions and to reestablish prayer in public schools, without success. The double supermajority feature of the amendment process usually prevents such uses by special interest and political groups, reserving amendments for the expression of the overwhelming desires of the vast majority.

Updating the Constitution by Judicial Interpretation

The Constitution has managed to remain vibrant and current even though it has been amended only twenty-seven times. Its survival has to do both with the brilliant ambiguity built into the Constitution and the power of the Supreme Court to interpret it.

But where did the Court obtain such power? As you will learn in Chapter 6, in the 1803 case of *Marbury* v. *Madison,* the Court under Chief Justice John Marshall ruled that because the Supreme Court interprets laws and the Constitution is a law, the

MakeItReal

Primary Source: *Marbury* v. *Madison*

Questions for Reflection

What role should the Constitution and the Bill of Rights play during times of crisis?

How much of that determination should reflect the Constitution's role in earlier times of crisis?

Court has the power to be the final interpreter of the Constitution. This power, judicial review, enables the Court to overturn acts of the other two branches of government if it rules that those acts violate the Constitution. In doing so, the Supreme Court interprets the Constitution, giving new meaning to the phrases and provisions written in 1787. This occurred in 2004 when the Supreme Court overruled two Bush administration actions. First was the designation of Yaser Esam Hamdi, an American citizen captured in the Afghanistan war, as an "enemy combatant" and holding him incommunicado for nearly three years. Second, the Court ruled that the government could not detain terrorism suspects without granting them legal hearings.

Since a Supreme Court constitutional ruling can be overturned by only the Court itself or through a constitutional amendment, these rulings, in effect, change the meaning of the Constitution. In exercising this power, the justices take on the role of modern constitutional framers, trying to define what the document should mean in the modern age. Throughout American history, scholars have debated the Court's role, with some believing that the justices should uphold the framers' original meaning of the Constitution and others maintaining that they should continue to update the document using a modern perspective.

THE GETTYSBURG ADDRESS AND AMERICA'S APPROACH TO DEMOCRACY

The most remarkable feature of the Constitution is how it has adapted to the times, changing along with an ever-changing nation. The world has changed dramatically since 1787, when it took four days for German immigrant Jacob Shallus to write the Constitution by hand on four pieces of stretched vellum with a quill pen and ink made from oak galls and dyes. Now we can create a version of the same document in just a few seconds using computer software. We have gone from a population of 3 million to one of over 290 million people, from a geographic base of thirteen seashore colonies to fifty states spread across a continent. In 1787, wars took months to develop as ships crossed vast oceans; now, one press of a button can mean instant annihilation. Yet, as Supreme Court Justice Byron White has argued, the Constitution still survives because, "From the summer of 1787 to the present the government of the United States has become an endeavor far beyond the contemplation of the Framers. But the wisdom of the Framers was to anticipate that the nation would grow and new problems of governance would require different solutions."[38]

Over time, actions taken by the different branches of government have changed the nature of the government's structure without changing the Constitution. The framers originally gave Congress the power to declare war, but the speed of modern warfare has created the need for quicker responses. Now the president has the power to make war. The Korean and Vietnam wars, along with a host of other conflicts, were presidential wars. The framers also intended, despite the system of checks and balances, for Congress to be the predominant branch. But certain presidents have enlarged the executive powers. Thomas Jefferson directed the purchase of the Louisiana Territory; Abraham Lincoln imposed martial law and freed the slaves; Woodrow Wilson and Franklin D. Roosevelt extended the powers of their offices during world wars; and a host of other presidents exercised powers well beyond those delegated to them by Congress. Thus President George W. Bush could commit troops to Afghanistan, Iraq, and the "war on terrorism" without congressional declarations of war. It is doubtful that Madison and Franklin would recognize much of today's government, but they would appreciate the fact that their handiwork allowed this evolution to take place.

As you have seen, the original Constitution was hardly a testament to full participatory democracy. It begins with the words, "We the People," but the "we" who drafted the document were the fifty-five delegates to the Constitutional Convention in Philadelphia and the elite landowners they represented. The Constitution did not fully protect the rights of all citizens, and the framers did not seek to use their 4,400-word document to advance social or political equality. Slavery was not banned; in fact,

Great Speeches: Franklin Delano Roosevelt, "The Great Arsenal of Democracy" (December 29, 1940)

it seemed to be condoned. The feminine pronoun never appeared in the document, and women had no more rights under the Constitution than they had under the Articles of Confederation. Most Americans could not vote and had essentially no voice in the operation of their government. Perhaps for this reason some of the framers anticipated that this document would need revision within a generation as the nation expanded. In that sense, as Vaclav Havel said so eloquently, democracy in America only began in 1787, and the approach to democracy would have to continue.

President Abraham Lincoln continued that evolution in 1863 when he ventured to Gettysburg, Pennsylvania, to dedicate the new Civil War cemetery there. In his short 271-word speech, Lincoln began by referring to the Declaration of Independence: "Fourscore and seven years ago our fathers brought forth on this continent a new nation, conceived in liberty and dedicated to the proposition that all men are created equal." But now, he argued, by the men who had given their "last full measure of devotion" on the battlefield, that promise had become "that this nation, under God, shall have a new birth of freedom—and that government of the people, by the people, for the people, shall not perish from the earth." This concept represented a "Second Declaration of Independence." Suddenly, the governmental vision created by free, white, landowning men over the age of twenty-one had become a more inclusive democracy promising a vision of democracy for all people. As author Garry Wills argued, "If all men are created equal, they cannot be property. They cannot be ruled by owner-monarchs. They must be self-governing in the minimal sense of self-possession. Their equality cannot be denied if the nation is to live by its creed, and voice it, and test it, and die for it."[39] Applying this new concept of a "people's government" to the Constitution allowed the American government to better approach democracy.

The framers hoped that their Constitution would lead to a stable republic, an improvement over the Articles of Confederation. They did not seek to establish a system of pure democracy, relying instead on the notion of a representative government. That task would be left to the government itself, the people it represented, and the Supreme Court's interpretation of the Constitution. Yet the constitutional convention was truly "the Miracle" described by Catherine Drinker Bowen, not only because these men were able to reach compromise on the shape of a new government but also because the compromise they reached would create a system of government that continues to govern, even in times of crisis such as we now face, in ways that the framers could not fully anticipate.

MakeItReal

Visual Literacy: The Election of 1860

Question for Reflection

How might legislators field-test potential acts to weigh the long-term constitutional ramifications of their implementation prior to approval?

Summary

1. The governments of some American colonies were based on the idea of a compact, an agreement legally binding two or more parties to enforceable rules. Other colonies evolved from royal grants of land that gave governing rights to a lord or baron, who became the colony's proprietor.

2. Frequent conflicts between the governors and the colonial legislatures made the colonists highly suspicious of executive power. The colonists were also influenced by the ideas of Charles de Montesquieu, who saw the separation of executive, legislative, and judicial powers as the best way to counteract any tendency toward despotism, and by the ideas of social contract theorists such as Thomas Hobbes and John Locke—especially the latter, who asserted the importance of limited government based on popular consent.

3. Slowly American colonists recognized the need for cooperation. Benjamin Franklin proposed a plan that called for a self-governing confederation, a league of

sovereign states that would delegate specific powers to a central government. However, in 1754, both the Crown and the colonial assemblies rejected Franklin's plan.

4. After 1763, Britain imposed a series of direct taxes on the American colonies. The Sugar Act retained a tax on molasses and extended duties to other goods imported into the colonies; the Stamp Act required that taxes be placed on all printed matter and legal documents. The Townshend Revenue Acts imposed taxes on glass, lead, tea, and paper imported into the colonies.

5. The tax on tea especially irritated the colonists. The most famous protest against this tax was the Boston Tea Party of December 16, 1773, in which colonists dumped chests of tea into Boston Harbor. Parliament responded by passing the Coercive Acts, which closed Boston Harbor and required the quartering of British soldiers in private homes. In September 1774, representatives of twelve colonies met in Philadelphia to demand restoration of their English rights.

6. Hostilities broke out in the spring of 1775 when British troops attempted to destroy ammunition stored by colonial militias. Three weeks after the battles at Lexington and Concord, the Second Continental Congress convened, becoming in effect a revolutionary government. The next year, the Continental Congress approved and signed the Declaration of Independence.

7. On November 15, 1777, the Continental Congress adopted the Articles of Confederation. Under the Articles, the central government lacked the power to impose taxes, raise an army, or regulate commerce. Hence it was unable to protect either citizens or private property.

8. Although the stated goal of the Constitutional Convention was to revise the Articles of Confederation, some delegates believed that the Articles needed to be scrapped altogether and replaced by an entirely new document. Debate at the convention centered on two major proposals. The Virginia Plan called for a system of proportional representation in which the legislature would consist of two chambers, or "houses," and each state's representation in both houses would depend on its population. The New Jersey Plan proposed a unicameral (one-house) legislature in which each state would have one vote. The delegates voted to use the Virginia Plan as the basis for further discussion.

9. A key debate at the Convention dealt with representation in the two houses of Congress. States with large populations sought proportional representation in both houses, whereas those with smaller populations called for an equal number of votes for each state. In the Great (or Connecticut) Compromise the delegates decided that representation in the House of Representatives would be based on each state's population, while each state would have two votes in the Senate.

10. Another important debate was over slavery. The southern states wanted slaves to be counted as part of the population when determining representation in Congress; the northern states wanted slaves to be excluded from the count. The outcome of the debate was the three-fifths compromise: Each state's representation would be determined by adding three-fifths of the number of slaves to the number of free citizens in that state.

11. The delegates were also divided over the nature of the presidency. Some favored a single national executive with the power to veto legislative acts, while others were concerned that a single executive would hold too much power and called instead for a board of executives. Eventually they agreed on a single executive.

12. The new Constitution created a republican form of government, in which the people hold an indirect voting power over elected officials. Originally, only members of the House of Representatives would be elected directly by the people; senators would be chosen by the state legislatures, and the president by an electoral college. Over the years the people have gained a more direct voice in the government through a series of constitutional changes such as popular election of senators and extension of the right to vote to all people over the age of eighteen.

13. The Constitution established a system of separation of powers in which different powers are granted to the three major branches of government. In addition, it set up checks and balances, giving each branch the power to approve, disapprove, or alter what the other branches do. It also distributed powers between the central government and the state governments. The powers of the central government are delegated—expressly granted and limited in nature—while all remaining powers are reserved to the states. The supremacy clause states that the dictates of the national government take precedence over those of any state government.

14. Supporters of the Constitution called themselves *Federalists*; opponents took the name *Antifederalists*. The Federalists claimed that the new government was designed to represent the sovereignty of the people, while the Antifederalists believed that the states should remain independent of the central government. The Constitution was finally ratified after the Federalists agreed to the addition of the Bill of Rights.

15. The Constitution can be amended through a two-stage process. First, there must be a proposal for a change, which requires either a two-thirds vote of both houses of Congress or a request by two-thirds of the states for a constitutional convention. Then the amendment must be ratified by a vote of three-quarters of the state legislatures or a three-quarters vote of specially created state ratifying conventions. The primary source of constitutional change, however, is judicial interpretation in response to political and social changes.

Review Questions

1. Analyze the factors that led to the Revolutionary War.
2. Explain the influence of the French and Indian War on the creation of the Albany Plan, the need for Britain to increase colonial taxation, and the American Revolution.
3. Describe the historical background of the Constitution, highlighting the democratic forces as well as the aristocratic ones that were at work in 1787.
4. Explain the political strategies and tactics of the Federalists from the Constitutional Convention through ratification of the Constitution. Discuss whether these tactics were justified by the need for order and stability.
5. What was the importance of the three-fifths compromise? What were the ramifications of this compromise for the country?
6. What were the features of the Constitution that contributed to its longevity? Why has it only required twenty-seven amendments in over two hundred years?

Key Terms

Suggested Readings

COLLIER, CHRISTOPHER, and JAMES LINCOLN COLLIER. *Decision in Philadelphia: The Constitutional Convention of 1787.* New York: Random House, 1986. A popular account of the Constitutional Convention using all of the latest scholarship to bring it to life.

ELLIS, JOSEPH. *Founding Brothers: The Revolutionary Generation.* New York: Alfred A. Knopf, 2000. A study of the founders' views on, and actions in, the democracy that they created during the remainder of their lives.

FLETCHER, GEORGE P. *Our Secret Constitution: How Lincoln Redefined American Democracy.* New York: Oxford University Press, 2001. A study of the meaning of the Gettysburg address for the expanding nature of American democracy.

FONER, ERIC. *The Story of American Freedom.* New York: W.W. Norton, and Company, 1998. A wonderful history of the evolution of American democracy through the study of key events in American political history.

HAMILTON, ALEXANDER, JAMES MADISON, and JOHN JAY. *The Federalist Papers.* New York: New American Library, 1961. The compelling arguments by three framers on behalf of the Constitution, representing the document's handbook.

LAZARE, DANIEL. *The Velvet Coup: The Constitution, the Supreme Court, and the Decline of American Democracy.* London: Verso, 2001. An analysis of the nature of the effect of the 2000 presidential election on the Constitution and American democracy.

MAIER, PAULINE. *American Scripture: Making the Declaration of Independence.* New York: Vintage Books, 1997. A complete analysis of the Declaration of Independence, including its change from the original draft, and its meaning for America.

McCULLOUGH, DAVID. *John Adams.* New York: Simon and Schuster, 2001. A sweeping Pulitzer-prize winning biography of the Founder whom some believe to be just as important, if not more so, than Thomas Jefferson.

RAKOVE, JACK. *Original Meanings: Politics and Ideas in the Making of the Constitution.* New York: Vintage Press, 1996. The Pulitzer Prize-winning analysis of the making of the Constitution and the "original intent" of the framers.

WOOD, GORDON S. *The Creation of the American Republic, 1776–1787.* Chapel Hill: University of North Carolina Press, 1969. A fascinating study of political thought in America during the time of the framing.

The Constitution of the United States

THE PREAMBLE

We the People of the United States, in Order to form a more perfect Union, establish Justice, insure domestic Tranquility, provide for the common defence, promote the general Welfare, and secure the Blessings of Liberty to ourselves and our Posterity, do ordain and establish this Constitution for the United States of America.

"We, the people." Three simple words, yet of profound importance and contentious origin. Every government in the world at the time of the Constitutional Convention was some type of monarchy, wherein sovereign power flowed from the top. The Founders of our new country rejected monarchy as a form of government and proposed instead a republic, which would draw its sovereignty from the people.

The Articles of Confederation that governed the U.S. from 1776 until 1789 started with: "We the under signed Delegates of the States." Early drafts of the new constitution started with: "We, the states . . ." But again, the Founders were not interested in another union of states but rather the creation of a new national government. Therefore, "We, the states" was changed to "We, the people." The remainder of the preamble describes the generic functions of government. These would apply to almost any type of government. Some have proven more critical than others. For example, "promote the general welfare" has been cited as the authority for social welfare programs of the federal government.

ARTICLE I—THE LEGISLATIVE ARTICLE

Legislative Power

The very first article in the Constitution established the legislative branch of the new national government. Why did the framers start with the legislative power instead of the executive branch? Under the Articles of Confederation, the legislature was the only functional instrument of government. Therefore, the framers truly believed it was the most important component of the new government.

Section 1 All legislative Powers herein granted shall be vested in a Congress of the United States, which shall consist of a Senate and House of Representatives.

Section 1 established a bicameral (two-chamber) legislature, or an upper (Senate) and lower (House of Representatives) organization of the legislative branch.

House of Representatives: Composition; Qualifications; Apportionment; Impeachment Power

Section 2 Clause 1. The House of Representatives shall be composed of Members chosen every second Year by the People of the several States, and the Electors in each State shall have the Qualifications requisite for Electors of the most numerous Branch of the State Legislature.

This section sets the term of office for House members (2 years) and indicates that those voting for Congress will have the same qualifications as those voting for the state legislatures. Originally, states limited voters to white property owners. Some states even had religious disqualifications, such as Catholic or Jewish. Most property and religious qualifications for voting were removed by the 1840s, but race and gender restrictions remained.

Clause 2. No Person shall be a Representative who shall not have attained to the Age of twenty five Years, and been seven Years a Citizen of the United States, and who shall not, when elected, be an Inhabitant of that State in which he shall be chosen.

This section sets forth the basic qualifications of a representative: at least 25 years of age, a U.S. citizen for at least 7 years, and a resident of a state. Note that the Constitution does not require a person to be a resident of the district he or she represents. At the time the Constitution was written, life expectancy was about 43 years of age. So a person 25 years old was middle aged. Considering today's life expectancy of about 78 years, the equivalent age of 25 would be about 45. The average age of a current representative is 53. Because of the specificity of the Constitution as to the qualifications for office, the U.S. Supreme Court ruled that term limits could not be imposed.

Clause 2 does not specify how many terms a representative can serve in Congress. One provision of the Republican House *Contract with America,* "The Citizens Legislature Act," called for term limits for legislators. This provision was not enacted. Subsequently, some states passed legislation to limit the terms of their U.S. representatives. Because of the specificity of the qualifications for office, the Supreme Court ruled in *U.S. Term Limits, Inc. v. Thornton*, 514 U.S. 779 (1995), that term limits for U.S. legislators could not be imposed by any state but would require a constitutional amendment.

Clause 3. Representatives and direct Taxes[1] shall be apportioned among the several States which may be included within this Union, according to their respective Numbers, which shall be determined by adding to the whole Number of free Persons, including those bound to Service for a Term of Years, and excluding Indians not taxed, three fifths of all other Persons.[2] The actual Enumeration shall be made within three Years after the first Meeting of the Congress of the United States, and within every subsequent Term of ten Years, in such Manner as they shall by Law direct. The Number of Representatives shall not exceed one for every thirty Thousand, but each State shall have at Least one Representative; and until such enumeration shall be made, the State of New Hampshire shall be entitled to chuse three, Massachusetts eight, Rhode-Island and Providence Plantations one, Connecticut five, New-York six, New Jersey four, Pennsylvania eight, Delaware one, Maryland six, Virginia ten, North Carolina five, South Carolina five, and Georgia three.

This clause contains the Three-Fifths Compromise, wherein American Indians and Blacks were only counted as 3/5 of a person for congressional representation purposes. This clause also addresses the question of congressional reapportionment every 10 years, which requires a census. Since the 1911 Reapportionment Act, the size of the House of Representatives has been set at 435. This is the designated size that is reapportioned every 10 years. Based on changes of population, some states gain and some states lose representatives. This clause also provides that every state, regardless of population, will have at least one (1) representative. Currently, seven states have only one representative.

Clause 4. When vacancies happen in the Representation from any State, the Executive Authority thereof shall issue Writs of Election to fill such Vacancies.

This clause provides a procedure for replacing a U.S. representative in the case of death, resignation, or expulsion from the House. Essentially, the governor of the representative's state will assign a successor. Generally, if less than half a term is left, the governor will appoint a successor. If more than half a term is remaining, most states require a special election to fill the vacancy.

Clause 5. The House of Representatives shall choose their Speaker and other Officers; and shall have the sole Power of Impeachment.

Only one officer of the House is specified—the Speaker. All other officers are decided by the House. This clause also gives the House authority for impeachments (accusations) against officials of the executive and judicial branches.

Senate: Composition; Qualifications; Impeachment Trials

Section 3 Clause 1. The Senate of the United States shall be composed of two Senators from each State, *chosen by the Legislature thereof,*[3] for six Years; and each Senator shall have one Vote.

This clause treats each state equally—all have two senators. Originally, senators were chosen by state legislators, but since passage and ratification of the 17th Amendment, they are now elected by popular vote. This clause also establishes the term of a senator—6 years—three times that of a House member.

Clause 2. Immediately after they shall be assembled in Consequence of the first Election, they shall be divided as equally as may be into three Classes. The Seats of the Senators of the first Class shall be vacated at the Expiration of the second Year, of the second Class at the Expiration of the fourth Year, and of the third Class at the Expiration of the sixth Year, so that one third may be chosen every second Year; *and if Vacancies happen by Resignation, or otherwise, during the Recess of the Legislature of any State, the Executive thereof may make temporary Appointments until the next Meeting of the Legislature, which shall then fill such Vacancies.*[4]

To prevent a wholesale election of senators every six years, this clause provides that one-third of the Senate will be elected every two years. Senate vacancies are filled in the same way as the House—either appointment by the governor or by special election.

Clause 3. No Person shall be a Senator who shall not have attained to the Age of thirty Years, and been nine Years a Citizen of the United States, and who shall not, when elected, be an Inhabitant of that State for which he shall be chosen.

This clause sets forth the qualifications for U.S. senator: at least 30 years old, a U.S. citizen for at least nine years, and a citizen of a state. The equivalent age of 30 today would be 54 years old. The average age of a U.S. senator at present is 58.3 years.

Clause 4. The Vice President of the United States shall be President of the Senate, but shall have no Vote, unless they be equally divided.

The only constitutional duty of the vice president is specified in this clause—president of the Senate. This official only has a vote if there is a tie vote in the Senate; then the vice president's vote breaks the tie.

Clause 5. The Senate shall chuse their other Officers, and also a President pro tempore, in the Absence of the Vice President, or when he shall exercise the Office of President of the United States.

---

[1]Modified by the 16th Amendment
[2]Replaced by Section 2, 14th Amendment

[3]Repealed by the 17th Amendment
[4]Modified by the 17th Amendment

One official office in the U.S. Senate is specified—temporary president, who fills in during the vice president's absence (which is normally the case). All other Senate officers are designated and selected by the Senate.

Clause 6. The Senate shall have the sole Power to try all Impeachments. When sitting for that Purpose, they shall be on Oath or Affirmation. When the President of the United States is tried, the Chief Justice shall preside: And no Person shall be convicted without the Concurrence of two thirds of the Members present.

Clause 7. Judgment in Cases of Impeachment shall not extend further than to removal from Office, and disqualification to hold and enjoy any Office of honor, Trust or Profit under the United States: but the Party convicted shall nevertheless be liable and subject to Indictment, Trial, Judgment and Punishment, according to Law.

The Senate acts as a trial court for impeached federal officials. If the accused is the president, the Chief Justice of the U.S. Supreme Court presides. Otherwise, the vice president normally presides. Conviction of the charges requires a 2/3 majority vote of those senators present at the time of the vote. Conviction results in the federal official's removal from office and disqualification to hold any other federal appointed office. Removal from office does not bar further prosecution under applicable criminal or civil laws, nor does it apparently bar one from elected office. A current representative, Alcee L. Hastings, was removed as a federal district judge. He subsequently ran for Congress and now represents Florida's 23rd Congressional District.

Congressional Elections: Times, Places, Manner

Section 4   Clause 1. The Times, Places and Manner of holding Elections for Senators and Representatives, shall be prescribed in each State by the Legislature thereof; but the Congress may at any time by Law make or alter such Regulations, except as to the Places of chusing Senators.

Clause 2. The Congress shall assemble at least once in every Year, *and such Meeting shall be on the first Monday in December, unless they shall by Law appoint a different Day.*[5]

The states determine the place and manner of electing representatives and senators, but Congress has the right to make or change these laws or regulations, except for the election sites. Congress is required to meet annually, and now, by law, annual meetings begin in January.

Powers and Duties of the Houses

Section 5   Clause 1. Each House shall be the Judge of the Elections, Returns and Qualifications of its own Members, and a Majority of each shall constitute a Quorum to do Business; but a smaller Number may adjourn from day to day, and may be authorized to compel the Attendance of absent Members, in such Manner, and under the Penalties as each House may provide.

---

[5]Changed by the 20th Amendment

This clause enables each legislative branch to essentially make its own rules. Normally, to take a vote, a quorum is necessary. But if no votes are scheduled, fewer than a quorum can convene a session.

Clause 2. Each House may determine the Rules of its Proceedings, punish its Members for disorderly Behaviour, and, with the Concurrence of two thirds, expel a Member.

Essentially, each branch promulgates its own rules and punishes its own members. The ultimate punishment is expulsion of the member, which requires a 2/3 vote. Expulsion does not prevent the member from running again.

Clause 3. Each House shall keep a Journal of its Proceedings, and from time to time publish the same, excepting such Parts as may in their Judgment require Secrecy; and the Yeas and Nays of the Members of either House on any question shall, at the Desire of one fifth of those Present, be entered on the Journal.

An official record called the Congressional Record, House Journal, etc., is kept for all sessions. It is a daily account of House and Senate floor debates, votes, and members' remarks. However, a record is not printed if a proceeding is closed to the public for security reasons. Many votes are by voice vote, and if at least 1/5 of the members request, a recorded vote of Yeas and Nays will be conducted and documented. This procedure permits analysis of congressional role-call votes.

Clause 4. Neither House, during the Session of Congress, shall, without the Consent of the other, adjourn for more than three days, nor to any other Place than that in which the two Houses shall be sitting.

This clause prevents one branch from adjourning for a long period of time or to some other location without the consent of the other branch.

Rights of Members

Section 6   Clause 1. The Senators and Representatives shall receive a Compensation for their Services, to be ascertained by Law, and paid out of the Treasury of the United States. They shall in all Cases, except Treason, Felony and Breach of the Peace, be privileged from Arrest during their Attendance at the Session of their respective Houses, and in going to and returning from the same; and for any Speech or Debate in either House, they shall not be questioned in any other Place.

This section ensures that senators and congressional representatives will be paid a salary from the U.S. Treasury. This salary is determined by no other than the legislature. According to the Library of Congress legislative Web site THOMAS: "The current salary for members of Congress is $145,100. A small number of leadership positions, like Speaker of the House, receive a somewhat higher salary." In addition, members of Congress receive many other benefits: free health care, fully funded retirement system, free gyms, 26 free round trips to their home state or district, etc. This section also provides

immunity from arrest or prosecution for congressional actions on the floor or in travel to and from the Congress. For example, few members of Congress have ever been charged with drunk driving.

Clause 2. No Senator or Representative shall, during the Time for which he was elected, be appointed to any civil Office under the Authority of the United States, which shall have been created, or the Emoluments whereof shall have been encreased during such time; and no Person holding any Office under the United States, shall be a Member of either House during his Continuance in Office.

This section prevents the U.S. from adopting a parliamentary democracy, since congressional members cannot hold executive offices and members of the executive branch cannot be members of Congress.

Legislative Powers: Bills and Resolutions

Section 7   Clause 1. All Bills for raising Revenue shall originate in the House of Representatives; but the Senate may propose or concur with Amendments as on other Bills.

This clause specifies one of the few powers specific to the U.S. House—revenue bills.

Clause 2. Every Bill which shall have passed the House of Representatives and the Senate, shall, before it becomes a Law, be presented to the President of the United States; If he approve he shall sign it, but if not he shall return it, with his Objections to that House in which it shall have originated, who shall enter the Objections at large on their Journal, and proceed to reconsider it. If after such Reconsideration two thirds of that House shall agree to pass the Bill, it shall be sent, together with the Objections, to the other House, by which it shall likewise be reconsidered, and if approved by two thirds of that House, it shall become a Law. But in all such Cases the Votes of both Houses shall be determined by yeas and Nays, and the Names of the Persons voting for and against the Bill shall be entered on the Journal of each House respectively. If any Bill shall not be returned by the President within ten Days (Sundays excepted) after it shall have been presented to him, the Same shall be a Law, in like Manner as if he had signed it, unless the Congress by their Adjournment prevent its Return, in which Case it shall not be a Law.

The heart of the checks and balances system is contained in this clause. Both the House and Senate must pass a bill and present it to the president. If the president fails to act on the bill within 10 days (not including Sundays), the bill will automatically become law. If the president signs the bill, it becomes law. If the president vetoes the bill and sends it back to Congress, this body may override the veto by a 2/3 vote in each branch. This vote must be a recorded vote.

Clause 3. Every Order, Resolution, or Vote to which the Concurrence of the Senate and House of Representatives may be necessary (except on a question of Adjournment) shall be presented to the President of the United States; and before the Same shall take Effect, shall be approved by him, or being disapproved by him, shall be repassed by two thirds of the Senate and House of Representatives, according to the Rules and Limitations prescribed in the Case of a Bill.

This clause covers every other type of legislative action other than a bill. Essentially, the same procedures apply in most cases. There are a few exceptions. For example, a joint resolution proposing a new congressional amendment is not subject to presidential veto.

Powers of Congress

Section 8   Clause 1. The Congress shall have Power To lay and collect Taxes, Duties, Imposts and Excises, to pay the Debts and provide for the common Defence and general Welfare of the United States; but all Duties, Imposts and Excises shall be uniform throughout the United States.
Clause 2. To borrow Money on the credit of the United States;
Clause 3. To regulate Commerce with foreign Nations, and among the several States, and with the Indian Tribes;
Clause 4. To establish an uniform Rule of Naturalization, and uniform Laws on the subject of Bankruptcies throughout the United States;
Clause 5. To coin Money, regulate the Value thereof, and of foreign Coin, and fix the Standard of Weights and Measures;
Clause 6. To provide for the Punishment of counterfeiting the Securities and current Coin of the United States;
Clause 7. To establish Post Offices and post Roads;
Clause 8. To promote the Progress of Science and useful Arts, by securing for limited Times to Authors and Inventors the exclusive Right to their respective Writings and Discoveries;
Clause 9. To constitute Tribunals inferior to the supreme Court;
Clause 10. To define and punish Piracies and Felonies committed on the high Seas, and Offences against the Law of Nations;
Clause 11. To declare War, grant Letters of Marque and Reprisal, and make Rules concerning Captures on Land and Water;
Clause 12. To raise and support Armies, but no Appropriation of Money to that Use shall be for a longer Term than two Years;
Clause 13. To provide and maintain a Navy;
Clause 14. To make Rules for the Government and Regulation of the land and naval Forces;
Clause 15. To provide for calling forth the Militia to execute the Laws of the Union, suppress Insurrections and repel Invasions;
Clause 16. To provide for organizing, arming, and disciplining, the Militia, and for governing such Part of them as may be employed in the Service of the United States, reserving to the States respectively, the Appointment of the Officers, and the Authority of training the Militia according to the discipline prescribed by Congress.

These clauses establish what are known as the "expressed" or "specified" powers of Congress. In theory, they serve as a limit or brake on congressional power.

Clause 17. To exercise exclusive Legislation in all Cases whatsoever, over such District (not exceeding ten Miles square) as may, by Cession of particular States, and the Acceptance of Congress, become the Seat of the Government of the United States, and to exercise like Authority over all Places purchased by the Consent of the Legislature of the State in which the Same shall be, for the Erection of Forts, Magazines, Arsenals, dock-Yards, and other needful Buildings;—And

This clause establishes the seat of the federal government, which was first started in New York.

It eventually was moved to Washington, D.C., when both Maryland and Virginia ceded land to the new national government, which then established the District of Columbia.

Clause 18. To make all Laws which shall be necessary and proper for carrying into Execution the foregoing Powers, and all other Powers vested by this Constitution in the Government of the United States, or in any Department or Officer thereof.

This clause, known as the "Elastic Clause," provides the basis for the doctrine of "implied" congressional powers, which was first introduced in the U.S. Supreme Court case of *McCulloch v. Maryland*, 1819. This doctrine tremendously expanded the power of Congress to pass legislation and make regulations.

Powers Denied to Congress

Section 9   Clause 1. The Migration or Importation of such Persons as any of the States now existing shall think proper to admit, shall not be prohibited by the Congress prior to the Year one thousand eight hundred and eight, but a Tax or duty may be imposed on such Importation, not exceeding ten dollars for each Person.

This clause was part of the Three-Fifths Compromise. Essentially, the new Congress was prohibited from stopping the importation of slaves until 1808, but it could impose a head tax not to exceed ten dollars for each slave.

Clause 2. The Privilege of the Writ of Habeas Corpus shall not be suspended, unless when in Cases of Rebellion or Invasion the public Safety may require it.

Congress cannot suspend the writ of habeas corpus except in cases of rebellion or invasion. The writ of habeas corpus permits a judge to inquire about the legality of detention or deprivation of liberty of any citizen.

Clause 3. No Bill of Attainder or ex post facto Law shall be passed.

This provision prohibits Congress from passing either bills of attainder (forfeiture of property in capital cases) or ex post facto laws (retroactive crimes after passage of legislation). Similar restrictions were enshrined in many state constitutions.

Clause 4. No Capitation, or other direct, Tax shall be laid, unless in Proportion to the Census or Enumeration herein before directed to be taken.[6]

This clause prevents Congress from passing an income tax. Only with passage of the 16th Amendment in 1913 did Congress gain this power.

Clause 5. No Tax or Duty shall be laid on Articles exported from any State.

---

[6]Modified by the 16th Amendment

This section establishes free trade within the U.S. The federal government cannot tax state exports.

Clause 6. No Preference shall be given by any Regulation of Commerce or Revenue to the Ports of one State over those of another; nor shall Vessels bound to, or from, one State, be obliged to enter, clear, or pay Duties in another.

This clause also applies to free trade within the U.S. The national government cannot show any preference to any state or maritime movements among the states.

Clause 7. No Money shall be drawn from the Treasury, but in Consequence of Appropriations made by Law; and a regular Statement and Account of the Receipts and Expenditures of all public Money shall be published from time to time.

This provision of the Constitution prevents any expenditure unless it has been specifically provided for in an appropriations bill. At the beginning of most fiscal years, Congress has not completed its work on the budget. Technically, the government cannot spend any money according to this provision and would have to shut down. So Congress normally passes a Continuing Resolution Authority providing temporary authority to continue to spend money until the final budget is approved and signed into law.

Clause 8. No Title of Nobility shall be granted by the United States: And no Person holding any Office of Profit or Trust under them, shall, without the Consent of Congress, accept of any present, Emolument, Office, or Title, of any kind whatever, from any King, Prince, or foreign State.

Feudalism would not be established in the new country. We would have no nobles. No federal official can accept a title of nobility (even honorary) without permission of Congress.

Powers Denied to the States

This section sets out the prohibitions on state actions.

Section 10   Clause 1. No State shall enter into any Treaty, Alliance, or Confederation; grant Letters of Marque and Reprisal; coin Money; emit Bills of Credit; make any Thing but gold and silver Coin a Tender in Payment of Debts; pass any Bill of Attainder, ex post facto Law, or Law impairing the Obligation of Contracts, or grant any Title of Nobility.

This particular clause is a laundry list of denied powers. Note that these restrictions cannot even be waived by Congress. States are not to engage in foreign relations or acts of war. A letter of marque and reprisal was used during these times to provide legal cover for privateers. The federal government's currency monopoly is established. The sanctity of contracts is specified, and similar state prohibitions are specified for bills of attainder, ex post facto, etc.

Clause 2. No State shall, without the Consent of the Congress, lay any Imposts or Duties on Imports or Exports, except what may be absolutely necessary for executing its inspection Laws: and the net Produce of all Duties and Imposts, laid by any State on Imports or Exports, shall be for the Use of the Treasury of the United States; and all such Laws shall be subject to the Revision and Control of the Congress.

This section establishes the monopoly control of the national government in matters of both national and international trade. The only concession to states is health and safety inspections.

Clause 3. No State shall, without the Consent of Congress, lay any Duty of Tonnage, keep Troops, or Ships of War in time of Peace, enter into any Agreement or Compact with another State, or with a foreign Power, or engage in War, unless actually invaded, or in such imminent Danger as will not admit of delay.

This final section of the Legislative article establishes the war monopoly power of the national government. The only exception to state action is actual invasion or threat of imminent danger.

ARTICLE II—THE EXECUTIVE ARTICLE

This article establishes an entirely new concept in government—an elected executive power.

Nature and Scope of Presidential Power

Section 1 Clause 1. The executive Power shall be vested in a President of the United States of America. He shall hold his Office during the Term of four Years, and, together with the Vice President, chosen for the same Term, be elected as follows

This clause establishes the executive power in the office of the president of the United States of America. It also establishes a second office—vice president. A four-year term was established, but not a limit on the number of terms. A limit was later established by the 22nd Amendment.

Clause 2. Each State shall appoint, in such Manner as the Legislature thereof may direct, a Number of Electors, equal to the whole Number of Senators and Representatives to which the State may be entitled in the Congress: but no Senator or Representative, or Person holding an Office of Trust or Profit under the United States, shall be appointed an Elector.

This paragraph essentially establishes the electoral college to choose the president and vice president.

Clause 3. The Electors shall meet in their respective States, and vote by Ballot for two Persons, of whom one at least shall not be an Inhabitant of the same State with themselves. And they shall make a List of all the Persons voted for, and of the Number of Votes for each; which List they shall sign and certify, and transmit sealed to the Seat of the Government of the United States, directed to the President of the Senate. The President of the Senate shall, in the Presence of the Senate and House of Representatives, open all the Certificates, and the Votes shall then be counted. The Person having the greatest Number of Votes shall be the President, if such Number be a Majority of the whole Number of Electors appointed; and if there be more than one who have such Majority and have an equal Number of Votes,

then the House of Representatives shall immediately chuse by Ballot one of them for President; and if no Person have a Majority, then from the five highest on the List the said House shall in like Manner chuse the President. But in chusing the President, the Votes shall be taken by States, the Representation from each State having one Vote; A quorum for this Purpose shall consist of a Member or Members from two thirds of the States, and a Majority of all the States shall be necessary to a Choice. In every Case, after the Choice of the President, the Person having the greatest Number of Votes of the Electors shall be the Vice President. But if there should remain two or more who have equal Votes, the Senate shall chuse from them by Ballot the Vice President.[7]

This paragraph has been superseded by the 12th Amendment. The original language did not require a separate vote for president and vice president. This resulted in a tied vote in the electoral college in 1800 when both Thomas Jefferson and Aaron Burr received 73 electoral votes. The 12th Amendment requires a separate vote for each. Only one of the two can be from the state of the elector. This means that it is highly unlikely that the presidential and vice presidential candidates would be from the same state. This question arose in the 2000 election when Dick Cheney, who lived and worked in Texas, had to reestablish his residence in Wyoming.

The original language provided for a House election in the case of no majority vote or a tie vote among the top five candidates. The amendment lowered the number of candidates to the top three. The Senate is to select the vice president if a candidate does not have an electoral majority or in the case of a tie vote. The Senate considers only the top two candidates. The amendment also clarifies that the qualifications of the vice president are the same as those for president.

Clause 4. The Congress may determine the Time of chusing the Electors, and the Day on which they shall give their Votes; which Day shall be the same throughout the United States.

Congress is given the power to establish a uniform day and time for the state selection of electors.

Clause 5. No Person except a natural born Citizen, or a Citizen of the United States, at the time of the Adoption of this Constitution, shall be eligible to the Office of President; neither shall any Person be eligible to that Office who shall not have attained to the Age of thirty five Years, and been fourteen Years a Resident within the United States.

The qualifications for the offices of president and vice president are specified here—at least 35 years old, 14 years' resident in the U.S., and a natural-born citizen or citizen of the U.S. The 14th Amendment clarified who is a citizen of the U.S., a person born or naturalized in the U.S. and subject to its jurisdiction. But the term "natural-born citizen" is unclear and has never been further defined by the judicial branch. Does it mean born in the U.S. or born of U.S.

---

[7]Changed by the 12th and 20th Amendments

citizens in the U.S. or somewhere else in the world? Unfortunately, there is no definitive answer.

Clause 6. In Case of the Removal of the President from Office, or of his Death, Resignation, or Inability to discharge the Powers and Duties of the said Office, the Same shall devolve on the Vice President, and the Congress may by Law provide for the Case of Removal, Death, Resignation or Inability, both of the President and Vice President, declaring what Officer shall then act as President, and such Officer shall act accordingly, until the Disability be removed, or a President shall be elected.[8]

This clause has been modified by the 25th Amendment. Upon the death, resignation, or impeachment conviction of the president, the vice president becomes president. The new president nominates a new vice president, who assumes the office if approved by a majority vote in both congressional branches. The president is also now able to notify the Congress of his inability to perform his office.

Clause 7. The President shall, at stated Times, receive for his Services, a Compensation, which shall neither be encreased nor diminished during the Period for which he shall have been elected, and he shall not receive within that Period any other Emolument from the United States, or any of them.

This section covers the compensation of the president, which cannot be increased or decreased during his office. The current salary is $400,000/year.

Clause 8. Before he enter on the Execution of his Office, he shall take the following Oath or Affirmation:—"I do solemnly swear (or affirm) that I will faithfully execute the Office of President of the United States, and will to the best of my Ability, preserve, protect and defend the Constitution of the United States."

This final clause in Section 1 is the oath of office administered to the new president.

Powers and Duties of the President

Section 2 Clause 1. The President shall be Commander in Chief of the Army and Navy of the United States, and of the Militia of the several States, when called into the actual Service of the United States; he may require the Opinion, in writing, of the principal Officer in each of the executive Departments, upon any Subject relating to the Duties of their respective Offices, and he shall have Power to grant Reprieves and Pardons for Offences against the United States, except in Cases of Impeachment.

This clause establishes the president as Commander-in-Chief of the U.S. armed forces. George Washington was the only U.S. president to actually lead U.S. armed forces, during the Whiskey Rebellion. The second provision provides the basis for cabinet meetings that are used to acquire the opinions of executive department heads. The last provision provides an absolute pardon or reprieve power from the president. The provision was controversial, but

legal, when former President Clinton pardoned fugitive Marc Rich.

Clause 2. He shall have Power, by and with the Advice and Consent of the Senate, to make Treaties, provided two thirds of the Senators present concur; and he shall nominate, and by and with the Advice and Consent of the Senate, shall appoint Ambassadors, other public Ministers and Consuls, Judges of the supreme Court, and all other Officers of the United States, whose Appointments are not herein otherwise provided for, and which shall be established by Law: but the Congress may by Law vest the Appointment of such inferior Officers, as they think proper, in the President alone, in the Courts of Law, or in the Heads of Departments.

This clause covers two important presidential powers: treaty making and appointments. The president (via the State Department) can negotiate treaties with other nations, but these do not become official until ratified by a 2/3 vote of the U.S. Senate. The president is empowered to appoint judges, ambassadors, and other U.S. officials (cabinet officers, military officers, agency heads, etc.) subject to Senate approval. The Congress can and does delegate this approval to the president in the case of inferior officers. For example, junior military officer promotions are not submitted to the Senate, but senior officer promotions are.

Clause 3. The President shall have Power to fill up all Vacancies that may happen during the Recess of the Senate, by granting Commissions which shall expire at the End of their next Session.

This provision allows recess appointments of the officials listed in Clause 2 above. These commissions automatically expire unless approved by the Senate by the end of the next session. Presidents have used this provision to fill jobs when the nomination process is stalled. Some of these appointments have been very controversial. The regular nomination was stalled because the Senate did not want to confirm the nominee.

Section 3 He shall from time to time give to the Congress Information of the State of the Union, and recommend to their Consideration such Measures as he shall judge necessary and expedient; he may, on extraordinary Occasions, convene both Houses, or either of them, and in Case of Disagreement between them, with Respect to the Time of Adjournment, he may adjourn them to such Time as he shall think proper; he shall receive Ambassadors and other public Ministers; he shall take Care that the Laws be faithfully executed, and shall Commission all the Officers of the United States.

This section provides for the annual State of the Union address to a joint session of Congress and the American people. The president is also authorized to call special meetings of either the House or Senate. If there is disagreement between the House and Senate regarding adjournment, the president is empowered to adjourn them. This would be extremely rare. The president formally receives other nations' ambassadors. The next to last provision to faithfully execute laws provides the basis for the whole administrative apparatus of the presidency. All officers of the U.S. receive a formal commission

---

[8]Modified by the 25th Amendment

from the president (most of these are signed with a signature machine).

Section 4 The President, Vice President and all civil Officers of the United States, shall be removed from Office on Impeachment for, and Conviction of, Treason, Bribery, or other high Crimes and Misdemeanors.

This section provides the constitutional authority for the impeachment and trial of the president, vice president, and all civil officers of the U.S. for treason, bribery, or other high crimes and misdemeanors (the exact meaning of this phrase is unclear and is often more political than judicial).

ARTICLE III—THE JUDICIAL ARTICLE

Judicial Power, Courts, Judges

Section 1 The judicial Power of the United States, shall be vested in one supreme Court, and in such inferior Courts as the Congress may from time to time ordain and establish. The Judges, both of the supreme and inferior Courts, shall hold their Offices during good Behaviour, and shall, at stated Times, receive for their Services, a Compensation, which shall not be diminished during their Continuance in Office.

This section establishes the judicial branch in very general terms. It specifically provides only for the Supreme Court. Congress is given the responsibility of creating the court system. It initially did so in the Judiciary Act of 1789, when it established 13 district courts (one for each state) and 3 appellate courts. All federal judges hold their offices for life and can only be removed for breaches of good behavior—a very nebulous term. Federal judges have been removed for drunkenness, accepting bribes, and other misdemeanors. To date, no justice of the U.S. Supreme Court has ever been removed.

The salary of federal judges is set by congressional act but can never be reduced. Although the American Bar Association and the Federal Bar Association consider federal judges' salaries inadequate, most Americans would probably disagree. Federal district judges earn $145,100/year, appellate judges $153,900, and Supreme Court justices $178,300. The Chief Justice is paid $186,300. These are lifetime salaries, even upon retirement.

Jurisdiction

Section 2 Clause 1. The judicial Power shall extend to all Cases, in Law and Equity, arising under this Constitution, the Laws of the United States, and Treaties made, or which shall be made, under their Authority;—to all Cases affecting Ambassadors, other public Ministers and Consuls;—to all Cases of admiralty and maritime Jurisdiction;—to Controversies to which the United States shall be a Party;—to Controversies between two or more States—between a State and Citizens of another State;[9]—between Citizens of different States;—between Citizens of the same State claiming Lands under Grants of different States, and between a State, or the Citizens thereof, and foreign States, Citizens, or Subjects.

_____
[9]Modified by the 11th Amendment

Clause 2. In all Cases affecting Ambassadors, other public Ministers and Consuls, and those in which a State shall be Party, the supreme Court shall have original Jurisdiction. In all the other Cases before mentioned, the supreme Court shall have appellate Jurisdiction, both as to Law and Fact, with such Exceptions, and under such Regulations as Congress shall make.

Clause 3. The Trial of all Crimes, except in Cases of Impeachment, shall be by Jury; and such Trial shall be held in the State where the said Crimes shall have been committed; but when not committed within any State, the Trial shall be at such Place or Places as the Congress may by Law have directed.

This section establishes the original and appellate jurisdiction of the U.S. Supreme Court. With the Congress of Vienna's 1815 establishment of "diplomatic immunity," the U.S. Supreme Court no longer hears cases involving ambassadors. Since 1925, the Supreme Court no longer hears every case on appeal but can select which cases it will accept, which is now only about 150 cases per year. This section also establishes the right of trial by jury for federal crimes.

Treason

Section 3 Clause 1. Treason against the United States, shall consist only in levying War against them, or in adhering to their Enemies, giving them Aid and Comfort. No Person shall be convicted of Treason unless on the Testimony of two Witnesses to the same overt Act, or on Confession in open Court.

Clause 2. The Congress shall have Power to declare the Punishment of Treason, but no Attainder of Treason shall work Corruption of Blood, or Forfeiture except during the Life of the Person attainted.

Treason is the only crime defined in the U.S. Constitution. Congress established the penalty of death for treason convictions. Note that two witnesses are required to convict anyone of treason. Even in cases of treasonable conduct, seizure of estates is prohibited.

ARTICLE IV—INTERSTATE RELATIONS

Full Faith and Credit Clause

Section 1 Full Faith and Credit shall be given in each State to the public Acts, Records, and judicial Proceedings of every other State. And the Congress may by general Laws prescribe the Manner in which such Acts, Records and Proceedings shall be proved, and the Effect thereof.

This section provides that the official acts and records of one state will be recognized and given credence by other states, e.g., marriages and divorces.

Privileges and Immunities; Interstate Extradition

Section 2 Clause 1. The Citizens of each State shall be entitled to all Privileges and Immunities of Citizens in the several States.

This clause requires states to treat citizens of other states equally. For example, when driving in another state, a driver's license is recognized. One area not so clear is that of charging higher tuitions for out-of-state students at educational institutions.

Clause 2. A person charged in any State with Treason, Felony or other Crime, who shall flee from Justice, and be found in another State, shall on Demand of the executive Authority of the State from which he fled, be delivered up, to be removed to the State having Jurisdiction of the Crime.

Extradition is the name of this clause. A criminal fleeing to another state, if captured, can be returned to the state where the crime was committed. But this is not an absolute. A state's governor can refuse, for good reason, to extradite someone to another state.

Clause 3. No person held to Service or Labour in one State, under the Laws thereof, escaping into another, shall, in Consequence of any Law or Regulation therein, be discharged from such Service or Labour, but shall be delivered up on Claim of the Party to whom such Service or Labour may be due.[10]

This clause was included to cover runaway slaves. It has been made inoperable by the 13th Amendment, which abolished slavery.

Admission of States

Section 3   Clause 1. New States may be admitted by the Congress into this Union; but no new State shall be formed or erected within the Jurisdiction of any other State; nor any State be formed by the Junction of two or more States, or Parts of States, without the Consent of the Legislatures of the States concerned as well as of the Congress.

Clause 2. The Congress shall have Power to dispose of and make all needful Rules and Regulations respecting the Territory or other Property belonging to the United States; and nothing in this Constitution shall be so construed as to Prejudice any Claims of the United States, or of any particular State.

This section concerns the admission of new states to the Union. In theory, no state can be created from part of another state without permission of the state legislature. But West Virginia was formed from Virginia during the Civil War without the permission of Virginia, which was part of the Confederacy. With fifty states now part of the Union, this section has not been used for many decades. The only future use may be in the case of Puerto Rico or perhaps Washington, D.C.

Republican Form of Government

Section 4   The United States shall guarantee to every State in this Union a Republican Form of Government, and shall protect each of them against Invasion; and on Application of the Legislature, or of the Executive (when the Legislature cannot be convened) against domestic Violence.

This section commits the federal government to guarantee a republican form of government to each state and to protect the states against foreign invasion or domestic insurrection.

---

[10]Repealed by the 13th Amendment

ARTICLE V—THE AMENDING POWER

The Congress, whenever two thirds of both Houses shall deem it necessary, shall propose Amendments to this Constitution, or, on the Application of the Legislatures of two thirds of the several States, shall call a Convention for proposing Amendments, which, in either Case, shall be valid to all Intents and Purposes, as Part of this Constitution, when ratified by the Legislatures of three fourths of the several States, or by Conventions in three fourths thereof, as the one or the other Mode of Ratification may be proposed by the Congress; Provided that no Amendment which may be made prior to the Year One thousand eight hundred and eight shall in any Manner affect the first and fourth Clauses in the Ninth Section of the first Article; and that no State, without its Consent, shall be deprived of its equal Suffrage in the Senate.

Amendments to the U.S. Constitution can be originated by a 2/3 vote in both the U.S. House and Senate or by 2/3 of the state legislatures asking for a convention to propose amendments. Proposed amendments, by either route, must be approved by 3/4 of state legislatures or by 3/4 of conventions convened in the states for purposes of ratification. Only one amendment has been ratified by the convention method—Amendment 21 to repeal the 18th Amendment establishing Prohibition.

Thousands of amendments have been proposed; few have been passed by 2/3 vote in each branch of Congress. The Equal Rights Amendment was one such case, but it was not ratified by 3/4 of state legislatures. There have only been 27 successful amendments to the U.S. Constitution.

ARTICLE VI—THE SUPREMACY CLAUSE

Clause 1. All Debts contracted and Engagements entered into, before the Adoption of this Constitution, shall be as valid against the United States under this Constitution, as under the Confederation.

This clause made the new national government responsible for all debts incurred during the Revolutionary War. This was very important to banking and commercial interests.

Clause 2. This Constitution, and the Laws of the United States which shall be made in Pursuance thereof; and all Treaties made, or which shall be made, under the Authority of the United States, shall be the supreme Law of the Land; and the Judges in every State shall be bound thereby, any Thing in the Constitution or Laws of any State to the Contrary notwithstanding.

This is the National Supremacy Clause, which provides the basis for the supremacy of the national government.

Clause 3. The Senators and Representatives before mentioned, and the Members of the several State Legislatures, and all executive and judicial Officers, both of the United States and of the several States, shall be bound by Oath or Affirmation, to support this Constitution; but no religious Test shall ever be required as a Qualification to any Office or public Trust under the United States.

This clause requires essentially all federal and state officials to swear or affirm their allegiance to and support of the U.S. Constitution. Note that a religious test was prohibited for federal office. However, some states used religious tests for voting and office qualification until the 1830s.

ARTICLE VII—RATIFICATION

The Ratification of the Conventions of nine States, shall be sufficient for the Establishment of this Constitution between the States so ratifying the Same.

Done in Convention by the Unanimous Consent of the States present the Seventeenth Day of September in the Year of our Lord one thousand seven hundred and Eighty seven and of the Independence of the United States of America the Twelfth. *In Witness whereof We have hereunto subscribed our Names.*

AMENDMENTS

Realizing the unanimous ratification of the new Constitution by the 13 states might never have occurred, the framers wisely specified that only 9 states would be needed for ratification. Even this proved to be a test of wills between Federalists and Anti-Federalists, leading to publication of the great political work *The Federalist Papers.*

THE BILL OF RIGHTS

[The first ten amendments were ratified on December 15, 1791, and form what is known as the "Bill of Rights."]

The Bill of Rights applied initially only to the federal government and not to state or local governments. Beginning in 1925 in the case of *Gitlow v. New York,* the U.S. Supreme Court began to selectively incorporate the Bill of Rights, making its provisions applicable to state and local governments. There are only three exceptions, which will be discussed at the appropriate amendment.

AMENDMENT 1—RELIGION, SPEECH, ASSEMBLY, AND POLITICS

Congress shall make no law respecting an establishment of religion, or prohibiting the free exercise thereof; or abridging the freedom of speech, or of the press; or the right of the people peaceably to assemble, and to petition the Government for a redress of grievances.

This is the godfather of all amendments in that it protects five fundamental freedoms: religion, speech, press, assembly, and petition. Note that the press is the only business that is specifically protected by the U.S. Constitution. Freedom of religion and speech are two of the most contentious issues and generate a multitude of Supreme Court cases.

AMENDMENT 2—MILITIA AND THE RIGHT TO BEAR ARMS

A well-regulated Militia, being necessary to the security of a free State, the right of the people to keep and bear Arms, shall not be infringed.

This amendment is the favorite of the National Rifle Association. This amendment also has not been incorporated for state/local governments; that is, state and local governments are free to regulate arms within their respective jurisdictions. There is also controversy as to the meaning of this amendment. Some believe that it specifically refers to citizen militias, which were common at the time of the Constitution but now have been replaced by permanent armed forces. Therefore, is the amendment still applicable? Do private citizens need weapons for the security of a free state?

AMENDMENT 3—QUARTERING OF SOLDIERS

No Soldier shall, in time of peace be quartered in any house, without the consent of the Owner, nor in time of war, but in manner to be prescribed by law.

It was the practice of the British government to insist that colonists provide room or board to British troops. This amendment was designed to prohibit this practice. Today, military and naval bases provide the necessary quarters.

AMENDMENT 4—SEARCHES AND SEIZURES

The right of the people to be secure in their persons, houses, papers, and effects, against unreasonable searches and seizures, shall not be violated, and no Warrants shall issue, but upon probable cause, supported by Oath or affirmation, and particularly describing the place to be searched, and the persons or things to be seized.

This extremely important amendment is designed to prevent the abuse of state police powers. Essentially, unreasonable searches or seizures of homes, persons, or property cannot be undertaken without probable cause or a warrant that specifically describes the place to be searched, the person involved, and the suspicious things to be seized.

AMENDMENT 5—GRAND JURIES, SELF-INCRIMINATION, DOUBLE JEOPARDY, DUE PROCESS, AND EMINENT DOMAIN

No person shall be held to answer for a capital, or otherwise infamous crime, unless on a presentment or indictment of a Grand jury, except in cases arising in the land or naval forces, or in the Militia, when in actual service in time of War or public danger; nor shall any person be subject for the same offence to be twice put in jeopardy of life or limb; nor shall be compelled in any criminal case to be a witness against himself, nor be deprived of life, liberty, or property, without due process of law; nor shall private property be taken for public use, without just compensation.

Only a grand jury can indict a person for a federal crime. This provision does not apply to state/local governments. This amendment also covers double jeopardy, or being tried twice for the same crime in the same jurisdiction. Note that since the federal government and state governments are different jurisdictions, one could be tried in each jurisdiction for essentially the same crime. For example, it is a federal crime to kill a congressperson. It is also a state crime to murder anyone. Further, this amendment also covers the prohibition of self-incrimination. Pleading the 5th Amendment used to be common in Mafia cases but recently was used by Enron witnesses. The deprivation of life, liberty, or property by any level of government is prohibited unless due process of law is applied. Finally, private property may not be taken under the doctrine of "eminent domain" unless the government provides just compensation.

Amendment 6—Criminal Court Procedures

In all criminal prosecutions, the accused shall enjoy the right to a speedy and public trial, by an impartial jury of the State and district wherein the crime shall have been committed, which district shall have been previously ascertained by law, and to be informed of the nature and cause of the accusation; to be confronted with the witnesses against him; to have compulsory process for obtaining witnesses in his favor, and to have the Assistance of Counsel for his defence.

This amendment requires public trials by jury for criminal prosecutions. Anyone accused of a crime is guaranteed the rights to be informed of the charges; to confront witnesses; to subpoena witnesses for their defense; and to have a lawyer for their defense. Currently, the government must provide a lawyer for a defendant unable to afford one.

Amendment 7—Trial by Jury in Common Law Cases

In Suits at common law, where the value in controversy shall exceed twenty dollars, the right of trial by jury shall be preserved, and no fact tried by a jury shall be otherwise re-examined in any Court of the United States, than according to the rules of the common law.

This amendment is practically without meaning in modern times. Statutory law has largely superseded common law. Federal civil law suits with a guaranteed jury are now restricted to cases that exceed $50,000. The Bill of Rights, which includes the right to trial by jury, applied originally only to the national government. Beginning in 1925, the Supreme Court began a selective process of incorporating provisions in the Bill of Rights and making them applicable to state/local governments as well. There are just a few provisions that have not been thus incorporated. Trial by jury is one. Some state/local governments have trials by judges, not by juries.

Amendment 8—Bail, Cruel and Unusual Punishment

Excessive bail shall not be required, nor excessive fines imposed, nor cruel and unusual punishments inflicted.

Capital punishment is covered by this amendment, which also prohibits excessive bail. But this is relative. Million-dollar bails are not uncommon in some cases. One federal judge offered voluntary castration for sex offenders in lieu of jail time. Higher courts held this to be a cruel or unusual punishment. But it is the death penalty that generates the most heated controversy. Court cases challenging the constitutionality of capital punishment cite this amendment's language prohibiting cruel and unusual punishment. For a period of 4 years, the Supreme Court banned capital punishment. When states modified their statutes to provide a two part judicial process of guilt determination and punishment, the Supreme Court allowed the reinstitution of capital punishment by the states.

Amendment 9—Rights Retained by the People

The enumeration in the Constitution, of certain rights, shall not be construed to deny or disparage others retained by the people.

This amendment implies that there may be other rights of the people not specified by the previous amendments. Indeed, the Warren Court established the right to privacy even though it is not specifically mentioned in any previous amendment. Some would claim that persons have a right to adequate medical care and education.

Amendment 10—Reserved Powers of the States

The powers not delegated to the United States by the Constitution, nor prohibited by it to the States, are reserved to the States respectively, or to the people.

The 10th Amendment was seen as the reservoir of reserved powers for state governments. If the national government had been limited only to expressed powers in Article 1, Section 8, of the Constitution, this would have been the case. But the doctrine of implied national government powers, which was established by the U.S. Supreme Court in *McCulloch v. Maryland* in 1819, made the intent of this amendment almost meaningless. Any reserved powers that were retained by the states were virtually removed by the U.S. Supreme Court's decision in the *Garcia v. San Antonio Metropolitan Transit Authority* case in 1985, which basically told state/local governments not to look to the courts to protect their residual rights but rather to their political representatives. In subsequent cases, the Supreme Court has retreated somewhat from this position when the court found the federal government encroaching in state jurisdictional areas.

Amendment 11—Suits against the States

[Ratified February 7, 1795]

The Judicial power of the United States shall not be construed to extend to any suit in law or equity, commenced or prosecuted against one of the United States by Citizens of another State, or by Citizens or Subjects of any Foreign State.

Article 3 of the U.S. Constitution originally allowed federal jurisdiction in cases of one state citizen against another state citizen or state. This amendment removes federal jurisdiction in this area. In essence, states may not be sued in federal court by citizens of another state or country.

AMENDMENT 12—ELECTION OF THE PRESIDENT

[Ratified June 15, 1804]

The Electors shall meet in their respective states, and vote by ballot for President and Vice-President, one of whom, at least, shall not be an inhabitant of the same state with themselves; they shall name in their ballots the person voted for as President, and in distinct ballots the person voted for as Vice-President, and they shall make distinct lists of all persons voted for as President, and of all persons voted for as Vice-President, and of the number of votes for each, which lists they shall sign and certify, and transmit sealed to the seat of the government of the United States, directed to the President of the Senate;—The President of the Senate shall, in the presence of the Senate and House of Representatives, open all the certificates and the votes shall then be counted;—The person having the greatest number of votes for President, shall be the President, if such number be a majority of the whole number of Electors appointed; and if no person have such majority, then from the persons having the highest numbers not exceeding three on the list of those voted for as President, the House of Representatives shall choose immediately, by ballot, the President. But in choosing the President, the votes shall be taken by states, the representation from each state having one vote; a quorum for this purpose shall consist of a member or members from two-thirds of the states, and a majority of all the states shall be necessary to a choice. And if the House of Representatives shall not choose a President whenever the right of choice shall devolve upon them, *before the fourth day of March next following*, then the Vice-President shall act as President, as in the case of the death or other constitutional disability of the President.[11] The person having the greatest number of votes as Vice-President, shall be the Vice-President, if such a number be a majority of the whole numbers of Electors appointed, and if no person have a majority, then from the two highest numbers on the list, the Senate shall choose the Vice-President; a quorum for the purpose shall consist of two-thirds of the whole number of Senators, and a majority of the whole number shall be necessary to a choice. But no person constitutionally ineligible to the office of President shall be eligible to that of Vice-President of the United States.

This was a necessary amendment to correct a flaw in the Constitution covering operations of the electoral college. In the election of 1800, Thomas Jefferson and Aaron Burr, both of the same Democratic-Republican Party, received the same number of electoral votes, 73, for president. Article II of the original Constitution specified that each elector would cast two ballots. It did not specify for whom. This amendment clarifies that the electoral vote must be specific for president and vice president. The original Constitution provided that if no candidate received a majority of electoral votes, the House would decide from the candidates with the top five vote totals. This amendment reduces the candidate field to the top three vote totals. If the House delays

in this selection past the fourth day of March, the elected vice president will act as president until the House selects the president. The original Constitution provided that the candidate with the second highest number of electoral votes would become vice president.

This amendment, which requires a separate vote tally for vice president, provides for selection by the U.S. Senate if no vice presidential candidate receives an electoral vote majority.

AMENDMENT 13—PROHIBITION OF SLAVERY

[Ratified December 6, 1865]

Section 1 Neither slavery nor involuntary servitude, except as a punishment for crime whereof the party shall have been duly convicted, shall exist within the United States, or any place subject to their jurisdiction.

Section 2 Congress shall have power to enforce this article by appropriate legislation.

This is the first of the three Civil War amendments. Slavery is prohibited under all circumstances. Involuntary servitude is also prohibited unless it is a punishment for a convicted crime.

AMENDMENT 14—CITIZENSHIP, DUE PROCESS, AND EQUAL PROTECTION OF THE LAWS

[Ratified July 9, 1868]

Section 1 All persons born or naturalized in the United States, and subject to the jurisdiction thereof, are citizens of the United States and of the State wherein they reside. No State shall make or enforce any law which shall abridge the privileges or immunities of citizens of the United States; nor shall any State deprive any person of life, liberty, or property, without due process of law; nor deny to any person within its jurisdiction the equal protection of the laws.

This section defines the meaning of U.S. citizenship and protection of these citizenship rights. It also establishes the Equal Protection Clause that each state must guarantee to its citizens. It extended the provisions of the 5th Amendment of due process and protection of life, liberty, and property and made these applicable to the states.

Section 2 Representatives shall be apportioned among the several States according to their respective numbers, counting the whole number of persons in each State, excluding Indians not taxed. But when the right to vote at any election for the choice of electors for President and Vice President of the United States, Representatives in Congress, the Executive and Judicial officers of a State, or the members of the Legislature thereof, is denied to any of the male inhabitants of such State, being twenty-one[12] years of age, and citizens of the United States, or in any way abridged, except for participation in rebellion, or other crime, the basis of representation therein shall be reduced in the proportion which the number of such male citizens shall bear to the whole number of male citizens twenty-one years of age in such State.

---

[11]Changed by the 20th Amendment

[12]Changed by the 26th Amendment

This section changes the Three-Fifths Clause of the original Constitution. Now all male citizens, 21 or older, will be used to calculate representation in the House of Representatives. If a state denies the right to vote to any male 21 or older, the number of denied citizens will be deducted from the overall state total to determine representation.

Section 3   No person shall be a Senator or Representative in Congress, or elector of President and Vice President, or hold any office, civil or military, under the United States, or under any State, who, having previously taken an oath, as a member of Congress, or as an officer of the United States, or as a member of any State legislature, or as an executive or judicial officer of any State, to support the Constitution of the United States, shall have engaged in insurrection or rebellion against the same, or given aid or comfort to the enemies thereof. But Congress may by a vote of two-thirds of each House, remove such disability.

This section disqualifies from federal office or elector for president or vice president anyone who rebelled or participated in an insurrection against the Constitution. This was specifically directed against citizens of southern states. Congress by a 2/3 vote could override this provision.

Section 4   The validity of the public debt of the United States, authorized by law, including debts incurred for payment of pensions and bounties for services in suppressing insurrection or rebellion, shall not be questioned. But neither the United States nor any State shall assume or pay any debt or obligation incurred in aid of insurrection or rebellion against the United States, or any claim for the loss or emancipation of any slave; but all such debts, obligations and claims shall be held illegal and void.

Section 5   The Congress shall have power to enforce, by appropriate legislation, the provisions of this article.

Sections 4 and 5 cover the Civil War debts.

AMENDMENT 15—THE RIGHT TO VOTE

[Ratified February 3, 1870]

Section 1   The right of citizens of the United States to vote shall not be denied or abridged by the United States or by any State on account of race, color, or previous condition of servitude.

Section 2   The Congress shall have power to enforce this article by appropriate legislation.

This final Civil War amendment states that voting rights could not be denied by any states on account of race, color, or previous servitude. Unfortunately, it did not mention gender. Accordingly, only male citizens 21 or over were guaranteed the right to vote by this amendment.

AMENDMENT 16—INCOME TAXES

[Ratified February 3, 1913]

The Congress shall have power to lay and collect taxes on incomes, from whatever source derived, without apportionment among the several States, and without regard to any census or enumeration.

Article I, Section 9, of the original Constitution prohibited Congress from enacting a direct tax (head tax) unless in proportion to a census. Congress in 1894 passed an income tax law, levying a 2 percent tax on incomes over $4,000. In 1895, the U.S. Supreme Court in a split decision (5–4) found that the income tax was a direct tax not apportioned among the states and was thus unconstitutional. Thus, Congress proposed an amendment allowing it to enact an income tax. Once this amendment was ratified, the flow of tax money to Washington increased tremendously.

AMENDMENT 17—DIRECT ELECTION OF SENATORS

[Ratified April 8, 1913]

The Senate of the United States shall be composed of two Senators from each State, elected by the people thereof, for six years; and each Senator shall have one vote. The electors in each State shall have the qualifications requisite for electors of the most numerous branch of the State legislatures.

When vacancies happen in the representation of any State in the Senate, the executive authority of such State shall issue writs of election to fill such vacancies: Provided, That the legislature of any State may empower the executive thereof to make temporary appointments until the people fill the vacancies by election as the legislature may direct.

This amendment shall not be so construed as to affect the election or term of any Senator chosen before it becomes valid as part of the Constitution.

Prior to this amendment, U.S. senators were selected by state legislatures. Now U.S. senators would be selected by popular vote in each state. Further, the governor of each state may fill vacancies, subject to state laws.

AMENDMENT 18—PROHIBITION

[Ratified January 16, 1919. Repealed December 5, 1933 by Amendment 21]

Section 1   After one year from the ratification of this article the manufacture, sale, or transportation of intoxicating liquors within, the importation thereof into, or the exportation thereof from the United States and all territory subject to the jurisdiction thereof for beverage purposes is hereby prohibited.

Section 2   The Congress and the several States shall have concurrent power to enforce this article by appropriate legislation.

Section 3   This article shall be inoperative unless it shall have been ratified as an amendment to the Constitution by the legislatures of the several States, as provided in the Constitution, within seven years from the date of the submission hereof to the States by the Congress.[13]

This amendment was largely the work of the Women's Christian Temperance Union and essentially banned the manufacture, sale, or transportation of alcoholic beverages. Unintended consequences

---

[13]Repealed by the 21st Amendment

of this attempt to legislate morality were the brewing of "bathtub gin" and moonshine liquor, the involvement of the mob in importing liquor from Canada, and the "Untouchables" of Eliot Ness. Fortunately, this ill-fated social experiment was corrected by the 21st Amendment. This is also the first amendment where Congress fixed a period for ratification—7 years.

AMENDMENT 19—FOR WOMEN'S SUFFRAGE

[Ratified August 18, 1920]

The right of the citizens of the United States to vote shall not be denied or abridged by the United States or by any State on account of sex.

Congress shall have power to enforce this article.

At long last, women achieved voting parity with men.

AMENDMENT 20—THE LAME DUCK AMENDMENT

[Ratified January 23, 1933]

Section 1 The terms of the President and Vice President shall end at noon on the 20th day of January, and the terms of the Senators and Representatives at noon on the 3d day of January, of the years in which such terms would have ended if this article had not been ratified; and the terms of their successors shall then begin.

Section 2 The Congress shall assemble at least once in every year, and such meeting shall begin at noon on the 3d day of January, unless they shall by law appoint a different day.

Section 3 If, at the time fixed for the beginning of the term of the President, the President elect shall have died, the Vice President elect shall become President. If a President shall not have been chosen before the time fixed for the beginning of his term, or if the President elect shall have failed to qualify, then the Vice President elect shall act as President until a President shall have qualified; and the Congress may by law provide for the case wherein neither a President elect nor a Vice President elect shall have qualified, declaring who shall then act as President, or the manner in which one who is to act shall be selected, and such person shall act accordingly until a President or Vice President shall have qualified.

Section 4 The Congress may by law provide for the case of the death of any of the persons from whom the House of Representatives may choose a President whenever the right of choice shall have devolved upon them, and for the case of the death of any of the persons from whom the Senate may choose a Vice President whenever the right of choice shall have devolved upon them.

Section 5 Sections 1 and 2 shall take effect on the 15th day of October following the ratification of this article.

Section 6 This article shall be inoperative unless it shall have been ratified as an amendment to the Constitution by the legislatures of three-fourths of the several States within seven years from the date of its submission.

Called the Lame Duck amendment, this amendment fixes the dates for the end of presidential and legislative terms. A new president is elected in November, but the current president remains in office until January 20 of the following year. Thus,

the term "lame duck." Legislative terms begin earlier, on January 3.

AMENDMENT 21—REPEAL OF PROHIBITION

[Ratified December 5, 1933]

Section 1 The eighteenth article of amendment to the Constitution of the United States is hereby repealed.

Section 2 The transportation or importation into any State, Territory, or possession of the United States for delivery or use therein of intoxicating liquors, in violation of the laws thereof, is hereby prohibited.

Section 3 This article shall be inoperative unless it shall have been ratified as an amendment to the Constitution by conventions in the several States, as provided in the Constitution, within seven years from the date of the submission hereof to the States by the Congress.

This unusual amendment nullified the 18th Amendment. The amendment called for the end of Prohibition unless prohibited by state laws.

AMENDMENT 22—NUMBER OF PRESIDENTIAL TERMS

[Ratified February 27, 1951]

Section 1 No person shall be elected to the office of the President more than twice, and no person who has held the office of President, or acted as President, for more than two years of a term to which some other person was elected President shall be elected to the office of the President more than once. But this article shall not apply to any person holding the office of President when this article was proposed by the Congress, and shall not prevent any person who may be holding the office of President, or acting as President, during the term within which this article becomes operative from holding the office of President or acting as President during the remainder of such term.

Section 2 This article shall be inoperative unless it shall have been ratified as an amendment to the Constitution by the legislatures of three-fourths of the several states within seven years from the date of its submission to the states by the Congress.

This amendment could be called the Franklin D. Roosevelt amendment. It was FDR who broke the previously unwritten rule of serving no more than two terms as president. Democrat Roosevelt won an unprecedented four terms as president. When the Republicans took control of the Congress in 1948, they pushed through the 22nd Amendment, limiting the U.S. president to a lifetime of two full four-year terms of office.

AMENDMENT 23—PRESIDENTIAL ELECTORS FOR THE DISTRICT OF COLUMBIA

[Ratified March 29, 1961]

Section 1 The District constituting the seat of government of the United States shall appoint in such manner as the Congress may direct:

A number of electors of President and Vice President equal to the whole number of Senators and Representatives in Congress to which the District would be entitled if it were a state, but in no event more than the least populous state; they shall be in addition to those appointed by the states, but they shall be considered, for the purposes of the election of President and Vice President, to be electors appointed by a state; and they shall meet in the District and perform such duties as provided by the twelfth article of amendment.

Section 2   The Congress shall have power to enforce this article by appropriate legislation.

This amendment gave electoral votes to the citizens of Washington, D.C., which is not a state and thus not included in the original scheme of state electoral votes. Currently, Washington, D.C., has 3 electoral votes, bringing the total of presidential electoral votes to 538. Puerto Ricans are citizens of the U.S. but have no electoral votes.

Amendment 24—The Anti-Poll Tax Amendment

[Ratified January 23, 1964]

Section 1   The right of citizens of the United States to vote in any primary or other election for President or Vice President, for electors for President or Vice President, or for Senator or Representative in Congress, shall not be denied or abridged by the United States or any state by reason of failure to pay any poll tax or other tax.

Section 2   The Congress shall have power to enforce this article by appropriate legislation.

The poll tax was a procedure used mostly in southern states to discourage poor white and black voters from registering to vote. Essentially, one would have to pay a tax to register to vote. The tax was around $34/year. But for a poor white or black voter, this might not be disposable income. As part of the assault against disenfranchisement of voters, the poll tax was abolished. Literacy tests, another device to disqualify voters, were abolished by the Voting Rights Act of 1965.

Amendment 25—Presidential Disability, Vice Presidential Vacancies

[Ratified February 10, 1967]

Section 1   In case of the removal of the President from office or of his death or resignation, the Vice President shall become President.

Section 2   Whenever there is a vacancy in the office of the Vice President, the President shall nominate a Vice President who shall take the office upon confirmation by a majority vote of both Houses of Congress.

Section 3   Whenever the President transmits to the President pro tempore of the Senate and the Speaker of the House of Representatives his written declaration that he is unable to discharge the powers and duties of his office, and until he transmits to them a written declaration to the contrary, such powers and duties shall be discharged by the Vice President as Acting President.

Section 4   Whenever the Vice President and a majority of either the principal officers of the executive departments, or of such other body as Congress may by law provide, transmit to the President

pro tempore of the Senate and the Speaker of the House of Representatives their written declaration that the President is unable to discharge the powers and duties of his office, the Vice President shall immediately assume the powers and duties of the office as Acting President.

Thereafter, when the President transmits to the President pro tempore of the Senate and the Speaker of the House of Representatives his written declaration that no inability exists, he shall resume the powers and duties of his office unless the Vice President and a majority of either the principal officers of the executive department, or of such other body as Congress may by law provide, transmit within four days to the President pro tempore of the Senate and the Speaker of the House of Representatives their written declaration that the President is unable to discharge the powers and duties of his office. Thereupon Congress shall decide the issue, assembling within forty-eight hours for that purpose if not in session. If the Congress, within twenty-one days after receipt of the latter written declaration, or, if Congress is not in session, within twenty-one days after Congress is required to assemble, determines by two-thirds vote of both Houses that the President is unable to discharge the powers and duties of his office, the Vice President shall continue to discharge the same as Acting President; otherwise, the President shall resume the powers and duties of his office.

President Woodrow Wilson's final year in office was marked by serious illness. It is rumored that his wife acted as president. There was no constitutional provision to cover an incapacitating illness of a president. This amendment provides a procedure for this eventuality. The president can inform congressional leaders of his incapacitation, and the vice president then takes over. When the president recovers, he can inform congressional leaders and resume office.

The amendment also recognizes that the president may not be able or wish to indicate this debilitation. In this case, the vice president and a majority of cabinet members can inform congressional leaders, and the vice president takes over. When the president informs congressional leadership that he is back in form, he resumes the presidency unless the vice president and a majority of the cabinet members disagree. Then Congress must decide who is to be president. The likelihood that this procedure will ever be used is relatively small.

The most immediate importance of this amendment concerns the office of vice president. The original Constitution did not address the issue of a vacancy in this office. The 25th Amendment established the procedure just in time! This amendment was ratified in 1967. In 1973, the sitting vice president, Spiro Agnew, resigned his office. Under the provisions of this amendment, President Nixon nominated Gerald Ford as vice president. As a former member of the House, Ford was quickly approved by the Congress. But a year later, President Nixon also resigned. Now Vice President Ford became President Ford, and he in turn appointed Nelson Rockefeller as the new vice president. For the first time in our history, we had both a president and vice president, neither of whom was elected by the electoral college.

AMENDMENT 26—EIGHTEEN-YEAR-OLD VOTE

[Ratified July 1, 1971]

Section 1   The right of citizens of the United States, who are 18 years of age or older, to vote, shall not be denied or abridged by the United States or by any state on account of age.

Section 2   The Congress shall have power to enforce this article by appropriate legislation.

During the Vietnam War, 18 year olds were being drafted and sent out to possibly die in the service of their country. Yet they did not even have the right to vote. This incongruity led to the 26th Amendment, which lowered the legal voting age from 21 to 18.

AMENDMENT 27—CONGRESSIONAL SALARIES

[Ratified May 7, 1992]

No law varying the compensation for the services of the Senators and Representatives shall take effect until an election of Representatives shall have intervened.

This is a "sleeper" amendment that was part of 12 amendments originally submitted by the first Congress to the states for ratification. The states only ratified 10 of the 12, which collectively became known as the Bill of Rights. But since Congress did not set a time limit for ratification, the other two amendments remained on the table. Much to the shock of the body politic, in 1992, 3/4 of the states ratified original amendment 12 of 12. This reflected the disgust of seeing Congress continuing to increase its salary and benefits. The amendment delays any increase of compensation for at least one election cycle.

★ CHAPTER 3 ★

FEDERALISM

CHAPTER OUTLINE

Approaching Democracy

From Wheat to Marijuana

When federal agents showed up at Diane Monson's house in Butte County, California in August 2002, seeking to destroy her six home-grown marijuana plants, and agents in Oregon sought to prevent Dr. Peter A. Rasmussen and pharmacist David M. Hochhalter from prescribing lethal doses of drugs to patients seeking physician-assisted suicides, both cases raised issues linked to a sixty-year-old ruling about an Ohio farmer and 239 bushels of wheat.

Monson had the right to grow and smoke the marijuana to ease her severe back spasm under California's Compassionate Use Act, overwhelmingly passed by voters in 1996, which allowed doctors to prescribe small amounts of home-grown marijuana. Ten other states, mainly in the West, also permitted the prescribed medical use of marijuana. On a separate issue, the state of Oregon, under its 1997 Death with Dignity Act, passed by voters, permitted doctors to prescribe and administer lethal doses of drugs to patients with terminal illnesses.

However, the federal government considered both medical use of marijuana and prescription of drugs for euthanasia violations of the Controlled Substances Act of 1970. Under this act, the federal government classifies drugs of all kinds within five schedules and regulates their distribution. The Drug Enforcement Agency (DEA) administers the act. So the question became whether or not the national drug enforcement policy superseded the state policies.

But just where did Ohio farmer Roscoe Filburn and his wheat fit in? Back in 1942, Roscoe Filburn grew 239 bushels of wheat to be eaten by his family, on his own farm. However, at that time the New Deal Agricultural Adjustment Act controlled all agricultural production, including production quotas for farm products to keep prices high during recovery from the Depression. Filburn argued that because all of his wheat was grown and used on his own farm and never entered interstate commerce, the national government had no control over it. However, a unanimous Supreme Court disagreed in *Wickard* v. *Filburn*, arguing that even though this wheat was grown and used on one farm, it "compete[d] with wheat in commerce," since growing his own wheat kept Filburn from buying other farmers' wheat. The Court ruled that Filburn's action would affect interstate commerce and was thus subject to national regulation under the "interstate commerce clause" of Article I, Section 8 of the Constitution. In the Court's words, the wheat "supplies a need of the man who grew it which would otherwise be reflected by purchases in the open market."

The Court turned to the Filburn case in ruling on the marijuana case, asking whether or not Monson's homegrown marijuana, like Filburn's wheat, competed with other products on the open market and was subject to federal regulation. The difference, of course, is that wheat is sold legally, whereas in many states selling marijuana is illegal. So the Court needed to decide whether the commerce clause gave the DEA, a federal agency, the right to undercut California's Medical Marijuana Act and Oregon's Death with Dignity Act.

★ Angel Raich, left, and Diane Monson at the Supreme Court for arguments in their medical marijuana case.

By a 6–3 vote, the Court ruled that the federal government's power to ban certain drugs did preempt states' power to eliminate penalties for the use of those drugs in certain circumstances. But the justices' voting pattern defied their political labels. Liberal John Paul Stevens wrote that Congress had a "firmly established" power to control these types of economic activity under the Filburn case because they were "purely local activities . . . that have a substantial effect on interstate commerce." On the other hand, states' rights advocate Sandra Day O'Connor dissented. She opposed the federal government limiting the "express choice by some states, concerned for the lives and liberties of their people, to regulate medical marijuana differently." Chief Justice William Rehnquist, a states' rights jurist who nonetheless normally voted in support of a national drug control policy, also dissented. But the dissenter who was least happy with the Court's decision was Clarence Thomas, who pointed out that the marijuana in this case had neither been bought nor sold and therefore did not constitute interstate commerce. He argued that if "Congress can regulate this under the Commerce Clause, then it can regulate virtually anything," including "quilting bees, clothes drives and potluck suppers throughout the fifty states."

When the Court ruled on whether the Oregon "Death With Dignity" law could be limited by the federal Controlled Substances Act (CSA) in January 2006, though, there was no mention of the *Wickard* v. *Filburn* case and the vote went the other way. Six Justices, speaking through Anthony Kennedy, upheld the Oregon law, arguing that while the Attorney General had the authority to regulate the use of drugs placed on the federal list of controlled substances, the federal CSA law was intended to control only "illicit drug dealing and trafficking" while allowing for state drug control for other reasons as well. Thus, there was no provision permitting the Attorney General to prevent doctors in Oregon to prescribe the federally-regulated drugs for use in physician-assisted suicide that was permitted under state law. In dissent, Justice Thomas disagreed, arguing that the CSA statute in fact regulated the prescription of drugs for "legitimate medical purposes." Given the conflicting nature of these two decisions, it remains to be seen whether in the future the Court will support efforts by the federal government to impose a uniform national policy in commerce clause cases dealing with medical issues, or whether it will remain open to state experimentation on these questions.[1]

★ Dr. Jack Kervorkian (right), nicknamed "Dr. Death," assisted over 100 terminally-ill patients in ending their lives, such as here, when Marjorie Wantz sought to end her life because of severe pelvic pain. After four attempts to convict him for various assisted suicides, when Kervorkian gave Thomas Youk, who suffered from Lou Gehrig's disease, a lethal injection on the show "60 Minutes," he was convicted in 1999 in a Michigan Court of second-degree murder and sentenced to 10–25 years in prison.

QUESTIONS FOR REFLECTION

What roles should federal and state government play in determining medical policy?

Under what circumstances should the national government seek to impose one overarching policy on all of the states?

Introduction
FEDERALISM AND DEMOCRACY

This case study illustrates the interaction of issues that cross state boundaries, the classic partnerships within Congress in search of a broad vision of national interests, states' efforts to preserve **states' rights**, and the challenges of trying to resolve any differences between those visions while applying the larger policies to a particular region. At the heart of these negotiations over policy is the concept of **federalism**.

Few subjects in American government are as likely to serve as a cure for insomnia as federalism, yet few subjects are more important. If you doubt this, glance at the daily newspaper and see how many articles deal with relations among national, state, and local governments. A typical local front page might cover the new national education bill that provides funding for local teachers; a new crime bill defining a new federal crime, a state road that lost funding because of changes in a bill dealing with the national highway system; or national assistance efforts after a hurricane or tornado has hit a local town. All of these are examples of federalism in action.

This chapter begins with a definition of federalism. It then looks at federalism as outlined in the Constitution and how it has developed over the years. Finally, it examines the dynamic and changing nature of the federal structure. As you will see, a series of Supreme Court decisions and public policies have made our government system far different from that envisioned by the framers. Federalism is one of America's unique contributions to democratic theory and republican government. Only by understanding how the system works can you come to understand how it has helped the United States approach democracy.

FEDERALISM DEFINED

Federalism is a political system in which governmental powers are shared between a general government with nationwide responsibilities and nationwide powers and decentralized regional governments with local responsibilities and local powers in their respective regions. In the uniquely American form of federalism, both the overarching national government, frequently called the *federal government,* and the fifty decentralized state governments share power on the basis of each one's sovereignty as outlined in the United States Constitution.[2]

To understand the nature of the federal system in America, it is important to know the framers' intentions in constructing it. The framers rejected the *unitary* system of government, in which all power is vested in a central authority that could compel the state governments to respond. This was the relationship between the English monarchy and the American colonies. The framers also rejected the *confederation* system of government, in which the power to govern is decentralized among sovereign states, and the national government has such limited powers that it must respond to state dictates. This was the system of government under the Articles of Confederation. Instead, the framers sought to create a structure that combined the best features of both systems—a central government strong enough to deal with the larger national problems, and decentralized state governments able to address the needs of the people in those territories.

The federal structure should be flexible, too, according to the framers. They wanted to delegate enough powers to the central government to allow it to govern the entire nation, thus correcting the weaknesses inherent in the Articles of Confederation. But they also saw functional reasons for maintaining powerful states

states' rights Rights the U.S. Constitution neither grants to the national government nor forbids to the states.

federalism The relationship between the centralized national government and the individual state governments.

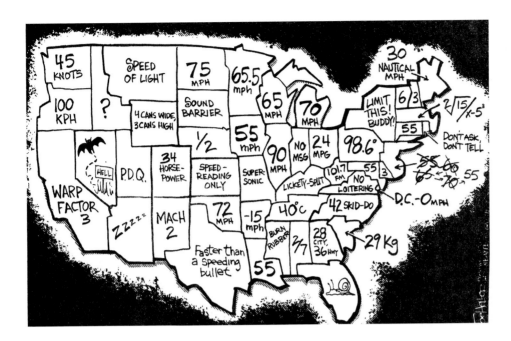

◄ When Congress allows states to set their own speed limits.

Hiller's View, The Boston Globe.

within that system. As James Madison explained in *The Federalist*, no. 10: "The federal Constitution forms a happy combination in this respect; the great and aggregate interests being referred to the national, the local and particular, to the state legislatures."[3] In other words, the federal system was designed to consist of a national government limited to areas of common concern, while the power to make particular policy would remain with the states. Over the years, the gaps deliberately left in the Constitution regarding allocation of powers between the two types of government have been filled by the experience of dealing with political problems. As a result, a new relationship was forged, leaving the national government as the controlling partner in the structure.

Federalism: Advantages and Disadvantages

National policy is the same for everyone, but state and local policy vary widely by region. Variations arise in tax policy, public programs, services such as police and education, and also the form of individual rights. While the Massachusetts Supreme Judicial Court ruled that same-sex marriages were constitutional in that state, and Vermont and Connecticut now allow same-sex civil unions, in 2004 Ohio and twelve more states voted either to legally or constitutionally ban same-sex marriages and thus joined thirty-five other states as well as the federal government in adopting a "defense of marriage" law. This removal of legal and constitutional protections for same-sex couples illustrates the slow development toward an overarching national governmental policy on this question. On the other hand, giving the states a chance to experiment with policy, as has been the case with affirmative action, education, and welfare programs, has in the past produced programs adopted by the national government.

Advantages Federalism has many advantages. Rather than one uniform policy for everyone, the large number of different governments ensures diversity among policies and programs. We need diverse policies to accommodate a diverse populace across a vast country.

Policy diversity also minimizes policy conflict. If groups fail to pass their programs in the federal government, they can try again in the state or local governments, thus minimizing pressure on the national government for action. But should action fail at the state government, attention can shift back to the national government. More centers

Quick Review

Advantages of Federalism

- Large number of different governments ensures diversity among policies and programs.
- Policy diversity minimizes policy conflict.
- Results in a healthy dispersal of power.
- Enhances prospects for governmental experimentation and innovation.

▲ Alabama governor George Wallace blocks the doorway of the all-white University of Alabama in 1963 to prevent two African American students from enrolling. The photo was all for publicity. With Deputy U.S. Attorney Nicholas Katzenbach looking on, Wallace then quietly stood aside, allowing the two students to enter. At the end of his life, Wallace, who had benefited from African American votes in later election successes, apologized.

of power for implementing policy allow more opportunity for government to respond to the needs and desires of the people. One example of this pattern can be seen in the area of health-care reform. When, in the 1960s and 1970s, successive efforts failed to pass a national health insurance program covering everyone, Vermont, Massachusetts, and Oregon passed their own programs. However, these state programs and others failed because of lack of financial resources and various political problems, thus shifting pressure for action back to the national government. As a result, President Bill Clinton pushed for national health-care reform in 1994.[4] After Clinton's comprehensive proposal failed to pass, several states established their own health-care programs. Now, with declining amounts of federal money for health care, various states have been restricting, tailoring, and sometimes even cutting their Medicaid programs for economically disadvantaged people in an attempt to meet the needs of more people.[5] Federalism also produces a healthy dispersal of power. The framers, concerned about a national government with too much power, reserved certain powers for the states. This dispersal of political power creates more opportunity for political participation. Individuals or political parties that lack national power have the opportunity in the federal structure to establish bases of power in the states and localities. Thus, the Republican party, which had no foothold in the national government in the early 1960s, managed to build a power base in many states and in 2000 became the nation's predominant party.

America's system of federalism also enhances the prospects for governmental experimentation and innovation. Justice Louis D. Brandeis described this possibility when he wrote: "It is one of the happy incidents of the federal system that a single courageous state may, if its citizens choose, serve as a laboratory and try novel social and economic experiments without risk to the rest of the country."[6] Thus, the national government can observe which experimental programs undertaken by various states are working and perhaps adopt the best of those ideas for the rest of the nation. The Social Security Act, for example, passed in 1935 to provide economic security for those over age sixty-five and unemployment insurance for the millions thrown out of work by the Depression. It was based on a Wisconsin unemployment program in use at the time. A more recent example came in December 2001 when President Bush signed into law his "No Child Left Behind Act," an education reform act modeled on that of the president's home state of Texas, which tests students yearly to measure public school performance. Under this plan, states were promised $26 billion in federal funds for education programs for low-income children, tied to the implementation of additional student testing to measure school performance. While some praised the law's intention to improve educational quality, critics called the law an underfunded federal mandate, imposing new regulations on the states without providing necessary funding.[7]

Disadvantages   But federalism has its disadvantages, as well. The federal structure's dispersed power and opportunities for participation allow groups in certain regions to protect their interests and sometimes obstruct and even ignore national mandates. For example, into the 1960s, the southern states tried to perpetuate segregationist policies by citing states' rights. Ultimately, legal discrimination in civil rights, housing, voting, and schools came to an end by federal law. In 2005, though, the discussion over whether or not to renew the Federal Voting Rights Act of 1965, set to expire in 2007, raised the specter of a possible damaging return to the patchwork quilt of regulations in state voting requirements that often excluded minority voters in the South.[8]

Inequities arise in a federal system. Poor regions cannot afford to provide the same services as wealthier ones. Rural regions have different needs from urban regions. Coastal regions and regions with significant waterways have different concerns from Midwestern plains states. Thus, governmental programs in localities can vary dramatically. It takes a proper balance of national and state powers to realize the benefits of federalism and minimize its drawbacks. What, then, constitutes this proper balance? That question has been debated since the Framers' day.

FEDERALISM IN THE CONSTITUTION

Let us now look at the vertical powers the framers outlined in the Constitution and their effect on the relationship between the national and state governments. Three constitutional provisions are particularly important—the interstate commerce clause, the general welfare clause, and the Tenth Amendment—because they continually shift the balance of power between the national and state governments. We refer to these three provisions as the **triad of powers**.

The Triad of Powers

Each power in the triad has a specific function. Two of them—the interstate commerce clause and the general welfare clause—have been used to expand the powers of the national government. The third—the Tenth Amendment—has been used to protect state powers.

The Interstate Commerce Clause   In Article I, Section 8, the Constitution's Framers gave Congress the power "to regulate Commerce with foreign Nations, and among the several States." This clause sought to rectify the national government's inability under the Articles of Confederation to control movement of goods across state lines. But it really did much more. The interstate commerce clause led to a national government able to provide basic uniformity of policy among the states. A broad interpretation of this clause—and changes over time from self-contained states to an economy that included commercial enterprises linked across state lines—ultimately provided the means for expanding national power even within state borders. Using this power, the national government could keep the states from penalizing each other while encouraging them to work together.

To demonstrate how the national government can use the commerce clause to achieve uniform policy, let's say that restaurateur Joe Bigot is determined to discriminate against minorities in his world-famous, fast-food hamburger business. "Joe's Best Burgers" franchises are sold everywhere. One franchise is located on a train club car that travels between New York and Connecticut, another on an interstate highway between Texas and Oklahoma. Clearly, the national government would be able to bar discrimination in these restaurants because the restaurants serve interstate travelers, and thus affect interstate commerce.

Thoroughly dismayed, Joe is so determined to do business his way that he sells his franchise, moves to his hometown high in the Rocky Mountains, and opens a restaurant in an area that hasn't seen an interstate customer since the wagon trains brought the gold rush settlers to California in the 1800s. Can the federal government bar discrimination here, too? The answer is yes, because the meat Joe serves, his kitchen machinery, and his eating implements were all imported from out of state. Since those purchases affect interstate commerce, federal regulations apply. This example reflects two Supreme Court cases that upheld Congress's use of its interstate commerce power as the basis for the 1964 Civil Rights Act. That act expanded the rights of African Americans and barred discrimination in public accommodations.[9]

MakeItReal

ABC News Video: *The Fix—Prescription Drugs in Canada*

triad of powers Three constitutional provisions—the interstate commerce clause, the general welfare clause, and the Tenth Amendment—that help to continually shift the balance of power between the national and state governments.

As you can see from this example, a broad interpretation of the interstate commerce clause can give the national government tremendous power to reach policy areas previously reserved to the states. Using the interstate commerce clause, the national government can, if it so desires (and it invariably does), regulate the wages and work hours on your campus; the admissions and scholarship rules, including the apportionment of scholarships between men and women on college sports teams; campus housing regulations; and campus codes of conduct. Off campus, the food you eat in a restaurant, local government operations, and practices in businesses you patronize all face regulation when the national government uses its interstate commerce power.

Questions for Reflection

What potential pitfalls do you see in this "carrot and stick" approach?

How might the general welfare clause help forward a particular social agenda?

Is there a balance to this power?

The General Welfare Clause　The Constitution, in Article I, Section 8, also grants Congress the power to "lay and collect Taxes, Duties, Imposts and Excises, to pay the Debts and provide for the common Defense and general Welfare of the United States." The combination of this spending power with the necessary and proper clause (also known as the *elastic clause*) in Article I, Section 8, enabled the national government to indirectly influence state policy through the power of the pocketbook. This power has expanded the national government's reach into formerly state-controlled areas via "carrot-and-stick" programs. The "carrot" is the money that the federal government provides for states that abide by national programs; the "stick" is the threatened loss of money if they do not. This approach to spending was evident in 1974, when Congress passed a law that states could receive national highway funds only if they abided by the fifty-five-mile-an-hour speed limit (a law repealed in 1987), and again, in 2001, when states could have more education funding money if they adopted the student achievement testing program. Should the national government ever try to ban cell phone use on the highways, they would likely have to apply pressure through the states, with lost highway funds as the "stick."

The most visible carrot-and-stick approach to policy making is the manner in which the legal drinking age was changed around the country. Before 1984, the drinking age varied from state to state, sometimes even from county to county. In 1984, however, Mothers Against Drunk Driving (MADD) demanded that the drinking age be raised nationwide to twenty-one. MADD pointed out that 9,500 Americans under the age of twenty-five were dying annually in alcohol-related driving accidents. Imposing a uniform national drinking age of twenty-one, they argued, was critical in discouraging drinking and driving among young people. But liquor sales meant big business in various states, a formidable obstacle to a policy change. Congress used the carrot-and-stick approach to prevail. States that did not raise their drinking age to twenty-one would lose 5 percent of their 1986 federal highway funds and 10 percent of the 1987 total. Not surprisingly, near uniformity on the new legal drinking age occurred almost immediately.[10]

▲ After Congress allowed states to raise the speed limit on interstate highways to sixty-five miles per hour, state workers changed signs on Interstate 80 in Vacaville, California.

The Tenth Amendment　What kept the national government from dominating the federal structure from the beginning? The answer lies in the Tenth Amendment, which states: "The powers not delegated to the United States by the Constitution, nor prohibited by it to the States, are reserved to the States respectively, or to the people." Thus the framers intended to preserve states' individuality and restrict the national government to its delegated powers.

This amendment has been at the center of the shifting balance of power between the national government and the state governments. Between 1877 and 1937, state-centered federalism advocates on the Supreme Court used the Tenth Amendment to bar national intrusion into state activities. Because manufacturing and mining took place entirely within state boundaries, the national government was assumed to have no power to reach them.[11] The Supreme Court changed direction, however, after Roosevelt's "court-packing plan," and the new Roosevelt appointees declared that the Tenth Amendment could not restrict Congress's desire to control commerce and economic activities within state boundaries.[12]

The Tenth Amendment has gained new prominence in recent years as a basis for the *devolution* of power from the national government to the states. Both the Congress since 1995 and a five-person conservative Supreme Court majority since 1994 have tended to use this amendment to shift power to the states, in line with their commitment to reduce Washington's role in administering and funding local programs.[13]

THE DIVISION OF POWERS

The framers were careful to express in the Constitution a series of powers that keep the two forms of government independent. You will recall from Chapter 2 that the **supremacy clause** upholds national laws and treaties as the "supreme Law of the Land." This clause establishes the predominance of national laws whenever national and state legislation overlap. The states also receive both powers and limits to power. Those provisions are outlined in Table 3.1. The Constitution carefully details the powers delegated to the national government, the powers reserved to the states, and the powers that apply to the two governments concurrently (see Figure 3.1).

First are the **delegated powers**, those delegated specifically to the national government. Generally, the framers saw these powers lacking in the old Articles of

supremacy clause A clause in Article IV of the Constitution holding that in any conflict between federal laws and treaties and state laws, the will of the national government always prevails.

delegated powers Powers expressly granted or enumerated in the Constitution and limited in nature.

Question for Reflection

In considering the dispute in both state and federal governments over the nature of marriage, which government should have the predominant power in determining how people lead their lives?

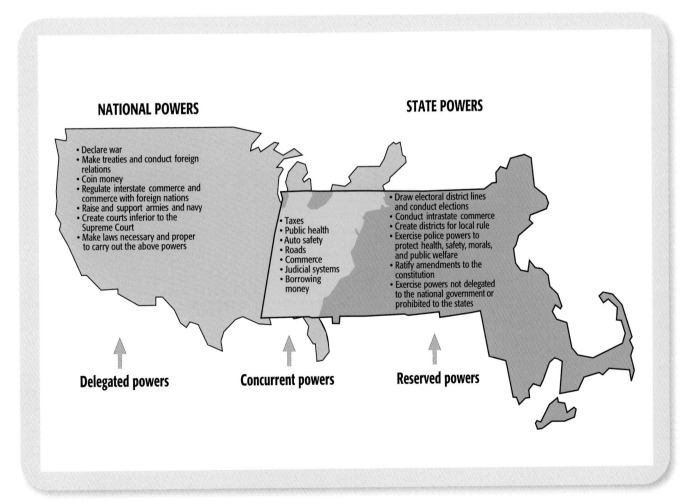

NATIONAL POWERS

- Declare war
- Make treaties and conduct foreign relations
- Coin money
- Regulate interstate commerce and commerce with foreign nations
- Raise and support armies and navy
- Create courts inferior to the Supreme Court
- Make laws necessary and proper to carry out the above powers

- Taxes
- Public health
- Auto safety
- Roads
- Commerce
- Judicial systems
- Borrowing money

STATE POWERS

- Draw electoral district lines and conduct elections
- Conduct intrastate commerce
- Create districts for local rule
- Exercise police powers to protect health, safety, morals, and public welfare
- Ratify amendments to the constitution
- Exercise powers not delegated to the national government or prohibited to the states

Delegated powers **Concurrent powers** **Reserved powers**

Figure 3.1 The Division of Powers in the Federal System.

Table 3.1 ▪ Constitutional Guarantees of and Limits on State Power

Guarantees	Limits
1. State Integrity and Sovereignty	
No division of states or consolidation of parts of two or more states without state legislative consent (Art. IV, Sec. 3)	States cannot enter into treaties, alliances, or confederations (Art. I, Sec. 10)
Guarantee of republican form of state government (Art. IV, Sec. 4)	No interstate or foreign compacts without consent of Congress (Art. I, Sec. 10)
Protection against invasion and against domestic violence (Art. IV, Sec. 4)	No separate coinage (Art. 1, Sec. 10)
Powers not delegated to national government reserved for states (10th Amend.)	National constitution, laws, and treaties are supreme (Art. VI)
State equality in Senate cannot be denied (Art. V)	All state officials bound by national Constitution (Art. VI)
	No denial of privileges and immunity of citizens (14th Amend.)
	No abridgment of right to vote on basis of race (15th Amend.)
	No abridgment of right to vote on basis of sex (19th Amend.)
2. Military Affairs and Defense	
Power to maintain militia and appoint militia officials (Art. I, Sec. 8, 2d Amend.)	No maintenance of standing military in peacetime without congressional consent (Art. I, Sec. 10)
	No engagement in war without congressional consent, except in emergency (Art. I, Sec. 10)
3. Commerce and Taxation	
Equal apportionment of direct federal taxes (Art. I, Secs. 2, 9)	No levying of duties on vessels of sister states (Art. I, Sec. 9)
No export duties imposed on any state (Art. I, Sec. 9)	No legal tender other than gold or silver (Art. I, Sec. 10)
No preferential treatment for ports of one state (Art. I, Sec. 9)	No impairment of the obligations of contract (Art. I, Sec. 10)
Reciprocal full faith and credit among states for public acts, records, and judicial proceedings (Art. IV, Sec. 1)	No levying of import or export duties without congressional consent, except the levying of reasonable inspection fees (Art. I, Sec. 10)
Reciprocal privileges and immunities for citizens of different states (Art. IV, Sec. 2)	No tonnage duties without congressional consent (Art. I, Sec. 10)
Intoxicating liquor may not be imported into states where its sale or use is prohibited (21st Amend.)	
4. Administration of Justice	
Federal criminal trials to be held in state where crime was committed (Art. III, Sec. 2)	No bills of attainder (Art. I, Sec. 10)
Extradition for crimes (Art. IV, Sec. 2)	No ex post facto laws (Art. I, Sec. 10)
Federal criminal juries to be chosen from state and district where crime was committed (6th Amend.)	Supreme Court has original jurisdiction over all cases in which state is a party (Art. III, Sec. 2)
Federal judicial power extends to controversies between two or more states, between a state and citizens of another state, and between a state or its citizens and a foreign nation or its citizens (Art. III, Sec. 2)	No denial of life, liberty, or property without due process of law (14th Amend.)
	No denial of equal protection of state laws to persons within its limits (14th Amend.)

Source: From Table 2.2, pp. 42–43 in *American Federalism: A View from the States,* 3rd ed., by Daniel J. Elazar. Copyright © 1984 by Harper & Row Publishers, Inc. Reprinted by permission of Pearson Education, Inc.

Confederation. They reasoned that a nation must speak with one voice when negotiating with foreign countries; it also needs a uniform monetary system for its economy to function. Thus, only the national government can declare war, raise and support an army, make treaties with other nations, and coin money.

Another category of powers comprises the **implied powers**, those not specifically enumerated in the Constitution but inferred from the delegated powers. Many can be justified through the elastic clause. For example, the national government's power to tax and spend can be extended by the necessary and proper clause to cover construction of a national system of roads. In addition, the **inherent powers** do not appear in the Constitution but are *assumed* because of the nature of government. Thus, only the national government has the power to conduct foreign relations, make war even in the absence of a formal declaration, and protect its officials against bodily harm or threats.

Those powers not assigned to the national government are left with the states. These **reserved powers**, guaranteed in the Tenth Amendment, protect the states' role in the federal system. Among the reserved powers are the so-called **police powers**, or the ability to regulate the health, morals, public safety, and welfare of state citizens. Such regulations include speed limits on highways, but they also involve education, marriage, criminal law, zoning regulations, and contracts.

Over time, some of these powers have shifted, by necessity, to the national government. For example, certain state criminal law powers have been supplemented by congressional acts and Supreme Court decisions to provide more uniformity among the states and prevent criminals from escaping punishment simply by crossing state boundaries. The "Lindbergh" law gave the national government power to investigate and prosecute kidnapping cases that involve the crossing of state lines.

Powers *shared* by both the national and state governments are known as **concurrent powers**. Both types of government can regulate commerce, levy taxes, run a road system, establish their own elections, and maintain their own judicial structure. Sometimes these overlapping powers give citizens an additional forum in which to seek support or to secure their rights. For instance, when the national government tried to discourage the move toward same-sex marriages, civil unions, and gay adoptions through the 1996 Defense of Marriage Act, couples sought recourse in state judicial systems such as that of Massachusetts, which ruled gay marriages constitutional in 2003.

The national government can bypass concurrent powers, if it chooses, and use the supremacy clause to force upon states policies in the best interests of the entire nation or to *preempt* state action in areas where both governments have legislative authority.[14] Over the years, the federal government, looking to impose uniform policies over the entire country, has devised laws that have superseded state action in areas such as pollution control, transportation, nutrition labeling, taxation, and civil rights. In 2002, President Bush and Congress decided, over objections from Nevada's state government and U.S. senators, to approve the burial of seventy-seven thousand tons of high-level radioactive waste, currently stored around the country, under Yucca Mountain, near Las Vegas. The national government also, in reaction to the attacks of September 11, 2001, used its preemption power over foreign affairs to prevent state and local governments from revealing the names of alleged terrorism suspects and witnesses being held in jail without legal representation.[15] And, as mentioned in the case study, the Bush administration unsuccessfully challenged a federal court judge's decision to deny the United States Attorney General the power to use federal drug laws to prevent the state of Oregon from implementing its assisted-suicide program under its "death with dignity" law, by threatening to prosecute doctors for prescribing lethal doses of controlled drugs.[16]

In addition to granting powers, the framers *denied* certain powers to both national and state governments. Fearful of creating an all-powerful central government that would override the rights of the states and the people, the framers withheld from the national government powers that might have that result. For example, Article I, Section 9, denies the national government the right to place an export tax on products

implied powers Powers not specifically stated in the Constitution but inferred from the express powers.

inherent powers Powers that do not appear in the Constitution but are assumed because of the nature of government. Also refers to a theory that the Constitution grants authority to the executive, through the injunction in Article II, Section 1, that "The Executive power shall be vested in a President of the United States of America."

reserved powers Powers not assigned by the Constitution to the national government but left to the states or to the people, according to the Tenth Amendment.

police powers The powers to regulate health, morals, public safety, and welfare, which are reserved to the states.

concurrent powers Powers shared by both national and state levels of government.

 **MakeItReal**

Primary Source: The Morrill Act (1862)

 **MakeItReal**

Primary Source: The Bill of Rights

from the states and the power to impose a direct tax on the people unless it was levied proportionally to each state's population (a provision overridden by the Sixteenth Amendment, allowing for the creation of a national income tax). The Bill of Rights, beginning with the words "Congress shall make no law . . ." can also be seen as a long list of powers denied to the national government in areas such as freedom of speech, freedom of religion, freedom of the press, and defendants' rights.

Denying certain powers to the states helped keep their functions separate from those of the newly established national government. Limits on state powers, some of which can be overridden by Congress, are outlined in Article I, Section 10, of the Constitution. Among the prohibited powers are those delegated exclusively to the national government: powers to declare war, make treaties, and coin money. In addition, states cannot impair the obligations of contracts, thus preventing them from wiping out any debts, including those that existed prior to the formation of the Constitution. In the case of states that support gay marriage and civil unions and those that do not, it remains to be seen how the Supreme Court will rule under the "obligation of contracts" and the "full faith and credit" provision of Article IV, Section I, on the question of whether same-sex couples from one state can require other states to provide them with the benefits of marriage.

Finally, the framers denied to both national and state governments certain powers deemed offensive based on their British experience. These include the power to grant titles of nobility, pass bills of attainder (which legislate the guilt of an individual without the benefit of a trial), and pass *ex post facto* laws (which declare an action to be a crime *after* it has been committed).

THE DEVELOPMENT OF FEDERALISM

Despite this enumeration of powers in the Constitution, the framers omitted many problem areas in mapping out the relationship between the national and state governments. National and state policy makers and the judicial system have had to develop that relationship over time. Many of those decisions were made in response to national crises.

Debating the National Role: Hamilton Versus Jefferson

The debate about how much leeway Congress would have to legislate beyond its enumerated constitutional powers began in the Washington administration over the creation of a national bank. At issue here was Article I, Section 8, Clause 18, of the Constitution (the elastic clause), which grants Congress the power "to make all Laws which shall be necessary and proper for carrying into Execution" its enumerated powers. Thus, Secretary of the Treasury Alexander Hamilton argued in 1791 that the national government could build on its power to coin money, operate a uniform currency system, and regulate commerce by chartering a national bank. Secretary of State Thomas Jefferson, however, opposed this idea, arguing that since no explicit power to charter banks was written into the Constitution, that power was reserved to the states.

This debate over the constitutionality of creating a bank represented two distinct visions of federalism. Hamilton's argument favoring a national bank suggested a whole new series of implied powers for the national government. Jefferson's argument was that such broad interpretation of the clause would give Congress unlimited power to, in his words, "do whatever evil they please," with the result that the national government would "swallow up all the delegated powers" and overwhelm the states. In the end, President Washington was more persuaded by Hamilton's vision of expansive national powers, and the bank was chartered in 1791. But was the bank constitutional?

Asserting National Power: *McCulloch v. Maryland*

After a second national bank was chartered in 1816, the state of Maryland challenged the bank's operation by imposing a state tax on it. The bank refused to comply, and the Supreme Court was asked in 1819 to rule, in ***McCulloch v. Maryland***, on two points: the constitutionality of Congress's chartering the national bank and the constitutionality of a state's tax on that bank.[17]

Chief Justice John Marshall, an advocate of strong, centralized national power, wrote a resounding unanimous opinion supporting the power of Congress to charter the bank. Marshall turned to the necessary and proper clause of the Constitution and found there the implied power for the national government to do what was convenient to carry out the powers delegated to it in Article I, Section 8. According to Marshall, the powers of the national government would now be broadened considerably: "Let the end be legitimate, let it be within the scope of the Constitution, and all means which are appropriate, which are plainly adapted to that end, which are not prohibited, but consistent with the letter and spirit of the Constitution, are constitutional."

This was indeed the broadest possible definition of national power. Now Congress could justify any legislation simply by tying it to one of the delegated national powers in the Constitution. The national government could potentially expand its powers into many areas that had previously been thought to be reserved to the states.

Having established the constitutionality of the national bank, the Court also declared Maryland's tax on the bank unconstitutional, reasoning that states have no power to impede congressional laws. In this case, Marshall argued, "the power to tax involves the power to destroy" the bank, and thus limit congressional power. The Court's reading of the supremacy clause made the national government "supreme within its sphere of action," meaning that it was the dominant power in areas where its power overlaps with that of the states. It seemed that Jefferson was right in fearing that the national government was well on the way to "swallowing up" the states.

Expanding National Power Further: *Gibbons v. Ogden*

The Constitution states quite clearly that Congress has the power "to regulate Commerce . . . among the several States." But does such power to control commerce extend to control of commerce entirely within a state? And, if so, how extensive would that power be? In the 1824 case of ***Gibbons v. Ogden***, John Marshall once again interpreted the Constitution broadly, ruling in favor of expanding national power.[18]

This case involved a license to operate steamboats in the waters between New York and New Jersey. One man, Aaron Ogden, had purchased a state-issued license to do so in New York waters, while his former partner, Thomas Gibbons, had gone to the national government for a federal coasting license. It was left to the Supreme Court to decide whether the central government's power over *interstate* commerce (commerce among states) predominated over an individual state's power to regulate *intrastate* commerce (commerce within a state boundary). Marshall used this opportunity to give the interstate commerce clause the broadest possible definition, holding that the national government had the power to regulate any "commercial intercourse" having an effect in two or more states. This meant that the national government could now reach activities that affect interstate commerce even within state boundaries. The states, then, had only the power to regulate commerce wholly within one state. But with the growth of industries such as mining and food production, it would soon be hard to find such enterprises. This ruling made states' rights advocates unhappy. Slaveholders in the South, for example, feared national incursion into their peculiar form of labor "commerce."

MakeItReal

Primary Source: *McCulloch v. Maryland*

McCulloch v. Maryland The 1819 decision by Chief Justice John Marshall that expanded the interpretation of the "necessary and proper" clause to give Congress broad powers to pass legislation and reaffirmed the national government's power over the states under the supremacy clause.

Gibbons v. Ogden The 1824 decision by Chief Justice John Marshall that gave Congress the power, under the "interstate commerce" clause, to regulate anything that "affects" interstate commerce.

Asserting State Power: Nullification

Inevitably, an organized response emerged to Marshall's strong central power position in the *McCulloch* and *Gibbons* cases. In the 1820s and early 1830s, southerners such as John Calhoun of South Carolina objected to the national government raising tariffs on raw materials and manufactured goods, thereby protecting northern industries but forcing southerners to pay higher prices. Lacking the numbers in Congress to reverse this direction, Calhoun adopted the theory of **nullification**, initially proposed by Jefferson and Madison in 1798 in opposition to the Alien and Sedition Acts. Nullification theory held that states faced with unacceptable national legislation could declare such laws null and void and refuse to observe them. South Carolina, for example, declared the national tariffs null and void in 1832 and threatened to *secede* (leave the Union) over the issue. A crisis was averted when President Andrew Jackson lowered the tariff while also threatening to use military force to prevent secession.

However, nullification reared its head again over attempts by the national government to restrict slavery. This time the South did secede, and the Civil War ensued. This war was a turning point in American federalism, because the North's victory ensured that the Union and its federal structure would survive. No longer could states declare national laws unconstitutional or threaten to secede.

This has not prevented states and localities from trying to do this on occasion. Since the passage of the U.S.A. Patriot Act in 2001, nearly 350 towns and localities, such as Des Moines, Iowa, and five states, such as New Hampshire, have considered nullifying the law in their regions. By this action they would refuse to enforce or implement the provisions of the law.[19] Another form of nullification followed a May 2005 Supreme Court decision to allow localities to seize private property in the name of other private financial interests in order to improve the economic development prospects on that property. Seventeen states immediately considered passing laws to reverse that decision in their region, with Alabama the first to pass the provision. Meanwhile, another seven states considered similar laws and a half-dozen other states considered constitutional provisions to reverse the judgment. Of course these laws and state constitutional provisions would eventually be subject to Supreme Court review.[20]

Developing a System of Separation: Dual Federalism

After the Civil War, the prevailing view of federalism was one of **dual federalism**, in which each type of government remained supreme in its own jurisdiction, thus keeping the states separate and distinct from the national government. Dual federalism prevailed during this period as a result of two factors. Supreme Court rulings between 1877 and 1937 fueled a state-centered view of federalism. In addition, industrial expansion created an economic environment opposed to government interference and regulation, thereby limiting the national government's power over industry and giving states the upper hand in the federal structure. For instance, in 1895 the Court ruled that the national government had no power to regulate the monopoly of the sugar-refining industry, which, although national in scope, had factories located in Pennsylvania. The Court ruled in *United States* v. *E. C. Knight* that the national government had the power to regulate shipment of sugar, which constituted interstate commerce, but it did not have the power to regulate manufacture of sugar, because that was local in nature and thus wholly within the supreme power of the states.[21]

In a 1918 ruling, the Court placed additional restrictions on national power. The 1916 Keating Owen Act sought to limit child labor, but, in overturning this act in *Hammer* v. *Dagenhart*, Justice William R. Day indicated just how state-centered the Court had become. He wrote: "The grant of authority over a purely federal matter

Question for Reflection

Think about efforts by states and localities to limit enforcement of the U.S.A. Patriot Act and the Supreme Court's *eminent domain* decision. How much leeway should localities now have to refuse to follow federal policies?

nullification A nineteenth-century theory that upholds that states faced with unacceptable national legislation can declare such laws null and void and refuse to observe them.

dual federalism A system in which each level of power remains supreme in its own jurisdiction, thus keeping the states separate and distinct from the national government.

Approaching Democracy Around the Globe

Federalism and the Iraq Constitution

Who would have thought that the concept of federalism would be the potential "deal breaker" in drafting the Iraqi Constitution? As the August 15, 2005, preliminary deadline for drafting the new constitution approached, how to apportion power among Iraq's three major factions, the Sunnis, Shiites, and Kurds, became the central issue. The Kurds in the north had large oil reserves and in 1991 had developed so successful a regional self-rule democratic system that they were seeking local self-rule under the new government. The Shiites, a religious Islamic group with ties to the Iranian theocracy, included more than 60 percent of the nation's twenty-seven million people and had been oppressed during Saddam Hussein's regime. They controlled most of the major oil regions as well as the nation's only seaport. But the Sunnis, a more secular Islamic people who had ruled the country for years under Saddam Hussein, had no such oil reserves, natural wealth, or local governmental structure. As a result, they opposed the federal structure favored by the Kurds and the Shiites. Many of the disputes involved apportionment of the other regions' oil wealth as well as the power afforded to each region.

During the debates over the new constitution, each faction made demands about the nature of the relationship between the new national government and each of the regions. The Shiites called for their own autonomous and self-ruled federated region, ruled by Islamic law. The Sunnis, worried that a system of local rule within a federal structure would break up the country, urged their followers to vote against the new constitution. Although the Kurds and the Shiites had enough votes in the National Assembly to approve the new draft of the constitution, the people would vote on the final draft, and supporters of the constitution feared that the Sunnis could block the popular vote.

When the August 15 deadline passed, discussions were extended for an additional week. Although some hoped the major differences could be bridged in that time, others realized that failure to do so would represent major problems for the Bush administration's hopes of restructuring post-war Iraq. When the vote finally took place in October 2005 the constitution won narrow approval. Two Sunni provinces overwhelmingly voted it down, but although more than half of the voters in a third province opposed it, the negative votes failed to reach the two-thirds threshold needed to reject the charter. However, similar to ratification of the U.S. Constitution, which was accepted only with the promise of immediate amendments, it was agreed that the following year the Iraqi government would consider changes to make the constitution more acceptable to the Sunni population. Indeed, by January 2006, after the Sunnis' strong showing in the December 15 popular parliamentary election, all three groups continued to negotiate governmental changes that would protect the rights of all. Clearly, the future of the national Iraqi government will depend on both the Sunnis' federalism concerns and the Kurds' and Shiites' willingness to accomodate them. By March 2006, though, the violence in the region made clear that successful negotiations would be difficult.

Source: Richard A. Oppel Jr. "Sunni Group Near Deal with Kurds on Iraqi Government," *New York Times*, January 3, 2006; Isorzou Daraghi and Solomon Moore, "Sunnis Accept Deal on Charter," *Los Angeles Times*, p. A1; Slobodan Lekic, "Shiite Negotiator Says Parliament Will Get Draft Shortly But No Agreement Yet with Sunni Arabs," *Boston Globe*, August 22, 2005; Jonathan Finer and Omar Fekeiki, "On Eve of Deadline, Charter Isn't Ready," *Washington Post*, August 15, 2005, p. A12; Robert H. Reid, "Federalism Emerges as Deal-Breaker in Iraq," August 15, 2005; Rory Carroll, "Clerics Push for Shiastan in Southern Iraq," *London Guardian*, August 12, 2005, p. 14; Ashraf Khalil, "The Conflict in Iraq," *Los Angeles Times*, August 13, 2005, p. 8.

---

was not intended to destroy the local power always existing and carefully reserved to the States in the Tenth Amendment to the Constitution."[22] In this classic statement of dual federalism, the states' reserved powers now represented a limitation upon the national government.

Creating a Cooperative System: The New Deal Era

The Great Depression of the 1930s and President Franklin D. Roosevelt's New Deal eventually put an end to dual federalism. In 1932, the country struggled with the worst economic depression in its history. To relieve the suffering, Roosevelt promised Americans a "New Deal," which meant taking immediate steps to restart the economy and create jobs. At Roosevelt's behest, Congress passed programs

Question for Reflection

If Roosevelt had carried out his "court-packing plan" and almost doubled the size of the Supreme Court, what impact would this have had on dual federalism and the country in other areas of law?

 **MakeItReal**

Primary Source: Franklin Roosevelt Unveils the Second Half of the New Deal (1936)

involving tremendous new powers for the national government, such as creating large national administrative agencies to supervise manufacturing and farming. These programs produced an increase in spending by the national government, numerous regulations, and hordes of bureaucrats to administer them.

Initially, the Supreme Court used the rulings of the dual federalism era to restrict Roosevelt's programs, arguing that the problems they addressed were local in nature and not in the province of the national government.[23] But the nation's needs were so great that the Supreme Court's position could not endure. A highly critical President Roosevelt proposed a "court-packing plan," whereby he sought to add one new justice for each one over the age of seventy up to a total of fifteen justices. While the plan was before Congress, the Supreme Court, in what became known as "the switch in time that saved nine," suddenly began ruling in favor of the New Deal programs, with Chief Justice Charles Evans Hughes and Justice Owen Roberts changing their mind about federalism to allow the national government to prevail over the states.

In a 1937 case, *National Labor Relations Board (NLRB)* v. *Jones and Laughlin Steel,* the Court upheld the national government's right to impose collective bargaining by unions and ban certain unfair labor practices. The Court was now willing to support the use of national power and allow the national government to control manufacturing, production, and agricultural activities through the interstate commerce powers. As a result, the court-packing plan dissolved.[24]

But what of the Tenth Amendment, which reserves to the states powers not delegated to the national government? A Supreme Court that was in the process of being completely remade by eight new Roosevelt appointees seemingly put an end to dual federalism in 1941. In *United States* v. *Darby Lumber Co.,* which upheld the national government's power to regulate lumber industry wages and hours under the interstate commerce power, the Court ruled that the Tenth Amendment "states but a truism that all is retained which has not been surrendered."[25] In short, this amendment was no longer seen as a limitation on the national government or a bar to the exercise of its power, even wholly within state boundaries.

The New Deal ushered in a new era in the federal relationship, one of cooperation between the national and state governments. This system is known as **cooperative federalism.** Solutions for various state and local problems were directed and sometimes funded by the national government and were then administered by the state governments according to national guidelines, as was the case in the rebuilding of New York City after the attacks of September 11, 2001.[26]

The national government was supreme in the federalism partnership despite the fleeting return of dual federalism in response to a 1976 Court challenge overturned nine years later. In 1976 the Supreme Court signaled a possible return to dual federalism in the case of *National League of Cities* v. *Usery,* which dealt with extending national wages and hours legislation to state and municipal workers. Writing for a slim majority, Justice William Rehnquist banned national regulation of "core" state functions. Nine years later, however, the Court overturned *Usery* in the case of *Garcia* v. *San Antonio Metropolitan Transit Authority,* which also dealt with wages and hours legislation. The Court shifted its position back to favoring national predominance, arguing that states must rely on Congress rather than the Court to decide which of their programs should be regulated by the national government. This ruling was reaffirmed by the Court in *South Carolina* v. *Baker.*[27] But, as you will see at the end of the chapter, the Supreme Court is once again reassessing and redefining the nature of the relationship between the national and state governments.

This partnership between the national and state governments encouraged states to look to the national government for help and funding to deal with problems seemingly beyond their means. Similarly, citizens began to look to Washington for solutions to their problems rather than to their state and local governments. The result was an increase in the power of the national government and a drive to achieve uniformity of programs throughout the country, often at the expense of state power and innovation.

cooperative federalism A cooperative system in which solutions for various state and local problems are directed and sometimes funded by both the national and state governments. The administration of programs is characterized by shared power and shared responsibility.

Seeking Uniformity:
Federalism in the Post–New Deal Era

A major judicial movement in the 1950s and 1960s created a new role for the national government in the federal system, that of protector of personal rights guaranteed by the Constitution. Prior to the 1930s, defendants' rights had been a power reserved to the states, leading to policy variations that, for example, allowed certain states to deny minorities personal liberties and legal protection. The Supreme Court ruled to extend most of the protections of the Bill of Rights to the states (the Bill of Rights originally applied to the national government only) to ensure uniformity from one state to another and help end inequality. The Court did this by ruling that certain guarantees in the Bill of Rights are part of the due process right guaranteed by the Fourteenth Amendment against state government intrusion. This process was called the **incorporation** of the Bill of Rights.

This established a uniform judicial process around the country. For instance, in the 1932 *Scottsboro* case, in which a group of young African Americans had been convicted of rape and sentenced to death without a fair trial, the Supreme Court ruled that the Sixth Amendment right to counsel should extend to all future state capital trials like this one to ensure fairness.[28] States could still operate their judicial systems, but to guarantee personal rights they had to adhere to national standards regarding constitutional protections. In Chapter 13 we discuss the full extent of this incorporation process in detail.

The national government also sought to impose national standards regarding equality. Social equality gained ground through a series of Court decisions, such as *Brown v. Board of Education of Topeka* in 1954, which called for the end of segregation in public schools,[29] and later cases that promoted integration. Political equality was sought through a series of cases, such as *Reynolds v. Sims* in 1964. This case established the "one-person, one-vote" standard in which the number of voters in each district was made roughly the same, thus giving people an equal say in the operation of their government.[30] Personal equality was guaranteed by a series of First Amendment cases granting citizens the same rights of speech, press, assembly, religion, and thought no matter where they live. The Johnson administration initiated the "War on Poverty" program in the 1960s that led Congress to adopt a series of welfare, educational, and social programs to improve economic equality. These judicial decisions and political actions establishing uniformity of rights have helped America approach democracy by guaranteeing to residents in all states a final recourse for seeking constitutional rights.

Federal Grants and Federal Mandates:
Federalism since 1930

The Depression in the 1930s spurred vast increases in federal spending and power. When the Supreme Court ruled during the New Deal that the national power to spend was not limited to the enumerated grants of power in the Constitution, further growth was inevitable.[31] Since then, national power has continued to grow, particularly in the past three decades. At issue in this federal system is how much money the national government will spend and under what conditions the states may use federal funds (with the answers usually being "lots" and "according to specific guidelines"). We now look at the different types of federal grants and at how various administrations have worked with the grant-in-aid system.

Federal Grants   National spending programs vary. The most frequently used is the **grant-in-aid**, money paid to states and localities to induce them to implement policies in accordance with federally mandated guidelines. Money moves through an *intergovernmental transfer*, but only if the states spend it in certain policy areas. If the states do not wish to abide by the **conditions of aid** or national requirements, they

incorporation The process whereby the Supreme Court has found that Bill of Rights protections apply to the states.

grant-in-aid Money paid to states and localities to induce them to implement policies in accordance with federally mandated guidelines.

conditions of aid National requirement that must be observed to receive benefits.

Quick Review

Incorporation of the Bill of Rights
- Judicial decisions and political actions established uniformity of rights and partnership between the national and state governments.
- States had to adhere to national standards of constitutional protections.
- Social equality was promoted through an end to segregation.
- Political equality was established through the "one-person, one-vote" standard.
- Personal equality was guaranteed, granting citizens the same rights regardless of where they live.
- Economic equality was the goal of programs that were part of the "War on Poverty" program in the 1960s.

Federal Grants
- Money is spent by the national government and under certain conditions it may be used by the states.
- Money paid to states and localities to induce them to implement policies in accordance with federally mandated guidelines.
- Congress can exercise considerable control over the states by attaching to federal money certain federal mandates.
- The number of such grants is vast and has been rising steadily for the past fifteen years.

can refuse federal funds. These conditions come in various forms. Some require that a grant be spent in a certain fashion, while others try to accomplish additional policy goals. For instance, in October 2000, President Bill Clinton signed into law a bill requiring all states to pass, by September 2003, a uniform .08 blood alcohol standard for driving "under the influence" applicable to first-time offenders, or lose an increasing amount of their federal highway funding assistance. Usually, the deep pockets of the national government and tight state budgets ensure acceptance. For example, although sixteen states initially retained their different blood alcohol standards, when they began losing tens of millions in federal highway funds because they had not passed the uniform national standard into state law, they capitulated. Minnesota became the last of the fifty states and the District of Columbia to comply with the law.[32]

The number of such grants is vast and has been rising steadily for the past fifteen years. National grants to states and localities rose from 594 to nearly 660 between 1993 and 1999. The number had dropped to 608 in 2004. Simultaneously, the size of grant outlays rose by 1998 to $251 billion, an increase of 29 percent from the $194 billion in 1993.[33] By 2006, though, that overall figure would rise to $435.7 billion, or 17 percent of the federal budget.[34] Medicaid growth was the principal cause of increase (more than doubling in cost from $75.8 billion in 1993 to $171 billion by 2006), but another large outlay went for the disaster assistance programs of the Federal Emergency Management Agency (see Figure 3.2).[35] President Bush's fiscal year 2002 budget called for a nearly 7 percent reduction in grant-in-aid spending, with eventual plans to reduce that spending by another 11.2 percent by fiscal year 2011. Some of the largest cuts, revealing the administration's new policy choices, were proposed in the environmental protection, highway aid, and state criminal alien assistance programs. Coinciding with these domestic cuts, and just two months after the September 11, 2001, attacks, President Bush signed Congress's anti-terrorism package providing another $20 billion in emergency funding and security programs, with $10.4 billion alone in federal aid promised to New York City and state for their recovery efforts. When much of this aid ended up going to areas in no danger of terrorist attack, in early 2006 discussions began about targeting the grants for areas most at risk.[36]

Grants-in-aid come in a wide variety of types. **Categorical grants** are the most common and address specific purposes, usually with strict rules attached. Most categorical grants cover only part of the costs and usually require the state or local government or a nonprofit organization to partially match funds. In this way, the grants induce states to increase spending for desired programs and encourage cooperation. Approximately 89 percent of national aid to the states and localities comes in the form of categorical grants. This is such a fast-growing form of national assistance that we now have the largest number of categorical grants in history, with the "catalog of federal domestic assistance" listing in 2006 approximately 1,628 different forms of federal assistance programs to the states and localities.[37] Categorical grants come in three types: **formula grants, project grants**, and combined **formula/project grants**.

Formula grants are federal monies allocated to states and localities based on a prescribed legislative distribution formula. They support continuing activities and are not confined to a specific project. Depending on their policy aim, such formula grants can reflect many factors, such as total population, median family income, miles of coastline, total enrollment in education, and miles of highways and railways. Governmental units that meet the strict rules for distribution automatically qualify for the grant.[38]

The *project grant* is not based on a formula but is distributed for specific purposes after a fairly competitive application and approval process for a fixed period. These are sometimes called *discretionary grants* because they are distributed at the discretion of a designated legislator or administrator. Given the desire of legislators to maintain more control over the operation of these programs, the majority of categorical grants, 56.9 percent in 2006, are project grants.[39]

In recent years a *combined formula/project grant* has been developed in which competitive grants are awarded but also are restricted by the use of a formula. For

categorical grant The most common type of federal grant, given for specific purposes, usually with strict rules attached.

formula grant A grant based on a prescribed legislative formula to determine how money will be distributed to eligible governmental units (states or major cities).

project grant A grant not based on a formula, but distributed for specific purposes after a fairly competitive application and approval process.

formula/project grant A grant in which competitive grants are awarded but also restricted by use of a formula.

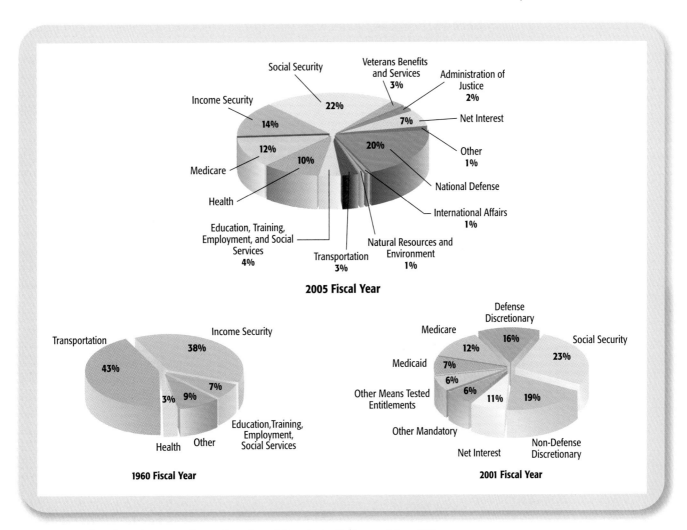

Figure 3.2   The Changing Functions of National Grants to States and Localities
Over the last forty years, there has been a dramatic shift in the purposes for national grants. In short, national funding for transportation and welfare programs has been replaced by a system of health care programs and funding for job training.

Sources: "Total Federal Outlays, FY 2005—"National Priorities Project" at http://nationalpriorities.org/charts/proposed_total_federal U.S. Advisory Commission on Intergovermental Relations, Characteristics of Federal Grant-in-Aid Programs to State and Local Governments, 1995 (Washington, D.C.; ACIR, January 1996), p. 16 and Lawrence Mishel, "Changes in Federal Aid to State and Local Governments," as proposed in the Bush Administration FY 2002 Budget, Economic Policy Institute, found at http://www.epinet.org/briefingpapers/.

example, Congress may limit the amount of grant money that can be awarded to a state or region of a state.

In 1966, President Lyndon Johnson created **block grants**, which simplified the process, consolidating several smaller grants into one large grant that provides money for broad functional program areas. The funds may be used at the recipient government's discretion. Federal government grants to states in localities for fiscal year 2006 amounted to $435 billion, or about 17 percent of the federal budget (well up from 7.6 percent in 1960). Compared with the 608 categorical grants available in 2004, 17 block grants were available, up from 15 in 1993 and covering such diverse areas as state and local homeland security, low income home energy assistance, community development assistance, institutions assisting Hispanic people and communities, Native American housing, and preventive health and health services.[40] One new program, created in October 2004, was the Innocence Protection Act, making law enforcement funds available to states and localities for the analysis of DNA evidence for both crime scenes and appeals of prisoners seeking to establish their innocence.

block grant A federal grant that provides money to states for general program funding with few or even no strings attached.

Similarly, that year, Congress promised to pay 40 percent of the cost of educating schoolchildren with disabilities.[41]

Examining all of these types of federal grants in specific issue areas, reveals clearly Congress's shifting spending priorities. In recent years, Congress has shifted its spending priorities toward people rather than places, directing nearly two-thirds of federal money toward aid to individuals, up from nearly 32 percent in 1978. As a result, although institutional programs have been allowed to decline, grants to people have meant that states and localities often must budget matching grants for these programs. For example, a Congressional Budget Office study of federal spending on the elderly and children concluded that in fiscal year 2000 the federal government spent just more than one-third of its budget, or about $615 billion, on the elderly and just under 10 percent, or $175 billion, on children. If present spending rates hold, though, by 2010 about half of the federal budget will be spent on these two groups, with four-fifths of that amount being devoted to the elderly. This spending priority's increasing importance, traceable to the aging Baby Boomer population, is apparent when we examine governmental spending programs for the elderly. These numbered only 46 in 1971, rose to 360 in 1990, nearly doubled to 615 in 2000, and are expected to rise to a staggering 1,050 (equal to the number of all current domestic programs now) by 2010.[42]

One anticipated major change in the welfare area was the **devolution revolution**, a term signifying the shift in policy-making responsibility to the states. In this way, Speaker of the House Newt Gingrich argued in the mid-1990s, "power" could be restored to the individuals first, then to state and local governments as the next best option. Noted federalism expert John Kincaid's research has suggested that political opposition negated most such devolution, but where devolution by law failed, a process of *de facto* devolution has occurred. The federal government's funding of urban programs as policies is no longer directed toward places, such as aid for state and local transportation and redevelopment programs, but instead is directed more toward people and the rights of individuals, such as social welfare programs. In the words of Senator Carl Levin (D.-MI), "There's no political capital in intergovernmental relations. Helping out mayors or county officials gets me very few votes."[43]

Great debate surrounds the extent to which grants-in-aid help this country approach democracy. When certain regions of the country fail to spend in a manner that reflects the needs of their citizens, the national government can take their tax money and redistribute it to other regions. Dictating the spending of governmental resources in this way has helped to remove inequalities, but it has political costs for the states. More than that, states quickly grow to depend on national money, thus further impelling them to allow the national government to dictate their policy direction. Some argue that grants detract from democracy because they decrease democratic accountability for government spending, decrease governmental efficiency, increase governmental spending, and change state and local spending priorities. For this reason, some students of fiscal federalism argue for minimizing intergovernmental transfers.

Federal Mandates—Funded and Unfunded   Congress can exercise considerable control over the states by attaching to federal money certain **federal mandates**. States may be required to create programs that accord with federal policy goals. For example, a program to increase employment might have a provision setting aside 10 percent of the grant dollars for minority hirings, or a national health grant may place restrictions on teenage smoking. Because the national government imposes these mandates uniformly, they lead to unusual policy choices in different regions. In order to receive federal funding for its water supply, the city of Chicago was compelled to test its water for two pesticides present only in the Hawaiian water supply, where they are used on pineapple crops.

States frequently complain that federal mandates are underfunded or unfunded, meaning that the federal government imposes requirements without providing the funds to make compliance possible. Thus the national government controls policy but shifts the financial burden to the states.[44] State officials object to

devolution revolution A trend initiated in the Reagan administration and accelerated by then-Speaker of the House Newt Gingrich to send programs and power back to the states with less national government involvement.

federal mandates A direct order from Congress that the states must fulfill.

these unfunded mandates because it means they must raise the tax revenue to support them. By 1995, state and local governments found that they were spending approximately 25 percent of their budgets to meet federal mandates. Voter backlash often aimed at local officials rather than the members of Congress who voted the policy into effect but did not pay for it. In response to state and local officials' complaints that the national government's use of unfunded mandates was overburdening their budgets, the Republican Congress in 1995 passed the Unfunded Mandates Reform Act of 1995 (UMRA) as part of its Contract with America. This bill said that Congress had to assess the fiscal effect of a federal mandate on state and local governments, and if it amounted to more than $100 million annually, any member of Congress could challenge it with a point of order that could lead to a separate vote on the mandate and consideration of its possible funding by Congress.[45] In addition, Congress asked the Advisory Commission on Intergovernmental Relations (ACIR) to review the impact of particularly controversial unfunded mandates. Of the first fourteen reviewed, half were suggested for elimination and the rest faced proposed modifications. More than two hundred other mandates were then proposed for review.[46]

The effort to eliminate federal mandates has not been totally successful. In May 2005, Congress passed as part of its $82 billion military-spending budget the REAL ID Act, a national ID card that amounts to a sort of super-driver's license and is designed to prevent illegal immigrants from obtaining drivers' licenses and government identification. The states must implement the act and determine citizenship status for more than 220 million driver's license applicants, which will cost the states about $13 billion in the next five years.[47] In November 2005, President Bush called on Congress to commit to a $7.1 billion program to develop and distribute a vaccine and medicines to combat the possibility of an avian flu pandemic. The proposal required the states to budget about $510 million to stockpile enough anti-flu medicines to treat thirty-one million people.[48] The National Conference of State Legislatures estimates that in 2004 and 2005 alone the cost of all unfunded mandates was $50 billion.[49]

BALANCING FEDERAL–STATE RELATIONS: POLICY INNOVATION AND PROTECTING RIGHTS

State Policy Initiatives

When Justice Louis D. Brandeis described states as the "laboratories of democracy," he could not have known how those laboratories might operate in the conservative federal governmental era of the late twentieth and early twenty-first centuries. State programs and federal programs act in a kind of harmonious balance. As one governmental structure expands or withdraws its support for programs, the other tends to move in the opposite direction. During the 1980s, when the federal courts and Reagan administration withdrew support for certain defendants' rights and civil rights, many state Supreme Courts and appeals courts expanded their interpretations of state constitutions to increase the protection of individual rights. As the national government withdrew its support for unemployment and job training programs in the 1990s, some states compensated by increasing their own programs.

The question then becomes where policy innovation can occur in the federal system.[50] The states' ability to create new policy programs is a function of different factors: First, there is the question of each state's budget. Because all but one state are required to balance their budgets, states are at the mercy of larger economic forces. In times of recession, they take in less money in taxes and have higher costs for programs such as welfare and health care. The second factor is the amount of support the states receive from federal funding programs. In the past, federal grants programs often made up the shortfall for state funding, but since the Reagan

Questions for Reflection

What criteria would you propose for evaluating unfunded mandates attached to federal funding?

How would you determine whether or not the national government should impose policy without accounting for the financial burden to the state that the policy generates?

U.S.A. Yesterday and Today

Cyber-Federalism and Shipping Wine

When the Constitutional framers debated by day whether or not federal control over interstate commerce would improve the Articles of Confederation and drank wine by night at the City Tavern in Philadelphia, they could never have imagined that one day their handiwork would determine whether or not Juanita Swedenburg could, in 2004, ship wine ordered by Internet from her Middleburg, Virginia, winery to customers in New York. Although the American domestic wine industry generated more than $18 billion in revenues a year, in 2004 twenty-four states had laws that banned direct shipment of out-of-state wines to customers in their regions, ostensibly to protect state wineries, preserve local tax revenues, and protect against alcohol sales to minors.

To many local wineries and to wine lovers around the nation, these state bans represented an unconstitutional restriction on interstate commerce. The case was also of interest to the thousands of microbreweries around the nation, which stood poised to market their product over the Internet. Dozens of such cases worked their ways through the federal courts, and Swedenburg's reached the Supreme Court in 2004.

Advocates of ending the restrictions pointed to the interstate commerce clause, which grants the national government the power to dictate the flow of commerce across state lines using the Internet. However, supporters of state restrictions argued that the Twenty-First Amendment, which ended Prohibition, also stated, "The transportation or importation into any State . . . for delivery or use therein of intoxicating liquors, in violation of the laws thereof, is hereby prohibited." This seemed to say that the power to dictate whether liquor could be shipped into a state was now a sovereign state power.

By a narrow 5–4 vote, the Supreme Court sided with the federalists and put an end to what it termed an "ongoing low-level trade war" that the interstate commerce

▲ Juanita Swedenburg, of Middleburg, Virginia, could not ship her premium family vineyard wine to New York or 23 other states in 2004 until the Supreme Court ruled state bans on out-of-state internet wine sales to be a violation of interstate commerce. Her victory pleased wine sellers and wine lovers everywhere.

administration those programs have diminished rapidly. President Bush's budget for fiscal year 2006 proposed cutting $10.7 billion, or 4.5 percent of the budget for all federal grants to the states with the exception of Medicaid. And the situation will not improve as the costs of defense and homeland security increases. With twenty-four states facing budget deficits of nearly $35 billion, making up this shortfall is going to present a new challenge.[51]

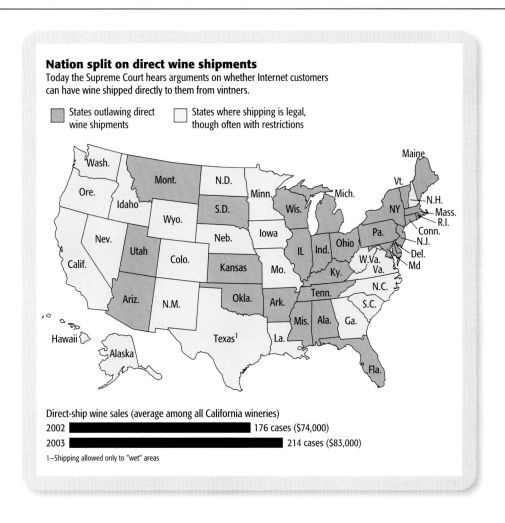

Nation split on direct wine shipments
Today the Supreme Court hears arguments on whether Internet customers
can have wine shipped directly to them from vintners.

☐ States outlawing direct   ☐ States where shipping is legal,
   wine shipments   though often with restrictions

Direct-ship wine sales (average among all California wineries)
2002 ████████████████████ 176 cases ($74,000)
2003 ████████████████████████ 214 cases ($83,000)
1–Shipping allowed only to "wet" areas

clause was designed to stop. The Court noted that with more than three thousand small wineries but few national wholesalers, it was not possible for "many small wineries [to] produce enough wine or have sufficient consumer demand for their wine to make it economical for wholesalers to carry their products." To Justice Anthony Kennedy, who authored the majority opinion, the Twenty-First Amendment could not deprive "citizens of their right to have access to other states' markets on equal terms." He later added, "Time and again, this Court has held that, in all but the narrowest circumstances, state laws violate the Commerce Clause if they mandate 'differential treatment of in-state and out-of-state economic interests that benefits the former and burdens the latter.' This rule is essential to the foundation of the Union." The Court decided the sale

and shipment of these wines around the country clearly affected commerce in a positive way.

As a result of this decision, states can no longer ban *only* out-of-state wine sales over the Internet, but they can still restrict or ban *all* wine sales in-state and out-of-state if they so choose. But in many states, wine lovers will now be able to buy Juanita Swedenburg's wine, or that of any other small winery they choose.

Source: Swedenburg v. Kelly, Granholm v. Heald 125 S. Ct. 1885 (2005); Fred Barbash, "Supreme Court Strikes Down Shipping Ban," *Washington Post,* May 16, 2005; Joan Biskupic, "Wineries That Sell Vino Via the Internet Stand to Gain," *USA Today,* May 17, 2005, p. 2B; Theresa Howard and Jerry Shriver, "Supreme Court: Let Those Wine Sales Flow," *USA Today,* May 17, 2005, p. B1; Richard Willing, "Justices to Debate Mail-Order Wine," *USA Today,* December 7, 2004, p. 3A.

The third factor is policy promises to citizens. When the government promises to educate its citizens, make them healthier, support them economically during troubled times, and keep them secure, if the national government does not provide funding, states must. After the September 11, 2001, attacks, the Bush administration promised, through the new Homeland Security Act, to provide money for securing the homeland, but many states found that the difficulty of

▲ After the Vermont Supreme Court ordered lawmakers to provide gay couples with the same rights as married people, demonstrators marched in Montpelier to oppose the civil union bill then under consideration in the state capitol. The bill was eventually passed.

obtaining those funds impelled them to create and fund new protection programs on their own. Similarly, increased costs of health care, increased demands for Medicaid services, and large projected cuts in federal funding for these programs have led the states to cut or reform their programs. One study found that if the federal budget had funded Medicaid at the same rate in 2006 as in 2001, $31 billion more would have been allocated to the program. If the states do not make up that gap, fewer citizens will receive aid.[52]

Finally, fourth, the federal government chooses to avoid certain policy areas, opening the door to policy innovation by the states. For example, when President Bush announced that the national government would not fund additional stem-cell research, California passed an initiative providing three billion dollars for developing such research programs. New Jersey and Wisconsin quickly followed.

Protection of Rights

Like innovation, protection of individual rights creates a complex relationship between state and federal levels. In numerous instances the federal judiciary has imposed the Bill of Rights on state courts to protect defendants being denied rights. Examples are civil rights cases and cases involving public school desegregation. In response to these federal pressures, many states have tried to restrict rights in their region. This process continues. When the Supreme Court created the right to abortion in *Roe* v. *Wade*, it also allowed the states to regulate the health of the woman in the second trimester of her pregnancy. In response, states including Pennsylvania, Missouri, and Texas searched for ways to restrict the right to abortion. Again, when the Supreme Court banned prayer and other forms of religious activities in public schools, Alabama created the moment of silent meditation, Texas allowed prayer by students before high school football games, Louisiana permitted the teaching of creationism and later "intelligent design" in science classes, and Rhode Island allowed nondenominational prayers at graduations. All of these were later overturned by the Court.

The grant-in-aid system has spiraled out of control, spurred by states' continual demands for national funding, the national government's willingness to provide it, and increasingly complicated restrictions on spending it. An examination of the history of this system will illustrate how presidents in the past sixty years initially used federal grants to change the relationship between the national and state governments and then sought to bring that system under control.

PRESIDENTS AND FEDERALISM

Roosevelt, Truman, and Eisenhower: The Era of Cooperative Federalism, 1930–1963

As you have learned, the system of cooperative federalism began during the Great Depression in the 1930s, when Congress authorized many new grants-in-aid beyond the fifteen that already existed for state support. By 1939, total federal outlays were fifteen times greater than they had been in 1933.

As public demands for greater government action increased following the New Deal, the national grant-in-aid became the major tool for responding. The Truman administration created seventy-one separately authorized grant programs involving areas

Chapter 3 Federalism **113**

▲ A group of young doffer and spinner boys comprised the labor force in a textile mill in Fall River, Massachusetts, in January 1912. In the early 1900s over 1.5 million children worked for as little as twenty-five cents for a twelve-hour day, and many exhausted young workers fell asleep on the job and were mutilated by their machines.

such as education, health, and transportation. The increase in grants-in-aid even continued through the conservative Eisenhower administration. By 1960, 132 grants were consuming $6.8 billion—a 250-percent increase in federal outlays. As the number and size of national grants grew, so did the conditions attached to these grants.[53]

Lyndon Johnson: The Era of Creative Federalism, 1963–1968

In the 1960s, President Lyndon B. Johnson launched his Great Society program, which involved using federal programs to create a smoother-functioning social welfare system. Johnson used **creative federalism**, an initiative that expanded the concept of partnership between the national government and the states. The national government would now work with cities, counties, school districts, and even nonprofit organizations to provide social services.

Creative federalism thrust the central government into areas neglected by the states. Johnson directed his administration to attack poverty, promote equal opportunity in education, solve the "urban crisis" through direct aid to the big cities (bypassing the states), and guarantee equal rights for minority groups. His Great Society initiative led to a rapid increase in new programs, most significantly Medicare and Medicaid, which provided national health care assistance for the aged and the impoverished; the Elementary and Secondary Education Act (ESEA), which provided national funding for public education; and Model Cities, which aimed at rejuvenating the inner cities. Broad national guidelines accompanied these programs, but the states and localities were left to implement them. For instance, national guidelines for Medicaid directed the level of income that qualified a person for assistance, but the states determined who would be eligible, how broad health coverage would be, and how health-care providers would be reimbursed.

In the 1960s, the grants-in-aid program shifted focus from needs the states pressed on the national government to needs the national government pressed on

Quick Review

Creative Federalism

- Partnership between the national government and the states.

- National government worked with localities to provide social services.

- Central government was thrust into areas neglected by the states.

- National guidelines were attached to programs; states and localities implemented the programs.

- Grants aimed at improving the quality of life for the handicapped, migrant workers, and neglected children.

creative federalism An initiative that expanded the concept of the partnership between the national government and the states under President Lyndon Johnson in the 1960s.

the states. In addition, national spending increased dramatically. Between 1960 and 1967, the number of grants increased from 132 to 379. Public as well as private resources were mobilized and pooled in an effort to meet a variety of goals, including improving farming, combating drug abuse, securing disaster relief after a flood or a storm, and improving education. As a result of these programs, the national government became bloated and overloaded. Bureaucracies to administer the spending programs were enlarged by both the national and state governments. States engaged in the "grantsmanship game," tailoring their applications to fit national requirements rather than their own policy needs. Moreover, the American people became accustomed to looking to the national government for solutions to their problems.

This effort to use federalism creatively helped the nation to approach democracy by empowering groups that had been voiceless for years. Grants went to programs aimed at improving quality of life for handicapped people, migrant workers, and neglected children. Other programs promoted bilingual education and desegregation. States that had previously ignored the needs of certain groups found that they could attract additional national funds by attending to their needs. In short, it was now in the states' financial interest to promote democracy.

As you will learn in Chapter 15, despite their laudable aims, the very nature of the American federal structure served to thwart the goals of creative federalism. Program bulk, sharp disagreements among groups about their goals, and lack of proper governmental oversight doomed them to failure. For instance, the Model Cities program, originally designed for twelve major cities, could not be passed until members of Congress from around the country secured a piece of the pie for their own region, thus expanding the program to an unmanageable 150 cities.[54]

By the end of the 1960s, widespread disenchantment hobbled the Great Society and the national government's efforts to make sweeping social changes.[55] However, many programs from that era still exist, such as the Head Start program, which provides preschool instruction for poor children; the Legal Services program, which provides legal assistance for the indigent; and food stamps, which provide national funding to feed the poor. But while poverty remains an enduring problem in America, the question of whether the benefits of the Great Society exceeded its administrative costs continues to be debated.[56]

Richard Nixon's New Federalism, 1969–1974

President Nixon's **New Federalism** program, so labeled because it was designed to return fiscal power to the states and localities, was, in essence, a reaction to the excesses of Johnson's creative federalism. The cornerstone of this policy was **general revenue sharing (GRS)**, which distributed money to the states with no restrictions on how it could be spent. Also important was **special revenue sharing**, in which groups of categorical grants-in-aid in related policy areas such as crime control or health care would be consolidated into a single block grant.

After the passage of revenue sharing in 1972, $30 billion was distributed among the states and local governments, but the program was not a complete success. One-third of the funds were given to the states according to a complicated formula taking into account poverty levels and city size; the remaining two-thirds were paid directly to local governments, such as the cities of New York, Dallas, and San Francisco. The list of allowed expenditures was so general that rather than using the revenue-sharing money to replace old grant-in-aid programs, many states and localities began using it to cover their basic operating expenses, such as the salaries of public officials. As a result, many program areas once funded by categorical grants-in-aid now went unfunded.

Paradoxically, although intended to return power to the states, the GRS in fact further extended the national government's influence. Even though GRS money had few funding restrictions, putting it into each jurisdiction's general treasury made states subject to national regulations in such areas as civil rights, affirmative action, and fair wages.

In the area of special revenue sharing, Nixon tried to create several block grants in community development, employment and training, and social services to replace the increasing number of more specific categorical grants. Contrary to his conservative image, Nixon spent freely in the domestic area, with the amount rising from 10.3 percent of the gross national product (GNP) at the beginning of his term of office to 13.7 percent six years later. Seeking to induce state and local officials to support his New Federalism initiatives, he added extra block grant money on top of that available from bundled categorical grants. Nixon was engaged in an ambitious process of grouping all of the operating and capital categorical grants into a handful of block grants in such areas as welfare and health care, and moving responsibility for income transfers (welfare, health care, school lunches, and food stamps) to the national government, when Watergate ended his effort.[57]

The movement toward the national government's increased dominance in the federal structure could not be reversed. Although Presidents Richard Nixon and Gerald Ford attempted through consolidation to slow the growth of national grants, by 1976 the total number of federal aid programs actually increased by 250 percent. The layer of unrestricted revenue-sharing money in addition to an increasing number of categorical grant programs kept national spending expanding. Unhappy with its lack of control over both the amount and nature of this spending, Congress abolished revenue sharing to the states in 1981, then did the same for revenue sharing to the localities in 1986.

With more time in the White House, the state-oriented Republican party might have been able to carry out its plan to reform and reduce the categorical grants program. But the Democrats returned to the White House in 1976.

Creative Federalism Returns under Jimmy Carter, 1977–1980

President Carter tried to combine the best aspects of Johnson's creative federalism and Nixon's New Federalism to more precisely target federal aid to the most hard-pressed communities. He also sought to use public funds to encourage private investment for certain problems. With these two goals, Carter hoped to mount a full-fledged attack on governmental red tape. These efforts leveled out federal aid to states and localities and, in the last years of Carter's term, even began to decrease it. But although Carter had begun to reverse the trend toward increased national involvement in the American federal system, once more failure to win reelection cut short a reform effort.

Ronald Reagan's New New Federalism, 1981–1988

When Ronald Reagan ran for president in 1980, he promised to restore the power and authority of the state governments. In his first inaugural address, Reagan vowed "to curb the size and influence of the federal establishment and to demand recognition of the distinction between the powers granted to the federal government and those reserved to the States or to the people."[58] Reagan's logic was simple: Why should the national government tax the people and then ship the money back to the states? Why not simply let the states do the taxing and administer the programs?

Reagan's crusade approached big government from several different angles. In a speech to Congress several weeks later, Reagan presented his economic recovery strategy in an Omnibus Budget Reconciliation Act, which consisted of tax cuts, vast budget cuts, and cuts in federal regulations—all of which were designed to give "local government entities and states more flexibility and control."[59] The president faced stiff opposition from those who would be affected by the cuts. State governors began to balk when the cuts proved deeper than anticipated. Interest groups speaking for the recipients of grant money also pressed for continued funding. Nevertheless, Congress consolidated seventy-seven categorical programs into nine block

Quick Review

Reagan's New New Federalism
- Economic recovery strategy consisted of tax cuts, vast budget cuts, and cuts in federal regulations.
- Designed to give local government entities and states more flexibility and control.
- Reordered national spending priorities.

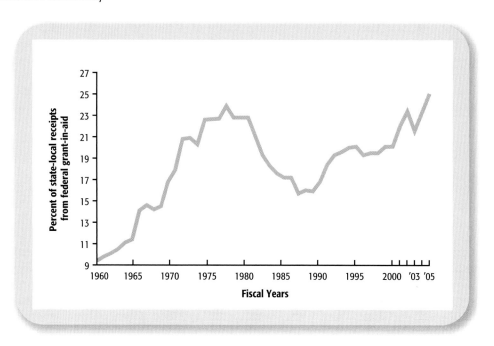

Figure 3.3   National Aid to States, 1960–2005

Sources: The Book of the States, vol. 34 2002, p. 269, vol. 35 2003, p. 27, vol. 37 2005, p. 26; "Giving Power to Fifty Little Washingtons," *Newsweek,* February 6, 1995, pp. 18–19; *The Book of the States, 1994–1995,* vol. 30 (Lexington, Ky.: Council of State Governments, 1996), pp. 580–581; *The Book of the States, 1988–1989,* vol. 24, p. 439; *The Book of the States, 1996–1997,* vol. 31, p. 494; *The Book of the States, 1998–1999,* vol. 32, pp. 287–289; *The Book of the States, 1997–1999,* vol. 32, pp. 287–89; and *The Book of the States, 2000–2001,* vol. 33, pp. 312–321.

grants. Although funding for the national programs was cut by less than half of what the administration had requested, Reagan's first year in office marked a significant break with the past. Figure 3.3 illustrates the rise and fall in national funding of state and local budgets from 1960 to 2003.

To further his reforms, in January 1982, Reagan proposed a complete reordering of the national spending priorities. First, the national government would use a "swap and turnback program" to take over Medicaid, and the states, in turn, would take over sixty programs, including Aid to Families with Dependent Children (AFDC) and food stamps. Relying on its budget estimates, the White House promised that the swap would not increase states' expenditures and that, because the health costs assumed by the national government were destined to rise sharply, the result would likely represent future savings for the states.

Additional resistance quickly developed over these new reforms. Although states wanted greater control over program spending, they also wanted the security of guaranteed national funding. And although the national government wanted to reduce its level of spending, transferring program responsibilities to the states would mean a loss of control over tax revenues. In short, this attempt to move away from national dominance in the federal partnership threatened to send a hesitant government into uncharted waters.

As a result, Reagan's new brand of New Federalism achieved mixed results. While the swap and turnback program never reached Congress, the budget cuts produced an $8 billion absolute reduction in national spending and 140 national grant programs were cut or consolidated. However, the number of federal grants began rising again, from 400 in 1982 to 492 in 1988. Reagan also won adoption of nine new block grants in areas such as substance abuse prevention and treatment and maternal and child care. Just as in the Nixon years, these block grants lost dollar value over time as inflation increased faster than their rise in funding.

Reagan's New New Federalism created challenges and dilemmas for states now faced with doing more with less.[60] Although between the late 1970s and late 1980s overall national grant funding did indeed drop from 25 percent of state budgets to less than 17 percent, in fact real-dollar federal aid dropped only one year during the Reagan years. In every other year, real-dollar federal aid actually increased.[61] Other factors contributed to the appearance of declining federal aid to states. First, a 1978–1988 statistical increase in state and local revenues lowered the percentage of federal aid based on state and local governments' revenue, budgets and outlays. States such as New Jersey, California, Massachusetts, New York, and Pennsylvania found that despite their increased state revenue, the increased programmatic responsibilities delegated to them through the turnback program and increased costs from a down-turned economy led to rapidly escalating state budget deficits. In response, governors called for large tax increases to prevent significant cuts to important programs such as college education funding. Despite these problems, the potential for greater state innovation as a result of funding cuts did offer hope for the future of policy reform.

The George H. W. Bush Years, 1989–1992

President George H. W. Bush sought to continue Reagan's government downsizing. In a speech describing "the thousand points of light," he called for personal volunteerism to address social ills and encouraged state and local governments to pick up the costs of certain national programs, including wastewater treatment plants and mass transit. In addition, Bush tried to lower welfare spending and find other ways to pay for environmental protection and education programs. Despite these funding cuts, sharp increases in Medicaid costs, now the national government's responsibility after the Reagan reform, led to national grant increases from $101.2 billion to $166.9 billion, or an average increase of 9.2 percent per year.[62] Escalating costs and the huge budget deficits left the Bush administration unable to carry out its plans to refocus domestic initiatives.[63] In 1992, Bush tried to consolidate $20 billion in categorical grant programs into a single block grant and turn it back to the states, but the proposal failed.

The Bush administration's experience, like that of the Reagan administration, revealed the difficulty of reversing heavy national financial involvement in the federal partnership. Rising budget deficits, the public's demands for increased services and lower taxes, and the inability of financially strapped states to meet policy expectations made reforms difficult. The out of control budget deficit and rising Medicaid expenses led to hard choices about which grant programs to fund. Various interest groups remained ready to do battle over any cuts or reforms.

Bill Clinton and New(t) Federalism, 1993–2001

President Bill Clinton took office facing an escalating national budget deficit and the dilemma of a vast majority of Americans who wished to retain but were less willing to pay for the national programs they had come to expect over the years. Medicaid expenses alone amounted to 40 percent of the one-quarter trillion dollars that the federal government now paid to states and localities. Clinton, a former governor of Arkansas, knew the states' ability to devise new programs if given the funds.

Clinton was elected on a campaign promise to be a **"New Democrat"**—a conservative Democrat who supports states' rights as well as a less activist national government that provides people with tools such as job training to help themselves, rather than with an array of expensive social services. But Clinton's first two years in office left him looking more like an "Old Democrat" from the liberal wing of the party, which maintains that the national government should provide people with a safety net, even if it means that government will grow. National grant funding rose steadily in his term of office until it reached 23 percent of state budgets by the late 1990s.

"New Democrat" A conservative Democrat who supports states' rights and a less activist national government.

The election of a Republican House under Speaker Newt Gingrich and a Republican Senate under Majority Leader Bob Dole forced the president to devise ways to reorganize government in the direction of the states. Clinton's initial step, his 1994 health-care package, although aimed at reducing escalating health costs, failed largely because of the perception that it would foster big government. In 1996, Clinton signed into law a welfare bill that gave the states much more control over welfare and forced recipients back to work after a two-year period of assistance, with an overall limit of five years of support in one's lifetime. As a result, the nature and amount of welfare assistance varied from state to state, with millions of people being dropped from the rolls.[64]

But then, on May 1, 1998, Clinton went the other way by reversing a 1987 Reagan executive order designed to prevent federal meddling in state and local affairs. He quietly laid the groundwork for increased federal power by signing Executive Order 13803, which allowed federal agencies to consult more with state and local officials and also created nine justifications for federal intervention in policy matters. Local officials as well as conservative members of Congress immediately charged that this order seriously eroded federalism, leading the president to suspend the order pending further review.

The last eighteen months of the Clinton administration brought changes in the legal aspects of federalism, though not as great as some expected. On August 5, 1999, President Clinton issued an executive order requiring all departments in the executive branch to take into account the "fundamental federalism principles" in creating policies, including federal regulations that "can inhibit the creation of effective solutions" to societal problems. This action undermined the legal doctrine of "preemption" by which Congress can, under the supremacy clause, signal that it will be the only legislative body to govern in a policy area, a means of creating uniform policy. So Clinton's executive order was designed to allow states and local governments to develop their own policies to govern certain commercial enterprises. Critics of the executive order argued that this move away from a uniform policy could create enough diversity of regulations to become a national problem.

Congress's effort to play a role in encouraging such a diversity of policies failed. The House passed a Federalism Act, and a Senate Committee passed the Federalism Accountability Act of 1999, which would have required Congress to consult with state and local officials before considering any federal regulations that could interfere with traditional state and local rights and to spell out both how the new law might preempt state and local law and why it would be a good idea. The attempt to allow for diversity in governmental regulation, however, united three normal sets of foes—the Chamber of Commerce (small businesses), labor unions, and environmental protection advocates—in derailing the measure in the House because of the maze of governmental regulations that would result in their area.

ABC News/Prentice Hall Video Library

Moment of Crisis—System Failure
Hurricane Katrina and the Federal Government

Report Card
The No Child Left Behind Initiative

George W. Bush, 2001–Present

President George W. Bush's domestic agenda of promoting a states' rights agenda was initially derailed by the terrorist attack on September 11, 2001, thus turning the president away from domestic issues to foreign and military issues. The one major domestic initiative of the Bush administration during this period, the No Child Left Behind Act educational reform, had the appearance of a grand federal program. But although states had wide latitude to spend the federal money targeted for low-income students in a manner best suited for their region, they complained of insufficient funds and a need for greater spending latitude.

Since March 2003, the administration's preoccupation with the war and nation-building efforts in Iraq and homeland security has made it difficult to mount a sustained states' rights programmatic effort. The financial cost of the war and rebuilding effort, estimated at $5 billion a month, with a total price tag of more than $600 billion by 2010, leaves little money for supporting state programs.[65] On top of that, the enormous rising costs of Medicaid programs have strapped the states. With federal Medicaid dollars comprising 45 percent of overall state aid, President Bush's proposal to cut $45 billion in these programs over the next decade will have a serious effect on state budgets.[66]

With Republican control of not only the White House but also both Houses of Congress, the Supreme Court's likely shift further into conservatism, as a result of the two new Bush appointments, and early preparation for the 2008 presidential race, President Bush will be pressed to further reduce domestic spending and continue in a states' rights direction.[67] The groundwork for this shift has already been laid by the Rehnquist Court.

THE REHNQUIST COURT AND THE FUTURE OF FEDERALISM

What does the future hold for our federal system? In addition to presidential and congressional policies attempting to devolve power to the states, Supreme Court and lower court rulings have recently begun to redefine federalism in the direction of more state power. In 1992, the Supreme Court had ruled, in *New York* v. *United States,* that a 1985 congressional statute regulating the disposal of low-level radioactive waste should be struck down because of its "take title" provision. If states and localities did not provide for the disposal of all such waste created in their region by a specific date, they were required to take possession and responsibility for it. Justice Sandra Day O'Connor and the majority found this statute to be a violation of the Tenth Amendment: "Whatever the outer limits of [state] sovereignty may be, one thing is clear. The Federal Government may not compel the States to enact or administer a federal regulatory program. The Constitution . . . [does not] authorize Congress simply to direct the States to provide for the disposal of radioactive waste generated within their borders."[68]

In its 1994–95 term, ruling in the case of *United States* v. *Lopez,* a narrow five-person majority of the Supreme Court overturned a section of the 1990 federal Gun-Free School Zones law making it a crime to possess firearms within one thousand feet of a school zone. Congress argued that its power to regulate such behavior came from the interstate commerce clause, because violent crime around a school could affect the national economy through higher insurance costs and self-imposed limits on travel. Although this justification would have worked in the past, during oral argument, Justice David Souter warned: "Presumably there is nothing left if Congress can do this, no recognizable limit." In overturning the law, the Court appeared ready to establish new limits on congressional authority by requiring Congress, for the first time in fifty years, to justify the link between a law and the commerce clause. Speaking for what has become a hard five-person conservative Court majority in favor of state power, Chief Justice William Rehnquist said that this regulation "neither regulates a commercial activity nor contains a requirement that the possession be connected in any way to interstate commerce."[69] This decision represented a true shift in decision-making, because for more than fifty years the Court had not even pushed for a clear connection between a law and the commerce power in approving federal extensions of authority. In 1996, Congress resurrected the Gun-Free School Zones Act in its Omnibus Appropriations Act, but this time with one key difference—now it was a federal crime either to knowingly carry a gun within a thousand feet of a school or to fire a weapon in that area.

That this decision represented a watershed in the direction of more state power was made clear in a series of later rulings.[70] Shortly after the decision to overturn the 1990 federal Gun-Free School Zones law, the same five-person conservative majority limited Congress's power to make states subject to federal lawsuits because of the Eleventh Amendment. In this case, Florida was freed by the states' sovereign right of immunity from lawsuits by citizens from suit by a Seminole Indian tribe challenging negotiations over its desire to create gambling interests on its tribal lands.[71] Finally, in 1997, the Supreme Court invalidated those portions of the federal Brady handgun control law that required local sheriffs to perform background checks on handgun purchasers until a national investigation database could be established. In this case, although Justice Antonin Scalia could not find anything in the Constitution requiring such a decision, he still decided so based on the "historical understanding and practice, in the structure of the Constitution, and in the jurisprudence of this Court." Using the *Federalist Papers* and a study of early American history, Justice Scalia argued that the national government "at most" had been able to impose certain duties on state court judges, but had never been able to do more than "recommend" that state government officials perform other actions. That this reading of history is controversial, however, was made clear by Justice David Souter in dissent, who defended Congress's power to adopt the Brady bill by quoting from Alexander Hamilton in *The Federalist*, no. 27, that: "The legislatures, courts, and magistrates, of the [states] . . . will be incorporated into the operations of the national government as far as its just and constitutional authority extends, and will be rendered auxiliary to the enforcement of its laws."[72]

Only the Court's refusal in its 1999 term to allow states to sell personal information from motor vehicle records to commercial databases represented a restriction on state authority in this period. When states began selling personal information about car owners gained from the implementation of the Brady Bill to raise money, the federal government sought to end the practice by passing the Drivers' Privacy Protection Act. The Court determined that the public's privacy interests regarding computer databases appeared to take precedence over the states' interests in making millions of dollars.[73] Then, in 2000, the Court ruled unconstitutional the Violence Against Women Act (VAWA), which allowed women unable to secure legal recourse in state courts for sexual assault cases to take their cases to the federal courts, thus leaving it to states to prosecute "gender-induced" attacks.[74] Congress re-passed the VAWA, and expanded it to include date rape, but because of the Court's decision refused to allow victims to sue their attackers in federal court.

Since 2002, though, the Court's tendency to favor states' rights over federal power has eased. For example, the Court upheld the right of state employees to sue their states for relief under the federal Family and Medical Leave Act of 1993. It also upheld the federal Children's Internet Protection Act of 2001, which required the use of antipornography filters in school libraries as a condition of receiving federal aid, and allowed disabled persons to sue their states under Title II of the Americans with Disabilities Act to improve physical accessibility to state courts.[75] As seen in the case study, this trend continued in 2005 in the California medical use of marijuana case, when the Court upheld the federal government's Controlled Substances Act over the state's decision to provide relief for critically ill patients. However, in 2006, the Court ruled for the state of Oregon in determining the balance between the federal drug program and Oregon's Death with Dignity Act.

Lying at the heart of all of these Supreme Court cases is the determination of who decides—the national government or the states—and since 1994 that decision has lain with the swing justice on the Court, Justice Sandra Day O'Connor. Now, though, with her retirement and the death of Chief Justice Rehnquist himself, it remains to be seen whether the Court will continue to favor state powers. Seven other justices over the age of sixty-five, together with President Bush's expressed support for states' rights, make it likely that future

Supreme Court appointments during the Bush presidency will move the Court further in that direction. Should the Court choose in the future to rule against an overarching federal approach in many cultural issues, such as abortion, right to die, or gay marriage, the individual states must decide on the direction of those policies.

FEDERALISM AND APPROACHING DEMOCRACY IN THE TWENTY-FIRST CENTURY

MakeItReal

Census 2000: Balance of Power

The debate over federalism and the proper balance of power between national and state governments is ongoing. "We need a certain administrative discretion," argues political scientist Don Kettl, "You can't run everything from Washington."[76] That has been the nature of the debate for more than two centuries. Most agree that problems remain to be dealt with: commerce, crime, the economy, health care, individual rights, the environment, and now the fight against the terrorism threat. The disagreement, however, comes over which type of government, or whether any government at all, should address such matters. Generally, more and more people argue that the government closest to the people is the best government to handle these issues. But with the terrorist threat and the Internet, the question may well be how much financial support and political guidance the federal government will provide.

Where one stands in the federalism debate reveals a lot about one's political ideology. In this century, Franklin D. Roosevelt's New Deal firmly positioned the liberal Democrats as the nation-centered party, asserting that only the national government can provide a basic standard of living and uniform democratic rights for all citizens. Lyndon Johnson's Great Society is a classic example of this position. He used the powers of the national government to create a welfare state aimed at helping the underprivileged, solving civil rights problems, improving education, and so forth. Conservative Republicans, on the other hand, advocate a state-centered approach, arguing that solutions are best left either to the state governments or to the private sector. These conservatives were understandably overjoyed with Ronald Reagan's election in 1980; his platform opposing big government and advocating the return of power to the states was more to their taste. Reagan sought to dismantle the welfare state and to cut national spending. Now the Bush administration's renewed call for making permanent federal tax cuts in the face of huge bills to rebuild Iraq and leading the anti-terrorism fight is likely to result in further cuts in spending to states and localities. As a result, Democrats and liberals continue to express worries about the potential consequences of a shrunken national role while looking to the states to further many of their policy aims. To some, then, a stronger national government means more democracy, while to others stronger state governments accomplish the same.

America's experience with federalism has involved a continual shifting of power from the states to the federal government, and now, as a consequence of the Rehnquist Court's decisions and the policies of the Bush administration, power in many areas is shifting back to the states. The nature of the federal structure continues to change. Although the national government predominates, in recent years due to the costs of the war and Iraq rebuilding and homeland security there has been a growing budget deficit that has meant less money in its coffers, meaning less leverage over the states and a new role for the states in their own policy-making efforts. Through it all, in exercising its political role, each form of government plays an important part in ensuring that our federal structure, the result of a careful compromise forged by the framers in Philadelphia, continues to function and thrive in dealing with America's new policy needs.

Summary

1. The term *federalism* refers to a political system in which two or more distinct forms of government share power over the same body of citizens. Federalism differs from a *confederation,* in which the power to govern is decentralized among sovereign states.

2. Among the advantages of federalism are the ability to accommodate a diverse population, a tendency to minimize policy conflict, dispersal of power, and enhanced prospects for governmental innovation. Such a system also has disadvantages: Groups that wish to protect their interests may obstruct national mandates, and the system may produce inequities among different regions.

3. The most important powers shared by federal and state government are the ability to regulate commerce and the right to collect taxes to provide for the general welfare. Also important are the powers reserved to the states by the Tenth Amendment to the Constitution. These three constitutional protections help create a balance of power between the federal and state governments.

4. The Constitution delegates certain powers exclusively to the national government; these include the power to declare war, raise and support an army, negotiate with foreign countries, and coin money. The powers reserved to the states include regulation of the health, morals, public safety, and welfare of state citizens. The national and state governments share concurrent powers. In addition to the power to regulate commerce and impose taxes, these include the power to regulate elections and to maintain a judicial structure.

5. A few powers are denied both to the national government and to the states. These include the power to grant titles of nobility and to pass bills of attainder and ex post facto laws.

6. Efforts in the early 1800s to expand the power of the national government were hotly debated, leading to a Supreme Court decision upholding the dominance of the national government in areas where its powers overlapped with those of the states. One response was the theory of nullification, which held that states could refuse to observe national legislation that they considered unacceptable.

7. After the Civil War the concept of dual federalism prevailed—both the national and state governments were viewed as separate and supreme within their own jurisdictions. During the Great Depression the national government regained its dominance despite numerous Supreme Court rulings setting limits on its activities. Eventually a new approach, known as *cooperative federalism,* emerged. Since the 1930s, Supreme Court decisions have sought to ensure uniformity in policies involving the rights of individuals and to impose national standards to reduce inequality.

8. A grant-in-aid gives money to states and localities to induce them to implement policies favored by the national government. Categorical grants are given for specific purposes and are usually accompanied by strict rules. Federal mandates are national requirements that states must observe.

9. In the 1960s, creative federalism sought to address problems in areas neglected by the states, resulting in rapid growth in the size and cost of the federal bureaucracy.

10. President Nixon's New Federalism included the policy of general revenue sharing, by which the states received money with no restrictions on how it could be spent; and special revenue sharing, by which categorical grants in related policy areas were consolidated into a single block grant. President Carter attempted to combine this approach with creative federalism, whereas President Reagan attempted to do away with revenue sharing and restore power to the state governments, a policy continued by President Bush.

11. At present, federalism is caught in a dilemma resulting from conflicting desires—to reduce spending by the national government, on the one hand, and to maintain national assistance to the states, on the other.

Review Questions

1. Trace the evolution of federalism from Dual to New(t) Federalism. What were the goals of each type of federalism and how did federal–state relations affect national policies?

2. Discuss the elements of the *McCulloch* v. *Maryland* case. Why was this case so important? What was Thomas Jefferson's position? What was Alexander Hamilton's position?

3. How did the U.S. Constitution allow for so many different interpretations of federalism? What accounts for the tremendous flexibility of the U.S. Constitution?

4. What were the political and historical influences that led to creative federalism? Describe the impact of creative federalism.

5. How did Supreme Court rulings in the nineteenth and twentieth centuries influence the evolution of federalism in this country? Identify at least two important cases in each century and explain their significance.

6. How have recent Supreme Court rulings interpreted the commerce clause? Identify reasons for the current sentiment of Supreme Court majorities regarding federalism.

Key Terms

Suggested Readings

The Book of the States, 2005 Edition, vol. 37, Lexington, Ky.: Council of State Governments. The most comprehensive collection of information on state governments and the nature of federalism in America.

BEER, SAMUEL H. *To Make a Nation: The Rediscovery of American Federalism.* Cambridge, Mass.: Harvard University Press, 1993. A highly readable account tracing the philosophical origins of federalism from the British experience, through the constitutional founding, to the use of federalism today.

DYE, THOMAS R. *American Federalism: Competition Among Governments.* Lexington, Mass.: Lexington Books, 1990. An intriguing picture of American federalism as a system of competition among national and state governments.

ELAZAR, DANIEL J. *American Federalism: A View from the States.* 3d ed. New York: Harper & Row, 1984. A helpful and comprehensive examination of American federalism from the perspective of state governments.

FRANK, THOMAS, *What's the Matter with Kansas?* New York: Holt, 2004. A best-selling book exploring how Kansas has evolved from its liberal progressive history to an ultraconservative state that explains the "red state vs. blue state" nature of current American politics.

KINCAID, JOHN. "De Facto Devolution and Urban Defunding: The Priority of Persons Over Places," *Journal of Urban Affairs* 21, no. 2 (1999) pp. 135–167. A highly informative and well-researched analysis of what really became of the promised "devolution revolution."

OSBORNE, DAVID. *Laboratories of Democracy.* Boston: Harvard Business School, 1988. A highly readable series of case studies on state governors and governments operating to solve public policy problems.

PRESSMAN, JEFFREY, and AARON WILDAVSKY. *Implementation.* Berkeley: University of California Press, 1973. An excellent account of how the democratic processes in federalism thwarted the implementation of one of Johnson's economic development projects in Oakland, California.

REAGAN, MICHAEL D., and JOHN G. SANZONE. *The New Federalism,* 2d ed. New York: Oxford University Press, 1981. A comprehensive and classic analysis of fiscal federalism outlining both the grant-in-aid and revenue-sharing systems.

RIKER, WILLIAM H. *The Development of American Federalism.* Boston: Kluwer Academic, 1987. Essays on the continuity of American federalism, written over a thirty-year period by Riker and his colleagues.

STEWART, WILLIAM H. *Concepts of Federalism.* Lanham, Md.: University Press of America, 1984. A comprehensive dictionary on the meanings of and metaphors for federalism.

WALKER, DAVID B. *Toward a Functioning Federalism.* Cambridge, Mass.: Winthrop, 1981. An in-depth examination of the intergovernmental-relations system, offering a series of suggestions for reform.

Visualizing Democracy

From Cesar Chavez to Antonio Villaraigosa

Labor activist Cesar Chavez (center) talks with grape pickers in support of the United Farm Workers Union.

Cesar Chavez, United Farm Workers president, and Dolores Huerta, a union executive (right) march with some 4,000 field workers in Salinas, California, October, 1984. The UFW was protesting against Salinas Valley growers who refused to renew expired UFW contracts.

President Clinton, in posthumously awarding Cesar Chavez the Medal of Freedom in 1994, declared, "Cesar Chavez left our world better than he found it, and his legacy inspires us still. He was for his own people a Moses figure. The farm workers who labored in the fields…pinned their hopes on this remarkable man." The citation for the nation's highest civilian honor lauded Chavez for having "faced formidable, often violent opposition with dignity and nonviolence." Cesar Chavez dedicated his life to improving working conditions for those without the means or the ability to access levers of power. He fasted many times and led boycotts and pickets. He proved that through persistence, hard work, faith, and sacrifice, people can maintain their self-respect, build a union, and achieve a commitment to the struggle for justice through nonviolence. His cause was supported by organized labor, religious groups, minorities, and students. His struggle symbolized America's approach toward the democratic ideal, and his actions delineated a path for others to follow. At the age of fifteen, Antonio Villaraigosa began his lifelong involvement with the labor movement as

▲ Los Angeles mayoral candidate Antonio Villaraigosa celebrates the opening of his campaign headquarters in Los Angeles in February 2005.

Antonio Villaraigosa formally takes his oath as Los Angeles's 41st mayor, becoming the first Hispanic to hold the office since the 19th century.

a volunteer with the farm workers movement, volunteering for the first grape boycott organized by Chavez. He later served as a field representative/organizer with the United Teachers Los Angeles (UTLA). In the California Assembly, he wrote laws to improve health care for children, to expand educational opportunities, to protect workers from the danger of pesticides, and improve working conditions for all workers. When he was elected as the 41st mayor of Los Angeles on May 17, 2005, and sworn in to office on July 1, 2005, Antonio Villaraigosa reminded everyone that "Cesar Chavez said, 'Sí Se Puede,' and I believed." In his inaugural speech, Los Angeles's first Hispanic mayor since 1872 said that if his mother had been with him she would have said "Antonio, don't declare victory tonight, declare your purpose." The new mayor also quoted Rabbi J. Leonard Levy, who in 1903 penned a fifth question for the ritual of Passover. "Where," he asked, "where do we find civil, political, and religious liberty united today?" Levy offered this answer: "To us, the United States of America stands as the foremost among nations granting the greatest liberty to all who dwell there. Therefore, we grace our table with the national flag. That flag stands for equal liberty to all men. It means equal rights for all. It means free hands, and free lips, self-government." Today, there are over six thousand elected Latino leaders nationwide, including Republican Senator Mel Martinez of Florida and Democratic Senator Ken Salazar of Colorado. ★

▲ Attorney General Alberto Gonzales addresses the media.

▼ Rep. Loretta Sanchez, D.-Calif,. center and her sister Rep. Linda Sanchez, D- Calif., on Capitol Hill, stand with House Speaker Dennis Hastert of Illinois on Jan. 7, 2003 after the House was officially sworn into the 108th Congress.

Henry Cisneros, Housing and Urban Development Secretary under President Clinton, talks with Sen. Don Riegle, D-Mich. (left) during a bus tour of housing projects in Flint, Mich.

Rep. Silvestre Reyes, D-Texas and members of the Congressional Hispanic Caucus of the 107th Congress: from left to right, Rep. Xavier Becerra, D-Calif., Rep. Charles A. Gonzalez, D-Texas, Rep. Bob Menendez, D-NJ and Rep. Lucille Roybal-Allard, D-Calif.

★ CHAPTER 4 ★

CONGRESS

CHAPTER OUTLINE

APPROACHING DEMOCRACY
Negotiating the Legislative Labyrinth

INTRODUCTION: Congress and Democracy

- The Structure and Powers of Congress
- The Members of Congress
- How Congress Organizes Itself
- Congress in Session
- How a Bill Becomes a Law
- Additional Functions of Congress
- The Republican Revolution of 1994 and Beyond
- Congress Toward the 2006 Election

Approaching Democracy

Negotiating the Legislative Labyrinth

Something was wrong with the Campaign Finance Law, passed in 1974 to regulate money flow into the election process. Although the law regulated how much "hard money" contributors could donate directly to a candidate's election campaign, they could donate unlimited "soft money" to the candidate's party. Abuse of this loophole allowed President Bill Clinton to raise tens of millions of dollars in soft money from large contributors by allowing them to spend a night in the Lincoln bedroom. In 2000, the Democratic and Republican parties raised more than $500 million dollars in soft money and used it to fund "issue advocacy ads." Senators John McCain (R.-AZ) and Russell Feingold (D.-WI) criticized the use of soft money, but conservative senators, including Mitch McConnell (R.-KY) and Trent Lott (R.-MS), defended it as free speech protected under the First Amendment. In 1995, McCain and Feingold introduced reform legislation that went nowhere. They tried again in 1997, proposing a routine amendment to the Campaign Finance Law that limited or banned the use of the soft money and issue ads.

The McCain-Feingold bill, introduced to the Senate on January 21, 1997, was not considered that year because McCain and Feingold failed to secure sixty votes to end a three-day filibuster led by conservative Republicans. They reintroduced the bill the following February. Again it failed.

Meanwhile, in the House of Representatives, Christopher Shays (R.-CT) and Marty Meehan (D.-MA) tried to push their own campaign finance bill through the House. With Majority Whip Tom Delay (R.-TX) vocally opposing the bill, the Democrats could not move it out of committee. On October 24, 1997, House Democrats threatened to pass a rarely used discharge petition that would bring the measure out of committee and onto the floor of Congress for consideration. Republicans sidetracked this maneuver, promising to bring the measure to the floor by March 1998, but they later broke this agreement.

In mid-summer 1998, the House bill finally made it to the floor, despite opposition from fifty-three interest groups and conservative congressional members' attempts to kill the measure by forcing votes on nearly four dozen amendments, many designed to make even the bill's original supporters unwilling to vote for it. In August 1998 the measure passed the House, but a companion bill still had to pass in the Senate before the measure could be sent to President Clinton for signature. When the House-approved Shays-Meehan Bill made it to the Senate, it was replaced by the McCain-Feingold Bill. Mitch McConnell led another filibuster, and campaign finance reform died once again. By now it was clear that unless McCain, Feingold, Meehan, and Shays could muster sixty votes in the Senate, campaign finance reform would never pass in Congress.

The polarized legislative climate in Congress worked against passage. The antagonistic relationship of the two political parties, undue influence from political interest groups, media impact, and a presidency weakened by scandal all affected the bill's passage.

★ Sen. Mitch McConnell (R.-KY), center, promised to challenge the McCain-Feingold Bipartisan Campaign Reform Act (BCRA) in the Supreme Court, and, together with his lawyer, Jon Baran, left, and First Amendment expert, Floyd Abrams, right, he got his day in Court on September 8, 2003. The Court ruled against his position.

In addition, the Monica Lewinsky scandal turned into an impeachment struggle, making Bill Clinton a weak leader on legislative issues. When Clinton recommended that Congress pass campaign finance reform no one listened.

In 2001, the issue reemerged. House Democrats used the discharge petition to send the Shays-Meehan Bill to the floor and pass it. This means of success in the House angered Republicans, inspiring them to fight the bill even harder in the Senate. Yet another filibuster in the Senate ended reformists' hopes of keeping the bill alive that term. However, in 2001, the political climate changed. First, several of the bill's most vocal opponents did not return to Congress after the 2000 election. Second, Senator John McCain made clear his intention to force his colleagues to vote the measure up or down early in the Bush presidency. Third, Senator Jim Jeffords' decision to leave the Republican party and become an Independent moved Senate control to the Democrats, allowing Majority Leader Tom Daschle to push reform. Finally, in early 2002, the Enron Corporation, an energy company, collapsed after revelations that company officials sought help from political officials, some in the new administration, who had received significant amounts of soft money from energy interests during the 2000 election campaign. Recognizing the shifting political dynamic, President Bush signaled that he would not veto a reform bill.

But even with the changed climate, passing the Bipartisan Campaign Reform Bill was difficult. The prospect of Senate passage prompted a mighty fight from the bill's House opponents. Despite repeated efforts by Republicans and interest group lobbyists to alter the bill from the Senate measure, thus forcing a conference committee and allowing one more chance to kill it, the House measure passed in mid-February 2002 by a 240–189 vote.

The bill, which passed five weeks later by a 60–40 vote in the Senate, banned national political parties from raising soft money after the November 2002 election and reduced the amount of money individuals could contribute to candidates and state and local political parties. It also prohibited unions, corporations, and nonprofit groups from paying for issue advocacy ads that run within thirty days of a primary or sixty days of a general election.

But not even a successful journey through the legislative labyrinth could guarantee the future of campaign finance reform. Even in defeat Senator Mitch McConnell vowed, "Today is not the end. There is litigation ahead. I am consoled by the obvious fact that the courts do not defer to Congress on matters of the Constitution." In 2003, however, a narrow 5–4 Supreme Court majority upheld the major provisions of the act.[1]

★ Representatives Christopher Shays (R.-CT) and Marty Meehan (D.-MA) and Senator John McCain (R.-AZ) (l. to r.), along with Senator Russell Feingold (D.-WI) (not shown), led the successful fight to enact campaign finance reform in 2002.

QUESTION FOR REFLECTION

Consider the long journey to pass campaign finance reform. Should Congress be designed to pass laws efficiently, or should laws be difficult to pass, thus promoting democratic consideration of the issues involved?

Introduction
CONGRESS AND DEMOCRACY

 MakeItReal

Civic Participation: Center on Congress

The legislative journey of the 2002 Bipartisan Campaign Finance Reform law illustrates the complex route bills must follow to become law. Each newly introduced bill faces a daunting set of obstacles.

The legislative process has many stages. Countless actors play roles in the drama of lawmaking, and enemies of every proposal lurk in a dozen or more places. It seems amazing that any bill ever passes. Occasionally, however, a "breakthrough moment" arrives, such as that when the USA Patriot Act was rushed into law in a matter of weeks, and Congress finds the political will to work like a well-oiled machine. This chapter looks at how Congress has helped, and at times thwarted, America's approach to democracy as it transforms public demands into governmental action.

THE STRUCTURE AND POWERS OF CONGRESS

The U.S. Congress is among the world's most powerful legislatures. If the dominant congressional faction is large and determined enough, it can override presidential vetoes and make national policy entirely on its own. Presidents cannot force Congress to do their bidding. Neither can they simply ignore it. They cannot get rid of Congress by dissolving it and calling for new elections. In nondemocratic nations, executives can do all these things, and their legislatures are little more than puppets under authoritarian leadership.

The U.S. Congress is a major power within the American constitutional system, but it is also a democratic body. Its members are elected by the American people. These two attributes—power *and* democracy—may seem obvious, but they are worth stressing for their significant political implications. If Congress is powerful, then citizens should focus on this body if they wish to influence national policy outcomes.

Congress is pluralistic and decentralized.[2] Each of its 535 members has real power in the sense that each has *one* vote. That means, in essence, 535 power points. Thus, the decision-making process is much more complex than if power were concentrated in the hands of a few people. Those wishing to influence Congress must persuade many people who have different outlooks, who are found at different points in a complex structure, and whose impact on policy outcomes can vary dramatically.

What the Framers Had in Mind

Believing that Congress would become the predominant branch of national government, the framers took steps to prevent it from becoming the tyrannical force that the state legislatures had been under the Articles of Confederation. We have already seen in Chapter 2 the way the Constitution limits Congress's power (through the Bill of Rights, for example) and the way other institutions (the president and the Supreme Court) can check its actions.

But the framers went further. Through the Connecticut Compromise, which based state seating in the House on population but equalized Senate seats at two per state, the Constitutional Convention devised a way to make Congress check itself by striking a balance between the interests of the large states and the small states. They divided Congress into a **bicameral** (two-chambered) **legislature**, and gave each chamber the power to inhibit the other's actions. The houses would develop significantly different structures and purposes.

James Madison referred to the House of Representatives as "the great repository of the democratic principle of government," that is, the one most sensitive to public

bicameral legislature A legislative system consisting of two houses or chambers.

opinion. The House would be made up of popularly elected representatives serving two-year terms. The entire body would have to face the electorate every other year, so it would by nature reflect shifts in public opinion. This requirement was supposed to ensure that representatives would reflect the popular will. This requirement also places members of Congress in an eternal "election mode," making their need for campaign finances a constant necessity. And being based on population, this House would also favor the larger states.

The Senate, in contrast, was designed as a brake on the public's momentary passions, or as Madison put it, a "necessary fence" against the "fickleness and passion" of the people. The equal number of senators per state would give the small states more power, making it an adequate counterbalance to the overrepresentation of the large states in the House of Representatives. At first, senators were selected by the state legislatures, not by the voting public. The Senate was to be a more aristocratic group, an advisory council to the president—a judicious group of wise elder statesmen, one step removed from the passions and demands of the people. This distinction between the two chambers relied on British tradition, in which the House of Commons represents the masses and the House of Lords the aristocracy.

Until 1913, most Senate members were chosen by their state legislatures (some western states had direct elections), ensuring that they were, in fact, somewhat removed from the mass electorate. In our more democratic age, senators, like House members, are directly elected by their state's residents. It is unclear whether popular election has made the Senate more democratic or merely created a body more hostile to centralization and federalism.

Even though their six-year term would seem to remove senators further from popular desires, their reelection campaigns often are more competitive than those of the House, which increases their chances of being turned out of office and encourages incumbents to have ample campaign financing at their disposal. It also ensures that they will more closely reflect shifts in public thinking. However, Senate terms are staggered so that only one-third face election every two years, making

MakeItReal

Primary Source: Federalist Paper #52: The House of Representatives

Primary Source: Federalist Paper #62: The Senate

▲ Senator Ken Salazar (D.-CO.), one of only two Hispanic Senators (the other being Florida's Republican Mel Martinez) proved in beating Republican Beer magnate Pete Coors in 2004 that winning in a Red State was still possible for a Democratic candidate.

Table 4.1 ■ The Key Powers of Congress
To lay and collect taxes, duties, imposts, and excises
To borrow money
To regulate commerce with foreign nations and among the states
To establish rules for naturalization and bankruptcy
To coin money, set its value, and punish counterfeiting
To fix the standard of weights and measures
To establish a post office and post roads
To issue patents and copyrights to inventors and authors
To create courts inferior to the Supreme Court
To define and punish piracies, felonies on the high seas, and crimes against the law of nations
To declare war
To raise and support an army and navy and make rules for their governance
To provide for a militia
To exercise exclusive legislative powers over the District of Columbia and over places purchased to be federal facilities
To "make all Laws which shall be necessary and proper for carrying into Execution the foregoing Powers, and all other powers vested by this Constitution in the Government of the United States"

Table 4.2 ■ Differences Between the House and Senate

House	Senate
435 members	100 members
Two-year term	Six-year term
Smaller constituencies	Larger constituencies
Fewer personal staff	More personal staff
Proportional populations represented	States represented
Less flexible rules	More flexible rules
Limited debate	Virtually unlimited debate
More policy specialists	Policy generalists
Less media coverage	More media coverage
Less prestige	More prestige
Less reliance on staff	More reliance on staff
More powerful committee leaders	More equal distribution of power
Important committees	Less important committees
More partisan	Less partisan
Nongermane amendments (riders) not allowed	Nongermane amendments (riders) allowed

Senate membership more stable than that of the House. After any given election, two-thirds of the Senate remain in place.[3]

In allocating legislative powers, the Constitution carefully specifies Congress's powers to avoid the chaos that had prevailed in state legislatures under the Articles of Confederation. In Article I, Section 8, Congress receives authority in three broad areas: economic affairs, domestic affairs, and foreign affairs (see Table 4.1). The power to impeach and remove a high official from office is divided between the two chambers, with the House drafting and voting on articles of impeachment to be tried in the Senate. Additional differences between the two houses of Congress are outlined in Table 4.2.

Although the framers wished to limit the powers of Congress, they realized that they could not foresee all the issues and emergencies likely to arise in the future. Therefore, they included in Article I, Section 8, the so-called **necessary and proper clause**, also called the *elastic clause,* which grants Congress the power to "make all Laws which shall be necessary and proper" to carry out all the other powers specified in Article I, Section 8. This sweeping language has been interpreted by the Supreme Court to allow Congress to develop its role broadly with regard to regulating commerce, borrowing money, and collecting taxes.[4]

Limits on Congress's Power

Although extensive, Congress's powers are limited in many ways. As with every agency of the U.S. government, Congress is checked at the most essential level by what the public will tolerate. In addition to regularly scheduled elections, which force members of Congress to be responsive to the will of the people, voters can ignore hated laws or even force Congress to rescind them. Congress is also limited by important elements of the Constitution. It cannot infringe on certain state powers, beginning with an essential one: Congress cannot abolish or change the boundaries of any state without that state's consent.

necessary and proper clause
Article I, Section 8, Clause 18, of the Constitution stating that Congress can "make all Laws which shall be necessary and proper for carrying into Execution the foregoing Powers."

In theory, the enumerated powers of Article I, Section 8, are not just grants of power to Congress but also limits. The framers argued that Congress (and the federal government) could use particular delegated powers only when specifically granted such authority. In all other cases, the authority would remain in the states or in the people—a restriction made clear in the Ninth and Tenth Amendments.[5] Furthermore, in the exercise of its powers, Congress is subject to the Supreme Court, the final interpreter of the Constitution. Thus, under its judicial review power, the Supreme Court can legitimately void legislation that in its view is contrary to the Constitution. The Court has done this nearly three dozen times since 1995. For example, the Supreme Court overturned the Communications Decency Act of 1995, the line item veto legislation in 1998, and Section 3501 of the 1968 Omnibus Crime Control Act in 2000.[6] In the case of the Communications Decency Act, the Court ruled that the law was too vague to enforce constitutionally under the First Amendment freedom of speech guarantee. The Court ruled that the line item veto was an unconstitutional violation of the separation of powers by giving the president too much of Congress's lawmaking power.[7] In June 2000, the Court continued this trend by overturning the anti-Miranda ruling law, Section 3501 of the Omnibus Crime Control Act, which instructed judges to examine whether a defendant's confession to police was made before rather than after police warnings of the rights to silence and counsel.[8]

Beyond these checks, perhaps the most important day-to-day limit on Congress's power is the president. No matter what the party lineup, Congress and the president continually play complex games of power politics that involve competition and cooperation. They must work together if government is to operate, yet each can check the other quite dramatically. The president's array of powers can stymie the will of Congress, including the role of commander in chief of the military, appointment powers, control of the national bureaucracy, and veto powers.

MakeItReal

Civic Participation: Members of Congress

THE MEMBERS OF CONGRESS

Who Are the Members?

The First Congress, in 1789, included only sixty-five representatives and twenty-six senators—all from the most elite families in America. They were rich, white, and male. Superficially, members of Congress today differ little from that first group. They are still disproportionately rich, white, and male, and they come overwhelmingly from the fields of law, banking, and big business. A third of senators and one-seventh of House members are millionaires. In the past two decades, at least thirty times more millionaires have served on Capitol Hill than are found in American society in general. On the other hand, thirty years ago more than half the members of Congress had a law degree, but that number has dropped by half.[9] Some ask, "How can such a group claim to be a representative body?" Others respond, "Does it matter whether the country's representatives are rich or poor, white or black, male or female, as long as they support policies its citizens want and oppose those they don't?"[10]

Some of the wealthiest members of Congress, such as Ted Kennedy and Jay Rockefeller, claim to represent the interests of the poor. And many male members of Congress work diligently to promote the welfare of women. Still, it seems reasonable to conclude that a healthy democracy would include leaders from all social groups. How does Congress shape up in this regard?

Because of Supreme Court decisions and redistricting at the state level, Congress approached democracy in the twentieth century by increasing the gender and ethnic diversity of its membership. When we compare today's Congress with its counterpart a few decades ago, we see that the institution is becoming far more diverse. In 1952 the House included only two African Americans and ten women; the Senate had no African Americans and only one woman. In 2006, the Senate included a record number of fourteen women, with several serving as committee chairs and

▲ In 1916 Jeannette Rankin of Montana became the first woman to be elected to Congress.

▲ Senator Barack Obama, (D-Ill.), only the third African-American to serve in the Senate since the 1800s, and seen here delivering the keynote speech at the 2004 Democratic National Convention in Boston, MA., is considered one of the rising stars of the national Democratic party.

Question for Reflection

What, if any impact will campaign finance have on the number of millionaires found in Congress?

MakeItReal

Simulation: Running for Congress

party leaders; two Asian-Pacific Americans, Daniel K. Inouye and Daniel K. Akaka; one African American, Barack Obama (D.-Ill); and two Latinos, Mel Martinez and Ken Salazar. The 2006 House membership included forty-two African Americans, twenty-six Hispanics, sixty-nine women, one Indian American (Asian), and six Asian-Pacific Americans, as well as nine naturalized citizens from Cuba, Hungary, Taiwan, Japan, Pakistan, Canada, and the Netherlands. In the past five decades African Americans have increased their numbers on Capitol Hill by more than 2,000 percent. The twenty-six Hispanic Americans elected in 2004 brought the number of Hispanics in Congress to its highest level ever.[11] Although the 109th Congress is just as diverse as its predecessors, it still falls short of reflecting the population as a whole.

The increasingly diverse demographics of Congress do affect the legislative agenda. The large African American caucus has had an impact both on President Bush's policies toward affirmative action and limiting racial profiling in the war on terrorism. At the same time, the increasing number of women in Congress has addressed such questions as the role of females in the military, gun control, and inclusion of women in federally funded medical research projects. Table 4.3 suggests what Congress would look like if its members represented a true cross section of the nation.

Table 4.3 ▪ To What Extent Does the House Mirror Society?

Social Group	Number in the House if It were Representative of American Society at Large	Number in the 107th Congress	Number in the 108th Congress	Number in the 109th Congress
Men	184	376	376	373
Women	226	59	59	62
African Americans	52	34	37	42
Hispanics	30	18	19	26
People in poverty	65	0	0	0
Lawyers	2	234	228	160
Americans under age 45	300	140	154	166
Military veterans	57	155	154	141

Source: Figures calculated from *Congressional Quarterly and Statistical Abstract of the United States,* and Mildred L. Amer, "Membership of the 109th Congress: A Profile," CRS Report for Congress, May 30, 2005, at www.senate.gov.

▲ Fourteen women served in the 109th Congress (2005–2006), a record number, with many of them moving into leadership positions in the chamber.

Congressional Districts

The racial and ethnic makeup of Congress strongly reflects the nature of the districts that elect its members. Boundaries can determine a candidate's chances of election, making defining the size and the geographic shape of any legislative district a political act.

Article I, Section 2, of the Constitution arbitrarily set the size of the first U.S. House of Representatives at sixty-five members and apportioned those seats roughly by population. Later, after the 1790 census, the size of the House was set at 105 seats, with each state given one seat for each 33,000 inhabitants. As the nation's population grew, so did the number of representatives. By the early twentieth century, the House had expanded to 435 members, each with a constituency of approximately 200,000 people. At that point, members agreed that the House had reached an optimum size. The Reapportionment Act of 1929 formalized this sentiment; it set the total House membership at 435, a number that has remained stable to this day. But because the nation's population has almost tripled since then, each congressional district now contains about 635,000 citizens.

Population growth and shifts within each of these 435 districts vary dramatically over time. Keeping the numerical size of districts relatively equal requires redrawing district lines from time to time, and even adjusting the number of representatives allotted each state. This process is known as **reapportionment**. Each reapportionment of House seats reflects the nation's population shifts since the last census.[12]

reapportionment A process of redrawing voting district lines from time to time and adjusting the number of representatives allotted each state.

Approaching Democracy Around the Globe

Approaching Democracy in the Middle East?

One of the neoconservative justifications for the Iraq War in 2003 was that if democracy could be established in that nation, it would spread like a "benign virus" throughout the rest of the Middle East. But change has been slow, indeed.

In Iraq, the challenge for the new parliament, called the National Assembly, was to find a way to unite the nation's three major factions—the Kurds, Shiites, and Sunnis. Although the Sunnis once ruled under Saddam Hussein, they now hold a majority in only four of the nation's seventeen provinces. The United Iraqi Alliance, a coalition of Shiite Muslim parties, holds a narrow majority in the National Assembly. An alliance of Kurdish parties holds seventy-five seats. The interim prime minister, Ayad Allawi, belongs to a party that won only forty seats in the body. The Sunnis have few seats because they boycotted the national elections. So, the question was how the Assembly could rule the nation if one major group was not taking part and no Constitution had yet been written.

Progress toward democracy was evident elsewhere in the Middle East. Saudi Arabia allowed restricted votes for municipal councils. In Egypt, a governmental opposition movement called Kifaya ("Enough" in Arabic), demonstrated in the hopes of unseating President Mubarek, who has been in power for nearly a quarter of a century, and contested national elections were held for the first time. In Lebanon, a small group of student demonstrators, wearing gelled hair and bare midriffs, demonstrated in favor of government reforms. In Syria, the Middle East's first mass democratic movement, consisting largely of protesting students, sought to lobby the government. As a result of their protests the Lebanese government fell and Syria was forced to pull its army and intelligence agents out of Lebanon. In time, parties such as the Progressive Socialist Party, the Druze movement, and various Sunni Muslim parties may form a more democratic legislature.

On the other hand, Iran seems to have moved in the opposite direction. In mid-2005, Iran refused a package of economic incentives offered by the European Union in exchange for shutting down its nuclear weapons development program. Instead, Iran opened a uranium-conversion plant at Isfahan, and by January of 2006 the issue still remained unsettled. The future of this issue will determine the chances for long-term peace and the growth of democracy in the Middle East.

Caryle Murphy, "Opening Session Set for Iraq's Legislature," *Washington Post,* March 7, 2005, p. A16; Neil MacFarquhar, "Unexpected Whiff of Freedom Proves Bracing for the Mideast," *New York Times,* March 6, 2005, p. 1; Scott Wilson and Daniel Williams, "Across Middle East, A New Power Rises," *Washington Post,* April 17, 2005, p. A18; Niall Ferguson, "Iran's Revolution Isn't Going Away," *Los Angeles Times,* August 15, 2005, p. B11.

Reapportionment occurs every ten years, always producing "winners" and "losers." Population growth in the South and Southwest helped states such as California, Arizona, Texas, and Florida pick up seats after the 2000 census; population loss in the industrial North and Northeast has dropped the number of representatives from states such as New York, Pennsylvania, Connecticut, and Ohio.

The responsibility for redrawing a state's congressional districts falls to the legislature of the state, pending the approval of the Justice Department to ensure that election districts are drawn fairly. This means that the party composition of state legislatures and the state governorships after the 2000 census was central to the future makeup of Congress.

Within these 435 districts, one finds every imaginable variation. Each has its own character; none is an exact replica of the larger society. Their particular social composition leads some districts to view Democrats more favorably, whereas others lean toward Republicans. The social composition of a district relies on more than its financial and socioeconomic status. Rich districts might be liberal and poor districts might be conservative because of social factors such as religion, education, and cultural background.

An enormous political struggle ensues when a new census changes the number of seats a state will receive. State governments, either through their legislatures, judicial panels, or specifically designed commissions, must then redraw the boundaries of their congressional districts. This process requires more than counting voters and redrawing boundaries to make the districts equal. There are, after all, many ways to carve out numerically equal congressional districts. Some of those ways will help Democrats, while others will help Republicans. Boundary line changes can make a large ethnic group the majority within a single district or dilute that group's influence by dispersing its members into two, three, or more districts, where they can be outvoted by the majority in each era. **Redistricting**, as the process is called, therefore becomes intensely political. State legislators naturally seek to establish district boundaries that will favor candidates from their own party.

The term **gerrymander** describes the often bizarre district boundaries set up to favor the party in power. This word was coined in the early nineteenth century after Republican governor Elbridge Gerry of Massachusetts signed a redistricting bill that created a weirdly shaped district to encompass most of the voters who supported his party. One critic looked at the new district and said, "Why, that looks like a salamander!" Another said, "That's not a salamander, that's a gerrymander" (see Figure 4.1). The term is now used to describe any attempt to create a *safe seat* for one party, that is, a district in which the number of registered voters of one party is large enough to guarantee a victory for that party's candidate.

These battles, never easy, can position one party or the other for greater success in future elections. In 2003, Texas Republicans took control of their state legislature and, with the encouragement of House Majority Leader Tom Delay, redistricted their state a second time in an effort to create a half-dozen new Republican seats in Congress. With these new seats, Delay hoped to solidify his hold on the House in the 2004 election. The plan involved the creation of wholly Republican districts, breaking up longtime incumbent Democratic districts and creating districts with no incumbents but largely conservative voters. In four instances, the plan pitted Democratic incumbents against each other, thus ensuring Democratic losses. Texas Democratic representatives were so outraged that they fled the state to deny the legislature a quorum and thus prevent the vote. Texas state troopers were sent to find them. The plan worked just as the Republicans hoped: They picked up six new seats in the 2004 congressional election to

redistricting The redrawing of boundary lines of voting districts in accordance with census data or sometimes by order of the courts.

gerrymander Any attempt during state redistricting of congressional voting boundaries to create a safe seat for one party.

Figure 4.1   The Gerrymander
An 1812 cartoon lampooning the original "Gerry-Mander" of a Massachusetts district. This district was redrawn to guarantee a Republican victory, and gerrymander soon became a standard political term.

increase their margin in the state to 22–10 (see Figure 4.2). However, in 2006 the U.S. Supreme Court undertook a review of the redistricting plan, though it allowed the plan to remain in effect for the 2004 election. Under the Court's ruling in a Pennsylvania political redistricting case, judges would determine whether the partisan nature of the plan and its possible discriminatory effect were sufficiently "invidious."[13] The Republicans have figured out a way to solidify their hold on Congress: a suburban strategy. So many Americans have moved to the suburbs and the districts have been redrawn in such a way after the 2000 census that 51 percent of the 435 congressional districts, or 220 of them, are suburban in nature. The Republican party message is carefully crafted to appeal to these suburban voters, whereas the Democrats continue to hold a lock on the 90 urban districts. In the 2004 election, the Republicans won three out of every five suburban seats. But the significant Republicans gains have come in the fastest-growing distant suburbs, the so-called "exurbs." "It's going to be who controls the suburbs," says University of Chicago at Illinois political scientist Dick Simpson, in analyzing who will control the House in the future.[14]

Majority-Minority Districts and the Approach to Democracy

The redistricting process has occasionally been used to further social as well as political goals, such as increasing diversity in Congress—an interesting example of America's meandering approach to democracy. After the 1990 census, states with histories of racial discrimination were required by law to draw new district boundaries that would give minority candidates a better chance of election. The mandated redistricting was meant to ensure representation for nonwhites living in white-dominated areas. Such African American and Hispanic majority districts were called **majority-minority districts**. The redistricting added nineteen new black and Hispanic members to Congress in 1992. Proponents point to these gains as evidence that the new districts made Congress more representative of the general population, but critics claim that they constitute "racial gerrymandering."[15]

North Carolina's Twelfth Congressional District was one of those created to strengthen the voting power of African Americans. However, it was so narrow that in some places it spanned only one lane of Interstate Highway 85. The Supreme Court disallowed this district in 1993 in the case *Shaw* v. *Reno*. Although the Court sidestepped the general question of racial gerrymandering, it did prohibit racially based redistricting in the case of "those rare districts [like North Carolina's Twelfth] that are especially bizarre." It added acidly that the district "bears an uncomfortable resemblance to political apartheid."[16] In 1992, Cynthia McKinney, an African American, was elected to the House of Representatives from Georgia's Eleventh District. In a 1995 5–4 decision, the Supreme Court struck down the "race-based" redistricting plan in Cynthia McKinney's 260-mile-long district.[17] The Court asserted that this Justice Department–directed plan to create three black majority districts in the state out of the previous eleven such districts violated the equal protection rights of white voters because it was based predominantly on race. The decision put similar plans throughout the nation (mainly in the South) in jeopardy by ruling that they must all be "narrowly tailored to achieve a compelling [state] interest." In other words, although race can be a factor in redistricting, it cannot be the overriding consideration.

A year later, the Supreme Court upheld another redistricting scheme coming out of Georgia. The Court approved the plan by the district court to create a single black majority district for the 1996 elections, saying that a single such district is enough, because any attempt to create more of them would have to be based on race and would thus violate both the Voting Rights Act and the "one person, one vote" standard in *Reynolds* v. *Sims* for interpreting Article I, Section 2, of the Constitution. Speaking for the Court, Justice Anthony Kennedy reaffirmed that race "must not be a predominant factor in drawing the district lines."[18]

majority-minority district A congressional district drawn to include enough members of a minority group to greatly improve the chance of electing a minority candidate.

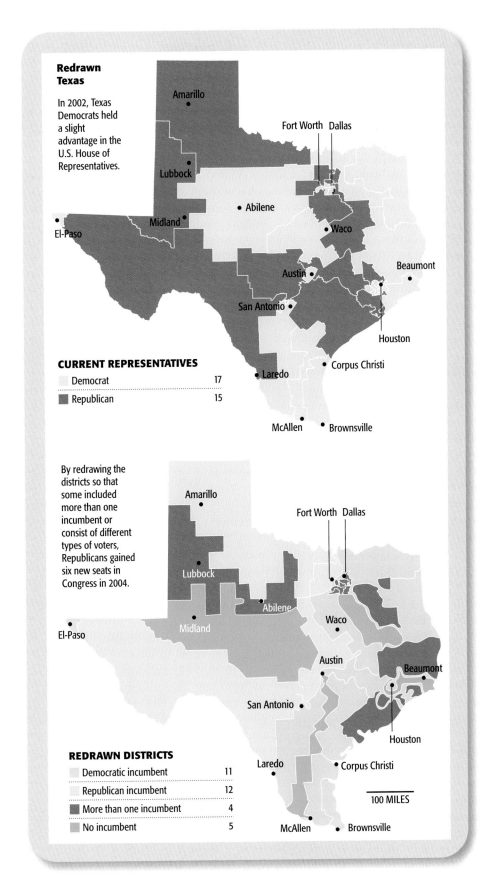

Redrawn Texas

In 2002, Texas Democrats held a slight advantage in the U.S. House of Representatives.

CURRENT REPRESENTATIVES

Democrat	17
Republican	15

By redrawing the districts so that some included more than one incumbent or consist of different types of voters, Republicans gained six new seats in Congress in 2004.

REDRAWN DISTRICTS

Democratic incumbent	11
Republican incumbent	12
More than one incumbent	4
No incumbent	5

100 MILES

Figure 4.2

Source: Texas Legislative Council

Since these rulings, electoral results in these areas have been interesting. Across the South in the 1996 election, McKinney and other redistricted minority candidates won reelection with huge majorities of black votes plus an average of 30 percent of white votes. Some argue that these results offer evidence that the traditional bias against voting for minority candidates in predominantly white districts is lessening, whereas others interpret the results as affirming the value of incumbency experience.[19] This issue continued after the 2000 elections. In a recent case, the Supreme Court unanimously offered the states "very significant breathing room" in redistricting, using the 2000 election results.[20] In Mississippi, the Bush administration stepped in, using the Voting Rights Act to block a state–court-ordered redistricting plan that would have created a congressional district with 37.5 percent African American voting age population in favor of one mandated by the federal court with only 30.4 percent African-American voters. The result was that the federal court plan was used for the 2002 election and approved by the U.S. Supreme Court the following year.[21] With so many federal, state, and local racially gerrymandered districts in existence, and nearly all of the Supreme Court decisions in this area being decided by a narrow 5–4 majority with the now retired Sandra Day O'Connor in the swing seat, the decisions of her replacement, Samuel Alito, will help to determine their future. With the Voting Rights Act of 1965 up for reauthorization in 2007, it is inevitable that the Court will revisit this question.

Delegates Versus Trustees

If Congress is to function as a representative institution, individual members must represent their constituents. In theory, legislators may view themselves as either delegates or trustees. **Delegates** feel bound to follow the wishes of a majority of their constituents; they make frequent efforts to learn voter opinions in their state or district. But how does a legislator represent district minority groups or raise issues of national importance but low priority for constituents? For example, should a representative with few minority constituents vote for an affirmative action program opposed by an overwhelming majority of voters in the district?

In these situations, many legislators see themselves not as delegates but as **trustees**, authorized to use their own judgment in considering legislation. The trustee role was best expressed by the English philosopher and member of Parliament Edmund Burke (1729–1797), who explained to his constituents that representatives should never sacrifice their own judgment to voter opinion. After hearing that Burke did not intend to follow their wishes, his constituency promptly ejected him from Parliament.

In Congress, the role of trustee, which often leads to policy innovations, is more likely to find favor with representatives from safe districts, where a wide margin of victory in the past makes future reelection likely by discouraging potential opponents and their contributors. Legislators from marginal districts tend to be delegates, keeping their eyes firmly fixed on the electorate. They apparently wish to avoid Burke's fate.

In practice, members of Congress combine the roles of delegate and trustee. They follow their constituency when voters have clear, strong preferences, but they vote their own best judgment either when the electorate's desire is weak, mixed, or unclear, or when the member has strong views on an issue. This approach to voting is called the *politico* role. Members of Congress frequently must balance votes on issues of national importance against votes on issues that are important to their constituents.[22]

A particularly poignant example of this dilemma arose during the early civil rights era. Lawrence Brooks Hays, an Arkansas moderate member of Congress from 1943 to 1959, was caught between his integrationist beliefs and his district's segregationist views. After he chose to act as a trustee—voting in favor of a civil rights bill—his constituents replaced him in the next election with someone closer to

delegates Congress members who feel bound to follow the wishes of a majority of their constituents; they make frequent efforts to learn the opinions of voters in their state or district.

trustees Congress members who feel authorized to use their best judgment in considering legislation.

their own views. This case illustrates a problem all elected officials ultimately face. Do they do what is popular or what they believe is right? Sometimes, when legislators do what they believe is right, it costs them so dearly that they lose their seat, a situation John F. Kennedy labeled "profiles in courage."[23]

Name Recognition and the Incumbency Factor

Incumbents are individuals who currently hold public office. From the 1950s through the early 1990s, an average of more than 92 percent of House incumbents and 80 percent of Senate incumbents who sought reelection were successful.[24] Despite the anti-incumbent sentiment of the 1994 election, since that time more than 95 percent of the House and 90 percent of the Senate incumbents who ran have won reelection.[25]

The advantage of incumbency is a relatively recent phenomenon. Before the Civil War, almost half of each new House and one-quarter to one-third of each entering Senate class included new members (a fact that can also be explained by the high number of members who voluntarily chose not to run for reelection). Despite high incumbency reelection rates, many members voluntarily leave office, either due to unhappiness with their jobs or a desire to turn the seat over to someone new. When combined with the change wrought by the so-called Republican Revolution in 1994, a majority of the members of the House and the Senate have been newly elected since 1990.

Incumbents enjoy a number of significant advantages in any election contest.[26] They nearly always enjoy greater name recognition than their challengers. They can hold press conferences for widespread publicity, participate in media events such as town meetings, and maintain offices back home that keep their names in the spotlight. Challengers must struggle for, and often fail to achieve, the kind of publicity and recognition that come automatically to an incumbent. Incumbents also often benefit from favorable redistricting during reapportionment.

Incumbents can increase their visibility through use of the **franking privilege**—free mailing of newsletters and political brochures to their constituents. These mailings solicit views and advice from constituents and serve to remind them of the incumbent's name and accomplishments. The use of franked mail has grown over the years. In 1994, House members seeking reelection sent out 363 million pieces of mail, nearly two items for every person of voting age. Excesses by members such as Dan Rostenkowski, former Democratic member from Illinois who served jail time for mail privilege violations, led to reforms such as caps on mailing and counting the franking privilege as part of the member's overall office expense allowance.

Incumbents have another advantage: Their staff helps them do favors for constituents. These services, known as **casework**, may involve arranging for pothole repairs, expediting Social Security benefit payments, or providing a tour of the Capitol. Casework is at the heart of the power of incumbents. Realizing that every voter remembers these little favors, members of Congress often have several full-time staff members who deal with cases involving individual constituents.[27] This kind of experience allows incumbents campaigning for reelection to "point with pride" to favors done for their districts. Although casework may have minimal direct impact on voting, it helps name recognition and avoids any negative backlash from constituents if requests are ignored. More than that, casework is a strategy to gain positive feedback from constituents, which enables members to take stands on legislative issues that might be unpopular with their constituents.[28]

Incumbents also have the advantage of legislative experience. They sit on committees with jurisdiction over issues of particular importance to their constituents. Former rock star turned representative, Sonny Bono of California's Palm Springs district became a member of the Judiciary Committee's Subcommittee on Courts and Intellectual Property because copyright issues are a significant issue for the

incumbents Individuals who currently hold public office.

franking privilege The free mailing of newsletters and political brochures to constituents by members of Congress.

casework Favors done as a service for constituents by those they have elected to Congress.

▲ Making a clean sweep of it? Republican candidates for Congress used this symbol in 1994 to symbolize their desire to pass term limits as part of their Contract with America. Once they were elected, however, their fervor cooled considerably. Term limits are yet to be passed by either house of Congress.

record and motion picture industry in his district. When Bono died in a skiing accident in early 1998, his wife Mary took advantage of reflected name recognition to win a special election for his seat and was then asked to take his seat on the Judiciary Committee.

Perhaps the greatest advantage incumbents hold is financial. Parties, interest groups, and individuals tend to back known candidates because they have the best chance of winning, whereas relatively unknown challengers have great difficulty raising money. In 2000, House incumbents spent about $400,000 more than their challengers, whereas Senate incumbents spent more than $2 million more than their challengers.[29] Just two years later, the average cost of a campaign was $891,000 in the House and $4.9 million in the Senate.[30] Incumbents can usually raise that kind of money with little difficulty, but few challengers can.[31] However, challengers usually need not raise as much money as incumbents just to be competitive in the election. All they really have to do is pass a threshold of about $400,000 for a House seat in order to make a credible run for the office.

Seeking to change this pattern, many voters now favor some form of **term limits**, usually a maximum of twelve years in each house. With polls in 1994 showing 80 percent of the public favoring term limits, twenty-three states passed legislation limiting the length of time their senators and representatives can serve in Congress. Underlying these measures is the growing public perception that incumbent legislators, feeling confident of reelection, become either complacent or corrupt.

In 1995, the Supreme Court overturned the power of the state of Arkansas—and thus *all* states—to impose term limits on congressional candidates (in this case a limit of no more than three terms for the House and two terms for the Senate). As a result, similar laws in twenty-two other states were voided. Justice John Paul Stevens explained that states could not add a new requirement for office to the three requirements for office—age, citizenship, and residency—specified in the Constitution. Any term limits on congressional candidates would have to be accomplished by constitutional amendment.[32] Two years later, the Court *disallowed* (by refusing to hear on appeal) Arkansas and eight other states' attempt to use a so-called scarlet letter provision to identify on the ballot congressional candidates who did not adhere to voluntary term limits.[33]

Despite the Supreme Court rulings, the term limits movement continues to have an effect. In 1995, the 104th Congress approved term limits for its leaders—four consecutive terms for the speaker and three consecutive terms for committee chairs. In addition, twenty states passed term limits for their state legislatures. These laws had such an impact that in California one entire house of its legislature has turned over since 1990.[34]

Although more than nine out of ten incumbents in the 2002 election were reelected, the actual turnover rate in Congress, including seats vacated because of deaths, retirements, and decisions to run for other offices, was well more than 15 percent—almost the same as it has been for more than two decades.

The movement seemed to be stalling when only Nebraska voted state legislative term limits into effect in 2000. Then, a year later, term limits were ruled unconstitutional in Oregon. When the Idaho legislature voted in early 2002 to become the first state to repeal its term limits law (a decision later ratified by voters in the 2002 election), only seventeen states still had term limits on their legislatures. However, term limits movements in the states refused to slip from view. This was made clear when a 2002 California special election defeated by 58–42 percent Proposition 45, which would have weakened the state's legislative term limits by allowing every legislator the chance to run for an additional four years in office.[35] The same happened in Arkansas and Montana in the 2004 election, when voters refused to extend the amount of time that legislators could serve by 50 to 100 percent.[36] Even without term limits, turnover in Congress in the past decade has been such that the average length of service is 9.3 years in the House and 12.1 years in the Senate.[37]

Question for Reflection

How might the next version of Campaign Finance Reform be written to deal with inequalities in campaign spending between incumbents and relatively unknown challengers?

term limits A legislated limit on the amount of time a political figure can serve in office.

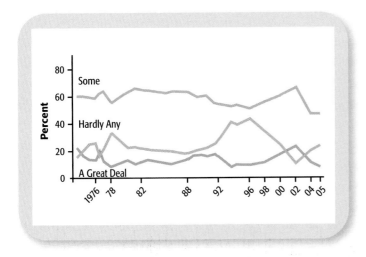

Figure 4.3   Confidence in Congress

Source: "Major Institutions," www.polling_report.com May 23–26, 2005. Gallup Poll, 5/21-23/04, accessed at www.//harrisinteractive.com/ harris poll/; see also National Opinion Research Center. Reported in *National Journal*, January 17, 1998, p. 111. http://www.polling_report polling_report.com/institut.htm

The Two Congresses: The Public's View of Congress

The American public has generally had a "Love my congressman, hate the Congress" view of the institution. Scholars in the field know this as the **Two Congresses** phenomenon. Congress as an institution generally has always drawn low public regard. Surveys conducted from the 1960s to the late 1990s revealed a steady decline in the proportion of respondents rating Congress positively. As you can see in Figure 4.3, by 2005 a Gallup Center poll revealed that the number of Americans saying that they had "a great deal" of confidence in Congress had dropped to 8 percent. But if Americans are negative about Congress as an institution, most still feel a strong sense of loyalty to their individual senators and representatives. In a 2005 poll, respondents approved of the performance of their individual member of Congress by a 61 to 32 margin, whereas that same poll's measurement of approval for Congress as a whole was virtually the reverse at 41 percent approval and 54 percent disapproval.[38]

Such a wide discrepancy between people's love of their own Congress member and disdain for the institution as a whole has many reasons. Individual members can serve constituents and act quickly, whereas the overall Congress tends to move much more slowly and focus on complicated national issues. Individual members are popular because they can direct government spending and projects to their home districts, whereas Congress as a whole is generally criticized for its overall spending practices. The national media are also much more critical of Congress as a whole, focusing on scandals and conflicts, whereas the local press tends to deal with the individual members in a much friendlier fashion. Finally, an individual member can speak on policy clearly and with one voice, whereas the overall Congress speaks with many voices, and sometimes no voice at all.[39] This paradox of the Two Congresses frequently leads even incumbent members from both parties seeking reelection to criticize their colleagues for going in the wrong direction or at the wrong speed.

Two Congresses A term denoting the differing views the public has toward Congress as a whole and their representative individual, noting that the opinions are more positive for the individual representative than for the body as a whole.

HOW CONGRESS ORGANIZES ITSELF

Since the Constitution says little about how each house of Congress should be organized, those structures have evolved over the decades. The result has been a tension between the centralizing influence of the congressional leadership and the decentralizing influence of the committees and the subcommittees.

MakeItReal

Visual Literacy: The House Chamber and House Leadership

Speaker of the House The only presiding officer of the House mentioned in the Constitution. The leader of the majority party in Congress and third in line for the presidency.

House majority leader The person elected by the majority party caucus to serve as the party's chief strategist and floor spokesperson.

party caucus A conference of party members in Congress.

Congressional Leadership

Leadership in the House   The Constitution designates only one presiding officer of the House, the **Speaker of the House**. One of the most powerful officeholders in the U.S. government, the speaker is usually seen as the voice of the House of Representatives, and sometimes even of the overall Congress. Though the Constitution does not specify that this person must be a member of Congress, he or she is, by tradition, leader of the majority party. The current Speaker is J. Dennis Hastert of Illinois.

The speaker's formal duties are to preside over the House when it is in session; to appoint all members to the Policy Committee, a representative body of the party conference that handles committee assignments and plans the legislative agenda;[40] to appoint the party's legislative leaders and senior staff members; and to control the assignment of bills to committees. When the House majority party is not the president's party, the speaker is often considered the minority party's national spokesperson.[41]

The speaker's power has varied over time. Around the turn of the twentieth century, Speakers Thomas Reed and Joseph Cannon were so powerful that they could personally appoint all committee chairs and determine committee membership and thus block legislation and punish those who opposed them. Cannon's powers, though, were diluted by a House revolution in 1910. Speaker Sam Rayburn of Texas exemplified, from 1940 until his death in 1961 (with the exception of four years when the Republicans controlled the House), the use of all the formal and informal powers of the office. Rayburn's powers, however, were limited by the competing interests of entrenched conservative committee chairs.

A series of reforms in the 1970s made the speakership of Thomas ("Tip") O'Neill (1977–87) even more powerful on paper. The speaker could now dictate the selection of the committee chairs, committee members from the speaker's party, and party members of the powerful Rules Committee. In addition, the office increased its power to refer bills to committees and dictate the order of the floor proceedings. O'Neill became far more powerful than any speaker since Cannon, but his powers had limits. O'Neill often failed to dissuade southern Democrats in Congress, the so-called "boll weevils," from backing President Ronald Reagan's conservative policies. On one occasion, in 1981, when Reagan's administration substituted a one-thousand-page bill that contained dozens of drastic funding cuts at the last moment before a vote, O'Neill could only use the "bully pulpit" of his position to object in a speech. Noticing that the "cut and paste" bill had the name of a woman and her phone number in the margin, a likely source for one of the cuts, O'Neill objected, "Why are we enacting this woman into law?" But no one listened, and the bill passed.[42]

Though the powers of the office had not changed, its prestige and effectiveness declined when O'Neill's successor, James Wright of Texas, tried to use his powers for partisan goals, only to be forced to resign by a House revolt, led by Newt Gingrich. Ironically, Gingrich thought he would restore the speaker's position to greater luster in 1995, but eventually he, too, contributed to its weakening. He voluntarily stepped down from the speakership after party members charged him with ethics violations and responsibility for the poor Republican showing in the November 1998 elections. When Bob Livingston of Louisiana was forced to resign almost immediately after being chosen to replace Gingrich, he was replaced with J. Dennis Hastert of Illinois.

Next in line after the speaker is the **House majority leader**. Although Tom Delay of Texas was elected majority leader in 2005, he stepped aside with the intention of returning after being indicted in Texas over ethics charges relating to a Texas political redistricting plan. Delay was temporarily replaced by Majority Whip Roy Blunt of Missouri, but early in 2006, in the wake of a growing scandal relating to lobbyist and former Delay aide Jack Abramoff, Delay announced that he would not return to the position, and John Boehner (R.-OH) won the election to replace him. The majority leader is elected by the **party caucus**, a conference of party members in

Congress, and serves as the party's chief strategist and floor spokesperson. The majority leader also schedules bills and attempts to persuade members of the majority party to vote according to the party's official position on pending legislation.

The minority party is headed by the **minority leader**, in 2006 Democrat Nancy Pelosi of California. Should the minority party become the majority in Congress, the minority leader is likely to be a candidate for speaker of the House.[43] When the Republicans gained a House majority in 1994 and minority leader Robert Michel retired, Newt Gingrich made the dramatic move from his former position as party whip.

Both the majority and minority party leaders work with the support of **whips**, members charged with counting prospective votes on various issues and making certain that members have the information they need for floor action. *Whip* is a fox-hunting term applied to the legislative process. During a fox hunt, the whipper-in keeps the sniffing dogs from straying by whipping them back into the pack. The majority whip in 2006 is Roy Blunt (R.-MO); the minority whip is Steny Hoyer of Maryland, who won the office in his second race for the position. Whips are aided by a complex system of more than ninety deputy whips, assistant regional whips, and at-large whips.

Leadership in the Senate   Other than making the vice president the **president of the Senate**, the Constitution does not specify a leadership structure for the Senate. The vice president presides over the Senate only on rare occasions—most commonly when a tie vote seems likely on a key piece of legislation. If a tie does ensue, the vice president can cast the deciding vote. Except for the occasional ceremonial event, the vice president rarely enters the Senate. To guide that body's day-to-day activities, the Constitution allows the election of a **president pro tempore**. This position is essentially honorary and goes by tradition to the majority party member with the longest continuous service. In 2006, Ted Stevens of Alaska, first appointed a senator in 1968, held the office. In theory, the president pro tempore presides over the Senate, although the position provides little political clout. The day-to-day task of the Senate presiding officer is usually farmed out to a wide range of senators, often junior ones who use the job to gain experience and "pay their dues."

The Senate party leadership structure differs only slightly from that of the House. The majority party selects a **Senate majority leader**—currently Bill Frist of Tennessee—whose functions resemble those of the Speaker of the House.[44] Senator Frist, a renowned former heart surgeon with limited Senate experience, has a conciliatory leadership style that has made it difficult for him to harness the diverging political views among Senate Republicans. The majority leader schedules legislation, directs committee assignments, and persuades members to vote along party lines. The Senate minority leader normally works with the majority leader to establish the legislative agenda, but these days incumbent Harry Reid of Nevada is largely left out of the process. Instead, Senator Reid has carved out a role as the public face of the Democrats, in offering his plainspoken homespun comments, in seek-

▲ Rep. Nancy Pelosi (D.-CA) received a whip from Rep. David E. Bonior (D.-MI) when she became the first woman elected House Minority Whip, and one year later she again made history by becoming the first woman to be elected House Minority Leader.

▲ Senator Bill Frist (R.-TN), has had a roller-coaster tenure as Majority Leader of the Senate. In trying to unite the conservative and moderate Republicans he frequently has clashed with Minority Leader Harry Reid (D.-Nev.) as he did here, objecting to Reid's invocation of a rule closing the Senate Chamber for a debate.

minority leader The leader of the minority party in Congress.

whips Congress members charged with counting prospective votes on various issues and making certain that members have the information they need for floor action.

president of the Senate The vice president of the United States.

president pro tempore The majority party member with the longest continuous service in the Senate; serves as the chief presiding officer in the absence of the vice president.

Senate majority leader A senator selected by the majority party whose functions are similar to those of the speaker of the House.

▲ Senator Harry Reid (D-NV), the Minority Leader of the Senate, has used his plain spoken ways and bare-knuckle style of leadership to embarrass Majority Leader Bill Frist (R.-TN.) and the Republicans. Here he displays a calendar at a press conference showing how many days of inactivity the Republicans have had in instituting their agenda for the American public.

ing to criticize the Republicans and put forward the Democrats' agenda. As in the House, the majority and minority leaders have party whips to help organize and count votes. In 2006, the majority whip is Mitch McConnell of Kentucky, and the Democrat whip is Dick Durbin of Illinois. Rick Santorum of Pennsylvania chairs the Republican Conference, the meetings of all GOP party Senate members. Minority Leader Harry Reid holds that position for the Democratic Conference. Another central leadership position is the chair of the campaign fundraising committees for the next Senate election, a person also in charge of distributing campaign funds for races deemed winnable and important. The chair of the National Republican Senatorial Committee (NRSC) in 2006 is Elizabeth Dole of North Carolina, and the chair of the Democratic Senatorial Campaign Committee (DSCC) is Chuck Schumer of New York.

The Senate majority leader is usually an influential politician. If the president is from the same party, the majority leader often can be a valuable ally and spokesperson on Capitol Hill. In 2005, though, as President Bush's popularity began to fall and Senator Bill Frist considered running for the White House, the two men split more frequently on policies such as stem-cell research. A majority leader from the opposing party can be among the president's toughest critics, as Robert Dole was for Bill Clinton from 1995 to 1997.

One of the most persuasive Senate majority leaders in recent history was Texas Democrat Lyndon Baines Johnson, who served from 1955 until he became vice president in 1961. In what became known as the "Johnson treatment," he would corner fellow senators in search of a vote and badger them with his charismatic charm and large size until he got an agreement.[45] Johnson always said that the Senate was like an ocean, with whales and minnows; if he could persuade the "whales" (powerful senators) to follow him, the "minnows" (weaker members) would follow along in a school. Nothing stood in Johnson's way. Once, when Senator Hubert Humphrey of Minnesota, caught in a holding pattern flying over Washington, was needed for a key vote, Johnson ordered air traffic controllers to clear the plane for immediate landing. On another occasion, when Senator Allen Frear of Delaware opposed a bill, Johnson stood up on the floor of the Senate and yelled, "Change your goddamn vote!" Frear immediately complied.[46]

Congressional leaders since the 1960s, particularly in the Senate, have been persuaders rather than dictators. The job requires give-and-take bargaining and consensus-building skills. Former Majority Leader Robert Byrd spoke of this difference from Johnson's world, describing the Senate in the 1970s and 1980s not as an ocean of whales and minnows to be led but rather a forest. "There are ninety-nine animals. They're all lions. There's a waterhole. They all have to come to the waterhole. I don't have power, but . . . I'm in a position to do things for others."[47] Years later, in an autobiography, Mississippi senator Trent Lott described his job as Senate majority leader in the 1990s as much like "herding cats."[48]

Congressional Committees: The Laboratories of Congress

A speaker or a Senate majority leader's success depends now on how well he or she works with leaders and members in the "laboratories of Congress"—its committees and subcommittees. Some of Congress's most important work is done in committee and subcommittee. As Woodrow Wilson put it, "Congress on the floor is Congress on public exhibition; Congress in committee is Congress at work."[49]

There are four types of congressional committees: standing, select or special, conference, and joint. Each party receives seats on all committees in proportion to its representation in the entire House or Senate. Thus, the majority party in each house generally controls a corresponding majority in each committee. The party leadership assigns members to committees. Table 4.4 lists the key committees in Congress.

The most important committees in both houses of Congress are the **standing committees**. These permanent committees—twenty in the Senate, twenty in the House—determine whether proposed legislation should be sent to the entire chamber for consideration. Virtually all bills are considered by at least one standing committee and often by more than one. When Congress considered Bill Clinton's proposals for health-care reform in 1994, the matter came before five standing committees: Ways and Means, Energy and Commerce, and Education and Labor in the House; Finance and Labor and Human Resources in the Senate. (The committees have been reorganized and the names changed since then.)

Table 4.4 ▪ Standing Committees in the House and Senate, 2006

House Committees	Senate Committees
Agriculture	Aging
Appropriations	Agriculture, Nutrition, and Forestry
Armed Services	Appropriations
Budget	Armed Services
Education and the Workforce	Banking, Housing, and Urban Affairs
Energy and Commerce	Budget
Financial Services	Commerce, Science, and Transportation
Government Reform	Energy and Natural Resources
Homeland Security	Environment and Public Works
House Administration	Ethics
International Relations	Finance
Judiciary	Foreign Relations
Resources	Health, Education, Labor, and Pensions
Rules	Homeland Security and Government Affairs
Science	Indian Affairs
Small Business	Intelligence
Standards of Official Conduct	Judiciary
Transportation and Infrastructure	Rules and Administration
Veterans' Affairs	Small Business
Ways and Means	Veterans' Affairs

standing committees Permanent congressional committees that determine whether proposed legislation should be sent to the entire chamber for consideration.

Select or **special committees** are temporary and conduct investigations or study specific problems or crises. These committees possess no authority to propose bills and must be reauthorized by each new Congress. Their creation and disbanding mirror political forces in the nation at large. When a given issue is "hot" (for example, concern about drug use or security), pressures on Congress grow. Congress may set up a special committee to investigate. When the problem seems solved or interest dies away, the committee also meets its end. On the other hand, if the original problem and the concerned constituency continue to grow, a new standing committee may be created, thus providing power and institutional permanence for those concerned with the issue.

Conference committees are formed to reconcile differences between the versions of a bill passed by the House and the Senate. A conference committee can be small, usually composed of the chairs of the relevant committees and subcommittees from each chamber.[50] Major bills, however, may have committees of as many as 250 representatives and senators. Conference committees rarely exist more than a few days.[51]

Since both houses jealously guard their independence and prerogatives, Congress establishes only a few **joint committees**. These groups, such as the Joint Economic Committee, include members from both chambers who study broad areas of interest to Congress as a whole. More commonly, joint committees oversee congressional functioning and administration, such as the printing and distribution of federal government publications.

Why Does Congress Use Committees?

Committees enable Congress to do its work effectively by allowing it to consider several substantive matters simultaneously. Because each committee addresses a specific subject area, its members and staff develop knowledge and expertise. Ideas can be transformed into policies based on research and expert testimony. Committees provide multiple points of access for citizens and interest groups, serving as mini-legislative bodies that represent the larger House or Senate.

Committees are major players in congressional business, and members actively seek seats on particular ones with three goals in mind: to be reelected, to make good public policy, and to gain influence within the chamber.[52] The ideal committee helps them do all three. A seat, for instance, on the House Ways and Means Committee or the Senate Finance Committee, which pass on tax legislation, or on the House or Senate Appropriations Committees, which dictate spending priorities, ensures internal influence and authority.[53] The House Rules Committee and the Judiciary Committees of both houses were once considered powerful and thus desirable. Now, though, the House Rules Committee is merely a tool of the speaker, and the Judiciary Committees of the House and Senate handle such controversial legislation that serving on them often creates only trouble for members.

The changing role of committee chairs also demonstrates the approach to democracy in Congress. In the 1950s and 1960s, when conservative southern Democrats had the most seniority and controlled the chairs, they blocked liberal civil rights legislation by bottling it up in committee. That power diminished after the 1974 "post-Watergate class" of legislators enacted a series of reforms lessening the discretionary power of the chairs to block legislation and determine the number and membership of subcommittees. However, the chairs still had enough power to keep the speaker from working his will, if they so desired.

After the 1994 election, Newt Gingrich moved quickly to take back much of the speaker's power by slashing the number of committees and delegating much of the power of the chairs to the speaker. This move allowed him to direct the fight for his proposed Contract with America. After personal problems weakened his leadership in 1996, power returned to the chairs, and once again they began to dictate the direction and pace of legislation.[54]

select committees (or special committees) Temporary congressional committees that conduct investigations or study specific problems or crises.

conference committees Committees that reconcile differences between versions of a bill passed by the House and the Senate.

joint committees Groups of members from both chambers who study broad areas that are of interest to Congress as a whole.

Although this appeared a return to the all-powerful chairs of earlier decades, the Republicans in 1995 enacted term limits for chairs and other congressional leaders of no more than three consecutive terms. This reduced their power to control legislation and has led to a periodic changeover in congressional leadership. As a result, Republican Tom Delay of Texas faced the loss of his majority whip seat but instead became majority leader when Dick Armey (R.-TX) retired, and the Republicans maintained control of the House after the 2002 election.

Various committees help members serve their districts directly. A representative from rural Illinois or California, both large agricultural states, might seek a seat on the Agriculture Committee. Membership on such a committee would increase the legislator's chances of influencing policies that affect constituents, a helpful move at election time. As a former member who was on the Public Works Committee (now Public Land and Resources) explains, "I could always go back to the district and say, 'Look at that road I got for you. See that beach erosion project over there? And those buildings? I got all those. I'm on Public Works.'"[55]

The committee system also provides opportunities for career advancement and name recognition. A strong performance at televised hearings can impress constituents, increase name recognition, and convey a positive image. But such visibility can also backfire. Consider the House Judiciary Committee, which received tremendous national visibility in 1998 during President Bill Clinton's impeachment hearings. California Republican James Rogan, a member of that committee and the one who led the House fight against Clinton, lost his 2000 reelection bid after spending more than $10 million in one of the most expensive congressional campaigns ever.

The Rise of Subcommittees

Much of Congress's legislative work occurs in **subcommittees**, the smaller working groups that consider and draft legislation. In 2004, the twenty House standing committees included eighty-eight subcommittees, whereas the twenty Senate standing committees had sixty-eight.[56] Subcommittees provide a further division of congressional labor. By narrowing the topic on which members focus, these groups allow for greater specialization. They also provide more opportunities for public access to the legislative process. Subcommittees hold hearings to obtain a broad range of testimony from local administrators, group leaders, and individuals. Such hearings would be impossible for the whole House and difficult for a large committee, but they are ideally suited to the smaller arena of the subcommittee.

Before 1970, congressional committees operated largely behind closed doors. Legislative decision-making power concentrated in a few powerful chairs usually appointed on seniority and not representative of rank-and-file members. In the 1970s, a revolution of sorts occurred. Younger rank-and-file members of Congress demanded and won more control over the policy agenda. In a crucial change, House Democrats made it technically possible to replace committee chairs by a secret ballot of the entire caucus. They proceeded to strengthen that newly gained power by voting to replace three long-standing conservative chairs deemed seriously out of touch with the national party's much more liberal perspectives. Most Democratic chairs responded quickly to that lesson. They became remarkably open to rank-and-file concerns; only a handful got into trouble again while Democrats controlled the House. But Speaker Gingrich also learned this lesson, and upon taking power in 1994, he bypassed seniority to place his ideological allies in chairs of key committees, including Robert L. Livingston (R.-LA) for Appropriations and Henry J. Hyde (R.-IL) for Judiciary, bypassing more senior members such as twenty-two-year veteran Carlos J. Moorhead (R.-CA).

Another crucial change adopted in the 1970s reform era radically decentralized power in the House. Usually referred to as the "Subcommittee Bill of Rights," it created additional subcommittees and seats on existing subcommittees.[57] Each House committee with more than twenty members had to create at least four standing

subcommittees The subgroups of congressional committees charged with initially dealing with legislation before the entire committee considers it.

U.S.A. Yesterday and Today

Forgive and Remember:
Playing Hardball in the Republican Congress

The late Senator Daniel Patrick Moynihan (D.-NY) used to say that life in the U.S. Senate, indeed in the whole Congress, was governed by a single Golden Rule: "forgive and remember." By that he meant that members of Congress never forgot the slights they suffered when in the minority and were always looking to pay them back when in the majority.

This may be happening now as the Republicans control both houses of Congress. Long-serving Republicans remember when their proposals were ignored under Democratic speakers and when Democratic committee chairs withheld sufficient staff from Republican colleagues. Powerful committee chairmen such as Dan Rostenkowski (D.-IL) of the House Ways and Means Committee acted in ways contrary to the institution's rules and even federal law, even as they launched ethics charges and investigations against Republican colleagues.

But now the Republicans are wielding their power with a heavy hand. Committee chairmen such as David Dreier (R.-CA) of the House Rules Committee and James Sensenbrenner (R.-WI) of the House Judiciary Committee have been known to gavel hearings closed and even shut off the microphones to prevent Democrats and their witnesses from testifying. Legislation, including the Medicare Reform Act of 2003 and the Energy Bill of 2005, is drafted only by Republicans, their staff members, White House staffers, and even lobbyists. Rules are added to bills to prevent Democrats from adding any amendments. And, when the vote is close, Speaker J. Dennis Hastert and former Majority Leader Tom Delay developed a new tactic: The speaker continues the normal fifteen-minute voting period for as long as it takes to win a vote, and then gavels the vote closed when the victory is secured. For the 2003 Medicare Bill, the vote did not begin until 3 a.m. and lasted nearly three hours, while the president worked the phones to cut deals, until two Republican members finally switched their votes.

Two years later, the same thing happened when Congress considered the Central American Free Trade Agreement (CAFTA). This time, the Democratic opposition initially held enough votes to defeat the bill, so the vote held off until 11:50 p.m. on July 27, 2005. With President Bush and Vice President Cheney lobbying reluctant Republicans all day, and many Cabinet secretaries bargaining in the hallways over provisions to be added to other bills, one vote after another changed. After an hour of arm-twisting, and members leaving without voting at key times, a 214–211 vote against the treaty became a 217–215 vote in favor.

This pattern of open-ended voting passes legislation, but whether or not these tactics come back to haunt the Republicans when the Democrats retake power in Congress remains to be seen.

"Deal Making, Washington Style," *San Francisco Chronicle*, August 1, 2005, p. B4; Sherrod Brown, "GOP Arm-Twisters Forced Agreement to Pass," *Columbus Dispatch*, August 6, 2005, p. 12A; Janet Hook and Vicki Kemper, "A Long Night's Journey into Yes in the House," *Los Angeles Times*, November 23, 2003, p. 28; Andrea Stone, "GOP Comes Around to a Majority View," *USA Today*, June 17, 2004, p. 15A.

▲ President George W. Bush beams with pride as he signs into law the Central American Free Trade Agreement (CAFTA) opening up trade with that region. The legislators watching this occasion did not hesitate to use hardball tactics to secure passage of the measure over Democratic Party objections.

subcommittees, and the committee chair could not easily tamper with subcommittee powers. Each subcommittee had its own chair, based largely on seniority, not political favoritism. Subcommittees had the right to hire permanent staff, and they could not be disbanded at the whim of the committee chair. All bills had to be referred to a subcommittee within two weeks of reaching the chair, thus preventing the chair from killing bills by ignoring them. This reform made subcommittee chairs powerful, owing their position to no one person, heading groups not easily dissolved, and commanding staff resources to support their work.

One additional fact ensured further decentralization of power in the House. No one was allowed to head more than one subcommittee. Thus, instead of the handful of powerful barons who ran Congress in the 1950s, in the 1980s scattered knights held power as heads of the more than one hundred House and eighty Senate subcommittees. A more recent reform in 1997 reduced the number of subcommittees by nearly one hundred panels and limited the number of panels on which an individual member could serve.

The proliferation of subcommittees has had effects beyond decentralizing congressional power. For one thing, interest groups can now influence bills by supporting and persuading only the legislators on a particular committee or subcommittee. For example, the tobacco industry targeted its campaign contributions to give it a favorable hearing. In 1998, the most campaign support, $159,416 over a six-year period, went to Thomas J. Bliley Jr. (R.-VA), the new House Commerce Committee chair, a man in a position to affect legislation on smoking. On the other hand, Henry A. Waxman (D.-CA), a vocal critic of the industry, received nothing.[58]

At the same time, these changes made the legislative process more unwieldy, giving many individual members a veto over legislation. For example, thirty committees and seventy-seven subcommittees played a role in shaping the 1992 defense budget. Moreover, as the number of subcommittees has grown, so has the amount of time a legislator must devote to committee business. Many find it impossible to even read the bills and instead rely on staff members and lobbyists to provide them with information about pending legislation.[59] These drawbacks brought subcommittee government's decentralized power, once heralded as an important reform, under strong attack by the 1995 Republican Congress.

Decline of the Congressional Committees

In recent years, congressional committees have become less important in the lawmaking process. Says Richard E. Cohen, "From the scant handful of major bills passed by the House and Senate [in 1999], one unmistakable fact emerges: The congressional committees have lost their long-standing pre-eminence as the center of legislative ideas and debates."

In 1999 alone, both the House and the Senate considered major gun control bills neither written nor reviewed by the Judiciary Committee of either chamber. When Senate Democrats pressed then–Majority Leader Trent Lott (R.-MS) to act on a patients' rights bill, he selected a bill written by key Democrats rather than one by a Republican dominated committee. The Republicans' version of the bill came from a Senate Republican task force, rather than a standing committee. And in the area of tax cuts, both houses considered measures reviewed by the tax-writing committees but written instead by a minority of members in consultation with their senior aides. Complained moderate Republican Michael N. Castle, of Delaware, "There was virtually no discussion of the bill with members."

Although committees were, in the past, as Woodrow Wilson said, a representation of "Congress at work," now the kind of ad hoc legislating that uses task forces and individual members belies the textbook model for congressional lawmaking. No longer are legislative compromises forged in committees. No longer are members of those committees recognized for their seniority and expertise. No longer are committee chairs recognized for their growing and continual power. No longer do committees have independent effects on the lawmaking process.

Instead, over the past three decades committee power has eroded to the point that committees have largely collapsed. The committees began to lose power during the Democratic control era, but the death warrant came in 1995 with the reforms instituted under Speaker Newt Gingrich. Once he began reforming committees with term limits for chairpersons, and with his top-down management style of creating task forces to draft bills that reflected the wishes of the congressional leadership rather than the committees, the committee structure began to collapse.

When J. Dennis Hastert took over as speaker in 1999, he promised to restore the committee structure, but it has not worked out that way. He tried to follow a return to "regular order" whereby the committees would be set free to consider legislation in their own way. Indeed, one member said, "There is a stronger sense that our members are charting their own course." But time and again, Hastert has found that a return to legislating-as-usual has not worked out well.

In the Senate, where many former House members now reside and Majority Leader Bill Frist has sought to impose leadership control over the lawmaking process, Senate committees found, like their House counterparts, that their lack of deliberation on issues, or their ineffectiveness, led the Senate leadership to ignore them. Committees "will become increasingly irrelevant from the standpoint of legislation" argued conservative political activist Gordon S. Jones. Whenever committee chairs have tried to assert independence they have been quickly brought into line by threats of the loss of their position. Following the 2004 election, Senator Arlen Specter (R.-PA) endangered his chances for succeeding Senator Orrin Hatch as Judiciary Committee chairman by saying that he would not necessarily demand that judicial candidates proclaim their opposition to the *Roe* v. *Wade* abortion decision to be approved. He also said that he might not guarantee a hearing for all such candidates, raising protests from far-right-wing interest groups and objections from his Republican colleagues and forcing him to retract those statements. Only when Specter promised to bring every nominee to a vote on the Senate floor was he allowed to remain in his position. But once there, he reasserted his independence by failing to fully back the nuclear option proposed by the Republicans to end the Senate's right to filibuster on judicial nominations.

This trend away from committee involvement brought to the House and Senate floors legislation neither properly reviewed nor carrying the necessary support from a majority of the members because of the compromises forged therein.

Indeed, these insufficiently backed and prepared bills were increasing the number of measures filibustered in the Senate. This constant hamstringing of measures has limited both parties' abilities to present a coherent platform to the voting public. In the 109th Congress, the Republicans seemed more than willing to continue bypassing their committee structure.[60]

Question for Reflection

Consider the changes that reduced 1950s–60s senior chairpersons' power to control the flow of legislation and the current decentralized system based on more power of individual committee members. Has the committee system approached or receded from democracy?

CONGRESS IN SESSION

A combination of House and Senate procedures and the power and influence of congressional leaders and committee and subcommittee chairs shapes the outcomes of the legislative process.[61]

The Rules and Norms of Congress

The formal rules of Congress can be found in the Constitution, in the standing rules of each house, and in Thomas Jefferson's *Manual of Parliamentary Practice and Precedent*. Congressional rules, for example, dictate the timing, extent, and nature of floor debate. Imagine what might happen without such rules. If, for example, each of the 435 members of the House tried to rise on the floor and speak for just one minute on just one bill, debate would last at least seven hours, not taking into account the time needed for amendments, procedural matters, and votes.

The House Rules Committee   As noted earlier, the House Rules Committee plays a key role, directing the flow of bills through the legislative process. Except for revenue, budget, and appropriations bills, which are *privileged legislation* and go directly to the House floor from committee, bills approved in committee are referred to the Rules Committee. The House Rules Committee issues **rules** that determine which bills will be discussed, how long the debate will last, and which amendments will be allowed.[62] Rules can be *open*, allowing members to freely suggest related amendments from the floor; *closed*, permitting no amendments except those offered by the sponsoring committee members; or *restrictive*, now the most commonly used procedure, which limits amendments to certain parts of a bill and dictates which members can offer them. By refusing to attach a rule to a bill, the Rules Committee can delay a bill's consideration or even kill it.

During the 1950s, conservative members dominated the Rules Committee and succeeded in blocking civil rights, education, and welfare legislation, even bills favored by a majority of House members.[63] Today, however, democratizing reforms have made the Rules Committee what one member of Congress has called "the handmaiden of the Speaker," directing the flow and nature of the legislative process according to the majority party's wishes.[64] If the speaker favors a bill, the rule is passed; if not, the rule is denied. If a long debate would prove embarrassing to the majority party, the speaker will likely allow only a short debate under a closed rule. Thus, contrary to earlier days when whole sessions of Congress would pass without a vote on a key issue, Speaker Newt Gingrich used his total control over the Rules Committee to direct the House to vote on each point of the Contract with America in the first one hundred days of the 104th Congress.

Because the Senate is smaller and more decentralized than the House, its rules for bringing a matter to the floor are much more relaxed. There is no Rules Committee; instead, the majority leader has the formal power to make the schedule. Until recently, the schedule was formed through informal agreements with the minority leader and finalized by **unanimous consent agreements**, a waiver of the rules for consideration of a measure by a vote of all of the members. Increasingly, decisions have been made by Senator Frist alone. With no central traffic cop to control the flow of legislation, some bills remain on the Senate floor for weeks, often at the expense of the substance, and chances for passage, of the measure.

Amendments to a Bill   A key procedural rule in the House requires that all discussion on the floor and all amendments to legislation must be *germane*, that is, relevant to the bill being considered. The Senate, in contrast, places no limits on the addition of amendments to a bill.

The ability to attach unrelated **riders** to a bill can sometimes help a senator secure passage of a pet project by attaching it to a popular proposal. Another important consequence of riders is that committees cannot serve the gatekeeper function on legislative wording, as in the House; Senate committees are less important in this function than their counterparts in the House. However, heavy use of riders has led to problems. When budget bills were considered, members sometimes added so many riders, each containing spending provisions desired by those individual members, that the result was known as a "Christmas tree bill," laden with financial "ornaments." The president had to either sign or veto a bill in its entirety, a requirement that led to spending bills containing expensive pet projects inserted by legislators. When Congress passed the **line item veto** in 1996, it allowed specific provisions of select taxing and spending bills to be vetoed independently of the rest of the bill. When the Supreme Court ruled the line item veto unconstitutional in 1998, the power of riders returned, leading President Bush to ask for its reinstitution.

Quick Review

Rules Committee

- Directs the flow of bills through the legislative process.
- Receives bills that have been approved in committee.
- Issues rules that determine which bills will be discussed, length of the debate, and which amendments will be allowed.
- Can delay or kill a bill by refusing to attach a rule to it.

rules The decisions made by the House Rules Committee and voted on by the full House to determine the flow of legislation—when a bill will be discussed, for how long, and if amendments can be offered.

unanimous consent agreement The process by which the normal rules of Congress are waived unless a single member disagrees.

rider An amendment to a bill in the Senate totally unrelated to the bill subject but attached to a popular measure in the hopes that it too will pass.

line item veto The power given to the president to veto a specific provision of a bill involving taxing and spending. Previously the president had to veto an entire bill. Declared unconstitutional by the Supreme Court in 1998.

Filibusters and Cloture   Senate debate has few restrictions. Opponents can derail a bill by **filibuster**. This technique allows a senator to speak against a bill—or just talk about anything at all—to "hold the floor" and prevent the Senate from moving forward with its business. Examples include the repeated filibusters used to derail the campaign finance reform legislation. He or she may yield to other like-minded senators, and the marathon debate can continue for hours or even days.

The record for the longest individual filibuster belongs to Senator Strom Thurmond of South Carolina, who spoke against the Civil Rights Act of 1957 for an uninterrupted twenty-four hours and eighteen minutes.

Over time, the Senate has made filibusters less onerous, first by interrupting them when the Senate's workday ended, and then by allowing them to be interrupted by a vote to consider other work. In recent years, senators have begun using a scheduling rule called a **hold** on legislation to stall a bill. This century-old practice was once a courtesy used specifically to keep a piece of legislation from being debated until a member could return to the chamber for the discussion. In recent years, however, senators have used holds to secretly indicate that any debate on a bill was pointless; they intended to filibuster it either because of objections to it or because the bill's supporters had not yet offered concessions in its wording.[65] Senator Jesse Helms (R.-NC) used this tactic as chair of the Senate Foreign Relations Committee to block forty-three ambassadorial appointments because he disagreed with the State Department's policies. By the end of 1999, Senator Herb Kohl (D.-WI) announced that he would place a hold on all legislation, including spending bills, unless dairy legislation that he opposed was allowed to die. At one point, several members threatened a hold on the adjournment vote unless legislation they wanted was supported.[66]

A hold can block several bills indefinitely, with the rule now in effect that requires sixty votes, rather than a simple majority, for passage. After witnessing the use of this tactic to block a $145 billion highway bill in late 1997, Majority Leader Trent Lott explained, "This is the Senate. And if any senator or group of senators want to be obstructionist, the only way you can break that is time."[67]

Between 1940 and 1965, only nineteen filibusters were employed for major legislation, but between 1992 and 1994 the Republicans conducted twenty-eight filibusters to derail the Democrats, who outnumbered them in the Senate. In fact, this period had more filibusters than the previous sixty years, reflecting the increasingly partisan nature of the body.

After Majority Leader Trent Lott took control of the Senate in 1996 and contended with Democrats who were returning what Republicans had done to them four years earlier by filibustering everything, he complained: "We are completely balled up and it's not my fault. I want us to sober up here now and get on with the business of the Senate."[68] But when Senate control changed over to the Democrats in May 2001, Trent Lott and the other Republicans were back using the same tactics to slow down the agenda of Tom Daschle and the Senate Democrats. Figure 4.4 shows that the number of filibusters dropped from thirty-five in 1999 to twenty-three in 2004.

How does the Senate accomplish anything under these conditions? In 1917, it adopted a procedure known as **cloture**, through which senators can vote to limit debate and stop a filibuster. Originally, cloture required approval of two-thirds of the senators present and voting (sixty-seven members if all were present), but when such a vote proved too difficult to achieve, the required majority was reduced to three-fifths of the members, or sixty votes.

Although the majority required for a cloture vote can be difficult to muster, the number of successful cloture votes has increased in recent years. Even if cloture has been voted, however, a postcloture filibuster can continue for thirty more hours.[69] The value senators place on this technique was evident in the 104th Congress when, despite the continual bogging down in concurrent filibusters, the members refused to reform the technique further. As a result, cloture votes occurred in the double

filibuster A technique in which a senator speaks against a bill or talks about nothing specific just to "hold the floor" and prevent the Senate from moving forward with a vote. He or she may yield to other like-minded senators, so that the marathon debate can continue for hours or even days.

hold A request by a senator not to bring a measure up for consideration by the full Senate.

cloture A procedure through which a vote of sixty senators can limit debate and stop a filibuster.

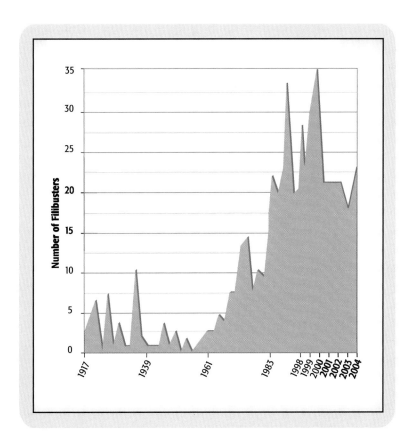

Figure 4.4   Senate Filibusters, 1917–2004
Source: Courtesy of Senate Historical Office, 6/14/02, post-2001 calculations drawn from number cloture votes & determination of formal filibusters senate historical office website, virtual Reference Desk www.senate.gov last checked 8/22/05.

digits throughout the rest of the 1990s, many unsuccessful, as with the Campaign Finance Reform bill.

Liberals who objected to the use of filibusters to stall civil rights legislation took advantage of that same tactic to combat and sometimes defeat key measures of the Contract with America. Some argue that cloture and filibusters empower minorities, whereas others claim they are stalling tactics that obstruct the will of the majority. This very debate led to the pivotal effort by Republicans in 2005 to vote into effect the so-called "nuclear option" eliminating the filibuster for judicial nominations. As outlined in the case study for Chapter 2, only after moderate and maverick senators, seven from each party, brokered a deal to avoid the vote, retaining the right to filibuster nominations in "extreme circumstances," and arranged for immediate votes on several disputed judicial candidates, was the crisis averted and the filibuster retained—for the moment.

To place the filibuster in perspective, remember that although it is abused on occasion, senators use it only on major issues where a large minority intensely opposes the majority's plan. Unhappy minorities should not necessarily win all they want, but neither should any political system systematically neglect the demands of a large minority. Filibusters force the majority to hear the minority and perhaps respond to certain demands. All in all, the filibuster's ability to give voice to minorities probably outweigh the frustrations it creates for the majority.

Informal Rules and Norms   In addition to its formal rules, Congress, like most large organizations, has informal, unwritten rules that facilitate its day-to-day operations. High among these has been the traditional rule of **seniority**, in which a member's rank in the House or Senate depends on length of service there. In the past, seniority was key to committee membership, and the only way to become a committee chair was to accumulate more years of continuous service on that committee than any other majority party member.

Question for Reflection

Few congressional rules raise such interesting questions about Congress's ability to approach democracy as the Senate's filibuster and cloture devices. Does the ability to talk a bill to death, or to silence those seeking to do so, promote or hinder the democratic process?

seniority An informal, unwritten rule of Congress that more senior members (those who have served longer than others) are appointed to committees and as chairpersons of committees. This "rule" is being diluted in the House as other systems are developed for committee appointments.

Apprenticeship was another traditional norm, whereby younger members were expected to sit quietly and learn their legislative craft from their elders. "To get along, go along" was the wisdom that Speaker Sam Rayburn once preached to junior members in persuading them to follow his lead.

Yet another traditional norm, designed to keep friction to a minimum, has been that debates on the floor and in committees are conducted with the utmost civility. One member never speaks directly to another; instead, members address the presiding officer, who may deflect damaging comments by ruling them out of order. In addition, whenever debates occur between members, titles, not names, are used, as in "I would like to commend the Representative from State X." Political scientist Donald Matthews has labeled such adherence to unwritten but generally accepted and informally enforced norms as "the folkways of the Senate."[70] Even the most bitter of political rivals still refer to each other as "the distinguished senator from . . ." or "my good friend and esteemed colleague" before proceeding to attack everything the other holds dear.

In recent years, however, increasing breakdowns in this norm lead some to wonder if it still exists. As the two parties have become more partisan and their ideologies have drifted further and further apart, members of Congress have increasingly stooped to trading insults with, or shouting at, each other in hearings or in debates on the floor. In 1996, a highly agitated Representative Sam Gibbons (D.-FL) called his Republican colleagues "a bunch of fascists" and "dictators" before stalking out of a hearing room and yanking on the necktie of a California colleague. In 1997, one debate on the House floor ended with House Majority Whip Tom DeLay (R.-TX) forcibly shoving Representative David R. Obey (D.-WI) before the two men were separated.[71] This lack of civility has persuaded many of the more moderate members to leave their positions early.[72] In November 2003, after Majority Leader Bill Frist led an all-night demonstration filibuster by his Republican colleagues on their perception that the Democrats were holding up President Bush's judicial nominees by filibuster, Minority Leader Harry Reid broke the usual civility rule when he said, "I've never seen such amateur leadership in all the time I've been in Congress, 21 years."[73]

These differences have increased since Speaker Newt Gingrich and the Republicans took power in 1994 and changed the way that Congress operated. The sharp differences in partisanship, the unwillingness to accept legislative compromise or defeats, and the increasing number of legislators who have few relationships with their colleagues because their weekends are spent going home to raise money, consult their constituents, and see their families, have broken the past bonds of civility in the chambers.

Such trends, according to congressional scholar Burdett Loomis, have meant change for the Senate, as we saw in the Bipartisan Campaign Finance Reform case study. Regarding the prospects of legislative passage Loomis has said, "However much we may want to romanticize the world's greatest deliberative body, the cold fact remains that the 1980s and 1990s have witnessed a consistent growth in partisan behavior and position-taking in the U.S. Senate." Fewer and fewer members of Congress in general, he charges, seem to put the national interests ahead of those of their own party, making it harder for the two parties to find a point of compromise.[74]

When more than half of the freshmen members in the 104th Congress made their maiden floor speech in the opening session in January 1995, it was clear that the apprenticeship norm was dying in the House, and it has been long since dead in the Senate. Thus, a new norm, political party loyalty, might be replacing seniority, apprenticeship, and civility, at least in the House.[75]

The Senate is currently more traditional than the House in its regard for seniority. Dilution of seniority rights began in 1953 when Senate Minority Leader Lyndon Johnson instituted what became known as the "Johnson rule," which provided that no Democratic senator would receive more than one major committee assignment until everyone had one. Republicans adopted a similar rule in 1965. Thirty years later, however, when Republicans once again controlled the Senate, Majority Leader Bob Dole decided instead to let seniority determine every committee chair, even though several Republican colleagues were uncomfortable with certain results—most notably, archconservative Jesse Helms of North Carolina chaired the Foreign Relations Committee, and ninety-two-year-old Strom Thurmond of South Carolina chaired the Armed Services Committee.

Two other norms used to push legislation through Congress are *specialization* and *reciprocity*. Legislators are expected to develop a certain expertise on one or more issues as a way to help the body in its lawmaking role. Members who lack expertise in a particular policy area defer to policy specialists with more knowledge, with the understanding that the favor will be reciprocated.

When reciprocity is applied to votes on key measures the result is called **logrolling**, which helps legislators cooperate effectively. The term comes from a competition in which two lumberjacks maintain their balance on a floating log by working together to spin it with their feet. In congressional logrolling, legislators seek the assistance of colleagues by offering to support legislation the colleagues both favor. For example, a Democratic senator from California might support a flood control project in Mississippi that has no relevance to West Coast voters, provided the Republican senator from Mississippi promises to support a measure delaying the closing of an army base in California.[76] The House leadership's "Freedom to Farm" Act in the 104th Congress, which continued farm subsidies for sugar, peanuts, and milk, passed without trouble because it was paired with a food-stamp program that brought it the votes of the liberal Northeast representatives.[77] In an era of government spending cuts, however, the notion of reciprocity has faded somewhat.

A traditional form of the logrolling norm is called **pork-barrel legislation**, special-interest spending for members' districts or states. It is named for the practice of distributing salt pork as a treat to sailors on the high seas. In this case, members of Congress see their job as "bringing home the bacon" in the form of support for jobs and programs in their districts: dams and highways, military bases, new federal buildings, high-tech company support, or even research grants for local colleges and universities. The distribution of district or state pork-barrel spending tends to follow power. Thus it is not surprising that Mississippi, the home state of former majority leader Trent Lott, got the most pork in 1997, receiving nearly $850 billion, or an average of $310 per capita. The state of Wyoming, with no powerful legislators, received only an average of eighty-three cents per capita. But these benefits are not limited by party. Leetown, West Virginia, hometown of Senate Appropriations Committee ranking Democrat Robert Byrd, was awarded $6 million for the National Center for Cool and Cold Water Aquaculture, winning it a 1998 annual "oinker" award from the Citizens Against Government Waste.[78]

It is not uncommon for revenue bills to contain their own version of pork: tax loopholes and breaks for companies in specific districts. Given Congress's program-cutting mood in recent years, a new form of "negative pork" has developed to distribute the cuts in different areas. Sometimes the cuts have been so contentious, for example, military base closings, that Congress had to create special bipartisan commissions to recommend them.

Although many people criticize these spendthrift ways, attracting federal spending is the traditional way members of Congress represent their districts. In many districts, federal buildings and roads are named for local members of Congress, thus solidifying their reelection support. The deadlock over the 1997 Omnibus Highway Spending Bill was eventually broken by an agreement with House Transportation Committee Chair Bud Shuster (R.-PA) to secretly dole out more than $9 billion for highways and bridges in states and districts around the country. One legislator labeled it "a pork barrel bill—I fear—to end all pork barrel bills for the decade."[79] As "Tip" O'Neill explained, "All politics is local." The line item veto was designed to eliminate such expensive practices. But, given the Supreme Court's

logrolling A temporary political alliance between two policy actors who agree to support each other's policy goals.

pork-barrel legislation Policies and programs designed to create special benefits for a member's district, such as bridges, highways, dams, and military installations, all of which translate into jobs and money for the local economy and improve reelection chances for the incumbent.

1998 decision, this option is no longer available, unless it is passed in a more acceptable fashion by Congress or approved by constitutional amendment.

How Members Make Voting Decisions

Political scientists have long sought to understand why members of Congress vote as they do. Their research suggests seven major sources of influence.

Personal Views   Personal views and political ideology are the central variables in determining members' voting decisions. When legislators care deeply about a policy matter, they usually vote their own preferences, sometimes risking their political careers in the process. Party leaders recognize the importance of personal convictions. "I have never asked a member to vote against his conscience," said former speaker of the House John McCormack. "If he mentions his conscience—that's all. I don't press him any further."[80]

Sometimes such votes show the best aspects of congressional representation. In early 1995, Republican senator Mark Hatfield offered to resign rather than provide his party with the winning vote to pass the Balanced Budget Amendment, saying he opposed "tinkering with the Constitution." Majority Leader Robert Dole declined his offer. These personal views, however, can reflect other factors as well—most notably the desires of a member's constituents.

Constituents   In votes with high visibility, constituents have a significant influence on their representative's voting decisions.[81] No representative wants to lose touch with the district or appear to care more about national politics than about the people back home. This was why Oklahoma Representative Mike Synar—a four-term liberal Democrat who supported gun control and the Family Leave Act and opposed a measure requiring parent notification if a teenage daughter has an abortion—was defeated in a 1994 primary in his conservative district. A former supporter explained that Synar had "lost touch." To avoid these situations, members regularly conduct surveys and return to their districts to learn constituents' opinions about issues on the congressional agenda.

On votes of lesser importance, or everyday activities in which the general public pays little attention, the members tend to follow other cues. However, they remain aware that opponents or a rival interest group might cite their votes in the next election.

Party Affiliation   A member's vote can often be explained by political party affiliation. The frequency of legislators voting based on party position steadily increased from below 60 percent by members in both parties in 1970 to more than 80 percent in the late 1990s and through 2002.[82] Sometimes, though, members vote against their party.[83] In the 104th Congress, six Democrats, including Alabama senator Richard Shelby and Colorado senator Ben Nighthorse Campbell, found themselves voting so many times with the opposition party that they switched to the Republican party.

If the national party leadership or the president is committed to a particular vote, the chances increase for a vote along party lines. If the party's position runs counter to the member's personal views, however, it is less likely to influence the way he or she votes.[84]

The President   Sometimes the president seeks to influence a member's vote by calling him or her to the White House for a consultation. The president may offer something in return (support for another piece of legislation or a spending project in the member's district) or threaten some kind of punishment for noncompliance. If the Supreme Court had accepted the line item veto, the president's influence over members' votes might have been strengthened. Without it, the president cannot negotiate votes from members who oppose him by threatening to eliminate a favorite piece of pork-barrel legislation. Sometimes the consultation with the president aims simply to make the member look important to the voters back home, but even that serves as a political favor, inducing the member to look more kindly on presidential requests for legislative support.[85]

Presidential lobbying of undecided or politically exposed members can be key in a vote. First-term Democratic representative Marjorie Margolies-Mezvinsky of Pennsylvania learned this lesson in the summer of 1993, when her party's congressional leadership pressed her to support a deficit-reduction bill that would raise taxes and offend her mainly Republican constituents. On the day of the vote Margolies-Mezvinsky decided to oppose the bill. However, when the vote tied at 217–217 (which meant that the bill would fail), President Clinton implored her to back the bill for the good of the country and the party. After casting the deciding vote in favor of the bill, she lost the 1994 election to the same Republican she had beaten two years earlier.[86]

Interest Groups Important interest groups and political action committees that have provided funds for past elections try to influence a member's vote by lobbying intensely on key issues. In addition, lobbying organizations seek access to members of Congress through personal visits and calls. Sometimes they apply pressure by generating grass-roots campaigns among the general public, jamming members' phone lines and fax machines, and filling their mailbags. In the end, interest groups and their financial political action committees (PACs) are much less relevant on votes than on access to the members to influence their thinking on an issue.

In considering tax legislation, for instance, so many prominent and well-dressed financial lobbyists prowl the Capitol seeking to influence the outcome that the halls are nicknamed "Gucci Gulch," for the fancy leather shoes lobbyists wear in the hallway button-holing members to lobby them.[87] But in certain extraordinary cases interest groups have been highly influential in final votes. In 1987, both liberal and conservative groups prevailed on followers to pressure the Senate concerning controversial Judge Robert Bork's nomination for the Supreme Court. So many calls came in during this debate that some members' telephone switchboards literally broke down.

Congressional Staff One job of congressional staff members is to sort through the various sources of pressure and information. In so doing, they themselves may pressure members to vote in a particular way. Staff members organize hearings,

▲ The Coalition for a Fair and Independent Judiciary protested the Senate's consideration of the "nuclear option" restricting the use of filibusters on judicial confirmations by delivering petitions containing one million signatures in April 2005 supporting the filibuster. Because of the compromise of the "Gang of 14" moderate and maverick Senators from both parties, the issue never came to a vote.

conduct research, draft bill markups and amendments, prepare reports, assist committee chairs, interact with the press, and perform other liaison activities with lobbyists and constituents. As important players in the political game, they have their own preferences on many issues. Their expertise and political commitments often help them convince members of Congress to vote for favored bills. Most often, staff people's political views echo and reinforce their legislator's, and they simply help members of Congress be more efficient at meeting their main goals, to please their constituents, promote their party, and vote their convictions.[88]

Congressional staffs proliferated in the 1960s as the federal government grew in size and complexity. Members of both houses of Congress became increasingly dependent on staff for information about proposed legislation. Moreover, in an effort to stay closer to voters, members established district-based offices staffed by aides.[89]

Colleagues and the Cue Structure   What do legislators do when all these influences—personal convictions, voters, party leadership, the president, interest groups, and staff—send contradictory messages about how to vote on a particular bill? And what do they do when time is too short to gather necessary information about an issue before a vote? They develop a personal intelligence system that scholars label a *cue structure*. The cues can come from various sources: members of Congress who are experts, knowledgeable members of the executive branch, lobbyists, or media reports.[90] Sometimes the cues come from special groups within Congress, such as the Black or Women's Caucuses, the Democratic Study Group, or the Republicans' Conservative Opportunity Society. Members also seek cues from their particular "buddy system:" other members whom they respect, who come from the same kinds of districts, and who have similar goals. In voting, members generally look first for disagreement among their various cues and then try to prioritize the cues to reach an acceptable vote. This "consensus model" suggested by political scientist John Kingdon does seem to hold when members vote on issues of average importance, but on highly controversial issues that may affect their reelection prospects, members are far more likely to follow their own opinions.[91]

HOW A BILL BECOMES A LAW

Spread over several square blocks of Washington, D.C., are six buildings that house congressional offices. An underground subway carries members of Congress from their offices to the Capitol, a magnificent structure that includes the Senate and House chambers where the 535 elected senators and representatives work when Congress is in session.

As you know from the case study at the beginning of the chapter, transforming a bill into a law is a long and complicated process. In order to succeed, a bill must win 218 votes in the House, 51 votes in the Senate, and one presidential signature. The process may take years because of disagreements among the two houses or the need to muster sixty votes to break a filibuster in the Senate. In the most controversial cases, members know that if the president is adamantly opposed to a bill and will not negotiate, then a two-thirds vote of both Houses will be needed to override the anticipated veto. Conflicting policy goals, special interests, ideology, partisanship, and political ambitions often delay or obstruct the passage of legislation. Most bills never even reach the House or Senate floors for debate.[92] Yet some do manage to make their way through the administrative and political maze. Let's see how that can happen.

The Congressional Agenda

congressional agenda A list of bills to be considered by Congress.

When a member of Congress drafts and submits a piece of legislation dealing with a particular issue, that issue is said to be on the **congressional agenda**. Although much of the agenda consists of mandated business—such as reauthorizations of earlier actions or appropriations for government spending—a new issue must gain widespread public attention to be viewed as important enough to require legislative action.[93] National events may bring issues to prominence, such as terrorist attacks and homeland security costs. Other issues, such as health care or a balanced budget, build momentum for years before reaching the level of national consciousness that ensures congressional action. Idea sources for bills include the president, cabinet, research institutes, scholars, journalists, voters, and sometimes **lobbyists** (people paid to further the aims of some interest group among members of Congress).[94] Any citizen can draft legislation and ask a representative or senator to submit it. Only members of Congress can introduce a bill.

Congress Considers the Bill

Once a bill has been introduced in Congress, it follows a series of steps on its way to becoming law (see Figure 4.5). In the House, every piece of legislation is *introduced* by a representative, who hands it to the clerk of the House or places it in a box called the "hopper." In the Senate, a senator must be recognized by the presiding officer to announce the introduction of a bill. In either case, the bill is first *read* (printed in the *Congressional Record*) and then referred to the appropriate committee (or committees, if it is especially complex) by the speaker of the House or the Senate majority leader.

After a bill has been assigned to a committee, the committee chair assigns it to a subcommittee. The subcommittee process usually begins with **hearings**, formal proceedings in which a range of people testify on the bill's pros and cons. Witnesses are usually experts on the bill's subject matter; or they may be people affected by the issue, including various administration officials and highly visible citizens. Such was the case in March 2005, when Congress subpoenaed baseball players Mark McGuire, Sammy Sosa, Rafael Palmiero, and Curt Schilling, among others, to speak about steroid use in baseball. Subcommittee chairs can influence the final content of a bill and its chances of passage by arranging mostly either friendly or hostile witnesses or by planning for the type of testimony that will attract media attention.

ABC News/Prentice Hall Video Library

Price of Victory
The Medicare Bill

▲ Baseball players (L to R) Sammy Sato, Mark McGuire, Rafael Palmiero, and Curt Schilling testify before Congress in 2005 on the use of steroids in their sport.

lobbyists People paid to pressure members of Congress to further the aims of an interest group.

hearings Formal proceedings in which a range of people testify on a bill's pros and cons.

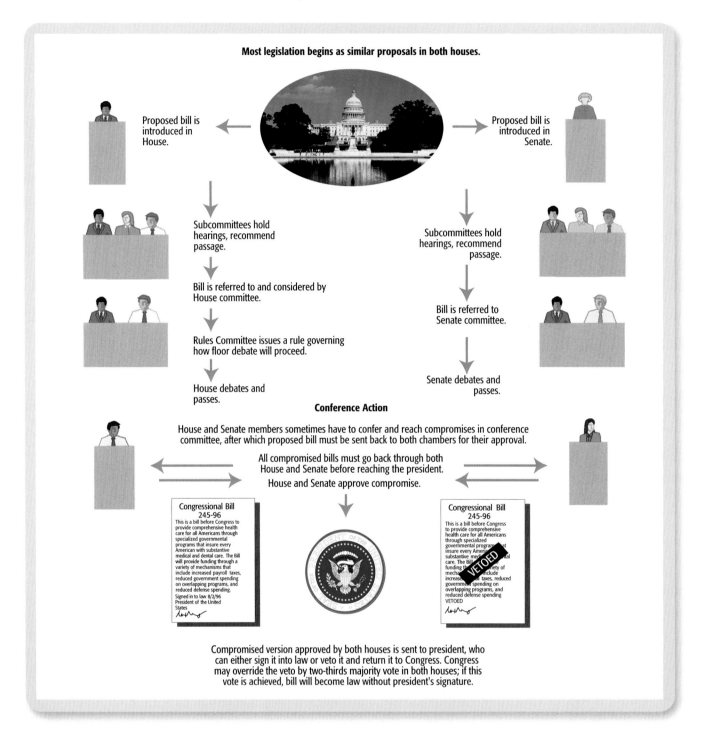

Most legislation begins as similar proposals in both houses.

Proposed bill is introduced in House.

Proposed bill is introduced in Senate.

Subcommittees hold hearings, recommend passage.

Subcommittees hold hearings, recommend passage.

Bill is referred to and considered by House committee.

Bill is referred to Senate committee.

Rules Committee issues a rule governing how floor debate will proceed.

House debates and passes.

Senate debates and passes.

Conference Action

House and Senate members sometimes have to confer and reach compromises in conference committee, after which proposed bill must be sent back to both chambers for their approval.

All compromised bills must go back through both House and Senate before reaching the president.

House and Senate approve compromise.

Congressional Bill
245-96

This is a bill before Congress to provide comprehensive health care for all Americans through specialized governmental programs that insure every American with substantive medical and dental care. The Bill will provide funding through a variety of mechanisms that include increased payroll taxes, reduced government spending on overlapping programs, and reduced defense spending.
Signed in to law 8/2/96
President of the United States

Congressional Bill
245-96

This is a bill before Congress to provide comprehensive health care for all Americans through specialized governmental programs that insure every American with substantive medical and dental care. The Bill provide funding through a variety of mechanisms that include increased payroll taxes, reduced government spending on overlapping programs, and reduced defense spending
VETOED

Compromised version approved by both houses is sent to president, who can either sign it into law or veto it and return it to Congress. Congress may override the veto by two-thirds majority vote in both houses; if this vote is achieved, bill will become law without president's signature.

Figure 4.5   How a Bill Becomes a Law

After hearings, the subcommittee holds a **markup session** to revise the bill. The subcommittee then sends the bill back to the full committee for additional discussion, markup, and voting. Approval at this level sends the bill to the full House, but most bills must first move through the House Rules Committee, which schedules the timing, length, and conditions of debate, such as whether or not amendments would be allowed, under which bills are debated on the House floor.

Once a bill reaches the House floor, its fate is still far from certain. Debate procedures are complex, and members take many votes (usually on proposed amendments) on measures containing almost indecipherable language before the bill

markup session A subcommittee meeting to revise a bill.

secures final acceptance. To expedite matters, the House or the Senate can act as a *committee of the whole* in which all members can function as a committee rather than as a formal legislative body. Committee rules are looser than those that apply to the full House. For instance, only 100 House members need be present when the House operates as the Committee of the Whole, whereas normally 218 representatives must be on the floor to conduct business. Opponents have numerous opportunities at this stage to defeat or significantly change the bill's wording, and thus its impact.

Being much smaller than the House, the Senate is an intimate body that operates with much less formality. After committee deliberation, bills are simply brought to the floor through informal agreements among Senate leaders. Individual senators can even bring bills directly to the floor, bypassing committees altogether. They do this by offering their bill as an amendment to whatever bill is then pending, even if the two are unrelated.

The House of Representatives uses an *electronic voting system* that posts each member's name on the wall of the chamber. Members insert a plastic card into a box attached to the chairs to vote "yea," "nay," or "present." The results of the vote then appear alongside each legislator's name. The electronic voting system has increased participation at roll calls, and watchdog groups have been known to keep a close eye on legislators who are frequently absent on important roll calls. In addition, legislators find the electronic system handy; it enables them to check how their colleagues are voting. But even if successful in the House and Senate, proposed legislation still faces hurdles. To become law, the bills passed in both houses of Congress must be worded identically. As mentioned earlier, a conference committee composed of both House and Senate members reconciles the differences in language and creates a single version of the bill.[95]

When the differences between versions of a bill have been ironed out, the final version returns to both houses for approval. If it is approved by both chambers, it becomes an **enrolled act, or resolution**, and goes to the White House for the president's signature or veto. Measures that require spending are offered in one of thirteen **appropriations bills**, based on authorized amounts passed by Congress. Thus, the Congress has two opportunities to debate a measure: first the measure itself, then its funding.

The President Considers the Bill   Once Congress has voted and sent a bill on to the president, four scenarios are possible. The president can sign the bill, making it law. Or the president can **veto** it; that is, return the bill to Congress with a statement of reasons for refusing to sign it. At that point, Congress can **override** the president's action with a two-thirds vote in both the House and Senate. Congress can rarely muster this level of opposition to a sitting president, so vetoes are overridden less than 10 percent of the time.[96] Of President Clinton's twenty-five vetoes in his first five years of office, only one was overridden. Although President Bush has repeatedly used the threat of a veto to try to enforce his spending priorities, by March, 2006, he had set a record in not issuing a single veto. Of course, his own party controlled both Houses of Congress during that time.[97] Still, such threats remind members that passage might now require a two-thirds vote. For example, in summer 2005, Senate Majority Leader Bill Frist announced his support for stem-cell research legislation "in the name of science," thus increasing the likelihood that Congress would fund it. But President Bush at the same time killed the measure when he vowed that he would veto this bill.[98]

Two other outcomes are possible. Once a bill reaches the president's desk, the president can simply do nothing, in which case the bill automatically becomes law after ten legislative days (not counting Sundays, and providing that Congress is still in session) in spite of remaining unsigned. The president can also refuse to sign a bill that Congress passes in the last ten days of its session. If Congress has adjourned, the unsigned bill automatically dies. This is called a **pocket veto**.

enrolled act (or resolution) The final version of a bill, approved by both chambers of Congress.

appropriations bill A separate bill that must be passed by Congress to fund spending measures.

veto Presidential power to forbid or prevent an action of Congress.

override The two-thirds vote of both houses of Congress required to pass a law over the veto of the president.

pocket veto Presidential refusal to sign or veto a bill that Congress passes in the last ten days of its session; by not being signed, it automatically dies when Congress adjourns.

From time to time, even if the president reluctantly signs a bill, a signing statement might also be released that seems to undercut aspects of the measure. This action is taken in anticipation of a Supreme Court challenge to the measure, knowing that the Court may use this statement in deciding whether to uphold the measure.

Obstacles to Passage of a Bill

This textbook approach to passing a bill rarely works smoothly because so many obstacles lie in the path of success. The backers of any bill must win support at each stage of the lawmaking process. They must find majorities in each committee, they must find enthusiastic backers during each formal discussion, and so forth. Opponents of the bill have a much easier job. They can kill it at any step along the way. Sometimes they do not even need a majority; one unfriendly legislator in the right place may be sufficient.

Imagine how you, as a member of Congress, might stop a bill you disliked. You might take any of the following actions:

1. Lobby members of your party conference or caucus to stop, or at least slow down, consideration of the bill.
2. Convince the speaker to stop, or slow down, consideration of the bill.
3. Lobby committee and subcommittee members to oppose the bill in committee hearings, deliberations, markups, and votes.
4. Lobby the Rules Committee to oppose giving the bill a rule, which dictates the timing and terms of a bill's debate.
5. Lobby colleagues on the House floor not to vote for the rule, thus preventing the bill from ever reaching floor discussion.
6. Call press conferences and give interviews trying to build a grass-roots or interest-group coalition against the bill.
7. Propose a series of amendments that weaken the bill or make it less attractive to potential supporters, then vote for unattractive amendments at every opportunity.
8. If the bill does gain passage in the House, use the same tactics to stop it in the Senate, mustering opposition in committees and on the Senate floor. Be sure to have senators also gain media attention against the bill, whipping up negative reaction to its possible passage.
9. Find senators who hate the bill and persuade them to filibuster, or place a hold on the bill yourself.
10. If both House and Senate pass the bill, work against it in the conference committee, if one convenes.
11. If Congress passes the bill, seek White House allies who might persuade the president to veto it.
12. Once the bill becomes law, use similar steps to prevent Congress from funding the measure.
13. If the bill becomes law and is funded, work to rescind the law or to keep funding so low it becomes ineffective. Or, lobby the executive branch to delay the bill's implementation.
14. If all else fails, have faith that some group opposed to the bill will mount a constitutional challenge to the law, going all the way to the Supreme Court if necessary.

This array of blocking options favors those who oppose change. What you think of this system depends on how you like the status quo. A majority of congressional liberals in the 1960s often felt frustrated by the difficulty in working their agenda through a conservative minority of Republicans and southern Democrats. Today, however, some of those same liberals find value in these legislative obstacles.

The best example of how all of these obstacles work is what happened to the Republican Congress's effort after the 1994 elections to pass the Contract with America.

Speaker Gingrich had vowed that the first one hundred days of the 104th Congress would be devoted to passing ten major items: a balanced-budget amendment, a line item veto, dealing with crime and closing loopholes in the death penalty, reforming welfare, dealing with "deadbeat parents" who failed to support children, creating school voucher programs, creating a middle-class tax cut, restricting the United Nations' ability to command U.S. troops, reforming Social Security, cutting capital gains taxes, reforming the legal system and product liability/malpractice suits, and establishing congressional term limits.

House Republicans were unified in passing nearly all of these promises, but the Senate considered these measures at a much more leisurely pace and greatly increased the time that it took to pass many of the measures. In addition, all of the measures had to be greatly watered down to have any chance of President Bill Clinton signing them. The balanced-budget amendment failed twice by a single vote. And the term limits proposal was defeated by a combination of amendments and vigorous lobbying.

Another example of legislative obstacles, as outlined in the case study, was the effort to block the reform of campaign finance by limiting soft money contributions and creating electoral spending limits. This measure was killed in 1998 and again in 1999 by then Majority Leader Trent Lott's substituting a less attractive amended bill and enforcing a cloture vote to shut off an anticipated filibuster. Campaign finance reform garnered only fifty-one votes in 1998, nine votes short of the sixty votes needed for cloture.[99] It lost again by a narrower margin in 1999, despite the fact that a majority in the Senate appeared willing to pass campaign finance reform. But in 2002, a combination of both the Jeffords party switch and the Enron scandal changed the climate, and the obstacles to passage were overcome.

Overcoming the Legislative Obstacles

In recent years, the Republican Congress has sought ways to overcome the traditional obstacles to passing legislation.[100] With all of the various blocking points that threaten to doom single pieces of legislation, party leaders in Congress have begun to package the biggest and most important legislation into so-called **omnibus legislation**, also known as "megabills" or "packages." The idea here is to hide controversial pieces of legislation inside packages of related bills most likely to pass. The president then must sign the entire bill. Members of Congress receive cover in supporting the controversial legislation, interest groups and their financial PACs are less likely to punish supporters for their votes, and the media sometimes lose track of the controversial issues. A symptom of this trend toward fewer but longer and more complex bills is the increase in the sheer size of the laws over the past half century, from averaging 2.5 pages to 16.2 pages.[101]

The Welfare Reform Bill of 1996, with all of its different provisions to limit the amount of time people could receive welfare and to encourage them to work, was an omnibus legislation. To pass this comprehensive measure, Republicans had to drop cutbacks in such "safety net" items as school lunches and turn to the more moderate Senate version of the bill before President Clinton would sign it. This strategy failed, however, with the health-care reform effort in 1994, when the bill's complex provisions offered multiple targets for medical interest groups to attack.

With many controversial appropriations measures to be passed each year under the budgeting procedure, leaders have had to resort to the passage of **continuing resolutions** that provide stop-gap funding to keep the government running. These resolutions must be passed by both houses of Congress and do not require a presidential signature, thus making them apparently veto-proof. Such resolutions were once common for temporary funding of one to three months for a handful of agencies. But learning from the late 1980s, when the procedure was used for all thirteen major appropriations measures, the Republican Congress used this technique to

omnibus legislation A large bill that combines a number of smaller pieces of legislation.
continuing resolution A bill passed by Congress and signed by the president that enables the federal government to keep operating under the previous year's appropriations.

overcome delays in approving the budget. The attempt backfired in late 1995 and early 1996 when disagreements between Congress and the president forced the government to shut down twice because even continuing resolutions could not be agreed upon and passed. To heal political damage, Republicans in 1997 pushed through an automatic continuing resolution to keep the government going in the event that the two parties disagreed on future funding. The same technique was used that year for emergency legislation that provided disaster relief for the states and funded the peacekeepers in Bosnia.[102]

From time to time, when faced with highly controversial legislative subjects, congressional leaders bypass the normal procedures for drafting bills, preferring instead to handle problems by creating special purpose **task forces**. Such task forces, groups of legislators charged with drafting legislation and coordinating strategy to forge a consensus on an issue, increase the communication among members and thus speed the passage of controversial legislation. Newt Gingrich used this means most successfully to push portions of the Contract with America along. In recent years, Speaker Hastert has abandoned the use of task forces in the House, while then-Majority Leader Trent Lott created in 2000 the bipartisan Senate National Security Working Group to examine possible legislation dealing with topics such as missile defenses and weapons control.

Even with all of these strategies, members of Congress often resort to presenting their cases directly to the media either to push or to block legislation. And, when all else fails, as outlined in the box above, members of the majority can use parliamentary tricks such as holding the vote open longer than normal in order to make enough deals to switch votes and win. One favorite strategy, employed frequently by Senator Robert Byrd of West Virginia, is to use a quirk in *Robert's Rules of Order* and vote for the majority, even though he did not support them, knowing that by rule he could later switch his vote and force the body to reconsider the measure (at which point different members might be present and voting or deals could be made to switch votes). In the old days, legislators used an *inside strategy* of lining up votes. But now they often resort to gaps in the body's rules, parliamentary tricks, and/or an *outside strategy* of giving speeches, press conferences, and interviews to try to mobilize public opinion and interest group assistance to work their will.

ADDITIONAL FUNCTIONS OF CONGRESS

Aside from enacting legislation, two of the most important functions of Congress are **oversight** and budget control. Congressional oversight involves monitoring the effectiveness of laws passed by Congress. The Legislative Reorganization Act of 1946 specifically directs congressional committees to exercise "continuous watchfulness" over executive branch agencies that carry out the laws, and to see that the laws are implemented as Congress intended. This oversight can be either *legislative* (in the form of pilot programs, special studies, or cost/benefit analysis) or *investigative* (in the form of hearings to examine possible legal or ethical infractions).[103] Examples of oversight investigations include the 1974 Watergate hearings, which toppled Richard Nixon, and the 1987 Iran-Contra hearings, which threatened Ronald Reagan.[104] More recently, the 2002 investigation by ten congressional committees into the causes of the Enron corporation collapse led to calls for changes in the government's regulation of businesses and energy corporations.

Congress oversees administrative implementation of its mandates without exercising day-to-day control by several means, including the **legislative veto**. The legislative veto allows the president or an executive agency to act, subject to later approval or disapproval of either one or both houses of Congress, or sometimes even the committees in one or both houses. In 1983, the Supreme Court ruled that many such legislative vetoes, in this case one dealing with the Immigration and Naturalization Service, are unconstitutional because they represent a violation of the separation of

Questions for Reflection

In considering the "red state versus blue state" political divide and the recent lack of civility in Congress, do you think that the group of moderate and independent legislators who saved the Senate filibuster power for judicial nominees indicate a movement toward compromise in the Senate or an aberration?

And, how might this process be spread to the House of Representatives?

task force An informal procedure used by Congress to assemble groups of legislators to draft legislation and negotiate strategy for passing a bill.

oversight Congressional function that involves monitoring the effectiveness of laws by examining the workings of the executive branch.

legislative veto A legislative action that allows the president or executive agencies to implement a law subject to the later approval or disapproval of one or both houses of Congress.

powers of the government branches and the presentation clause of the Constitution, which requires that all legislation must be presented to the president for signature.[105] In response, however, Congress eliminated some legislative vetoes and modified others but continued to pass new bills with this feature in them.

Congress's budget-control powers reside in the Constitution. Although all tax legislation (the raising of money) must originate in the House, both tax bills and appropriations (spending) bills need approval from both the House and Senate. This "power of the purse" is central to Congress's role. Through its influence on money matters, Congress can shape nearly every policy undertaken by the national government.

In 1974, Congress passed the Congressional Budget and Impoundment Control Act. This legislation created the **Congressional Budget Office (CBO)**, permanent budget committees in the House and Senate, and a new budget timetable. The act was intended to expand congressional control over the national budget at a time when the president usually dominated the process. The House and Senate Budget Committees review the president's annual budget in light of the projections made by the CBO. The CBO establishes budget totals and spending outlays, loan obligations, and deficit-reduction strategies.[106]

Congress's most extreme form of oversight is **impeachment**, by which the House can vote charges against the president, other executive officials, or members of the judiciary for committing "High Crimes and Misdemeanors." Only three times in our history have presidents faced impeachment—Andrew Johnson in 1868, Richard Nixon in 1974, and Bill Clinton in 1998. If the House votes articles of impeachment, a trial is held in the Senate, chaired by the chief justice of the United States. (Richard Nixon resigned after the House Judiciary Committee voted articles of impeachment.) When Special Prosecutor Kenneth Starr finished his investigation of President Bill Clinton and intern Monica Lewinsky, that information was turned over to Judiciary Committee Chair Henry J. Hyde (R.-IL). The committee and the full House decided to initiate an impeachment investigation. Although the House voted articles of impeachment, the president was not convicted in the Senate.

In the end, the entire process works more or less as the framers intended. With the Constitution silent on all but a few rules of Congress, this complex legislative system slowly evolved to ensure that no idea can break through the maze of political roadblocks without securing wide general support of both the short- and long-term interests from many segments of society. Observes congressional scholar Ross Baker, "If James Madison were to come back and sit in the gallery of the House and Senate, he'd be pretty pleased with the way things are working."[107]

THE REPUBLICAN REVOLUTION OF 1994 AND BEYOND

After leading the Republicans to retaking control of the House for the first time in more than fifty years, Newt Gingrich of Georgia took over as speaker of the House in 1995 for the 104th Congress. He had an overwhelming twenty-five seat majority in the House, while the Republicans also controlled the Senate under Majority Leader Robert Dole of Kansas. Everyone expected that the so-called "Republican Revolution" would endure for a generation to come: Even though Democrat Bill Clinton was in the White House, the congressional Republicans could successfully dictate the legislative agenda. And for one hundred days it looked like that would happen, as the Republicans passed a series of term limits on their speaker and committee chairs as well as ethical reforms to eliminate problems seen in the previous Democratic leadership.

A short time later, though, the body degenerated into much partisan and bitter wrangling. House ultraconservatives pushed their new speaker toward increasing conservatism at the same time that Clinton out-maneuvered Gingrich over shutting down the government to manage the growing national debt crisis. In time, the 1998 attempt to impeach Bill Clinton illustrated the partisan rancor in both houses of

Congressional Budget Office (CBO) A government office created by Congress in 1974 to analyze budgetary figures and make recommendations to Congress and the president.

impeachment The process by which government actors can be removed from office for "treason, bribery, or other high crimes and misdemeanors." The House of Representatives votes on the charges and then the trial takes place in the Senate.

Congress, when a unified and determined Democratic Senate minority led by South Dakota's Tom Daschle prevented Clinton's conviction. By 1999, Gingrich was gone, the Republicans held only a five-seat House majority, and Senate Democrats had successfully employed a variety of tactics to slow down the Republicans' legislative agenda. The partisan rancor in both houses had increased to the point that moderate legislators were leaving the body.

All in all, Congress in 1999 passed only thirty-nine bills into law, thirty-four of them on unanimous voice vote (of which nine were simply to rename federal buildings and three to reappoint the regents to the Smithsonian). And it did no better the following year as, rather than pass major laws, each party in Congress seemed determined to use its votes to highlight issues that created an agenda for the upcoming 2000 election.

The 2000 congressional elections produced during the 107th Congress the narrowest Republican majority in both Houses since the late 1950s. In the House, the Republicans took 222 seats, a four-seat majority. The Democrats took 211 seats, with two Independents (one who consistently voted with the Democrats and the other one with the Republicans). With the House poised for stalemate, the Senate became a Democrat-majority body in May 2001, when moderate Republican Jim Jeffords of Vermont changed his party affiliation to Independent. When Tom Daschle (D.-SD) became majority leader, he sought to advance his own party's agenda and to derail the Bush administration's legislative agenda. For a time after Jeffords' switch, moderate members from each party appeared ready to reach across the aisle in search of compromise. Daschle and Trent Lott even reached a unique power-sharing arrangement in the Senate. But not as much agreement between the parties could be reached as was hoped.

Then came September 11, 2001. Suddenly Congress united and spoke with one voice in support of the president. When members of Congress were forced to flee their buildings in response to the anthrax scare, it only further united the membership. Bonded together, members of Congress passed the USA Patriot Act of 2001, the sweeping "No Child Left Behind" Education Reform Act of 2002, and the McCain-Feingold Campaign Reform Act outlined in the case study. This short period of congressional bipartisanship was unique in the modern era. Said congressional scholar Thomas Mann of the Brookings Institution of the 107th Congress: "This is a session of Congress without historical precedent. Agendas changed as radically as I have ever seen them change."[108]

MakeItReal

Census 2000: Party Control in Congress

CONGRESS TOWARD THE 2006 ELECTION

Although the 2004 election seemed to dictate the Republican Revolution's next step toward long-term party control of the Congress, the 2006 election will show whether the Iraq war, the sputtering economy, the continuing and increasingly bitter partisan legislative wars, and the largely stalemated legislative gridlock will allow the Democrats to cut into the Republican margins in both houses or see their legislative influence continue to wane. The origins of this turning point, after more than a decade of Republican Party control of Congress, were seen in the 108th Congress (2003–05).

After the 2002 congressional election, for the first time in more than fifty years, the Republican Party controlled both Houses of Congress and the presidency. The Republicans widened their control of the House, taking 229 seats, with 205 going to the Democrats, and one Independent seat, leading to an expectation of a Republican agenda soon to be passed to set up President Bush's reelection effort. Meanwhile in the Senate, Democrats lost seats in Georgia, Missouri, and Minnesota (after the tragic death of Senator Paul Wellstone). Only the return to the Senate of seventy-eight-year-old Frank Lautenberg (D.-NJ) prevented them from losing that seat as well. In the end, the Republicans took fifty-one seats, while the Democrats took forty-eight, with one Independent (Jim Jeffords (I.-VT).

The Republicans found governing the Senate in the 108th Congress nearly impossible for three reasons. First, they lacked the necessary sixty votes to break repeated filibusters by a determined Democratic minority. Secondly, they could not develop a united voting force between ultraconservative party members and a half-dozen moderate Republicans, the so-called "Mod Squad," which included Lincoln Chafee (R.-RI), Olympia Snowe (R.-ME), Susan Collins (R.-ME), and Arlen Specter (R.-PA). Later, these members would add Minnesota's Norm Coleman and Ohio's George V. Voinovich to their numbers.[109] Ultraconservative members' efforts to broker deals with this group were thwarted by hard feelings remaining from earlier election campaigns. Repeatedly, whether they were running for office or not, Mod Squad members were attacked by ads in their home states placed by conservative interest groups. Some, such as Arlen Specter of Pennsylvania, found their campaigns put at risk by well-funded primary opponents, as these interest groups sought to replace moderate senators with even more conservative Republican candidates. Once the election was over, these independent members were unwilling to take up the agenda of right-wingers who had opposed them. And finally, it became impossible to develop a coherent policy agenda between these two groups and a small number of "mavericks," such as Arizona's John McCain (R.-AZ), who disagreed with the programs of both the Senate leadership and the White House.

These differences made the 108th Congress a disappointment for those who expected legislative action. Two years of partisan wrangling and legislative gridlock doomed this Congress to produce one of the least distinguished records in recent history. Although the Medicare Prescription Drug Improvement and Modernization Act of 2003 passed by the slimmest of margins, the House managed to pass only one of its thirteen appropriations bills and failed to deal with other issues such as whether to extend or pass the 2001 USA Patriot Act or create a new post of "Intelligence Czar." The Senate was no more productive, as increasing numbers of judicial appointments stalled (as detailed in Chapter 6). Rather, both parties seemed concerned only with partisan political issues that would position them for the 2004 election.

Realizing that their close seat margins in the 108th Congress came from a shift of fewer than fifty thousand votes nationwide, and that only about three dozen seats were competitive in the 2004 congressional election, Republican majority leader Tom Delay, together with presidential adviser Karl Rove, led a partisan redistricting of Texas that created six new Republican seats in their column while preventing re-election of long-time Democratic incumbents Charles Stenholm and Martin Frost. In the Senate, with Democrats defending nineteen seats, while the Republicans defended only fifteen seats, the narrowly divided Senate was expected to stay in Republican hands and even shift more toward the Republicans. When put together with the massive $125 million Republican "get out the vote" mobilization effort, President Bush's effective campaign, cultural issues such as opposing gay marriages to spur conservatives to vote, and political mobilization efforts of evangelical Christian leaders and churches, the Republicans managed to gain fifteen House seats and four Senate seats in the 109th Congress.

This meant that House Republicans increased their governing majority in early 2006 to 231 to 202, with one Independent and one vacancy. Senate Republicans picked up all five vacant Southern Democratic seats and inched closer to a sixty-vote filibuster-proof body. Senate margins changed to fifty-five Republicans, forty-four Democrats, and one Independent, Jim Jeffords of Vermont, who voted with the Democrats most often. The large number of new conservative members provided new allies for House majority leader Tom Delay. Meanwhile, a more experienced Majority Leader Bill Frist labored diligently to unite Senate party members into a more cohesive policy-making force.

The Democrats, however, erected two early roadblocks to that effort. In a crucial early decision, faced with the choice of electing as their new leader either a Ted-Kennedy–style, photogenic liberal, Christopher Dodd of Connecticut, or more plainspoken, less telegenic moderate Harry Reid of Nevada, they chose Reid. Although experts predicted that Reid would get along with the Republicans, when his early diplomatic efforts were rebuffed, he developed into a potent opposition force for the Democrats. By this time, the reforms of the conservative Gingrich era from 1994 had largely fizzled out. The eight-year term limit for the speaker's position had been eliminated, and the six-year term limit for committee chairs is occasionally waived, as it was in 2003 for then-congressional member Porter Goss (R.-FL).[110] Once more, Congress bogged down in cultural issues, forcing the federal judiciary to consider yet again the Florida dispute over the "right to die" issue and Terri Schiavo and attempting once more to pass an anti-flag-burning amendment to the Constitution. The two houses battled over competing versions of the bill renewing the USA Patriot Act, and major issues such as tax reform, balancing the budget and reforming Medicaid were left unattended.

In the Senate, Democrats used their newfound skill at filibustering to stall the appointment of John Bolton as ambassador to the United Nations, forcing President Bush to make another recess appointment to evade them. And although chief justice nominee John Roberts's impressive credentials and unflappable behavior during his nomination hearings ensured his confirmation, a major battle over Judge Samuel Alito's selection for Justice Sandra Day O'Connor's seat was narrowly averted.

As Congress prepared for the 2006 elections, Republican members of Congress were increasingly challenged in deciding how long to back lame-duck president George W. Bush over their own policies, the nature of their policy in the increasingly controversial Iraq rebuilding effort, Tom Delay's announcement that he would resign from the House, and the corruption investigation into the connection between indicted conservative lobbyist Jack Abramoff and other members of Congress. Democrats, seeing the near record lows in public support for Congress and increasing voter frustration on major political issues, began to set their sights on a takeover of both houses of Congress. Although that move would normally be hindered by the currently more conservative voting population, the large Republican majorities in both houses of Congress, and the paucity of vulnerable Republican seats, the flow of events in the Democrats' direction made them more hopeful.[111] But the Republicans did not find governing until that time easy, either. Republican majorities in the 109th Congress faced increased difficulty in passing legislation as members positioned themselves for their campaigns and the Democrats sought to derail legislation to establish their agenda for their own campaigns.

As the 109th Congress proceeds, and as the 2006 election approaches, questions about the stalemated Congress in an evenly balanced partisan voting environment continue. Will the bitter partisanship and stalemated chambers continue? Will the number of moderates in each party membership begin to grow and make policy negotiation more possible? Will the Republican Congress, spurred by what it views as an electoral mandate for its legislative agenda, unite to lead the nation in a more conservative direction? Will the leadership in both houses become less partisan and more effective? The passage of the 2002 Campaign Finance Bill showed that even the thorniest of legislative measures could move through the "legislative labyrinth." However, with voters for the upcoming 2006 election now expecting action on difficult issues such as the Iraq post-war transition, the war on terrorism, health care, economic programs such as relieving unemployment, balancing the budget, and social security reform, together with the more vigorous call for "moral values," it remains to be seen what course Congress will take. Only then will we see whether Congress can help the nation approach democracy in this time of crisis.

The strength of Congress, indeed its very constitutional purpose in American democracy, is its closeness to the people and its representational base. "To express the public views" remains the principal responsibility of the national legislature and its most pressing challenge, as Congress and America approach democracy during the twenty-first century.

Summary

1. The Constitution established a bicameral Congress consisting of a House of Representatives whose members serve two-year terms and a Senate whose members serve six-year terms. Congress received numerous major powers, including the power to collect taxes, declare war, and regulate commerce. The necessary and proper clause enables it to interpret these powers broadly.

2. A disproportionate number of Congress's members are rich, white males drawn from the fields of law, banking, and big business. Ethnic diversity in Congress increased in the twentieth century, but it still falls short of that of the population as a whole.

3. Today, each congressional district contains about 635,000 citizens. The number of representatives from each state is adjusted after each census (reapportionment). In states that gain or lose seats, district boundaries must be redrawn (redistricting). The term *gerrymander* describes the often-bizarre district boundaries drawn to favor the party in power.

4. Members of Congress sometimes find themselves torn between the role of delegate, in which they feel bound to follow the wishes of constituents, and the role of trustee, in which they use their best judgment regardless of the wishes of constituents. In practice, they tend to combine these roles.

5. Incumbents have several advantages over their challengers in an election, including greater name recognition, the franking privilege, services of staff members, legislative experience, and greater financial backing. These advantages have led critics to call for legislation limiting the length of time members may serve in Congress.

6. The presiding officer of the House is the leader of the majority party and is known as the speaker of the House. Next in line is the House majority leader, who serves as the party's chief strategist. The minority party is headed by the minority leader, and both party leaders are assisted by whips. In the Senate, the majority party elects a president pro tempore, but this is essentially an honorary position. As in the House, the Senate has majority and minority party leaders and whips.

7. There are four types of congressional committees: standing (permanent), select or special (temporary), conference, and joint. Much of the legislative work of Congress is done in subcommittees. The power of the subcommittees since the 1970s has made the legislative process rather unwieldy, prompting calls for reform.

8. In the House, the Rules Committee determines what issues will be discussed, when, and under what conditions. In the Senate, the majority leader does the scheduling in consultation with the minority leader. The Senate imposes no limits on floor debate. As a result, a bill can be derailed by filibuster, when a senator talks continuously to postpone or prevent a vote. Filibusters can be halted only by cloture, in which sixty or more senators vote to end the discussion.

9. Legislators' voting decisions are influenced by personal views, constituents, party affiliation, the president, interest groups, and congressional staff. Members also receive cues about how to vote from their "buddy system" of other members whom they respect.

10. A member of Congress places an issue on the congressional agenda by drafting a bill and submitting it to the House or Senate. The bill is then referred to the appropriate committee, whose chair assigns it to a subcommittee. After holding hearings on the proposed legislation, the subcommittee holds a markup session in which the language of the bill is revised. It then returns the bill to the full committee. If the committee approves the bill, it goes to the full House or Senate. If the two chambers pass different versions of a bill, it goes to a conference committee, which reconciles the differences and creates a single bill. If the final version is approved by both chambers, it goes to the president to be signed or vetoed.

Review Questions

1. Why does the design of Congress make it a suitable foundation for a representative democracy or republican form of government?

2. Describe the attitude toward one's office that might be held by a member of Congress representing constituents as a delegate. Describe the attitude that would be held by a trustee. When would it be most politically advantageous to act as a delegate? When would it be most politically advantageous to act as a trustee?

3. Describe all of the factors influencing a member of Congress's vote. Which of these influences are the most democratic? Which influences are the least democratic? Why?

4. How does Congress promote majority rule? How does it also provide for protection of minority rights?

5. What are the limitations on the powers of Congress? Were the founders successful in preventing this branch from becoming tyrannical? Why or why not?

6. How could one argue that the increasing number of women and minorities in Congress will make that body more sensitive to issues affecting these groups?

Key Terms

appropriations bill 163
bicameral legislature 130
casework 141
cloture 154
conference committees 148
congressional agenda 160
continuing resolution 165
Congressional Budget Office (CBO) 167
delegates 140
enrolled act (or resolution) 163
filibuster 154
franking privilege 141
gerrymander 137
hearings 161
hold 154
House majority leader 144
impeachment 167

incumbents 141
joint committees 148
legislative veto 166
line item veto 153
lobbyists 161
logrolling 157
majority-minority district 138
markup session 162
minority leader 145
necessary and proper clause 131
omnibus legislation 165
override 163
oversight 166
party caucus 144
pocket veto 163
pork-barrel legislation 157
president of the Senate 145
president pro tempore 145

reapportionment 135
redistricting 137
rider 153
rules 153
select (or special) committees 148
Senate majority leader 145
seniority 155
Speaker of the House 144
standing committees 147
subcommittees 149
task force 166
term limits 142
trustees 140
Two Congresses 143
unanimous consent agreement 153
veto 163
whips 145

Suggested Readings

BAKER, ROSS K. *House and Senate.* 2d ed. New York: Norton, 1995. An excellent study of the political and stylistic differences between two markedly different legislative bodies.

BARRY, JOHN N. *The Ambition and the Power: The Fall of Jim Wright—A True Story of Washington.* New York: Viking Press, 1989. An engagingly written account of the tenure of Democratic speaker James Wright and his downfall in 1989, revealing how Congress really operates.

BINDER, SARAH A., and STEVEN S. SMITH. *Politics or Principles? Filibustering in the United States Senate.* Washington, D.C.: Brookings Institution, 1997. A revealing study of the growing use of the filibuster and other delaying tactics to derail legislation in the Senate.

CARO, ROBERT A. *Master of the Senate.* New York: Alfred A. Knopf, 2002. The third volume, covering his majority-leader years, of the masterful four-volume series on Lyndon B. Johnson.

CWIKLIK, ROBERT. *House Rules: A Freshman Congressman's Initiation to the Backslapping, Backpedaling, and Backstabbing Ways of Washington.* New York: Villard Books, 1991. A window into the world of a member of Congress, tracking Nebraska Democrat Peter Hoagland's first year in office (1989).

DAVIDSON, ROGER H. *The Postreform Congress.* New York: St. Martin's Press, 1992. Readings examining how Congress changed as a result of reforms in the 1970s.

DAVIDSON, ROGER H., and WALTER J. OLESZEK. *Congress and Its Members.* 9th ed. Washington, D.C.: Congressional Quarterly Press, 2004. The finest comprehensive text on every aspect of Congress and its operations.

DEERING, CHRISTOPHER, and STEVEN S. SMITH. *Committees in Congress.* 3d ed. Washington, D.C.: Congressional Quarterly Press, 1997. A complete text on the operations of committees in Congress, showing their role as "laboratories" of the legislative process.

DODD, LAWRENCE C., and BRUCE I. OPPENHEIMER. *Congress Reconsidered.* 8th ed. Washington, D.C.: Congressional Quarterly Press, 2004. A revealing series of articles on facets of Congress's operations.

DREW, ELIZABETH. *Showdown: The Struggle Between the Gingrich Congress and the Clinton White House.* New York: Simon & Schuster, 1996. A behind-the-scenes look at the titanic political battle in 1995 and 1996 between Bill Clinton and the Republican revolutionaries in Congress under Newt Gingrich and Bob Dole.

FENNO, RICHARD. *Congressmen in Committees.* Boston: Little, Brown, 1973. An analysis based on comprehensive interviews with members of Congress and their staffs, describing how committees are staffed and organized, and how they operate.

———. *Home Style: House Members in Their Districts.* Boston: Little, Brown, 1973. A study showing how members of the House deal with their constituents.

GOULD, LEWIS L. *The Most Exclusive Club: A History of the Modern United States Senate.* New York: Basic Books, 2005. A wonderful narrative history of the evolution of the U.S. Senate in the twentieth century that goes far in explaining the current disfunctionality of that institution.

KILLIAN, LINDA. *The Freshmen: What Happened to the Republican Revolution?* Boulder, Colo.: Westview Press, 1998. A highly readable account of the tribulations of the conservative members of Congress elected in 1994 to fulfill Newt Gingrich's legislative vision.

LOOMIS, BURDETT, ed. *Esteemed Colleagues: Civility and Deliberation in the U.S. Senate.* Washington, D.C.: Brookings Institution Press, 2000. An interesting collection of essays investigating the changing nature of the modern Senate away from civility and more toward partisanship.

LOTT, TRENT. *Herding Cats: A Life in Politics.* New York: Regan Books, 2005. A fascinating account of the life and congressional career of the Mississippi senator and the reasons for his eventual fall from power as Republican majority leader.

POLSBY, NELSON. *How Congress Evolves: Social Bases of Institutional Change.* New York: Oxford University Press, 2004. A classic work by one of the field's preeminent scholars, detailing how the nature of political party changes in Congress have first liberalized that body and then led to the sharply partisan institution of the modern era.

WALDMAN, STEVEN. *The Bill: How Legislation Really Becomes Law: A Case Study of the National Service Bill.* New York: Penguin, 1996. A highly readable and informative account of how Americorps was debated and passed in Congress, illustrating how tortuous this process can be.

ZELIZER, JULIAN. *On Capitol Hill: The Struggle to Reform Congress and Its Consequences, 1948–2000.* Cambridge, U.K.: Cambridge University Press, 2004. A wonderful study of the repeated attempts and failures to reform Congress and their impact on the current operations of that institution.

ZELIZER, JULIAN (ed.), with JOANNE BARRIE ZELIZER, JACK RAKOVE, and ALAN TAYLOR. *The American Congress: The Building of Democracy.* Boston, Mass.: Houghton Mifflin, 2004. A wonderful collection of essays written by major scholars in the field detailing the history of changes in Congress in all areas throughout American history.

★ CHAPTER 5 ★

THE PRESIDENCY

CHAPTER OUTLINE

APPROACHING DEMOCRACY
The Presidency of George W. Bush

INTRODUCTION: The Presidency and Democracy

- The Constitutional Design
- Functional Roles of the President
- Two Views of Executive Power
- Expanding Presidential Power: Moving Beyond the Constitution
- The Institutionalized Presidency

Approaching Democracy

The Presidency of George W. Bush

George W. Bush entered office as the forty-third president on January 20, 2001, amidst intense scrutiny. He had failed to win the popular vote, and the Supreme Court had halted a recount of disputed ballots in Florida, where his younger brother, Jeb, served as governor. The new president had no electoral mandate to govern, and many considered the election outcome tainted; others questioned whether the Texas governor was up to the job of president of the United States. One year later, President George W. Bush's legitimacy was unchallenged; his performance as a war leader had won great praise; his job approval rating hovered above 80 percent. The events of September 11, 2001, completely altered the presidential power equation. In the president's own words, "I had the responsibility to show resolve. I had to show the American people the resolve of a commander in chief that was going to do whatever it took to win. No yielding. No equivocation . . . It was also vitally important for the rest of the world to watch . . . I understand the job of the president. And the job of the president is to lead a nation in a long and difficult struggle, and this is going to be a very long and difficult struggle."[1]

By all standards of presidential power, this president has clearly expanded the prerogatives of the office. He has utilized his role as commander in chief during a period of unprecedented terrorist attacks worldwide as well as continued threats. He has claimed for the executive the power to set policy on detention and interrogation of suspected terrorists, to make rule changes in environmental policy, to refuse to allow Congress to call White House aides to testify at hearings, and to refuse the release of historic presidential documents and authorized the National Security Agency's domestic counterterrorism surveillance operation to spy on Americans.[2] The Bush administration has also moved toward greater secrecy by classifying documents at a rate greater than any previous administration.[3] In the wake of Hurricane Katrina, the president endorsed changes in federal law that allow the military to assume immediate responsibility when the nation confronts natural disasters.[4] As Carl Cannon explained, "Bush came to office determined to retrieve the executive power he believed his predecessor had forfeited in the crucible of impeachment."[5]

Four years following the controversial 2000 election, Bush was reelected in the first post–September 11 presidential election. While the margin was narrow in percentage terms—51 percent to 48 percent—it was historic in that Bush won more than 62 million votes, 3 million more than John Kerry and 7.5 million more than any winning candidate in history. Post-election analyses confirmed that President Bush won reelection for one main reason—he was perceived as being the stronger leader at a time when Americans felt threatened by terrorism. That is, national security concerns now dominated the political landscape, and the voters judged Bush's stand on these issues and his leadership as far more important than any other characteristic.[6]

★ President Bush visits residents of the Gulf Coast and tries to reassure them that the government will help rebuild their lives in the wake of Hurricane Katrina.

Yet, just a few months later, in January 2005, President Bush began his second term with an approval rating lower than that of Presidents Eisenhower, Johnson, Nixon, Reagan and Clinton at the same points in their presidencies (see Figure 5.1). The war in Iraq seriously eroded the president's approval rating at a time when the public's policy agenda seemingly wanted him focusing on election issues such as Social Security's financial stability, affordable health care, tax reform, and the budget deficit.[7] Then, in September 2005, Hurricane Katrina brought the Bush presidency face to face with responding to a major domestic challenge. "The challenge would be immense for any president, but it is especially so for Mr. Bush," wrote Richard Stevenson. "He is scrambling to assure a shaken, angry nation that not only is he up to the task but he also understands how much it disturbed Americans to see their fellow citizens suffering and their government responding so ineffectively."[8] By mid-September 2005, for the first time, just half of Americans approved of the president's handling of terrorism, his most consistent strength in previous approval polls (see Figure 5.2). By the end of February 2006, President Bush's approval ratings were down to 34%, the lowest level of his presidency. This reflected strong opposition to the agreement allowing a Dubai company to operate six American ports and increasing doubts about the situation in Iraq.[9] Only time will tell whether this determined president can reassure the public and thereby fortify his presidential legacy.

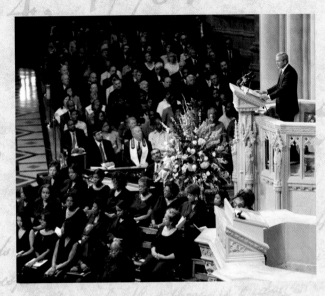

★ President Bush, at the National Cathedral in Washington, discussed themes of racial injustice and its impact in New Orleans and the devastation from Hurricane Katrina.

QUESTION FOR REFLECTION

How do you think history will evaluate the presidency of George W. Bush?

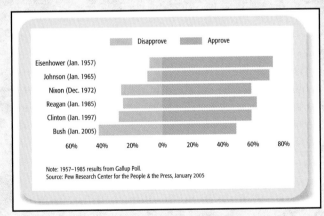

FIGURE 5.1
Presidential Approval Ratings at Start of Second Term (1957–2005).
Source: Pew Research Center for the People & the Press, January 2005

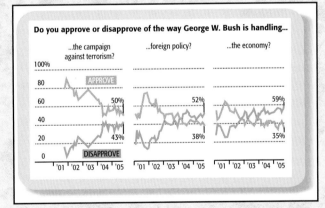

FIGURE 5.2
Public Perceptions of the President.
Source: New York Times, June 17, 2005 A. 14; The New York Times/CBS News Poll

Introduction
THE PRESIDENCY AND DEMOCRACY

MakeItReal

Simulation: Presidential Greatness: How Do We Judge Them?

Question for Reflection

How do the qualities of character, vision, leadership, and communication contribute to presidential success?

MakeItReal

Primary Source: Federalist #70: The Executive Department Further Considered

Quick Review

Design of the Presidency

• Executive power centered on one individual.

• Selection made by an independent body of individual electors.

• Serve a *fixed term of office* with the possibility of reelection.

• Removal from office by a *process of impeachment*.

• *Veto power* enabling the executive to say no to Congress.

• Allowed to act independently within the executive arena.

The great paradox of the presidency is that no other office in America unites so much power and purpose to help Americans approach their democratic potential, yet also poses the most serious threats to the ideals of democracy. The framers of our government designed the presidency so that its potential for energy would be encouraged and its potential for tyranny would be minimized. This entailed a complicated separation and distribution of powers. But, in the intervening two centuries, that distribution has been altered; presidents have gained power by formal grants of congressionally delegated power, court-sanctioned expansions of power, and popularly based assumptions of power.

Lord Acton, a British historian and political figure, noted that "Power tends to corrupt and absolute power corrupts absolutely." That belief has changed little since the eighteenth century; what has changed, however, is the role government plays in American life. Americans have delegated increasing amounts of power to the national government and to the presidency; their expectations of both the government and the chief executive have risen proportionately. The office of president lies at the center of countless demands, many of them contradictory, some impossible to achieve under any conditions. The mere energy required to hold the position and carry out its duties puts it far beyond the average person's capacity. The office has broken several presidents; many have been diminished by it and have diminished the office. Even those who have risen to its challenge, whose records from the distance of history we admire, faced scathing criticism and fought determined foes throughout their tenure in the White House. Still, some have thrived in the office, and certain presidents have achieved greatness. It is impossible to predict who will or will not succeed at the job, but one thing is certain: The presidency is at the core of the American democratic system.[10]

THE CONSTITUTIONAL DESIGN

The presidency may be the framer's most original contribution. In a world of kings and emperors, many of whom left office feet first or on the wrong end of a bloody revolution, the American president was to be unlike any other world leader. In creating this unique position, the framers avoided creating a monarchy like the one in England they had rebelled against, but they also wanted a strong, independent executive for the nation as a whole. They were appalled at the results of legislative omnipotence in the states, as had been the case under the Articles of Confederation.

In creating a source of power independent of the Congress but capable of balancing its powers, the framers based the presidency on seven key principles:

1. They set up a *single presidency*. Executive power would retain its strength and energy in an individual, not a council or a cabinet.

2. Neither Congress nor the people would elect the president. A president chosen by Congress could become its puppet; one chosen by the people could become a demagogue and tyrant. An independent body of individual electors selected by the state legislatures (the *electoral college*) would produce a president independent of the two branches.

3. The president was given a *fixed term of office*. The genius of this idea lies in its assurance of both stability and constraint. Executives serve four years, with the possibility of reelection. They cannot be forced from office by arbitrary "no-confidence" votes in Congress (votes that force the early resignation of entire

governments in parliamentary systems). On the other hand, no president would win reelection without broad popular support. Presidents who commit "Treason, Bribery, or other High Crimes and Misdemeanors" may be impeached and removed from office. This impending sequence forced President Nixon's resignation.

4. The president would be eligible for *more than one term of office,* making the executive a source of potential power to balance or check congressional power. (The Twenty-second Amendment now restricts the president to two terms.) If presidents remained popular and their policies successful, they could win reelection. Thus, Congress must always take the president into account when exercising its own powers and responsibilities.

5. The president could be removed from office only by a cumbersome *process of impeachment* involving both houses of Congress; thus, a president must continually be reckoned with. On the other hand, the House's impeachment of former President Clinton demonstrates that impeachment does indeed represent an ultimate check.

6. The president was given a *veto power,* enabling the executive to say no to Congress. This single provision makes the president a central player in the legislative process because Congress must consider a president's wishes in policy making.

7. The president was not required to appoint an advisory council. Thus, presidents were allowed to act on their own, at least within their own constitutional realm of the executive arena.

This set of principles pointed toward a strong but constrained executive—a single, symbolic head of the nation who holds serious means for exercising power but operates under law and is restricted in power by the countervailing institutions of Congress and the Supreme Court.

Who Is Eligible to Be President?

The Constitution specifies only three requirements for becoming president: a president must be at least thirty-five years old, must have lived in the United States for at least fourteen years, and must be a natural-born citizen.

The framers set the minimum-age requirement of thirty-five (which at that time represented middle age) to guarantee that a president would be reasonably mature and experienced in politics. The fourteen-year-residence condition was to guard against the possibility of a president with divided loyalties between England and the United States—an obvious concern in the years following the American Revolution. For the same reason, the framers stipulated that presidents be natural-born citizens (born in the United States or to American citizens abroad), which is why California Governor Arnold Schwarzenegger is ineligible. (See U.S.A. Yesterday and Today in Chapter 2.)

Presidential Powers

The Constitution has remarkably little to say on the president's powers to accomplish the office's broad range of responsibilities. Only one-third of Article II is devoted to formal presidential powers. This brevity reflects the framers' uncertainty on the subject. Trusting that George Washington would almost certainly be the first president, the framers assumed that he would establish precedents for the office.

What the framers did write into the Constitution can be categorized in two ways. First, in clear, simple language they gave the president specific powers. Second, and more important, they also gave the executive broad, even sweeping, powers written in vague language and subject to individual interpretation.

The Veto Power   Perhaps the president's most potent legal constitutional weapon is the **veto**, a Latin word meaning "I forbid." The power to forbid or prevent an

▲ There are no gender specifications for the job of president, but thus far all American presidents have been men. Victoria Woodhull, shown here, was the first woman presidential candidate. A stockbroker and newspaper editor from New York, Woodhull ran for president in 1872 as a member of the Equal Rights party.

 **MakeItReal**

Simulation: Who's Got the Power?

veto   Presidential power to forbid or prevent an action of Congress.

▲ Surrounded by a bipartisan coalition of supporters, President Bush signs a $26 billion education bill at Hamilton High School in Hamilton, Ohio.

action of Congress gives the president a central role in the legislative process. When Congress passes a bill or joint resolution, the legislation goes to the White House for presidential action. The president then has four options. First, the president can sign the bill, at which point it becomes law. Second, the president can do nothing, allowing the bill to become law without a signature in ten days. Third, if Congress adjourns before those ten days pass, the president can refuse to sign, killing the bill by what is known as a **pocket veto**. Finally, the president can veto the bill, returning it to the house of origin with a message stating reasons for the veto. Congress then has the option to override the veto by a two-thirds vote in each house.

The framers saw the veto as a bulwark of executive independence, a basic building block in their efforts to separate and check power. Alexander Hamilton made this position clear in *The Federalist,* no. 73: "The primary inducement to conferring [the veto] power upon the executive is to enable him to defend himself; the second one is to increase the chances . . . against the passing of bad laws, through haste, inadvertence, or design." The veto was thus conceived as a "negative" by which an executive could defend against legislative excesses.[11]

Presidents can sometimes affect a law's wording or passage by announcing ahead of time that they intend to veto a pending bill. The strategy is akin to the story of a farmer who used "friendly persuasion" to make his mule move but first had to whack it on the head "to get its attention." In 1985, President Ronald Reagan dared Congress to raise taxes. Borrowing from Clint Eastwood, he said such actions would "make my day" and be met by a quick veto. Using a similar tactic,

pocket veto Presidential refusal to sign or veto a bill that Congress passes in the last ten days of its session; by not being signed, it automatically dies when Congress adjourns.

President Bill Clinton warned Congress during a nationally televised State of the Union address: "If you send me legislation that does not guarantee every American private health insurance that can never be taken away, you will force me to take this pen [and] veto the legislation." Throughout his presidency, George W. Bush threatened Congress that he would veto any health-care legislation containing a patient's bill of rights unless the Senate made dramatic changes to legislation passed by the House. In July 2005, President Bush threatened to veto any legislation containing human embryonic stem cell research.[12] Table 5.1 shows presidential vetoes from 1789 through 2006. President Bush had not vetoed a single piece of legislation as of this writing.

The Appointment Power   This specific and important power affects the president's ability to staff the executive branch with trusted allies. Article II, Section 2, of the Constitution gives the president, "by and with the Advice and Consent of the Senate," the power to appoint ambassadors, public ministers, and consuls; judges of the Supreme Courts; and "other Officers of the United States, whose Appointments are not herein otherwise provided for, and which shall be established by Law."

The power of appointment allows a president to recruit people who will help promote his policies. Although appointment is an important administrative power, more than two thousand presidential appointments require Senate confirmation, which is sometimes difficult to obtain. President Bush used a "backdoor" procedure known as a *recess appointment* to bypass the Senate and install John R. Bolton as his ambassador to the United Nations. The constitution authorizes the president to fill vacant positions when the Senate is in recess. Appointees can serve without Senate confirmation until the congressional session ends at the year's end. However, a majority of senators can remove appointees at any time. Bolton was the highest ranking of the 106 people that President Bush has installed into positions by recess appointment. President Clinton had 140 recess appointments in his two terms.[13] The first President Bush made 77 recess appointments over one term, and President Reagan made 243 over two terms.

Perhaps the most important appointment presidents can make is a nomination to fill a Supreme Court vacancy. On average, a president names only two justices during any four-year term of office. Presidents rarely end up naming a majority of Court members. Nevertheless, since the Court is usually split ideologically, even one or two appointments can affect the outcome of important constitutional cases well beyond the president's term of office. Jimmy Carter had no opportunity to appoint a justice to the Supreme Court, but his successor, Ronald Reagan, appointed four. President Clinton appointed Ruth Bader Ginsburg (1993) and Stephen G. Breyer (1994) to the Court. President Bush has had John Roberts confirmed as Chief Justice, nominated Harriet Miers, who withdrew following a conservative revolt, and then nominated Federal Appeals Court Judge Samuel Alito Jr., who was confirmed as Associate Justice of the Supreme Court in January 2006.

The Treaty Power   The Constitution also gives presidents the power to negotiate treaties with other nations. **Treaties** are formal international agreements between sovereign states. But the framers foresaw a system that required consultation between branches—the executive's negotiation would involve the Senate's "advice and consent." When President George Washington went to Congress to solicit advice on an Indian treaty, however, he had to stay several hours and answer questions that he believed had little bearing on the treaty. Irked by this experience, Washington resolved not to repeat it. Henceforth, although he had to secure the Senate's consent in ratifying treaties, he did not encourage senators to contribute their sometimes dubious "advice"—and later presidents have followed that model.

Treaty approval can prove difficult, partly because it requires a two-thirds majority of senators present and voting. In addition, the Senate may attach amendments

treaties Formal international agreements between sovereign states.

Table 5.1 ■ Presidential Vetoes, 1789–2006

	Regular Vetoes	Pocket Vetoes	Total Vetoes	Vetoes Overridden
Washington	2	—	2	—
Madison	5	2	7	—
Monroe	1	—	1	—
Jackson	5	7	12	—
Tyler	6	3	9	1
Polk	2	1	3	—
Pierce	9	—	9	5
Buchanan	4	3	7	—
Lincoln	2	4	6	—
A. Johnson	21	8	29	15
Grant	45	49	94	4
Hayes	12	1	13	1
Arthur	4	8	12	1
Cleveland	304	109	413	2
Harrison	19	25	44	1
Cleveland	43	127	170	5
McKinley	6	36	42	—
T. Roosevelt	42	40	82	1
Taft	30	9	39	1
Wilson	33	11	44	6
Harding	5	1	6	—
Coolidge	20	30	50	4
Hoover	21	16	37	3
F. Roosevelt	372	263	635	9
Truman	180	70	250	12
Eisenhower	73	108	181	2
Kennedy	12	9	21	—
L. Johnson	16	14	30	—
Nixon	26	17	43	7
Ford	48	18	66	12
Carter	13	18	31	2
Reagan	39	39	78	9
Bush	29	17	46	1
Clinton	36	0	36	2
G. W. Bush	0	0	0	0

Sources: Statistical Abstract of the United States, 1986, p. 235; Senate Library, Presidential Vetoes (Washington, D.C.: Government Printing Office, 1960), p. 199; From The Paradoxes of the American Presidency by Thomas E. Cronin and Michael A. Genovese. Copyright © 1998 by Oxford University Press, Inc. Used by permission of Oxford University Press, Inc.; updated by authors.

to treaties. Most treaties are approved without modification, and the Senate has defeated only 1 percent of treaties submitted to it. However, that record of success is misleading; presidents have withdrawn 150 treaties that seemed headed for defeat.

The most dramatic example of a treaty rejection took place in 1919, when the Senate failed to ratify Woodrow Wilson's Treaty of Versailles, which ended World War I and included membership in Wilson's cherished League of Nations. Its defeat seemed a direct slap in the president's face by a hostile Congress and not only undermined Wilson's authority at home but also helped doom the league—the predecessor of today's United Nations—to ineffectiveness abroad.[14]

Although treaty rejection gives the Senate power similar to presidential veto power, its potential has declined as presidents have increasingly turned to less formal means for conducting foreign affairs. **Executive agreements**, diplomatic contracts negotiated with other countries, allow presidents or their agents to make important foreign policy moves without Senate approval. These agreements appeal to harried presidents in their role as world leader. Treaties generate media coverage and controversy and take time to ratify, but executive agreements are usually negotiated in secret, making them a particularly powerful foreign policy tool. William McKinley used executive agreement to end the Spanish-American War, and Theodore Roosevelt used it to restrict Japanese immigration to the United States.

Presidents may conclude an executive agreement on any subject within their constitutional authority as long as the agreement is consistent with legislation enacted by Congress in the exercise of its constitutional authority. Scholars agree that, although not explicitly outlined in the Constitution, the president's right to conduct foreign policy through executive agreement rests on several sound constitutional bases. These include the president's authority as chief executive to represent the nation in foreign affairs, the president's authority to receive ambassadors and other public ministers, the president's authority as commander in chief, and the president's authority to "take Care that the Laws be faithfully executed." Presidents are increasingly finding in executive agreements the flexibility they need to make foreign policy.[15]

In 1997, President Clinton sought "fast-track" authority to negotiate new trade agreements to open markets for U.S. exporters. Congress cannot amend these executive-negotiated trade agreements; Congress can only vote for or against the agreement. Former Republican President Gerald R. Ford strongly endorsed fast-track for a Democratic president because it "is essential for continued U.S. leadership on all issues . . . The United States must lead the world toward a more open, prosperous global economy. But without fast-track, the United States is relegated to the sidelines."[16]

In his 2002 State of the Union address, President Bush pushed for Senate passage of trade promotion authority (TPA), a fast-track authority that would allow the president to negotiate good trade deals that would open markets and increase opportunities for American farmers, workers, consumers, and business. Supporters of fast-track trade promotion see it as the key test of America's international leadership. Opponents argue that it undermines hard fought legislative protections. On August 6, 2002, President Bush signed into law the Trade Act of 2002, under which future international trade agreements will be subject to an up-or-down vote, but not amendment, in Congress.[17]

Executive Privilege   President Dwight Eisenhower once said that "any man who testifies as to the advice he gave me won't be working for me that night." He invoked executive privilege forty times in his eight years in office.[18] **Executive privilege** is the president's claim of implied or inherent power to withhold information on the grounds that to release such information would affect either national security or the president's ability to discharge his official duties. The important question is not necessarily whether the privilege should exist, but rather who should determine its extent—the president, the legislative branch, or the courts.

executive agreement
A government-to-government agreement with essentially the same legal force as a treaty. However, it may be concluded entirely without Senate knowledge and/or approval.

executive privilege   The president's implied or inherent power to withhold information on the ground that to release such information would affect either national security or the president's ability to discharge official duties.

MakeItReal

ABC News Video: Principles of Trial

The Constitution does not mention executive privilege; the first discussion of privilege occurred in 1792. A special House investigation committee requested that President Washington turn over materials pertaining to an Indian massacre of troops under the leadership of General Arthur St. Clair. Washington called a special cabinet meeting to establish standards for the executive branch's responses. The House committee had requested that Secretary of War Henry Knox turn over all original letters and correspondence pertaining to St. Clair's mission. In the first case of a president's refusing to supply Congress with a document, Washington denied the request, giving both constitutional and pragmatic reasons.

Several of George Washington's successors followed his precedent of withholding information. President Jackson refused to turn over documents that would have disclosed his reasons for removing government deposits from the Bank of the United States. The best-known case of executive privilege involved President Richard Nixon's claim that tapes of confidential conversations between himself and his aides were within the province of the White House. In a unanimous decision, the Supreme Court acknowledged a constitutional basis for executive privilege, but not in Nixon's case. The Court did not view the power to protect presidential communications as absolute. The privilege of confidentiality had to derive from the supremacy of the executive branch within its assigned areas of constitutional duties. Neither the doctrine of separation of powers nor the need for confidentiality of high-level communications can sustain an absolute, unqualified presidential privilege of immunity from judicial process under all circumstances. The president's need for complete candor and objectivity from advisers calls for great deference from the courts. However, when the privilege depends solely on the broad undifferentiated claim of public interest in the confidentiality of such conversations, a confrontation with other values arises. During the Clinton presidency, this involved controversies between the president and his attorney as well as the Secret Service during the Monica Lewinsky investigation and impeachment.

President Bush invoked executive privilege for the first time when he rejected a congressional subpoena for prosecutor's records on a thirty-year-old Boston mob case as well as for documents on the Clinton campaign finance probe. In both cases, Bush cited threats to "national interest" that disclosure might produce. The collapse of Enron brought another claim of privilege. The Bush administration refused to release details of energy policy meetings between energy corporation executives and a task force to set energy policy guidelines chaired by Vice President Cheney.[19] The Government Accountability Office (GAO), the legislative arm of Congress, filed suit to obtain that information, the first such action in history.[20] Most recently, the Bush administration has made the case for privilege over records of ex-presidents. Currently, eleven Reagan-era documents are at the center of a protracted court battle over the Bush order. Public Citizen, a group that advocates for openness and accountability in government, is challenging the executive privilege claim.[21]

Although democracy requires openness, legitimate needs for government secrecy can pertain to national security matters. Each of us can debate the extent of privilege over access to information and where or where not the national interest is truly at stake. The level of secrecy already demonstrated by the Bush presidency raises several important issues in thinking about our theme of approaching democracy.

Other Constitutionally Designated Powers   The Constitution gives the president additional specific powers. One is the right to grant pardons (President Ford pardoned Richard Nixon for any crimes he may have committed as president, and President Clinton issued, and later admitted regretting, controversial pardons during his last day in office). Another is the right to convene Congress in extraordinary circumstances. Perhaps the most important is the power of commander in chief of the armed forces.

Beyond these specific grants of power, the Constitution gives the president a vague mandate to run the executive branch of government. Different presidents have interpreted that mandate in different ways. We'll discuss the leeway that constitutional vagueness has allowed presidents in expanding chief executive powers during the two centuries since the framers wrote the Constitution. But first, we'll look at the various roles that define the job of chief executive.

FUNCTIONAL ROLES OF THE PRESIDENT

Presidential behavior depends only partly on laws that require action or prohibit it. Beyond formal legalities, all presidents are constrained and directed by informal or functional role expectations. When leaders are expected to take an action, they do it—whether or not permission for the action is contained somewhere in a legal document. As leader of a vocal, democratic people, the president stands at the center of a mass of such expectations.

The President as Chief of State   The president acts as a ceremonial chief of state, symbolizing the national government to people in this country and other nations. At world gatherings, the chief of state holds the same high protocol rank as kings. Presidents greet foreign ambassadors, pin medals on heroes, hold barbecues on the White House lawn, and give state dinners. Virtually all these opportunities help dramatize and personalize a presidency. From meeting astronauts to making an entrance to the tune "Hail to the Chief," presidents bask in the glory and often hide behind the pomp and circumstance of their office. Our favorite example can be seen in the picture of President Bush as "Hurler in Chief" throwing out the first pitch at the first home game for the Washington Nationals in April 2005.

The President as Commander in Chief   Presidents have more than ceremonial duties, however. They hold enormous powers, particularly in their military leadership role. As commander in chief, the president is charged with providing national security and defense. When necessary, the president must defend American interests by committing troops to combat. The war against international terrorism provides a case in point. This role is reinforced by the president's oath of office to "preserve, protect, and defend the Constitution of the United States." A president who fails to respond forcefully to a threat is seen as weak or indecisive, as was the case with President Carter's response, or lack thereof, to the seizure of the United States embassy in Tehran, which resulted in an extended hostage crisis. On the other hand, President Bush's decision to remove Saddam Hussein from power and liberate the people of Iraq from Saddam's tyranny continues to create heated debate on the president's war powers.[22]

The President as Crisis Leader   The president also comes to the forefront of the nation's attention during crises such as natural disasters, civil unrest, and military or terrorist attacks against the United States. After natural disasters or events such as the terrorist attacks of September 11, 2001, the nation turns to the president as the only leader capable of bringing about timely action in such circumstances. George W. Bush's September 14 visit to the site of the World Trade Center attack unified our nation and gave comfort to a people in mourning.

In times of crisis, Congress generally acquiesces to the president. Moreover, during such episodes, presidential actions are generally accompanied by a noticeable jump in popularity. For example, on the heels of the Persian Gulf War, former President Bush's popularity rating soared well above 85 percent, the highest rating of any president until his son's rating topped it in January 2002. This relationship between crisis and presidential support has become known as the "rally effect"—the country appears to around the president in response to a crisis.

The President as Chief Diplomat   Presidents must be international diplomats as well as warriors. Maintaining smooth relations with allies and a tough stance with

Quick Review

Functional Roles of the President

- Chief of State—ceremonial role.
- Commander in Chief—provide national security and defense.
- Crisis Leader—bring about timely action during periods of crisis.
- Chief Diplomat—serve as broker or mediator.
- Chief Legislator—forge legislation to improve the quality of life.
- Chief Executive—sign *executive orders* and presidential decrees.
- Moral Leader—set a high moral tone for the American people.
- Party Leader—chief architect of his political party.
- Manager of Prosperity—act as an economic superhero who will stave off both depression and inflation while keeping the economy at full employment.

MakeItReal

Primary Source: The Twenty-fifth Amendment to the U.S. Constitution

Primary Source: John F. Kennedy's Inaugural Address (1961)

Primary Source: State of the Union Messages

Primary Source: 1974 Budget and Impoundment Control Act

Visual Literacy: Lyndon Johnson and George Bush

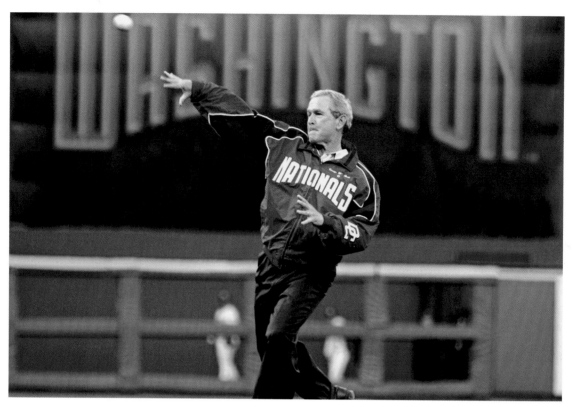

▲ Baseball has returned to the nation's capital. Among the President's many roles is the one Professor Berman dreams about—throwing out the first pitch at the Washington Nationals' home opener.

potential or real enemies is expected of all presidents. Presidents often serve as brokers or mediators between parties, as President Bush tried doing between Israel's Ariel Sharon and the PLO's Yasser Arafat. Indeed, foreign policy is so important that many presidents direct foreign relations from the Oval Office more than through the State Department. This power shift reflects the significance of the president's role as world leader. President John Kennedy once quipped, "The big difference [between domestic and foreign policy] is that between a bill being defeated and the country [being] wiped out."

The President as Chief Legislator   Despite numerous constraints, however, presidents do play a major role in domestic matters. Congress and the American public expect the president to send legislative initiatives to Congress and to work with congressional leaders in forging legislation that will improve the quality of life in America. Indeed, most legislation addressed by Congress originates in the executive branch, but when President Dwight Eisenhower chose not to submit a program in 1953 (his first year in office), he was chided by a member of Congress: "Don't expect us to start from scratch. . . . That's not the way we do things here. You draft the bills and we work them over."[23]

Besides proposing policies and lobbying for them, the president also has negative legislative power. As you've seen, presidents can thwart congressional attempts at legislation through the veto or threats of a veto.

The President as Chief Executive   As the nation's chief executive, the president signs *executive orders* and presidential decrees, setting the administrative direction and tone for the executive branch (see Table 5.2). As chief administrator or chief bureaucrat, the president oversees an army of officials, thousands of executive branch workers trying to administer presidential policies effectively and quickly. Presidents, of course, do not act in a vacuum but are closely monitored by interest groups throughout the country, all eager to see that the executive branch promotes policies and interprets laws to their liking. Table 5.2 shows only those executive orders not issued secretly. For

MakeItReal

Primary Source: Executive Order 10730: Desegregation of Central High School (1957)

Table 5.2 ■ Executive Orders Issued by President George W. Bush, thru March 2006

Date	Executive Order
2006	
Mar. 7	Executive Order: Responsibilities of the Department of Homeland Security with Respect to Faith-Based and Community Initiatives
Feb. 8	Executive Order: Blocking Property of Certain Persons Contributing to the Conflict in Côte D'Ivoire
Jan. 13	Executive Order: Designating the Global Fund to Fight Aids, Tuberculosis and Malaria as a Public International Entitled to Enjoy Certain Privileges, Exemptions, and Immunities
2005	
Dec. 22	Executive Order: Providing An Order of Succession Within the Department of Defense
Dec. 22	Executive Order: Adjustments of Certain Rates of Pay
Dec. 14	Executive Order: Improving Agency Disclosure of Information
Nov. 23	Executive Order: Blocking Property of Additional Persons Undermining Democratic Process or Institutions in Zimbabwe
Nov. 1	Executive Order: Creation of the Gulf Coast Recovery and Rebuilding Council
Nov. 1	Executive Order: Establishment of a Coordinator of Federal Support for the Recovery and Rebuilding of the Gulf Coast Region
Oct. 25	Executive Order: Further Strengthening the Sharing of Terrorism Information to Protect Americans
Oct. 14	Executive Order: 2005 Amendments to the Manual for Courts Martial, United States
Sept. 30	Executive Order: Further Amendment to Executive Order 13369, Relating to the President's Advisory Panel on Federal Tax Reform
Sept. 30	Executive Order: Continuance of Certain Federal Advisory Committees and Amendments to and Revocation of Other Executive Orders
Jul. 27	Executive Order: Assignment of Functions Relating to Original Appointments as Commissioned Officers and Chief Warrant Officer Appointments in the Armed Forces
Jul. 15	Executive Order: Amending Executive Orders 12139 and 12949 in Light of Establishment of the Office of Director of National Intelligence
Jun. 29	Executive Order: Blocking Property of Weapons of Mass Destruction Proliferators and Their Supporters
Jun. 28	Executive Order: Strengthening Processes Relating to Determining Eligibility for Access to Classified National Security Information
Jun. 17	Executive Order: Implementing Amendments to Agreement on Border Environment Cooperation Commission and North American Development Bank
Jun. 16	Executive Order: Amendment to Executive Order 13369, Relating to the President's Advisory Panel on Federal Tax Reform
May 12	Executive Order: Amendments to Executive Order 12788 Relating to the Defense Economic Adjustment Program
Apr. 13	Executive Order: Designating the African Union as a Public International Organization Entitled to Enjoy Certain Privileges, Exemptions, and Immunities

Source: http://www.whitehouse.gov/news/orders

example, President Bush by secret executive order directed the National Security Agency to eavesdrop on American citizens suspected of having terrorist ties.

The President as Moral Leader Increasingly, voters have shown that the president's character is important to their support. The president has always been expected to set a public, if not private, high moral tone for the American people. Even though few citizens see politics as a fair and moral game, and even though no one can become president except through politics, Americans still seem to hold the president to higher public standards than most politicians—or most citizens for that

▲ From the Oval Office, President Bush speaks with New York City Mayor Rudolph W. Giuliani and Governor George E. Pataki and pledges to visit New York on September 14, 2001.

MakeItReal

Census 2000: Party Affiliations in Congress and the Presidency: 1899 to 2003

matter. Presidents are expected to emulate George ("I cannot tell a lie") Washington and Abraham ("Honest Abe") Lincoln—to be truthful, to deal openly with problems, to keep their word—and even to set high standards in their personal lives. In 2004, people who identified moral values as a defining issue in their election choices voted overwhelmingly to reelect President Bush, whom they considered the candidate more likely to uphold morality and traditional values.

The President as Party Leader   Presidents are the chief architects of their political party's fortune. The Constitution makes no reference to party leadership—indeed, it makes no reference to parties at all—but today's presidents must never forget that their party put them in the Oval Office. A president's every action either helps or hurts that party, and its members keep a close eye on the president to make sure that its ideas and fortunes are promoted.

Still, in campaigning and speaking for the party, the president must be careful. If too zealous, the president will be perceived as narrowly partisan rather than the leader of the entire nation. President Clinton's fund-raising efforts on behalf of the Democratic party while in the White House raised questions of credibility, not to mention legality.

The President as Manager of Prosperity   The public expects the president to act as an economic superhero who will stave off both depression and inflation while keeping the economy at full employment. Presidents acting in this capacity adopt the role described by political scientist Clinton Rossiter as "Manager of Prosperity."[24] The chief executive is, in a sense, the nation's chief economist. The political lessons of the Great Depression are clear. No president can preside over hard times without being blamed. Herbert Hoover was soundly defeated after failing, in the public's eyes, to deal competently with the economic setbacks of that time. George H.W. Bush was sent into retirement because, in the words of political strategist James Carville, "It's the economy, stupid."[25] Democratic presidents seeking reelection, too, have suffered from the public's perception that they couldn't keep soaring inflation rates in check. Harry Truman lost his Democratic majority in Congress during the 1946 election, and Jimmy Carter's fate might have been different if he could have averted the double-digit inflation of his last years in office.

The President as Juggler of Roles   The president must play all of these roles—and others besides—a virtually impossible task because the roles often conflict. How can one be a partisan politician and still unify the nation? For that matter, can one be a politician at all and yet inspire the nation? Can one both legislate and administer laws? Can a president address world affairs as both soldier and diplomat? How can a president seem universally fair and effective to a multitude of constituencies? Finally, just finding the time and energy to carry out these expected tasks is surely beyond the capacity of any mortal. Political scientists Thomas Cronin and Michael Genovese have divided the job description into three "subpresidencies" (see Table 5.3).

The job of president is particularly daunting because the powers granted to carry out these multiple roles fall far short of any person's capacity to do so. In fact, we expect Herculean accomplishments of presidents, even though we hedge them with restrictions so that they look less like Captain Marvel and more like Gulliver, tied down by a thousand tiny ropes. How, then, can anyone fill all the expected

Table 5.3 ▪ The Presidential Job Description

Types of Activity	The Three Subpresidencies		
	Foreign Policy and National Security	Macroeconomics	Domestic Policy and Programs
Crisis management	Wartime leadership; missile crisis, 1962; Gulf War, 1991	Coping with recessions, 1982, 1992	Confronting coal strikes of 1978; LA riots, 1992; LA earthquake, 1992
Symbolic and morale-building leadership	Presidential state visit to Middle East or to China	Boosting confidence in the dollar	Visiting disaster victims and building morale among government workers
Priority setting and program design	Balancing pro-Israel policies with need for Arab oil	Choosing means of dealing with inflation, unemployment	Designing a new welfare program health insurance
Recruitment leadership (advisers, administrators, judges, ambassadors, etc.)	Selection of secretary of defense, UN ambassador	Selection of secretary of treasury, Federal Reserve Board governors	Nomination of federal judges
Legislative and political coalition building	Selling Panama or SALT treaties to Senate for approval	Lobbying for energy-legislation package	Winning public support for transportation deregulation
Program implementation and evaluation	Encouraging negotiations between Israel and Egypt	Implementing tax cuts or fuel rationing	Improving quality health care, welfare retraining programs
Oversight of government routines and establishment of an early-warning system for future problem areas	Overseeing U.S. bases abroad; ensuring that foreign-aid programs work effectively	Overseeing the IRS or the Small Business Administration	Overseeing National Science Foundation or Environmental Protection Agency

Source: From *The Paradoxes of the American Presidency* by Thomas E. Cronin and Michael A. Genovese. Copyright © 1998 by Oxford University Press, Inc. Used by permission of Oxford University Press, Inc.

roles of the presidency? Let us examine two reactions to this system: presidents who accept the restraints and live within them, and presidents who chafe at the restraints and invent ways to surpass or abolish them.

TWO VIEWS OF EXECUTIVE POWER

The Constitution is silent on how much actual power a president should possess. Article II begins with the ambiguous sentence, "The executive Power shall be vested in a President of the United States of America." What did the framers mean? Did "the executive Power" refer to a mere designation of office, or did it imply a broad and sweeping mandate to rule? Scholars and politicians alike have long debated the question without agreement. History has left it up to each president to determine the scope of executive powers, given a president's personality, philosophy, and the political circumstances of the time.

This executive power "wild card" has allowed many a president to outreach the Constitution's narrow prescriptions when conditions call for extraordinary action—or when the president thinks such action is necessary. Activist presidents find ways to justify sweeping policy innovations even if the Constitution has no specific language for those policies.

Franklin Roosevelt exemplified this approach in his March 4, 1933, inaugural address. With the Great Depression holding the country at the brink of economic

Questions for Reflection

How realistic are the expectations for the president to fulfill all these roles?

How would you amend the position to assure that democracy is best served?

collapse, Roosevelt declared in one of history's most memorable speeches, "Let me first assert my firm belief that the only thing we have to fear is fear itself—nameless, unreasoning, unjustified terror which paralyzes needed efforts to convert retreat into advance." Roosevelt then turned to the issue of means: "I shall ask the Congress for the one remaining instrument to meet the crisis—broad executive power to wage a war against the emergency, as great as the power that would be given to me if we were in fact invaded by a foreign foe."[26] Roosevelt then took dramatic actions that included closing the banks by executive order, forbidding payments of gold, and restricting exports.

Not all presidents have made as sweeping claims to executive power as Franklin Roosevelt. Their different approaches to use of power allow us to categorize presidents in office as either stewards or constructionists. Theodore Roosevelt articulated the **stewardship** approach to presidential power based on the presidencies of two of his predecessors, Abraham Lincoln and Andrew Jackson. Roosevelt believed that the president had a moral duty to serve popular interests as "a steward of the people bound actively and affirmatively to do all he could for the people." Roosevelt believed the president needed no specific authorization to take action:

> I did . . . many things not previously done by the President. . . . I did not usurp power, but I did greatly broaden the use of executive power. . . . I acted for the common well being of all our people . . . in whatever manner was necessary, unless prevented by direct constitutional or legislative prohibition.[27]

Teddy Roosevelt held an activist, expansionist view of presidential powers. In a classic example of the stewardship model, he engineered the independence of Panama and the subsequent building of the Panama Canal. As he put it, "I took the [Panama] Canal Zone and let Congress debate, and while the debate goes on, the canal does, too."[28] Over the years, activist or steward presidents have used their powers broadly. Thomas Jefferson presided over the Louisiana Purchase in 1803, which almost doubled the size of the country. Lincoln assumed enormous emergency powers during the Civil War, justifying them on the grounds of needing to take quick, decisive action during an extraordinary national crisis. During World War I, Woodrow Wilson commandeered plants and mines, requisitioned supplies, fixed prices, seized and operated the nation's transportation and communication networks, and managed the production and distribution of foodstuffs.

In contrast to this stewardship view of executive power is the **constructionist** view espoused by William Howard Taft. Taft believed that the president could exercise no power unless it could be traced to or implied from an express grant in either the Constitution or an act of Congress. He scoffed at the idea of some "undefined residuum of power" that a president can exercise "because it seems to him to be in the public interest." The president, he believed, was limited by a strict reading of the Constitution. Unless that document gave the executive a specific power, that power was beyond the scope of legitimate presidential activity. Taft cringed in horror at Theodore Roosevelt's view that the president could "do anything that the needs of the nation demanded."[29]

This restricted view of presidential power made Taft a passive executive, reluctant to impose his will or the power of his office on the legislative process. He neither exerted strong party leadership in Congress nor embarked on the ambitious exercises of power typical of Teddy Roosevelt. Other presidents besides Taft have pursued this constructionist line, at least in certain situations. For example, Herbert Hoover appeared strongly constructionist—at least in economic policy—in his reluctance to manipulate the economy during the Great Depression. Indeed, his reluctance caused many voters to see him as indifferent to their economic plight.

On the whole, Americans have sided with an activist interpretation of the presidency. They expect dynamic leadership from the office. Almost no president regarded as "great" by either historians or the public has adopted a passive, constructionist approach to the job (see Table 5.4). The men who largely created

stewardship An approach to presidential power articulated by Theodore Roosevelt and based on the presidencies of Lincoln and Jackson, who believed that the president had a moral duty to serve popular interests and did not need specific constitutional or legal authorization to take action.

constructionist A view of presidential power espoused by William Howard Taft, who believed that the president could exercise no power unless it could be traced to or implied from an express grant in either the Constitution or an act of Congress.

Table 5.4 ▪ How Historians Rank the Presidents

	Overall Ranking	Public Persuasion	Moral Authority	Crisis Leadership	International Relations	Vision/ Setting an Agenda	Economic Management	Administrative Skills
Abraham Lincoln	1	3	2	1	4	1	3	1
Franklin Delano Roosevelt	2	1	4	2	1	2	1	3
George Washington	3	6	1	3	2	3	2	2
Theodore Roosevelt	4	2	3	5	3	4	4	4
Harry S. Truman	5	12	7	4	5	7	7	5
Woodrow Wilson	6	9	6	6	6	5	6	6
Thomas Jefferson	7	8	8	12	16	6	13	8
John F. Kennedy	8	5	15	8	13	9	9	13
Dwight D. Eisenhower	9	10	5	10	9	18	8	7
Lyndon Baines Johnson	10	13	28	17	36	11	12	9
Ronald Reagan	11	4	11	15	14	8	21	32
James K. Polk	12	16	20	9	15	10	10	10
Andrew Jackson	13	7	14	7	19	12	24	23
James Monroe	14	17	17	18	7	14	20	14
William McKinley	15	14	16	14	17	17	14	15
John Adams	16	24	9	13	10	19	11	19
Grover Cleveland	17	15	18	16	18	16	19	12
James Madison	18	18	13	19	24	15	15	18
John Quincy Adams	19	33	12	21	11	13	16	22
George H. W. Bush	20	19	19	11	12	28	23	16
Bill Clinton	21	11	41	20	21	22	5	21
Jimmy Carter	22	30	10	28	20	20	33	26
Gerald Ford	23	31	21	22	23	31	25	24
William Howard Taft	24	25	22	25	22	26	18	20
Richard Nixon	25	28	40	23	8	21	17	17
Rutherford B. Hayes	26	23	26	26	26	23	22	27
Calvin Coolidge	27	20	23	31	30	33	26	28
Zachary Taylor	28	26	27	24	27	25	29	31
James Garfield	29	21	25	32	38	24	30	34
Martin Van Buren	30	32	29	34	28	27	34	25
Benjamin Harrison	31	35	30	33	29	30	28	30
Chester Arthur	32	34	33	29	34	29	27	29
Ulysses S. Grant	33	22	31	30	33	36	37	39
Herbert Hoover	34	37	24	39	25	37	41	11
Millard Fillmore	35	36	32	27	32	32	32	35
John Tyler	36	38	35	35	31	34	31	33
William Henry Harrison	37	29	34	36	41	35	39	36
Warren G. Harding	38	27	39	38	35	38	36	41
Franklin Pierce	39	39	36	40	39	40	38	38
Andrew Johnson	40	41	37	37	37	39	35	40
James Buchanan	41	40	38	41	40	41	40	37

Source: C-Span, reported in *The Washingtonian*, April 2000, p. 55.

our idealized view of the presidency—Washington, Jefferson, Lincoln, the two Roosevelts—did not reach lofty status by minding their own business. They crossed and stretched constitutional boundaries in the name of the national interest. Their achievements stand as models, if not monuments. Current presidents invoke their names and strive to fill their shoes, while voters measure current White House occupants against these past giants. Few hope that the next president will behave like William Howard Taft, and it is unlikely that anyone will seek that office promising "to govern in the spirit of Franklin Pierce." President George W. Bush is known to admire and even fashion his presidency after the active Republican steward Teddy Roosevelt. The controversy over domestic surveillance leads us to ask, what are the boundaries of presidential authority? Can the president ignore the law or unilaterally reinterpret it? Can constitutional protections endure pervasive official secrecy? Would Americans rather have a "strong leader" or a strong system of laws? In the view of Vice President Cheney, "I believe in a strong, robust executive authority, and I think the world we live in demands it."[30] Although not everyone may agree with Woodrow Wilson that "the President has the right, in law and conscience, to be as big a man as he can be," many now believe that the health of American democracy rests in the hands of an activist executive as described by the vice president.

Question for Reflection

How much activism is too much in the hands of the president?

Approaching Democracy Around the Globe

President Bush's Stalwart Ally:
Gloria Macapagal-Arroyo of the Philippines

President Gloria Macapagal-Arroyo of the Philippines arrived in Washington, D.C. for a state visit in May 2003. President Arroyo was among the first global leaders to join President Bush in the fight against terrorism. She was greeted with full military honors, a twenty-one-gun salute, and warm personal praise: "Madame President, for all you have done to make our world safer, America thanks you," Bush said. Arroyo responded that "the war is not yet won, but that it will be won, there can be no doubt. Terrorism is contagious, and it will not be contained unless we agree on a comprehensive approach for defeating it in Southeast Asia."

President Bush subsequently paid a state visit to the Philippines. But things soon went sour for the president of the Philippines, and she faced approval problems similar to those facing President Bush. After announcing in 2002 that she would not seek reelection in 2004, Arroyo changed her mind and decided to seek a new six-year term. Her popularity and credibility suffered, and the 2004 election was marred by questions of legitimacy. Although she won by more than a million votes over her closest rival, she faced accusations of cheating and of inappropriate use of taxpayers' money for her campaign funds. Congress proclaimed Arroyo the election winner more than a month after election day, making her only the fourth Philippine president to be reelected. She took her oath of office on June 30, 2004. By July 8, ten appointed cabinet officials filed their resignations and asked the president to do the same. Later that day, the Liberal Party and former

president, Corazon Aquino, both former allies of the president, joined calls for her resignation. Arroyo rejected these calls and sought to manipulate the democratic system by proposing a shift in her country's design from a presidential system to a parliamentary one, believing that she would more likely overcome a vote of no-confidence than impeachment, but also making the case that the country's problems needed a new political system. In a rather creative example of trying to approach democracy by changing the rules, President Arroyo in August 2005 argued that "in my experience, given the needs of the twenty-first century, especially now that our Asian neighbors are beginning to accelerate their recovery again, I believe we should have a parliamentary form of government." While some saw this tactic as a power grab, others rallied to the call. As of this writing, President Macapagal-Arroyo is as unpopular as any leader since polling began in the Philippines. In February, President Arroyo ordered suspected conspirators arrested and declared a state of emergency, banning all demonstrations against the government.

Source: www.mainearth.com/articles/Gloria_Macapagal-Arroyo; http://en.wikipedia.org/wiki/Gloria_Macapagal-Arroyo; Karina's Kolumn: "Driven By Faith And Overdue Reforms—Philippines President Gloria Macapagal-Arroyo Gives Karina Robinson a Glimpse of the Tenacity That Is Now Keeping Her in Power," *The Banker,* 8/1/2005. See Seth Mydans, "The Philippines Wages a Campaign of Intimidation Against Journalists," April 3, 2006, p. A10.

EXPANDING PRESIDENTIAL POWER: MOVING BEYOND THE CONSTITUTION

Conducting Foreign Policy and Making War

Although presidential power has grown in domestic affairs, leading the nation in an increasingly complex and dangerous world has most enlarged executive branch powers. When key diplomatic and military decisions must be made in hours, even minutes, a president, as one individual with great authority, has an enormous advantage over a many-headed, continuously talking institution such as Congress. At times, national survival itself may require nothing less than rapid and unfettered presidential action.

Congress, along with the rest of the nation, recognizes that reality and has delegated broad and sweeping powers that allow presidents to act in foreign affairs with few congressional restraints. In the days immediately following September 11, 2001, the Senate voted 96–0 and the House 422–0 to give President Bush $40 billion to help rebuild lower Manhattan and the Pentagon and to launch his global war on terrorism. The Senate voted 98–0 to give the president virtually unlimited powers to prosecute the war against terrorism.

Other governmental bodies also defer to the president in foreign affairs. The executive's preeminence in this field has been recognized and legitimized by the Supreme Court, which enunciated its position in the 1936 case of *United States* v. *Curtiss-Wright*. Associate Justice George Sutherland's opinion provides the rationale for an active presidential role by distinguishing between foreign and domestic affairs and the powers apportioned to each. Although domestic power comes only from an express constitutional grant, he argued, in foreign affairs the president is sovereign. Sutherland concluded that the president's foreign policy power depended not on any constitutional provision but rather on national sovereignty. In sweeping language Sutherland stated: "In this vast external realm, with its important, complicated, delicate and manifold problems, the President alone has the power to speak or listen as a representative of the nation."[31]

Presidential War Powers   In theory, then, both Court and Congress see the president as the dominant force in foreign policy. This perspective is bolstered by the president's constitutionally delegated role as commander in chief of the American armed forces. Presidents have used this military role in a variety of ways to achieve their policy ends and expand the power of their office.

Some presidents have left the actual conduct of war to professional military personnel, while using their role as commander in chief to set broad national and international policy. That policy often seemed far removed from urgent military matters. Abraham Lincoln, for instance, issued the Emancipation Proclamation "by virtue of the power vested in me as Commander-in-Chief of the Army and Navy" and "warranted by the Constitution upon military necessity." In short, Lincoln used his command over the military to abolish slavery. Although a worthy goal, his action represents a broad interpretation of the commander in chief powers.

In times of crisis, other presidents have gone even further than Lincoln. Following Japan's bombing of Pearl Harbor, Franklin Roosevelt ordered more than 100,000 West Coast Japanese Americans evacuated to internment camps, citing national security. He thus used his military powers to establish de facto concentration camps. Roosevelt also issued an ultimatum in a speech to Congress on September 7, 1942. Should legislators not repeal provisions within the Emergency Price Control Act, he stated that he would "accept the responsibility and act." Roosevelt's claim here is impressive: that acting in his capacity as commander in chief, he could free domestic policy from congressional restraint. Even more impressive, perhaps, is the fact that the American people strongly supported him on this matter.

U.S.A. Yesterday and Today

From Imperial, to Imperiled, to Impervious Presidency

Thomas Jefferson, in 1797, referred to the presidency as "a splendid misery." Other former presidents would no doubt concur. In the past four decades, eight men have served as president. Despite achievements such as winning the Cold War, landing on the moon, and establishing several beachheads of peace around the globe, Gerald Ford, Jimmy Carter, and former President George Bush were voted out of office; John Kennedy was assassinated; Ronald Reagan shot; Richard Nixon resigned in disgrace; Lyndon B. Johnson chose not to seek reelection fearing defeat; and Bill Clinton was impeached. With the Vietnam War raging and the Watergate scandal unfolding, historian Arthur M. Schlesinger Jr. described and deplored "the expansion and abuse of presidential power" in his 1973 book, *The Imperial Presidency*. In several respects, however, that vivid, cautionary phrase, "imperial presidency," has today become anachronistic, as formal and informal measures have sought to curb what Schlesinger referred to as the "runaway presidency."

The 1973 War Powers Act, the 1974 Budget and Impoundment Control Act, and the 1978 Independent Counsel Act all notified the executive branch that other government entities were monitoring military involvement in hostile situations, the spending of appropriated money, and the conduct of the presidents and their appointed subordinates.

Moreover, Supreme Court decisions (notably *United States* v. *Nixon* in 1974 and *Clinton* v. *Jones* in 1997) made it clear to presidents that their standing in potentially criminal matters was the same as any other citizen's. In the Nixon case, claims of executive privilege did not prevent surrender of his Oval Office tapes about Watergate. Bill Clinton's argument of presidential immunity against an allegation of sexual harassment before taking office failed to delay court proceedings that involved Paula Corbin Jones and, ultimately, Monica Lewinsky.

While the high court and Congress were imposing various checks on the presidency and on individual presidents, the news media was dramatically changing its approach to and attitude toward White House coverage. In the post–Watergate climate of unblinking scrutiny, any suggestions of scandal or personal peccadilloes received sustained attention. As journalists became more probing and, at times, adversarial, previously taboo subjects such as health or sex partners became fair yet controversial game. A loose-lipped coterie of White House officials and assistants added to the tell-all atmosphere by leaking anonymous insider information to willing reporters and by leaving government service and writing revealing, behind-closed-doors memoirs about their former bosses still in office.

Considered collectively, the governmental, journalistic, and cultural changes of the past twenty-five years produced more of an investigated or imperiled presidency rather than an imperial one. Although the United States is the world's only superpower, whoever occupies the Oval Office faces new constraints that, to a degree, weaken the institution. The presidency remains a combination of chief executive, head of state, commander in chief, principal diplomat, legislative agenda setter, crisis manager, and party leader, but these roles have become more difficult since Vietnam and Watergate. The two-hundred-year-old system of checks and balances between the executive and legislative branches deliberately limit the powers of each branch of government. Theodore Roosevelt once remarked, "Oh, if I could only be president and Congress too for just 10 minutes." That lament could serve as the hopeful wish of any president, but none more appropriately than the current White House occupant, George W. Bush.

Source: Excerpted and adapted from Robert Schmuhl, "The Presidency: Full of Peril or Possibility?" *Boston Globe*, January 2, 2000. Reprinted by permission of the author.

Presidents have also used the commander-in-chief role to make war, and expanded its reach through congressional delegation. Lyndon Johnson, for example, committed ground troops to Vietnam on the basis of a loosely worded congressional resolution. The 1964 Southeast Asia Resolution, remembered now as the Tonkin Gulf Resolution, stated that "the Congress approves and supports the determination of the President, as Commander in Chief, to take all necessary measures to repel any armed attack against the forces of the United States and to prevent further aggression." President Johnson later described the resolution as being like grandma's nightshirt—it covered everything! And as you will learn in Chapter 16, we now know that the Tonkin Gulf intelligence was skewed.[32]

Using his powers as commander in chief, Richard Nixon later ordered the Vietnam War expanded into Laos and Cambodia, neutral countries at the time.

Hundreds of enemy sortie reports were falsified to justify the president's actions. Congress and the public were kept in the dark. The House Judiciary Committee considered an article of impeachment against Nixon that cited his deliberate misleading of Congress "concerning the existence, scope, and nature" of the American operation in Cambodia. This article was dropped, however, suggesting Congress's strong reluctance to curb presidential powers, as long as the president, even an unpopular one, appears to be acting as commander in chief.

Still, military power does not make the president a dictator, and various commanders in chief have been restrained by both Congress and the Supreme Court. In *Youngstown Sheet and Tube Company* v. *Sawyer* (1952), the Supreme Court struck down President Truman's seizure of the domestic steel industry. Truman claimed that his powers as commander in chief in wartime (the Korean War) allowed him to seize and run the steel mills to preserve the war effort. The Court ruled that only a pressing national emergency, which in its opinion did not exist at the time, could justify such a sweeping action in the domestic sphere without approval of Congress.[33]

Primary Source: The War Powers Resolution of 1973

Congress, too, has challenged presidents in military affairs. After all, the Constitution assigns Congress the power to declare war, order reprisals, raise and support armies, and provide for the common defense. Many legislators in the Vietnam War era, believing that confers legal authority to commit American forces to combat and oversee their actions, worked to assert Congress's constitutional prerogatives. As a result, the War Powers Resolution passed in 1973, over President Nixon's veto.[34]

The resolution requires that the president "in every possible instance" report to Congress within forty-eight hours after committing U.S. troops to hostile action if no state of war has been declared. If Congress disagrees with the action, the troops must be removed within ninety days. Actually, the troops must be withdrawn within sixty days unless the president requests thirty additional days to ensure their safety. Congress can no longer stop the military commitment by *concurrent resolution* (a resolution passed by both houses in the same form).

The first test of the new War Powers Resolution occurred in May 1975, when President Gerald Ford ordered the marines and navy to rescue the U.S. merchant ship *Mayaguez* without prior consultation with members of Congress. The ship, carrying both civilian and military cargo, was seized by Cambodian ships for being in Cambodia's territorial waters. In his report to Congress, submitted *after* the troops had been withdrawn, President Ford cited both his inherent executive power and his authority as commander in chief.[35]

These examples illustrate that a president no longer needs a congressional declaration of war to send American troops into combat. Although the Constitution grants Congress the power "to declare War," history, practice, precedent, and popular expectation have given the president authority to "make war." Presidents have often ordered troop actions, leaving Congress with few options but to support them. Appropriations cutoffs expose legislators to charges of having stranded soldiers in the field. Perhaps these facts explain why presidents have committed troops abroad in dozens of combat situations, while Congress has declared war only five times.[36]

As the war on terrorism escalates, the president's war-making powers are once again expanding. After much debate over the president's need to seek congressional approval for a war on Iraq, President Bush introduced a bill to Congress that would give him the power to use military force if necessary to rid Iraq of its chemical and biological weapons and to dismantle its nuclear weapons program. The House approved Joint Resolution 114 with a vote of 296–133 (3 not voting), and the Senate in a 77–23 vote the following day. The resolution was signed into effect on October 16, 2002. House Joint Resolution 114 requires the president to notify Congress before or within 48 hours of an attack, explaining its necessity and how military action will not hurt the war on terror, but allows the president to act unilaterally. President Bush then received unanimous backing from the UN Security

Council, which approved a resolution he formulated in his September 12 speech entitled "A Decade of Deception and Defiance." In it, Bush outlined sixteen Iraqi violations of UN regulations over the past decade and asked the Security Council to mandate new weapons inspections whose failed compliance could trigger military action.[37] Chapter 16 discusses at length the road to war and the justifications involved, but suffice it to say that many now see this as a presidential war and an imperial presidency.

Going Public

We have seen that the growing importance of America's role in the world has helped increase the president's power; an American president is a world leader. Given the singular nature of the office, a president can use modern means of communication to curry public support for his policies. As individuals in an age of personality, they are in a position to manipulate the media to enhance their reputation, which most members of Congress cannot do.

During the early years of the Republic, presidents promoted themselves through the prevailing means of communication: public speeches, pamphlets, and articles. Although nearly all of the early presidents had some experience in mass persuasion, it was by no means considered vital to the office.

Throughout the nineteenth century, most presidents, with the conspicuous exception of Andrew Johnson, communicated to Congress in formal, written addresses. Public speeches were suspect, to be avoided as demagoguery. Indeed, one impeachment charge against Johnson read that he "did . . . make and deliver with a loud voice certain intemperate, inflammatory, and scandalous harangues . . . particularly indecent and unbecoming in the chief Magistrate of the United States."

▲ Former President Clinton is joined by James Roosevelt and Anna Eleanor Roosevelt for the unveiling of a statue of the thirty-second President in his wheelchair.

These charges seem laughable today, when effective speechmaking has become a requirement of the presidency.

Not until the twentieth-century presidency of Theodore Roosevelt, in fact, did presidents ascend to what Roosevelt called "the bully pulpit." Great American oratory—what there was of it—had always come from Congress, out of the mouths of speakers such as Stephen Douglas, Daniel Webster, and Henry Clay. Roosevelt changed all that, at least for the duration of his term. He spoke loudly and often, but only compared to presidents of his day, not presidents of ours.

Woodrow Wilson was the first twentieth-century president to use mass persuasion for a particular policy goal. Facing serious opposition in Congress after World War I, Wilson toured the country in search of support for the League of Nations. He was unsuccessful, but the presidency thereafter became a national theater with the chief executive the most visible actor on the stage. That supreme thespian, Franklin D. Roosevelt, would soon expertly develop the presidency as a forum for mass persuasion.

A master of public communication, Roosevelt used that expertise to increase the power of the national government and in particular the presidency. He did this in part by personalizing the office. Listening to his "fireside chats" on radio, people felt that they knew and understood the president as a person, not just as a chief executive. What Roosevelt began, other presidents continued. Although varying widely in their skill as communicators, no president since Roosevelt has attempted to govern without also attempting to create and maintain mass support.

Presidents see popular opinion as both a source of power and a constraint. Presidents must attend to their approval ratings and dedicate increasing amounts of time to the public side of their office. As a result, the office has become more ceremonial and less deliberative than the framers ever intended.

Nonetheless, presidents have long recognized the advantages of what political scientist Samuel Kernell calls **going public**, promoting themselves and their policies to the American people. The strategy includes televised press conferences, prime-time addresses, White House ceremonies, and satellite broadcasts. Rather than bargain directly with Congress, presidents appeal to the American public, hoping to generate popular pressure for their policy aims. In one nationally televised speech, for example, President Ronald Reagan appealed to the public to "contact your senators and congressmen. Tell them of your support for this bipartisan [tax] proposal."[38] During the 2002 midterm elections, President George W. Bush used his extraordinary approval ratings, as well as the perks of his office (Air Force One), to campaign for Republican candidates throughout crucial battleground states. The strategy worked, bringing Republican control to the Senate and increasing the Republican majority in the House. Going public secured great political advantage for the president.

Going public may seem an easier strategy than bargaining or negotiation, but it is far riskier. Members of Congress may feel ill disposed toward a president who bypasses them and goes directly to the people. Going public thus risks the often tenuous lines of communication between the White House and Capitol Hill. Generally, negotiators must be prepared to compromise, and bargaining proceeds best behind closed doors. By fixing a firm presidential position on an issue through public posturing, however, the strategy of going public may serve to harden a president's bargaining position and make later compromise with other politicians difficult.

going public Actions presidents take to promote themselves and their policies to the American people.

▲ Ronald Reagan was an expert at communicating with the American people, and no president better understood how to make the best of a photo opportunity. The former movie actor was ideally suited for television.

THE INSTITUTIONALIZED PRESIDENCY

The bureaucratic aspects of the president's job are daunting. One individual, the president, is expected to manage both a permanent staff and a national government of about two million employees.[39]

Before 1939, presidents relied on a few clerks for general staff assistance. One of President Washington's first decisions was to hire his nephew Lawrence Lewis as a clerical assistant. Lewis, the president's sole employee, was paid out of Washington's own pocket. That tradition continued for seventy years until Congress appropriated funds for the president's household staff in 1833.

Andrew Jackson was the first president to receive an allowance for a departmental clerk, authorized only to sign land patents. For day-to-day functions such as writing letters or speeches, however, the president was still left to his own resources. Not until 1857 did Congress fund the first official household staff budget, including a private secretary ($2,000 a year), an executive mansion steward ($1,200), messengers ($900), and a contingency fund ($750).

Little had changed by 1937, when the administrative aspects of an expanded modern government and the proliferation of New Deal agencies overwhelmed Franklin Roosevelt, who had a secretary, a press secretary, and a handful of aides. Believing that expanded government requires management tools equal to the task, Roosevelt commissioned the Committee on Administrative Management, usually referred to as the Brownlow Commission. This group recommended that the president have a permanent staff for managing the executive branch. Its report began with a clarion call, "The President needs help," and recommended that the president receive both personal and institutional assistance.

The Brownlow Report displayed keen insight and sensitivity with regard to the potential dangers of installing unelected and anonymous staff in a White House office. It recognized that presidential assistants could be effective in direct proportion to their ability to discharge their functions with restraint. Therefore, they were to remain in the background, make no decisions, issue no orders, make no public statements, and never impose themselves between cabinet officers and the president. These assistants were to have no independent power base and should "not attempt to exercise power on their own account." In the famous words of the Brownlow Report, they were to have a "passion for anonymity."[40]

As presidential aides have multiplied, the Brownlow Report's admirable goals have become difficult to maintain. Staff members have grown in power, along with the presidency, and in an open democracy few people with power can maintain anonymity for long. Many of them have come to hold important powers, despite being unmentioned in the Constitution. The number of people working directly for the president has become so large that we need complex organizational charts merely to keep track of them.

The White House Office

MakeItReal

Civic Participation: White House Internships

Closest to the president are those who work in the White House, at 1600 Pennsylvania Avenue NW, Washington, D.C., where the president both lives and works. The first family sleeps upstairs; the president works downstairs in the West Wing Oval Office. Presidential staff members also work downstairs in both the East and West Wings. The president's chief lieutenants operate nearby in the West Wing. Also located in the West Wing are the Situation Room, the Oval Office, the National Security Council staff, the vice president's office, assistants to the president, and the Cabinet Room.

All presidential assistants in the White House tread a thin line between the power they derive from being close to the president and their actual role as assistants and underlings. Jack Valenti, a special assistant to President Johnson from 1963 to 1966, explains the temptations:

You sit next to the Sun King and you bask in his rays, and you have those three magic words, "the President wants." All of a sudden you have power unimagined by you before you got in that job. And if you don't watch out, you begin to believe that it is your splendid intellect, your charm and your insights into the human condition that give you all this power. . . . The arrogance sinks deeper into their veins than they think possible. What it does after a while is breed a kind of insularity that keeps you from being subject to the same fits of insecurity that most human beings have. Because you very seldom are ever turned down. You are seen in Washington. There are stories in *Newsweek* and *Time* about how important you are. I'm telling you, this is like mainlining heroin. And while you are exercising it, it is so blinding and dazzling that you forget, literally forget, that it is borrowed and transitory power.[41]

The size of the staff has increased with the growth of government. As presidents are expected to solve more and more problems, the number of specialists on the White House staff has come to look like "a veritable index of American society," in political scientist Thomas Cronin's words.[42] These men and women come from every imaginable background. Because their loyalty is solely to the president and not to an administrative agency, they seem more trustworthy to the president than cabinet members or high-level officials from the civil service. The president therefore puts them to work running the everyday operations of the presidency. White House staff members often end up usurping the policy-making power normally held by cabinet secretaries, their staffs, and the staffs of various independent executive agencies.

The Chief of Staff   The White House **chief of staff** is now the president's de facto top aide. Often earning a reputation as assistant president, this individual is responsible

chief of staff The president's top aide.

◄ On September 11, 2001, in Sarasota, Florida, Chief of Staff Andrew Card whispers news of the attacks to President Bush. On March 28, 2006, President accepted the resignation of Card and appointed OMB Director Joshua Bolten as the new Chief of Staff. "No person is better prepared for this important position, and I'm honored that Josh has agreed to serve," said the President.

for White House operations and acts as gatekeeper to the president. The chief of staff also plays a key role in policy making. During the Eisenhower years, Chief of Staff Sherman Adams was so influential that the following joke became popular: "Wouldn't it be awful if Ike died, then we'd have Nixon as president?" Response: "But it would be even worse if Sherman Adams died. Then Eisenhower would be president." In like manner, H. R. Haldeman, Nixon's chief of staff, was once described as "an extension of the President."[43] President George W. Bush's chief of staff, Andrew Card, had a firm idea about the way things should work in the White House. He did not want the president referred to as POTUS, the long-used acronym for President of the United States. Card also established dress codes for staffers in the West Wing. It's not quite as casual as during the Clinton years. Mr. Card is in the office every morning by 5:30 A.M. and after five years on the job admits, "my entire life has been exhaustion."[44] Only Sherman Adams served longer in the job. In February 2005, President Bush named Karl Rove White House deputy chief of staff in charge of coordinating domestic policy, economic policy, national security, and homeland security.

The Executive Office of the President

This title is somewhat misleading. The federal government has no single executive office building. Instead, the **Executive Office of the President (EOP)** consists of staff units that serve the president but are located away from the White House, such as the National Security Council, the Council of Economic Advisers, and the Office of Management and Budget, among others. The Bush administration made two significant additions to the EOP: the Office of Strategic Initiatives and the Office of Faith-Based and Community Initiatives.

The National Security Council   The National Security Council (NSC) was established in 1947, and its formal membership consists of the president, vice president, and secretaries of defense and state. The special assistant to the president for national security affairs is the council's principal supervisory officer. The NSC advises the president on all aspects of domestic, foreign, and military policy that relate to national security.

The Council of Economic Advisers   The Council of Economic Advisers (CEA), a product of the Employment Act of 1946, gave the president professional, institutionalized,

Executive Office of the President (EOP) Created in 1939, this office contains all staff units that support the president in administrative duties.

▲ The morning after the September 11 attacks, President Bush meets with his National Security Council and begins the strategic planning for striking back.

economic staff resources. Today, the CEA is responsible for forecasting national economic trends, making economic analyses for the president, and helping to prepare the president's annual economic report to Congress. The CEA chair is appointed by the president with the advice and consent of Congress. The recently created National Economic Council is responsible for coordinating high-priority economic policy matters for the president.

Although the CEA is a valuable resource, the president actually receives most economic advice from a group referred to as the "troika"—a functional division of labor among the secretary of the treasury (revenue estimates), the CEA (the private economy), and the Office of Management and Budget (federal expenditures). When the chair of the Federal Reserve Board is included in the group, it is referred to as the "quadriad."

Office of Management and Budget   Observers of American politics have long recognized the central role that the Office of Management and Budget (OMB) plays. The OMB's primary responsibility is to prepare and implement the budget, but the office also evaluates federal program performance. It reviews management processes within the executive branch, prepares executive orders and proclamations, plans the development of federal statistical services, and advises the president on the activities of all federal departments. The OMB also helps promote the president's legislative agenda with Congress. As the most highly developed coordinating and review unit in the Executive Office, the OMB is also the most powerful. It acts as the central institutional mechanism for imprinting (some would say inflicting) presidential will over the government.[45]

The OMB began as the Bureau of the Budget (BOB) in 1921. It acted at first only as a superaccountant, keeping track of the executive branch's books. Over the years, BOB's powers continued to grow until, in 1970, a major executive office reorganization transformed BOB into OMB, with greatly expanded powers. Given its array of responsibilities and powers, OMB's influence now extends into every nook and cranny of the executive branch.

The Cabinet

Cabinet officers act as a link between the president and the rest of the American political system. Congress creates cabinet departments, giving them specific legal responsibilities and political mandates. Department heads are confirmed by the Senate and are frequently called to testify before congressional committees (see Table 5.5).

A cabinet is an unusual institution. It is mentioned in neither the Constitution nor in statutory law, yet it has become a permanent part of the presidency. The framers considered but eventually rejected adding a council of any kind to the executive. Thus, the cabinet as such does not legally exist. Nevertheless, the idea of a cabinet surfaced early. Newspapers began using the term in the 1790s to describe the relationship between President Washington and his executive officers.

In its most formal meaning, the **cabinet** refers to the secretaries of the major departments of the bureaucracy and any other officials the president designates (such as the OMB director). An informal distinction is often made between the inner and outer cabinet. Members of the *inner cabinet* are the most visible and enjoy more direct access to the president. Typically, this inner cabinet is composed of the secretaries of state, defense, treasury, and justice. These being the most powerful positions, presidents tend to staff them with close political allies.

Cabinet officers are responsible for running their departments as well as advising the president on matters of policy. Although many of its members have been quite distinguished, the cabinet has rarely served as a collective source of advice. John Kennedy, for instance, scoffed at calling full cabinet meetings; he

---

Table 5.5 ■ The Second-Term Bush Cabinet, April 2006

Department of Agriculture
Secretary Mike Johanns

Department of Commerce
Secretary Carlos Gutierrez

Department of Defense
Secretary Donald Rumsfeld

Department of Education
Secretary Margaret Spellings

Department of Energy
Secretary Samuel W. Bodman

Department of Health & Human Services
Secretary Michael O. Leavitt

Department of Homeland Security
Secretary Michael Chertoff

Department of Housing & Urban Development
Secretary Alphonso Jackson

Department of the Interior
Secretary Gale Norton*

Department of Justice
Attorney General Alberto Gonzales

Department of Labor
Secretary Elaine Chao

Department of State
Secretary Condoleezza Rice

Department of Transportation
Secretary Norman Mineta

Department of the Treasury
Secretary John Snow

Department of Veterans Affairs
Secretary Jim Nicholson

Cabinet Rank Members

The Vice President
Richard B. Cheney

Office of Management and Budget
Rob Portman

Environmental Protection Agency
Stephen Johnson

White House Chief of Staff
Joshua Bolten

United States Trade Representative
Ambassador Rob Portman

Office of National Drug Control Policy
John Walters

Source: http://www.whitehouse.gov/government/cabinet.html

*Resignation submitted March 19, 2006.

cabinet Group of presidential advisers including secretaries of the major bureaucracy departments and any other officials the president designates.

vice president The second-highest elected official in the United States.

saw no reason to consult the postmaster general about matters of war and peace. Lincoln viewed his cabinet with something approaching disdain. On the occasion of signing the Emancipation Proclamation, he looked around his cabinet table and said, "I have gathered you together to hear what I have written down. I do not wish your advice about the main matter. That I have determined for myself."[46]

One president who took cabinet meetings most seriously was Dwight D. Eisenhower. Not only did his cabinet meet regularly with a set agenda, but Eisenhower also created the position of cabinet secretariat to serve as a liaison with the president. He also expanded the size of the official cabinet to include such important aides as U.S. ambassador to the United Nations, budget director, White House chief of staff, and a national security affairs assistant. Still, most presidents have followed a different pattern. Cabinet members end up as glorified bureaucrats, running their departments and consulting with the president individually about their specialized activities.

President Bush's most recent cabinet innovation was the creation of the "war cabinet" composed of the top national security officials in the White House, CIA, State Department, and Pentagon. The cabinet-level Office of Homeland Security (OHS), formerly headed by Governor Tom Ridge, is also an important innovation. Michael Chertoff was the director in 2005.

The Vice Presidency

The second highest elected official in the United States, the **vice president**, has few significant constitutional responsibilities. Indeed, the only such powers actually assigned to the vice president are to preside over the Senate (except in cases of impeachment) and to cast a vote when the Senate is deadlocked. Most vice presidents have shunned that job; few wish to spend all day listening to senators talk. The vice president's most important job is the one Americans hope he never takes—succeeding to the presidency in case of death, resignation, or removal. (Table 5.6 outlines the line of succession to the presidency.) As Woodrow Wilson once wrote, "There is very little to be said about the vice-president. . . . His importance consists in the fact that he may cease to be vice-president."

The actual work of the vice president ends up being whatever the president decides it will be. In recent years, presidents have bestowed more authority than they have removed. The growth in their own responsibilities has led them to turn to the vice president for help. Thus, the office of vice president, like that of the president, is becoming institutionalized. Between 1960 and 1980, vice-presidential staff increased from twenty to more than seventy and largely parallels the president's, with domestic and foreign policy specialists, speech writers, congressional liaisons, and press secretaries.

Recent occupants of the office have been deeply involved in substantive matters of policy. Nelson Rockefeller chaired President Ford's Domestic Council. Walter Mondale served as a senior presidential adviser on matters of Carter administration policy. President Reagan appointed George H. W. Bush to lead the administration's crisis management team. Dan Quayle played an important role as chair of the Bush administration's Council on Competitiveness. Al Gore Jr. led President Clinton's ambitious program to "reinvent government" by downsizing the bureaucracy, streamlining procedures, updating systems, and eliminating certain subsidies and programs.

Dick Cheney's experience in Washington, his formidable role during the 2000 presidential transition, and the support and counsel he offered President Bush in the period immediately after September 11, 2001, have elevated the vice presidency to new heights. Cheney, for example, recommended and formulated the plan to set up the Office of Homeland Security. More than any other vice president in

Question for Reflection

How would the role of vice president change if the Constitution were amended to include specific responsibilities for the office?

▲ Vice President Cheney has become the most influential power broker and presidential confidant in history. Cheney has had a distinguished career as a businessman and public servant, serving four Presidents.

Table 5.6 ■ Presidential Line of Succession
1. Vice president
2. Speaker of the House of Representatives
3. Senate president pro tempore
4. Secretary of State
5. Secretary of the Treasury
6. Secretary of Defense
7. Attorney General
8. Secretary of the Interior
9. Secretary of Agriculture
10. Secretary of Commerce
11. Secretary of Labor
12. Secretary of Health and Human Services
13. Secretary of Housing and Urban Development
14. Secretary of Transportation
15. Secretary of Energy
16. Secretary of Education
17. Secretary of Veterans Affairs

history, he has become the last voice the president wants to hear before making a decision; "What does Dick think?" counts. The vice president has also been one of the strongest advocates for promoting an expansive view of presidential power. On the domestic policy front, the vice president plays a pivotal role in such areas as Social Security and overhauling the tax code.[47]

The Executive Office of the President was created and expanded to help a twentieth-century president deal with managing a modern government. Yet despite this increase in the potential for power, presidents are seriously constrained by the context in which they function. While great, their powers are far from absolute. Except in rare cases of clear emergencies, presidents do not act alone. They must seek and obtain the approval of Congress, the courts, and the people, and they must lead their own federal bureaucracy. Each of these groups has high expectations. No other office of government represents the elements of democracy to Americans more than the presidency.

Summary

1. The framers designed the presidency to be independent of the legislature. This separation was achieved by creating a single executive who would be selected neither by Congress nor directly by the people. The president would serve a fixed term of office but be eligible to serve more than one term. The framers also made it difficult to remove the president from office.

2. The veto power gives the president a central role in the legislative process. The president also has the power to appoint officials of the executive branch and nominate justices of the Supreme Court. The president negotiates treaties with other nations, but the Senate must approve by a two-thirds majority. To avoid seeking Senate approval, modern presidents have made increasing use of executive agreements and executive privilege.

3. The president performs a variety of roles, both formal and informal. Among these are chief of state, commander in chief, crisis leader, chief diplomat, chief legislator, chief executive, moral leader, and party leader. The president is also viewed as the manager of the nation's prosperity.

4. Activist presidents go beyond the powers prescribed in the Constitution when they believe extraordinary action is required; this view of the presidency is referred to as stewardship. Constructionist presidents, in contrast, exercise no powers other than those expressly granted by the Constitution or an act of Congress. The theory of inherent powers holds that the Constitution grants broad authority to the executive during times of national emergency.

5. Congressional grants of power have greatly increased the power of the presidency. The greatest enlargement of executive branch powers has occurred in the areas of foreign and military policy. Bowing to the president's constitutionally delegated role as commander in chief of the armed forces, Congress has largely acquiesced to the president in matters related to war. In 1973, however, it passed the War Powers Resolution, which requires the president to report to Congress within forty-eight hours after committing U.S. troops to hostile action.

6. Advances in communications technology have increased the president's influence by enabling the president to reach ever-larger numbers of people more quickly. Modern presidents promote their policies to the people through televised press conferences, prime-time speeches, and the like.

7. In recent decades the president's staff has grown steadily and staff members have come to hold important powers. The White House chief of staff is responsible for White House operations but also plays a key role in policy making. The special assistant for national security affairs may also have considerable influence. The Office of Management and Budget plays a central role in executive policy because it is responsible for evaluating the performance of federal programs as well as budget formation.

8. Cabinet members include secretaries of the major federal departments and any other officials designated by the president. The inner cabinet consists of the secretaries of state, defense, treasury, and justice. Cabinet officials are responsible for running their departments as well as advising the president on matters of policy.

9. In the event of the death, resignation, or removal of the president, the vice president succeeds to the presidency. In recent administrations, vice presidents have become increasingly involved in substantive matters of policy.

10. One view of the presidency holds that the president's real power derives from the ability to persuade and bargain. Another view places more emphasis on the formal powers of the presidency but does not downplay the importance of leadership skills. As a result, modern presidents often go public, that is, attempt to persuade the people to put pressure on their legislators in support of the president's policies.

Review Questions

1. To what degree might it be argued that the framers of the Constitution pursued contradictory goals in establishing the American presidency?

2. In what way and why has Congress sought to limit the power of the Executive branch? How and why has the Executive branch actually increased its power despite specific attempts on the part of Congress to limit power?

3. What are the alternative or contrasting attitudes toward one's office that might be held by a President? Explain the impact that these attitudes might have on performance in office.

4. How and why have vice presidents become increasingly involved in matters of public policy?

5. What is meant by the presidential use of the "recess appointment"?

6. In a time of national crisis, how must a U.S. president reassure the American people? Comment on the necessary approaches after reviewing George W. Bush's moves on 9/11 and shortly thereafter.

Key Terms

cabinet 201	Executive Office of the	stewardship 190
chief of staff 199	President (EOP) 200	treaties 181
constructionist 190	executive privilege 183	veto 179
executive agreement 183	going public 197	vice president 202
	pocket veto 180	

Suggested Readings

BARBER, JAMES DAVID. *The Presidential Character: Predicting Performance in the White House.* Upper Saddle River, N.J.: Prentice Hall, 1985. rev. ed., 1992. A provocative proposal that from the pattern a person followed in political life, we can predict how that person will perform as president.

BRUNI, FRANK. *Ambling into History: The Unlikely Odyssey of George W. Bush.* New York: HarperCollins, 2002. *New York Times* reporter Frank Bruni's look at President George W. Bush from the campaign trail though the 9/11 tragedy.

COHEN, JEFFREY E. *Presidential Responsiveness and Public Policy-Making: The Public and the Policies That Presidents Choose.* Ann Arbor: University of Michigan Press, 1997. An examination of the way in which presidents have dealt with public opinion in policy making.

FISHER, LOUIS. *Military Tribunals and Presidential Power.* Lawrence: University of Kansas Press, 2005. A detailed and comprehensive discussion of these extra-legal courts that represent a dramatic expansion in presidential power during war.

GREENSTEIN, FRED. *The Presidential Difference: Leadership Style from FDR to Clinton.* Princeton, N.J.: Princeton University Press, 2005 ed. A fascinating account of the qualities that have served well in the Oval Office and those that haven't, from Franklin D. Roosevelt to George W. Bush.

IRONS, PETER. *War Powers.* New York: Metropolitan Books/Henry Holt, 2005. A valuable discussion of what the Constitution says and how presidents have interpreted its language on the power to make war.

KERNELL, SAMUEL. *Going Public: New Strategies of Presidential Leadership.* Washington, D.C.: CQ Press, 1993. rev. ed., 1997. Examination of presidential power in the context of political relations in Washington—particularly the strategy of bypassing bargaining on Capitol Hill and appealing directly to the American public.

MAYER, KEN. *With the Stroke of a Pen: Executive Orders and Presidential Power.* Princeton, N.J.: Princeton University Press, 2001. A lucid historical discussion of the evolution of executive orders and the rise of executive powers.

NEUSTADT, RICHARD E. *Presidential Power and the Modern Presidents.* New York: Free Press, 1990. A classic study of presidential bargaining and influence that has set the agenda for a generation of presidency scholars.

ROZELL, MARK. *Executive Privilege: Presidential Power, Secrecy, and Accountability.* Lawrence: University Press of Kansas, 2002. An authoritative account of the development of privilege and the claims made by presidents. This is a must read on the subject.

SKOWRONEK, STEPHEN. *The Politics Presidents Make: Leadership from John Adams to George Bush.* Cambridge, Mass.: Harvard University Press, 1993. An important and innovative book that chronicles fifteen presidents and how they continually transformed the political landscape.

★ CHAPTER 6 ★

THE JUDICIARY

CHAPTER OUTLINE

Approaching Democracy

Changing of the Guard?

Supreme Court Justice Sandra Day O'Connor's retirement on July 1, 2005, and Samuel Alito's appointment to replace her, opened the door for the next great shift on the Court. This new vacancy brought the "Red State–Blue State" partisan battle to the Court itself, and hanging in the balance stood the reputations of the Rehnquist Court, the president of the United States, and senators such as Pennsylvania Republican Arlen Specter.

As the 2004–2005 Court term drew to a close, everyone anticipated the retirement of Chief Justice William Rehnquist, who was seriously ill with thyroid cancer. The Court he led for nineteen years had been one of the most remarkable conservative activist courts in history. A reliable five-vote majority had cut down the rights of the accused in favor of state investigative and punishment powers, had used the Constitution's Tenth Amendment to increase states' powers as opposed to those of the federal government, and had forged new connections between the government and religious programs. The same five-vote majority confirmed George Bush as the winner of the 2000 presidential race when it stopped a recount of votes in Florida. Time and time again, the conservative Rehnquist Court overturned acts of Congress, including the Religious Freedom Restoration Act

and the Omnibus Crime Control Act of 1968, designed to reverse the Court's constitutional decisions. Not since the Burger Court of the 1970s and 1980s had the nation seen such an activist Court or one so willing to overturn the political branches in the federal and state governments. Not since the Hughes Court of the 1930s had the nation seen such conservative judicial decisions. But the Burger Court overturned Congress only thirty times, and the Hughes Court only fourteen times, whereas the Rehnquist Court overturned Congress thirty-nine times in nineteen years.

But this Court had a mixed record. It also upheld the constitutional right to privacy, personal rights of gays, the right to burn the flag, the right of abortion, the continued existence of the *Miranda* protections against self-incrimination, and affirmative action programs in law school admissions. In addition, it limited the states' right to impose capital punishment on mentally challenged and juvenile defendants and the rights of religious groups to place "Ten Commandments" monuments and plaques in public sites. These decisions, celebrated by liberals and abhorred by conservatives, led to the most aggressive political attacks on the Court since the 1930s.

Such attacks were sure to intensify when President Bush began to fill Court vacancies. But with Justice O'Connor's decision to retire, the first replacement involved a crucial swing vote on this closely divided Court. Throughout her career, O'Connor voted with the majority 77 percent of the time. But even more revealing, she was the pivotal fifth vote in 5–4 decisions 235 times, 146 of them since 1994. Voting along with a conservative majority, she upheld vouchers for parochial school tuition, allowed the Boy Scouts to exclude gays, struck down a congressional act prohibiting guns within one thousand feet of school grounds, and allowed George Bush to

Judge John Roberts

★ Chief Justice John Roberts displayed the dazzling argumentation skills that he learned in appearing before the Supreme Court 39 times, more than all the other Chief Justices combined, with his no notes, definitive answer-avoiding performance in testifying during his Senate confirmation hearings in September 2005, ensuring his confirmation for the position.

208

win the 2000 presidential election. On the other hand, voting with the liberals, she upheld women's right to abortion, allowed so-called partial-birth abortions, upheld affirmative action in law school admissions, overturned the death penalty of defendants who had inadequate legal defense, protected whistle-blowers in sex discrimination cases, and disallowed prayer at public high school graduations and the posting of the Ten Commandments inside a Kentucky courthouse.

In a strategy constitutional law expert Cass Sunstein calls "judicial minimalism," O'Connor created a legal test in each specific case and used it to incrementally change the law with her vote. "Closely tailored" programs designed to remedy personal racial discrimination became the test for the affirmative action area. "No endorsement" of religion by a state became the test for the establishment of religion cases. "Undue burden" on a woman's abortion-related right to choose was the test in abortion cases. In short, O'Connor, giving something to both sides, produced the Rehnquist Court's mixed political and legal legacy.

Then, with the death of Chief Justice William Rehnquist, President Bush decided to shift John Roberts' nomination to that position. But filling a conservative seat with a conservative appointee would keep the focus on Justice O'Connor's replacement. Any change in the political direction of that pivotal fifth vote would determine the direction of the Court.

When President Bush appointed relatively unknown White House staffer Harriet Miers to the seat, conservative interest groups, the Evangelical movement, and some liberals were unhappy. In a matter of weeks, so many objections were raised against Miers' appointment by conservative interest groups and conservative leaders that she withdrew her nomination. The president then appointed Third Circuit Court of Appeals Judge Samuel Alito. Alito was heartily endorsed by conservatives but faced significant objections by liberal interest groups owing to his memos as a member of the Reagan administration seeming to oppose the *Roe* v. *Wade* abortion decision and supporting strong presidential power. Many predicted that the confirmation of Alito, considered a more conservative judge than Sandra Day O'Connor, would shift the Court to the right. But that may not necessarily be the case.

Changes in the Court's membership may place Justice Anthony Kennedy in the swing seat long occupied by O'Connor. For eighteen years he has hovered close to Justice O'Connor. His decisions and opinions have determined the current state of the liberal rulings on gay rights. The change in O'Connor's seat will make him the pivotal fifth vote on the Court until one of the more liberal seats is changed or he leaves the Court. Kennedy had already deserted the conservatives on the gay rights cases, but in the 2004–2005 term he also voted against them in overturning

★ From 1994 to 2006, Justice Sandra Day O'Connor cast the tie-breaking vote nearly 150 times, and often wrote the majority opinion, in key 5–4 decisions, meaning that during this period the United States Supreme Court could more properly be labelled "The O'Connor Court" instead of "the Rehnquist Court." Whether the rules that she crafted in those decisions will last will depend on the decisions of her replacement, Samuel Alito, as well as the remaining justice in the swing position on the Court, Anthony Kennedy.

capital punishment for juvenile defenders, the right of local governments to expand their powers under the *eminent domain* power to take private property in order to promote economic development, and in voting for states' rights to allow marijuana use for medical purposes despite a federal law banning such a practice (though the overall decision backed federal power).

Long after the political appointment and confirmation battles are fought, the highly independent judicial actors will set the course for the Court, and almost never do they see it quite as the politicians and public expect. Beyond that, future elections will determine the future direction of this aging Court.[1]

QUESTION FOR REFLECTION

Should the Senate defer to presidents in appointing justices, or should the two branches share in the power to fill these vacancies?

Introduction
THE COURTS AND DEMOCRACY

The changing nature of Supreme Court appointments made by people such as George W. Bush and their impact on judicial decisions illustrate why we should attend to the workings of the American court system. Supreme Court judicial decisions produce fundamental changes in our society. William O. Douglas's decision in Estelle Griswold's 1965 case allowed married people and others to be counseled about contraceptive devices. Harry Blackmun's opinion in Jane Roe's 1973 case allowed women to choose to have an abortion. Tom Clark's 1961 opinion in Dolores Mapp's case and Earl Warren's 1965 opinion in Ernesto Miranda's case placed limits on police who search a residence or question an individual about crimes. Warren's 1954 opinion in Linda Brown's case outlawed segregation in public schools, while Warren Burger's 1971 opinion in James Swann's case legitimized busing as a means for achieving school integration.

All of these justices and the cases they decided produced fundamental societal change. The Court interprets the Constitution, and in the process the Court can create new rights or expand, and even dramatically alter, existing ones.

An irony in American democracy is that the Supreme Court, which interprets the Constitution, is the least democratic of the three branches of government. Operating in total secrecy, nine unelected, life-tenured jurists sit at the top of a complex legal structure designed to limit rather than encourage appeals, and they have almost total power to interpret the law. But as you will see, despite its undemocratic nature, in the past seventy years the Court has actually helped to expand and protect the rights of Americans. As a result, the Court has helped America approach democracy.

Nearly all issues that make their way to the Supreme Court begin in the lower federal courts or state judicial systems. The right of state courts and federal courts to disagree with each other makes necessary a single Supreme Court to resolve those differences.

In this chapter we examine the Supreme Court's developing powers and the organization of the American court system, appointment of justices, and means by which cases are appealed to and then decided by the Supreme Court. We also look at how judges arrive at decisions and, perhaps most important, how those decisions affect both public policy and democracy.

THE ORIGINS AND DEVELOPMENT OF JUDICIAL POWER

Of the three branches of government created by the framers of the Constitution, the judiciary is the least clearly defined, both in its organization and in the nature of its powers. Instead, the Court was left to define the nature of its power through its own rulings.

Creating the "Least Dangerous Branch"

The framers outlined the nature of the federal judicial branch in Article III of the Constitution: "The judicial Power of the United States shall be vested in one supreme Court, and in such inferior Courts as Congress may from time to time ordain and establish." As you can see, the framers were vague about court structure and about how powerful they wanted the courts to be. And in establishing only a Supreme Court, they left it to Congress to design a lower federal court system.

Neither did they clearly define the jurisdiction, or sphere of authority, of the federal courts. Article III establishes that the Supreme Court and the lower federal courts shall decide all legal disputes of a federal nature or those arising under the Constitution, U.S. law, and treaties. In cases such as those involving disputes between or among states of the union or involving foreign ambassadors, the Supreme Court will have **original jurisdiction**; that is, it will be the first court to hear the case. For all other disputes, such as those involving the United States as a party, admiralty or maritime claims, disputes between citizens of two or more different states, and between a citizen and a state, the Court will hear cases on **appellate jurisdiction**, or after the matter has been argued in and decided by a lower federal or state court.

Although they did not specify the full extent of the Supreme Court's powers, the framers designed the judiciary to be the least influential and weakest of the three branches of government. Some framers believed that in a representative government, the courts should have little power because they have no explicitly political or representative role. Alexander Hamilton made this argument in *The Federalist*, no. 78: "The judiciary . . . will always be the least dangerous to the political rights of the Constitution. . . . The judiciary . . . has no influence over either the sword or the purse . . . [and it] may be truly said to have neither FORCE nor WILL, but merely judgment."[2]

The framers left it to Congress to be more specific about the organization and jurisdiction of the judiciary. In the Judiciary Act of 1789, Congress established a three-tiered system of federal courts, consisting of district or trial courts, appellate courts, and one Supreme Court. The act also defined more fully the jurisdiction of the Supreme Court, granting it, among other things, the power to review state court rulings that reject federal claims.

Still, the Supreme Court remained weak, and often it had no cases to decide. Chief Justice John Jay (1789–95) was so distressed by the "intolerable" lack of prestige and power of his job that he quit to take a better one—as governor of New York. But the relative weakness of the Court changed in 1803 with the decision in *Marbury* v. *Madison*.[3]

Marbury v. *Madison*: The Source of Judicial Power

When the Federalist party lost the election of 1800, outgoing president John Adams made several last-minute political moves. With the help of a lame duck Congress that passed two judiciary acts and confirmed judicial appointments in the Senate, Adams tried to pack the federal courts with appointments from his own party by issuing several commissions the night before leaving office. When the incoming Jefferson administration denied one of those commissions, the appointment of William Marbury as justice of the peace for the District of Columbia, Marbury sued for his post. The case became the landmark *Marbury* v. *Madison* decision.

This case tested the Supreme Court's power to order federal officials to carry out their official duties—in this case to deliver a judicial commission—a power given to the Court by the Judiciary Act of 1789. Chief Justice John Marshall (1801–35), himself an Adams midnight appointee, wrote the Court's opinion. After conceding that the commissions were valid, he then proceeded to move beyond the issue to review the constitutionality of the Judiciary Act of 1789. Since no power to review the constitutionality of any law can be found in the Constitution, Marshall brilliantly used this case to establish just such a power. He argued that because courts interpret law, and the Constitution is a form of law, the Supreme Court can interpret the Constitution.

Thus, Marshall invoked the power of **judicial review**, the Supreme Court's power to overturn acts of the president, Congress, and the states if those acts violate the Constitution. In assuming the absolute and final power to say what the Constitution means, Marshall helped define the powers of the Court and placed it on an equal

---

original jurisdiction The authority of a court to be the first to hear a case.

appellate jurisdiction The authority of a court to hear a case on appeal after it has been argued in and decided by a lower federal or state court.

Marbury* v. *Madison The 1803 case in which Chief Justice John Marshall established the power of judicial review.

judicial review The power of the Supreme Court established in *Marbury* v. *Madison* to overturn acts of the president, Congress, and the states if those acts violate the Constitution. This power makes the Supreme Court the final interpreter of the Constitution.

MakeItReal

Primary Source: *Federalist #78: The Judiciary Department Federalist #79: The Judiciary Continued*

Primary Source: *The Federal Judiciary Act of 1789*

Primary Source: *Marbury* v. *Madison*

Quick Review

Marbury v. *Madison*

- Appointment of William Marbury as justice of the peace for the District of Columbia was denied by the incoming Jefferson administration.

- Marbury sued for his post, arguing that since courts interpret law, and the Constitution is a form of law, then the Supreme Court can interpret the Constitution.

- Chief Justice John Marshall established the power of judicial review, the power of the Supreme Court to overturn acts of the president.

- Landmark case helped to define the powers of the court.

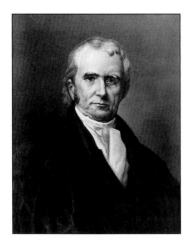

▲ Chief Justice John Marshall (1755–1835) served from 1801 to 1835. His ability to forge unanimous majorities for a series of Supreme Court decisions transformed America from a confederation of states into a nation.

MakeItReal

Primary Source: *Federalist #80: The Powers of the Judiciary*

Primary Source: *Federalist #81: The Judiciary Continued, and the Distribution of Judicial Authority*

statutory construction The power of the Supreme Court to interpret or reinterpret a federal or state law.

footing with the other branches. Marshall then used his newfound judicial review power to deny Marbury his commission. As a result, the Jeffersonians had no judicial order to reject, so Marshall's establishment of judicial review stood unchallenged.

Few decisions in the early years of the nation had such a tremendous impact on America's approach to democracy. The Supreme Court now had the power in the system of checks and balances to negate potentially oppressive majority actions the other political branches might take. Thus, minorities would have a place to go for relief. With the power of judicial review, the Supreme Court could bring various state government actions, both political and judicial, into harmony with the national Constitution, thus altering the federal structure.

Judicial Review: The Court's Ultimate Power

Judicial review has been called the Court's ultimate power because it is absolute. Professor Edward S. Corwin has called it "American democracy's way of hedging its bet," meaning that the Court has the means to correct wayward actions by political branches.[4] Moreover, judicial review has allowed the Supreme Court to update the Constitution by continually reinterpreting its words to fit new situations.

Over the years, judicial review has become a feature of American government accepted by the political branches, the lower judiciary, and the general public. Since 1803, the Supreme Court has declared unconstitutional approximately 1,200 provisions of state laws and state constitutions and exercised the same power with respect to 110 federal executive branch actions and the provisions of more than 160 out of the more than 95,000 federal laws passed.[5] Since 1986, the Rehnquist Court has overturned all or part of forty-one federal laws—an all-time record—many of them by a narrow five–four majority.[6]

Is judicial review a democratic power? Although advocates of judicial review hold that someone has to have the final say over the meaning of the Constitution, others argue that this power is undemocratic because life-tenured, appointed justices can, by a five-vote majority, overrule the collective will of the elected branches. Judicial review is indeed a significant power with few mechanisms to directly countermand it: Congress can pass new or modified legislation or amend the Constitution, or the Court can reverse its decision. However, although judicial review may appear to provide the Court with unlimited power, the political branches and the general public do possess considerable power to rein in the Court.

Other Powers of the Supreme Court

The Court has two other important powers in addition to the power of judicial review. Using its power of **statutory construction**, the Court can interpret or reinterpret a federal or state law. Because the wording of a law is sometimes unclear, the justices must determine the law's true meaning and apply it to the facts in a specific case. In 2005, the Supreme Court narrowly interpreted the so-called federal "felon-in-possession" law that makes it illegal for one "who has been convicted in any court of a crime punishable by imprisonment for a term exceeding one year" to possess a gun. Gary Small had served three years' imprisonment in Japan for smuggling guns and was arrested after buying a gun one week after his return to the United States. The Court ruled in Small's appeal that this law did not include foreign convictions because various nations had different versions of illegal behavior. By reading the law narrowly, the Court used its interpretation of Congress's real intentions to conclude that because the law did not mention foreign convictions, it referred only to domestic convictions.[7]

The Supreme Court's most frequently used power, though, is the power to do nothing, which it exercises by *refusing to review a case,* thus letting stand a lower-court judgment, even one from the states. The Court did this in 2005 when it refused to hear an appeal by reporters Judith Miller of the *New York Times* and

Mathew Cooper of *Time* magazine, who were ordered to jail for contempt by federal district court Judge Thomas Hogan when they refused to reveal to a federal grand jury their sources for an article revealing the identity of C. I. A. agent Valerie Plame. Because the Court refused to hear the case, Miller went to jail. *Time* magazine released Cooper's notes, revealing his source to be presidential adviser Karl Rove, and preventing Cooper from going to jail.[8]

Independence of the Judiciary

A court's power depends on its independence, that is, its ability to make decisions free of outside influences. The framers understood the importance of an independent court and placed several provisions in the Constitution to keep the Supreme Court free of pressures from the people, Congress, and the president:

1. Justices are appointed, not elected; thus, they are not beholden to voters.
2. The president and Senate share the power to appoint justices, leaving the Court beholden to no one person or political party.
3. The justices are guaranteed their position for life, as long as they exhibit "good Behaviour." Even in cases of bad behavior, justices can be impeached only for "High Crimes and Misdemeanors," thus ensuring that the Court cannot be manipulated by the political branches.[9]
4. The Constitution specifies that justices' salaries "shall not be diminished during their Continuance in Office," meaning that Congress cannot lower the Court's salary to punish it for its rulings.

▲ "Hi, I'm your court-appointed lawyer—whoa! Don't tell me you've been executed already."

The Court possesses a great deal of independence, but it is not completely shielded from outside influences. Presidents can change the direction of the Court with new appointments. Congress can attack the judiciary's independence through some or all of the following: passing laws attempting to overturn Court decisions (an action the Court itself can review), abolishing some or all lower federal courts (or refusing to create new courts), refusing to raise salaries, using its power to remove certain classes of cases from the appellate docket (thus leaving lower-court rulings in force), changing the number of justices on the Supreme Court, passing a law to reverse a Court decision, trying to impeach a sitting justice, and attacking the Court in speeches.

Only about a half-dozen times has Congress attempted to use any of these methods to threaten the Court's independence. In 1804, impeachment proceedings were brought against rabid Federalist Justice Samuel Chase for his intemperate political remarks against President Thomas Jefferson, but the Senate trial resulted in acquittal, further solidifying the independence of the judiciary. Another effort came in 1957, when a Congress, displeased with judicial limits placed on its investigative powers, considered the Jenner-Butler Bill, which would have weakened the Court by removing several classes of cases from its appellate docket. Only the efforts of powerful Senate Majority Leader Lyndon Johnson prevented passage of the bill.

At times, mere threats to judicial independence can have an impact on Court decisions. Franklin Roosevelt's court-packing plan failed but still produced a change of direction among the justices in favor of his New Deal programs. And although the Jenner-Butler Bill failed, Justices Felix Frankfurter (1939–62) and John Marshall Harlan (1955–71) changed their positions and began to uphold Congress's power to investigate. In 1968, Congress passed the Omnibus Crime Control Bill, one section of which sought to overturn the *Miranda* v. *Arizona* police interrogation restrictions by allowing federal investigators to use "voluntary" confessions as determined by the "totality of the circumstances" of the interrogation. In 2000, the Supreme Court overturned this provision under the Fifth Amendment.

Question for Reflection

Should any additional constitutional limits be placed on the Supreme Court's power of judicial review?

Since 1997, judicial independence has been under serious attack by congressional Republicans led by Congressman Tom DeLay (R.-TX) and senators led by Jefferson Beauregard Sessions (R.-AL), the latter a failed judicial nominee. Unhappy with what they see as the "liberal activism" of the federal judiciary, judicial nominees found their confirmations delayed or voted down first by the Republicans in the Clinton years and later by the Democrats in the Bush years. While Congress routinely delayed and even derailed President Clinton's court appointments, many of them stopped in the Senate Judiciary Committee by Chairman Orrin Hatch (R.-UT), Clinton, at the end of his eight-year term of office had 374 federal judges confirmed, comparable to the 382 for Ronald Reagan in his eight years and George H. W. Bush's 193 in his four-year term. While Senate consideration of the second President Bush's nominees, especially those with a conservative ideology, was slowed considerably during his first year in office by Democrats seeking political "payback," by mid-2005 a record 208 of the president's nominees to the federal court had been confirmed.

During this time, Court congressional critics searched for other means to influence the direction of the judiciary. Judges were threatened with impeachment; bills were introduced to end life tenure and split the liberal Ninth Circuit Court of Appeals into two circuits, thus giving conservative judges a chance to exercise more power. Other bills were introduced to remove classes of cases from the federal judicial docket, and for a time Congress passed no salary raises for the judiciary.[10] Another attack came in March 2005 when conservative members of Congress, unhappy about the Florida state supreme court decision not to review the order to remove feeding and hydration tubes supporting the life of Theresa Marie Schiavo, passed a private bill on behalf of her parents, placing the case back on the federal judicial docket. The case was subsequently heard in district court and denied once again. As seen in the Chapter 2 case study, by 2005 all of this led the Senate to consider eliminating the filibuster power in judicial confirmations. All of these battles, plus those over abortion, gay marriage, and the disputed "under God" phrase in the Pledge of Allegiance, are sure to be reflected in the confirmation fights for future Supreme Court justices.

Another new area of focus on Supreme Court independence deals with the nature of the justices' appointment process and their life tenure. Seeking to avoid the divisive partisan appointment and confirmation process, and the effect on the types of individuals selected for the Court, political scientist Richard Davis has suggested that justices be elected to eighteen-year terms of office.[11] The lingering, fatal illness of Chief Justice Rehnquist and attendant debate over his decision not to retire raised the question of limiting justices' life tenure. Many justices have remained on the bench in spite of terminal or even incapacitating illnesses.[12] Few leave the Court in relatively good health. Justice William O. Douglas remained on the Court so long after his crippling stroke in 1974 that his colleagues, one of whom was William Rehnquist, voted privately to delay consideration of any case that might turn on Douglas's vote until he retired.[13] Justices are reluctant to leave the Court for a variety of human and political reasons: realization of their own mortality, loss of power and public prestige, loss of control over policy, and hope of setting the Court longevity record for service. Justices also time their departure to make sure their seats are filled by a president from their own political party—Justice Byron White waited until President Clinton came to office in 1993. Modern justices realize that their retirement decision might cause a confirmation fight.

In the end, the Court's greatest protection from political threats to its independence has always come from the people themselves. As long as justices are careful not to outpace public opinion in their decisions, the public is generally supportive of this branch of government. An independent judiciary that secures the rights and liberties of citizens is a cherished part of the American political landscape. It is also one of the measures of true democracy, as you learned in Chapter 1. Thus, it remains to be seen how long the public will allow this Senate version of political payback to be accepted in the judicial confirmation process.

THE ORGANIZATION OF THE AMERICAN COURT SYSTEM

The American judicial system consists of two separate and parallel court systems: an extensive system of state and local courts in which the vast majority of cases are decided, and a system of national or federal courts. Figure 6.1 illustrates the structure of the American court system. Most of the time, these two judicial systems operate independently of each other. State courts deal with state laws and constitutions, and federal courts deal with federal laws and the U.S. Constitution. But when the state courts handle issues touching on the Constitution or federal laws, it is possible for a litigant to shift over to the federal system. The extensive lower-court system (all courts beneath the Supreme Court) functions as a gatekeeper, restricting the flow of appeals to the Supreme Court. Appeals come to the Supreme Court from both the highest courts in the fifty states and from the federal appellate courts.

Types of Courts

Federal and state courts are divided into trial and appellate courts. A **trial court** (also known as a *petit court*) is often a case's point of original entry in the legal system, with a single judge and at times a jury to decide matters both of fact and law. Deciding issues of fact involves determining what actually happened; deciding

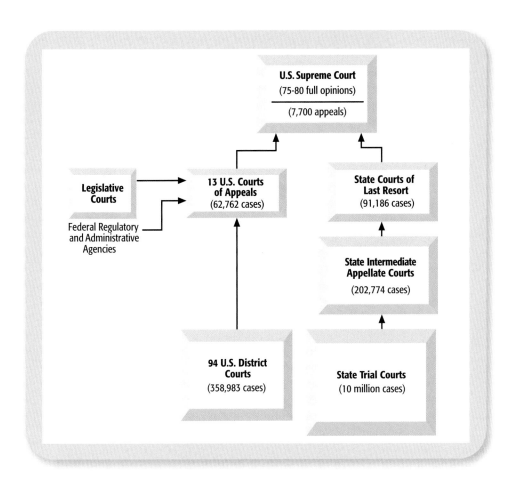

Figure 6.1   Structure of the American Court System

Sources: Federal Judicial Workload Statistics (Washington, D.C.: Administrative Office of the U.S. Courts, 2005) Judicial Caseload Profiles Administrative Office of the U.S. Courts Website, http://www. uscourts/gov; National State Caseload Highlights, National Center for State Courts, Williamsburg, VA, http://www.ncsonline.org; http://www.ncsc.dni.us/2003AnnlRept.htm/.

Question for Reflection

Should the length of service of Supreme Court justices have any limit?

---

trial court The point of original entry in the legal system, with a single judge and at times a jury deciding matters of both fact and law in a case.

Approaching Democracy Around the Globe

Democracy and Judicial Independence

In the United States, the concept of judicial independence means that judges are free to decide in support of civil liberties and press freedom based on the law and not on the wishes of powerful political leaders. But the degree of judicial independence varies in other nations.

As the accompanying map shows, a strong correlation exists between judicial independence, support of civil liberties and press freedom, and democratic government. Democratic countries usually select judges on merit rather than politics. Judges act in an independent fashion, apply constitutional rules to the political branches and the military, and cannot be removed from office because of the nature of their decisions. In contrast, judges in authoritarian regimes are more likely to follow the dictates of political leaders and to be disciplined if they do not.

The link between stable, democratic government and full judicial independence is apparent in nations such as Australia, Canada, Great Britain, Japan, Finland, and Taiwan. Nations such as Nigeria, the Ukraine, Turkey, and Nepal, while democratic, are less stable, and their judicial systems have less independence.

The least independent judicial systems are found in countries with authoritarian governments, such as China, North Korea, Saudi Arabia, Haiti, and many African nations. Their limited court systems make few decisions, and the decisions they do make can be overruled by military and party leaders. Judges who make unpopular decisions risk being removed, jailed, or even killed.

When governments reform, as they have recently in Mexico, Peru, Afghanistan, Hungary, the Czech Republic, Estonia, and Slovakia, one of the first signs of change is increasing independence of the judicial branch.

A historical comparison of this map over the past several years shows that the number of "free judicial" countries has risen more than 500 percent, to nearly half of the nations of the world, with the biggest geographical increases coming in South America. Although the number of countries that lack free judiciaries has remained roughly the same, the change of Russia to the "not free" category from the limited category has greatly increased the geographical coverage of this category.

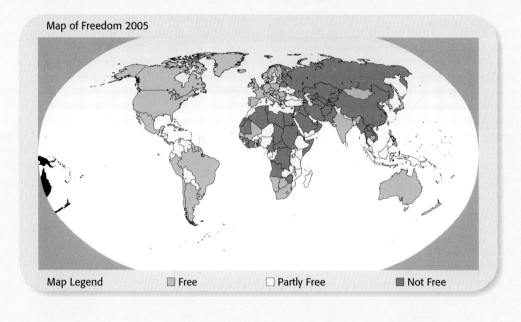

Map of Freedom 2005

Map Legend   ☐ Free   ☐ Partly Free   ■ Not Free

issues of law involves applying relevant statutes and constitutional provisions to the evidence and conduct of a trial. For instance, in a murder case, deciding a matter of fact would involve the jury's determining a defendant's guilt or innocence based on the evidence admitted into trial. Deciding a matter of law would involve the judge's determining whether certain pieces of evidence, such as a particular witness's testimony, should be admitted into the proceedings.

An **appellate court** reviews the proceedings of the trial court, often with a panel of judges and no jury. The appellate court considers only matters of law. Thus, in a murder case the appellate court would not be concerned with the jury's verdict of guilty or innocent; instead, it might reconsider the trial's legality, such as whether the judge was correct in admitting certain evidence into trial. An appellate court ruling could lead to a new trial if evidence is deemed inadmissible.

Types of Cases

Trial and appeals courts hear both criminal and civil cases. In **criminal cases**, decisions are made regarding whether to punish individuals accused of violating the state or federal criminal (or penal) code. Criminal law covers murder, rape, robbery, and assault, as well as certain nonviolent offenses such as embezzlement and tax fraud. The state courts handle the vast majority of criminal cases, though in recent years Congress, outraged at the nature of certain illegal actions, has passed laws creating more federal crimes. The 1994 Freedom of Access to Clinic Entrances Act made it a federal crime to prevent access to abortion clinics, and the 1996 Church Arson Prevention Act made burning a church a federal crime. The 2001 USA Patriot Act created a new category of federal crimes of terrorism against mass transit. In 2005, the Judicial Conference of the United States, the policy-recommending body for the judiciary, under the leadership of Chief Justice William Rehnquist, recommended that Congress resist the impulse to create new federal crimes to be enforced by the federal courts.[14] More than 90 percent of criminal cases never come to trial but instead result in private conferences called **plea bargains**, in which the state agrees to press for either a reduced set of charges or a reduced sentence in return for a guilty plea. Plea bargains eliminate the need for a time-consuming trial, thus helping to keep the court system from overload.[15]

In **civil cases**, courts resolve private disputes among individuals over finances, property, or personal well-being. Malpractice suits, libel suits, breach of contract suits, and personal injury suits are examples of civil cases. Judicial remedies in such cases often involve a judicial decree that requires a certain action or monetary award. Monetary awards can include both *compensatory damages,* which reimburse a litigant for the harm done by another's actions, and *punitive damages,* which go beyond compensation to punish intentional or reckless behavior that causes harm, seeking to discourage such action in the future. Large groups of people affected by an action can unite in a **class action suit**, a single civil case in which the results apply to all participants. Often class action suits are used to compensate victims of large corporations. In 2005, 20,000 former employees of the bankrupt Enron energy firm won a $356 million class action lawsuit to restore their lost 401(k) pension funds.[16] Sometimes, though, these cases have important policy implications as well. In 2002, a group of seven Bucks County, Pennsylvania, relatives of victims of the September 11, 2001, World Trade Center attack filed a multibillion-dollar class action lawsuit against Osama Bin Laden and his terrorist network, in seeking to dry up their monetary funds worldwide. When the American government froze $80 million, together with the $150 million already frozen, it seemed more possible to fight back against terrorism in this way.[17] As with criminal cases, a great many class action suits and civil cases never come to trial because they are settled out of court.

Organization of the Federal Courts

As you've seen, the federal judiciary is organized in three tiers—the U.S. district courts at the bottom, the courts of appeals in the middle, and the Supreme Court at the top. These are all **constitutional courts**, so called because they are mentioned in Article III of the Constitution, the judicial article. All federal constitutional courts are staffed by life-tenured judges or justices.

The **U.S. district courts** are the workhorses of the federal judicial system. These trial courts serve as the original point of entry for almost all federal cases. Roughly

appellate court The court that reviews an appeal of the trial court proceedings, often with a multijudge panel and without a jury; it considers only matters of law.

criminal cases Cases in which decisions are made regarding whether or not to punish individuals accused of violating the state or federal criminal code.

plea bargains Agreements in which the state presses for either a reduced set of charges or a reduced sentence in return for a guilty plea.

civil cases Noncriminal cases in which courts resolve disputes among individuals and parties to the case over finances, property, or personal well-being.

class action suit A single civil case in which the plaintiff represents the whole class of individuals similarly situated, and the court's results apply to this entire class.

constitutional courts Courts mentioned in Article III of the Constitution whose judges have life tenure.

U.S. district courts The trial courts serving as the original point of entry for almost all federal cases.

 **MakeItReal**

ABC News Video: *Elian, Abortion, and School Prayer*

Question for Reflection

If the majority of criminal and civil cases are settled out of court, how might the American court system be reorganized to accommodate this reality and improve the speed with which justice is rendered?

U.S. courts of appeals The middle appeals level of judicial review beyond the district courts; in 2006, consisted of 165 judges in 13 courts, 12 of which are geographically based.

360,000 civil and criminal cases are filed every year in ninety-four district courts—at least one in every state—staffed in 2006 by 679 judges. District courts hear cases arising under federal law, national treaties, and the Constitution, and they review the actions of various federal agencies and departments. Roughly half of the cases involve juries. Appealing cases to the next level is expensive and time consuming, therefore, in about 85 percent of cases decided in district court, the judgment is final.

The next rung on the federal judicial ladder is the **U.S. court of appeals**, consisting in 2006 of 165 judges and 88 retired senior judges in thirteen courts. Twelve of these appeals courts are geographically based, eleven of them in multistate geographic regions called *circuits* (see Figure 6.2), so named because Supreme Court justices once literally "rode the circuit" to hear cases. The U.S. Court of Appeals for the Ninth Circuit, for example, covers more than 50 million people in California, Arizona, Nevada, Oregon, Washington, Idaho, Montana, Alaska, and Hawaii. The twelfth circuit court is the U.S. Court of Appeals for the District of Columbia, which hears appeals from federal regulatory commissions and agencies. Because of the important nature of the cases arising from federal agencies and departments, many consider the Court of Appeals in the District of Columbia the second most important federal court after the Supreme Court. The U.S. Court of Appeals for the Federal Circuit is the thirteenth appeals court; it specializes in appeals involving patents and contract claims against the national government.

Decisions from various circuits vary widely, depending on the political orientation of their judges. As of January 2006, the Republicans had nearly 60 percent of the appointees on the Court of Appeals and had controlling majorities on nine of the thirteen appeals courts and were poised to take control of two others. The ninth circuit, however, has a two-to-one majority of liberal Carter and Clinton Democrats to Republicans. This balance affects the nature of the Supreme Court's acceptance of appeals and decisions. The conservative Rehnquist Court reversed the vast majority

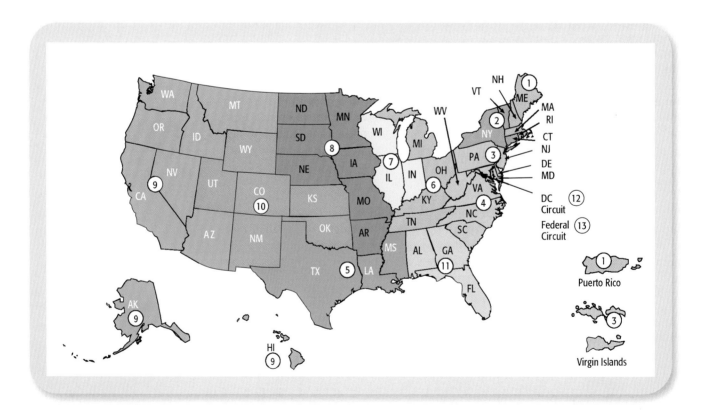

Figure 6.2 The Thirteen Federal Judicial Circuits
Source: Administrative Office of the United States Courts, September 1991.

of appeals from the ninth circuit, whereas those from the fourth circuit in the Virginia and Carolina regions, and the fifth circuit in Texas, Louisiana, and Mississippi, where highly ideological Reagan-Bush conservative judges predominate, were upheld.[18] Appeals courts usually hear cases in three-judge panels, although sometimes cases are decided in **en banc** proceedings, in which all of the appeals judges in a particular circuit serve as a tribunal. The court of appeals receives more than 62,000 appeals in a year. For the remaining cases, the district court's judgment is left in force.[19] Because so few cases proceed to the Supreme Court, the court of appeals has been described by one prominent judicial scholar as a "mini Supreme Court in the vast majority of cases."[20] This is important because the recent high volume of appeals has led judges to resolve cases with one-word opinions just to clear their dockets—thus creating a two-level justice system for tens of thousands of cases.[21]

In addition to these constitutional appeals courts, the federal judiciary includes **legislative courts** of appeal. Legislative courts are called Article I courts because they are established by Congress based on Article I, Section 8, of the Constitution. These courts are designed to provide technical expertise on specific subjects. Unlike life-appointed judges on constitutional courts, legislative court judges serve a fixed term. Legislative courts include the U.S. Court of Military Appeals, the U.S. Tax Court, the U.S. Court of Veterans Appeals, and various territorial courts. Any decision by legislative courts can usually be appealed to the constitutional court system. Some of these legislative courts are special courts consisting of already serving Article III judges who have specialized jurisdictions. The Foreign Intelligence Surveillance Act (FISA), established in 1978, is a secret court consisting of eleven federal judges who serve seven-year terms. These judges review federal intelligence agency requests for warrants to use electronic surveillance agencies in investigating terrorism. The newly created Alien Terrorist Removal Court, with federal judges appointed by the chief justice, reviews deportation orders for legal aliens suspected of terrorist acts.[22]

COURT APPOINTMENTS: THE PROCESS AND THE POLITICS

The process for appointing judges to the federal courts is stated clearly in Article II, Section 2, of the Constitution. The president is charged with making the appointments, and the Senate is charged with confirming those appointments by majority vote (its "advice and consent" role). Although the framers wanted only the most "meritorious" candidates selected, politics plays an important part in the process and helps determine which judges end up on the federal bench.

The Supreme Court Appointment Process

How does any one of the hundreds of people qualified for the Supreme Court rise to the top and secure an appointment? The process for appointing Supreme Court justices varies depending on the president and the candidate involved, but in general it begins with the collection and sifting of names. When a vacancy occurs, suggestions for the new appointment come into the White House and the Justice Department from politicians, senators, governors, friends of the candidates, the candidate themselves, and even sitting and retired federal judges. This list is then winnowed down to about two dozen top names. A member of the attorney general's staff or the White House staff oversees an information-gathering process that involves a background check by the Federal Bureau of Investigation (FBI) to determine suitability of character and to uncover any potentially damaging information that might lead to problems with confirmation. A short list of candidates is then forwarded to the president for consideration.

A seat on the Supreme Court is the juiciest plum in the presidential patronage garden. It can go to a highly visible candidate or to someone close to a president. But

en banc Proceedings in which all of the appeals judges in a particular circuit serve as a tribunal.

legislative courts Courts designed to provide technical expertise on specific subjects based on Article I of the Constitution.

Quick Review

Appointing Supreme Court Justices

- Process begins with the collection of names and creation of a short list of candidates.

- An information-gathering process involves a background check to determine suitability and to uncover any potentially damaging information.

- List of candidates is forwarded to the president for consideration and selection of a candidate.

- The Senate confirms Supreme Court appointments by majority vote.

▲ Ruth Bader Ginsburg signs the Supreme Court's oath card on October 1, 1993, with Chief Justice William Rehnquist and President Bill Clinton looking on. Ginsburg has proven less liberal on the Court than she had been in practicing law.

MakeItReal

Visual Literacy: Sandra Day O'Connor and Earl Warren

an equally important consideration is partisanship. Presidents tend to be partisan in their choices, seeking both to reward members of their own party and to see their own political ideology mirrored on the Court. In addition, ethnicity and gender come into play, as do various political interest groups such as the American Bar Association and the Senate.

The Role of Party   Well over 90 percent of Supreme Court appointees have been from the president's own political party. In general, Democrats tend to appoint judges who are willing to extend constitutional and legal protections to the individual and to favor government regulation of business. Republicans, on the other hand, tend to appoint judges who are less attentive to individual rights and more willing to defer to the government unless the issue is business, where they favor less government control. Republican George H. W. Bush appointed David Souter and Clarence Thomas to the Supreme Court, two jurists with philosophies inclined to uphold lower-court and regulatory agency decisions. Democrat Bill Clinton appointed Ruth Bader Ginsburg, a leader of the women's rights movement, and Stephen G. Breyer, a strong advocate of individual rights.

But presidents are sometimes unpleasantly surprised. What a person *was* can be a poor predictor of what he or she *will become* on the Supreme Court. Although some scholars estimate that more than 70 percent of the time appointees meet presidents' expectations, miscalculations do happen.[23] Conservative president Dwight Eisenhower appointed Earl Warren (1953–69) and William Brennan (1956–90) to the Court on the assumption that they were conservatives. Later he would call the two ultraliberal justices "the two biggest mistakes" in his career.[24] Richard Nixon thought he was appointing a conservative ally to Chief Justice

▲ Presidential Counsel Harriet Miers was nominated to the Supreme Court by President Bush on October 3, 2005 to replace retiring Justice Sandra Day O'Connor. Sharp and sustained objections to her nomination by conservative groups, who did not trust her conservative credentials, though, forced her withdrawal less than six weeks later, even before her Senate confirmation hearing.

Warren Burger in his childhood friend Harry Blackmun, but in time Blackmun became the liberal anchor on the Rehnquist Court. Sandra Day O'Connor was much more liberal than Ronald Reagan assumed at the time of her appointment. On the present Court, Anthony Kennedy and David Souter have come under fire by conservatives who once backed their appointments. Essentially, the immense responsibilities of the office, the lifelong freedom to decide issues, the weight of the history of a Court seat, the interaction with new colleagues on the bench, and the natural evolution of one's life, can all combine to create a jurist far different from expected.

Recently, presidents have tried to sharpen their ability to predict the ideology of their Supreme Court appointments and improve their chances for Senate confirmation by selecting candidates who are judges on the courts of appeals, where their prior judicial records might offer clues regarding future decisions. This changes the kind of Court assembled. For instance, although the 1941–42 Roosevelt Court consisted of a

Harvard law professor, two U.S. senators, a chair of the Securities and Exchange Commission, three former attorneys general, a solicitor general, and a U.S. attorney, the 2006 Court consists entirely of former U.S. court of appeals judges. The result is a Court that operates in a more bureaucratically judicial fashion as the justices take fewer cases, decide them in an incremental fashion, and write narrow opinions.

Aiming for a more ideologically suitable set of judicial appointments, President Bush initially put Alberto Gonzales, a Hispanic attorney now serving as attorney general, in charge of the Office of Legal Policy, which vets possible judicial nominees. When Gonzales became Attorney General Harriet Miers was placed in charge of the ad hoc group of fifteen to twenty staffers and Justice Department appointees who review the credentials of and interview possible nominees in order to prepare lists of appointment prospects for the attorney general and President Bush.

Seeking a More Representative Court   Over the years, the representative nature of the Court has become an issue. Presidents have used emerging categories such as geography, religion, race, and gender to create a sort of "balanced" Court that keeps various constituencies satisfied.

An effort has always been made to have all geographical regions of the country represented on the Court. "Wiley, you have geography," Franklin Roosevelt told Iowan Wiley Rutledge (1943–49) when explaining his impending appointment. The Roosevelt Court's only other "non-Easterner," William O. Douglas (1939–75), had been raised in Yakima, Washington, although he actually lived on the East Coast since his law school years.[25] Religion also plays a role. For more than one hundred years there was a so-called Catholic seat on the Court. The appointment of Louis Brandeis (1916–39) created a "Jewish seat" that remained until 1969 (and some believe was resumed in 1993). Thurgood Marshall's appointment (1967–91) established an "African American seat." Clarence Thomas (1991–present), also an African American, was appointed to fill that seat when Marshall retired. Sandra Day O'Connor's appointment (1981–06) seemed to have established a "female seat." It is widely anticipated that in time a new Hispanic seat will be created on the Court.

Judicial scholars continue to debate whether considering such representational factors is the proper way to staff the Court.[26] Many believe that merit should be the primary consideration. Some argue that given the small number of Court seats and the large number of interest groups, satisfying everyone is virtually impossible. Still, political considerations are unavoidable in an atmosphere dominated by sharp partisanship. Recent administrations have tried to appease their constituencies by mentioning during the initial winnowing-down process that candidates from various categories are "under consideration." President Bush undertook a series of consultations with senators from both parties in selecting John Roberts Jr., and then seemingly failed to consult widely in the choice of Harriet Miers to replace Justice Sandra Day O'Connor. But most often presidents end up selecting appointees based on other factors.

The Role of the American Bar Association   In the past, the president submitted a short list of judicial candidate names to the American Bar Association (ABA), a national association for the legal profession, for an informal review by its Standing Committee on the Federal Judiciary. Attorneys canvass judges and lawyers throughout the country regarding the nominees' qualifications. Based on these inquiries, Supreme Court nominees are rated "highly qualified," "not opposed," or "not qualified." Candidates for the lower courts are rated "well qualified," "qualified," or "not qualified."[27] Although the intent is to seek out information on the nominee's professional qualifications, personal and ideological considerations inevitably arise as well.

The president is not required to consult the ABA in the judicial appointment process.[28] Conservatives became unhappy with the ABA after it issued a mixed review for Robert Bork in 1987 and four years later gave its worst rating ever for Clarence Thomas. The Republican Senate's unhappiness with the ABA's judicial survey results led the Senate Judiciary Committee, under Republican Orrin Hatch (R.-UT), to stop

Question for Reflection

How might the 2006 congressional and 2008 presidential election results alter this judicial appointment process?

using their reports. Later, Republican president George W. Bush announced that, despite the half-century tradition, he would no longer use the ABA review process. Instead, the ABA sent its reports to the Senate Judiciary Committee for use by the Democrats in the hearings.

The Role of the Senate The Constitution charges the Senate with confirming Supreme Court appointments by majority vote. The Senate confirmation process begins with a Senate Judiciary Committee hearing designed to elicit views about a candidate. The committee then makes a recommendation for or against the candidate prior to a vote of the full Senate. Over the years, Senate confirmation has proven a significant hurdle, with nearly one in five presidential nominations rejected.

In general, the president initially has the upper hand in the appointment process, but the Senate can oppose a nominee for a variety of reasons, including unhappiness with the candidate's competence or political views. The Senate rejected G. Harrold Carswell in 1971, citing a lack of competence—but not before Nebraska senator Roman Hruska defended Carswell by saying: "Even if he is mediocre, there are a lot of mediocre judges and people and lawyers. They are entitled to a little representation, aren't they?"[29]

Other rejections have to do with partisan politics. In 1987, Republican president Ronald Reagan's appointee Robert Bork was confronted by a Senate Judiciary Committee controlled by the opposing Democratic party. After a massive media campaign by a coalition of liberal interest groups and vigorous questioning from the Judiciary Committee, and with the tide of public opinion turning against him, the intellectually qualified Bork was defeated because of his ultraconservative views, well documented in a trail of paper that spanned his entire career.[30] Some candidates are rejected through Senate opposition to the president or as a message of opposition to the current direction of the Court.

Timing seems important in the success of a nomination. A nomination that comes early in a president's term or during a period of presidential popularity is more likely to succeed. Those that come late in the term or are made by a weak president face greater potential for a difficult confirmation. For instance, Bork's troubled nomination came in the next-to-last year of Reagan's presidency, while neither of Bill Clinton's nominations, made in his first two years in office, met with significant opposition.

Sometimes a nominee is challenged because of information uncovered in the Judiciary Committee investigation. When George H. W. Bush nominated Clarence Thomas in 1991, law professor Anita Hill charged that Thomas had sexually harassed her while she worked for him at the federal Equal Employment Opportunity Commission (EEOC). The televised hearings were dramatic, with Senator Arlen Specter accusing Professor Hill of "flat-out perjury," and women's rights groups demanding that the nomination be defeated. In the end, Thomas was confirmed by a razor-thin 52–48 margin.[31]

In the late twentieth century, the Senate sought greater influence in the confirmation process. After approving all Supreme Court candidates for nearly forty years, the Senate began to use its "advice and consent" role to such an extent that since 1968 it has turned down four nominees (Abe Fortas, G. Harrold Carswell, Clement Haynsworth, and Robert Bork), forced the withdrawal of another (Douglas Ginsburg), and significantly attacked two other candidates (William Rehnquist for chief justice, and Clarence Thomas).[32] Since the Bork battle in 1987, the public has become more interested in Supreme Court confirmations, and the Senate's role has become more dramatic. Televising confirmation hearings and floor debates has made senators more conscious of the politics of the appointment process. Finally, the increased lobbying activity of highly partisan coalitions of interest groups, which now mount election-style media campaigns, has whipped up considerable public pressure on voting senators. The more than $100 million that interest groups spent during the confirmation of William Rehnquist's and Sandra Day O'Connor's successors created an "election style" environment for these debates.

To counter this newfound Senate willingness to question seriously and even reject nominees, presidents have devised new appointment strategies. First, they have searched for "safe" candidates—ones lacking a large body of writing or decisions that make easy targets for attack. Seeking to avoid the problems faced by highly visible and widely published legal scholar Bork, two years later President George H. W. Bush appointed a little-known court of appeals judge from Weare, New Hampshire, David Souter. The lack of a paper trail to provide any inkling of Souter's leanings helped dub him the "stealth candidate."

Presidents have also appointed friends and protégés of prominent senators, in hopes that the senator will lead the confirmation fight in the Senate. Clarence Thomas's nomination was greatly helped by his mentor, Republican Senator John Danforth of Missouri, while Stephen Breyer's nomination was helped along by the advocacy of a fellow Massachusetts resident, Senator Ted Kennedy. President Clinton consulted with powerful members of the Senate, including opposing party members, prior to any appointment, seeking to eliminate any names that might cause difficulty. Thus, Secretary of the Interior Bruce Babbitt was dropped from the appointment list in 1994, when conservative Republican Senator Orrin Hatch of Utah objected to his liberal philosophy.[33]

Presidents have looked to the court of appeals for appointees, believing that having been confirmed once by the Senate might bode well, and that their record on the bench might reveal the nature of their decision making on the Supreme Court. The practice became so common, as indicated by the appointments of both Ruth Bader Ginsburg and Stephen Breyer, that during discussions over Sandra Day O'-Connor's replacement, Court and Senate members suggested repeatedly, and without success, that the president look elsewhere to fill the vacancy.

This search for "safe" candidates could affect the nature of the Court. Highly qualified but also highly controversial legal scholars are now being passed over for appointment by presidents fearful of Senate rejection. In the past, controversial candidates such as Felix Frankfurter and William O. Douglas had tremendous impact on the Court's direction. Some judicial scholars wonder whether this avoidance of talented but risky candidates will produce a Court unwilling to expand its decision-making role or make controversial decisions. Such a trend is impossible to predict, of course, because of the politics of appointment and the ways jurists develop once on the Court. With the sharply partisan Senate debating elimination of the filibuster, and senators from both parties demanding a voice in the Court selection process, it remains to be seen what impact all of this will have on the judicial selection process.

The Impact of Presidential Appointments on the Supreme Court

Although every Court appointment is important, not every appointment changes the direction of the Court. Supreme Courts are commonly named after their chief justice, such as the Rehnquist Court, but philosophical directional changes within those years may make it better to categorize a Court according to the president who redirected it through judicial appointments.

In recent history, three presidents—Kennedy, Nixon, and Reagan—have dramatically changed the Court's direction. In 1962, Democratic president John F. Kennedy shifted an ideologically balanced moderate conservative Court to a more liberal one by replacing moderate conservative Justice Frankfurter with more liberal Arthur Goldberg (1962–65). In doing so, Kennedy assured a solid 5–4 vote in favor of civil rights and liberties cases. After Richard Nixon was elected on a "law and order" platform in 1968, his four conservative appointments to the Supreme Court—William Rehnquist, Lewis Powell, Harry Blackmun, and Warren Burger—moved the Court in a more conservative direction, away from individual rights. After his 1980 election, Ronald Reagan's four appointments—Sandra Day O'Connor, Antonin Scalia, Anthony Kennedy, and William Rehnquist as chief justice—created a Court able to

Questions for Reflection

How has the process of selecting Supreme Court Justices in the twenty-first century affected the types of candidates considered?

How does this approach conform with Article II, Section 2 of the Constitution and the framers' desire that the most "meritorious" candidates be selected?

reverse earlier rulings in such areas as defendants' rights. Thus, the rights of Americans can expand and contract as a result of their president's choices.

Presidents generally expect their legacy of Supreme Court appointments to remain long after them (with the exception of William Howard Taft, who appointed sixty-six-year-old Edward White as chief justice, hoping that he would die shortly and leave the opening for Taft himself—which, in fact, did happen). Fate sometimes dictates otherwise. The much-celebrated New Deal Court changed direction in late 1949 when liberals Frank Murphy (1940–49) and Wiley Rutledge (1943–49) died suddenly, to be replaced by moderate conservatives Tom Clark (1949–67) and Sherman Minton (1949–56). The Rehnquist Court was reshaped by two retirements in 1993–1994—conservative Democrat Byron White and Republican Harry Blackmun, a conservative who evolved into a liberal.

Bill Clinton's appointments of moderate liberals Ruth Bader Ginsburg and Stephen Breyer actually moved the Supreme Court in a more conservative direction. This conservative trend, often by 5–4 votes, occurred because Justices Anthony Kennedy and Sandra Day O'Connor shifted to the conservative side to vote frequently with Justices Rehnquist, Scalia, and Thomas. Now, with Chief Justice Rehnquist's death and Justice O'Connor retired, leaving all but 3 justices over the age of sixty-five, the Court composition is poised for dramatic change. Each new appointment can change the decision making of all the remaining members. For instance, while many expect that the new Court will shift to the right with the loss of O'Connor's moderate swing vote, it is equally possible that moderate Anthony Kennedy could shift slightly to the left, as he has already done on gay rights cases. His could then become the swing vote determining the Court's decisions.

Staffing the Lower Federal Courts

The real impact of the presidential appointment power comes not so much at the Supreme Court level as at the lower federal court level. With hundreds of appointments of life-tenured judges here, and more than 99.9 percent of all federal cases never reaching the Supreme Court, these appointments determine the direction of American law for many years to come. The legacy of a president's lower-court appointments will last for about two decades after the end of that president's term of office.[34]

The formal selection process for the lower federal courts is roughly the same as for the Supreme Court. Guided by officials in the Justice Department and White House Office of Legal Policy, the president nominates candidates first screened by the FBI. The candidates' names are then sent to the Senate Judiciary Committee, which consults the ABA report in beginning the confirmation proceedings. But there is one important difference in the selection process for lower-court judges. For federal district court appointments, presidents usually observe the practice of **senatorial courtesy** by submitting the names of nominees to senators from the same political party who are also from the nominee's home state. Failure to do so might lead to a senator declaring that a candidate is "personally obnoxious," dooming the appointment. Other senators, wishing to preserve the practice of senatorial courtesy for their own use in the future, will follow the first senator's lead and vote against the nomination. In these ways, senatorial courtesy has forced presidents to share their nomination power with the Senate.[35] In fact, in many cases the names of prospective candidates are forwarded to the White House by the senators from the president's party and the candidate's state (and sometimes even from powerful senators in the other party) prior to the nomination decision. These candidates often become the nominee.

A president's ability to use the appointment power to shape the lower federal court is determined by length of service in the White House, the number of vacancies that arise during that time, and whether or not the Senate confirms the nominees. In addition, Congress can expand the lower-court system, creating new seats to be filled. One-term president Jimmy Carter made 258 appointments, while two-term president Ronald Reagan made 382. When Republican George H. W. Bush's 193 appointments were combined with the holdovers from previous Republican administrations, we see

senatorial courtesy A procedure in which a president submits the names of judicial nominees to senators from the same political party who are also from the nominee's home state for their approval prior to formal nomination.

that the Republican party appointed approximately 65 percent of the lower federal judiciary. By the end of Bill Clinton's first term of office, he had filled more than one-fifth of the federal judiciary. By the end of Clinton's administration he had appointed 374 judges, or roughly 45 percent of the federal court judges. However, even at that time, well more than 40 percent of the appointees from the Reagan/Bush administrations remained on the federal bench. When added to the 208 appointees by George W. Bush, roughly 25 percent of the federal judiciary, more than half of the federal judiciary had been appointed by Republican presidents as of mid-2005. By this time, despite retirements by a great many conservative jurists, the conservatives controlled ten of the thirteen courts of appeals and needed only two more judges to control two more of them, with several vacancies yet to be filled.[36] Recent presidents have clearly sought to leave their mark on the composition of the federal bench. President Jimmy Carter sought to make the court system more representative of the general population. After years of largely white male appointments, in 1976 Carter created merit selection panels for choosing nominees to the appeals courts. Charged with searching for more diverse candidates as opposed to those merely politically well connected, these panels identified qualified female, African American, and Hispanic prospects. As a result, more than one-third of Carter's appointments were from these underrepresented groups.[37]

The Reagan administration abandoned the merit selection process, seeking instead to correct a perceived liberal bias on the federal courts. The President's Committee on Federal Judicial Selection was created to give the administration centralized ideological control over the selection process. In addition to the usual background checks, extensive written surveys and lengthy personal interviews were conducted to determine the nature and degree of the conservatism of the candidates. The result was, in the words of one judicial selection expert, "the most consistent ideological or policy-orientation screening of judicial candidates since the first term of Franklin Roosevelt."[38] And the change in the gender and ethnic composition of nominees was dramatic. Far fewer women, African Americans, and Hispanics were nominated (see Figure 6.3). Although the George H. W. Bush

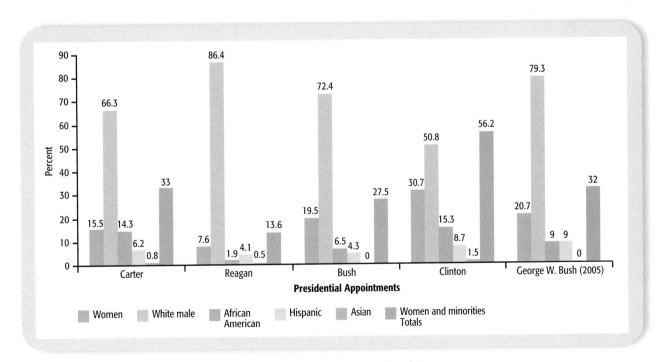

Figure 6.3   Presidential Appointments of Minorities on the Lower Federal Courts

Source: Sheldon Goldman, et al., "W. Bush's Judiciary: The First Term Record," *Judicature,* Vol. 88, No. 6, May-June, 2005, pp. 244–74; "W. Bush Remaking the Judiciary: Like Father, Like Son?" *Judicature,* Vol. 86, No. 6, May-June 2003, pp. 282–309. "Clinton's Judges: Summing Up the Legacy," *Judicature 84,* no. 5 (March/April 2001), pp. 228–54. Sheldon Goldman and Matthew D. Saronson, "Clinton's Nontraditional Judges: Creating a More Representative Bench," *Judicature 78,* no. 2 (September/October 1994), pp. 68–73; Sheldon Goldman and Elliot Slotnick, "Clinton's First-Term Judiciary: Many Bridges to Cross," *Judicature 80,* no. 6 (May/June 1997), p. 254; Sheldon Goldman and Elliot Slotnick, "Picking Judges Under Fire," *Judicature 86,* no. 6 (May/June 1999), pp. 265–78.

administration ended the overt screening of candidates for conservatism, ideology remained as much a consideration as under the Reagan administration. Nonetheless, the Bush administration appointed more women to the federal bench than even Carter had (20.7 percent to 15.5 percent). More than 30 percent of Bush's appointments to the federal bench were women and minorities.[39]

In his eight years of office, Clinton sought to make the courts even more representative, and in the process made history because of the highly representative nature of his federal judicial appointments. Compared with the past four presidential administrations, Clinton appointed the greatest percentage of African American and female judges, resulting in historic highs in each category. Well over one of every two of his appointments were women and minorities, resulting in a federal judiciary in which 32 percent of the judges in 2002 came from these groups (representing a 68 percent increase during Clinton's presidency).[40] Although these percentages do not mirror the proportion of these groups in the total population, the percentage of women on the federal bench is now much closer to the percentage of women in the legal profession, and the percentage of African Americans on the bench is more than two times the proportion of African Americans in that profession.[41]

George W. Bush's diversity in his appointments to the federal judiciary was far less than the previous administration. Only 20.7 percent of his federal court appointments

U.S.A. Yesterday and Today

The "Borking" of the Federal Judiciary

When conservative former appeals court judge Robert Bork was rejected for the 1987 Supreme Court vacancy created when swing Justice Lewis Powell retired, it had lasting effects on the confirmation process, the U.S. Senate, and, later, operation of the Supreme Court itself.

The Democrat–controlled Judiciary Committee, chaired by Senator Joseph Biden (D.-DE), used every weapon at its disposal to defeat the nomination. In confirmation hearings run on prime-time television, a coalition of liberal interest groups, called People for an American Way, under the chairmanship of Ralph Neas, and the Alliance for Justice, under Nan Aron, charged that Bork would move the Court in a conservative direction. The coalition used newspaper and television ads, creating a circus-like election atmosphere. At one point, journalists even attempted to secure the list of Bork's video rentals, seeking to make statements about his views and morals.

The rejection of Bork's nomination in a close vote did not end this new type of confirmation practice. Next, Democrats attacked Clarence Thomas's nomination to the Supreme Court in 1991, accusing him of sexually harassing Professor Anita Hill. After Thomas complained that he was being subjected to a "high-tech lynching," he was confirmed by a narrow four-vote Senate margin. Such events have forced presidents to make Supreme Court nominations based as much on "confirmability" as on merit, even sometimes to the point of nominating "stealth candidates" about whom little is known, to avoid a Senate

fight. The result has been surprising decision making by more centrist justices David Souter and Stephen Breyer. Without doubt, the Bork defeat affected Court relations. Former law clerk to Harry Blackmun, Ed Lazarus, writes that during the 1988–89 term, one conservative clerk wrote his colleagues in the early 1990s, "Every time I draw blood I'll think of what they did to Robert H. Bork."*

Following Robert Bork's failed confirmation and Clarence Thomas's narrow confirmation victory, presidents from both political parties have also had increasing difficulty in reshaping the lower federal judiciary because of partisan Senate opposition. The Democrat-controlled Senate Judiciary Committee refused to confirm fifty-two of George H. W. Bush's nominees, affording incoming president Bill Clinton the opportunity to immediately fill 13 percent of the judiciary seats. After the 1996 congressional elections, the Republican-dominated Judiciary Committee, led by Utah's Orrin Hatch, held up Bill Clinton's appointments even to the point of not allowing hearings on many nominees. By 2000, the lower federal judiciary had a backlog of eighty-two vacancies, nearly 10 percent of all judges. Senate Republicans urged newly elected president George W. Bush to send forward nominations as quickly as possible to staff the judiciary with conservatives.

When the Democratic party took control of the Senate in early 2001, Democratic senator Patrick Leahy led the Judiciary Committee in slowing down consideration of the president's nominations until, by early 2002, sixty-four were women, less than 10 percent have been African American, and less than 10 percent have been Hispanic.[42] With many vacancies yet to be filled, it remains to be seen whether those numbers increase as the appointments progress in Bush's second term of office.

HOW THE SUPREME COURT OPERATES

How many times have you heard someone involved in a legal dispute proclaim defiantly, "I'm going to appeal this case all the way to the Supreme Court"? In truth, a successful appeal to the Supreme Court is extremely rare, partly because many cases are decided on their way to and through the intermediate appeals level and partly because of the Supreme Court's methods in selecting cases it will hear.

Each year the Supreme Court receives roughly 7,700 appeals. Of these, about 1 percent, or roughly seventy-five cases, appear on the Court's **docket**, or agenda, after they are accepted for full review with oral argument. Nearly all of these cases are decided by a full written opinion. But a few will be decided *per curiam*, in a brief, unsigned, generally unanimous opinion by the Court. The lower-court judgment remains in effect for cases the Court does not accept for review.

Nearly all of the Court's cases come from its *appellate jurisdiction*, cases that have already been reviewed and decided by one or more federal or state courts. About

docket The Supreme Court's agenda of cases to consider.

Questions for Reflection

How is this politically motivated approach to appointing judges affecting our democracy?

What could be done to alter the "court blocking" strategy employed by the opposition party to presidential nominations?

MakeItReal

Civic Participation: Visitor's Guide to the Supreme Court

vacancies remained on the federal bench. This apparent "court-blocking" strategy, as it has been labeled by political scientists Sheldon Goldman and Elliot Slotnick, put great pressure on the independence of the judiciary, much in the fashion of Roosevelt's court-packing plan of 1937.[43] When the Republicans retook control of the Senate in 2003, confirmations appeared likely to speed up. However, the Democrats' continued willingness to filibuster and threaten to filibuster nominees derailed more than a dozen of President Bush's appointees, including Fifth Circuit Court of Appeals nominee Charles Pickering. But a presidential counselor, Karl Rove, made clear to the Family Research Council, a key Christian political action committee, that the administration was just beginning to fight: " . . . This is not about a good man, Charles Pickering. This is about the future. This is about the U.S. Supreme Court. And this is about sending George W. Bush a message that, 'You send us somebody that is a strong conservative, you're not going to get him.'" But, Rove added, defiantly, "Guess what? . . . They sent the wrong message to the wrong guy."

Five delayed nominees were subsequently confirmed, including Judges Pryor, Owens, and Brown, after Senate agreement to continue the possibility of a filibuster in judicial confirmation battles. But, with each senator retaining the right to filibuster "extreme candidates," more fighting seemed likely with the nominations of John Roberts and Harriet Miers to replace the retiring Sandra Day O'Connor and the deceased William Rehnquist. In an effort to avoid more divisive "borking" of his nominees, President Bush initiated an unprecedented round of consultations with senators from both parties before presenting his nomination of Roberts. However, whether his consultations were insufficient or not fully revealing, his nomination of Harriet Miers so thoroughly

failed to win the support of many of his own senatorial party members from the far right that she was forced to withdraw her nomination before it was even considered by the Senate Judiciary Committee. In the end, though, the process did seem to work for President Bush as, in replacing her, he returned to a name that had been mentioned frequently in consultations with conservatives, Court of Appeals Judge Samuel Alito, for a successful appointment. Even there, though, conservative Senator Lindsay Graham's (R.-SC) questions in the hearings, professed to be a summary of the Democratic senators' charges, moved Judge Alito's wife to tears.

▲ Judge Robert Bork testifies before the Senate Judiciary Committee in a nationally televised confirmation hearing in 1987, saying that serving on the Court would be an "intellectual feast." Bork was eventually denied his seat on the Court.

*Ed Lazarus, *Closed Chambers*. New York: Times Books, 1998, p. 265.

Source: Edward Walsh, "Confirmation Fight: Replay and Review," *Washington Post*, March 14, 2002; "Judicial Game Cycles On," *Los Angeles Times*, January 21, 2002; and Jay Bookman, "GOP 'Borkers' Righteously Slam 'Borking,'" *Atlanta Constitution*, March 21, 2002.

▲ The only known photograph of the Supreme Court hearing oral arguments was taken secretly in June 1932 by Dr. Erich Solomon, who smuggled a camera into the courtroom. From left to right are Justices Owen Roberts, Pierce Butler, Louis D. Brandeis, Willis Van Devanter, Chief Justice Charles Evans Hughes, George Sutherland, Harlan Fiske Stone, and Benjamin Cardozo. The empty seat was that of Justice James C. McReynolds.

90 percent of the appellate cases come from the lower federal courts, with most coming from the court of appeals. The 10 percent of cases from state courts must raise a *federal question* and have exhausted all possible state appeals in order to jump to the Supreme Court. This usually means that state cases come from the state court of last resort, though they need not do so. The second source of Court cases is its *original jurisdiction,* which, as you learned earlier, involves cases seeking to resolve disputes among states and cases affecting foreign ambassadors. The Court hears few original jurisdiction cases today.

Selecting Cases

The rules for appealing a case to the Court have been established by congressional legislation. Appellate cases come to the Court through a formal writ called a **writ of certiorari**, a Latin term meaning "to be made more certain." Established in 1925, this discretionary writ enables the Court to accept cases for review only if there are "special and important reasons therefore." Essentially, the Court will consider accepting a case for review if it raises issues that affect society or the operation of government. You will recall that the *Bush* v. *Gore* case was accepted for review to determine the winner of the 2000 presidential election, even though some considered it a "political question" best left to political bodies such as Congress. Following legislation passed by Congress in 1988, the Court now has virtually total discretion over the cases it will hear.

All of the justices (except John Paul Stevens, whose own clerks assist him) rely on a group of law clerks in a "cert pool" to screen appeals. The clerks divide up the petitions, summarize a portion of them in memo form, and then submit their recommendations for acceptance or rejection to the justices.[44] Some believe this makes the law clerks into an intermediate court of review, as the justices use these initial evaluations to form their own judgments about which cases are worthy of review (see Figure 6.4).

The justices meet twice weekly to decide which appeals to accept. To speed up the decision process, the chief justice places appeals deemed worthy of consideration on a "discuss list" at the request of any Court member. The remaining appeals go on a "dead list" and, unless at least one justice asks for further consideration, the Court denies them without further discussion. The Court then votes on the cases

writ of certiorari A Latin term meaning "to be made more certain"; this writ enables the Court to accept cases for review only if there are "special and important reasons therefore."

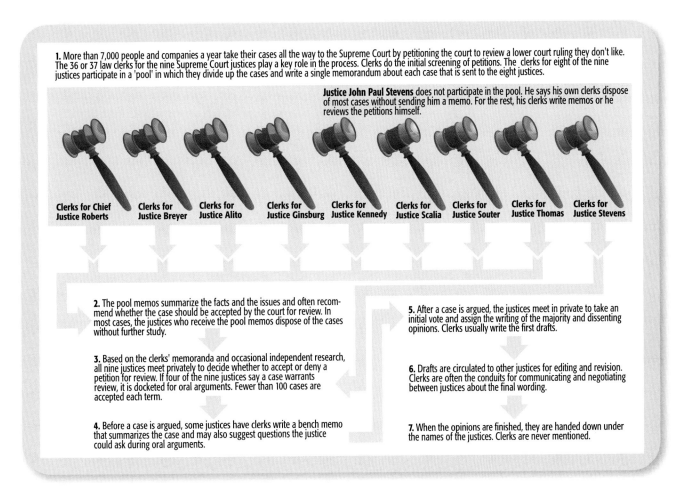

1. More than 7,000 people and companies a year take their cases all the way to the Supreme Court by petitioning the court to review a lower court ruling they don't like. The 36 or 37 law clerks for the nine Supreme Court justices play a key role in the process. Clerks do the initial screening of petitions. The clerks for eight of the nine justices participate in a 'pool' in which they divide up the cases and write a single memorandum about each case that is sent to the eight justices.

Justice John Paul Stevens does not participate in the pool. He says his own clerks dispose of most cases without sending him a memo. For the rest, his clerks write memos or he reviews the petitions himself.

Clerks for Chief Justice Roberts | Clerks for Justice Breyer | Clerks for Justice Alito | Clerks for Justice Ginsburg | Clerks for Justice Kennedy | Clerks for Justice Scalia | Clerks for Justice Souter | Clerks for Justice Thomas | Clerks for Justice Stevens

2. The pool memos summarize the facts and the issues and often recommend whether the case should be accepted by the court for review. In most cases, the justices who receive the pool memos dispose of the cases without further study.

3. Based on the clerks' memoranda and occasional independent research, all nine justices meet privately to decide whether to accept or deny a petition for review. If four of the nine justices say a case warrants review, it is docketed for oral arguments. Fewer than 100 cases are accepted each term.

4. Before a case is argued, some justices have clerks write a bench memo that summarizes the case and may also suggest questions the justice could ask during oral arguments.

5. After a case is argued, the justices meet in private to take an initial vote and assign the writing of the majority and dissenting opinions. Clerks usually write the first drafts.

6. Drafts are circulated to other justices for editing and revision. Clerks are often the conduits for communicating and negotiating between justices about the final wording.

7. When the opinions are finished, they are handed down under the names of the justices. Clerks are never mentioned.

Figure 6.4

Source: Copyright 1998, *USA Today.* Reprinted with permission.

on the discuss list. A vote by at least four justices to hear the case, known as the **rule of four**, will grant the petition for a writ of certiorari and put the case on the Court's docket.

Since the Court never explains why it accepts or rejects particular cases, political scientists have tried to discover what cues guide the Court's choices. Chief Justice Rehnquist reported, and political science research confirms, that if an issue receives a set of conflicting rulings in the courts below, a misapplication of an earlier Supreme Court ruling by a lower court, or a request from certain interest groups that a case be heard, the justices will be inclined to give serious consideration to the appeal petition.[45] New research, however, indicates that law clerks' value systems and inexperience may well be affecting the Court's appellate choices. For instance, far fewer important economic cases are being accepted for review (and far fewer cases overall as well) since the law clerks' cert pool has increased in importance.[46]

Using its agenda-setting power to decide what cases to hear, the Court frequently waits for the ideal case or cases raising precisely the constitutional or legal issue it wants to rule on. For example, the Court ruled in the 1964 case *Escobedo* v. *Illinois*[47] that criminal suspects have the right to have an attorney present during police questioning if they ask for one. The Court then considered sixty-six cases over the next two years before finding the one with just the right facts. *Miranda* v. *Arizona*[48] stated that police would have to inform suspects of the right to an attorney before custodial interrogation.[49]

rule of four A means of determining which cases the Supreme Court will hear; at least four justices must vote to hear a case and grant the petition for a *writ of certiorari* for the case to be put on the Court's docket.

solicitor general The third-ranking official in the Justice Department, appointed by the president and charged with representing the U.S. government before the Supreme Court.

amicus curiae briefs Legal briefs that enable groups or individuals, including the national government, who are not parties to the litigation but have an interest in it, to attempt to influence the outcome of the case; literally, "friend of the court" briefs.

Recent Trends in Case Selection   Since the late 1980s, the Supreme Court has been accepting and deciding fewer and fewer cases. Although the number of appeals to the Court has increased by 85 percent in the past twenty-five years, the percentage of cases actually accepted by the justices has dropped dramatically. In the late 1970s and early 1980s, several hundred cases were decided yearly by either full opinions or unsigned orders. Of the 7,700 appeals coming to the Court in 2004–2005, only 74 cases were decided by full opinion. Reflecting the narrow balance of the Court, nearly one-fourth of these decisions were made by 5–4 votes. Even with this small number of cases, though, the Court can impose its will through its selection process and the region of the country from which it takes cases. In the 1996–97 term, twenty-six of the eighty cases, or nearly 40 percent, came from the Ninth Circuit Court of Appeals, one of the most liberal judging panels in the country, and the conservative Rehnquist Court reversed an amazing twenty-five of those decisions.[50] On the other hand, many of that Court's most conservative decisions come from the highly conservative Fourth Circuit Court of Appeals, whose decisions the Court tends to uphold.

The Court's shrinking docket has several explanations. First, recent congressional legislation on federal jurisdiction eliminated nearly all categories of constitutional cases that the Court was once required to review. Second, the staffing of the vast majority of the lower federal courts with conservatives by the Reagan and Bush administrations has meant that a fairly conservative Supreme Court has had fewer lower-court opinions with which it disagrees. Third, political scientist David O'Brien discovered that an old practice called "Join 3" has recently been abandoned, whereby a justice would vote to review if three of his colleagues were willing to do so, thus increasing the number of appeals accepted.[51] But the most likely explanation is that the cert pool law clerks reviewing the petitions are far less interested in taking cases than were reviewing justices in the past. "You stick your neck out as a clerk when you recommend to grant a case," explains Justice John Paul Stevens. "The risk-averse thing to do is to recommend not to take a case. I think it accounts for the lessening of the docket."[52] Whether this is a long-term change or a cyclical trend remains to be seen.

The Solicitor General: "The Government's Lawyer"

One of the most important outside players influencing the Supreme Court's work, including its selection of cases, is the **solicitor general**. The third-ranking official in the Justice Department (after the attorney general and deputy attorney general), the solicitor general is appointed by the president and charged with representing the U.S. government before the Supreme Court. The solicitor general decides which federal cases to appeal from the lower courts, prepares those appeals, files briefs for accepted cases, and appears before the Court for oral argument. In cases that do not involve the national government as a party, the solicitor general may file **amicus curiae briefs**, or "friend of the court" briefs. Amicus briefs enable groups or individuals, including the national government, who are not parties to the litigation but have an interest in it, to attempt to influence the outcome of a case. All in all, the solicitor general is involved in about two-thirds of the cases before the Supreme Court.

The solicitor general has become so powerful and influential that the position is sometimes informally referred to as "the tenth justice." The willingness of the solicitor general to become involved in a case alerts the justices to the need to hear that appeal. In this way, the solicitor general serves as eyes and ears for the Court and can play a role in setting the Court's agenda.

The solicitor general is often pulled in two directions. As a presidential appointee, he or she must be sensitive to White House policy preferences and interests. At the same time, the solicitor general is an officer of the Court, representing the interests of both the judiciary and the entire national government. At times,

Quick Review

The Solicitor General

- The third-ranking official after the attorney general and deputy attorney general.
- Appointed by the president and represents the government before the Supreme Court.
- Decides which federal cases to appeal from the lower courts.
- Prepares appeals and files briefs for accepted cases.

politics prevails. During the Ronald Reagan and George H. W. Bush years, the solicitor general's office took hard-line conservative positions on controversial issues, such as abortion, favored by the administration. Bill Clinton's acting solicitor general in the 1996–97 term, Walter Dellinger (his name was never sent to the Senate for confirmation because of the opposition of Senator Jesse Helms), tried as an officer of the Court to represent the position of the national government and judiciary. However, the White House occasionally forced him to modify his liberal stance on certain issues for political reasons.[53] Dellinger's replacement, Seth Waxman, faced fewer challenges in presenting the Clinton administration's legal agenda because of his more moderate point of view.[54] It was President Bush's first solicitor general, Theodore Olson, who successfully argued the president's case in the *Bush* v. *Gore* litigation and who argued the war-on-terrorism cases, with the justices fully aware that his wife Barbara died in the plane hijacked and crashed into the Pentagon. When Olson left office he was replaced by his deputy, Paul Clement.

The Process of Deciding Cases

Once a case is accepted for review, it passes through several stages as it is considered. Each of these stages is designed to inform the jurists and to give them a chance to organize a final decision.

Filing Briefs   When a case is accepted for argument, the attorneys for all sides are asked to submit **briefs**. These are hundreds of pages of written arguments outlining not only all the facts and legal and constitutional issues in the case but also answering the anticipated arguments of the opposing side. Today so many groups file so many briefs that, together with the lower court opinions and Supreme Court precedents, the justices must read about 1,500 pages of material a day.[55]

These written arguments were originally strictly legal in nature, but now attorneys often present extensive sociological, psychological, scientific, and historical arguments to bolster their legal documentation. In the 1954 case of *Brown* v. *Board of Education*,[56] which raised the issue of desegregating public schools, the Court received evidence from social psychologist Kenneth Clark that African American youngsters were psychologically harmed by segregated school systems.[57] As you will see in Chapter 14, it was primarily this evidence that contributed to the Court's decision to ignore legal precedents and rule that segregated schools are inherently unconstitutional.

Oral Argument   Once briefs are submitted, oral arguments follow. One of the most exciting and impressive events in Washington, D.C., is the public oral argument before the Supreme Court. Typically, the arguments are heard during the first three days of the first two weeks of each month from October through April. Lawyers from all sides, occasionally the solicitor general, and in the most important cases other interested parties such as those who have submitted amicus curiae briefs, come before the justices and present their case. Each side usually has only thirty minutes to speak, with time limits kept so carefully by the chief justice that during one Court session, a lawyer was interrupted in the middle of the word *if*.

Although lawyers come prepared with statements, they must stop to answer questions from the justices. Justices have different questioning styles. Ruth Bader Ginsburg asks carefully sculpted questions designed to keep counsel from avoiding issues, while Stephen Breyer usually waits until the end of counsel's time before asking one or two lengthy questions designed to crystallize the central issue in the case. By contrast, Clarence Thomas asked no questions during his first eighteen months on the bench.

The most combative person currently on the bench is Antonin Scalia. Much as when he was a law professor, Scalia asks many rapid-fire questions—once as many as

MakeItReal

Primary Source: *Brown* v. *Board of Education of Topeka (1954)*

briefs Written arguments to the court outlining not only the facts and legal and constitutional issues in a court case, but also answering all anticipated arguments of the opposing side.

135 on a single case—and tries to lead the argument in his direction in an effort to educate his fellow justices. At one point in a case, Scalia appeared ready to argue the case himself for an attorney who would not answer his question to his satisfaction, only to have Chief Justice William Rehnquist interject: "I think he's capable of answering himself." "Well, he's not capable," Scalia responded. One attorney who has faced this barrage says of Scalia: "I've seen some lawyers really thrown off. At the end, they look dizzy." In responding to these questions, lawyers must be careful to pitch their arguments to the more centrist, swing justices in the voting—Anthony Kennedy and David Souter.[58]

The appellate and oral argument process is such a specialized skill that it can cost as much as $500,000 to take a case to the Supreme Court. For a solo practitioner to take a case to the Court *pro bono*, or for free, is a once-in-a-lifetime experience that comes with a cost, such as having to close down a practice for six months to prepare for the argument. More and more, corporations, states, and even other law firms are assigning this final step to an elite group of fewer than two dozen Washington, D.C., litigators who specialize in Supreme Court argumentation, some of them former U.S. solicitors general and Supreme Court law clerks.[59] Sometimes their willingness to take a case or not makes these attorneys further gatekeepers in deciding which appeals reach the Court.

What role does oral argument play in the decision-making process? Some justices find that oral presentations highlight problems with the issue raised by the written briefs and suggest possible avenues for decision. Others find that written briefs weigh more heavily. This makes it difficult to predict how the Court will rule based on the nature of its questioning during oral argument.

The Decision-Making Stage: The Conference   After the justices read the briefs and listen to oral arguments, the decision-making process begins with the *judicial conference*. These conferences take place on Wednesday afternoon for cases argued on Monday, and all day Friday for cases argued on Tuesday and Wednesday. At these meetings, the justices discuss both the cases under consideration and which appeals to grant in the future.

The meetings take place in total secrecy in an oak-paneled conference room, with only the justices present. Proceeding from the chief justice down to the most junior justice, the justices indicate both their views and how they will vote. Opinions expressed at this time constitute a preliminary vote.[60]

In recent years, the conference stage has changed dramatically. Harlan Fiske Stone (chief justice, 1941–46) conducted exhausting judicial conferences that went on for hours and often extended from Friday into Saturday. During these long meetings clerks recall hearing Felix Frankfurter and William O. Douglas screaming at each other so loudly that their voices carried down the hall. Recently, though, the conference stage has become briefer and less heated. "Not very much conferencing goes on," explains Justice Antonin Scalia. "In fact, to call our discussion of a case a conference is really something of a misnomer. It's much more a statement of the views of each of the nine justices, after which the totals are added and the case is assigned [for the drafting of the opinion]."[61] "Bam, bam, bam" is how one justice describes the current speed of voting in conference.[62]

Assignment of Opinions   Once the discussion and voting are over, if the chief justice is in the majority he assigns a member voting in the majority to draft an **opinion**, the written version of the decision. Sometimes the chief justice will write the opinion in the hope of expressing an even stronger view from the Court. If the chief justice is not in the majority, the senior justice in the majority makes the assignment or writes the opinion.

Assignments rely on several factors, including the expertise of certain Court members, their speed in drafting opinions, their ability to forge consensus, and their current workload. At times, personal and symbolic considerations govern the

opinion A written version of the decision of a court.

choice. Earl Warren liked to give the most interesting opinions to his colleagues; his successor, Warren Burger, was known to assign the least interesting opinions to the justices with whom he was unhappy. To the great annoyance of colleagues such as William O. Douglas, Burger occasionally tried to assign opinions even though he was not in the majority.[63] The assignment of opinions is important because such choices determine the tone of Court opinions and their reception by the public. Though he was a vocal critic of the *Miranda* police interrogation protections case, in 2000 Chief Justice Rehnquist assigned the *Dickerson* opinion upholding that decision to himself because of its historic importance and his desire to limit the scope of its holding.

Sometimes the voting lineup—and thus the decision in a case—hinges on who is assigned the opinion. In 1992, five justices—Thomas, Scalia, Rehnquist, White, and Kennedy—seemed ready to overturn the *Roe* v. *Wade*[64] abortion decision in the case of *Planned Parenthood of Southeastern Pennsylvania* v. *Casey*.[65] When conservative Chief Justice Rehnquist assigned the opinion to himself because of the importance of the case and drafted a harsh opinion toward the Roe precedent, Kennedy decided to vote in a more moderate direction, joining in an opinion with David Souter and Sandra Day O'Connor upholding the precedent.[66]

Marshaling the Court: The Opinion-Drafting Process

After the judicial conference, the justice assigned to write the opinion takes weeks, and sometimes months, to develop a draft to circulate among the other justices. This requires special care because conference votes are tentative, and justices will lobby to change their colleagues' positions. As Justice William Brennan used to say to his law clerks while wiggling all of the fingers of his hand in the air: "Five votes. Five votes can do anything around here."[67] And each side attempts to muster those five votes.

At any point, right up to public announcement of the opinion, a justice can change a vote. That occasionally happens, but changes to the language of opinions nearly always occur, sometimes dramatically in controversial cases, as a result of lobbying efforts. Each opinion goes through multiple drafts, with justices negotiating with each other over changes on which the final votes may depend. Such negotiations take time. For this reason, opinions for major cases argued in the fall of a judicial term might not be issued until the spring of the following year. Often, these negotiations come in the form of written comments on various opinion drafts, personal memos, and even personal lobbying by the justices or their assistants. Years ago such lobbying took place through personal interaction, but in recent years what little lobbying has taken place is usually done by argumentative memos. Despite such efforts, however, evidence suggests that votes change in fewer than 10 percent of the cases.[68]

Sometimes the final opinion reflects the frustration of these unsuccessful negotiations. In one abortion case, Justice Antonin Scalia, by all accounts a charming man in person, once described Justice Sandra Day O'Connor's opinion as "perverse," "irrational," and "not to be taken seriously."[69] When Scalia could not convince the Court to abandon its prevailing test in establishment of religion cases—the so-called *Lemon* test, taken from the case *Lemon* v. *Kurtzman*—he wrote: "Like some ghoul in a latenight horror movie that repeatedly sits up in its grave and shuffles abroad, after being repeatedly killed and buried, *Lemon* stalks our Establishment Clause jurisprudence once again, frightening little children and school attorneys."[70] These attacks, and similar attacks on Justice Anthony Kennedy, hurt Scalia's prospects for adding their support to his opinions, and in some cases caused him to lose control of the Court majority.

Only after all justices agree on the wording of the final opinion is it ready to be announced.

MakeItReal

Primary Source: *Lemon v. Kurtzman* (1971)

The Announcement of Opinions

The vote on any case is final only when the decision or opinion is announced in open court. The Court's opinion not only states the facts of a case and announces the decision, but since this will be the only public comment on the case, it contains supporting logic, precedents, and rationale to persuade the public of the merits of the judgment. In addition, the language used in an opinion is designed to be used later by lower courts, federal and state politicians, and the legal community to interpret similar cases in the future.

The Court makes its decision based on a majority (five votes out of nine), called a **majority opinion**, which represents the agreed-upon compromise judgment of all the justices in the majority. This opinion is almost always signed only by its authors.

In cases where less than a majority agrees on the wording, a **plurality opinion** is issued. This plurality opinion announces the opinion of the Court, but it lacks the same binding legal force as a majority opinion.

If a justice agrees with the majority decision of the Court but differs on the reasoning, a **concurring opinion** can be written. From this literary platform a single justice, or a small group of them, can show where the majority might have ruled. A careful reading of concurring opinions thus can reveal the true sentiments of the Court majority. In the landmark 1971 freedom of the press case *New York Times Co. v. United States*,[71] the Court allowed two newspapers to publish the Pentagon Papers, a classified study of the decision-making process of America's involvement in Vietnam. However, the six concurring opinions revealed that, had the government sought to punish the *Times* editors after publication rather than attempt to prevent publication through prior censorship, and if a statute had outlawed such a publication, a majority of the Court would have sided with the government.

When a justice disagrees with the Court's holding, frequently he or she will write a **dissenting opinion**, as an individual or for a few of the members of the Court. In the *Dickerson* case, Justice Scalia used his dissent to attack Chief Justice Rehnquist's majority opinion by using language from confession cases that Rehnquist himself had decided nearly three decades before. From the stewardship of Chief Justice Marshall until the early 1920s, justices avoided dissents, fearing a diminution of the public authority of the Court. The practice increased in the 1940s when dissents occurred in 70 percent of the cases, as opposed to 22 percent of the cases in the previous decade. Now many more dissents are being issued, either as a result of less personal conferencing by the justices, weaker leadership by the chief justice, the law clerks' greater role in the drafting process, or a greater desire by individual jurists to be heard.

One must pay attention to these statements; the dissents of today can become the majority opinions of tomorrow when the Court changes members. The Court's recent decisions on defendants' rights and federalism reflect earlier dissents by Associate Justice William Rehnquist. The decision rule proposed in dissents by Oliver Wendell Holmes and Louis D. Brandeis in the First Amendment free speech cases of the early twentieth century, and Justices Hugo Black and William O. Douglas in the 1950s, later became the law of the land.

Law Clerks: The Real Tenth Justices?

One of the most significant changes in the modern Supreme Court has been the justices' reliance on their law clerks. Each associate justice has four law clerks, and the chief justice has five. Clerks earn $45,823 per year and are selected during their second year of law school. Most graduate from the elite law schools and serve a year's clerkship with a federal court of appeals judge before moving to the Supreme Court. Certain appeals judges, such as Michael Luttig of the fourth circuit, Laurence Silberman of the D.C. circuit, and Alex Kozinski of the ninth circuit, have proven major "feeder judges" for Supreme Court law clerks. The overwhelming majority of clerks are white males. Once in the "cert pool," these assistants draft memos to aid in

majority opinion A decision of the Supreme Court that represents the agreed-upon compromise judgment of all the justices in the majority.

plurality opinion Less than a majority vote on an opinion of the Court; does not have the binding legal force of a majority opinion.

concurring opinion A written opinion of a justice who agrees with the majority decision of the Court but differs on the reasoning.

dissenting opinion A written opinion of a justice who disagrees with the holding of the Court.

selecting appeals heard by the Court for eight of the nine justices (John Paul Stevens being the exception). "When I tell clients who have cases with hundreds of millions of dollars on the line that a bunch of 25-year-olds is going to decide their fate, it drives them crazy," says Carter Phillips, who frequently argues before the Court and served as a law clerk for Chief Justice Warren Burger.[72]

Justice Louis D. Brandeis once said that the Supreme Court was respected because "the justices are almost the only people in Washington who do their own work," but that no longer appears to be true. More and more, the clerks' most important job is to draft opinions. Chief Justice William Rehnquist determined that it is "entirely proper" for clerks to draft opinions, because it is, in his words, a "highly structured task."[73] As a result, in recent years, the justices still make decisions, but they increasingly leave law clerks to write first drafts of opinions, a most influential part of the process determining the tone and direction of the final opinion. For instance, the decision by Justice Lewis Powell to back out of writing the majority opinion in a 1987 gay rights case, *Bowers* v. *Hardwick*, shifting the majority from the liberal to the conservative side, turned because the initial opinion was given to one of his clerks who was a married Mormon from Idaho, rather than to another clerk who was gay, but had not told the Justice.[74] Justice John Paul Stevens, who was a law clerk to Justice Wiley Rutledge in the 1940s, acknowledges this change: "I had a lot less responsibility than some of the clerks now. They are much more involved in the entire process now." It is not unusual for opinions to come through the writing process without significant change. Indeed, the private papers of former Supreme Court Justice Harry Blackmun, a justice thought to have done most of his own work, reveal that many of his most famous opinions and best known judicial turns of phrases were drafted by his law clerks.[75] Clerks are expected to sign and adhere to a "code of conduct" preventing them from revealing privileged information about their work, and were at one time instructed not to speak with any journalist for more than ninety seconds. Partially as a result of this delegation of the early drafting process, the lack of time arguing over cases in the judicial conference, and the relative lack of personal consultation among the justices, judicial opinions have become longer, more numerous, and more academic, whereas justices' decisions are more fragmented. The resulting opinions are often much less clear in their legal explanations than previously. Often times, negotiations during the drafting process are left to conversations among the law clerks, who serve as informal emissaries from the various justices' chambers, as they did during the *Bush* v. *Gore* deliberations in 2000.[76] Increasingly, students of the Court are becoming critical of the greater reliance by the Justices on law clerks for the production of their opinions.

The Chief Justice's Role   The chief justice is first among equals on the Supreme Court, with substantial powers to influence the Court's direction by assigning opinions, leading the judicial conference, and acting as the social and intellectual leader of the Court. In addition, he or she also heads, represents, and lobbies for the entire federal judiciary.

Chief justices vary widely in leadership styles. Some have been more effective leaders than others. The austere Charles Evans Hughes (1930–41) moved the Court along with military precision. His replacement, the gregarious Harlan Fiske Stone (1941–46), lost control of the Court during judicial conferences. Fred Vinson (1946–53) was mismatched with the high-powered, egocentric Roosevelt appointees, leading to considerable rancor on the Court in those years. On the other hand, relative harmony followed during the tenure of the politically skilled former governor of California, Earl Warren (1953–69), known to his admiring colleagues as "the Super Chief." This period contrasted to the sharply split Court under Warren Burger (1969–86), who was reputed to be an uninspiring leader.[77] The highly popular and respected William Rehnquist proved capable of forging and maintaining the Court's narrow conservative coalition. Now the challenge for John Roberts will be to find a way to lead a group that has been together since 1994, remains

Quick Review

The Chief Justice

- Appointed by the president upon confirmation of the Senate.
- Oversees the operation of the judiciary.
- Sets the tone and has a greater opportunity to influence the rest of the court.

sharply divided politically, all despite the fact that he is much younger and has no experience on the Court.

ANALYZING SUPREME COURT DECISIONS

To analyze and understand any Supreme Court decision we must consider the following: the Court's use of precedent and other legal factors, the mind-sets of the individual justices, the personalities of the justices, and the contemporary Court voting blocs.

The Use of Precedent and Other Legal Factors

Judges throughout the legal system often base decisions on the doctrine of *stare decisis*, which means "to let the decision stand" or to adhere if at all possible to previously decided cases, or **precedents**, on the same issue. Federal and state courts, for example, are supposed to follow Supreme Court precedents in making their own decisions. The Supreme Court often rules based on its own precedents. By following previous rulings all courts, including the Supreme Court, appear nonpolitical, impartial arbiters, making incremental changes based on past decisions.

But following precedent is not as restrictive as it sounds. Since in practice precedents need interpretation, judges can argue about the meaning of an earlier case or whether the facts of the current case differ substantially from those of past cases, thus requiring a different ruling. In one case, *Bowers* v. *Hardwick*, dealing with the privacy rights of gays in the bedroom, Justices Blackmun and White cited the same case of *Stanley* v. *Georgia*,[78] a privacy and pornography case, as a major precedent upholding their opposing positions on the constitutionality of the Georgia anti-sodomy law. Occasionally, justices will appear to uphold precedent, when in fact they are deliberately ignoring it or consciously reinterpreting it to reach a different result.

Only in the most extreme cases is the Court willing to overturn an earlier decision, thus declaring it invalid. Precedents are usually overturned if they prove unworkable from a public policy standpoint, outmoded, or just plain unwise. Sometimes, though, a change in Court personnel or in public opinion will lead to overturning a precedent. For example, in 1991 the Court overruled two earlier Eighth Amendment capital punishment decisions barring the use of statements by victims in the penalty phase of a capital trial. The arrival of new conservative members made these rulings possible but led frustrated liberal Thurgood Marshall to argue before retiring from the Court, "Power, not reason, is the new currency of this Court's decision making."[79] In actuality, however, the Court rarely overrules its own precedents. Out of tens of thousands of decisions it has issued, the Court has overruled its own precedents in fewer than three hundred.[80] In recent years, though, the practice has increased. Since 1946, the Court has overturned its own precedents an average of about three times a term.[81] A favorite technique for circumventing precedent without reversing a previous decision is to *distinguish* cases, that is, to claim that the earlier case and a more recent case are different (even if in fact similar), thus requiring different decisions. The Court has been able to dilute the original ruling in the 1973 *Roe* v. *Wade* case using such a technique. That case created a trimester system governing state regulation of abortions, allowing women an unfettered right to an abortion in the first trimester of their pregnancy. Although the decision has not been overruled, the Court has allowed the states to impose so many regulations that the original ruling is now much less protective of women's right to choose abortions.

Justices also look at a variety of factors beyond precedent to decide an issue, including the meaning of a law, the meaning of part of the Constitution, the lessons of history, and the possible impact on public policy. Using *strict construction*,

stare decisis A doctrine meaning "let the decision stand," or that judges deciding a case should adhere if at all possible to previously decided cases similar to the one under consideration.

precedents Previously decided court cases on an issue similar to the one being considered.

justices look carefully at a statute or a portion of the Constitution and interpret the law as closely as possible to the literal meaning of its wording. When the wording is vague, justices search for historical context—or for the so-called intent of the framers who wrote the law and the Constitution—to determine the true meaning of both. Proponents of *original intent,* such as Judge Robert Bork, argue that it is the Court's duty to adhere solely to the original meaning of the framers. The effect is to limit the power of Supreme Court justices to interpret the law. This method has come to be labeled "originalism," as legal theorists examine all of the writings and newspaper accounts of the founders to determine how they would decide current issues. Justice Antonin Scalia, though, has developed his own method of "textualism," looking at dictionaries from the early period to determine the meaning of the words in the Constitution at that time to determine how the founders would decide these issues. Others, however, argue that society has changed since the drafting of the Constitution, and that the Court's decisions should thus reflect the needs of a continually changing society in creating an evolving document. Sometimes justices examine an issue's general history and the public policy impact of their decision. In the *Bush* v. *Gore* case, the Court majority argued that many factors led them to rule that the initial certification of the presidential vote by the Florida Secretary of State should stand, thus effectively ending the election in Bush's favor.

The Mind-Set of Individual Justices

Personal factors also figure in analyzing judicial decisions. It is helpful to look at a judge's mind-set—his or her political ideology, jurisprudential posture, or a combination of the two.

Political Ideology   Although some Court observers would prefer that justices decide cases on the basis of neutral principles, the individuals sitting on the Court are human beings influenced by their own biases.[82] A comprehensive study by two political scientists found a strong correlation between justices' votes on the Court and their ideological views as expressed in newspaper articles written during the appointment process.[83]

Like members of political parties, justices tend to be grouped ideologically as conservative, liberal, or moderate. Conservatives tend to support the government's position instead of the individual's in civil rights and liberties, while liberals tend to defend or even expand the rights of the individual instead of the government. On economic questions, conservatives tend to oppose government regulation in favor of *laissez faire* business oversight, while liberals tend to vote for a more intrusive government regulatory role. Moderates often flip back and forth between these two positions, depending on the issues. On the Rehnquist Court, Justices O'Connor and Kennedy, both moderate conservatives, often switched back and forth in their votes on various issues, thus determining the direction of the Court's decision.

Labeling jurists this way is helpful but in no way definitive. Many varieties of liberals and conservatives and many legal issues fail to fit clearly into those groupings. Political ideology, then, is only a starting point for understanding a jurist's mind-set. We must also consider a justice's willingness to use power.

▲ Supreme Court Justice Anthony Kennedy, from California, who has served since 1987, will hold in his hands the direction of the Court with his swing vote after the retirement of fellow conservative moderate, Sandra Day O'Connor. He has the potential by his decisions to turn the "Roberts Court" into the "Kennedy Court" with his vote in key 5-4 decisions.

judicial restraint An approach in which justices see themselves as appointed rather than elected officials, who should defer to the legislature and uphold a law or political action if at all possible.

judicial activism An approach in which justices create new policy and decide issues, to the point, some critics charge, of writing their personal values into law.

Jurisprudential Posture   Justices have a certain jurisprudential posture, meaning how willing they are to use their power on the Court. Some practice self-restraint, others are activists. Justices who believe in **judicial restraint** see themselves as appointed rather than elected officials who should defer to the elected legislature and uphold a law or political action if at all possible. "If the legislature wants to go to hell, I'm here to tell them they can do it," said Oliver Wendell Holmes. Justice Felix Frankfurter pronounced the classic expression of judicial self-restraint in his dissent in a case forcing the children of Jehovah's Witnesses to salute the flag in contravention to their religious beliefs:

> One who belongs to the most vilified and persecuted minority in history [Frankfurter was Jewish] is not likely to be insensible to the freedoms guaranteed by our Constitution. . . . As a member of this Court I am not justified in writing my private notions of policy into the Constitution, no matter how deeply I may cherish them or how mischievous I may deem their disregard.[84]

Judges who practice **judicial activism** believe that they have a duty to reach out and decide issues even to the point, critics charge, of writing their own personal values into law. Judicial activists are more willing to strike down legislation, reject a presidential action, or create rights not specifically written in the Constitution. For example, William O. Douglas's ruling in the case of *Griswold* v. *Connecticut*[85] fashioned a right to privacy even though such a right is not explicitly in the Constitution. Douglas's classic description of the activist posture came in his dissent to a Court decision not to protect the environment in California's Sierra Nevada Mountains against Walt Disney Corporation, seeking to build a ski resort:

> Inanimate objects are sometimes parties in litigation. . . . So it should be as respects valleys, alpine meadows, rivers, lakes, estuaries, beaches, ridges, groves of trees, swampland, or even air that feels the destructive pressures of modern technology and modern life.[86]

For Justice Douglas, nature should have the right to sue, too. The activist posture often leads to conservative charges that the Court is acting as a "superlegislature," overruling duly elected bodies.[87]

Activists come in many varieties and receive many labels. *Result-oriented* justices begin with their intended result in mind and simply announce that judgment, paying little attention to justifying their decision in the opinion. Another kind of activist, the *absolutist*, believes that the rights in the Constitution are paramount, and no contrary interest of the state can be used to justify overruling them. New Deal justice Hugo Black (1937–71) once stated, in reference to the First Amendment's ban on any law abridging freedom of speech, "No law means NO law!"[88]

Figure 6.5   The Four-Cell Method for Classifying Justices
It is useful to assess justices by looking at their politics (whether they are liberal or conservative) and at their judicial philosophy (whether they are activist or self-restrained). We learn, as a result, that both types of self-restrained justices share an inclination to avoid innovation, while activists in the two camps can differ dramatically with regard to the goals of their activism.

The Four-Cell Method for Classifying Justices   It is often revealing to assess justices according to a four-cell categorization that considers both political ideology (whether a judge is liberal or conservative) and jurisprudential posture (whether a judge is self-restrained or an activist). This scheme, illustrated in Figure 6.5, helps us better understand that the Court's self-restrained liberals and self-restrained conservatives have much in common because neither will be inclined to break new ground. For instance, New Deal appointee Felix Frankfurter was frequently criticized by liberal colleagues because his self-restrained opinions upholding the letter of the law made him look too conservative. However, the activists on either side of the political spectrum can differ dramatically, as liberal activists are willing to reach beyond the law and write new individual rights into the Constitution, while conservative activists sometimes seek to substitute their vision of the constitution for that of the legislators. Thus, the conservative activists on the Rehnquist Court overturned over three dozen congressional laws between 1994 and 2006, oftentimes claiming to adhere to the "original intention" of the framers of the Constitution.

But concentrating solely on the political and judicial views of a justice is not enough to understand decisions. Instead, dealing with a life-tenured Court requires us to consider an additional angle: judicial character.

Judicial Character

The personalities of individual justices and how the justices interact with each other play a large role in the direction of the Court. Justice William Brennan explains: "In an institution this small, personalities play an important role. . . . How those people get along, how they relate, what ideas they have, how flexible or intractable they are, are all of enormous significance."[89] A justice can shade an opinion to secure a colleague's agreement or perhaps remain silent rather than write a dissent in the interest of interpersonal harmony. On the other hand, a justice can, for personal or professional reasons, simply chart a separate course, possibly creating friction on the Court.

Like any group, members of the Court can be characterized as leaders, team players, and loners. The leader does not necessarily have to be the chief justice. One political scientist argued that every Court has "task leaders" who see that the work gets done and "social leaders" who keep life on the Court harmonious.[90] Sometimes these two types of leaders can be rolled into one, as with Justice Brennan, who during his tenure became known as a "playmaker," or the justice who unites a ruling majority on the Court. That role continued even during the highly conservative Rehnquist Court years, where the liberal Brennan's elfin, affectionate style enabled him to continue amassing five-person majorities. Then there are the team players, those justices usually willing to go along with the majority. On the present Court, Justice Clarence Thomas, a team player, early in his career nearly always followed the conservative position of Justices Rehnquist and Scalia. In recent years, though, he has been evolving into a libertarian, non-governmental-power jurist who relies on his interpretation of the "inalienable rights" in the Declaration of Independence and religious doctrine to decide cases. In contrast are the loner justices, who are willing to take a stand even if it means issuing frequent sole dissents and angering colleagues. Justice William O. Douglas and, in his early years, Justice Rehnquist adopted this role with such frequency that each was called "the Lone Ranger." Now liberal Justice Stevens (taking over the far left position once occupied by Justice Harry Blackmun) and conservative Antonin Scalia appear willing to adopt this role, frequently issuing solo dissents on civil rights and liberties questions. Although the conservatives now lack the kind of vote-unifying playmaker the liberals had in Brennan, Justice Kennedy's increasing willingness to vote with them many times places him in the determinative playmaker role on such issues as affirmative action, federalism issues, and freedom of religion that Sandra Day O'Connor once occupied.

Voting Blocs

Another angle on analyzing Court decisions relies on grouping the Court into blocs of like-minded jurists. An example would be grouping justices by ideology as conservative, liberal, and moderate (see Table 6.1). Although justices sometimes shift within these blocs, change more frequently occurs when appointees alter the balance of the Court. For example, how will the replacements of Justice Sandra Day O'Connor and Chief Justice William Rehnquist affect the old voting blocs? O'Connor was the "swing vote" between three reliable conservatives (Rehnquist, Scalia, Thomas), one moderate conservative except on gay rights (Kennedy), and four relative liberals (Stevens, Ginsburg, Breyer, and Souter). While many believe that trading O'Connor for a more conservative replacement and keeping Rehnquist's seat as a conservative will immediately move the Court in a more

Table 6.1 ■ Judicial Voting Blocs

	Liberal	Moderate	Conservative
Eisenhower Court (1961)	Warren	Whittaker	Frankfurter
	Brennan	Harlan	Stewart
	Black		Clark
	Douglas		
Kennedy Court (1963)	Warren	Harlan	Stewart
	Brennan		Clark
	Black		White
	Douglas		
	Goldberg		
Johnson Court (1969)	Warren	Harlan	Black*
	Brennan		Stewart
	Douglas		White
	Fortas		
	Marshall		
Nixon Court (1974)	Brennan	Powell	Burger
	Douglas	Blackmun	Rehnquist
	Marshall		Stewart
			White
Ford Court (1976)	Brennan	Powell	Burger
	Marshall	Blackmun	Rehnquist
		Stevens	Stewart
			White
Reagan Court (1989)	Brennan	Kennedy	Rehnquist
	Blackmun†	O'Connor	Scalia
	Marshall	Stevens	White
Bush (41) Court (1993)	Blackmun	Kennedy	Rehnquist
	Stevens	Souter	Scalia
		O'Connor	White
			Thomas
Bush (43) Court (2006)	Stevens	Kennedy‡	Roberts
	Ginsburg		Scalia
	Breyer		Thomas
	Souter‡		Alito

*Liberal Hugo Black became conservative after a stroke.

†It is interesting to note that when appointed in 1970, Blackmun was strongly conservative. By 1973, he had become a moderate, and later in his career he became a liberal.

‡These moderate, swing justices have tended over the past several years to vote more frequently with these groups, thus accounting for the frequent 5–4 conservative votes.

conservative direction, it seems even more probable that the most moderate of the conservative bloc, Anthony Kennedy, might, with a slight shift to more liberal voting, become the tipping point on the new Court. Of course, if the new appointee votes more moderately, there could be no change on the Court. As Justice Byron White used to say, "When you change one justice, you change the whole court."[91] These blocs are not absolute determinants of votes, however, because a justice's views, and thus the justice's position within a bloc, frequently vary according to the issue under consideration. This is especially true when new members come to the Court, offering new arguments on cases and new potential alliances on all facets of an issue.

Bloc analysis can be helpful in predicting which justices may become the swing votes that determine the outcome in a case. Law firms appearing before the Court make this kind of analysis so they can pitch their oral argument to one or two justices they deem critical to their case.

Replacing a member of the Court's leading bloc with a member suited to the other bloc can sharply tip the decision balance. So while all Supreme Court appointments are important, some can change the entire direction of the Court. That was why the prospect of replacing Warren Burger with Antonin Scalia in 1986—a conservative for a conservative—had far less impact and was less controversial than the attempt to replace moderate Powell with highly conservative activist Robert Bork a year later. The new Court appointments raise the question of whether President Bush will succeed in turning Court decision making in a more conservative direction.

Limitations of Court Analysis

Although the preceding tools for analyzing Supreme Court decisions help us understand how the Court may have arrived at a decision, they have limitations as predictors of Court rulings. The Court's independent role, the shifting nature of its members and their constantly evolving philosophies, and the hidden role of law clerks produce a Court that may head in directions that experts neither expect nor predict. Harry Blackmun was expected to become a conservative on the Court like his friend Warren Burger, but instead he evolved into one of its most liberal members. John Paul Stevens was appointed by Republican president Gerald R. Ford, but, although his views altered little, when liberals William Brennan and Thurgood Marshall retired, he became known as the most liberal member of an increasingly conservative Court. Republican president George H. W. Bush's additions of conservatives David Souter and Clarence Thomas were expected to make the Court extremely conservative, but Souter teamed up with two Reagan appointees, Anthony Kennedy and Sandra Day O'Connor, to create a controlling centrist bloc that frequently thwarted the conservatives. Thomas, as expected, sided with the conservatives.

President Clinton's two moderate-liberal appointments—Ruth Bader Ginsburg and Stephen Breyer—were expected to move the Court left. Instead, two of the moderate-conservative swing justices—Sandra Day O'Connor and Anthony Kennedy—began in the 1996–97 term to ally with the three solid conservatives on the Court—Rehnquist, Scalia, and Thomas. By the 1998–99 term, they had formed a consistent but narrow 5–4 majority on key questions such as favoring states' rights, diluting defendants' rights, and opposing affirmative action. This same narrow majority, most often with Sandra Day O'Connor casting the determining vote, has decided most of the controversial cases over an eleven-year period. Will the two most recent appointments affect the ideological direction of the Court? A true shift in policy direction will likely occur only if a new vacancy is created by the loss of a member of the four-person liberal group, or the moderate conservative Anthony Kennedy, and if a conservative president, such as George Bush, makes the replacing appointment.

IMPLEMENTING SUPREME COURT DECISIONS

When the Supreme Court issues its judgments, in theory they become the law of the land, and one might expect compliance to be automatic. But that does not always happen. Some decisions are so controversial that they are often ignored. For example, judges in Northampton County, Pennsylvania, decided to leave the "Ten Commandments" plaque behind the witness stand in Courtroom 1, contrary to the 2005 decision banning the "Ten Commandments" plaque from inside a Kentucky Courthouse because it violated the First Amendment's Establishment of Religion clause. In the Pennsylvania judges' opinion, the plaque in their courtroom promoted history rather than religion.[92]

Possessing neither "sword" nor "purse," the Supreme Court must maintain the support of political actors such as the president, the Congress, the state and local governments, and public opinion to implement its decisions. This means that the Court, although an unelected body, cannot make its decisions in a political vacuum.

The President and the Court

The president can influence compliance with a decision by choosing whether or not to lend the weight of the office to mobilize favorable public opinion. When state and local officials in Little Rock, Arkansas, resisted the *Brown* v. *Board of Education* school desegregation decision in 1957, President Eisenhower sent federal troops to help implement it.[93] Catholic president John F. Kennedy's support for the Court's 1962 decision outlawing school prayer helped build public support on behalf of that decision.[94]

While most often presidents have nothing to say about Court decisions, their occasional opposition can have an impact. The classic expression came in 1832 with a Supreme Court ruling in favor of the legal rights of the Cherokee Indians. The old frontier fighter President Andrew Jackson was reputed to have said: "Well, John Marshall has made his decision, now let him enforce it!"[95] Since the state of Georgia also opposed the rights of the Cherokee Indians, the federal judiciary and Congress were left to safeguard their rights.

In the long run, however, presidents who do not support the direction of Court rulings can have a greater impact on the Court through appointments than through direct confrontation.

Congress and the Court

Congress often says nothing about Court rulings, the majority of which interpret or define their laws. But if Congress disagrees with the Court's statutory ruling, it has four routes to convey its discontent:

1. It can pass a new law or a revised version of an old law restating its original intentions.
2. It can pass resolutions expressing disagreement with the Court.
3. It can threaten to use one of its constitutional powers to attack the Court directly.
4. It can propose a constitutional amendment.

Generally, Congress will choose to overturn statutory interpretations by passing another version of the law that has been struck down. For instance, in response to six anti-civil rights decisions by the Court in 1991, Congress passed new versions of the same laws guaranteeing those civil rights to citizens.

Less frequently, Congress attempts to reverse constitutional decisions by passing new laws limiting their effect. Section 3501 of the 1968 Omnibus Crime Control Law, reviewed in the *Dickerson* case, was just such an example of Congress trying to overrule the Court by substituting the old "voluntariness" rule for the *Miranda* warnings in determining the admissibility of confessions. In 1993, Congress sought to use legislation to overturn a 1990 case that ruled that the state of Oregon could deny unemployment compensation to two Native Americans who, in smoking peyote in a religious ritual, violated state antidrug laws.[96] When this ruling was then applied in more than sixty other cases to restrict free exercise of religion, Congress passed, and President Clinton signed into law, the Religious Freedom Restoration Act (RFRA), which required the states to show a "compelling state interest," or a high level of proof, before it could interfere with freedom of religion.[97]

Those and similar efforts to overturn a constitutional decision by the Court through legislative means risk review by the Court in the future. Indeed, in the 1996 term, the Supreme Court did overturn RFRA, arguing that "the power to interpret the Constitution in a case or controversy remains in the Judiciary."[98] Indeed, an activist conservative majority on the Rehnquist Court overturned thirty-nine federal laws between 1995 and 2005. When the Court strikes down a law, Congress always retains the option of proposing a constitutional amendment. While a lack of congressional support can weaken or undermine Supreme Court rulings, congressional displeasure with Court rulings is also apparent during confirmation hearings for judicial vacancies.

Court Impact at State and Local Levels

Implementing Supreme Court decisions, especially controversial and complex ones, requires the cooperation of many state and local officials. Compliance often lags while decisions filter through the system and become a workable part of everyday life.

Lower courts have tremendous power to establish how a Supreme Court ruling will be applied. Lower federal and state court judges are empowered to apply Supreme Court rulings to new cases in their jurisdiction. Because Supreme Court decisions are sometimes couched in vague language, they are open to significant interpretation.

Governors, state legislatures, local governments, and even school boards also affect how Supreme Court decisions are implemented. Even local law enforcement has considerable impact. Decisions limiting the power of the police to search for evidence are implemented only if police and prosecutors choose to observe them and state judges decide to enforce them. Although the vast majority of decisions are implemented without question, a handful of highly controversial ones are not, illustrating the problems the Court faces when issuing decisions. More than four decades after the *Brown* desegregation ruling, many American school systems remain segregated. And three decades after the decision striking down prayer in public schools, students in many public schools still participate in some form of devotional service. Although *Roe* v. *Wade* legalized abortion, state legislatures around the country have placed a wide variety of restrictions on that right.

Public Opinion and the Supreme Court

Finally, supportive public opinion plays an important part in implementation. Although the Supreme Court is an unelected body and need not consult public opinion polls when making its rulings, the views of the American people do play a role in its decision making. Should the Court fail to capture the public's conscience with persuasive reasoning, the decision might never be fully implemented. The sharp public division over the abortion decision in *Roe* v. *Wade*, for example, has affected its level of acceptance.

Research has revealed the Court's general willingness to adhere to majority public sentiment in nearly 60 percent of its decisions.[99] In addition, the Court often signals an accounting for public opinion by counterbalancing bold, innovative decisions with later, more conservative judgments to encourage acceptance. The Court is aware that if it strays too far ahead of public opinion, it risks losing support

▲ Supporters of the Presidential candidates, George Bush and Al Gore, hold their own "oral argument" outside the United States Supreme Court Building while the disputed Florida voting case is being argued inside.

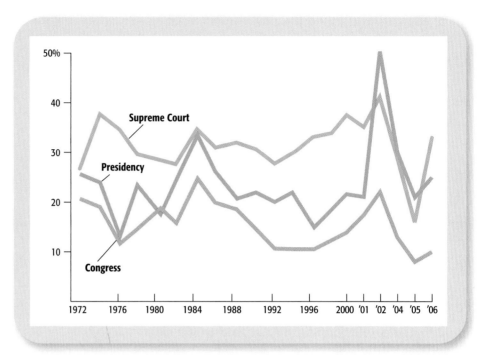

Figure 6.6 Confidence in Political Institutions
Although a higher percentage of the public has consistently expressed a "great deal of confidence" in the Supreme Court than in the presidency and Congress, since the terrorist attacks on September 11, 2001, for the first time in 2005 the president had been outpolling the Supreme Court in the public's level of confidence. By early 2006, though, the Court resumed its leadership position.

Source: Compiled from Harris Poll, Feb 7–14, 2006, www.pollingreport.com, last checked on 3/8/06; Harris Poll #6, January 30, 2002, Harris Poll Library, harrisinteractive.com/ harris_poll/ and data by John R. Hibbing and James T. Smith "What the American Public Wants Congress to Be," in *Congress Reconsidered,* 7th ed., by Lawrence Dodd and Bruce I. Oppenheimer, eds., Congressional Quarterly Press 2001, as it appeared in *National Journal,* June 10, 2000, p. 1818.

(see Figure 6.6). Thus, the Court will change the law, and thereby public policy, incrementally to encourage implementation. Since 2001 the Court's level of public support has dropped dramatically, possibly a reaction to the Court's increased politicization, liberal reaction to the *Bush* v. *Gore* presidential vote case, and conservative reaction to some of the Court's more controversial decisions in cultural issues. Although 68 percent of the people expressed support for the Court in January 2001, by June 2005 that number had dropped to 57 percent. Even more telling, 30 percent of the public now express a negative reaction to the Court.[100] Should the Court lead or follow public opinion? Ideally, it should do both. In general, it is best to be attentive to the views of those implementing the decisions and to the general public, but at times the Court must lead when others in the political arena are unwilling to take the initiative. In this respect, the Court's independence is indispensable if it is to help America approach democracy.

Question for Reflection

Under what conditions, if ever, should public or political figures refuse to follow or implement Supreme Court decisions?

THE COURT'S INDEPENDENCE IN APPROACHING DEMOCRACY

The Supreme Court, said political scientist (and later president) Woodrow Wilson, is "the balance wheel of our whole constitutional system."[101] Like the balancing middle wheel that keeps a machine running smoothly, the Supreme Court takes into consideration the demands of the president, Congress, the bureaucracy, the fifty states and its protectorates, and the American public, and attempts to arrive at decisions that bring them all into harmony.

The paradox is that this vital balancing role is being filled by one of the least democratic institutions in the world. In other countries, nonelected leaders who hold office for life and rule in complete secrecy are either kings or dictators; in America they are Supreme Court justices. In theory, the justices can make any decisions they like, but as you have seen, in reality the judiciary is restrained by the possibility that its decisions will meet resistance or not be implemented at all.

What, then, is the role of an independent Supreme Court in the American system of democracy? Attempts to answer this question have led to a long-standing debate about whether the Court should actively make policy or practice judicial restraint. Should the Court adhere to the letter of the law and leave policymaking to the elected Congress and president? Should it be an architect of public policies that advance human rights or simply reflect the desires of the populace?

Over the years, the Supreme Court and the lower federal courts have varied in their willingness to fully use their power based on the nature of the legal issues, the number of cases heard, the political situation, and who's on the bench. Recalling the negative reaction to the 1954 *Brown* v. *Board of Education* desegregation decision and the 1973 *Roe* v. *Wade* abortion decision, it remains to be seen whether the Court, faced with today's cultural issues and wartime posture of the terrorism crisis, back off of issues that they would otherwise like to resolve now. Whatever happens, judiciary actions in America's democracy will continue to have powerful implications for both government and individual rights.

Summary

1. The federal courts decide all legal disputes arising under the Constitution, U.S. law, and treaties. In cases involving disputes between states or involving foreign ambassadors, the Supreme Court has original jurisdiction. For all other federal cases, it has appellate jurisdiction.

2. In the 1803 case of *Marbury* v. *Madison*, Chief Justice Marshall argued that the Supreme Court has the power to interpret the Constitution. This power, known as judicial review, enables the Court to overturn actions of the executive and legislative branches and to reinterpret the Constitution to fit new situations. The power of statutory construction enables the Court to interpret a federal or state law.

3. The power to appoint justices to the Supreme Court is shared by the president and Congress. The justices are appointed for life and can be impeached only for "High Crimes and Misdemeanors." The president can influence the Court by appointing justices who support a particular philosophy. Congress can change the number of justices or pass a law to reverse a Court decision.

4. Most cases enter the judicial system through a trial court consisting of a single judge and, at times, a jury. The proceedings of the trial court are reviewed by an appellate court consisting of a panel of judges but no jury. Criminal cases involve violations of state or federal criminal law; civil cases involve private disputes. Most criminal cases are resolved by plea bargains, in which the state agrees to reduce the charges or sentence in return for a guilty plea.

5. The federal judiciary is organized in three tiers. At the bottom are the ninety-four district courts, with at least one in each state. At the next level are the courts of appeals, which hear cases from thirteen circuits, or regions, usually in three-judge panels. District and circuit courts are constitutional courts, but the federal judiciary also includes legislative courts, courts established by Congress.

6. Candidates for the Supreme Court are suggested by senators, governors, the candidates themselves, their friends, and federal judges, and they are screened by the FBI and the American Bar Association. Most nominees to the Court are members of the president's party and share the president's political philosophy.

7. The confirmation process begins with a hearing by the Senate Judiciary Committee, which makes a recommendation prior to a vote by the full Senate. These procedures can constitute major hurdles, resulting in the rejection of nearly one in five presidential nominations.

8. In nominations to district courts, the tradition of senatorial courtesy gives senators what amounts to a veto power. Often, however, candidates are suggested by senators in the president's party. Recent presidents have attempted to make the federal judiciary more representative of the population as a whole.

9. The solicitor general decides which federal cases to appeal from the lower courts, prepares the appeals, and represents the United States before the Supreme Court. Appellate cases come to the Supreme Court through writs of certiorari. If at least four justices vote to hear a case, it is placed on the docket. In recent years the Court has decided fewer cases, even though the number of appeals reaching it has increased dramatically.

10. When the Court accepts a case, attorneys for all sides submit briefs, or written legal arguments. They then present oral arguments before the Court. The justices

hold a conference to discuss and vote on the case, and one of the justices voting with the majority is assigned to draft the opinion, or written version of the decision. The opinion must be approved by at least five justices. A justice who agrees with the majority decision but differs on the reasoning may write a concurring opinion. When a justice disagrees with the Court's ruling, he or she may write a dissenting opinion.

11. Interpretation of a law or a portion of the Constitution as closely as possible to the literal meaning of the words is known as *strict construction*. When the wording is vague, justices may attempt to determine the original intent of the framers. Justices may consider the effect a ruling would have on public policy. Some justices believe in judicial restraint—deferring to the other branches of government whenever possible—others are judicial activists, believing that judges have a duty to further certain causes.

12. Decisions of the Supreme Court become the law of the land. However, compliance with a decision is influenced by the extent to which the president supports it. It may also be circumvented by Congress, which can pass a new law or propose a constitutional amendment restating its original intentions.

Review Questions

1. Why has the Supreme Court been the institution that has extended existing rights and even created new ones?

2. In what ways and when has the Supreme Court protected us against tyranny of the majority?

3. Why did the founding fathers view the judiciary as the "least dangerous" branch of government?

4. What factors limit the Supreme Court's actions? What factors enhance its independence?

5. What is the role of the law clerks on the "cert pool"? How have they affected the docket? How have they affected the independence of the court? Does this represent an approach to democracy? Why or why not?

6. What factors influence the court's docket in a given year? How have these factors changed over time?

7. Describe the political and legal roles of the "Tenth Justice" or Solicitor General. In what ways has this individual been influential?

Key Terms

amicus curiae briefs   230
appellate court   217
appellate jurisdiction   211
briefs   231
civil cases   217
class action suit   217
concurring opinion   234
constitutional courts   217
criminal cases   217
dissenting opinion   234
docket   227

en banc   219
judicial activism   238
judicial restraint   238
judicial review   211
legislative courts   219
majority opinion   234
Marbury v. *Madison*   211
opinion   232
original jurisdiction   211
plea bargains   217
plurality opinion   234

precedents   236
rule of four   229
senatorial courtesy   224
solicitor general   230
stare decisis   236
statutory construction   212
trial court   215
U.S. courts of appeals   218
U.S. district courts   217
writ of certiorari   228

Suggested Readings

ABRAHAM, HENRY J. *Justices, Presidents and Senators: A History of the U.S. Supreme Court Appointments from Washington to Clinton.* Lanham, Md.: Rowman and Littlefield, 1999. A complete history of presidential appointments to the Supreme Court and the decision making that resulted.

BLACKMUN, HARRY. *The Harry Blackmun Papers at the Library of Congress,* Manuscript Division, Library of Congress, Washington D.C.: www.loc.gov/rr/mss/blackmun/. The most revealing primary source examination of the Justice and the recent courts available.

BREYER, STEPHEN. *Active Liberty: Interpreting Our Democratic Constitution,* New York: Knopf, 2005. A thoughtful and clearly expressed explanation of the Justice's theory of "Policing the Boundaries" of Constitutional governmental power.

DAVIS, RICHARD. *Electing Justice: Fixing the Supreme Court Nomination Process.* New York: Oxford University Press, 2005. An interesting argument about possible changes in the Supreme Court appointment process.

EPSTEIN, LEE, and JACK KNIGHT. *The Choices Justices Make.* Washington, D.C.: CQ Press, 1998. An analysis of the strategically political manner in which justices decide cases.

FOSKETT, KEN. *Judging Thomas: The Life and Times of Clarence Thomas.* New York: William Morrow, 2004. An inside look at the Court's most enigmatic justice.

GOLDMAN, SHELDON. *Picking Federal Judges: Lower Court Selection from Roosevelt Through Reagan.* New Haven, Conn.: Yale University Press, 1997. Findings from thirty years of study by the nation's expert on the lower federal court judicial selection process into how nine presidents have undertaken this process.

GREENHOUSE, LINDA. *Becoming Justice Blackmun: Harry Blackmun's Supreme Court Journey.* New York: Times Books, 2005. A wonderfully readable biography of both Justice Blackmun and the Rehnquist Court.

LAZARUS, EDWARD. *Closed Chambers.* New York: Times Books, 1998. Not only a revealing look inside the Court in the 1998–89 term by a former Blackmun law clerk, but a potentially damaging account of the increased role of law clerks in the Court's work.

LEVIN, MARK. *Men in Black: How the Supreme Court is Destroying America.* Washington, D.C.: Regnery, 2005. A best-selling critique of the behavior, philosophy, and decisions of the Court.

LEWIS, ANTHONY. *Gideon's Trumpet.* New York: Vintage Press, 1964. A study of the *Gideon* v. *Wainwright* case. Still the best short, single volume on the progress of a case through the Supreme Court.

MURDOCH, JOYCE, and DEB PRICE. *Courting Justice: Gay Men and Lesbians* v. *the Supreme Court.* New York: Basic Books, 2001. A highly readable history of the Supreme Court's effort to avoid and then mishandle the issue of gay rights in cases throughout the decades.

MURPHY, BRUCE ALLEN. *Wild Bill: The Legend and Life of William O. Douglas.* New York: Random House, 2003. A revealing study of the real person behind the legend and the sources of his judicial decision-making.

O'BRIEN, DAVID. *Storm Center: The Supreme Court in American Politics.* 7th ed. New York: Norton, 2005. A highly revealing text on the internal politics of the Supreme Court using sources from justices' papers in historical archives.

SAVAGE, DAVID. *Turning Right: The Making of the Rehnquist Supreme Court.* New York: Wiley, 1992. The *Los Angeles Times* court reporter's inside account of the people who make up the Rehnquist Court and the ways their personal views and interactions shape public policy.

TUSHNET, MARK. *A Court Divided: the Rehnquist Court and the Future of Constitutional Law.* New York: Norton, 2005. A learned and informative analysis of the justices and legal topics that made the Rehnguist Court so interesting.

WOODWARD, BOB, and SCOTT ARMSTRONG. *The Brethren: Inside the Supreme Court.* New York: Avon Books, 1979. A highly controversial study of the inside workings of the Supreme Court from 1969 through 1975. Uses anonymous law clerk interviews and Court papers.

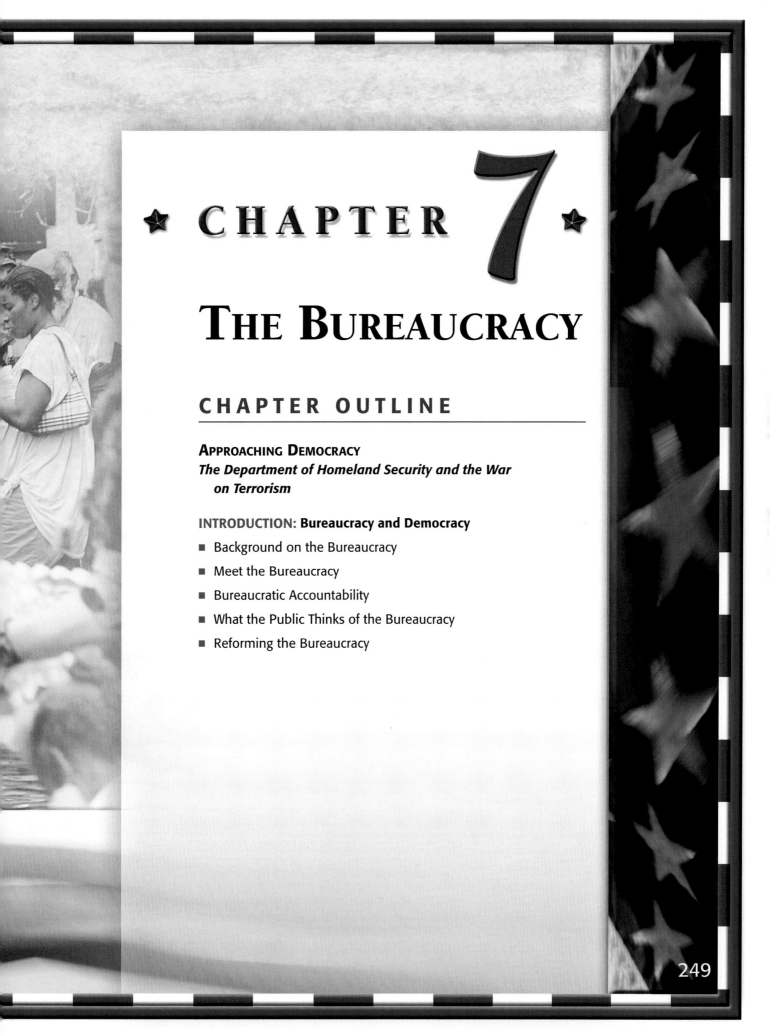

★ CHAPTER 7 ★

THE BUREAUCRACY

CHAPTER OUTLINE

APPROACHING DEMOCRACY
*The Department of Homeland Security and the War
on Terrorism*

INTRODUCTION: Bureaucracy and Democracy

- Background on the Bureaucracy
- Meet the Bureaucracy
- Bureaucratic Accountability
- What the Public Thinks of the Bureaucracy
- Reforming the Bureaucracy

Approaching Democracy

The Department of Homeland Security and the War on Terrorism

Following the September 11, 2001, attack on the World Trade Center and the Pentagon by al-Qaeda operatives, President Bush used an executive order to create the Office of Homeland Security. The president selected Tom Ridge, a former prosecutor, congressman, and two-term Republican governor of Pennsylvania (and a close friend and political supporter of both Bush presidents), to run the new office as Assistant to the President for Homeland Security.

Ridge received a high-profile office in the West Wing, an initial staff of eighty, and a broad agenda for overseeing eleven major subject areas. The new office was mandated to protect twenty thousand miles of U.S. borders and to coordinate forty-six separate federal agencies to fight terrorism. The challenge was to streamline the organizational coherence of the new cabinet post without creating another management or supervisory bureaucratic unit.

Considering the creation of the Office of Homeland Security within the context of the September 11 attacks reveals the complex challenges our democracy faces. In the weeks following September 11, Ridge helped coordinate a remarkable infrastructure involving the Federal Bureau of Investigation (FBI), Federal Emergency Management Agency (FEMA), Department of Energy (DOE), Environmental Protection Agency (EPA), Coast Guard, Army National Guard, and the Departments of Justice, Transportation, and other agencies of the federal government. "I think one of the challenges that the Office of Homeland Security has is to make sure that it becomes a permanent part of how the federal government does business," said Ridge.[1]

By June 6, 2002, we learned just how permanent a structure President Bush envisioned for homeland security when he proposed a new cabinet department for domestic defense. In the president's words, "We have concluded that our government must be reorganized to deal more effectively with the threats of the twenty-first century. So tonight I ask the Congress to join me in creating a single permanent mission—securing the homeland and protecting the American people. . . . Tonight I propose a permanent cabinet-level Department of Homeland Security to unite essential agencies that must work more closely together. . . . What I am proposing tonight is the most extensive reorganization of the federal government since the 1940s."[2]

In the aftermath of the 2002 Republican electoral victory, the House and Senate passed legislation establishing a new department to oversee homeland security. President Bush, soon thereafter, signed the bipartisan bill into law, thereby creating the Homeland Security Department—the most comprehensive reorganization of the federal government in more than fifty years. Yet, this very reorganization came under intense scrutiny in September 2005 when Hurricane Katrina hit New Orleans and surrounding areas. As the nation looked on in shock and dismay at the failed federal response to Katrina,

★ President George W. Bush and guests applaud Secretary Michael Chertoff after he was sworn in as the second Secretary of Homeland Security, Thursday, Mar. 3, 2005. White House photo by Paul Morse.
Source: www.whitehouse.gov/homeland

it became apparent that the problem rested in leadership as well as the bureaucracy itself.[3] Stephen Flynn, author of *America the Vulnerable: How Our Government is Failing to Protect Us from Terrorism*, perhaps best summed up the situation in observing, "I would argue that the Department of Homeland Security is not prepared to deal with an act of terror, and it's obviously been shown not to be able to deal with a natural disaster. These agencies that were pulled together into a department are agencies that were treated as orphans in the departments that they came from—the Coast Guard, which is from the Department of Transportation; Customs Service, which came out of the Department of Treasury; INS from Justice. They did not get much care and feeding..."[4]

To make matters even worse, the department's workers ranked the least satisfied in a survey of federal employee attitudes. (See Figure 7.1) Only 12 percent of employees working in the government agency most responsible for protecting the country against terrorism and responding to natural disasters said they felt strongly that they were

★ In the aftermath of Hurricane Katrina, Michael D. Brown, Under Secretary of Emergency Preparedness and Response for FEMA, briefed the President and Homeland Security Secretary Michael Chertoff. Brown was under fire for the federal government's slow response to the storm that destroyed much of the Gulf Coast region, and he was soon removed from his role in managing the Bush administration's hurricane relief efforts.

"encouraged to come up with new and better ways of doing things."[5] In the aftermath of Hurricane Katrina, Homeland Security Secretary Chertoff vowed to reshape the 180,000-worker department. He plans to reshape FEMA's emergency logistics, communications, and operations systems in order to bolster the nation's preparedness for future natural disasters.

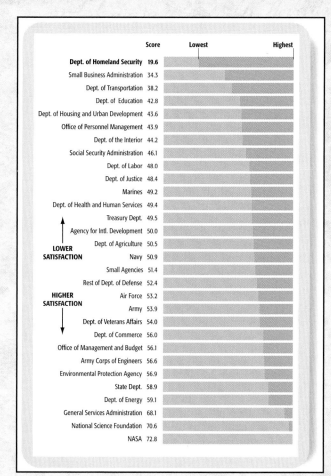

	Score
Dept. of Homeland Security	**19.6**
Small Business Administration	34.3
Dept. of Transportation	38.2
Dept. of Education	42.8
Dept. of Housing and Urban Development	43.6
Office of Personnel Management	43.9
Dept. of the Interior	44.2
Social Security Administration	46.1
Dept. of Labor	48.0
Dept. of Justice	48.4
Marines	49.2
Dept. of Health and Human Services	49.4
Treasury Dept.	49.5
Agency for Intl. Development	50.0
Dept. of Agriculture	50.5
Navy	50.9
Small Agencies	51.4
Rest of Dept. of Defense	52.4
Air Force	53.2
Army	53.9
Dept. of Veterans Affairs	54.0
Dept. of Commerce	56.0
Office of Management and Budget	56.1
Army Corps of Engineers	56.6
Environmental Protection Agency	56.9
State Dept.	58.9
Dept. of Energy	59.1
General Services Administration	68.1
National Science Foundation	70.6
NASA	72.8

LOWER SATISFACTION ↑
HIGHER SATISFACTION ↓

FIGURE 7.1
High Profile, Low Satisfaction
Workers in the Department of Homeland Security ranked the lowest in a survey of employee attitudes in the federal government. On this scale, a theoretical score of 200 would indicate complete satisfaction by every worker; a score of –200 would indicate complete dissatisfaction by everyone.
Source: Scott Lilly, Center for American Progress.

QUESTION FOR REFLECTION

Early in the twentieth century, the United States developed agencies to combat threats to our way of life both at home and abroad. The Federal Bureau of Investigation (FBI) and Central Intelligence Agency (CIA) were established to fight crime and coordinate intelligence data. Based on the evolution of these two agencies, what predictions might you make for the future of the Department of Homeland Security?

Introduction
BUREAUCRACY AND DEMOCRACY

In this chapter we look at contradictions that arise between bureaucratic necessity and democratic ideals. We want you to consider how necessary but inherently secretive bureaucratic organizations such as the Department of Homeland Security gain legitimacy and function without public disclosure of their activities. After all, democracy requires plurality; traditional bureaucracy requires unity. Democratic society is organized around the principle of equality, while bureaucratic organization is hierarchical. A fundamental element in any democracy is openness, but bureaucratic operations often demand secrecy, especially when national security is involved. A democratic political system ensures equal access to participation in politics, but bureaucratic participation depends on institutional authority. Finally, democracy assumes the election and subsequent public accountability of all officials, but bureaucrats are appointed, and the agencies they lead are often created without congressional action and thus not subject to public accountability.

Though the bureaucracy is an institution often scorned for its enormous size and lack of responsiveness or accountability, this "fourth branch" of government has an important function that makes it indispensable in America's approach to democracy: carrying forth the work of the federal government. The Department of Homeland Security has the responsibility of developing and coordinating a national strategy to secure the United States from terrorist threats or attacks. The president's most important job is to protect and defend the American people. The Coast Guard has assumed expanded duties to safeguard our shores and ports. The National Guard has increased its surveillance. A new agency, the Transportation Security Administration (TSA) was created to shield the nation's airports and transportation systems from attack. New licensing requirements have been instituted to ensure safer transportation of hazardous materials. New federal antiterrorism laws, particularly the USA Patriot Act, have been passed, giving law enforcement officers tools to fight terrorists. Tighter immigration controls are being instituted. Many of these actions challenge core values such as freedom and liberty. Most if not all of us are willing to compromise some of our democratic principles if it means achieving the greater good—the survival of our nation and the eradication of terrorist networks. Thinking about these issues will help you to conceptualize the challenge of approaching democracy.

MakeItReal

ABC News Video: *Department of Homeland Security*

BACKGROUND ON THE BUREAUCRACY

Although Americans usually measure the performance of bureaucratic agencies by the impact of their failures rather than by their routine successes, it is difficult to imagine a world without bureaucracy. "Bureaucracy is the cod-liver oil of social institutions. It smells bad and leaves a nasty aftertaste, but sometimes it is just what you need."[6] In part Americans suspect their bureaucracy because they realize that government agencies mostly function with little or no citizen restraint. Indeed, the bureaucracy, sometimes called the "fourth branch of government"—as powerful as Congress, the president, and the Supreme Court—operates without the regular elections and/or oversight committees that keep these institutions responsive to public opinion.

A **bureaucracy** is a large and complex organizational system in which tasks, roles, and responsibilities are structured to achieve a goal. The term is rooted in the eighteenth-century French word for a woolen cloth (*burel*) used to cover a writing

bureaucracy A large and complex organizational system in which tasks, roles, and responsibilities are structured to achieve a goal.

◀ On November 19, 2001, President Bush signed into law the Aviation and Transportation Security Act (ATSA), which among other things created a new Transportation Security Administration (TSA) within the Department of Transportation. This act established a series of challenging but critically important milestones toward achieving a secure air travel system. The improvements include that by November 19, 2002, screening of individuals and property in the United States will be conducted by TSA employees and companies under contract with TSA. This requires enhanced qualifications, training, and testing of individuals who perform screening functions. It also requires that federal law enforcement officers be present at screening locations.

desk, or *bureau*. **Bureaucrats**, the people who work in a bureaucracy, include not only the obscure, faceless clerks normally disparaged by critics of government but also "street-level" bureaucrats, such as police officers, social workers, and schoolteachers.

German sociologist Max Weber (1865–1920) is considered the father of modern bureaucracy. He modeled his "ideal type" of bureaucratic organization on the Prussian government of the early twentieth century. He believed that a bureaucracy should improve efficiency by three means—through specialization, hierarchy, and a system of formal rules.[7]

The principle of **specialization** rests on delegating specific tasks to individuals whose training and experience give them the expertise to execute them. As government responsibilities increase, so too does the need for specialization, or more experts in various areas. Bureaucratic organization also requires **hierarchy**, a clear chain of communication and command running from an executive director at the top down through all levels of workers, such as the mailroom clerks in the middle and janitors at the bottom. The hierarchy facilitates decision making and establishes clear lines of authority within a large, complex organization. As we create new bureaucratic organizations in which multiple agencies coordinate and collaborate, such as the Department of Homeland Security, we need new approaches to hierarchy.

In addition to specialization and hierarchical authority, bureaucratic organizations use **formal rules**, clearly defined procedures for executing their assigned tasks. Sometimes called *standard operating procedures* (*SOPs*), these rules simplify and establish routines for complex procedures, curtail favoritism, and improve the decision-making process by allowing bureaucrats to respond to a broad array of situations with a minimum of delay and confusion. Such formal rules also apply to the professional lives of bureaucrats. There are clearly defined steps for job advancement, specific descriptions of duties, and specific qualifications for salary increases.

Problems Inherent in the Bureaucratic Form Specialization, hierarchy, and formal rules are all designed to improve the performance of bureaucracy. Usually this structure works. For example, although we sometimes hear horror stories

bureaucrats People who work in a bureaucracy, not only the obscure, faceless clerks normally disparaged by critics of government but also "street-level bureaucrats" such as police officers, social workers, and schoolteachers.

specialization A principle that, in a bureaucracy, specific tasks should be delegated to individuals whose training and experience give them the expertise to execute them. Also refers to a norm used to push legislation through Congress in which members who lack expertise in a particular policy area defer to policy specialists with more knowledge.

hierarchy A clear chain of communication and command running from an executive director at the top down through all levels of workers.

formal rules In a bureaucracy, clearly defined procedures governing the execution of all tasks within the jurisdiction of a given agency.

Question for Reflection

What type of hierarchy would be effective for the Department of Homeland Security?

about mail going undelivered, the U.S. Postal Service remains one of the most efficient public bureaucracies in the world. And for all of our moaning and groaning about taxes and the Internal Revenue Service, most of us receive our tax returns from the IRS promptly—through the U.S. mail. In fact, during the anthrax scare in Fall 2001, the United States Postal Service continued to process thirty billion pieces of mail daily. Postal employees took extra precautions, but they came to work and did their jobs, always knowing that another contaminated letter could arrive at any time at any postal facility within the United States.[8]

The very nature of specialization within a bureaucracy can sometimes impede rather than improve performance, rendering an agency relatively efficient in certain tasks but inflexible in others. Weber warned that bureaucratic organization might turn workers into "specialists without spirit," motivated only by narrowly defined tasks and unable to adapt to changing circumstances. You can probably think of an applicable case from your own daily dealings with bureaucracy at college, local government, or even during a summer vacation at your favorite national park administered by the National Park Service.

Growth of the Federal Bureaucracy

The bureaucracy commands the most attention when problems arise—when sacks of undelivered mail are discovered in a musty Chicago basement, or when a natural disaster such as Hurricane Katrina reveals ineptitude at all levels. Despite their problems, bureaucracies are necessary and characteristic parts of modern industrialized societies. Large-scale bureaucratic organizations allow high productivity and complex coordination of government programs such as road building, air traffic control, environmental management, the postal system, and telecommunications. Nevertheless, bureaucracies pose serious problems in terms of accountability and power. For example, how can organizations such as the Federal Bureau of Investigation (FBI), the Central Intelligence Agency (CIA), or the National Security Agency (NSA) gather sufficient enforcement power to thwart terrorism without compromising the rights of innocent civilians whose phones are wiretapped or e-mails read without court approval? How can the Internal Revenue Service (IRS), responsible for processing several million tax returns annually, be sufficiently restrained not to prey on innocent citizens by terrifying them into paying taxes they don't owe or by ruining them financially if they cannot pay what they do owe?

America's early bureaucracy hardly resembled today's Leviathan. George Washington's budget for the entire bureaucracy in 1790 was just under $1.5 million, and the money funded just three departments—state, war, and treasury. The largest of these, the Department of the Treasury, employed seventy workers, minuscule by modern standards. The federal government's rapid growth began in the late nineteenth century. At that time, industrial expansion was increasing the U.S. economy in size and complexity and destabilizing American social life. As corporations became more powerful, the popular call intensified for a larger government role in business regulation and protecting citizen welfare. Among those calling for change were the Progressives, and in the early twentieth century they became successful advocates for increased popular participation in government and administrative reform at the local level. The Progressives thought government ought to assume broad regulatory powers over corporations, thus initiating the modern trend toward viewing government involvement in a positive light.

Public commitment to activist government paved the way for the astonishing growth of the federal bureaucracy in the twentieth century. This new faith in the power of government peaked during the thirty years in which the government mobilized the nation's resources to fight the Great Depression, wage World War II, and combat domestic poverty and racial discrimination. The greatest growth was evident in the 1930s and 1940s, during the emergence of what has become known as the "welfare state."

The Welfare State   Beginning in 1933, Franklin D. Roosevelt's New Deal involved the government in everyday economic affairs. Its programs dramatically increased the government's workforce and the scope and power of federal responsibilities. The New Deal emerged in response to the Great Depression, which brought massive unemployment—at times as much as a quarter of America's labor force was out of work—and a growing awareness of the need to provide more security for American citizens, both on the job and after retirement.

The New Deal consisted of a series of legislative acts, executive orders, and proclamations that created large-scale federal programs offering retirement insurance, health care, economic security, and poverty relief for Americans. New Deal programs created jobs and jump-started a stagnant economy. They also laid the legislative foundation for liberal Democratic policies. The Civilian Conservation Corps (CCC) granted millions of dollars to the states to pay young people to work at forestry, irrigation, and land projects; by 1935 more than 500,000 youths were at work under the auspices of the CCC. The Tennessee Valley Authority (TVA) provided funds to build dams and reservoirs, creating thousands of jobs and bringing electricity to new areas. The Wagner Act established the National Labor Relations Board (NLRB) and gave workers the right to unionize and bargain collectively. The Social Security Act established a federally funded financial safety net for the elderly, infirm, and unemployed.

Roosevelt built on his cousin President Theodore Roosevelt's earlier progress in using government power to increase regulation of finance and commerce. Responding to a wave of bank failures and lost deposits, Roosevelt's administration established the Federal Deposit Insurance Corporation (FDIC) to insure most bank deposits. Roosevelt's administration also created the Securities and Exchange Commission (SEC), the Federal National Mortgage Association (FNMA, or "Fannie Mae"), and the Federal Communications Commission (FCC) to regulate the stock exchanges, the interstate mortgage market, and the public airwaves, respectively.

The New Deal programs became the core of the modern **welfare state**. Although designed as temporary emergency programs to relieve Depression-era suffering, most New Deal agencies became a permanent part of the dramatically enlarged federal bureaucracy. In addition to expanding the bureaucracy, the New Deal era led to a growing dependence on that bureaucracy to administer and regulate many essential functions of modern American life.

Similarly, during World War II the federal government hired hundreds of thousands of temporary employees to plan and coordinate the vast assembly of personnel and machinery used to defeat the Axis Powers. After World War II, many of these "temporary" employees remained at work in government and were absorbed by agencies that redefined their civilian missions more broadly. But neither the growth of the bureaucracy nor the dependence on it by increasing numbers of Americans stopped with the end of the Great Depression and World War II. Since then the size of the federal bureaucracy has been relatively stable, although hardly stagnant.

In the 1960s, President Johnson's Great Society, an ambitious assault on racial injustice and poverty, created scores of new government agencies and slight overall growth. At the president's request, Congress enacted programs to provide medical care, job opportunities, and business loans to the poor and to improve the quality and availability of education at all levels. In addition, Congress enacted programs to conserve water, air, and natural resources.

During the 1970s, growing citizen awareness of the problems of consumer safety and environmental degradation led to creation of the Consumer Product Safety Commission (CPSC) and the Environmental Protection Agency (EPA), and, thus, more bureaucratic growth. In the wake of the OPEC oil embargo, the old Office of Emergency Preparedness was systematically expanded. First it became the Federal Energy Office (FEO), then the Federal Energy Administration (FEA), and finally

   **MakeItReal**

Primary Source: National Labor Relations Act (1935)

Primary Source: The Social Security Act (1935)

welfare state   A social system whereby the government assumes primary responsibility for the welfare of citizens.

the cabinet-level Department of Energy (DOE). Mounting concern over safety in the workplace, coupled with evidence that corporations were not willing to adopt appropriate safety measures without government prodding, led to creation of the Occupational Safety and Health Administration (OSHA).

Expansion of government responsibilities during the 1960s and 1970s brought major increases in the federal budget, largely because of increases in *transfer payments*—that is, money paid to individuals in the form of Social Security benefits, welfare payments, and the like—thereby "transferring" money from one segment of society to another.

Virtually all presidential candidates since the 1970s have pledged to reduce the size and scope of the federal government. Throughout their campaigns, candidates attack big government, but once in office they find it difficult to reduce the number of federal workers. Former president Ronald Reagan made one of the most dramatic attempts at downsizing, but even this conservative icon found it difficult to reduce the scope of bureaucratic power. Reagan, like presidents throughout American history, had to accept that bureaucracy is a constantly evolving, growing, largely independent realm of government. Perhaps the final irony of the bureaucracy's vengeance on the Reagan legacy came in 1997 with the opening of the largest new federal building in Washington, D.C. Taking up the size of several football fields and housing thousands of federal workers, the new federal building is named the Ronald Reagan Building and International Trade Center. Only the Pentagon building is larger.[9]

Evolution of the Bureaucracy: Creating the Civil Service

The federal bureaucracy has grown enormously since the early days of the republic. There has also been a corresponding change in its character. Prior to the presidential election of Andrew Jackson in 1828, a small, elite group of wealthy, well-educated white males dominated the bureaucracy. Jackson, a populist, was determined to make the federal workforce more representative by opening up jobs to the masses. He instituted

"H.U.D. called the F.A.A. The F.A.A. called the S.E.C. The S.E.C. called G.S.A. G.S.A. called O.M.B. O.M.B. called Y-O-U."

a new system based on the declaration of his friend, Senator William Marcy: "To the victor go the spoils."[10] The emergence of this **spoils system** meant that Jackson and his subordinates would award top-level government jobs and contracts on the basis of party loyalty rather than social or economic status or relevant experience.

Jackson's opponents in the Whig party recognized the advantages of using government jobs for patronage purposes, and when Jackson's Democrats were voted out of office, the bureaucracy was restaffed by those loyal to the Whigs. Later on, as the government grew, supporters of the spoils system found that if a thousand patronage jobs were beneficial, ten thousand or twenty thousand would be even more welcome.

The spoils system survived until the 1881 assassination of President James Garfield by Charles Guiteau, who was bitter about his inability to find a job in Garfield's administration. In response, Congress passed the Pendleton Act of 1883, which created a **civil service**, a system of hiring and promoting employees based on professional merit, not party loyalty. Such a system was designed to protect government employees from political threats to their job security. The act also created a three-person Civil Service Commission to oversee the merit system throughout the federal work force. The Civil Service Commission evaluated job applicants based on their performance on civil service examinations. Employees achieved permanent status after a probationary period and were promoted only with strong performance evaluations from supervisors. The Civil Service Commission functioned until 1978, when the Civil Service Reform Act replaced it with two agencies: The Office of Personnel Management administers civil service recruitment and promotion procedures, and the independent Merit Systems Protection Board studies the merit system and holds grievance and disciplinary hearing for federal employees.

Today, merit-based hiring and advancement have eliminated much of the corruption and cronyism of the old patronage system. The civil service system encourages hiring of highly skilled experts and provides procedures for evaluating federal workers' qualifications and job performance. The civil service has a downside, however. For one thing, it insulates federal employees from many pressures of a competitive private sector job market. For example, federal employees are hard to fire or even discipline. The employee must receive written notice at least thirty days in advance, detailing the reasons for, and specific examples of, the conduct prompting the action. The employee may then appeal the action to the Merit Systems Protection Board (MSPB), which must grant a hearing, at which point the employee has the right to legal counsel. If the MSPB rejects the appeal, the employee may take the case to the U.S. Court of Appeals. The process has become so burdensome that, rather than attempt to fire unproductive employees; supervisors have learned to live with them. Debate on the Homeland Security legislation centered on President Bush's push for greater freedom from civil service rules versus union opposition to political management control over federal employees.

Civil service guidelines not only insulate the federal workforce, they also tend to give some agencies a sense that they are "untouchable," whatever the periodic changes in the political climate of the country. One common remark associated with career civil servants when they are asked about a change in presidential administration is that while presidents are temporary employees, careerists in the bureaucracy stay for life. Research has shown that most civil servants tend to conform to the policy directives of administrations as they come and go, but determined resistance to presidential initiatives can hamper a president's agenda considerably.

The Hatch Act Congress passed the **Hatch Act**, named for its author, New Mexico senator Carl Hatch, in 1939. The act works to make the bureaucracy more responsive to the policy directives of changing presidential administrations and to move it in the direction of greater political neutrality with a list of political dos and don'ts for federal employees. The Hatch act was designed to prevent federal civil servants from using their power or position to influence elections, thereby creating a nonpartisan, nonpolitical, professionalized bureaucracy. Under the act, bureaucrats may express

▲ In this political cartoon by Thomas Nast, President Andrew Jackson is riding the hog of political patronage, implying that those who win office can help those who support them with jobs, money, and power.

spoils system A system in which government jobs and contracts are awarded on the basis of party loyalty rather than social or economic status or relevant experience.

civil service A system of hiring and promoting employees based on professional merit, not party loyalty.

Hatch Act Approved by Congress in 1939 and named for its author, Senator Carl Hatch of New Mexico, a list of political dos and don'ts for federal employees; designed to prevent federal civil servants from using their power or position to engage in political activities to influence elections, thereby creating a nonpartisan, nonpolitical, professionalized bureaucracy.

MakeItReal

Primary Source: Navigating The Hatch Act

opinions about issues and candidates and contribute money to political organizations, but they cannot distribute campaign information, nor can they campaign actively for or against a candidate. A federal employee may register and vote in an election but cannot run as a candidate for public office.

Although the authors of the Hatch Act believed it necessary to restrict the political liberties of government employees to preserve the neutrality of the growing maze of federal agencies and programs, these restrictions illustrate one area where bureaucracy clashes with democratic ideals. Nearly three million American civilians who work for the federal government have their rights to full participation in the nation's political process sharply curtailed. In the box "Know Your Grasp of the Hatch Act," test your knowledge of what federal employees are allowed to do. Although many civil servants and constitutional scholars have denounced the Hatch Act as unconstitutional, the Supreme Court has disagreed with them.

Critics of the law have found some sympathy in Congress. In 1993, it amended the act to allow federal employees to participate more actively in partisan politics, with several restrictions. They cannot be candidates for public office in partisan elections, use official authority to influence or interfere with elections, or solicit funds from or discourage the political activity of any person undergoing an audit, investigation, or enforcement action. However, federal workers can register and vote as they choose, assist in voter registration, participate in campaigns when off duty, and seek and hold positions in political parties or other political organizations. At times, the line between what federal employees can and cannot do is a thin one. For example, when President Bush arrived at an August 2004 campaign rally in Albuquerque, employees at nearby Kirtland Air Force Base were invited to attend. They had received the following e-mail: "The White House has extended an invitation to TEAM KIRTLAND to attend President Bush's speech downtown at the Convention center. . . ." Photos of the event appeared in many newspapers and on the television news. The American Federation of Government Employees said the invitation violated the Hatch Act.

Question for Reflection

How would you amend the Hatch Act to enable federal workers greater involvement in their democratic system of government?

Know Your Grasp of the Hatch Act

Test your Hatch Act IQ. Knowing the right answers could keep you from losing your job, being fined or suspended, or maybe even going to jail.

Federal employees may do the following (true or false):

1. Sign a nominating petition for a partisan candidate.

2. Assist in voter registration drives.

3. Hold office in a political club or party.

4. Contribute money to a political organization and attend political fund-raisers.

5. Wear a political button at work.

6. Distribute political party literature at a polling place on election day.

7. Solicit contributions to a partisan political fund-raiser.

8. Park a car with a political bumper sticker in a federally owned or subsidized parking lot.

9. Participate in partisan political activity if employed by the Office of Personnel Management, the Commerce Department, the Bureau of Indian Affairs, or the Health Care Finance Administration.

10. Participate in partisan political activity if employed in a low-level job by the Central Intelligence Agency, the National Security Council, the FBI, or the Contract Appeals Boards.

11. Wear a political button on a government-issued uniform if off duty or on vacation or other approved leave.

Answers

1. True
2. True
3. True
4. True
5. False
6. True
7. False
8. True
9. True
10. False
11. False

All these changes in the Hatch Act are intended to allow federal workers to exercise more of the rights and privileges of political participation open to other American citizens. But giving federal employees more freedom to participate in politics raises the potential for the kinds of partisanship that prompted passage of the Pendleton and Hatch Acts in the first place. Yet, during the 2004 presidential election the U.S. Office of Special Counsel warned federal employees working in national parks, monuments, and other facilities that they could be breaking the law by allowing candidates to campaign at the Grand Canyon, for example. It would be a violation of the Hatch Act to allow photo opportunities at the Grand Canyon, and the counsel warned federal employees they could be suspended or fired for approving these actions.

MEET THE BUREAUCRACY

What does the federal workforce look like? *Civilians* employed by the federal government work in more than fifteen thousand official job categories, ranging from electricians to paperhangers, from foreign service officers to postal service workers. There are nearly 100,000 regulators; 150,000 engineers; hundreds of thousands of analysts, clerks, and secretarial staff; 15,000 foresters; 2,300 veterinarians; 3,000 photographers; and 500 chaplains. Surprisingly, nearly 90 percent of federal employees work outside Washington, D.C. California alone has almost as many federal employees as does the nation's capital.

MakeItReal

Census 2000: Federal Government Civilian Employment by Function

The federal civilian workforce is spread among departments, agencies, commissions, and government corporations in more than 400,000 government-owned buildings throughout the United States and abroad. Today's federal worker is better educated and better compensated than at any time in history. Shifts are occurring in their work, as well. A Congressional Budget Office study showed that, from 1985 to 2000, employment in clerical jobs dropped from 377,400 to 135,000.[11] The upper tier of Figure 7.2 shows the new percentage of workers by occupation categories. You can notice the increase in professional, management, and administrative jobs.(See Figures 7.2 and 7.3.)

Although bureaucrats are appointed rather than elected, the evidence shows that they and the public share similar demographic characteristics and general values. Those allegedly "faceless bureaucrats," in fact, tend to be more diverse than private industry. Congress requires the Office of Personnel management to compile a report every year on minorities in the federal workforce. Minorities made up 31.5 percent of nonmilitary federal employees in 2004, contrasted with 27.5 percent of all workers in comparable occupations in the national civilian labor force (see Figure 7.4).

What the Bureaucracy Does

Americans today share a tradition as old as their government: animosity toward "those faceless bureaucrats" in Washington, their state capital, or their local city hall. Yet those bureaucrats perform many essential functions that we take for granted. Bureaucrats direct air traffic, patrol U.S. borders to control the flow of people and drugs, and deliver the mail. Civil servants are typical working Americans whose jobs, although hardly glamorous, are important to the smooth functioning of society. Whenever a letter is delivered on time, an application for governmental financial aid is processed, or a highway is repaired, the bureaucracy has done its job.

Because bureaucrats have been facing pressure from private competitors, they have found it in their interest to be more attentive to public opinion and more open to useful suggestions from within the organization. This development has occurred in spite of the fact that their institutional authority is based on professional

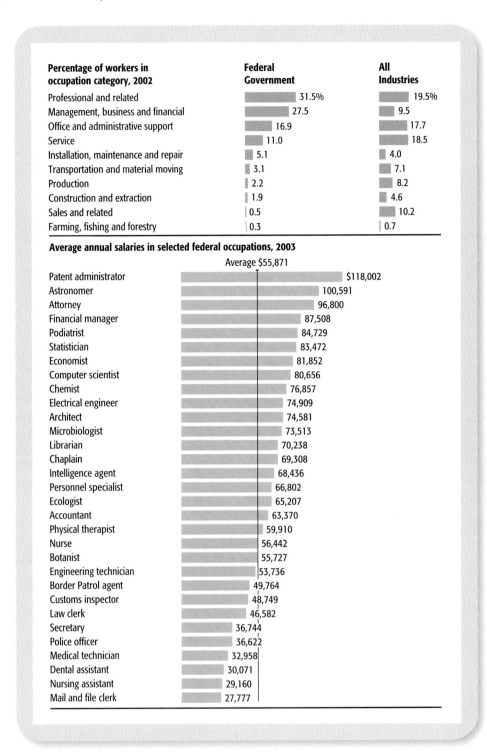

Figure 7.2   Government Salaries
The federal government has about 1.8 million civilian employees, not including postal workers. These employees were far more likely to hold management or professional jobs than private sector workers. Top-paying federal occupations include patent administrators and astronomers. Among the lowest paid are nursing assistants and mail clerks.

Source: Office of Personnel Management.

Secretary
Chief of staff to the secretary
Deputy chief of staff to the secretary
Deputy secretary
Chief of staff to the deputy secretary
Deputy chief of staff
Deputy deputy secretary
Principal associate deputy secretary
Associate deputy secretary
Deputy associate deputy secretary
Assistant deputy secretary
Undersecretary
Chief of staff to the undersecretary
Principal deputy undersecretary
Deputy undersecretary
Chief of staff to the deputy undersecretary
Principal associate deputy undersecretary
Associate deputy undersecretary
Principal assistant deputy undersecretary
Assistant deputy undersecretary
Associate undersecretary
Assistant undersecretary
Assistant secretary
Chief of staff to the assistant secretary
Deputy chief of staff to the assistant secretary
Principal deputy assistant secretary
Associate principal deputy assistant secretary
Deputy assistant secretary
Chief of staff to the deputy assistant secretary
Principal deputy deputy assistant secretary
Deputy deputy assistant secretary
Associate deputy assistant secretary
Chief of staff to the associate deputy assistant secretary
Deputy associate assistant secretary
Assistant deputy assistant secretary
Principal associate assistant secretary

Associate assistant secretary
Cheif of staff to the associate assistant secretary
Deputy associate assistant secretary
Principal assistant assistant secretary
Assistant assistant secretary
Chief of staff to the assistant assistant secretary
Deputy assistant assistant secretary
Administrator
Chief of staff to the administrator
Deputy chief of staff to the administrator
Assistant chief to staff to the administrator
Principal deputy administrator
Deputy administrator
Chief of staff to the deputy administrator
Associate deputy administrator
Deputy associate deputy administrator
Assistant deputy administrator
Deputy assistant deputy administrator
Senior associate administrator
Associate administrator
Chief of staff to the associate administrator
Deputy executive associate administrator
Deputy associate administrator
Assistant administrator
Chief of staff to the assistant administrator
Deputy assistant administrator
Associate assistant administrator
Associate deputy assistant administrator

The list includes all positions defined in statute as Executive Level I–V. Some titles such as assistant assistant secretary may sound odd, but they actually refer to positions such as assistant inspector general and assistant general counsel.

Figure 7.3   The Titled Bureaucracy
The number of executive titles in the top layer of the federal bureaucracy has more than tripled, from 17 in 1960 to 64 in 2004, according to a study by the Brookings Institution. The titles are for 2004, with the ones that also existed in 1960 in bold.

Source: Washington Post, July 23, 2004, p. A27. Paul C Light of New York University for the Brookings Institution.

Race	Federal workers	Percentage of workforce	
Black	292,752	17.4	
Hispanic (non-white)	123,207	7.3	
Asian/Pacific Islander	82,219	4.9	
Native American	32,251	1.9	
White	1,154,361	68.5	

Figure 7.4   Minorities in Government Jobs
Congress requires the Office of Personnel Management to compile a report every year on the representation of minorities in the federal workforce. This reflects the end of fiscal 2004.
Source: Office of Personnel Management.

expertise. Most bureaucratic specialists feel—often rightly—that they know more than other bureaucrats and more than the general public about an issue.

The bureaucracy performs three key governmental tasks: implementation, administration, and regulation.[12]

MakeItReal

Simulation: Bureaucracy: The Place Where Ideals Meet Reality

Implementation   A primary task of the bureaucracy is to implement the policies established by Congress and the executive. Think back to the opening case study and the task of homeland defense. **Implementation** means providing the necessary organization and expertise to put into action any policy that has become law. When, for example, Congress passed legislation establishing the Head Start early childhood care and education program in the 1960s, a new agency was established to "flesh out" the program guidelines, hire and train employees, and disburse appropriated federal monies.

Implementation can involve a considerable amount of bureaucratic autonomy. Administrators exercise **administrative discretion**—the latitude an agency, or even a single bureaucrat, has in interpreting and applying a law. When passing legislation, Congress often does little more than declare policy goals, assign their implementation to an agency, and make money available to the agency. Lack of statutory specificity may help a bill over the legislative hurdles, but after a bill is passed, bureaucratic managers must step in and, exercising administrative discretion, draft detailed guidelines for all the various procedures required to turn policies into workable programs.

Despite good intentions, implementation can go awry. Frequently, state and local interest groups resist new policies or raise questions—for example, about clean air and water laws—that make implementation difficult if not impossible. In 1994–95, citizens in Maine, Pennsylvania, and Texas protested the implementation of strict auto emissions tests ordered by the Environmental Protection Agency. As a result, legislatures in all three states suspended the programs, preferring the wrath of the EPA to the wrath of their constituents.

implementation The act of providing the organization and expertise required to put into action any policy that has become law; also refers to the actual execution of a policy.

administrative discretion The latitude that an agency, or even a single bureaucrat, has in interpreting and applying a law.

administration Performance of routine tasks associated with a specific policy goal.

Administration   Another bureaucratic task is **administration**, performing the routine tasks associated with a specific policy goal. Bureaucrats exercise a lot less administrative discretion at this stage. If we look at the federal government's post–September 11 activities we can see that virtually every agency contributed to the relief effort. In New York alone the Federal Emergency Management Agency (FEMA) had eight sixty-two-member urban search and rescue teams working closely with the Army Corps of Engineers, the General Services Administration, and the Environmental Protection Agency.

The federal government had to determine if the water was safe to drink, if other structures were safe from collapse, and whether or not that section of New York City should be declared a Superfund site, thereby providing additional clean-up money.

Health and Human Services provided grants for child care, elder assistance, mental health care, and other services for those left homeless or bereft following the collapse of the two towers. The Departments of Justice and Treasury were called in to administer improved airport security. U.S. Customs administered additional scrutiny at U.S. borders. The Internal Revenue Service extended income tax filing deadlines for all involved in the search and rescue efforts. The Department of Housing and Urban Development processed FHA loans to thousands in need of assistance. The so-called "simple" administrative tasks of bureaucracy became the vital survival link to those immediately affected by the terrorist attack in New York. If we expand this list to include services provided at the Pentagon, we begin to sense the responsibilities given to our fourth branch of government.

Regulation   Another important bureaucratic task is **regulation**. Regulation involves making rules, enforcing them, and adjudicating disputes about them. In many areas of American life, the bureaucracy establishes and enforces guidelines regulating behavior and enforcing punishments for violation of those guidelines.[13]

Administrative regulation is pervasive in America. The U.S. Department of Agriculture regulates the quality of our breakfast food, including organically grown products. The Food and Drug Administration (FDA) regulates labeling rules that apply to, for example, the booming diet supplement industry. After a hard day, Americans often watch television programming whose content must fall within guidelines established by the Federal Communications Commission. Finally, at the end of the day, Americans crawl into bed and snuggle under blankets certified as fire resistant by the Consumer Product Safety Commission. Americans drive cars that reduce pollution by using catalytic converters mandated by the Environmental Protection Agency. They buckle their car seat belts because it is the law, and it is the law because the Federal Highway Administration withholds federal funds from states that do not require seat belt use. At work, Americans conform to antidiscrimination guidelines established by the Equal Employment Opportunity Commission. Some watchdog groups are wary of adverse effects that will accompany decreases in funding and support in such areas as air traffic control and food safety inspection.

Whether implementing, administering, or regulating, bureaucrats exercise a great deal of autonomy and have power over our lives. Given the complex demands on the bureaucracy, such power is inevitable. But, some ask, whose interests do the bureaucrats serve? Are they responsive to the needs of the public? In fact, many bureaucrats do heed the voices of ordinary citizens and seek to stay in the good graces of the two government institutions most responsive to public opinion: Congress and the presidency. Yet federal morale is clearly down and federal employees are reporting less satisfaction with their own work and the work of their agencies.

The Structure of the Federal Bureaucracy

The four institutions that constitute the federal bureaucracy are part of the executive branch. They are cabinet departments, independent agencies, independent regulatory commissions, and government corporations.

Cabinet Departments   **Cabinet departments** are major administrative units responsible for conducting a broad range of government operations. Originally, the heads of these departments—usually called *secretaries*—were the president's closest advisers, though today the president's personal White House staff is more likely to command the president's attention. Each department is subdivided into smaller units called divisions, sections, agencies, and offices. Although each department has jurisdiction over a specific policy area, sometimes their responsibilities overlap, as when the State and Defense Departments address diplomatic and strategic aspects of U.S. foreign policy.

regulation A rule-making administrative body must clarify and interpret legislation, its enforcement, and the adjudication of disputes about it.

cabinet departments Major administrative units whose heads are presidential advisers appointed by the president and confirmed by the Senate. They are responsible for conducting a broad range of government operations.

 **MakeItReal**

Primary Source: Keating-Owen Child Labor Act of 1916

► Secretary of Labor Elaine L. Chao is responsible for carrying out the department's mission of inspiring and protecting the hard-working people of America.

Independent Agencies   **Independent agencies** usually are smaller than cabinet departments and have a narrower set of responsibilities. Generally, they exist to perform a service. Congress may establish an independent agency so that it can keep particularly tight control over that agency's functions. For example, Congress may establish an independent agency when interest groups demand a government function performed with care and attention rather than by an indifferent department. Among the major independent agencies are the Central Intelligence Agency (CIA), the Environmental Protection Agency (EPA), the National Aeronautics and Space Administration (NASA), the Small Business Administration (SBA), the Peace Corps, and the General Services Administration (GSA), which manages federal property.

Independent Regulatory Commissions   **Independent regulatory commissions** regulate sectors of the nation's economy in the public interest. For example, an independent regulatory commission might guard against unfair business practices or unsafe products. They generally are run by a board whose members have set terms, although some newer regulatory bodies are headed by a single individual, making the label "commission" something of a misnomer. These bodies establish rules, enforce rules, and adjudicate disputes about rules, all of the traditional functions of government—legislative, executive, and judicial. These agencies develop a great deal of expertise in a particular policy area, although sometimes they become too closely identified with the businesses they are charged with regulating. Congress and the courts rely on their expertise and are usually loath to overrule them. Among the more important independent regulatory commissions are the Federal Communications Commission (FCC), which regulates radio and television; the Federal Reserve Board (FED), whose members function as a central bank for the United States; the Federal Trade Commission (FTC), which regulates advertising and labeling; the National Labor Relations Board (NLRB), which enforces the laws governing labor-management disputes; and the National Transportation Safety Board (NTSB). The NTSB investigates every civil aviation accident in the United States and significant accidents in other modes of transportation—railroad, highway, marine, and pipeline—and issues safety recommendations aimed at preventing

independent agencies Agencies established to regulate a sector of the nation's economy in the public interest.

independent regulatory commissions Agencies established to regulate a sector of the nation's economy in the public interest.

future accidents. The NTSB maintains the government's database on civil aviation accidents and also conducts special studies of transportation safety issues of national significance.

Government Corporations   A **government corporation** is a semi-independent government agency that administers a business enterprise and takes the form of a business corporation. Congress creates such agencies on the assumption that they will serve the public interest and gives them more independence and latitude for innovation than it gives other government agencies. A government corporation can raise its own capital and devise its own personnel system; it can, within the limits of its congressional charter, determine the kind of services it provides; and when the occasion seems favorable, it may develop new services. The Tennessee Valley Authority (TVA), a government corporation originally set up to control flooding and provide electricity to the area within the Tennessee River watershed, now manages the artificial lakes it created for recreational purposes, runs economic development programs, and experiments with alternative energy development.

In addition to possessing much of the flexibility of a private company, a government corporation also has the authority of government. It can take land, levy fees, and make rules that govern the public. Though these agencies have more leeway in establishing the nature and cost of the services they provide, they generally remain subject to more regulation than private corporations do. Besides the TVA, other major government corporations include the Postal Service, the Corporation for Public Broadcasting, the Federal Deposit Insurance Corporation, the Export-Import Bank, and Amtrak.

Constraints on the Bureaucracy and Bureaucratic Culture

The bureaucracy faces three major constraints that shape its behavior: Bureaucratic agencies do not control revenue; decisions about how to deliver goods and services must be made according to rules established elsewhere; and other institutions mandate goals. Because of these constraints, bureaucrats and bureaucracies behave differently from private-sector employees and companies. Certain *norms,* or unwritten rules of behavior, have developed, creating a unique bureaucratic culture.

First, Congress does not allow agencies to keep money left over when the fiscal year ends. Furthermore, an agency that ends the year with a surplus demonstrates to Congress that it can run on less than the current year's budget. As a consequence, bureaucrats have no incentive to conserve funds. In fact, they have every incentive to spend with abandon as the fiscal year draws to a close on September 30, in hopes of showing Congress that they have no surplus and, in fact, need more money for the next year. In addition, because bureaucrats are not supposed to profit from their dealings with government, they focus on nonmonetary incentives such as prestige. The bigger the budget and the larger the agency, the more prestige a bureaucrat acquires, providing managers with another reason to put political pressure on Congress to allow their agencies to grow.

Second, to ensure fairness, efficiency, and comprehensive program coverage, decisions about hiring, purchasing, contracting, and budgeting must follow rules established by Congress and the president. Since the end of World War II, Congress has passed an array of such rules: For example, the Administrative Procedure Act of 1946 governs the way an agency makes rules, publicizes its operations, and settles disputes; the Freedom of Information Act of 1966 assures that most agency records are available to interested citizens on demand; the National Environmental Policy Act of 1969 requires federal agencies to prepare environmental impact statements for all actions that significantly affect the environment; the Privacy Act of 1974

government corporation A semi-independent government agency that administers a business enterprise and takes the form of a business corporation.

U.S.A. Yesterday and Today

The Space Shuttle Program

The successful April 1981 launch of the first space shuttle began a new era for the National Aeronautics and Space Administration (NASA), a long-established but somewhat neglected public bureaucracy. The shuttle was designed to cut the cost of delivering various hardware payloads such as satellites into space and to encourage public support for future research projects in space. The shuttle's first twenty-four missions went off almost flawlessly. Their success revived NASA's image and led to increased federal funding. However, mission number twenty-five proved different. Early on the morning of January 28, 1986, with temperatures well below freezing, NASA launched the space shuttle *Challenger* from the Kennedy Space Center in Florida.

Seventy-three seconds after lift-off, *Challenger* exploded before millions of television viewers and stunned NASA officials. All seven astronauts on board died. One was Christa McAuliffe, a grade-school teacher whose training for the mission had been followed by schoolchildren all over the United States. It was the worst disaster in the history of the space program. President Ronald Reagan appointed a commission, headed by a former secretary of state, William Rogers, to investigate the disaster. The Rogers Commission concluded that most of the blame lay with NASA's bureaucratic culture. NASA's "can-do" atmosphere and its strict adherence to the principles of engineering had produced a string of historic accomplishments in aerospace exploration—the *Apollo* flights, the moon landings, and the first shuttle missions—but that same culture sometimes led the agency to push too far too fast.

The Rogers Commission discovered that on the bitterly cold night before the fateful launch, officials from NASA and Morton Thiokol Industries (MTI), the designer of the shuttle's solid rocket booster system, debated the wisdom of launching *Challenger*. MTI engineers in Utah tried desperately to convince NASA officials in Florida and at the Johnson Space Center in Houston, Texas, to scrub the *Challenger* mission because the rocket booster system was not designed to withstand subfreezing temperatures. The O-ring seals that joined sections of the fuel tanks had never been used below 53 degrees Fahrenheit. In laboratory experiments performed at freezing temperatures, the seals had disintegrated. Given the warnings from MTI officials, how could NASA have allowed the disaster to happen? The decision to ignore MTI's advice and launch *Challenger* arose from a combination of problems within NASA that are all too common in large public bureaucracies. NASA officials were overconfident in light of previous successes. They worried about public image problems that might arise from a scrubbed mission and insinuations of technical failure. They wanted to guard against possible budget cutbacks if Congress concluded that technical flaws threatened the shuttle program. And they were concerned about costs. A postponed shuttle mission would be enormously expensive; scrubbing the launch would have cost a half million dollars in wasted solid rocket fuel alone.

More than two decades have passed since the *Challenger* disaster, but concerns about NASA culture and the space

limits the circumstances in which information about individuals can be released to other agencies and to the public; and the Government in the Sunshine Act of 1976 mandates open meetings of most regulatory decision-making bodies.

Such a system breeds rule-following managers, not managers who take initiative. It is no wonder that, surrounded by such a thicket of regulations and laws, bureaucratic managers worry more about violating procedure than about marching boldly ahead to promote the public good. After all, managers can always explain poor outcomes by claiming that they were just following the rules.

Finally, bureaucratic agencies do not control their own goals, which are set by Congress and the president. Congress has told the United States Postal Service that it must charge one rate to deliver a first-class letter no matter where the letter goes. Furthermore, the Postal Service must deliver newspapers, magazines, and junk mail below cost, and it must keep small post offices open even though they may not be economical to operate.

Despite such constraints, some administrative institutions flourish. A determined leader can instill a sense of mission even in employees of an organization whose offices are scattered across the nation. The Social Security Administration is such a shuttle safety remain. First, there was the space shuttle *Columbia* tragedy in February 2003, in which failed heat shielding led to the space shuttle's destruction on reentry, killing all on board. A post-tragedy assessment found that politics, budgets, schedule pressure, and managerial complacency all played roles in the *Columbia* tragedy. The *Columbia* Accident Investigation Board (CAIB) said in its final report: "The organizational causes of this accident are rooted in the space shuttle program's history and culture, including the original compromises that were required to gain approval for the shuttle, subsequent years of resource constraints, fluctuating priorities, schedule pressures, mischaracterization of the shuttle as operational rather than developmental, and lack of agreed national vision for human space flight . . . the NASA organizational culture had as much to do with this accident as the foam." The board compared the *Columbia* tragedy with that of the *Challenger* seventeen years earlier: "For both accidents there were moments when management definitions of risk might have been reversed were it not for the many missing signals—an absence of trend analysis, imagery data not obtained, concerns not voiced, information overlooked or dropped from briefings."

Then, in July 2005, the shuttle *Discovery* roared back into space after two and a half years of planning. During liftoff, a piece of foam could be seen breaking away from the fuel tank air load ramp. It was soon discovered that NASA engineers had discounted a 2004 internal NASA report warning that this could occur. Fortunately, the protruding strips were removed during a spacewalk, and *Discovery* and its crew returned safely. In December 2005, NASA announced that such sections of insulating foam would be eliminated from future fuel tanks to remove the hazard. The shuttle program is scheduled to

▲ The space shuttle Challenger exploding seventy-three seconds after lift-off on January 28, 1986.

keep flying until 2010 in order to complete construction of an international space station.

Sources: www.space.com/missionlaunches/sts109_update_020128.html 8/20/02; http://cbc.ca/news/indepth/background/ spacetourist. html 8/20/02; and www.nytimes.com/aponline/arts/AP-Russia-Space-Lance-Bass.html 8/20/02. James Q. Wilson, *Bureaucracy: What Government Agencies Do and Why They Do It* (New York: Basic Books, 1989), pp. 104–5. Brian Berger, "Columbia Report Faults NASA Culture, Government Oversight," *Space News Writer,* August 26, 2003. John Schwartz, "2004 Report Found Faults in Use of Shuttle Foam," *New York Times,* August 4, 2005, A1. John Schwartz, Andrew C. Revkin, and Matthew L. Ward, "For NASA, Misjudgments Led to Latest Shuttle Woes," *New York Times,* July 31, 2005, A1. Warren E. Leary, "NASA Plans to Remove Some Foam From Shuttle," *New York Times,* December 16, 2005, A32.

mission-driven agency. Its personnel officers recruit potential employees who show an orientation to customer satisfaction, and managers constantly invoke an ethic of service when they talk to employees. Bureaucrats who work for the Social Security Administration take pride in their jobs and do them well, unlike, as we saw earlier, the employees in the Department of Homeland Security.

BUREAUCRATIC ACCOUNTABILITY

The story of late twentieth-century American politics is in large part the story of attempts by the White House and Congress to control the powerful federal bureaucracy and make it more accountable to the people. Perhaps the most disturbing example of this challenge occurred in 1997 when the nation's attention focused on congressional hearings concerning the Internal Revenue Service. We learned of horrifying instances of taxpayer harassment and intimidation and a culture of abusive tax collection methods and abuse by individual agents within the organization. Witnesses before the congressional investigating committee told of IRS agents who

MakeItReal

Primary Source: Freedom of Information Act (1966)

Approaching Democracy Around the Globe

The French Bureaucracy

Although American citizens constantly complain about excessive red tape and believe that civil servants are both too numerous and too lazy, the French regard their bureaucrats as competent, efficient, and highly ethical. This is particularly striking in light of the inflexible and autocratic nature of the French bureaucracy.

Part of the explanation for this difference can be found in French culture, which assumes that the answer to every particular question can be found by deduction from general principles (as opposed to experimentation with different solutions). A French bureaucrat decides each individual case by reasoning deductively from a legal premise. When the deduction is done properly, the citizen has no basis for disagreement with the decision. Pleading individual circumstances to bend the rules is not done.

The French bureaucracy is less attentive to public opinion than its American counterpart. Civil servants are recruited from the families of the political elite and educated in national schools of public administration, called *grandes écoles*. They tend to develop a sense of superiority that occasionally translates into contempt for the masses. On occasion they have deliberately made life difficult for citizens on the theory that it is good for citizens to spend time in the *marais*, or swamp. An American bureaucrat who showed such contempt for citizens would stand a good chance of receiving an irate call from a congressional office.

Despite its elitist quality, French citizens hold their civil service in high esteem. One reason for this is the bureaucracy's long history of success in providing benefits to the public. Whereas the American bureaucracy did not achieve its considerable size and power until the New Deal and World War II era, France has had strong bureaucratic institutions since the early nineteenth century, including medical and dental and retirement benefits for generations. During the Napoleonic era, the French civil service built a national highway system radiating from Paris to every single provincial city; the United States did not even plan such a system until the 1950s. Furthermore, throughout almost two centuries of weak monarchies and confused republics that proved incapable of governing, the civil service has always managed the day-to-day operations of government.

The French bureaucracy is regarded as amongst the most professional and efficient in the world. It is not surprising that the French bureaucrats enjoy a level of social prestige that is rare among their American counterparts.

Sources: William Safron, *The French Polity*, New York: Longman, 1995, pp. 243–44; B. Guy Peters, *The Politics of Bureaucracy*, New York: Longman, 1995, pp. 49–50; Udom, Udoh Elijah, "The International Civil Service: Historical Development and Potential for the 21st Century," *Public Personnel Management* 32, no. 1 (2003).

sought out lower-income individuals for audits, destroyed credit ratings, and sought to punish people through the audit process. We heard stories of IRS agents snooping through computer files to read the tax forms of the famous, their neighbors, their former spouses, and even prospective dates. President Clinton quickly jumped aboard a congressional plan to create a citizen oversight board that would monitor IRS activities. On July 22, 1998, Clinton signed into law a major IRS overhaul. Yet, in February 2000, Clinton was calling for more tax revenue and asking IRS agents to be more aggressive in identifying tax cheaters.

Still, American bureaucracy has made major strides toward democratic accountability. Today, few bureaucracies operate outside the law as the FBI did under J. Edgar Hoover in the 1950s and 1960s. Today's administrators, influenced by modern business management techniques, spend as much time listening to their employees and to their customer, the public, as they do giving orders. Although few administrative rules are made according to a democratic voting process, the policy-making process has broadened to include a variety of perspectives in recent years. Rule-making agencies take care to notify not only businesses subject to regulation about upcoming hearings, but also to invite consumer and civil rights groups to testify.

On secrecy, the picture is less clear. Although the Administrative Procedure Act, the Freedom of Information Act, and the Government in the Sunshine Act have opened up routine administrative decisions to public scrutiny, the national security establishment continues to operate behind closed doors. The terrorist attack on America has only created more layers of official secrets in the name of national and homeland security. As we saw in Chapter 5, the Bush administration has done virtually everything it can to claim the privilege of confidentiality and maintain official secrets.

Presidential Control

One of the most common complaints of presidents is the difficulty of aligning the federal bureaucracy's objectives with the administration's priorities. President Harry Truman once complained, "I thought I was the president, but when it comes to these bureaucrats, I can't do a damn thing." Truman may have been exaggerating, but presidential control of the bureaucracy is more difficult than most incoming chief executives either thought or hoped.[14]

As the federal bureaucracy has grown, so, too, has the amount of energy presidents expend to rein in agencies that oppose their objectives. After a grueling election, the president enters office with a policy agenda presumably supported by at least a plurality of the American people. To pursue that policy agenda, the president must convince not only Congress but also the various federal agencies to cooperate with the White House. Presidents have four main strategies at their disposal: the appointment power, reorganization, the budget, and the power of persuasion.

The Appointment Power   Every president requires a clear agenda of policy goals. To advance that agenda, the president has a powerful weapon, the **appointment power**. As we learned in Chapter 5 on the presidency, the president can nominate approximately three thousand agency officials, of whom about seven hundred are in policy-making positions, such as cabinet and subcabinet officials and bureau chiefs. The rest are lower-level appointees who can provide the president with valuable information and a source of political patronage hearkening back to the old spoils system. A president who can secure loyalty from these appointed bureaucrats has overcome a major obstacle in pursuing the White House policy agenda.

But a president who uses the appointment power to control the bureaucracy must know what is going on within it. One president who did just that was Franklin Roosevelt. He filled federal agencies with people who were more loyal to him than to each other. Although his appointees battled each other over policy questions, they ultimately referred their disagreements to the president, who resolved them and in doing so exercised effective control over bureaucratic policy making. Roosevelt's administration funneled information and decision-making authority to the top, and because Roosevelt had the intellectual capacity to understand the arguments of the specialists, he was able to settle their disputes with dispatch. This form of management is impossible today, given the size of government.

Reorganization   Presidents also have the power to move programs around within specific agencies—**reorganization**. For example, a president opposed to pesticide regulation might shift that program from the EPA, which favors regulation, to the Department of Agriculture, where pro-agriculture forces would tend to limit such regulation.

A president may also choose to elevate an agency to cabinet level, thereby expanding its scope and power, as President Bush did with the Department of Homeland Security. This department involves numerous agencies within the federal government, and its evolution may lead to agency reorganization. In 1979, President Carter elevated one office of the Department of Health, Education, and Welfare to cabinet level, creating the Department of Education. He hoped that this reorganization would improve the office's prestige and status and underscore

appointment power The president's power to name agency officials. Of the current approximately three thousand, about seven hundred are in policy-making positions, such as cabinet and subcabinet officials and bureau chiefs.

reorganization Having the power to move programs around within specific agencies.

Office of Management and Budget (OMB) The unit in the Executive Office of the President whose main responsibilities are to prepare and administer the president's annual budget. A president and the OMB can shape policy through the budget process; the process determines which departments and agencies grow, are cut, or remain the same as the year before.

education's importance as a national priority. Conversely, as we noted previously, a president can remove an agency's cabinet status and thus potentially reduce its power and prestige. Upon succeeding Carter, Reagan sought several ways to reduce the power of the Department of Education, including an unsuccessful attempt to demote the agency from the cabinet level. The Reagan administration saw the department as wasteful and inefficient and as an inappropriate extension of federal government into state and local realms. But the department dug in its heels and outlasted Reagan.[15]

The Budget Another formidable tool for presidential control of the bureaucracy is the **Office of Management and Budget (OMB)**. The OMB was established in 1921, transferred to the newly created Executive Office in 1939, and renamed OMB as part of the major executive office reorganization in 1970. Its main responsibilities are to prepare and administer the president's annual budget. A president and the OMB can shape policy through the budget process, determining which departments and agencies grow, are cut, or remain the same as the year before. During the budget-preparation cycle, officers from OMB—all specially trained to assess government projects and spending requests—remain in constant touch with government agencies to make sure that the agencies are adhering to the president's policies. Because the budget has a profound effect on an agency's ability to function and survive, it is rare for an administrator to defy the OMB.

The Power of Persuasion Presidents have another tool: the power to persuade in an attempt to control the bureaucracy. Certain presidents, such as John F. Kennedy, have sought to inspire the bureaucracy with a vision of public service as a noble activity. Even though he was frequently thwarted by and frustrated with bureaucratic procedures, Kennedy saw the bureaucracy as capable of innovation. He reorganized the space program and convinced its employees that despite the string of failures in attempting to launch unmanned rockets, NASA would put a man on the moon before the decade was out, which it did. But persuasion has limits, and most turn to their marginal command powers for moving the bureaucracy—or they shift responsibility into the Executive Office of the President—creating yet another bureaucratic layer.[16]

Congressional Control

Congress provides much of the oversight that keeps bureaucratic power in check (see also Chapter 4). To perform this task, Congress has several mechanisms at its disposal. Most important is the *power of the purse*. Congress appropriates all funding for each federal agency. If problems arise, Congress can, and occasionally does, curb funds or even eliminate entire projects.

Congress also has the power of *administrative oversight*, the practice of holding hearings and conducting investigations into bureaucratic activity. As a consequence of these hearings, Congress can rewrite agency guidelines to expand or narrow its responsibilities. Finally, through its "advice and consent" role, the Senate can shape the direction of federal agencies by confirming or rejecting presidential nominees for top positions in the bureaucracy.

One classic example of Congress asserting control over a runaway program is its treatment of the Department of Energy's (DOE) superconducting super-collider project. In 1982, the huge particle accelerator, designed to allow scientists to learn more about atomic structure, had a projected budget of $4.4 billion; by 1993 the total budget had topped $11 billion. When the DOE investigated the Texas-based project, officials discovered a history of free-spending waste of taxpayers' money, including $56,000 for potted plants to adorn the project's offices. Finally, in late 1993, and after the expenditure of $2 billion, Congress canceled the entire program.

Although Congress has many tools to fulfill its oversight functions, it often chooses not to use them. Why would Congress not want to keep the bureaucracy under close control? One answer can be found by examining the mutually beneficial political relationship between federal agencies and members of Congress.

Federal agencies provide goods and services—such as contracts, exemptions, and assistance—that members of Congress use to please their constituents. In return, legislators have the ability to keep federal agencies alive and funded. Legislators from agricultural states, for example, work hard to keep crop subsidies in the federal budget, thus ensuring a future for the Department of Agriculture and its employees. In turn, the department can give special consideration to the crops grown in a member's district, thus helping to ensure a member's reelection.

These relationships have been characterized as **iron triangles**. An iron triangle is a strong interdependent relationship among three crucial actors in policy making: legislators, particularly those on the relevant subcommittees with jurisdiction over the policy in question; lobbyists for specific interests affected by the policy; and bureaucrats at the agencies with jurisdiction over the implementation and administration of relevant policies. Iron triangles resist democratic accountability. Their interlocking interests are so strong that few presidents and few members of Congress who are not a part of them ever try to bring them under control.

▲ Standing on the agency seal, President George W. Bush speaks to the media inside the CIA headquarters Thursday, Mar. 3, 2005, as CIA director Porter Goss listens in. White House photo by Paul Morse. www.whitehouse.gov/response/

Similar to but broader than iron triangles are **issue networks**, composed of political actors in a particular policy area. These networks usually include bureaucrats, congressional staffers, interest groups, think tank researchers or academic experts, and media participants, all of whom interact regularly on an issue. Issue networks dominate the policy-making process, and different issue networks exist for different policy areas.

WHAT THE PUBLIC THINKS OF THE BUREAUCRACY

Americans tend to be suspicious of the administrative state, and politicians often exploit the public's distrust of government. A few years ago, members of Congress made headlines with stories about Defense Department purchases of $435 hammers and $91 screws. The stories, though exaggerated, confirmed long-held suspicions about government waste. But following the bombing of the Federal Building in Oklahoma City, many critics of government began to see their antigovernment statements as delegitimizing the very idea of government.

iron triangles Informal three-way relationships that develop among key legislative committees, the bureaucracy, and interest groups with a vested interest in the policies created by those committees and agencies.

issue networks Networks composed of political actors in a particular policy area, usually including bureaucrats, congressional staffers, interest groups, think-tank researchers or academic experts, and media participants, all of whom interact regularly on an issue.

► As Hurricane Katrina approaches, thousands lined up outside the Superdome in New Orleans waiting for buses to take them out of the city. Most of the people in line were the poor, mostly black and Creole, who did not have a car to escape or a place to go.

Many Americans believe that government is expensive and wasteful. Each year, the federal government spends a good deal of money unwisely. Highly publicized examples of government waste include the Department of Agriculture sending subsidy checks to wealthy recipients in Beverly Hills, Chicago, and Manhattan. Retired federal employees have been found to live in luxury far beyond that of the ordinary taxpayer because the government guarantees them cost-of-living adjustments pegged to exaggerated calculations of the rate of inflation. And although the Commerce Department helps tobacco growers market their products, the surgeon general works toward the goal of reducing the number of smokers in society. As a consequence of such stories, Americans have an exaggerated notion of the extent of government waste.

One of the most common complaints is that government is unresponsive to citizens. In implementing policies, agencies should attend to the needs and circumstances of individual taxpayers. But too often, red tape prevents such flexibility. **Red tape** refers to the excessive number of rules and regulations that government employees must follow. While many employees chafe under the burden of these regulations, others welcome them. Rigid adherence to the rules relieves bureaucrats of the burden of thinking about individual cases and shelters employees from being criticized by their supervisors for making wrong decisions. One consequence of the proliferation of red tape in government is that citizens with unusual circumstances encounter delays while their cases are bumped up to higher levels for official rulings. Businesses complain that the bureaucracy hobbles them with unnecessary regulations and paperwork. Every time a company wants to expand its operations or use a new method for manufacturing its products, it must apply for permission from a host of government agencies and fill out many forms.[17]

Are the Criticisms Justified?

Bureaucracy is a modern-day inevitability. And despite criticisms, many Americans rely on goods and services the bureaucracy provides. Although many criticisms are

red tape The excessive number of rules and regulations that government employees must follow.

valid, there are two sides to every story about an institution as large as the federal government. Bureaucratic waste is real, but it is less prevalent than the public believes. And it is important to keep in mind that government expenditures exist for reasons that many Americans would support. For example, most citizens want to stop officials awarding contracts based on personal friendship or bribery, so agencies must use costly bidding procedures on federal contracts. Most citizens would support programs that give people skills to find jobs in the public sector. Such policies add to the cost of government, but ultimately many citizens agree with the rationale for the expenditures. Although some agencies never accomplish the tasks Congress gives them, the Social Security Administration has sustained a remarkable record for competence. It assigns a number to, and maintains a lifetime earnings record for, each taxpayer in the country, then mails a benefit check for everyone who becomes eligible for Social Security.

Although businesses resist government rules and regulations, those guidelines almost always serve an important purpose. Automobile manufacturers complain that the government's requirement of rear-window brake lights on cars adds $100 million to production costs, but that requirement prevents $900 million in property damage and a great deal of human suffering. We feel safer knowing that chemical manufacturers must fill out government forms specifying where they dump hazardous materials.[18]

REFORMING THE BUREAUCRACY

Ideas for reforming the federal bureaucracy are plentiful. Some advocate for a partial return to the patronage system in use until passage of the 1883 Pendleton Act. These political observers argue, just as Andrew Jackson did nearly two centuries ago, that patronage appointments improve efficiency and democratic accountability by translating popular support for an incoming president's objectives into actual policy. But, as reformers in the 1880s pointed out, patronage leads to widespread corruption, disorganization, and under-qualified personnel in the bureaucracy.

Other reforms seek to address charges of an inert, unproductive work force in federal agencies. One effort to improve innovation and productivity was the Civil

 **MakeItReal**

Primary Source: Pendleton Act (1883)

Primary Source: 1974 Budget and Impoundment Control Act

◄ In March 2006 Interior Secretary Gale Norton announced her resignation, ending a controversional five year term for the first woman to head the 153-year-old department.

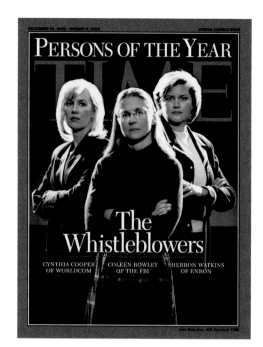

▶ They took huge professional and personal risks to blow the whistle on what went wrong at WorldCom, Enron and the FBI. In so doing Cynthia Cooper of Worldcom, Colleen Rowley of the FBI and Sherron Watkins of Enron helped remind us what American courage and American values are all about.

Service Reform Act in 1978, which created the *Senior Executive Service* (*SES*), a group of upper-management bureaucrats with access to private-sector incentives such as bonuses but also subject to measurable job-performance evaluations. Those who failed to achieve high ratings could be fired. The idea was that the senior bureaucrats would respond positively to productivity incentives and become more responsive to presidential policy leadership. The program's effects have been unclear. Innovation has occurred, but some career officers find exposure to political pressure uncomfortable. Few members of the SES have been fired, but many have left their jobs with a bad taste in their mouths.

Another reform aimed at making the bureaucracy more effective and accountable is the 1989 **Whistleblower Protection Act**. This act encourages civil servants to report instances of bureaucratic mismanagement, financial impropriety, corruption, and inefficiency. It also protects civil servants from retaliation—from being fired, demoted, or relocated, for example. The act has been effective in helping to identify and root out problems in the bureaucracy. In February 1998, the FBI agreed to pay a settlement of $1.16 million to a whistle-blower whose report brought about an overhaul of its crime laboratory. Frederick Whitehurst exposed the FBI lab for flawed scientific work and inaccurate, pro-prosecution testimony in many cases, including the Oklahoma City and the 1993 World Trade Center bombings. Still, the U.S. Court of Appeals for the Federal Circuit has often given the Whistleblower Act a narrow interpretation to "exclude employees who first take their allegations to supervisors or coworkers."[19]

The very people who have grown comfortable with the status quo—relevant legislators and the bureaucrats themselves—are responsible for developing, implementing, and administering the programs that would improve bureaucratic performance, democratize the bureaucracy, and enhance accountability. For this reason more than any other, attempts at dramatic reform have encountered bristling opposition and only partial success.

Some have proposed drastically reducing or even eliminating inefficient functions through privatization. **Privatization** involves turning over public responsibilities for regulation and for providing goods and services to privately owned and operated enterprises. Some economists argue that private enterprises could do a superior and less costly job of implementing, administering, and regulating government programs. Advocates of privatization point to the success of United Parcel

Whistleblower Protection Act
This act encourages civil servants to report instances of bureaucratic mismanagement, financial impropriety, corruption, and inefficiency. It also protects civil servants from retaliation, such as being fired, demoted, or relocated.

privatization The turning over of public responsibilities to privately owned and operated enterprises for regulation and for providing goods and services.

Service and Federal Express, and compare these two private companies with the more costly and less efficient U.S. Postal Service. They view this comparison as evidence that shifting services from governmental to private hands will greatly improve both quality and cost effectiveness. But defenders of the Postal Service argue that such comparisons are unfair when the Postal Service, unlike private firms, must meet costly congressional policy mandates.

In conclusion, bureaucratic organizations are inherently undemocratic. Democracy requires plurality; traditional bureaucracy requires unity. Though the bureaucracy is often scorned for its enormous size and lack of responsiveness or accountability, the intent behind this "fourth branch" of government is indispensable in America's approach to democracy.

The Department of Homeland Security typifies many of the problems facing the U.S. bureaucratic system. Developing federal plans for preventing and responding to terrorist attacks and then coordinating those blueprints with state and local governments is an enormous undertaking. It will take much more than a presidential stroke of a pen to achieve the appropriate response, and the true test lies in personal leadership and response of a bureaucratic entity charged with ensuring the safety of our democratic policy. That is the lesson we can draw from the Katrina response, and hope that next time the federal government will be ready with an effective bureaucratic response.

Summary

1. A bureaucracy is a large and complex organizational system in which tasks, roles, and responsibilities are structured to achieve a goal. Bureaucracies are characterized by specialization, hierarchy, and a system of formal rules. Bureaucratic failures often result from too-rigid adherence to one or more of these characteristics.

2. The federal bureaucracy began growing rapidly in the late nineteenth century, spurred by industrial expansion. The size of the bureaucracy has increased dramatically during the twentieth century, largely as a result of efforts to create a welfare state. Recent growth has resulted from legislation to address racial injustice, environmental degradation, and other problems in American society.

3. Before 1828, the federal bureaucracy was dominated by a small elite of wealthy, well-educated white males. Under the "spoils system" instituted by President Andrew Jackson, government jobs were awarded on the basis of party loyalty. In 1883, Congress passed the Pendleton Act, which created a civil service—a system that hires and promotes employees on the basis of professional merit and protects them from political threats to their job security.

4. The Hatch Act of 1939 established standards for federal employees. The political liberties of government employees were restricted to preserve the neutrality of federal agencies. Recent amendments allow federal employees to participate more actively in partisan politics, although they cannot run for office.

5. One of the primary tasks of the bureaucracy is to implement the policies established by Congress and the president. Administrators have considerable discretion in implementing legislation, which can produce a policy impact quite different from the original intention.

6. Policy administration involves routine tasks associated with a specific policy goal. Bureaucracies also regulate: make rules, enforce them, and adjudicate any disputes that arise.

7. Cabinet departments are major administrative units responsible for conducting a broad range of government operations. Each department has jurisdiction over a specific policy area and is headed by a secretary who is also a member of the president's cabinet.

8. Independent agencies are smaller than cabinet departments and have a narrower set of responsibilities; they generally perform a service such as space exploration or intelligence gathering. Independent regulatory commissions regulate a sector of the nation's economy in the public interest and are generally run by a board whose members have set terms.

9. A government corporation is a semi-independent government agency that administers a business enterprise. It takes the form of a business corporation but possesses the authority of government.

10. Agencies of the federal bureaucracy are subject to three major constraints. They lack control over their revenues, over decisions about how to deliver goods and services, and over the goals they must attempt to achieve.

11. Presidents attempt to control the bureaucracy through the appointment power, which enables them to appoint agency officials who will support their policies. Reorganization is another tool available to presidents

seeking to control the bureaucracy. The Office of Management and Budget, which administers the federal budget, can be used to control government agencies. Presidents can also seek to influence the bureaucracy through persuasion.

12. Congressional oversight of the bureaucracy occurs largely through the power of the purse, which gives Congress the power to appropriate all funding for federal agencies. Congress also has the power of administrative oversight, and the Senate can confirm or reject presidential nominees for top positions in the bureaucracy.

13. The term *iron triangle* refers to a strong interdependent relationship among legislators, lobbyists, and bureaucrats concerned with a particular area of public policy. Iron triangles are resistant to democratic accountability.

14. The American public has a negative view of the bureaucracy, believing that government is expensive and wasteful and that the bureaucracy is incapable of achieving its goals. It is widely believed that the bureaucracy hobbles businesses with unnecessary regulations, that government is unresponsive to citizens, that federal bureaucrats take advantage of the taxpayer, and that bureaucracy growth is out of control.

15. Efforts to reform the bureaucracy led to creation of the Senior Executive Service, which was intended to increase innovation and productivity in the federal work force. Another proposed reform is privatization, or turning over certain governmental responsibilities to private enterprises. Current reform efforts focus on "reinventing" government: shrinking agencies, reducing budgets, and making the bureaucracy more efficient.

Review Questions

1. Compare the bureaucracy under Washington to the current federal bureaucracy. Explain the reasons for change and growth.

2. Use the iron triangle and issue network models to explain how bureaucracies and the legislature have been forced to increase access to public policy formation and implementation.

3. What accounts for the durability of negative American attitudes toward the bureaucracy? What would be the most effective way to change public opinion in this area?

4. What are the advantages and disadvantages of the Hatch Act? Why was it amended? Should it have been amended?

5. Why is the bureaucracy called the "fourth branch of government?" What would the founding fathers have said about this new branch of government? How might it check and balance the other three branches?

6. How does the bureaucracy resist both presidential and congressional control?

7. Do Americans have an exaggerated notion of the extent of government waste? Why or why not?

Key Terms

administration 262
administrative discretion 262
appointment power 269
bureaucracy 252
bureaucrats 253
cabinet departments 263
civil service 257
formal rules 253
government corporation 265
Hatch Act 257

hierarchy 253
implementation 262
independent agencies 264
independent regulatory
   commissions 264
iron triangles 271
issue networks 271
Office of Management and
   Budget (OMB) 270
privatization 274

red tape 272
regulation 263
reorganization 269
specialization 253
spoils system 257
welfare state 255
Whistleblower Protection
   Act 274

Suggested Readings

ABRAMSON, MARK, and PAUL LAWRENCE. *Learning the Ropes: Insights for Political Appointees.* Lanham, Md.: Rowman & Littlefield, 2005. A valuable guide for understanding the dilemma of permanent government and what to do about it.

BOZEMAN, BARRY. *Bureaucracy and Red Tape.* Upper Saddle River, N.J.: Prentice Hall, 2000. A useful guide to understanding the complexity of government regulations as well as solutions for making government more efficient.

DOWNS, ANTHONY. *Inside Bureaucracy.* Prospect Heights, Ill.: Waveland Press, 1994. Interesting theories and insights into bureaucratic decision making.

GAY, PAUL DU. *The Values of Bureaucracy.* New York: Oxford University Press, 2005. This book highlights the positive attributes of bureaucracy and shows why bureaucratic organization should be valued, both by those engaged in business and commerce, and those responsible for running states and delivering public services.

NEIMAN, MAX. *Defending Government: Why Big Government Works.* Upper Saddle River, N.J.: Prentice Hall, 2000. This book addresses the benefits of well-designed, democratically inspired public policies. It provides a thoughtful analysis of the public sector, economic performance, and personal liberty.

TESKE, PAUL. *Regulation in the States.* Washington, D.C.: Brookings Institution Press, 2004. An insightful study of government regulation of economic activity.

WILSON, JAMES Q. *Bureaucracy: What Government Agencies Do and Why They Do It.* New York: Basic Books, 1989. A lively, "bottom-up" view of bureaucracy and an explanation of why some agencies work well whereas others fail.

Visualizing Democracy

Presidential Wars and Crises and Their Challenge to Democracy

▲ President Abraham Lincoln with generals and other military leaders outside the tent serving as headquarters for General George McClellan at Antietam, Maryland, 1862.

Photographer Mathew Brady provided the first photographic record of the devastation of the Civil War, as seen on this hillside in the aftermath of a battle.

Japanese-American men and women wait in line at a desk in a Japanese internment camp, and rest in the barracks of a relocation camp in California.

Members of Congress often tell a story about the origins of government: "Once upon a time, there was a powerful king who lived in a forest. But, having all of this power bored him and he decided to give some to his followers, who eventually became judges and legislators. But the 'indefinite residuum,' or *executive power*, he kept for himself." Such has been the president's approach to democracy when the nation's security was perceived as being at risk. As holder of a broadly defined inherent executive power, Abraham Lincoln linked the president's commander-in-chief role with the presidential oath to preserve and protect the Union. He blockaded southern ports, enlarged the army and navy, spent treasury funds without congressional authorization, closed the mails to treasonable correspondence, created special military tribunals where courts were operating, and suspended habeas corpus. Following the bombing of Pearl Harbor, President Franklin D. Roosevelt ordered 120,000 Japanese Americans living on the West Coast evacuated to internment camps. When attempting to repeal a farm parity provision in the Emergency Price Control Act, FDR declared that if Congress did not act, he would do so alone and "when the war is won, the powers under which I act automatically revert to the people—to whom they belong." When Lyndon Johnson decided to commit major ground troops to Vietnam, he did so on the loosely worded Tonkin Gulf resolution, based on dubious reports of attacks on American destroyers. "For all I know, our navy was shooting at whales out there," Johnson later quipped. No congressional declaration of war was ever issued. Following the September 11, 2001 terrorist attacks on America, President Bush endorsed the Patriot Act and claimed broad executive power to set policy on the detention and interrogation of suspected terrorists and utilized the National Security Agency (NSA) in domestic counterintelligence surveillance. One common theme runs through all of these cases—in times of national emergency or crisis, presidents have claimed broad executive powers to protect and defend the Constitution, even if those actions might come at the cost of violating some of our long fought-for civil liberties. ★

▲ President Lyndon Johnson signed the Tonkin resolution, giving him power to escalate the Vietnam War after the Gulf of Tonkin incident in which it was alleged that American vessels had been attacked by the North Vietnamese.

▼ President Johnson visits the troops in Vietnam in 1966.

▼ Americans in fatigues stand over handcuffed Taliban and Al-Qaeda detainees in orange suits and masks in a holding area at Guantanamo Bay in Cuba.

▼ President Bush stands on a burned fire truck surrounded by fire fighters in front of the World Trade Center during a tour of the devastation three days after the attack.

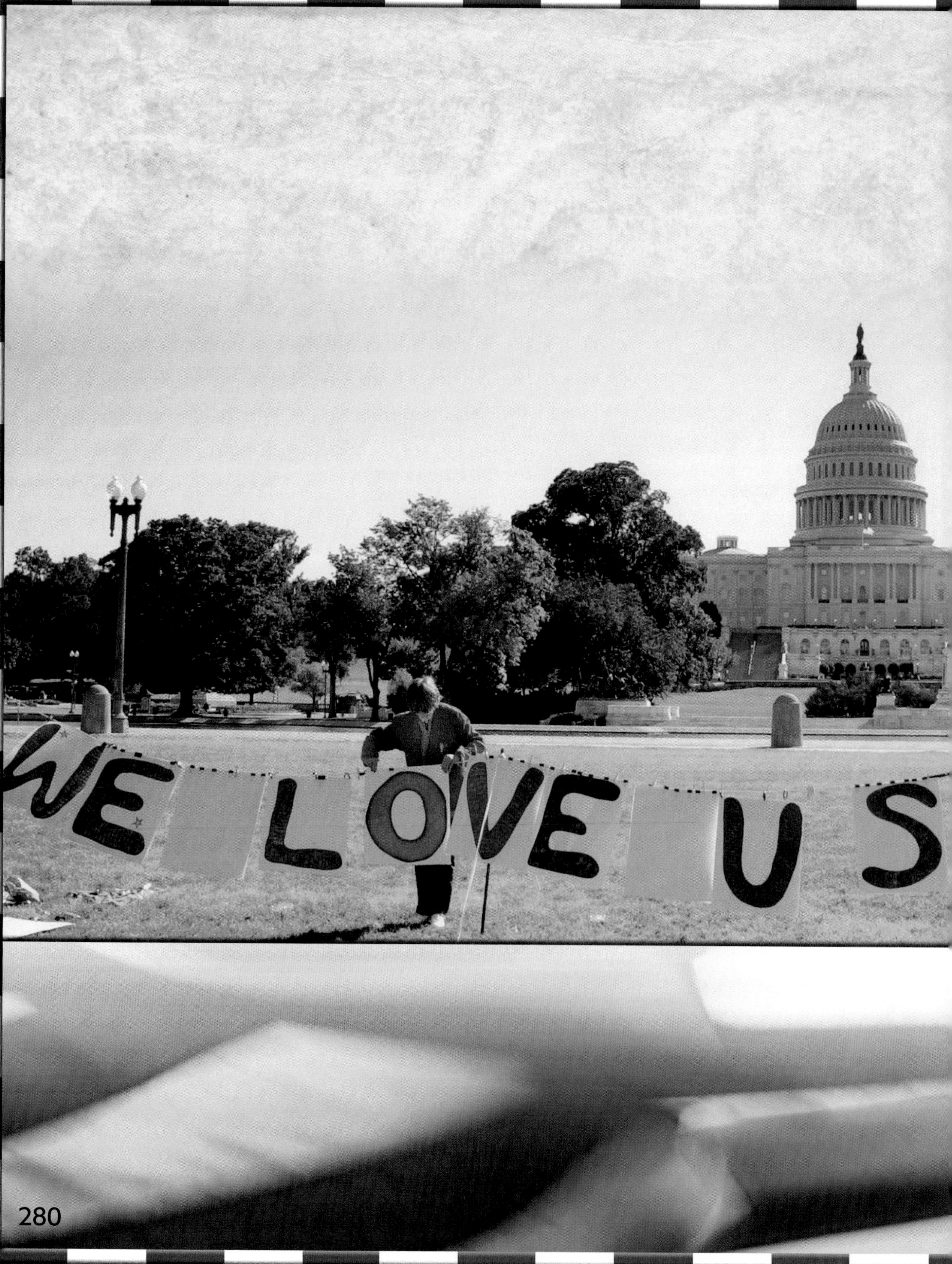
WE LOVE US

★ CHAPTER 8 ★

PUBLIC OPINION

CHAPTER OUTLINE

Approaching Democracy

Landon Defeats Roosevelt

Beginning about 1916, the magazine *Literary Digest* made the most sophisticated use of polling for political data of the time. The magazine mailed surveys to a large number of Americans asking for opinions on a host of important issues. Using their responses, the magazine claimed a high degree of accuracy in predicting election outcomes. Indeed, in 1932 the *Literary Digest* poll came within 1 percent of the actual vote in predicting Roosevelt's victory over Herbert Hoover. So impressive was this predictive ability that Democratic national chair James Farley proclaimed just prior to the election: "I consider [the poll results] conclusive evidence as to the desire of the people of this country for a change in the national government. The *Literary Digest* poll is an achievement of no little magnitude."[1] This was high praise for a magazine whose editorial policy and readership were decidedly sympathetic to the Republican party.

But a major mistake by the *Literary Digest* in 1936 changed everything and signaled the beginning of a new era in how polling is done. Today we take for granted that the New Deal was generally popular, that Roosevelt's policies were widely supported, and that Roosevelt himself was beloved by millions. Nothing is clearer than hindsight. But at the time, before the advent of sophisticated polling techniques, the outcome of the 1936 election was unclear to most political observers. Indeed, *Literary Digest,* the most respected polling outfit of the day, predicted incumbent Roosevelt's sound thrashing by Republican opponent and Kansas governor, Alfred Landon.

Before the election that year, the *Literary Digest* poll predicted a landslide win for Landon and claimed Roosevelt would gain only 41 percent of the vote to Landon's 55 percent, with 4 percent going to a third-party candidate, William Lemke. A disgusted James Farley, who had praised

★ President Franklin D. Roosevelt during inauguration ceremonies, January 20, 1937. The president is pictured on the porch of the Hermitage, a replica of the home where Andrew Jackson lived.

282

the *Digest* only four years earlier, now entirely discounted the poll results, predicting instead a Roosevelt sweep of all but eight electoral votes. His prediction was exactly right, and the rest is history. Landon carried only two states, while FDR garnered 61 percent of the popular vote. Landon promptly faded into obscurity, and Roosevelt went on to win two more presidential elections in the next eight years.

How could *Literary Digest* have been so wrong? The answer is simple. The *Digest* worked with a biased sample. As with its earlier polls, in 1936 the magazine sent out millions of informal surveys to people whose names had been culled from automobile registration lists and telephone books. Altogether 10 million ballots were sent out, and nearly 2.4 million were returned—large numbers, but a response rate of under 25 percent. In 1936, however, these respondents were no longer as representative of the total American public as they had been in 1932. They were wealthier, for one thing. In a period of grinding economic depression, they could still afford the luxury of an automobile and a telephone. They were also better educated than the average American in 1936. These two factors ensured a built-in bias against Roosevelt—wealth and education have long been correlated with support for Republicans. Many people in this group were motivated to return their ballots because they wanted to get rid of Roosevelt. Despite their large numbers, they were hardly typical of the American public as a whole.

In addition to these problems, poll participants were self-selected. They were picked not at random but simply because they chose to return the questionnaire. Because the individuals most motivated to respond to a political survey are almost never representative of the wider population, the results from such a self-selected survey are unreliable. This incident marked an end to the era of unscientific polling and pushed survey researchers to fine-tune their methods. It opened the door to today's much more sophisticated—and reliable—survey models.

★ Census 2000 was the largest peacetime effort in the history of the United States. Information about the 115.9 million housing units and 281.4 million people across the United States was obtained in the manner depicted above by a census-taker doing a survey.

QUESTION FOR REFLECTION

If the individuals motivated to respond to a political survey almost never represent the wider population, how might pollsters attract a broader percentage of the general populace to participate in surveys?

Introduction
PUBLIC OPINION AND DEMOCRACY

 **MakeItReal**

Primary Source: Planning to err? Then do it as publicly as possible

Simulation: The Great American Divide, Parts I and II

Public opinion is the keystone of democracy. No government can claim to be the legitimate voice of a people unless public opinion plays an integral role in the choice of political leaders and the development of public policy. Thus, gathering information about public opinion becomes a vital task for a democracy. Today, survey analysts use sophisticated polling techniques to provide a relatively accurate snapshot of what Americans think and feel about specific issues, events, and candidates. At the same time, those in government use similarly sophisticated means in attempts to shape and guide public opinion on issues (see Figure 8.1).

Although not all Americans are politically active and informed, all have the opportunity to be, and millions do take advantage of that opportunity. Leaders are continually made aware of what citizens are thinking; they are particularly well informed about voter desires through a constant barrage of scientific public opinion polls and a never-ending series of popular elections. Leaders who know what citizens want are likely to heed the public's wishes, a result central to any idea of democracy.

Americans are sufficiently informed and participatory to keep leaders in touch with their desires, sufficiently open and tolerant to live together peacefully within a diverse and complex culture. To gauge the strength of democracy, leaders need to know what citizens desire, how well they communicate those desires through political activity, and how well political leaders respond to those desires. For any political system in the world to be democratic, its leaders must at the very least hear "the voice of the people." The leader–follower connection is central to democratic theory in democratic societies. Citizens in a democracy express their preferences through informed political activity, and leaders listen with a keen interest to those expressed preferences. If the masses are inactive or if the leaders consistently ignore their desires, democracy falters. To begin to understand the impact of public opinion, we examine how it is measured, sources of opinions on political issues, and the nature of public opinion in America.[2]

WHAT IS PUBLIC OPINION?

Public opinion is the collective expression of attitudes about the prominent issues and actors of the day. The concept of a "public" holding "opinions" on various issues is almost as old as politics itself. Plato, for instance, saw public opinion as a danger if it meant the mass of citizens could freely express individual desires. According to Plato, popular opinions were good only when they reflected the will of the state and its rulers. Centuries later, John Stuart Mill expressed a significantly different view in his

public opinion The collective expression of attitudes about the prominent issues and actors of the day.

▶ © 1995 Creators Syndicate Inc. *Richmond Times-Dispatch* 11/95. Bob Gorrell.

Most See a More Divided Nation

	TOTAL	PARTY IDENTIFICATION		
		REP.	DEM.	IND.
THE COUNTRY IS ...	%	%	%	%
More politically divided	66	61	77	64
Not more divided	26	32	16	29
Don't know	8	7	7	7
	100	100	100	100
PEOPLE YOU KNOW ARE ...				
More divided over politics	53	44	65	52
Not more divided	40	51	29	40
Don't know	7	5	6	8
	100	100	100	100

What's Dividing America?

	ALL	PARTY IDENTIFICATION		
		REP.	DEM.	IND.
	%	%	%	%
Foreign policy (net)	36	35	39	33
War in Iraq	32	31	36	28
Terrorism	3	4	2	3
Domestic issues (net)	19	15	22	18
Economy/jobs	13	10	17	11
Taxes	2	1	2	*
Moral values and issues (net)	14	15	15	13
Morals, values	3	5	2	3
Religion	5	5	5	5
Gay marriage, gay rights	2	4	3	1
Abortion	2	2	2	1
Leaders (net)	11	7	13	13
Bush	6	3	8	8
Republicans/conservatives	1	—	2	*
Democrats/liberals	1	2	*	*
Rich-poor gap	3	1	5	2

Note: Based on respondents who said that America is more divided politically or that people they knew were more politically divided.

Figure 8.1

Source: Pew Research Center for the People & the Press, December 2004.

MakeItReal

Primary Source: *Federalist #10: The Same Subject Continued: The Union as a Safeguard Against Domestic Faction and Insurrection*

essay *On Liberty* (1859), when he argued in favor of a populace free to express its diverse political views. Only by giving all individuals the maximum liberty to state their opinions, said Mill, could a society ever arrive at the "truth." Whereas Plato wanted to shape and control opinions, Mill advocated free rein to their expression.

James Madison took a middle stance between Plato and Mill. In *The Federalist,* no. 10, Madison acknowledged the inevitable diversity of opinion that would develop in a free society but feared that competing opinions could lead to hostile factions that would divide rather than unify or improve society:

> A zeal for different opinions . . . [has] divided mankind into parties, inflamed them with mutual animosity, and rendered them . . . disposed to vex and oppress each other.[3]

Like most of the framers, Madison was concerned that an overzealous majority might inflict its irrational, prejudiced, or uninformed wishes on a political minority. Hence, the framers made sure to install what they envisioned as constitutional safeguards (such as the electoral college, the Senate, and the Supreme Court) against too easy implementation of public passions. On the other hand, they also allowed many outlets for the expression of public opinion: voting, a free press, the right of assembly, and other forms of political participation.

How deeply public opinion should be taken into account, then, has long been the subject of intense political debate, but today we have clear parameters for this debate. No longer can a legitimate public figure argue, as Plato did, that the public should be ignored or manipulated in political decision making. The only real argument now is whether the public's will should prevail "all of the time," "most of the time," or "some of the time." The public, in short, is a key player in the democratic game of politics. For that reason, discovering and publicizing the public's opinion has become a key political activity in modern democracies.

MEASURING PUBLIC OPINION

Although the notion of public opinion has been with us for centuries, we have only recently developed reliable ways to measure it. The first attempts at measuring public opinion began in the mid-1800s, with a variety of straw polls. A **straw poll** is a nonscientific method of measuring public opinion. It springs from the farmer's method of throwing straw up into the air to gauge the strength and direction of the prevailing breeze. In a straw poll, one wishes to measure which way and how strong the political breezes are blowing.

As we saw in the case study, straw polls have inherent flaws that make them inappropriate as scientific indicators of public opinion. Their main problem is that they fail to obtain a **representative sample** of the public. A valid sample must be representative, meaning it must include all the significant characteristics of the total population. A sample of Americans that included no women, for instance, would obviously be invalid. A nonrepresentative sample like the infamous *Literary Digest* poll of 1936, which underrepresented poor and average-income people, is worthless.

After the 1936 fiasco, professional pollsters began a determined effort to make their work more scientific. George Gallup and Elmo Roper, among others, helped meet the growing demand for information about public attitudes. Applying modern statistical techniques, they succeeded, through interviews with small but representative samples of voters, in predicting the behavior of the overall voting population.

Obtaining a representative sample poses several requirements. First, the sample should include at least several hundred people. Second, the people to be polled must be chosen through a technique known as *random sampling*. In addition, pollsters must guard against sampling bias.[4]

Sample Size Most pollsters produce results of high reliability. Their findings are accurate at least 95 percent of the time, within a margin of error of about 3 percent. **Margin of error** reflects the validity of the results obtained by a poll given the

straw poll A nonscientific method of measuring public opinion.

representative sample A sample that includes all the significant characteristics of the total population.

margin of error The measure of possible error in a survey, which means that the number for the entire population of voters will fall within a range of plus or minus several points of the number obtained from the small but representative sample of voters.

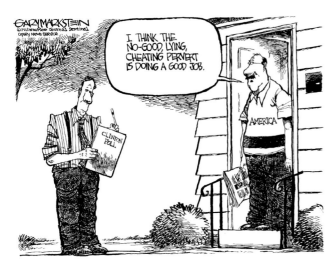

I THINK THE NO-GOOD, LYING, CHEATING PERVERT IS DOING A GOOD JOB.

◀ Gary Markstein, Copley News Service © *The Milwaukee Journal Sentinel.*

sample size. For example, a poll with a 3 percent margin of error suggests that, on average, the results of the poll would differ by plus or minus 3 percent if the entire population were polled, rather than just a sampling of that population.

Another component of a good poll is sample size. Generally, the larger the sample the better, because larger samples reduce the margin of error. Most reputable national polls have sample sizes of 1,500 to 2,000 respondents, a size that reduces the margin of error to plus or minus 3 percent. Using statistical methods, pollsters have determined that information from a sample of that size can be projected onto the entire population. The method does work, but it places a heavy burden on pollsters: "What's critical is that we all act with care—gathering our data honestly and well: examining them fully and thoughtfully; chasing bias and conventional wisdom out the door; reaching for new, independent approaches and fresh understandings; keeping sight of the limitations as well as the possibilities of our work; and, ultimately, producing the best, most thoughtful analysis of public opinion we can. The times demand no less," observed Gary Langer, when he worked as director of polling for ABC news.[5]

Random Sampling   The second requirement for a good poll, random sampling, is harder to achieve. In a **random sample**, every member of the population must have an equal chance of appearing in the sample. Advancements in technology have reduced the problems associated with randomness. Pollsters increasingly rely on *random digit dialing* (RDD), which uses computers to automatically select phone numbers at random. The use of this technique includes both listed and unlisted phone numbers, ensuring that all individuals have the same chance of being selected for inclusion in a poll.

Pollsters make every effort to guard against **sampling bias**. They try to ensure that no particular set of people in the population at large—rich or poor, of any ethnicity, from any region—is any more or less likely to appear in the final sample than any other set of people. Recall that the major flaw in the *Literary Digest* poll of 1936—the disproportionately high percentage of respondents who were relatively wealthy and well educated—led to biased results.

Good polling leaves little room to interviewer discretion. Most polling organizations divide the U.S. population into categories based on the location and size of the city in which they live. Interviewers are sent into randomly selected neighborhood areas or blocks. Using another technique, pollsters carry out a survey using computer-generated lists of telephone numbers. Because people are selected completely at random, these lists will reflect an approximation of the entire nation. The result is that polls today come relatively close to meeting the crucial requirement that every American have an equal chance of appearing in any given pollster's sample.

Problems still occur, however. The reliance on telephones, although convenient and inexpensive, does introduce a modest degree of sampling bias. For example,

random sample A strategy required for a valid poll whereby every member of the population has an equal chance of appearing in the sample.

sampling bias A bias in a survey whereby a particular set of people in the population at large is more or less likely to appear in the final sample than other sets of people.

almost 20 percent of Native American households lack telephone service of any kind, as do 15 percent of African American and Hispanic households; by contrast, only about 5 percent of white households have no telephone. Since a statistical correlation exists between poverty and lack of telephone facilities, it would appear that most "phoneless" housing units are in areas of urban poverty. Polls based on telephone ownership are therefore likely to underrepresent the urban ethnic poor. Also, the increasing number of young people who have only cellular phone service has caused concern about balance since these numbers are not part of the sample.

Reliability   Another major concern of polling is reliability. Pollsters want meaningful and consistent results. Attention to *question wording* is essential for reliable results. Respondents can often be led into answers by the way a question is worded. For example, in 1992 Independent presidential candidate Ross Perot commissioned his own poll, which asked: "Should laws be passed to eliminate all possibilities of special interests giving huge sums of money to candidates?" Here was a case of a candidate framing a poll question to obtain the answer he wanted—99 percent of the respondents answered "yes." But if the question had been rephrased to ask, "Do groups have the right to contribute money to candidates they support?" the response likely would have been different.[6]

The type of answers pollsters solicit can also affect the results. Generally, questions are either *open-ended,* where respondents are free to offer any answer to a question ("What do you think is the biggest problem facing the country today?") or *close-ended,* where the pollster provides a set of possible answers ("Would you consider welfare, crime, or environment the biggest problem facing the country?").

Pollsters confront additional problems as they set out to conduct their polls. Interviewers must be carefully trained to avoid interviewer bias. They must be courteous, businesslike, and neutral so as to elicit open and honest responses. Interviewers must also be persistent. Some people are rarely home; others may hesitate to answer questions. Interviewers must make every effort to contact potential respondents and draw them out; they must learn how to extract truthful answers from shy, hostile, or simply bewildered members of the voting public.

The Importance of Polls   Public opinion polls have emerged as an integral part of American politics. Accurate polls are one of the most important sources of information political leaders use in the decision-making process. Polls today, conducted by reputable national polling organizations, provide a reasonably accurate picture of the American public's beliefs and desires that would otherwise be difficult to achieve. Virtually every news organization works with a polling company as well as an in-house polling team. The president has professional pollsters on his staff—always prepared to check the pulse of the people and even to shape that pulse when necessary. Lobby groups constantly release the results of polls they have commissioned to "prove" that the public supports their particular policy preferences.

The media use polls during campaigns to track support for candidates over time. These types of polls are called **tracking polls**. The media also utilize **exit polls**, which target voters as they leave the voting booth in an effort to gauge the likely winner of an election before the results are announced. The polling places are a scientifically selected sample that collectively represent a state or the nation. The use of exit polls is sometimes criticized for lowering voter turnout, particularly in western states, because the media or more recently the bloggers, have used exit polls to project winners well before voting booths have closed across the nation. Indeed, the results are often on the Internet and blog sites before they appear on television.

On election night 2000, the television networks, basing their announcement on exit polling in Florida, erroneously projected Al Gore as winning the election. Voter News Service (VNS), a consortium of news organizations that provide exit polls, erred in its statistical projections, not unlike *Literary Digest's* prediction of the 1936 presidential election results. VNS was disbanded after the 2002 election.

MakeItReal

Simulation: Public Opinion: Spin Detection

Visual Literacy: Dewey Defeats Truman

MakeItReal

ABC News Video: *Conspiracy Theory*

tracking polls Polls used by the media to track the support levels for candidates over time.

exit polls Polls that question voters as they leave the voting booth to predict the outcome of an election.

In 2003, the National Election Pool (NEP), a consortium of ABC News, Associated Press, CBS News, CNN, Fox News, and NBC, provided information on election night about the vote count and projections. NEP retained the Associated Press to conduct a tabulation of the vote and contracted with the firm Edison Media Research and Mitofsky International (Edison/Mitofsky) to make projections and provide the exit poll releases.[7]

The 2004 presidential election did not go well for exit polling. The first round of exit polls was leaked to the bloggers, and, based on early projections, John Kerry was projected as the winner. Richard Morin, the *Washington Post*'s director of polling, observed that "it seems now that the 2004 exit polls were rife with problems, most of them small, but none trivial. Skewed samples, technical glitches, and a woefully inept question that included the undefined term 'moral values' in a list of concrete issues all combined to give exit polling its third black eye in as many elections."[8] (See Figure 8.2). Why were Bush voters underrepresented in the precinct samples? Perhaps they were busier than Democrats and did not have time to be interviewed; perhaps they disliked the media's coverage of Bush and chose to snub pollsters. As we look to the future of exit polling, perhaps the advice offered by the *Post*'s Morin is best: "In a perfect world, early exit poll results would be treated just like early vote returns or the score at the end of the first quarter of the Redskins game. . . . [S]ometime soon, I suspect that the electorate will come to see these early exit poll results the same way. The view of exit polls also will change, from blind awe and acceptance to respect tempered by a healthy skepticism. Thanks to the 2004 election and my new best friends the bloggers, we're closer to that day."[9] The emergence of bloggers is the focus of Chapter 10's case study.

POLITICAL SOCIALIZATION

Where do our ideas about politics come from? **Political socialization** refers to the process by which we learn about the world of politics and develop our political beliefs. Learning about politics begins early in childhood. Political thinkers have long observed that parent–child and sibling relationships shape the social and political outlook of future citizens. Other institutions—schools, peer groups, mass media—also serve as agents of socialization.

The Role of Family

Family influence is especially powerful in the development of political knowledge, understanding, and participation. Whether we grow up poor or rich, for instance, shapes our view of the world and bears heavily on the likelihood of our developing an interest in politics. Other family traits—education level, race, even geographic location—deeply affect our perspectives on the political world.

About the age of ten, children begin to form their worldview, based significantly on family views toward politics. The role of family in political socialization is mostly informal. Parents rarely sit their children down and inform them that they are Democrats, supply-siders, or isolationists. In this sense, the family unit has a unique advantage for influence. Children absorb the casually dropped remarks of their parents and, over time, unthinkingly adopt those views as their own.[10]

Family influence also derives from the strong emotional bonds forged by the family connection. Children want to adopt the views of their beloved mentors. Close-knit families produce offspring whose views differ little from those of the parents. The family power structure provides an additional key to the early political socialization of children. Strong parental authority figures have an enormous impact on a child's values and attitudes. Many scholars believe, for instance, that harsh, punitive parents produce children who are more authoritarian, intolerant, and ultraconservative than the average American.

Because many variables affect political attitudes, it is difficult to trace the precise effects of family on the political opinions of adult Americans. In one area, however,

---

political socialization The process by which we learn about the world of politics and develop our political beliefs.

Questions for Reflection

Have you ever been contacted by pollsters for your opinion on political issues on a national, state, or local level?

Did you comply with their request for your feedback?

If not, why, and would you reconsider your decision based on the impact polls have on our democratic system?

Quick Review

Political Socialization

- Where we live, our age, occupation, education level, and religion all affect how we vote.
- Large individual differences sometimes exist within socioeconomic and demographic categories.
- More striking are the consistent differences that pollsters find in the political opinions of men and women.

 **MakeItReal**

Simulation: Political Survey: What Do You Believe?

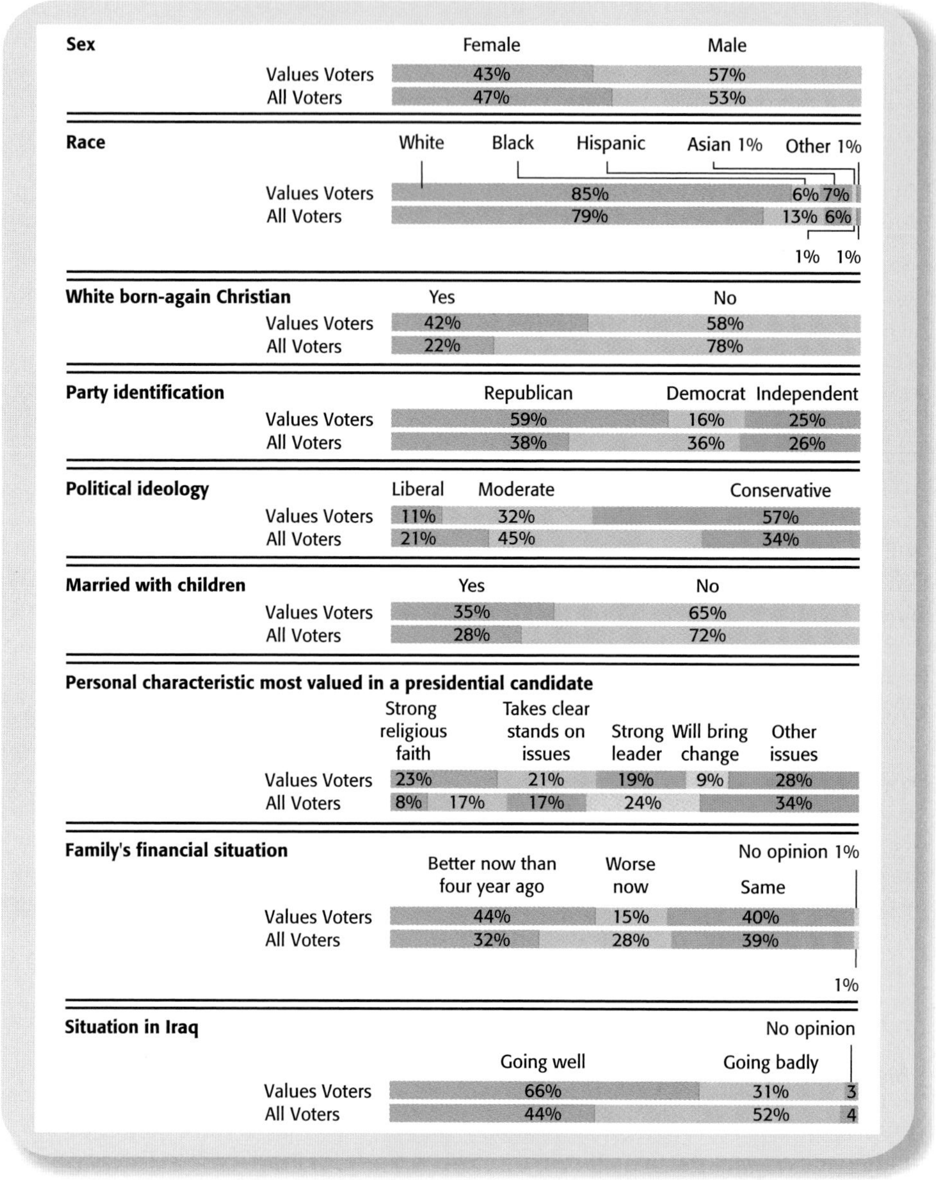

Sex

	Female	Male
Values Voters	43%	57%
All Voters	47%	53%

Race

	White	Black	Hispanic	Asian 1%	Other 1%
Values Voters	85%			6%	7%
All Voters	79%			13%	6%

1% 1%

White born-again Christian

	Yes	No
Values Voters	42%	58%
All Voters	22%	78%

Party identification

	Republican	Democrat	Independent
Values Voters	59%	16%	25%
All Voters	38%	36%	26%

Political ideology

	Liberal	Moderate	Conservative
Values Voters	11%	32%	57%
All Voters	21%	45%	34%

Married with children

	Yes	No
Values Voters	35%	65%
All Voters	28%	72%

Personal characteristic most valued in a presidential candidate

	Strong religious faith	Takes clear stands on issues	Strong leader	Will bring change	Other issues
Values Voters	23%	21%	19%	9%	28%
All Voters	8%	17%	17%	24%	34%

Family's financial situation

	Better now than four year ago	Worse now	Same	No opinion 1%
Values Voters	44%	15%	40%	
All Voters	32%	28%	39%	1%

Situation in Iraq

	Going well	Going badly	No opinion
Values Voters	66%	31%	3
All Voters	44%	52%	4

Figure 8.2   Who Were the Values Voters?

Moral values led the list of issues that most influenced the 2004 presidential vote, and 8 in 10 values voters supported President Bush. These voters, who made up 22 percent of the electorate, tended to be politically, socially, and religiously conservative. More than four in 10—or 42 percent—were white, born-again Christians, compared with 22 percent of all voters.

Source: Washington Post, November 5, 2004, p. A3.

parental impact seems clear and pronounced. Children tend to adopt their parents' party loyalty. That's significant, because *partisan identification* helps people make sense of the political world and predicts their behavior within it. Interestingly, when parents identify with different political parties, children generally embrace their mother's partisan affiliation. We are not certain why this is, but one possible explanation, which would certainly reinforce the importance of family socialization, is that children feel closer to their mother, from whom they received much early nurturing and affection.

Children, however, must adjust their values so they can adapt to a changing world. The concept of a *generation gap* describes the potential decline in family influence over children's values. It postulates that when children reach adulthood they break away and may condemn their parents' political beliefs. The rebellious 1960s gave new credence to this theory. However, follow-up studies during the 1970s suggest that as the children of the 1960s grew older, many adopted some of their parents' political beliefs. What accounts for this transition? Among other things, we know that as people age, they settle down and grow slightly more conservative. The day-to-day responsibilities of a job, a family, and a home move individuals in the direction of preserving the status quo of society and politics. One cannot, after all, remain a rebellious youth forever.

Still, no generation simply mimics its parents' views. Analysts have observed a strong **generational effect** in American socialization patterns. The generation of adults who grew up during the 1960s does appear to have its own outlook, different from that of the previous generation. Its views reflect weaker ties to political institutions, weaker partisan identification, and a higher incidence of political independence or nonpartisanship. This pattern results from a host of factors, including the social dislocations of the 1960s, the Vietnam War, and the Watergate scandal—all of which made Americans more critical of their political system.

Schooling

Outside the family, the most powerful institutional influence on political socialization is education. In school, children first learn the formal rules of social interaction and come face-to-face with institutional authority: teachers, staff, and principals. More specifically, they learn to develop positive attitudes toward citizenship through history and civics courses. Early primary education leads children to recognize the name and image of the president. Most children are taught to look at the president as a benevolent symbol of government and politics. This early socialization carries over strongly into adult life. Even after Richard Nixon's resignation from office in the midst of the Watergate scandal, most American adults still placed enormous faith in the office of the presidency and believed in the notion of a strong political leader in the White House.

Schools' central role in the socialization process has made them the center of political controversy, as different sides of the political spectrum struggle to control what schools teach. The issue of prayer in the public schools, for example, has sharply divided the American public and led to heated debate. This clash fits into a larger debate between educational conservatives and liberals on the role of schools in modern American society. Both sides wish to use schools to socialize students to the perspectives they hold dear. Conservative critics charge that schools are failing to provide students with the traditions and norms of American culture. Liberal critics fault the schools for perpetuating class, race, and gender divisions and for failing to teach about "diversity" and "multiculturalism." As these arguments suggest, Americans live in a complex and increasingly divided society. Debate about the way schools should socialize young Americans is therefore likely to continue for some time.

University training also represents a key element in the process of socialization. Most people believe that the experience of attending a university somehow "makes people more liberal." In fact, recent years have witnessed an increase in the number of self-identified conservatives among university students. Historically, university students were every bit as likely to be Republicans as Democrats; however, those who obtain both a university education and high socioeconomic status tend to be moderate or conservative, not liberal.

Peers

A child's peers make up another important source of political socialization. We all absorb the ideas and outlook of our contemporaries, especially close friends. However, studies have found that although teenage peer groups significantly influence taste, dress, and style, they do little more than reinforce parental and community

generational effect Socialization patterns in which a generation of adults who grew up during a certain decade or period appears to have its own outlook, differentiating itself from the previous age.

values, at least when it comes to politics. Peer groups do appear to affect political attitudes on the rare public issues of special relevance to young people. The decision to resist the draft or to enlist in the 1960s, for example, would have been influenced by one's peer group. And "Generation X," young people of the 1990s, through a political action committee representing their political and economic needs (XPAC), identify Social Security reform as the core issue for this group.

In recent decades, many observers have described the emergence of a "youth culture." Urie Bronfenbrenner, for instance, has argued that children's peers and television are much more influential in American culture than they were in the past, due in large part to the breakdown of the family and the decrease in its traditional influence.[11] The youth culture, he fears, stresses immature, violent, and commercialized perspectives on life, shielded as it is from the more responsible perspectives of an adult world and deeply influenced by images on the television screen. A landmark study by Robert Putnam suggests these consequences: Americans today are less prone to engage in civic activities, less trusting of others, and more cynical about the institutions of American society than those in previous generations. The values propagated in young adult peer groups may have a role in this trend.[12]

Television

Perhaps more than anything else in American culture, television has emerged to dominate the social and political landscape. Americans' societal language, habits, values, and norms seem to derive as much from exposure to television imagery as from any other socializing force.

Despite a considerable literature devoted to the effects of television on political attitudes and behavior, no consensus exists regarding just how and to what degree television affects Americans. Television has come under severe scrutiny because of its ubiquity, its demonstrated power to absorb viewer time for several hours a day, and its unique blend of immediacy, proximity, and audiovisual appeal. Perhaps the major criticism of television focuses on its power to divert our attention from the serious to the trivial.

Because the vast majority of television shows are devoted to amusement rather than information, and most people watch television for entertainment, its effect in shaping political attitudes must be indirect. One study concludes that "politically relevant issues are now raised in virtually all types of programming."[13] The values conveyed by television—commercialism, tolerance for sex and violence, encouragement of an extreme form of rugged individualism—become, in other words, an unthinking part of the general culture. Viewers absorb these values and subconsciously draw on them when thinking about politics.

Despite all the criticism of television, however, many studies reveal a surprise. Although children watch an average of twenty-seven hours of television per week—close to the amount they spend in class—a significant amount of viewing actually increases exposure to and knowledge of politics and government. So although Americans are undoubtedly bombarded with huge daily doses of advertising, sports, and entertainment, television watching does at least expose young viewers to a considerable amount of political information as well.

SOCIAL VARIABLES THAT INFLUENCE OPINION FORMATION

In learning about politics, we are all subject to the same general influences that shape our society's mind-set. We learn from our families a common set of norms and values; together we live through major political and economic events; we go to school; and we are bound together by the unifying force of television. Still, even within the same culture, people differ from each other in important ways. Different social circumstances—class and income, race and ethnicity, religion, region, and gender—produce significantly different life experiences undoubtedly reflected in differing political opinions.

Class

Our relative standing in society shapes many of our social and political values. Class, or social status, rests high on every social scientist's list of the forces that mold behavior. Unfortunately, class is a complex and difficult variable to measure; no two analysts and no two citizens agree on its precise definition. In March 2005, the *New York Times* conducted a nationwide survey to discover how Americans regard class and where they place themselves. The poll uncovered optimism about social mobility and found important differences between rich and poor, including the likelihood of achieving the American dream. The authors of the study observed that even though social diversity has erased many traditional markers of status (that is, it is harder today than twenty years ago to determine status by a person's car, clothing, religion, or race), class remains a powerful force in American life. Over the past three decades, it has come to play a greater, not lesser, role in important ways. At a time when education matters more than ever, success in school remains linked tightly to class. At a time when the country is increasingly integrated racially, the rich are isolating themselves more and more. At a time of extraordinary advances in medicine, class differences in health and lifespan are wide and appear to be widening. And new research on mobility, the movement of families up and down the economic ladder, shows far less of it than economists once thought and less than most people believe.[14]

Income

Income, a key element in the concept of class, is far easier to define and study. People in different income groups often see the political world in different ways. The impact of both class and income, however, is mitigated through education. That is, those with higher education are more likely to be wealthy and of a higher class than those who are poorly educated. This relationship has a particularly strong impact on voting behavior. Better–educated people, usually the wealthier too, are much more likely to vote than less–educated people, who are predominantly poor. We saw evidence of this connection in the *Literary Digest* presidential election poll of 1936, which represented opinions of the wealthier and better-educated segments of the U.S. population.

As a general rule, the less money one makes, the more inclined one is to favor liberal economic policies that provide benefits to the poor. These policies include a Social Security system, progressive taxation, minimum wage laws, generous unemployment benefits, and welfare payments to the disadvantaged. The more money one makes, the more one is likely to oppose such policies. Both positions reflect a degree of economic self-interest. Lower-income groups benefit from liberal economic policies, whereas higher-income groups supply the money to pay for these policies. Nevertheless, these are only tendencies. Many individuals in each income category take positions opposite to what we would expect. Some millionaires are liberals, and some individuals at the lower end of the economic spectrum are conservatives. Income level strongly influences voting patterns in the United States. Roughly stated, poor people tend to vote for Democrats (the more liberal party on economic policy); rich people tend to vote for Republicans (the more conservative party on economic policy); and middle-income people split their votes, depending on circumstance.[15]

Race and Ethnicity

Income is but one of many social influences that produce different perspectives on politics. In addition, racial and ethnic background strongly affect the attitudes a person is likely to develop. Imagine how different your life experiences

Census 2000: Projected Population of the United States, by Race and Hispanic Origin: 2000 to 2050

would have been, and how different the political attitudes you would have developed, had you been born into this world with a different skin color or a different ethnic heritage.

Most cultures discriminate against minorities in their midst. Hence, members of minorities can grow up feeling distrustful of and alienated from their society and its public authorities. They may express these attitudes in politics in various ways. In the United States, for instance, blacks are clearly more alienated from the political process than are whites. As a result, they vote less frequently in elections and participate at a lower level in other areas of the political process. African Americans vote in large numbers for the party most associated with economic benefits for minorities and the less well off—that is, the Democrats. Race, America's most enduring social cleavage, produces the clearest of all social delineations between the two major political parties. The vast majority of black voters consider themselves Democrats, whereas white voters are more closely divided in party identification. Blacks consistently identify former President Bill Clinton as the greatest president in their lifetime.

Hispanics, too, tend to take a liberal position on economic issues and vote heavily for the Democratic party. However, the different groups within the Hispanic population are not as unified on issues as African Americans tend to be. Cuban Americans, for example, are wealthier than average and are among the more conservative of American voting blocs.

As a general rule, ethnic groups become conservative as they rise in social status. Asian Americans, whose income levels have risen significantly in recent decades, are now among the most conservative groups in the nation. The same is true for so-called white ethnic voters, people whose ancestors immigrated from Ireland, Italy, or Poland. This group was heavily Democratic for decades, but as members rose into the middle class, they developed more conservative outlooks.

▲ Bob Jones University has been a traditional stop for Republicans during the South Carolina primary. In 2000, however, George W. Bush's visit prompted outcries from John McCain and others because of the university's position on interracial dating and the founder's statements about Catholics.

Religion

Religious differences produce serious political differences in the United States, as in all countries. Three general principles help explain the effect of religion on political attitudes. First, the less religious you are, the more liberal or "left" you are likely to be. In the United States, people with few religious connections are likely to take liberal stands on most social and economic questions and to vote Democratic. This pattern is not numerically significant, however, because most Americans profess religious belief of one kind or another.

More important for its political ramifications is the second principle: Members of any country's dominant religion tend to be more conservative. This stand makes sense, because these people have more investment in the status quo. By comparison, minority religious groups, especially the more oppressed ones, tend to favor liberal perspectives. This pattern is clear in the United States. Protestantism has long been the majority religion. Catholicism and Judaism were generally the religions of minority groups discriminated against when they first immigrated to this country. As we would expect, over the years, Protestants have been the most conservative religious group, whereas Catholics and Jews have been more liberal, and thus more likely to support Democrats. The Catholic

Church's handling of issues related to sexual abuse of children by priests now threatens to undercut the church's influence on its members' political views.

These are, of course, broad generalizations; many individuals within each category deviate significantly from the pattern. Furthermore, changing social circumstances are changing this pattern. Many Catholics have entered America's mainstream and have become conservatives. But Catholics who still belong to minority ethnic groups are still more liberal and more likely to support Democrats than are Protestants—or other Catholics for that matter. Jews remain the most liberal of all religious groups, but even they have made modest moves in a conservative direction as their economic situation has improved.

A final principle helps further explain the effect of religion on political outlook. Generally, the more religious one is, the more conservative one is likely to be. Thus, ardent churchgoers and committed believers take a conservative outlook on life; in politics they gravitate toward the right side of the political spectrum. This tendency helps explain a key trend of this age: White evangelical Protestants, along with right-to-life supporters, have moved in significant numbers toward the Republican party and are moving the GOP more to the right. Fourteen percent of Bush voters identified their candidate's "strong religious faith" as the major factor in their vote, compared with 1 percent of Kerry supporters. In the 2004 presidential election, President Bush owed much to the support he received from white evangelical Protestants. The president received 78 percent of the vote of white evangelicals, an increase of 10 percent from 2000. "The election underscored the importance of white evangelical voters to the GOP. In 2004, they constituted 36 percent of Bush voters. By comparison, African Americans, the most loyal of Democratic constituencies, constituted only about one-fifth (21 percent) of Kerry's voters."[16] President Bush also increased his share of the Catholic vote by five percentage points (52 percent in 2004 and 47 percent in 2000). The president gained among white, non-Hispanic Catholics (56 percent in 2004 compared with 52 percent in 2000.)

Region

People's political outlooks often reflect where they grew up and where they now live. Certain sections of the United States have conservative traditions; other areas are more liberal. People from conservative areas are likely to be conservative, and those from liberal areas, liberal. Nothing better illustrates this than the concept of "blue" and "red" states that we discuss in Chapter 9, Political Parties.

The South has always been America's most conservative region. Strongest among the many reasons for this pattern was that disheartened southern whites after the Civil War rejected all "northern" values, including industrial-age liberalism. A firm emphasis on tradition, on order and hierarchy, and of course on religious fundamentalism have all helped keep the South a bastion of social—and now political—conservatism, especially for white residents of that area. By a quirk, however, the South remained Democratic for decades, a reaction against the Republicanism of Abraham Lincoln and the victorious North. In recent decades, however, the South has moved increasingly into the Republican camp, a trend especially strong during presidential elections and among white Protestant fundamentalists.

From a more general perspective, rural areas everywhere tend toward social and political conservatism. The reasons for this tendency are complex. It may have to do with the traditionalism associated with longtime, stable communities, along with a sense, developed from years of working on the land, that permanence and stability are the most desirable patterns of life. For whatever reason, conservatives and Republicans are more numerous than average in smaller communities, in rural areas, and increasingly in the South (except among minorities). In contrast, one is much more likely to find liberal voters and Democrats in the urban areas of America, especially outside the South. In suburban areas, the two parties are closely matched and compete intensely for the moderate, middle-class vote.

Gender

1980	Reagan	Carter	Anderson Carter
Men	55%	36	7
Women	47%	45	7

1984	Reagan	Mondale	
Men	62%	37	
Women	56%	44	

1988	Bush	Dukakis	
Men	57%	41	
Women	50%	49	

1992	Bush	Clinton	Perot
Men	38%	41	21
Women	37%	45	17

1996	Dole	Clinton	Perot
Men	44%	43	10
Women	38%	54	7

2000	Bush	Gore	
Men	52%	42	
Women	42%	54	

2004	Bush	Kerry	
Men	55%	44	
Women	48%	51	

Figure 8.3   The Gender Gap
The difference between a candidate's votes from men and his votes from women in presidential elections. Percentages may not add up to 100 because of other candidates.

Sources: From *The New York Times,* March 26, 2000. Copyright © 2000 by The New York Times Co. Reprinted by permission. Updated by authors.

Few forces shape one's world outlook as powerfully as gender. It should surprise no one that men and women differ in the way they see the world. That difference carries over into politics. Of all trends in American public opinion, few are more striking than the consistent differences that pollsters find in the political opinions of men and women. In a pattern known as the **gender gap**, women have consistently been more supportive of so-called "compassion issues" such as school integration and social welfare programs than have men (see Figure 8.3). Compared with men, women "are more supportive of arms control and peaceful foreign relations; they are more likely to oppose weapons buildups or the use of force. They much more frequently favor gun control and oppose capital punishment."[17] Men, in contrast, are more likely than women to support military, police, and other sources of government force. In most cases, men take the tougher, more conservative stands. For instance, men are more likely than women to oppose environmental and consumer protection, busing and other forms of desegregation, and most programs to aid the sick, the unemployed, the poor, and ethnic minorities.

As we will see in Chapter 10's detailed discussion of the gender gap, the ultimate difference between men and women shows up at election time. Where candidates or parties show clear differences on issues of force and compassion, women vote, on average, 4 to 8 percentage points further "left"—that is, for the more liberal position, candidate, or party (usually the Democrats). Thus, in the 1980 election between President Jimmy Carter and challenger Ronald Reagan, men voted strongly for Reagan, whereas women split their vote almost evenly. Indeed, the perception that Reagan was wildly popular relied largely on his enthusiastic backing by one key group in American society—white men. Women were frequently divided in their feelings about Reagan, and black men were clearly hostile. This gender gap continues to show itself in presidential elections. About 45 percent of women supported Bill Clinton in 1992, compared with 40 percent of male voters. This trend continued in the 1996 election. In the 2000 election, a majority of women (54 percent) voted for Gore; a majority of men (53 percent) for Bush. This trend continued in 2004.

In 1992, Clinton received overwhelming support from women voters often referred to as "soccer moms." Soccer moms—predominantly white suburban women between the ages of thirty-five and forty-five—replaced "angry white men" as the swing vote in 1996. Candidates of both parties woo them because they vote but not along party lines. They are busy but not disinterested. Exit polls in 1996 showed soccer moms favored Clinton over Dole by 49 percent to 41 percent, with 8 percent for Perot. "Soccer dads" preferred Dole by 56 percent, Clinton by 34 percent, and Perot by 9 percent.

On certain issues, however, men and women hold similar views. One finds almost no difference at all in their views on abortion. Interestingly, where male and female opinions do begin to converge, the direction of change follows the prevailing opinion preferences of women rather than men. This has been the case on issues ranging from environmental protection to defense spending. For various reasons, men have become more supportive of historically "female" positions. These findings may point to women's increasing political clout.

A New Political Typology   In December 2004 and March 2005, the Pew Research Center conducted two nationwide public opinion surveys that helped develop a new political typology for 2005. The political typology study sorted voters into homogeneous groups based on values, political beliefs, and party affiliation. The major difference between this post–September 11, 2001, study and its predecessors is the importance of national security issues on the typology. "Foreign affairs assertiveness now almost completely distinguishes Republican-oriented voters from Democratic-oriented voters; this was a relatively minor factor in past typologies. In contrast, attitudes relating to religion and social issues are not nearly as important in determining party affiliation."[18] Perhaps most interesting among the typology study's

gender gap A difference in the political opinions of men and women.

U.S.A. Yesterday and Today

Polls of the Past

From a 1939 poll: Which of these do you think is the main thing holding back greater prosperity in this country?

The New Deal
The leaders of business
Labor
Events abroad over which we have no control
Don't know

This question, from the Roper Poll for *Fortune* magazine in 1939, gives a compact view of the main forces in American society and the growing fear of war.

From 1943: During World War II, the War Department conducted many surveys of soldiers. The questions they asked make for an interesting insight into those running and fighting in the war:

In general, how well do you think the army is run?

It is run very well
It is run pretty well
It is not run so well
It is run very poorly
Undecided
No answer

The vast majority responded #1.

What kind of work is needed to win the war? What kind of work would you prefer to do?

I would rather be a soldier
I would rather be a civilian doing some kind of work needed to win the war

Undecided

Most of those surveyed answered #2.

From 1949: As things look now, do you think that within the next two years, at least a moderate depression with considerably more unemployment than we have now is likely or unlikely?

The pollsters provided explicit instructions for the staff: "Read this question slowly and carefully to give the respondent a good chance to understand it all. Obviously, what we are trying to describe is a depression that may be less severe than that of the early 1930s, but still one severe enough to cause a good deal of unemployment."

Source: Roper *Fortune* #75, Security/Insecurity: Optimism/ Pessimism about Country and the Individual, February 28, 1949.

From 2000: Although it would be inaccurate to draw grand conclusions from the subject of one poll, it's interesting to note that among the Roper Center for Public Opinion Research's files is the Law and the Media Survey. The subject matter is not exactly what you'd imagine—no views on journalistic ethics, media influence and law enforcement. Instead it's the intersection of two great twenty-first-century American obsessions, television and crime.

Question: Some shows on television feature police officers and prosecutors such as *NYPD Blue* and *Law and Order*. How often do you watch shows like these . . . ?

Sources: This feature and poll questions are from Bill Moyers at www.pbs.org/now/politics/polling.html.

findings are the significant cleavages that exist within parties. This runs counter to the prevailing notion of a nation divided between two unified party camps.

Along with the emergence of national security issues, the typology reveals that both Democrats and Republicans are currently experiencing a fundamental reevaluation of government—in an era of unified GOP control. This has "produced new alignments within each of the two parties and caused once-relevant groups to disappear. Moreover, religious and social issues continue to divide both within and across party lines, creating challenges to party leaders as they seek to build or maintain their majorities."[19]

AMERICAN POLITICAL CULTURE

Scholars have pored over huge amounts of data on public opinion and built up a picture of the American public's perspectives, or its **political culture**. They have discovered that American political culture is shaped by three key variables: core values, political ideology, and culture and lifestyle.

 **MakeItReal**

Civic Participation: American Political Landscape

political culture A political perspective based on core values, political ideology, culture, and lifestyle.

Quick Review

American Values

- The protection of basic individual rights that ensure freedom.
- The guarantee of equal access to the political system, universal voting rights, and equality under the law.
- The guarantee of equal economic opportunities and economic activity that is free from coercion.

Question for Reflection

How might our democracy change if Americans supported economic equality as strongly as they now support the concepts of free enterprise and a capitalistic economy?

MakeItReal

Visual Literacy: Japanese Internment

Primary Source: The Chinese Exclusion Act (1882)

Primary Source: Dawes Act (1887)

Core Values

At the deepest level, American values are remarkably homogeneous. Surveys reveal broad consensus on the core issues and ideals of government: individual liberty, political equality, and the rule of law. These values ensure the stability of the political system. Support for them is rock solid, in sharp contrast to the vacillating winds of change evident on everyday political issues. The genius of the Constitution rests in its embodiment of these core ideals. The framers wrote them in, recognizing that the Constitution must elicit strong support. Those three basic principles have been held in high esteem by generations of Americans who have sought to approach the democratic ideal.

Perhaps the leading American value is liberty. Central to the function of American government is the protection of basic individual rights that ensure freedom. Americans can, in theory, speak and act as they wish. These rights are legally guaranteed by the Bill of Rights clauses that protect freedom of speech, assembly, and religion. Liberty is also central to the American economic system. Americans overwhelmingly support the concept of a free enterprise, capitalistic economy.

The American belief in equality represents another key American value. Americans place enormous importance on the ideas of *political equality* and formal political rights, seeking to guarantee equal access to the political system, universal voting rights, and equality under the law. Americans do not particularly support *economic equality*, especially if defined as a guarantee of equal economic outcomes. They do, however, support equality of another kind, namely, *equality of opportunity*. Americans have even been willing to use government to achieve this goal—to level the playing field, so to speak. Yet recent years have seen a backlash against affirmative action. Americans want government to guarantee equal economic opportunities and to ensure that economic activity is free from coercion, but they definitely do not want government to guarantee that economic outcomes will be the same for all.

Public support for the Constitution and the democratic institutions it created represents another core American value, although support for this ideal may be weakening. Part of this decrease in confidence derives from a paradox of this era: Americans expect government to provide increasing services in an age of decreasing resources. Americans want lower taxes and blame government for their high tax bills, and yet complain about poor government service. The one government agency insulated from the public's increasing political negativism is the least democratic of all American institutions—the U.S. Supreme Court. Continued respect for that institution illustrates the value we place on the concept of rule of law.

Americans and Intolerance   Is tolerance a core American value? Many Americans believe it is, yet evidence is mixed regarding how open Americans are to a wide range of political viewpoints. Even before the Revolution, American political thinkers and European counterparts such as Tocqueville feared the "tyranny of the majority." They worried that the "inflamed passions" of the majority might sweep away the opinions—and also the fragile liberty—of the minority, thus threatening the very core of American democracy. Think about how mobs in the aftermath of the September 11, 2001, terrorist attacks pursued, attacked, and harassed Arab Americans in this country. In a few cases, innocent people were killed by angry mobs seeking vengeance against someone who looked like Osama Bin Laden.

How valid were the framers' fears? Public opinion data on intolerance gives some credence to anxieties about the tyranny of the majority. Statistically, Americans remain among the least tolerant of all people in industrialized democratic societies. Many Americans remain reluctant to allow those with whom they disagree, or whom they simply dislike, the same liberties and opportunities—including those protected by government institutions. Racism, homophobia, gender discrimination, and fear of foreigners are still powerful forces in American culture. And many Americans still feel reluctant or even afraid to speak out against prevailing majority opinion. How dangerous is this pattern of conformity and intolerance?[20]

◄ In the post–9/11 climate, tolerance and respect for diversity often proved to be elusive. This group had its sign torn down and chose to gather at a New York State thruway exit ramp in order to send their message.

Political scientists studying the consequences of cultural conformity argue that intolerance in America constrains "the freedom available to ordinary citizens." Studies have found, for instance, that blacks are much more likely to feel "unfree" than are whites. Compared with Americans as a whole, African Americans feel less comfortable expressing unpopular opinions and more worried about the power of government, including the police.[21]

Similar studies also reveal a "spiral of silence" and a "spiral of intolerance" in America. Individuals sensing the prevailing opinions of those around them echo those opinions to avoid social ostracism.[22] Their silence has a reinforcing effect. An initial reluctance to express opinions counter to the majority continues in an ever-tightening spiral, with the result that many Americans are pressured into conforming to the dominant opinion, whether they agree with it or not. Public opinion thus becomes a form of social control.

Intolerance does constitute a serious problem, but it need not remain an inevitable feature of American society. Studies show that as socioeconomic status and level of education increase, so does tolerance for conflicting points of view and alternative lifestyles. Perhaps a "spiral of tolerance" will develop in which family, peers, community, and institutions reinforce rather than suppress tolerance. Over the years, programs such as school busing to break down segregation, and affirmative action to ameliorate its negative impact, have attempted to foster socioeconomic and educational improvements that might, in time, reverse the spiral of intolerance. Teaching about diversity (different perspectives) and multiculturalism (different ways of life) represents another attempt to combat intolerance, although this approach is meeting increased resistance in many communities.

Political Ideology

A second set of deep-seated public attitudes makes up our ideology. **Political ideology** is a coherent way of viewing politics and government. Ideological perspectives include beliefs about the military, the role of government, the proper relation between government and the economy, the value of social welfare programs, and the relative importance to society of liberty versus order. Our political ideology provides an overarching frame on which to organize our political beliefs and attitudes.

Ideologies of every kind abound. Each one offers a coherent and unified body of ideas that explain the political process and the goals sought by participants within

political ideology A coherent way of viewing politics and government; ideological perspectives include beliefs about the military, the role of government, the proper relation between government and the economy, the value of social welfare programs, and the relative importance for society of liberty and order.

Approaching Democracy Around the Globe

Poll of 27 Countries: Most Significant Events of 2005 Were Iraq War, Tsunami, U.S. Hurricanes

As 2005 came to an end, a BBC World Service poll asked 32,439 citizens in twenty-seven countries, "In the future, when historians think about the year 2005, what event of global significance do you think will be seen as most important?" The countries surveyed were Afghanistan, Argentina, Australia, Brazil, Canada, Congo (DRC), Finland, France, Germany, Ghana, Great Britain, India, Indonesia, Iraq, Italy, Kenya, Mexico, Philippines, Poland, Russia, Saudi Arabia, South Africa, South Korea, Spain, Sri Lanka, Turkey, and the United States.

The war in Iraq was the most frequently cited event by 15 percent worldwide. It was most prominent among Iraqis (43 percent), but also quite prevalent in South Korea (31 percent), Spain (28 percent), the United States (27 percent), and Turkey (26 percent). Most surprising is that only 9 percent of Britons mentioned the war as the most important event.

The other most widely cited events were the Asian tsunami (15 percent) and the U.S. hurricanes (9 percent). Asia-Pacific countries most focused on the tsunami—Sri Lanka (57 percent), Indonesia (31 percent), Australia (28 percent), South Korea (24 percent) and the Philippines (21 percent). Hurricanes Katrina and Rita were cited by 9 percent worldwide, although were not mentioned as most significant by Americans (15 percent). Larger percentages were found in Afghanistan (18 percent) and Argentina (18 percent).

The poll was conducted for BBC World service by the international polling firm GlobeScan in partnership with the Program on International Policy attitudes (PIPA) at the University of Maryland. Perhaps most interesting in the findings is how similar assessments were across countries. Steven Kull, director of PIPA, observed that "the extent to which people in different countries perceive the same events as significant is a sign of how much the world has become globalized."

Contrary to the image of the United States as unconcerned about global warming (see Chapter 15), 4 percent mentioned it, slightly more than the worldwide average of 3 percent. Finally, and surprisingly, although Americans identified the war in Iraq as one of most important events, (27 percent), other countries, including South Korea (31 percent), Spain (28 percent), and Iraq (43 percent), were higher. The complete poll results and methodology can be found at www.pipa.org.

Source: This feature is based on materials provided in "Poll of 27 Countries: Most Significant Events of 2005 Were Iraq War, Tsunami, US Hurricanes." at www.pipa.org.

---

that process. The most common ideologies among politically aware Americans are liberalism and conservatism. Although these two outlooks capture only part of the American public's diversity of political attitudes, they do serve to categorize most people in the mainstream; they also offer a useful introduction to political differences at the national level.

These terms often are associated with political party affiliations—Democrats with liberalism, and Republicans with conservatism—but they go well beyond party allegiance. They express a political philosophy, a view of human nature and the proper role of government in society. On the whole, liberals support government intervention to minimize economic inequality. They support progressive taxes and minimum wage laws, for example, but oppose government actions that restrict cultural and social freedoms, such as censorship, prayer in school, and restrictions on abortion. Conservatives take precisely the opposite positions.

Political observers have long debated whether or not Americans are becoming more conservative. Many saw Ronald Reagan's success in 1980 and 1984 as a clear signal that the nation had turned to the right. Scholars have questioned this claim, however, by pointing out that although Reagan enjoyed high personal popularity (he left office with 67 percent approval rating), the policies and ideas he advocated throughout his presidency had only limited success and modest public backing. His attempts to cut government, balance the budget, and implement school prayer all failed. On the day Reagan left office, polls showed that although the president remained enormously popular, more and more Americans favored a decrease in military spending and diverting that money to social programs, an outlook directly opposed to Reagan's own.

Still, Reagan's legacy of tax cuts and reforms, a strong military, and a reinvigoration of support for the presidency stands in contrast to his failures. Some believed the 1994 Contract with America signaled renewed support for Reagan's conservative ideals, but by election time in 1996 that tide had ebbed. Today, President George W. Bush champions "compassionate conservatism," which blends Reagan's defense budgets with a commitment to education and welfare reform.

The very terms *liberal* and *conservative* mean little to many Americans, so their voting decisions may not reflect an ideological preference. Indeed, some scholars argue that the real trend of this age is alienation and a general withdrawal from politics. The terms *liberal* and *conservative,* then, may have little more than symbolic meaning to most Americans. At the political-leadership level, these terms work well to define people, but average citizens adopt a variety of political stands covering all points on the political spectrum. How does one categorize, for instance, an individual who favors conservative positions such as deregulation of business and cuts in the capital gains tax, but who also supports the liberal stand of a woman's right to choose an abortion? Many Americans defy easy classification. How can we accurately describe public opinion, then, if ideology proves a weak guide? Moreover, most Americans view themselves as neither liberals nor conservatives, but as moderates. The implication of this self-perception for governing is significant. Given that most voters see themselves in the center of the political spectrum, it should not surprise us that President Clinton, lagging in the polls, positioned himself as a "New Democrat" for the 1996 election—right in the shifting center of American politics. Likewise, it is clear that President Bush based his selection of John G. Roberts Jr. as Chief Justice on the assumption that no one side of the spectrum could view Roberts as an extremist.

Culture and Lifestyle

Culture theory argues that individual preferences emerge from social interaction. A way of life designates a social orientation, a framework of attitudes within which individuals develop preferences based on how they relate to others and to the institutions of power. Recall the earlier discussion of intolerance that indicated that blacks tend to trust government less than whites do and to feel less free to express different opinions. In light of the disproportionately high number of African Americans arrested and imprisoned, the tendency to distrust and even fear government authority seems hardly surprising. This orientation is neither liberal nor conservative; rather, it reflects an outlook on life that might be characterized as suspicion of the law enforcement system and alienation from government in general. This explanation of political attitudes is cultural rather than ideological.[23]

THE STATE OF AMERICAN PUBLIC OPINION

We now have some idea of what lies at the heart of the average American's perspective on political life. But how interested are citizens in politics? How much do they know about politics, and how likely are they to participate? And how do Americans form their opinions on political issues? Polling data helps us answer these and other questions about the current state of American public opinion.

Political Awareness and Involvement

Knowledgeable insiders have often been appalled at the average citizen's poor grasp of public affairs. Respected journalist Walter Lippmann once wrote that the average American "does not know for certain what is going on, or who is doing it, or where he is being carried. . . . He lives in a world which he cannot see, does not understand

culture theory A theory that individual preferences "emerge from social interaction in defending or opposing different ways of life."

and is unable to direct."[24] And scholar Joseph Schumpeter's view of citizens was even more caustic: "The typical citizen drops down to a lower level of mental performance as soon as he enters the political field. He argues and analyzes in a way he would readily recognize as infantile within the sphere of his real interests. He becomes a primitive again."[25] Lippmann and Schumpeter join a host of social scientists who have portrayed American voters as apathetic and poorly informed, their opinions unstable or even irrational.

Polling research from the 1940s and 1950s revealed that Americans knew little about important issues and that they tended to confuse the issue positions of various candidates during campaigns. At the height of the cold war, for instance, many Americans believed that the Soviet Union—the foremost ideological enemy of the United States—was in fact part of the North Atlantic Treaty Organization (NATO), the military alliance to which the United States and its allies belonged. Today, in poll after poll, more than half of Americans fail to make a single correct statement about either major political party, despite both parties having been at the core of American history for more than a century. In tests on knowledge of the Constitution and Bill of Rights, only a few respondents correctly identify the preamble of the Constitution and the contents of the Bill of Rights. Typically, most Americans cannot even identify their own representatives and senators.

The American public indeed falls short of the ideal advocated by democratic theorists—a well-informed citizenry. Their interest in politics is minimal. No more than a third of the electorate ever claims to be seriously active in electoral politics. Even smaller percentages take part in political activities that influence those in power: writing to an elected official, joining a political group, attending a political rally. The general public seems to show little interest in the issues most hotly debated by politicians. Over time, such issues as abortion rights, crime and violence, AIDS, racism, the environment, and arms control have dominated the political agenda of elected officials, party leaders, and interest group activists. During the same period, no more than five percent of the general public ever ranked any of these issues as "the most important problem" facing the nation. Even when issues do catch the public's attention, citizens do not always assign them the same importance and commitment as do political activists. For example, America's concern with drugs, although significant, skyrocketed briefly after former President George Bush's declaration of a "war on drugs," only to drop to relatively low levels within a matter of months. The public's interest in economic issues such as the deficit, unemployment, and the general health of the economy is similarly unstable, mirroring the ebbs and flows of the business cycle. Until September 11, 2001, surveys found that college freshmen were less interested in politics and participated less than any group of freshmen in the previous three decades. One of the great paradoxes of democracy was that the information age had produced a relatively indifferent and apathetic group of young people.

Some scholars counter this image of the ignorant, apathetic citizen by asserting that American people are generally well informed and that their opinions are as sensible as those of their leaders. These scholars see the public as more rational than many observers are willing to concede, arguing that, although Americans may not know all the names of political people and places or the intricate details of every issue of the day, they do recognize and rationally distinguish between the alternatives presented to them, especially when they step into the voting booth. In *The Rational Public*, political scientists Ben Page and Robert Shapiro find that "public opinion as a collective phenomena is stable, meaningful, rational and able to distinguish between good and bad."[26] Indeed, surveys show that when presented with a list of names, rather than having to rely on their own recall of such names, most Americans can accurately identify their regional and national leaders.

Nonetheless, scholars continue to debate if average citizens are politically informed and involved enough to make democracy work. We cannot supply a definitive answer here. Certainly few Americans live up to the ideal image of the fully informed citizen, ever alert, and deeply involved in the political process. Still, most citizens may be informed enough to make simple decisions on the few options presented to them on election day. Besides, the American system has built-in safeguards in case citizens, for lack of information or other reasons, make a poor decision. If people elect a candidate or party they come to dislike, they can "turn the rascals out" at the next election. And no matter who is elected, no position within the U.S. government carries overwhelming power, and all positions are checked by other positions and institutions. Given this system of multiple checks and frequent elections, the American public may well be sufficiently informed to keep the system working and reasonably democratic.

How Are Political Opinions Formed?

If people know little about politics and have little interest in it, how is it that they develop seemingly strong opinions on various political issues? How do they know for whom to vote on election day? The answer is surprising. Average citizens develop broad orientations toward their world, including ways of thinking about politics, based on their entire set of life experiences. They then use these broad intellectual frameworks as shortcuts for processing new information.

These intellectual frameworks for evaluating the world, often called **schemas**, act as efficient filters or cues. When people encounter new issues or ideas, they frequently lack the time or energy to study them in detail. It is simpler just to fit them into a preexisting perspective. Studies show, for instance, that Americans know nothing about the actual level of spending for foreign aid, nor do they have any idea which countries receive most U.S. foreign aid; nevertheless, they remain convinced that the United States spends too much abroad. That's because they have already developed a general orientation (opposition to government spending and fear or distrust of non-Americans, perhaps) that allows them to take a stand on foreign aid while knowing almost nothing about the subject.

As this example suggests, facts are often irrelevant in the development of opinions. Changing a deeply ingrained set of beliefs is psychologically painful. That's why people often avoid facts and resort to preexisting schemas. These schemas allow individuals to sift and categorize new information, so that it can be made "safe"—that is, congruent with an existing framework of attitudes. People ignore or explain away evidence that would undermine their carefully constructed world views.

Party Identification as a Schema   Despite the declining number of Americans who identify with one of the major parties, **party identification** remains the strongest predictor of an individual's political behavior. Partisan identification provides a cue that individuals use to evaluate candidates and acts as a filter through which individuals view the political world. These party ties represent one of the most enduring of all political attitudes Americans hold. However, even this apparently stable indicator of opinion can change over time or under the impact of dramatic events.

A broad-based change in partisanship is known as **realignment**. In a period of realignment, large groups of people shift allegiance from one party to another.[27] A realignment occurred in the 1932 election, when many people took their support—and their votes—from the Republican to the Democratic party. The resulting New Deal coalition was a strong electoral force that kept Democrats the majority party for decades. However, recent evidence suggests that grand realignments of this kind are rare. A more useful approach to understanding shifts in partisan identification suggests that a gradual, continual process is taking place through generational replacement. Specifically, this theory suggests that as a new generation reaches maturity and becomes involved in the political process, it will have been socialized around a set of values and issues different from those of the parent and grandparent generations. As each new generation becomes a larger

schemas Intellectual frameworks for evaluating the world.

party identification A psychological orientation, or long-term propensity to think positively of and vote regularly for, a particular political party.

realignment A shift in fundamental party identification and loyalty caused by significant historical events or national crises.

segment of the electorate, it replaces older generations and produces shifts in the identification of certain groups within the party around the new issues and values (see Figure 8.4).

Partisan identification and general political orientation can also change across generations. Several studies revealed a sharp decline of support for and trust in the institutions and actors of government following the Vietnam War and the Watergate

	2000		2002		2004		2004
	REP.	DEM.	REP.	DEM.	REP.	DEM.	N
	%	%	%	%	%	%	
Total	28	33	30	31	30	33	29,092
Men	30	28	32	27	31	29	13,699
Women	26	38	29	35	28	37	15,393
White	32	29	35	27	34	29	23,828
Black	6	65	6	63	6	63	3,005
Hispanic	21	42	22	36	20	40	1,915
Conservative	49	23	50	22	51	22	10,908
Moderate	21	39	24	35	22	36	11,289
Liberal	9	52	9	47	8	51	5,365
18-29	25	30	27	27	25	29	4,855
30-49	29	32	32	30	31	32	10,869
50-64	28	35	30	33	29	35	7,313
65+	30	40	32	38	32	40	5,642
<H.S. grad	19	39	20	36	21	40	2,304
H.S. grad	26	34	29	32	28	33	8,355
Some college	31	32	34	30	32	31	8,106
Coll. grad+	34	30	36	29	33	32	10,178
White Catholic	29	34	32	30	31	32	4,934
White Protestant	39	27	42	24	41	26	12,490
Evangelical	43	26	47	23	49	22	6,313
Mainline	34	29	35	27	32	29	6,177
Jewish	16	52	18	51	17	55	561
No religion	16	28	16	27	15	31	2,751
<$20,000	19	43	20	39	19	42	4,384
$20,000–$30,000	26	37	26	35	24	37	3,281
$30,000–$50,000	29	34	31	32	30	34	6,155
$50,000–$75,000	34	31	35	29	36	29	4,421
$75,000+	37	27	39	27	38	29	6,768

Figure 8.4   Party Identification Trend, By Demographic Groups

scandal. At that time pollsters began to track a decline in partisan identification, the rise of political *independents*—people declaring no allegiance to either party—and a growing suspicion of government in general.

Even with periodic realignments and generational change, political partisanship remains the most stable indicator of political preference. It is not, of course, the only schema to affect people's political thinking. Others include ideology, ethnic consciousness, and regional identification. And people occasionally change their minds or ignore "the party line" when it comes to specific issues, events, and actors. Nevertheless, to understand how any citizen feels about a host of political matters, begin by learning that individual's partisan allegiance.

Stability and Change in Public Opinion

Though many of our opinions remain stable over long periods others do change. Many scholars believe that people are flighty and changeable; others point to the deep-seated, long-lasting nature of our opinions. To understand this difference in perspective, it helps to look at three factors: intensity, latency, and salience.

Intensity Opinions are not all equal. People feel some things more intensely than others, and that affects the strength and durability of their opinions. **Intensity** is a measure of the depth of feeling associated with a given opinion. It affects the way people organize their beliefs and express their opinions on a wide variety of issues. Some react most intensely to the issue of a woman's right to choose an abortion; others express their most intense political sentiments for or against gun control. Try visiting a local senior center and suggest cutting Social Security benefits! On

intensity In public opinion, a measure of the depth of feeling associated with a given opinion.

Quick Review

Change in Public Opinion

- Intensity is a measure of the depth of feeling associated with a given opinion.
- Latency describes feelings that are hidden or unspoken, suggesting the *potential* for an opinion or behavior, but only when the right circumstances occur.
- Salience is the extent to which people see an issue as having a clear impact on their own lives. Salient issues stir up interest and participation.

◀ The World Economic Forum is an independent international organization committed to improving the state of the world. The Forum provides a collaborative framework for the world's leaders to address global issues, engaging particularly its corporate members in global citizenship. In February 2002 the International A.N.S.W.E.R. (Act Now to Stop War and End Racism) coalition called a teach-in and street demonstrations in New York City coinciding with the meeting of the Forum at the Waldorf-Astoria Hotel. These demonstrators displayed their concerns dressed as Lady Liberty.

the other hand, try getting just about anyone to speak out on soybean subsidies. Some issues elicit more intense reaction than others.

Issues that provoke intense feelings are often called *hot-button issues,* because they strike a nerve, a "hot button" that can elicit strong reactions and affect voting choices. In the 2000 election, abortion was just such an issue. The more intensely an opinion is felt, the more likely it is to endure and to influence policy decisions. Thus, we can assume that attitudes about race (a subject most Americans have intense opinions about) will not change much over the next decade or two. Attitudes about U.S. foreign policy toward Belize, on the other hand, could prove extremely volatile. Few Americans hold intense feelings about Belize, so short-term events (a communist takeover) or the sudden pronouncements of respected American leaders ("Let's help Belize, our democratic neighbor to the south") could dramatically affect how Americans feel about that nation.

Latency   Public opinion is not always explicit. **Latency** describes feelings that are hidden or unspoken, suggesting the *potential* for an opinion or behavior, but only when the right circumstances occur. Ross Perot's bid for the presidency in 1996 unleashed an avalanche of latent feeling. The American public's long-standing but often dormant distrust of government and politicians—and its admiration for successful entrepreneurs—leapt to the fore following a series of scandals, a sagging economy, and a burgeoning federal budget deficit. Those latent opinions gave Perot the highest third-party vote since Theodore Roosevelt in 1912, even though Perot withdrew and then reentered the race.

Salience is the extent to which people see an issue as having a clear impact on their own lives. Salient issues stir up interest and participation. Proposition 209, which banned affirmative action programs in California, is an example. Similarly, the issue of base closings is more salient to residents of states such as California, where local, regional, and state economies rely on the proximity of military bases or lucrative contracts for the production of military hardware. Politicians decrying base closures might garner a strong following in California but be ignored in Chicago, where the issue lacks salience. To understand public opinion and how that opinion will affect citizen actions, one must know how salient a given issue is to a given population.

How Changeable Is Public Opinion?

Some research findings have suggested that individual political opinions are not firmly held.[28] When respondents are asked the same questions again and again over relatively brief periods, their responses tend to vary and even to contradict earlier responses. Does this indicate that we tend to offer random, meaningless answers when asked our opinions? Many scholars see this pattern as proving the "irrationality" of the American voter. However, much of the apparent irrationality may actually stem from faulty polling methods. When the same question is asked differently, or when questions are worded vaguely, respondents are more likely to change their answers. This does not so much suggest irrationality as indicate that people are trying to make the best sense of what they are asked, even when questions are difficult to understand. On the other hand, when researchers phrase questions so that they contain the information necessary to formulate firm opinions, results show that individuals actually do have stable, "rational" opinions. Although Americans may not be particularly intimate with political specifics, they nonetheless harbor enduring and meaningful political beliefs. It is up to the pollster to find the best way to elicit these opinions.

Yet we do know that people's opinions sometimes change. Changing circumstances trigger corresponding changes in public opinion. As incomes rise, so does support for shorter workweeks, higher minimum wages, and increasing expenditure for workplace safety and environmental protection. As more women join the workforce, more calls emerge for women's rights. And awareness of rising crime produces a demand for tougher laws and more police officers in the street. Sudden events can

latency In public opinion, unspoken feelings, suggesting the potential for an attitude or behavior, but only when the right circumstances occur.

salience In public opinion, the extent to which people see an issue as having a clear impact on their own lives.

also cause a change in opinions. In time of national crisis, Americans are likely to feel more patriotic, to "rally around the flag" and the president; they are also likely to lower their levels of criticism of the government and national leadership.

Although Americans appear to respond in an almost knee-jerk fashion to appeals from popular figures or to images presented in the media, it's unwise to overestimate the malleability of public opinion. On many issues Americans maintain a deep-seated set of attitudes that they don't want to change, making them a "tough sell" when leaders solicit approval for unpopular actions.

FROM PUBLIC OPINION TO PUBLIC POLICY

Public opinion is a crucial element in the political process. It can dramatically affect both the government policies and government's legitimacy in the mind of the people. After all, the ultimate test of a democracy comes down to this: Do government actions, over the long run, reflect what citizens want?

At first glance, we are struck by a significant gap between what Americans say they want and what their leaders are doing. The United States would be quite a different place if public opinion set public policy. Over the years, polls have shown consistent support for proposals that American political leaders do little to implement. For instance, the following policies would all have been in force today if American public opinion were translated into the law of the land.

- Individuals would have the "right to die."
- Members of Congress would be limited to twelve years in office, and term limits would be placed on most other political offices as well.
- Stricter limits would be imposed on campaign spending.
- The death penalty would consistently be imposed for murder.
- Prayer would be permitted in public schools.
- Financial aid to other nations would be severely curtailed.
- Most affirmative action programs would be banned.
- Trigger locks would be installed on most handguns.

Why hasn't American public policy reflected these majority preferences? Translating the public will into public policy within a complex framework of divided powers takes time—often a good deal of time. Further slowing down the entire process is the Constitution framers' persistent view that the "common will" of the people does not always stand for the "common good" of society.

How well has the U.S. government reflected its people's will over the past few decades? Has the United States approached democracy, in the sense that government is doing Americans' bidding? There are no easy answers to these questions. Clearly, American government policy does not always reflect popular desires. But a perfect reflection of popular desires is surely beyond the capability of any government. Some aspects of the public will are simply unrealistic ("more services, lower taxes!"). Others are opposed by most political actors because they contradict the spirit of the Constitution. For example, a constitutional amendment allowing school prayer in public schools has been widely popular but until recently was opposed by most decision makers.

On many issues we find government policies reasonably close to the general direction of public opinion. The United States has been an activist world power in accordance with, not in opposition to, the will of the American people. Laws and policies designed to ensure gender equality have gradually been implemented as public attitudes shifted to favor them. Tough crime laws have increased in response to growing demands on government officials to "do something" about alarming crime rates. On the whole, if a significant majority of the American people indicate over time that they believe government should act in a particular manner, chances are good to excellent that government will accede to those wishes. For that reason, Americans remain loyal to their democratic political system.

Summary

1. Public opinion is the collective expression of attitudes about the prominent issues and actors of the day. Discovering and publicizing the public's opinion has become a key political activity in modern democracies.

2. Political polling began in the mid-1800s with informal straw polls. These failed to obtain a representative sample of the population, which must be chosen through random sampling. In a random sample, every member of the population must have an equal chance of appearing in the sample. Efforts must be made to avoid sampling bias, in which particular population subsets are over- or underrepresented in the sample.

3. Political socialization refers to the process by which we learn about the world of politics and develop our political beliefs. It begins early in childhood, starting with the family. Children tend to adopt their parents' party loyalties and, to some extent, their political ideology. Political socialization continues in school, where children learn about citizenship, and in college, where students may modify their political ideology. Other important sources of political socialization are peers and the mass media.

4. Numerous social variables influence opinion formation. They include social class as represented by income and educational level, race and ethnicity, religious differences, region and place of residence, and gender.

5. The leading core values of Americans are liberty and equality. Although Americans generally are untroubled by economic inequality, they do support equality of opportunity. Another important value is rule of law. Americans are much less tolerant than citizens of other industrialized democratic societies; intolerance is expressed in the form of racism, homophobia, gender discrimination, and fear of foreigners.

6. The most common ideologies among politically aware Americans are liberalism and conservatism. In general, liberals support government intervention to minimize economic inequality but oppose government actions that restrict cultural and social freedoms; conservatives take the opposite positions.

7. Culture theory argues that culture and lifestyle create a framework of attitudes within which individuals develop preferences. Lifestyle orientations explain more about political behavior than do ideological preferences.

8. Political opinions appear to be based on schemas—broad orientations toward the world based on previous life experiences. Schemas serve as cues for judging new issues or ideas. Among the strongest schemas is political partisanship. Even with periodic realignments and generational change, political partisanship remains the most stable indicator of political preference.

9. Intensity is a measure of the depth of feeling associated with a given opinion; issues that provoke intense feeling are often called hot-button issues. In contrast, latent feelings are unspoken, suggesting the potential for an opinion under the right circumstances. Whether an opinion is intense, latent, or nonexistent depends on the salience of the issue, that is, the extent to which people see it as having a clear impact on their lives.

10. The media's portrayal of events and actors can significantly influence public opinion.

Review Questions

1. Why did the framers of the American Constitution fear public opinion? Should we fear public opinion today for the same or for different reasons?

2. What role do you think the Internet will play in political socialization?

3. How can question wording lead to unreliable results? What else can lead to unreliable poll results?

4. What types of issues are likely to produce a gender gap? Why?

5. What are exit polls? What key role did they play in the Bush–Gore 2000 race?

6. What do public opinion polls reveal about the attitudes younger Americans have toward government since 9/11?

Key Terms

Suggested Readings

ASHER, HERBERT. *Polling and the Public.* Washington, D.C.: Congressional Quarterly Press, 1988. An explanation of the meaning and methods of public opinion research, using contemporary examples.

BERINSKY, ADAM. *Silent Voices: Public Opinion and Political Participation in America.* Princeton, N.J.: Princeton University Press, 2004. An excellent analysis of how polls are flawed by exclusion bias to a sizeable portion of the public.

BISHOP, GEORGE. *The Illusion of Public Opinion: Fact and Artifact in American Public Opinion Polls.* Lanham, Md.: Rowman & Littlefield, 2004. A detailed analysis of how particular wording and order of questions influences respondent's answers and how certain questions lead respondents to make up answers.

ERIKSON, ROBERT S., NORMAN R. LUTTBEG, and KENT L. TEDIN. *American Public Opinion: Its Origins, Content, and Impact.* 4th ed. New York: Macmillan, 1991. A comprehensive overview of major aspects of American public opinion, including opinion formation, opinion distribution within society, and the influence of public opinion on public policy.

GINSBERG, BENJAMIN. *The Captive Public: How Mass Opinion Promotes State Power.* New York: Basic Books, 1986. An examination of the thesis that public opinion, as it becomes a more prominent force in American politics, actually enhances the power of American government over its citizens.

GROSSMAN, LAWRENCE K. *The Electronic Republic: Reshaping Democracy in the Information Age.* New York: Viking, 1995. An examination of changes in our democratic political system that have shrunk the distance between the governed and those who govern.

HUNTINGTON, SAMUEL. *Who Are We: The Challenges to America's National Identity.* New York: Simon & Schuster, 2004. A discussion on the nature and role of Anglo-Protestant values and culture with specific reference to the values and behaviors of Latin American immigrants.

PAGE, BENJAMIN I., and ROBERT Y. SHAPIRO. *The Rational Public: Fifty Years of Trends in America's Policy Preferences.* Chicago: University of Chicago Press, 1992. A challenge to the assumption that American public opinion is "irrational" based on data revealing relatively steady public preferences over time, changing only under logical circumstances.

STIMSON, JAMES A. *Public Opinion in America.* Boulder, Colo.: Westview Press, 1991. A major study of public opinion research and its link with major issues in American politics.

★ CHAPTER 9 ★

POLITICAL PARTIES

CHAPTER OUTLINE

Approaching Democracy

Evangelicals and the 2004 Election

When the Reverend Rod Parsley, an evangelical Christian minister and senior pastor of the World Harvest Church in Ohio, titled his new book *Silent No More* he was speaking for the entire conservative Christian movement and its role in the political party structure. The manner that both major political parties choose to deal with the newly vocal population of evangelical Christians will dictate their success in future national elections.

In the 2004 election, the evangelical Christian movement succeeded in placing anti-gay marriage initiatives on eleven state ballots, and all of them passed. So many conservative voters turned out for the elections that a CNN exit poll found that "moral values" was the deciding issue for the presidential vote of 22 percent of the electorate. This was the most popular choice of issues, leading economy/jobs (20 percent), terrorism (19 percent), and Iraq (15 percent).

Since 80 percent of the voters who chose "moral values"—issues related to gay marriage, abortion, government and religion, and government funding for stem-cell research—voted for President Bush, the election turned on these issues. Based on their pre-election polling data, President Bush's advisers believed that to win he would need to attract four million more evangelical voters than he did four years before. He did that and more: He won 79 percent of the 26.5 million evangelical voters and 52 percent of the 31 million Catholic voters.

While a debate later raged as to whether moral values did in fact tip the presidential election nationally, with some saying that the major issues were partisanship and the economy, none doubted the effect of the evangelical movement in Ohio, the most crucial battleground state. President Bush won Ohio by less than 120,000 votes, and fully 25 percent of the vote came from evangelical Christians.

Evangelical Christians considered this a significant victory, following a campaign that differed from those in the past. Throughout the 1970s and 1980s, evangelicals were organized into major groups such as the Moral Majority or the Christian Coalition. The 2004 election produced more of a grassroots effort, with leadership coming from individual evangelical churches. Large constellations of churches led by nationally oriented ministers and pastors included Reverend Ted Haggard's National Association of Evangelicals, Reverend James Dobson's Focus on the Family, former Louisiana state legislator Tony Perkins's Family Research Council, and Reverend Richard Land's Southern Baptist Convention with its sixteen million registered members. However, most voters responded to grassroots efforts—sermons from ministers and educational literature provided in churches and on the Web—encouraging them to register and vote on their cultural values. Throughout the campaign, officials such as Karl Rove kept in close touch with religious leaders.

★ Dr. James Dobson, the leader of the evangelical Christian group "Focus on the Family" and a Christian radio talk show host, is seen by many as one of the main leaders of the religious right in its quest for political power in promoting "family values."

The question remained as to how these groups would use their newfound power. Many also demanded that President Bush appoint an ultraconservative Supreme Court justice at the earliest opportunity. They pushed for passage of a constitutional amendment banning gay marriage, continued ban of government funding for stem-cell research, laws against euthanasia, government funding of religious education in public and private schools, and teaching "intelligent design" alongside or in place of evolutionary biology. Many saw President Bush's endorsement of the "intelligent design" theory in mid-2005 as an effort to appeal to these voters in the future.

These tens of millions of religious voters represent the tipping point in an evenly balanced electorate for future presidential elections. The challenge for Republicans is to make sure these groups do not sit out future elections, as they did in 1992 and 1996. On the other hand, if Republican candidates move far to the right on cultural issues, it may well cost them significant numbers of moderate voters. For their part, the Democratic party must figure out an electoral strategy that will appeal to these voters in 2006 and beyond. Senator Hillary Rodham Clinton (D.-NY), an expected 2008 presidential candidate, has begun taking more and more conservative positions. The Democrats have also tried to moderate their stance on social issues. During the 2005 confirmation hearings for Chief Justice John Roberts, the Democrats distanced themselves from a harsh NARAL ad that claimed that Roberts once supported violent protests at abortion clinics. Meanwhile, right-wing conservatives aligned solidly behind Roberts's nomination. That support, together with his skilled performance in the Senate Judiciary Committee hearings, ensured his confirmation. President Bush's second nominee to the Court, Harriet Miers, did not have the same easy road toward confirmation. Although Reverend Dobson and a few other evangelical leaders initially supported her appointment, a great many other right-wing groups allied against her, creating Web sites opposing her confirmation. As a result, when it became clear that conservative groups would not support her in the Senate Judiciary Committee hearings, Miers withdrew her nomination and resumed her White House duties, and Judge Samuel Alito was nominated and confirmed to replace Justice O'Connor.[1]

★ Pro-life activists stage their own counter-protest, while hundreds of thousands of pro-abortion members in the annual January March for Women's Lives Rally fill the Washington Mall in Washington D.C.

QUESTION FOR REFLECTION

What challenges might be posed to American democracy when religious leaders take such an active role in political lobbying and election activities?

313

Introduction
POLITICAL PARTIES AND DEMOCRACY

MakeItReal

Simulation: The Political Horizon, Parts I and II

A s the evangelical Christian vote in the last presidential election shows, the balance of powers among political parties lies at the heart of democracy, representing the crucial link between what citizens want and what government does.[2] That is why parties must continually change, adapt, and adjust to the popular forces of their time. They must stay in touch with the voters—from whom they derive their support and power—so that they can gain control of government and the policy-making process. Competitive and democratic political parties allow a wide range of groups to enter peacefully into politics that might otherwise have to turn to illegitimate measures to gain their ends.

Political parties are a relatively new phenomenon, nonexistent until less than two hundred years ago. Charlemagne needed no party nomination before heading the Holy Roman Empire. Parties did not vie for power under Henry VIII. The framers did not even mention political parties in the U.S. Constitution. Parties played little role in history because the general public played little role in the political process. For most of human history, politics was a game for elites. It consisted of power struggles among a small inner circle of leaders, people trying to become rulers or currying favor with those in power. Broad-based political parties began to form with eighteenth-century attempts to implement political equality, when the number of people participating in the governing process began to grow. Parties became helpful in organizing the legislative factions and in finding effective ways to seek power and influence. Today, political parties are massive, complex institutions, incorporating large numbers of citizens into the political process. By their very nature, parties are forces of democratization.

Political parties, then, are nongovernmental institutions that organize and give direction to mass political desires. They bring together people who think alike or who have common interests to work toward common goals. The clearest goal of any political group is power to control government and thus implement its policy preferences. In an age of mass participation, power goes to those elites who can connect with the masses. Today, the Democratic and Republican parties appear to frequently have trouble making that connection.

In this chapter we look at party history, as well as at the functions, development, role, and future of American political parties. First, let's look at the history of American parties to see how the development of democracy is inextricably tied to the activity of political parties.

A BRIEF HISTORY OF THE AMERICAN PARTY SYSTEM

Many of the framers, beginning with George Washington, feared the development of a political party system. James Madison, the strongest influence on the Constitution's final shape, saw them as a direct threat to the common good because their promotion of specialized interests would subvert the general welfare.

Despite the framers' fears, political parties quickly developed in the United States and by 1800 were already playing a major role in elections and governance. A party system began to emerge during the divisive and continuing debate between Alexander Hamilton, President Washington's secretary of the treasury, and Thomas Jefferson, his secretary of state. Hamilton, a supporter of a strong federal government, argued for a manufacturing sector that would allow the United States to become a wealthy and self-sufficient trading partner in the world economy. A strong

political parties Organizations that exist to allow like-minded members of the population to group together and magnify their individual voices into a focus promoting individual candidates and government action.

federal government would have a national bank with sufficient power to borrow and spend money, develop international agreements, and protect the domestic economy. Conversely, Jefferson wished to see a United States that remained largely rural. He envisioned a nation that retained its republican roots built upon a large working, agrarian class. These two visions for the country divided other leaders and the general public into *factions*—"the spirit of party" the framers had feared.

In the first few years of the republic, many of the framers denounced party divisions. Hamilton, for instance, declared that a faction dominated by Madison and Jefferson was "decidedly hostile to me and my administration . . . and dangerous to the union, peace and happiness of the country."[3] George Washington warned "in the most solemn manner against the harmful effects of the spirit of party." This spirit, he asserted, demands "uniform vigilance to prevent its bursting into a flame." Washington's cautionary remarks about political parties may seem extreme by today's standards, but he was surely correct when he said that the "spirit of party" was "a fire not to be quenched."[4] Although the U.S. party system has undergone many changes, political partisanship has remained from his day to ours.

Scholars have identified five historical eras in which party influence, allegiance, and control have changed. These eras always begin with a party **realignment**, in which significant historical events or national crises cause a shift in fundamental party identification and loyalty. Realignments are the result of a change in public attitudes about the political system and the ability of each party to deliver favorable candidates and policies. They usher in new eras, which tend to be stable and lengthy in duration.[5]

The First Party System (1790s–1820s)

The Federalists, followers of John Adams and Alexander Hamilton, and the Republicans, led by Jefferson (also called the Jeffersonian Republicans and later the Democratic-Republicans), represented two competing groups. As such, they constituted America's first parties. Today's Democratic party, the direct descendant of Jefferson's party, is the oldest political party in the world. This party originally sided with rural and small-town forces in the struggle between promoters of agriculture and promoters of manufacturing. Its followers resisted the trend toward nationalization of power. They promoted Jefferson's belief that a nation of small property owners represents the best society, one likely to be virtuous and egalitarian.

The elections of 1789 and 1792 went smoothly, since parties had yet to be formally established. On the first Wednesday of February in 1789, the newly established electoral college chose George Washington as the nation's first president. Washington was easily reelected in 1792. With his departure from the political scene after his second term, however, political tensions emerged as distinct factions.

Federalist John Adams and Democratic-Republican Thomas Jefferson opposed each other in the closely contested elections of 1796 and 1800. Adams barely won the initial contest, but Jefferson triumphed in the rematch in 1800. The pivotal 1800 election became known as the **Revolution of 1800**, because it was the first time anywhere in the world that the ruling elite in a nation changed without a death or a revolution and the loser left office voluntarily. But this election also illustrated how the party system affected the electoral system. All of the Jeffersonian party electors in the electoral college followed their instructions and voted for both Jefferson and his running mate, Aaron Burr, causing a tie and throwing the decision into the House of Representatives. Fears of further intrigue and deals that might overturn the will of the electorate, produced the Twelfth Amendment, which mandated separate votes for the presidency and the vice presidency.

With Jeffersonians clearly dominating after Jefferson's reelection in 1804, Federalist support rapidly declined, and following the War of 1812, the party fell apart. In fact, during the presidency of James Monroe (1817–25), distinctions between the two parties disappeared. This so-called "Era of Good Feelings" was characterized by a lack of divisive issues and the rapid recovery of the American economy.

realignment A shift in fundamental party identification and loyalty caused by significant historical events or national crises.

Revolution of 1800 The first election in world history in which one party (the Federalist party of John Adams) willingly gave up power because of a lost election to another party (the Republican party of Thomas Jefferson) without bloodshed.

Questions for Reflection

What do you think would be the impact on the current U.S. government and economy if the distinctions between the two parties suddenly disappeared?

Would the result warrant the label "Era of Good Feelings"?

"King Caucus" The process of selecting candidates for president in the early nineteenth century in which the members of each party's delegation in Congress did the nominating.

Table 9.1 ■ Results of the Presidential Election of 1824

Candidate	Popular Votes		Electoral College Votes	
	Number	Percent	Number	Percent
Jackson	155,872	42.2	99	37.9
Adams	105,321	31.9	84	32.2
Crawford	44,282	12.9	41	15.7
Clay	46,587	13.0	37	14.2

The election of 1824 was the first in which popular votes were counted and the last to be settled by the House of Representatives. Four regional candidates could produce no electoral college winner (see Table 9.1). To become president took more than winning the most electoral college votes—as Andrew Jackson clearly did in this election. According to the Constitution, a candidate must win a *majority* (more than 50 percent) of those electoral college votes; otherwise, the U.S. House of Representatives chooses from among the top three contenders. The winner and eventual president must receive a majority of state delegations, that is, thirteen out of twenty-four states in Jackson's day, and twenty-six out of fifty states in our time. Jackson won only 37.9 percent of the electoral college vote (more than anyone else, but short of a majority); therefore, the election went to the House of Representatives for resolution.

Jackson found his popularity with the public did not help him there, where he was viewed as a political outsider and demagogue. Henry Clay—Jackson's weakest election rival but a power in the House, where he served as speaker—threw his support behind the second-place candidate, John Quincy Adams. Clay's influence gave Adams his thirteen states, making him president by the slimmest of margins. In return, Adams named Clay secretary of state. This "deal" came to be widely resented in the nation at large, a fact Jackson exploited as he continued to campaign for president over the next four years. Adams soon proved an unpopular leader. A National Republican who favored major increases in the power of the federal government to encourage domestic economic development, he met tremendous opposition in Congress and thereby contributed to the rebirth of the two-party system (see Figure 9.1).[6]

The Second Party System (1820s–1850s)

After having the election of 1824 "stolen" from them, Jackson's outraged followers organized to take power in the next election. Their grassroots activism, under the energetic leadership of Jackson himself, reenergized the old Jeffersonian party and sent it forth in the modern format of the populist Jacksonian Democrats. Formalized by Jackson's presidential victory in 1828, the Jacksonian Democrats sought to revive Jefferson's egalitarian principles. The party drew support from urban workers, westerners, and southern nonslaveholders.

Symbolic of this new democratic spirit, in 1832 the party chose Jackson as a second-term presidential candidate at a national convention in which delegates, chosen by local party members throughout the country, selected a candidate by a two-thirds vote, adopted a statement of party principles, and generated party spirit. This nomination differed from the old system of nomination by a small group of national legislative leaders, known as the "**King Caucus**."

When President Jackson sought to dismantle the national bank, business interests joined with slaveholding southerners

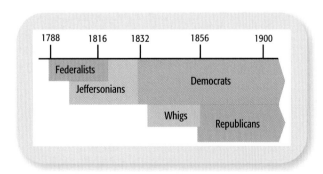

Figure 9.1   The Five Major American Political Parties
Five political parties have achieved a successful and competitive role in American politics. The Democrats and the Republicans have succeeded over the last 150 years where others have failed.

to form the Whig party. Much like the Hamiltonian Federalists, Whigs supported an active federal government. Their ranks included Senators Henry Clay and Daniel Webster and Illinois lawyer Abraham Lincoln. This was an era of real two-party competition, with each party capturing a significant portion of political offices. The Whigs were particularly successful in winning congressional elections. Ultimately, the Civil War and the issues of slavery and the nature of the Union would lead to the disintegration of this second party system.

primary system The system of nominating candidates in which voters in the state make the choice by casting ballots.

The Third Party System (1850s–1890s)

Slavery splintered not only the party system, but American society as well. The Supreme Court's Dred Scott decision established that a slave who resides in a free state or territory is still a slave. Denying African Americans the rights of citizenship added fuel to the fire, as did acrimonious congressional debates over the spread of slavery and actual clashes between proslavery and antislavery forces in the new western territories. Northerners, progressive whites, and many of those settling in the West, along with activists from former minor parties such as the Liberty and Free Soil parties, came together in 1854 to form the Republican party, dedicated to abolishing slavery.

Lincoln, elected president in 1860 as part of this new political alignment, came to the Republican party from the Whigs. He and other Republican leaders developed policy platforms that stressed issues of moral conscience more than had previous political parties. The Whigs dropped from sight, while the Democratic party, weakened by its connection to the losing Confederate cause, kept its base in the South and Midwest, primarily among agricultural, rural voters. The Republican party dominated national politics until the 1890s by winning six consecutive presidential elections (1860–84). Grover Cleveland, in the close elections of 1884 and 1892, was the lone Democrat to capture presidential office in this period. Critics at the time charged that Democratic nominations were being made by middle-aged, cigar-chewing, white male party bosses, wheeling and dealing in "smoke-filled back rooms."

The Fourth Party System (1896–1932)

The late nineteenth and twentieth centuries are frequently characterized as a time of party government. Democratic and Republican parties became highly developed and well organized, attracting a loyal body of voters. The huge influx of immigrants helped change the shape of domestic politics, leading to the growth of urban party "machines" and creating long-term alliances between various ethnic groups and political parties.

The Democrats lost ground over an 1893 economic depression during Democrat Grover Cleveland's presidency. Already the stronger party, Republicans in 1896 held off the combined challenge of the Populists and Democrats, both of whom nominated "the Silver-Tongued Orator," William Jennings Bryan, for president. Republican William McKinley's victory ended the Populist party and solidified a fundamental and long-term shift in Democratic and Republican constituencies. Republicans consolidated their control of the North and West, while Democrats continued to control the South.

Certain Populist issues found support among the Progressives, reformers from both parties who argued that the process of nominating candidates should be shifted from the leaders in the "smoke-filled rooms" to the voters. Although some states did adopt a **primary system**, and hold elections to nominate candidates, not enough of them did so to dictate the outcome of the process. Between 1896 and 1932, only one Democrat, Woodrow Wilson (1913–21), became president. Economic expansion, industrialization, immigration, and the United States' emerging status as a world power brought great prosperity in the early decades of the twentieth century. However, Republican domination ended abruptly in 1932, as the Great Depression brought the next realignment in party identification and power.[7]

▲ William Jennings Bryan, the "boy orator of the Platte," delivered his classic "Cross of Gold" speech in 1896 about the harm the monetary system did to farmers. His loss to William McKinley in 1896 ushered in a new period of Republican control of the White House.

The Fifth Party System (1932–1968)

By the summer of 1932, the Great Depression had left millions without work or economic relief. The incumbent president, Republican Herbert Hoover, did his best to assure a frightened American citizenry that prosperity was forthcoming; people just had to trust his leadership. Hoover clung relentlessly to faith in the gold standard, the need for a balanced budget, and no government handouts. Meanwhile, New York governor Franklin Delano Roosevelt accepted the Democratic party's nomination for president claiming, "I pledge you, I pledge myself, to a new deal for the American people."

On November 8, 1932, Governor Roosevelt defeated President Hoover. "A frightened people," wrote James David Barber, "given the choice between two touters of confidence, pushed aside the one they knew let them down and went for the one they prayed might not."[8] Roosevelt amassed a 472–59 electoral college majority and a popular vote margin of 22,809,638 to 15,758,901.

To gain this massive victory, Roosevelt brought together an alliance of Americans that came to be known as the **New Deal coalition**. The key components of this successful amalgam consisted of the urban working class, most members of the newer ethnic groups (especially Irish, Poles, and Italians), African Americans, the bulk of American Catholics and Jews, the poor, southerners, and liberal intellectuals. This broad-based coalition allowed Roosevelt to forge scores of new government programs that increased government assistance and brought him immense popular support. It also brought about a new set of beliefs and attitudes toward government.

Riding a wave of New Deal enthusiasm, Democrats dominated national politics between 1932 and 1968. The nation chose only one Republican president during this period: World War II hero Dwight Eisenhower. Each of Roosevelt's Democratic successors kept the New Deal coalition alive. Lyndon B. Johnson (1963–69), in particular, gave renewed impetus to New Deal philosophy by expanding government economic assistance programs with his "Great Society."[9] In the pivotal 1968 election, however, conservative Richard Nixon beat Vice President Hubert H. Humphrey, whose election was hampered by the bitter split in the Democratic party, and the Republicans took control of the White House.

A Sixth Party System? 1968 to Present

Since 1968, the Republican party has won seven of ten presidential elections. The two Democratic winners were southern conservative party members. Yet until recently, scholars have been reluctant to describe the post–1968 period as another realignment. Republican presidents Richard Nixon, Gerald Ford, Ronald Reagan, and George H. W. Bush failed to dismantle the New Deal and Great Society programs, which had proven broadly popular. Democrats retained majority control of the U.S. House of Representatives from January 1955 to January 1995. In past realignments, the emerging dominant party rode a highly controversial issue to broad election victories in both Congress and the presidency and then took control in the majority of American states as well. But Republicans remained the minority party in state and local elections throughout the 1960s and 1970s.

Many signs indicate, however, that partisan strengths are shifting. After taking control of both houses of Congress in 1994 for the first time in forty years, Republicans succeeded in retaining control of both bodies in 1996 and 1998. But in 2001, Senator Jim Jeffords (R.-VT), because of differences with the Bush administration over education and other policies, defected to become an Independent who would vote Democrat, denying Republicans control of the Senate until the 2002 election. However, party results in 1998 and 2000 state races were mixed. Middle-of-the-road, pragmatic Republican conservatives won the governorships of twenty-three of the thirty-four contested races in 2000. In 2002, the Democratic party picked up three governorships nationwide, including Pennsylvania, Michigan, and Illinois. The 2004 gubernatorial races were a virtual stand-off, with Democrats winning six races and

New Deal coalition Brought together by Franklin Roosevelt in 1932, a broad electorate made up of the urban working class, most members of the newer ethnic groups, the bulk of American Catholics and Jews, the poor, the South, and liberal intellectuals.

◀ Who gets the "sound bite" this time? While Senator Trent Lott (R.-Miss.) announces the Republican party's "hunt for bills" in the Democratic party-led Congress, Senator Bill Frist (R.-Tenn.) tries unsuccessfully to wrest a boom microphone out of the mouth of one of the bloodhounds brought in to lead the "search."

Republicans winning five. The Republicans also picked up an additional four Senate seats, giving them a substantial 55–44 margin over the Democrats. One Independent, James Jeffords of Vermont, voted with the Democrats most frequently. Some Democratic senators were so dispirited by the Republicans' near filibuster-proof voting margin that they considered leaving the Senate to run for their state governorships. Although New York's Chuck Schumer decided to stay in the Senate to chair the Democratic Senatorial Campaign Committee (DSCC), New Jersey's Jon Corzine left and won his state's governorship in 2005.

"RED V. BLUE": THE CURRENT BALANCED POLITICAL PARTY SYSTEM

Since 1977, the Democratic party has experienced a substantial loss of voter support. When Ronald Reagan took control of the White House in 1981, the percentage of people identifying with the Democratic party dropped below 40 percent for the first time. With the steady rise in Republican support during Reagan's presidency, the lead held by the Democratic party fell from 27 percent to only 9 percent in 1985; by 2001 the Democratic party lead was a mere 5 percent. By 2003, the two parties were roughly equal.[10] As Table 9.2 shows, through 2004 the Democratic

Table 9.2 ■ Trends in Party Identification

	1988	1989	1991	1992	1993	1994	1996	1998	2001	2004	2005
Republicans	27%	33%	31%	28%	27%	29%	28%	28%	29%	30%	31%
Democrats	30	33	32	34	34	33	39	38	34	33%	34%
Independents	38	34	33	34	34	35	33	34	37	37%	35%

Source: "Beyond Red vs. Blue," Pew Research Center for the People and Press, http://people-press.org/commentary/display.php37.analysisID=95, May 10, 2005; Times Mirror Center for the People and the Press, *The New Political Landscape*, October 1994, p. 43; *American National Election Studies,* Center for Political Studies, University of Michigan; and Gallup Poll Election Survey, 1998.

Table 9.3 ■ Results of the Presidential Elections of 2000 and 2004					
		Popular Votes		**Electoral College Votes**	
Year	Candidate	Number	Percent	Number	Percent
2000	George W. Bush	50,456,002	47.87%	271	50.37%
	Al Gore	50,999,897	48.38%	266	49.44%
	Ralph Nader	2,882,955	2.74%	0	
2004	George W. Bush	62,040,606	51%	286	51%
	John Kerry	59,028,109	48%	252	49%
	Ralph Nader	411,304	1%	0	

party began to gain new members and by mid-2005, perhaps as a result of the war in Iraq or plummeting public support for the Bush presidency, the Democrats held a 3 percent lead over the Republicans in party identification, with independents still registering as the largest group.

This shifting balance between the parties made the 2000 and 2004 elections two of the closest back-to-back presidential elections in American history. As Table 9.3 shows, although Al Gore had more than 500,000 more popular votes than George W. Bush, a shift of 269 votes in Florida gave that state's electoral college votes (with help from the U.S. Supreme Court) to George W. Bush. Four years later, although President Bush topped Senator John Kerry by 3 million votes—with the help of millions of new voters from the evangelical Christian movement—his victory hung on a 120,000-vote margin in Ohio, mainly in the conservative western part of the state, which gave him that state's 20 electoral college votes and the victory.

Another indication of the Republican party's rise can be seen in the balance of state legislative seats. Prior to the 2000 election, the Democrats controlled both houses of the states legislatures in nineteen states and the Republicans in seventeen. After the 2000 election, Republicans and Democrats each controlled both houses of the legislature in seventeen states. Another fifteen states were split, with each party controlling one house, with Nebraska having a nonpartisan, single-chamber legislature. In 2000, the Republicans held a fourteen-state margin in governorships (31–17, with one reform governor). The difference in party control was much closer after the 2004 election, with the Republicans holding a 21–19 margin. More revealing of the close national party balance is the fact that of 7,382 state legislative seats, both parties hold an identical 3,660 seats, with the rest held by candidates from minor parties or no party affiliation.[11]

As a result of these gains in state legislatures and their control of the governorships, the Republicans managed the 2000 congressional redistricting, which made it easier for them to defend and increase their margin in the House of Representatives in 2002 and 2004.[12] And the strategy worked, as the Republicans, aided by a partisan redistricting of Texas, made President Bush the first incumbent since the nineteenth century to increase his majority in Congress in his second term reelection. By early 2006, the Republicans held a 231–202–1 margin, with one vacancy, in the House and a 55–44–1 margin in the Senate. These trends will become clearer in the 2006 election, when thirty-three Senate seats are up for election, with the Democrats defending eighteen of them (including Independent Senator Jim Jeffords' seat in Vermont), five in states that voted for President Bush, whereas the Republicans will defend fifteen seats.

The reasons for this trend toward republicanism over the past three decades are varied. The number of young conservatives entering the electorate has steadily increased. The number of Democratic voters has slowly declined for several years,

Table 9.4 ■ Top Five Values Related to Party Identification

1999	Index of Influence	2004	Index of Influence
Government is almost always wasteful and inefficient.	10	The best way to ensure peace is through military strength.	24
Government regulation of business is necessary to protect the public interest.	10	We should all be willing to fight for our country, whether it is right or wrong.	12
Homosexuality is a way of life that should be accepted by society.	10	As Americans we can always find ways to solve our problems.	10
Poor people today have it easy because of government benefits.	9	Poor people today have it easy because of government benefits.	8
The government should do more to help needy Americans.	8	The government should do whatever it takes to protect the environment.	8

Index numbers reflect the relative impact of each item in explaining party identification. Based on multiple regression analysis.

Source: Pew Research Center for the People and Press, 1/24/05 found at http://people-press.org/.

in part because its constituency is aging and labor unions are losing influence, whereas the number of Independents has steadily risen. With the electorate so evenly divided, and the only difference in the past two presidential elections being the evangelical Christian vote in the key electoral college states of Florida and then Ohio, the question is when and how one party or the other will take control of the political scene.[13]

The last election showed that the reasons people give for identifying with certain parties was in the process of changing. As Table 9.4 shows, in 1999 the main reasons that people chose parties came from their views on government wastefulness, business regulation and gay rights. By 2004, people chose parties based on war issues and the choice of military over diplomatic options in foreign policy.[14] The Democratic party built its base on liberals, African Americans, Jews, women, and lower-income voters. Republican support comes from conservatives, middle- and upper-income Caucasians, and evangelical Protestants. Although conservative African Americans and Hispanics have been shifting to the Republican party, those two groups still overwhelmingly vote Democrat, with a 2–1 majority for Hispanics and a 10–1 majority for African Americans.[15]

After the 2004 election, the Republican party appeared to gain ground. Based on extensive polling, however, the Pew Research Center for the People and the Press was uncertain this process would continue: "The GOP had extensive appeal among a disparate group of voters in the middle of the electorate, drew extraordinary loyalty from its own varied constituencies, and made some inroads among conservative Democrats. . . . Looking forward, however, there is no assurance that Republicans will be able to consolidate or build upon these advantages."[16] Within months, obstacles were mounting: growing problems in the Iraq War, a failure to deal quickly and adequately with the aftermath of Hurricane Katrina and other natural disasters on the Gulf Coast, an investigation into an apparent administration leak of CIA operative Valerie Plame's identity, the Texas indictment of House Majority Leader Tom Delay on campaign election issues relating to that state's redistricting (leading to his stepping down from that leadership position and decision not to return to it), and the conservatives' political in-fighting over the Supreme Court nomination of Harriet Miers. In addition, the growing scandal relating to the investigation into the government corruption investigation into the actions of lobbyist Jack Abramoff, a former aide to Rep. Delay, made it even less likely that the Republicans would build support for their party. In upcoming elections, Republicans face the problem of uniting their new ultraconservative and religious voters with more moderate party members. This will be especially true as they choose a 2008 presidential candidate. On the other hand, the Democrats, having been out of the White House for the past two election cycles and lost considerable ground in Congress, will find it difficult to unite their diverse constituency on social and cultural issues. In addition, the weak voter identification with the major parties, coupled with increasing numbers of Independents and third-party voters, might well lead to a system of relatively balanced political party strength, making any election predictions based solely on party identification uncertain.

FUNCTIONS OF AMERICAN POLITICAL PARTIES

The governing institutions of the United States were designed to fragment and decentralize power, and they have succeeded at that task. The only political institutions that work to pull people together—that exert a coherent, unified perspective on public affairs and attempt to govern in a reasonably cohesive manner—are the two major political parties.[17] Their functions within American society are varied and crucial for the health of our democracy.

Parties Organize the Election Process

A party's most basic role is to nominate candidates and win elections.[18] True, citizens need not belong to a political party to run for office, but to win high elective office a candidate must, with few exceptions, belong to one of the two major American political parties. Every president since 1853 has been either a Democrat or a Republican. In 2006, Vermont's Jim Jeffords and Bernard Sanders were the only senator and House member not in one of those two parties. All of the state governors belonged to major parties. The stability of this pattern is impressive. For more than a century, the rule for any ambitious politician has been simple: To build a serious career in public life, first join either the Democratic or the Republican party. When dissatisfied, however, an elected politician can always switch parties. Senator Richard Shelby of Alabama in 1994 switched to the Republican party after finding that, in the early Clinton years, he lacked the White House influence he had expected. But this change, which gave the Republicans a six-vote margin in the Senate, failed to equal the profound policy-making impact of Jim Jeffords' 2001 switch, which changed the party balance of the entire Senate body.

Winning office is crucial to party fortunes. Party members spend much time and energy on the election process. Parties select candidates, provide money to local, state, and national races and arrange administrative support at all levels of electoral competition. They begin this work with the vital function of **recruitment**. Parties continually look for effective, popular candidates to help them win votes and offices. Since 2000, both parties have had increasing difficulty persuading rising political figures to run for Congress, even for open or highly winnable seats, because of the need to raise large campaign war chests and the stresses such service places on their families. In some states term limits for state legislators have seemed to improve this prospect, as state politicians were forced to run for federal office to stay in public life.

Parties' search for successful campaigners serves another key function: *representation*. To win free and democratic elections, parties follow a crucial axiom: Find out what voters want and promise to give it to them. No matter who is elected, the winners attempt to remain committed to the popular programs on which they campaigned. Following this logic, parties must *act responsibly* and legislate the policies they promised. Parties elected under pledges to carry out a specific set of policies know that voters will judge them at the next election. Did they do what they promised? If not, voters can (and often do) reject them in favor of

Question for Reflection

What role has voters' frustration with Republican and Democratic "politics as usual" played in reshaping the party system in the past decade?

recruitment The process through which parties look for effective, popular candidates to help them win votes and offices.

their rivals. The potential for punishment of this sort keeps parties under serious pressure when writing their platforms. Backing away from or even flip-flopping on a public commitment can often produce a devastating backlash.

In the long run, this open competition for power serves the voting public. By recruiting good candidates, representing voter wishes, and being held responsible for their actions in office, the two parties help Americans approach the democratic ideal of government.[19]

Parties Represent Group Interests

In their struggle for power, parties speak for and unite different groups and their varied interests. Parties find that it pays to discover what groups want, then work with those groups to fulfill their desires. Thus, Republicans often work closely with business groups to articulate pro-business positions; Democrats do the same with labor union leaders. But parties must do more than speak for one narrow interest if they wish to gain majorities needed to win public office; they must appeal to a wide range of social groups. In so doing, they learn to meld individual group interests into a larger whole with a coherent philosophy of governing.[20]

The need to combine varied and complex interests forces parties to become broad political coalitions. Republicans, for instance, must bring together the interests of multinational corporations and small businesses, rural evangelical Protestants and pro-life Catholics. Democrats, too, must unite a diverse set of factions that include small-town white southerners, urban black workers, and ethnic white suburbanites. In the process of building a coalition from social subgroups, both parties perform another democratic function—integrating various groups into public life and the democratic process. Parties thus help mute the conflicts that might arise if each interest group had its own separate party and fought the others at every election.

Parties Simplify Political Choices

By bringing groups together and creating a coherent platform for voters at election time, parties simplify political choices for voters. Most voters do not study every issue in depth, nor do they know where each candidate stands on every issue. Parties help them make rational decisions at the ballot box by melding a series of complex issues into a broad, general perspective and explaining that perspective in simple, direct ways. By election day, most voters have been educated enough to know that their choices are not merely between two individual personalities but between two differing philosophies of governance. Consider what the alternative would be: a ballot listing only a long series of names unconnected to any party and without any hint of the candidate's position.

Parties Organize Government and Policy Making

Once elections are over, parties help organize the country's political institutions for governing. Public officials work together as organized members of the winning party to carry out their party's aims and election pledges. The Republican takeover of Congress after the 1994 elections, for example, produced a set of policies different from when Democrats were in the majority. In early 2005 the increase in margin of seats held by the Republicans in the House of Representatives allowed Republican Speaker J. Dennis Hastert (IL) and Majority Leader Tom Delay (TX) to use more hardball tactics with their members, such as threatening to change their committee assignments, to help promote the legislative agenda of President Bush. At the same time, in the Senate, Pennsylvania's Arlen Specter had to fight for his chairmanship of the Judiciary Committee by promising not to delay any ultraconservative Bush administration judicial nominees who might oppose the *Roe* v. *Wade* abortion decision. U.S. policy decisions emerge from party

Quick Review

State and Local Parties

- Local party organizations provide entry for people seeking involvement in politics as volunteers, organizers, or candidates.

- State party organizations organize elections and provide electoral college votes needed to win the presidency.

- Committee leaders supervise the various functions vital to state parties.

- State parties work with state governments to conduct primary elections or caucuses.

- Party structure varies dramatically from state to state.

local party organization The initial point of entry for those seeking involvement in politics as volunteers, organizers, or candidates.

leaders' attempts to govern in the spirit of their party's philosophy. This works in both parties' interest. After all, the party that solves political problems wins mass support at the next election.

PARTY ORGANIZATION

Despite recent trends toward strengthening national party organizations, political parties are still relatively decentralized institutions. The flow of power moves upward—from local to state organizations, and from there to the national committees and conventions.

Parties at the Grass Roots

Parties at the grass roots consist of city, county, and state organizations. Party operations begin at the local level. The **local party organization** provides an initial point of entry for people who want to participate in politics as volunteers, organizers, or candidates. Each local party is highly dependent on the level of community interest—high in some places and low in others. Party faithful in active areas

Approaching Democracy Around the Globe

From Bullets to Ballots

Although Mexico's Zapatistas and their leader, a man known only by his nickname of "Marcos," have come a long way, no one yet knows where or how far they are going. Mexico's governmental system was dominated through much of the twentieth century by the Institutional Revolutionary Party (PRI). The domination broke only when former Coca-Cola executive and regional governor Vicente Fox Quesada, representing the competing National Action Party (PAN), surprised everyone in 2000 by winning the presidential election, becoming the first non-PRI president since Francisco Madero won in 1910. Neither of these parties, though, appeared to do much for the native peoples in Mexico.

In 1994, the Zapatistas declared war on the Mexican government and launched a separatist revolt in the Chiapas state that left 150 people dead. Their twin issues—a socialist government and rights for the country's native Indian tribes—were not as glamorous as the mystery of the group's future plans. Because no one knew what the group was likely to do next, or even the full name of its charismatic, pipe-smoking leader, rumored to be a former university professor, all Mexican political parties found it necessary to address its issues. But after leading a weeklong march of 100,000 people in Mexico City in 2001 to bring attention to its cause, and being treated like rock stars, the group withdrew to the jungles and maintained silence.

Now Marcos has said that the group will launch a national tour that might last for years and include a run for the country's presidency. "Now that the 'we' is bigger,

and not just the Zapatista National Liberation Army, this is so that other people outside who are not in these meetings can say if they want to enter the 'we.'"

All of this creates problems for the presumed leader in the 2006 presidential election, leftist former Mexico City mayor Andres Manuel Lopez Obrader. Says one member of the Mexican Congress, Janet Ovando, "They already . . . and will continue to influence what the candidates are saying, talking about Indian rights. That will affect the people who are going to vote." But some believe that the move from a protest organization to a mainstream political party will not work. Juan Antonio Gordillo, also a member of Congress, argues: "They have found a way to pressure the government as guerillas. As a political party like any other, they will be easy to ignore."

For a movement numbering near a quarter of a million people, many living in wooden shacks without water or electricity, the chance to become a more influential political party is an exciting one. But it is also quite uncertain. Whether this group can successfully make the transformation from gun-toting revolutionaries to campaigning political party figures will help to determine whether the group's political agenda is taken more seriously within the Mexican government.

Source: Will Weissert, "Zapatista Rebels Eye 2006 Mexico Election," *Boston Globe,* August 13, 2005; "Zapatista Leader Emerges to Scorn Mexican Candidates," *Los Angeles Times,* August 7, 2005, p. 4; Danna Harman, "It Will All Be Made Clear in the Next Zapatista Memo," *Christian Science Monitor,* August 2, 2005, p. 1.

eagerly fill slots as precinct chairs and election organizers, volunteer for administrative posts, and even run to participate in state conventions. Where interest is low, party structures remain skeletal, with many posts unfilled or a few party faithful keeping the organization going.

Although linked to the national apparatus, local and state political parties have significant independent power, often more than the national party. Local parties enjoy higher personal interaction with members, base their platforms on significant local issues, and can perform their duties without seeking huge monetary donations. Citizens can more easily become involved at the local level by donating money or working for a campaign.

Political activists are vital in a democracy; they exert important influence on the party platform and on political decision makers. Party activists differ from the population at large in that they tend to be wealthier and better educated. Reforms in Democratic party methods to select delegates to nominating conventions have encouraged increased activism for women, minorities, and youth. And the Republican party has also opened its doors to these newer activists.[21] So although party activists show socioeconomic differences from the population at large, party reform has produced a more demographically representative group.

The fifty **state party organizations** have strikingly different systems. Through their two key roles as election organizers and providers of electoral college votes, state party organizations play a critical part in American national politics. They also play a significant role in state politics. The leaders in each state party's central committee supervise various vital functions such as raising funds, identifying potential candidates, providing election services, offering advice on reapportionment, and developing campaign strategies. State parties also work with state governments to conduct the primary elections or caucuses most states use to register preferences for presidential candidates.

Party structure varies dramatically from state to state. Some party organizations, like that of Pennsylvania, have permanent headquarters, a regular calendar of events, frequent meetings with local officials, and a central committee staffed with professional administrators, strategists, and fund raisers. Some states, such as California, have weak political parties. From these differences follows a common political rule: Where parties are weak, interest groups are strong.

George Bush's 2004 election succeeded in part through the Republican party's comparative victory over the Democratic party in grassroots party and interest-group organization in the battleground states. Although ministers in local evangelical Christian churches were motivating and registering their parishioners to vote, the Republican party put $125 million into a massive ground game, organized by presidential adviser Karl Rove and campaign director Ken Mehlman, to make sure that these voters voted on election day. For their party, the Democrats relied on the ground game organized by a new interest group called "America Coming Together," based on $200 million raised from financier George Soros and Hollywood figures, among others, to motivate millions of people to register and vote. In the end, though, a comparison of the 2004 election results with those four years earlier made clear that the Republican grassroots operation was much more effective.[22]

state party organizations Party organizations at the state level; they organize elections and provide the electoral college votes needed to win the presidency; they also supervise the various functions vital to state parties, such as fund raising, identifying potential candidates, providing election services, offering advice on reapportionment matters, and developing campaign strategies.

▲ Ken Mehlman (C), the chairman of the Republican National Committee, rose to power as President Bush's campaign manager in the 2004 election, planning the "ground game" for the election and "spinning" reporters to see his party's view of the issues.

The Party Machine

From the final decades of the nineteenth century to the early or middle part of this century, a political party organizational

machine politics An organizational style of local politics in which party bosses traded jobs, money, and favors for votes and campaign support.

national party organization Party organization at the national level whose primary tasks include fund raising, distribution of information, and recruitment.

style called **machine politics** flourished in New York City, Chicago, Philadelphia, Kansas City, and elsewhere. At the heart of the system lay an ingenious scheme of reciprocal influence. Party leaders (bosses) traded jobs, money, and favors for votes and campaign support. Once in office, the party bosses had jobs to distribute to party workers who had helped them to victory. Voters who supported the winning party could be assured of good local service, the occasional handout, the odd favor. The bosses regularly reached into the public till for party funds, personal enrichment, and to keep voters and party workers happy.[23]

The system worked for a time to ensure strong, organized parties. It was based largely on an urban landscape of impoverished workers, often recent immigrants more concerned with immediate benefits and simple economic survival than with ideals such as effective and honest government. Poor, hungry, and uneducated urban dwellers found that supporting the party boss and the machine could ensure a job or at least an economic safety net in tough times. The party machine acted as a combination employment agency, social work provider, and welfare state. Naturally, the machine and the party bosses did not undertake these tasks merely for humanitarian reasons. They sought power, wealth, and privilege—primarily through the public coffers. Eventually their venality and corrupt behavior produced a backlash that swept them into oblivion.

The boss and the machine fell to several modernizing forces of the twentieth century. To begin with, increasingly wealthy and educated Americans supported government that served people's interests and were less inclined to accept corrupt machine behavior. People needed fewer of the favors that the bosses typically had at their disposal. Candidates who ran against party bosses started winning elections.

Four additional developments doomed the old machine system. First, the new civil service system robbed the party machine of those tangible and valued rewards for potential followers—government jobs. Second, the developing modern welfare state provided a safety net for the poorest citizens, who no longer needed bosses to serve that purpose. Third, the proliferation of primary elections removed decision making about candidates and nominations from the hands of party bosses and gave it to a mass electorate. With little power to control the struggle for high office and few rewards to dole out to anyone, party boss influence crumbled, and nearly all of the traditional machines ground to a halt. Finally, the secret ballot helped speed the decline of party bosses' ability to intimidate voters.

Still, good organizations know how to adapt to changing circumstances. As the 2004 presidential nomination campaign revealed, party machines have not been dismantled but streamlined. Amid intense focus on the increased money in the campaigns, it was the millions of campaign workers in both parties "pounding the pavement"—some carrying on a partisan family tradition handed down over generations—that got the vote out for President George Bush and Senator John Kerry. In the end, the better-organized Republican national campaign generated three million more voters than the Democrats, especially in key swing states such as Ohio and Florida, to tip the electoral college in President Bush's favor.

MakeItReal

Visual Literacy: 1976 Republican Convention
Democratic Party Platform
Republican Party Platform

National Party Organization

The strength of the **national party organization** is most apparent during presidential elections. Even with the increasingly democratic nominating process and proliferating interest groups and political action committees, the national party organization remains a crucial source of coordination and consensus building for both Republicans and Democrats.

Although the national organization is supposedly the highest authority for each political party, in fact it has always been weak. For decades, the national organization's primary task was to organize the **national party convention** once every four years. The convention symbolizes the party's existence as a national institution. At this festive affair, party delegates from around the country come together to select presidential and vice presidential candidates for the coming election and to write the party's platform. At no other time is the national party much in evidence to the American public.[24]

A **party platform** is a statement of principles and policies, the goals that a party pledges to carry out if voters give it control of government. The platform announces positions on prominent issues of the day such as gun control, abortion, taxation, and social spending. The platform is also an important way of setting the tone for each party and distinguishing one party from another. As you can see in Table 9.5, Democrats and Republicans differ from each other ideologically. These differences show up clearly in platform statements.

Although many people assume that party platforms have little relationship to the party's actual performance in government, this is not the case. Platform positions tend to mirror subsequent government expenditures quite closely. At times, though, in search of votes, candidates such as George W. Bush find that they must differentiate their campaign rhetoric from the party platform. For the Republicans, often the platform's strong anti-abortion stance forces them to take this approach.

The day-to-day operations of the national party fall to the *national chair.* Each chairperson, selected by the presidential nominee of the party, is the actual administrator. The chair is

▲ Howard Dean, the Chairman of the Democratic National Committee, rolls up his sleeves in search of votes just as he did as presidential candidate in 2004 and Governor of Vermont.

responsible for personnel, fund raising, scheduling, and the daily activities of the party. Modern fund-raising techniques, such as computer-derived mailing lists and direct mail, have made both state and national party units more effective in recent years. Parties become better able to target specific voters—based on geography, demographics, previous financial support, and precinct location—with each election. Given the administrative responsibilities of the national chair's job, holders of this office tend to be relatively unknown rather than popular national political figures. However, it is not uncommon after a national presidential election to choose visible figures from those races to galvanize future supporters. The Democrats' choice of ultraliberal former Vermont Governor Howard Dean, himself an early leading candidate for the presidential nomination, and the Republicans' appointment of highly successful former 2004 Bush campaign director Ken Mehlman, are evidence of this point. Party chairs, besides organizing and running the party machinery, are the party's public face as it raises money and prepares for the next presidential primary season.

Party Similarities and Differences

Although the parties have similar organizational structures, each bases its structure on different goals. The Republican party emphasizes creating and maintaining effective administrative structures, especially at the national level, to supply assistance and raise funds for candidates. As a result, Republicans tend to be more bureaucratically oriented than Democrats, but also benefit from less ideological discord. Conversely, Democrats emphasize representation by promoting voter mobilization, activism, and debate. Because it encourages pluralistic participation, the Democratic party ensures acrimonious argument regarding policy and the selection of candidates.

The Republican party seems more effective at fund raising. In a typical election year, Republicans raise and distribute to candidates about 250 percent more money than Democrats do.[25] In 2002, President Bush scheduled so many fund raisers for the spring and summer to fund the upcoming congressional elections that by June he had raised more than $100 million. Providing a sense of the magnitude of this fund-raising effort, President Bill Clinton worked ten years, from 1992 on, to raise

national party convention The national meeting of the party every four years to choose the ticket for the presidential election and write the party platform.

party platform The statement of principles and policies; the goals that a party pledges to carry out if voters give it control of the government.

Table 9.5 ■ Party Platforms: How They Compared in the 2004 Election

	Democrats	Republicans
ABORTION	We will defend the dignity of all Americans against those who would undermine it. Because we believe in the privacy and equality of women, we stand proudly for a woman's right to choose, consistent with Roe v. Wade, and regardless of her ability to pay. We stand firmly against Republican efforts to undermine that right. At the same time, we strongly support family planning and adoption incentives. Abortion should be safe, legal, and rare.	. . . the unborn child has a fundamental individual right to life which cannot be infringed. We support a human life amendment to the Constitution and we endorse legislation to make it clear that the Fourteenth Amendment's protections apply to unborn children. . . . We oppose using public revenues for abortion and will not fund organizations which advocate it.
SAME-SEX "MARRIAGE"	We support full inclusion of gay and lesbian families in the life of our nation and seek equal responsibilities, benefits, and protections for these families. We repudiate President Bush's divisive effort to politicize the Constitution by pursuing a "Federal Marriage Amendment." Our goal is to bring Americans together, not drive them apart.	We strongly support President Bush's call for a Constitutional amendment that fully protects marriage, and we believe that neither federal nor state judges nor bureaucrats should force states to recognize other living arrangements as equivalent to marriage.
HEALTH CARE	We will attack the health care crisis with a comprehensive approach. Our goal is straightforward: quality, affordable health coverage for all Americans to keep our families healthy, our businesses competitive, and our country strong . . . every expectant mother should get quality prenatal care; every child should get regular check-ups; every senior should be able to get safe, affordable prescription drugs; and no hardworking family should ever lose everything because illness strikes a loved one. We will strengthen Medicaid for our families and expand the children's health program created under President Clinton so no child goes without medical care. We will enact a real Patient's Bill of Rights to put doctors and nurses back in charge of making medical decisions with their patients—instead of allowing HMO bureaucrats to decide what a patient needs.	The cost of providing health care for employees is a major burden for American businesses. . . . We must attack the root causes of high health care costs by: aiding small businesses in offering health care to their employees; empowering the self-employed through access to affordable coverage; putting patients and doctors in charge of medical decisions; reducing junk lawsuits and limiting punitive damage awards that raise the cost of health care; and seizing the cost-saving and quality-enhancing potential of emerging health technologies. We reject any notion of government-run universal health care . . . And we applaud efforts by President Bush and the Republican Congress to reform the broken medical liability system that is raising health care costs and limiting patients' access to doctors—doctors who are being driven out of their practices by excessive medical liability costs. We support continued efforts to make health care more affordable, more accessible, and more consumer-driven.
HOMOSEXUALS IN THE MILITARY	We are committed to equal treatment of all service members and believe all patriotic Americans should be allowed to serve our country without discrimination, persecution, or violence.	We affirm traditional military culture, and we affirm that homosexuality is incompatible with military service.
STEM CELL RESEARCH	We will push the boundaries of science in search of new medical therapies and cures. . . . We will secure more funding for aggressive biomedical research seeking affordable and effective therapies based on real science.	We strongly support the President's policy that prevents taxpayer dollars from being used to encourage the future destruction of human embryos. In addition, we applaud the President's call for a comprehensive ban on human cloning and on the creation of human embryos solely for experimentation.
NATIONAL SECURITY AND COMBATING TERRORISM	. . . we need a new national security policy guided by four new imperatives: First, America must launch and lead a new era of alliances for the post-September 11 world. Second, we must modernize the world's most powerful military to meet the new threats. Third, in addition to our military might, we must deploy all that is in America's arsenal—our diplomacy, our intelligence system, our economic	We endorse the efforts of President Bush and Republicans in Congress to keep our homeland safe by taking action on multiple fronts, all aimed at stopping terrorists before they strike. . . . Defeating terrorism requires the United States to: • help establish stable and democratic governments in nations such as Afghanistan and Iraq that once supported terrorism;

Table 9.5 ▪ (Continued)

	Democrats	Republicans
	power, and the appeal of our values and ideas. Fourth and finally, to safeguard our freedom and ensure our nation's future, we must end our dependence on Mideast oil. . . . Finally, we must win the war on terror without losing the values of freedom and justice for all that make us so proud to be Americans.	• support front-line states and coalition partners; • deepen counterterrorism, intelligence, and law enforcement cooperation with allies and friends; and • energetically promote democracy, especially in the Broader Middle East.
APPOINTMENT OF JUDGES	We support the appointment of judges who will uphold our laws and constitutional rights, not their own narrow agendas.	We believe that the self-proclaimed supremacy of . . . judicial activists is antithetical to the democratic ideals on which our nation was founded.
SCHOOL CHOICE AND VOUCHERS	Instead of pushing private school vouchers that funnel scarce dollars away from the public schools, we will support public school choice, including charter schools and magnet schools that meet the same high standards as other schools.	. . . we support state efforts to expand school choice, as well as . . . funding for new and existing charter schools . . . The Republican Party supports the efforts of parents who choose faith-based and other nonpublic school options for their children.
EDUCATION	We believe schools must teach fundamental skills like math and science, and fundamental values like citizenship and responsibility. We believe providing resources without reform is a waste of money, and reform without resources is a waste of time. . . . we will offer high quality early learning opportunities, smaller classes, more after school activities, and more individualized attention for our students, particularly students with special needs, gifts, and talents. The federal government will meet its financial obligations for elementary and secondary education and for special education. We must raise pay for teachers . . . We must improve mentoring, professional development, and new technology training for teachers . . . At the same time, we must create rigorous new incentives and tests for new teachers. . . . . . . we will expand and improve preschool and Head Start initiatives with the goal of offering these opportunities to all children. . . . we will work on a bipartisan basis to reform foster care.	Now is the time to extend the progress we've made. The No Child Left Behind Act is already showing gains in elementary school . . . Our next mission is to take the reforms that we know are working in elementary schools and apply them up and down the education ladder—starting in early childhood education, so that children enter school ready to learn, and finishing in high school, so that every young adult who graduates has the skills he or she needs to succeed in the 21st century economy. . . . We pledge to bring real reform to high schools. . . . state and local governments must assume most of the responsibility to improve the schools, and the role of the federal government must be limited as we return control to parents, teachers, and local school boards. . . . reading is the new civil right. Every child must be able to read by the end of the third grade.
CIVIL RIGHTS	Our commitment to civil rights is ironclad. We will restore vigorous federal enforcement of our civil rights laws for all our people, from fair housing to equal employment opportunity, from Title IX to the Americans with Disabilities Act. We support affirmative action to redress discrimination and to achieve the diversity from which all Americans benefit. We believe a day's work is worth a day's pay, and at a time when women still earn 77 cents for every dollar earned by men, we need stronger equal pay laws and stronger enforcement of them. . . . We will enact the bipartisan legislation barring workplace discrimination based on sexual orientation.	The Republican Party favors aggressive, proactive measures to ensure that no individual is discriminated against on the basis of race, national origin, gender, or other characteristics covered by our civil rights laws. We also favor recruitment and outreach policies that cast the widest possible net so that the best-qualified individuals are encouraged to apply for jobs, contracts, and university admissions. We believe in the principle of affirmative access—taking steps to ensure that disadvantaged individuals of all colors and ethnic backgrounds have the opportunity to compete economically and that no child is left behind educationally.

Source: Based on selections taken from the 2004 party platforms in "Party Platform-Comparison Resource" at ivotevalues.com

$113 million for the Democratic party. As a result of the Bipartisan Campaign Finance Reform Act, this kind of "soft money" fund-raising ended after the 2002 election.[26] The "issue ads" that this money often funds are illegal for thirty days before the election primaries or sixty days before the general election. But this did not slow down the fund-raising. In the 2004 election season, President Bush raised more than $367 million to Senator John Kerry's $326 million.[27] However, as outlined in Chapter 11, additional hundreds of millions of "soft money" dollars were raised by so-called 527 organizations, tax-exempt political lobbying organizations that work with the political parties to place issue ads not related specifically to either candidate and thus not controlled by campaign finance law restrictions.

NOMINATING A PRESIDENT: PARTIES AND ELECTIONS

Before a party can run the government and make public policy, it must win control of the top political offices. In the United States, parties vie for the presidency in particular. Let us examine the process by which a Democrat or a Republican becomes a candidate for president of the United States.

Nominating Candidates

Before candidates can be elected to public office, they must first be nominated. **Nomination** is the political party's endorsement of a candidate. Party endorsement carries legal weight. Only one candidate per position can appear on any ballot with the word Democrat or Republican after his or her name. Since other names on a ballot have next to no chance of election, the nomination process matters a great deal. In the past, a small group of party leaders controlled nominations. The process is now more democratic, with major political consequences.

In the current American system, a candidate gains a party's nomination for president by winning a majority of delegates at the party's national convention, held the summer before the November presidential election. By tradition, the party currently holding the White House holds the later convention, usually in August. The challenging party holds its convention a month or so earlier, usually in July—perhaps on the theory that its candidate needs a running start to win the presidency.

Delegates in the past were often *uncommitted,* or under the control of party leaders who frequently withheld any commitments until a politically opportune moment at the convention itself. Even on the convention's opening day, the race might remain wide open. Today, however, nearly all delegates are *committed* long before the convention convenes. In fact, the nominee's identity is clear long before the convention, which acts primarily as a formal ratifier of the obvious. Convention activities now aim less at choosing a candidate than at unifying the party faithful and gearing up for the fall election struggle. It is left to the state political parties to choose how to select their delegates to the national political party conventions. They use one of two selection methods, or sometimes a combination of these: caucuses—meetings of the party faithful—and primaries—public elections by the voters.

nomination A candidate's "sponsorship" by a political party.

caucus Meeting of party adherents who gather to discuss, to deliberate, and finally to give their support to a candidate for president. They then select delegates who will represent their choices at higher-level party meetings; eventually, their votes are reflected at the national convention itself. Also means a conference of party members in Congress.

Caucuses   Caucuses are meetings of party adherents who gather in precinct halls or private homes to discuss, deliberate, and finally throw their support to a candidate for president. They then select delegates who will represent their choices at higher-level state party meetings; eventually their votes are reflected at the national convention. Candidates or their representatives often attend caucuses to discuss issues and make appeals.

Caucus meetings may be all-day affairs that require a heavy investment of time. For that reason, although any party member may by law attend, generally only the most active and devoted—usually wealthier and better educated—party members participate.

▲ The Bushes and the Cheneys celebrated their win at the Republican National Convention.

For that reason, as American society approaches democracy, it has tended to prefer primary elections, which are more inclusive and democratic in nature than caucuses.

Primaries   Primary elections date from the beginning of the twentieth century. The Progressives, tired of seeing their candidates pushed aside by political bosses and party machines, argued that it was undemocratic to allow party elites to choose candidates. Under pressure, party leaders buckled, and the primary system slowly developed. A **primary election** is essentially a preelection that allows all party members, not just leaders, to select the party's candidates for the general election in the fall.

Today, political parties in about three-quarters of the states employ primaries to select candidates for national elections. Voters in presidential primaries vote for a specific candidate, and these votes are converted into delegates for that candidate. The delegates then attend the party's national convention, where they vote for the candidate they represent.

States that use primaries employ various systems for parceling out delegates. Republicans allow greater variation than Democrats. Some states use a **winner-take-all system** in which the primary winner receives all the state's convention delegates. Other states distribute delegates by congressional district, using a winner-take-all system for each district; thus, a state might split its delegates among several candidates. Finally, in some states Republicans distribute delegates through various systems of **proportional representation**. Candidates who win, say, 20 percent of the statewide vote in the party primary will win about that same proportion of the state's delegates to the national convention.

In contrast to Republicans, Democrats employ a mandatory system of proportional representation to distribute delegates. Any candidate who wins at least 15 percent of the vote in any statewide primary must be allocated delegates to the national convention, and those delegates must reflect the exact percentage of primary votes received.

These generalizations about the delegate selection process only suggest the complexity of rules governing the winning of delegates. The arcane nature of the rules makes them comprehensible only to political insiders and specialists in the party organizations.[28]

Although primaries vary, most states use the closed primary system. In **closed primaries** only citizens registered as members of a political party may participate in that party's primary. A registered Republican, for instance, cannot cast a ballot in the

primary election A pre-election that allows all members of a party, not just its leadership, to select the party's candidate for the general election in the fall.

winner-take-all system A system in which the winner of the primary or electoral college vote receives all of the state's convention or electoral college delegates.

proportional representation A system of representation popular in Europe whereby the number of seats in the legislature is based on the proportion of the vote received in the election.

closed primary A system of conducting primary elections in which only citizens registered as members of a particular political party may participate in that party's primary.

Democratic primary. Conversely, **open primaries** allow all registered voters to vote in whichever party's primary they choose. Few states use open primaries because such cross-party voting may allow voters from one party to help pick their rival party's nominee. An organized effort could produce crossover votes that select the opposition party's weakest candidate. This appeared to be the case in the 2000 campaign, when Democratic voters crossed over to vote for McCain in an effort to defeat George W. Bush before the general election. Two states, Washington and Alaska, have *blanket primaries,* which allow voters to choose either party on an office-by-office basis.

For nearly half a century the New Hampshire primary was the first big test of a candidate's legitimacy. Indeed, in ten straight presidential elections (from 1952 through 1988), nobody became president without first winning the party's presidential primary in New Hampshire. Why should this small and atypical American state assume a dominant role in the presidential selection process? Much of New Hampshire's influence stems from a simple fact: It always holds the first primary of each presidential election year. This race shows how a candidate fares in the "retail politics" of actually meeting the voters. The Iowa caucus also is important; it tests candidates in the farm belt and precedes New Hampshire's primary. In 2004, Iowa ended the presidential ambitions of Vermont Governor Howard Dean, as his loss to Senator John Kerry effectively doomed his candidacy.

Being first has a powerful effect on voter and media perceptions, and thus on candidates' fund-raising ability. For instance, Bill Clinton overcame questions about his personal life and his draft status to place second to Massachusetts Senator Paul Tsongas in the 1992 New Hampshire primary and thus save his candidacy. Then, in the 1996 nominating process, Republican favorite Bob Dole barely defeated conservative candidate Pat Buchanan in the Iowa caucuses and lost to him in New Hampshire. As a result, Dole briefly considered dropping out of the race entirely. In 2000, George W. Bush's nineteen-point loss to McCain in New Hampshire nearly derailed him.

The traditional importance of Iowa and New Hampshire is diminishing, however. Many states, including some of the large ones, came to resent their power in selecting the nominee. To give themselves more political clout, many states changed the dates of their primaries. More than 75 percent of both parties' convention delegates are now chosen from one to six weeks after New Hampshire's primary, a process known as **frontloading**. Thus, ambitious candidates must campaign in numerous states, in addition to New Hampshire, to have any chance of gaining their party's nomination. They cannot count on putting all their effort into winning New Hampshire and having a month or more, as they once did, to bask in that limelight and build national support. It is now harder for a dark horse to come out of nowhere, do well in New Hampshire, and go on to win a major party's nomination, as George McGovern did in 1972.

In 2000, the primary landscape changed dramatically. California decided to move its presidential primary from mid-June to March 7, when New York, Maryland, Colorado, Ohio, and five New England states were also holding their contests. March 7 is just one week before "Super Tuesday," when Florida, Texas, and the southern states hold their primaries. Predictions that as a result of these moves the nomination process would move closer to one big presidential primary, seemed to be borne out in 2002 when the Democratic party announced that any state would be able to hold primaries at any time after February 2, 2004. As a result, states such as Missouri and Wisconsin moved their primaries from March and April respectively, to February, and Iowa and New Hampshire moved their delegate selection process to late January and early February 2004. This front-loaded process, with more than two-thirds of the delegates allocated in the first six weeks of the race, seemed to favor candidates with the most early name recognition and prior fund-raising. But then, to everyone's surprise, relatively unknown Vermont Governor Howard Dean, a vocal opponent of the Iraq War, became the front-runner in the race. When he failed to win the Iowa caucus, largely through press coverage critical of a campaign rally in which he, unable to hear himself, appeared to be yelling out-of-control, Senator

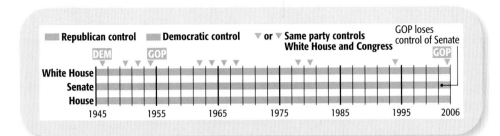

Figure 9.2 Taking Control
When George W. Bush became the first new President since Franklin D. Roosevelt in 1934 to add seats in Congress, he restored control of both Houses of Congress that was lost when Sen. Jim Jeffords deserted the Republican party in 2001.
Source: The Washington Post, May 25, 2001. Updated to 2006 by the authors.

John Kerry became the front-runner. The compressed schedule did not allow Dean to recover, and Kerry won twenty-seven of the first thirty caucuses and primaries, securing the Democratic nomination in just six weeks.[29] (See Figure 9.2).

As the 2008 presidential election season approaches, states begin to reposition their primaries to improve their influence on the process. Some states, such as Pennsylvania and North Carolina, discussed the possibility of moving their primaries to the early part of the primary season to make their states more relevant to the process. On the other hand, California, which had front-loaded the entire process in 2004 by moving its primary from June to March, reversed this decision and returned its primary to June for 2008.[30] As the state-by-state nomination process has become further compressed, in September 2005 the Commission on Federal Election Reform, led by former President Jimmy Carter and former Reagan secretary of state James Baker, recommended the creation of a series of four regional multistate primaries. In March 2006 the Democrats endorsed scheduling several state primaries and caucuses by early February to reduce the impact of Iowa and New Hampshire.

After the long caucus and primary season (February to June), prospective nominees have several weeks before the parties meet for their national party conventions. If the race is still close, candidates use that time to keep pushing their nomination prospects. They seek to keep their committed delegates in line and to convince uncommitted delegates to declare for them. Negotiation, conciliation, and planning characterize this period.

Question for Reflection

What impact will twenty-first century changes to the primary system have on party selection of a presidential candidate and our approach to democracy?

Reforming the Nominating Process

Since 1968, the presidential selection process has been radically altered. The Democrats' disastrously divisive 1968 convention in Chicago fueled change in the party's nomination process for presidential candidates.

◄ Can you locate the presidential candidate? Bill Bradley, standing at far right, looks unhappy campaigning among commuters on a ferry boat near Seattle as he tries, unsuccessfully, to save his race for the Democratic nomination from certain defeat to Al Gore.

The nomination race itself had foretold the problems. Senator Eugene McCarthy's anti-Vietnam War stance and narrow second-place finish in the New Hampshire primary had convinced President Lyndon B. Johnson to end his reelection campaign. Then Senator Robert F. Kennedy entered the race, and though he was far behind, his victory in the winner-take-all primary in California seemed to indicate that he would be nominated. However, his assassination by Sirhan Sirhan right after the primary narrowed the race to McCarthy and Vice President Hubert Humphrey, who had entered no primaries at all but was amassing significant support from the caucuses and party leaders behind the scenes.

At the Democratic National Convention during several hot days in Chicago, holders of opposing perspectives clashed dramatically in front of the television cameras. Inside the convention hall, party leaders, led by Chicago machine boss Mayor Richard Daley, tried to direct the party's nomination to their candidate, Hubert Humphrey. But outside, Vietnam War protesters, led by Tom Hayden, Jerry Rubin, and a group later known as the "Chicago Seven," clashed violently with police as they shouted, "The whole world's watching! The whole world's watching!" The party leaders could not contain the rising force of the next generation of political activists, who demanded more opportunity to participate in the nomination process. As the news broadcasts switched back and forth between the two scenes, clashes broke out inside the convention hall itself, and NBC national broadcaster John Chancellor was escorted out when he tried to report on events Democratic party leaders did not want exposed.[31] As a result of this disaster, Humphrey received the nomination but was too far behind in the election to win in November, as many party faithful sat out the early part of the campaign.

The Chicago convention was a watershed in American politics. Its most important accomplishment was to create widespread agreement that future party nominees had to depend on a deeper base of support than just the party hierarchy. Candidates at all levels in American politics since then have increasingly had to pass muster with the party rank-and-file in primaries before gaining the right to wear the party label in a general election.

Before the Chicago convention adjourned, activists succeeded in passing a resolution that by 1972 all state parties would "give all Democrats a full, meaningful, and timely opportunity to participate" in the selection of delegates. To create guidelines for compliance, the Democratic National Committee created the Commission on Party Structure and Delegate Selection, usually called the **McGovern-Fraser Commission** (after its chair, Senator George McGovern of South Dakota, and its vice chair, Representative Donald Fraser of Minnesota). This commission had far-reaching effects on the character of American politics. Its recommendations, largely adopted by the Democratic party, opened up meetings and votes to a large variety of party activists, made primaries rather than caucuses the common means of choosing convention delegates, weakened the power of party leaders, and set up rules to ensure that a wide range of party members—especially women, young people, and minority group representatives—could participate fully in all party operations.

Although Republicans did not adopt these same reforms in all the details, they did follow Democrats on the essential points. Most of their delegates to the national convention, as well as their nominees for most lower-level offices, are now also chosen through party primaries. No longer can a handful of leaders in either party dictate whom the party will nominate for any office or what the party will stand for in an upcoming election.[32]

The Results of Reform   It is often said that every reform creates a series of unintended consequences, some of which may prove even less popular than the system the reform was designed to improve. States were so frustrated by the confusion and expense of implementing the many rule changes that they simply adopted a primary system. As a result, George McGovern, who did not represent

McGovern-Fraser Commission
Democratic party commission that after the 1968 national convention opened up meetings and votes to a broad variety of party activists, made primaries rather than caucuses the common means of choosing convention delegates, weakened the power of party leaders, and set up rules to ensure that a wide range of party members could participate fully in all party operations.

the mainstream of the Democratic party, won the 1972 nomination by bypassing the party and going directly to the voters. Many observers are dissatisfied with the post–1968 party reforms; they level particularly harsh criticism against the current dominance of primaries in the party nomination process.

As a result of this criticism, in 1984 the Democratic party revised its rules to bring elected and party officials back into the nominating process. They did this by creating "independent" delegate spots (in the 2004 campaign season these were 802 of the 4,353 delegates) and allowing party and elected officials to attend the convention as unpledged **superdelegates** who could change their minds about their votes at any time. Democrats hoped that these superdelegates would attract more media attention and provide a display of party unity. Because the delegates were not bound by primary elections, a candidate would still need the support of national party leaders to win the nomination. This process had unexpected results in 2004, as Senator John Kerry received the commitments of the vast majority of these delegates in advance, giving him a tremendous advantage over all of his other rivals in the primary race.

The winds of reform that swept through the presidential nomination system touched party processes at every level in both parties. In the past, candidates gained party nominations by working within the party hierarchy, rising through party ranks, and demonstrating party loyalty to the inner circle of leaders. Anyone who now wishes to run for office in a partisan election anywhere in the United States must first win a party primary or caucus, one likely to be contested by other ambitious party figures. The implications of this change are enormous. Politicians stopped working within the party to please a small group of leaders and now work outside party structures to please a large mass of relatively uninformed voters.

This shift in focus from party elites to party masses made money increasingly important in American politics, another unexpected and unintended consequence of making candidate selection more democratic. Yet it costs more to sway many people than a few. In the past those who desired party nominations needed to influence at most a few hundred, more typically a few dozen, and in some cases a handful of party leaders. Today decision makers (that is, registered party voters) number in the millions.

The change is so great that nomination races are now decided well before the national conventions, which have become so reduced in importance that the national networks are debating whether to cover them on television. To reach today's decision makers, a prospective candidate needs to hire a team of campaign specialists, conduct polls, create and mail out an impressive array of literature, and, most important, buy time on television.

In addition, the electronic media have taken on a new and important role in American politics. To impress the large mass of the electorate that votes in primaries, candidates must invade their consciousness by appearing on the dominant media of the age. The centrality of television in modern political campaigns raises campaign costs and also changes politicians' behavior. Those who can craft clever sound bites and look attractive are not guaranteed a win, but they surely have an advantage over those who lack them.

And increasingly, interest groups have become powerful and influential. Candidates need workers, support services, and money. They have found those resources in the varied strong interest groups that have sprung up to promote specialized causes. Symbolic of this development is the growing influence of **political action committees (PACs)**, which promote specific interest groups' agendas. Those who won elections in the past owed much to the traditional party hierarchy; now they owe much to their numerous interest group backers. Interest group and PAC lobbying has grown to such an extent that in the 2000 election the Democratic party raised $520 million, with about half of that coming from "soft money" donations, and the Republican party raised $716 million, with a third of that as "soft money." With no limits placed on soft money fund-raising until after

superdelegates Delegates to the Democratic National Convention not bound to vote for any particular candidate; usually prominent members of the party or elected officials.

political action committees (PACs) Committees formed as the fund-raising and financial distribution arm of specific interest groups.

U.S.A. Yesterday and Today

Chicago, 1968, to Boston and New York, 2004: The Vanishing Presidential Convention

The presidential nomination process changed forever after the 1968 Democratic National Convention in Chicago. The result of the 2008 election may change the process once again. National party conventions were once the centerpiece of American politics. Today they are merely extended party political infomercials.

In 1940, citizens captured the Republican convention with chants of "We Want Willkie," granting Wendell Willkie the opportunity to lose to Franklin D. Roosevelt. The same happened to Adlai Stevenson in 1952, who, after not even running in the presidential primaries, became the Democrats' choice to run against Dwight Eisenhower. By 1968, though, the Democratic party was deeply divided between southern conservatives with their states' rights agenda and peace advocates opposing the Vietnam war and protestors opposing the lack of civil rights for African Americans. The opportunity to carry out their battle on national television made the Chicago convention a recipe for political party disaster.

The nomination field appeared wide open after a turbulent nomination season. President Lyndon Johnson, stung by the intense criticism of his Vietnam and civil rights policies and by his narrow margin of victory over antiwar Senator Eugene McCarthy in the New Hampshire primary, had announced on March 31 that he would not run for reelection. Although Senator Robert Kennedy of New York seemed on his way to making a serious challenge for the nomination after winning the "winner-take-all" primary in California, his assassination reopened the nomination. So the race was left to the Es-

▲ As police and anti–Vietnam demonstrators, led by Tom Hayden, Abbie Hoffman, and the "Chicago Seven," clashed violently outside the 1968 Democratic party convention, onlookers began chanting, "The whole world's watching! The whole world's watching!"

tablishment candidate, liberal Vice President Hubert Horatio Humphrey of Minnesota, and antiwar Senator Eugene McCarthy.

While African Americans, antiwar delegates, women, and young people prepared to vote and lobby in Chicago for McCarthy and the antiwar movement, Mayor Richard Daley prepared his own plan. Though Humphrey had entered no primaries (some said be-

MakeItReal

Primary Source: Dwight D. Eisenhower's Farewell Address

the November 2002 election by the new Bipartisan Campaign Finance Reform Act of 2002, the huge fund-raising efforts from these sources continued. Planning for the 2002 Congressional elections, three different Republican fund-raising committees raised $204 million, which was $86 million more than that raised by the parallel Democratic party fund-raising committees. When combined with the $100 million campaign war chest raised by President Bush, the Republicans were able to mount their successful 2002 Congressional and state government electoral campaign.[33]

The Campaign Finance Law did not change the size of the fund-raising efforts, just the sources. Unlike earlier elections, only a small part of the fund-raising for each candidate in the 2004 election came from the PACs: about $3 million, or about 1 percent of President Bush's campaign funds, and less than 1 percent for Senator John Kerry. However, the so-called 527 single-issue groups enabled supporters of President George Bush and Senator John Kerry to raise more than $175 million for their campaigns and to place "issue ads" supporting their candidate or attacking their opponent in the media.[34] Individual candidates also learned from the successful efforts of Democratic presidential candidate Howard Dean that they could raise millions of dollars on their own on the Internet.

cause he missed filing deadlines; others believed that he did so deliberately to avoid defeats), he had won enough votes in the party elite-dominated caucus states, where the delegates are chosen only by meetings, many of which were secret, that he had the advantage going into the convention. Then Daley and the leaders excluded some state delegations and many activists for McCarthy. In addition, members of the press such as Tom Brokaw and Dan Rather were prevented from reporting on events while the process was rigged for Humphrey. Meanwhile, in Grant Park, about two miles from the convention hall, Daley was keeping antiwar protesters bottled up with city policemen. The American public was so horrified by the clashes that the Democrats were terribly split in their support. Humphrey won the nomination, but his candidacy for the presidency in the weeks following never left the ground, and he narrowly lost a presidential election to Richard Nixon that the Democrats could have easily won. Some in fact believe that if the election season had gone just two weeks longer, the Democrats would have won. The controversy continued as William Kunstler defended the leaders of the antiwar convention protest—including Tom Hayden, Jerry Rubin, and Abbie Hoffman—the so-called "Chicago Seven," in a turbulent political trial.

Having seen the damage done by closing the convention and by its presidential selection process, the Democratic party created the McGovern-Fraser Commission, named for South Dakota Senator George McGovern and Minnesota Congressman Don Fraser, to reform the nomination process by opening it up. Women, minorities, and young people would now be included in a much more open process. The adopted rules were so complicated, though, that many states simply created a state primary system. As a result, more than 70 percent of the delegate votes would now be chosen directly by the people. And, not coincidentally, the first choice of those voters for the Democrats in 1972 would be the man who knew the rules best—George McGovern. His grassroots campaign was led by a young director named Gary Hart, who refined the process of mobilizing circles of voters for a candidate. One day Hart would try to do the same for himself, but fail when scandal overtook him.

For years, this reformed nomination process settled beforehand the candidates, choices for running mates, and lengthy party platforms. By 2004, lagging viewer interest spurred network executives to greatly reduce national convention coverage. More and more, each convention became a lengthy infomercial as the parties sought to spin their own candidate and platform while attempting to damage the image of their opposition. Each network covered the meeting for only a couple of hours a night, focusing late at night on a few key speeches, the selection of a vice presidential candidate, and the presidential candidates' acceptance speeches.

"These conventions are no longer what they used to be," said veteran news anchor Bob Schieffer. "There was a time when all of these delegates came together, and you really saw something being decided at the convention. [Now] they're almost like a boat show. Both parties come along, they roll out the new model, we come out, look them over, listen to them, write stories about them, and that's about it."

The question is, with additional television networks such as CNN, MSNBC, and FOXNEWS, together with Internet coverage, if conventions will garner any extended television coverage in the future. Even more, with the advent of electronic communication technology, will such meetings continue, when parties can gather by satellite uplink, or perhaps on computers?

Sources: Rick Hampson, "Today's Delegates do Less Work, More Partying," *USA Today*, August 31, 2004, p. 8A; James Endrst, "Conventions Suffer Low Viewer Turnout," *Hartford Courant*, July 27, 2000; and Robert Dallek, "The Real Race to the White House Begins," *Australian Financial Review*, July 21, 2000.

Finally, with the destruction of the old party leadership that once provided continuity and cohesion, politicians who win high office now do so on their own and see themselves as independent of the discipline of party structures. In particular, the Democratic party in recent years has appeared to many observers like an uneasy coalition of squabbling individualists rather than a unified group of like-minded team players. Politicians' ability to secure their own campaign money, and their desire to work for their own political ambition in pursuing higher office, has enabled them to go their own way.

In recent years the Republican party has developed splits among ultraconservatives such as Orrin Hatch of Utah and Mitch McConnell of Kentucky, mavericks such as John McCain of Arizona, and moderates such as Arlen Specter of Pennsylvania and Olympia Snowe and Susan Collins of Maine. The conservative establishment is challenged to unite party members behind the Bush administration's conservative cultural positions. Majority Leader Bill Frist (R.-TN), thinking toward a presidential run in 2008, split from President Bush's position to call for federal government funding for stem-cell research. Similarly, "new Democrat" progressive reformers such as Minority Leader Harry Reid (D.-NV) and his assistant leader Dick Durbin (D.-IL) have had to seek unity with more liberal members such as both Massachusetts senators, Ted Kennedy and John Kerry, and Christopher Dodd of Connecticut. This trend seems likely to lead to further party fragmentation.

WHY A TWO-PARTY SYSTEM?

Throughout American history, two political parties have been the rule rather than the exception. Yet most democratic nations are characterized by a **multiparty system** in which five, ten, and sometimes even more parties regularly compete in elections, win seats, and have some chance of gaining power. Why is it that only two parties flourish in the United States?[35]

Institutional Factors

The most frequent explanation for the emergence and survival of the two-party system is the way the United States elects public officials. Known as the *single-member district electoral system*, it is widely believed to inhibit the development of third parties. In other democratic nations, districts are often, but not always, large enough to contain many representatives, and each party elects about as many representatives as its proportion of the vote in that large district. In a ten-member district, for instance, a party obtaining 10 percent of the vote has one elected legislator. If that party averages 10 percent of the vote across the country, it will end up with 10 percent of the members of the national legislature. Then, if it maneuvers sensibly, it may be asked to form part of a governing coalition. The upshot of such a multimember district, or proportional representation system, is that small parties can gain seats and power, providing an incentive for minor parties to form and contest elections.

In the United States, the incentives all favor the two large parties. The entire country is divided into **single-member districts**, and each district seat is awarded to the candidate with the most votes. Small parties that, say, win 10 percent in every district across the nation, receive no seats in the legislature. With that performance, they would lose in each district to one of the two big parties. Small parties that end up with no seats and no power gradually fade away as supporters grow discouraged. Potential supporters for a third party simply join one of the two big parties and promote their policy aims within a successful political grouping where those aims have some chance of being implemented.[36]

This system not only prevents third parties forming but also inhibits breakaway factions of the two major parties from setting up shop on their own. Disgruntled party subgroups have no incentive to leave and form their own parties, because doing so will lead to political impotence. Another institutional element favoring two-party competition is the **electoral college**. By its very design, the electoral college puts smaller parties at a disadvantage. The system produces, in effect, fifty-one winner-take-all state (including the District of Columbia) contests. Each state is allotted a certain number of electoral college votes, depending on its representation in Congress. Votes for president are then counted by state, and in all but two small states (Maine and Nebraska), whichever candidate comes in first in that state gains *all* of that state's electoral votes, no matter how close the contest, even if the winning candidate falls short of a majority of the ballots cast. There is no consolation prize for finishing second, much less third or fourth, in American politics. A candidate comes in first or not at all. For that reason, many voters are reluctant to "throw their vote away" on a candidate outside the mainstream. They tend, in the end, to align with one of the two major parties.

Question for Reflection

Should the United States move to a series of regional multistate primaries or even a national primary, and why?

multiparty system A political system in which five to ten or more parties regularly compete in elections, win seats, and have some chance of gaining power. Promoted by systems with proportional representation and characteristic of most democratic nations.

single-member districts Districts in which a seat goes to the candidate with the most votes. In this system, a small party, say, one that wins 10 percent in every district across the nation, would fail to secure a single seat in the legislature.

electoral college The group of 538 electors who meet separately in each of their states and the District of Columbia on the first Monday following the second Wednesday in December after a national presidential election. Their majority decision officially elects the president and vice president of the United States.

Occasionally, a significant portion of the electorate will cast off such inhibitions and risk supporting a third-party candidate, as in the case of Ross Perot. But consider the result of Perot's 1992 campaign. Although he captured about twenty million votes—close to 19 percent of the total—he did not receive a single vote in the electoral college. The same was true in 1996, when Perot's overall support fell to 9 percent of the voting electorate, and his nearly eight million votes again gained him no electoral college votes at all. What matters, then, is where those votes are located. And remember that citizen votes do not make a president; only electoral college votes do. It is hardly surprising, then, that Perot-style candidacies have been the exception rather than the rule. Nevertheless, although the 2000 Green party candidate Ralph Nader received no electoral college votes, his nearly three million votes, especially the 97,421 votes in Florida, might well have given George Bush the presidential win. In the 2004 campaign, though, Nader and the other third party candidates had no impact on the presidential election.

Cultural Factors

Some scholars believe that the American two-party system is built into prevailing cultural norms and values. They point to the United States' supposed traditions of moderation, deliberation, and compromise. Whereas the French or Italian political cultures—out of which have sprung vigorous multiparty democracies—are often described as volatile and fragmented, American culture is supposedly centrist, devoid of the ideological extremes, class divisions, and group hatreds that produce political fragmentation elsewhere. This theory suggests that with most citizens clustering at the center of the spectrum, the United States has no room for a variety of parties. These conditions produce a natural setting for a two party system, with each vying for the largest constituency of moderate voters.

Although this was the accepted cultural explanation for decades, in recent years scholars have begun to question it.[37] Particularly since the 1960s, American political culture appears to be fragmenting. Bitter struggles over civil rights, Vietnam, women's rights, and abortion have shattered the country's veneer of consensus and may help explain what many see as a weakening in the pattern of stable two-party dominance. In recent years, as shown in the 2000 and 2004 elections, some of the most volatile issues tearing at the fabric of the two-party system and its stability have been essentially cultural—abortion, gay rights, race, and family values.

Party Identification

Another attempt to explain the two-party system centers on electorate psychology. Explanations of this type emphasize the deep-seated, enduring nature of party attachments. Many voters develop lasting loyalty to a political party, often because that party served their needs on a crucial issue. Thus, Republicans gained the loyalty of millions in the 1860s by standing for national unity and the abolition of slavery. Democrats gained lifelong supporters in the 1930s with their attempts to mitigate the worst aspects of the Depression. Furthermore, voters have long memories. They stay faithful to their party for years, even for life, often passing these loyalties on to their children.

Political scientists call this long-term propensity to think positively of and vote regularly for a political party **party identification**. It does not explain the origins of the U.S. two-party system, but it does help explain its persistence. The intense psychological ties that keep party voters faithful ensure both parties of long-term support. These old attachments hamper any new party trying to break through the status quo to gain followers.[38]

party identification A psychological orientation or long-term propensity to think positively of and vote regularly for a particular political party.

MINOR PARTIES

Despite the power of the two major American parties, **minor** or **third parties** have made appearances in every decade of American history. Why do they appear, how have they performed, and what do they accomplish?[39]

Why Minor Parties Appear

With most Americans clustering in the middle range of the ideological spectrum, the two major parties take relatively moderate positions on most controversial policies. Any clear ideological stand far to the right or left of the average voter would alienate a large portion of the potential electorate. Since the major parties aim at winning votes and gaining office, they cast their nets as widely as possible for broad inclusiveness. Both major parties end up focusing on the same central segment of the electorate but do not necessarily give equal emphasis to the same issues. Frequently, the emergence of a third party talking about issues the major parties seek to avoid will signal a realignment of the voters, or at the very least a restructuring of the major parties.

In like fashion, the major parties cannot aim their appeals too obviously at just one subgroup of the population, be it farmers, union members, or gun owners. Focusing on one minority can easily leave many other minorities alienated.

This lack of ideological purity and the absence of narrow group promotion directly affect the character and formation of the minor American parties. Third parties form when an issue arises that leaves some Americans dissatisfied with the relatively moderate stands of both Democrats and Republicans. They also form when a group feels totally ignored and left out of the mainstream political process. But third parties that organize under such circumstances almost always remain minor, or sometimes have their platforms co-opted by one or both of the major parties.

Minor Party Performance

Third parties do, on occasion, make waves, usually when an issue or set of issues unite with a popular or charismatic leader. Under these conditions, minor party efforts have done remarkably well. Theodore Roosevelt, a former president, turned in the best performance of any minor party candidate. In 1912 he ran on the Progressive ticket and garnered 27 percent of the popular vote, along with 88 electoral votes out of 531. Most remarkable about his achievement was placing second in the balloting ahead of an incumbent president, William Howard Taft.

Another significant minor party candidacy occurred in 1968, when Alabama's segregationist governor, George Wallace, a Southern Democrat, ran as an American Independent. Wallace captured 14 percent of the popular vote and forty-six electoral votes. In 1980 a former Republican and member of the House of Representatives, John Anderson, ran as an independent candidate, receiving 7 percent of the popular vote but no electoral votes.

Texas billionaire H. Ross Perot stunned many observers when he ran in 1992 without any party affiliation, and after dropping out and later reentering the race, still won 19 percent of the popular vote. His organization, United We Stand America, however, was little more than a label attached to a group of amateur enthusiasts; at that time it was nothing like an organized party. In 1995 Perot's organization held a three-day national convention that once again raised the possibility of a third party, and by 1996 it had become the Reform party. Today Reform party members are frequently identified as a new "radicalized center" in American politics that Democratic and Republican party leaders cannot afford to ignore.

Since 2000, the major third party in the United States has been the Green party, represented by Ralph Nader in the 2004 presidential election. This party, which has

MakeItReal

2004 Green Party Platform

◄ While consumer advocate Ralph Nader's campaign for the presidency in 2000 as the candidate for the Green Party is credited and blamed by many for tipping the election to the Republican party, he had no impact on the final vote in the 2004 election.

been in existence since 1984, has an agenda of redistributing wealth, lessening global warming, improving the environment, and controlling genetic engineering in agriculture. Ralph Nader represented this group in both the 1996 and 2000 presidential elections. But, in 2004, seeking to build their party and not antagonize supportive liberals still angry with Nader over his effect on the 2000 election results, the Green party nominated Texas attorney David Cobb.[40] As of mid-2005, the Greens held more than 225 state and local political offices in 27 states.

Despite these modest successes, third-party candidates have rarely been a significant force in American national elections. As we have seen, they face the major psychological hurdle of party identification. Most voters already feel an emotional link to one of the two major parties; few are eager to wrench themselves away from their traditional voting habits to support a new, little-known group with no governing track record.

Beyond psychology, candidates outside the two-party mainstream face serious procedural obstacles. To be listed on local and state ballots, minor party candidates must obtain a certain number of signatures that demonstrate a minimal level of support. With few activists and little public recognition, minor parties frequently can't even get on the ballot. At the national level, they have enormous difficulty meeting eligibility requirements for federal election campaign funds. They also face a key difficulty in simply making people aware of who are and what they stand for. To capture national attention, candidates with little more than local or regional notoriety must court a national press often intent on following only the major candidates.

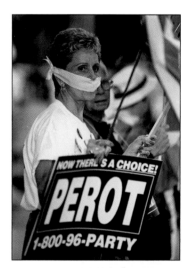

▲ A supporter of Ross Perot, the candidate for president from the Reform party in 1996, protested when he was excluded from the second debate between President Clinton and Republican nominee Robert Dole. Perot had been allowed to participate in the 1992 debates, but his successor, Patrick Buchanan, was not allowed into the 2000 debates.

The 2000 election provided a vivid example of these procedural obstacles when the Reform and Green parties were denied permission to appear in the presidential debates unless they had 15 percent support in the public opinion polls. Four years later, these candidates were again ruled ineligible for the presidential debates because of their lack of public support.

Overall, the barriers to the creation of a successful third party are enormous.[41] Both the Reform party and the Green party are now minor grassroots public-interest parties. Knowing this, many of the people who might be inclined to work in such parties devote their energies to lobbying interest groups such as the conservative judicial organization, the Federalist Society, and the ultraliberal Internet lobbying organization, MoveOn.org. The challenge for political parties will be to find ways to become more responsive to the American people.

Functions of Minor Parties

Although minor parties rarely attain power in the United States, they do perform important functions in a democracy. In a way, they act as wake-up calls to the two major parties. If enough dissatisfaction exists to fuel a third-party movement, both Democrats and Republicans quickly pay close attention. Almost always one, and often both, parties adopt enough of the third party's proposals to defuse the grievances the third party represents—and incidentally deflate the chances of that third party ever gaining power.

A prime illustration of this process can be seen in the "radical" platform that Socialist Eugene Debs endorsed in his 1904 campaign for the presidency. It included such "subversive" promises as support for women's right to vote, an eight-hour day for factory workers, and an end to child labor. All of these ideas, and many others from the Socialist agenda of that era, have long since become mainstream concepts, accepted by both major parties and most of the American electorate. The same was true of George Wallace's 1968 "Law and Order" campaign for the American Independent party, which held strong conservative views about the control of crime and the dismantling of civil rights programs. Richard Nixon adopted many of these views, becoming increasingly conservative in his campaign rhetoric and promising to appoint more strictly constructionist federal judges to accomplish these goals. He soon discovered that he was losing significant voter support to Democrat Hubert H. Humphrey, forcing him to tack back to the moderate position at the end of the election race. Finally, Ross Perot's constant call through the Reform party for budget deficit reduction led to the adoption of this proposal by both major parties.

By being the first to champion original ideas that may later become widely endorsed, minor parties perform a vital service for the democratic process. But even ideas that fail to prosper at least encourage open discussion of new proposals, force mainstream groups to rethink and justify the status quo, and give life to key democratic norms, such as free speech and the right of all citizens to organize to promote their interests.

THE PARTY IN GOVERNMENT

Although the Constitution says nothing about political parties, and the framers hoped that parties would play no role in the emerging republic, today's government institutions at all levels are organized through the party system. Party leaders run administrations at the state and national levels. Many act as city or town mayors or hold other executive offices in a variety of political settings. Members of Congress and legislators in each state hold party caucuses practically every day. These meetings help them decide the direction of party policy and the best tactics to gain their ends. In Congress and in most state legislatures, the leadership of the chamber, the committee chairs, and committee membership rolls all result from partisan votes, and party members usually sit together on opposite sides of the main aisle. Party is simply the first and dominant force in all of the upper-level institutions of American political life.

Among other things, party significantly influences the behavior of individual politicians. It proves to be, for instance, the single most powerful variable

Question for Reflection

How might a third-party candidate for president win the election?

Quick Review

The Party in Government

- The legislative branch is highly partisan.
- Partisanship is also important in presidential appointments.
- Although the judicial branch is designed to be nonpartisan, the appointment process for judges has always been partisan.

for predicting how American legislators will vote. The number of times that members of Congress vote based on party affiliation has steadily increased from below 60 percent in 1970 to more than 80 percent in the 1990s. This was clearly seen during the Clinton impeachment battle of 1998 when the two parties voted as a unified group more than 90 percent of the time. Since 2000, Republican members of Congress have voted based on party affiliation more than 85 percent of the time, whereas Democrats did so more than 80 percent of the time.[42] Simply put, party ideology matters. Democrats vote differently from Republicans.

The Importance of Party Ideology

Many people outside the political system are surprised to learn just how much party matters in governance. Yet why should we be surprised? We already know that Democrats and Republicans hold different ideologies and represent different segments of society. Given the reasonably clear party differences, we should logically expect the parties to create different public policies when they control government. That has indeed been the case. Government changes sharply when power clearly shifts from one party to the other. Democrats create liberal policies; Republicans create conservative ones.

An excellent way to illustrate party difference is to compare the voting records of Republicans and Democrats. For this purpose, we can make use of a device called an *interest group rating scheme*. Many interest groups routinely rank members of Congress on a scale from 0 to 100, based on votes that reflect the group's position, to publicize each member's level of support for issues related to the group's agenda. (The closer to 100, the higher the level of support.) The best known of these groups, and indeed the one that started this practice back in the 1940s, is the liberal Americans for Democratic Action. The ADA, as it is known, each year gives each member of Congress a rating that represents the percentage of times that member voted as the ADA desired on the thirty or forty most important bills taken up by Congress that year. The resulting number provides a rough idea of how "liberal" a member of Congress is. Ratings of 60 or higher indicate a clear liberal. Ratings of 40 or lower suggest a conservative. Middle numbers delineate moderates. Although in 1972 senators from the two parties showed considerable overlap on their liberal ratings, since that time the Senate has become increasingly polarized. By 2004, Senate members were more polarized than at any time since World War II, with Democrats largely voting with high liberal scores and the Republicans almost entirely confined to conservative scores.

No scheme of this sort can be perfectly precise. A difference of 5 or 10 points between two legislators may reflect little more than a vote or two missed because of illness. Still, major differences over time clearly indicate different voting patterns and different philosophies. Year after year, Democrats score between 60 and 100 on the ADA scale, whereas Republicans rank in the 0 to 20 range. Although some moderates can be found in both parties, the bulk of Republicans are conservative, whereas the bulk of Democrats are liberal.

So, it really matters which party gains control of government. Today, conservative Republican committee chairs in Congress have a major impact on policy. They shepherd bills they like through the legislature and find ways to kill those they do not. For example, when liberal Democrats tried to air their opposition to renewal of sixteen expiring provisions of the U.S.A. Patriot Act in 2005, Republican Chairman James Sensenbrenner of the House Judiciary Committee simply shut off the microphones, turned out the room's lights, and left, ending the hearing. The policies that emerge from the actions of partisan politicians greatly affect how the public views the two major parties (see Figure 9.3).

Question for Reflection

The framers did not envision political parties in their original approach to democracy. How have parties affected the way democracy is shaped?

MakeItReal

Civic Participation: Voting Records

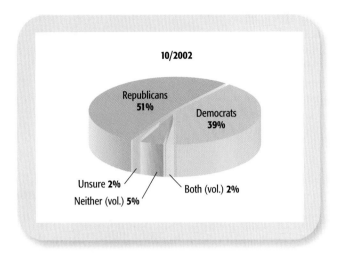
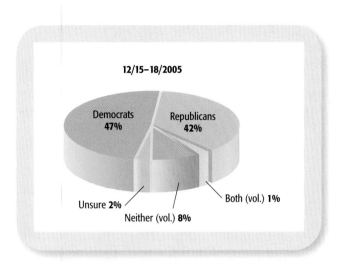

Figure 9.3   The Public Shifts on Which Party They Trust to Solve the Nation's Problems
Overall, which party, the Democrats or the Republications, do you trust to do a better job in coping with the main problems the nation faces over the next few years?

*Source: The New York Times/*CBS News Poll, October 27–31, 2002, reported in *The New York Times,* November 3, 2002, p. 1, and ABC News/Washington Post poll, Dec.15–18, 2005, found at www.pollingreport.com, last accessed, March 11, 2006.

POLITICAL PARTIES AND THE 2008 ELECTION

David Broder, a leading American journalist, wrote a grim analysis several years ago of America's party system entitled *The Party's Over.*[43] He claimed that American political parties were disintegrating, that they had lost their traditional stabilizing power over the electoral and governmental processes and were being replaced by a proliferation of special interest groups and the imagery of television.

Is the party really over? Many argue that declining rates of party identification, voter apathy, and the lack of formal constraints to ensure party allegiance all indicate that American political parties are headed toward extinction. Political party optimists, however, see hope for the future of parties and even a role for them in the revival of a more participatory and stronger democracy. They argue that parties have responded reasonably well to the many sources of change over the past three decades. After all, despite social upheavals, new forms of technology and communications, changing attitudes toward politics, institutional reforms in government, generational shifts in support for politics, and major crises in government, parties have stayed afloat and even maintained their hold over a large percentage of the American electorate. Could dying institutions have such staying power?

The 2004 election once again showed that political parties are crucial democratic structures that link the popular will to governmental outcomes. Just two years earlier, one congressional election poll revealed that the American people, when asked what issue they considered "the number one problem," were most concerned about the economy (27 percent) and terrorism (13 percent), with education (6 percent) a distant third. But for the 2004 election the issues had changed to "moral values" (22 percent), the economy/jobs (20 percent), the "war on terrorism (19 percent), and Iraq (15 percent). (See Figure 9.4.) These were policies on which the two political parties disagreed. As mentioned above, in the end, it was the Republican party's "ground game," masterminded by presidential counselor Karl Rove, funded by $125 million from the Republican National Committee, and enlisting more than 1.5 million volunteers in a massive national "get-out-the-vote" operation, that generated more than 8 million voters and won the election for the Republicans. This effort, especially effective in key swing states such as Ohio and Florida, overwhelmed the independent system of so-called 527 interest groups working for the Democrats through America Coming Together, the Media Fund, MoveOn.org, and such groups. Although the Democrats got five million new votes, the uncoordinated and comparatively underfunded nature of

Survey of Voters: Who They Were...

PERCENTAGE OF VOTERS		FOR BUSH	FOR KERRY
100	Total	51%	48%
46	Men	55	44
54	Women	48	51
17	18 to 29 years old	45	64
29	30 to 44 years old	53	46
30	45 to 59 years old	51	48
24	60 or over	54	46
77	White	58	41
11	Black	11	88
8	Hispanic/Latino	44	53
2	Asian	44	56
54	Protestant	59	40
27	Catholic	52	47
3	Jewish	25	74
10	None	31	67
23	White evangelical or born-again Christian	78	21
37	Republican	93	6
26	Independent	48	49
37	Democrat	11	89
4	Gay, lesbian or bisexual	23	77

... And What Was on Their Minds

ISSUE THAT MATTERED MOST

		FOR BUSH	FOR KERRY
22	Moral values	80	18
20	Economy/jobs	18	80
19	Terrorism	86	14
15	Iraq	26	73
8	Health care	23	77
5	Taxes	57	43
4	Education	26	73

WAR WITH IRAQ

		FOR BUSH	FOR KERRY
51	Approve of decision to go to war with Iraq	85	14
45	Disapprove	12	87
46	War with Iraq has improved long-term security of U.S.	90	10
52	Has not	19	80

THE STATE OF THE NATIONAL ECONOMY IS

		FOR BUSH	FOR KERRY
47	Excellent/good	87	13
52	Not so good/poor	20	78

Figure 9.4   A Picture of Partisanship: Voters and Issues in the 2004 Presidential Election

Source: Edison/Mitofsky nationwide surveys of voters leaving the polls on Tuesday. Those who voted for other candidates or had other answers are not shown. New York Times, November 4, 2004, p. 4.

this structure relative to the Republican party effort put John Kerry at a disadvantage in the election.

The point is clear, then, that no matter what the issue or the era, each party will do its best to fashion a position in the voters' minds that they hope will secure electoral support and then motivate those voters to go to the polls.[44] As the nation moves toward the next set of elections in 2006 and 2008, the questions will be whether the Republican party can institutionalize its gains or can the Democratic party restructure its organization to incorporate lessons from its 2004 defeat and regain lost seats in 2006. Although the party in power normally loses congressional seats in off-year elections, the large Republican majority in both the House and the Senate makes it unlikely that the Democrats will retake control in either house in 2006. Senate Democrats will be defending more seats than the Republicans (18 to 15), with five of them in "red" states that President Bush won in 2004. However, if the war in Iraq continues to go poorly, or the nation-building and constitutional process stalls, and the Democratic candidates persuade the voters that a change in the Senate or the House will improve the process, it could change the calculation.

As for the presidential election in 2008, normally the party out of power would be most interested in positioning itself for the race. The Democrats will face just such a challenge in choosing between candidates such as the more liberal, but increasingly moderate Senator Hillary Clinton of New York, possibly once again liberal Senator John Kerry, and more conservative candidates such as former senator John Edwards. But in 2008, with the presidency open, the Republicans will also be challenged to broker the selection of a candidate between the ultraconservative, religiously oriented candidates such as Senators Sam Brownback of Kansas and Bill Frist of Tennessee, and the more pragmatic, moderate candidates such as Senator Mark Warner of Virginia and Governor George Pataki of New York. Through it all, the Republicans might well be grappling with the maverick, independent candidacy of Senator John McCain of Arizona. As the United States approaches democracy, power has shifted from the few to the many, but sometimes even the few matter greatly. Still, recent changes in the way parties operate are merely part of the ongoing process of democratization central to the current pattern of American political development.

Summary

1. Political parties have played a role in American democracy since 1790. The first party system pitted Federalists (led by Hamilton) against Democratic-Republicans (led by Jefferson) and was so unstable that it disappeared between 1816 and 1824. The second party system began with the formation of the Jacksonian Democrats, actually an outgrowth of the Jeffersonian party. Seeking to make the electoral process more democratic, the Jacksonian Democrats replaced the system of nomination by party leaders with a national party convention. Opposition coalesced around a new party, the Whigs.

2. The third party system arose during the 1850s out of conflict over the issue of slavery. The new Republican party was devoted to abolishing slavery, whereas one branch of the Democratic party supported the Confederate cause. By this time, the Whigs had dropped from sight. The fourth party system began with a realignment in party constituencies in the 1890s and lasted until 1932. During this period the Democratic and Republican parties became highly developed and well organized.

3. The fifth party system began in 1932 with the realignment in party identification known as the New Deal coalition. This broad-based coalition supported the Democratic party and enabled it to dominate national politics until 1968. Although Republicans have won five out of seven presidential elections since then, it is unclear whether another realignment is taking place.

4. Political parties organize the election process by recruiting candidates for public office, representing the desires of voters, and attempting to ensure that their candidates carry out specific policies once in office. They also speak for and unite different groups and their varied interests through the formation of political coalitions. Other important functions of parties are to simplify political choices and organize government and policy making.

5. The local party provides the point of entry for those seeking involvement in politics. At the next level is the state party organization, which acts in conjunction with the state government to conduct primary elections. The national party organization is most active during presidential elections.

6. From the end of the nineteenth century to the middle of the twentieth, local parties often engaged in machine politics, in which party bosses traded jobs, money, and favors for votes and campaign support. Machine politics declined when the civil service and the modern welfare state emerged and primary elections proliferated.

7. At the national party conventions, delegates from the state parties meet to select presidential and vice presidential candidates and write the party's platform—a statement of principles and policies that it will carry out if its candidates are elected.

8. Some state party organizations select candidates for presidential elections at a caucus, or meeting of party adherents. Other state parties hold primary elections that allow all of the party's members to vote for a candidate. In a closed primary, the most common kind, only registered members of a political party may participate in that party's primary. Open primaries allow registered voters to vote in whichever primary they choose, thus permitting cross-party voting.

9. Since 1968, the presidential selection process has been radically altered as a result of demands for "democratization." Reforms adopted by the Democratic party included selecting candidates by means of primaries rather than caucuses and increasing the diversity of delegates to national conventions. The Republican party also adopted some of these reforms.

10. The greater power of rank-and-file party members has reduced the power of party bosses, increased the cost of conducting a campaign, reinforced the dominance of the electronic media in American politics, increased the power of interest groups and political action committees, and brought about a decline in party cohesion.

11. The single-member district system inhibits the development of third parties and thus produces and maintains a two-party system. In nations with systems of proportional representation, in which more than one member of the legislature can come from the same district, small parties can gain legislative seats and a multiparty system results. The electoral college favors a two-party system because the candidate who wins the most popular votes in a state receives all of that state's electoral votes.

12. Other explanations of the U.S. two-party system include cultural factors. Some believe that the two-party system is built into prevailing cultural norms and values; the tendency toward party identification leads voters to deep-seated, enduring affinity for the major parties.

13. Although minor or third parties usually have no hope of gaining real power, such parties occasionally arise when an issue is not adequately addressed by the major parties. When a minor party has a popular or charismatic leader, it can affect the outcome of elections and force the major parties to adopt or at least consider some of its proposals.

14. Although political parties are not mentioned in the Constitution, government institutions at all levels are organized through the party system. Party membership influences the behavior of individual politicians and leads to the creation of different public policies depending on which party is in control of the government.

The result is a trend toward candidate-centered, rather than party-centered, politics.

Review Questions

1. How and when have realignments affected the American party system since its inception?

2. Which structural, historical, and cultural factors account for the endurance of the two-party system?

3. Why don't third parties gain in power and influence? Has the two-party system in this country helped or hindered our approach to democracy?

4. What are the relative benefits of proportional representation versus the single member district, winner-take-all system? Which is more democratic and why?

5. Why have American political parties declined in influence?

6. How did the use of primary elections decrease the influence of political parties?

Key Terms

caucus 331
closed primary 331
electoral college 338
frontloading 332
"King Caucus" 316
local party organizations 324

machine politics 326
McGovern-Fraser
    Commission 334
minor or third parties 340
multiparty system 338
national party convention 327

national party organization 326
New Deal coalition 318
nomination 330
open primary 332
party identification 339
party platform 327

Suggested Readings

CEASAR, JAMES W., and ANDREW E. BUSCH. *Red Over Blue: the 2004 Elections and American Politics.* Lanham, Md.: Rowman and Littlefield, 2005. A comprehensive analysis of the effects of the balanced partisan structure on the 2004 presidential and congressional elections.

DICLERICO, ROBERT E. *Political Parties, Campaigns, and Elections.* Upper Saddle River, N.J.: Prentice Hall, 2000. A fine up-to-date textbook dealing with the state of political parties in the election process.

DREW, ELIZABETH. *Showdown: The Struggle Between the Gingrich Congress and the Clinton White House.* New York: Simon & Schuster, 1996. A wonderful recounting and analysis of how party politics has shaped the national political agenda in this study of the policy battles between Democrat President Clinton and the Republican Congress elected in 1994.

FRANK, THOMAS. *What's the Matter with Kansas?* New York: Owl Books, 2004. An informative and highly readable analysis of the sources of the red state versus blue state divide in the midwest and the entire nation.

GREEN, JOHN, and DANIEL SHEA. *The State of the Parties: The Changing Role of Contemporary American Parties.* 3d ed. Lanham, Md.: Rowman & Littlefield, 1999. An interesting study of the future of American political parties in a changing democratic system.

JEFFORDS, JAMES M. *My Declaration of Independence.* New York: Simon and Schuster, 2001. A readable account of why and how Senator Jeffords decided to leave the Republican party.

JOHNSON, HAYNES, and DAVID BRODER. *The System: The American Way of Politics at the Breaking Point.* Boston: Little, Brown, 1996. Two of America's finest political journalists examine how well the American political system is operating in a review of the political party dispute over the Clinton administration's efforts to create a system of universal health care.

KAYDEN, XANDRA, and EDDIE MAHE JR. *The Party Goes On: The Persistence of the Two Party System in the United States.* New York: Basic Books, 1985. The first full-scale assessment of the strength of political parties and their impact on national political life.

KEY, V. O. *Southern Politics.* New York: Knopf, 1949. A classic account of one-party politics in the South.

POLSBY, NELSON. *Consequences of Party Reform.* New York: Oxford University Press, 1983. An excellent account of changes in party rules and the impact of those changes on party roles in government.

RANNEY, AUSTIN. *Curing the Mischief of Faction: Party Reform in America.* Berkeley: University of California Press, 1975. A detailed account of the effect of party reforms on politics, with a special focus on the 1972 changes. Should be read with Shafer, *Quiet Revolution: The Struggle for the Democratic Party and the Shaping of Post-Reform Politics.*

SHAFER, BYRON E. *Quiet Revolution: The Struggle for the Democratic Party and the Shaping of Post-Reform Politics.* Washington, D.C.: Brookings Institution, 1983. The story of party reform in 1968–72, which produced a new era in national politics. The changes altered the very character of presidential politics, from campaign organization to grassroots participation.

SUNDQUIST, JAMES L. *Dynamics of the Party System: Alignment and Realignment of Political Parties in the United States.* Washington, D.C.: Brookings Institution, 1973. An analysis of the party system and the meaning of realignments in American history.

THOMAS, EVAN, et al. *Back from the Dead: How Clinton Survived the Republican Revolution.* New York: Atlantic Monthly Press, 1997. The story of how the once-liberal Democratic president Bill Clinton repositioned himself in the American political landscape to forge an electoral victory in 1996.

WATTENBERG, MARTIN. *The Decline of American Political Parties, 1952–1996.* Cambridge, Mass.: Harvard University Press, 1989. A scholarly analysis of declines in party identification, the rise in ticket splitting, and the challenges facing American political parties today.

★ CHAPTER 10 ★

PARTICIPATION, VOTING, AND ELECTIONS

CHAPTER OUTLINE

$\mathscr{A}$pproaching $\mathscr{D}$emocracy

The Motor-Voter Law, 1995–2005

In a democracy, the people govern themselves—or at the very least, they play a major role in the governing process. In modern representative democratic systems, the core of popular participation is the vote. If all citizens can easily register to vote and exercise that right, elected candidates will represent the people's choice. Conversely, if most citizens have no chance to vote, leaders will ignore them, leading to mass discontent and long-term disaffection from the political system.

President Bill Clinton signed the National Voter Registration Act (NVRA, P.L. 103–31), known as the Motor-Voter Law, in 1993, and it went into effect on January 1, 1995. More than eleven million citizens, the largest single increase in history, registered to vote or updated their voting addresses by the time of the 1996 presidential election. The Motor-Voter Law was designed to encourage voter registration by simplifying the registration process and, thus, it was hoped, increase voter turnout for elections. The law required states to provide registration services through driver's license agencies and public assistance and disability offices, and by mail-in registration. No citizen can vote without being registered, but in the past the registration process in most states was cumbersome, time consuming, and unpublicized. As a result, many citizens lost their right to vote by failing to enroll on the voting list. In all but a few states, Americans must register several weeks before an election if they wish to vote in it. If, on election day, they suddenly decide that they want to vote, it is too late. Opponents of the law claimed that the new law would impose excessive expenses on financially strapped state governments and that it would increase opportunities for voter fraud. Underlying the opposition was the belief that the law would benefit Democrats more than Republicans by making it easier for more inner-city and lower-income people to register. Winning over enough

★ Millions of voters have been added to the rolls since 1992, but the great challenge for democracy is to get these voters to actually go to the voting booth.

Republican support to pass the bill required Democratic concessions, including new language that tried to ensure that welfare agency employees did not pressure recipients of public benefits into registering to vote or registering for a particular party.[1] Opposition continued after the law passed, with some states challenging its constitutionality. Republican Governor Pete Wilson of California refused to implement the act, claiming that it would cost more than $35 million. Wilson argued that states should not have to pay for unfunded mandates issued by the federal government. Wilson also claimed that the law would increase voter fraud by encouraging ineligible voters, such as undocumented immigrants, to vote. The Justice Department responded by filing lawsuits against California and two other states to force compliance. The U.S. Supreme Court later ruled that the Motor-Voter Law was not an infringement on the states' rights to govern, not an unfunded mandate, and not a tool for increasing voter fraud.

Unfortunately, the Motor-Voter Law did not produce an immediate increase in voter turnout, only in registrations to vote. In fact, turnout in the 1996 presidential election was less than 50 percent—the lowest since 1924. Four years later, in November 2000, more than 105 million people cast a vote for president—9.5 million more votes than in 1996—but this was a mere increase from 49 percent to 51 percent in overall turnout. Perhaps when citizens must expend little energy to register, they are less likely to vote. Yet, according to the U.S. Census Bureau, 64 percent of U.S citizens ages eighteen and older voted in the 2004 presidential election. Most encouraging was the fact that 126 million people voted in November 2004, a record high for a presidential election year. Voter turnout increased by 15 million voters from the 2000 year election. The registration rate of the voting age population was 72 percent, higher than the 70 percent registered in the year 2000.[2]

★ Rhode Island Secretary of State Matt Brown, left, is given a demonstration of the new electronic voter registration system for the Rhode Island Department of Motor Vehicles by RIDMV clerk Kathy Lussier, center, and administrator Charles Dolan. This system, the first system of its kind in the nation, simplifies voter registration and reduces voter registration fraud.

QUESTIONS FOR REFLECTION

Did you vote in the 2004 or 2005 elections? What factors accounted for your decision to vote or not to vote in these two elections?
Do you plan to vote in the 2006 and 2008 elections?

Introduction
POLITICAL PARTICIPATION AND DEMOCRACY

In this chapter we consider an issue that goes to the very heart of the democratic ideal. Democracy simply cannot work without mass political involvement, or **participation**. Citizens who have a say in the national decision-making process show greater levels of satisfaction with the political system as a whole. The very act of participation makes them feel a part of the system; in addition, citizens feel good when they see that policy decisions, over the long run, reflect their desires. Although mass participation can produce political tension, as participants argue their various interests, in the long run it leads to democratic outcomes and acceptance of the system. A 2001 bipartisan National Commission on Federal Election Reform, co-chaired by former presidents Gerald R. Ford and Jimmy Carter, concluded that, "for Americans, democracy is a precious birthright. But each generation must nourish and improve the processes of democracy for its successors."[3] Four years later, the Commission on Federal Election Reform issued a final report titled "Building Confidence in U.S. Elections." Co-chaired by Jimmy Carter and James A. Baker III, the report began with the observation that "elections are the heart of democracy. They are the instrument for the people to choose leaders and hold them accountable. At the same time, elections are a core public function upon which all other government responsibilities depend. If elections are defective, the entire democratic system is at risk. Americans are losing confidence in the fairness of elections, and while we do not face a crisis today, we need to address the problems of our electoral system." The committee offered many challenging proposals, including the controversial proposal to require photo identification cards for voters.[4]

Active citizen participation can move the United States closer to the ideal of a democratic political system. Through voting and other forms of political participation—campaigning, gathering information, joining groups, and protesting—Americans can involve themselves in the democratic process. American government, closed to the vast majority in the framers' day, has opened to the input of millions, representing every conceivable point of view. Any citizen who makes even a marginal effort can find dozens of outlets for effective political participation. Still, the 2000 presidential election reminds us that we remain on the road to democracy; the 2004 election reminds us of issues that might help our polity approach the democratic ideal—electronic voting machines, an improved absentee ballot system, early voting, making election day a holiday, and the need for upgraded voting machines with improved ballot designs.

WHO PARTICIPATES?

Since the ancient Greek theorists first debated various types of government, political thinkers have held that a citizen's informed participation represents the highest form of political expression within democracy. Indeed, the Greek word *idiot* originally described someone who did not participate in politics—a definition showing how much importance the ancient Greeks placed on democratic involvement. In Athens, citizens not only discussed politics but served in government as well. They held no elections as such; instead, everyone eligible regularly drew lots to serve in the legislature and fill other posts.

In a nation as large as the United States, the Athenian kind of *direct* democracy is logistically impossible. Instead, the United States has evolved a *representative* form of government in which all eligible citizens may participate in electing officeholders

participation Mass political involvement through voting, campaign work, political protests, civil disobedience, among many others.

to represent their opinions in government. And Americans have the opportunity to go to the polls frequently. The United States has more elections than any nation in the world, with more than 500,000 offices filled in any four-year election cycle!

The standards of self-governance assume most citizens participate in some form of political activity and that they base their participation on a reasoned analysis of ideas, options, and choices. This link between widespread and informed participation, voting, elections, and public policy constitutes the fundamental component of democracy. Voting is but one form of political behavior essential to a democracy. Indeed, the right to choose *not* to vote is also essential to the workings of a successful democracy.

The ancient Greeks regarded participation in a democratic society a full-time job for males who had full citizenship and owned property. Citizens would spend a good deal of time familiarizing themselves with the issues of the day, then make policy decisions based on informed reason and factual knowledge. This ideal is clearly difficult to achieve in a modern, large-scale mass democracy where citizens spend much of their time earning a living. Also, individuals' interests vary, and it is unrealistic to expect that in their spare time all citizens will participate in political activity. On the other hand, not all Americans are apathetic and uninvolved. Many come close to the ideal of full-time political involvement, and many others meet various criteria for democratic citizenship.

A classic study of political participation levels of the American electorate by Sidney Verba and Norman Nie found that citizens fall along a continuum of political engagement, ranging from those totally uninvolved in politics to those who make it a full-time occupation.[5] About a tenth of the population is deeply involved in the political process. Nearly half of American citizens engage in political activities of which the ancient Greeks would have approved—they work for candidates or issues at election time or in groups that support social issues, or both. Almost 46 percent of the population engages in some kind of serious, politically oriented activity. In addition, another quarter of the population votes or contacts public officials for one purpose or another, leaving only about a fifth of American citizens completely inactive in the political process. We can debate if this record could be improved upon, but it does not appear as lamentable a performance as many social commentators would make it.

The disturbing element in the varying participation rates concerns the different types of people likely to be found in each category. Generally speaking, fewer low-income people and minority group members participate at the higher activism levels. Activists, for instance, are largely well-educated, middle- and upper-income voters. Inactives are disproportionately poorly educated and low-income. This is not to say that all active citizens are rich and educated, or that all inactive ones are poor and uneducated. The issue here is one of tendency. These findings, replicated in study after study, lead many observers to wonder how well American society is approaching the democratic ideal of equal political participation by all.

▲ For days before national elections in India, this billboard reminded voters of the scorn the ancients felt toward nonvoters.

A Brief History of Voting in the United States

Historically, American politics has been notable for the steady erosion of barriers to democratic participation. Voting in particular, and other avenues of participation more generally, were closed for many years to minorities, women, and young people. Today, many barriers to participation have been broken.

Politics in the United States began as an activity reserved for white, property-holding, tax-paying, middle- and upper-class males. Perhaps a quarter of the American adult population met those criteria. Thus, poor whites and women were disenfranchised. Slaves remained "property," retaining none of the citizenship rights that whites enjoyed; in fact, slaves were not even considered whole human beings. A compromise forged during the Constitutional Convention resulted in each slave being counted as three-fifths of a person for purposes of taxation and of representation in the U.S. House of Representatives.

Question for Reflection

Would you favor implementing a photo identification card as a prerequisite to vote?

Quick Review

The Fifteenth Amendment

- Passed in 1870 as part of the Civil War amendments.
- Guaranteed right to vote could not be denied because of race, color, or previous servitude.
- Goal was to extend voting privileges to former slaves.

MakeItReal

Primary Source: The Fifteenth Amendment
Primary Source: The Voting Rights Act (1965)
Primary Source: Seneca Falls Declaration

Quick Review

Voting Rights

- The Fifteenth Amendment, 1870: right to vote to African American males.
- The Nineteenth Amendment, 1920: right to vote to women.
- The Twenty-third Amendment, 1961: right to vote to citizens of the District of Columbia.
- The Twenty-fourth Amendment, 1964: outlawed the poll tax.
- The Voting Rights Act of 1965: provided protection to African Americans wishing to vote.
- The Twenty-sixth Amendment, 1971: right to vote to citizens eighteen years of age or older.

poll tax A fee that had to be paid before one could vote; used to prevent African Americans from voting; now unconstitutional.

literacy test A requirement that voting applicants had to demonstrate an understanding of national and state constitutions. Primarily used to prevent African Americans from voting in the South.

good-character test A requirement that voting applicants wishing to vote produce two or more registered voters to vouch for their integrity.

Property requirements for voting gradually relaxed over the decades, disappearing by the middle of the nineteenth century, when virtually all white males were enfranchised. The Fifteenth Amendment, passed in 1870 as part of the Civil War Amendments, guaranteed that "The right of citizens of the United States to vote shall not be denied or abridged by the United States or by any State on account of race, color, or previous condition of servitude." The amendment's aim was to extend voting privileges to former slaves—and to African American males in general. Though it seemed to pave the way for broader political participation, by the end of the nineteenth century the spirit underlying the Fifteenth Amendment had been perverted to the narrow perspective of southern state and local interests intent on keeping African Americans from voting.

Racism led government officials in the South to devise techniques that kept African Americans from the polls. First and foremost was the simple tactic of intimidation. Local African Americans were victims of threats, beatings, home burnings, or in many cases were lynched by anonymous mobs. Naturally, when people live under the constant fear of violence, an unsubtle "suggestion" that they not exercise their right to vote will be enough to deter all but the bravest of them.

Southern officials also devised formal ways to keep the African American vote down. First, they required payment of a **poll tax**, a fee paid before one could vote. In several states, an unpaid fee continued to accrue from one election to the next until it became a sum beyond the means of poor African Americans. Southern election officials also made selective use of the **literacy test**, a requirement that voting applicants demonstrate ability to read and write. African American college graduates might be asked to read and explain complex passages of the Constitution, whereas white citizens received simple grade-school paragraphs to read. A third device was the **good-character test**, requiring those wishing to vote to find two or more registered voters to vouch for their integrity. Because African Americans found it difficult to register, they also had trouble finding registered friends to vouch for them, and registered whites were unwilling to come to their aid. Southern states used a variety of other devices as well to limit African American political power.

These prohibitions were extremely successful. Because most African Americans lived in the South until well into the 1950s, southern interference with African American political rights effectively disenfranchised the vast majority of African Americans for decades. For the first half of the twentieth century, African Americans rarely participated in politics, few held public office, and less than 10 percent voted regularly.

Change came as the civil rights movement gained momentum in the 1950s and 1960s. The Voting Rights Act of 1965, providing protection to African Americans who wished to vote, and the Twenty-fourth Amendment (1964), outlawing the poll tax in federal elections, helped seal a new national commitment to equal opportunity in the political arena. The U.S. Supreme Court erased many barriers to African American participation, striking down state poll tax laws in 1966.

The movement for women's political equality has a lengthy history, beginning with the first women's rights convention at Seneca Falls, New York, in 1848. After decades of pressuring for suffrage and other legal rights, women finally won the right to vote with passage of the Nineteenth Amendment in 1920. This was a rather slow approach to democracy—minority males won the vote in 1870—twenty-two years after Seneca Falls. Fifty years later, the Nineteenth Amendment guaranteed that "The right of citizens of the United States to vote shall not be denied or abridged by the United States or by any State on account of sex."

Further expansion of political participation came with ratification of the Twenty-third Amendment in 1961, which gave residents of the District of Columbia the right to vote in presidential elections, and the Twenty-sixth Amendment in 1971, which gave the right to vote to all citizens of the United States eighteen years of age or older. Extending suffrage rights is a key step toward approaching the democratic ideal of equal political participation by all and the primary reason why former presidents Ford and Carter co-chaired the 2001 National Commission on Federal Election Reform.

VOTING

As we have seen, political participation may take many forms, but the most central act in a democracy is the citizen's decision to vote. All other political acts cost more in terms of time, effort, and money, and none produces such a level of equality as the vote. In the 2000 presidential election, more than 105 million ballots were cast and Vice President Al Gore received 539,897 more votes than George W. Bush, who won the electoral vote 271–266, but only after the Supreme Court, in a 5–4 decision, overruled the Florida Supreme Court order that would have allowed manual counting of ballots. An examination of more than 175,000 uncounted Florida ballots revealed that the ballots of those in Florida's black neighborhoods were most likely to go uncounted. "Overall, 136 out of every 1,000 ballots in heavily black precincts were set aside—a rate of spoiled ballots three times higher than in predominantly white precincts."[6]

The disenfranchisement of black voters poses a challenge for a system like ours that rightfully prides itself in the great progress made in enfranchising voters in America. A joint study conducted by Caltech/MIT in July 2001 found that four to six million presidential votes were lost in 2000. Another 1.5 million votes were not

Question for Reflection

Would allowing ex-felons to vote lead us closer to the democratic ideal?

 **MakeItReal**

Civic Participation: Registering to Vote

Approaching Democracy Around the Globe

The Iraqi People Vote

On January 30, 2005, an historic event occurred—during wartime and with an insurgency mounting every day, the Iraqi people chose representatives for a new national assembly. The voting represented the first general election since the 2003 invasion and marked an important step in the transition to Iraqi self-rule. Nothing symbolized the pride of Iraqis more than showing their fingers, marked with ink by election workers, after casting ballots.

Iraq's historic ballot garnered votes from 8.6 million out of an eligible 14 million people in the country, and nearly 310,000 Iraqis abroad. They chose a 275-member interim national assembly along with a new regional 111-member parliament in the north. Turnout was estimated at 58 percent in the country and more than 90 percent for those living abroad. Sunni Arabs boycotted the election, which the United Alliance party, backed by Shi'ite cleric Grand Ayatollah Ali al-Sistani, won with 48 percent of the vote. The Kurdish parties followed with about 26 percent of the vote. The Independent Electoral Commission of Iraq (IECI) gave a breakdown of seats: Shi'ite alliance—141 seats, Kurdish alliance—75 seats, interim prime minister Iyad Allawi's list—40 seats, and interim Iraqi president Ghazi Yawar—5 seats. "Today marks the birth of a new Iraq and free people," said Farid Ayar, an IECI spokesman. UN Secretary-General Kofi Annan said the results reflected not only the courage and determination of the Iraqi people but also their commitment to the political transition process that their country was undergoing.

The new national assembly was charged with writing a permanent constitution. By late August, the Iraqis had completed a draft constitution. "I want to congratulate our people who struggled against dictatorship for democracy and freedom," said Iraqi President Jalal Talabani. On October 15, the Iraqi people voted in a referendum on whether or not to approve the draft constitution. When the votes were tabulated, 78 percent of voters backed the charter and 21 percent opposed it. Elections for a constitutional government were held on December 15, 2005. Seventy percent of registered voters turned out, the highest participation level recorded in any of the three post-Saddam Hussein elections. The Iraqi electoral commission reported that 10.9 million of the 15.6 million registered voters cast ballots in the election for a new four-year Iraqi parliament. "There's a lot of joy, as far as I am concerned, in seeing the Iraqi people accomplish this major milestone in the march to democracy," said President Bush. "I was struck by how joyous they were to be able to vote for a new constitution. We take it for granted in America because we vote quite often in this country."

Sources: Elisabeth Bumiller, "'A Lot of Joy' for Bush as Iraqis Make the Most of Chance to Vote," *New York Times*, December 16, 2005, p. A15; Edward Wong, "Turnout in the Iraqi Election Is Reported at 70 Percent," *New York Times*, December 22, 2005, p. A10; Dexter Filkins, "Iraqis, Including Sunnis, Vote In Large Numbers on a Calm Day," *New York Times*, December 16, 2005, p. A1. The Independent Electoral Commission of Iraq (IECI) home page is quite instructional: www.ieciraq.org/English/Frameset_english.htm; see also Dexter Filkins and John F. Burns, "Iraqis Cast Votes on Constitution to Shape Future," *New York Times*, October 16, 2005, p. A1; David Sanger and Steven R. Weisman, "Vote Over, Iraq Faces Task of Forming a Government," *New York Times*, February 1, 2005, p. A1; "A Guide to Iraq's Elections," *Washington Post*, p. A17.

voter turnout The percentage of eligible voters who actually show up and vote on election day.

counted because of difficulties using voter equipment. The U.S. Census Bureau reported that 2.8 percent of registered voters who did not vote (one million people) did so because of long lines, inconvenient hours, or the location of their polling place.[7]

A major study conducted by the California Voter Foundation on "Voting Incentives and Barriers" (www.calvoter.org) found that nonvoters are "disproportionately young, single, less educated and more likely to be of an ethnic minority than infrequent voters. Forty percent of California's nonvoters are under the age of thirty, and only 34 percent of nonvoters are married. Seventy-six percent of nonvoters have less than a college degree, and 54 percent are white or Caucasian, compared to 60 percent of infrequent voters. Though California's population grows increasingly younger and more diverse, California's voting population continues to be dominated by older, white voters," said Kim Alexander, director of the CVF.[8]

Voter Turnout

Many political observers define the health of a representative democracy by the degree to which its citizens participate in elections. **Voter turnout** expresses the percentage of eligible voters who actually show up and vote on election day. Thus, a turnout rate of 80 percent for a given election means that 80 percent of all citizens legally entitled to vote actually did vote in that election. Scholars have traced voter turnout in the United States over the years (see Figure 10.1). The 2004 presidential election showed promising signs for those concerned with participation: A record number of voting-age citizens turned out, and turnout rates were 67 percent for non-Hispanic whites, 60 percent for blacks, 44 percent for Asians, and 47 percent for Hispanics. These rates topped the previous presidential election by 5 percentage points for non-Hispanic whites and 3 points for blacks. The voting rates for Asian and Hispanic citizens remained the same. Those ages eighteen to twenty-four had the lowest voting rate (47 percent), whereas those forty-five and older had the highest turnout (close to 70 percent.) Turnout was higher for women (65 percent)

▶ Activists in nineteen states held rallies in July 2005 against the use of error-prone electronic voting machines.

Source: National Journal, September 11, 2004, p. 2720.

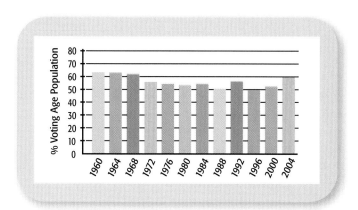

Figure 10.1   Voter Turnout in Presidential Elections (1960–2004)

Source: http://www.bettercampaigns.org/documents/turnout.htm.

than for men (62 percent). Turnout for those with bachelor's degrees or higher was 80 percent; with a high school diploma, 56 percent.[9]

Explaining Turnout

How can we explain turnout rates in the world's oldest democracy? Nations such as Italy, the Netherlands, Belgium, Sweden, Australia, Germany, and Norway boast an average turnout of more than 80 percent in national elections (see Table 10.1). Some experts argue, however, that these figures are deceptive. Turnout data are not comparable from one nation to the next. Many nations make voting compulsory, and they fine people who do not vote. Naturally, their turnout will be higher than in nations where voting is voluntary. Furthermore, many foreign nations report turnout as a percentage of all registered voters, whereas turnout rates in the United States are usually given as a percentage of all adult citizens eligible to vote.[10]

To explain voting, let us start with a simple axiom: Nothing in this life is free. Even the simplest political action has costs. Consider what it takes to exercise the right to vote in America. First, a citizen must register to vote. Unlike other democracies, registration in the United States is the individual's responsibility, requiring a conscious decision and the expenditure of time and energy, although less of both since implementation of the Motor-Voter Law. Why vote? The benefits must outweigh the costs to ensure that people will vote, so it helps to know the benefits as well as the costs of voting. There are few concrete benefits in voting; that is, a single vote is unlikely to determine the election outcome, so we must look at the intrinsic benefits, what political scientists Wolfinger and Rosenstone describe as "the feeling that one has done one's duty to society, to a reference group, and to oneself; or the feeling that one has affirmed one's allegiance to or efficacy in the political system." In addition, some people enjoy the simple act of voting in the same way others enjoy the opera or going to the baseball game.[11]

The costs of voting are much easier to measure. Registering can be cumbersome. It usually means taking time to contact a government agency during business hours. Voters must reregister when they move to a new address. Thus, when they move out of a district, citizens lose the right to vote unless they make another conscious decision to register in their new community. One explanation for low voter turnout may be that the average American moves often—about every five years—and registering

Quick Review

National Voter Registration Act

* Motor-Voter Law signed by President Bill Clinton in 1993.
* Over 11 million citizens registered to vote or updated voting addresses.
* Simplified registration process to help increase voter turnout.
* States provide registration services through driver's license agencies, and public assistance and disability offices, and by mail-in registration.

▲ American's recent experience with poor voting equipment, ambiguous registration rules, and poorly trained pollworkers demonstrate that we are still approaching the democratic ideal.

Source: National Journal, September 11, 2003, p. 2721.

Table 10.1 ■ International Voter Turnout, 1991–2000

International voter turnout per year

Country	1991	1992	1993	1994	1995	1996	1997	1998	1999	2000	Average	System
Argentina	89%		78%		80%			78%			81%	PR
Australia		83%				82%					83%	PR***
Austria	80%		76%	79%							78%	PR
Belgium	85%				83%						84%	PR
Bolivia			50%				62%				56%	Mixed**
Brazil				77%							77%	PR
Canada			64%				56%				60%	District#
Chile			82%								82%	PR
Colombia	26%			29%				40%			32%	PR
Denmark				82%				83%			83%	PR
Dominican Republic				31%		62%					47%	PR
Ecuador				66%		68%		48%			61%	PR
Finland	71%				71%						71%	PR
France			61%				60%				61%	District$
Germany				72%							72%	PR*
Greece			86%			84%					85%	PR
Guatemala				14%	33%						24%	PR
Iceland	89%				88%						89%	PR
Ireland		74%					67%				71%	PR***
Italy		92%		91%		87%					90%	Mixed**
Luxembourg				60%							60%	PR
Mexico	50%			66%			54%			60%	58%	Mixed**
Netherlands				75%							75%	PR
Norway			74%				77%				76%	PR
Peru					58%						58%	PR
Portugal	78%				79%						79%	PR
Spain			77%			81%					79%	PR
Sweden	83%			84%							84%	PR
Switzerland	40%				36%						38%	PR
Thailand		58%			64%	65%					62%	District&
Turkey	80%				79%						80%	PR
United Kingdom		75%					69%				72%	District#
United States		55%		39%		49%		36%		47%	45%	District#
Venezuela			50%								50%	Mixed**

Data is based on Voting Age Population (VAP).
Blank spaces indicate missing data or no elections held that year.

* 50% by single-seat, plurality election $ Single-seat districts, with majority provision
** 75% by single-seat, plurality election   & Multi-seat districts, elected by plurality
*** Choice Voting   ‾ Indicates compulsory voting
# Single-seat districts, elected by plurality

Source: International Institute for Democracy and Electoral Assistance, as found on The Center for Voting and Democracy Website, www.fairvote.org/turnout/intturnout.htm. Reprinted by permission of The Center for Voting and Democracy. Updated data unavailable at website.

to vote is often a low priority when moving into a new home and adapting to a new community.

Registration laws in most states seem designed to depress election turnout rates. Well more than 90 percent of Americans live in states where they must register to vote in advance, up to several weeks before the actual day of the election. Since many people pay little heed to an election until the campaign is in high gear two or three weeks before voting day, many of them lose the right to vote because by the time it occurs to them to register, it is too late. As you would expect, states that do allow same-day registration and voting (such as Maine, Minnesota, and Wisconsin) have much higher turnout rates.

Motor-voter laws, of course, ease the registration process. Even registered voters, however, may fail to reach the polls. Most detrimental to election turnout in the United States is the traditional day of voting—Tuesday. Most states keep their polls open from 8:00 A.M. to at least 7:00 P.M., but busy citizens with jobs, families, and errands to run often have difficulty finding the time to vote on a weekday.[12]

In recent years, most states have taken steps to minimize the costs of registering and voting. Registration can now be done closer to election day than in the past, and polls stay open longer than in the past. In some states, such as California, employers must give employees paid time off to vote. In Oregon, voters may cast their ballots by mail or at drop boxes. Frequently, civic groups target universities and colleges, grocery stores, shopping malls, and other crowded areas to register people. Other creative suggestions have been put forth by various citizen groups: keeping polls open for twenty-four or forty-eight hours, same-day registration in all states, making election day a national holiday, holding elections on weekends, and Internet voting.[13]

All in all, voting involves costs, but the costs have been declining. Understanding nonvoting, then, requires looking beyond institutional factors. We must also look at subjective, psychological explanations.

Nonvoting

People have numerous reasons for failing to vote, and one is the possibility that they are satisfied with the way things are going and see no particular need to become involved politically. Today's nonvoters may decide to vote when a public controversy sears their consciences and forces them to act, as former Supreme Court justice Felix Frankfurter once argued. Thus, nonvoters may start showing up on election day if they become unhappy enough. This option of nonvoters to vote also keeps politicians relatively honest. They know that truly unpopular actions could bring out hordes of formerly silent citizens eager to vote them out at the next election. Thus, from this perspective, nonvoting does not threaten the survival of democratic processes in America. It simply maintains the status quo.

Another school takes issue with this perspective. It claims that nonvoting and nonparticipation in general undermine the health of democratic politics. Citizens who remain outside the political process may come to feel little connection with the laws of the land and the government that administers those laws. They feel alienated—that their vote makes no difference, that the process of voting is too difficult, and that the parties do not offer true alternatives.

A 1996 poll conducted by the League of Women Voters found that nonvoters were no more alienated than voters. This survey concluded that people do not vote because they do not grasp the significance or importance of elections to them, because the process of voting seems difficult and cumbersome, or because the costs of becoming informed are just too steep. This survey showed that nonvoting was not a product of alienation, but rather that nonvoters merely fail to see voting as particularly important. When asked what they would do, given a choice between a once-a-year sale at their favorite store and voting, 30 percent of nonvoters chose the sale, compared with 6 percent of voters. When asked to choose between watching a new episode of their favorite television show and voting, 27 percent of nonvoters chose watching television; only 3 percent of voters would stay at home. Voters and nonvoters were equally distrustful of government, but nonvoters saw their participation as irrelevant to the outcome.[14]

The 2004 California Voter Foundation Survey on "Voting Incentives and Barriers" concluded that "millions of Californians are eligible to vote but not registered. Millions more vote infrequently."[15] The two reasons for voting cited most often are "to make your voice heard/express your opinion" and "to support a particular candidate." More than 90 percent of infrequent voters surveyed agreed that "voting is an important part of being a good citizen" and "voting is an important way to voice your opinions on issues that affect your family and your community." The two reasons for not voting cited the most often were "I'm too busy to vote" and "there are no candidates I believe in." The widely held perception that politics are controlled by special interests represents a significant barrier to participation. Job hours were the biggest factor leading infrequent voters to say they are too busy to vote, and more than half of those surveyed said they work more than forty hours a week. More than half also said they are unfamiliar with absentee voting. Eighteen percent of nonvoters surveyed said they thought they were registered to vote through the Department of Motor Vehicles (DMV). Twenty-three percent of nonvoters surveyed said they do not want to register to vote because they want their information to be private. The logistics of the voting process were more of a barrier for Spanish-speaking infrequent voters, who cited difficulty in locating their polling places, obtaining help from pollworkers, and accessing voting materials in their preferred language at a much higher rate than infrequent voters generally.

The survey found that infrequent voters' family members were as influential as newspapers when it comes to deciding how to vote. However, only half of nonvoters said their friends vote or said they grew up in families that discuss political issues and candidates. Latino, African American, and Asian Pacific Islander nonvoters were less likely to live in a pro-voting culture than other nonvoters.

Nearly half of the infrequent voters surveyed said election information is hard to understand, whereas 29 percent called it untrustworthy. Among nonvoters, 39 percent said it is hard to understand and the same number said it was untrustworthy. The survey results indicated that African American infrequent voters and nonvoters are more distrustful of election information than infrequent voters and nonvoters generally.[16]

Who Votes?

The answer to the question "Who votes?" is crucial for understanding the political process, because political leaders, quite naturally, pay more attention to voters (who determine politicians' fates) than to nonvoters (who play only a potential role in making or breaking governments). As we pointed out earlier in the discussion of the 2004 election, many variables affect who votes. Schooling increases one's ability to understand the intricacies of politics and, in turn, see the benefit of taking a political action, such as voting for a favorite cause or candidate.

Social status is another crucial variable that determines the likelihood of voting. Simply stated, the higher one's socioeconomic level, the more likely one is to participate in politics, especially to vote.

Education and income frequently go together, of course, since it is becoming more difficult in modern society to gain economic success without an education. People who have both education and income possess two strong motivators of political activity.

Social connections in general make political participation more likely. The more ties citizens have to their community, the more reason they see for participating in politics. They work to keep their property taxes low, help support a new school for their children, or promote their next-door neighbor's city council campaign. Older people are more likely to vote than younger people, and longtime community residents are more likely to vote than newcomers. Similarly, married people are more likely to vote than those who are single.

These variables describe tendencies, of course, not iron laws. Not all young people ignore politics, but as a group the pattern is clear: Eighteen- to twenty-year-olds vote less than any other age group, followed by twenty-one- to twenty-five-year-olds, then twenty-six- to thirty-year-olds, and so on. People in their sixties, seventies, and even eighties, though they vote slightly less than middle-aged people do, are still far more likely to vote than people in their early twenties. This tendency helps explain the powerful influence of the senior-citizen lobby and its chief representative, the American Association of Retired Persons (AARP).

The continuing modest level of U.S. voting rates puzzle social observers. For four or five decades, Americans have been gaining in education, wealth, and age. These demographic trends would suggest a pattern of increasing political participation and voting that has not materialized.

The Gender Gap

Political races for president, senate, gubernatorial, and house offices often reflect an iron-clad gender divide—10 percent more women vote for the Democratic candidate than for the Republican candidate. The reverse is true among men, who give the preference to Republican candidates. This gender gap holds regardless of the gender of any candidate. This gap is wide enough to sway elections in all major contests. What does this mean for candidates, campaign managers, and special interest groups involved in the complex process of campaigning and election in a modern democracy?

The gender gap has been widening for the past decade. In the 1990s, the gender gap in presidential support was about four percentage points. But in 1996, this jumped to 11 percent. In 2000, the figure was 10 percentage points, with 43 percent of women and 53 percent of men voting for George W. Bush. In contrast, 42 percent of men and 54 percent of women voted for Al Gore. Race, class, and ethnic background fail to alter the disparity between male and female voters. The gender gap narrowed but persisted in the 2004 presidential election: Women were 7 percent less likely than men to support President Bush, and John Kerry received a smaller share of women's votes than Al Gore did 2000. In 2004, 48 percent women and 55 percent of men voted for President Bush.[17] Figure 10.2 illustrates President Bush's ratings with both men and women.

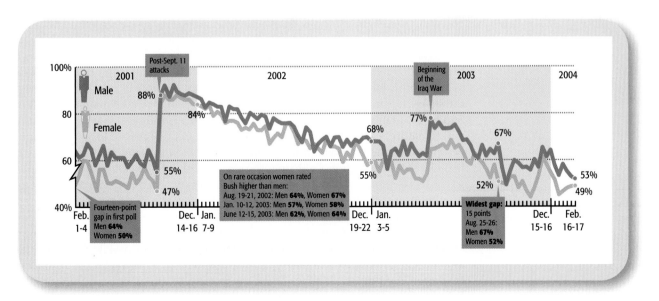

Figure 10.2 President Bush and the Gender Gap

U.S.A. Yesterday and Today

Phantom Voters

The right to vote is not guaranteed in the U.S. Constitution; each state's standards have evolved separately aside from federal laws that apply to all states. At the time of our constitutional founding, only white men with property were routinely permitted to vote (although freed African Americans could vote in four states). Women and most people of color were denied the franchise. Enslaved people could not vote, and each slave counted as three-fifths of a person for the purpose of apportioning representation in Congress. This provision inflated slave owners' power and gave them more influence in legislative matters than their numbers warranted. Of course, none of us would tolerate these arrangements today. In 1866, the Fourteenth Amendment guaranteed citizenship to the former slaves; in 1869, the Fifteenth Amendment guaranteed the right to vote to black men; the Nineteenth Amendment in 1920 extended the vote to women. The federal Voting Rights Act of 1965 banned literacy tests and provided federal enforcement of voting registration and other rights in several Southern states and Alaska. The Voting Rights Act of 1970 provided language assistance to minority voters who did not speak English fluently. The Americans with Disabilities Act of 1990 provided for ballot and poll access for those with disabilities.

Yet the system still has an important glitch, in that census methods that inflate populations of certain legislative districts have created inequities in representation. It involves counting prison inmates in the district where they are confined rather than where they actually live. The census counts prison inmates as "residents" even though they cannot vote in all but two states. Thus, inmates count as voters when state legislatures draw up their legislative districts. This mattered little when the national prison population was small, but today U.S. prisons hold more than 1.4 million people, numbers that can shift political power within a state from one district to another. One study by Peter Wagner of the Prison Policy Initiative found that seven upstate New York senate districts had met their population requirements only because inmate populations were included in the census. The study found "21 counties nationally where at least 21 percent of so-called residents lived behind bars." Counting nonvoting inmates as residents offends the principle of one person/one vote and alters political power with a state.

Sources: "Phantom Voters, Thanks to the Census," *New York Times*, December 22, 2005, p. A22. The Prison Policy Initiative study can be found at www.prisonpolicy.org/.

A Voting Trend: Direct Democracy

Those dissatisfied with American voting levels continue to explore creative ways to encourage voters to the polls. In recent years, support has increased for the use of initiatives and referenda. **Initiatives** are policy proposals placed on the ballot for voter consideration at the instigation of a group of citizens. Often they are ideas unsuccessful in a state's legislature or even contradictory to existing laws. Issues such as term limits have raised voter ire in recent years, leading to popular initiatives in the states. The initiative was designed to allow the public to take matters into its own hands. To qualify for the ballot, the initiative process requires that proponents obtain signatures—usually representing 10 percent of all registered voters—that must be verified by the secretary of state. Once verified, the initiative is placed on the ballot. The 2004 election in California to recall Governor Gray Davis is an example of grassroots democracy. The two million signatures on recall petitions was the largest number ever gathered.[18]

    A **referendum** is a proposal submitted by the legislature to the public for a popular vote, often focusing on whether a state should spend money in a certain way. For example, in California the legislature often places bond issues before the voters, asking them to approve the sale of state bonds to finance various programs, such as education and prisons. At other times, the legislature will place a referendum on the ballot to determine the public's sentiment on an issue.[19]

initiative A proposal submitted by the public and voted upon during elections.

referendum A proposal submitted by a state legislature to the public for a popular vote, often focusing on whether a state should spend money in a certain way.

These two methods of consulting citizens on issues, like the primary system, grew out of attempts to broaden political participation and decrease the influence of special interests. Many people see these options as ways to approach direct democracy. But initiatives and referenda have met with mixed success, and in recent years criticism of both methods has emerged. "Where direct democracy becomes a more dominant force than representative government the result is whipsaw, without any long-term coherence," observed Brian Weberg, of the National Conference of State Legislatures.[20] Some critics find that issues end up on the ballot even though they are too complex for simple yes or no decisions. Both initiatives and referenda have become costly, requiring expensive television campaigns, and are therefore subject to the influence of big business and special interest groups. Lastly, by involving people directly, these methods bypass the considered deliberations of representative political institutions.

Although the idea of direct democracy is appealing, studies have shown that even when given the opportunity to vote by initiative or referenda, voter turnout does not dramatically increase. Is direct democracy, then, an answer to the problems of voter turnout? In the 2004 elections, many states had ballot initiatives ranging from gay marriage, to stem-cell research, to casino gambling. It is likely that more and more states will begin to utilize this approach to democracy.

VOTING CHOICE

Although not everyone votes in every election, millions of Americans do vote with some regularity. When voters show up at the polls to make political choices, what determines their actual vote? Political scientists have long been studying the electoral process and the reasons why citizens vote as they do. We now have a good idea of the key influences on American voters: party, candidate appeal, policies and issues, and campaigns.[21]

Party

More than five decades of study of the American electorate have shown one overwhelming influence on voting decisions: party. Other things being equal, voters show up on election day and vote for candidates from the party to which they feel most connected. We explored this idea of connection, **party identification**, in Chapter 9. Party identification is a psychological phenomenon, a deep-seated feeling that a particular party best represents one's interests or best symbolizes one's lifestyle. Once party attachments develop, especially if they develop early, they tend to remain in place for a lifetime; it is psychologically painful to change party allegiance.

Not all voters have strong party ties. Some are registered as Independents, and others are weak party identifiers. These voters bring other considerations to the voting decision. Frequently, they cast **split-ticket ballots**, meaning that they vote for candidates from more than one party. Those with strong party connections, however—still 25 to 30 percent of the electorate—can be counted on to vote, and to vote for one party only, known as a **straight-party ticket**. Only in exceptional circumstances (say, a friend is running on the other party's ticket, or a key issue of the day turns them temporarily away from their party) do party loyalists break their longstanding commitment to their own party in an election.

But party is far from the only determinant of voter choice. For one thing, some elections (usually local) are *nonpartisan*, so voters must choose among candidates whose party affiliation is unknown. Other elections involve primary contests. In a party primary, all candidates on the ballot belong to the same party and vie to represent that party in the general election. Hence, party primary voters often must choose among candidates without party to guide their decisions. Finally, many elections—for example, state constitutional amendments and referenda questions—involve issues.

MakeItReal

Civic Participation: Supporting Federal Candidates—A Guide For Citizens

---

Quick Review

Factors Affecting Voting Choice

- Voters' connection to the candidate's party.
- The candidate's message and policy positions.
- Issue voting is a central part of the political process.
- How well an incumbent or party in power has performed in office.
- Effectiveness of a political campaign.

---

party identification A psychological orientation, or long-term propensity to think positively of and vote regularly for, a particular political party.

split-ticket ballots Ballots on which people vote for candidates from more than one party.

straight-party ticket Ballots on which people vote for only one party.

Party positions on these policy matters are not indicated on the ballot, and often parties take no clear position during the campaign. For a full understanding of how voters make electoral decisions, we must go beyond the useful but still limited variable of party preference.

Candidate Appeal

Personality has always played a major role in the individualist culture of the United States. Our political system has been deeply touched by key personalities of the day: George Washington, Thomas Jefferson, Andrew Jackson, Abraham Lincoln, Theodore Roosevelt, Woodrow Wilson, Franklin Roosevelt, and Ronald Reagan, to name just a few. Colorful, authoritative, or charismatic individuals at the local, state, or national level have often won office by drawing voters away from longstanding party loyalties and by picking up the bulk of the Independent vote as well. Republican Dwight Eisenhower, for instance, traded on his status as war hero to gain the votes of many Democratic loyalists in the 1950s. Ronald Reagan's movie star charisma and charm, combined with a clear message of change, helped draw many traditionally Democratic voters into the Republican camp in 1980 and 1984.

Strong or popular personalities have a major advantage in any political campaign. Through force of personality they can grab a voter's attention, and even support, at the ballot box. After all, most voters know little about the specifics of political life, except their own party preferences, the top issues of the day, and the names of just a few of the top political leaders of the time. Thus, in a typical election, whatever the office being contested, neither candidate is likely to make much of an impact on average voters, who simply vote their usual party allegiances. Gaining name recognition means that candidates have a stronger chance of picking up support.

What attributes help a candidate attract the voting public? Likeability is surely important to Americans. Next-door-neighbor friendliness and casual informality go a long way toward pleasing the American voter. It also helps to exude self-confidence, and especially to show a calm assurance when speaking in public. It does not hurt, of course, to be attractive. Studies show that although people vigorously deny it, they are clearly influenced to think better of individuals whose looks are above average. This finding may explain why celebrities, who are well known at least in part because of their good looks, often have an advantage if they choose to run for office.

Another important attribute is the candidate's message. No matter how attractive the candidate, or how folksy or self-assured, if he or she takes unpopular policy positions, the battle for office will be uphill. No election for public office is a simple popularity contest. Candidates cannot survive a campaign without stating where they stand on the issues or explaining what they will do once elected.

MakeItReal

ABC News Video: *Vote 2004—* Bush and Kerry

Policies and Issues

Ultimately, elections hinge on what government is going to do. Despite many observers' cynicism about voters choosing candidates on the basis of their teeth or hairstyle, the electorate does make decisions quite regularly on the basis of issues. Issue voting is a central part of the political process, although that is not always clear because issue voting is a complex matter.

Let's say a voter feels strongly about ten issues. He or she then looks for a candidate who takes the "right" stand on those issues. It may turn out, however, that one of the two leading candidates for the contested office takes the voter's favored position on just five of those issues, while the other candidate takes the preferred stand on the other five. This situation leaves the issue-oriented voter without much direction on how to vote. He or she may then consider other factors (such as party or personality) to make a voting choice.

Issue voting, then, depends on several factors existing at the same time and in the same election:

1. The voter must care intensely enough about one or more issues to become informed about which positions each candidate takes on these issues.
2. Issue differences on these specific policy matters must exist between the leading candidates for the office.
3. These issue differences must be communicated clearly to all voters.
4. The voter's preferred positions on issues must not split between the candidates but rather should fall mostly toward one candidate and away from the other.
5. Other factors, such as party and personality, should not detract from the voter's focus on issues.

Because these elements rarely all come together in elections, observers often conclude that issues are irrelevant to average voters. In fact, issues are relevant to voters, but the structure of the voting situation may make issue voting difficult.

Those who criticize the American electorate for failing to take issues into account when voting may be missing another key point. Party voting, the key determinant of voting, relates closely to policy preferences and issue voting. Parties take positions on dozens, even hundreds, of current policy questions, so a party vote is a vote to support those positions. Party-line voters may not agree with everything their party stands for, but studies show that, by and large, party identifiers agree much more often with their own party on the key issues of the day than with any other party. Thus, a party vote is in many ways an issues vote.

A particularly powerful form of issue voting occurs when voters look back over the past term or two to judge how well an incumbent or the party in power has performed in office. This is known as **retrospective voting**. Generally, retrospective voting reflects voters' judgment of the incumbents' handling of the economy. The elections of 1992 and 1996 provide strong support for the retrospective voting model. In 1992, following the Persian Gulf War, former President Bush had the highest approval rating of any president in history. Unfortunately for Bush, the economy was perceived as sluggish in late 1991 and into the 1992 election year, and Bush, the incumbent, was held responsible. The economy became the dominant issue of the 1992 campaign. In 1996, President Clinton, benefiting from a sound economy, easily defeated Bob Dole. Conversely, Gerald Ford's defeat in 1976 and Jimmy Carter's in 1980 represented negative voter evaluations.[22] If voters feel generally positive, if policy problems have been solved, if one's personal economic situation is good, if foreign or domestic crises have been skillfully addressed, then they reward incumbents by returning them or their party successors to office.

Campaigns

A final influence on voting choice is the campaign itself. At least one-third, and sometimes as much as one-half, of the electorate makes up its mind during political campaigns. With fewer Americans holding deeply rooted attachments to parties, campaigns can take on special significance. Many voters can be swayed during the months leading up to election day. Issues and personalities of the day can move uncommitted voters in one direction or another with relative speed.

Campaigns also take on special significance for their ability to arouse voters' interest and send them to the polls. The candidate or party that inspires its supporters to vote on election day is the most likely to win, and citizens are most likely to turn out to vote after a well-organized and stimulating campaign. For these reasons, the past two decades have seen the rise of *campaign specialists*—public relations people, media consultants, and fund-raising experts. With the decline of the old party machine, a new world of political entrepreneurs has arisen to provide advice and direction to any candidate with the money and desire to hire them.

retrospective voting A particularly powerful form of issue voting in which voters look back over the past term or two to judge how well an incumbent or the "in party" has performed in office.

We should not conclude, however, that money and a strong public relations campaign alone can make a winning candidate. Remember that party and issues play key roles in voter decisions. There is not enough money in existence to catapult into office a minor party candidate taking unpopular positions on key issues. That assumes, of course, that such a candidate's opponent is reasonably competent and does not self-destruct through scandal or incompetence. Finding a clever way to package a message or present a candidate are surely important, but the content of that message and the substance of a candidate's personality are even more important. If those do not impress voters, chances of winning, despite all the slick packaging imaginable, are slim.

OTHER FORMS OF POLITICAL PARTICIPATION

Voting in elections is the most common but not the only form of participation. Political participation takes many other shapes in the United States, including campaign work, seeking information, protesting, civil disobedience, and even violence. In Chapter 11, we discuss participation through interest groups, but here we examine other ways in which individuals become involved in the political process.[23]

Campaign and Election Activities

Unlike the pattern in most countries, Americans do not expect to join political parties and become dues-paying members who regularly attend monthly meetings. Still, some Americans do volunteer to work for their party in election campaigns, although the work is hard, the hours long, and the material benefits negligible. Even with the increasing use of sophisticated electronic media, the backbone of most campaigns remains people. Successful campaigns require volunteers to answer telephones, handle mail, canvass the electoral district, distribute candidate or party literature, and discuss the candidates and issues with people in the neighborhood. Other interested citizens participate by displaying signs or bumper stickers or handing out literature of a favored party or candidate, hoping to induce others to echo such support at the polls. Still others work as party volunteers in voter registration drives.

▲ A Democratic party worker talks on the telephone at the Kerry campaign headquarters in Columbus, Ohio.

Why do people volunteer? They likely believe in what they are doing, feel an obligation to participate actively in the political process, or simply enjoy the game of politics. When all is said and done, relatively few people become involved in campaign activities. In recent years, the number of people who wear a campaign button or put a bumper sticker on their car always falls below 10 percent of the adult population, as does the number who claim to have attended a political meeting in the past year. Even so, 5 percent of the voting-age population is close to ten million people. Thus, millions of Americans regularly work at election time to influence other voters and elect policy makers.

Seeking Information

Political knowledge is important. The World Wide Web provides that information, and, as the photo shows, candidates use the Web. No one can exercise an effective citizenship role without being well informed. For that reason, the simple act of gaining knowledge about public affairs constitutes a form of political activity. Certainly, a person who attends a meeting of public officials or the local government is participating in politics. In addition, every time a person reads a newspaper or news magazine, watches a news broadcast or political program, or enrolls in a political science class, he or she is actively seeking information that will assist in formulating political preferences and opinions. By just learning about politics, a citizen contributes to the overall knowledge base of the American political system. And each time a person discusses political events and issues of the day with friends and family or writes a letter to the editor to express an opinion on those events and issues, that person is participating in the continuous process of politics. Thomas Jefferson acknowledged the importance of information in democracy in remarking that, given the choice between a government without newspapers or newspapers without government, he would without hesitation choose the latter.

The most recent innovation in outlets for political information is the myriad television stations and programs that focus on political affairs, such as the C-SPAN channels as well as local cable television channels that air state legislature sessions and city council meetings. The World Wide Web and Internet have helped individuals obtain in seconds complete texts of candidate speeches, position papers, and analyses of these positions by political experts. Those especially interested in politics can join online bloggers or even create their own blog site.

Quick Review

Political Participation

- Volunteer work for candidates in election campaigns.
- Learning about politics and the political system.
- Discussing and expressing opinion on political events and issues of the day.
- Organized protests and acts of civil disobedience.

Question for Reflection

Technological advances have brought an unprecedented level of access to information to American voters. What are some of the best ways to analyze this material to determine its accuracy and bias?

◄ The use of Websites by candidates has become one of the hottest ways of getting information out to potential voters.

▲ Protest and civil disobedience are characteristics of a free society. Here, demonstrators march to the Capitol urging debt forgiveness for poor countries.

Protest, Civil Disobedience, and Violence

When governments produce public policy, groups, institutions, and individuals in society invariably respond. This response may be simple support, such as accepting and participating in government-sponsored programs, voting in elections, paying taxes, or complying with new laws. But sometimes government actions may provoke strong expressions of dissatisfaction. Occasionally, these expressions take the form of organized protests and acts of civil disobedience, either against existing policies or conditions or as a response to actual or threatened change in the status quo.

Protest may take the form of demonstrations, letters to newspapers and public officials, or opting out of the system by failing to vote or participate in any other way. **Civil disobedience** is a more specific form of protest in which disaffected citizens openly but nonviolently defy existing laws that they deem to be unjust. Civil disobedience was in common use in the 1960s by citizens protesting continued U.S. involvement in the Vietnam War. Draftees burned their Selective Service cards, and students organized boycotts of classes and "die-ins." Even disillusioned veterans marched on the Pentagon and the 1968 Republican and Democratic National Conventions to call attention to their opposition to the war. In late summer 2005, dozens of war protesters camped near President Bush's ranch to protest the war in Iraq, led by Cindy Sheehan, who started the camp to protest her son's death in Iraq. Although the president said he sympathized with Sheehan's personal loss, he did not meet with her or the protesters.

Civil rights protestors in the 1950s and 1960s often actively violated existing segregation laws, on the basis that these laws were unjust, exclusionary, and racist. Martin Luther King Jr. used civil disobedience as a principal means of demanding equal justice in the political system. African Americans asked for service at "whites-only" lunch counters and sat quietly on the lunch counter stools, knowing that these actions would provoke a reaction. By violating laws they believed wrong—and that were ultimately abolished as morally unjust—they drew attention and support to their cause.

Discussions about political participation seldom include the phenomenon of **political violence**, violent action motivated primarily by political aims and intended to have a political impact. When radical opponents of abortion bomb abortion clinics or shoot clinic workers, they claim that their actions are aimed at stopping the "murder of unborn citizens." It is often difficult to tell the true motives behind supposedly political acts of violence. The rise of white supremacist and neo-Nazi movement is certainly, in part, a response to social conditions. We know that violent intolerance follows in the wake of sustained economic downturns, when competition for jobs and scarce governmental resources are most troubling.

In the summer of 1992, residents of south-central Los Angeles rioted after four policemen were acquitted of assault charges stemming from the videotaped beating of black motorist Rodney King. Not all of them were looters and vandals—some sought an outlet for genuine frustration over the system's apparent failure to mete out appropriate justice, not only in the King case but in its treatment of minorities and the poor in general. Although most political violence appears triggered by a combination of economic problems and political events, the vast majority of Americans strongly condemn criminal actions involving injury and property damage.

CONGRESSIONAL ELECTIONS

Our Constitution calls for House and Senate elections every two years. Each of the 435 House members is up for reelection every two years, as are one-third of the senators (who serve six-year terms). Most candidates for Congress are not nationally known; they may not even be widely known within their own state or district. Although the U.S. Senate has included a former astronaut and a former movie actor, most national legislators come from somewhat less conspicuous, if equally wealthy, backgrounds. For that and other reasons, many constituents may have little infor-

protest Expression of dissatisfaction; may take the form of demonstrations, letters to newspapers or public officials, or simple "opting out" of the system by failing to vote or participate in any other way.

civil disobedience Breaking the law in a nonviolent fashion and being willing to suffer the consequences, even to the point of going to jail, in order to publicly demonstrate that the law is unjust.

political violence Violent action motivated primarily by political aims and intended to have a political impact.

mation about who their elected representatives are, what they stand for, or even what sort of work they actually do.

Congressional elections generally receive less national media attention and voter turnout than does the national contest for the presidency. In off-year or **midterm elections**, with no presidential contest to galvanize press and voter attention, voter turnout usually hovers around one-third of registered voters, far below even the relatively modest turnout in recent presidential election years. Because of this, and because congressional elections are not federally subsidized like presidential elections, the race for House and Senate seats takes on a form decidedly different from a presidential campaign. The 2002 midterm election, however, proved an exception to this rule, when President Bush nationalized the election and the issues. In 2004, Republicans increased their majority in both House and Senate elections, allowing the president to claim a mandate to govern.

Presidential Coattails

Over the years, an interesting pattern has emerged in congressional elections. Typically, in presidential elections, the winning presidential candidate's party gains seats in Congress; conversely, in off-year elections, the incumbent president's party loses seats. This phenomenon varies somewhat over time, depending on the president's fortunes, the state of the economy, and possible flare-ups of controversy or scandal. President George Bush's Republicans gained seats in the midterm elections of 2002, and in 1994 another midterm election ushered in the Contract with America and brought the Republicans to power in Congress for the first time since 1952.

When representatives or senators of a successful presidential candidate's party unseat incumbents, they are said to "ride the president's coattails" into office. Sometimes this **coattails effect** can be quite dramatic. For example, in 1980, when Ronald Reagan defeated Democratic president Jimmy Carter, he brought enough Republican senators into office on his coattails to wrest control of the Senate from the Democrats for the first time since 1955. But the coattails effect is rarely so dramatic. Despite Republican George H. W. Bush's presidential victory in 1988, Democrats retained control of both House and Senate. The same result occurred in the 1968 and 1972 presidential victories of Republican Richard Nixon. Thus, the coattails effect is not an absolute guarantee in American politics, and many scholars believe its importance is waning as voters become less predictable, less tied to party, and more willing to vote a split ticket.

During off-year elections, with voter turnout low and the public able to look back on two years of presidential performance with a skeptical eye, the sitting president's party typically loses seats in the House and Senate. The 1994 midterm election offered a dramatic example of that pattern, as the Democratic party saw itself ejected from its longtime control of Congress by an electorate motivated, at least in part, by unhappiness over a widespread perception of incompetence on Democratic president Clinton's part. The 1998 election was atypical in that Republicans lost five seats in the House and broke even in the Senate. This was the first time since 1934 that the president's party gained seats in a midterm election and the first time since before the Civil War that a president gained seats in the sixth year in office.

PRESIDENTIAL ELECTIONS

Every four years, after a summer of national party conventions, the nation turns its attention to the presidential election. The pack of presidential contenders has usually been narrowed to two, although occasionally a serious third candidate competes.

The rules of the game at this stage differ markedly from those of the nomination phase (see Chapter 9 for more on the nomination process). The timetable is compressed from two years to two months, and the fight is usually Democrat against

MakeItReal

Simulation: Election in Action: 2008 Presidential Election

midterm elections Elections in which Americans elect members of Congress but not presidents; 2002, 2006, and 2010 are midterm election years.

coattails effect "Riding the president's coattails into office" occurs in an election when voters also elect representatives or senators belonging to a successful presidential candidate's party.

MakeItReal

ABC News Video: *Monday Night Politics*

Quick Review

The Electoral College

- Chooses the president.
- Written into the Constitution from the beginning.
- Provided an indirect election method of electors from each state.
- Electors would be an elite group of state leaders.
- The Twelfth Amendment called for separate ballots for president and vice president.

---

electoral college The group of 538 electors who meet separately in each of their states and the District of Columbia on the first Monday following the second Wednesday in December after a national presidential election. Their majority decision officially elects the president and vice president of the United States.

Republican. Candidates who previously spent all their efforts wooing the party faithful to gain the nomination must now broaden their sights to the less committed party voters and Independents who will determine the election outcome. The fall campaign involves successfully juggling numerous political balls in the air. Candidates must use federal funds strategically, define a clear campaign theme, anticipate any last-minute "October surprises" by opponents, avoid self-inflicted gaffes, attack opponents without seeming to mudsling, monitor the pulse of the nation, and manage a successful media campaign.

The Electoral College: The Framers' Intention

Until the 2000 presidential election, many voters were unaware that not they but the **electoral college** actually chooses the president. That's how George W. Bush was elected president and why the outcome of the popular vote in Florida was so important. How did this little-understood institution come into being? The design for the electoral college was written into the Constitution from the beginning. The framers wanted to ensure that exactly the right type of person was chosen for the job, and they sought to clone the best aspects of the first presidential role model—George Washington. Rather than voting in ambitious demagogues who cater only to the whims of the electorate or act as the mouthpiece of Congress, the framers wanted to ensure the selection of a statesman, someone wise enough to unify the people behind a program that served their best interest. After considerable discussion, the framers chose not to have Congress select the president, fearing that the president would then become dependent on that body. They also decided not to let the people choose the executive, hoping thus to insulate that office from what they considered the popular passions and transitory fancies of the electorate.[24]

Instead, they designed a system unlike any in the world, the electoral college, which provided an indirect election method. Legislators from each state would choose individuals known as *electors,* the number to be based on the state's representation in Congress. (A state with two senators and five representatives, for instance, would be allotted seven electors to the electoral college.) The framers expected that electors would be individuals with experience and foresight who would meet, discuss in a calm, rational manner the attributes of those candidates who were best suited for the presidency, and then vote for the best person to fill that post. Thus, presidents would be chosen by an elite group of state leaders in a sedate atmosphere unencumbered by political debts and considerations.

In practice, the electoral college has never worked as the framers planned because the framers had not anticipated the emergence of political parties. Originally, the electors had nearly absolute independence. They had two votes to cast and could vote for any two candidates, as long as one of their two votes went for someone from outside their state. Today, this requirement ensures that the president and vice president cannot both be residents of the same state.

This odd system worked well only in the first two presidential elections, when victories by George Washington were foregone conclusions. After his departure, the beginnings of the first party system had, by 1796, ensured that electors were not, in fact, disinterested elder statesmen. They were instead factional loyalists committed to one of the two leading competitors of the day, John Adams or Thomas Jefferson. Thus, in a straight-line vote after the 1796 election, the electoral college chose Adams for president by a scant three votes over Jefferson. This made Adams president but Jefferson, his chief rival, vice president. A modern-day equivalent of this situation would be if Bob Dole, who came in second to Bill Clinton in the electoral voting of 1996, served under Clinton as vice president.

Matters worsened in the election of 1800. By then, strong political parties with devoted loyal followers had arrived to stay, ensuring that members of the electoral college would vote the party line. Jefferson and Adams opposed each other again, but this time both chose running mates to avoid the anomaly of another Adams-Jefferson presidency. Jefferson's vice presidential selection was Aaron Burr, and their ticket combined to win more electoral votes than either Adams or Charles Cotesworth Pinckney, Adams' running mate. However, all of Jefferson's supporters in the electoral college had been instructed by party leaders to cast their ballots for Jefferson and Burr, and when they did, the two men ended up in a tie vote for the presidency. This result threw the choice of president into the House of Representatives. It took a good deal of intrigue in the House before Jefferson finally emerged the winner and was named president.

The absurdity of these two elections brought cries for reform. The Twelfth Amendment was quickly proposed and ratified, directing the electoral college to cast separate ballots for president and vice president. Under this system, the party that wins a majority of electors can first elect the party's nominee for president, then go on to choose the party's nominee for vice president. No longer can a president from one party and a vice president from another be elected, nor can there be tie votes between two candidates from the same party. In a way, this early reform preserved the electoral college system, since in nearly all subsequent American elections it has worked to give Americans the president who received the most votes. To this day, the electoral college remains a central part of the American political system.

How the Electoral College Works Today   When Americans go to the polls in a presidential election, most believe they are casting their ballots for president. In fact, they are voting for a slate of electors, individuals selected by state party leaders who are expected to cast ballots for their respective state's popular vote winner. Still, electoral college votes produce the occasional **faithless elector**, who casts his or her electoral vote for someone other than the state's popular vote winner. In 1988, for example, one of the electoral delegates from West Virginia cast a vote for Republican Robert Dole rather than for the party's nominee, George H. W. Bush.

The electors selected in the presidential election meet in their respective state capitals on the first Monday after the second Wednesday in December. The term *electoral college* is deceptive, since the 538 electors never actually assemble en masse to cast their votes for president. Title 3, Chapter 1, of the U.S. Code provides that on the sixth day of January after every meeting of the electors—usually referred to as Certification Day—the electoral vote (which had been sent by registered mail to Washington) will be announced by the vice president before both houses of Congress. Not until that moment are the election results considered official—although the whole world has known these results unofficially for several weeks.

In January 2005, Congress officially ratified President Bush's election victory after a rare challenge to the electoral votes in Ohio.

To become president, the winning candidate needs to receive a majority, or 270, of the 538 electoral votes. The 538 votes consist of 1 vote for each of the 435 members of the U.S. House of Representatives, plus one vote for each of the 100 senators, plus 3 votes for the District of Columbia. If no candidate receives the required electoral college majority, a **contingency election** is held in the House. The House chooses among the top three candidates, with each state casting a single vote.

The Electoral College and Strategies for Campaigning

Presidential campaigns are shaped by the rules governing electoral college operations. The name of the game is winning 270 electoral votes to become president, which means parties must campaign to improve their chances of winning those votes. That leads to a simple strategy: Go where the votes are. Thus, the "big" electoral states are at the heart of a presidential contest (see Figure 10.3).

MakeItReal

Primary Source: The Electoral College Home Page

faithless elector Member of the electoral college who casts his or her vote for someone other than the state's popular vote winner.

contingency election An election held in the House if no candidate receives the required majority in the electoral college.

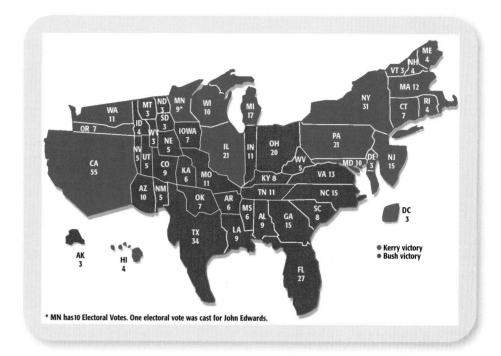

* MN has10 Electoral Votes. One electoral vote was cast for John Edwards.

Figure 10.3   2004 Electoral Vote Distribution
States are drawn in proportion to number of electoral votes. President Bush received 286 electorial votes; John Kerry 251 electorial votes.

Going Where the Votes Are   The strategy of "going where the votes are" is crucial because of a voting system that gives the large states extraordinary influence in presidential elections. All but two small states (Nebraska and Maine) choose electors on a winner-take-all basis. Whichever candidate wins the highest number of popular votes wins all of a state's electors. The consequences can be dramatic. A 54–46 percent victory, for example, in a large state like Ohio would give a candidate all of Ohio's important twenty-one electoral votes and hence a 21–0 lead over an opponent. If electors were allocated by proportional representation with this same popular vote outcome, a candidate would hold a minuscule one vote (11–10) electoral college lead over a rival.

Most states long ago decided to adopt this winner-take-all system to bolster their political importance, so it has become ingrained in American political habits and seems unlikely to change. The result is to exaggerate the power of the large states, where all rational candidates will end up spending most of their campaign time, effort, and money.

Electoral College Reform?

The most favored alternative to the electoral college is a direct vote to elect the president. Four American presidents—Lyndon Johnson, Richard Nixon, Gerald Ford, and Jimmy Carter—endorsed a constitutional amendment that would replace the electoral college with direct election. The direct vote plan has its critics. What would happen, for instance, if four or five candidates ran for president, and someone with, say, 31 percent of the vote came in first? Would Americans accept someone for whom less than a third of the electorate had voted? To remedy that problem, most direct election proposals would require 40 percent of the vote to win. If no candidate won 40 percent, a run-off election between the top two candidates would be held.[25]

Critics then argue that such rules would encourage many candidates to enter the race, some representing single-issue parties, hoping to come in first or second, even with a relatively small percentage of the votes. The winner of a run-off election might have gained minimal national support on the first ballot and still emerge as president. The adverse consequences for political legitimacy, and perhaps even political stability, would be significant in a nation unaccustomed to the idea of a runner-up winning the presidency.

Question for Reflection

Would abolishing the electoral college take us closer to or farther from the democratic ideal?

MakeItReal

Census 2000: Presidential Election Results

Interpreting Presidential Elections

The day after the election, virtually every politically interested citizen, including the president-elect, asks the same question: What message did voters send to their new (or reelected) leaders? The answer to that question is usually unclear.

Election outcomes are notoriously difficult to interpret. For one thing, never in U.S. history has a president been elected with a majority of those eligible to vote. As we know, only 50 to 55 percent of the electorate turn out to vote for president. Nearly every one of them would have to vote for the same candidate for that person to obtain a majority of all adult Americans as supporters. Naturally, this has never happened in a free society and never will. Indeed, more citizens choose "none of the above" by staying at home on election day than vote for the winning presidential candidate.

In an attempt to make more sense of presidential contests, political scientists use party realignment theory to classify elections as maintaining, deviating, or realigning (or critical) elections. In **maintaining elections** the majority party of the day wins both Congress and the White House, maintaining its long-standing control of government. In **deviating elections**, the minority party captures the White House because of short-term intervening forces, and the country experiences a deviation from the expectation that power will remain in the hands of the dominant party. **Realigning elections** are characterized by massive shifts in partisan identification, as in 1932 when the New Deal coalition was forged. Recent trends have been toward regional realignment in the South, with Republican gains in 1992 and 1996.

The size of Ronald Reagan's 1984 electoral victory led many to speculate that it, too, represented a realignment that changed the electoral landscape. This interpretation weakened, however, with the Democratic congressional victories of 1986, 1988, and 1992 and with Bill Clinton's triumph in the presidential races of 1992 and 1996. The realignment thesis revived with the dramatic takeover of the House and Senate by the Republicans following the 1994 midterm elections, but the voters in 1998 did not continue a revolt against politics as usual. Analysts will need a few more years to assess the true nature of the voting changes occurring within the American electorate, but most do agree on one thing: Regional realignment has undoubtedly occurred in the South, particularly among white males. That group, as shown in the 2000 and 2004 presidential elections, formerly a bastion of support for the Democratic party, can now be safely categorized as solidly Republican.

maintaining election Election in which the majority party of the day wins both Congress and the White House, maintaining its control of government.

deviating election Election in which the minority party captures the White House because of short-term intervening forces, and thus a deviation from the expectation that power will remain in the hands of the dominant party.

realigning election Election characterized by massive shifts in partisan identification, as in 1932 with the New Deal coalition.

◀ It seems that every election has its share of pranksters and good humor.
Source: Washington Post, October 17, 2004, front page.

 **MakeItReal**

Primary Source: *Federal Election Commission—Summary Financial Information for 2000 Presidential Campaigns and past Presidential Campaigns*

Quick Review

Federal Election Campaign Act

- Created the Federal Election Commission (FEC) in 1971.
- Limited individual contributions.
- Instituted a system of public financing through an income tax checkoff.

 MakeItReal

Primary Source: Federal Election Campaign Act of 1974

MONEY AND ELECTIONS

It is often said that money is the mother's milk of politics. The 2004 presidential and congressional elections were the most costly in history, with a total price of $4 billion, an increase from $3 billion in 2000, $2.2 billion in 1996, and $1.8 billion in 1992.[26]

For the most part, a simple rule holds: Spend more money than your opponent, and you are likely to win the election. Candidates therefore spend a good deal of time and effort raising campaign dollars. Still, exceptions to the rule do occur. In the 1998 California gubernatorial primary, millionaire Al Checci spent $40 million of his personal fortune, but it did not buy him his party's nomination. Steve Forbes spent millions of his own funds in 2000, but failed to capture the Republican nomination for president.

Presidential elections are conducted under the guidelines of the Federal Election Campaign Act of 1971. Before this campaign finance law was enacted, candidates could raise as much money as possible, with no limits on the size of individual contributions. Most of the money came from the large contributions of wealthy individuals, corporations, and organized labor. For example, in the 1952 presidential contest, at least two-thirds of all the money raised and spent at the national level came from contributions of $500 or more (equivalent to $2,000 in 1996 dollars). This was the era of the political "fat cats," the wealthy capitalists who, along with rapidly growing labor unions, contributed most of the money and exerted most of the influence during campaigns.

The aftermath of the Watergate scandal led to the most significant election reform in history. The Federal Election Campaign Act of 1971 created the Federal Election Commission (FEC), limited individual contributions, and instituted a new system of public financing through an income tax checkoff. The 1974 amendments were immediately challenged, leading to an important judicial ruling. On January 30, 1976, in *Buckley* v. *Valeo,* the Supreme Court struck down the limits an individual can spend on his or her own campaign for political office. The Court ruled that the First Amendment gives each citizen the right to spend his or her money, no matter how much, in any lawful way, as a matter of freedom of speech. In a later ruling, the Court also struck down legal limits on the amount of money an interest group can spend on behalf of a candidate, as long as the group spends its money independently of the candidate's campaign organization. Despite these rulings, however, the fundamentals of the act remained intact.[27]

The Court did back reformers on several crucial issues. It upheld contribution limits, disclosure rules, and public financing. Thus, individuals can give only modest

▶ Large segments of the American populace favor campaign finance reform. One of the most well-known protesters is Doris Haddock, known as "Granny D," who walked from California to Washington, D.C., to protest soft money.

amounts of money to campaigns, limiting the political power of the wealthy—in theory. Furthermore, the names of all who give money to any campaign are placed on public record through the disclosure provisions, meaning that under-the-table "buying" of political candidates seems unlikely to occur, given the certainty of publicity. These reforms, along with the public financing of presidential campaigns, led some to assume that American elections are approaching closer to the democratic ideal than in the days when a few wealthy groups and individuals surreptitiously paid for most of the candidates' expenses. However, the system is in crisis because of the ways that the law can be circumvented.

Federal Matching Funds

On the long road to the nomination before the convention, presidential candidates can opt for **federal matching funds**. That is, once they raise a certain amount of money in the required way, they apply for, and are given, a matching sum of money from the federal government. The rules that govern qualifying for these funds are relatively simple. A candidate must raise $100,000 in individual contributions of $250 or less, with at least $5,000 collected in each of twenty states. Once this is accomplished, the federal government will match all individual contributions of $250 or less, dollar for dollar. Individual contributions over the $250 limit are not matched. This stipulation has led candidates to concentrate on raising $250 from as many contributors as possible. The result is an increase in small contributors ("kittens"), compared with the large contributors ("fat cats") who had previously dominated campaign financing.

In return for federal funds, candidates must accept a total preconvention spending limit plus a percentage limit on fund raising, as well as spending limits in each state. A state's spending limit is calculated at sixteen cents for each resident of voting age, plus an adjustment for inflation. Thus, candidates who accept matching funds must develop careful strategies for where and when to spend.

Not all candidates accept matching funds. In 1996, Steve Forbes refused to accept the limitations on spending and therefore did not request federal funds. In 2000, Bush and Forbes chose not to accept federal matching funds and, in 2004, Bush and John Kerry chose not to accept the funds. But this did not mean that either candidate was free of all financial restrictions. Although legally permitted to spend as much as they wanted of their own money in each state, they were prohibited by federal law from accepting donations higher than the legal limit from individuals and from political action committees (PACs).

Matching funds are cut off if a candidate does not receive 10 percent of the vote in two consecutive primaries. To re-qualify for funds, a candidate must receive 20 percent of the vote in another primary. The FEC requires twenty-five days' advance notification that a candidate is not participating in a particular primary. Candidates who run unopposed in the primaries, as Ronald Reagan did in 1984, are allowed to spend the legal limit anyway.

During the general election, candidates from each major political party are eligible for public funds for presidential elections. The money source is a three-dollar income tax check-off to the Treasury's Presidential Campaign Fund.

Campaign Finance Reform

The 1996 and 2000 election cycles highlighted the need for reform, based in part on efforts by both political parties to take advantage of loopholes in election laws. In 1996, the Democrats raised $123.9 million and the Republicans $38.2 million in soft money contributions. Another distinguishing component of the 1996 election was the role of foreign contributions, particularly those brought in by John Huang, a former Commerce Department official who raised millions of dollars from overseas donors.

federal matching funds System under which presidential candidates who raise a certain amount of money in the required way may apply for and receive matching federal funds.

State and local party organizations may use **soft money** contributions for "party-building" activities. These include party mailings, voter registration work, get-out-the-vote efforts, recruitment of supporters at the grassroots level, and so forth. This money is considered "soft" because it does not go directly into a specific candidate's campaign and is unrestricted. Therefore, it does not count toward the legal limits imposed on every presidential candidate who accepts federal matching funds. This provision allows candidates to evade legal spending limits, since the money, although intended to strengthen state and local parties, ends up (more than coincidentally) helping the party's national ticket as well. The soft-money loophole has allowed corporations, unions, and wealthy individuals to contribute as much as they want to political parties.

Issue advocacy, the process of campaigning to persuade the public to take a position on an issue, has become, like soft money, a mechanism for channeling huge amounts of money into the system. Moreover, these funds need not be disclosed publicly and do not face FEC regulation.

Another loophole in the campaign finance law involves **independent expenditures**, funds dispersed independently by a group or person in the name of a cause, presumably not by a candidate. Thus, a group or even an individual can spend unlimited sums of money on advertising and TV time to promote policies favored by a particular candidate. Although these actions help that candidate's chance of success in the political campaign, they are entirely legal as long as the group and the candidate maintain separate organizations. The Supreme Court has ruled that in such cases, there can be no restrictions on individual or interest group spending.

In June 2002, the FEC approved a major new campaign finance law known as the McCain-Feingold law, named for its primary sponsors, Senators John McCain (R.-AZ) and Russell Feingold (D.-WI). The law completely changed the way political parties spend soft money contributions from companies, labor unions, and donors. McCain-Feingold banned soft money—unlimited contributions to the national political parties for "party-building" activities. The bill also placed restrictions on outside groups airing so-called "issue ads" that promote or criticize a candidate's position on an issue, but refrain from explicitly telling viewers to vote for or against that candidate. After vigorous debate in the House and Senate, Congress passed the McCain-Feingold bill. President Bush signed the bill into law in March 2002, and the U.S. Supreme Court upheld the law's major provisions in a December 2003 decision.[28]

During the debate over McCain-Feingold, supporters and opponents alike knew that a ban on soft money would have a significant impact on the campaign finance system. After all, the Democratic and Republican parties raised nearly half a billion dollars in soft money for the 2000 and 2002 elections. Because it could be given in unlimited amounts of $100,000, $250,000, or more, soft money allowed corporations, labor unions, and wealthy individuals to wield tremendous influence over the political process—much more influence than the average voter. Many hoped their contributions would pay off later in the form of a policy decision or a bill endorsement. Supporters of reform say soft money made large contributors indispensable to the political parties and reduced the power of the broader electorate. The parties used soft money to help pay for critical voter-registration campaigns, get-out-the-vote drives, and the all-important "issue ads." But donors didn't have to give their money to their party of choice to influence an election. They could spend it themselves—or give it to an interest group to spend—on "issue ads."

The McCain-Feingold campaign finance law has produced great debate. Despite its new restrictions, presidential candidates and political parties raised significantly more money in 2004 than in previous years (see Figure 10.4). A loophole in the law allowed groups known as 527 committees to raise hundreds of millions of dollars in soft money. These 527 committees, named after the section of the tax code that created them, raised more than $350 million. According to the IRS, a Section 527

soft money Campaign contributions directed to advancing the interests of a political party or an issue in general, rather than a specific candidate.

issue advocacy The process of campaigning to persuade the public to take a position on an issue.

independent expenditures Funds dispersed, as allowed by a loophole in campaign finance law, by a group or person not coordinated by a candidate, in the name of a cause.

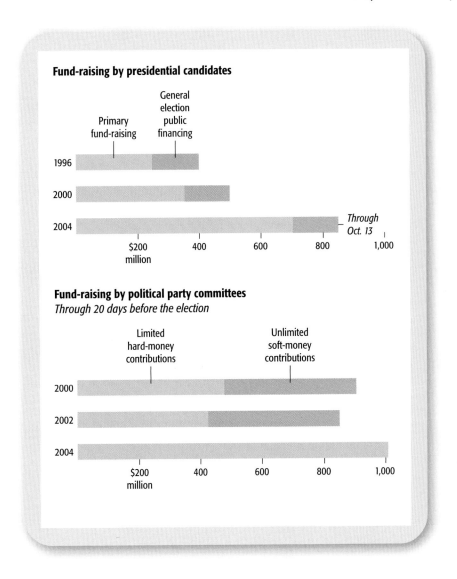

Fund-raising by presidential candidates

Primary fund-raising

General election public financing

1996

2000

2004   Through Oct. 13

$200 million   400   600   800   1,000

Fund-raising by political party committees
Through 20 days before the election

Limited hard-money contributions

Unlimited soft-money contributions

2000

2002

2004

$200 million   400   600   800   1,000

Figure 10.4   The Money Finds a Way

Sources: Federal Election Commission; Center for Responsive Politics; The New York Times.

(§527) organization is created to receive and disburse funds to influence or attempt to influence the nomination, election, appointment, or defeat of candidates for public office. A §527 organization sounds like a PAC, but it is a PAC by another name and with one key difference—a §527 organization falls outside the regulator realm of the Federal Election Commission and therefore does not have the same limits as FEC-regulated PACs.[29]

As we write, legislation to reform the 527 committees is under consideration. Known as the "527 Reform Act of 2005," the legislation would close the major loophole in campaign finance rules that allowed the exploitation of unlimited soft money. The legislation would require that all 527s register as political committees with the FEC. The exceptions would include organizations with annual receipts of less than $25,000, tax-exempt organizations, and those raising money for nonfederal elections, state referendums, and local initiatives. Lining up to support the legislation is the League of Women Voters, who say, "Section 527 groups are self-declared political organizations. They should be regulated as political organizations. They should register as a federal political committee and abide by federal campaign finance laws. Such groups should not be operating free from the federal campaign finance laws that apply to candidates, political parties and others that participate in federal elections."[30]

Summary

1. About one-tenth of American citizens are deeply involved in the political process, but nearly half engage in political activities such as campaigning for candidates or working in groups to support social issues. Another 20 percent vote but do not participate in other ways.

2. Today, all citizens who are eighteen years of age or older are eligible to vote. Over the years, many barriers to voting have been removed, including property requirements, poll taxes, literacy and good-character tests, and prohibitions based on gender and age.

3. Voter turnout rates for presidential elections have been declining since the mid-nineteenth century and are now below 50 percent.

4. Education is the leading influence on whether people vote, followed by social status; people with more education and income are more likely to vote. Social connections in general increase rates of political participation; thus, older people, married people, and people with ties to their community are more likely to vote.

5. In recent years, state-level support has increased for use of initiatives and referenda as ways to return to direct democracy. Initiatives are proposals the public places on the ballot for a popular vote; referenda are submitted by the legislature to the public for a popular vote.

6. The most important factor in voters' choices is identification with a political party. Voters who do not strongly identify with a party may cast split-ticket ballots, but those with strong party loyalty usually vote a straight-party ticket.

7. Other influences on voters' choices are the candidates' attractiveness, personalities, and positions on key issues. Issue voting is likely to take the form of retrospective voting, in which voters judge how well the incumbent performed during the previous term. The skill with which the campaign is conducted also influences voter choice.

8. In presidential election years, the winning presidential candidate's party often also gains power in the legislature; this effect is known as "riding on the president's coattails." In off-year elections, the president's party tends to experience losses.

9. In a presidential election, voters cast their ballots for a slate of electors who are expected to cast their ballots for the candidate who wins the most popular votes in their state.

10. To become president, the winning candidate must receive a majority of the 538 electoral votes (1 for each member of Congress, plus 3 for the District of Columbia). If no candidate receives a majority, a contingency election is held in the House of Representatives, in which each state casts a single vote.

11. Under the winner-take-all system, all of a state's electoral votes go to the candidate who wins the most popular votes in that state. Presidential campaigns therefore focus on the states with the largest numbers of electoral college votes.

12. Presidential elections are conducted under the guidelines of the Federal Election Campaign Acts of 1971 and 1974, which limit the amounts of money that may be contributed to candidates by individuals and interest groups. The system today is in crisis because of loopholes involving soft money, independent expenditures, and issue advocacy.

13. In March 2002, President Bush signed into law new campaign finance legislation that sought to ban soft money in politics.

14. The Bipartisan Campaign Reform Act of 2001 passed the Senate 59–41 on April 2, 2001. The McCain-Feingold legislation, named after co-sponsoring senators John McCain (R.-AZ) and Russell Feingold (D.-WI), sought primarily to ban soft money contributions to national parties.

15. Despite its new restrictions, presidential candidates and political parties raised significantly more money in 2004 than in previous years. A loophole in the law allowed groups known as 527 committees to raise hundreds of millions of dollars in soft money.

Review Questions

1. What is important about political participation? What are the implications of low voter turnout?

2. What is the relationship between alienation, voters, and nonvoters? What do these results suggest about the American political system?

3. What are the reasons for lower voter turnout in off-year elections in the United States?

4. What were the intentions of the framers in creating the electoral college? What function does it fulfill today?

5. How does the electoral college affect the way presidential candidates campaign for office?

6. Explain the methods used in the South to prevent African Americans from voting after the Fifteenth Amendment to the Constitution was passed. How were voting rights in the South eventually ensured for African Americans?

7. Why has the Motor-Voter Law failed to increase voter turnout significantly in presidential elections since 1995?

Key Terms

civil disobedience   370
coattails effect   371
contingency election   373
deviating election   375
electoral college   372
faithless elector   373
federal matching funds   377
good-character test   356
independent expenditures   378

initiative   364
issue advocacy   378
literacy test   356
maintaining election   375
midterm elections   371
participation   354
party identification   365
political violence   370
poll tax   356

protest   370
realigning election   375
referendum   364
retrospective voting   367
soft money   378
split-ticket ballots   365
straight-party ticket   365
voter turnout   358

Suggested Readings

BERNS, WALTER, ed. *After the People Vote: A Guide to the Electoral College.* Lanham, Md.: University Press of America, 1992. An exceptionally useful guide to the operations of the electoral college.

CAMPBELL, ANGUS, PHILIP E. CONVERSE, WARREN E. MILLER, and DONALD STOKES. *The American Voter.* New York: Wiley, 1960. The classic study of voting, which even today should be the starting point for study of elections and politics.

CORRADO, ANTHONY, THOMAS MANN, DANIEL ORTIZ, and TREVOR POTTER. *The New Campaign Finance Sourcebook.* Washington D.C.: Brookings Institution Press, 2005. A completely revised and updated sourcebook; the definitive resource on federal campaign finance regulation.

GOFF, MICHAEL. *The Money Primary: The New Politics of the Early Presidential Nomination Process.* Lanham, Md.: Rowman & Littlefield, 2004. This book examines the "money primary" and fund-raising's instrumental role in candidate visibility and success.

GRANT, J. TOBIN, and THOMAS J. RUDOLPH. *Expression vs. Equality: The Politics of Campaign Finance Reform.* Columbus: Ohio State University Press, 2004. A systematic study of attitudes toward campaign finance reform and the role of pubic opinion in shaping reform measures.

MATSUSAKA, JOHN G. *For the Many or the Few: The Initiative, Public Policy, and American Democracy.* Chicago, Ill.: University of Chicago Press, 2004. An economist addresses the question of whether the presence of initiatives benefits the many or the few.

NIE, NORMAN H., SIDNEY VERBA, and JOHN R. PETROCIK. *The Changing American Voter.* Cambridge, Mass.: Harvard University Press, 1976. An important study offering a fresh look at the classic 1960 study of the American voter.

PIVEN, FRANCIS FOX, and RICHARD CLOWARD. *Why Americans Don't Vote.* New York: Pantheon, 1988. A starting point for understanding the problems associated with the decline of voting in America.

POLSBY, NELSON, and AARON WILDAVSKY. *Presidential Elections,* 10th ed. New York: Scribner's Sons, 2000. An important book that provides a history and analysis of elections and American politics.

SMITH, DANIEL A., and CAROLINE J. TOLBERT. *Educated by Initiative: The Effects of Direct Democracy on Citizens and Political Organizations in the American States.* Ann Arbor: University of Michigan Press, 2004. A valuable discussion on the extent to which ballot-measure decisions educate citizens about the workings of democracy and interest them in democratic processes.

TEIXEIRA, RAY A. *The Disappearing American Voter.* Washington, D.C.: Brooking Institution, 1992. The reasons Americans don't vote and the effects of nonvoting on political life.

WOLFINGER, RAYMOND E., and STEVEN J. ROSENSTONE. *Who Votes.* New Haven, Conn.: Yale University Press, 1980. An important empirical analysis of voting, the results of which are then unified into a theory of voting behavior.

CHAPTER 11

INTEREST GROUPS

CHAPTER OUTLINE

Approaching Democracy

Supreme Cyber-Battle

On July 19, 2005, when President George W. Bush announced his choice of Judge John G. Roberts for a vacant seat on the Supreme Court, he launched an election-year–style "cyber war" among dozens of interest groups willing to spend more than $100 million to determine who would replace the "swing justice," Sandra Day O'Connor.

The confirmation battle started even before Bush made his nomination, as conservative interest groups lobbied against the possible appointment of moderate Attorney General Alberto Gonzales. They argued that he would not be a reliably conservative judge and would be forced to recuse himself from cases he had been involved in at the Justice Department. This led the president to tell the press, "I don't like it when a friend gets criticized. I'm loyal to my friends." But in the end, word leaked out from the White House saying "message received," and Gonzales's name was struck from the list of candidates.

Then, just forty-five minutes after Justice Sandra Day O'Connor announced that she was retiring, Progress for America Inc., a conservative interest group established by former members of the Bush campaign staff, sent e-mails to 8.7 million Americans warning against possible liberal "smear tactics" used against President Bush's nominee. Meanwhile, interest groups began reserving Web site names and booking television and radio advertising time in anticipation of the upcoming confirmation battle. This was quite a difference from the state of the electronic war just eighteen years before, in the Robert Bork confirmation battle of 1987. During that fight, also over the replacement of the "swing seat" on the Court then held by Justice Lewis Powell, so many phone calls came to the Senate offices that they incapacitated the phone system, and Senator Alan Simpson (R.-WY) complained from the Judiciary Committee bench on national television that he was being buried by phone messages and faxes.

Now faxes and phones are the least of the senators' problems. There are Web sites, blogs, Internet news and magazine sites, twenty-four-hour-a-day cable news channels, PDAs, e-mails, Blackberries, and even iPods, not to mention enormous national interest groups using massive voter contact lists and millions of dollars.

As soon as Roberts's name was announced, groups such as Progress for America launched a Web site about the candidate, judgeroberts.com, containing

★ David Frum (right) a conservative former special assistant for economic speechwriting for George W. Bush, used his computer to help persuade Harriet Miers to withdraw her nomination for the Supreme Court in 2005 when he launched his "Alliance for Better Justice" website, arguing that she was not conservative enough to fill Sandra Day O'Connor's swing seat on the Court.

biographical information and supportive comments from both conservatives and liberals. Another site, UporDownVote.com, included a "rage gauge," seeking to discourage a bruising Senate confirmation fight. These sites contained the current television ads, a new online ad, and critiques of the opposition's charges and media ad campaign.

Other conservative groups appealed for a "fair and speedy" confirmation hearing for Roberts. James Dobson's evangelical Focus on the Family group mobilized his religious followers, while former Bush campaign staffer Gary Marx's Judicial Confirmation Network mobilized constituents of Democratic senators up for reelection in 2006 in states that voted for Bush in 2004.

The liberal opposition also had its tool in place for challenging the nomination. Nan Aron of the liberal, pro-civil-rights Alliance for Justice pronounced the appointment an "outrage." Ralph Neas, president of People for the American Way, a coalition of liberal interest groups, sent out 400,000 e-mails urging senators to be cautious before supporting Roberts because of "sizable questions about his legal writings." NARAL Pro-Choice America launched its own Web site opposing the appointment, and then aired two television ads highly critical of Roberts, both of which were quickly withdrawn at the insistence of other liberal groups who found them too hard-hitting. Moveon.org, a liberal Web organization uniting small donors, started an anti-Roberts national petition drive. But, in the end, the Roberts appointment seemed so likely to be confirmed that the liberal groups largely held their fire for the next appointment.

When Harriet Miers was nominated to replace Sandra Day O'Connor, conservative groups engaged in the initial interest group debate and discussion on blogs, while liberal groups largely sat back and watched. Former Bush speechwriter David Frum and others created the "Alliance for Better Justice" Web site to criticize the appointment. Then another group of conservatives launched the WithdrawMiers.org Web site revealing their complaints against the appointment, and seeking anonymous tips against the appointee. In the end, conservative cyber-lobbyists dominated. The conservatives forced Miers to withdraw her nomination by complaining about her lack of knowledge of constitutional law and her friendship with President Bush. Although Samuel Alito's nomination prompted cyber-groups to create sites such as the liberal Think Progress group's "Samuel Alito's America" site and the conservative Progress for America group's "JudgeAlito.com" site, Alito's impressive testimony before the Senate Judiciary Committee and the voting public's general lack of interest in opposing his nomination left cyber-lobbying with little effect on the confirmation.

The number of cyber-lobbying groups, their size, the millions of dollars funding them, and the technological means of persuasion at their disposal all ensure that they will be a factor in future Supreme Court nominations. But more than that, they will continue to be a factor in lobbying for every cultural and other issue that such justices will eventually decide. In a sense, then, the election-year interest group battles will never end.[1]

QUESTION FOR REFLECTION

The framers did not explicitly include lobbying groups in their outline for government. What impact has the public's increased participation in the crafting of laws and the confirmation battles over appointments had on approaching democracy?

Introduction
INTEREST GROUPS AND DEMOCRACY

Interest groups are formal organizations of people who share a common outlook or social circumstance and who band together in the hope of influencing government policy.[2] Americans often see corporate interest groups as sinister, selfish, high-pressure outfits that use illegitimate means to promote narrow ends at the expense of the public interest. Interest groups as a whole really do not run anything; they struggle against each other for influence over those who do run things. Each group has wins and losses.

In truth, we *all* belong to interest groups, whether we recognize it or not. Many of us are members of churches or synagogues, or perhaps we work in a unionized job. Students in colleges and universities might be surprised to learn that part of their student fees may support lobbying efforts. Even if you do not belong to any such organizations you may recall signing petitions in the malls or on the streets supporting such causes as environmentalism. In such ways, millions of people can band together and persuade political candidates, and thus governing officials, to make their agenda the new governmental agenda.

American suspicion toward interest groups is especially curious, given the evidence that they are a natural and inevitable presence in free societies. Interest groups are here to stay, and they play a key role in American politics. In fact, interest groups are crucial to democratic society. They provide an easy means for average citizens to participate in the political process, thereby allowing all Americans to approach the democratic ideal. In this chapter we will look closely at interest groups to see how they broaden the possibilities for political participation. We also will examine why these agents for democratic influence often are accused of distorting and even undermining the democratic system.

INTEREST GROUPS: A TRADITION IN AMERICAN POLITICS

Foreign and domestic observers have long noted the propensity of Americans to form and join groups. "Americans of all ages, all stations in life, and all types of disposition," wrote Alexis de Tocqueville in 1831, "are forever forming associations."[3] This tendency has been attributed to causes ranging from calls for religious conformity to the need for community cohesion imposed by the rugged conditions of the country's early history. For whatever reasons, the desire to come together in social groups for common ends has been deeply embedded in American culture.

This value is enshrined politically in the First Amendment's freedom of association clause: "Congress shall make no law . . . abridging . . . the right of the people peaceably to assemble, and to petition the government for a redress of grievances." These simple words provide the legal framework for all citizen-based political activity in the United States. They ensure the existence of a vast array of interest groups, because government can literally do nothing ("Congress shall make no law") to interfere with people joining together ("peaceably to assemble") to try to influence government policies ("petition government for a redress of grievances"). Deeply ingrained in American culture, then, as well as in an entire body of legal precedents, is the norm that citizens may form any kind of group they please to try to influence government, as long as that activity is undertaken "peaceably."

To help Americans in their efforts to influence government, the Constitution also provides, in the same sentence in the First Amendment, the rights of assembly

interest groups Formal organizations of people who share a common outlook or social circumstance and who band together in the hope of influencing government policy.

and petition, the right to say what they want (freedom of speech), and to publish what they want (freedom of the press). And Americans have not been shy about using these rights. From the earliest days of the republic, they have formed groups of every type and description to defend common interests and obtain favorable government policies. The result has been a complex array of competing and cooperating interests that practically defines modern democracy. If you find a political regime today that does not allow competing interest groups, you will have found a political system that is *not* democratic.

What Is an Interest Group?

If interest groups are central to the democratic process, what precisely are they? Interest groups can take a wide variety of forms. One example is a labor union such as the United Auto Workers (UAW), which formed in 1935 to secure improvements in wages and working conditions for automobile factory workers. Another example is the National Rifle Association, a large affiliation of firearms owners who have organized a powerful lobby for the Second Amendment right to "keep and bear Arms." Groups may be large organizations with diffused goals, like the American Association of Retired Persons (AARP), with its thirty-five million members and its broad aim of promoting the interests of the elderly, or small outfits with specific goals, such as the American Women's Society of Certified Public Accountants.

Some political scientists have found it useful to distinguish between actual and potential interest groups. **Actual groups** have already been formed; they have a headquarters, an organizational structure, paid employees, membership lists, and the like. **Potential groups** are interests that could gather under the right circumstances but as yet have no substantive form—and may never have one. Still, political participants cannot discount them. Whenever substantial numbers of people share a common outlook or socioeconomic condition, they might well decide to join together to promote their mutual interests. Politicians who ignore potential groups for long may, in fact, be encouraging their formation.

Strongly held policy preferences are essential for interest group formation. Interest groups provide individuals who hold strong policy preferences with a way to disseminate information to legislators, make their preferences known, and work within the system to influence legislation.

Often it takes little more than one or a few dynamic leaders, called **policy entrepreneurs**, to create the conditions whereby a potential group becomes an actual interest group. Ralph Nader, a Green Party candidate for president in 2000 and an independent candidate in 2004, is one such policy entrepreneur. Nader's untiring efforts were instrumental in forming consumer-oriented interest groups such as the Public Citizen Litigation Group and the Health Research Group, as well as various other public interest research groups (PIRGs) in the 1970s, with a major impact on both national and state legislation. They provide oversight on auto safety, consumer issues, health issues, and the environment. Today more than two hundred such groups claim among their victories nonsmoking rules on airlines, nutrition labels, and laws requiring smoke detectors in apartment buildings.

A classic example of a potential interest group becoming an actual group can be seen in the establishment of Mothers Against Drunk Drivers (MADD). For decades children had been killed or maimed by intoxicated motorists. The potential existed for the parents of those children to gather and push for stricter laws to prevent and punish drunk driving. Yet no such group appeared until one woman, Candy Lightner, who had lost a child to a drunk driver, decided to form such a group and devote her life to this work.

In a free society actual groups may form and even become powerful on short notice. United We Stand America, an interest group formed to support Ross Perot's 1992 presidential candidacy, in a few short months went from nonexistence to major-player status in national politics and then became a full-fledged political

actual groups Interest groups that have already been formed; they have headquarters, an organizational structure, paid employees, membership lists, and the like.

potential groups Interest groups that could form under the right circumstances; as yet, they have no substantive form and may never have one, but they cannot be discounted by political participants.

policy entrepreneurs Leaders who invest in, and who create the conditions for, a potential group to become an actual interest group. Ralph Nader stands as a classic example of a policy entrepreneur.

party. Thus, politicians and observers of politics must always be aware of potential groups "out there" in the public.

Some groups are more likely to form and to gain political clout than others. In making policy, politicians consider numerous factors without constantly worrying whether an action they decide to take today could cause the formation of a group that will punish them tomorrow. Still, that possibility can never be wholly ignored and must play at least a modest role in the policy-making process.

A Long History of Association

From the very beginning of the republic, national leaders have wrestled with the idea of interest groups. In *The Federalist*, no. 10, James Madison wrote, "Liberty is to faction what air is to fire."[4] To put it in modern terms, he saw that the development and proliferation of interest groups were inevitable in a free society. But Madison also saw a basic flaw in democratic politics when it came to interests. He worried that one set of interests (a **faction**), whether a majority or a minority of the population, might gain control of the levers of power and rule society for its own aims, to the detriment of the collective good.

Madison worked to control their potential negative effects, while warning against any effort to eliminate factions altogether—an action he knew would undermine Americans' precious liberties. He reasoned that the power of factions could be moderated by *diffusing* their influence. This diffusion would occur in two ways. First, the very act of joining the individual states into a large and diverse country undercut the power of any one faction. What group could successfully unite the industrial interests of the Northeast and the plantation interests of the South, small independent farmers, indentured servants, urban workers, artisans and merchants, hired hands, and all of the other groups in America at that time? Its size and complexity would guard the new nation against any one faction controlling government.

Madison's second hedge against the triumph of any given faction was to make government complex. By *dividing* political power among several institutions that represented different interests chosen at different times by different elements of the population, he strove to ensure that no one faction could ever gain control of all the key levers of power. As we know, Madison and the other framers were hugely successful at their task. Indeed, a major criticism of the American political system is that the framers were too successful. America's national government is so hedged with restrictions on its powers and so open to the input of every imaginable faction or interest group that it can rarely develop a coherent set of national policies.[5]

As Madison saw it, the causes of faction are "sown in the nature of man." Given the human tendency toward disagreement and disharmony, factional differences will always exist. Thus, government can never eliminate the causes of faction; government can only eliminate or suppress faction itself. Madison and the framers' choice to allow diverse factions within a complex system of political and social pluralism ensured that all interests could be heard, but made it difficult for any one interest to gain tyrannical control of power.

From a modern perspective, Madison's view of faction was both wise and prescient. Tens of thousands of interest groups have formed and thrived since the early days of the republic, allowing widespread input into the policy process from millions of average citizens, yet no one group has ever gained full control of all the levers of political and social power. Setting group against group in relatively peaceful competition within a complex system of divided powers seems to have been a successful vision of the way to deal with the fissures and stresses that are inevitable in a free society.

Political parties formed in the early years of the republic, and groups of every type and description began to flourish soon thereafter. Revivalist religious groups, social reform groups, peace groups, women's rights groups, abolitionist groups, temperance groups—these and hundreds of others that sprang up in the first half

factions According to James Madison in *The Federalist*, no. 10: "A number of citizens, whether amounting to a majority or a minority of the whole, who are united and actuated by some common impulse or passion or . . . interests."

of the nineteenth century bore witness to Madison's expectation that the air of liberty would do nothing but nourish a swarm of factional organizations. It is hardly surprising that American political history is in many ways a history of diverse and competing interest groups.

The organizational ease with which groups form in the United States is generally attributed to its democratic culture. Americans, who often see themselves as equals, usually find it easy to work together in groups toward common ends. As Tocqueville wrote, "[I]n no other country of the world has the principle of association been more successfully used, or more unsparingly applied to a multitude of different objects, than in America."[6] Although all modern democracies exhibit interest-group activity, few have achieved the level of vibrant nongovernmental group life apparent in the American system.

Recent Trends

Even though interest groups have been central to American political history, the number of groups trying to pressure government has grown dramatically in the past three decades. The reasons for this development are complex. For one, government policies since the 1960s have produced greater regulation of society. Responding to demands that Washington "do something" about the problems of civil rights, the environment, education, conditions in the workplace, health, women's rights, and so forth, the national government has developed policies that affect all sectors of society. Government regulations now touch all Americans. Naturally, people whose livelihoods and values are affected by government actions find it expedient to work together to influence those actions. Thus, as government's power to affect society grows, so, too, does the number of groups that aim to influence and pressure government.

Another explanation for the growth of interest groups stems from the success liberal interest groups experienced starting in the 1950s. In the past, conservative groups rarely relied upon group activity to advance their aims because conservatives were already active in civic affairs, being on the average wealthier, better educated, and more likely to participate in politics than average citizens. Thus, they were already well represented in government and believed that it adequately responded to their needs. Conversely, those groups most underrepresented in political institutions were most likely to use interest groups to pursue policy goals. These groups tended to promote the liberal aims of civil rights groups, environmentalists, the poor, and women.

By the 1970s, liberal groups had gained many victories by exerting pressure on Congress, the executive branch, and the courts. Moreover, the federal government actually sponsored citizen-group involvement by reimbursing participants with seed money or outright grants. Federal domestic legislation included provisions for citizen participation that spurred group organizations such as environmental action councils, legal defense coalitions, health care organizations, and senior citizen groups.[7] Manufacturing and business leaders, along with ideological conservatives of every type, responded by forming their own interest groups. These conservative groups developed their own dynamism in reaction to the social-policy gains made previously by liberals. As Planned Parenthood,

▲ From Seattle to Washington, D.C., protests against the World Bank continued in April 2000. While remaining much more peaceful than the Seattle protests (shown here), Washington saw occasional clashes.

► The Federalist Society, a conservative educational and lobbying group on legal issues, hears from conservative speakers such as former Bush Attorney General John Ashcroft in seeking to influence the selection process for more conservative federal judges.

MakeItReal

Primary Source: Federal Election Campaign Act (FECA)

political action committees (PACs) Committees formed as the fund-raising and financial distribution arm of specific interest groups.

the American Civil Liberties Union, and other liberal groups fought for abortion and privacy rights, political conservatives countered in the late 1970s and 1980s with groups such as Operation Rescue and the Moral Majority.

The success of liberal interest groups led to the rise of conservative counterpart groups, especially in economic and legal areas. One of the most successful on the economic side was the Club for Growth. Economist and lobbyist Stephen Moore organized nearly three dozen conservative financial advisers to back the Reagan administration's "supply side" economic policy of lowering income taxes, reducing the size of the national government, and cutting government spending. Since that time, the group has grown to more than ten thousand members. It funnels millions of dollars to economically conservative Republican candidates in the primaries and ads for anti-tax congressional candidates.[8]

The Federalist Society lobbying organization focuses more on legal issues than on raising campaign funds. Founded in 1982 at schools such as Yale Law School and the University of Chicago Law School, the Federalist Society was designed to be an academic think tank and debating society and to provide a forum for conservative ideas and legal philosophies. It was intended to counter a perceived liberal bias in legal education. Now, though, many appointees to the federal judiciary, including John Roberts, and to cabinet and executive branch positions have connections to this group. The group's ability to organize disparate individuals to keep them on the same message shows how an organized lobbying group can work to affect public opinion. For example, the Federalist Society can post a notice on its Web site and almost immediately engage a group of experts who can provide media commentary on relevant issues, such as court appointments.[9] A major boost to group involvement in politics came in the early 1970s with campaign finance reform. Two acts (the Federal Election Campaign Act (FECA) of 1971 and its amendments in 1974) changed the nature of money in American politics. As you saw in Chapter 9, these laws, and the amending Bipartisan Campaign Reform Act (BCRA) of 2002, more popularly called the McCain-Feingold Act, limited the role of individual "fat cats" and expanded **political action committees (PACs)**. Rather than seeking large donations from a small number of wealthy individuals, these groups raised small amounts of money from large numbers of contributors and combined them for maximum effectiveness.

Finally, increasing income and education levels have led to increased levels of political activity in the United States over the past sixty years. The United States now has a large middle class and upper middle class of educated, affluent voters who are vitally

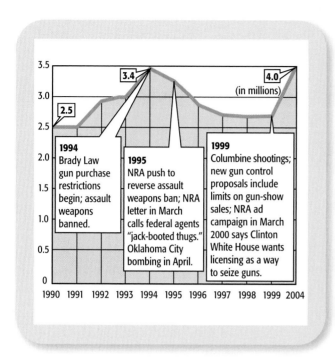

Figure 11.1   How NRA Membership Has Risen
Source: USA Today, May 18, 2000, p. 4A. Copyright © 2000 *USA Today*. Reprinted with permission. Updated Nedra Pickler, "Kerry Faces opposition from NRA members," May 21, 2004, found at www.esgv.org/news/headlines/ap5_21_04.cfm

aware of the political process and how it affects them. Many of these people have become deeply involved in politics—especially in groups that promote their interests and concerns. No theory seeking to explain the rise in the number and power of American interest groups can fail to take into account this important social development. Figure 11.1 shows how membership in the NRA has risen over the years.

FUNCTIONS OF INTEREST GROUPS

Interest groups help people band together to influence public policy and are therefore central to democracy. They also provide policy makers with information; indeed, members of Congress have come to depend on expertise and information provided by interest groups as part of their deliberative process.

Interest Groups Allow for Collective Action

People form and join interest groups because **collective action** (the action of many) is stronger, more credible, and more likely to influence policy outcomes than the isolated actions of individuals.[10] Imagine, for example, the modest influence you would have if you alone wrote a letter to your congressional representative to protest a new law. You would probably receive a form letter from a staff member expressing concern about the issue, to be followed later by another letter asking for a campaign donation. Your individual letter would not change policy. But what if you joined a group and several thousand of you write and complain about this law? Collective action of that sort is taken more seriously than the actions of one or a few individuals.

A new form of collective action has begun with Internet use such as personal blogs and even personal video sites on the Web. "Cyber action" in 2004 exposed the fraudulent nature of the CBS News Report on President Bush's service in the Alabama air national guard. Increasing numbers of **netizens** organizations—groups of people joined in a cyber-society for political purposes—are uniting individual Internet lobbying actions. This form of collective action lobbied successfully to eliminate portions of the Communications Decency Act of 1996 and expose practices such as unethical spamming and the existence of unknown surveillance cameras.[11]

As outlined in the U.S.A. Yesterday and Today box below, effective collective actions include the early 1970s protests, when tens of thousands of students temporarily

collective action The political action of individuals who unite to influence policy.

netizens Groups of people joined in a cyber-society for political purposes.

shut down many colleges across the nation as part of their protest against the Vietnam War, and the 1960s civil disobedience of thousands of African Americans that helped change our civil rights policies. Collective actions include groups of people demonstrating at environmental sites such as Thoreau's Walden Pond in Massachusetts or the giant redwood forest in northern California, or collecting money to buy threatened land areas, such as the Civil War and Revolutionary War battlefields, to save them from development. Not all of these groups are large ones, or even completely serious, relying instead on the symbolic nature of their messages. Recently, a small group in tiny Weare, New Hampshire, the home of Justice David Souter, joined other protestors in Los Angeles and elsewhere in threatening to raise funds to protest a 2005 eminent domain decision by the Supreme Court that allowed cities and localities to seize a person's property if they can show that economic development will benefit the community by increasing the property tax base. The group planned to take

U.S.A. Yesterday and Today

Students with a Cause

In April 2005, seven students, members of the World Worker Justice Committee at the University of Colorado, began a hunger strike designed to persuade their school to stop purchasing school clothing produced in foreign sweatshops. In that same year, Emerson College students gathered on Boston Common in support of their teachers' union, and Boston College students boycotted classes seeking protection of gay rights. Meanwhile, in reaction to student protests at their schools, Harvard decided to sell off its investments in Sudan, Georgetown University increased wages for its janitorial corps, and U-Mass Amherst canceled plans to charge international students a fee for its homeland security policy and also changed its picketing policy that restricted student protests. The upsurge in protests stems from the reaction to the September 11, 2001, attacks and the Iraq War, says Liz Hollander, the executive director of Campus Compact, a nonprofit student protest support group. "We're emerging from an era where students didn't think anything going on in the world would affect their lives."

Few people realize that America's approach to democracy over the past fifty years has been fueled, and at times actually led, by college student protests. Americans have a proud history of student protests over the past half century. In the 1940s and 1950s labor unions mobilized student-run groups such as the American Student Congress to help fight labor issues such as inadequate pay and racial discrimination. At the same time, the American Communist party recruited student chapters on campuses. In time, professional activists in the National Association for the Advancement of Colored People (NAACP) began to recruit students to help in the fight for civil rights.

On February 1, 1960, student protests reached a crossroads as four African American students in North Carolina engaged in a sit-in, protesting the lack of civil rights for African Americans, by refusing to leave a segregated lunch counter at F. W. Woolworth's in Greensboro, North Carolina. By May of that year the Student Nonviolent Coordinating Committee (SNCC) was formed to lobby for civil rights, naming as its president Marion Barry of Fisk University, later the mayor of Washington, D.C. This group helped to register minority voters in the South, often in spite of bloody riots. In June 1962, Tom Hayden of the University of Michigan, later a California state senator, held a retreat in Port Huron, Michigan, and drafted the manifesto for the Students for a Democratic Society (SDS). This group later protested against the Vietnam War and participated in the riots at the 1968 Democratic Convention in Chicago.

In March 1965 SNCC members and leaders were beaten as they marched for civil rights from Montgomery to Selma, Alabama. The photos of the students being attacked, as they used Gandhi's nonviolent resistance technique, spurred passage of the 1965 Voting Rights Act. When civil rights progress seemed too slow, new SNCC leaders advocated a more violent protest approach, and another group, the Black Panthers, formed to achieve change "by any means possible." In time, an even more radical group of student dropouts formed a group called the Weather Underground to "make revolution."

By 1968, student protest changed focus from civil rights to ending America's involvement in the war in Vietnam. College-age students, too young to vote yet old enough to be drafted to fight in Vietnam, began to vigorously protest against the war. Student protests continued across the nation until on May 2, 1970, four students were killed and nine were injured by National Guardsmen at Kent State University in Ohio. Many were over the Weare Board of Selectmen and use the eminent domain power to seize Justice Souter's two-hundred-year-old family homestead to turn it into either a bed and breakfast called the Lost Liberty Hotel or a museum on the U.S. Constitution.[12] In time, if enough people join them, such interest groups could have important consequences for election outcomes.

Group action allows citizens to promote their specialized concerns. In representing specific points of view, interest groups can project precise citizen demands into politics, bringing both government and political parties closer to the people and democratizing the national agenda. Interest group activity enfolded the perspectives of the abolitionist movement, which sought to end slavery, into the political outlook of the pre–Civil War Republican party. In similar fashion, post–New Deal Democrats absorbed the perspective of the twentieth-century civil rights movement.

Question for Reflection

Given our history and the success of the student protest movement, how will student actions affect America's approach to democracy in the twenty-first century?

the same age as the student protestors. As a result, many colleges across the nation decided to close and end their semesters. Eventually, America ended its participation in the war, but before that, the Twenty-sixth Amendment had extended voting rights to include Americans ages eighteen to twenty-one.

By 1985, student groups across the nation were back at work protesting the connection between the investment portfolios of their colleges and universities and the segregation-promoting apartheid government in South Africa. Cornell and Penn State students built cardboard and tin buildings on their campuses to protest the shantytowns in which the blacks were forced to live in that country. Although a thousand students were arrested at Cornell, eventually colleges and universities, as well as American companies, were forced to divest themselves of holdings in South Africa and eventually, thanks to Nelson Mandela, Bishop Desmond Tutu, and their followers, apartheid ended.

The 1990s represented a return to the links between student protestors and labor unions as students joined the AFL–CIO's Union Summer to learn protest tactics. In the summer of 1998 Union Summer launched United Students Against Sweatshops to protest the cheap labor shops in foreign countries that produce the logo-bearing clothing so popular on campuses throughout the United States. More than one hundred chapters of this group and their work against such companies as Nike obliged many colleges and universities to change their policies for dealing with these businesses.

The end of the millennium saw students in December 1999 join protestors in Seattle who sought to disrupt the meeting of the World Trade Organization in Seattle. When as many as fifty thousand people marched in protest of the monetary gap between the industrialized countries and the Third World and the lack of attention given to poverty by the World Trade Organization, a riot ensued. Six hundred protestors were arrested, compromising the peaceful intentions of the majority. In the end, the meeting produced no new agreements and analysts declared it a failure.

▲ Students at Harvard University engage in a sit-in protest in 2001 on behalf of raising the hourly wage for the school's janitors.

In the early fall of 2004, across the nation, students became the central participants in numerous anti-Iraq War and anti-Bush administration protests. Hundreds of thousands of protestors occupied New York City in early September 2004 to signal this message. Meanwhile, hundreds of students in the Boston Student Mobilization to End the War organized an antiwar rally in that city. Now, so many students use the Internet, pagers, PDAs, and other technological advances that protest groups find it much easier to organize them. What will the next student protest be?

Source: Based on Jenna Russell, "Campuses with a Cause," *Boston Globe,* April 18, 2005; and Stephanie Gutmann, "Half a Century of Student Protest," *New York Times,* "Education Life" section, November 11, 2001, p. 29; Also, Berny Morson, "Students Protest Foreign Sweatshops," *Rocky Mountain News,* April 29, 2005.

Interest Groups Provide Information

Interest groups possess the expertise to provide relevant information about policy goals to party leaders, public officials, and bureaucrats. This function allows interest group members an important avenue for broader participation in the actual policy-making process.

Interest groups also provide government officials with a constant, reliable source of information about popular sentiment, albeit information always slanted toward a group's chosen outcome. The information may be technical in nature, educating public officials about the details of a topic, or perhaps political in nature, educating public officials about potential consequences of voting one way or another. Thus, interest groups serve as vital transmitters of the system's responsiveness to citizen demands. The more public officials hear the varied voices of the people, the more likely they are to take those voices into account in formulating government policies.

Although interest groups are an important element in American democratic life, many observers fear that their effects are not all positive. Because interest groups focus only on their own cause, some believe they downplay or ignore the public good and their proliferation of competing demands and divisive rhetoric may drown out moderate voices of compromise and cooperation. Their information can be biased, leaving officials and the public with just one perspective on an issue. Furthermore, interest groups are not all equal. The powerful groups tend to be those already in control of the major resources in society, especially money and property. Large corporations tend to dominate the sphere of interest group activity, and their activities often overwhelm groups trying to promote consumer safety, workers' welfare, and environmental protection.[13]

Interest groups thus represent a peculiar irony of democracy. While stimulating citizen action and political involvement, they can also create confrontation instead of cooperation, diatribe in place of reasoned debate. Although they allow average citizens a role in promoting their democratic goals, interest groups can also skew the political process to favor the already powerful and well off. The "factions" that so concerned Madison are now powerful, well-financed organizations. Can a modern democratic system preserve liberty—allowing groups free rein to promote their goals—without sacrificing the very essence of the democratic ideal—widespread access to power for all citizens? That is one of the central questions that American society continually confronts as it struggles to approach democracy.

TYPES OF INTEREST GROUPS

Nearly twenty thousand organized groups of every imaginable kind regularly seek to influence American governmental policies. These groups take a wide variety of forms, but for simplicity we can divide them into a few major types: economic, public interest, government, ideological, religious, civil rights, single-issue, state, and local interest groups. Table 11.1 shows the different types of groups that participated in world trade protests in Washington, D.C., in April 2000.

Economic Interest Groups

Most observers would say economic interests dominate in democratic politics. The old saying, "Most people vote their pocketbooks," applies to group activity as well. Most people take political action to protect or enhance their economic well-being. Thus, groups that aim to help their members make money or keep money will always play a central role in the political process of any democracy. Economic interest groups include business, organized labor, and similar groups.

Question for Reflection

Will the Internet diminish the number and type of interest groups, or increase them, and how might it change their operation?

Quick Review

Economic Interest Groups

- Goal is to help their members make or keep money.
- Some represent single businesses or groups of businesses as trade associations.
- Some organizations, like the AFL–CIO, represent workers.

Table 11.1 ■ World Trade Protest Groups

	Religious Groups	Environmental Groups	Organized Labor	Student Groups	Ad Hoc Coalitions
Some of the Main Groups	A movement known as Jubilee 2000, backed primarily by Catholics and Protestant churches.	Friends of the Earth, the Sierra Club, and the Rainforest Action Network.	The AFL-CIO, the United Steel-workers of America, and the Teamsters Union.	United Students Against Sweatshops and the U.S. Student Association.	Global Exchange, 50 Years Is Enough, and the Ruckus Society.
Among Their Main Complaints	Many of the poorest nations are overburdened with international debt and deserve debt forgiveness.	The spread of free market capitalism is damaging forests, silting rivers, contributing to greenhouse gas emissions, and destroying the natural resources of poor nations.	Global trade will have a negative effect on workers' jobs in wealthy countries. Labor groups have pushed for stricter trade and labor standards worldwide.	U.S. companies that make consumer products sometimes tolerate poor working conditions in overseas factories.	Globalization worsens social injustice, poverty, and animal rights, and speeds the erosion of indigenous cultures.
Why They Are Protesting the World Bank and the IMF	The World Bank and the IMF are among the leading lenders to the poorest countries. Many religious groups criticize these lenders for a slow and half-hearted response to the push for debt relief.	Some accuse the World Bank of funding energy and road projects that hasten environmental degradation. These groups contend that the IMF encourages governments to curtail spending on environmental protection in return for aid.	Some say the lenders encourage poor nations to develop big export-oriented industries, costing U.S. jobs. Labor's main goal, however, is to rewrite trade rules enforced by the World Trade Organization.	Some student groups accuse the World Bank and the IMF of protecting the interests of corporations over the rights of workers abroad and of forcing Third World corporations to open their doors to investment by multinational companies.	The World Bank and the IMF are seen as the main villains of globalization, capitalist enforcers trying to make the world safe for big corporations.

Source: From *New York Times,* April 15, 2000, p. 8. Copyright © by The New York Times Co. Reprinted by permission of *The New York Times.*

Business   Corporations have long dominated interest-group activity in American politics, as clearly seen in the lobbying efforts of failed Texas energy corporation Enron. That pattern is hardly surprising in an environment of entrepreneurial capitalism. Calvin Coolidge made the point concisely: "The business of America is business." The United States' political process almost seems designed to illustrate Coolidge's observation. More than half the lobbies operating in Washington today represent corporate and industrial interests.[14] Sometimes those groups represent single businesses, but other times groups of businesses unite in trade associations that lobby on a much broader range of issues. Trade associations give individual business members additional clout from other allied companies and also increase access to the political system at both federal and state levels.

Heading the list of business-oriented trade associations is the U.S. Chamber of Commerce, which represents 225,000 businesses across the nation, including manufacturers, retailers, construction firms, and financial, insurance, and real estate companies. With an annual budget of more than $65 million and a full-time staff of fourteen hundred, the Chamber of Commerce carries considerable political clout. Other major business interest groups in this category include the National Association of Manufacturers (NAM) and the Business Roundtable. These groups led the fight against Clinton's health-care reforms in the mid-1990s. However, individual health maintenance organizations (HMOs) also played a role.

▶ Looking for work? The collapse of the huge energy corporation Enron in 2002 threw thousands of highly qualified people out of work, stripped them of their pensions consisting entirely of company stock, and caused chaos in the political world. It also led to lobbying efforts for corporate reforms.

In addition to group memberships, many large and medium-sized companies, about five hundred in Washington alone, including IBM, Ford, General Motors, Exxon, and Xerox, maintain their own lobbyists to ensure that their voices are heard. Before Enron's failed efforts, the tobacco lobby offered one of the best examples of how individual business lobbying works. Various tobacco businesses spent tens of millions of dollars seeking to influence federal and state tobacco-control legislation. Corporate executives from the U.S. tobacco industry testified that smoking does not cause cancer. Later internal documents proved that their own research indicated that smoking causes cancer as well as other serious physical maladies such as emphysema and heart disease. And, like the problems faced by the Enron executives, the tobacco companies and their executives faced lawsuits and legislative control efforts across the country.

MakeItReal

Census 2000: Union Membership

Organized Labor Despite its power, business is not the only voice of organized economic interest. From the late nineteenth century until the middle of the twentieth, labor played a major role in American politics. Indeed, the influential economist John Kenneth Galbraith once called labor unions an important "countervailing power" that could stand up to and dilute the power of business.[15] But their power has declined in recent years. Unionized workers once represented nearly 36 percent of the workforce, now they account for less than 15 percent of it. Still, the American Federation of Labor–Congress of Industrial Organizations (AFL-CIO), labor's umbrella organization, continues to represent millions of workers and put intense pressure on politicians for better wages, improved working conditions, job protection, social programs, and health insurance. Other major labor groups include the United Auto Workers, the United Mine Workers, and the Teamsters (a union representing workers in the transportation industry).

Although business and labor often appear at odds, they occasionally join forces. For instance, when the Chrysler Corporation sought government loans in 1981, the United Auto Workers were ardent backers of the loan program, hoping to preserve the tens of thousands of jobs its workers held in Chrysler plants.

Recently, though, the news for labor unions has not been so good. Less than 10 percent of private industry workers belong to the labor union movement. The Service Employees International Union (SEIU) decision to split from the overarching AFL-CIO in mid-2005 threatens to greatly lessen the impact of labor on the direction of political policy and elections.[16]

Other Economic Interest Groups   Practically every group of people who make their living in the United States has some kind of interest group to protect and promote its interests. Beyond workers and businesspeople, groups exist to advance the interests of lawyers (the American Bar Association), doctors (the American Medical Association), teachers (the National Education Association), and so forth.

Farmers were once among the most powerful groups in the United States and are still solidly represented by such organizations as the American Farm Bureau Federation, the National Corn Growers Association, and the National Farmers Union. The power of agricultural interests has inevitably diminished as the number of farmers has steadily declined, mirroring a pattern in all industrial nations. People who make more than half their income through farming now represent less than 2 percent of the U.S. workforce. Still, given the importance of this segment of the population, which provides food for Americans and many others around the world, it is safe to say that farm groups will continue to wield major political power for some time to come. In mid-2002, for example, members of the Black Farmers and Agriculturist Association protested in hopes of receiving the fifty-thousand-dollar payments promised them by a successful $2-billion-dollar 1999 class action suit as remedy for allegations that the U.S. Department of Agriculture had been racially biased in awarding agricultural grants. Despite their efforts, though, years later, tens of thousands of claimants still sought their payments, leading to further complaints that the Agriculture Department was fighting payment of the claims.[17]

Public Interest Groups

Economic self-interest, though a powerful force, represents just one reason why people come together in groups to secure collective action from government. One of the most interesting developments in American government since the 1960s is the dramatic increase in **public interest groups**. These groups represent the interests of average citizens as consumers, as holders of individual rights, as proponents of various causes, and as the disadvantaged. Public interest groups focus not on members' immediate economic livelihood but on achieving a broad set of goals that represent their members' vision of the collective good. Their members and leaders seek substantive policy goals ("clean air"), not specific increments of economic well-being ("twenty cents more an hour for minimum wage workers").

Some of the best-known public interest groups include Citizens for Tax Justice, the Nature Conservancy, the Natural Resources Defense Council, the National Taxpayers Union, the National Organization for Women, the League of Women Voters, and Common Cause. Pursuing policy favorable to all citizens, public interest groups recruit widely and welcome the support of the general public.

Perhaps the best-known public interest group is Common Cause, which promotes campaign reform, abolition of political action committees (PACs), elimination of unneeded bureaucratic institutions, and in other ways aims to achieve "good government." Common Cause has more than 250,000 members and an $11-million annual budget. Its central target has been the abuse of money in the political process.[18] Common Cause has been especially outraged by the cozy relationship between interest group contributions and political influence. It points, for instance, to the fact that the National Rifle Association can contribute money to members of the Senate Judiciary Committee, which has the job of reviewing firearms legislation, and that the American Medical Association and American Dental Association can

public interest groups Groups that focus not on the immediate economic livelihood of their members, but on achieving a broad set of goals that represent their members' vision of the collective good. Examples include the National Taxpayers Union, the League of Women Voters, and Common Cause.

▶ Environmental protesters dressed in various ways for former Utah Governor Michael O. Leavitt's confirmation hearing as Administrator of the Environmental Protection Agency (EPA). Despite their efforts, he was confirmed and later became Secretary of Health and Human Services.

contribute millions to members of Congress who serve on committees that consider regulations that affect business practices in these professions. Emphasizing that PAC expenditures on congressional races are at an all-time high, Common Cause recently sought to organize People versus PACs, a campaign designed to clean up the financing of congressional elections. Common Cause's longtime efforts to reduce or eliminate the influence of money in politics eventually led to the passage of the Bipartisan Campaign Finance Reform Act of 2002.

Government Interest Groups

A recent addition to the interest group mix has been government itself. Today, the National Conference of Mayors, the National League of Cities, the National Governors' Association, and other organizations composed of government officials compete alongside traditional interest groups for funding, policies, and attention.

Although questions have been raised about whether government interest groups should compete for scarce resources, these groups are well funded, influential, and easily able to gain access to the halls of Congress. Their right to act as interest groups was affirmed in an important 1985 Supreme Court case, *Garcia* v. *San Antonio Metropolitan Transit Authority*. The opinion's author, Justice Harry Blackmun, refused to grant states authority to set their own compensation rates for municipal employees. States, he said, like private employers, must abide by the regulations governing wages established in the federal Fair Labor Standards Act. Blackmun argued that states were inherently well represented in Congress—through automatic representation in the Senate and secondary representation in the House—and were responsible for petitioning Congress to make laws in accordance with their wishes.[19] Immediately following the *Garcia* decision, several government interest groups successfully lobbied Congress to grant exemptions from the Fair Labor Standards Act to public employees. Government agencies and officials are under no constitutional restraints when it comes to forming their own interest groups to

Questions for Reflection

Interest groups give citizens' concerns a stronger voice. Is this better accomplished if various groups band together in a new, more unified, multi-issue approach to democracy?

And, during an election year, would we better off to approach democracy by offering public funding to candidates who bypass those interest groups?

place pressure on other agencies and officials of our government, thereby strengthening the concept of federalism.

Ideological Interest Groups

Some people enter politics to promote deep-seated ideological beliefs, seeking nothing less than to transform society and the political process along the lines of some broad philosophical perspective. Such people form ideological interest groups. The best known is Americans for Democratic Action (ADA). Founded in 1947 by Hubert Humphrey, John Kenneth Galbraith, and Eleanor Roosevelt to oppose the more centrist policies of President Harry Truman, ADA has been pushing ever since for an entire set of policy proposals that would create a coherently liberal society. A few years after the ADA's advent, a group known as the American Conservative Union (ACU) sprang up to counter ADA efforts and promote a conservative agenda. Other ideologically oriented groups include the American Civil Liberties Union (ACLU) on civil liberties issues, People for the American Way (liberal) on legal issues, and the Concord Coalition (conservative) on tax and budget issues.

In keeping with our American culture's tendency toward pragmatism, ideological interest groups have always been few and consisting primarily of small numbers of dedicated activists. Still, because these activists are energetic, well educated, well connected, and adept at raising money, ideological interest groups frequently wield relatively strong clout. A prominent example of this clout came in 1987 when a group of liberal interest groups, including the People for the American Way and the National Association for the Advancement of Colored People, united to defeat Robert Bork's nomination to the Supreme Court.

Religious Interest Groups

A variant of the ideological interest group is the group that wishes to transform society along the lines of its religious beliefs. As you would expect in a society where most people take religion seriously, groups seeking to bring religious values into the political arena have at one time or another had powerful effects on American politics. Perhaps the most famous example of religion's impact was the Prohibition movement, which in the nineteenth and early twentieth century sought to ban the sale and consumption of alcohol. Church and religious groups throughout the nation drove the movement. Among the more powerful religious groups today are the Christian Coalition, the Catholic Alliance, the National Council of Churches (mainstream Protestantism), B'nai B'rith's Anti-Defamation League (Judaism), and the Council of Catholic Bishops. These religious organizations' influence on politics has grown to the point that many believe that they tipped the balance of the 2004 presidential election, as discussed at the end of this chapter.

Sometimes these groups oppose each other, but when they unite on questions of freedom of religion, as they did in seeking to overturn a Supreme Court decision to create the Religious Freedom Restoration Act (RFRA) and to secure government vouchers for students to attend religious schools, they can be particularly effective with governing officials (see Chapter 13).

ABC News/Prentice Hall Video Library

God and Country

Civil Rights Interest Groups

Civil rights interest groups, similar to ideological interest groups, seek to promote the legal rights of minorities and others who have suffered discrimination. They focus on creating an egalitarian society in which their members have equal opportunities for advancement and move in mainstream society without denigration. One of the best known of these groups is the National Association for the

Approaching Democracy Around the Globe

Lobbying for Democracy in Hong Kong

What happens when the people in a region want one course of action and the government wants another? In the case of Hong Kong, it has meant turning over the argument for universal suffrage to the Civil Human Rights Front, a coalition of activist lobbying groups.

Britain's 1997 turnover of Hong Kong to the Chinese government left Hong Kong's democratic system in uncertainty. Although a clear majority (60 percent) of the nearly seven million residents want universal suffrage, the Chinese government has adopted a "take it slow" attitude toward change. China announced no direct elections for a chief executive or the sixty members of the Legislative Council until 2007, a date that has since been pushed back to some time after 2008. Until then, the chief executive will be chosen by an eight-hundred-member committee guided by the Chinese government, and the Legislative Council chosen partly by the people and partly by various groups.

Seeing that change was not forthcoming, the Civil Human Rights Front, an alliance of fifty nongovernmental groups, organized a huge demonstration of more than a half million people on July 1, 2003, the anniversary of the handover of Hong Kong to the Chinese government. Some predicted that the democracy movement would take over the Legislative Council in the near future. But such was not to be.

Just two years later, on July 1, 2005, only 21,000 protesters marched in the streets seeking universal suffrage and democracy, while more than 30,000 marched in a counter-protest organized by the government to celebrate the handover of the region. Showing just how little the region was interested in this march, at the same time nearly 190,000 people lined up to see an exhibition of dinosaur fossils found on mainland China.

The poor turnout for the pro-democracy march caused the lobbying alliance to reconsider its goals. Perhaps, it was argued, the group's main agenda should not be the annual march, or on seeking universal suffrage, but rather on other issues such as economic conditions and the new national security proposals, known as Article 23. But although the march had failed to draw a huge crowd that day, it did attract the nation's attention.

The Chinese government retracted the security proposals, fearing that it might not win support in the Legislative Council.

This new defeat at the hand of the pro-democracy supporters gained sufficient attention in Beijing that Hong Kong chief executive Tung Chee-hwa was replaced. Without the former chief executive's unpopularity as a unifying target, and with improved economic conditions, for a time various groups in the alliance began to splinter away as each one sought to push for its own individual concerns.

But even as the alliance hovered on the verge of fragmenting, hope for its future existed in the activity of these individual groups and the development of new generations of democratic activists and lobbyists in the region. In time, it seemed that these pro-democracy groups might re-form and renew their quest for universal suffrage.

That hope was realized on December 22, 2005, when the pro-democracy supporters in Hong Kong's Legislative Council defeated a Beijing-supported governmental plan for the region. It marked the first time a government-supported bill had been defeated in the legislature since the Chinese had taken over the region from Great Britain. For two months, the new Beijing-supported chief executive of the region, Donald Tsang, had lobbied for a "democratic" program that would have expanded both the Legislative Council and the voting group for the chief executive. While a protest group of 2,100 waited outside the legislature, the measure was defeated because it contained no specific timetable for moving the island toward universal suffrage. This action left the pro-democracy groups and mainland Chinese communist government at "an impasse" over the questions of whether and when to further democratize the government. Hong Kong's "approach to democracy" appeared to be still underway.

Source: Keith Bradsher, "Hong Kong Democrats Defeat Beijing-Backed Political Changes," *New York Times*, December 22, 2005, www.nyt.com; "Activists Must March to a New Tune," *South China Morning Post*, July 19, 2005; Edward Cody, "Democracy Movement is Stalled in Hong Kong," *Washington Post*, August 13, 2004; and Gary Cheung, "21,000 March for Democracy," *South China Morning Post*, July 2, 2005.

Advancement of Colored People (NAACP), which for decades was the driving force behind the black civil rights movement. Other well-known groups of this sort include the National Organization for Women (NOW), the American Indian Movement (AIM), the Mexican-American Legal Defense and Educational Fund (MALDEF), and various organizations that protect and seek to advance the rights of gay Americans.[20]

Single-Issue Interest Groups

As the name implies, single-issue interest groups represent citizens primarily concerned with one particular policy or social problem. Their members often enter political activity to pursue one issue so important in their value scheme that all other issues seem insignificant by comparison. Hence, group members are both intense and uncompromising in promoting their aims.

Groups of this type currently powerful in American politics include the National Rifle Association (NRA), the National Coalition to Ban Handguns, the National Right to Life Committee, and NARAL, now known as NARAL ProChoice America. Sometimes the single issue that inspires an interest group can expand to encompass a series of related issues, all with a single goal. Such is the case with the Sierra Club and the Environmental Defense Fund (EDF), both of which fight for environmental preservation. The multimillion-member Sierra Club began in the early 1970s in response to the threat of Walt Disney Corporation to create a ski resort on the edge of the Sequoia National Forest in California. The group won this fight, and since has saved countless other areas.

Given their uncompromising beliefs, single-issue activists present a prickly problem for politicians, whose usual job consists of balancing competing demands and reaching judicious compromise solutions. Single-issue groups do not look kindly on compromise. Their supporters often have a polarized view of the world: If you're not with them, you're against them—an enemy to be crushed and defeated. Inevitably, single-issue groups raise political temperatures and exacerbate conflict whenever they engage in politics. Many politicians shudder at the prospect of having to deal with them.

CHARACTERISTICS OF INTEREST GROUPS

Although each interest group is unique, most share characteristics that distinguish them from other organizations in society. For instance, interest groups, unlike political parties, rarely try to elect their leaders to political positions, but they do target elected officials unsympathetic to their interests and support those who are sympathetic. Interest groups want to influence government, not *be* government, and they seek a government of policy makers who support their goals.

In addition, interest groups do not usually focus on business, trade, or making money. They may promote business interests, and they may incidentally make money (often through the sale of books, maps, insurance policies, or other items for members), but profit is not their main focus. Interest groups are quintessentially government-influencing institutions. Their goal of pressuring government decision makers sets them apart from the other major structures of American society: government itself, political parties, business enterprises, and run-of-the-mill social groups that do not undertake political activities (such as the Lions or Masons).

Interest Group Membership

Interest groups need members to survive and prosper, and in a democratic society, the more members a group has, the more political clout it will wield. Scholars have long sought to learn why some interest groups outpace others in attracting members. Closely related to that question is another: Why do some groups form and prosper while others never start, or if they do, falter and disappear?

Maintaining Interest Group Membership   An interest group forms when citizens, be they few or many, believe the political arena is failing to provide their preferred policy outcomes, or when citizens feel adversely affected by technological change or by government policies. Many other factors influence the development of a particular interest group: the presence of strong, dynamic leaders; the group's financial and educational resources; and its geographic concentration (it is easier to unite workers in one large factory than people who clean individual homes across a large city). Many factors help determine the likelihood that a group will become cognizant of itself and band together in a formal organization to promote a common interest.

Perhaps the central question about why people form and join interest groups follows from our earlier discussion about the likelihood of a potential group becoming an actual group. Just because people share a common interest, they won't necessarily form a group and actively promote its aims. No one is obliged to become an interest group member. As with all life choices, people must choose to spend the time, money, and effort to join. And no one is obliged to remain a group member, as the ACLU learned when nearly half its members resigned over the group's decision to support the free speech rights of the American Nazi party to march in Skokie, Illinois, a region populated by survivors of the Holocaust. Some groups that share common economic interests and goals, such as businesses, unions, and trade associations, avoid problems of organizing and maintaining memberships since they speak for people who are already in their group.

Groups that represent interests external to their members, such as rainforest protection rather than worker safety, must devote a major portion of their time to **group maintenance**; that is, they must constantly canvass for new members and provide benefits—both psychological and material—for current members to their specific issue. For example, the group Habitat for Humanity, which builds affordable housing for homeless people, launched a new fund-raising campaign after Hurricane Katrina in 2005 by sending attractive house ornaments for Christmas trees to their top donors hoping for additional house-building donations. Although the interest group originally forms to advance favorable policies, policy efforts soon become just one part of the equation when the group considers how best to use its resources. The Sierra Club devotes a good deal of time, money, and energy to pleasing current members and recruiting new ones; the club organizes singles vacations to scenic areas and family package cruises, and offers discounts of many types for purchases of environmentally conscious products and subscriptions to its magazine. The same is true of the American Association of Retired Persons (AARP), which represents senior Americans on a wide variety of legislative issues. Only by offering benefits such as discount cards, insurance policies, and trips has that group been able to build its organization into a powerful legislative force. Finally, some groups represent interests of individuals whether the individuals are members or not. The American Association of University Professors (AAUP), for instance, monitors a wide range of educational issues to the benefit of all academics, even though some professors are not formal dues-paying members.

The Free Rider   The need to keep current and potential group members happy stems from an issue known as the *free rider.* Mancur Olson Jr., a leading social theorist, has identified and described this issue.[21] To achieve a collective good, groups call upon their members for resources, time, expertise, and participation. But if everyone benefits anyway, why should people feel the need to put in any time or money? Members who do not invest but still share in the collective benefits of group action are known as **free riders**. Some union members, for instance, may reason that they need not go to interminable union meetings, since they will end up with the same pay hikes and improved working conditions as members who do attend. The problem, of course, is that if everyone in the union thinks that way, management will realize that the union is ineffectual and will reduce, not increase, employee benefits. Too many free riders may cause all members of a group to suffer, undermining the group's very reason for being.

If group benefits extend to nonmembers, an additional free-rider problem exists. The Sierra Club, for instance, has more than a half million members, and its work to preserve the national parks benefits all Americans. So why should you join the club

Questions for Reflection

Check your postal and electronic mailboxes. How many pieces of mail are from interest groups?

Why did you receive a mailing from this particular group?

How actively are you involved in any interest group's activities?

group maintenance Activities by an interest group designed to affect policy. Includes enrolling new members and providing benefits for them.

free riders Members who invest no money or time in an interest group but still share in the collective benefits of group action.

if you're guaranteed the benefits of its work anyway? In another example, all citizens will benefit if the National Taxpayers Union persuades Congress to lower tax rates. Why, then, put in the time and money to join the National Taxpayers Union?

However, the free-rider theory may be exaggerated. It rests heavily on the argument that most people join groups for material gain. In fact, people undertake voluntary group activity for many reasons, and few calculate the economic benefits before deciding if joining is "worth it." Feelings of moral obligation drive many Americans to contribute to a cause or join a group. And when people strongly commit themselves to political action, most likely the rewards they gain are psychological rather than material. Thus, dedicated activists may have a variety of psychological incentives, including desires to make social contacts or advance political career chances, opportunity to participate in a fascinating game (politics), and the urge to help improve the quality of government. Most groups, then, can gain both supporters and active members without necessarily offering them a material reward for their participation.[22]

Other Characteristics of Interest Groups

Interest groups differ from each other in many ways. These differences help to explain why groups succeed or fail, use or reject a grassroots strategy, or choose to operate at the state rather than the national level. One key difference centers on *resources*. Naturally, groups with money, connections, social prestige, and access to political elites have great advantages in the struggle to influence government. On the other hand, zeal and numbers can go a long way toward overcoming financial deficiencies. Any group that can inspire large numbers of people to write letters, call political leaders, and march in the street can have a serious impact on the policy-making process.

Group *cohesion* is important. A neighborhood association trying to block construction of a nearby prison will have a greater chance of success than a broad potential group of people who have recently lost jobs due to American free-trade policies. The *level of government* at which a group needs to exert pressure is also crucial. Results may come easier at the local level than at the national level. Group *leadership skill* often affects outcomes. Naturally, the more forceful and persuasive the group leader, the more successfully that person can advance the group's cause and keep it in the public eye. Whether a skilled, dynamic leader will emerge for any given group is, of course, subject to circumstance. One wonders, for instance, if the American civil rights movement could have been as successful without Martin Luther King Jr. These days, interest group organizations and medical research endeavors often try to attract attention by using movie stars as spokespeople in their advertising

◄ Gun-rights advocates march in support of their rights to maintain their guns and their constitutional protections.

campaigns and congressional testimonies. After President George W. Bush banned the use of federal funds for stem-cell research, actors Michael J. Fox, who suffers from Parkinson's disease, and the late Christopher Reeves supported a successful 2004 California election initiative to spend $3 billion on stem-cell research. A year later, their work had produced several effects: Nancy Reagan, whose husband President Ronald Reagan suffered from Alzheimer's disease at the end of his life, showed public support for stem-cell research, as did Senator Arlen Specter (R.-PA), suffering from Hodgkin's disease, and Majority Leader Bill Frist (TN), a former heart surgeon, who split with President Bush to support federal funding for stem-cell research "in the name of science."

INTEREST GROUP STRATEGIES

Interest groups must constantly make decisions about strategy: Where should it focus its energies? What issues should it push? With whom should it align itself? Should the group target a House subcommittee, the Senate majority leader, the president, a deputy undersecretary, or key governors and mayors? Issues cut across political arenas at local, state, and national levels, which may leave the best place to apply pressure unclear. Groups must also consider whether to push at the grass roots to create a populist groundswell for their ideas or to go directly to powerful public officials.

Lobbying

Lobbying represents the most common and effective way to influence public policy. **Lobbying** is a formal, organized attempt to influence legislation, usually through direct contact with legislators or their staffs. The political use of the term *lobby* in the United States was first recorded in the annals of the Tenth Congress; in 1829 the term *lobby-agents* was used to describe favor seekers. President Ulysses S. Grant (1869–77) frequently walked from the White House to the Willard Hotel on Pennsylvania Avenue, and when he was relaxing with legislators in the Willard's comfortable lobby, individuals seeking jobs or favors would visit him there—hence the term *lobbyists*.[23]

Lobbyists have never ranked high in the eyes of the public. However, the distasteful caricature of a fat-cat special interest lobbyist who buys a vote by bribing a legislator is a gross distortion of what most lobbyists do. Outright bribery is rare; so, too, are other illegal attempts to gain the favor of political officials. The reason is simple. The rewards for corrupt behavior rarely outweigh the risks. After all, money leaves a trail that investigators can follow. Besides, people talk (especially people in politics), so keeping a political secret is no easy task. Astute reporters, hundreds of them hoping to expose some juicy scandal, can ultimately uncover most bribery episodes. Furthermore, bribery is illegal, so not only are reporters out to uncover corruption, so are state and federal legal officers.

Who Are the Lobbyists? Lobbyists are key players in the game of politics. Some are prominent Washington figures and major power brokers. Many are former government officials who have discovered that their expertise, access, influence, and good name are valuable assets, particularly to major industries. More than one public official has learned that it pays much better to be a lobbyist influencing policy from the outside than to be a public servant making policy on the inside. Interest groups particularly value former members of Congress for their knowledge of government operations and their many contacts with the politically powerful. They command salaries well above those paid in Congress, although ex-members are barred from lobbying Congress for a year after leaving that institution.

In 1961, 365 lobbyists were registered in Washington, D.C. By mid-2005, lobbyists registered there numbered more than 34,750, double the number that existed just

MakeItReal

Simulation: Lobbying America

Quick Review

Lobbying

- Formal, organized attempt to influence legislation.
- Lobbyists are prominent Washington figures, major power brokers, or former government officials.
- Lobbyists seek to win tax breaks and federal grants.

lobbying The formal, organized attempt to influence legislation, usually through direct contact with legislators or their staff.

five years earlier. "Everybody in America has a lobby," declared former House Speaker Thomas (Tip) O'Neill. The leading lobby registrants are businesses and corporations, trade associations, state and local governments, citizen groups, and labor unions. Even foreign governments lobby, as seen in the case of Kazakhstan, a republic in Central Asia. Japanese companies and the Japanese government spend more than $100 million to hire hundreds of lobbyists in Washington.[24]

Indeed, the rapid increase in Washington lobbyists may relate to rapid growth in government, receptivity of Republican leaders who control both the White House and the Congress to lobbying, and a widespread belief by the corporate world that lobbying help is indispensable. Whereas lobbying began as a tool to prevent passage of laws that might hurt a business, now lobbyists seek to aid organizations win tax breaks and federal grants that will aid their business.[25]

Lobbying Tactics   How do lobbyists work with politicians to achieve their aims? The relationship between lobbyists and politicians is one of the least understood in politics. Most lobbyists neither bribe nor threaten politicians. Both tactics are self-defeating. What they do instead is inform, persuade, and pressure. And since most people dislike pressure, the smart lobbyist does as little of that as possible, and only as a last resort.

Persuasion starts (and often ends) with information, a lobbyist's most valuable resource. Legislators, whose staffs are small and usually stretched thin, often need help locating vital information to make decisions about the possible impact of pending legislation. A good lobbyist gains access by providing this information. Naturally, the information will be skewed to favor the lobbyist's point of view. Still, it must never be an outright lie, or the interest group loses all credibility for future lobbying efforts. And even if lobbyists do not provide legislators with a well-rounded perspective on the issue, the information they do provide can be helpful. At a minimum it lets politicians know how key groups feel about the way pending legislation will affect their interests. And sensible politicians listen to a variety of groups and take a range of information into account before putting the final package of a given bill together.

A lobby exists to achieve results, and most Washington-based lobbies seek to influence policy in similar ways. To begin, the interests represented by the lobby will make campaign contributions to members of Congress. They hope thereby to elect

◄ A group of disabled activists from twenty-six states gathers at the Lincoln Memorial prior to rolling across the Memorial Bridge to Arlington National Cemetery to lobby in favor of health care reform.

representatives who see the world as they do and who will vote for the issues they support. Failing that, they hope that campaign contributions will at least buy them access: time to present their case to the members whose campaigns they supported. That explains why many large interests donate money to both parties. By hedging their bets, they hope to gain an audience with whatever group ends up controlling Congress.

Access is crucial; lobbyists can't influence people if they can't grab their attention. Lobbyists are salespeople. If they can make their case one-on-one, they will be effective. Good lobbyists get to know the members of Congress and their key staff people so that they can talk to influential politicians when the need arises. In some cases, lobbyists and legislators work together so closely that lobbyists actually draft the legislation and submit it to Congress through their legislative contacts.

Beyond pushing their legislative aims in Congress, lobbyists spend a good deal of time presenting their case formally and publicly. They put out reports, pamphlets, and press releases, all aimed at presenting arguments and evidence to support their group's policy goals. They also give speeches, appear on television and radio and at other public forums, and provide interviews—all in the hope that their message will be noticed and viewed favorably by those who have power or by those who can influence power holders. Among their many activities, lobbyists often testify before congressional committees about the policies they hope to persuade Congress to adopt. They often write *amicus curiae* briefs to the Supreme Court. Interest groups have also successfully used the lower courts to sue government and private industry and have had an impact on public policy in this way, especially in the environmental arena.

Grassroots Activity

Rallying the public behind their cause is a central element in most lobbyists' work, a strategy known as **grassroots activity**.[26] As we see in Table 11.2, 80 percent of lobbyists engage in this activity. The reason is simple: Just as nations with no army participate little in world affairs, lobby groups with no popular support participate little in a democracy. Those who make our laws gain office in a mass democratic election, so they pay particularly close attention to matters that the mass of the people in their electoral districts seem to care about. A lobbyist is just one person, but a lobbyist with the backing of hundreds or thousands of voters in a legislative district is a power to be reckoned with. Thus, the most effective lobbyists are those who can clearly show an ability to rally grassroots support for their proposals.

Grassroots pressure "greases the wheels" of the policy-making process. Lobbyists create this pressure by rousing constituents back home in a variety of ways: through political advertisements in newspapers, radio, and television, through speeches in local and national forums, and through rallies or letter-writing campaigns. These activities aim to let politicians know that numerous voters agree with the lobbyist, so that the politicians will decide that supporting the lobby group's goal is the only sensible and expedient action. Certain groups are especially adept at grassroots activism. For example, in the fall of 2004, the National Rifle Association successfully prevented Congress from renewing the assault weapons ban in the Brady Bill. As pointed out in this chapter's case study, the high-tech cyber methods various interest groups use to reach and mobilize their followers on issues of importance to them rank among the most effective grassroots campaigns in recent years.

Women's groups have recently gained prominence in the political arena. From the National Organization for Women (NOW) to the conservative antifeminist group Concerned Women for America, women have been making their policy positions on issues known, and in so doing they have influenced legislation. In addition, two women's PACs have been increasingly important in funding female candidacies: EMILY's List (*Early Money Is Like Yeast;* it makes the dough rise) for Democrats, and WISH (*Women In the Senate and House*) for Republicans.

grassroots activity The rallying of group members, as well as the public, behind a lobby's cause.

Table 11.2 ■ What Lobbyists Do

Activity	Percent Who Use Technique
Testify at hearings	99%
Have formal contact with public officials	98
Have informal contact with public officials	95
Present research information	92
Send letters to group members to update them on group activities	92
Enter into coalitions with other organizations	90
Attempt to shape policy implementation	89
Talk with the media	86
Consult with public officials to devise legislative strategy	85
Help draft legislation	85
Sponsor letter-writing campaigns	84
Help shape the government's agenda by calling attention to problems	84
Mount grassroots lobbying efforts	80
Have influential group members contact legislative offices	80
Help draft agency regulations, rules, and guidelines	78
Serve on advisory commissions and boards	76
Alert legislators to the effects of legislation on their districts	75
File suits or otherwise engage in litigation	72
Make financial contributions to campaigns	58
Assist officials by doing favors for them	56
Attempt to influence appointments to public office	53
Publicize candidates' voting records	44
Engage in direct-mail fund raising for the interest group	44
Use media advertisements to publicize the group's position on an issue	31
Contribute work, personnel, or services to electoral campaigns	24
Publicly endorse candidates for office	22
Engage in protests or demonstrations	20

Source: "Activities of Professional Lobbyists," from *Organized Interests and American Democracy* by Kay Lehman Schlozman and John T. Tierney. Reprinted by permission of Pearson Education, Inc.

Interest groups use various strategies to appeal directly to group members or potential members for support and action. A group might use a letter-writing campaign asking group members to "write your representative" and "express your support" for the group's position on a given issue. Congressional offices are periodically inundated by cards, letters, telegrams, e-mail, and faxes from concerned group members and sympathizers—testimony to the effectiveness of this tactic.

The group may also use *direct mail* to target citizens with mailings describing the group's cause, presenting its arguments, and requesting support or money. An important political function of the direct-mail campaign is to send recipients valuable information, although most mailings are decidedly skewed toward the group's avowed position. The group often provides voting cues by giving voters a checklist to take with them into the voting booth. Another grassroots technique is to stage free concerts, speaking engagements, or even demonstrations. These events are often effective at raising both funds and citizens' consciousness of the group's cause, and they have the added advantage of attracting attention through news coverage.

Using the Courts and Lobbying the Political Branches

Although grassroots strategies can often ignite large-scale popular support, interest groups must still reach the institutions of government—Congress and the executive branch—to meet their objectives. Even large-scale grassroots movements sometimes fail to impress policy makers in Congress. Members of Congress may simply disagree with the group's goals; or the constituents who voted them into office may not support these goals; or policy makers may be influenced by other powerful groups with opposing aims; or members of Congress may be listening to other, more powerful interest groups. Many grassroots campaigns have failed to persuade Congress to produce desired legislation. Recent failed efforts include campaigns to limit congressional terms of office, to declare abortion illegal nationally, and to reform the health-care system.

The difficulty of lobbying Congress has caused interest groups to direct increasing attention to the executive branch. Groups may seek an appointment with the president or a member of the cabinet, or at least mount a letter-writing campaign in that direction. Far more likely, though, these groups will direct their efforts toward lower-level bureaucrats.

Despite the inevitability of setbacks, interest group leaders rarely give up easily. Groups unsuccessful with one institution often turn to another. The civil rights movement of the 1950s and 1960s is perhaps the best example of group persistence. Unable to persuade either Congress or southern state legislatures to eliminate discriminatory laws and practices, civil rights groups turned to the courts and to the executive branch, where they achieved great success. Ultimately, the Supreme Court, not Congress, declared school segregation unconstitutional, and it took a series of presidents willing to use federal troops to enforce that decision. These judicial and executive actions, initiated by interest group pressures, finally forced states to dismantle their segregated school systems and eliminate other previously legal forms of racial discrimination.

Today, conservative interest groups such as Operation Rescue, which seeks to restrict abortion, use the courts nearly as frequently as did liberal groups of the past, a strategy that makes sense given the growing conservative inclination of the courts. Operation Rescue has combined traditional grassroots strategies with more aggressive tactics such as blockades of abortion clinics and the intimidation of clinic workers and patients. But the group also has a third and quite effective strategy— continued appeal to state and federal courts in an attempt to eliminate all laws permitting abortion. Coupled with the publicity garnered from their aggressive tactics, Operation Rescue has become a political force that even the supposedly nonpolitical courts can no longer ignore. The federal judiciary, then, has once again become a key target for interest group activity.[27]

POLITICAL ACTION COMMITTEES

Of all the trends related to interest groups, the most dramatic new development has been the proliferation of political action committees (PACs). The first PAC was created as early as 1948, when the AFL-CIO founded its Committee on Political Education (COPE) to channel union funds to pro-labor candidates. In 1963, the Business-Industry Political Action Committee (BIPAC) became the first business

Quick Review

Political Action Committees

- First PAC was created as early as 1948.

- PACs could donate up to five thousand dollars to any single campaign.

- Added a new way to gain access and influence by donating tremendous amounts of money in relatively small increments to congressional election campaigns.

PAC. But because campaign contributions were relatively unlimited until the 1970s, and recipients of large contributions needed not report either the names of donors or the amount of money donated, most large industries and corporations simply funneled the money from corporate coffers directly to the campaigns of their chosen candidates or causes.

Matters changed dramatically by the mid-1970s with passage of the Federal Election Campaign Act (FECA) of 1971, which placed a thousand-dollar limit on donations from individuals to any single campaign. The act did, however, allow labor unions, corporations, and other entities to create PACs that could donate up to five thousand dollars to any single campaign. The newly formed Federal Election Commission (FEC) provided regulation and oversight. By 1976, the FEC had granted authority for universities, museums, trade associations, cooperatives, and eventually for private citizens to form PACs, bringing on a virtual explosion in PAC formation and activity. More than four thousand PACs have since registered with the FEC.

PACs have taken the traditional lobbying role of interest groups and added a new way to gain access and influence: donating tremendous amounts of money in relatively small increments to congressional election campaigns. In the 1996 elections, the top fifty PACs donated nearly $64 million in unregulated **soft money** to the Clinton and Dole campaigns, both national political parties, and all federal congressional election campaigns. All of these groups carefully hedged their bets by donating to candidates from *both* parties, thus giving them access no matter who won the election.

Because PACs can legally donate more money than individuals, campaign fund raising has shifted away from seeking individual contributions to seeking money from PACs. As a result, interest group power has increased, while political party power has weakened. Politicians seeking elective office now turn to PACs for support rather than to party organizations. A Michigan Democrat running for the U.S. Senate, for instance, will be equally concerned with gaining the backing of state party officials as with soliciting support from the political action committees of the various unions that wield power in that state, beginning with the United Auto Workers. As PACs decide which candidates receive support, they usurp one of the traditional roles reserved for parties: the recruitment and selection of candidates for office.

This growth of PAC influence in the candidate selection process has created problems for American politics.[28] Most PACs focus on a narrow range of issues or even on a single issue. Candidates seeking scarce political resources for their increasingly expensive campaigns often court the favors of influential PAC groups with narrow agendas while giving short shrift to political parties, with their moderating perspective, broad-based public agendas, and amorphous ideologies. The result, as we saw in Chapter 9, is the candidate-centered campaign, the subsequent weakening of traditional party power, and a growing number of elected officials with narrow viewpoints and confrontational operating styles.

In fact, concern among political observers and insiders alike about increasing PAC influence led to the campaign finance reform effort. And PAC power kept the legislation from being passed year after year. Although the 2002 Bipartisan Campaign Reform Act (BCRA) limited the power of PACs, by eliminating the use of "soft money" to benefit party-building activities directed to supporting political candidates outside of the legal federal limits, before long those groups found loopholes in the legislation to allow their continued lobbying. As outlined below, in the 2004 election, so-called "527 groups," named for the federal Internal Revenue Service regulation that allows certain nonprofit tax-exempt groups to raise and spend money for educating the public on certain political issues, raised and spent just under $500 million dollars supporting candidates for election. As Table 11.3 shows, the top fifteen 527 groups raised and spent a substantial portion of this money. And yet, although the top three fund-raising groups—America Coming Together, the Joint Victory Campaign 2004, and the Media Fund—all liberal 527s, raised and

MakeItReal

Primary Source: The FEC and the Federal Campaign Finance Law

soft money Campaign contributions directed to advancing the interests of a political party or an issue in general, rather than a specific candidate.

Table 11.3 ■ Top Ten 527 Committee Activity in the 2004 Elections

Committee	Total Receipts	Expenditures
America Coming Together (L)	$79, 795,487	$78,040,480
Joint Victory Campaign 2004 (L)	$71,811,666	$72,588,053
Media Fund (L)	$59,414,183	$57,694,580
Service Employees International Union (N)	$48,426,867	$47,730,761
Progress for America (C)	$44,929,178	$35,631,378
American Federation Of State/County/ Municipal Employees (N)	$25,537,010	$26,170,411
Swift Boat Veterans & POWs for Truth (C)	$17,008,090	$22,565,360
MoveOn.org (L)	$12,956,215	$21,565,803
College Republican National Committee (C)	$12,780,126	$17,260,655
New Democrat Network (L)	$12,726,158	$12,524,063
Citizens for a Strong Senate	$10,853,730	$10,228,515
Club for Growth (C)	$10,645,976	$13,074,256
Sierra Club (L)	$8,727,127	$6,261,811
EMILY's List (L)	$7,739,946	$8,100,752
Voices for Working Families (N)	$7,466,056	$7,202,695

(L = liberal group, C = conservative group, N = nonpartisan group)

Source: Adapted from information on the www.opensecrets.org Web site, January 22, 2006.

spent more than $200 million on the election, one of the less lucrative groups, the so-called Swift Boat Veterans and POWs for Truth, spending only $22 million, exerted the most election influence with their ads raising questions about Democrat John Kerry's Viet Nam service. This fund-raising has continued; as of January 2006, the 527s had already raised more than $60 million for the congressional elections.[29]

So, although the campaign finance law was designed to limit uncontrolled "soft money" funding of candidates, and even party-building activities, large amounts of 527 money went to issue advocacy. Many of these "issue ads" were perfectly clear about which candidate would benefit from the ad, thus remaining legal under the restrictive campaign-finance provisions of the McCain-Feingold law. This loophole greatly influenced the outcome of the 2004 election, because groups independent of the political party system still raised and spent money on behalf of particular candidates. The future effect of this finance system on the electoral process is described further below. As these groups continue to spend money to influence election results, Madison's admonition that removing the causes of faction reduces liberty still rings strong.

REGULATION OF INTEREST GROUPS

Interest group activity is protected by the First Amendment, making politicians cautious about proposals to regulate interest groups and their lobbyists. But the poor image many citizens have of special interests has produced periodic attempts at regulation. Some of these efforts have borne fruit and produced the occasional law aimed at reducing the scope of interest group influence. For the most part, however, these laws have been few and weak, leaving interest groups relatively unfettered.

The 1946 Federal Regulation of Lobbying Act stipulated that lobbyists seeking to influence congressional legislation must list all contributions, expenditures, and the names of anyone who received or contributed five hundred dollars or more. When the act was challenged on First Amendment grounds, the Supreme Court upheld the legislation but interpreted the registration requirement to apply only to groups whose "primary purpose" was to influence legislation.[30] Many large outfits such as the National Association of Manufacturers use this argument to avoid registering altogether. They claim no need to register as lobbyists, since influencing legislation is not their principal reason for existing as a group. For that reason and others, the 1946 act was virtually useless. It also lacked enforcement powers and failed to address lobbying the executive branch, grassroots organizing, or indirect lobbying.

The 1971 and 1974 Federal Campaign Finance laws were much more effective in their efforts to regulate donations, but they also ensured an increase in the power and proliferation of PACs, which represent many citizens, thereby reducing the power of individual fat-cat financiers. The 1978 Ethics in Government Act, which codified rules governing conflict of interests, had some effect on lobbying behavior. A key section of this law was meant to prevent the kind of "revolving-door" activity in which government officials leave their posts and immediately use their insider knowledge and contacts to lobby the very people for whom they had just been working. The law prohibited former government employees from lobbying their former agency for a period of one year after leaving office and prohibited them from lobbying any department on an issue for which they clearly had direct responsibility for two years.

Efforts to regulate the operations and impact of lobbying have continued with varying degrees of success. Realizing that the 1971 Federal Election Campaign Act covered only lobbyists who seek to influence members of Congress, in December 1995 Congress passed the Lobbying Disclosure Act, which regulated those who sought to lobby members of the congressional staffs and policy-making members of the executive branch, including the president and staff, even if they worked only part-time at lobbying. Lobbyists now must register within forty-five days of either being hired or making their first contact with such officials and file reports twice a year about their activities. These reports must list the special interests for which they are lobbying and the offices they have contacted (but not the names of the people contacted), and specify whether they are undertaking any action for a foreign government; the only groups exempt are grassroots lobbying and tax-exempt religious organizations.[31]

MakeItReal

Primary Source: Lobbying Disclosure Act of 1995
Primary Source: Lobbying Registration Guidance for Lobbying Disclosure Act of 1995

ASSESSING THE IMPACT OF INTEREST GROUPS

The growth of interest groups presents new challenges and problems for the U.S. political system. As more interest groups participate in the political arena, do they open or close opportunities for individual influence? As groups continue to increase in number, will they become the only legitimate channel for political expression?[32]

Scholars have devoted much effort to understanding the role groups play in American politics. Nearly a century ago political scientist Arthur Bentley argued that groups lie at the very heart of the political process.[33] Indeed, in his eyes *all* political phenomena could be understood in terms of group activity. He saw politics as a perpetual struggle for power. Groups compete endlessly for public goods and services, and only the fittest prosper and survive. Government is simply the agency that sorts out which groups are winning or losing at any given time. From this perspective, interest group activity is synonymous with politics itself.

Another leading scholar, political scientist David Truman, argued in 1951 that groups play a stabilizing role in American politics.[34] Echoing both Madison and Bentley, Truman wrote that politics is best understood as a complex network of groups, each striving for access to government. In response to critics who believed that powerful economic interests have an advantage, Truman countered with two responses. First, most Americans have overlapping group memberships and are likely to belong to at least one group that benefits from government policies. Second, he pointed to the idea of potential groups. Certain issues could arise and galvanize unorganized citizens into cohesive groups, as exemplified by the pro-gun control Million Mom March and the anti-gun control Second Amendment Sisters. Formerly disadvantaged people would thus be represented in the halls of power, and these new groups would provide a vital balancing mechanism to counter the influence of groups already representing the wealthier elements of society.

In yet another critique of the pluralist vision of group activity, political scientist Theodore Lowi maintained that contemporary group politics has fundamentally altered how the United States functions.[35] Lowi described a new political system, which he called *interest group liberalism,* in which interest groups have proliferated, expanding their control of legislative politics. Real policy making stems from neither voter preference nor Congress. Instead, it flows from a set of tight connections among the bureaucracy, selected members of Congress (especially subcommittee chairs), and special interest groups representing the upper stratum of American society. Lowi and others have used the term **iron triangles** to characterize the typically cozy relationship among congressional elites, lobbyists, and bureaucrats.

The rapid proliferation of interest groups, all competing for influence over policy, could place excessive and conflicting demands on public officials. In the face of massive political pressure, government might grind to a halt or continue to implement the status quo, as all efforts at change or reform are stymied by the many competing claims of powerful interest groups. This produces **gridlock**, a condition in which major government initiatives are impossible because existing groups can veto any effort at change and will do so, for fear of losing their own already established connections and privileges.

Not all interest group specialists accept such pessimism. More optimistic scholars raise several points of objection. First, they claim that gridlock may derive less from the proliferation of interest groups than from American society's lack of consensus about which direction government policy should take. That lack of consensus has been a standard condition in American history, as one would expect in a diverse and complex culture. But when Americans do reach consensus on political aims, government can take dramatic action with amazing speed, despite all the talk about interest groups causing gridlock. That situation occurred in 1933 with the rapid approval of a vast range of New Deal programs, in 1941–42 with the United States' entry into World War II, in 1965 with passage of the Great Society programs, and in 1995 with the acceptance of many Republican "Contract with America" proposals. Group pressures did little to prevent those dramatic changes in national public policy. Perhaps interest groups do not create gridlock but merely take advantage of its existence in a complex and diverse society.

The *iron triangle* idea also has been criticized. As early as 1978, political scientist Hugh Heclo pointed to the rise of a range of issue experts who forced legislators, bureaucrats, and lobbyists to pay attention to other information and actors, thus undermining their cozy triangular relationship.[36] As a result, **policy networks** have formed. These networks feature discussion of a wide range of options in the effort to resolve issues and convey a more inclusive and less conspiratorial image of the policy process than do *iron triangles.*[37]

Other scholars have noted the vast array of new groups that have entered the political arena in recent years. This influx of groups has created conditions of uncertainty and unpredictability, helping to break up established connections among the principal actors of the old triangles. As the number of groups and interests

iron triangles Informal three-way relationships that develop among key legislative committees, the bureaucracy, and interest groups with a vested interest in the policies created by those committees and agencies.

gridlock A condition in which major government initiatives are impossible because a closely balanced partisan division in the government structure, accompanied by an unwillingness to work together toward compromise, produces a stalemate.

policy networks Networks characterized by a wide-ranging discussion of options as issues are resolved, conveying a more inclusive and less conspiratorial image of the policy process than iron triangles do.

operating in American society has dramatically expanded, political life has become more complex, making any generalization about how policies evolve more difficult to substantiate.

Finally, we must remember that many of the new groups represent public interest activists, political participants who stand up for those segments of society not usually represented in the ongoing group struggles for power. Public interest lobbyists may be middle class, but their aims, at least in theory, would benefit all citizens, particularly those at the lower ends of the socioeconomic spectrum. Thus, the argument that the less well-off are disadvantaged by interest group activity, while retaining a strong kernel of truth, is less accurate today than it might have been two or three decades ago.

GROWTH OF THE EVANGELICAL CHRISTIAN LOBBYING MOVEMENT

Since 1978, one of the biggest changes in the interest group landscape has been the growth of both conservative political and conservative religious interest groups. In 1978, spurred by an Internal Revenue Service investigation into the evangelical movement's tax-exempt status, the Reverend Jerry Falwell of Virginia along with evangelical leader Robert Billings cofounded the Moral Majority, a conservative group based on evangelical religious teachings that lobbied to change IRS policies, support conservative policies, and elect conservative leaders. This organization's 2.5- million-person mailing list helped to revolutionize the direct-mailing grassroots lobbying efforts and, after the 1980 election of President Reagan, made it one of the most visible political movements in the country. The Moral Majority's focus on cultural issues, including opposition to abortion and gay rights, somewhat limited its ability to attract a broader base of citizen support.

The visibility and success of this movement led Pat Robertson, who ran for president in 1988, to hire a young conservative activist, Ralph Reed, to organize and lead the Christian Coalition, a highly effective national interest group that lobbied on a full range of cultural and religious issues. Reed's approach was to organize a decentralized system of state and local lobbying chapters united in a single conservative message. Just seven years later, the group had more than two thousand local chapters with nearly two million members. Rather than focusing on lobbying inside the Washington Beltway, this group sought to organize the general citizenry on cultural issues. The conservative Family Research Council, started by Gary Bauer, a former Reagan administration member, aided this movement.

By the 1990s, the Christian Coalition's influence began to decline because of Ralph Reed's willingness to moderate the group's message. By then, however, other evangelical ministers and conservative leaders had organized their own groups. Reverend James Dobson of Colorado created the Focus on the Family group through his successful radio broadcasts. Reverend Ted Haggard organized the National Association of Evangelicals umbrella lobbying group, with nearly thirty million members organized by their churches around the country. The largest single group of evangelicals is the sixteen-million-member Southern Baptist Convention, led by Richard Land, president of the Southern Baptist Ethics and Religions Liberty Commission. This group was so important to the 2004 Bush reelection campaign that campaign director Karl Rove consulted weekly with Reverend Land. Former Louisiana state legislator Tony Perkins took over the Family Research Council to lobby for a national heterosexual marriage amendment opposing the gay rights movement. Former Nixon administration aide Reverend Charles Colson created the Breakpoint Ministries, initially bringing his ministry to the prisons. And Reverend Jim Wallis led the Sojourners, an organization of Christians seeking ethics, justice, and peace, in arguing at hundreds of town meetings that eliminating poverty, rather than debating cultural issues, should head the national agenda.

All of these groups had a tipping influence on the outcomes of the 2000 and 2004 presidential elections when they overwhelmingly backed George W. Bush and the Republican Party. They have helped set the Republican Party agenda, mainly on the cultural issues of abortion, gay rights, drug use, and the right to die. These groups have combined with highly visible political leaders such as Senators Sam Brownback (R.-KS) and Rick Santorum (R.-PA), Senators John Cornyn and James M. Inhofe (R.-TX), and Senator Tom Coburn (R.-OK). The influence of these groups motivated President Bush, grateful for their support, to choose John Roberts and Samuel Alito as his Supreme Court nominees in 2005.

The challenge for this vast network of perhaps as many as fifty million people and their powerful leaders will be to find a way to institutionalize their message to solidify their impact on politics. Whether or not they continue to work as lobbying groups outside of the system, whether or not their messages are slowly co-opted by existing political parties seeking to extend their influence, or whether or not they eventually seek to create their own political party, remains to be seen.[38]

LOBBYING IN THE TWENTY-FIRST CENTURY

The world of lobbying seemed to be changing in the twenty-first century as a result of new technology, the vast amounts of money available, and the highly partisan nature of politics in an evenly balanced political world. As pointed out in this chapter's case study, the Internet and other technologies have enabled interest groups to develop new strategies, develop grassroots movements, and lobby politicians. Web sites, blogs, and mass-generated e-mails help groups develop a seeming groundswell of public opinion. Although such movements can resemble direct democracy, it is important to remember that they are actually just high-tech lobbying.

Another change is the "rotating door" aspect of the lobbyist's job, as more and more ex-congressional members simply move to the center of the lobbying world, K Street in Washington, and use their contacts to become highly paid lobbyists. Because former members retain their privileges to visit the floors of Congress and enter the "members only" areas of the Capitol, their access to former colleagues makes them potentially successful lobbyists. A 2005 study revealed that of the 198 Senate and the House members who left government from 1998 to 2005, 43 percent registered to become lobbyists (50 percent for ex-senators). This is quite a change; as recently as the mid-1980s, former members of Congress rarely became lobbyists. Beyond the problems raised by former officials using insider skills to give certain groups more access to government than they otherwise might have, the notion that sitting members of Congress might one day become lobbyists could affect the way they deal with lobbyists. Is a member of Congress who gives access to a lobbyist seeking a future job prospect? The congressional revolving door resembles one that has always existed in the executive branch, with outgoing administration officials moving to think tanks and academic positions to wait for the next compatible administration to be elected, thus allowing them to return to government. The congressional revolving door allows members of Congress to remain inside the Washington Beltway, earning a living and maintaining their contacts while they assess future runs for elected office.[39]

The nature of this "revolving door" relationship and its possible corrupting influence in Washington became a central focus in late 2005 with investigation into the lobbying of Jack Abramoff, former aide to Majority Leader Tom Delay. Abramoff was believed to be involved in a kind of "pay-for-government policy" program, raising tens of millions of dollars from various interest groups, such as from casino operations run by Native Americans, as well as certain foreign entities, funneling that to specific congressional candidates both for their campaigns and for personal benefit, such as in certain vacations and vacation trips in Scotland, and getting legislation, as well as federal grants added to other legislation, passed in return. After one of Abramoff's top assistants, Michael Scanlon, pled guilty and began cooperating with federal officials, Abramoff pled guilty on January 3, 2006, to fraud, tax evasion and conspiracy to bribe federal public officials, making it clear that he would also cooperate with federal officials investigating bribery of government officials. As of mid-January 2006 it was rumored that as many as two dozen members of Congress, from both parties in both the Senate and the House, but mainly from the Republican party, would become the focus of the probe.[40]

Owing to this investigation, Tom Delay gave up his effort to retake the House majority leader position. Ohio Congressman Robert Ney gave up his chairmanship of the powerful House Administration Committee, which had jurisdiction over drafting lobbying regulation reforms.[41] Also caught up in the investigation and embroiled in certain charges against Abramoff was former evangelical movement leader and Christian Coalition head Ralph Reed, who was running for lieutenant governor of Georgia on what appeared to be an escalator to national political office. Questions of just how far this investigation will spread led the *New York Times* to wonder if Abramoff would become the "new Monica."[42]

TOWARD THE 2006 ELECTION: INTEREST GROUPS AND 527s

A 1996 Supreme Court decision has dramatically changed the nature of interest group advertising in elections. The dispute arose from Colorado's Democratic senator Timothy Wirth's 1986 reelection campaign, when that state's Republican Federal Campaign Committee exceeded spending limits on independent campaign contributions by political parties as outlined in the Federal Election Campaign Act of 1971. The Republicans, who had not yet picked their candidate when they ran $15,000 in radio ads against Wirth, claimed that they had a First Amendment freedom of speech right to spend what they wished on the election. Speaking for a seven-person majority, Justice Stephen Breyer agreed, arguing, "We do not see how a Constitution that grants to individuals, candidates, and ordinary political committees the right to make unlimited independent expenditures could deny the same right to political parties."[43] Only if the party and the candidates worked together in the campaign spending would the federal limits apply. As a result, interest groups that helped the Republicans win back Congress in 1994 proliferated in the elections in the years ahead.

This loophole in the campaign expenditure law spurred political parties and interest groups to continue to collect soft money, unregulated donations directed for "party building activities," and not specific candidates. The funds covered campaign costs and national **issue advertisements** that address issues rather than candidates directly. Such ads made clear the organization's position about a particular issue rather than a specific candidacy, thus avoiding federal regulation.[44] Various national interest groups funded such ads, almost completely bypassing the candidates themselves. In June 2001, the Supreme Court, by a narrow 5–4 decision, ruled in a Colorado campaign finance reform case that limits on coordinated campaign spending by political parties and candidates for federal office were constitutional. The Court reasoned that if they did not exist, it would be impossible to establish spending limits for individual candidates' campaigns. This decision gave supporters of campaign finance reform hope.[45] The Bipartisan Campaign Finance Reform Act of 2002, the so-called McCain Feingold law, now bans raising of unregulated soft money and limits the use of issue advertisements thirty days before an election primary and sixty days before the general election. In late 2003, the Supreme Court upheld most of the law's provisions by a 5–4 majority, supporting the limit of political corruption.

issue advertisements
Advertisements in a political campaign funded by an interest group advocating a position on an issue but technically not supporting a specific candidate.

Interest groups provide a vital link between citizens and public officials. This was certainly true in the 2004 election campaigns at all levels, with more than $4 billion spent on the 2004 presidential race alone, up a billion dollars from the 2000 election. Despite efforts in the Campaign Finance Reform Act of 2002 to limit use of soft money, in the 2004 race, more than a billion dollars was spent, a 40 percent increase over 2000. The McCain-Feingold law said nothing about so-called 527s, tax exempt organizations much like political action committees (PACs) created under section 527 of the federal Internal Revenue code to lobby for political issues.[46] Therefore, forty-six people contributed more than a million dollars apiece to 527s, up from six such donors in 2002, with some contributing more than $20 million apiece. The 527s also spent hundreds of millions in unregulated money on "get out the vote" campaigns and issue advocacy on behalf of their candidates.

Democrats got the early start with this strategy, raising twice as much as Republicans. One such group was the "get out the vote" operation of America Coming Together. An issue advocacy group called The Media Fund, organized by former Clinton Aide Harold Ickes Jr. for John Kerry, received millions of dollars from liberal philanthropist George Soros and others. Indeed, Soros went beyond the campaign finance limits to contribute nearly $25 million to nine 527 organizations in the 2004 campaigns. The television and Internet ads of liberal MoveOn.org, which raised small contributions from large numbers of donors and used the money to challenge the administration and candidacy of George W. Bush, received much attention. On the Republican side, the ads by the Swift Boat Vets group, who challenged John Kerry's Vietnam war record, were particularly effective. Similarly, the Republican Club for Growth 527 lobbying group spent millions of dollars on behalf of conservative candidates who favored cutting taxes and reducing the size of government, even if this meant opposing moderate Republicans in the primaries to determine the party's representatives on the fall ballots.[47] All in all, 527 organizations raised and spent more than $400 million dollars in the 2004 presidential campaign.

A new liberal group called Citizens for a Strong Senate raised more than $12 million to fund television ads in 2004 Senate races in six states, opposing Republican candidates who failed to support social services programs. The move was particularly effective in defeating candidates such as Republican Pete Coors of Colorado.[48] Government's decision on whether or not these 527s will be regulated will determine the level of their impact on the 2006 election. Even if they are regulated, though, money, like water, tends to seek its own level, and well-funded groups desiring to influence the political process will still find a way to raise funds legally.

As of mid-January 2006, the Democrats seemed to focus on this issue as a major plank in their platform for the upcoming Congressional election campaign. Seeing the developing Jack Abramoff scandal, Democrats began talking about the Washington, D.C. "culture of corruption," and the issue of morality in politics. Senator Harry Reid of Nevada brought together his colleagues for an "Honest Leadership/Open Government" photo opportunity in the Great Hall of the Library of Congress, calling for a "commitment to change, change to a government as good and as honest as the people that we serve."[49] This effort, much resembling 1994 Republican anticorruption attacks against the Democrats, began to shape the Democratic party's 2006 election campaign posture as it sought to add to attacks on the Iraq War and nation-rebuilding effort. As mentioned above, the outcome of the 2006 congressional elections and the 2008 presidential election to follow may largely reflect the lobbying, campaigning, and voting behavior of the armies of organized evangelical Christians. As in 2004, at least six to eight million voters, motivated to vote by messages from their pastors in the pulpit, could tip the balance in future elections. Because these groups and their leaders had "moral values" as their agenda, particularly opposition to abortion and gay marriage, the Bush campaign's successful get-out-the-vote ground war targeted them with voter initiatives seeking to ban gay marriages on the ballots of eleven states. As a result, "moral values" became the top issue for many voters, tipping the elections in the key swing states of Ohio and Florida and giving President Bush a national 3.5-million-vote margin. But whether or not this large bloc of voters will continue to turn out for the Republican party in future elections, or if the Democratic Party can restructure its message to appeal to some of these groups, remains to be seen.

Summary

1. Interest groups are formal organizations of people who share a common outlook or social circumstance and who band together in the hope of influencing government policy. Actual groups have a headquarters, an organizational structure, paid employees, and so forth; potential groups are interest groups that could form under the right circumstances. Those circumstances are often created by dynamic leaders known as *policy entrepreneurs.*

2. Although all modern democracies exhibit interest-group activity, few have achieved the level of nongovernmental group life found in the United States. The number of groups trying to pressure government has grown dramatically in recent years, partly owing to the growth and increased activity of the government and partly owing to higher average levels of education.

3. People form interest groups because collective action is stronger, more credible, and more likely to influence policy outcomes than the isolated actions of separate individuals. However, because interest groups focus on their own cause, they are said to skew or ignore the public good.

4. Economic interest groups include those representing big business, organized labor, farmers, and other economic interests. Public interest groups represent the interests of average citizens; they focus on achieving a broad set of goals that represent their members' vision of the collective good. Government interest groups compete alongside traditional interest groups for funding, policy goals, and attention. Other interest groups include ideological groups, religious groups, civil rights groups, and single-issue groups.

5. Interest groups are most likely to form when citizens have been adversely affected by technological change or by government policies. Other factors, such as dynamic leaders and geographic concentration, also influence the development of an interest group.

6. Group leaders must devote much of their time to group maintenance—canvassing for new members and providing benefits for current members. In doing so, they face the so-called "free-rider issue," the tendency of individuals to share in the collective benefits of group action even if they do not themselves contribute to the group.

7. Lobbying is the formal, organized attempt to influence legislation, usually through direct contact with legislators or their staff. Lobbyists provide legislators with needed information and attempt to persuade and sometimes pressure them to support the interest group's goals. They also publicize the group's cause to the general public through published materials, speeches, television appearances, and the like.

8. A key aim of lobbying is to rally group members, as well as the public, to the cause—that is, to gain grassroots support for the group's proposals. An often-used tactic is the direct-mail campaign, in which targeted citizens receive mailings describing the group's cause and requesting their support.

9. Leaders of interest groups learn that when they fail to gain a hearing for their cause in one branch of government, success may be achieved by looking for help elsewhere. Thus, in times when Congress and the president are unsympathetic, requests for help can be directed toward the Supreme Court, and vice versa.

10. An important trend is the proliferation of political action committees, groups whose main aim is to promote the political goals of particular interest groups. PACs donate large amounts of money to political campaigns, thereby undermining the role of political parties in recruiting and selecting candidates for office.

11. Interest groups face few legal restrictions. Lobbyists must list their contributions and expenditures, but only if their "primary purpose" is to influence legislation. The Ethics in Government Act bars former government employees from lobbying their former agency for a year after leaving office and for two years on specific policy issues.

12. Interest group activity during congressional elections has evolved to the point that issue advertising sometimes proceeds without any reference to the candidates in the race. Such ads alert voters to the importance of the issues but sometimes blur candidate identities.

13. Some political scientists believe that policy making stems from comfortable and resilient connections among the bureaucracy, selected members of Congress, and interest groups—so-called "iron triangles." The rapid proliferation of interest groups has led to what some political scientists call "gridlock," or a harmful excess of competing demands. Policy networks, more broad-based than iron triangles, now characterize the process. The number of groups and interests now operating in American society has dramatically expanded, adding to the complexity of political life.

Review Questions

1. In what way do interest groups serve as links between citizens and their representatives?

2. How has the use of independent expenditures affected the way political parties and interest groups attempt to influence policy? Do unlimited independent expenditures enhance our approach to democracy or detract from it? Why?

3. What was the intent of the Lobbying Disclosure Act of 1995?

4. How have student protests in American history resulted in political and social change in the nation?

5. What are some typical examples of world trade protest groups?

6. What is *cyber-lobbying* and how will it help or hinder American democracy?

Key Terms

actual groups 387
collective action 391
factions 388
free riders 402
grassroots activity 406
gridlock 412
group maintenance 402

interest groups 386
iron triangles 412
issue advertisements 415
lobbying 404
netizens 391
policy entrepreneurs 387
policy networks 412

political action committees (PACs) 390
potential groups 387
public interest groups 397
soft money 409

Suggested Readings

BERRY, JEFFREY M. *The Interest Group Society*. 3d ed. New York: Longman, 1997. An interesting examination of the development of interest group politics in American society.

CIGLER, ALLAN J., and BURDETT A. LOOMIS, eds. *Interest Group Politics*. 4th ed. Washington, D.C.: Congressional Quarterly Press, 1995. An excellent collection of readings on American interest groups.

DYE, THOMAS R. *Who's Running America? The Clinton Years*. 6th ed. Upper Saddle River, N.J.: Prentice Hall, 1995. A description of the dominant political institutions of our time and the individuals who control them.

HEINZ, JOHN P., EDWARD O. LAUMANN, ROBERT L. NELSON, and ROBERT H. SALISBURY. *The Hollow Core: Private Interests in National Policy Making*. Cambridge, Mass.: Harvard University Press, 1993. A scholarly examination of connections among interest groups, members of Congress, and bureaucrats that sheds doubt on the theory of iron triangles.

LOWI, THEODORE J. *The End of Liberalism: The Second Republic of the United States*. 2d ed. New York: Norton, 1979. A provocative perspective on American government, arguing that the tight connections between interest groups and government officials have created a new kind of American political system.

OLSON, MANCUR, Jr. *The Logic of Collective Action*. Cambridge, Mass.: Harvard University Press, 1965. An influential work that argues that rational citizens have few incentives to join groups, and consequently the interests of nonjoiners are poorly represented in politics.

RAUCH, JONATHAN. *Demosclerosis: The Silent Killer of American Government*. New York: Random House/Times Books, 1994. A popularization of the Lowi–Olson thesis that interest groups dominate American politics and create a government of institutionalized gridlock.

TRUMAN, DAVID B. *The Governmental Process*. New York: Knopf, 1951. A classic book presenting the pluralist vision of how interest groups operate in American politics.

WALKER, JACK L., Jr. *Mobilizing Interest Groups in America: Patrons, Professions, and Social Movements*. Ann Arbor: University of Michigan Press, 1991. An excellent and wide-ranging discussion of interest groups in modern American political life.

WOLPE, BRUCE C., and BERTRAM J. LEVINE. *Lobbying Congress: How the System Works*. 2d ed. Washington, D.C.: Congressional Quarterly Press, 1996. An in-depth examination of how interest groups successfully influence the direction of Congress.

WRIGHT, JOHN R. *Interest Groups and Congress*. Boston: Allyn & Bacon, 1996. A well-written study of how political action committees and interest group lobbies influence congressional policy making.

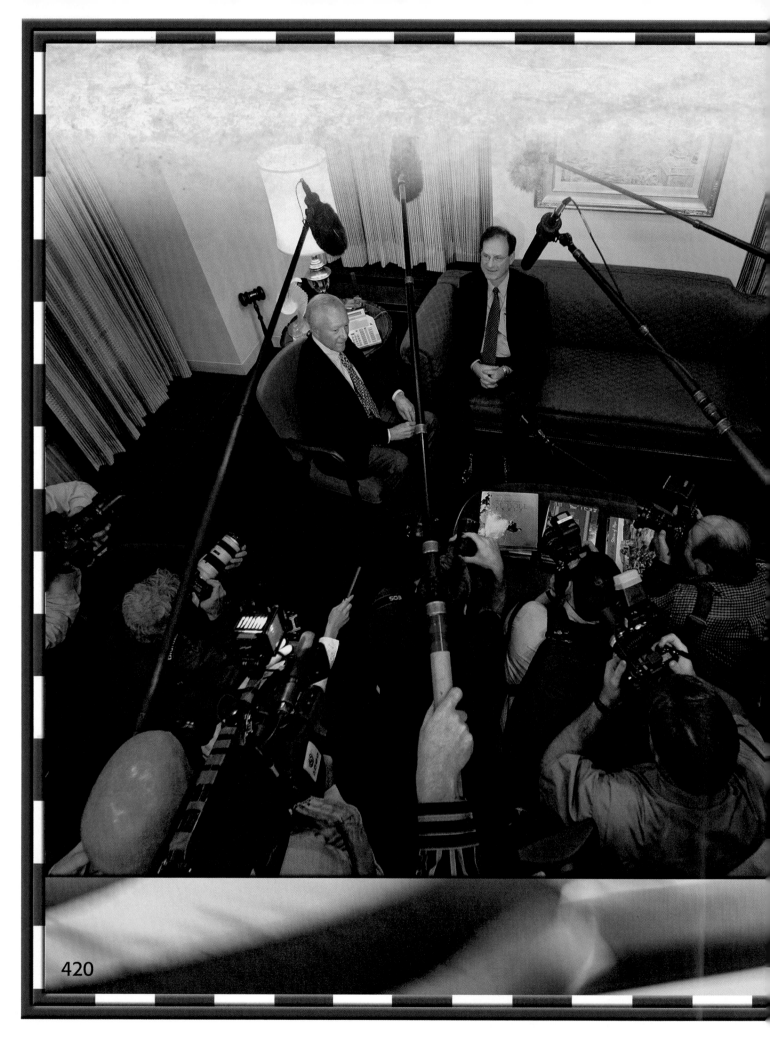

★ CHAPTER 12 ★

THE MEDIA

CHAPTER OUTLINE

APPROACHING DEMOCRACY
A New Web of Influence: Bloggers Rewrite the Rules of Journalism

INTRODUCTION: The Media and Democracy

- The Emergence of the Media
- Functions of the Media
- Limits on Media Freedom
- Ideological Bias and Media Control
- The Media and Elections

$\mathcal{A}$pproaching $\mathcal{D}$emocracy

A New Web of Influence:
Bloggers Rewrite the Rules of Journalism

Millions of online diarists known as bloggers now share their opinions daily online, interacting with a global audience. Bloggers see themselves as "the single most transformative media technology since the invention of the printing press."[1] Two Pew surveys in 2005 showed that 16 percent or thirty-two million U.S. adults are now blog readers. Blogs, short for weblogs, are online journals with which people develop from readers into writers of news and in doing so increase their civic participation. In 1999, approximately fifty blogs appeared on the Web; today there are almost ten million. The significance of this development cannot be overestimated: "Drawing upon the content of the international media and the World Wide Web, they weave together an elaborate network with agenda-setting power on issues ranging from human rights in China to the U.S. occupation of Iraq. What began as a hobby is evolving into a new medium that is changing the landscape for journalists and policymakers alike."[2]

The term *blogosphere* describes the universe of blogs. Political blogs have led to national mainstream media discussions on such topics as racial profiling at airports,

Dan Rather, bribery at the United Nations, the war in Iraq, and *Newsweek's* retracted story on the flushing of the Qur´an. When former Senate majority leader Trent Lott commented at Senator Strom Thurmond's one hundredth birthday party that the country would have been better off had Thurmond won his segregationist campaign for president in 1948, the remarks went virtually unnoticed in the mainstream media. Blogs immediately picked up the story. Soon the mainstream could not ignore Lott's words, and Lott subsequently resigned his leadership position. During the initial period of Hurricane Katrina in New Orleans, the first news about the levels of devastation came from bloggers, some of whom remained in high rise offices in downtown New Orleans.[3] Indeed, bloggers provided much-needed information and relief aid in the wake of Hurricane Katrina, and, according to one report, "a few on-the-scene and remote bloggers are emerging as unique sources of information in an area where electricity, Internet connections, and telephone communications have been severely compromised."[4] Intelliseek's BlogPulse (www.blogpulse.com/), which analyzes daily posts from 15.6 million blogs, found that CNN.com and Yahoo! News were the most cited news sources for Katrina-related information, while the Irish Trojan blog (www.brendanloy.com/), written remotely by Brendan Loy from South Bend, Ind., is the most frequently cited hurricane-related blog (see Table 12.1 for a list of Hurricane Katrina–related blogs).[5] "Just as they did during the 2004 tsunami, bloggers are emerging as unique and very necessary sources of information, especially from areas where access and communications are so adversely affected," said Pete Blackshaw, Intelliseek's chief marketing officer.[6]

★ Ana Marie Cox, announced her retirement as Wonkette's editor on January 5, 2006. Under her tenure, Wonkette was known for its mixture of heady political discourse and satire.

Other blog highlights

- Pre-hurricane article creating the most blog conversation: Chris Mooney's May 23 article, "Thinking Big About Hurricanes, It's Time to Get Serious about Saving New Orleans," in *The American Prospect* online edition, www.prospect.org/web/page.ww?section=root&name=ViewWeb&articleId=9754) created the most blog conversation before the hurricane made landfall (as determined by BlogPulse's Conversation Tracker).

- Post-hurricane articles creating the most blog conversation: MSNBC's "Nightmare Worsens: More Flooding, and Death" (www.msnbc.msn.com/id/9063708) and the *Washington Post's* "Looting, Fires and a Second Evacuation" (www.washingtonpost.com/wp-dyn/content/article/2005/08/30/AR2005083000689.html).

- Blog entries most likely to be shared: LiveJournal Blogger Insomnia's "New Orleans Stories—Hurricane Katrina" (www.livejournal.com/users/insomnia/599039.html) and New Orleans–based Wizbang Blogger Paul's reports from within the Superdome, "Riding Out Katrina in the Superdome,"(http://wizbangblog.com/archives/006917.php) have been shared more frequently among bloggers than other entries.

Source: Intelliseek web site, www.intelliseek.com, http://www.blogpulse.com

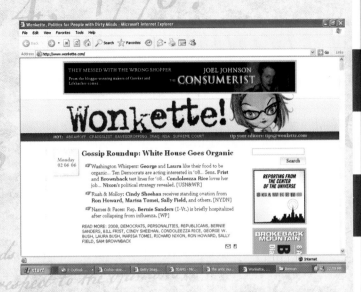

★ Wonkette blog web site.

Table 12.1 TOP HURRICANE-RELATED BLOGS 2005

While traditionally popular bloggers discussed the hurricane, many lesser-known but hurricane-specific blogs emerged after Katrina slammed ashore. On-the-scene and remote blogs that provide information about Katrina and the relief effort include the following:

1. Irish Trojan Blog (www.brendanloy.com/) by Brendan Troy of South Bend, IN

2. Metroblogging New Orleans (http://neworleans.metblogs.com/) by nine New Orleans-area residents

3. Eyes on Katrina (http://eyesonkatrina.blogspot.com/) from the Biloxi *Sun Herald*

4. Kaye Trammel's Hurricane Katrina blog (http://hurricaneupdate.blogspot.com/) written from Louisiana State University

5. Ernie the Attorney blog (www.ernietheattorney.net/about.html) written by a New Orleans lawyer

6. Stormtrack (http://stormtrack.breitbart.com/) written by two scientists from the University of Massachusetts

7. A LiveJournal group blog called Katrinacane (www.livejournal.com/users/katrinacane/friends)

8. Dancing With Katrina (http://dancingwithkatrina.blogspot.com/) from two Gulfport bloggers

Introduction
THE MEDIA AND DEMOCRACY

Perhaps no other chapter in this text raises issues that deal so directly with democracy. President John Kennedy once said, "The flow of ideas, the capacity to make informed choices, the ability to criticize, all of the assumptions on which political democracy rests, depend largely on communications."[7] Democracy requires an *informed* citizenry, and the communication of political information is an essential prerequisite for political participation. A free press stands as one of the defining features of any democratic political system and, as the case study suggests, bloggers are transforming this communication process.

The tension between freedom of the press and government restrictions on that freedom is one of several key issues related to the role of the mass media in a democratic society. Indeed, one of the central components of a society's approach to democracy is whether or not the government allows freedom of the press—a press free to criticize the government without fear of being shut down and its editors thrown into prison. As George Orwell observed, censorship in "free" societies is necessarily more complex and calculated than in dictatorships; the latter merely issues an official ban backed by armed force to halt coverage, while the former must find more thorough means to ensure that "unpopular ideas can be silenced."[8]

At a minimum, democracy requires that citizens receive objective information so they can make informed decisions about candidates, policies, and government actions. Yet the media responsible for transmitting that information are often characterized by bias, distortion, and sensationalism. The job of the media entails simplifying complex and detailed realities into symbols and images. Thus, the information reaching the citizen often consists primarily of sound bites and pictures that greatly simplify the definition of political reality for millions of Americans. Indeed, it is no exaggeration to say that for most people, politics has little reality apart from its media version. Perhaps it is this very frustration that has fueled the bloggers. New opinion surveys consistently show that a large and expanding gap exists on many media issues between journalists and the general public.[9]

In the United States, information about politics routinely reaches the public through the electronic and print media as well as through faxes, electronic mail, and online information sources. Americans can read local, regional, national, and international newspapers; and twenty-four-hour news stations and coverage of local, state, and national public officials on television provide a firsthand look at the political process. But in a democratic polity, the media must do more than bring political information to a broad audience. They must report events accurately and truthfully, free from control or censorship by government agencies and also free from the taint of their own ideological biases. Freedom of the press and other media is essential in a free society. Yet, just 14 percent of the public can name "freedom of the press" as a guarantee in the First Amendment to the constitution, and six in ten adults believe that the media is biased in its reporting.[10]

No other nation in the world, even among the industrialized democracies, enjoys the degree of media freedom found in the United States. Yet, a variety of limits constrict media independence. They range from government-imposed restrictions, both foreign and domestic, to more subtle forms of censorship resulting from the symbiosis between reporters and "official sources" within the government. Nothing captures this dilemma more than the case of *New York Times* reporter Judith Miller who spent eighty-five days in jail for refusing to testify before a grand jury investigating the leak of CIA covert officer Valerie Plame's identity. Thus, although media

Approaching Democracy Around the Globe

Bloggers Challenge Censors' Control in China: A Party Girl Leads China's Online Revolution

China has almost two million blogs, which poses a challenge for China's government censors, who have attempted to thwart this online freedom of expression by prohibiting access to pro-democracy and human rights sites. The Chinese government requires Internet providers to police and restrict access on their sites to any controversial or provocative material. It is not uncommon for the government to shut down blogs, as happened to Isaac Mao, a Shanghai investment banker whose blog discussed both education and technology. When he displayed a diagram showing how government censors utilized a firewall, his site isaacmao.com was blocked. He later went back online, but censors once again succeeded in shutting down the site.

China is experiencing significant change, and at the forefront are communities of bloggers who utilize personal diaries. "The new bloggers are talking back to authority, but in a humorous way," said Xiao Qiang, director of the China Internet Project at the University of California, Berkeley. "People have often said you can say anything you want in China around the dinner table, but not in public. Now the blogs have become the dinner table, and that's new. The content is often political, but not directly political, in the sense that you are not advocating anything, but at the same time you are undermining the ideological basis of power." Symbolic of these currents is China's most popular Web blog created by a twenty-five-year-old Shanghai woman using the

pseudonym Mu Mu. A dance girl and communist party member, Mu Mu provides commentary on sexuality, intellect, and political identity. Other instances abound. For example, after the government announced that it had selected five cartoon mascot figures for the 2008 Olympics, hosted in Beijing, the official press praised the mascots. The blogs ridiculed them: "It's not too difficult to create a mascot that's silly and ugly. The difficulty is in creating five mascots, each sillier and uglier than the one before it," wrote one blogger.

The bloggers are helping change China by offering free expression and discussion on subjects traditionally under government control. Perhaps the best example of the use of satirical style that touches on the political is commentary provided by journalist Wang Xiaofeng, known to bloggers by his nickname, Dai San Ge Biao. When the Chinese government commemorated its defeat of the Japanese in World War II with unbridled stories of patriotism, Wang asked who had really fought the Japanese, since only two communist generals had been killed in fighting, but more than one hundred of their nationalist counterparts had died. "In blogging I don't need to be concerned about taboos," said Mr. Wang.

Source: This feature is based on an article written by Howard W. French, "A Party Girl Leads China's Online Revolution," *New York Times*, November 24, 2005, p. A1.

freedom in the United States represents a closer approach to democracy than any other nation has achieved, it is far from absolute, evidenced by the limited access allowed the press during the early stages of the war on terrorism. As a point for comparison, French prosecutors shut down blogs and arrested scribes for what they described as *moblogging*—rallying and inciting rioters with incendiary language—during the riots that plagued France in late 2005.

THE EMERGENCE OF THE MEDIA

A *medium* (plural, *media*) is a means of transferring or conveying something. By **mass media**, we mean the various means—newspapers, magazines, radio, television, the Internet—through which information is transferred from its sources to large numbers of people. Perhaps more than any other nation, the United States has become a mass media society. Where citizens seek their news—a newspaper, the Internet, television—influences their views on candidates and the election process. For most of the past two hundred years, newspapers and television have dominated the mass communication of political information; radio and magazines have played a less influential yet meaningful role in the development of Americans' political

mass media The various media—newspapers, magazines, radio, television, and the Internet—through which information is transferred from its sources to large numbers of people.

attitudes. Because the media occupy such a central place in political affairs today, it is important to understand how they evolved over the course of American history, especially as newspaper readership is down, as is interest in news from all sources except the Internet.

Newspapers

The importance of the press in American politics dates from the revolutionary period, when newspapers served as effective tools for mobilizing public opinion. They were also the primary vehicle for the debate over ratification of the Constitution. The *Federalist Papers,* written by Alexander Hamilton, James Madison, and John Jay, were originally published as articles in the *New York Independent Journal.*

Early political leaders saw the press as the key to public education about the new political system. Thomas Jefferson believed that the success of a participatory democracy depends on preventing citizens from making unwise decisions: "Give them full information of their affairs through the channel of the public papers, and . . . contrive that those papers should penetrate the whole mass of the people." In an address to Congress, President George Washington stressed the "importance of facilitating the circulation of political intelligence and information" through the press.[11]

In the period following revolution and independence, political leaders sought allies among newspaper publishers. As secretary of the treasury, Hamilton encouraged a staunch Federalist, John Fenno, to establish a newspaper that would espouse the administration's partisan positions. In return, Fenno was guaranteed financial assistance and printing jobs. Fenno moved from Boston to New York and then Philadelphia, publishing the *Gazette of the United States* from the national capital.

Not to be outdone, Jefferson and other Democratic Republicans urged Philip Freneau to publish a Democratic Republican newspaper, the *National Gazette.* Although neither paper was a financial success, a relationship was forged between editors and their benefactors. As late as 1860, the superintendent of the census classified 80 percent of the nation's periodicals, including all 373 daily newspapers, as "political in their character."[12]

The mass media revolution more or less began with the September 3, 1833, issue of the *New York Sun,* which sold on the streets for one cent, thereby earning the name "penny press." The paper targeted the masses and offered news of local events, along with human-interest stories and entertainment. Low price (most newspapers at the time cost six cents) and availability helped it achieve mass circulation; it could be purchased on virtually every street corner in New York.

Between 1850 and 1900, the number of daily papers multiplied from 254 to 2,226. Total circulation increased nearly sevenfold, from 758,000 to more than 15 million. Today, about 60 percent of a typical newspaper's space is allotted to advertising; human-interest stories, sports, reviews, recipes, and other features account for most of the remainder. The portion devoted to news and editorial coverage amounts to about 4 percent of the total. As you will see shortly, newspapers' evolution as mass communicators influenced the way in which news was presented and even the definition of what constituted news.

Muckraking and Yellow Journalism   During the nineteenth century, journalistic style changed significantly, both in the way stories were reported and in the events considered newsworthy. The mass journalism that developed during that period included much less political and foreign affairs reporting and more local news and sensationalism. In particular, newspapers began to feature coverage of dramatic court cases and criminal activity, along with a strong dose of sex or violence or both. The new journalism also spawned two trends whose effects continue today: muckraking and yellow journalism.

The term **muckraking** is derived from the Man with the Muckrake, a character in John Bunyan's *Pilgrim's Progress* who could look only downward and rake the filth on

muckraking A word used to describe a style of investigative reporting that uncovered many scandals and abuses.

the floor. The word is used to describe a style of reporting that preceded today's investigative journalism. Muckraking journalists such as Lincoln Steffens and Ida Tarbell and photographer Lewis Hine came to prominence during the early 1900s, a period characterized by reform movements and populist politics known as the Progressive era. They attempted to expose the power and corruption of the rich while championing the cause of workers and the poor. Their stories of political fat cats, machine politics, evil slumlords, and heartless millionaire industrialists enraged the political and social elite. Although these exposés inevitably suffered from subjectivity, not to mention bias, the muckrakers set a trend that continues today.

The darker side of the new journalism drew less on social conscience and more on the profit motive. **Yellow journalism**—named after the controversial "Yellow Kid" comic strip—is usually associated with the big-city daily newspapers of Joseph Pulitzer and William Randolph Hearst. In the late nineteenth century, Pulitzer and Hearst transformed the staid, rather dull publications of their predecessors into brash, colorful, well-illustrated, often lurid and sensationalized organs of half-truth, innuendo, and sometimes outright lies. The writing style became more casual and colloquial and the stories more dramatic, with emphasis on sex and violence. Facts became less important than impact. Yellow journalists often left the onus of proving a story's truth or untruth on those most damaged by its publication, having little to fear from the ineffective libel and slander laws of the time. The legacy of yellow journalism can be seen in many of today's daily papers and in the sensationalism of news Web sites like the Drudge Report. More and more, newspapers are printing stories formerly reserved to tabloids such as *The National Enquirer.*

Magazines

Although they are less prominent than newspapers as a source of political information, magazines enjoy wide circulation, attentive readership, and an important place in the political education of Americans. Of all the major mass media, magazines as a whole offer the widest variety of subject matter and ideological opinion because each targets certain groups of readers on the basis of socioeconomic status, education, political views, or consumer habits. The proliferation of specialized magazines covering everything from aerobics to zoology is evidence of this strategy.

Of the major news magazines, the most widely read is *Time.* Originally, *Time* was the flagship of the publishing empire founded by Henry Luce. The son of a Presbyterian minister, Luce brought to the magazine his strident faith in the "American Century" and the exalted place of Western culture. According to journalist David Halberstam, Luce "was one of the first true national propagandists; he spoke to the whole nation on national issues, one man with one magazine speaking with one voice, and reaching an entire country."[13] Luce's domineering editorial stance revealed magazines' far greater potential for ideological extremes than the other mass media offered. For decades, Luce's control of *Time* made him one of the most important and influential political forces in America.

Luce's impact on mass-readership magazines extended beyond politics. In addition to *Time,* his growing company published *Look, Life, Fortune,* and *Sports Illustrated.* But *Time* created an explosive popular appetite for news coverage. Luce's formula for the "modern" news magazine featured dramatic photographs, information, analysis, and opinion on the dominant issues of the day. *Time's* success soon produced a host of competitors, including *Newsweek* and *U.S. News & World Report.* These and similar publications continue to serve as "sources of record" for elected officials, corporate executives, and informed citizens who pay close attention to political affairs. Besides the news magazines, numerous magazines offer political opinion, including the conservative *National Review,* the liberal *New Republic,* and the progressive *Nation.* The ideological differences among these publications testify both to the targeting of readership and to the breadth of political opinion among magazine readers.

yellow journalism Brash, colorful, generously illustrated, often lurid and sensationalized organs of half-truth, innuendo, and sometimes outright lies, usually associated with the big-city daily newspapers of Joseph Pulitzer and William Randolph Hearst.

▲ President Franklin D. Roosevelt is shown here during a radio broadcast in 1938. Millions of Americans came to trust their president because of his extremely personal radio broadcasts, known as "fireside chats."

 **MakeItReal**

Primary Source: Roosevelt's Radio Address on the New Deal

Radio

Radio enjoyed a brief but important heyday as a significant source of political information for the American public. Developed in the early twentieth century, radio technology underwent a revolution during World War I. From the 1930s until after World War II, radio was the dominant popular medium. Today's three major television networks—NBC, ABC, and CBS—began as radio networks.

Unlike print media, radio broadcasts could report events as they happened. This quality of immediacy produced some of the most dramatic live reporting in history, including the horrifying account of the explosion of the German zeppelin *Hindenburg* in 1937. The degree to which radio had become a trusted medium was revealed in October 1938, when Orson Welles and his Mercury Theatre of the Air broadcast "War of the Worlds," a fictionalized invasion of the earth by Martians. So convincing were the dramatization's simulated "live" news reports that many Americans believed that the invasion was real.

Radio journalism picked up where print journalism left off. Many of radio's early news reporters had begun as newspaper or magazine reporters. The most successful of them combined the journalistic skills of print reporters with the effective speaking voice required by a medium that "spoke" the news. One of radio's premier news reporters, Edward R. Murrow, established standards of integrity and reportorial skill that continue to this day. He combined the investigative traditions of the early muckrakers with concise writing and a compelling speaking voice. Murrow's career would outlast the peak of radio's popularity; he enjoyed equal fame as a television journalist.

Probably the most successful use of radio by a politician was President Franklin Roosevelt's famous series of "fireside chats." An impressive public speaker, Roosevelt used these brief broadcasts to bolster American confidence—and his own popularity—as he pushed for major legislative reforms to combat the Great Depression. The immediacy of radio also served demagogues such as the arch conservative Father Charles Coughlin of Michigan. Although Coughlin never ran for public office, his broadcast "sermons" included strident attacks on communists and Jews, even implying support for the Nazi regime at a time when the United States was seriously contemplating entering the war against Germany.

Radio's popularity began to ebb after World War II. Its chief competition came not from newspapers and magazines but from a new, even more immediate and compelling medium—television. By 1948, three networks were broadcasting regular programming on television. But radio has not been entirely eclipsed. In recent years, radio talk-show hosts such as Rush Limbaugh, Don Imus, and Al Franken have become important sources of news, opinion, and entertainment for the listening public, and politicians often seek to appear on these shows.

Television

Unlike newspapers, magazines, and radio, television developed primarily as a commercial medium, designed not so much to provide information or opinion but to entertain and stimulate mass consumerism. Thus, most Americans tend to think of television as a low-cost leisure resource rather than as a source of political information. Television is more pervasive and effective than any other form of mass communication in the United States. Advances in broadcast technology have made possible virtually instantaneous transmission of information and have greatly expanded the range of program choices for viewers. As a result, according to political scientist Richard Neustadt, television is "at once the primary news source for most Americans, the vehicle for national political competition, a crucial means to sell consumer goods, and an almost universal source of entertainment."[14] Yet network television news viewing has declined in recent years. In fact, people appear to be less inclined to believe television news and less inclined to watch it. Over the years, news viewership has been in a steady decline. Indeed, Fox News cable channel proved a bigger draw for viewers during the Republican convention than any of the broadcast networks. More recently, shows such as "The Daily Show with John Stewart" and "The Colbert Report" have gained immense popularity with younger audiences because of the manner in which they mock real newscasts and political speeches.[15]

New Media Technologies

During President Ronald Reagan's vacations at his ranch in Santa Barbara, California, CBS News assigned two technicians to sit in a truck parked on a hilltop three miles away for the sole purpose of monitoring a television screen. The screen was wired to a camera with a lens three feet long and weighing more than four hundred pounds, custom-made for photographing the president when he appeared outdoors. "I'm going to fake a heart attack and tumble off this horse to see how quickly they get down the mountain with the news," Reagan joked.[16]

High-tech cameras are just one of many innovations that have greatly changed the nature of television reporting. The 1962 taping of "A Tour of the White House with Mrs. John F. Kennedy" required nine tons of lights, cameras, and cables put into place by fifty-four technicians. In contrast, the 1990 NBC special, "A Day in the Life of the White House," was produced by a handful of technicians. It was filmed on a Monday, edited on a Tuesday, and broadcast that Wednesday.

Satellites   An especially significant technological advance has been the satellite. Satellite technology has made television an instantaneous means of worldwide communication. The cost of satellite relay links between the East and West Coasts of the United States has dropped significantly, and the cost of transmission links to formerly remote areas in the Far East and Middle East has been reduced by half. One effect has been expanded coverage of the president's activities, both in Washington and abroad. In the early 1980s, the number of local news stations with Washington bureaus grew from fifteen to more than fifty. Today, that number has tripled.

In the 1970s, fewer than half of all television news stories were shown on the day they occurred. Today, new technology makes it rare for any news story other than special features to be more than a few hours, if not minutes, old. The use of videophones during the early stages of the war on terrorism brought live visual images back from distant Afghanistan.

Satellites have also affected the political process. Senators and members of the administration, as well as candidates for office, are making increasing use of direct satellite links to bypass network news and appear on local television newscasts.

Cable Television   Cable television was developed in the 1950s to bring television programming to remote areas beyond the reach of normal VHF and UHF broadcast signals. By transmitting television signals through coaxial cable to individual receivers, cable television avoided the environmental and atmospheric disturbances that often plagued regular broadcast signals. Since the 1980s, cable television has become almost universal throughout the United States; although in recent years it has faced a serious challenge from satellite dish systems. Both systems are more popular than regular broadcasting because they provide superior signal definition and a wider variety of programming choices than any single broadcast market could provide. Channels such as C-SPAN, Cable News Network, and CNN Headline News, as well as specialty channels for sports, cooking, feature films, and cultural programming, compete vigorously with the established broadcast networks for viewers' attention.

Collectively, these advances have produced what media expert Austin Ranney calls *narrowcasting*. Network television broadcasts television signals over the air to be picked up by wireless receivers in the homes of a huge, heterogeneous audience. Narrowcasting, in contrast, is a mass communications system "in which television signals are transmitted either by air or by direct wires to people's homes and are aimed at smaller, more narrowly defined, and more homogenous audiences."[17]

Narrowcasting involves more than a move toward greater programming efficiency; it has developed largely as a way to boost profits in an increasingly competitive media

▲ The Internet brings the world, and democratic ideals, to even the most closed societies. Here an Azad University student in an Internet café in Tehran, Iran, uses the Internet to research a term paper.

MakeItReal

Census 2000: The Internet

market. It is based on the idea that a more carefully targeted viewing audience is also a more homogeneous buying audience. Among the most successful experiments in narrowcasting are CNN (twenty-four-hour programming devoted exclusively to news and information), ESPN (twenty-four-hour sports programming), Nickelodeon (programming for children), and MTV (twenty-four-hour music and entertainment).

World Wide Web   As we have already seen, the World Wide Web and the Internet are playing an increasingly important role in obtaining and disseminating political information. News organizations now have their own home pages on the Web, and in the 2004 presidential nomination election, every Republican and Democratic challenger in the 2004 primaries constructed a home page on the Web where their platforms, programs, and information could easily be viewed. The Democratic and Republican National Committees did the same. Virtually every government agency, lobbying group, interest group, newspaper, and television station have Web pages with easily available information. Indeed, much of the updated information for the textbook comes from reliable Web sites. The Web has become the great equalizer in American politics, what one political analyst described as "keypad democracy."[18] A recent Pew study on the 2004 presidential election documents this "Internet difference." Especially for young Americans, the Internet has become a means of empowerment for acquiring political information. Television is still the most widely used source, but the Internet is now second, far outpacing radio, newspapers, and magazines.[19]

FUNCTIONS OF THE MEDIA

Social scientists are in general agreement that the mass media perform three basic functions: (1) surveillance of world events, (2) interpretation of events, and (3) socialization of individuals into cultural settings. "The manner in which these . . . functions are performed," writes political scientist Doris Graber, "affects the political fate of individuals, groups, and social organizations, as well as the course of domestic and international politics."[20]

Surveillance

In their surveillance role, the media function, as Marshall McLuhan observed, as "sense extensions" for people who do not participate directly in events. From the media we learn about world conditions, cultural events, sports, weather, and much else. In many respects, the mass media have helped transform the world into a global community. Citizens of the now-united Germany and citizens of the United States watched the dismantling of the Berlin Wall at the same time. Millions of viewers worldwide watched the changing of the millennium. And when President George W. Bush inadvertently referred to the Japanese *devaluation* rather than *deflation*, the yen immediately fell and did not correct itself until the White House issued a retraction.

Every afternoon, television news anchors and their staffs sift through myriad stories, tapes, and bits of information funneled to them during the day to identify the most important information and events. What they select will be relayed to the public in evening news broadcasts. Thus, the news anchors actually define what is newsworthy.

The ability of the media to decide what constitutes news is a controversial aspect of their surveillance role. "There are few checks on the media's surveillance role," writes Doris Graber. "The power of the media to set the civic agenda is a matter of

U.S.A. Yesterday and Today

Internet News and the Mainstream Media

It started late Saturday night, when Web-newsie Matt Drudge filed this breathless report on his site: "At the last minute, at 6 P.M. on Saturday evening, *Newsweek* magazine killed a story that was destined to shake official Washington to its foundation: A White House intern carried on a sexual affair with the President of the United States!" Drudge explained that "reporter Michael Isikoff developed the story of his career, only to have it spiked by top *Newsweek* suits hours before publication."

The scandal moved to television Sunday morning. *Weekly Standard* editor William Kristol strategically inserted it in a discussion of the Paula Jones case during the roundtable section of ABC's *This Week with Sam and Cokie.* It was approximately 12:45 P.M., EST, about a half-day after the Drudge eruption. Other "incidents" of Clinton philandering may surface, Kristol said, and "the media is going to be an issue here." He continued, "The story in Washington this morning is that *Newsweek* magazine was going to go with a big story based on tape-recorded conversations, which a woman who was a summer intern at the White House, an intern of Leon Panetta's—"

Monday brought more postings on various Web sites: The *Drudge Report* updated the story—and the story behind the story. Drudge named Monica Lewinsky as Clinton's alleged paramour. *Slate* mentioned the ABC News exchange in "Pundit Central" and the alleged spiking of the *Newsweek* story in "In Other Magazines." Webzine *The Underground* made it the day's feature story. CNBC's *Rivera Live* aired a few choice rumors about the scandal. By Tuesday, Matt Drudge spoke his piece on CBS Radio's *Mary Matalin Show* and kept filing on the Web. Tuesday night, Drudge wrote that federal investigators possessed taped phone conversations that substantiated the rumors of a presidential affair. And from the print media? Not a peep until Wednesday morning.

Matt Drudge earned his reputation by posting unconfirmed reports of political skullduggery and sex in the Clinton White House. Whether you think that Matt Drudge is Walter Winchell reincarnated or just the class gossipmonger of American politics, DrudgeReport.com has long been a site to be reckoned with. The *Drudge*

▲ Internet political reporter Matt Drudge has helped to change the face of reporting with his online columns.

Report is one of the best-known political news and gossip sites on the Internet. The Drudge Report Web site is a model of simplicity and has billions of yearly visitors. Drudge is often described "as a new kind of journalist, made possible by personal computers and the Internet. Some people say Drudge is not any kind of journalist." Still, he is not only widely known, he is widely quoted and debated; millions of Internet news junkies visit his Web site each month to read his Drudge Report.

Source: Seth Stevenson, "How the Story Everyone Is Talking About Stayed Out of the Papers," www.drudgereport.com; and Marty Beard, "Matt Drudge's Rise as a Hot Ad Domain," *Media Life,* www.medialifemagazine.com/pages/templates/scripts.prfr.asp; See also http://vikingphoenix.com/public/rongstad/bio-0002/MattDrudge.htm.

concern because it is not controlled by a system of formal checks and balances as is power at various levels of government. It is not subject to periodic review through the electoral process. If media emphases or claims are incorrect, remedies are few."[21] Surveillance can occur at the private as well as public level. Despite the appeals from many in the administration and slain *Wall Street Journal* reporter Daniel Pearl's family, CBS decided to show the nongraphic portions of the amateur video showing Pearl's murder, determining that the U.S. public had a right to understand the depth of the propaganda war against the United States. The complete graphic soon turned up on the Internet.

The media not only bring certain matters to public attention but also doom certain others to obscurity. During election campaigns, for example, the press is the "great mentioner," repeating the names of certain individuals who are being mentioned as possible candidates, or applying labels such as "dark horse" or "long shot." "At any given time in this country," writes journalist David Broder, "there are several hundred persons who are potential candidates for nomination. . . . Who is it that winnows this field down to manageable size? The press—and particularly that small segment of the press called the national political reporters."[22]

Interpretation

The media do much more than provide public and private surveillance of events. They also interpret those events by giving them meaning and context, and in the process often shape opinions. Psychologist Hadley Cantril illustrates this point with the following example:

> Three umpires describe their job of calling balls and strikes in a baseball game. First umpire: "Some's balls and some's strikes and I calls 'em as they is." Second umpire: "Some's balls and some's strikes and I calls 'em as I sees 'em." Third umpire: "Some's balls and some's strikes but they ain't nothin' till I calls 'em."[23]

According to Cantril, few journalists are like the first umpire, believing that the "balls and strikes" they count represent what is happening in the real world. Some journalists may admit to the second method of umpiring, using their judgment to "call them as they see them." The third umpire's style is the most controversial when applied to mass media coverage of significant events. For if, like the third umpire, journalists in print and television actually make the decisions regarding which actors or events are in or out of the "strike zone" or even determine their own "strike zone" or context for news, the potential power of the media becomes immense, and assertions of media "objectivity" sound rather hollow.

Actually, the process of gathering, evaluating, editing, producing, and presenting news involves each of the three umpiring styles. Some reporters may pursue a case against a prominent public figure or institution in the belief that their article will finally expose the "reality" of corruption, scandal, or wrongdoing. And every journalist—from reporters on the street to editors behind desks—exercises judgment over which events are most "newsworthy;" an event is neither a curve ball in the dirt nor a fastball on the outside corner until some journalistic "umpire" makes the decision to cover it.

Political scientist Shanto Iyengar has developed a theory of media "framing effects" particularly relevant to television news coverage. In a series of carefully controlled experiments, Iyengar and his colleagues found that the way television portrays events and actors exerts a significant influence on the opinions of those who watch the coverage. For example, coverage of terrorism that emphasizes the violence and brutality of a terrorist act without attempting to explain the motivations behind it is likely to influence viewers to consider all such actions brutal and violent, regardless of the motivations or historical explanations. This is an important point. Since the constraints of time tend to dictate relatively brief, often superficial coverage of important news, viewers are likely to form equally superficial opinions.[24]

investigative journalism The uncovering of corruption, scandal, conspiracy, and abuses of power in government and business; differs from standard press coverage in the depth of the coverage sought, the time spent researching the subject, and the shocking findings that often result from such reporting.

Investigative Journalism Journalism may have changed since the days of the muckrakers, as the technology and political culture of America have changed, but the spirit of the muckraker lives on in the practice of **investigative journalism**. Investigative journalism differs from standard press coverage in the depth of coverage sought, the time spent researching the subject, and the shocking findings that often result from such reporting. Like their muckraking predecessors, today's investigative journalists turn their reportorial skills to uncovering corruption, scandal, conspiracy, and abuses of power in government and business.

The most familiar historical example of such reporting occurred during the 1970s Watergate scandal, revealed through extensive interviewing and analysis by two *Washington Post* reporters, Carl Bernstein and Bob Woodward. *Post* editor Ben Bradlee risked his professional reputation and the reputation of his paper by running a series of investigative articles on the Watergate break-in and its connection to the White House. Although the *Post* articles, which began raising questions in the months before the 1972 presidential election, did not affect its outcome, they eventually uncovered a scandal that led to the resignation of President Richard Nixon. Not until June 2005 was the paper's information source, Deep Throat, revealed as former FBI assistant director Mark Felt.

Socialization

The media play an important role in **socialization**, the process by which people learn to conform to their society's norms and values. As we noted in Chapter 8, children acquire most of their information about their world from the mass media, either directly, or indirectly through media influence on parents, teachers, or friends. The mass media also provide information that helps young people develop their own opinions. MTV provides a forum, "Choose or Lose," that informs young people about politics, issues, and candidates. It also served as a forum for Secretary of State Colin Powell to urge condom use—only to meet criticism from conservatives who argued that this was inconsistent with the president's position of promoting abstinence.

Studies of the effects of mass media exposure have found that higher reliance on television as the primary source of information seems to correlate with a greater fear of crime and random violence, even when controlling for individual socioeconomic status, education, and living conditions. Although such findings are tentative and subject to interpretation, they indicate that the medium on which most Americans rely for the bulk of their global information—television—may contribute to a growing sense of unease. Yet more Americans feel that television news, as compared to newspapers, is the most reliable and honest source of news.

The power of the media as a socializing agent is reflected in public concern about media violence, particularly in children's television programming. Although analysts remain sharply divided about the actual effects of violent programming, efforts have been made to regulate the frequency and intensity of violent and sexually explicit media content. For example, in the wake of the assassinations of Robert Kennedy and Martin Luther King Jr., television programmers canceled several popular but violent shows or changed the programs to reflect less explicit violence.

In recent years, the television networks have begun to voluntarily rate their shows for violent or adult content. Televised screenings of feature films containing explicit violence or sexual content have adopted the motion picture precedent of rating these programs and including viewer discretion warnings. Cable stations that air films "uncut" provide the original film rating and generally restrict the airing of such programming to the late evening, when children are more likely to be asleep. Although such attempts to regulate the socializing influence of mass media are controversial, they demonstrate widespread agreement that freedom of expression must sometimes be limited to avert social harm.

LIMITS ON MEDIA FREEDOM

The First Amendment to the Constitution states that "Congress shall make no law . . . abridging the freedom . . . of the press." Ideally, the media would investigate, report, provide information, and analyze political events without government-imposed restrictions. Such restrictions are commonplace in many other nations, where the media experience various degrees of restraint, prohibition, or censorship. Americans take pride in the tradition of a free press, yet that freedom is not absolute. Laws protect against libel, slander, and obscenity, the **Federal Communications Commission (FCC)** regulates media behavior, and the judiciary imposes

socialization The process by which people learn to conform to their society's norms and values.

Federal Communications Commission (FCC) A government commission formed to allocate radio and television frequencies and regulate broadcasting procedures.

equal time rule A requirement that radio and television stations allow equal time to all candidates for office.

MakeItReal

Primary Source: Federal Communications Act, 1934

certain limitations as well. The nature of media ownership also plays a role in limiting media freedom.

Regulating the Media

Regulation of the media began after World War I, in the heyday of radio. During that period, the Radio Corporation of America (RCA) and other large consortiums established networks to broadcast news, information, and entertainment, and millions of amateur "radio hams" were buying or building simple broadcast receivers and sending their own gossip, sermons, monologues, and conversations over the increasingly congested airwaves. In 1927, the federal government stepped in to clean up the chaotic radio waves. Congress created the five-member Federal Radio Commission (FRC) to allocate frequencies and regulate broadcasting procedures. Essentially, the FRC worked to organize radio broadcasting and constrain the growing radio broadcast industry to prevent monopolization and other unfair practices.

In 1934, Congress passed the Federal Communications Act, which expanded the FRC's jurisdiction to include telephone and telegraph communications, enlarged the panel to seven members (eventually reduced again to five in 1982), and renamed the agency the Federal Communications Commission (FCC). As broadcast and cable television (CATV) developed, they too came under FCC scrutiny and jurisdiction. The most recent communications innovations—multipoint distribution service (MDS), direct broadcast satellites (DBS), and satellite master antenna television (SMATV)—have also come under the umbrella of FCC regulation.[25]

Four sets of guidelines regulate the electronic media:

1. Rules that limit the number of stations owned or controlled by a single organization
2. Examinations of station goals and performance as part of periodic licensing
3. Rules that mandate public service and local interest programs
4. Rules that guarantee fair treatment to individuals and protect their rights

Supreme Court has consistently upheld regulation of the electronic media under the scarcity doctrine. Although the law does not limit the number of newspapers that can be published in a given area, two radio or television stations cannot broadcast signals at the same time and at the same frequency without jamming each other. Thus it is clearly in the public interest that government allocate frequencies to broadcasters. Broadcasting is viewed as a public resource, much like a national park, and the government establishes regulations designed to promote "the public convenience, interest, or necessity."

The scarcity doctrine, with its implications for the public interest, underlies FCC regulation of political content in radio and television broadcasts. This regulation takes the form of three rules of the airwaves often referred to as the equal time rule, the fairness doctrine, and the right of rebuttal.

The Equal Time Rule   Although a station is not required to give or sell airtime to a candidate seeking a specific office, whenever it provides time to one candidate—whether for a price or for free—it must give equal time to all candidates running for the same office. This **equal time rule** holds whether two or two hundred candidates run for the office; each is entitled to equal time. Section 315(a) of the Federal Communications Act stipulates:

> If any licensee shall permit any person who is a legally qualified candidate for any public office to use a broadcasting station, he shall afford equal opportunities to all other such candidates for that office in the use of such broadcasting station.

The equal time rule has become important in recent presidential campaigns. In the 1992 presidential elections, when Ross Perot bought large blocks of time for his "infomercials" on various campaign issues, the networks involved were required to

Quick Review

The Federal Communications Commission (FCC)

- Regulation of the media began after World War I.
- Federal Radio Commission (FRC) was created in 1927 to monitor the growing radio broadcast industry.
- The Federal Communications Act of 1934 expanded the FRC to include telephone and telegraph communications.
- The FRC was renamed the Federal Communications Commission (FCC).
- Jurisdiction expanded to include broadcast and cable television and, most recently, communications innovations.

Scarcity Doctrine

- Comprised of three rules of the airwaves for the FCC's regulation of the political content of radio and television broadcasts.
- The equal opportunities rule held that a station must give equal time to all candidates.
- The fairness doctrine, now abandoned, required a percentage of programs on issues of public interest.
- The right to rebuttal provided airtime to refute allegations made against a person or group, free of charge, within a reasonable time.

make similar blocks of time available to George Bush and Bill Clinton. However, the rule does not require that the candidates actually take advantage of the available time, only that they have the opportunity to purchase it on an equal basis with all other candidates.

The Fairness Doctrine   The **fairness doctrine**, now abandoned, required radio and television stations to provide a reasonable percentage of time for programs dealing with issues of public interest. Stations were also required to provide time for those who wished to express opposition to any highly controversial public issue aired or discussed on the station. Defining what is controversial had traditionally been left to the administrative courts, but the FCC has ruled that "two viewpoints" satisfies the licensee's obligation. The Supreme Court upheld the fairness doctrine in 1969 in *Red Lion Broadcasting* v. *FCC*. A federal court of appeals later ruled that the doctrine was not law and could be repealed without congressional approval. Congress then passed a bill that would have made the fairness doctrine permanent. But President Ronald Reagan vetoed the bill on grounds that federal policing of editorial judgment of journalists was an outrage. Following the veto, the FCC negated the doctrine.[26]

The Right of Rebuttal   When the honesty, integrity, or morality of persons or groups is attacked on a station, they have the **right of rebuttal**—the right to refute the allegations, free of charge, within a reasonable time. The FCC operates under the assumption that a maligned person deserves a chance to reply, and the public has a right to hear that response. The rule does not apply to attacks on foreign groups or leaders, to personal attacks made by legally qualified candidates or their representatives, or to live, on-the-spot broadcasts.

Prior Restraint Versus the Right to Know

In 1971, former government employee Daniel Ellsberg gave the *New York Times* copies of classified documents on the Vietnam War. The documents had been prepared in 1968 during the presidency of Lyndon Johnson, and they revealed the concerns of senior Defense Department officials during the Kennedy and Johnson years. The government sought to suppress publication of the documents by obtaining a judicial restraining order, an action known as **prior restraint**. President Richard Nixon maintained that publishing the papers would threaten the lives of servicemen and servicewomen, intelligence officers, and military plans still in operation in Vietnam.

The case eventually reached the Supreme Court, which decided in favor of the *Times*. In his concurring opinion on the case, Justice Hugo Black offered a strong argument for absolute freedom of the press:

> Paramount among the responsibilities of a free press is the duty to prevent any part of the Government from deceiving the people and sending them off to distant lands to die of foreign fever and foreign shot and shell. . . . The *New York Times* and the *Washington Post* and other newspapers should be commended for serving the purpose that the Founding Fathers saw so clearly. In revealing the workings of government that led to the Vietnam War, the newspapers nobly did precisely that which the Founders hoped and trusted they would do.[27]

fairness doctrine A policy, now abandoned, that radio and television stations provide time to all sides in programs of public interest.

right of rebuttal The right to refute the allegations presented on a radio or television station, free of charge, within a reasonable time.

prior restraint An action in which the government seeks to ban the publication of controversial material by the press before it is published; censorship.

▲ In July of 2005 Judith Miller was jailed for contempt of court by refusing to testify before a federal grand jury investigating a leak naming Valerie Plame as a covert CIA agent. After spending 85 days in jail, Miller was released and testified before a federal grand jury investigating the leak.

Source: New York Times, October 1, 2005, front page.

In another case, when CNN broadcast recorded phone conversations involving Panamanian general Manuel Noriega as he awaited trial in Miami in 1990, the Supreme Court refused to block a lower court's injunction banning all future broadcasts that CNN planned to air. The controversy raised important constitutional questions. At issue were Noriega's right to a fair trial as well as freedom of the press. What made the issue more intriguing was that the Court decided to suppress publication despite the fact that the U.S. government was responsible for taping the phone conversations in the first place.

Other cases have been concerned with the media's right to cover a trial and whether that coverage would threaten the fairness of the trial. In January 2002, a federal judge rejected cable television's *Court TV* request to broadcast the trial of Zacarias Moussaoui, believed to be the twentieth hijacker on September 11, 2001. In his ruling, Judge Leonie M. Brinkema cited procedural and security reasons for denying the request to overturn a ban on television broadcasts of federal criminal trials.

The case of *Miami Herald Publishing Co. v. Tornillo* (1974) brought up the issue of whether or not statutory guidelines implemented by Florida state law require newspapers to publish specific replies from political candidates attacked in their columns rather than merely publishing retractions. The Court ruled against the "right to reply" law, stating that it "turns afoul the elementary First Amendment proposition that government may not force a newspaper to print copy which, in the journalistic discretion, it chooses to leave on the newspaper floor." That is, even when accused of publicly defaming a political figure, newspapers could not be required by law to print the responses of the defamed figure, since this was to "force a newspaper to print copy" in violation of the constitutional guarantee of a free press. As Chief Justice Warren E. Burger noted, "A responsible press is an undoubtedly

MakeItReal

Primary Source: *Miami Herald Publishing Co., Division Of Knight Newspapers, Inc. v. Tornillo.*

▲ The Pentagon blacked out the faces and identifying information in some photos showing honor guards for coffins lining the interiors of C-17 transports. Thomas Blanton of the National Security Archive called the edited images "an outrage and an insult."

Source: Washington Post, April 29, 2005, p. A10.

desirable goal, but press responsibility is not mandated by the Constitution, and like many other virtues, it cannot be legislated."[28]

Even with a relatively broad guarantee of freedom, certain laws restrict how the press may cover news. Journalists are allowed wide latitude in levying charges against whomever they choose and may even print facts or accusations that subsequently prove untrue, as long as they do not *knowingly* publish untruths or print intentionally damaging statements known as **libel**. Anyone attempting to sue a newspaper for libel must also prove that the publication in question actually caused damage. As you will see in Chapter 13, libel is difficult to prove, especially for public figures whose reputation may be affected by numerous factors besides a single journalistic "hit piece" and who have an opportunity to make a reply. In general, as long as journalists do not set out to attack a public figure with malice, they are not subject to prevailing laws against libel.

libel Published material that damages a person's reputation or good name in an untruthful and malicious way. Libelous material is not protected by the First Amendment.

IDEOLOGICAL BIAS AND MEDIA CONTROL

First, we must recall that the word *media* is plural. Differences among the various communications media make lumping them together inaccurate. For example, print media tend to offer considerably more breadth of opinion than television. Although newspapers and magazines can boast of numerous popular conservative and liberal publications, television tends to offer a much more homogeneous, mainstream view. Diversity occurs, however, even within the relatively narrow ideological parameters of television, particularly on the cable stations. But for the most part, television aspires to represent a mainstream, status quo perspective.

Many observers believe that the mass media display bias in the way they select and present news, and recent survey evidence documents this as well. Although the majority of reporters in both print and electronic media are fairly liberal, their bosses— the magazine and newspaper publishers and network executives—tend to be more conservative, some decidedly so. Most statistical evidence supporting conservative charges of a liberally biased "media elite" fails to clearly differentiate between the reporters, the editors, and the publishers and owners of media outlets; some analyses examine only the reporters, a peculiarly well-educated, well-paid, and liberal cohort of the American public. In the often-cited studies of Robert Lichter, Linda Lichter, and Stanley Rothman, for example, the "media elite" includes reporters, editors, and executives, but only as an aggregate population with no distinctions regarding the differences that might exist within this elite. Simply establishing the liberal leanings of reporters does not prove liberal press bias.[29]

In 2002, a book by former CBS journalist Bernard Goldberg engendered heated debate. In *Bias,* Goldberg argues that real media bias is the result of how those in the media see the world and how their bias directly affects how we all see the world. Goldberg maintains that an elitist culture at the networks is out of touch with conservative America. According to research surveys, 55 percent of journalists consider themselves liberal, compared with about 23 percent of the population as a whole. And the media's liberal attitudes are pervasive on numerous issues, such as government regulation, abortion, and school prayer. Do these attitudes affect news coverage?[30]

In a *Times Mirror* survey of more than 250 members of the press, a substantial majority (55 percent) of American journalists who followed the 1992 presidential campaign believed that former President George H. W. Bush was harmed by press coverage. "Only 11 percent felt that Bill Clinton's campaign was harmed by press coverage. Moreover, one out of three journalists (36 percent) thought that the media helped Clinton win the presidency, while a mere 3 percent believed that the press coverage helped the Bush effort." During the waning days of the campaign, President Bush frequently waved a red bumper sticker that stated, "Annoy the Media: Reelect Bush."[31]

▲ Here's a presidential photo opportunity: President Bush leaves the White House carrying one of his favorite books, *Bias,* by former CBS reporter Bernard Goldberg, which claims that a liberal bias permeates the news media.

A widely circulated May 2005 poll by the University of Connecticut Department of Public Policy revealed a substantial gap between journalists and the public, but even more disturbing is the finding that six in ten Americans perceive bias in reporting and 22 percent favor government censorship of news. When journalists were asked for whom they voted in the 2004 election, reporters overwhelmingly picked Kerry over Bush. In the sample of 300 journalists, registered Democrats outnumbered registered Republican by three to one.[32]

Media Ownership and Control

One reason to avoid making too much of evidence of media "bias" concerns the economics of mass communication—specifically, the ownership and control of mass media outlets. Many recent analyses suggest that the mass media's overwhelming bias is neither liberal nor conservative but corporate. William Greider maintains that the dissemination of information is so dominated by large media conglomerates and lobbyists for special interests who can afford to spend huge amounts of money that no real dialogue can exist because those without money, for example, the far left, have little chance of bringing their viewpoints into the public debate.[33]

Media scholar Ben Bagdikian has written extensively on the development of what he calls a "private ministry of information" created by the formation of a "media monopoly." Bagdikian's studies reveal that most of America's daily newspapers, magazines, television broadcasting, books, and motion pictures are controlled by only twenty-three corporations. As media control slips into fewer and fewer hands, Bagdikian argues, the content of those media becomes increasingly similar because the overall interests of corporate executives tend to coincide, especially since many of them sit on the boards of directors of the same companies. The result is a disturbingly homogenous version of "reality," tempered by the priorities of large corporations that own and advertise through major media outlets. Consequently, the media are reluctant to attack their own corporate masters. An example is the refusal of NBC's *Today* show to include in its story on national boycotts of large corporations one of the largest—General Electric—which happens to own NBC. The same was true when ABC news programs refused in 1999 to report negative stories on Disney Corporation, its parent company.[34]

Since World War II, news media business profits have steadily increased. This increase has been accompanied by a decrease in competition. With the exception of CNN, Fox, and a few cable programs, the three major television networks enjoy a monopoly over news and commercial sponsorship. The same process is at work in the newspaper industry, where large groups such as Gannett, Thomson,

MakeItReal

Primary Source:
Telecommunications Act, 1996

▶ After angry Afghans took to the streets to protest a Newsweek story that U.S. interrogators had desecrated the Qur'an while interrogating Muslim terror suspects, protests like this one occured outside many news organizations. The NEWSWEEK story was wrong and this led to angry partisan protest at home.

Source: New York Times, May 23, 2005, p. C1.

and Knight-Ridder control more than 80 percent of the daily circulation of all newspapers.

More recently, cross-ownership of media has increased—newspapers, television networks, book publishing, and Internet service providers all owned by conglomerates. For example, Time merged with Warner Brothers to form Time Warner. The conglomerate then acquired Turner Broadcasting (CNN, Headline News, and TNT cable networks). And then Time Warner, in turn, was acquired by America Online. In the same vein, Disney purchased Capital Cities, which owns ABC, which in turn owns a host of cable stations, including ESPN. By 1989, Capital Cities/ABC owned the ABC television network, twenty-nine affiliated radio and television stations, as well as ten daily newspapers, seventy-seven weeklies, and eighty specialized periodicals. NBC and CBS are owned by major conglomerates anchored by General Electric and Westinghouse, respectively.

These mergers have been highly beneficial to media autonomy. By putting themselves on solid financial footing, the mass media need not fear dependency on others, most notably politicians. In addition, this independence has increased news-gathering capabilities. However, some contend that the high concentration of media in the hands of a few can limit the expression of alternative views, further dilute news coverage, and limit criticism of the status quo. In February 2002, the Court of Appeals for the District of Columbia nullified the FCC's cross-ownership rule, which prevents one company from owning a cable system and local broadcast station in the same market. This may open a door to a new wave of mergers among cable conglomerates and broadcast companies. The ruling was a huge victory for media giants such as AOL, Time Warner, Viacom, and News Corporation, which have long maintained that the regulation prevented expansion. "This is earth shattering," said Gene Kimmelman, codirector of the Washington office of the Consumers Union. "The end result could be the most massive consolidation in media this nation has ever seen."[35]

Media-Government Symbiosis

A final problem with establishing a basis for ideological bias involves the symbiotic, or interdependent, relationship between the press and government. Just as the media have close ties with the largest American—and certain international—corporations, so are they closely tied to the very government they are so often accused of attacking or treating unfairly. Reporters in all media rely overwhelmingly on "official sources," usually well-placed public officials, when reporting government events. Journalist Philip Weiss has observed that, when such "official" sources are consulted, reporters commonly allow these sources considerable approval privileges over how their statements are used in stories. Certainly the practice of "quote approval" is not restricted to government officials alone, and it may be an attempt to ensure journalistic "objectivity" by allowing interviewees to verify the intentions as well as the language behind what they express in interviews. But, as the Judith Miller case illustrates, practices such as quote approval can draw reporters into an uncomfortably intimate relationship with the very individuals about whom they must remain unbiased. Only rarely are strong opponents of a government's foreign and domestic policy ever granted significant coverage in the mass media.

THE MEDIA AND ELECTIONS

No discussion of the media and politics would be complete without an examination of the uses of mass communication in elections. It is important here to distinguish between two types of media use in elections: media coverage of the campaign, and media exploitation by candidates in the form of political advertising and "infomercials."

ABC NEWS/PRENTICE HALL STUDENT LIBRARY
Air Wars

▲ How often have you heard a reporter say, "According to an anonymous administration source. . . ." Former White House Press Secretary Mike McCurry decided to parody that dodge by showing up at a briefing wearing a bag over his head: "A briefing today from an anonymous source. . . . This is what they call . . . a senior White House official who is so helpful to so many of you all the time. I just thought I'd bring him out here."

 **MakeItReal**

Visual Literacy: Press Conferences

Press Coverage

The amount of media coverage can influence the outcome of an election campaign. By focusing on particular candidates or issues, the media often ignore others. Indeed, the media have been accused of focusing on the "horse race" nature of politics. Most of the coverage in any given campaign is devoted to the race itself rather than to the policies and issues around which the race revolves. As primary campaigns unfold, the media often focus on reporting candidates' standing in the race, limiting coverage to the front-runners, and thereby delivering the message that only the front-runners are worthy of public attention.

As we discussed in Chapter 8, over the past fifteen years use of opinion polls has expanded dramatically. Not only are newspapers and television networks increasing their use of polls from the larger survey organizations such as Gallup, Harris, and Roper; major media outlets are conducting more of their own surveys. Large-circulation newspapers and magazines including the *New York Times, the Washington Post, USA Today,* and *Newsweek,* as well as CNN and the major broadcast television networks, frequently conduct public opinion surveys on numerous national issues. Much subsequent news coverage relies on these in-house polls. How significant is the impact of such coverage?

No solid evidence suggests that media polling significantly affects public opinion; that is, such polling does not appear to change opinions. However, published accounts of consistently high or low public responses or sudden shifts of opinion can affect the political process. If candidates do not do well in published polls, they have much more trouble raising the contributions necessary to run expensive campaigns. And elected legislators, ever watchful for trends within their constituencies, obviously pay close attention to published opinion data concerning their states or districts. If we recall that polling techniques can sometimes distort public opinion simply by the way questions are worded, we face the possibility that campaign contributors and legislators may sometimes take their cues from data that inaccurately reflect public preferences.

Likewise, controversy has been growing regarding published results of early exit polls during the national elections aired before the polls close. Many of Jimmy Carter's supporters complained that network broadcasting of early exit polls, which projected an easy victory for Ronald Reagan, actually discouraged Carter's West Coast supporters from voting. The 2000 election exit polls created one of the great embarrassments when NBC, CBS, and CNN announced that Al Gore had won Florida. ABC and FOX quickly followed suit. All of this was based on the Voter News Service (VNS) statistical analysis, which was corrected for 2002.

Yet, the 2002 midterm elections brought embarrassment and questions for Voter News Service. Just hours before the polls were scheduled to close, VNS abandoned its state and national exit poll results of voter attitudes. Projections were based on actual returns and not voter attitudes from exit polls. Citing server and system overload, faulty operator data input, and inadequately trained precinct workers, VNS pulled the plug. Networks and viewers did not know how the economy or the possibility of war affected voter decisions. This was a major setback for a system redesigned and rebuilt after the 2000 election fiasco.

The networks then terminated VNS and established the National Election Pool (NEP) consortium to provide tabulated vote counts and exit-poll surveys for 2004. This consortium appointed Edison Media Research and Mitofsky International as sole providers of exit polls. Shortly after 1 P.M. on election day, the national networks' raw exit-poll data was posted on the Internet showing Kerry winning the election in a landslide. The bloggers were running with these reports, which fueled mass confusion.

Talk Shows

The proliferation of call-in radio and television talk shows presents an interesting bridge between press coverage of campaigns and media utilization by the candidates. Today, more than ten thousand radio stations and eleven hundred commercial television stations broadcast in the United States, 99 percent of all households have a radio, 95 percent of all cars have a radio, and 57 percent of all adult Americans have a radio at work.

During the 1992 election, radio and television talk shows emerged as a new campaign platform and as the primary mode of discourse between candidates. Independent candidate H. Ross Perot decided to bypass journalists and appeal directly to the people on *Larry King Live.* By the end of the 1996 campaign, candidates had appeared on MTV, MSNBC, the three network morning shows, CNN, and radio talk shows.

Radio talk shows are believed to have significantly influenced the results of the 1994 congressional elections that ushered in a Republican majority. With their call-in format and no-holds-barred commentary, they provided an outlet where Americans dissatisfied with the Clinton administration and a Congress controlled by Democrats could vent their frustration.

Rush Limbaugh, the most successful of the talk-show hosts, is broadcast over nine hundred radio stations. Calling the press "willing accomplices to the liberal power base in Washington," Limbaugh and other hosts (70 percent of whom label themselves conservative) led the movement to transform Congress into a Republican stronghold. Listeners turned out to vote in droves. Polls showed that more than half the voters surveyed at polling places said they listened to talk radio, and frequent listeners voted Republican by a 3–1 ratio. Other surveys found that although dedicated listeners make up only about 10 percent of the population, they have the highest level of voter registration.

More than that, however, some analysts believe talk radio may be performing a function formerly the domain of political parties, unions, and civic groups, giving people a feeling of connection with the political process. With a simple phone call, they have an opportunity to express their views to a wide audience. Talk radio is, in short, a forum for political discussion. Often, however, the discussion is one-sided and opposing views are not presented.

Television and Presidential Elections

Presidential candidates gear their television use toward a major goal: spreading their message on the evening news. They accomplish this through various means—the most effective is the sound bite. A sound bite is a brief statement, usually a snippet from a speech that conveys the essence of a longer statement and can be inserted into a news story. Lines such as "You're no Jack Kennedy," uttered by Lloyd Bentsen during the 1988 vice-presidential debate with Dan Quayle, and "Are you better off now than you were four years ago?" asked by Ronald Reagan in his 1980 debate against Jimmy Carter, have entered political lore because of their effectiveness in targeting a specific issue or sentiment. Today, candidates come to debates prepared with one-liners they hope will be turned into sound bites and reported in the next day's news.[36]

Over the years, sound bites have become progressively shorter. In 1968, presidential candidates averaged forty-three seconds of uninterrupted speech on the evening news. The average sound bite during the 1984 presidential campaign was only 14.79 seconds. By 1988, the average was down to 9 seconds, and by 1992 it was 8.4 seconds. A voter rarely hears a potential president utter a complete paragraph on the evening news. How much useful information about a policy or issue can a candidate relay to the viewer in a nine-second sound bite? Not much.

In addition, many politicians have played the entertainment media card in their campaign bids to attract attention. Political satire had such a definite impact on the voters that during the 2000 election Gore's advisers actually had him watch Darrell Hammond's adept impersonation of him in the presidential debate to help improve his performance. The 2004 presidential campaign was notable for its movement into popular entertainment culture. Seeking to mobilize young and "undecided" voters to their side, John Kerry appeared regularly with Bruce Springsteen and other entertainers, and both candidates made multiple appearances on

MakeItReal

ABC News Video: Vote 2004

Quick Review

Negative Campaign Advertising

- Usually involves a harsh attack on a political opponent.
- Voters are more willing to believe negative information about public officials than positive information.
- Negative ads are more memorable than positive messages.
- Recent studies suggest that negative advertising decreases voter turnout.
- Tends to further increase feelings of distrust and lower individual levels of efficacy.

late-night television shows hosted by Jay Leno and David Letterman. Although both candidates resisted the offer to appear on the World Wrestling Foundation, other appearances made clear that for better or worse the presidential candidates have now become entertainers plugging their product on various television shows.

Political Advertising

The use of sound bites on television news contributes to the increasing focus on the candidates themselves at the expense of major issues facing the nation. This tendency is carried over into political advertising, which may refer to issues but is geared primarily to depicting the positive qualities of the candidate and the negative—even sinister—characteristics of opposing candidates.

In political advertising, everything hinges on image, and the image-maker's playground is the television commercial, or "spot." Image-makers have produced some of the most memorable, and infamous, images of recent campaigns. In 1964, for example, an anti-Goldwater spot was produced in which a little girl counted daisy petals. When she finished counting, the frame froze, a nuclear device was detonated, and a giant mushroom cloud dominated the television screen, with a voice-over: "These are the stakes, to make a world in which all God's children can live, or to go into the darkness. Either we must love each other or we must die." The ad was aired only once, but that was more than enough. The impression had been established that Goldwater was a danger to the future.[37]

Such gripping, even terrifying, imagery is risky. Usually, therefore, media consultants try for a balance between their negative and positive political spots. Thus, not all political spots are as intensely negative as the one just described. The 1960 presidential campaign featured spots showing John Kennedy sailing his yacht, riding horses, and frolicking with his family to demonstrate his "common" appeal, despite his uncommon wealth and social position. President Jimmy Carter made use of similar spots in 1976 and 1980; they showed him helping his daughter Amy with her homework and toiling away in shirtsleeves behind his desk in the Oval Office. Even the normally stiff, formal Richard Nixon tried to infuse his image with more warmth by allowing a film crew to capture him casually strolling along a California beach. The effect became unintentionally hilarious when reporters noticed that Nixon was wearing dress shoes.

Some of the most compelling positive advertising appeared in 1984, when incumbent Ronald Reagan ran under the theme "Morning in America." Hiring the same advertising agency that had produced a successful series of Coca-Cola commercials, Reagan's image management team crafted a series of spots showing smiling small-town men and women going about their daily business, secure in the knowledge that America was "back." The implication that America had to "return" from some worse place constituted a hint of negative advertising within an otherwise positive spot. These elegantly filmed, carefully designed spots are generally conceded to have played a major part in reinforcing Reagan's already formidable public support. Candidates expect that undecided voters will watch positive ads, with their warm, homey images of these potential national leaders, and embrace the leaders not as abstract political ideas but as people. George W. Bush tried to use this strategy in the 2000 nomination race when, upon seeing the success of reformer John McCain, he began touting a new theme called "Reform with Results."

As often as not, however, media consultants employ more combative imagery. Negative advertising usually involves a harsh attack on a political opponent, implying that the opponent is dishonest, corrupt, ignorant, or worse. In the 2004 election, this was most notable in the Swift Boat veterans' attacks on John Kerry's war record. This kind of political mudslinging is as old as American politics itself. Research shows that voters are more willing to believe negative information about public officials than positive information. Negative ads are also more memorable than positive messages.

Perhaps the most damaging negative ad in recent elections, aside from the 2004 Swift Boat attacks, aired in the 1988 Bush campaign. It portrayed Willie Horton, a convicted rapist who had committed murder while on parole, and implied that Democratic candidate Michael Dukakis was so soft on crime and criminals that the public safety was endangered. Later, however, Bush himself fell victim to negative advertising by Bill Clinton in 1992.

No other nation in the world, even among the industrialized democracies, enjoys the degree of media freedom found in the United States. A major study released by Freedom House in April 2005, *Freedom of the Press 2005: A Global Survey of Media Independence*, revealed that gains outnumbered setbacks, as measured by shifts among the survey's three main categories: free, partly free, and not free (see Figure 12.1). Improvements occurred in countries that experienced new or burgeoning democratic openings, such as in Ukraine and Lebanon. Several countries in the Middle East showed positive trends. Nevertheless, the report notes, "the overall level of press freedom worldwide—as measured by global average score—worsened, continuing a three-year downward trend." Notable setbacks occurred in Pakistan, Kenya, Mexico, Venezuela, and the United States, stemming from legal cases in which prosecutors sought to compel journalists to reveal sources or turn over notes or other material they had gathered in the course of investigations. "Additionally, doubts concerning official influence over media content emerged with the disclosures that several political commentators received grants from federal agencies, and that the Bush administration had significantly increased the practice of distributing government-produced news segments." This led Freedom House executive director Jennifer Windsor to observe, "even in established democracies, press freedom should not be taken for granted. It must be defended and nurtured."[38]

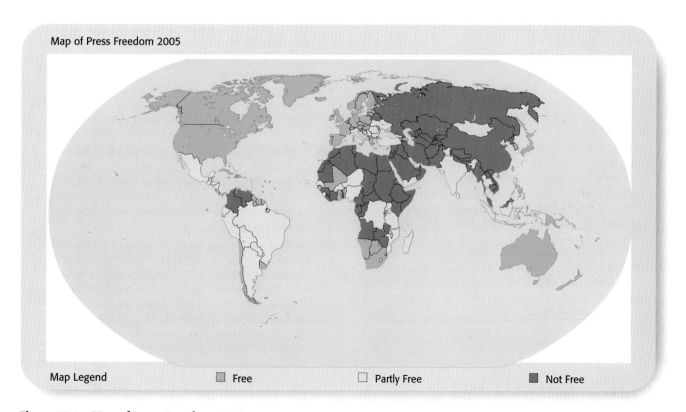

Map of Press Freedom 2005

Map Legend   □ Free   □ Partly Free   ■ Not Free

Figure 12.1   Map of Press Freedom 2005
Source: Reprinted by permission of The Freedom House.

As we have seen in this chapter, a variety of limits curb media independence. They range from government-imposed restrictions, both foreign and domestic, to more subtle forms of censorship resulting from the symbiosis between reporters and "official sources" within the government. Thus, although media freedom in the United States represents a closer approach to democracy than any other nation has achieved, it is far from absolute.

Summary

1. The mass media consist of the various means, such as newspapers, radio, and television, through which information is transferred from its source to large numbers of people.

2. Early political leaders saw newspapers as the key to educating the public about political affairs and gaining support for their parties' positions. Mass-circulation newspapers first appeared in the 1830s. At the end of the nineteenth century, the desire for dramatic stories led to muckraking, which attempted to expose the power and corruption of the rich, and yellow journalism, which sought to entertain the masses with little regard for the truth.

3. Of all the mass media, magazines offer the widest variety of subject matter and political opinion. The most successful news magazine is *Time*; there are also numerous magazines of political opinion.

4. Radio was popular between the two world wars, largely because events could be described as they were happening. Politicians and public officials soon learned the value of speaking directly to the American people in radio broadcasts.

5. Television is more persuasive and effective than any other form of mass communication. It is an almost universal source of entertainment and the primary source of news for most Americans. New technologies such as satellites have expanded television coverage to permit instantaneous reporting of events throughout the world. Cable television has made possible a much wider range of programming choices, including entire channels aimed at specially targeted audiences.

6. One function of the mass media is surveillance of events throughout the world. This means that the media decide what events are newsworthy. The media also interpret events by giving them meaning and context, and thereby shape opinions. The third major function of the media is socialization, in which the members of a society learn to conform to society's norms and values. In general, the media serve to reinforce existing values rather than create new ones.

7. The electronic media are regulated by the Federal Communications Commission, which establishes regulations designed to protect the public interest. The FCC's rules of the air include the equal opportunities rule (for political candidates), the fairness doctrine (now abandoned), and the right of rebuttal.

8. On occasion the government has attempted to prevent publication of information on the grounds that it would pose a threat to national security. This is done through a judicial restraining order, an action known as prior restraint. The media are also restricted by laws against libel and slander.

9. It is often said that the media have a liberal bias. However, numerous conservative publications, and many radio and television commentators, as well as publishers and network executives, are distinctly conservative. Corporate control of the media tends to produce middle-of-the-road coverage tempered by the concerns of advertisers. Another factor is the symbiosis between reporters and "official sources" within the government.

10. Media coverage of campaigns can influence election outcomes. The media are often accused of focusing on the "horse race" aspect of campaigns, implying that only front-runners are worthy of coverage. The increasing use of data from opinion polls can also affect the political process.

11. In recent campaigns, radio talk shows have taken on increasing importance. This was especially true in 1994, when conservative talk show hosts led the movement to replace many Democrats in Congress with Republicans.

12. Television takes center stage in presidential elections. Candidates travel throughout the country giving speeches in settings designed to make them look good on the evening news. The news broadcasts usually contain only snippets of candidates' speeches, known as *sound bites*.

13. Political advertising takes the form of commercials designed by image makers. The right image can have a tremendous impact on the voting public. Media consultants try to balance positive and negative images, but because negative advertising appears more effective, its use is increasing. A recent variant on the commercial is the infomercial, which combines commercial advertising with an informational discussion.

Review Questions

1. In what ways do the mass media shape the ways in which Americans think about and participate in the democratic process?

2. Is there a bias to press coverage? If yes, what is that bias and how does it affect our democracy? If no, how does the media maintain unbiased coverage?

3. How has the electronic media been generally regulated in this country?

4. What was the fairness doctrine and why was it abandoned? Will changes in electronic technology weaken or add impetus to strengthening this regulation? Why?

5. What impact does negative advertising have on the political process? What are a candidate's options in dealing with false and/or negative advertising by an opponent?

6. In a democracy, how would you characterize the responsibilities of the media during wartime?

7. What is the significance of the "international proliferation" of the Internet?

Key Terms

equal time rule 434	investigative journalism 432	prior restraint 435
fairness doctrine 435	libel 437	right of rebuttal 435
Federal Communications	mass media 425	socialization 433
Commission (FCC) 433	muckraking 426	yellow journalism 427

Suggested Readings

ALTERMAN, ERIC. *What Liberal Media? The Truth About Bias and the News.* New York: Basic Books, 2005. An analysis of how conservatives monopolize the resources and create an unfair playing field for objective news reporting.

ANDERSON, BRIAN C. *South Park Conservatives: The Revolt Against Liberal Media Bias.* New York: Regency, 2005. An editor of the Manhattan Institute's *City Journal* tracks the rise of what he calls "anti-elitist" right-wing thought in America's public dialogue, spearheaded by Rush Limbaugh in the late 1980s.

BAGDIKIAN, BEN H. *The Media Monopoly.* 4th ed. Boston: Beacon Press, 1994. A fascinating analysis of the continuing concentration of ownership of mass media outlets into fewer hands.

GOLDBERG, BERNARD. *Bias: A CBS Insider Exposes How the Media Distort the News.* Washington, D.C.: Regency, 2001. Former Emmy-award-winning broadcast journalist reveals a corporate news structure that responds to liberal opinions.

HALBERSTAM, DAVID. *The Powers That Be.* New York: Dell, 1979. A classic account of the rise of major media figures in America, written by one of America's foremost political journalists.

HAMILTON, JAMES. *All The News That's Fit to Sell: How Market Transforms Information Into News.* Princeton, N.J.: Princeton University Press, 2005. A valuable study of how sensationalism creates competition and polarization. The more news sources that exist, the more intense the struggle for an audience.

IYENGAR, SHANTO. *Is Anyone Responsible? How Television Frames Political Issues.* Chicago: University of Chicago Press, 1991. A scholarly analysis of the power of television to "frame" political issues and influence the way viewers respond to and think about those issues.

KUYPERS, JIM A. *Press Bias and Politics: How the Media Frames Controversial Issues.* New York: Praeger, 2005. An excellent discussion of how partisans consciously and unconsciously attempt to shape public perceptions of the world.

Visualizing Democracy

Straddling the Red State/ Blue State Divide

Since the 2000 Presidential Election, the American electoral map has been defined by the amazingly even division between the Red States, symbolizing the conservative Republican states, and the Blue States, symbolizing the more liberal Democratic states.

Since that time, the nation has split down the middle in a political civil war over the so-called "cultural issues" such as the rights of abortion, gay rights, gay marriage, privacy rights, stem-cell research, and sex education. Others have debated the issue of religion in politics, such as prayer in schools; the "under God" provision in the Pledge of Allegiance; the posting of Ten Commandments monuments in courtrooms, public schools, and outside public buildings; and the teaching of creationism and intelligent design in public school science classes. Still others debate policy questions such as homeschooling, the right to die with dignity, and the death penalty.

Pro-choice and pro-life signs at the March for Life rally in Washington, DC.

Ten Commandments monument supporters pray near the monument in the State Judicial Building rotunda on August 20, 2003 in Montgomery, Alabama. About 20 supporters who refused orders to leave the building during a protest were removed by authorities.

Christian Coalition leader Ralph Reed's new book is promoted at the Conservative Political Action Conference

446

The Red State proponents, led by the Evangelical Christian movement and highly conservative Republicans, have sought to restore religion to American governmental institutions and life, ban gay marriages and pass laws restricting gay life, restrict and even end the right of abortion, prevent euthanasia, and increase the use of the death penalty. The Blue State advocates, however, led by liberal groups such as the American Civil Liberties Union (ACLU) and the People for the American Way (PFAW), who have often linked up with conservative libertarians, have sought to expand personal rights for abortion, gay rights, and the right to die, and also to limit the appearance of religious symbols in publicly-funded American institutions as well as the use of the death penalty. The result is a sharply divided partisan environment, as evidenced in the battles over the appointments to the Supreme Court and federal judiciary.

The winner of the battle between the Red States and the Blue States will determine the political direction of this country for decades to come. ★

▼ Two women announce their recent marriage in Oregon during a gay pride parade Sunday, June 27, 2004, in Oklahoma City.

JuST LEGALLY MARRIED

▼ Supporters gather outside the U.S. Supreme Court in Washington, March 24, 2004, as the court heard arguments in a case deciding whether the words "under God" must be removed from the Pledge of Allegiance during its recitation in public schools, an important case on church-state separation.

▼ Protesters pray next to picture of Terri Schiavo in front of the hospice where Schiavo was being cared for in Pinellas Park, Florida, March 30, 2005. A U.S. appeals court rejected a bid by her parents to reconnect her feeding tube.

KEEP U.S.A. 1 NATION UNDER GOD

Apostle Building Company ☆ P.O. Box 74 ☆ Jacksonville, Alabama 36265 ☆ 256-231-61

★ CHAPTER 13 ★

CIVIL LIBERTIES

CHAPTER OUTLINE

Approaching Democracy

Reconsidering the Patriot Act

"The Patriot Act defends our liberty. It's essential law," said President George W. Bush to an audience in Hershey, Pennsylvania, in April 2004. Bush added, "It's a law that is making America safer. . . . It doesn't make any sense to scale it back." Bush made these assertions on a tour of the country seeking to persuade Congress to reauthorize and expand the 2001 Uniting and Strengthening America by Providing Appropriate Tools Required to Intercept and Obstruct Terrorism Act, better known by its acronym, the USA Patriot Act. This law, signed by President Bush after a speedy congressional passage on October 26, 2001, significantly curtailed civil liberties in the interests of security.

The impetus behind the new law was constitutional limitations on the FBI's search and seizure and arrest powers in search of information regarding the terrorists implicated in the attacks of September 11, 2001. In response, the attorney general asked for broad powers to conduct investigations: "one stop shopping" for a "roving wiretap" search warrant that covered all telephones in all jurisdictions used by a suspect rather than separate warrants for each one (thus dealing with the problem of tracking throwaway cell phones); computer searches for Internet activity; seizure of suspects' voice mail, searches of medical files, business records, and library files; "sneak and peek" or "black bag" searches in which the suspect is never informed of a search of home or office; indefinite detention of suspects; and monitoring the communications between a suspect and his or her attorney. Many people feared that this law would create a modern version of the old British "writ of assistance," which the authorities could use to search indiscriminately for evidence of criminal activity. The Bush administration argued compellingly that only speed and certainty of investigations could prevent future attacks on American soil.

After minimal congressional discussion, the act passed the House of Representatives by an overwhelming 357–66, only forty-five days after the September 11 attacks. The bill was negotiated behind closed doors by House Judiciary Committee chairman F. James Sensenbrenner Jr. (R-WI), House speaker J. Dennis Hastert (R-IL), and members of the Bush administration. Many House members had not yet read it at the time of the vote. The Senate, equally hasty, bypassed the Judiciary Committee, sending to the floor a measure hammered out by a group of top committee members from both parties, the administration, and the Senate leadership. The full Senate debated a scant four hours before passing the measure 98–1.

The result was a law that gave authorities almost everything that the attorney general had requested, except for unlimited detention of suspects before filing charges. However, if authorities determine that a suspect represents a threat to national security, he or she can be detained indefinitely. One of the most controversial provisions approved "sneak and peek" searches, even on computer files, without notice to the suspect, as long as authorities could argue that they had "reasonable cause to believe" that giving notice would have an

★ While Senator Patrick Leahy (D.-VT) recorded the moment for history, President George Bush signed the "U.S.A. Patriot Act" into law on October 26, 2001, thus launching the domestic legal war on terrorism.

"adverse" result on future investigations. In addition, rather than obtaining a search warrant from a judge to conduct electronic surveillance, authorities can secure warrants from a secret Foreign Intelligence Surveillance Act (FISA) court. FISA courts are made up of federal judges who serve in secrecy and use a lower probable-cause standard to determine the legality of a search request. Under the Patriot Act, this court can also permit the FBI to seize "tangible things," such as library records and bookstore sales records, during antiterrorism investigations. In one year, 2004–2005, this court approved more than seventeen hundred searches and seizures, which exceeded all of the search warrants issued by other courts in the federal or state system.

By 2005, four years after it was passed, the Patriot Act dominated the news once again as Congress considered whether to renew sixteen provisions that would expire at the end of 2005. By now, the public debate over liberty versus security was raging among the general public. Frequently, critics of the Patriot Act would quote Ben Franklin: "They who would give up an essential liberty for temporary security, deserve neither liberty or security." More than 250 cities and towns had passed ordinances symbolically nullifying enforcement of the Patriot Act in their regions. Polling data showed that 71 percent of the American people opposed Section 213, which allowed sneak and peek searches, and 50 percent opposed access to library and bookstore records. On the other hand, the deadly July 2005 bombings in London raised new issues supporting the Patriot Act's electronic surveillance provisions. What could America learn from these attacks in its effort to make itself even more secure?

Despite President Bush's calls to make all of the Patriot Act provisions permanent, Congress initially could not agree on a course of action. Spurred by Judiciary Committee chairman James Sensenbrenner (R.-WI), Congress renewed fourteen of the sixteen provisions permanently, making the provisions that dealt with the seizing of tangible records and the national roving wiretaps subject to a ten-year renewal. It also proposed twenty new federal death penalty offenses relating to terrorist acts. The Senate, however, was more restrictive, permanently renewing the same fourteen provisions but restricting the ability to search financial and business records and placing a four-year renewal deadline on the records and national wiretap provisions. When the House and the Senate could not agree by the end of 2005 on a compromise bill, largely because of a threatened bipartisan filibuster against it, the act was extended for several weeks while negotiations continued. Those negotiations were made more difficult by revelations that President Bush had approved electronic surveillance of American citizens by the National Security Agency outside of the FISA process. FISA judge James Robertson, also a U.S. District Judge, subsequently resigned.

★ Zacarias Moussaoui, a French citizen from Morocco, was convicted in 2006 for his role as the so-called "20th hijacker" in the 9/11 attacks.

In mid-March 2006, after two renewal extensions and just one day before 16 provisions of the Patriot Act were about to expire, President Bush signed into law a compromise Patriot Act that looked much more like the strict House version. All of the contested provisions that were about to "sunset", or go out of existence, were renewed permanently except for two of them. Ignoring objections by the Democrats, Congress renewed the ability to search for "tangible things" such as library, bookstore, and business records. However, one significant change allowed individuals who faced searches of such records to be able to discuss and challenge such requests in legal proceedings. But the debate over civil liberties in the "war on terrorism" battle will never end, as shown when Democratic Senator Russell Feingold (D.-WI) sought shortly thereafter to get a Senate vote on the question of censuring President Bush, something that had not been done since President Andrew Johnson in the Reconstruction era in the 1860s, for his role in the extra-legal electronic surveillance program.[1]

QUESTION FOR REFLECTION

How much have the Bill of Rights civil liberties protections been reduced by the war on terrorism as outlined in the USA Patriot Act, and how much should those protections be reduced during wartime or a time of crisis?

Introduction
CIVIL LIBERTIES AND DEMOCRACY

MakeItReal

Simulation: Civil Liberties: The Great Balancing Act

Primary Source: The Bill of Rights

civil liberties The individual freedoms and rights guaranteed to every citizen in the Bill of Rights and the due process clause of the Fourteenth Amendment, including freedom of speech and religion.

civil rights The constitutionally guaranteed rights that the government may not arbitrarily remove. Among these rights are the right to vote and equal protection under the law.

The debate over the renewal of the USA Patriot Act illustrates the challenge of defining and interpreting civil liberties, especially in times of crisis. The quality of a democracy can be measured by the degree to which it protects the rights of all its citizens, including those with unpopular views. Frequently, this task falls to the Supreme Court of the United States, which may find itself safeguarding the rights of individuals charged with carrying out heinous crimes or engaging in socially unpopular acts. In a democracy, the fundamental rights of such individuals have the same protection as those of any other citizen.

The fundamental rights of U.S. citizens are set forth in the Bill of Rights—the first ten amendments to the Constitution—and we often speak of the "protection" provided by that document. However, individual rights are always in jeopardy if they are not zealously safeguarded by all the institutions of society. When local authorities place a Ten Commandments monument inside a courtroom or on the Texas state capitol grounds, freedom of religion is at issue. When Congress bans "indecent material" transmitted over the Internet, freedom of speech is at issue. When the Supreme Court says that students can grade one another's papers, the right to privacy is at issue. And, when a police officer stops you in your car and asks to search the trunk, the Fourth Amendment search and seizure provision is at issue. All of these situations and hundreds more are governed by the Bill of Rights.

In this chapter, we explore the historical development of civil liberties. We begin with the framers' vision of the Bill of Rights, which was much less protective of individual freedoms than you might realize. We then explore the gradual expansion of civil liberties to the states over the course of our nation's history. We also analyze how civil liberties have been defined and how they have expanded and contracted over the past sixty-five years. These topics provide a dramatic demonstration of how the United States has approached democracy in the area of individual rights.

DEFINING AND EXAMINING CIVIL LIBERTIES AND CIVIL RIGHTS

Although the terms *civil liberties* and *civil rights* are often used interchangeably, they are not synonymous. **Civil liberties** are the individual freedoms and rights guaranteed to every U.S. citizen by the Bill of Rights and the due process clause of the Fourteenth Amendment. They include Americans' most fundamental rights, such as freedom of speech and religion. **Civil rights** concern protection of citizens against discrimination because of characteristics such as gender, race, ethnicity, or disability; they derive largely from the equal protection clause of the Fourteenth Amendment.

One way to distinguish between civil liberties and civil rights is to view them in terms of governmental action. Civil liberties are best understood as *freedom from* government interference with, or violation of, individual rights. This is a "negative" freedom in the sense that we understand people to have a right to certain liberties, such as freedom of speech, which they can exercise without government interference. For this reason, the First Amendment begins with the words, "Congress shall make no law. . . ."

In contrast, civil rights may be understood as *freedom to* exercise certain rights that are guaranteed to all U.S. citizens under the Constitution, and which the government cannot remove. This is a "positive" freedom in that we expect the government to provide the conditions under which certain rights can be exercised. Examples include the right to vote, the right to equal job or housing opportunities, and the right to equal education. We look more closely at civil rights in Chapter 14; in this chapter, we focus on civil liberties.

One reason the terms *civil liberties* and *civil rights* have become almost interchangeable in popular speech is that many issues involve aspects of both positive and negative freedom.[2] For example, consider the abortion issue, in which a woman seeks to terminate a pregnancy—a civil liberty—while others seek to preserve the life of the potential being, a civil right.

Cases involving civil liberties nearly always come down to a conflict between the individual, seeking to exercise a certain right in a democracy, and the state, seeking to control the exercise of that right so as to preserve the rights of others. The judiciary is charged with drawing the lines between acceptable individual actions and permissible governmental controls.

But how are those lines drawn? You will recall from Chapter 6 that "activist" jurists tend to uphold the rights of individuals over those of the state, while "self-restraint" jurists tend to defer to the state. The activists are also inclined to overturn acts of Congress, while the self-restraint jurists are inclined to defer to Congress in upholding the laws. Under these definitions, the Rehnquist Court was an activist court. Before 1994, the Court overturned congressional acts an average of once every two years. During 1994–2005, the Court overturned all or portions of thirty-nine such acts. One recent study concluded that the most "activist" member of the current Court is Clarence Thomas, who votes to overturn congressional acts 65.6 percent of the time. On the other hand, more liberal justice Stephen Breyer voted to overturn laws only 28.1 percent of the time. This same study concluded that the most restrained jurists on this Court are all liberals: Ruth Bader Ginsburg, David Souter, and John Paul Stevens.[3] The great majority of jurists fall in neither camp and are called "balancers" because they attempt to balance the rights of the individual with the rights of society.

The Dawn of Civil Liberties and Civil Rights in America

Many think that America's history of civil liberties and civil rights protection began in 1791 with the ratification of the Bill of Rights to the Constitution, but in fact the process did not begin in earnest until 1938, and it accelerated in the 1960s. Prior to that time, the Supreme Court did not consider the Bill of Rights a tool for protecting individual liberty, and before 1897, none of the Bill of Rights applied to the states. The Court's interest in civil liberties and civil rights began with these words in the footnote of an obscure 1938 economics case called *United States v. Carolene,* which dealt with Congress's regulation of "filled milk," the amount of additives added to milk to make the product more profitable to sell during the Depression. After explaining that the Court would continue to defer to the legislative body in matters of economic regulation, in a three-paragraph footnote, the Court sent a billboard to those attorneys and litigants seeking justice under the Constitution:

> There here may be narrower scope for operation of the presumption of constitutionality when legislation appears on its face to be within a specific prohibition of the Constitution, such as those of the first ten amendments, which are deemed equally specific when held to be embraced within the Fourteenth. . . . It is unnecessary to consider now whether legislation which restricts those political processes which can ordinarily be expected to bring about repeal of undesirable legislation, is to be subjected to more exacting judicial scrutiny under the general prohibitions of the Fourteenth Amendment than are most other types of legislation. . . . Nor need we enquire whether similar considerations enter into the review of

Quick Review

Civil Liberties Versus Civil Rights

- Distinguish between civil liberties and civil rights in terms of governmental action.
- Civil liberties are *freedom from* government interference with, or violation of, individual rights—negative freedom.
- Civil rights are *freedom to* exercise certain rights guaranteed to all U.S. citizens under the Constitution and cannot be removed by the government—positive freedom.
- Terms *civil liberties* and *civil rights* have become almost interchangeable in popular speech because many issues involve aspects of both positive and negative freedom.

double standard The varying level of intensity by which the Supreme Court considers cases by which it protects civil liberties claims while also deferring to the legislature in cases with economic claims.

statutes directed at particular religious, or racial minorities, whether prejudice against discrete and insular minorities may be a special condition, which tends seriously to curtail the operation of those political processes ordinarily to be relied upon to protect minorities, and which may call for a correspondingly more searching judicial inquiry.[4]

This may read like incomprehensible gibberish, but it actually tells us which kinds of cases the Court might be willing to accept on appeal and consider seriously ruling in favor of the individual in litigation against the government and other actors. The first sentence says that any dispute that touches on the Bill of Rights or the Fourteenth Amendment may receive special protection from the Supreme Court. The second sentence promises that any case that touches on the political process will receive special protection. Finally, the third sentence promises that any case that touches on "discrete and insular minorities" may receive special protection. In short, the Court is promising the launching of a **double standard** in which civil liberties will be judicially protected, but in economic cases the Court will defer to the legislature. The reason is that without Court protection politically disenfranchised or minority people cannot protect themselves through the voting process or the legislature.

Since the United States' approach to democracy in the area of civil liberties is relatively recent, we will focus on how these rights were created and expanded by the Warren Court (1953–69), partially cut back by the Burger Court (1969–86), and finally placed under full attack by the Rehnquist Court (1986–2005). First, however, we will explore the history of the development of civil liberties and their application to the states and to the national government.

A HISTORY OF THE APPLICATION OF CIVIL LIBERTIES TO THE STATES

The history of civil liberties is one of gradually expanding protection of personal rights guaranteed by the Bill of Rights. This evolution occurred through a series of Supreme Court decisions that applied portions of the first ten amendments to the states, thereby protecting citizens from state action in relation to specific individual rights. This evolutionary process, summarized in Table 13.1, illustrates that it did not begin until 1897 and did not really take hold until the 1960s.

In the early years of the nation's history, the Bill of Rights provided far less protection for individual rights than is the case today. For example, the guarantee of freedom of speech did not prevent the Federalist party from passing the Alien and Sedition Acts in 1798, which jailed opponents of John Adams's administration. And the right to counsel guaranteed by the Sixth Amendment did not prevent passage of the Federal Crimes Act of 1790, which instructed courts to provide defendants with counsel for capital offenses only.

But narrow as these individual protections were, in the 1833 case of *Barron* v. *Baltimore* the Supreme Court severely limited their collective impact.[5] Rains and swollen rivers washed silt unearthed by excavation and construction for the city of Baltimore into Baltimore harbor, rendering a wharf owned by John Barron unusable. Barron claimed that he was entitled to money damages under the Fifth Amendment's "eminent domain" clause, which guarantees "just compensation" from the state when government takes private property for public use.

▲ Protestor Lance Powers of Rochester, N.H. responds to the Supreme Court's 2005 eminent domain ruling extending the power of local governments to take private property for public use by suggesting that Justice David Souter's Weare, N.H. family farm be taken to create the "Lost Liberty Hotel."

Table 13.1 ■ The Incorporation of the Bill of Rights

Case	Issue	Incorporated
Chicago, Burlington and Quincy Railway Co. v. *Chicago* (1897)	Taking of private property by the state for public use without just compensation	Fifth Amendment guarantee of eminent domain
Gitlow v. *New York* (1925)	Arrest for speech threatening the state government	First Amendment guarantee of free speech
Near v. *Minnesota* (1931)	Prior restraint (censorship) of press	First Amendment guarantee of free press
Powell v. *Alabama* (1932)	Right to counsel in capital crimes. This was the famous *Scottsboro* case, in which seven young black males were accused and convicted without the aid of counsel of raping two white females	Sixth Amendment guarantee of right to counsel in capital cases where a "fair hearing" was lacking
Hamilton v. *Regents of the University of California* (1934)	Challenged public institution's mandatory military drills on basis of religious objections	First Amendment guarantee of freedom of religion
De Jonge v. *Oregon* (1937)	Peaceful assembly of Communist party members in Oregon	First Amendment guarantees of free assembly and of right to petition the government for a redress of grievances
Palko v. *Connecticut* (1937)	Twice being tried for same offense. In this case, Justice Cardozo devised his famous "honor roll of superior rights"	None, but Cardozo's insistence that superior rights should be incorporated begins "selective incorporation"
Cantwell v. *Connecticut* (1940)	Whether or not religious groups (Jehovah's Witnesses) should have to be licensed to promote their religion	First Amendment guarantee of free exercise of religion
Everson v. *Board of Education of Ewing Township* (1947)	State aid to bus children to parochial schools	First Amendment requirement that church and state be separate
In re Oliver (1948)	Whether or not a judge can act simultaneously as a grand jury and a trial judge to find a defendant guilty without a proper trial	Sixth Amendment guarantee to a public trial
Louisiana ex. rel. Francis Resweber (1947)	Whether or not a convicted man could be executed again after an electric chair failure	Cruel and unusual punishment
Wolf v. *Colorado* (1949)	Whether patient names from an appointment book of a suspected abortionist gained by illegal search of doctor's office can be used in trial	The "core" of the Fourth Amendment, defined as "arbitrary invasions of privacy by the police"
NAACP v. *Alabama* (1958)	Whether groups must register with the state and file membership names and addresses	First Amendment guarantee of freedom of association
Mapp v. *Ohio* (1961)	Use of the fruits of an illegal search and seizure without a proper search warrant in trial	Fourth Amendment prohibition on unreasonable search or seizure, and its exclusionary rule
Robinson v. *California* (1962)	A California statute providing a mandatory ninety-day jail sentence for conviction of addiction to narcotics without any evidence of drug use	Eighth Amendment guarantee against the infliction of cruel or unusual punishment
Gideon v. *Wainwright* (1963)	Legal counsel availability when someone is on trial for a misdemeanor, noncapital offense	Sixth Amendment guarantee of counsel was expanded to include all felony-level criminal cases

(Continued)

Table 13.1 ■ The Incorporation of the Bill of Rights (Continued)

Case	Issue	Incorporated
Malloy v. *Hogan* and *Murphy* v. *Waterfront Commission of New York* (1964)	Whether or not investigation into gambling offenses after serving a jail sentence for the crime resulted in self-incrimination	Fifth Amendment prohibition against self-incrimination
Pointer v. *Texas* (1965)	Whether or not the accused has the right to confront witnesses against him or her instead of a transcript of their earlier testimony during a trial	Sixth Amendment guarantee that the accused shall be confronted by the witnesses against him or her
Griswold v. *Connecticut* (1965)	Legality of use and counseling on the use of birth control by married couples	First, Third, Fourth, Fifth, Ninth, and Fourteenth Due Process Amendments (and their penumbras) right of privacy
Parker v. *Gladden* (1966)	Whether or not bailiff statements rendered the jury unable to produce an impartial verdict	Sixth Amendment guarantee that the accused shall be judged by an impartial jury
Klopfer v. *North Carolina* (1967)	Whether or not a state can place a live case on inactive status only to take the case up again when it has more time and resources	Sixth Amendment guarantee of a speedy trial
Washington v. *Texas* (1967)	Whether or not a defendant can compel witnesses in his or her favor to appear in trial	Sixth Amendment right to compulsory process for obtaining witnesses
Duncan v. *Louisiana* (1968)	Whether or not state must offer trial by jury in noncapital cases	Sixth Amendment guarantee of a trial by jury in all criminal cases above the petty level
Benton v. *Maryland* (1969)	Whether a state must provide a guarantee against two trials for the same crime	Fifth Amendment guarantee against double jeopardy

Even the normally nationalist-oriented Chief Justice John Marshall refused to extend Bill of Rights protections to the states in denying Barron's claim. The Bill of Rights, he ruled, "contains no expression indicating an intention to apply them to the state governments [so] this Court cannot so apply them." The First Amendment, by stating that "Congress shall make no law. . . ," indicates that the Bill of Rights applies *only* to the national government. Unable to use the Fifth Amendment to sustain his claim, Barron had no case. The entire Bill of Rights would not be applied to the states for another century. During that time, civil liberties varied from state to state, depending on the protections afforded by that state's constitution and existing laws.

The Fourteenth Amendment

Passage of the Fourteenth Amendment in 1868 again raised the issue of state responsibility relative to civil liberties. The Fourteenth Amendment was one of the so-called *Civil War Amendments*, designed to free the slaves and protect their rights as citizens. It reads: "No State shall make or enforce any law which shall abridge the privileges or immunities of citizens of the United States; nor shall any State deprive any person of life, liberty, or property, without due process of law; nor deny to any person . . . the equal protection of the laws."

Because the Fourteenth Amendment began with the words "No State shall make or enforce any law . . . ," some believed that it was intended to reverse the Barron ruling and extend the Bill of Rights to the states. Initially, the Supreme Court was asked to rule on whether the "privileges or immunities" clause of the amendment would accomplish this aim. However, the Court ruled that this language did not protect state rights of citizenship, such as property rights, but only national rights of

MakeItReal

Primary Source: Fourteenth Amendment Due Process Clause

Quick Review

The Fourteenth Amendment

- Passed in 1868.
- One of the Civil War Amendments.
- Designed to free slaves and protect their rights as citizens.

citizenship, such as petitioning Congress for a redress of grievances and being protected from piracy on the high seas.[6]

In later cases the Court was asked if part or all of the Bill of Rights could be defined as "due process" of law and thus extend to the states under the language of the Fourteenth Amendment. This approach, in which by redefinition the Bill of Rights would be absorbed into the due process clause, was called the **incorporation** of the Bill of Rights.[7] The argument ran thus: Under the Fourteenth Amendment the states must protect due process, and because some or all of the Bill of Rights could be defined as due process, the states must also protect those portions of the Bill of Rights.

However, in the late 1800s and early 1900s the conservative jurists who dominated the Court were more concerned with protecting property rights than with making this definitional leap to extend personal civil rights. Did California violate due process of law by using a list of evidence called a bill of information to indict people rather than the grand jury proceeding promised in the Fifth Amendment? No, said the Court, ruling that the "new" procedure can be just as fair as the "old" grand jury guarantee.[8] Did New Jersey's practice of allowing a judge to comment on a defendant's unwillingness to take the stand in self-defense, which a jury might interpret as an indication of guilt, violate the Fifth Amendment's guarantee that no person shall be "compelled . . . to be a witness against himself"? No, ruled the Court, because this was not a "fundamental" right that must be applied to the states.[9]

The Court's position became known as **no incorporation**, because it was unwilling to define the Bill of Rights as part of the Fourteenth Amendment and thus to apply its amendments to the states. The states would be bound only by the dictates of due process contained in the Fourteenth Amendment. The one exception came in an 1897 case involving a railroad company's objection to the city of Chicago's seizure of its land without just compensation. Here the Court ruled that the Fifth Amendment's right of eminent domain extended to the states.[10] Opposing the majority was Justice John Harlan, who argued that Bill of Rights protections were so fundamental that all of them should be applied to the states, thus creating the position known as **total incorporation**.

The Clear and Present Danger Test

The battle over application of the Bill of Rights to the states resumed during World War I, when the government was anxious to restrict certain individual liberties. Concern with wartime treason, spying, and obstruction of the military draft led in 1919 to *Schenck* v. *United States,* the first important case involving freedom of speech. Charles T. Schenck had been convicted of circulating pamphlets against the draft. In upholding the conviction, Justice Oliver Wendell Holmes argued that the state could restrict speech when "the words used are of such a nature as to create a clear and present danger that they will bring about the substantive evils that Congress has a right to prevent." In short, certain cases, such as falsely shouting "Fire!" in a crowded theater, may justify restriction of this liberty. In ignoring the fact that no evidence indicated that Schenck's "speech" had affected the draft, Holmes was saying that a wartime crisis was sufficient cause for restrictions on freedom of speech.[11]

Two other 1919 cases that came to the Supreme Court, dealing with federal restrictions of freedom of speech, revealed the problems of applying the **clear and present danger test** to other circumstances. When Jacob Frohwerk was convicted for writing scholarly articles on the constitutionality and merits of the military draft for a German-language newspaper in Missouri, the Court upheld the conviction in *Frohwerk* v. *United States.*[12] And when socialist Eugene Debs spoke out against the draft after signing an Anti-War Proclamation and Program in St. Louis, the conviction was upheld by the Court. The Court ruled in *Debs* v. *United States* that Debs was impeding the war effort.[13] Thus, the Court had convicted one man for writing for a tiny minority and another for the thoughts he might have had while speaking, and neither had any demonstrable effect on the draft.

incorporation The process whereby the Supreme Court has found that Bill of Rights protections apply to the states.

no incorporation An approach in which the states would be bound only by the dictates of due process contained in the Fourteenth Amendment.

total incorporation An approach arguing that the protections in the Bill of Rights were so fundamental that all of them should be applied to the states by absorbing them into the due process clause of the Fourteenth Amendment.

clear and present danger test A free speech test allowing states to regulate only speech that has an immediate connection to an action the states are permitted to regulate.

 **MakeItReal**

Primary Source: Fifth Amendment Due Process Clause

Primary Source: *Schenck* v. *United States,* 1919

Question for Reflection

How does the 1919 Supreme Court ruling on restriction of freedom of speech when "the words used are such a nature to create a *clear and present danger* . . ." compare with the 2001 USA Patriot Act, which allows for covert searches without notice to the suspect if the authorities can argue that they have "*reasonable cause to believe*" that giving notice would have an adverse result on future investigations?

Seeing the censorship effect of his test, Holmes changed his views. In the fall of 1919, when an anarchist named Jacob Abrams appealed his conviction for circulating pamphlets imploring American workers to go on strike in sympathy with Russian workers hurt by the revolution there, seven members of the Court upheld the conviction in *Abrams* v. *United States* because Abrams's actions posed a *clear and present danger* to the war effort. However, Holmes, the inventor of the test, together with Louis D. Brandeis, dissented. They argued that Abrams was nothing more than a "poor and puny anonymity" whose "silly leaflet" represented no clear and present danger to the state.[14] Thus America's approach to freedom of speech began, but it still had a long way to go.

The Beginnings of Incorporation

Whereas the federal government passed laws against certain actions resulting from speech but did not attempt to control speech directly, some states, including New York, chose to outlaw the words themselves. In 1925, a radical named Benjamin Gitlow was convicted under New York's Criminal Anarchy Act of advocating the overthrow of the government. In *Gitlow* v. *New York*, the Supreme Court ruled for the first time that the First Amendment guarantee of freedom of speech could be applied to the states; however, it upheld Gitlow's conviction, deferring to the state of New York's belief that certain speech had a "bad tendency."[15]

Why would the Court be willing to apply the free speech guarantee to the states but not use it to protect Gitlow himself? Because it had learned that the right of free speech could be used to protect businesses—for example, when a business refuses to give reasons for firing an employee. The Court was therefore setting a precedent that could be used to protect the status quo without actually condoning speech aimed against these same interests.

In the early 1930s, the Court applied three other parts of the Bill of Rights to the states. In 1931, when the Minnesota legislature passed a law censoring the *Saturday Press*, a muckraking tabloid printed by Jay Near, the Court in a landmark case called *Near* v. *Minnesota* incorporated the guarantee of freedom of the press into the Fourteenth Amendment, thus applying it to the states, and overturned the Minnesota law.[16]

A year later, the Court was called upon to rule in the case of the "Scottsboro Boys," in which a group of black youths had been unjustly accused of raping two white women on a train. The young men had been convicted in a trial in which, instead of assigning a defense attorney, the judge asked "the entire bar of the county" to defend them. (In other words, they had no defense.) The Court's decision incorporated and applied to the states the notion of a "fair hearing" implied in the Sixth Amendment, thus guaranteeing the right to counsel, but only for capital crimes such as this one.[17]

Finally, in 1934, when the University of California required that all students, including religious pacifists, take courses in military training, the Court incorporated the freedom of religion provision and applied it to the states but left the program intact.[18]

The Court made clear in all of these cases that extending rights to the states did not necessarily mean increased rights for individuals. States remained free to punish the press after publication rather than before, to deny the right to counsel in noncapital criminal cases, and to require even pacifist students to take courses in military training. Thus, the question remained whether or not a more general rule could be established that applied the Bill of Rights to the states in a meaningful way.

Selective Incorporation of the Bill of Rights

Not until 1937, the year of FDR's failed court-packing plan and one year before the Carolene Products footnote in the landmark case of *Palko* v. *Connecticut*, could the first step be taken toward establishing a rule about incorporating a right into the Fourteenth Amendment due process clause and applying it against the states.[19] Frank Jacob Palko had been convicted of the second-degree murder of two police officers,

MakeItReal

Visual Literacy: The Scottsboro Boys

and he objected to the state's plan to retry him because of procedural errors in the earlier trial for first-degree murder, which carried the death penalty. Palko claimed that a retrial would deny him the Fifth Amendment's protection against **double jeopardy**, that is, the guarantee that a person may not be tried twice for the same crime. However, the Supreme Court had not yet applied this right to the states. The Court ruled that only rights "implicit in the concept of ordered liberty" would be applied to the states. According to Justice Benjamin Cardozo, those rights were fundamental freedoms such as freedom of speech, the right to fair trial, and freedom of thought; the double jeopardy protection did not qualify. Palko lost his appeal, and, with no double jeopardy right to worry about, the state retried him, convicted him, and put him to death. It was surely little comfort to him that his name was now associated with a new incorporation standard, **selective incorporation**, in which certain portions of the Bill of Rights, but not all, became part of the Fourteenth Amendment's due process clause and thus guaranteed against invasion by the states.

Over the next forty-five years, all but a handful of the provisions contained in the Bill of Rights were applied to the states by way of the Fourteenth Amendment. This judicial redefinition of civil liberties, particularly during the 1960s, was the greatest expansion of national government power in the federal structure since the 1930s decisions that extended interstate commerce power to the states.

Several amendments or portions thereof—including the Second, Third, and Seventh, the grand jury provision of the Fifth, and the excessive bails and fines provision of the Eighth—have not been, and probably will not be, incorporated. Because other rights not contained in the Bill of Rights, such as the right to privacy, have also been applied to the states, the best characterization of the Court's current approach might be "selective incorporation plus."

Incorporating a Bill of Rights provision raised the question of whether or not these provisions meant the same at both the federal and state levels. For example, once the right to trial by jury in the Sixth Amendment was applied to the states, must states and national government observe the same twelve-person, unanimous-verdict rules? In this case, the Court decided that they did not.[20] Additional questions such as exactly what a provision means and how much protection it extends to the individual must be resolved. In the case of freedom of religion, for example, are religious practices protected if they violate other laws, such as the ban on polygamy? In the case of freedom of speech, is only actual speech protected, or is symbolic speech such as flag burning protected as well?

FREEDOM OF RELIGION

Few issues lay closer to the framers' hearts than those involving religion. Many of the nation's earliest European settlers were religious zealots seeking independence from the state-run Anglican Church of England. Accordingly, they either established state religions of their own or supported various religions without giving preference to any of them. State laws often disenfranchised various religious groups, such as Catholics, Jews, agnostics, or atheists. Since the new nation's potential for fragmentation into different religious communities fighting for governmental control was too dangerous to be ignored, the guarantee of freedom of religion appeared early in the Bill of Rights.

The framers considered religion a matter of personal choice and conscience, not an area for governmental control. However, by restricting government's "establishment" of religion while simultaneously guaranteeing the "free exercise" of religion, they created contradictory goals.[21] For example, if the government provides tax-exempt status for religious organizations, as it does for other charitable institutions, thus promoting "free exercise of religion," does this constitute an "establishment of religion"? On the other hand, if government fails to grant such tax relief, would this force some churches to close, thus restricting the free exercise of religion?[22] Questions like these have led the Supreme Court to rely more on the establishment clause rather than on the free exercise clause.

Quick Review

Incorporation of the Bill of Rights

- Provisions contained in the Bill of Rights applied to the states by the Supreme Court.

- Judicial redefinition of civil liberties expanded power of the national government.

- Several amendments have not been, and probably will not be, incorporated.

- Other rights not contained in the Bill of Rights, such as the right to privacy, have also been applied to the states by the Court.

---

double jeopardy Trying a defendant twice for the same crime; banned by the Fifth Amendment.

selective incorporation An incorporation standard in which some portions of the Bill of Rights, but not all, were made part of the Fourteenth Amendment's due process clause, and thus guaranteed against invasion by the states.

ABC NEWS/PRENTICE HALL VIDEO LIBRARY

Church & State, And Pledge Of Allegiance

Voices Of Dissent

Establishment of Religion

In deciding whether particular governmental practices would have the effect of "establishing" a religion, the Court has searched for the proper balance between two opposing views of the relationship between government and religion. These are known as the *high wall of separation* position and the *government accommodation* position.

The high wall of separation position originated with the author of this constitutional provision, James Madison, who was reacting to the fact that half the colonies had adopted laws that provided support for religious institutions and practices.[23] Fearing that such laws could lead to religious persecution, he called for strict separation between church and state. However, connections between church and state were too numerous to bar them all. In the government accommodation view, the government would be allowed to assist religion, but only if the aid was indirect, available to all other groups, and religiously neutral.

The government accommodation position was first articulated in 1947 in the case of *Everson* v. *Board of Education of Ewing Township*. A local school board, spurred by the desire to aid Catholic parochial schools, had provided funds to enable children to travel to parochial school on city buses. The Court ruled that the state's policy did not violate the establishment clause because the children, not the church, received the benefit. According to Justice Hugo Black, the transportation assistance resembled other basic services, such as police and fire protection. Black was unpersuaded by dissenters' arguments that such assistance helped children to attend the church schools, thereby indirectly aiding religion.[24]

The high wall of separation doctrine was best described in 1962 in the case of *Engel* v. *Vitale,* in which the Court ruled that a brief nondenominational prayer led by a teacher in a public school was unconstitutional. For the Court, the mere chance that a student might feel compelled to worship a God in which he or she did not believe was precisely the kind of establishment of religion the framers had sought to avoid.[25]

Partly because of public outcry after the *Engel* decision, the Court began to search for a middle ground between separation and accommodation. It took a step in this direction one year later in the case of *Abington School District* v. *Schempp*. In ruling on this case, which involved Bible readings in Pennsylvania public schools, the Court adopted a *strict governmental neutrality* rule, under which a state was barred from doing anything that either advanced or inhibited religion. Since school-directed Bible reading clearly advanced religion, the practice was ruled unconstitutional.[26]

During the 1960s, the Court continued to search for the proper test for judging cases involving state aid to religious schools. If parochial school students could receive bus money, could they receive books? Because the books were loaned, the Court found this practice constitutional. Could the same be said for state aid to parochial school teachers teaching nonreligious subjects? This question was raised by the 1971 case of *Lemon* v. *Kurtzman*. In deciding that case, the Court created a new test, called the **Lemon test**, for determining the permissible level of state aid for church agencies. Such aid was considered constitutional, if the state could prove that (1) the law had a secular purpose, (2) the primary purpose and effect of the law were neither to advance nor to inhibit religion, and (3) the law did not foster an "excessive governmental entanglement with religion." Aid for teachers of nonreligious subjects met the first two conditions. However, the only way the state could judge if the funded teachers were aiding religion would be to monitor their classes; the law therefore violated the "excessive entanglement" provision of the test.[27]

During the past three decades, this three-pronged *Lemon* test has been applied in all cases involving the establishment of religion. However, its application has varied over the years depending on the composition of the Court. During the early years of the Burger Court, the justices were sharply divided on the question of state aid to religious schools. States could supply standardized tests to parochial schools[28] and provide grants to all colleges, even church-related ones.[29] But in 1973, the Court

Lemon test A test from the 1971 Supreme Court case *Lemon* v. *Kurtzman* for determining the permissible level of state aid for church agencies by measuring its purpose on three counts: is it nonreligious in nature? does it either advance or inhibit religion? and/or does it produce excessive entanglement of church and state?

ruled in the *Committee for Public Education* v. *Nyquist* case that the state of New York could not offer tuition reimbursement of between sixty and one hundred dollars to impoverished students because there was no effort "to guarantee the separation between secular and religious educational functions and to ensure that State financial aid supports only the former," thus potentially causing religious strife.[30] Later, it ruled that the government could also not reimburse students for taking the New York State Regents exams,[31] or provide auxiliary services, such as counseling and speech therapy, to parochial school students.[32]

In the early 1980s, changes in the makeup of the Court produced a shift toward a more accommodationist position. The parents of Minnesota private, public, and parochial school students were permitted in *Mueller* v. *Allen* to take an income tax deduction for the costs of tuition, textbooks, and transportation;[33] a chaplain could open the daily proceedings of the Nebraska legislature;[34] and a crèche could be placed in a public park in Pawtucket, Rhode Island, as part of a larger Christmas display. It was here that Justice Sandra Day O'Connor offered her suggestion for replacing the *Lemon* test, saying that the Christmas display was permissible for her because it offered "no endorsement" of a particular religion or religion in general.[35] On the other hand, certain practices were disallowed: The state of Kentucky was barred from posting the Ten Commandments in school classrooms;[36] the state of Alabama was barred from requiring a moment of silent meditation in public schools if the teacher suggested that students use the time to pray or even suggested the wording of a prayer;[37] public school teachers could not be sent to parochial schools to teach secular subjects;[38] and the state of Louisiana could not require the teaching of creationism, a religious theory that the Earth was created according to the biblical book of Genesis as a way of providing a perspective different from Darwin's theory of evolution.[39] Twice in the 1980s, the Court considered and rejected state public school curricula that required the teaching of both creationism and evolution. Religious groups around the country mounted the "Hang Ten" movement, seeking to post the Ten Commandments on the walls of public schools and public buildings. In 2002, for the second time in a year, a deeply divided court refused to hear an appeal by Indiana Governor Frank O'Bannon, whom a lower court had prevented from placing a seven-foot stone monument containing the Ten Commandments on the statehouse lawn, a situation reminiscent of a similar effort by Justice Roy Moore in the Alabama Supreme Court building rotunda. These cases have led to the removal of memorials around the country.[40] In November 2002, the federal court also ordered that the Alabama monument be removed.

In June 2005, the Court weighed in once more on the Ten Commandments issue with two rulings on the erection of Ten Commandments monuments on state grounds, one inside a Kentucky courtroom and the other on the grounds of the Texas State Capitol. In a pair of narrow 5–4 decisions, the Court ruled that these monuments were constitutional only if they did not "endorse" religion by the state. According to the Court, this made the Texas state capitol grounds monument acceptable because it celebrated only the history of the relationship between state and religion. The monument inside the Kentucky courtroom, however, was unconstitutional because it "endorsed" religion by the state. In the words of Justice David Souter in the Kentucky case: "sacred text can never be integrated constitutionally into a governmental display on the subject of law, or American history."[41] The Rehnquist Court stood ready to modify or reverse many of its other religion decisions. The crèche declared acceptable in Pawtucket five years earlier was now unacceptable on the grand staircase of the Allegheny County Courthouse in Pittsburgh. On the other hand, the placing of a menorah next to a Christmas tree and a sign saluting liberty just outside the City-County Building in the same city was acceptable.[42] A nondenominational prayer at a Rhode Island graduation was ruled unconstitutional in an opinion by Justice Anthony Kennedy because, in his alternative to the *Lemon* test, it might have a "psychological coercion" effect on nonbelievers who were present, and might even induce some students not to attend their

MakeItReal

Primary Source: Statement by U.S. Secretary of Education Richard W. Riley regarding "Religion in Public Schools: A Joint Statement of Current Law"

▲ Alabama Supreme Court Chief Justice Roy Moore showed what he thought of the First Amendment's call for the separation of church and state when he moved this Ten Commandments granite monument into the lobby of the state's Supreme Court building. Federal District Court Judge Myron Thompson ordered its removal.

graduation for religious reasons.[43] While five members of the current Court saw the test as too separationist in its impact, it remained to be seen whether they could agree on a more accommodationist test.

In the 2001 term, the current Court plumbed the full limits of the *Lemon* test when it heard an appeal from Cleveland, Ohio, raising the question of whether school vouchers were constitutional. This voucher program, passed by the Ohio legislature, offered $2,250 in state aid to impoverished students, 99 percent of whom would use the money to attend religious schools. In a narrow 5–4 ruling, Chief Justice Rehnquist upheld the Cleveland program, arguing that because it gave parents the option of sending their children to public charter or magnet schools as well as nonreligious private schools, it did not coerce them into subjecting children to religious instruction. Justice David Souter, in an unusual denunciation of the Court's decision delivered orally from the bench, called it a "major devaluation" of the Court's church–state rulings and "not only mistaken, but tragic."[44] This ruling gave energy to the Bush administration's effort to fund "faith-based initiatives," such as soup kitchens and day care centers run by religious organizations that might seek government funding.

This decision did not end the fight over government spending for religious schools, but merely shifted the legal battle to the state level. Thirty-seven or so states have Blaine Amendments, named for the anti-Catholic Maine Republican Congressman of the 1850s, James G. Blaine, who tried to secure passage of a constitutional amendment banning any government funding for parochial schools. When that failed, states used it as a model for their own anti-religious-school funding amendments to their constitutions, sometimes barring both direct and indirect financial aid. After the school voucher decision, states renewed their examination of the legality of state aid to religious schools, and by mid-2005, thirty-eight states had passed restrictions on this practice. The Florida Supreme Court also announced that it would hear a case challenging the state's merit-based Opportunity Scholarships Program because they provided aid to a religious school.[45]

Recently, another establishment-of-religion issue has again arisen when public schools have required the teaching of another religious theory, "intelligent design," in science classes. Intelligent design explains the gaps perceived by some in Darwin's evolutionary theory as being the result of the "intelligent design" of God, thus once again basing the instruction on the book of Genesis in the Bible.[46] While advocates in these schools argue that intelligent design is as much a scientific theory as is Darwin's theory of evolution, others argue that it is a means of inserting religious doctrine that lacks scientific proof into the schools' science curriculum. Since 2001, just under half of the states, twenty-four, have considered changing the way evolution is taught in their state by either including this creationism theory or using it in the curriculum to critique the Darwinian evolutionary theory. President Bush's public support for the intelligent design theory in mid-August 2005 raised the prospect that more states would add this religiously connected theory to their science education curriculum. That fall, the intelligent design curriculum in the Dover, Pennsylvania public schools was tested in federal court, and was struck down in December 2005. All eight school board members who had supported the curriculum were voted out of office in the 2005 election. However, across the country in that same election, the Kansas State Board of Education adopted this curriculum for science classes throughout the state. The Court will no doubt consider once again if this course represents state establishment of religion.

Free Exercise of Religion

Issues involving the free exercise of religion are particularly vexing because they most often involve disputes of liberty versus liberty, or the right of one person to practice religion in the face of another who seeks to avoid religion. One look at certain government practices—the "In God We Trust" motto on its currency, the chap-

MakeItReal

Primary Source: *Lemon v. Kurtzman,* 1971

Question for Reflection

How much religion in public schools and what kind of religious references in public observances and public places are consistent with the First Amendment of the Constitution?

◄ The United States Senate, meeting in a special session held in New York City in 2002, offered its dissenting opinion to 9th Circuit Court of Appeals Court Judge Alfred T. Goodwin's decision to ban the recitation of the Pledge of Allegiance in public schools because it contains the words "one Nation under God."

lain's invocation that opens sessions of Congress, and even the admonition "God save this honorable Court" that opens each session of the Supreme Court—tells us that religion is pervasive in American politics. But do these practices place limits on the free exercise of religion? And, even if they do, is it politically possible to change them? These questions over the symbolic use of religious symbols in state-funded locations became clear in June 2002 when a three-judge panel of the Ninth Circuit Court ruled that the "under God" provision of the Pledge of Allegiance made its use in public schools unconstitutional because it coerced nonreligious students to express a religious belief that they did not hold. The nationwide storm of controversy that resulted from this decision caused the entire Court of Appeals to announce that it would reconsider its decision. If the case should ever reach the Supreme Court, it will almost certainly be reversed.[47]

Free exercise cases usually involve a law that applies to everyone but is perceived as imposing a hardship on a particular religious group. For example, can laws against mail fraud be used to prosecute religious groups that make dubious claims in letters to potential donors? In such cases the Court will not inquire into the nature of the religion, but it will examine whether the actions that result from that belief contravene the law. This so-called **secular regulation rule** holds that no constitutional right exists to exemption on free exercise grounds from laws dealing with nonreligious matters. This rule was applied in 1878 in a case involving the Mormon practice of polygamy (taking multiple wives) in Utah Territory. The Court ruled that religious beliefs did not provide immunity from the law, in this case the law enforcing monogamy.[48]

Subsequently, it became clear that the secular regulation rule did impose undue hardship on religious groups in certain instances. For example, the so-called "blue laws," that required all businesses to close on Sunday, put Muslim or Jewish business owners who observed the Sabbath on Friday or Saturday at a competitive disadvantage because their businesses had to be closed on Sunday as well. Accordingly, the Court invented a new test—the **least restrictive means test**—in which the state was asked to find another way, perhaps through exemptions, to enforce its regulations while still protecting all other religions.[49]

This "live and let live" position on issues of free exercise prevailed until 1990, when the Rehnquist Court decided a case in which two Native Americans working as unemployment counselors in Oregon were held to have violated the state's antidrug laws by smoking peyote, a hallucinogenic drug, as part of a religious observance.

secular regulation rule Rule denying any constitutional right to exemption on free exercise grounds from laws dealing with nonreligious matters.

least restrictive means test A free-exercise-of-religion test in which the state was asked to find another way, perhaps through exemptions, to enforce its regulations while protecting all other religions.

The Court chose in this instance to defer to the state's efforts to control drug use rather than protect the free exercise of religion.[50] Although the Court refused to use this precedent to allow the state of Florida to rely on its public health and animal anticruelty laws to specifically ban religious sacrifices of animals,[51] government authorities used it to justify even greater incursions into religious behavior: Autopsies were ordered contrary to religious beliefs, and an FBI agent who refused a work assignment for religious reasons was fired.[52]

Congress reversed the Oregon peyote-use ruling in the Religious Freedom Restoration Act (RFRA), and in 1997 the Supreme Court overturned this law in the case of *City of Boerne* v. *Flores*. In this case, the congregation of the St. Peter Catholic Church in Boerne, Texas, wanted to expand its beautiful historic stone structure to accommodate its growing membership, but was blocked by the city's Historic Landmark Commission. This decision was challenged under RFRA, and the Court overturned the law, thus returning the standard to the *secular regulation rule for state cases*, saying that it was not within Congress's power to legislatively void judicial decisions:

> When the Court has interpreted the Constitution, it has acted within the province of the Judicial Branch, which embraces the duty to say what the law is. When the political branches of the Government act against the background of a judicial interpretation of the Constitution already issued, it must be understood that . . . the Court will treat its precedents with the respect due them under settled principles . . . and contrary expectations must be disappointed. RFRA was designed to control cases and controversies, such as the one before us; but as the provisions of the federal statute here invoked are beyond congressional authority, it is this Court's precedent, not RFRA, which must control.[53]

Eventually, the city and the church reached an agreement that allowed the church to expand the structure.

In sum, the principle of freedom of religion appears straightforward on the surface, but in practice it raises complex issues resolved in various ways throughout our history. It appears impossible to erect a high wall of separation between church and state, but we accommodate government practices that involve religious organizations that may vary depending on Supreme Court composition and the specific test applied in each instance. The same is true in the area of free exercise, where the Court composition determines the degree of freedom religious groups have against state regulations. In the past several years, the Court signaled its willingness to protect the free speech and free exercise rights of religious organizations. In 2001, the Court ruled that public schools that allowed nonreligious groups to meet for activities in their buildings after school hours must also open their building to religious groups for their meetings, in this case an after-school Bible club for young children.[54]

This direction continued with the Court's 2002 8–1 ruling that protected Jehovah's Witnesses from the town solicitation regulations of Stratton, Ohio. The law required door-to-door advocates to secure a permit and reveal the names of missionaries before going door-to-door to proselytize.[55]

FREEDOM OF SPEECH

One hallmark of a democratic state is the guarantee of freedom of speech. But just where does the state draw the line between a person's right to speak and other rights, such as the speech rights of others? Over the years, the Supreme Court has taken two different approaches in attempting to solve this dilemma. One approach was suggested by Alexander Meiklejohn, a legal theorist who argued that although public, or political, speech on matters of public interest must be absolutely protected to preserve a democratic society, private speech, or speech intended for one's own purposes, can be restricted to protect the interests of other members of society.[56] On the other hand, Justice Oliver Wendell Holmes argued that democracy requires a "free marketplace of ideas" in which *any* view may be expressed, allowing the audience to decide what to believe. Holmes believed that limits on freedom of speech were justified only when the consequences of speech endangered the state.[57]

Caught between these absolutist and balancing approaches, the Court has ruled in ways that protect certain kinds of speech but not others. All speech is afforded First Amendment protection unless it is offensive or obscene or poses a threat to national security. Such utterances either convey no worthwhile ideas or do more harm to society than good and are deemed unworthy of protection. Despite these guidelines, however, the degree of protection afforded to particular forms of speech has varied considerably.

Political Speech

Where does the government draw the line between promoting full political discussion and protecting the government's right to exist? The Court faced this challenge in the early 1950s, when cold-war tensions led to fears that Communist party members in the United States were actively seeking to overthrow the government. These were no "poor and puny anonymities," the government argued in prosecuting twelve Communist party leaders, but members of a worldwide organization calling for full-scale revolution.

In *Dennis* v. *United States,* the Court reviewed in 1951 the convictions of Communist party leaders under the Smith Act, which made it a crime to teach or advocate overthrow of the government or to organize and conspire with those who do so. Did these actions pose a clear and present danger to the nation? In view of the tiny and disorganized nature of the American Communist party, the Court concluded that its actions created no such a danger. However, the Court was anxious to uphold the convictions, and therefore it invented a new *sliding-scale test* in which the state needed to prove less about the probable results of speech if the potential threat involved was significant enough. In this case, since the Communists aimed to overthrow the government, the government could convict if it found only their names on a party membership list and evidence that they were involved in the organization's activities, not that they were actively plotting the government's overthrow.[58]

Not until 1957 did the Court become willing to protect the speech of Communists as long as they were not actively plotting to overthrow the government.[59] By 1967, the Court had made it virtually impossible to deny First Amendment rights to someone for merely being a Communist.[60] At the time of Earl Warren's retirement in 1969, the Court had moved a considerable distance toward absolutism in protecting political speech. For example, when Ohio's Ku Klux Klan leader was convicted for advocating unlawful methods of terrorism because television cameras caught him with a gun at a cross-burning rally, the Court invented a new test. It would uphold convictions only for speech that incited "imminent lawless action" and was "likely to produce such action." On this basis, the conviction was reversed.[61]

In the 1999 term, the Supreme Court opened the door for further campaign finance reform by ruling in a Missouri case that limits on individual contributions are constitutional. The limits of $1,075 for contributions to statewide candidates, similar to laws in two-thirds of the states, were ruled not a limit on free speech.[62] The following term, the Court indicated once more its concern about the effect of money on political campaigns when it ruled against the Colorado Republican party's request for exemption from federal limits on how much money political parties can spend to assist their candidates' campaigns.[63] These campaign finance reform decisions took on added importance in 2002 given passage of the Bipartisan Campaign Finance Act banning soft money and "issue ads." When the Supreme Court upheld the constitutionality of nearly all provisions of the McCain-Feingold campaign finance law a year later, the legal battle shifted to the question of ads funded by non-political-party interest groups called "527s." These groups are named for the IRS provision that allowed for such speech by tax-exempt organizations, a practice sure to be tested in court as well.

 **MakeItReal**

Primary Source: Official Program for the March on Washington (1963)

Public Speech

States have passed many laws to protect those who might be offended or threatened by certain kinds of speech. Disturbing the peace, disorderly conduct, inciting to riot, terrorist threats, and fighting-word statutes are designed to preserve public order and safety. The main problem with such statutes is that sometimes they are crafted or enforced specifically to exclude certain ideas or groups.

Laws involving public speech require the Supreme Court to weigh the speaker's right to say what he or she wishes against the state's right to maintain law and order. Over the years, the Court has developed three standards in this area. First, it asked if a particular form of speech comes under the protective umbrella of the First Amendment. Thus, although controlled protests in public places such as the state library and state capitol are protected, calling a police officer "a goddamned racketeer" and "a damned fascist" is not; such expressions are considered fighting words.[64] The Court looked next at the nature of the statute itself. Is the law overbroad, including certain protected forms of speech among the proscribed ones? Or is it underinclusive, failing to regulate forms speech that should be barred? For instance, a "disturbing the peace" law was used to arrest an anti-Semitic priest for making an inflammatory speech. The conviction was overturned because the law was used to punish speech that merely "invited dispute" or created "a condition of unrest;" it did not actually cause a riot.[65] The same standard is used today in determining the degree of protection available to **hate speech**—speech and symbolic actions, such as cross-burning, laced with negative views toward certain groups of people. In two cases the Court ruled that government cannot selectively ban such speech based on its content, but it can increase punishment for those who physically assault minorities.[66]

Finally, assuming that a particular form of speech is protected and the statute is precisely and narrowly drawn, the Court will examine the facts of the case to see if the state's interests override those of the speaker. Can the state demonstrate that the speech posed dangers significant enough to override the free speech interests involved (meaning that the regulation would be upheld)? Or did the police make arrests because of their objection to the speech itself rather than the resulting action (meaning that the arrest would be overturned)? Thus, picketing on state-owned jailhouse grounds, which risked causing a riot inside the jail, would constitute trespassing, and the picketers' arrests would be upheld.[67] But, arresting a civil rights leader the day after he had made a protest speech in front of a courthouse and claiming that he might have caused a riot would not be allowed.[68]

Symbolic Speech

Not all speech involves words. Some actions, such as burning the American flag, take the place of speech and are commonly called **symbolic speech**. In a 1971 case, *Cohen* v. *California,* the Court expanded its protection to these types of protests. Paul Cohen had appeared in a courthouse wearing a leather jacket bearing the words "F——K THE DRAFT. STOP THE WAR." The Court might have argued that these were **fighting words**—controllable actions or obscenity forced upon a captive audience—but instead it ruled that because the offensive speech was meant to convey a larger symbolic meaning, the behavior was protected under the First Amendment. This protective view of symbolic speech led the Court in 1989 to uphold Gregory Lee Johnson's right to burn the American flag, even though many people found the action objectionable.[69]

Some symbolic speech, however, crosses the line into objectionable conduct, which can be regulated under the Constitution. In a series of cases dealing with so-called hate speech, including actions and protests that tend to defame or are intended to intimidate ethnic or religious groups, the Court ruled that although symbolic speeches such as burning crosses or painting swastikas were objectionable,

hate speech Speech or symbolic actions intended to inflict emotional distress, to defame, or to intimidate people.

symbolic speech Some actions, such as burning the American flag, that take the place of speech because they communicate a message.

fighting words Certain expressions so volatile that they are deemed to incite injury and are therefore not protected under the First Amendment.

state laws had to be carefully drawn to proscribe them. A unanimous Court over-turned a St. Paul, Minnesota, city ordinance that banned any symbol likely to arouse "anger, alarm, or resentment in others on the basis of race, color, creed, religion or gender" as both underinclusive, because it banned too few kinds of speech, and overinclusive, because it banned too many kinds.[70] However, a unanimous Court up-held state laws that enhanced penalties for such hate speech behavior.[71]

In the 1990s, this issue of symbolic protests and whether they become regu-latable conduct or are protected free speech led the Court to examine the behavior of antiabortion protesters. In an effort to protect women seeking abortion counsel-ing and procedures at abortion clinics from antiabortion protesters demonstrating and sometimes trying to block their entry, the Rehnquist Court in 1995 upheld a thirty-six-foot "no approach buffer zone" around a Florida clinic that excluded an-tiabortion protesters.[72] Two years later, the Court revisited this issue when a lower court (1) created a fifteen-foot "fixed buffer zone" around a New York clinic's door-ways and parking lot entrances in which no protesting would be allowed, (2) per-mitted two antiabortion "sidewalk counselors" to enter the zone at any time unless the target of their conversation asked them to "cease and desist," and (3) created a fifteen-foot "floating buffer zone" around anyone entering or leaving the facility—a sort of "no-protest bubble." The Supreme Court struck down the floating no-protest bubble as a violation of protesters' free speech, but upheld the fifteen-foot "fixed no protest" zone around the clinic.[73]

In 2000, the Court took another step in protecting abortion rights by upholding an unusual Colorado "bubble" law that established a one-hundred-foot "no ap-proach" zone around a "health-care facility" and prevented people from approach-ing others within eight feet to protest or pass out literature. The Court agreed that individuals had a "right to be left alone."[74]

FREEDOM OF THE PRESS

Decisions in cases that involve freedom of the press must establish a balance between the public's right to know and (1) the government's right to secrecy, (2) an indivi-dual's right to personal reputation and/or privacy, (3) a defendant's right to a fair trial, or (4) an individual's personal and moral sensibilities. To illustrate this point, ask yourself whether the public's "right to know" about a controversial criminal trial like that of Sean "P. Diddy" Combs or Kobe Bryant overrides both the defendant's right to receive a fair trial and society's right to maintain law and order. Some see the press as a critical "fourth branch," keeping a watchful eye on the government. But what if revealing certain government activities could damage national security?

Prior Restraint

Often the balance between these two sets of rights depends on the kinds of laws used to restrict the press. **Prior restraint** (censorship) laws prevent the press from revealing information *before* the government chooses to publish it. Prior restraint cases generally involve issues of national security, but they may also involve "gag or-ders" intended to preserve the right to a fair trial. In contrast, **subsequent punish-ment** laws punish writers and editors *after* they publish certain information. Such laws are used to ban libel and obscenity because they are harmful to reputations or public sensibilities. The framers were more concerned with prior restraint than with subsequent punishment, believing that a trial by a jury of peers could deal with the latter, but in reality both can be equally harmful. A threat of significant enough punishment after publication can lead the press to censor itself before publication.

Probably the most significant case involving prior restraint was the 1971 *Pentagon Papers* case. Defense Department researcher Daniel Ellsberg, who had worked on a study called "A History of the United States Decision-Making Process on Vietnam

Question for Reflection

Should people be permitted to protest anywhere they want, on any topic that they choose, given the First Amendment's mandate that "Congress shall make no law . . . abridging Freedom of Speech?"

prior restraint An action in which the government seeks to ban the publi-cation of controversial material by the press before it is published; censorship.

subsequent punishment Laws that would punish someone for an action after it has taken place. For ex-ample, laws such as those banning li-bel and obscenity because they are harmful to reputations or public sensi-bilities punish writers, editors, and pub-lishers after an item appears in print.

Policy" (the Pentagon Papers), had leaked almost all of the forty-seven-volume report to the *New York Times*, which in turn eventually passed excerpts on to the *Washington Post*. When the newspapers planned to publish excerpts from the study, the government took the extraordinary step of seeking a court injunction to prevent their publication, claiming that it would damage national security. Because of its controversial nature, the case went through the federal courts and reached the Supreme Court in the extraordinarily brief time of fifteen days. The Court ruled against prior restraint. In a concurring opinion, Justice Potter Stewart argued that prior censorship can be justified only when publication "will surely result in direct, immediate, and irreparable damage to our Nation or its people." Since the Pentagon papers were strictly historical documents, Stewart failed to see the potential for such harm.[75]

However, a closer analysis of the four concurring and three dissenting opinions reveals that the decision was not so great a victory for the press as it seemed. Five of the justices implied that if the government had tried to punish the press after publication, using laws barring the release of secret documents, the convictions would have been upheld. Accordingly, later administrations passed and enforced a series of administrative regulations and laws to prevent the divulging of secret information.

The press also faces restraints in its coverage of criminal proceedings. Judges sometimes issue gag orders barring the media from publishing information about an ongoing criminal case. In 1976, the Court declared a gag order issued by a Nebraska court in the pretrial hearing of a multiple-murder case prior restraint of the press and a First Amendment violation.[76] Because the Court extended its ruling in 1980 to open criminal trials to the press and public "absent an overriding interest to the contrary," gag orders are far less common today.[77]

Libel

The free flow of ideas in a democracy must sometimes be prevented or limited when it is untruthful, malicious, or damaging to a person's reputation or good name. Speech that has these effects is **slander**; if it appears in written form, it is **libel**. The Supreme Court has ruled that slander and libel are not protected by the First Amendment. But how does one determine whether a published statement is libelous? Some published statements may be intended to defame a person's reputation, but defamation also may stem from negligence or failure to take reasonable care in verifying information before publication. Do the latter instances also constitute libel?

The Court addressed this question in 1964, when the *New York Times* printed an advertisement critical of the racial views of unnamed public officials in Alabama. An elected commissioner in Montgomery, Alabama, L. B. Sullivan, filed suit in an Alabama court, claiming that the ad libeled him personally; he won the case under an Alabama law requiring newspapers to establish the truth of material before publishing it. The *New York Times* appealed the case to the Supreme Court. Seeking to balance the newspaper's right to publish against Sullivan's right to maintain his reputation, the Court took careful notice of Sullivan's status as a public official. Unlike private individuals, public officials can respond to published statements through such means as press conferences. On the other hand, if the press were prevented from publishing statements critical of political figures, it could not fulfill its role as a watchdog of government. So the Court ruled that convictions in cases involving libel against public officials—expanded in later cases to public figures—could be upheld only if the defamatory article had been printed with "knowledge that it was false or reckless disregard whether it was false or not." In short, the untrue and defamatory piece would have to be printed without any effort to check the facts.[78] Making only the most minimal effort to check facts, supermarket tabloids can print outrageous articles about movie stars and public figures, generally without fear of legal retribution.

Seeking to restrict the press, the Burger and Rehnquist Courts launched a two-pronged attack against the Sullivan standard. The class of people defined as "public

 **MakeItReal**

Primary Source: *The New York Times* v. *Sullivan,* 1964

slander Speech that is untruthful, malicious, or damaging to a person's reputation or good name and thus not protected by the free speech clause of the First Amendment.

libel Published material that damages a person's reputation or good name in an untruthful and malicious way. Libelous material is not protected by the First Amendment.

figures" was narrowed,[79] and the press was instructed to turn over materials indicating its "state of mind" when publishing an article claimed as libelous.[80] These changes had the effect of increasing the burden on the press to prove that it had not been negligent or malicious in publishing a statement challenged as libelous.

One trend to watch in the future is the willingness of companies to resort to libel-like suits to attempt to silence their critics. The Food Lion grocery chain sued ABC's *Primetime Live* for a report on the chain's sales of spoiled food. Rather than sue for libel, the firm sued for fraud, breach of loyalty, and trespass because the reporters were undercover. Although the grocery firm won $5.5 million in damages, most of it was reversed on appeal, leaving Food Lion with a $2 award. The Court ruled against such an end run of the First Amendment.[81] Yet another type of case will likely arise from the Internet, where statements in various Web sites might cause damage to named people or businesses. Court decisions will need to explore what kind of speech exists in this format and whether it is protected.

Obscenity

Although the First Amendment does not protect publication of obscene material, it is difficult to establish a definition of obscenity and thus judge whether or not a particular publication is obscene. In a 1957 case, *Roth* v. *United States,* the Supreme Court stated that material could be judged obscene if "the average person, applying contemporary community standards, [determines that] the dominant theme of the material, taken as a whole, appeals to the prurient interest."[82] Thus, books such as *Lady Chatterley's Lover* or *Peyton Place* could not be declared obscene because of a few scattered passages that might be offensive to a few highly susceptible people. In 1966, the Court added to the *Roth* standard the requirement that a work could be banned only if it was "utterly without redeeming social value."[83]

During the 1960s, the Warren Court developed a *variable obscenity test* in which the definition of obscenity changed according to the circumstances of the material's use or sale. Material was judged obscene if it was thrust upon a "captive audience"—for example, a pornographic outdoor drive-in movie visible from the street—or sold to unsuspecting customers such as children. In addition, material geared specifically toward customers with alternative sexual lifestyles could be banned.[84]

The confusion and uncertainty resulting from this variable standard led the Burger Court to attempt a clearer standard in the 1973 case of *Miller* v. *California.* Henceforth, the definition of material as obscene would depend on "whether the average person applying contemporary community standards would find the work taken as a whole, appeals to the prurient interest; whether the work depicts or describes, in *a patently offensive way,* sexual conduct specifically defined by the applicable state law; and whether the work taken as a whole *lacks serious literary, artistic, political, or scientific value.*"[85] In contrast to the *Roth* standard, the *Miller* standard considered local tastes. But this distinction did not solve the problem of defining obscenity. Each locality now had its own standard and applied it in varying ways to nationally distributed work. For example, the movie *Carnal Knowledge,* which depicted no sexual activity but contained a great deal of dialogue on the subject, was judged obscene in Georgia but not elsewhere.[86]

The Rehnquist Court made little progress toward establishing a clear definition of obscenity. The only clarity came in the area of child pornography, for which the Court has so little tolerance that it has permitted convictions for even the possession of obscene videos of clothed children.[87] The question of how to determine if a particular book or other published material is obscene, and thus to prevent or punish the publication of such material, remains unanswered.

One question the Court has answered for the moment, however, concerns attempts to regulate alleged pornography on the Internet; such regulation will not be allowed. In 1996, Congress passed the Communications Decency Act (CDA) seeking to protect those under the age of eighteen from "obscene or indecent" messages or "patently offensive" communications "knowingly" sent over the Internet. Although the Court in the case testing this act was committed to "protecting children from harmful materials," it found the definition of speech restricted by the Communications Decency Act too vague and the law so vague that parents could be prosecuted for how their own children used the family computer. Justice John Paul Stevens wrote for the majority that the First Amendment protects the Web's "vast democratic fora . . . where any person with a phone line can become a town crier." Thus, he explained, "in the absence of evidence to the contrary, we presume that governmental regulation of the content of speech is more likely to interfere with the free exchange of ideas than to encourage it."[88]

But Congress was not finished with its efforts to regulate the Internet to shield children from pornography. Neither was the Court with its determination to make difficult this form of restricting free speech. In 1996, Congress passed the Child Pornography Prevention Act, which made it a crime to create or distribute on the Internet virtual images of child pornography, that is, simulated computer images rather than real children engaging in sexual acts. In the 2001–2002 term, the Supreme Court struck down this law, ruling that the law was so broad that it could be used to block the simulated teen-aged sexual acts found in movies such as *Titanic* and *Traffic*.[89]

Whether this Supreme Court posture will continue remains to be seen. In 1998, Congress passed the Child Online Protection Act, which required all commercial Web sites, not just those marketing pornography, to use some form of service to protect children under age seventeen from material deemed "harmful to minors." After a Philadelphia federal appeals court blocked enforcement of this law, the Supreme Court ruled in its 2001 term that the lower court had not correctly applied the "contemporary community standards" provision of the obscenity test because the Web is worldwide. So, the lower court was instructed to reexamine the substantive provisions of the law, a ruling that will likely be revisited by the high court.[90] Then, Congress went beyond the regulation of an individual's use of the Web to pass the Children's Internet Protection Act of 2000, which requires all schools and libraries to place filters on their computers in order to protect child users from pornographic Web sites, or face the loss of millions of dollars in federal funding. In 2003, the Supreme Court upheld the law by a 6–3 majority, arguing that it did not violate the First Amendment rights of the children, the first time the Court upheld a law limiting child access to the Internet.[91] The interesting part of this battle, given the difficulty of defining pornography on the Web in a manner acceptable to the federal courts under the First Amendment, will come if Congress moves to expand its Internet regulatory efforts to deal with sites believed harmful to national security.

Confidentiality of Sources

MakeItReal

ABC News Video: *On Trial*

A major issue arose in 2005 on the confidentiality of reporters' sources after reporter Bob Novak revealed the identity of an undercover CIA agent. A government special prosecutor, Patrick Fitzgerald, began investigating if this CIA leak violated a 1982 law against revealing the identity of intelligence agents. The civil liberties question was raised when *Time* magazine reporter Matthew Cooper and *New York Times* reporter Judith Miller both faced jail for contempt of court when they refused to reveal their sources for stories they were developing on this same issue. In finding them in contempt of court, the judge relied on a 1972 Supreme Court decision that denied confidentiality of press sources when the opposing interest was a criminal investigation.[92] As it turned out, Miller did not even publish the name of the agent, yet she ended up going to jail. Cooper avoided jail time when *Time* released his notes, following the Supreme Court's refusal to hear the reporters' appeals. The notes revealed that his source had been presidential adviser Karl Rove. By mid-2005, with the grand jury still considering its evidence, President Bush said that he would fire anyone convicted of a crime for leaking this secret information. After eighty-five days in jail, Judith Miller was finally released when she secured the permission of her source, Lewis Libby, chief of staff to Vice President Dick Cheney, to reveal his name to the grand jury. Shortly thereafter, Libby was indicted on charges of making false statements to the grand jury and obstruction of justice and resigned from his position. After the *New York Times* published an extensive examination of this controversy, Ms. Miller retired from the newspaper. But seeing that the question of reporters and source confidentiality when writing about the government would not disappear, Congress began to consider the possibility of passing a federal shield law to legally create confidentiality for such sources.[93]

Question for Reflection

Should the federal government pass a national "shield law" making reporters' sources confidential, or should the names of sources of government leaks continue to be available to government investigators?

THE RIGHTS OF DEFENDANTS

The framers, fearful of the kinds of abuses that had prevailed under British rule, considered protection of the rights of defendants vital. The Bill of Rights therefore contains several safeguards against government oppression, including the right to be left alone in one's home (Fourth Amendment), the right to remain silent (Fifth Amendment), and the right to be represented by counsel (Sixth Amendment). Remarkably, despite many changes in the technology of police work, these guarantees remain as vital today as they were two hundred years ago. Whether searches involve ransacking one's belongings under a writ of assistance or using technology to monitor one's computer or conversations, the balance remains between the rights of the individual and the rights of society. However, as in many other areas involving civil liberties, this balance depends on the Supreme Court's composition at any given time. No issue better illustrates this fact than the shifting nature of Fourth Amendment protection over the past three decades.

The Fourth Amendment

The Fourth Amendment tries to balance two rights: the individual's reasonable expectation of privacy and society's right to control crime and protect the public. Over the years, the Supreme Court has devised different rules for establishing this balance. During the 1960s, the Warren Court "revolution" greatly expanded the protection provided by the expectation of privacy, but in subsequent decades the Burger and Rehnquist Courts shifted the balance back toward the state (that is, the police). These shifts have had significant effects on both the nation's approach to, and recession from, democracy as expressed by the constrained and then increased power of the state to investigate and imprison people.

Many issues related to Fourth Amendment protections stem from the amendment's lack of an explicitly written remedy. What can a judge do if the police go too far in conducting a search? Can the evidence uncovered by such an illegal search be used in a trial? In other words, can the police break the law to uphold the law? As Justice Benjamin Cardozo put it, should "the criminal . . . go free because the constable had blundered"?[94] Debates over this issue center on the creation of an **exclusionary rule**, whereby evidence gathered by illegal means cannot be used in later trials. Likewise, under another doctrine, the *fruit of the poisonous tree*, no other evidence can be used that was gathered as a result of other searches or investigations based on an initially illegal search.

The exclusionary rule was created in 1914 in the case of *Weeks* v. *United States*,[95] which prevented federal courts from using illegally gathered evidence in a trial. This rule, it was argued, not only protected the privacy rights of the individual defendant but also deterred the authorities from conducting illegal searches in future cases. However, the rule gave rise to problems both legal and symbolic. In certain cases, it prevented the use of hard, observable evidence, thus possibly allowing guilty individuals to go free.[96]

Since the Fourth Amendment did not yet apply to the states, the exclusionary rule could be used only in federal cases. In ruling on the admissibility of illegally

exclusionary rule Rule whereby evidence gathered by illegal means, and any other evidence gathered as a result, cannot be used in later trials.

Approaching Democracy Around the Globe

Beyond London: Securing Liberty in the European Union

Within days of the terrorist bombings in London on July 7, 2005, British authorities had figured out who was responsible, thanks to an extensive system of surveillance cameras. Set up because of the earlier terrorists' threat of the Irish Republican Army, this surveillance system was so extensive that for years the government had used it to fine people for dropping gum on the streets. But for all its ability to solve the crime, Great Britain was all but powerless to prevent this or future terrorist attacks because Parliament and the courts forbid wiretapping or electronic eavesdropping that would alert authorities to crimes ahead of time. In contrast, other countries, such as the United States and France, lean more toward security, allowing an early warning system of detection using extensive electronic surveillance.

With the London attack coming on the heels of the 2004 Madrid train attacks, European Union countries began to review their terrorism security procedures to decide whether to follow the English "protecting liberty" model or the American/French "increasing security" model. Under the Schengen Agreement of 1990, citizens of European Union countries are entitled to free passage between member nations. However, in 2005, France decided to resume checking passports at what had long been an open border with the other European nations. Italy announced that it would beef up its northern border guards and, just two weeks after the London attacks, approved a new set of security laws that allowed authorities to obtain DNA samples from terrorism suspects, to imprison anyone who teaches how to use explosives, and to detain terrorism suspects for twenty-four hours without being charged or having access to their attorneys. Acting at the request of Interior

Minister Giuseppe Pisanu, more than three hundred terrorism suspects were rounded up for questioning. Germany began plans to create an antiterrorism database. For the first time, all of the European nations began, at the request of the British, to compel telecommunications firms to store all e-mails, text messages, Internet logs, and phone records for up to three years. Cell phone records were crucial in tracing the London bombers.

The major problem has been to find a way to encourage the nations to cooperate. "You're not going to have a European FBI. But these bombings are making people think seriously about European security as an EU-wide problem," says Rolf Tophoven, of the Institute for Terrorism Research and Security Policy in Germany. But this will be difficult, with each nation having a different intelligence service, a different kind of judicial system, and varying kinds of national structures. While some complained at the loss of liberty implied by these changes, British Home Secretary Charles Clarke said of the balancing process: "I absolutely accept that civil liberty is a genuine concern for any democrat. The point I want to make is that the human right to travel on the underground in London on a Thursday morning without being blown up is also an important right." With all of these changes, it was clear that the London and Madrid attacks had changed the political calculation of the liberty versus security balance forever.

Based on Mark Rice-Oxley, "How Far Will Europe Go to Stop Terror?" *Christian Science Monitor*, July 15, 2005; Natasha Bita, "Freedom in a Wrestle with Security Reform," *Nationwide News*, July 16, 2005; Author interview with Edward Turzanski, National Security, Intelligence, Political Analyst, LaSalle University, July 18, 2005 (by phone).

seized evidence in state cases, the Supreme Court used the Fourteenth Amendment's due process clause. It held that only the results of searches that "shocked the conscience" of the justices could be barred from use in trials. The problem here was that different justices were shocked by different things. Justice Felix Frankfurter, the inventor of this test, was shocked by a case in which police officers broke into the office of a doctor suspected of performing abortions to find his patient book to use in making up a list of witnesses and by a case in which a man's stomach was pumped to retrieve two morphine capsules.[97] He was not, however, shocked by a case that involved taking blood from an unconscious man to determine whether he was drunk.[98] Many of Frankfurter's fellow justices disagreed with his views. Not until after Frankfurter's retirement in 1962 did the Court begin to consider extending the Fourth Amendment exclusionary rule guarantee to defendants in state courts.

The Due Process Revolution   In the case of Dollree Mapp in 1961, the Warren Court made its landmark ruling on the nature of the Fourth Amendment and its application to the states. The case began when the Cleveland police received a tip from a "reliable authority" that a "suspected bomber of a house porch and bookmaker" was in Mapp's home. When Mapp refused to let the police in, three officers broke into the house, waving a blank piece of paper in the air and claiming that it was a search warrant. After Mapp stuffed the "warrant" inside her blouse, the officers tried to retrieve it and handcuffed Mapp for resisting their search. The search through the house produced no bomber or bookmaker, but the officers arrested and the court convicted Mapp for possessing obscene materials.[99]

While this episode might have "shocked the conscience" of the justices in an earlier day, in this case the Court made the *Weeks* exclusionary rule part of the Fourth Amendment and then incorporated it into the Fourteenth Amendment to apply it to the states. Thus the exclusionary rule was made uniform among the states and between the state and federal levels of government. Mapp's conviction was reversed and her case was sent back to the state court for a retrial, but with the pornographic materials now excluded from the new trial, the state had no choice but to drop the charges.

Limiting the Exclusionary Rule   During the Burger Court years, the justices were unhappy that under the exclusionary rule even the most minor police violations led to loss of all the evidence. The Court began to argue that the exclusionary rule should be restricted or eliminated, saying that it had little or no deterrent effect on police.[100] It began to question if any possible deterrent effect of the rule outweighed the possible harm to society from allowing guilty individuals to go free because improperly gathered evidence was excluded from the trial.

After limiting the use of the exclusionary rule in various criminal justice proceedings, such as the grand jury[101] and habeas corpus proceedings in which convicted defendants were seeking a new trial,[102] the Court greatly reduced its application in the 1984 case of *United States* v. *Leon*. Federal authorities had received a warrant to search certain houses and cars for drugs, based on an unreliable informer's outdated tips. The Warren Court would have voided the search and excluded the use of its evidence, but the Burger Court ruled that since the police believed they had a valid search warrant, the resulting evidence could be used in a trial.[103] This reasoning became known as the *good faith exception* to the Fourth Amendment. "Good faith" was not defined, but the watering-down effect on the exclusionary rule was clear. Evidence that once could have been excluded could now be allowed if the Court was persuaded through "reasonably objective" criteria that the police believed the search to be valid.

The Rehnquist Court appeared willing to extend the good faith exception to cases in which no search warrant was issued. In *Illinois* v. *Rodriguez,* for example, officers relied on the word of a woman who said that she had a right to enter her ex-boyfriend's apartment. Searching the apartment with her consent, they found illegal drugs. Despite the fact that the woman actually had no right to admit the police, the Court ruled that since the police had relied on her word in good faith, the search was permissible.[104] In 1995, the Court allowed as evidence a bag of marijuana found after police searched a car based on a faulty computer report of a misdemeanor charge against the driver.[105]

Warrantless Searches   Another way in which the Court can affect Fourth Amendment rights is by broadening or contracting the nature of searches for which judges have not issued warrants. The Fourth Amendment defines a proper search as one in which a proper search warrant has been issued after the police have demonstrated to a neutral judge **probable cause**. Probable cause means that there is enough evidence to convince a reasonable person that a search should be undertaken because a crime has been or is about to be committed, and investigators are likely to find evidence of such a crime at a particular location. Only then will the judge issue a warrant stating specifically where and for what police can search. But in cases where there isn't time to obtain a warrant, the amendment protects people against unreasonable searches. What, then, is a "reasonable search"?

probable cause A reasonable belief that a crime has been, is being, or is about to be committed. Searches also require a belief that evidence of that crime may be located in a particular place. Police must establish this to a judge to secure a search warrant or retroactively justify a search that has already taken place.

▲ Not all unwarranted searches and seizures are illegal or suspect. In many states it is implied that drivers have to take a breathalyzer test to check possible impairment from alcohol.

Suppose a police officer stops a car, suspecting that it is carrying illegal weapons. Obviously, the officer has no time to obtain a warrant. If the officer can later demonstrate that the search was "reasonable," it will be allowed under a *movable automobile exception* to the Fourth Amendment.[106] The rationale in such a case is that delaying for a warrant may place the officer's safety in jeopardy or allow the car and evidence to escape, or both. On the other hand, what if a police officer enters a private house to speak with the occupant about a problem in the neighborhood and sees a Sidewinder missile hanging above the mantel? As long as the officer can give a valid reason for being there, justifiably believes what she sees is incriminating, and can legally proceed to it, she can seize what is in "plain view" as evidence, even without a warrant.

In all Fourth Amendment cases, then, the central issue is whether or not a suspect's "expectation of privacy" is outweighed by the state's need to control crime by preserving evidence and ensuring the safety of police officers. As the Court said in *Katz* v. *United States,* a case ruling electronic surveillance of public phone booths to be unconstitutional: "The Fourth Amendment protects people, not places. What a person knowingly exposes to the public, even in his own home or office, is not a subject of Fourth Amendment protection. . . . But what he seeks to preserve as private, even in an area accessible to the public, may be constitutionally protected."[107] However, many other exceptions to the Fourth Amendment have been created, including searches incident to a lawful arrest (on the person and within the person's reach), consent searches (if the suspect permits the search, the Fourth Amendment protection is waived), searches of fleeing suspects who might destroy evidence, and various kinds of administrative searches (for example, in airports and at national borders).[108] The 2001 USA Patriot Act gave significant latitude to civil authorities in their investigations of alleged terrorism, enabling them to search multiple locations using "one-stop shopping" warrants and wiretaps for all phones used by suspects (including public phones).

The evolution of the *stop-and-frisk exception* shows clearly the pattern of expanding and contracting Fourth Amendment rights. A stop-and-frisk case is one in which the police detain a person and conduct a *pat-down search* of that person's outer clothing without a warrant or an arrest, basing their action on observed, potentially criminal conduct. The Warren Court first defined the constitutional limits of such searches in 1968 in *Terry* v. *Ohio,* in which an experienced Ohio police officer had observed two men apparently planning to burglarize a store. The officer approached the men, asked them some questions, and then patted down their clothing; the search revealed revolvers and bullets concealed under their jackets, and the officer thereupon arrested the men. The Court ruled that even though the officer lacked probable cause to arrest the suspects for the robbery until after he had conducted a full search, the initial frisk was legal because he could justify stopping the suspects in the first place.[109]

The Burger and Rehnquist Courts have watered down individual protections under the Fourth Amendment. First, the Court has developed a notion of *reasonable suspicion* or reasonableness of a search, balancing the expectation of privacy interests of the defendant against the investigation interests of the state. In the 1985 case *New Jersey* v. *T.L.O,* the Supreme Court lowered the standard for searching in public schools in a case involving the search of a female student's purse. She was suspected of smoking because a school administrator stopped her as she left a women's rest room that had smoke billowing out of its vents into the hallway. At the same time as he saw the cigarettes, the administrator saw a package of rolling papers that led him to search further for drugs. Further search of her purse revealed other drug paraphernalia and a large amount of money. The purse's zipped-shut side pocket yielded lists of student names with dollar amounts next to them. The student was suspended for drug sales. The Court held that this search was justifiable because the vice principal had "reasonable suspicion." In response to the Court's holding that two searches were made here, one justified by smoke and the other by the rolling papers, Justice William Brennan argued that a third search occurred, of the zipped pocket, where the student had a greater "expectation of privacy."[110]

In 1991, the Rehnquist Court decided two cases involving stop-and-frisk searches. In the first, the Court ruled that police need only make a "show of authority" by ordering a person to halt; if the person runs away, the police have the right to "seize" the person and "search" his or her possessions.[111] In the second case, the Court allowed the practice of "working the buses," in which police officers board a bus on which a person suspected of possessing drugs is a passenger and announce that they are going to search the belongings of everyone aboard. According to Justice Sandra Day O'Connor, as long as each of the passengers feels free to decline the officers' request for a search "or otherwise terminate the encounter," such a search is legal.[112]

By 1995, the Court, speaking through Antonin Scalia, expanded the *T.L.O.* case to uphold the random drug-testing of all student athletes in Vernonia, Oregon, public schools. School administrators had determined that this was the only way to root out the drug culture they believed existed in the athletic community. In dissent, Justice Sandra Day O'Connor argued that the appellant, Jamie Acton, had absolutely no personal history of drugs, meaning that the school lacked the "individualized suspicion" to require this test.[113] Schools across the nation began expanding their drug-testing programs beyond athletes to students in extracurricular activities, and even to students seeking parking privileges on school grounds. The breadth of the Court's holding was tested in 2002 in a challenge involving a small town near Oklahoma City that randomly drug tested all students in any competitive extra-curricular activity (including debate, choir, school plays, and the Future Homemakers of America). Said Lindsey Earls, now a student at Dartmouth but tested in high school because she was in the marching band, "I know the Supreme Court, in the *Vernonia* case, talked about how athletes have a risk of physical harm. But we're not going to hurt ourselves in choir."[114] Here the Court ruled by a narrow 5–4 margin that such drug testing was constitutional because school officials believed it was the only way drugs could be controlled in their school district.[115] This ruling takes on even more importance given some communities' policy of drug testing all public school students. The Court's allowance of such sweeping searches, citing a "war on drugs," resembles similarly sweeping searches, using other techniques, approved by the 2001 USA Patriot Act and conducted in the U.S. war on terrorism.

Seeking to expand police searching powers, the Court relied on the wording of the concurring opinion by Justice John Harlan in the *Katz* case to develop another exception to the *expectation of privacy standard*. In trying to explain why a person could justifiably expect privacy in a glass-enclosed, public phone booth, Harlan argued: "There is a twofold requirement, first that a person have exhibited an actual (subjective) expectation of privacy and, second, that the expectation be one that society is prepared to recognize as 'reasonable.'" Harlan was only trying to say that the phone booth was "a temporarily private place whose momentary occupants' expectations of freedom from intrusion are recognized as reasonable."[116] In recent years, conservative jurists have been seizing on that concept of societal expectation of privacy to argue that society would not accept the claims of other privacy rights to be reasonable.

In cases that focus on crime control, almost every scenario can somehow be justified using these standards of societal expectation of privacy or reasonable suspicion. This was made clear in 2000 when the Court ruled that running at the mere sight of a police officer in a high-crime area justifies police in stopping and searching the suspect because the act of running constituted "reasonable suspicion."[117] In

Quick Review

The Fourth Amendment

- Tries to balance two rights: the individual's reasonable expectation of privacy and society's right to control crime and protect the public.
- The Supreme Court has devised different rules for establishing this balance.
- The Warren Court of the 1960s greatly expanded the protection provided by the expectation of privacy.
- The Burger and Rehnquist Courts shifted the balance back toward the state.

2002, the Court used these concepts of reasonable suspicion and societal expectation of privacy to rule on the practice of police sweeps for drugs and weapons on buses, with one officer kneeling at the front of the bus while two others worked their way forward questioning and searching passengers without first informing them that they had the right to refuse permission to be searched. The Court ruled that this practice was constitutional because under the "totality of circumstances" rule such a search would be permissible if the police wished to make a similar kind of search of a suspect off the bus. In the future, police might be able to use this ruling to justify their educated guesses in selecting suspects to search in cases such as antiterrorism searches.[118] Another case that might add to the search arsenal in antiterrorism cases is a Nevada case in which the Supreme Court upheld a state statute that people must identify themselves to police who request their names, even though that name might then be entered into a computer database to search for outstanding warrants. This decision led to the creation of the REAL ID national identification card by 2008 to aid in national efforts to search for potential terrorism suspects.[119]

When combined with a 2001 case involving the use of technology to search, this ruling made for a potentially powerful tool in the effort to combat terrorism. In a Florida case, *Kyllo* v. *U.S.*, a man named Kyllo was arrested for growing marijuana in his home after police used a thermal imaging device to discover the "hot" portions of his home where the plant was grown. The Supreme Court overturned this search because, as Justice Scalia explained for the majority, this device was not yet in common use and seemed to be measuring heat inside the house from outside. However, it was clear from the opinions that in time this kind of search might become acceptable under the Fourth Amendment (especially because fire departments routinely use such devices to find lost firefighters in burning buildings).[120] Thermal imaging and other new technologies, such as "puffer devices" that can test the air around a person for the smell of explosive devices, offer new potential for successful searches but also raise vexing questions about the balance between liberty and security.

All of these decisions have led to discussions between the federal government and the judicial system as to the reach of their Fourth Amendment powers dealing with electronic surveillance for antiterrorism investigations. In October 2002, a review of just three months of the FISA court's handling of FBI requests for wiretap surveillance search warrants on terrorist suspects revealed that seventy-five such warrants were based on misrepresented information and that some of these searches extended to citizens not under suspicion. A month later, though, a special federal appeals court ruled that under the Patriot Act the Justice Department could apply for counterintelligence wiretaps on "agents of a foreign power," including e-mail–monitoring programs, and use them in prosecutions. Legal testing of this practice began in a 2005 prosecution of a Florida university professor, Sami al-Arian, who was charged with but not convicted of aiding the Palestinian Islamic Jihad terrorist group based on evidence including more than twenty thousand hours of monitored phone calls and faxes, authorized by the FISA court.[121] (See Figure 13.1.)

The Fifth and Sixth Amendments

The safeguards contained in the Fifth and Sixth Amendments were designed to prevent the worst practices of early English criminal law, such as secret interrogation and torture. In addition to guaranteeing the right not to be compelled to witness against oneself in a criminal trial, the Fifth Amendment provides the right to a grand jury, protection against double jeopardy (being tried twice for the same offense), and a guarantee against state government's taking of one's property for public use without due process of law and just compensation. To the guarantee of a right to counsel in criminal cases, the Sixth Amendment adds the rights to a speedy and public trial by an impartial jury, to be informed of the nature of the charges against oneself, to be confronted with the witnesses against oneself, and to compel the appearance of wit-

Quick Review

Fifth Amendment

- Provides the right to a grand jury.
- Protection against double jeopardy (being tried twice for the same offense).
- Guarantee against state government's taking of one's property for public use without due process of law and just compensation.

AMERICAN PUBLIC SUPPORT FOR THE WAR ON TERRORISM
"Here are some increased powers of investigation that law enforcement agencies might use when dealing with people suspected of terrorist activity, which would also affect our civil liberties. For each, please say if you would favor or oppose it. . . ."

	Favor %	Oppose %	Unsure %
"Stronger document and physical security checks for travelers"			
2/7–14/06	84	15	1
9/19–24/01	93	6	1
"Expanded under-cover activities to penetrate groups under suspicion"			
2/7–14/06	82	17	1
9/19–24/01	93	5	1
"Closer monitoring of banking and credit card transactions, to trace funding sources"			
2/7–14/06	66	33	1
9/19–24/01	81	17	2
"Expanded camera surveillance on streets and in public places"			
2/7–14/06	67	32	1
9/19–24/01	63	35	2
"Adoption of a national I.D. system for all U.S. citizens"			
2/7–14/06	64	34	2
9/19–24/01	68	28	4
"Law enforcement monitoring of Internet discussions in chat rooms and other forums"			
2/7–14/06	60	39	1
9/19–24/01	63	32	5
"Expanded government monitoring of cell phones and e-mail, to intercept communications"			
2/7–14/06	44	55	1
9/19–24/01	54	41	4

Harris Poll. Feb. 7-14, 2006. Reported *www.pollingreport.com*, last accessed on February 28, 2006.

Figure 13.1
Notice in this comparison of polling data on various aspects of the government's "War On Terrorism" recorded from just after the 9/11 attack and later in February, 2006 in a sea of public support for the use of investigative powers for the "war on terrorism" how the public support has flipped on the issue of intercepting cell phone and email communications. Likely this is the result of the revelations about the Bush Administration's warrantless National Security Administration interception of phone communications. Harris Poll. Feb. 7–14, 2006.
Reported www.pollingreport.com, last accessed on February 28, 2006.

nesses in one's defense. Such safeguards are vital to a democratic society and constitute a basic difference between democracies and totalitarian governments.

Like all the other civil liberties discussed in this chapter, the rights of accused persons have been subject to interpretation by the Supreme Court. Before the Fifth and Sixth Amendments were applied to the states, the Court used the due process clause of the Fourteenth Amendment in deciding cases involving police interrogations.[122] In such cases, the justices examined the totality of circumstances of an interrogation to determine the "voluntariness" of a confession. If the "totality of circumstances" (the conditions under which the defendant had been questioned) indicated that a confession was involuntary, it would not be allowed in a trial. If, on the other hand, the suspect had flagged down a police car or walked into a station house and started to confess before a question could be asked, or even after police had made the statements, the confession would be considered voluntary. Voluntariness was an elusive concept, defying clear measurement, however. In one case, the court judged that a defendant had been compelled to confess because he had been refused the right to call his wife before talking to the police.[123]

Quick Review

Sixth Amendment
- Guarantees right to counsel in criminal cases.
- Provides the right to a speedy and public trial by an impartial jury.
- Right to be informed of the nature of the charges against oneself.
- Right to be confronted with the witnesses against oneself, and to compel the appearance of witnesses in one's defense.

After the protections of the Fifth and Sixth Amendments were extended to the states, the Court began to explore whether a person could be compelled to confess simply by being confronted by the police. This question was the central issue in a 1964 case, *Escobedo* v. *Illinois,* in which a man had been arrested for the murder of his brother-in-law and questioned by police without being allowed to see his attorney, who was then in the police station. The Supreme Court ruled that police questioning of suspects for the purpose of gaining a confession was just as important as the trial itself. Once the police had gone beyond the general investigation phase of their interrogation by seeking to secure a confession, they had shifted "from the investigatory to the accusatory" phase, and, under the Sixth and Fourteenth Amendments, the suspect had the right to have counsel present.[124]

But should defendants be warned of their right to silence, and just how far may the police go in their questioning? The answers came two years later in the case of *Miranda* v. *Arizona.* If you watch movies or television you have surely seen police officers recite the so-called **Miranda warning** to a suspect before questioning:

> You have the right to remain silent. Anything you say can and will be used against you. You have the right to an attorney. If you cannot afford an attorney, one will be provided for you. Do you understand these rights, and are you willing to speak with us?

The requirement to inform suspects of their rights stems from the *Miranda* case, in which a slightly psychotic produce worker given to flights of fantasy had confessed to a kidnapping and rape after only two hours of questioning in which the police lied in saying that the victim had identified him. The Court ruled that all police questioning was "inherently compulsory" and that confessions were therefore "inherently untrustworthy." Before questioning a suspect who had been taken into custody or "deprived of his freedom in any significant way," the police had to offer the warning just described. Otherwise, statements made by the accused could not be used in a trial or to gather related evidence.[125]

This ruling was highly controversial. It looked as if the Court was legislating new rules that would make convicting known felons impossible. In reality, the Court merely applied to the states the practices that the Federal Bureau of Investigation had long used in interrogating suspects. Still, the outcry against the "criminal-coddling Warren Court" did serious damage to the Court's prestige and led critics to demand that the decision be reversed.

Rather than overturning *Miranda* directly, the Burger and Rehnquist Courts chipped away at its underpinnings to such an extent that little of it remains in force. The Burger Court increased the range of situations in which confessions could be used in a trial even if the suspect had not been read the Miranda warning, such as to impeach the credibility of a witness.[126] Hints of the Court's future direction seemed apparent in a 1974 case called *Michigan* v. *Tucker,* in which a suspect was convicted partly based on an alibi witness he had named to police in a statement offered without full observance of the *Miranda* guarantees. In the majority opinion upholding use of the evidence, William Rehnquist argued that the Fifth Amendment right against self-incrimination did not require Miranda; it was merely a "prophylactic standard," or protective device, replaceable by other means to safeguard the voluntariness of a suspect's statements to police. Rehnquist seemed to be saying that if he had the votes, *Miranda* could be overturned. In later cases, police also received more leeway to encourage a suspect to confess, such as by making statements in his presence rather than questioning the suspect directly;[127] asking a suspect only where his or her weapon was located for the purposes of securing "public safety;"[128] and questioning a suspect twice, reading him or her the warning after a "voluntary" confession had been secured.[129]

After William Rehnquist's ascension to the chief justiceship, overturning the *Miranda* precedent seemed to become his personal odyssey. The Rehnquist Court seemed on the road toward overturning *Miranda* in the 1991 case of *Arizona* v.

Miranda warning A warning that must be recited by police officers to a suspect before questioning: "You have the right to remain silent; anything you say can and will be used against you. You have the right to an attorney. If you cannot afford an attorney, one will be provided for you. Do you understand these rights and are you willing to speak with us?" Established in *Miranda* v. *Arizona,* 1966.

Fulminante, in which a prisoner confessed to murdering his stepdaughter to a fellow inmate who offered to protect him from harm but was in fact working as an FBI informer. The Court ruled that such confessions could be used in trials, even this arguably involuntary one in which the defendant did not realize that he was speaking to an agent of the police.[130]

In 2000, the Court and Chief Justice Rehnquist had the opportunity to reconsider *Miranda* directly in the case of Charles Thomas Dickerson. Dickerson was interrogated by an FBI agent in January 1997 about a bank robbery in Alexandria, Virginia. After a few hours of questioning, Dickerson admitted that he knew about the robbery. Although the officer said that the *Miranda* warnings had been given before the incriminating statement was made, Dickerson said that the warnings came after he had made his statement—meaning that the confession should be invalidated.

This case tested the constitutionality of Section 3501 of Title 18 of the United States Code, called the Omnibus Crime Control and Safe Streets Act, passed just two years after *Miranda.* The law stated that confessions could be admitted into federal trials if they were given "voluntarily," based on an examination of the "totality of circumstances" of the questioning. Although this contradicted Chief Justice Earl Warren's argument that any questioning by police was "inherently compulsory," it was widely anticipated that Chief Justice Rehnquist and the conservative majority would take this opportunity to overturn *Miranda.*

To the surprise of many, the Court upheld the *Miranda* case by a 7–2 vote, with even its most vocal critic, Chief Justice Rehnquist, voting with the majority and writing the opinion. In overturning Section 3501, Justice Rehnquist argued, as the Court did in the *City of Boerne* free exercise of religion case, that "*Miranda,* being a constitutional decision of this Court, may not be in effect overruled by an act of Congress." Rehnquist further explained that the *Miranda* warnings should continue because they "have become part of our national culture" and have "become embedded in routine police practice." Because the warnings caused no measurable difficulties for prosecutors, the Court saw no reason to overturn the case.[131] Just why the Chief Justice wrote the majority opinion in this way is unclear, but although *Miranda* still exists as a legal precedent, studies have found that police continually search for ways to avoid having suspects "lawyer up" in their questioning.[132]

MakeItReal

ABC News Video: *American Justice*

Although the Fourth, Fifth, and Sixth Amendments protect most basic rights of accused persons, the full nature and precise limits of those rights are subject to judicial interpretation. This tension between public safety and the rights of the accused that makes defendants' civil liberties a source of continuing debate also applies to the rights of accused terrorists. In July 2005, U.S. District Court judge Audrey B. Collins of Los Angeles struck down the Patriot Act ban on providing "expert advice" or "training" to foreign terrorist organizations as being unconstitutionally vague. In this case, Judge Collins ruled in favor of groups seeking to aid Sri Lankans displaced by the December 2004 tsunami but fearing prosecution if the Justice Department declared them terrorist organizations. This decision, and future decisions dealing with the nature of the Fifth Amendment's protections against certain types of questioning of terrorist suspects, will help to refine the meaning of this clause.[133]

The Eighth Amendment

ABC NEWS/PRENTICE HALL VIDEO LIBRARY

Crime & Punishment

Debate over whether the death penalty violates the Eighth Amendment's "Cruel and Unusual Punishment" clause has existed since the Supreme Court ruled in 1976 in the case of *Furman* v. *Georgia* that this form of punishment cannot be implemented in an "arbitrary and capricious manner." As of January 2006, 1,004 prisoners had been put to death and 3,383 people sat on death row, a disproportionate number of them minorities. However, the standards for determining who will live and who will die vary widely around the nation (see Figure 13.2). In July 2000, President Bill Clinton postponed the first federal execution in nearly forty years when a

U.S.A. Yesterday and Today

Civil Liberties in Wartime

When Chief Justice William Rehnquist wrote in his book *All the Laws But One* that during wartime the government and its judges in interpreting the Constitution generally operated under the Roman rule of *"Inter arma silent leges,"* or "In time of war, the laws are silent," it seemed that the current Supreme Court might be unwilling to protect civil liberties. Rehnquist also pointed out that "Generally, Chief Executives in wartime are not very sympathetic to the protection of civil liberties." On another occasion, he added that the laws in such times "speak with a muted voice." But although the Bush administration has followed the historical pattern in moving toward increasing security, the federal courts have not been so willing to do the same.

Throughout American history, the government during times of crisis has generally responded by restricting liberties first, backing off from those restrictions after the crisis had passed, and later apologizing for those actions. The 1798 Alien and Sedition Acts that jailed opponents of John Adams' Federalist administration were repealed in Thomas Jefferson's following administration. The Supreme Court ruled Lincoln's imposition of martial law at the beginning of the Civil War unconstitutional after the war ended. The 1920s "Red Raids" of Attorney General A. Mitchell Palmer and the McCarthy "witch hunts" for Communists in the 1950s were later overturned by the federal courts and criticized by historians. The World War II internment of 120,000 Japanese American citizens so embarrassed the nation that in 1988 Congress ordered reparations to be paid to survivors. In the 2004 case of *Hamdi* v. *Rumsfeld* the Court dealt with the case of a Louisiana-born Saudi American who was seized while fighting with the Taliban in the Afghanistan War. Military authorities declared Yaser Esam Hamdi an "enemy combatant," making him subject to military and not civilian courts, and held him in prison for two years. The Court ruled that "a state of war is not a blank check for the president" and that Hamdi was entitled to a hearing before a "neutral decision maker." Justice Sandra Day O'Connor wrote: ". . . .[I]ndefinite detention for the purpose of interrogation is not authorized." She later added, "History and common sense teach us that an unchecked system of detention carries the potential to become a means for oppression and abuse of others." The government was required to grant Hamdi a civilian court hearing where the charge that he was an "enemy combatant" could be answered. After the ruling, the government moved to deport Hamdi to Saudi Arabia rather than try him.

The Supreme Court has been supportive of civil liberties in its handling of civil liberties cases emerging from the current war on terrorism. In the case of *Rasul* v. *Bush*

federal study determined that more than three-quarters of the defendants in federal capital cases belonged to minority groups.

Rules were changing in certain states, too. In March 2000, outgoing governor George Ryan of Illinois placed a moratorium on use of the death penalty in his state when thirteen men were cleared by discovery of new evidence and released from death row. Many of these cases were developed by classes of undergraduate students of David Protess, a journalism professor at Northwestern University, who found evidence clearing these men and even at times pointing toward the real criminals. Meanwhile, nationally, as of January 2006, 122 people had been cleared of death-penalty sentences, many on the basis of DNA evidence. Although only two states—Illinois and New York—grant inmates the right to have their DNA tested, the vast majority of the American people want that right guaranteed to suspects. In June 2000, the most extensive U.S. study of the death penalty found that nearly two out of every three death penalty convictions were overturned on appeal because of incompetent lawyers or overzealous police investigators. The study examined nearly 5,800 death penalty convictions and found that 75 percent of those whose death penalties were set aside were later

▼ Northwestern journalism professor David Protess shares a laugh with Anthony Porter, a former death row inmate who was freed as a result of investigations by Professor Protess's class. As of December 2005 that class has helped to clear 19 prisoners.

the Court dealt with whether federal courts had jurisdiction over terrorism suspects held incommunicado without being charged and without limits on their detention in Camp X-Ray in Guantanamo Bay, Cuba. Here the Court ruled that the federal courts did have jurisdiction to hear appeals from prisoners who claimed that they were being wrongly held. Justice John Paul Stevens suggested that the federal courts had jurisdiction in the Guantanamo Bay camp and perhaps even in foreign countries. This led Justice Antonin Scalia to complain in dissent that "the court boldly extends the scope of the habeas statute to the four corners of the earth."

Eventually, more cases will be brought before the Supreme Court to test the extent of civil liberties during the war on terrorism. Beyond the question of presidential and government powers in wartime will be the question of who defines when this country is at war and how long that war will continue. And now that the Supreme Court has two new conservative members appointed by President Bush, and has shown itself increasingly willing to inject itself into such questions, it surely will decide the constitutionality of those matters.

▲ American Army Pfc. Lynndie R. England was sentenced to three years in prison and dishonorably discharged for her role in the torturing and humiliation of prisoners at the Abu Ghraib prison near Baghdad during the Iraq war. This photo and others like it triggered waves of anti-American sentiment in Arab and Muslim countries.

Jerry Markon, "Consider Padilla Case," *Washington Post,* July 18, 2005; Linda Greenhouse, "Access to Courts," *New York Times,* June 29, 2004; Linda Greenhouse, "Detention Cases Before Supreme Court Will Test Limits of Presidential Power," *New York Times,* April 18, 2004.

given a lesser sentence on retrial. Only 18 percent of those overturned cases resulted in another death sentence.[134]

In mid-2002, the Supreme Court issued a major ruling on the death penalty indicating that this sentence was now under review. The Court ruled 6–3 in *Atkins* v. *Virginia* that executing a mentally retarded defendant would constitute "cruel and unusual punishment" in violation of the Eighth Amendment. In their view, when eighteen of the thirty-eight states with death penalty laws recently passed provisions banning the execution of mentally challenged defendants, those moves indicated "evolving standards of decency that mark the progress of a maturing society" against this practice. Justice Scalia countered with a vigorous dissent: "Today's decision is the pinnacle of our Eighth Amendment death-is-different jurisprudence. Not only does it, like all of that jurisprudence, find no support in the text or history of the Eighth Amendment; it does not even have support in current social attitudes regarding the conditions that render an otherwise just death penalty inappropriate." Labeling the Court's majority opinion as "merely the subjective views of individual Justices," Scalia challenged their use of foreign legal sources to support their argument: "But the Prize for the Court's Most Feeble Effort to fabricate 'national consensus' must go to its appeal (deservedly relegated to a footnote) to the views of assorted professional and religious organizations, members of the so-called 'world community,' and respondents to opinion polls. . . . I agree with

Figure 13.2   Executions by State, 1976–2005

Source: The Death Penalty Information Center, found at http://www.deathpenaltyinfo.org/, last accessed on February 28, 2006

the [chief justice] that the views of professional and religious organizations and the results of opinion polls are irrelevant."[135]

Three years later, a narrow majority ruled in 2005 in *Roper* v. *Simmons* that executing a minor was "cruel and unusual punishment" and should be banned under the Constitution. Once more, the Court, led by Anthony Kennedy, relied on "foreign sources" and their version of the "evolving standards of decency" to overturn this practice. Again, Justice Scalia objected that "the Court thus proclaim[ed] itself [the] sole arbiter of our Nation's moral standards," an action that would "crown arbitrariness with chaos." The question, with the changing Supreme Court, is whether decisions to limit use of the death penalty will continue or this trend will be reversed.[136]

And the larger question is whether or not the U.S. Congress and more states will choose to follow this direction.

THE EXPANDING NATURE OF IMPLIED RIGHTS

Do rights exist beyond those set forth in the language of the Bill of Rights that should be safeguarded against governmental intrusion? If so, what are they, and what are their limits? These difficult questions involve moral and ethical positions as well as legal and constitutional judgments.

MakeItReal

ABC News Video: *No Place to Hide*

Civic Participation: Freedom of Information

Privacy

The Constitution does not explicitly mention the right of privacy. Is this right implied in the Fourth Amendment's protection against "unreasonable searches and seizures"? Or did the framers intend it to be one of the "rights retained by the people" in the Ninth Amendment? Or was it so obvious and important that it did not need to be mentioned at all? And, assuming that such a right exists, what exactly does it encompass?

These issues were explored in a landmark 1965 case, *Griswold* v. *Connecticut*, in which Estelle T. Griswold, director of a New Haven birth control clinic opened by the Connecticut Planned Parenthood League, was charged with violating a state statute that prohibited the use of and medical counseling regarding birth control. This law had been passed in response to the concerns of its author, entrepreneur P. T. Barnum, who wished to control the spread of adultery and unsavory diseases. Private citizens, however, argued that the state had no business regulating personal conduct in the bedroom, especially the marital bedroom.

The Supreme Court ruled that the right of privacy protects the behavior of married people in their bedrooms. According to Justice William O. Douglas, such a right, which he had argued as early as 1952, was a "right to be let alone." While not explicitly stated in the Bill of Rights or the Constitution, it could be found in the "penumbras, formed by emanations," or shadows of shadows, of the First, Third, Fourth, Fifth, Ninth, and Fourteenth Amendments; these, he said, create several "zones of privacy." To dissenting justices and students of law, this statement was somewhat confusing, in that the right of privacy could be glimpsed in several amendments but was not stated in any of them. Many believed that Douglas was inserting his own value preferences into the Constitution. Three months after the decision, Griswold and Dr. Lee Buxton reopened their New Haven birth control clinic. The Griswold decision has stood as the basis for the expansion of privacy rights, to the dismay of judicial conservatives and self-restraint advocates such as Robert Bork, who do not support rights not explicitly written into the Constitution and its amendments.[137]

Once privacy became an accepted part of constitutional interpretation, many additional rights could be created. It was not long before the right of privacy was extended to unmarried persons.[138] This constitutional privacy right became a central element in debates over rights related to abortion, homosexuality, AIDS, drug testing, and euthanasia. Soon, states began the process of threatening this right to privacy by trying to remove legal and constitutional protection for those pursuing alternative lifestyles.

Gay Rights

After years of failing to bring their appeals to the Supreme Court, gay rights advocates, arguing for a protected "right to privacy" under the equal protection of the laws and due process clauses of the Fourteenth Amendment, received a setback. In 1987, twenty-eight-year-old Michael Hardwick was arrested for having sexual relations with another man in violation of the Georgia anti-sodomy statute. When *Bowers* v. *Hardwick* reached the deeply divided Burger Court, the result hinged on the vote of centrist Justice Lewis Powell. The initial vote was five to four to overturn the law, and liberal justice Harry Blackmun was assigned to write the opinion. The Blackmun majority viewed this as a privacy case, arguing that an individual's private, consensual sexual activity should be left to the individual, not to the government. The minority, led by Byron White, viewed this not as a privacy case but as a criminal one, arguing that sodomy was banned as a criminal activity in twenty-four states.

Powell had provided the fifth vote for overturning the law, saying he was troubled by the prospect of a twenty-year jail sentence for Hardwick. Several days later, though, Powell changed his vote, believing that Hardwick's criminal case had been dropped and he was merely suing to test the anti-sodomy law. As a result, the vote swung to the conservatives, and White, now speaking for the majority, upheld Georgia's law, arguing that the Constitution does not confer a fundamental right of privacy to homosexuals engaging in sodomy. The four-justice dissent, led by Blackmun, responded that if the constitutional right to privacy means anything, it

▲ These signs outside the State House in Boston, Mass, show the range of opinions of gay marriages since that state's Supreme Court ruled them to be constitutional. When the state legislature could not agree on its response to the decision, the state allowed gay marriages.

means that Georgia cannot prosecute its citizens for private consensual sexual activity.[139] A few years later, Justice Powell admitted to an audience that he now regretted his decision in this case: "I think I probably made a mistake in that one. When I had the opportunity to reread the opinions. . . . I thought the dissents had the better of the arguments."[140]

Eight years later, the Court, with Justice Anthony Kennedy sitting in the retired Justice Powell's seat, seemed more supportive of gay rights when it reviewed "Amendment 2" of the Colorado constitution, which prohibited all governmental protection at either the state or the local level for gays and lesbians. The Court overturned the provision. Persuaded by a legal brief from Harvard law professor Laurence Tribe that the Ninth Amendment might protect gay rights, Justice Kennedy argued in the majority opinion that "the amendment imposes a special disability upon those persons alone," an action "unprecedented in our jurisprudence."[141] Fearing that the issue was heading toward the Court's endorsement of gay marriages, in 1996, Congress, acting at the behest of conservative Congressman Bob Barr (R.-GA), passed the Defense of Marriage Act (DOMA), which defines marriage as "a legal union between one man and one woman as husband and wife." In addition, states were not required "to give effect of any public act, record, or judicial proceeding" in any other state or territory that allowed marriage between members of the same sex. Just whether or not this violates the Constitutional provision in Article IV, Section I, stating, "Full Faith and Credit shall be given in each State to the public Acts, Records, and judicial Proceedings of every other State" awaits the Court's test.

Freedom to Associate Having now ruled in both directions, the road to democracy for gays continued in the 1999 Supreme Court term when it accepted the New Jersey case, *Boy Scouts of America* v. *Dale.* The New Jersey Supreme Court had ruled that the Boy Scouts could not exclude a gay troop leader because it would violate state laws that prohibit discrimination, making it the first state high court to so rule. The state court had ruled that the Boy Scouts were a public enterprise, open to all boys, and as such could not discriminate based on sexual orientation. The Boy Scouts responded that their code of conduct requires "morally straight" behavior, so the exclusion of gays is included in their First Amendment right to establish the message of their organization and freely associate as they wish. The court ruled that the Boy Scouts could exclude people based on sexual orientation because forcing them to do otherwise against the tenets of the organization would violate the group's freedom of association. For Chief Justice Rehnquist, it was "the freedom not to associate."[142]

Civil Unions and Gay Marriages Adding to the confusion in this area of law, states began taking different approaches to the question. In Hawaii, after the state had allowed gay marriages, the state supreme court upheld a 1998 amendment to the state constitution barring them. In California, the voters did the same by approving an initiative called Proposition 22 in the 2000 election, which barred the state from recognizing same-sex marriages, even those legalized by other states. While supporters of the California measures claimed the initiative supported "family values," their vote effectively banned same-sex marriages and denied same-sex couples a series of benefits of marriage available to heterosexual married couples.

Going in the other direction, however, in 2000 Vermont passed a civil union law for gays, allowing them to enjoy all of the rights and benefits of marriage without formally being legally married. Under the Vermont law, only marriages are "sanctified" by clergy or justices of the peace, whereas civil unions are to be "certified." To end a marriage requires a divorce; same-sex couples can end their relationship by "dissolution." But the benefits of civil union are clear. Same-sex partners can make decisions about their partner's health care and apply for spousal benefits from employers. The new relationship would likely have an effect on custody fights and adoption requests. Couples in civil unions receive breaks in inheritance and property taxes but must pay the increased "marriage penalty" that heterosexual couples pay for income taxes.

This new law resulted in significant changes, both in that state and elsewhere. From July 1, 2000, to January 4, 2002, 3,471 civil union licenses were issued in the state of Vermont. In early 2002, the Vermont Supreme Court rejected a legal challenge claiming that the law forced town clerks to issue such licenses in violation of their religious beliefs. The American federal system of government had to face the question of how a law promising traditional marriage benefits to same sex couples in one state would affect other governmental structures at local, state, and national levels.[143] Meanwhile, at the federal level, in July 2001 a group called the Alliance for Marriage proposed a "Federal Marriage Amendment," which reads: "Marriage in the United States shall consist only of the union of a man and a woman. Neither this Constitution or the constitution of any state, nor state or federal law, shall be construed to require that marital status or the legal incidents thereof be conferred upon unmarried couples or groups."

The New Battleground over Gay Rights

In 2003, the Supreme Court continued the discussion of gay marriages in the landmark case of *Lawrence* v. *Texas,* which reversed the 1987 *Bowers* v. *Hardwick* case when it overturned a Texas anti-sodomy law that resembled the earlier Georgia version. Justice Anthony Kennedy wrote for the five-justice majority that the Court would protect privacy, which he defined as: "Freedom presumes an autonomy of self that includes freedom of thought, belief, expression, and certain intimate conduct." While he argued that the Texas law, which sought to safeguard morality, had no "rational basis" for restricting gays, in dissent Justice Antonin Scalia argued that the majority position could also be used to uphold gay marriages, which he opposed.[144] Justice Kennedy said nothing about the issue in his opinion, but Justice O'Connor, in the majority, wrote that in her opinion the Court was not then supporting gay marriages. So, the issue remained in doubt.

The movement toward same-sex marriage accelerated at the state level. In late 2003, the Massachusetts Supreme Judicial Court ruled that gay marriages were constitutional, a decision that remained in force when the state legislature failed to meet the court's 180-day deadline to either legislate on the issue or allow gay marriages to become legal in the state. Initially, the state legislature failed to reach an agreement on a new law in this area, and so the Court's gay marriage ruling went into effect in 2004. When Massachusetts became the first state in the union to allow gay marriages, gay and lesbian couples from all over the country traveled to the state to be married.

The impact on American politics was profound and may have helped to turn the presidential election in 2004 in George Bush's favor. Republican strategists, working in concert with other conservative interest groups, placed initiatives on the ballots of eleven states, including a highly restrictive Ohio provision rejecting gay marriages, and all eleven passed. When Republican candidates, including President Bush, did better than expected in all eleven states, it became clear that the higher turnout of conservative voters to vote on the "anti-gay marriage" ballot initiatives

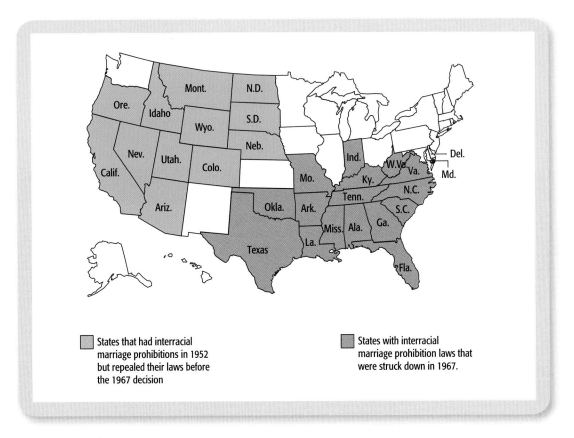

States that had interracial marriage prohibitions in 1952 but repealed their laws before the 1967 decision

States with interracial marriage prohibition laws that were struck down in 1967.

Figure 13.3

A comparison of the states banning interracial marriages in 1967 and the states seeking to ban gay marriages either by law or Constitutional Amendment illustrates the similarity in the volutionary process of these policies.

Source: For the interracial marriage map New York Times, March 17, 2004, p. A22 and for the Anti-Gay Marriage bans at http://www.thetaskforce.org/downloads/marriagemap.pdf

had worked in the party's favor. Immediately these conservative groups put out a renewed call for passing the Federal Marriage Amendment making the gay marriage ban national.

By late 2005, the gay marriage map had changed considerably (see Figure 13.3). Connecticut had become the second state to pass a "civil unions" law along the lines of Vermont's. On the other hand, Texas that year overwhelmingly passed Proposition 2, a constitutional ban on same-sex marriages, making it the nineteenth state to do so. In all, forty states have constitutional amendments or laws limiting marriage to one man and one woman. On the other hand, Maine in that same election renewed its support for an anti-gay bias law.[145]

The gay marriage issue appeared headed for the Supreme Court when states began to go their separate ways on the issue. Nebraska federal judge Joseph Bataillon struck down that state's constitutional amendment banning gay marriages and civil unions. Nebraska attorney general Jon Bruning appealed the decision to the Eighth Circuit Court of Appeals, while Senator Ben Nelson (D.-NB) called for consideration of the federal marriage amendment, seeking to make the gay marriage ban nationwide. Meanwhile, in the fall of 2005, the Massachusetts legislature tried again to reach an agreement on the question of gay marriages, this time proposing a state constitutional amendment supporting civil unions only. When this was voted down overwhelmingly, a popular petition movement began seeking to force a statewide vote in 2008 on a proposed constitutional ban against gay marriages.[146] As various states continue to develop and enforce their

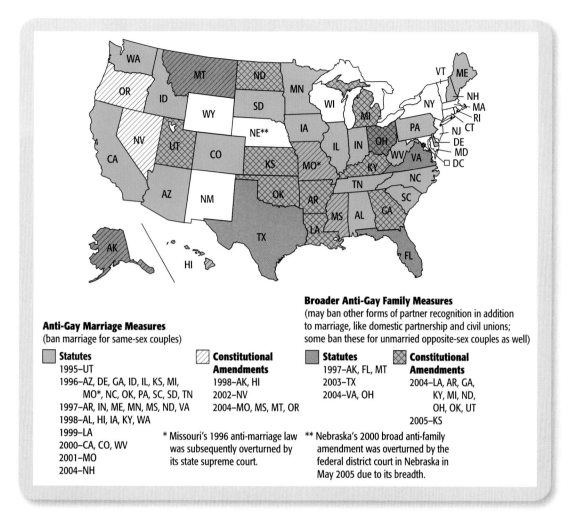

Anti-Gay Marriage Measures
(ban marriage for same-sex couples)

▆	**Statutes**

1995–UT
1996–AZ, DE, GA, ID, IL, KS, MI,
    MO*, NC, OK, PA, SC, SD, TN
1997–AR, IN, ME, MN, MS, ND, VA
1998–AL, HI, IA, KY, WA
1999–LA
2000–CA, CO, WV
2001–MO
2004–NH

▨	**Constitutional Amendments**

1998–AK, HI
2002–NV
2004–MO, MS, MT, OR

* Missouri's 1996 anti-marriage law was subsequently overturned by its state supreme court.

Broader Anti-Gay Family Measures
(may ban other forms of partner recognition in addition to marriage, like domestic partnership and civil unions; some ban these for unmarried opposite-sex couples as well)

▆	**Statutes**

1997–AK, FL, MT
2003–TX
2004–VA, OH

▩	**Constitutional Amendments**

2004–LA, AR, GA,
    KY, MI, ND,
    OH, OK, UT
2005–KS

** Nebraska's 2000 broad anti-family amendment was overturned by the federal district court in Nebraska in May 2005 due to its breadth.

Figure 13.3   **(Continued)**

own policies, leading to a patchwork of proposals throughout the country, it is only a matter of time before the Court hears additional cases exploring the issue of gay rights.

Abortion

If the constitutional right of privacy allows people to choose to prevent conception, does it also allow them to terminate a pregnancy after conception? Before 1973, states were free to set restrictions on a woman's right to obtain an abortion, and many banned abortion entirely. Differences in state laws sent vast numbers of women across state lines or out of the country to obtain abortions, and many others placed themselves in the hands of dangerous "back-alley" abortionists to terminate unwanted pregnancies.

In the 1973 case of *Roe* v. *Wade,* the Supreme Court reviewed a Texas law that limited a woman's right to obtain an abortion. The Court ruled that the right of privacy gave a woman the right to obtain an abortion. But, as with all rights, the exercise of this right could be limited. In this case, those limitations were dictated by the state's right to protect the health of the mother and the rights of the unborn fetus.[147]

The rights of the unborn fetus were the focal point in the *Roe* case. Some religious groups argue that the fetus is a living human being; for them, therefore, abortion constitutes murder. Other groups use the findings of medical science to argue

that life begins when a fetus can be sustained by medical technology outside the mother's womb, an argument that leads to a different set of limitations on the abortion procedure. Opposed to both of these arguments are those who claim that the right of privacy gives a woman the unfettered right to control her own body—and a right to choose abortion.

In his majority opinion, Justice Harry Blackmun attempted to strike a balance among these competing arguments by segmenting the pregnancy term into three trimesters. In the first three months, the woman has an absolute right to obtain an abortion, and the state has no legitimate interest in controlling a routine medical procedure. In the second trimester, the interests of the state become more important as the abortion procedure becomes more risky; thus, states may regulate abortions to ensure the woman's safety, but not to the extent of eliminating them. In the final three months, when the fetus has become viable and has interests that must be safeguarded, abortions can be banned completely.

Roe left open several questions. As medical technology advances and fetuses can survive outside the womb earlier, can abortions be banned at an earlier stage of pregnancy? On the other hand, will the line move in the other direction as medical technology also makes abortions safer at later stages of pregnancy? And what will happen as new reproductive technologies permit a fetus to develop outside of the womb?

Since the *Roe* decision, certain states including Louisiana, Utah, Ohio, and Pennsylvania, have limited and regulated abortions in various ways, including requiring notification of the parents of minors seeking abortions, establishing rules for determining which physicians and facilities are qualified to perform abortions, requiring notification of prospective fathers, and requiring a woman to follow a series of steps to inform herself about the nature of abortions before undergoing the procedure.

At the federal level, the debate has centered on whether government medical assistance to the poor should cover the cost of abortions. Opponents of abortion argue that public funds should not pay for a procedure that some taxpayers find objectionable. Since 1976, Congress has passed various measures limiting federal assistance for abortions except in cases of rape or incest and when the health of the mother is in jeopardy. Some states have followed suit. In 1980, the Supreme Court upheld these restrictions, essentially denying low-income women their constitutional right to obtain an abortion.[148]

Initially, the Burger Court was inclined to strike down restrictions such as the requirement that a woman's husband, or her parents if she is a minor, be informed if she seeks an abortion.[149] In 1983, the Court further reaffirmed the *Roe* decision in a case involving regulations passed by the city of Akron, Ohio. The Court ruled that laws regulating abortion must be designed to protect the health of the mother. Justice Sandra Day O'Connor dissented, arguing that the Court should be concerned only with whether the law represents an "undue burden," or a severe obstacle, on the right to obtain an abortion.[150]

The Rehnquist Court considered several cases involving abortion, beginning with the 1989 case of *Webster* v. *Reproductive Health Services*. The state of Missouri had passed one of the most restrictive of all state abortion laws: physicians performing abortions more than five months into the pregnancy were required to determine whether the fetus was viable; public employees or facilities could not be used to perform abortions; and public funds could not be spent to counsel women to seek abortions. The appointments of Justices Antonin Scalia and Anthony Kennedy had created an activist-conservative Court that seemed to have the votes to overturn the *Roe* decision; however, Justice O'Connor remained unwilling to do so. Thus, the Court upheld all the components of the Missouri law but allowed *Roe* to remain in force.[151]

In 1992, the abortion issue again came before the Court, this time in a case dealing with a restrictive Pennsylvania statute. In a surprising action, three jurists—O'Connor, Kennedy, and Souter—broke from their conservative colleagues and wrote a centrist opinion upholding *Roe* because of its long-standing value as a precedent.[152] Shortly thereafter, two judges who seemed to support abortion rights—Ruth Bader Ginsburg and Stephen Breyer—were appointed to the Court. For the moment, the right to obtain an abortion, though restricted in some instances, seemed safe. This was further demonstrated in 1998, when the Supreme Court refused to rule on a federal court decision voiding a ban in Ohio on late-term abortions. Thus, the federal courts blocked state versions of legislation twice passed by Congress and twice vetoed by President Clinton.[153] Pro-abortion advocates won a major victory in June 2000 when the Court declared a Nebraska law, similar to ones in thirty other states, banning partial-birth (late-term) abortions, unconstitutional as well. Still, the narrow 5–4 vote and specific problems with the wording of this law, extending into a broad range of abortion decisions, make it uncertain whether the Court would strike down similar future laws.[154]

In 2003, Congress passed the Partial-Birth Abortion Ban Act, using language that nearly duplicated the already overturned Nebraska law. In early 2006, the Supreme Court agreed to review the decision of federal district court judge Richard G. Kopf, who had overturned the new federal law because it did not allow for an exception to protect the health of the woman and could also be interpreted to ban other earlier term abortions. At the same time, South Dakota launched a frontal attack on *Roe* by declaring abortion illegal in that state. When the abortion issue returns to the Supreme Court in the fall of 2006 on the Partial Birth Abortion case, and eventually on the South Dakota law, the addition of John Roberts and Samuel Alito to the Court will place Justice Kennedy in the swing vote on the issue.[155]

The Right to Die

As advances in medical technology allow people to live longer, questions arise about the quality of life experienced by those kept alive by artificial means. Should relatives and loved ones be allowed to turn off the life-support systems of critically ill patients? On another front, the efforts of a Detroit doctor, Jack Kevorkian, to assist the suicides of terminally ill patients raised the question of whether people have a right to conduct their own mercy killing.

▲ Demonstrators outside the hospice in Pinellas Park, Florida, housing the comatose Terri Schiavo demanded that her feeding tube be reattached after a court order allowing it to be detached. Despite Congressional efforts to force judicial action, both federal and Florida state courts later refused to intervene and Schiavo died.

Source: New York Times, March 22, 2005, front page.

ABC NEWS/PRENTICE HALL VIDEO LIBRARY

Life or Death Decision, Part 2

During its 1989 term the Supreme Court heard arguments in the case of a Missouri woman, Nancy Cruzan, who had been in a coma for several years and was being kept alive by life-support equipment. No hope remained that she would recover, and her parents sought to have life support removed. The Court ruled that because the state of Missouri requires clear and convincing evidence that a person maintained on life support would not wish to be kept alive by such means, the life-support system could not be disconnected in the absence of such evidence. However, Chief Justice Rehnquist noted, "[T]he principle that a competent person has a constitutionally protected liberty interest in refusing unwanted medical treatment may be inferred from our prior decisions."[156]

Are physician-assisted suicides equivalent to murder, or do they simply represent the ultimate individual right stemming from the right of privacy? The Court refused in two 1997 cases to find in the Constitution a "fundamental liberty" of the right to die. Thus states were permitted to decide for themselves whether or not to allow physician-assisted suicides. Laws in Washington and New York forbidding this practice were allowed to stand.[157] However, a majority of the Court seemed to indicate in these cases that they might in the future be willing to hear an appeal from a terminally ill patient who is suffering greatly and is seeking the right to end his or her life.

The issue was raised again in March 2005. Theresa Marie Schiavo had suffered irreparable brain damage, and her feeding tube had been removed at the request of her husband, Michael. However, Schiavo's parents sought for the third time to have the case reviewed by the Supreme Court. When the Court denied the appeal, conservative members of Congress passed, and President Bush signed, a private bill giving the U.S. District Court jurisdiction over the case once again. Despite this effort, both the Florida state courts and the federal courts denied a series of requests to have the tube reinserted. This political and legal battle, and the public uproar that ensued, made clear that this issue would return to the Supreme Court in the near future.[158]

This area of law took a new turn in January 2006 when the Supreme Court, under the chief justiceship of John Roberts, ruled in *Gonzales* v. *Oregon*[159] on a controversial attempt by former Attorney General John Ashcroft to supersede Oregon's "Death with Dignity" law, which permits physician-assisted suicides. Ashcroft argued that the federal Controlled Substances Act empowered the federal government to jail any Oregon doctor who prescribed lethal doses of restricted drugs at the request of terminally ill patients who sought to end their lives under state law. Their actions were, in his opinion, not a "legitimate medical purpose." The Supreme Court ruled 6–3 (with the retiring Justice Sandra Day O'Connor still on the Court and participating in the case) in favor of Oregon's position, arguing through Justice Anthony Kennedy's majority opinion that "Congress did not have this far-reaching intent to alter the federal–state balance."[160] Beyond the decision itself, the vote here might offer clues as to the future decisions of the Roberts Court. With Chief Justice Roberts ruling on behalf of the Bush administration, and if Samuel Alito were to adopt a similar posture upon replacing the retiring swing-voter Justice O'Connor, the decision making on this issue and many others would remain in the hands of more moderate conservative Justice Anthony Kennedy.

In the area of civil liberties, the United States has traveled a considerable distance in approaching democracy, but with each new controversy we can see that it has some way to go. Only citizens' continued interest in their constitutional rights, by their votes for the president and senators who choose and confirm the judges, and their continued interest in the Court's rulings, help ensure that the evolution toward democracy over the past two centuries (but mainly the past sixty-five years) will continue.

Summary

1. Although the terms *civil liberties* and *civil rights* are often used interchangeably, they are not synonymous. Civil liberties are the individual freedoms and rights guaranteed to every citizen by the Bill of Rights and the due process clause of the Fourteenth Amendment. Civil rights are concerned with protection of citizens against discrimination because of characteristics such as gender, race, ethnicity, or disability and are derived largely from the equal protection clause of the Fourteenth Amendment.

2. The history of civil liberties is one of gradually expanding protection provided by the Bill of Rights. This evolution occurred initially through a series of Supreme Court decisions that applied portions of the first ten amendments to the states, thereby protecting citizens against state action in relation to specific individual rights. Those decisions centered on the question of incorporation of the Bill of Rights into the Fourteenth Amendment. Later cases expanded the protection of these guarantees by judicial interpretation.

3. The Court's process of applying the Bill of Rights to the states by incorporating some, but not all, into the Fourteenth Amendment due process clause was a slow one. Between 1884 and 1925 the Court refused to apply most of them, saying that they were not "fundamental principles lying at the base of our civil and political institutions." In 1937, the Court began the process of "selective incorporation" by ruling that some of these rights were "implicit in the concept of ordered liberty." The real incorporation revolution, though, did not occur until the 1960s. Now, all but five parts of the Bill of Rights have been incorporated.

4. Issues involving freedom of religion are of two main types: those involving establishment, or governmental preference for one religion over others, and those involving free exercise of individual religious practices. In deciding if certain governmental actions would have the effect of establishing a religion, the Supreme Court has searched for the proper balance between complete separation of church and state, known as the high wall of separation doctrine, and government accommodation, in which the government would be allowed to assist religious organizations indirectly and in a neutral manner. In deciding free exercise cases, the Court's protection of religious freedom against state regulation has varied depending on which justices have been on the Court when various cases were considered.

5. In cases involving freedom of speech, the Court has ruled in ways that protect certain kinds of speech but not others. Political speech is protected if it is not likely to incite imminent lawless action. Public speech is protected unless it consists of fighting words or can be shown to create a dangerous situation. Symbolic speech such as flag burning is also protected.

6. Issues involving freedom of the press hinge on the balance between the public's right to know and other rights, such as the government's right to secrecy or an individual's right to personal reputation. The Supreme Court has tended to rule against the state in cases of prior restraint, or censorship before publication, but not in cases of punishment after publication. In ruling on charges of libel, or the publication of statements that are untruthful and damaging to a person's reputation, the Court requires evidence of actual malice or reckless disregard for the truth. Cases involving obscenity have been most problematic because of the extreme difficulty of defining obscenity.

7. Many early debates over the Fourth Amendment's ban on unreasonable searches centered on creation of an exclusionary rule whereby evidence gathered by illegal means cannot be used in later trials. Later, by defining "unreasonable searches" the Supreme Court has alternately expanded and limited the application of the Fourth Amendment; while generally protecting suspects against unreasonable searches, it has permitted a variety of exceptions that give the police leeway in the methods used to obtain evidence.

8. The Fifth and Sixth Amendments contain several provisions designed to protect the rights of defendants. Of these, the most controversial have to do with the right to silence governing confessions resulting from police questioning. Since 1966, police officers have been required to read the so-called Miranda warning to suspects before questioning them; if they do not, statements made by the accused cannot be used in a trial. In recent years, however, the Court has increased exceptions to this rule, and the absence of the Miranda warning will no longer result in the automatic overturning of a conviction.

9. The right of privacy is not explicitly mentioned in the Constitution, but the Supreme Court has ruled that such a right is implied by the wording of several provisions in the Bill of Rights. This right has been extended to cover a woman's right to obtain an abortion in the first three months of pregnancy. The Court has, however, allowed states to place certain restrictions on abortion. The right of privacy has also been extended to cover the right to die in cases involving patients kept alive by life-support equipment, provided that evidence indicates that the patient would not have wished to be kept alive by such means.

Review Questions

1. Outline the incorporation of the Bill of Rights at the state level. In what way can we explain this long process of incorporation? Did the addition of the Bill of Rights to the American Constitution help this country more closely approach democracy?

2. What were the origins and implications of the *Lemon* test?

3. Explain the evolution of the rights of defendants in this country. Which cases have been primary in establishing these rights? Explain the significance of recent Court rulings in the areas of "reasonable suspicion" and a "reasonable expectation of privacy."

4. What new judicial trends are affecting the status of the death penalty in America?

5. What was the significance of the June 2002 Ninth Circuit Court ruling on the "under God" statement contained in the pledge of allegiance? Also, what was significant about the Supreme Court's 2002 ruling regarding Jehovah's Witnesses and town solicitation regulations?

6. What was the Children's Internet Protection Act of 2000? Why did a federal court declare the Act unconstitutional?

7. What is the current Supreme Court position on drug testing of student athletes?

Key Terms

civil liberties   452
civil rights   452
clear and present danger test   457
double jeopardy   459
double standard   454
exclusionary rule   471
fighting words   466

hate speech   466
incorporation   457
least restrictive means test   463
Lemon test   460
libel   468
Miranda warning   478
no incorporation   457

prior restraint   467
probable cause   473
secular regulation rule   463
selective incorporation   459
slander   468
subsequent punishment   467
symbolic speech   466
total incorporation   457

Suggested Readings

ABRAHAM, HENRY J., and BARBARA A. PERRY. *Freedom and the Court: Civil Rights and Liberties in the United States.* 7th ed. New York: Oxford University Press, 1998. A comprehensive and highly readable survey of the Supreme Court's development of civil rights and liberties in the United States since the 1930s.

ALDERMAN, ELLEN, and CAROLINE KENNEDY. *In Our Defense: The Bill of Rights in Action.* New York: Avon Books, 1991. A timely journalistic account of the background and outcome of several cases covered by the first ten amendments.

CRAY, ED. *Chief Justice: A Biography of Earl Warren.* New York: Simon & Schuster, 1997. An eminently readable and informed biography of one of the greatest chief justices of all time, the man who presided over the Court responsible for many of our civil liberties and rights today.

FRIENDLY, FRED W., and MARTHA J. H. ELLIOTT. *The Constitution, That Delicate Balance: Landmark Cases That Shaped the Constitution.* New York: Random House, 1984. A fascinating account of sixteen major cases in civil liberties. Designed as a companion volume to the excellent PBS videotape series by the same name.

GARROW, DAVID, JR. *Liberty and Sexuality: The Right to Privacy and the Making of* Roe *v.* Wade. New York: Macmillan, 1994. A superb historical study of the Supreme Court's development of the right to privacy from *Griswold* v. *Connecticut* through *Roe* v. *Wade.*

GREENHOUSE, LINDA. *Becoming Justice Blackmun: Harry Blackmun's Supreme Court Journey.* New York: Holt, 2005. A fine biography based on the Library of Congress's newly released Justice Blackmun papers showing his evolution from conservative to liberal.

IRONS, PETER. *War Powers: How the Imperial Presidency Hijacked the Constitution.* New York: Holt, 2005. An excellent examination of the cases and doctrines that will be used to decide the antiterrorism war powers cases.

JEFFRIES, JOHN C., JR. *Justice Lewis F. Powell: A Biography.* New York: Scribner's, 1994. A wonderful biography of the justice who served as the "swing member" on the contentious Burger Court and was responsible for so many crucial decisions and nondecisions.

KECK, THOMAS M. *The Most Activist Supreme Court: The Road to Modern Judicial Conservatism.* Chicago: University of Chicago Press, 2002. A comprehensive and readable history of the evolution of conservative philosophy on the Court.

LAZARUS, EDWARD. *Closed Chambers.* New York: Times Books, 1998. A fascinating account by a Blackmun law clerk of life on the Supreme Court in the 1988–89 term, revealing the clerks' role in producing opinions that year.

LEE, FRANCIS GRAHAM. *Church–State Relations.* Westport, CT: Greenwood Press, 2002. A superb summary and analysis of the Court's meandering path in freedom of religion cases.

LEWIS, ANTHONY. *Gideon's Trumpet.* New York: Vintage Press, 1966. Still the best one-volume account of a single Supreme Court case, in this instance the *Gideon* v. *Wainwright* case, which extended the right to counsel protections of the Sixth Amendment to state criminal defendants.

————. *Make No Law: The Sullivan Case and the First Amendment.* New York: Random House, 1991. An account of the development of the *New York Times* v. *Sullivan* case, in which the Supreme Court established standards for libel by the press in cases involving public figures.

MURDOCH, JOYCE, and DEB PRICE. *Courting Justice: Gay Men and Lesbians* v. *The Supreme Court.* New York: Basic Books, 2001. A highly readable history of the Supreme Court's effort to avoid and subsequent mishandling of the issue of gay rights in cases throughout the decades.

MURPHY, BRUCE ALLEN. *Wild Bill: The Legend and Life of William O. Douglas.* New York: Random House, 2003. A biography of the most controversial justice and advocate of civil liberties ever to have served on the Supreme Court.

NEWMAN, ROGER. *Hugo Black: A Biography.* New York: Pantheon Books, 1994. A fine biography of the justice who fought for so many years to implement his vision of an absolute and literal reading of the Bill of Rights.

O'BRIEN, DAVID M. *Constitutional Law and Politics.* Vol. 2, *Civil Rights and Civil Liberties.* New York: Norton, 1997. An excellent casebook containing cuttings of Supreme Court cases mixed with historical information and comprehensive charts showing the development of case law.

PRITCHETT, C. HERMAN. *Constitutional Civil Liberties.* Englewood Cliffs, N.J.: Prentice Hall, 1984. A complete survey of civil liberties case law broken down by amendment and subcategories within each amendment.

REHNQUIST, WILLIAM H. *All the Laws But One: Civil Liberties in Wartime.* New York: Alfred A. Knopf, 1998. A readable history of the Supreme Court's unwillingness to protect civil liberties and civil rights during times of crisis, because "In time of war the laws are silent."

ROSEN, JEFFREY. *The Unwanted Gaze: The Destruction of Privacy in America.* New York: Random House, 2000. An interesting and disturbing examination of our loss of privacy and control over the use of our personal information on the computer and in cyberspace.

SAVAGE, DAVID G. *Turning Right: The Making of the Rehnquist Supreme Court.* New York: Wiley, 1992. A well-researched behind-the-scenes journalistic account by the *Wall Street Journal's* court reporter on Rehnquist Court efforts to shape legal doctrine regarding civil rights and liberties.

THOMAS, ANDREW PEYTON. *Clarence Thomas: A Biography.* San Francisco: Encounter Books, 2001. An expansive full-length biography of the most elusive and enigmatic justice now on the Supreme Court.

★ CHAPTER 14 ★

CIVIL RIGHTS AND POLITICAL EQUALITY

CHAPTER OUTLINE

Approaching Democracy

Divided We Stand: Whither Affirmative Action?

Barbara Grutter and Jennifer Gratz just wanted to attend the University of Michigan, but they claimed that the school's admissions policies prevented them from doing so. Grutter, a white professional woman with children, applied to the University of Michigan law school, and Jennifer Gratz, a white co-ed, applied to the undergraduate program. When they were denied admission and similarly credentialed minority students were accepted, Grutter and Gratz filed lawsuits alleging race discrimination. Their lawsuits gave the Supreme Court a chance in 2003 to rule for the first time since 1978 on whether or not affirmative action programs should continue in educational institutions across the nation.

The University of Michigan created one of the strongest affirmative action admissions programs in the nation even though it had no past history of discrimination. Indeed, a 1995–2000 study showed that a minority student had a 234.5 times greater chance of being admitted to the University of Michigan law school than a majority student. The undergraduate school's new affirmative action program gave minority students an extra 20 points out of 150 required in the admissions process.

The federal district courts disagreed on how to rule in the Michigan cases. One federal district court judge ruled in Grutter's suit that the law school's affirmative action program violated the Constitution because "a racially diverse student population . . . is not a compelling state interest," and "even if it were, the law school has not narrowly tailored its use of race to achieve that interest." Meanwhile, another federal district court judge ruled in Gratz's case that the undergraduate affirmative action program was constitutional because it provided diversity in the class that benefited the educational process. Both cases were then sent to the sixth circuit court of appeals. The federal Sixth Circuit Court of Appeals heard the case *en banc* and voted 5–4 in May 2002 that the University of Michigan affirmative action program for its law school was constitutional because it allowed for needed diversity in educational programs. Once the cases were accepted for Supreme Court review, eighty organizations, including the U.S. military and thirty-one Fortune 500 companies, filed thirty-two *amicus curiae* briefs on behalf of the University of Michigan's affirmative action policies.

By the time that both cases had worked their way to the Supreme Court, legal precedents across the nation had greatly limited or ended affirmative action programs. In 1999, Washington voters passed a civil rights act that ended affirmative action in that state for both African Americans and women. The Federal Appeals Court in the Fifth Circuit voted in 2001 in the case of Cheryl Hopwood to end affirmative action in the University of Texas law school, saying that race could not be considered a factor in admissions. Following that, Texas attorney general Dan Morales ruled that race would no longer be a basis for admissions to undergraduate schools or for scholarship programs in that state. Shortly thereafter, California voters passed Proposition 209, which ended affirmative action based on race, sex, or ethnic origins in state hiring, education programs, and govern-

★ Jennifer Gratz's suit against the University of Michigan, challenging its affirmative action undergraduate admissions program, had historic consequences.

ment contracts. Seeking "to restore true color-blind fairness," the regents of California's state university system eliminated affirmative action programs in graduate and, later, in undergraduate admissions decisions.

Politicians moved quickly to adjust to the new legal climate. Then-governor of Texas George W. Bush and Governor Gray Davis of California both announced that affirmative action programs in state schools would end in favor of guaranteed admission for varying percentages of top students from the state regardless of race. In November 1999, Florida governor Jeb Bush inaugurated by executive order his "One Florida" program. This program would guarantee admission to state colleges and universities to the top 20 percent of graduating seniors in the state, increase financial aid and test preparation assistance for poor students, and end the "racial set-aside" programs for minorities seeking government contracts. "The time has come to eliminate these legally suspect practices, that never fully achieved their purpose to begin with," said Governor Jeb Bush. By doing this, the governor derailed the statewide vote on affirmative action.

Bush's action caused a storm of controversy in Florida. African-American leaders protested, two African-American legislators staged a sit-in in the lieutenant governor's office, and in March 2000 thousands of protesters marched at the Capitol while Bush was giving his State of the State address. But the governor was undaunted. "By September," said Jeb Bush, "what you will see is an increased number of students attending our university systems and an increased number of African Americans and Hispanics attending the university system. That's the synthesis of what this rule is about." Indeed, by the early fall of 2004, the "One Florida" program appeared to be sustaining the minority admissions rate in the Florida state school system, with the ten universities and New College enrolling 5 percent more minority students. But at the same time, when the University of Florida decided to stop awarding any race-based scholarships, the school was running nearly 5 percent behind its normal rate of admission of minority students when the affirmative action programs were in effect.

In 2003, a narrow 5–4 Supreme Court majority upheld these affirmative action programs but with certain limitations, arguing the need for a "critical mass" of minority students in order to achieve diversity in the educational experience. Although seven justices upheld the University of Michigan's law school admission program without changes, a much narrower five-vote Court majority ruled that the undergraduate procedure represented an unconsti-

★ Students at the University of Michigan celebrated in June 2003 when the Supreme Court upheld the affirmative action admissions programs at the law school and slightly modified the one in the undergraduate school.

tutional quota. Sandra Day O'Connor wrote: "In order to cultivate a set of leaders with legitimacy in the eyes of the citizenry it is necessary that the path to leadership be visibly open to talented and qualified individuals of every race and ethnicity." With the retirement of swing-voter Justice O'Connor in 2005, and her replacement by more conservative Court of Appeals Judge Samuel Alito, the question will become whether or not affirmative action court decisions will change direction in the future.[1]

QUESTION FOR REFLECTION

Established in 1965, affirmative action programs attempted to provide a "boost" to minority applicants competing against white applicants with roughly the same qualifications. How will eliminating this assistance, with added emphasis on academic achievement and introduction of education assistance for minorities, affect America's search for racial equality?

Introduction
CIVIL RIGHTS AND DEMOCRACY

The fight over civil rights and affirmative action did not begin with Jennifer Gratz and Barbara Grutter. When Rosa Parks refused to move from her seat on a bus in Montgomery, Alabama, in 1955, she set off a boycott that eventually led to a federal court ruling, affirmed by the Supreme Court, that the city of Montgomery could not maintain its policy of segregated transportation. Despite the resolve and bravery of those involved in the boycott, however, the legal process took almost thirteen months before culminating in the decision that African Americans would be allowed to sit at the front of a bus. Nor did the story end there; in fact, it was only beginning.

More than fifty years after the Supreme Court told the nation's public schools to desegregate "with all deliberate speed" in the landmark case of *Brown* v. *Board of Education of Topeka, Kansas*,[2] we see that the goal still seems out of reach. Today, we debate about trying to equalize rights, even at the expense of someone else's job or college admission. With such acrimonious debate over affirmative action programs, can we hope to approach a democratic system of "equal rights for all" and "full participation by all" in the government?

In this chapter, we trace the history of civil rights in the United States, a history that began only in the second half of the nineteenth century, when the nation, recovering from devastating civil war, sought to establish equality of rights under the Constitution. But real change did not come until nearly a century later. The period from 1896 to 1954 was spent debating the notion of legal equality; then from 1954 to 1968 the debate turned to achieving actual equality through governmental policies. In the nearly thirty years that followed, the debate centered on whether actual equality should be achieved, and if so, how. But for the past decade, the discussion over a "color-blind" policy has raised questions as to whether those policies will be reversed or even abandoned.

Before discussing the history of civil rights, however, we need to clarify exactly what we mean by civil rights, equality, and discrimination.

DEFINING CIVIL RIGHTS

Most people agree that to truly approach democracy it is necessary to eliminate **unfair discrimination**, that is, unequal treatment based on race, ethnicity, gender, and other distinctions. The primary means for achieving equal treatment is ensuring full protection of civil rights, constitutionally guaranteed and protected rights that may not be arbitrarily removed by the government. These rights are often referred to as personal, natural, or inalienable rights; they are believed to be granted by God or nature to all human beings. Thomas Jefferson had these rights in mind when he wrote in the Declaration of Independence, "We hold these truths to be self-evident, that all men are created equal, that they are endowed by their Creator with certain unalienable Rights, that among these are Life, Liberty and the pursuit of Happiness." These rights become statutory when they are established by legislation.

Several groups within the U.S. population have suffered from discrimination at various periods in the nation's history, and many still do today. Although in much of this chapter we focus on the civil rights of African Americans and women, we also discuss the efforts of other groups, such as Hispanics and Native Americans, to obtain equal treatment. Not all of these groups are minorities. Women, for example, are not a numerical minority, but they have experienced discrimination throughout the nation's history and continue to encounter unequal treatment in the workplace and elsewhere.

unfair discrimination Unequal treatment based on race, ethnicity, gender, and other distinctions.

▲ Compare the two drinking fountains established under the Supreme Court's 1896 doctrine of "separate but equal" facilities in the segregated South, and ask yourself about the fairness of that policy.

de jure equality Equality before the law. It disallows legally mandated obstacles to equal treatment, such as laws that prevent people from voting, living where they want to, or taking advantage of all the rights guaranteed to individuals by the laws of the federal, state, and local governments.

de facto equality Equality of results, which measures real-world obstacles to equal treatment. For example: Do people actually live where they want? Do they work under similar conditions?

Civil rights are closely linked with the ideal of equality. There are two basic forms of equality: equality before the law (legal equality) and actual equality. Equality before the law, also called **de jure equality**, requires no legally mandated obstacles to equal treatment, such as laws that prevent people from voting, living where they want to, or taking advantage of all the rights guaranteed to individuals by the laws of the federal, state, and local governments. Actual equality, also called **de facto equality**, looks at results: Do people live where they choose? Do they work under similar conditions? In a diverse and complex society like that of the United States, it is often difficult to achieve de jure equality; it is even more difficult to create the conditions that will lead to de facto equality. The nation's history includes many turns along the road to equality, and although de jure equality has been achieved in several respects, de facto equality remains a distant objective.

Quick Review

Fugitive Slave Act

- Passed by Congress in 1793.
- Allowed runaway slaves to be captured, even where slavery was outlawed.
- Captured slaves could be returned to slave owners.

ESTABLISHING CONSTITUTIONAL EQUALITY

Although the Constitution was written to "secure the Blessings of Liberty to ourselves and our Posterity," those blessings did not extend to African American slaves. This was not surprising; all references to slavery had been stricken from the Declaration of Independence, written eleven years before. Why did the Constitution's framers ignore the plight of the slaves? And why did they choose to count "other persons"—that is, slaves—as only three-fifths of a person, with no rights at all? As we saw in Chapter 2, to create a constitution that would be ratified by a majority of the states, the framers were forced to compromise. To preserve the economic position of the southern states, they allowed slavery to continue. But in doing so, they also ensured that future battles would be fought over slavery.

Even for free African Americans, legal status varied in different regions of the country. By 1804, many northern states had either banned slavery or passed laws under which the children of slaves would be free. However, the right to vote, generally granted on the basis of property qualifications, remained beyond the reach of most African Americans as well as landless white males. In the South, legal measures made the release of slaves extremely difficult.[3] At the federal level, Congress passed the Fugitive Slave Act (1793), which allowed runaway slaves to be captured (even in parts of the nation that outlawed slavery) and returned to slave owners. Even Article VI, Section 2, of the Constitution mandated the return of fugitive slaves. African Americans were excluded by law from a procedure that enabled immigrants to become citizens (1790), from service in militias (1792), and from the right to carry the mail (1810).

In 1820, the *Missouri Compromise* was passed when the proposal to introduce Missouri as a slave state threatened to upset the equal division of slave and free states. Missouri was admitted as a slave state along with the free state of Maine, and slavery was prohibited in the remainder of the Louisiana Purchase territory north of Missouri's southern border.

Although some African Americans submitted to their condition, many others did not. The most famous slave revolt occurred in August 1831, when Nat Turner led a rebellion of about seventy slaves in Southampton County, Virginia. In twelve hours of turmoil, Turner's men killed dozens of whites. Eventually the insurgents were defeated by hundreds of soldiers and militiamen, and Turner was executed, along with scores of other slaves.

The *Compromise of 1850*, which admitted California as a free state, eliminated the slave trade in the District of Columbia, but continued to permit slavery there, while the territories of New Mexico and Utah were given no federal restrictions on slavery. As part of the compromise, Congress passed a stronger Fugitive Slave Act and provided for hundreds of additional federal officials to enforce it. The political prospects for equality seemed more remote than ever.

The *Dred Scott* Case

In 1857, the Supreme Court decided a case with far-reaching implications for the civil rights of African Americans. A slave named Dred Scott had been taken by his master from Missouri into the free state of Illinois and the free territory of Wisconsin. When his master died and Scott was returned to Missouri, he claimed that because he had lived in areas where slavery was illegal, he was now a free man.

The case of *Dred Scott* v. *Sandford* reached the Court at a time when the justices were seeking to define the legality of slavery, particularly in the territories, as a means of solving the political dispute between the North and the South. In a highly controversial decision, the Court ruled that Scott could not sue in federal court because no African American, free or enslaved, could ever become a citizen of the United States. According to Chief Justice Roger Taney, even if Scott were free, he could not sue because African Americans were "not included, and were not intended to be included, under the word 'citizens' in the Constitution" and therefore had no rights under that document. Finally, the chief justice ruled that the Missouri Compromise was unconstitutional because Congress could not deprive people of their property rights, in this case their slaves, under the due process clause of the Fifth Amendment.[4]

The Civil War and Reconstruction

The *Dred Scott* case closed the door to judicial remedies for African Americans seeking legal protection. Political remedies were still open, however. By freeing the slaves in the areas still in rebellion, President Abraham Lincoln's Emancipation Proclamation of 1863 renewed the possibility of "equality for all." But for Lincoln's executive order to be implemented, the Union had to win the Civil War and Congress had to apply legal authority to support freedom for slaves. Thus, following the Civil War, Congress played a pivotal role in efforts to establish equality for African Americans.

In one series of actions, Congress drafted three constitutional amendments, known as the Civil War Amendments. The Thirteenth Amendment, which abolished slavery, was ratified in 1865. It reads as follows:

> Section 1. Neither slavery nor involuntary servitude, except as a punishment for crime whereof the party shall have been duly convicted, shall exist within the United States, or in any place subject to their jurisdiction.
>
> Section 2. Congress shall have power to enforce this article by appropriate legislation.

Quick Review

The *Dred Scott* Case

- Scott was a slave taken by his master into the free state of Illinois and the free territory of Wisconsin.
- Upon the death of his master, Scott claimed he was now a free man because he lived in free territories.
- Supreme Court ruled that Scott could not sue in federal court because no African American, free or enslaved, could ever become a citizen of the United States.
- Court concluded that African Americans were not included under the word "citizens" in the Constitution and therefore had no rights under that document.

Congress had already passed legislation allowing African Americans to testify against whites in federal courts (1864), granting equal pay and benefits to all soldiers (1864), and establishing the Freedmen's Bureau (1865), an agency of the War Department authorized to assist the newly freed slaves in making the transition to freedom.

But southern states were already passing laws, known as the **black codes**, that restricted the civil rights of blacks and enforced oppressive labor practices designed to keep them working on plantations. Led by the so-called Radical Republicans, Congress undertook to counteract these measures. Over President Andrew Johnson's vetoes, the Radical Republicans gave the Freedman's Bureau additional powers to settle labor disputes and nullify oppressive labor contracts. It also passed the Civil Rights Act of 1866, which made African Americans U.S. citizens and empowered the federal government to protect their civil rights.

Many members of Congress feared that the new law might not stand up in court. They drafted the Fourteenth Amendment to the Constitution, making African Americans citizens and giving them rights of that citizenship. Section 1 of the amendment states:

> All persons born or naturalized in the United States, and subject to the jurisdiction thereof, are citizens of the United States and of the State wherein they reside. No State shall make or enforce any law which shall abridge the privileges or immunities of citizens of the United States; nor shall any State deprive any person of life, liberty, or property, without due process of law; nor deny to any person within its jurisdiction the equal protection of the laws.

Section 5 of the amendment gave Congress the "power to enforce, by appropriate legislation, the provisions of this article." The new citizens were thus supposed to have the same rights as others, as well as be treated with fairness and equality under law.

Congress acted quickly. It required southern states to ratify this amendment, and later the Fifteenth Amendment, before they could rejoin the Union. The Fifteenth Amendment, granting African Americans **suffrage**, or the right to vote, reads:

> The right of citizens of the United States to vote shall not be denied or abridged by the United States or any State on account of race, color, or previous condition of servitude.

Again, Congress was given the power to "enforce this article by appropriate legislation." To break the power of the Ku Klux Klan and other terrorists who attacked, beat, and sometimes killed African Americans who tried to vote or otherwise claim their rights, Congress also passed the Ku Klux Klan Acts of 1870 and 1871, making it a federal offense for two or more persons to conspire to deprive citizens of their equal protection and voting rights.

But the legislative branch of government could only create the tools for establishing legal equality. It remained to be seen whether the executive branch would enforce them and how the judicial branch would interpret them.

CREATING LEGAL SEGREGATION

After the Civil War, the Supreme Court showed little interest in the rights of African Americans. In *United States* v. *Cruikshank* (1876), for example, the Court considered the constitutionality of the Ku Klux Klan Act of 1870. William Cruikshank was part of a white mob that had murdered sixty African Americans in front of a courthouse. Since murder was not a federal offense and the state authorities had no intention of prosecuting anyone for the crime, mob members were indicted on federal charges of interfering with the murdered men's right to assemble. However, the Court ruled that under the Fourteenth Amendment only **state action**, or action by the state government under the color of law to deprive rights, was subject to decisions

black codes Laws restricting the civil rights of African Americans.

suffrage The right to vote.

state action Action taken by state officials or sanctioned by state law.

by the federal court.[5] In other words, the federal government could not prosecute private individuals. This ruling left the states free to ignore lynchings, assaults, and mob actions against African Americans within their borders.

Separate but Equal?

Primary Source: *Plessy v. Ferguson, 1896*

In the *Civil Rights Cases* (1883), the Supreme Court applied its new *state-action doctrine* to overturn the Civil Rights Act of 1875, which prohibited racial segregation in transportation, inns, theaters, and other places of public accommodation and amusement.[6] The southern states thereupon passed a series of **Jim Crow laws**, which separated the races in public places. This legal separation was challenged in the 1896 case of *Plessy v. Ferguson*.[7]

Homer Adolph Plessy, who was one-eighth African American, had sought to ride in a railroad car designated as "whites only," rather than in the car at the end of the train designated for "coloreds only," as required by law, and had been arrested. The Supreme Court upheld the arrest, stating that the Fourteenth Amendment regulated only political equality and not social equality.

The logical consequences of the Plessy ruling were revealed in *Cumming v. County Board of Education* (1899), in which the Court approved "separate but equal" public schools in Georgia. Though the facilities were not really "equal," by claiming that public schools were a subject for state rather than federal jurisdiction, the Court could let segregation stand.[8] Soon, legally enforced segregation pervaded every other area of social life.

The Disenfranchisement of African American Voters

Seeking to disenfranchise African American voters, southern politicians invented loopholes in the voting laws, thus circumventing the Fifteenth Amendment. Because many freed slaves owned no land, *property qualifications* kept some off the voting rolls; *literacy tests* did the same for those who could not read. When these loopholes were found to exclude many poor whites, an *understanding clause* was used: People were permitted to vote only if they could properly interpret a portion of the state constitution. (Of course, examiners used different sections of the constitution and different standards for "proper interpretation," depending on the race of the test taker.)

Another loophole was the *grandfather clause*, which exempted from property qualifications or literacy tests anyone whose relatives could have voted in 1867, thus excluding the freed slaves. Some southern states also implemented a **poll tax**, that is, a fee for voting, which would exclude poor African Americans. Finally, with the Democratic party, in effect, the only party in the South, states utilized *whites-only primaries* to select the Democratic candidate, making African-American votes in the general election irrelevant.[9] Thus, the law denied African Americans, although citizens of the United States, a voice in its government.

ESTABLISHING LEGAL EQUALITY

African Americans reacted to end discrimination and oppression in a variety of ways. In 1895, Booker T. Washington, a former slave who had founded Tuskegee Institute, argued that racism would eventually end if African Americans would accept their situation, work hard, and improve their education. On the other hand, W.E.B. DuBois, the first African American to earn a Ph.D. from Harvard, argued that all forms of racial segregation and discrimination should be aggressively attacked and eradicated.

In 1909, DuBois, with other African Americans and concerned white people, formed the National Association for the Advancement of Colored People (NAACP)

Jim Crow laws Laws passed by southern states that separated the races in public places such as railroads, streetcars, schools, and cemeteries.

poll tax A fee that had to be paid before one could vote; used to prevent African Americans from voting; now unconstitutional.

to litigate on behalf of racial equality. In a series of cases decided between 1905 and 1914, the NAACP convinced the Court to use the Thirteenth Amendment to strike down **peonage**, in which employers advanced wages and then required workers to remain on their jobs, in effect enslaving them, until the debt was satisfied.[10]

Encouraged by these successes, the NAACP challenged Oklahoma's law effectively exempting whites from the literacy test required for voting. In *Guinn* v. *United States* (1915), the Supreme Court struck it down using the Fifteenth Amendment.[11] Then, in 1927, the Court found that Texas's white-primary law violated the equal protection clause of the Fourteenth Amendment.[12] Still, the southern states continued to disenfranchise blacks by reenacting the offending laws or inventing new loopholes. Clearly, a more general approach to protecting the civil rights of African Americans was needed.

The White House and Desegregation

During World War II, the obvious inequity of expecting African Americans to fight for a country that did not afford them full protection of their civil rights gave rise to new efforts to achieve equality. This time the White House took the lead. President Franklin D. Roosevelt issued an executive order prohibiting discrimination in defense businesses and creating a temporary wartime agency, the Fair Employment Practices Committee (FEPC), to investigate allegations of, and provide compensation for, such discrimination. In 1946, spurred by a spate of racial lynchings, President Harry Truman established a panel of citizens to examine the problem and recommend solutions.[13] He also issued an executive order making the FEPC a permanent executive branch agency.

But Truman's most significant action in relation to **desegregation** came in 1948, when he issued an executive order prohibiting segregation in the military and in federal employment. Truman also asked Congress to ban discrimination by private employers and labor unions, outlaw poll taxes, pass a federal anti-lynching law, create a permanent civil rights commission, and compel fair elections. However, these efforts were doomed by the opposition of conservative southerners who had split from the Democratic party under the leadership of South Carolina's Strom Thurmond to form the Dixiecrats. The struggle for equality now turned to the public school system.

Seeking Equality in the Schools

NAACP attorneys had long been planning a comprehensive legal attack on segregation in the public schools. Initially, their strategy was to work within the separate but equal standard, using a series of test cases to show that certain educational facilities were not, in fact, equal. In 1938, the NAACP challenged a Missouri statute that met the state's separate but equal requirement by offering tuition refunds to African Americans who attended an out-of-state law school. The Supreme Court overturned the law, stating that students required to go to out-of-state schools would be burdened by inconveniences and costs not imposed on students who attended law schools in their home state.[14]

In 1950, under the leadership of Thurgood Marshall, the NAACP challenged the University of Texas law school's separate but equal plan, in which African American students were taught in the basement of an Austin office building rather than at the highly regarded state university. The justices agreed that the two "separate" schools were not "equivalent" in any respect, and for the first time the Court went beyond such physical differences to point out the constitutional importance of the intangible psychological differences represented by the differing academic environments, such as the differences in the prestige of the faculty, the students, the library, and the law review.[15] On the same day, the Court ruled that Oklahoma could not satisfy its separate but equal requirement for graduate

---

Question for Reflection

What impact did creation of the Dixiecrats have on the Democratic party's strength and its attempts to achieve racial equality for African Americans?

 MakeItReal

Primary Source: *Brown v. Board of Education of Topeka, Kansas,* 1954

peonage A system in which employers advance wages and then require workers to remain on their jobs, in effect enslaving them, until the debt is satisfied.

desegregation The elimination of laws and practices that mandate racial separation.

◄ Lawyers George E. C. Hayes, Thurgood Marshall, and James M. Nabrit of the NAACP Legal Defense Fund congratulate each other outside the Supreme Court Building on May 17, 1954, after the announcement that they had won the case of *Brown* v. *Board of Education.*

schools by forcing an African American student to sit in the doorway during class, study in a special section of the library, and eat at a table in the cafeteria labeled "For Colored Only."[16]

Now that the Court had ruled that psychologically "separate" facilities could not be considered equal in graduate education, Marshall and the NAACP were ready to take direct aim at overturning the separate but equal doctrine as applied to public schools. Suits were initiated to challenge the segregated school districts of four states (Kansas, Delaware, South Carolina, and Virginia) and the District of Columbia. The NAACP's strategy was to attack the *Plessy* decision by focusing on the intangible psychological effects of separate but equal public school facilities.

Because so many of the precedents supported *Plessy,* the most effective way to convince the Court to change its position was to present evidence from social science research on the effects of segregation. An example was a series of studies by psychologist Kenneth Clark, who discovered that when African American schoolchildren were shown white and black dolls and asked which one they would prefer to be, they invariably chose the white doll. On the basis of such findings, Marshall argued that segregation had a devastating effect on African American children's self-esteem, and that therefore the education received in separate educational facilities could never be equal.

In 1952, the Supreme Court decided to combine the four state cases and rule on them under *Brown* v. *Board of Education of Topeka, Kansas.* Rather than handing down a decision, however, it called for reargument of the case. At about this time, Chief Justice Fred Vinson, who was totally unsympathetic to the attack on segregation, died suddenly. The new chief justice, former California governor Earl Warren, who was appointed to the Supreme Court as part of an election deal with President Dwight D. Eisenhower, was far more willing to use his political skills to persuade all of the justices, even Kentuckian Stanley Reed, to rule against segregation.

On May 17, 1954, Warren announced the Court's unanimous decision that the separate but equal standard was henceforth unconstitutional. Warren argued that the importance of education in contemporary society was greater than it had been at the time of the *Plessy* ruling. Because segregated schools put African American children at a disadvantage, he stated, they violated the equal protection clause of the Fourteenth Amendment.[17] On the same day, relying on the Fifth Amendment's due process clause to deal with schools under federal government supervision, the Court also struck down segregation in Washington, D.C.'s, public schools.[18]

A year later, the Court issued a second statement on *Brown* v. *Board of Education* (commonly referred to as *Brown II*) dealing with implementation of the decision.[19] All of the cases were ordered back to the lower federal courts, which in turn would supervise plans for desegregation, or the elimination of laws and practices mandating segregation "with all deliberate speed." Missing from the Court's statement was a direct order to compel **integration**, efforts to balance the social composition of the schools.

▲ Nine-year-old Linda Brown and her family in Topeka, Kansas, in 1954, who became the subject of the landmark Supreme Court case *Brown* v. *Board of Education.* The case began when Linda's father, a clergyman, took her to the all-white school, where she was denied admission.

State and Federal Responses

State governments responded to the *Brown* decision in a variety of ways. Washington, D.C., Kansas, and Delaware largely eliminated legalized segregation. In the Deep South, however, violence grew against African American activists who tried to implement this ruling. In some places, mobs gathered to block African Americans from attending previously segregated public schools and universities. State legislatures also took steps to fight the *Brown* decision. Some forbade state officials to enforce the decision, while others closed the public schools in certain districts and paid the private school tuitions of white children.[20] Any uniform progress toward desegregation in the South would be up to the federal government.

Initially, with the exception of fifty-eight courageous federal district court judges in the South, the federal government was no more willing to take desegregation action than the states had been.[21] Southern politicians took President Dwight Eisenhower's ambivalence as a signal to continue their discriminatory practices without White House interference. Only reluctantly did the president decide to send federal troops to Little Rock, Arkansas, to help nine African American students desegregate the region's Central High School in the face of strong opposition, which included the deployment of state National Guard units to prevent the students from entering the school.

President Eisenhower signed into law the Civil Rights Act of 1957, which created a Civil Rights Commission to recommend legislation and gave the Justice Department the power to initiate lawsuits on behalf of African Americans who were denied the right to vote. Then, in the Civil Rights Act of 1960, the attorney general was authorized to call in federal officials to investigate voter registration in areas where discrimination may be occurring. Although the Eisenhower administration did not use its new power vigorously, it did demonstrate that the federal government could be effective, if it wished, in protecting civil rights. In the meantime, however, the struggle for equality fell to the people most affected—African Americans themselves.

integration Government efforts to balance the racial composition in schools and public places.

MakeItReal

Simulation: Travel The Civil Rights Timelines, Parts I and II

▲ A young Reverend Martin Luther King, Jr., is arrested in Montgomery, Alabama in 1958 for "loitering" near the courthouse where one of his civil rights allies was being tried. King later charged that once out of sight of the cameras he was beaten and choked by the arresting officers.

civil disobedience Breaking the law in a nonviolent fashion and being willing to suffer the consequences, even to the point of going to jail, in order to publicly demonstrate that the law is unjust.

boycott Refusal to patronize any organization that practices policies perceived as politically, economically, or ideologically unfair.

protest march March in which people walk down a main street carrying signs, singing freedom songs, and chanting slogans.

sit-in A protest technique in which protesters refuse to leave an area.

THE CIVIL RIGHTS MOVEMENT

The modern civil rights protests began with Rosa Park's refusal to give up her seat on a bus, which led to the bus boycott in Montgomery, Alabama, in 1955–56. Shortly afterward, African American activists founded the Southern Christian Leadership Conference (SCLC), which was headed by a charismatic leader, the Reverend Martin Luther King Jr. Like Mahatma Gandhi of India, King preached **civil disobedience**, that is, breaking the law in a nonviolent fashion and being willing to suffer the consequences, even to the point of going to jail, to publicly demonstrate that a law is unjust. For example, in the Montgomery bus case, protesters might **boycott**, or refuse to patronize, a business that practices segregation. Another kind of demonstration is the **protest march**, in which people walk down a main street carrying signs, singing freedom songs, and chanting slogans. During the early years of the civil rights protests, counter protesters frequently lined the streets to jeer at the marchers, and law enforcement officials, blaming the protesters for the disturbances, would break up the protest, using everything from clubs to fire hoses.

The concept of civil disobedience was not confined to the SCLC. Inspired by the Montgomery boycott, in 1958 Oklahoma City's NAACP Youth Council decided to protest the segregation of lunch counters by sitting down on the stools and refusing to leave when they were not served. This protest technique became known as a **sit-in**, and it proved to be highly effective. In 1960, four African American students used this technique, entering a Woolworth store in Greensboro, North Carolina, and sitting down at the segregated lunch counter. When they were refused service, they simply sat there and studied until the store closed. During the following days others, both African American and white, joined the protest, and soon more than a thousand people were sitting-in at segregated eating establishments in Greensboro. The Greensboro protest gained national attention, and college students throughout the South

▲ Fifteen-year-old Elizabeth Eckford calmly ignores the taunts of the jeering crowd as she becomes one of the "Little Rock 9" in 1957 who integrated Central High School. "I tried to see a friendly face somewhere in the mob—someone who maybe would help me. I looked into the face of an old woman and it seemed a kind face, but when I looked at her again, she spat at me."

began engaging in sit-ins. Many of the protesters were arrested, convicted, and jailed, thereby drawing further attention to the movement. The tide of public opinion turned, and eating establishments throughout the South began to desegregate.

Beginning in 1961, civil rights activists, called **freedom riders**, began traveling throughout the South on buses to test compliance with the Supreme Court's mandate to integrate bus terminals accommodating interstate travelers. In Anniston, Birmingham, and Montgomery, Alabama, the freedom riders were attacked by mobs while local police made themselves scarce.

During the same period, the federal government worked with civil rights leaders to register African American voters in the hope of creating a legal revolution from within the system. With the aid of the Justice Department, the privately funded Voter Education Project began a campaign to enforce the voting rights provisions of the Civil Rights Act of 1957. As a result of these efforts, African American voter registration in the South rose from 26 percent in 1962 to 40 percent in 1964.[22]

Meanwhile, the civil rights movement was encountering increasingly violent resistance. When extremists began harassing and even killing civil rights activists, the White House was forced to act. In the spring of 1963, Martin Luther King Jr. decided to protest segregation in Birmingham with a series of demonstrations and marches designed to trigger a response from the segregationist police commissioner, Theophilus Eugene "Bull" Connor. The protest began with marches and sit-ins at segregated businesses, to which Connor responded by arresting protesters, including King himself, and obtaining a court injunction to prevent further demonstrations. Finally, after Connor attacked nonviolent protesters with vicious police dogs and fire hoses, President John F. Kennedy sent Justice Department officials to Birmingham to work out a compromise, and business leaders agreed to desegregate their establishments. However, the night after the compromise was announced, bombs went off at the hotel where King was staying. Riots broke out, and peace was not restored until President Kennedy sent federal troops to a nearby fort and threatened to dispatch them to Birmingham if the violence continued.

freedom riders Civil rights activists who traveled throughout the American South on buses to test compliance with the Supreme Court's mandate to integrate bus terminals and public facilities accommodating interstate travelers.

▲ The brutality with which state authorities dealt with civil rights protestors, shown here as firefighters turned the full blast of their hoses on them, served to galvanize public sentiment in favor of the civil rights cause.

Primary Source: Civil Rights Act (1964)

Quick Review

Civil Rights Act of 1964

- Increased the federal government's ability to fight discrimination.
- Government could withhold funds from segregated schools and the attorney general could initiate school desegregation suits.
- Equal Employment Opportunity Commission (EEOC) and the Commissioner of Education put the power of the federal bureaucracy behind efforts to end discrimination.

Primary Source: Voting Rights Act (1965)

Primary Source: Fair Housing Act of 1968

The Civil Rights Acts

The civil rights movement made great progress toward equality in the early 1960s, but there was still a long way to go. To succeed, it needed more effective legal tools. In 1963, President Lyndon Johnson urged Congress in the name of the assassinated President Kennedy to "enact a civil rights law so that we can move forward to eliminate from this nation every trace of discrimination and oppression that is based upon race or color." And Congress responded. The Twenty-fourth Amendment, which prohibited the use of poll taxes in federal elections, was passed by Congress in 1962 (ratified 1964). Then, after a fifty-seven-day filibuster led by southern senators that was finally broken by the arm-twisting of President Johnson, Congress passed the Civil Rights Act of 1964.

The 1964 act was extremely comprehensive and greatly increased the federal government's ability to fight discrimination. Because the government could withhold funds from segregated schools and the attorney general was empowered to initiate school desegregation suits, African Americans would no longer have to rely on the slow, case-by-case approach to end school segregation. Moreover, by creating the Equal Employment Opportunity Commission (EEOC) and placing authority in the hands of the Commissioner of Education, the act put the power of the federal bureaucracy behind efforts to end discrimination.

The Voting Rights Act of 1965 was another step toward racial equality. Areas where less than 50 percent of the population had been registered to vote or had voted in the 1964 presidential election were automatically found to be in violation of the law. Literacy tests and similar devices were prohibited in those areas, and no new voting qualifications could be imposed without approval of the attorney general. The law also mandated that federal examiners be sent to those areas to assist in the registration of voters and to observe elections.

In addition to calling for this legislation, President Johnson, a former Texas senator, issued executive orders that brought the federal bureaucracy into the fight for civil rights. Among other actions, Johnson instructed the Civil Service Commission to guarantee equal opportunity in federal employment, directed the secretary of labor to administer nondiscrimination policies in the awarding of government contracts, and ordered the attorney general to implement the section of the Civil Rights Act of 1964 that withdrew federal funds from any racially discriminatory programs.

By 1965, the federal government was clearly at the forefront of the struggle to end discrimination and guarantee the civil rights of all Americans. However, it remained to be seen whether the provisions of the new laws were constitutional.

The Supreme Court and Civil Rights

Less than six months after Congress passed the Civil Rights Act of 1964, two cases challenging its constitutionality reached the Supreme Court. In *Heart of Atlanta Motel* v. *United States,* the proprietor of a motel claimed that, as a private businessman and not a "state actor," he was not subject to Congress's power to enforce the Fourteenth Amendment. The Court ruled that because the motel was accessible to interstate travelers and thus was engaging in interstate commerce, Congress could regulate it under the interstate commerce clause of Article I.[23] In *Katzenbach* v. *McClung,* the justices noted that although Ollie's Barbecue (in Birmingham, Alabama) had few interstate customers, it obtained supplies through interstate commerce; therefore it, too, was subject to congressional regulation.[24] After these decisions, private businesses began voluntarily ending their discriminatory practices rather than risk losing costly lawsuits.

In 1966, in the case of *Harper* v. *Virginia Board of Elections,* the Court held that all poll taxes, even those imposed by states, violated the equal protection clause of the Fourteenth Amendment.[25] By the end of the 1960s, the number of African American voters in the Deep South had almost doubled.[26] This new voting bloc eventually defeated segregationist candidates, changed the views of politicians who had formerly favored segregation, and elected many African Americans to office at all levels of government. But although African Americans were gaining de jure equality, they were still far from de facto equality.

De Jure Versus De Facto Discrimination

The "War on Poverty" declared by President Johnson in 1964 was in part an attempt to address the problem of racial inequality. But African American communities continued to be plagued by poverty, and it became evident to people throughout the nation that discrimination and its effects were not limited to the South. When civil rights groups began to concentrate on the discrimination that existed in the North, their arguments changed considerably. In the South, segregation had been de jure, or sanctioned by law. In the North, however, segregation was more likely to be de facto; that is, it had developed out of social, economic, and other nongovernmental factors.

As efforts to fight discrimination continued, a major tragedy, the assassination of Martin Luther King Jr., was turned into a dramatic achievement. One week after King's death on April 4, 1968, President Johnson signed into law the Civil Rights Act of 1968, which banned housing discrimination of all types. A few weeks later, the Supreme Court upheld the government's power to regulate private housing by relying on the Civil Rights Act of 1866, which guaranteed all citizens the rights "to inherit, purchase, lease, sell, hold, and convey real and personal property." Justice Potter Stewart linked this law to the Thirteenth Amendment's guarantee to eliminate "badges and incidents of slavery," saying that discrimination in housing "herds men into ghettos and makes the ability to buy property turn on the color of their skin."[27] As a result, a homeowner who wished to sell a house was required to sell it to any financially qualified buyer. But the question of what could be done about the racially divided neighborhoods that already existed, and about the segregated schools that resulted from those divisions, remained.

◀ Some of the most violent and protracted fights against integration took place in northern cities such as Boston, Detroit, and Denver. In this powerful image, a white protester against busing white students in South Boston into Roxbury to integrate the school system turns his flag on an African-American man who was just on his way to work.

affirmative action Programs that attempt to improve the chances of minority applicants for jobs, housing, employment, or education by giving them a "boost" relative to white applicants with similar qualifications.

In 1969, the Supreme Court, tired of the continuing delay in school desegregation fifteen years after the *Brown* decision, ruled in *Alexander* v. *Holmes County Board of Education* that every school district must "terminate dual school systems at once and . . . operate now and hereafter only unitary schools."[28] In other words, they must desegregate immediately. School districts in the South complied within eight years, becoming the most integrated schools in the nation.[29] But northern cities, where de facto segregation still existed, made little progress.

How far would a school district have to go to end segregation? Did the Court's command require that school districts undertake to integrate schools? Did it mean that schools would have to bus children of different races to schools outside their neighborhoods to achieve racial balance? In 1971, the Court considered these questions in the case of *Swann* v. *Charlotte-Mecklenburg Board of Education*. It held that busing, numerical quotas for racial balancing, and other techniques were constitutionally acceptable means of remedying past discrimination.[30] Two years later, in *Keyes* v. *School District #1, Denver, Colorado,* the Court ruled that even in the absence of a law mandating segregation in the schools, school districts could be found to have discriminated if they had adopted other policies that led to segregation.[31]

In the early 1970s, the political and legal climate changed, and the civil rights movement suffered a setback. After ruling unanimously in every racial case since *Brown,* the Supreme Court became increasingly divided. Encouraged by this division, people who believed their neighborhood schools were threatened by busing and other integration programs made their views known, and political opposition to desegregation grew. In 1972 and 1974, congressional efforts to restrict the use of busing to remedy segregation were narrowly defeated. In 1976, however, opponents of busing managed to remove the power of the Department of Health, Education, and Welfare (HEW) to cut off federal funds for school districts that refused to use busing as a remedy.

Amid the turmoil surrounding busing, the Supreme Court heard the case of *Milliken* v. *Bradley* (1974), which asked whether or not the courts could go beyond the city limits of Detroit—in other words, outside an individual school district—in requiring busing programs to remedy segregation. In Detroit as in many other cities, whites had left the inner city to live in the suburbs, and only a plan that bused suburban children to inner-city schools or inner-city children to suburban schools would achieve racial balance. However, arguing that the local operation of schools is a "deeply rooted" tradition, the Court ruled that because the suburban school districts had not been found guilty of official acts of discrimination (though the city schools and the state had), the Detroit desegregation plan need not include the suburban school districts.[32]

During the 1980s, busing remained so controversial that the Justice Department turned instead to other measures, such as the creation of "magnet schools," or schools with special curricula designed to attract interested students from all parts of a city. But the struggle for de facto equality was not limited to public schools. Discrimination in other areas of social life, such as employment and higher education, was coming under increased public scrutiny. Much of that scrutiny focused on efforts to make up for past discrimination through an approach known as affirmative action.

Question for Reflection

Many parents in poor urban school districts with low academic success enroll their children in the more academically successful religious schools in their neighborhoods. Might this be seen as an attempt at de facto equality and should the government support this placement financially?

AFFIRMATIVE ACTION

We now turn to one of the most controversial aspects of the search for equality: programs that seek to increase equality but create temporary inequalities in the process. Such programs are collectively known as **affirmative action**, or programs that make exceptions to the standard operating procedures for the benefit of a previously discriminated against minority.[33] They attempt to improve the chances of minority applicants for jobs, housing, employment, government contracts, or school admissions by giving them a "boost" relative to white applicants with roughly the same qualifications. This action seeks to correct for past discrimination that held members of minority groups at a competitive disadvantage. The problem, of course, is that such efforts appear to discriminate against white applicants. Affirmative action thus raises difficult questions about the nation's commitment to equality and the extent to which the civil rights of all citizens can be protected.

Seeking Full Equality: Opportunity or Result?

At the beginning of the chapter we distinguished between legal equality and actual equality. Much of the discussion so far has described the history of efforts to remove obstacles to legal equality. We have seen that removing legal obstacles does not automatically result in actual equality; often, doing so gives rise to a new set of questions. In particular, does "actual equality" mean **equality of opportunity** or equality of result?

Underlying the goal of equality of opportunity is the idea that "people should have equal rights and opportunities to develop their talents."[34] This implies that all people should begin at the same starting point in a race. But what if life's circumstances make that impossible, placing members of different groups at different starting points, some much farther behind others? For example, a person born into a poor minority family in which no one has ever graduated from high school is likely to be much less prepared for admission to college than a person born into a highly educated family. Because of such differences, many people believe that the nation should aim instead for **equality of result**. All forms of inequality, including economic disparities, should be completely eradicated. This may mean giving some people an advantage at the start so that everyone will complete the race at the same point.

These two forms of equality—opportunity and result—are often in conflict. In a democracy, does providing rights or resources for one group take away rights from others? And if it does, would the action be undemocratic, or would it further approach democracy by improving the well-being of all? For example, the court can order the Piscataway, New Jersey, school system to integrate its high school business department, but can it force the creation of integrated public housing and schools in an effort to seek actual equality? Even if it does take this action, the justices cannot personally change the attitudes of those who think that protecting the civil rights of others will diminish their own rights.

Affirmative action was a logical extension of the desegregation effort. Its proponents argued that in allowing minority candidates to compete on a more level playing field by first tilting the field in their favor, affirmative action would eventually produce equality. In **quota programs**, the concept went a step further to guarantee a certain percentage of admissions, new hires, or promotions to members of minority groups. Opponents of affirmative action, however, labeled this "reverse discrimination" and argued that providing benefits solely on the basis of membership in a minority group would deny those benefits to other, more deserving candidates who had not themselves discriminated against minorities. In other words, equality of result for minorities took away equality of opportunity for majority applicants.

Affirmative action programs began with an executive order issued by President Johnson in 1965 requiring that federal contractors in the construction industry and later in the business community give a slight edge to minority applicants at a disadvantage compared to nonminority applicants. Between 1968 and 1971, the newly created Office of Federal Contract Compliance Programs (OFCCP) issued guidelines for federal contractors establishing certain "goals and timetables" if the percentages of African Americans and women they employed were lower than the percentages of those groups in similar positions in the local workforce. Although the OFCCP's requirements originally dealt only with federal contractors, in 1972 Congress passed the Equal Employment Opportunity Act, which gave the Equal Employment Opportunity Commission the power to take private employers to court if they did not eliminate discrimination in their hiring practices.

Quick Review

Affirmative Action Programs

- Sought to increase equality but created temporary inequalities in the process.
- Made exceptions to the standard operating procedures for the benefit of a previously discriminated against minority.
- Attempted to improve the chances of minority applicants for jobs, housing, employment, government contracts, or school admissions.

equality of opportunity The idea that "people should have equal rights and opportunities to develop their talents," that all people should begin at the same starting point in a race.

equality of result The idea that all forms of inequality, including economic disparities, should be completely eradicated; this may mean giving certain people a starting advantage so that everyone has fair chances to succeed.

quota programs Programs that guarantee a certain percentage of admissions, new hires, or promotions to members of minority groups.

Primary Source: *Regents of the University of California* v. *Bakke* (1978)

Those who supported affirmative action hailed these actions; they believed that such measures could eliminate discrimination unrelated to job performance. Those who opposed affirmative action believed that these "guidelines" and "goals" amounted to quotas that would exclude more-qualified white applicants. They argued that the Constitution was, and should be, "color-blind." Even the ultraliberal William O. Douglas expressed the opinion that the Fourteenth Amendment should be used "in a racially neutral way."[35]

The issue of affirmative action and quota programs reached the Supreme Court in 1978 in the case of *Regents of the University of California* v. *Bakke*. At issue was a voluntary policy of the University of California at Davis medical school, in which sixteen of the school's one hundred openings were set aside for minorities, who received an advantage in admissions. Allan Bakke, a white male, claimed that the policy had deprived him of admission, even though he was more qualified than some of the minority candidates who had been admitted. Four of the justices wanted to rule that the University of California's policy violated the Civil Rights Act of 1964 because the use of quotas discriminated on the basis of "race, color, religion, sex, or national origin." Four other justices wanted to uphold the university's policy of affirmative action as an appropriate remedy for the nationwide scarcity of African American doctors. The deciding vote was cast by Justice Lewis Powell, who agreed in part with both groups. Powell argued that the university's admissions policy violated both the Civil Rights Act and the Fourteenth Amendment's equal protection clause, because its quota program provided specific benefits for students solely on the basis of race. However, Powell also argued that since schools had "a substantial interest" in promoting a diverse student body, admission policies that took race, ethnicity, and social and economic factors into account, while not employing strict quotas, could be constitutional.[36]

Confusion reigned after the *Bakke* decision. The Court tried a year later to refine its mandate in a case involving the use of affirmative action in employment. In *United Steelworkers* v. *Weber*, it considered an affirmative action program at the Kaiser Aluminum Chemical Corporation, which had previously discriminated against African Americans. The program provided training that guaranteed that African Americans would fill half of the openings at its Gramercy, Louisiana, plant until the proportion of minority workers matched their proportion in the local labor force. The Court ruled that the Kaiser plan did not violate the Civil Rights Act, since the purpose of the act was to remedy the effects of past discrimination.[37] In 1980, the Court reinforced this judgment in upholding a program that set aside 10 percent of the grants in the 1977 Public Works Employment Act for minority-owned businesses.[38]

Almost forty years after its inception, affirmative action remains controversial. Even some who might benefit from the policy oppose it, believing that it stigmatizes individuals who wish to compete on their own merits. According to one critic, affirmative action programs "entail the assumption that people of color cannot at present compete on the same playing field with people who are white."[39] Nevertheless, proponents of affirmative action continued to argue that the effects of past discrimination will prevent true equality until overcome by transition programs that give minorities a temporary advantage. Thus, the approach to democracy related to affirmative action is hampered by lack of agreement not only over which goal is most democratic but also over which means represent the best approach.

Affirmative Action in the Reagan-Bush Era

Shortly after coming to office in 1981, President Ronald Reagan appointed officials who challenged many of the nation's civil rights policies. In reexamining affirmative action, his administration took the position that the various civil rights acts prohibited all racial and sexual discrimination, including discrimination against white males. It further argued that only employers found to have discriminated should be required to remedy their discriminatory practices and that they should be required to hire or promote only individuals who could prove that they had been discriminated against.

Programs that protected recently hired minority employees from "last-hired/ first-fired" union layoff rules raised a key issue. White workers with more seniority who now faced layoffs argued that such protections violated their civil rights. In 1984, the administration persuaded the Supreme Court to overturn a federal district court ruling that required a fire department to suspend seniority rules when laying off employees.[40]

In 1986, the Court overturned a program in which a district with no history of discrimination laid off public school teachers with more seniority in favor of minority teachers.[41] However, it rejected the Reagan administration's position that race should never be a criterion for layoffs, ruling that such a plan may be justified in situations where *intent* to discriminate can be shown.[42]

Shortly thereafter, in another case, the Court accepted the use of a 29 percent hiring quota, which reflected the percentage of minorities in the local workforce in that case, because it was being used to remedy blatant past discrimination by the local sheet metal union.[43] And in a 1987 case involving state troopers in Alabama, where not a single African American had reached the rank of corporal, the Court ruled that quotas could be used in promotion decisions where blatant discrimination had occurred in the past.[44]

In general, the Court was saying that affirmative action could be used in states and localities only in cases with demonstrable evidence of specific discrimination and where the program was "narrowly tailored" to meet that offense. A similar pattern prevailed during the George H. W. Bush administration, as can be seen in the Rehnquist Court's rulings on six cases:

1. In *Martin* v. *Wilks* the Court held that even affirmative action programs acceptable to employees and minority workers could later be challenged by nonminority workers.[45]
2. In *City of Richmond* v. *Croson* the Court held that a state contract with a set-aside affirmative action plan could be designed only to remedy specific instances of past discrimination.[46]
3. In *Patterson* v. *McLean Credit Union* the Court held that once a private employment contract was made, employers could not be held liable for issues such as racial harassment and discrimination, because such issues were subsequent to the "making" of that contract.[47]
4. In *Lorance* v. *AT&T Technologies* the Court reduced the amount of time available to plaintiffs wishing to bring employment discrimination suits.[48]
5. In *Independent Federation of Flight Attendants* v. *Zipes* the Court limited the right of recovery of attorneys' fees in employment discrimination cases.[49]
6. In *Wards Cove Packing Co.* v. *Antonio* the Court held that employees claiming employment discrimination had the burden of proving that employment qualifications were not necessary for the jobs they sought.[50]

Seeing the resegregating pattern of these judicial decisions, civil rights leaders turned for help to Congress, dominated by a combination of liberal Democrats and southerners who depended on the African American vote for reelection. In February 1990, a bill was introduced that sought to overturn the Court's decisions in the six cases just described. Both houses of Congress passed the law, but President Bush vetoed it, claiming that it would support "quotas." However, after extensive negotiations, a few minor changes in wording, and passage of the new bill, the president agreed to sign it into law as the Civil Rights Act of 1991.

The Future of Civil Rights

The direction of the government's policy toward civil rights during the Clinton administration was difficult to determine. Although Clinton's initial rhetoric indicated a sensitivity toward further integrating American society, when the congressional Republicans' hostility toward affirmative action programs became clear, the president placed all of these programs "under review," leading several women's groups to march in Washington shouting "No retreat! No retreat!" The president later pledged full support for such programs, perhaps with an eye toward the 1996 election.

At the same time, in early 1995, the federal courts sent mixed messages on racial equality. The nation had thirty-eight historically black state-funded colleges in nineteen states that had histories of segregated higher education systems. In a case referred to as the *Brown* v. *Board of Education* of higher education, the federal court considered whether Mississippi's system of three of these historically black universities was constitutional. District court judge Neal B. Biggers Jr. ruled the state's practice of historically different admission standards for the all-white as opposed to all-black schools unacceptable and ordered the state to spend more money to upgrade the black colleges. With similar legal challenges under way in states such as Alabama, Louisiana, and Tennessee, however, it was unclear how widespread the effect of this ruling would be.[51] The Supreme Court let stand a lower federal court ruling that overturned the University of Maryland's program of blacks-only scholarships despite the school's admission that this program was designed to remedy its past discrimination. (One of those discriminated against was Thurgood Marshall.) Once again, just what effect this ruling would have on similar programs in the rest of the nation's other historically black colleges remained unclear.

Then, in a key 1995 decision, the Supreme Court for the first time refused to uphold the federal program. The case involved a small business administration program in Colorado that gave a Hispanic-owned company an affirmative action advantage in bidding for a highway contract. Instead, the Court ruled that in deciding such cases it would now use the *strict scrutiny test,* meaning that federal programs must serve a compelling governmental interest and must be designed to remedy specific instances of past discrimination by this institution, rather than just overall societal discrimination. This test will make it much more difficult to uphold federal affirmative action programs.[52]

In 1997, the Court's unwillingness to review key actions and lower court decisions led to reduction of affirmative action programs. As the case study makes clear, the fifth circuit court of appeals ruled in the case of Cheryl Hopwood that such race-based preference admissions programs were unconstitutional. Shortly thereafter, California voters passed Proposition 209 by an overwhelming majority.[53] When the Supreme Court refused to accept either of these appeals, thus leaving the lower-court and government actions in force, affirmative action appeared in jeopardy. These rulings, other refusals to make rulings by the Court, voter initiatives, and actions by governors such as Jeb Bush in Florida made clear that America's approach to democracy in the area of civil rights would continue to be debated year after year.

After the election of President George W. Bush, the debate continued, but with a couple of new twists. On the one hand, a year after the Michigan affirmative action cases it became clear that schools' reactions to the decisions had a great impact on their minority admissions efforts. Michigan's African American student composition in its first-year class dropped 13 percent a year after the decisions, and the University of California at Berkeley saw its numbers drop by 60 percent, while Texas A & M saw its numbers increase a staggering 57 percent. Although not all reasons for this change were clear, Michigan's decision to add another written essay in which applying students discuss hardships they had endured and the ways that they would improve campus diversity hurt the school's minority admissions program. On the other hand, Texas A & M, situated in a state that had long before ended affirmative action programs, increased its efforts to recruit low-income students, in the process improving its minority numbers. The school also eliminated its only existing affirmative action program, one that gave an advantage to children of alumni, more than three-quarters of whom were white.[54]

With literally thousands of racial preference laws hanging in the balance at local, state, and national levels, the Supreme Court was narrowly balanced 5–4, as it has been for curbing some such programs, as it did with the undergraduate affirmative action admissions program at the University of Michigan. With Sandra Day O'Connor holding the swing vote, court observers anticipate a change here as a result of her retirement in 2006 and replacement by the more conservative Court of Appeals Judge Samuel Alito. But in fact, it remains to be seen where the new appointee will stand in future cases. Beyond that, even if Alito opposes affirmative action, a slight shift could put Anthony Kennedy, the other moderate swing justice, in the pivotal voting spot on new programs.

MakeItReal

ABC News Video: *Politics of Race*

WOMEN'S RIGHTS

MakeItReal

Primary Source: Seneca Falls Declaration

Civic Participation: State Abortion Rights Policies

In the early 1800s, women in the United States were not permitted to vote, serve on juries, find profitable employment, attend institutions of higher education, or own land in their own name. Moreover, the English common law notion of *coverture,* which held that upon marriage a woman lost her separate legal identity, had been adopted in the United States. As a consequence, married women could not sue in their own name, divorce an alcoholic or abusive spouse, own property independently, or enter into contracts.

When Elizabeth Cady Stanton and Lucretia Mott were not seated as duly elected delegates at an international antislavery meeting in London in 1840, they decided to take action. They organized a movement to attain full legal rights for women. At an 1848 convention in Seneca Falls, New York, the movement borrowed the language of the Declaration of Independence in issuing a Declaration of Sentiments concerning the "natural rights" of women:

> We hold these truths to be self-evident: that all men and women are created equal; that they are endowed by their Creator with certain inalienable rights; that among these are life, liberty, and the pursuit of happiness.[55]

The convention passed twelve resolutions calling for political and social rights for women.

In response to lobbying by women activists, the New York State legislature passed the Married Women's Property Act of 1848. The law gave women control even after marriage over property they received through gifts and inheritance. Encouraged by this success, Stanton, Susan B. Anthony, and other feminist leaders began to lobby for further reforms in New York and other states. Their efforts bore fruit in 1860, when New York passed a civil rights law that gave women control over their wages and inheritances, guaranteed them an inheritance of at least one-third of their husband's estate, granted them joint custody of their children, and allowed them to make contracts and sue in their own name.[56]

Two Steps Forward, One Step Back

After the early successes of the women's rights movement came several setbacks. In 1862, the New York State legislature rescinded and modified the earlier women's rights laws. Realizing the necessity of maintaining constant pressure on legislators, Anthony and Stanton tried to further link their cause with that of African Americans; they formed the National Woman's Loyal League to advocate a constitutional amendment to prohibit slavery. Soon thereafter they joined with supportive men to form an abolitionist alliance called the American Equal Rights Association.

The new group put aside its feminist goals to promote the Fourteenth Amendment. This move proved to be a tactical error, as the amendment introduced the word "male" into the Constitution for the first time. When language giving women the vote was not included in the Fifteenth Amendment, Stanton and Anthony decided to form another organization designed to push solely for women's suffrage.

▲ Susan B. Anthony and Elizabeth Cady Stanton, shown in 1870, were early leaders of the fight for women's rights and women's suffrage. As a result of their efforts, women got the vote in 1920 with the ratification of the Nineteenth Amendment.

In 1869, they formed the National Woman Suffrage Association and began a campaign for a constitutional amendment giving women the right to vote. Meanwhile, Lucy Stone, another longtime activist, formed the American Woman Suffrage Association, which sought to achieve suffrage state by state.

The still-long journey to women's equality became clear in 1873, when the first women's rights case reached the Supreme Court. In sustaining a law that barred women from practicing law, Justice Joseph Bradley stated:

> Man is, or should be, woman's protector and defender. The natural and proper timidity and delicacy which belongs to the female sex evidently unfits it for many of the occupations of civil life. . . . [The] paramount destiny and mission of women are to fulfill the noble and benign offices of wife and mother. This is the law of the Creator.[57]

That "law" became the law of the land as well.

The Struggle for Suffrage

The question of whether the Fourteenth and Fifteenth Amendments were inclusive enough to permit women to vote still remained. In a test case that reached the Supreme Court in 1875, *Minor* v. *Happersett*, Virginia Minor's husband (women still could not sue in their own names) argued that the new "privileges and immunities" clause protected his wife's right to vote. However, the Court disagreed, arguing that the Constitution and state laws reserved this privilege to men only.[58]

Despite such setbacks at the federal level, gradual progress continued at the state level. In 1869 and 1870, the Wyoming and Utah Territories granted full suffrage to women. Nebraska (1867) and Colorado (1876) gave women the right to vote in school elections. In 1890, Alice Stone Blackwell brought together the two rival suffrage organizations to form the National American Woman Suffrage Association, and lobbying for women's suffrage became more organized. By 1910, though, only four states (Colorado, Idaho, Utah, and Wyoming) had provided for full women's suffrage.

The new president of the National American Woman Suffrage Association, Carrie Chapman Catt, advocated the use of a coordinated grass-roots strategy, that is, decentralized action by ordinary citizens, to seek suffrage. This strategy paid off, and by 1918 more than fifteen states, including New York and California, had given women the vote.

This progress was too slow for some. For five years, Alice Paul had been running the Congressional Union (later to become the National Woman's Party) to fight for a constitutional amendment permitting women's suffrage. Arguing that the party in power should be held accountable for the continued disenfranchisement of women, the Congressional Union began picketing the White House and putting pressure on Congress to pass an amendment by touring the country with a replica of the Liberty Bell wrapped in chains. But World War I finally put the suffrage movement over the top. Women argued that their wartime service to the nation should be rewarded with the right of suffrage, and Congress agreed, passing the amendment in June 1919. The Nineteenth Amendment was ratified by the states in 1920, fifty-two years after ratification of the Fourteenth Amendment granting African American males the right to vote and eighty years after Elizabeth Cady Stanton and Lucretia Mott began their quest for full legal rights.

The Road to Equality

MakeItReal

Primary Source: Chronology of the Equal Rights Amendment, 1923–1996

Women successfully used their new electoral clout to secure congressional passage of the Married Women's Independent Citizenship Act of 1922, which granted women citizenship independent from their husbands. However, having achieved its main goal of suffrage, the lobbying coalition fell apart, and actual equality for women would have to wait for decades.

Sex discrimination, also called **sexism**, could be seen in many areas of American society, but especially in education and employment. In 1961, the uproar that resulted when President Kennedy appointed only two women to governmental positions spurred him to issue an executive order creating the President's Commission on the Status of Women, chaired by Eleanor Roosevelt. At the commission's suggestion, Congress passed the Equal Pay Act of 1963, which mandated equal pay for equal work—that is, salaries for men and women performing the same job had to be the same. Although this was a victory for women, the law had limited effectiveness because employers were still free to create different job classifications with varying rates of pay.

The Civil Rights Act of 1964, originally intended to bring about equality for African Americans, represented the greatest advance for women's rights. This was perhaps poetic justice because the movement for full legal rights for women did much to further the causes of African Americans in the 1800s. Ironically, the change came at the behest of a southern congressman, who proposed adding sex to the bill's language in the hope of killing the bill, only to see the measure passed with the language intact. The act barred discrimination against any person on the basis of "race, color, religion, sex, or national origin."

Overburdened by an immense caseload, however, the EEOC was slow to enforce the provisions of the 1964 act. In 1966, outraged by the EEOC's inaction, several women organized the National Organization for Women (NOW). Borrowing techniques from the civil rights movement, NOW organized demonstrations and even picketed the *New York Times* because of its policy of printing a separate section advertising jobs for women. NOW also pressured the EEOC to hold hearings on regulations concerning sex discrimination. In the 1972 Federal Education Amendments, Congress amended the 1964 Civil Rights Act with Title VI, threatening a denial of federal funds to public and private programs that discriminated against women, and Title IX, which called for equal athletic opportunities for women in schools. As the U.S.A. Yesterday and Today box shows, this law has resulted in great changes in college sports.

Leaders of the women's movement still hoped for a constitutional standard establishing equality for women. In 1967, NOW proposed the Equal Rights Amendment (ERA). Women's rights advocates entered the 1970s with the hope that the amendment would be passed and quickly ratified. However, despite congressional approval of the amendment in 1972 and the support of Presidents Nixon and Carter, the ERA fell three states short of the thirty-eight required for ratification. As a result, people often are surprised to learn that women are not specifically mentioned in, and thus not specifically protected by, the Constitution.

Seeking Equality Through the Courts

The quest for equal rights now turned to the courts, focusing on the Fourteenth Amendment, which states that "No state shall . . . deny to any person within its jurisdiction the equal protection of the laws." It seemed reasonable that a woman could be defined as a person and thus be included in the equal protection clause. The key to this strategy would be the Supreme Court's interpretation of *equal protection,* or treating people in different categories equally unless the state can demonstrate some constitutional reason for doing otherwise.

For many years, sex discrimination cases had been decided by the **test of reasonableness**, or whether or not a reasonable person would agree that law had a *rational basis,* thus making it constitutional. The woman had to prove that a law that discriminated by gender was arbitrary, capricious, and totally unjustifiable. Under this test, women rarely won discrimination cases, because the state could so easily find or invent an acceptable rationale for the law. Thus, when the state of Michigan in the 1940s barred women from obtaining a bartender's license unless they were "the wife or daughter of the male owner," the Supreme Court accepted the state's

sexism Prejudice against the female gender.

test of reasonableness Test in court cases of what reasonable people would agree to be constitutional because the law has a rational basis for its existence.

 **MakeItReal**

Visual Literacy: Civil Rights Movement and Women's Suffrage

Quick Review

Title IX, 1972
- No one could be excluded from participation in any education program on the basis of sex.
- Federally funded college or university had to provide opportunities for men and women in varsity sports.
- Schools had to give scholarships to male and female varsity athletes in the same proportion as those participating in the sports.
- A "three-prong test" was created to enforce this provision.

 **MakeItReal**

Primary Source: Equal Rights Amendment

U.S.A. Yesterday and Today

Leveling the Playing Fields

When the University of Connecticut women's basketball team won the NCAA championship in 2002, after a perfect 39–0 season, people somewhat seriously suggested them as a formidable opponent in the men's tournament. The championship was the culmination of thirty years of change at UConn. Alumni recalled the days in the 1970s when women competed without scholarships, for the fun of the game, in a field house with a leaky roof. In those days, the men's basketball team got all the perks while the women's team got none. But a federal law passed in 1972 changed everything for women's collegiate sports.

Title IX of the Federal Education Amendments, passed in 1972, promised that "No person in the United States shall, on the basis of sex, be excluded from participation in, be denied the benefits of, or be subjected to discrimination under any education program or activity receiving federal financial assistance." As a result, every federally funded college and university had to provide opportunities for men and women in their varsity sports roughly equal to the proportion of each gender in the school, unless they could prove an overriding reason for not doing so. In addition, the school had to award scholarships to male and female varsity athletes in substantially the same proportion as those participating in the sports. A "three-prong test" was created to enforce this provision: The percentage of women in college sports must correspond to the percentage of women enrolled in college (currently about 56 percent), progress must be made to improve athletic opportunities for women, and schools have the burden of proving that they provide athletic opportunities for women on their campus.

But change takes time. Despite the promise afforded by this law, in the 1991–92 academic year Donna Lopiano, the women's athletic director at the University of Texas, noticed that the school's football team had more athletes than did the entire women's athletic program. And Texas was hardly the only school in this situation.

▲ Continuing the positive legacy of Title IX of the 1972 Federal Education Amendments, the University of Connecticut's undefeated women's basketball team celebrates its 2002 national championship victory over the University of Oklahoma.

rationale that it wanted to protect the sensibilities of women.[59] And when the state of Florida in the late 1950s declined to put women on jury lists unless they specifically asked to be included, the Court upheld the law because a "woman is still regarded as the center of home and family life" and had "special responsibilities" in this capacity.[60]

Women's rights advocates moved to change the legal standard by which the Court decided cases involving sex discrimination, to shift the burden of proof to the state, thus helping women win their suits. Ruth Bader Ginsburg, a lawyer for the American Civil Liberties Union (ACLU), designed a campaign modeled on that led by Thurgood Marshall twenty years earlier for the NAACP to end racial segregation in the public schools. The idea was to move the Court incrementally, on a case-by-case basis, toward replacing the reasonableness test with a new test more favorable to the women's cause.

Seeking a remedy, Lopiano left her position to direct a national group promoting women in sports. A class action lawsuit against the school, successfully settled out of court in July 1993, brought the University of Texas within four years to its goal of devoting 44 percent of its varsity athletic rosters to women's sports.

Across the nation, schools began adding women's sports, such as softball, soccer, lacrosse, and field hockey, to meet the goal of equality. Sometimes, when funding was tight, men's college athletic programs that generated little or no income were cut or trimmed, such as gymnastics, wrestling, swimming, or track. Certain schools with large football programs that made it difficult to achieve equality created unisex rifle teams in an effort to achieve the goals of the legislation.

This drive for women's equality has produced dramatic results. Female athletes not only have the same chance to compete as men, many now receive athletic scholarships. The number of girls playing competitive sports in high school has increased tenfold, from 300,000 to 3 million. In the past decade, the number of women's college athletic teams has risen from 2,159 to 2,613, and the total number of female athletes has risen from 35,557 to 47,124.

The positive results are most clearly evident in women's basketball. Women's basketball was once a barely noticed sport, with only a handful of college teams. Today, women's collegiate basketball is played on national television to sold-out audiences. We have a women's U.S. Olympic basketball program and the world-ranked U.S.A. women's soccer team draws huge crowds and also competes in the Olympics.

And this progress is not being eroded. In 1996, a federal rule clarifying the 1972 Title IX law dictated that equality in team sports would be judged by numbers of actual athletes rather than spots allotted to a team, or money allocated to men's and women's sports. The following year, the Supreme Court, by refusing to take an appeal, affirmed a decision that Brown University had to equalize its sports funding based on gender. In 2000, with 80 percent of the people supporting Title IX, schools everywhere were being compelled to equalize funding for sports based on gender. Georgia Governor Roy Barnes signed a gender equity law ensuring that Title IX would equal funding for genders in state high schools. One indication of the progress was the new trend by male wrestlers and their coaches to sue in federal court, alleging the elimination of men's programs to equalize sports participation in itself constituted gender discrimination. In June 2002, the Bush administration announced the creation of a Commission on Opportunity in Athletics to review Title IX and recommend ways the law could be changed to ensure "fairness for all college athletes." Women's groups immediately objected, and a year later the group recommended almost no changes in the law.

In 2005, the Supreme Court refused to reinstate the appeal of the National Wrestling Coaches Association, which claimed that Title IX was discriminating against male athletes by forcing their programs to disband. In Colorado, three women sued the University of Colorado under Title IX, alleging sexual harassment by the school's football team. Their cause may have been aided when the Supreme Court ruled in 2005, speaking through Justice Sandra Day O'Connor, that a person who "whistle blows" about violations of Title IX will be protected against retaliation. This case involved Roderick Jackson, a girl's basketball coach in Birmingham, Alabama, who revealed that the boys' teams were being better funded and equipped and was later fired for doing so. Another indication of Title IX legislation success came in 2005 when American women so dominated Olympic softball competition that the sport was eliminated from future Olympic Games.

Sources: Eileen McNamara, "They Fought Just to Play," *Boston Globe,* June 8, 2005; Charles Lane, "High Court Supports Title IX Protection," *Washington Post,* March 30, 2005; Chuck Plunkett, "Release of Report May Aid Women's Title IX Lawsuit," *Denver Post,* March 1, 2005; "Common Sense about Title IX," *Tampa Tribune,* July 22, 2003; Erik Brady, "Bush Picks Panel to Review Title IX," *USA Today,* June 28, 2002, p. C. 1; Darryl Campagna McGrath, "Pioneer Players of the '70s Set Stage for Women's Basketball Today, *Buffalo News,* April 7, 2002; Amy Shipley, "Playing Field Levels at Texas," *Washington Post,* July 6, 1997, p. 1; David Nakamura, "Equity Leaves Its Mark on Male Athletes," *Washington Post,* July 7, 1997, p. 1; and Derrick Gould, "LSU Women Win Court Ruling," *New York Times,* June 2, 2000, p. 1.

The first case, decided by the court in 1971, involved an Idaho law requiring that in naming the executor of a will a male must be chosen over equally qualified females. Under this law a divorced mother named Sally Reed had been prevented from supervising the will of her deceased son. It seemed likely that the law would be upheld under the reasonableness test. The state's "rational basis" for the law was that men know more than women about business, and it was unnecessary for the courts to hold additional hearings to prove this fact.[61]

Ginsburg decided to use the *Reed* v. *Reed* case to persuade the Supreme Court to use the **strict scrutiny test** in dealing with cases of sex discrimination. Under this test, laws that discriminate on the basis of a characteristic "immutable [or unchangeable] by birth," such as race or nationality, are considered "suspect." In cases involving such laws, the burden of proof shifts from the plaintiff to the state, which must demonstrate a "compelling state interest" to justify the discriminatory law.

strict scrutiny test Test of laws that discriminate on the basis of a characteristic "immutable (or unchangeable) by birth," such as race or nationality; in such cases, the burden shifts from the plaintiff to the state, forcing the government to show the compelling reasons for the law.

heightened scrutiny test A middle-level standard that would force the state to prove more than just the reasonableness of a law, though not its compelling nature, in order to justify it. For women's rights cases this means proving the important governmental objectives of the law's goals and linking it to the wording of the law.

That is, the state must show the absence of other means to accomplish a goal than to treat these classes of people unequally.

Because sex, like race and national origin, is "immutable by birth," Ginsburg hoped that the Court would add it to the list of suspect categories. She was only partially successful. The Court still used the reasonableness test to decide the case, but for the first time it could not find an acceptable justification for the state's discriminatory policy. The law thus violated the equal protection clause of the Fourteenth Amendment. The *Reed* v. *Reed* case has been called the women's rights equivalent of the *Brown* v. *Board of Education* case for African Americans.

In 1973, the Court considered the case of Sharron Frontiero, a married air force lieutenant, who objected to a federal law that automatically provided benefits to dependents of married men in the armed forces while the husbands of women in the military received benefits only if they could prove that they were dependent on their wives. Four of the justices were now ready to expand the strict scrutiny test to include women. However, just as he would do later for homosexual rights, the "swing justice," Lewis Powell, was not yet ready to do so, because the Equal Rights Amendment was then being considered for ratification. Thus, the less protective reasonableness test continued as the standard, which became even more important when the ERA failed to be ratified.[62]

In an unusual turn of events, the next case in this area involved a man, Mel Kahn, who claimed to have been discriminated against on the basis of his sex by a Florida law that provided $500 more in property tax exemption for widows than for widowers. Although the ACLU lost the case, it had made an important step forward. Rather than pressing for the strict scrutiny test or accepting the reasonableness test, Ginsburg asked the Court to create an intermediate **heightened scrutiny test**, which would be used for laws that created benevolent forms of discrimination. Such a standard would force the state to justify the law by proving more than its mere "reasonableness," though not its "compelling" nature. Thus, a law would now be upheld if the rights of the plaintiff were deemed on balance more important than the state's interests as represented in the law.[63]

The current legal status of women was finally achieved in a 1976 case called *Craig* v. *Boren* that on the surface did not look like material for a landmark constitutional decision. An underage fraternity boy and the Honk 'n' Holler convenience store had teamed up to challenge an Oklahoma statute under which eighteen-year-old girls could buy weak 3.2 beer (3.2 percent alcohol, as opposed to the 3.5–6 percent), but boys could not do the same until they were twenty-one. The state justified the law on the basis of differential driving records for the two groups. Ginsburg called this a "nonweighty interest pressed by thirsty boys," but it nonetheless led to a legal victory. In striking down the law as an unconstitutional violation of the equal protection clause, the Supreme Court applied the heightened scrutiny test. Under this test, laws that classify people according to their sex must now "serve important governmental objectives and must be substantially related to the achievement of those objectives."[64]

More progress for women's rights occurred in 1996, when the Supreme Court ruled that the Virginia Military Institute (VMI), a state-run, all-male military college, had to admit women or lose state funding. VMI had argued that its 157-year tradition of single-sex education—highlighted by its "rat line" whereby new cadets

▲ Members of the senior class at the previously all-male Virginia Military Institute, standing in their "rat line," greet new cadet Megan Smith, properly attired with her military-style crew cut, as she becomes one of thirty women in the school's first coeducational class under court order.

Approaching Democracy Around the Globe

Women's Rights in Iraq and Afghanistan

In legislative assemblies around the world, women's roles are a matter of "where you stand, depends on where you sit." The clearest evidence of political effects wrought by the American military operation in Afghanistan and Iraq is the number of women in the legislatures of each country.

As a result of the successful American war in Afghanistan, more than 160 seats in the 1,500 person assembly are now guaranteed for women, women clothed in brightly colored attire without veils, with daughters admitted to local schools. "Our endeavor has been aimed at ensuring the rights of the Afghan people to freely choose their own destiny and political future," said Ismael Qasimyar, head of the independent commission in charge of planning the new nationwide assembly. Meanwhile, in Iraq, changes occurring in the adoption of the new Constitution based on the "sharia," or Islamic law, may negatively affect the rights of women in that country. Under the earlier regime of Saddam Hussein, the government guaranteed women's equality. After the Iraq war, their rights were further safeguarded as many women continued to pursue professional careers and wear Western clothing. Much of the impetus for these changes was the addition of ninety women to the United Iraqi Alliance, the national assembly charged with implementing Iraqi law. The addition stemmed from a constitutional quota adopted in 2004. Over time, this large group of female representatives, then 31 percent of the assembly, began to debate the nature of their political agenda. "When you have a fairly large number of women [in a legislature], it brings women's rights to the forefront," said Marina Ottaway of the Carnegie Endowment for International Peace. Still, lacking a majority in the alliance and realizing that, like all large groups in that society, they were deeply divided on many issues, women in Iraq found that they had to rely on the support of other groups, such as the Kurds in the north, the Shiites in the

south, and the supporters of Prime Minister Iyad Allawi, in order to solidify their gains in the new Iraq constitution as well as government.

By late July, the draft constitution for Iraq seemed to indicate that women's rights would not advance, and might well regress significantly. Article 14 of the draft left definition of divorce and inheritance rights for women to the family's religion or sect. And, women's rights would only be guaranteed so long as they did not "violate Sharia." Discussions also suggested eliminating an early constitutional draft requirement, overseen by the Americans, guaranteeing women at least a quarter of the seats in parliament.

When the constitution was narrowly voted into effect on October 15, the nature of women's rights in the country remained deeply in doubt. Moving the government toward a more religious orientation increased chances that a future conservative government might diminish women's rights. The popular elections for the new parliament on December 15, 2005, and discussions over constitutional changes in 2006 in response to Sunni demands may influence whether or not women's rights will be improved or sacrificed as a condition for making the new government more permanent.

Sources: Olivia Ward, "Secular Freedoms in Jeopardy," *Toronto Star,* October 16, 2005, p. A14; Edward Epstein, "New Government Will Face Big Challenges After Constitution Settled," *San Francisco Chronicle,* October 18, 2005, p. A10; Isobel Coleman and Mehlaqa Samdani, "Promote Iraqi Women's Rights Within an Islamic Framework," *Christian Science Monitor,* October 14, 2005, p. 9; Edward Wong, "Iraqi Constitution Draft Includes Curbs to Women's Rights," *New York Times,* July 20, 2005; Sarah Lyall and Jill Carroll, "Iraqi Women Eye Islamic Law," *Christian Science Monitor,* February 25, 2005; Pamela Constable, "Afghans Enjoy a Gala No Longer Banned," *Washington Post,* March 22, 2002; and "Panel Unveils Rules for Afghan Assembly," *Washington Post,* April 1, 2001.

get crew cuts and face the taunts and face-to-face inquisitions of upperclassmen—justified the single-sex approach. But Justice Ginsburg ruled, "We find no persuasive evidence in this record that VMI's male-only admission policy 'is in furtherance of a state policy of diversity.' . . . Rather," she added, "neither the goal of producing citizen-soldiers nor VMI's implementing methodology is inherently unsuitable to women."[65] Although VMI and the Citadel, a formerly all-male military academy in South Carolina, both admitted women to their incoming classes, the tradition of the "rat line" has continued.[66] The progress of women in the service academies became even more evident in 2002 when George W. Bush spoke to the graduating class at West Point, which included a female valedictorian. The nation's only three all-male colleges—Hampden-Sydney in Virginia, Wabash in Indiana, and Morehouse in Georgia—are private ones.

Much progress has been made toward equal rights for women in the United States, but much progress is yet to be made. Many gains have been evident in the political world. In the past five presidential administrations, twenty cabinet heads have been women. The first term of the Bush administration benefited from the advice of more influential women in top executive branch levels than ever before. National Security Adviser Condoleeza Rice, "the most powerful woman to work on a White House staff," helped shape foreign policy, Karen Hughes was one of the most influential presidential counselors before leaving the staff to return to Texas, and Harriet Miers, President Bush's counsel, is consulted on issues ranging from judicial nominations (though not her own unsuccessful one to the Supreme Court) to the "war on terrorism." With more than fifty congressional seats, 19,000 elective posts nationwide, 22.6 percent of the state legislative posts (up from only 4.5 percent in 1971), and twenty-five hundred state and federal judicial posts (not to mention numerous college presidencies and state governorships) all filled by women, progress seems evident when measured against the days when Sandra Day O'Connor and Ruth Bader Ginsburg were only offered positions as legal secretaries after their distinguished law school careers.

This progress became even clearer in 1998 when the Supreme Court clarified its rules on sexual harassment. Confusion had reigned in the federal courts for years after the 1986 Supreme Court ruling that sexual harassment was a form of sex discrimination covered by Title VII of the 1964 Civil Rights Act. In time, lower federal courts required that alleged victims prove loss of a job or an anticipated promotion—a difficult task—in order to win restitution.

In June 1998, the Court handed down two 7–2 decisions, one involving a lifeguard in Boca Raton, Florida, and the other a marketing representative for Burlington Industries in Chicago. The Court ruled that employers were responsible for supervisors' sexual misconduct, even if they had no knowledge of it. Moreover, victims of abuse should not have to prove loss of promotion or job because they rejected a boss's advances; rather, pervasive or continued threats or abuse were enough for a lawsuit. In some cases, though, companies could defend themselves by proving that they took reasonable steps to prevent workplace harassment. As Justice David Souter wrote: "It is by now well recognized that . . . sexual harassment by supervisors (and, for that matter, co-employees) is a persistent problem in the workplace."

In the same term, the Court also ruled that sexual harassment claims can be filed even in same-sex situations. And finally, students in public school who claimed sexual harassment by teachers were ruled unable to sue the school district unless school officials had direct knowledge of the harassment and were deliberately indifferent to it.[67]

In 2000, the Court ruled it unconstitutional for a college student who had been raped in her Virginia college dorm room by two football players to sue the alleged perpetrators under the 1994 Violence Against Women Act in federal court. The states were left to provide criminal and civil remedies for such attacks.[68] Although Congress, in the same year, reauthorized VAWA and expanded it to include date rape, those victims still could not sue their attackers in federal court.

CIVIL RIGHTS AND OTHER MINORITIES

Hispanic Americans

Immigrants to the United States from Mexico, Cuba, Puerto Rico, and other Spanish-speaking countries throughout South America and the Caribbean islands have experienced forms of discrimination similar to those faced by African Americans, though to different degrees. Mexican Americans have been robbed of their land, attacked by the Ku Klux Klan and rioting mobs, excluded from labor unions, and discriminated against in employment, housing, and education. Puerto Ricans,

---

Question for Reflection

What, if any, impact would it have on our approach to democracy if women were represented in leadership positions in government and business at the levels equivalent to their percentage of the total U.S. population?

MakeItReal

Census 2000: The Foreign-Born Population, 2000

Census 2000: Immigrants to the United States, 2002

Cubans, and Colombians have also suffered from discrimination and de facto housing segregation.

In 1929, Mexican Americans founded the League of United Latin American Citizens (LULAC), seeking to gain more equal treatment in American society. Then in the 1950s, they formed organizations that stressed electoral politics and attempted to reclaim lost lands in New Mexico. Perhaps the most famous aspect of the movement was the formation of a union of migrant Mexican American farmworkers under the leadership of Cesar Chavez. Through strikes, boycotts, pickets, and political action, the United Farm Workers drew national attention to the conditions endured by migrant farmworkers.

In the late 1960s, the Mexican American Legal Defense and Education Fund (MALDEF) used litigation and lobbying to campaign for integration, equal school financing, and full protection of voting rights and against discrimination in employment. MALDEF's success led to creation of the Puerto Rican Legal Defense Fund. Other Hispanic American groups, such as the National Council of La Raza, also have fought for increased voter registration and electoral participation.

Along with African Americans, Hispanic Americans benefited from Supreme Court rulings on segregation, the Civil Rights Act of 1964, and the Voting Rights Act of 1965. In *Katzenbach* v. *Morgan,* for example, the Court upheld a portion of the Voting Rights Act of 1965 that outlawed the use of an English literacy test in New York.[69] MALDEF and other groups helped extend the Voting Rights Act to protect Hispanic Americans and "other language" minorities.

The effort to achieve greater education equality for Hispanic and other minority children living in poor communities suffered a setback in 1973 in the case of *San Antonio Independent School District* v. *Rodriguez.*[70] The Court was unwilling to overturn the use of property taxes to finance state school systems, despite the resulting inequality in educational resources between wealthy and poor Texas communities. Nevertheless, several other state supreme courts subsequently used their state constitutions as a basis for requiring equal financing of education. Then, in 1982, the Court ordered that all children must be provided with schooling regardless of whether or not their parents were legal immigrants.[71]

Hispanic Americans continue to struggle against discrimination and poverty. Now the nation's largest majority, numbering more than forty-one million people, or 14.1 percent of the population, an increase of nearly 100 percent over the twenty-two million present in this country in 1990, and with half having been born outside this country, it is predicted that by the mid-twenty-first century Hispanic Americans will make up nearly one-third of the U.S. population.[72] So achievement of legal and actual equality for this group deserves high priority. Evidence of this demand was seen in the Bush administration discussion as to who should replace Chief Justice William Rehnquist and Justice Sandra Day O'Connor. Two Hispanic Americans, Attorney General Alberto Gonzalez and Emilio Garza of the U.S. Court of Appeals for the Fifth Circuit, received prominent mention for the vacancies.[73]

Native Americans

The discrimination and segregation against Native Americans is well known but virtually ignored throughout America's history. Native American tribes have been removed from their land, treaties have been broken, and Native Americans have been denied the basic right of citizenship. In 1884, the Supreme Court ruled that Native Americans were not citizens of the United States and therefore were neither protected by the Fourteenth Amendment nor granted the right to vote.[74] In the early 1900s, Native Americans strove to attain both citizenship and tribal autonomy, while during the 1920s they struggled against attempts to open reservations to miners' exploitation. Finally, in 1924 Congress passed the Indian Citizenship Act, which gave Native Americans the right to vote.

Quick Review

Hispanic Americans
- Now the nation's largest minority.
- Nearly 40 million people, half born in the United States, up nearly 100 percent since 1990.
- By the mid-twenty-first century, Hispanic Americans will make up nearly one-third of the U.S. population.

▶ Descendants of Chief Spotted Elk and his people commemorate the one-hundredth anniversary of the Battle of Wounded Knee, South Dakota, where on December 29, 1890, some three hundred women, children, and elderly people were massacred by the U.S. Army Seventh Regiment, Custer's old regiment, which was seeking revenge for the Battle of the Little Bighorn.

Native Americans have resisted various attempts to assimilate them into the mainstream culture of American society over the years. In the 1940s, the National Congress of American Indians formed to fight for education and legal aid. During the 1960s, Native Americans engaged in acts of civil disobedience such as delaying dam construction, occupying government offices, and holding sit-ins and other demonstrations to fight against discrimination. The American Indian Movement (AIM) occupied buildings and staged demonstrations, and in 1973, AIM played a major part in the well-publicized occupation of Wounded Knee on the Pine Ridge Reservation in South Dakota. Unfortunately, however, the Native American cause has yet to generate the support found for other minority groups.[75]

Native Americans face a challenge that most other minorities do not: They are divided into two movements with different aspirations. The ethnic movement shares the aspirations of other ethnic minorities to achieve equality in American society. In contrast, the separatist tribal movement seeks separate citizenship and a system of government based on the tribe, the Indian culture decimated by the United States' growth. Whereas the ethnic movement wishes to participate in American democracy, the tribal movement seeks to create its own concept of democracy, removed from a democratic government that in the past too often failed to live up to its treaties.

During the 1960s, Native Americans advanced tribal sovereignty and treaty rights and changed public perceptions of "Indians." In recent years, tribes in Rhode Island,

▶ Native American activist Eloise Cobell stands in front of one of the oil wells on land owned, according to treaty, by her Blackfeet Nation, but whose mineral rights profits have been going elsewhere, leading to her $137-billion law suit against the United States government. In February 2006, while tribal leaders sought to settle the case, the government was ordered to pay $7 million in legal fees.

Connecticut, and elsewhere have used state law exemptions to create highly profitable gambling enterprises on reservation lands, thus raising money for their communities and creating political clout. This success, however, is relatively isolated, and discrimination has not been eliminated. Equality remains elusive as the Native American population remains among the poorest and least represented in government in the nation.

MakeItReal

Primary Source: The Americans with Disabilities Act (1990)

EMERGING MINORITY GROUPS SEEK PROMINENCE

Americans with Disabilities

Unlike other minority groups, Americans with disabilities, who by some definitions now number forty-three million, have been extremely successful in persuading Congress to pass legislation barring discrimination against them. However, since 1999, Supreme Court rulings have been making it more and more difficult for these people to obtain federal government protection.

In 1948, likely stirred by the memory of the wheelchair-bound late president, Franklin D. Roosevelt, Congress passed a law prohibiting discrimination against the physically handicapped in the civil service. The 1968 Architectural Barriers Act required that all buildings constructed with federal money or leased by the federal government be made accessible to the handicapped. Congress acted again in 1973, when it mandated that federal contractors and programs that received federal funds adopt policies of nondiscrimination and affirmative action for the disabled. When Congress passed the Civil Rights Restoration Act of 1988, it barred any institution that discriminated on the basis of race, sex, age, or handicap from receiving federal funds.

Despite passage of these and other statutes that protect the rights of the disabled, Americans with disabilities continue to be deprived of many basic civil rights. For example, they still face discrimination by private employers and establishments. Some progress occurred in 1990, when Congress passed the Americans with Disabilities Act (ADA). Under the provisions of this act, firms with more than twenty-five employees

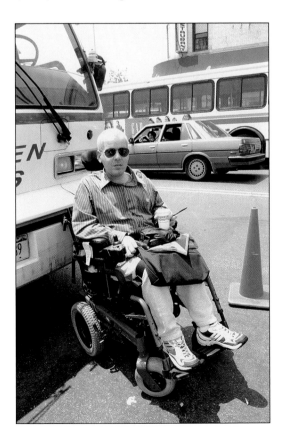

◄ Seeking to protest the lack of access to some New York City buses for wheelchair-bound passengers, Anthony Trocchia led a spontaneous sit-in blocking the bus. When the bus was ordered by police to leave in reverse, they blocked the back as well.

are barred from discriminating against disabled individuals in hiring or promotion. In addition, companies must make "reasonable accommodations" for disabled employees, such as providing readers for blind workers or wider doors for those in wheelchairs. Interestingly, the Court is interpreting these laws that bar unlawful discrimination against people with disabilities as saying that government and industry must make exceptions in favor of those groups. The law thus becomes the largest and most expensive affirmative action program in the nation. Recent studies have shown, however, that this law rarely helps the disabled seeking jobs. Instead, more than one-third of the complainants are using it to address such relatively minor problems as back pain, psychological stress, and substance abuse.[76]

As we discussed in Chapter 3, the Supreme Court in 1999 ruled in five separate cases that the ADA would have a much narrower reach than many expected. Noting that Congress intended to reach 43 million people with the law, the Court ruled that this law did not apply to people with correctable impairments, such as high blood pressure or bad eyesight, which would have expanded the law's influence to 160 million people. As a result, attorneys seeking disabilities protection will now turn to the states, such as California, for greater protection.[77] In the 2001–02 term, the Court continued the states' rights direction of its rulings by deciding against disabled litigants who were seeking federal judicial protection in four separate cases. Among these decisions, the Court ruled that states are constitutionally immune from lawsuits for damages under the ADA. The Court ruled that Congress had not sufficiently demonstrated in the legislative record for the law that states discriminated against handicapped persons, and that Congress had no power to require states to implement such a law.[78] This issue was revisited in 2004 after a wheelchair-bound criminal defendant, George Lane, was forced to crawl up two flights of stairs to reach a courtroom on the second floor because the building had no elevator. Lane and a similarly disabled certified court reporter, Beverly Jones, sued the state of Tennessee under Title II of the Americans with Disabilities Act, arguing that parts of the Tennessee courthouse were inaccessible to them. Although the state claimed immunity from such suits under the Eleventh Amendment, the Supreme Court ruled 5–4 that Congress had the power to compel states to "take reasonable measures to remove architectural and other barriers to accessibility" for public services such as the state court system.[79] Because Tennessee had failed to do so, citizens seeking, and being denied, access to these facilities could sue for damages.

Why has the struggle for equality been relatively easy for the disabled, compared with other minority groups? One reason is that laws requiring access to facilities provide equality of opportunity, a goal on which most Americans agree. Another reason is that many of us, including politicians such as Franklin D. Roosevelt and Robert Dole, either have disabilities or have relatives with disabilities, which brings the experiences of the disabled close indeed. The ADA demonstrates how far the United States can travel along the road to democracy when it is unified about the direction it wants to take.

Other Groups Seeking Representation   Inevitably, more minority groups that face discrimination will demand greater equality. Two such groups are the elderly and homosexuals. With an ever-increasing percentage of Americans in the oldest age groups as Baby Boomers retire, demands will increase for protection of the civil rights of the elderly. Although the Age Discrimination in Employment Act (ADEA) covers many of the elderly, new issues will undoubtedly arise and will be pressed on the government by the thirty-million-member American Association of Retired Persons (AARP). In 2000, this group lost ground because of a narrow 5–4 Supreme Court ruling that Congress lacked the power to make state governments liable to federal lawsuits brought under the Age Discrimination in Employment Act to remedy discrimination against older workers.[80]

The challenge for the gay and lesbian community, as seen by the controversy in 2002 when talk show host Rosie O'Donnell announced that she was gay, is unique in American society. A high percentage of the estimated 25–30 million homosexual Americans live their lives in secret, undetected and unsuspected by a "straight" society prone to homophobia. Although some states and localities attempt to protect the civil rights of homosexuals, the federal government and many states do not. Vermont now has a civil union law protecting same-sex couples and Massachusetts allows gay marriages, but the 2004 decision by eleven states to ban same-sex marriages illustrates how these rights vacillate. Even with the 2003 *Lawrence* v. *Texas* decision upholding the privacy rights of gays, as outlined in Chapter 13, one wonders if one day a judicial decision will have the same impact on legal equality for this community as *Brown* had for racial minorities.

CIVIL RIGHTS AND THE WAR ON TERRORISM

ABC NEWS/PRENTICE HALL VIDEO LIBRARY

Muslims In America

Facing discrimination demands greater equality, but the immediate question facing the nation is whether or not we can preserve the civil rights of any individual under investigation during a time of crisis. Although Chapter 13 considered how to preserve legal and trial safeguards for people arrested in the "war on terrorism," what of those under investigation simply because of their ethnic background?

Perhaps the greatest test of America's approach to democracy with respect to civil rights since September 11, 2001, is the issue of ethnic profiling in conducting antiterrorism investigations, airport searches, immigration interviews, and secret detentions of Muslim men who came from nations where the al-Qaeda network is considered active. Within days after the attacks on the World Trade Center and the Pentagon, more than twelve hundred Muslim men were arrested on minor immigration violations, such as overstaying their visas, and jailed without legal representation or their names being released. The passage of the USA Patriot Act later allowed for this kind of detention of others. Two months after the attack, nearly five thousand Arab men, between the ages of eighteen and thirty-three who entered the United States after January 1, 2000, on nonimmigrant visas, were requested to "voluntarily" present themselves for interviews by Justice Department and Immigration and Naturalization Service representatives. "We are merely seeking to solicit their assistance to obtain any information they may have regarding possible terrorists or potential terrorist acts," explained Attorney General John Ashcroft. Nearly twenty-five hundred of the men could not be found, and these interviews, which produced fewer than two dozen arrests, revealed minimal information. Still, the Justice Department was encouraged by the level of cooperation of those interviewed and the nature of the information it gathered. So, early in 2002, over the objections of civil rights groups who feared that these interviews carried with it the dual risks of racial profiling and potential deportation, the government requested that another three thousand visitors who had entered this country more recently present themselves for interviews. Years of dealing with charges of "racial profiling" in New Jersey, California, and wherever police have used their discretion in stopping and questioning African Americans now took a twist as authorities in airports and mass transportation centers began targeting Arab Americans, persons of Arabian descent, and Arab visitors for questioning, searching, and even detention. Although authorities tried to use random search techniques, thousands of complaints were lodged nationwide concerning racial profiling. Profiled individuals were forced to leave planes, one of them a Secret Service agent for President Bush, because of pilots', flight attendants', or even passengers' fears about traveling with them.[81]

These actions eventually led to challenges in federal court. Realizing that by mid-February 2002 more than three hundred men were still detained in federal prisons without legal representation, many of them in northern New Jersey, a New Jersey state judge set a deadline for release of their names. The Immigration and Naturalization service ordered the state and local governments not to release the names, saying that the move could endanger both national security and the welfare of those being detained. By the middle of April, a civil rights group sued the federal government on the detainees' behalf, alleging that hundreds of Muslim men were being held in prison on minor immigration violations, being subjected to harsh treatment, and not receiving hearings to determine their legal status. When the case reached District Court Judge Gladys Kessler in the District of Columbia Circuit in August 2002, she ordered the names of these prisoners released. "The requirement that arrest books be open to the public is to prevent any 'secret arrests,' a concept odious to a democratic society."[82] In short, this practice receded from, rather than approached, democracy. Despite this ruling, the United States government continued to refuse to release the names of prisoners. By October 2002, a few prisoners deemed to have little intelligence value were released from the Guantanamo Bay holding facility. Still, one controversial government practice was the decision to seal the records of hundreds of deportation hearings if they were deemed of "special interest" after the September 11 attacks. The sixth circuit court of appeals ruled the Bush administration's policy of holding secret deportation hearings unconstitutional. "Open proceedings, with a vigorous and scrutinizing press, serve to ensure the durability of our democracy," ruled the Sixth Circuit judges, who relied on the First Amendment's right of access to government proceedings.[83] In March, 2006, with nearly 500 prisoners still being held at Guantanamo Bay, some prisoners were being released and others were being named amid calls by some in the European Union to close the facility.

As other lawsuits work their way through the courts the question is whether the government can show that the benefits to the security of the nation of such law enforcement supercedes the civil rights of the people under investigation. Lessons will be drawn from the civil rights fights of African Americans and women, the 1940s Japanese internment policy, and the "red scare" period in the 1950s, as the federal courts and the American people decide the nature of civil rights in times of crisis. In the end, the question will be asked whether the actions taken to preserve security will preserve the democratic goals of the nation or lead instead to a nation which no longer approaches the very democratic vision that it claims to be seeking.

CIVIL RIGHTS AND APPROACHING DEMOCRACY

After two hundred years of civil rights battles, how much farther must we go to achieve full equality for all Americans? Clearly, the disputes over affirmative action, women's rights, and the war on terrorism illustrate that the struggle goes on. Another set of questions deals with just how inclusive society should be in approaching democracy.

We have seen that at various times civil rights protection has fallen to the Supreme Court, at other times to the Congress, and at still other times to the president. Throughout the struggle, the force behind the effort to achieve equal rights had been the "people power" of the civil rights movement, the women's movement, and others. Yet much work remains. America will continue to approach democracy by guaranteeing legal and actual rights, but the road will not be a straight or smooth one.

Summary

1. Discrimination is unequal treatment based on race, ethnicity, gender, and other distinctions. The primary means for achieving equal treatment is ensuring full protection of civil rights, constitutionally guaranteed rights that government may not arbitrarily remove.

2. Equality before the law, or de jure equality, forbids legally mandated obstacles to equal treatment. Actual equality, or de facto equality, refers to results—the actual conditions of people's lives.

3. Although black slaves were freed during the Civil War, they had no legally protected civil rights. By the end of the nineteenth century, the races were strictly segregated by Jim Crow laws, and in *Plessy* v. *Ferguson* the Supreme Court ruled that separate but equal facilities did not

violate the Fourteenth Amendment. Although African Americans had the right to vote, state voting laws contained many loopholes that effectively disfranchised blacks. In the early decades of the twentieth century, the NAACP won several lawsuits that advanced the cause of racial equality.

4. During and after World War II the White House issued executive orders prohibiting discrimination in the defense business and the military. The NAACP led the battle to desegregate the public schools, which culminated in the historic *Brown* v. *Board of Education of Topeka, Kansas,* ruling that struck down the separate-but-equal doctrine.

5. Beginning with the Montgomery bus boycott in 1955, the civil rights movement employed techniques such as boycotts, protest marches, and sit-ins to publicly demonstrate the injustice of unequal treatment based on race. During the 1960s, Congress passed several laws designed to eliminate discrimination, including the Civil Rights Act of 1964 (which focused on discrimination in public accommodations, voter registration, and employment), the Voting Rights Act of 1965, and the Civil Rights Act of 1968, which focused on discrimination in housing. Several cases decided by the Supreme Court during this period dealt with the specific means used to desegregate schools.

6. Affirmative action programs attempt to improve the chances of minority applicants for jobs, housing, employment, and graduate admissions by giving them a slight advantage over white applicants with similar qualifications. Such programs seek to increase equality but can create temporary inequalities in the process, and therefore are controversial. Underlying the controversy is a disagreement over the meaning of actual equality; some believe that the goal should be equality of opportunity, whereas others believe that the nation should strive for equality of result.

7. The Reagan administration challenged many of the nation's civil rights policies, claiming that the various Civil Rights Acts prohibited all racial and sexual discrimination, including discrimination against white males. In a series of cases, the Supreme Court set specific limits on the use of affirmative action.

8. The movement for women's rights began with the Declaration of Sentiments drawn up at a convention held in Seneca Falls, New York, in 1848. Progress toward equality was slow and uneven throughout the next several decades; women gained control over their property but could not vote. Not until 1920 did the Nineteenth Amendment to the Constitution grant women the right of suffrage.

9. In response to complaints of sex discrimination in education and employment, Congress passed the Equal Pay Act of 1963, which required equal pay for equal work. The Civil Rights Act of 1964 also barred discrimination on the basis of sex. However, efforts failed to pass the Equal Rights Amendment to the Constitution, which would have given full protection to the civil rights of women.

10. In the 1970s, efforts to gain equal protection for women's rights turned to the courts and focused on the standard used to determine whether a state law is constitutional. Supreme Court decisions gradually shifted from favoring a reasonableness test, which upheld a law if the state could provide an acceptable rationale for the law, to favoring a heightened scrutiny test, in which laws that classify people according to their sex must serve important governmental objectives and be substantially related to the achievement of those objectives.

11. Hispanic Americans have made considerable progress toward equal treatment, particularly in the area of voting rights, but they continue to struggle against discrimination and poverty. Native Americans also have organized to demand the basic rights of citizenship and to fight against discrimination. In contrast to these and other minority groups, Americans with disabilities have been extremely successful in persuading Congress to pass legislation barring discrimination against them.

12. The ongoing investigation in the war on terrorism has raised the question of racial profiling of people of Middle Eastern descent. Although the government has tried to use random searches to avoid complaints, future litigation must determine if the proper balance is maintained between civil rights and national security. The federal courts have ruled unconstitutional the Bush administration's practice of holding secret deportation hearings.

Review Questions

1. Explain how the intervention of the Supreme Court in both the nineteenth and twentieth centuries as well as amendments to the Constitution have changed the lives of African Americans in this country.

2. In what way can *Brown* v. *Board of Education* be seen as a turning point in civil rights cases? Which important actions have been taken since to further implement civil rights for African Americans?

3. Explain the evolution in civil rights for Native Americans in this country. Why do you think it took so long for this group to gain citizenship and voting rights?

4. What is affirmative action and why might even beneficiaries oppose it?

5. Explain the ways in which southern states kept their African American populations from voting. What were the legislative and judicial developments that

finally allowed African Americans to politically participate?

6. Discuss the evolution of women's rights in the United States. What was the significance of the failure of the ERA to this movement?

7. How did Title IX transform the nature of women's sports in America?

8. What is the status of civil rights for "Americans with Disabilities"?

Key Terms

affirmative action 510	equality of result 511	quota programs 511
black codes 501	freedom riders 507	sexism 517
boycott 506	heightened scrutiny test 520	sit-in 506
civil disobedience 506	integration 505	state action 501
de facto equality 499	Jim Crow laws 502	strict scrutiny test 519
de jure equality 499	peonage 503	suffrage 501
desegregation 503	poll tax 502	test of reasonableness 517
equality of opportunity 511	protest march 506	unfair discrimination 498

Suggested Readings

ABRAHAM, HENRY J., and BARBARA A. PERRY. *Freedom and the Court: Civil Rights and Liberties in the United States.* 7th ed. New York: Oxford University Press, 1998. An analysis of the Supreme Court and lower federal courts' development of American civil rights and liberties.

BOK, DEREK, and WILLIAM BOWEN. *The Shape of the River: Long-Term Consequences of Considering Race in College and University Admissions.* Princeton, N.J.: Princeton University Press, 1998. A powerful critique of the affirmative action program in American education.

BRANCH, TAYLOR. *Parting the Waters: America in the King Years, 1954–63.* New York: Simon & Schuster, 1988. A Pulitzer Prize winner, this is the first of three volumes on Martin Luther King Jr. and the civil rights movement in the United States.

BRANCH, TAYLOR. *Pillar of Fire: America in the King Years, 1963–65.* New York: Simon & Schuster, 1998. The second of three planned volumes on the life and times of Martin Luther King Jr., covering events in the civil rights movement from the March on Washington to the demonstrations in Selma, Alabama.

BRANCH, TAYLOR. *At Canaan's Edge: America in the King Years, 1965–68,* New York: Simon & Schuster, 2006. The final volume in this groundbreaking life and times of Martin Luther King Jr. covers the Civil Rights movement from the 1965 Selma protest march through Reverend King's assassination in 1968.

BROWN, DEE ALEXANDER. *Bury My Heart at Wounded Knee: An Indian History of the American West.* New York: Holt, Rinehart & Winston, 1971. A highly readable history of the sad treatment of Native Americans by the United States government and its people.

CARTER, STEVEN L. *Reflections of an Affirmative Action Baby.* New York: Basic Books, 1991. A learned critique of the affirmative action programs by an African-American law professor from Yale who benefited from them.

GARROW, DAVID J. *Bearing the Cross: Martin Luther King, Jr., and the Southern Christian Leadership Conference.* New York: Morrow, 1986. This landmark biography of King won a Pulitzer Prize.

HALBERSTAM, DAVID. *The Children.* New York: Random House, 1998. Offers a dramatic account of the young civil rights freedom riders who desegregated the buses and restaurants in 1961 and tracks what happened to them in later life.

KEYSSAR, ALEXANDER. *The Right to Vote: The Contested History of Democracy in the United States.* New York: Basic Books, 2000. A groundbreaking study of the meandering expansion of voting rights throughout this nation's history.

KLUGER, RICHARD. *Simple Justice.* New York: Knopf, 1976. The compelling story of the cases that made up the landmark *Brown* v. *Board of Education* case. Included is the remarkable story of legendary NAACP attorney Thurgood Marshall.

MANSBRIDGE, JANE J. *Why We Lost the ERA.* Chicago: University of Chicago Press, 1986. An examination of reasons why the Equal Rights Amendment failed.

NIEMAN, DONALD G. *Promises to Keep: African-Americans and the Constitutional Order, 1776 to the Present.* New York: Oxford University Press, 1991. An informative history of the development of legal rights for African Americans.

ROWLAND, DEBRAN. *The Boundaries of Her Body: The Troubling History of Women's Rights in America.* Naperville, Ill.: Sphinx, 2004. A wonderfully complete history and analysis of the evolution of women's rights in America.

VERBA, SIDNEY, and GARY R. ORREN. *Equality in America: The View from the Top.* Cambridge, Mass.: Harvard University Press, 1985. An analysis of how close the United States has come to achieving true racial equality.

WILLIAMS, JUAN. *Eyes on the Prize: America's Civil Rights Years, 1954–1965.* New York: Penguin, 1987. The companion book to the PBS series on the history of the civil rights movement in the United States.

Visualizing Democracy

Minority Rights in America

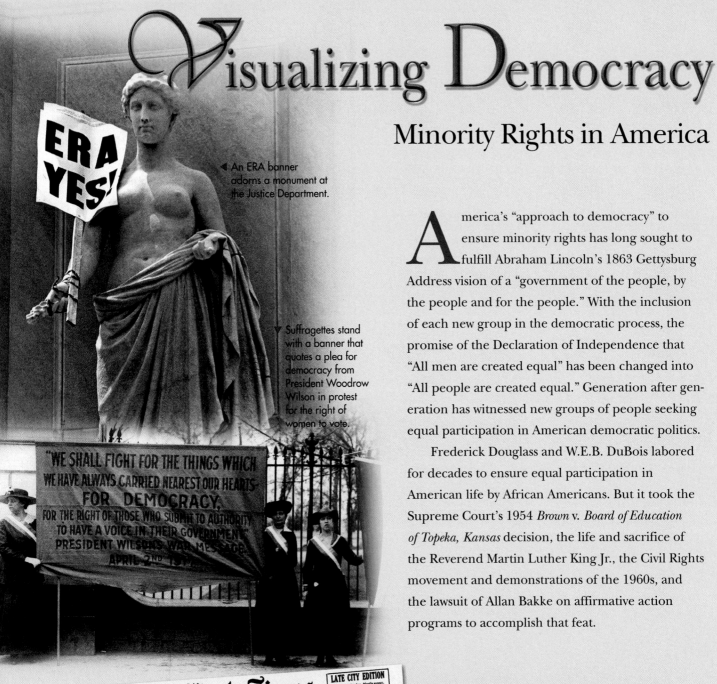

◀ An ERA banner adorns a monument at the Justice Department.

ERA YES!

▼ Suffragettes stand with a banner that quotes a plea for democracy from President Woodrow Wilson in protest for the right of women to vote.

"WE SHALL FIGHT FOR THE THINGS WHICH WE HAVE ALWAYS CARRIED NEAREST OUR HEARTS— FOR DEMOCRACY, FOR THE RIGHT OF THOSE WHO SUBMIT TO AUTHORITY TO HAVE A VOICE IN THEIR GOVERNMENT" PRESIDENT WILSON'S WAR MESSAGE APRIL 2ND 1917

America's "approach to democracy" to ensure minority rights has long sought to fulfill Abraham Lincoln's 1863 Gettysburg Address vision of a "government of the people, by the people and for the people." With the inclusion of each new group in the democratic process, the promise of the Declaration of Independence that "All men are created equal" has been changed into "All people are created equal." Generation after generation has witnessed new groups of people seeking equal participation in American democratic politics.

Frederick Douglass and W.E.B. DuBois labored for decades to ensure equal participation in American life by African Americans. But it took the Supreme Court's 1954 *Brown* v. *Board of Education of Topeka, Kansas* decision, the life and sacrifice of the Reverend Martin Luther King Jr., the Civil Rights movement and demonstrations of the 1960s, and the lawsuit of Allan Bakke on affirmative action programs to accomplish that feat.

◀ The front page of *The New York Times* on May 18, 1954 announces the Supreme Court's historic decision in the Brown v. Board of Education school segregation case.

▼ Native American men from the American Indian Movement stand guard with rifles outside a church building in Wounded Knee, South Dakota.

The New York Times

LATE CITY EDITION

"All the News That's Fit to Print"

FIVE CENTS

VOL. CIII...No. 35,178.

NEW YORK, TUESDAY, MAY 18, 1954.

HIGH COURT BANS SCHOOL SEGREGATION; 9-TO-0 DECISION GRANTS TIME TO COMPLY

McCarthy Hearing Off a Week as Eisenhower Bars Report

A young girl and her mother participate in a vigil in which Muslims protest treatment of Iraqi detainees. ▶

Elizabeth Cady Stanton, Susan B. Anthony, Carrie Chapman Catt and other women's suffragettes lobbied Woodrow Wilson and the Congress in the early twentieth century for the Nineteenth Amendment guaranteeing women's right to vote. But it would take until the late twentieth century to realize their dream, when Condoleezza Rice and Madeleine Albright served as Secretary of State, Hillary Clinton and others served as U.S. Senators, and Ruth Bader Ginsburg and Sandra Day O'Connor served on the U.S. Supreme Court.

As the decades passed, other groups sought inclusion in the political process. Cesar Chavez protested for the inclusion of Hispanics and migrant farm workers. Young people protested in the early 1970s for their voice to be heard while their generation was being sent to fight in Vietnam. Native Americans protested on reservations and at Wounded Knee in South Dakota.

Whether it be the Gray Panthers and other senior citizens protesting for better health-care benefits, gay Americans seeking the right to marry, documented and undocumented immigrants asking for the right to become citizens, or Muslim Americans arguing against stereotyping in the war on terrorism, the efforts by groups to be included equally in the American political process never ends. The ability of America to maintain an open democracy and thus come closer to Abraham Lincoln's ideal will help to define the true nature of our democracy. ★

▶ Pro-affirmative action demonstrators gather outside the U.S. Supreme Court in Washington on April 1, 2003, in a civil rights march.

▼ The Rev. Martin Luther King Jr. acknowledges the crowd at the Lincoln Memorial during the March on Washington, D.C., on Aug. 28, 1963. The march was organized to support proposed civil rights legislation and end segregation.

The Gray Panthers protest in Washington, DC.

★ CHAPTER 15 ★

DOMESTIC AND ECONOMIC POLICY

CHAPTER OUTLINE

$\mathscr{A}$pproaching $\mathscr{D}$emocracy

The First Major Achievement of a New Era

In a moment of major political success, on June 7, 2001, President Bush signed into law a $1.35-trillion-dollar tax cut, the third largest since World War II. The signing took place in a public ceremony in the East Room and was steeped in the type of tradition reserved for important moments of national legislative history. As the Marine Corps band played "Hail to the Chief," President Bush signed the tax cut (see Figure 15.1), using a different pen to sign each letter of his name.[1]

In signing the bill, President Bush fulfilled a campaign promise that many observers believed he could not achieve—"the first major achievement of a new era," as President Bush optimistically described the tax cut. "Today, for the first time since the landmark tax relief championed twenty years ago by President Ronald Reagan, and forty years ago by President John F. Kennedy, an American President has the wonderful honor of letting the American people know significant tax relief is on the way," President Bush said.[2]

In addition to $300 for adults filing single tax returns and $600 for joint returns, the tax cut called for gradual reductions in the tax rate and a new 10 percent tax bracket at the bottom of the income scale. Tax filers also could

★ Taxes rose after Lyndon B. Johnson signed the Medicare and Medicaid law in 1965, and fell slightly with President Ronald Reagan's tax cut in 1981.

increase the amount of money contributed to retirement plans, 401(k)s, and education-related savings accounts.

No doubt recalling the lessons of his father who lost his second bid for office by breaking the "big" promise of "read my lips: no new taxes," the younger Bush intended to implement what he said—a major tax break for the American people. The new law was also a victory for conservatives who believed "cutting taxes is the public policy precondition to expanding freedom, limiting government growth and promoting prosperity."[3]

★ "Tax relief is a great achievement for the American people. Tax relief is the first achievement produced by the new tone in Washington, and it was produced in record time," said President Bush at a White House ceremony for signing the historic $1.35-trillion tax cut bill in June 2001.

Not everyone agreed. Former Senate democratic leader Thomas Daschle warned that "the policy implications . . . will be felt for decades to come. What this means is that the Social Security and Medicare trust funds are no longer viable. What this means is that we won't have the resources to make the commitment to education, prescription drug cost, and the other priorities of the American people. But most sadly what this means is that we could be back into the days of debt in the not too distant future, all because many could not find the prudence and the balance to limit their appetite for tax cuts."[4]

Congress attached a caveat to the tax bill—the tax cut expires on December 31, 2010. This was in keeping with rules passed by Congress to limit spending bills that reach more than a decade into the future. The Bush tax cuts were followed by additional cuts in 2003. In all, they have reduced individual tax rates, provided breaks for married couples, set a 15 percent rate on dividends and capital gains, phased out the estate tax, and increased the child tax credit to $1,000. In his 2006 budget, the president proposed permanently extending the 2001 and 2003 tax cuts, even in light of record budget deficits.[5]

★ President Bill Clinton signed a deficit-reduction bill in 1993 that, along with the booming economy, sparked a steady rise in the national tax take. President George Bush reversed that course with a series of tax cuts in 2001, 2002, 2003, and 2004.

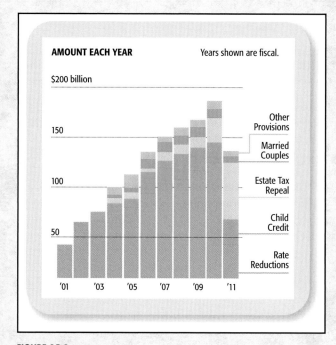

FIGURE 15.1
The Tax Cut Becomes Law
Note: Does not include an accounting change that shifts some corporate tax payments from one fiscal year to another.

QUESTIONS FOR REFLECTION

What relationship exists between taxes and public policy?

What conditions need to be in place for adequate social programs as well as reasonable taxing policies to coexist?

Introduction
PUBLIC AND ECONOMIC POLICY

Public policies are the decisions, actions, and commitments of government. They are the means by which government attempts to solve problems and make life easier and safer for its citizens. Regulation of the national economy is one of the most crucial roles for modern government. This responsibility is important not only for the multiple benefits it yields to specific corporations and entrepreneurs, but also because a stable, growing economy provides an environment for a stable, orderly, and healthy democratic society.

By looking more closely at public policies, we can better understand both how government operates and how well it does so. In this chapter we begin by outlining the policy-making process. We then consider the politics of policy making and explore recent trends in American public policy, asking if these policies are leading in an increasingly democratic direction. Finally, we will look at the world of taxing and spending policy to see how politics and economics are intertwined.

TYPES OF POLICIES

Public policies enacted by the national government have four aims:

1. To regulate key industries and aspects of American life, such as the tobacco industry, savings and loan industry, or the meatpacking industry, in the interests of public safety.
2. To protect Americans from actual or potential enemies at home and abroad by providing a powerful national defense.
3. To encourage the accomplishment of important social goals by providing such programs as Head Start for preschool children and Pell grants for college students.
4. To assist a wide range of American citizens such as farmers (through grain subsidies), low-income families (through Temporary Assistance for Needy Families), and state and local governments (through highway construction funds).

Public policy can be divided into two major categories: regulatory policy and social welfare policy. **Regulatory policy** involves use of federal police powers to supervise the conduct of individuals, businesses, and other governmental agencies. It is essentially a set of *negative incentives* the government establishes to prevent certain kinds of behavior. For this reason, regulatory policy often focuses on social "villains"—industrial polluters, crooked savings and loan executives, unscrupulous railroad barons, meat packers, and tobacco companies.[6] An interesting example of regulators moving into a new area involves the Federal Trade Commission's efforts toward requiring cigar and chewing tobacco manufacturers to report how much they spend on advertising and promotions as well as mandating that all cigars and chewing tobacco packages carry a health warning from the U.S. surgeon general. These are early moves to narrow the regulatory gap between cigars, chewing tobacco, and cigarettes.

In contrast to regulatory policy, **social welfare policy** uses *positive incentives*—cash assistance, stipends, entitlements, grants—to promote or encourage basic social fairness. Long-standing American social welfare objectives include aiding disadvantaged groups, including people living below the poverty line, older Americans, people of color, women, military veterans, and people who are educationally, emotionally, or physically challenged.

MakeItReal

Civic Participation: Federal Programs

public policies The decisions, actions, and commitments of government.

regulatory policy Policy that involves the use of police powers by the federal government to supervise the conduct of individuals, businesses, and other governmental agencies.

social welfare policy Policy that uses positive incentives (cash assistance, stipends, entitlements, grants, etc.) to promote or encourage basic social and economic fairness.

THE POLICY-MAKING PROCESS

Policy scholars have developed several process models that try to capture the flavor and substance of policy making. One such model views the policy-making process as a *life cycle*. This model is especially useful in analyzing how an issue can be moved into the spotlight of the national agenda. These concepts of a public policy agenda and a policy life cycle are part of a relatively new approach to studying public policy that centers on the *process* by which the agenda of public policy is established. It seeks to discover how we come to view certain conditions, events, or situations as political problems requiring a policy response from government.[7]

Stated differently, how do public policies arise? How are they "born"? How long do they live? Why do some have long "lives," whereas others "die" quick deaths? Why do some ideas never become policies at all, whereas others travel quickly through the early stages of the policy life cycle, only to be stopped later in the process? The policy life cycle consists of eleven steps or stages, which can be illustrated by utilizing the evolution of federal funding for AIDS research.[8]

The Life Cycle of Policy Making

1. ***Redefinition of a public or private "condition" as a public "problem."*** In the case of the AIDS crisis—involving a disease that, in the United States, mostly affected certain population subgroups the Reagan administration considered largely unsupportive—six years passed after information surfaced regarding the disease's appearance in the United States before it was defined as a problem to be addressed by public policy.

▲ During a stop in St. Louis, President Bush spent time with fourth graders at the inner-city Pierre Laclede Elementary School. On the chalkboard is a reference to the No Child Left Behind Act signed by President Bush on January 8, 2002. The law has expanded the federal role in education and set requirements in place that affect every public school in America. At the core of No Child Left Behind are measures designed to close achievement gaps between different groups of students.

U.S.A. Yesterday and Today

Where Have You Gone, Joe Camel?

"We are here to announce what we believe is the most historic public health achievement in history," said Michael Moore, attorney general for Mississippi, in June 1997, announcing a global settlement with the tobacco industry. "This is really the beginning of the end for the way the tobacco industry has treated the American public and probably the people of the world," observed Moore. The terms of the deal between the tobacco industry and the states were truly historic. The tobacco companies agreed to pay $363 billion over the next twenty-five years, as well as to dramatically overhaul their marketing practices aimed at youth. In return, the industry would receive protection against future lawsuits bearing on tobacco-related diseases.

Just four years earlier, tobacco executives had vehemently denied the existence of any research that might suggest that their product was hazardous to anyone's health or even addicting. At 1993 congressional hearings, for example, James W. Johnston, then chief executive officer of R. J. Reynolds, laughed that the word "addiction" could be associated with cigarettes, going so far as to say that smoking was a pleasurable habit, like eating sweets or drinking.

The tobacco industry also lost credibility when released internal documents from the 1970s showed how tobacco companies had targeted children as potential users for their products. These previously secret documents were part of a California lawsuit alleging that the Joe Camel advertising campaign was an unlawful and unfair business practice because it targeted minors and led them to purchase cigarettes illegally. The Joe Camel cartoon icon is recognized almost as readily by schoolchildren as is Mickey Mouse. The documents showed that in states where the Joe Camel campaign was introduced, cigarette purchases by minors increased dramatically. One internal R. J. Reynolds memo focused on young smokers as representing "tomorrow's cigarette business." T-shirts and other promotional items with brand-name logos were sold and given away on beaches. The secret documents also revealed that even when the tobacco companies had given public assurances that they would market cigarettes with lower nicotine, tobacco researchers were secretly involved in projects that would increase nicotine potency.

In July 2000, a Miami-Dade County jury awarded the largest damage award in U.S. history—$145 billion—in punitive damages to 500,000 Florida smokers. The Florida decision opened the floodgates and eventually five out of seven plaintiffs were awarded damages. The tobacco industry, previously successful in defeating lawsuits brought by individual smokers, began to suffer significant setbacks.

On June 11, 2002, a Miami, Florida, jury ordered three cigarette makers to pay $37.5 million in damages to a lawyer who lost his tongue to cancer. Also in June 2002, a California judge ruled that R. J. Reynolds had violated its 1997 agreement to overhaul its marketing practices aimed at adolescents by continuing an advertising campaign that still promoted youth smoking. The

2. *Placement of the problem on the national policy agenda.* In the case of AIDS, this did not happen until the death of President Ronald Reagan's close friend, Rock Hudson.

3. *Emergence of the problem as a "public issue" requiring government action.* Only when Surgeon General C. Everett Koop announced that the problem was widespread did AIDS become a public issue. Prior to this, Reagan administration budget cutters were disinclined to allocate funds to fight a disease they believed afflicted only drug users, Haitian immigrants, and the gay community.

4. *Formulation of a public policy response, usually followed by a pledge of action.* President Reagan announced that he would appoint a commission to study the epidemic.

5. *One or more reformulations of the proposed policy.* Every year the question of how much funding would be provided for AIDS research led to a policy reformulation.

6. *Placement of the proposed policy on the formal agenda of government.* Despite the Reagan administration's unwillingness to push for major funding for AIDS research, the public, the press, and Congress would not let the issue die.

company was fined $20 million. On June 20, 2002, a Miami jury awarded $5.5 million in damages to Lynn French, a nonsmoking flight attendant who suffered from chronic sinus problems after spending years in smoke-filled planes. The judgment was the first defeat in a secondhand case for the nation's largest tobacco companies, paving the way for future secondhand smoke cases. In October 2002, a Los Angeles jury awarded a sixty-four-year-old woman $28 billion after she developed lung cancer from Philip Morris cigarettes. The $28 billion in punitive damages was calculated by multiplying one million dollars times the twenty-eight thousand people in the United States who die each year from lung cancer linked to smoking.

By 2004, in the largest civil racketeering trial in U.S. history, representatives of the tobacco industry argued that they never purposely lied to the American public about the dangers of smoking, but that individual tobacco company officials made mistakes and showed poor judgment in dismissing evidence of health risks. "We do not concede in any shape or form that there was a [racketeering] conspiracy," said Ted Wells, a Philip Morris lawyer who led the defense arguments in federal court. "Some of the conduct by individuals in the past . . . was wrongheaded, mistaken and even regrettable, but it wasn't a . . . conspiracy." R. J. Reynolds Tobacco Co. lawyer Robert McDermott denied any conclusive proof that secondhand smoke causes disease. Then, after eight months of courtroom argument, Justice Department lawyers asked for less than 8 percent of the expected penalty. "As he concluded closing arguments in the six-year-old lawsuit, Justice Department lawyer Stephen D. Brody shocked tobacco company representatives and anti-tobacco activists by announcing that the government will not seek the $130 billion that a government expert had testified was necessary to fund smoking-cessation programs. Instead, Brody said, the Justice Depart-

ment will ask tobacco companies to pay $10 billion over five years to help millions of Americans quit smoking." The Justice Department offered little explanation for the figure. "It feels like a political decision to take into consideration the tobacco companies' financial interest rather than health interests of 45 million addicted smokers," said William V. Corr, director of the Campaign for Tobacco-Free Kids. "The government proved its case, but the levels of funding are a shadow of the cessation treatment program that the government's own expert witness recommended."

Sources: "Florida Smoker Awarded $37.5 million," AP, *Washington Post,* June 12, 2002, p. A2; Greg Winter, "Tobacco Company Reneged on Youth Ads, Judge Rules," *New York Times,* June 7, 2002; Quoted in Robert Weissman, "The Great Tobacco Bailout," *Multinational Monitor* 18, nos. 7–8 (July/August 1997); *Washington Post* editorial; quoted in Steven F. Goldstone, "Don't Let the Tobacco Deal Go Up in Smoke," *Wall Street Journal,* February 20, 1998, p. 1; See Saundra Torry and John Schwartz, "Contrite Tobacco Executives Admit Health Risks before Congress," *Washington Post,* January 30, 1998, p. A14; See also "Tobacco Execs Urge Lawsuit Immunity," *USA Today,* January 29, 1998, p. 1; See "Court Papers Reveal Teen Smoking Targets," *USA Today,* January 15, 1998, p. 1; "Hundreds of Tobacco Industry Documents Released," *USA Today,* January 15, 1998, p. 8; "Cigarette Makers Manipulated Nicotine," *USA Today,* January 29, 1998, p. 1; Barry Meier, "Cigarette Maker Manipulated Nicotine, Its Record Suggests," *New York Times,* February 23, 1998, p. A1; "Clinton Pushes Anti-Tobacco Measures," *USA Today,* February 13, 1998, p. 1; See also Sandra Sobieraj, "Cigarette Tax May Cut Teen Smoking," *Washington Post,* February 13, 1998, p. 1; "Feds Vow to Push Anti-Tobacco Legislation," *USA Today,* April 12, 1998, p. 1; Greg Winter, "Jury Awards $5.5 Million in a Secondhand Smoke Case," *New York Times,* June 20, 2002, p. A16; Carol D. Leonnig, "Tobacco Escapes Huge Penalty: U.S. Seeks $10 Billion Instead of $130 Billion," *Washington Post,* June 8, 2005, p. A01; Carol D. Leonnig, "Tobacco Industry Admits Mistakes: But Cigarette Makers Never Purposely Lied to Public, Attorneys Say," *Washington Post,* September 23, 2004, p. A03.

7. *Enactment of part or all of the proposed policy.* In 1986, Surgeon General C. Everett Koop released a report that made AIDS the key item on the administration's legislative agenda.

8. *Implementation of the policy.* Funding for AIDS research continued to grow. The government was now committed to fighting the disease—some six years following the first article on the mysterious disease.

9. *Effects of policy implementation.* Activist groups ranging from coalitions of celebrities to congressional members emerged to help raise funds.

10. *Evaluation of policy impact.* During the 1992 presidential nominating convention, AIDS funding was one of the many issues challenger Bill Clinton used to attack Bush administration policies.

11. *Termination or continued implementation and evaluation of the policy.* Although the government continues to fund AIDS research at high levels, the disease remains the primary cause of death for men between the ages of twenty-five and forty-five in cities throughout the United States. Successfully attacking the HIV/AIDS epidemic requires a full-scale approach, which includes funding for prevention, research, housing, and care. We have come a long way but have a long road ahead, as AIDS remains in epidemic proportions in Africa and other countries.

policy elites Members of Congress, the president, Supreme Court justices, cabinet officers, heads of key agencies and departments, leading editorial writers, and influential columnists and commentators.

public agenda The set of topics that concern policy elites, the general public, or both.

formal agenda The policies actually scheduled for debate and potential adoption by Congress, the president, the Supreme Court, or executive departments and agencies.

triggering mechanism A critical development that converts a routine problem into a widely shared, negative public response.

policy entrepreneurs Leaders who invest in, and who create the conditions for, a potential group to become an actual interest group. Ralph Nader stands as a classic example of a policy entrepreneur.

MakeItReal

Visual Literacy: Influencing Policy Making

Quick Review

Formulating Policy

- Policy is constructed, debated, and put into effect by all branches of the federal government.

- Congress formulates and reformulates policy in committees and subcommittees and during the process of debate and amendment in the House and Senate.

- Courts formulate and reformulate public policy by adopting a policy position.

- Government agencies formulate policy by issuing regulations explaining how the agency will enforce and interpret a new law.

JOINING THE PUBLIC AGENDA

Why do certain issues and not others become subjects for governmental action? That is, how do they join the agenda of the political world? Before they can enter the policy-making process, potential subjects of public policy must undergo a radical redefinition in the eyes of **policy elites**—members of Congress, the president, Supreme Court justices, cabinet officers, heads of key agencies and departments, leading editorial writers, and influential columnists and commentators. Such a redefinition changes the way the topic is viewed and places it on the **public agenda**, the set of topics of concern to policy elites, the general public, or both.

The public agenda can be viewed as the informal agenda of government. It should not be confused with the **formal agenda**, that is, policies actually scheduled for debate and potential adoption by Congress, the president, the Supreme Court, or executive departments and agencies. For example, nicotine's harmful effects have also been on the public agenda for quite some time, but only after recent legal challenges and released documents did it reach the current threshold.

From Problems to Issues How do social concerns become translated or redefined into matters important enough to be placed on the public agenda? The distinction between *problems* and *conditions* is critical for understanding public policy making. Citizens and policy makers are willing to live with various *social conditions*—pollution, high crime rates, low voter turnout, high rates of unemployment, or poverty rates—as long as they do not see those conditions as immediate threats to safety or financial security. When a condition is redefined as a problem, however, we expect the government to do something about it.

Before a *condition* is redefined as a *problem*, it must eventually be framed as an *issue*. Social conditions become redefined as problems that require governmental policy responses in two key ways. First, a dramatic event may serve as a **triggering mechanism**. A triggering mechanism is a critical development that converts a routine problem into a widely shared, negative public response. It can transform a *condition* into a *problem* in the minds of the American public and political leadership alike. The tragic killings at Columbine High School triggered a national debate on gun control. The destruction of the World Trade Center buildings triggered a national debate on airline passenger screening and student visas for foreign students.

A potential policy can also reach the public agenda through the activities of **policy entrepreneurs**, individuals or groups instrumental in "selling" a program or policy to a policy-making body. American political history offers many examples of policy entrepreneurs who succeeded in placing a potential policy issue on the public agenda. In the 1950s and 1960s, Martin Luther King Jr., the Congress on Racial Equality, the Southern Christian Leadership Conference, the Student Non-Violent Coordinating Committee, and the National Association for the Advancement of Colored People used nonviolent tactics that successfully placed the issue of civil rights on both the public agenda and the formal agenda of the national government.[9]

In the case of the civil rights movement, the policy entrepreneurs used a variety of tactics. Lawsuits challenged the separate but equal doctrine in public education. Confrontational demonstrations such as the civil rights marches in Montgomery, Birmingham, Selma, and Washington, D.C., and rallies and speeches such as the famous "I Have a Dream" speech, given on the steps of the Lincoln Memorial by Martin Luther King Jr., made the civil rights movement more visible to the American public. The assassinations of President John F. Kennedy, Martin Luther King Jr., and Robert Kennedy served as triggering mechanisms for passage of additional civil rights acts covering other areas of life. Thus, the efforts of a dedicated core of organizers and advocates stimulated actions and events that underscored existing problems in American society; the policy entrepreneurs then worked to promote specific solutions to those problems in the form of proposed policies.[10]

Reaching the Formal Agenda

A policy reaches the formal agenda when it is actually scheduled for debate and potential adoption by policy-making bodies such as Congress. In the process, it is generally formulated and reformulated several times. In a formal sense, Congress actually enacts or passes legislation, but policy is "enacted"—constructed, debated, and put into effect—by all branches of the federal government.

Courts also formulate and reformulate public policy. Abortion is a case in point. In 1973, the Supreme Court adopted a policy position in the case of *Roe* v. *Wade*, arguing that women have an absolute right to choose an abortion in the first trimester of a pregnancy. More recently, in cases such as *Webster* v. *Reproductive Health Services* (1989), the Court modified the earlier *Roe* policy in favor of a more restrictive policy on abortion. It is possible that the Bush Supreme Court may overturn *Roe*, in which case abortion will surely return to the public agenda.[11]

Policies often are formulated and reformulated in the committees and subcommittees of Congress, as well as during debate and amendment on the floor of the House and Senate. For example, in 1998 the Senate decided not to rush into a vote on whether or not to ban human cloning. The issue of cloning raised questions ranging from the specter of genetic engineering of a master race to the cloning of specific tissue types or organs that could help in treating and possibly curing Alzheimer's, heart disease, leukemia, diabetes, and other diseases. As a policy, cloning involves ethical, moral, medical, and, of course, political concerns, which, at the moment, few members of Congress fully understand.[12]

Policy formulation also occurs in the government agencies that implement laws enacted by Congress. Those agencies often issue regulations explaining how the agency will enforce and interpret the new law. These regulations are issued in draft form and subsequently modified as part of a regular hearing and appeal process. For example, the Environmental Protection Agency will develop new microbiological testing criteria for coastal waters and then discuss them in public forums or provide analysis on the causes and effects of global warming.

Implementing a Policy

Once a policy has been enacted, it must be implemented. **Implementation** is the actual execution of a policy. Some policies are relatively easy to implement. For example, when Congress enacted a national highway speed limit of fifty-five miles per hour to conserve gasoline, the government quickly achieved full implementation of the policy by denying federal funds for highway construction to any state that did not enforce the new speed limit.

Other policies, however, are more difficult to implement. An example is court-mandated school desegregation, first ordered in 1954 by the Supreme Court in *Brown* v. *Board of Education of Topeka*. The next year, the Court ordered that desegregation should proceed "with all deliberate speed," in part to soften the blow for the conservative and historically segregationist southern states, which were powerfully represented in Congress. However, it soon became apparent that the ambiguous phrase "all deliberate speed" meant one thing to the justices of the Supreme Court and another to state and local officials who were reluctant to implement the policy.[13]

Difficulty in implementing federal policies relates to the "three Cs of implementation": *complexity*, *cooperation*, and *coordination*. Desegregating public schools is a far more complex process than changing the highway speed limit. Efforts to achieve full desegregation of public schools have encountered racial and ethnic hostilities in the American public, "white flight" to suburban communities surrounding urban areas, and declining funds for public schools.

Another obstacle to implementation of the *Brown* decision was that the actual plans for desegregating the schools required the cooperation of local and state officials. The involvement of more individuals and groups with the power to stop or delay a policy, such as officials of school districts and elected school boards, means

Quick Review

Clean Air Act of 1990

- Set strict limitations on pollution from utilities and automobile emissions.
- Mandated the use of less polluting fuels.
- Authorized inspections of potential polluters.
- Set standards for allowable pollutants by industries and to limit emissions of sulfur dioxide.

Old Age Survivors Disability Insurance

- Key provision of the Social Security Act of 1935.
- Provided a *contributory* program of retirement and unemployment benefits.
- Payments were available to workers upon retirement at age sixty-two or later, or to dependents in the event of death.
- Funded through a *payroll tax* shared equally by employers and employees.
- Each state administered a separate unemployment insurance system.
- Benefits are paid to *any* eligible recipient, regardless of financial status.

implementation The act of providing the organization and expertise required to put into action any policy that has become law; also refers to the actual execution of a policy.

policy evaluation The required period of monitoring and analysis of federal policies following their implementation.

more obstacles to full implementation of the policy. Some school districts, including those in Los Angeles and Boston, were actually turned over to "federal masters" appointed by federal courts to supervise desegregation in their areas.[14]

As the difficulty of desegregating public schools increased, so did problems of coordination. In the cases of Los Angeles and Boston, coordination among the federal courts, the court-appointed "masters," the elected school boards, as well as the parents and students, presented one of the greatest implementation challenges ever faced by the federal government.

As the examples of highway speed limits and school desegregation illustrate, public policy implementation is far from automatic. Complex policies requiring extensive cooperation and a great deal of coordination have much less chance of achieving full implementation than simpler policies.

Evaluating a Policy

All policies have impact of some kind, though not all achieve the impact intended by those who proposed and enacted them. It is difficult to generalize about which policies have greater impact and why, but scholars have identified characteristics that contribute to the effectiveness of public policies: (1) a clearly written law or policy statement, (2) strong presidential support for the policy, and (3) local cooperation in the implementation of the policy. Policies that combine all three of these basic ingredients have the greatest chance of achieving their full impact. Most federal policies require a period of monitoring and analysis following implementation, known as **policy evaluation**. Policy evaluation at the federal level is a mixture of scientific and political considerations. A good example is the Environmental Protection Agency (EPA) decision to relax clean air enforcement rules governing coal-fired power plants and refineries that would preclude government lawsuits when costly antipollution equipment to control smog, acid rain, and soot was not installed. The industry had been complaining that aggressive enforcement hindered or discouraged investment in power-generating plants. Environmentalists see the EPA decision as a rollback of the 1970 Clean Air Act.[15]

Terminating a Policy

Following evaluation, policies are either terminated or continued. Termination ends the policy life cycle. If they are continued, they enter what social scientists call the *feedback loop*. Information about the policy's consequences can be "fed back" into the cycle to help in the formulation of new policies. Policies may be terminated when they lose the political support of the general public, the president, the Supreme Court, or members of Congress. But, to be enacted in the first place, policies require strong support from government policy entrepreneurs and interest groups outside the government, all, presumably, its beneficiaries. As a result, public policies, once enacted, are rarely terminated.[16]

In the rare cases in which policies are terminated, one of three scenarios usually takes place. First, the policy or program may become out of date and no longer important in light of new developments. An example is the nuclear-targeting policy of "mutual assured destruction" (MAD). The targeting of civilian areas such as Moscow as part of a strategy to protect the United States against the threat of a nuclear strike by the Soviet Union was rendered obsolete after the breakup of the Soviet Union in 1991.

Second, the policy or program may fail to perform effectively, or an alternative policy may perform better than the original policy. An example is the Aid to Families with Dependent Children (AFDC) program, a sixty-year-old entitlement to federal cash assistance for mothers and children at the poverty level redesigned by the 1996 Welfare Reform Law. Today, block grants to states, designated as Temporary Assistance for Needy Families (TANF), provide assistance, but with a five-year lifetime limit on benefits.

 **MakeItReal**

Primary Source: The Aid to Families with Dependent Children Program (AFDC)

Continuing a Policy

Some policies have been in effect for a long time. They are implemented, evaluated, and continuously refined or modified by key actors in the national policy-making process—the president, Congress, or the courts. Policies that survive the early stages of the policy life cycle and are actually implemented are still subject to periodic review and possible modification over time. For example, the basic mission of the National Aeronautics and Space Administration (NASA) has changed over time, from catching up with the Soviets (during the 1950s), to space exploration (1960–90), to analysis of the earth's weather and environmental patterns from space.

Several factors make public policy making a highly political process. They include the fragmentation created by a federal system of government; temporary political alliances (*logrolling*); policies that benefit particular states or districts (*pork barrel legislation*); *iron triangles*, or informal relationships among legislative committees, executive agencies, and interest groups; and *issue networks*, in which large numbers of participants take an active interest in a particular policy.

REGULATORY POLICY

Regulatory policies are designed to regulate conduct and protect the health and welfare of all Americans. As political scientist Kenneth Meier has noted, "Regulation is any attempt by the government to control the behavior of citizens, corporations, or sub-governments."[17]

The national government engages in six different kinds of regulatory activity. It may regulate (1) the price that can be charged for a good or service; (2) franchising or licenses granted to individuals or businesses; (3) performance of safety standards; or (4) resources such as water or electricity from federal dams and hydroelectric projects available to citizens or businesses. It may also (5) provide or withhold operating subsidies; or (6) use regulatory commissions such as the Federal Trade Commission (FTC) or the Securities and Exchange Commission (SEC) to regulate vital industries and promote fair competition among individuals and businesses.

Regulatory activity by the federal government has increased gradually during the past century after being almost nonexistent during the first hundred years of the nation's history. The first significant regulation occurred in response to the political pressures of the Granger and muckraker movements in the late 1800s and early 1900s. Another surge of regulatory activity occurred in the 1930s as a result of the problems created by the Great Depression. The highest levels of regulation were reached in the 1960s and 1970s in response to the consumer, civil rights, and environmental movements.

Beginning in the mid-1970s, regulatory activity by the federal government declined and a movement toward *deregulation* emerged. The government sold ("privatized") government-owned railroads to private investors and acted to deregulate the trucking, banking, and airline industries. Beginning in the late 1980s, however,

MakeItReal

Primary Source: National Labor Relations Act, 1935

◄ Government tests such as this one, a side impact test on a Ford Taurus, are part of the effort to regulate public safety.

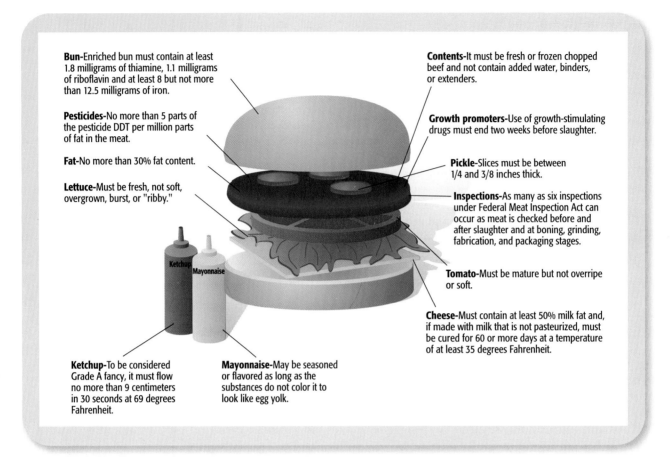

Bun-Enriched bun must contain at least 1.8 milligrams of thiamine, 1.1 milligrams of riboflavin and at least 8 but not more than 12.5 milligrams of iron.

Pesticides-No more than 5 parts of the pesticide DDT per million parts of fat in the meat.

Fat-No more than 30% fat content.

Lettuce-Must be fresh, not soft, overgrown, burst, or "ribby."

Ketchup-To be considered Grade A fancy, it must flow no more than 9 centimeters in 30 seconds at 69 degrees Fahrenheit.

Mayonnaise-May be seasoned or flavored as long as the substances do not color it to look like egg yolk.

Contents-It must be fresh or frozen chopped beef and not contain added water, binders, or extenders.

Growth promoters-Use of growth-stimulating drugs must end two weeks before slaughter.

Pickle-Slices must be between 1/4 and 3/8 inches thick.

Inspections-As many as six inspections under Federal Meat Inspection Act can occur as meat is checked before and after slaughter and at boning, grinding, fabrication, and packaging stages.

Tomato-Must be mature but not overripe or soft.

Cheese-Must contain at least 50% milk fat and, if made with milk that is not pasteurized, must be cured for 60 or more days at a temperature of at least 35 degrees Fahrenheit.

Figure 15.2   Your Hamburger: 41,000 Regulations
Source: U.S. News & World Report, February 11, 1980, p. 64. Copyright 1980. U.S. News and World Report, Inc.

policy began a swing back toward increased regulation, a pattern that continues to this day (see Figure 15.2).

Regulating the Environment

Environmental policy provides a good illustration of regulatory policy making. Americans became vitally interested in environmental issues in the 1960s and 1970s, and the federal government responded by enacting several key pieces of environmental legislation. The triggering mechanism for environmental policy making at the federal level was the 1962 publication of Rachel Carson's *Silent Spring.* In this groundbreaking book, Carson argued that the widely used pesticide DDT was poisoning fields, streams, fish, and wildlife, and ultimately the American consumer. The book spurred a scientific search to develop less hazardous pesticides, as well as a search by federal policy makers for environmentally sensitive policies and programs.[18]

In a landmark piece of legislation, the National Environmental Policy Act of 1969, Congress required that government agencies issue an environmental impact statement listing the effects that proposed agency regulations would have on the environment. In 1970, Congress created the Environmental Protection Agency (EPA) to administer environmental programs and issue environmental regulations. It also enacted the Clean Air Act of 1970, which directed the EPA to monitor industrial air pollution and enforce compliance with existing pollution laws. The Department of Transportation was assigned the responsibility for monitoring and reducing pollution associated with automobile emissions (see Figure 15.3).

In 1972, Congress passed the Water Pollution Control Act, aimed at reducing pollution in the nation's rivers and lakes. Congress soon added ocean dumping of

Question for Reflection

Historically, regulatory activity was most often spurred by social need. What impact do you think the deregulation activity of the 1970s–80s had on America's approaching democracy?

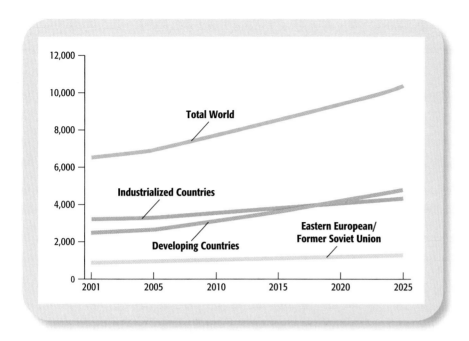

Figure 15.3
Carbon Emissions and the Economy

Source: Energy Information Administration. *International Energy Outlook,* 2003 (Washington, DC 2003). http://www.eia.doe.gov/oiaf/1605/ggccbro/chapter1.html.

wastes to the policy agenda with the Marine Protection Research Act, followed in 1976 by legislation regulating the dumping of hazardous waste. The 1976 Resource Conservation and Recovery Act not only regulated the disposal of hazardous waste but also sought to reduce the volume of waste by encouraging recycling, on-site disposal, incineration, and disposal of hazardous waste in safe landfills. The enormous expense associated with cleaning up hazardous-waste sites led to the enactment in 1980 of the Superfund Law, which created a fund to pay for toxic-site cleanups and authorized the EPA to order polluters to clean up sites where necessary. Congress later enacted the Safe Water and Toxic Enforcement Act of 1986, regulating discharges into surface water and groundwater; the Toxic Substances Control Act of 1987, requiring the removal of carcinogenic material such as asbestos from buildings; and the Clean Air Act Amendments of 1990, which resolved a long-running conflict between coal-producing and auto-manufacturing states, such as West Virginia and Michigan, and states such as Maine and California, whose residents and local economies were more favorably inclined toward environmental protection.

The Clean Air Act of 1990 set strict limitations on pollution from utilities and automobile emissions, mandated use of less-polluting fuels, and authorized inspections of potential polluters ranging from automobiles to wood-burning stoves. In addition, the 1990 act authorized the EPA to set standards for allowable industrial pollutants and to limit sulfur dioxide emissions, the primary cause of acid rain. Still, many American cities have yet to meet the air quality standards established in the original Clean Air Act of 1970. Much future progress will depend on the EPA's willingness to enforce the regulations aggressively.

A second set of concerns has to do with the fact that pollution and the need for environmental regulation spill over state and national borders into the arena of international politics. The first international conference on the environment was held in 1992 in Rio de Janeiro, Brazil. The United States was the only major nation that refused to sign the Rio Accords, which committed nations to strict environmental goals and required them to allocate a fixed percentage of their national budgets to take action on environmental concerns. The United States did not sign because pro-business interests did not like international entanglements that would cut into their profits, and conservative politicians had a general suspicion of multinational agreements such as this one.

In late 1997, representatives of more than 150 nations gathered in Japan to discuss how best to counter the threat of global warming. The meeting produced the

poverty level The federally determined income below which a family of four is considered poor.

entitlements Government-sponsored benefits and cash payments to those who meet eligibility requirements.

Kyoto Protocol—a commitment by developed nations to bring their emissions down to specific levels by specific dates. The parties agreed to reduce greenhouse gas emissions; the specific limits vary from country to country, but the framework and targets were based largely on U.S. proposals.[19]

In June 2002, the fifteen-member European Union ratified the Kyoto Protocol, even though the United States, the world's largest emitter of greenhouse gases, opposed it. The Bush administration specifically opposed mandatory cuts in emissions that would cost billions of dollars and five million lost jobs. At the treaty's implementation in February 2005, the agreement had been ratified by 141 countries representing more than 61 percent of global emissions; the United States still had no intention of signing. By August 2005, 153 countries had ratified the protocol, including Canada, People's Republic of China, India, Japan, New Zealand and Russia and the twenty-five countries of the European Union, as well as Romania and Bulgaria. Six countries had not ratified the protocol: Australia, Mexico, the United States, Croatia, Kazakhstan, and Zambia. At the December 2005 United Nations meeting on global warming held in Montreal, the United States and China, "the world's current and projected leaders in emissions of greenhouse gases," refused to accept any mandatory reductions.[20]

A third challenge facing environmental regulation is the increasing complexity of regulatory policy. *Offset policies* are a case in point. A potential polluter can build a facility otherwise not allowable by "offsetting" the increased pollution with lower pollution elsewhere. For example, the 1990 Clean Air Act created *pollution credits.* Industries and companies that fail to meet their emission standards can buy extra pollution credits from companies whose emissions are below the allowable level. Although the overall level of pollution in a particular area must remain below the established limit, industries and businesses emit significantly different amounts of polluting substances. How should such a market in pollution credits be regulated, and will it require further monitoring and regulation as it develops?[21]

SOCIAL WELFARE POLICY

The second major category of public policy, social welfare policy, is intended to alleviate the numerous problems associated with poverty in contemporary American society. Although America has had poverty conditions since early colonial days, poverty first reached the public agenda in the early 1900s as a result of works by muckraking journalists (see Chapter 12). Two books, Lincoln Steffens' *Shame of the Cities* and Robert Hunter's *Poverty*, both published in 1904, were influential in elevating poverty to the status of a political issue. In his study of tenement dwellers in Boston and New York, Hunter shocked turn-of-the-century readers by estimating that between 12 and 25 percent of all Americans lived in poverty.[22]

Before we consider the sources of poverty and the government's attempts to improve **poverty levels**, it is necessary to understand the history of social welfare policy in the twentieth century, beginning with the Social Security Act of 1935.

The Social Security Act

The Social Security Act was the centerpiece of President Franklin D. Roosevelt's New Deal legislative program. Even today, Social Security—the largest single nondefense item in the federal budget—is at the heart of social welfare policy in the United States. The Social Security Act established a safety net to catch those falling into poverty. It did so through a system of **entitlements**—government-sponsored benefits and cash payments—for which individuals might qualify by virtue of being poor, elderly, disabled, or a child living in poverty. The act created four major programs: Social Security retirement benefits, unemployment compensation, a public assistance or welfare program, and a series of aid programs for blind, disabled, or otherwise ineligible senior citizens.

▲ Saving Social Security is perhaps the most important issue on the minds of all citizens and politicians.

Approaching Democracy Around the Globe

Social Security Around the World: As the United States Considers Private Accounts, Experiences in Chile and Britain Provide Some Inspiration and Offer Cautionary Tales

As Congress considers moving toward voluntary private accounts, it is important to know that more than a dozen nations have converted their traditional, government-financed pension systems to programs that involve various types of financing through personal accounts invested in the private sector. In a *Washington Post* study, Chile and Britain's, experiences with private accounts serve as both a model and a cautionary tale for Bush administration reformers. In Chile, for example, private accounts "have given participants a sense of ownership of their retirement fortunes. However, many Chileans who transitioned out of the old system received inadequate pensions, leaving retirees dissatisfied and the government worried about its fiscal future." In the case of Britain, "surging management fees for private accounts turned into a political scandal, and many contributors were left worse off than if they had stayed with the state system." The graphic provides details for the comparative cases:

Source: "Social Security Around the World: As U.S. Considers Private Accounts, Experiences in Chile and Britain Provide Some Inspiration and Offer Cautionary Tales," *Washington Post*, April 11, 2005, p. A11.

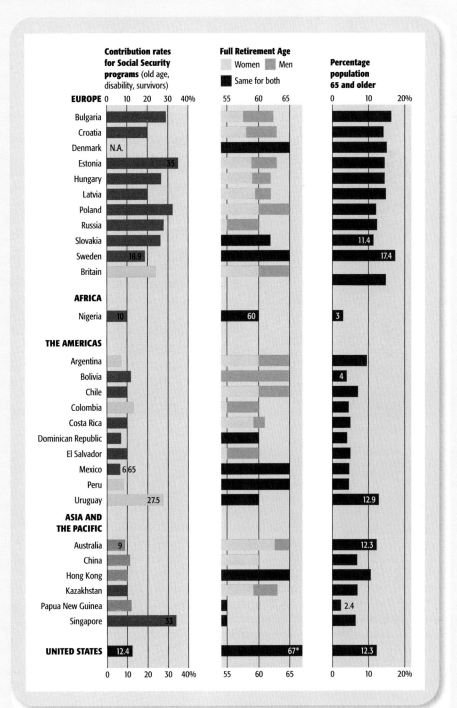

The key provision of the act was Old Age Survivors Disability Insurance (OASDI), which provided a *contributory* program of retirement and unemployment benefits. The payments were available to workers who retired at age sixty-two or later, or to their dependents in the event of death. The money to fund the program came from a *payroll tax* shared equally by employers and employees. In subsequent years the act was modified to include self-employed persons, certain state and local government employees, agricultural workers, and other workers not protected under the original act. Each state administers a separate unemployment insurance system. Workers who lose their jobs are eligible for twenty-six weeks of payments, although Congress has,

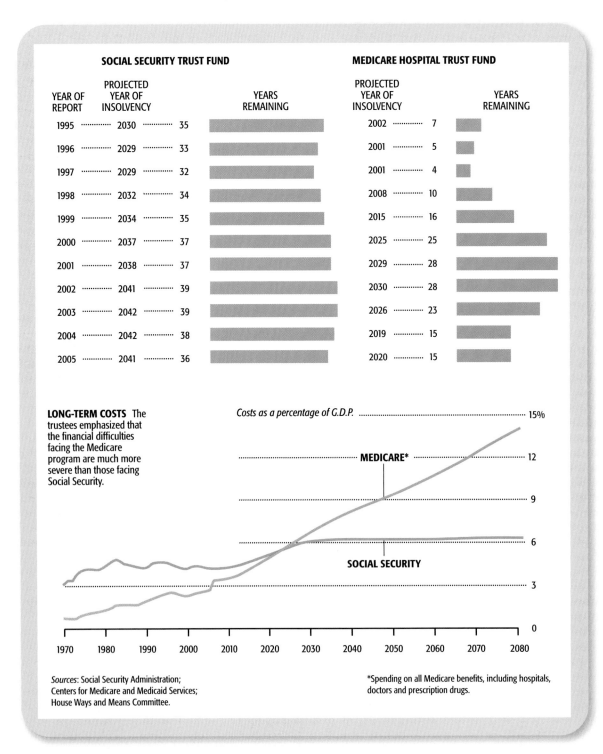

Figure 15.4   Outlook for Medicare and Social Security

on occasion, extended the eligibility period in times of high unemployment. Congress has made several efforts to apply **means testing** to Social Security entitlements—that is, to link benefits to income and provide payments only to the "truly disadvantaged"—but such efforts have failed owing to successful lobbying by senior citizen groups. Social Security benefits therefore are not means-tested entitlements; they are paid to *any* eligible recipient, regardless of his or her financial status.

Social Security was established as a pay-as-you-go system, but recent projections of the ratio of working people to retirees indicate that the trust fund will be unable to meet its obligations in the future, when the majority of baby boomers will be entitled to collect full benefits. The Social Security system's long-term viability has become the focus of intense political debate. President Bush's top legislative priority in 2005 was to transform Social Security from a government program that uses tax money to pay guaranteed benefits to retirees and disabled workers into one that allows workers to put their taxes into individual investment accounts.[23] The trust funds will be exhausted by 2041, and after that time government will be able to pay only 74 percent of scheduled benefits; by 2017, annual benefits will begin to exceed annual revenues from Social Security taxes, and the government will have to borrow money or tap into general reserves to meet the system's obligations. The impending retirement of the baby-boom generation has raised much concern about the very viability of the system. "The number of Americans over age 65 is expected to reach 20 percent by the year 2030, when the nation as a whole will have a higher percentage of older people than Florida does today (see Figure 15.4)."[24]

A third program created by the 1935 act was a public assistance program, Aid to Families with Dependent Children (AFDC). Commonly referred to as "welfare," this program proved far less popular and more controversial than OASDI. AFDC was a *noncontributory* entitlement program that provided cash assistance to families below the official poverty line; this program was terminated by federal legislation as part of the Clinton administration's welfare reforms of 1996.

The fourth program created by the Social Security Act of 1935 was actually a series of programs, now known as Supplemental Security Income (SSI), that provide aid to needy senior citizens who did not contribute to Social Security payroll taxes, as well as to blind or disabled citizens. Unlike the other programs just described, SSI is funded entirely by the federal government.

means testing The changing of eligibility for entitlement benefits from everyone receiving benefits to only those with earnings and savings below a predetermined level, in an attempt to save money.

MakeItReal

Primary Source: Social Security Act Amendments (1965)

The War on Poverty

Along with other New Deal legislation, the Social Security Act was spurred by the massive economic dislocation caused by the Great Depression. In other words, the Depression acted as a triggering mechanism to translate the economic *condition* of poverty into a political *issue* to be addressed by policy makers in the national government. Three decades later, poverty again reached the formal agenda of national government, influenced by the civil rights movement—in particular, by Martin Luther King Jr.'s call for civil rights and jobs for black Americans and also by Michael Harrington's description of the "invisible poor" in *The Other America*. President John F. Kennedy called for the creation of a "New Frontier" in which poverty would be attacked and overcome. Kennedy was assassinated before his program could be enacted, but his successor, Lyndon Johnson, launched a "War on Poverty" with two major pieces of legislation: the Economic Opportunity Act (1964) and the Medicare Act (1965).

The Economic Opportunity Act created the Job Corps to train long-term unemployed people, the

▲ President Lyndon Baines Johnson, shown here with former President Harry S Truman, who first proposed the measure, signs the legislation that creates Medicare, part of his War on Poverty.

Neighborhood Youth Corps to provide job training for neighborhood and inner-city unemployed youth, literacy programs to help adults learn to read and prepare for the job market, Head Start preschool programs to help poor children gain the skills necessary to do well in school, and work-study programs for low-income college students. Unlike Social Security, these community action programs (CAPs) were designed to generate "maximum feasible participation" of people in poor neighborhoods.

"Maximum feasible participation" proved highly controversial. Many members of Congress believed the federal government had too little control over vast sums of CAP money; mayors and other local officials believed they should control funds targeted for their cities; local community activists running CAP programs complained of insufficient funding and interference by local and federal officials. In the words of one key participant, Senator Daniel Patrick Moynihan of New York, maximum feasible participation quickly evolved into "maximum feasible misunderstanding."[25] Congress responded by passing the Hyde Amendment, which gave more control to local officials in deciding how CAP money would be spent.

The other major thrust of the war on poverty was the Medicare Act, enacted in 1965, which added health insurance to the Social Security program. Medicare provides basic health-care and hospitalization coverage for people over age sixty-five. A related program, Medicaid, provides health-care coverage for needy individuals under age sixty-five. The federal government pays a percentage of Medicaid costs, with state and local governments sharing the balance. Medicaid covers people not covered by Medicare, especially the blind, the disabled, and children living in poverty. In his 1998 State of the Union Address, President Clinton proposed opening Medicare to people fifty-five to sixty-four years old. A fierce political battle followed over whether this proposal to widen Medicare would pay for itself or eventually need subsidies (see Figure 15.5).[26]

In 1988, in a major revision of social welfare policy, Congress enacted the Family Support Act. The act's chief legislative architect, Senator Daniel Patrick Moynihan of New York, described it as "a new social contract" between the poor—who agree to work in exchange for benefits—and society—which agrees to support the poor at a livable wage.

The Family Support Act attempted to address the trend toward the feminization of poverty, produced by increasing numbers of working women, higher divorce rates, higher rates of illegitimate births, and a dramatic increase in single-parent households. The act promoted **workfare**—programs to assist welfare recipients in making the transition into the workforce. It provided federal assistance in obtaining child support payments from absent parents. It also created the Jobs program, designed to eventually replace AFDC with a program in which recipients (except mothers with children under three years old) must work in exchange for cash assistance. Recipients must be willing to engage in job training and job search activities as a condition for receiving benefits.

The Family Support Act was but the first step in welfare reform, which culminated on August 22, 1996, when President Clinton signed perhaps the most controversial legislation of his presidency—welfare reform legislation that signaled the end of cash assistance to dependent children by the federal government. "This is not the end of welfare reform, this is the beginning," said President Clinton when signing the legislation that "ended welfare as we know it." The new welfare reform law—the Personal Responsibility and Work Opportunity Reconciliation Act of 1996—ushered in a national commitment to the concept "from welfare to work." The new program did much more than redesign AFDC; it made broad changes in federal programs and policies. Under the terms of the legislation, each state must submit a state plan to the Department of Health and Human Services for certification in order to receive Temporary Assistance for Needy Families (TANF) block grant funds. The law restricted recipients to five years on federal benefits in their lifetime and required states to enroll recipients in work programs.[27]

In 2005, HHS Secretary Mike Leavitt announced that caseloads for both families and individuals receiving cash assistance under the TANF program declined

MakeItReal

Primary Source: Medicare and Medicaid

ABC News Video: *Sticker Shock*

MakeItReal

Primary Source: Welfare Reform Act of 1996

Census 2000: Government Payments to Individuals

workfare The requirement that recipients of welfare programs such as AFDC work on public works unless they find employment elsewhere.

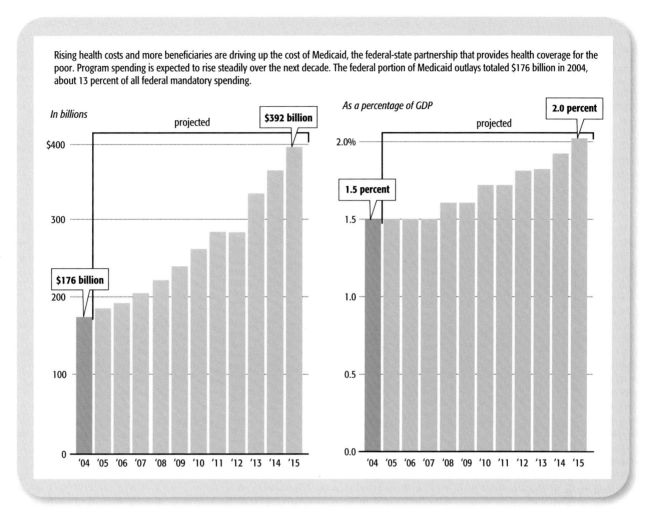

Rising health costs and more beneficiaries are driving up the cost of Medicaid, the federal-state partnership that provides health coverage for the poor. Program spending is expected to rise steadily over the next decade. The federal portion of Medicaid outlays totaled $176 billion in 2004, about 13 percent of all federal mandatory spending.

Figure 15.5   Medicaid Spending's Steady Rise
Source: Congressional Budget Office

between the first and second quarters of calendar year 2004. "Throughout the first four years of the Bush administration, we have seen caseloads decline continuously," Secretary Leavitt said. "Now it is important to work with Congress to reauthorize welfare reform so more families can be strengthened by work instead of weakened by welfare dependency."[28] Between March and June 2004, TANF caseloads for families dropped 1 percent, from 1,992,143 to 1,969,909. For individuals, the caseload declined 1.3 percent, from 4,798,986 to 4,729,291. "More Americans are leaving welfare and entering the economic mainstream," said Dr. Wade F. Horn, HHS assistant secretary for children and families. "The Bush administration is dedicated to welfare reform because it replaces dependency with self-sufficiency."[29] In February 2006 President Bush signed the deficit reduction act of 2005 which reauthorized the TANF program.

Still, the federal poverty rate—the dollar amount of annual earnings below which a family is considered poor—has not been significantly reduced. This figure is established by the Census Bureau and used to generate official government estimates of the number of Americans living in poverty. The federal poverty measure actually has two slightly different versions: *poverty thresholds* and *poverty guidelines.* The thresholds have statistical value for estimating the numbers of Americans in poverty each year; the guidelines have administrative value in determining financial eligibility for certain federal programs (see Table 15.1).[30]

ABC NEWS/PRENTICE HALL VIDEO LIBRARY

On The Edge
Illegal Immigrant Workers

   **MakeItReal**

Primary Source: AFDC before and after the Personal Responsibility and Work Opportunities Act of 1996

Table 15.1 ▪ What Is Poverty?

Computations for the 2005 Annual Update of the HHS Poverty Guidelines for the 48 Contiguous States and the District of Columbia

(1) Persons in Family Unit	(2) Poverty Thresholds for 2003 - Published Aug. 2004[a]	(3) Column 2 Multiplied by 1.027 Price Inflator[b]	(4) Difference between Successive Column 3 Entries	(5) Average Difference in Column 4[c]	(6) February 2005 Poverty Guidelines
1	$9,393	$9,647			$9,570
			$2,692	$3,260	
2	12,015	12,339			12,830
			2,737	3,260	
3	14,680	15,076			16,090
			4,242	3,260	
4	18,810	19,318			19,350[d]
			3,528	3,260	
5	22,245	22,846			22,610
			2,954	3,260	
6	25,122	25,800			25,870
			3,515	3,260	
7	28,544	29,315			29,130
			3,127	3,260	
8	31,589	32,442			32,390

Notes:

a: Column 2 entries are weighted average poverty thresholds from U.S. Census Bureau, Current Population Reports, Series P60-226, *Income, Poverty, and Health Insurance Coverage in the United States: 2003,* Washington, D.C.: U.S. Government Printing Office, August 2004, p. 39.

b: Price inflation calculated from Table 1A of U.S. Department of Labor, Consumer Price Index press release (USDL-05-99), January 19, 2005. The Consumer Price Index (CPI-U) for all items was 184.0 for calendar year 2003 and 188.9 for calendar year 2004, an increase of 2.7 percent.

c: The arithmetic average of Column 4 entries, rounded to the nearest multiple of $20.

d: Obtained by multiplying the average poverty threshold for a family unit of four persons for 2003 ($18,810, from Column 2) by the price increase factor from 2003 to 2004 (1.027) and rounding the result upward to the nearest whole multiple of $50. All other entries in Column 6 are obtained by successive addition or subtraction of the average difference ($3,260) to the size–4 2005 guideline entry ($19,350).

http://aspe.hhs.gov/poverty/05computations.shtml.

Social-welfare policy making, like regulatory policy making, has a long political history and faces tremendous challenges. We have no easy formula for providing equal resources for all, a fair chance for all to succeed, and opportunity for all to flourish financially and personally. How well national policy makers respond to these challenges—and how democratic the policies are—remain crucial questions as American government continues its task of approaching democracy.

For Alaska and Hawaii, where the cost of living is traditionally believed to be significantly higher than in other states, scaling factors of 1.25 and 1.15, respectively, are applied to the 2005 guideline for a family of four for the 48 contiguous states, and the results (if not already a multiple of $10) are rounded upward to the nearest whole multiple of $10. (These scaling factors were based on Office of Economic Opportunity administrative practice for these two states beginning only in the 1966–70 period.) These scaling factors are applied to the average difference for the

48 contiguous states (Column 5) to obtain average differences for Alaska and Hawaii for deriving guidelines for other family sizes; these average differences for Alaska and Hawaii are rounded to the nearest multiple of $10. For families with more than 8 persons, add the following amount for each additional person: $3,260 (48 contiguous states and the District of Columbia); $4,080 (Alaska); $3,750 (Hawaii).

MakeItReal

Census 2000: *Income, Poverty, and Health insurance Coverage in the United States: 2003*

ECONOMIC POLICY

One of the most crucial roles for modern government is regulation of the national economy. When we look at the world of taxing and spending policy, we see clearly that politics and economics are fundamentally intertwined. In studying American politics, then, we need to understand how politics and economics interweave to present opportunities and obstacles in the United States' continuing approach to democracy. Both Republicans and Democrats believe in a strong, healthy economy. Where they differ is on how best to achieve this goal. Within each party, differences exist regarding broad goals and specific policies, differences that have important consequences for government's ability to make coherent budgetary policy and for the lives of every American citizen (see Figure 15.6).

The federal government influences the economy in many ways, both directly and indirectly. Government policies that affect the economy are categorized as fiscal policy, monetary policy, regulatory policy, and international economic policy.

Fiscal policy has the clearest impact through budget-related decisions. Government budgetary choices concerning when and how much to tax, spend, subsidize, and borrow affect the economic lives of all citizens.

Economic freedom index

The index of economic freedom is based on 21 criteria, including freedom of personal choice, protection of private property and freedom of exchange.

Political freedom ratings

Free

Partially free

Not free

The top-ranked countries:	Index number	Quality of life rank
1. Hong Kong	9.4	24
2. Singapore	9.3	22
3. New Zealand	8.9	18
4. Britain	8.8	10
5. United States	8.7	3
6. Australia	8.5	7
7. Ireland	8.5	20
8. Switzerland	8.5	12
9. Luxembourg	8.4	17
10. Netherlands	8.4	8
11. Argentina	8.3	39
12. Bolivia	8.3	112
13. Canada	8.2	1
14. Finland	8.1	13

0 1 2 3 4 5 6 7 8 9 10

Other selected countries:	Index number	Quality of life rank
20. Japan	7.9	4
62. Mexico	6.5	50
72. Indonesia	6.2	105
81. China	5.8	98
92. India	5.3	132
Some of the lowest-ranked countries:		
110. Rwanda	4.4	164
114. Gabon	4.3	124
114. Syria	4.3	111
117. Russia	3.9	71
118. Romania	3.8	68
119. Sierra Leone	3.5	174
121. Congo	3.0	141
122. Algeria	2.6	109
123. Myanmar	1.9	128

0 1 2 3 4 5 6 7 8 9 10

Figure 15.6 Freedom and Prosperity

[1]Political freedom rankings are based on Freedom House's Freedom in the World survey, which provides an annual evaluation of political rights and civil liberties.

[2]Quality of life ranking is based on the Human Development Index, which ranks nations based on criteria that include health, life expectancy, education and economic data.

Sources: Cato Institute, Freedom House, U.N. Development Program.

Monetary policy is the range of actions taken by the Federal Reserve Board to influence the level of the gross domestic product (GDP) or the rate of inflation. In an open economy, monetary policy affects the level of imports, such as Japanese cars to the United States.

Regulatory policy is also pervasive. Government regulates aspects of the workplace to achieve health, safety, and environmental goals.

International economic policy influences economic relations with other countries through exchange rates, trade negotiations, and international economic institutions such as the World Bank, the International Monetary Fund (IMF), and the World Trade Organization (WTO) and its predecessor, the General Agreement on Tariffs and Trade (GATT).

The Goals of Economic Policy

The primary goal of **economic policy** is to produce a vibrant, healthy, and growing economy. The federal government's role in making economic policy has increased since World War II. Conditioned by the experience of 25 percent unemployment rates during the Great Depression of the 1930s and the high *inflation rates* (rate of increase in prices) and commodity shortages of the war years of the 1940s, Congress adopted the Employment Act of 1946, which formalized the federal government's responsibility to guide the economy to achieve three primary economic goals: *stable prices* (low or zero inflation), *full employment* (an unemployment rate of 4 percent or less), and *economic growth* (substantial and sustained growth in the economy as measured by increases in the gross domestic product). The conditions necessary to achieve these three goals, as the postwar record shows, were often lacking, and the U.S. economy experienced periods of high unemployment, high inflation, and slow or even negative economic growth.

Developing an economic policy that can achieve these goals is difficult and complex, because actions that affect one goal also affect the others, often in undesirable ways. Policies that raise interest rates to push inflation down, for example, may discourage spending, which can raise unemployment rates and may also reduce investment spending and the adoption of new technology, which can, in turn, affect the rate of economic growth. Economic trade-offs must thus be considered in addition to political trade-offs.

To make matters worse, it appears that to achieve the goals of stable prices, full employment, and economic growth, we also need to attain a secondary set of economic goals, such as low and stable interest rates, stable exchange rates, and reduced federal budget **deficits** (annual shortfalls between what government takes in and spends) and balance-of-trade deficits. Progress toward these secondary economic goals seems necessary to achieve the rising living standards embodied in the nation's principal economic goals.

MakeItReal

Primary Source: Budget of the United States 2006

economic policy Policy aimed at producing a vibrant, healthy, and growing economy.

deficit A shortfall between the monies a government takes in and spends.

THE POLITICS OF THE FEDERAL BUDGET

There is perhaps no better place to observe how economic policy and political factors intertwine than the case of the federal budget. We have already discussed some of the ways government uses its power to tax and spend to influence the economy. Yet government also taxes and spends to provide services for its citizens. How policy makers attempt to provide these services—and, more important, who pays for them and who receives them—touches the very heart of federal budget politics.

The President Proposes, Congress Disposes

Stated simply, the national budget is a document that proclaims how much the government will try to collect in taxes and how those revenues will be spent on various

	2005	2006	2007	2008	2009	2010	2011
Budget Totals:							
Receipts	2,154	2,285	2,416	2,590	2,714	2,878	3,035
Outlays	2,472	2,709	2,770	2,814	2,922	3,061	3,240
Deficit	**-318**	**-423**	**-354**	**-223**	**-208**	**-183**	**-205**
Gross Domestic Product (GDP)	12,290	13,030	13,761	14,521	15,296	16,102	16,955
Budget Totals as a Percent of GDP:							
Receipts	17.5%	17.5%	17.6%	17.8%	17.7%	17.9%	17.9%
Outlays	20.1%	20.8%	20.1%	19.4%	19.1%	19.0%	19.1%
Deficit	**-2.6%**	**-3.2%**	**-2.6%**	**-1.5%**	**-1.4%**	**-1.1%**	**-1.2%**

Figure 15.7   Budget Totals

Note: (Dollar amounts in billions)

Source: http://www.whitehouse.gov/omb/budget/fy2007/tables.html

federal programs. Yet, despite this seemingly simple definition, the preparation of the budget and its subsequent passage are both complex and profoundly political activities. The budget sets policy priorities by establishing the amount of money each program is slated to receive. Some programs are created, some receive more support than others, and still others are reduced or eliminated. The budget thus provides a policy blueprint for the nation.[31]

The law requires that by the first Monday in February, the president submit to Congress his proposed federal budget for the next fiscal year. Only after the Congress passes and the president signs the required spending bills does the government have a budget. Figure 15.7 shows budget projections made in President Bush's 2007 federal budget.

How the Budget Is Prepared

Budgetary politics involves many actors, the most important being the president and Congress. Although in a strict constitutional sense Congress has sole power to authorize spending of any federal monies, the modern-day practice is for Congress to follow the president's lead. The Budget and Accounting Act of 1921 conferred this responsibility upon the president, greatly enhancing the president's power in domestic affairs. First, the law requires government agencies to send their budget requests to the president for consideration. The president ultimately decides whether or not to include these requests in the budget plan. Second, the act created an executive budget office, the Bureau of the Budget (BOB), which became the **Office of Management and Budget (OMB)** under President Richard Nixon. The director of the OMB has cabinet-level status and is one of the president's top advisers and policy strategists.[32]

The OMB provides each agency with budgeting instructions and guidelines reflecting presidential budgetary priorities and then analyzes the agencies' budget requests. This process takes place during the spring and fall of the year, after which the OMB director goes to the president with a budget—a set of estimates for both revenues and expenditures. But this procedure is more than a matter of adding up numbers. Agency heads submit budgetary figures that represent their goals, their

Quick Review

Office of Management and Budget (OMB)

- Director of the OMB has cabinet-level status and is one of the president's top advisers and policy strategists.
- Provides each agency with instructions and guidelines reflecting presidential budgetary priorities.
- Analyzes the budgetary requests made by the agencies.
- Director presents a budget that represents the goals, ideologies, and personal ambitions of the agencies.
- With the help of the OMB, the president submits to Congress a budget plan that outlines the president's vision for the policy agenda of the country.

Office of Management and Budget (OMB) The unit in the Executive Office of the President whose main responsibilities are to prepare and administer the president's annual budget. A president and the OMB can shape policy through the budget process; the process determines which departments and agencies grow, are cut, or remain the same as the year before.

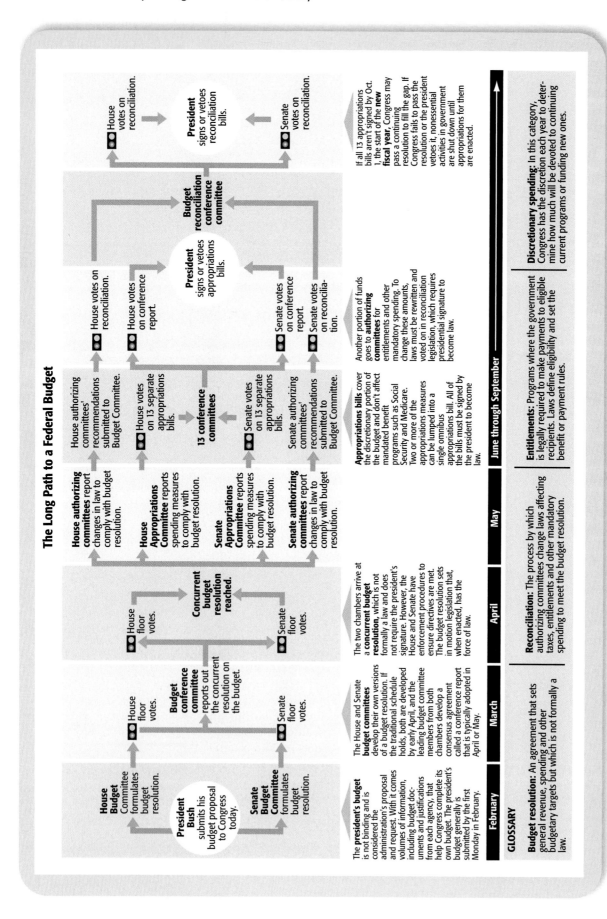

The Long Path to a Federal Budget

President Bush submits his budget proposal to Congress today.

House Budget Committee formulates budget resolution.

Senate Budget Committee formulates budget resolution.

House floor votes.

Budget conference committee reports out the concurrent resolution on the budget.

Senate floor votes.

Concurrent budget resolution reached.

House floor votes.

Senate floor votes.

House authorizing committees report changes in law to comply with budget resolution.

House Appropriations Committee reports spending measures to comply with budget resolution.

Senate Appropriations Committee reports spending measures to comply with budget resolution.

Senate authorizing committees report changes in law to comply with budget resolution.

House authorizing committees' recommendations submitted to Budget Committee.

House votes on 13 separate appropriations bills.

13 conference committees

Senate votes on 13 separate appropriations bills.

Senate authorizing committees' recommendations submitted to Budget Committee.

House votes on reconciliation.

House votes on conference report.

President signs or vetoes appropriations bills.

Senate votes on conference report.

Senate votes on reconciliation.

House votes on reconciliation.

Budget reconciliation conference committee

President signs or vetoes reconciliation bills.

Senate votes on reconciliation.

The **president's budget** is not binding and is considered the administration's proposal and request. With it comes volumes of information, including budget documents and justifications from each agency, that help Congress complete its own budget. The president's budget generally is submitted by the first Monday in February.

The House and Senate **budget committees** develop their own versions of a budget resolution. If the traditional schedule holds, both are developed by early April, and the leading budget committee members from both chambers develop a consensus agreement called a conference report that is typically adopted in April or May.

The two chambers arrive at a **concurrent budget resolution**, which is not formally a law and does not require the president's signature. However, the House and Senate have enforcement procedures to ensure directives are met. The budget resolution sets in motion legislation that, when enacted, has the force of law.

Appropriations bills cover the discretionary portion of the budget and don't affect mandated benefit programs such as Social Security and Medicare. Two or more of the appropriations measures can be lumped into a single omnibus appropriations bill. All of the bills must be signed by the president to become law.

Another portion of funds goes to **authorizing committees** for entitlements and other mandatory spending. To change these amounts, laws must be rewritten and voted on in reconciliation legislation, which requires presidential signature to become law.

If all 13 appropriations bills aren't signed by Oct. 1, the start of the **new fiscal year**, Congress may pass a continuing resolution to fill the gap. If Congress fails to pass the resolution or the president vetoes it, nonessential activities in government are shut down until appropriations for them are enacted.

February	March	April	May	June through September

GLOSSARY

Budget resolution: An agreement that sets general revenue, spending and other budgetary targets but which is not formally a law.

Reconciliation: The process by which authorizing committees change laws affecting taxes, entitlements and other mandatory spending to meet the budget resolution.

Entitlements: Programs where the government is legally required to make payments to eligible recipients. Laws define eligibility and set the benefit or payment rules.

Discretionary spending: In this category, Congress has the discretion each year to determine how much will be devoted to continuing current programs or funding new ones.

Figure 15.8
The Long Path to a Federal Budget

Sources: House Budget Committee, Office of Management and Budget, Congressional Research Service.

ideologies, and even their personal ambitions. This is an extremely political undertaking, with plenty of political maneuvering and overt lobbying geared toward protecting and enhancing each agency's share of the budgetary pie. Finally, in January, after adjustments by the president, the budget of the U.S. government is submitted to Congress. With the help of the OMB, the president submits a budget plan that outlines the national priorities, the president's vision for the policy agenda of the country. It is in this context that we see the workings of the old budgetary adage: "The president proposes and Congress disposes"—Congress must approve the budget, turning the president's vision into tangible law. Congress uses its oversight authority to assess the performance of government agencies but also to check the president's power (see Figure 15.8).

However, by 1973 it had become increasingly difficult for Congress to formulate a comprehensive, substantive alternative to the president's plan. Congress was often left with little control over the budget, making only incremental and marginal adjustments to what is clearly the president's plan for the nation. As we saw in Chapter 4, Congress is a highly decentralized and fragmented institution, one that allows its individual members to pursue their personal policy and reelection goals. Although the institutional setup of Congress works to the advantage of individual members, it diminishes Congress's ability to produce a collective vision of national priorities to balance that of the president.

Partly in response to recurring budget battles with President Richard Nixon and partly to reassert its constitutional mandate to use the budget as an expression of its own policy vision, Congress passed the Budget and Impoundment Control Act of 1974. **Impoundment** refers to either the president's refusal to spend appropriated funds or his deferral of such expenditures. The first executive impoundment occurred in 1803, when Thomas Jefferson refused to spend $50,000 appropriated by Congress for gunboats on the Mississippi. From 1969 to 1973, Richard Nixon impounded approximately 20 percent of controllable funds appropriated by Congress, arguing that he would be unfaithful to his oath to take care that the laws are faithfully executed if spending money appropriated by Congress would create an inflationary spiral.

In essence, the Impoundment Control Act sought to provide Congress a procedure, independent of the president, to gain more control and give it the ability to make comprehensive appropriations and spending decisions. The act modified the budget process by allowing Congress to establish overall levels for taxing and spending, including breakdowns for national defense, foreign aid, health, infrastructure, and agriculture. Congress established budget committees in the House and Senate to carry out these tasks and to hold hearings on the president's proposed budget. Congress set up the Congressional Budget Office (CBO), a staff of budgetary experts to provide both houses with their own source of budgetary data, enhancing their independence from the executive branch OMB. The House and Senate Budget Committees examine the president's budget. The committees send a budget to each chamber in the form of resolutions, and a conference committee then hashes out a single congressional budget that can reward or punish different agencies.

The reform worked well for several years, increasing the congressional role in budget formation. For the most part, recent budgets have reflected multiyear commitments to agencies and programs. At the same time, budgets have been more sensitive to macroeconomic changes.

By the mid-1980s a new problem was emerging, one that eventually led to further reform of the budgetary process. The combined tax cuts and increased military spending of the Reagan administration dramatically increased the existing budget deficit. In the same period, the percentage of the budget committed to *entitlement programs* (benefits to which people are entitled because they fall into a particular category, such as Medicaid or Medicare) also grew, taking much of the budgetary flexibility away from both the White House and Congress.

impoundment The president's refusal to spend funds appropriated by Congress.

MakeItReal

Primary Source: Budget and Impoundment Control Act of 1974

Quick Review

Budget and Impoundment Control Act of 1974

- Sought to provide Congress with an independent procedure to make comprehensive appropriations and spending decisions.

- Modified the budget process by allowing Congress to establish overall levels for taxing and spending.

- Congress established Budget Committees to hold hearings on the president's proposed budget.

- Congress set up the Congressional Budget Office (CBO) to provide a source of budgetary data.

tariffs The imposition of import taxes on foreign goods in an attempt to protect a nation's industry and/or labor.

progressive taxes System of taxation in which those who make more money are taxed at a higher rate. An example is the income tax.

regressive taxes System of taxation in which taxes take a higher fraction of the income of lower income taxpayers; examples are taxes on gasoline, cigarettes, and alcohol.

TAXING

Although all citizens want their fair share of the budgetary pie—whether for better highways or more police protection—almost nobody wants to foot the bill for these services. Therein lies the strain in the politics of taxing and spending, a profoundly political strain. The president's ideas about where government revenues should be spent and who should shoulder the burden of paying lead to serious battles. Policy makers decide who will benefit from government programs and who will pay for them, and neither these benefits nor the burden of paying for them are distributed evenly across society. The 2001 tax cut, with its standard rebates, was the Bush administration's attempt at giving back money to the highest percentage of the tax-paying U.S. population.

Governments have never been able to meet public needs by relying on voluntary contributions alone. Most of us want—and in fact, expect—government to provide us with certain things. From highly targeted benefits such as farm subsidies to broad intangibles such as national security, we look to our government as a provider. Most Americans fail to realize that "government money" is predominantly the accumulated tax dollars collected annually. So when the government reaches into our pockets to pay for these services, we balk, we complain, and some of us even risk stiff penalties by trying to evade paying our "fair share." Such is the relationship between a government and its people where taxes are concerned.[33]

This unwillingness to fork over hard-earned dollars is understandable. The idea of a free, democratic society is challenged when governments demand and take private property, including portions of the profits of corporations and the modest wages of workers. The federal government did not collect taxes from private corporations until 1909 and from individuals until 1913. Before these new tax levies, money to run the government came primarily from **tariffs**, taxes on goods imported into the country.

Many U.S. citizens have had trouble swallowing taxation, leading to periodic "tax revolts." In 1978, the citizens of California staged one such revolt when they passed Proposition 13, a measure designed to permanently cap local property taxes. Anti-tax sentiment has appeared since then, as well. Tax cuts were a central feature of the Reagan administration and led subsequently to President George H. W. Bush's now infamous pledge of "Read my lips. No new taxes." And the case study made clear that George W. Bush understood better than anyone the lesson of embracing and signing the historic tax cut.[34]

Sources of Tax Dollars

At least a partial answer to these questions comes from examining the sources and outlays of federal revenues. The government relies to a significant degree on the personal income tax. This puts the federal government in a position to benefit from the increases in personal income that accompany a healthy economy. The better the economy, the more income tax revenues. Interestingly, reliance on the income tax can also act as a buffer during economic downturns, in that the national pool of taxpayers means that economic slumps affecting certain parts of the country are at least partially offset by greater prosperity in other parts. This heavy reliance on individual taxpayers rather than large corporations can impose severe—some argue unfair—tax burdens, particularly for middle-class citizens (see Figure 15.9).

When we evaluate the importance of income taxes, it is important to recognize that not all taxes are created equal. Different types of taxes affect different groups of people. One way to judge taxes, therefore, is according to whom they affect and how much. **Progressive taxes**, which tax those who make more money at a higher rate, are often considered the fairest, as they place a larger burden on those people with the greatest ability to pay. In general, the greater the number of tax brackets—steps in which the percentage rate of tax increases—the more progressive the tax. **Regressive taxes**, on the other hand, tax all people by the same amount, thereby

Question for Reflection

The government relies to a significant degree on the personal income tax for federal revenues. What implications does this decision have for taxing and spending policy?

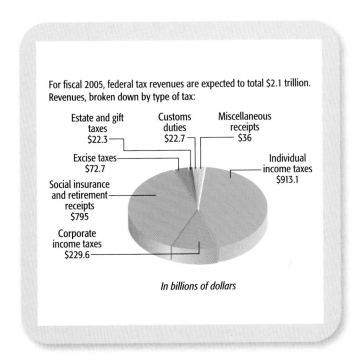

For fiscal 2005, federal tax revenues are expected to total $2.1 trillion. Revenues, broken down by type of tax:

Estate and gift taxes
$22.3

Customs duties
$22.7

Miscellaneous receipts
$36

Excise taxes
$72.7

Individual income taxes
$913.1

Social insurance and retirement receipts
$795

Corporate income taxes
$229.6

In billions of dollars

Figure 15.9
All the Federal Tax Dollars
Source: Office of Management and Budget

taking a higher fraction of the income of lower-income taxpayers. These rates are generally seen as less fair. The **capital gains tax** (tax on unearned income from rents, stocks, and interest) is an example of a progressive tax, since most of the revenue it gathers comes from a tiny portion of the wealthiest Americans. Taxes on consumer goods such as gasoline, cigarettes, and alcoholic beverages are generally regressive, because most of their consumption—hence most of the taxes paid—comes from the relatively larger group of middle-and lower-class Americans.

Tax Reform

Periodic attempts to reform the tax structure typically relate to the issue of fairness. After prolonged political battles over who would benefit and who would pay, Congress passed the Tax Reform Act of 1986. The purpose of the reform was to simplify an unwieldy tax structure and promote greater fairness. Toward the first goal, the number of tax rates decreased from fifteen categories to three, including a zero rate for low-income individuals. The remaining brackets dropped the highest rate from 50 to 28 percent and the lowest rate to 15 percent. Thus, on the face of things, tax rates fell for higher-income individuals, suggesting that the tax structure actually became even more regressive.

Yet the tax reform of 1986 included another important aspect, one that helped increase revenues and retain a degree of progressivity. In addition to changing tax rates, the reform also eliminated many tax deductions, or what are technically called **tax expenditures**. Tax expenditures are amounts taxpayers have spent for items that they can subtract from their income when filing their tax returns. These deductions (some call them "loopholes") reduce the amount of income actually subject to taxes, resulting in losses of government revenue. Some of the most common tax expenditures are interest paid on home mortgages or business equipment and business-related entertainment. Critics of tax expenditures argue that they are a drain on the federal treasury and specifically benefit the relatively wealthy. After all, only those who can afford to buy a home can benefit from the mortgage interest reduction.

In the end, the 1986 reforms changed many of these deductions, eliminating deductions for state sales taxes, interest paid on credit card and other personal debt, and

capital gains tax Tax on unearned income from rents, stocks, and interest.

tax expenditures Deductible expenses that reduce the amount of income subject to taxes; for example, home mortgages, business equipment, or business-related entertainment.

▲ "I've been thinking about the flat tax and how it would inflict hardship on the poor, and I can live with that."

MakeItReal

Simulation: Balancing the Nation's Checkbook: What Can You Get for $4 Trillion?

excise taxes Charges on the sale or manufacture of products such as cigarettes, alcohol, and gasoline.

discretionary spending The spending Congress actually controls; 33 percent of all spending.

mandatory spending Spending that must be allocated by law rather than by appropriations, for entitlements such as Social Security, Medicare, and Medicaid; 67 percent of the budget.

interest on mortgages on third or fourth homes, while reducing deductions for medical expenses and business entertainment, among others. The result was a simplified, more progressive tax code, in which many taxpayers paid lower taxes and a greater burden was placed on upper-middle-income individuals. Critics argue, however, that the reform did not go far enough and that as deductions were eliminated, new deductions sprang up to take their place, effectively reducing the impact of any attempts to increase the progressiveness or fairness of the reforms.

Unfortunately for George H. W. Bush, these tax reforms had another effect. They did not bring in enough revenue to cover federal spending. The result was further increases in the annual budget deficit. Thus, in 1990, former president Bush was forced to renege on his "Read my lips. No new taxes" promise and enact a modest tax increase on wealthier Americans. Republicans who had supported Bush in 1988 were enraged by this tax increase, and it is likely that Bush paid a price for reneging on his pledge, as many Republicans voted for Ross Perot in 1992.

One major goal of President Clinton's tax strategy was to make the tax structure more equitable, to make good on his campaign promise to make wealthier people "pay their fair share." Clinton introduced a greater degree of progressiveness in income taxes by changing the tax structure: Individuals making more than $115,000 saw their tax rates rise from 31 to 36 percent; those making more than $250,000 became subject to a 10 percent surcharge, making their tax-effective rate 39.6 percent. Clinton's plan resulted in actual income tax increases for fewer than 2 percent of all taxpayers, with the greatest hit being taken by the wealthiest, and tax cuts going to the poorest Americans.

The next largest source of federal revenue comes from Social Security taxes paid by employers and their employees. Although it did not raise the effective tax rate for these taxes, Clinton's plan did tax a larger percentage of Social Security benefits from relatively wealthy recipients. Finally, Clinton's plan placed greater emphasis on a traditionally small part of federal revenue raised from excise taxes. **Excise taxes** are charges on the sale or manufacture of certain products, such as cigarettes, alcohol, and gasoline. Despite the concern of members of Congress from oil-producing states, Clinton won passage of an increased excise tax on gasoline.

SPENDING

Just as deciding who pays taxes and how much is a profoundly political question, so is deciding where to spend those revenues. Although most of us balk at picking up the bill, we are also quite ready to hold out our hands for our fair share (or more) from the federal treasury. Be it low-cost student loans, government-subsidized health care, or cleaning up the environment, everyone wants his or her program to receive funding, and the more funding the better.

Federal tax revenue spending choices often signal a government's priorities. Ronald Reagan sought to boost the prestige and visibility of the U.S. military, and he achieved this goal by dramatically increasing spending for national defense, with much of the money coming from cuts in social programs and an increase in the deficit. Of course, priorities change from year to year and administration to administration (see Figure 15.10).

Discretionary spending accounts for 33 percent of all federal spending; this is what Congress and the president must decide to spend for the next year through thirteen annual appropriations bills. Examples of discretionary money are funding for the Federal Bureau of Investigation and the Coast Guard, housing and education, space exploration and highway construction, defense and foreign aid.

Mandatory spending accounts for approximately 70 percent of all spending and is authorized by permanent laws, not the appropriations bills. It includes entitlements such as Social Security, Medicare, food stamps, and veterans' benefits that

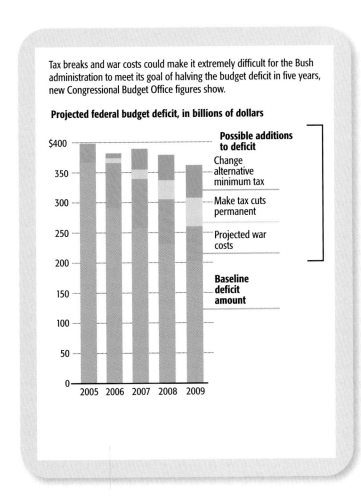

Tax breaks and war costs could make it extremely difficult for the Bush administration to meet its goal of halving the budget deficit in five years, new Congressional Budget Office figures show.

Projected federal budget deficit, in billions of dollars

**Figure 15.10
Continued
Deficits**

Note: 2005 figures do not include President Bush's $80 billion emergency spending request.

Source: Congressional Budget Office

benefit individuals eligible based on age, income, or other criteria. Mandatory spending also includes the interest on the **national debt**—the cumulative unpaid total of all annual budget deficits. By law, any legislation that raises mandatory spending or lowers revenues from levels in existing laws must be offset by spending cuts or revenue increases. This requirement is known as "pay as you go" because it is designed to prevent new legislation from increasing the deficit.

THE POLITICS OF INTERNATIONAL ECONOMIC POLICY

The increasingly integrated global economy is making nations increasingly interdependent. To a greater extent than ever before, the United States must take account of global forces in making economic policy. International economic policy deals with international trade, international monetary problems (including exchange-rate policy), international finance and debt problems, and the actions of international economic institutions such as the World Bank, the International Monetary Fund (IMF), and the World Trade Organization (WTO). Some economic issues are global in scope; others are multilateral, involving groups of nations; still others are bilateral, between two nations. In the area of trade, for example, U.S. policy influences global trade policy through the General Agreement on Tariffs and Trade (GATT) and the WTO, and regional trade policy through the North American Free Trade Agreement (NAFTA). The United States also engages in bilateral trade negotiations with many nations, most notably Japan.

national debt The cumulative total of all budget deficits.

▲ On February 1, 2006, Ben S. Bernanke replaced Alan Greenspan as Chairman and a member of the Board of Governors of the Federal Reserve System. Bernanke also serves as Chairman of the Federal Open Market Committee, the System's principal monetary policymaking body. He was appointed as a member of the Board to a full 14-year term, which expires January 31, 2020, and to a four-year term as Chairman, which expires January 31, 2010. Before his appointment as Chairman, Dr. Bernanke was Chairman of the President's Council of Economic Advisers, from June 2005 to January 2006.

ABC NEWS/PRENTICE HALL VIDEO LIBRARY

Outsourcing

International economic policies, like their domestic counterparts, are influenced both by political concerns and by broad philosophical and theoretical concerns. When policy makers determine their support for international policies, they must consider both how their constituents will be affected and whether or not the policy is broadly beneficial, given their understanding of the way the international economy works.

The politics of international economic policy illustrate that these types of decisions rely on a mix of economic theories and on local as well as national political concerns. As the U.S. economy becomes less distinctly national and more firmly connected to the global web of commercial enterprises, the United States must take the policies of other nations into account when setting its own, and attempt, when possible, to coordinate its policies with the European Union, Japan, and other nations.

To see why policy coordination is more important now among nations, consider for a moment this simple analogy. Think of the economy as a bathtub. In previous years, each nation had its own small bathtub, which connected to others in only a few ways. Governments could use monetary and fiscal policy like water faucets, to regulate the flow of water in their own bathtub economy without much regard to what other nations did. Domestic economic policy reigned supreme.

These days, however, the economies are increasingly global in scope. Markets span national borders through trade, finance, and telecommunications. People buy goods from around the world, invest money around the world, and participate in global culture. *Globalization* means that all the nations are, to a certain extent, now part of one big bathtub economy. A large nation like the United States can affect the flow of economic activity, but much less than before. It is difficult to raise the water in its end of the bathtub without raising the level for everyone else. The effective economic policies of, say, France, depend increasingly on the corresponding economic policies of Germany, Great Britain, and the United States.

In these days of "global bathtubs," the most effective way individual nations can change the economy is to coordinate their economic policies with those of other nations. Such coordination, however, conflicts with the ideal of an independent democratic process within nations.

The tension between domestic democratic processes and global economic forces was illustrated in 1995, when Mexico experienced sudden and unanticipated foreign debt problems, which caused the peso's value to fall from about thirty to fifteen cents over the course of a few days. Recognizing the interdependence of the U.S. and Mexican economies, the Clinton administration quickly organized a plan to help finance part of Mexico's debt. His plan had to be withdrawn, however, when congressional leaders made it clear that they would not support this program because of negative voter sentiments. Ten years later, President Bush attended a summit meeting of world leaders of thirty-four Western Hemisphere nations in Argentina aimed at agreement on a free-trade compact known as the Free Trade Area of the Americas. President Bush and such staunch allies as President Vicente Fox of Mexico and President Ricardo Lagos of Chile hoped to persuade their counterparts to endorse the plan. The meeting ended without agreement.[35]

The fact of international economic interdependence has not destroyed the concept of domestic democracy, but it has changed it. On critical matters of economic policy, the fundamental nature of the relationship among voters and elected officials, together with the policies they enact and the impact of those policies, has changed in subtle and important ways.

Economic policy making is a vital role of government. The decisions made by elected and nonelected officials can influence the economic well-being of the nation as a whole, as well as every single individual, whether rich or poor, Republican or Democrat. Moreover, these decisions are often rooted in those officials' conception of the proper role of government in the lives of citizens—who should be taxed and how these revenues should be spent—and thus policies are likely to change as individuals representing different philosophies and political constituencies assume the reins of government. Managing the economy takes you to the very heart of the relationship between a government and its people. Voters know this, and they make their feelings known come election time.

The politics of economic policy have changed in recent years due to the rising importance of international economic policy. As economic matters have become increasingly global, the very nature of democracy has changed with respect to international economic policies. These forces make the political analysis of international economics more complex, even as they become more important in our daily lives.

Summary

1. Public policies are the decisions, actions, and commitments of government. They have four key aims: to regulate key industries and aspects of American life, to protect citizens from foreign powers and other potential enemies, to encourage the accomplishment of important social goals, and to assist citizens and state and local governments.

2. The policy life cycle consists of eleven stages: (1) redefinition of a condition as a public problem, (2) placement of the problem on the public agenda, (3) emergence of the problem as an issue that requires government action, (4) formulation of a public policy response, (5) reformulation of the proposed policy, (6) placement of the policy on the government's formal agenda, (7) enactment of the policy, (8) implementation of the policy, (9) effects of implementing the policy, (10) evaluation of the effects, and (11) termination or continued implementation and evaluation of the policy.

3. To reach the public agenda, a potential subject of public policy must undergo a radical redefinition in the eyes of policy elites; that is, it must be labeled as a problem that the government must solve. A potential policy reaches the issue stage when it is framed in terms of a yes-or-no policy option. A dramatic event may serve as a triggering mechanism that causes a condition to be redefined as a problem, or an issue can reach the public agenda through the activities of policy entrepreneurs who "sell" it to a policy-making body. A policy reaches the formal agenda when it is actually scheduled for debate and potential adoption by a policy-making body.

4. Implementation is the execution of a policy. Some policies are difficult to implement because of their complexity, the cooperation required, and the need for coordination. Most federal policies require a period of monitoring and analysis known as policy evaluation. Following evaluation, policies are either terminated or continued. Once a policy has been enacted, however, it is often difficult to terminate.

5. Regulatory policy involves the use of federal police powers to supervise the conduct of individuals, businesses, and other governmental agencies. The national government may regulate prices, franchising or licenses, performance or safety standards, and resources available to citizens or businesses. It may also provide or withhold operating subsidies or use regulatory commissions to regulate vital industries and promote fair competition.

6. Regulatory activity by the federal government began in the late 1800s and increased during the Great Depression. The highest levels of regulation were reached in the 1960s and 1970s and were followed by a movement toward deregulation. The late 1980s saw a swing back toward increased regulation.

7. Social welfare policy uses positive incentives to promote or encourage basic social fairness. Much social welfare policy is intended to alleviate problems associated with poverty. The federal poverty level—the dollar amount of annual earnings below which a family is considered poor—is used to generate official government estimates of the number of Americans living in poverty.

8. The first major piece of social welfare legislation was the Social Security Act of 1935, which created four major sets of entitlements: Old Age Survivors Disability Insurance, unemployment insurance, Aid to Families with Dependent Children, and Supplemental Security Income. Additional social welfare legislation enacted during the 1960s formed part of the "War on Poverty."

9. Entitlements increased during the 1970s and 1980s, only to be scaled back during the Reagan administration. The Family Support Act of 1988 introduced work requirements for recipients of welfare benefits. The Personal Responsibility and Work Opportunity Reconciliation Act of 1996 ended the welfare system as we knew it and set the stage for ongoing state-by-state reforms.

10. Government policies that affect the economy can be organized into four groups: fiscal policy (decisions to tax and spend), monetary policy (the Fed's influence over the rate of inflation), regulatory policy (policies designed to achieve health, safety, and environmental goals), and international economic policies (policies dealing with exchange rates, trade negotiations, and international economic institutions).

11. The three main goals of economic policy are stable prices, full employment, and economic growth. Achieving these goals involves achieving certain secondary goals as well, such as low and stable interest rates, stable exchange rates, and reduced federal budget deficits and balance-of-trade deficits. The complex interactions among these goals often lead economic policy makers to trade off one goal against another.

12. The federal budget is prepared by the Office of Management and Budget, which analyzes the budgetary requests

made by every government agency. The president submits the budget to Congress in February of each year. The budget committees in the two houses consider the president's proposals and establish overall levels for taxation and for various areas of government spending.

13. The federal personal income and capital gains taxes are progressive; that is, those who make more money are taxed at a higher rate. Taxes on consumer goods such as gasoline and cigarettes are regressive because they take a higher fraction of the income of lower-income taxpayers. Periodic attempts to reform the tax structure typically give rise to major political battles over who will benefit and who will pay more.

14. Discretionary spending covers appropriations for government operations. The largest proportion of federal spending consists of mandatory spending or direct payments to individuals through entitlement programs such as Social Security.

15. When policy makers consider international economic policies, they must consider both how their constituents will be affected and whether the policy is beneficial to the country as a whole. Increasingly, the United States must take the policies of other nations into account when making economic policy and must try to coordinate its policies with those of the European Union, Japan, and other nations.

Review Questions

1. Describe the "life cycle" of public policy making.

2. What were the politics and goals of the Social Security Act of 1935 and the manner in which it sought to achieve those goals?

3. Why do media, individuals, and books have such a strong influence on the public agenda? Do they have the same influence on the formal agenda? Why or why not?

4. What were the circumstances surrounding President Clinton's approval of the Personal Responsibility and Work Opportunity Reconciliation Act of 1996? How is this an example of the interaction between real world politics and legislative priorities? Will the Personal Responsibility and Work Opportunity Reconciliation Act of 1996 reduce poverty in the long run?

5. How does the budget process work and how do projections of surpluses/deficits affect budget planning by the federal government (president and Congress)?

6. What factors and events have led to the increasingly global nature of the U.S. economy? How is it changing the nature of democracy with respect to international economic policies? Do these events represent an approach to democracy? Why or why not?

Key Terms

capital gains tax   561
deficit   556
discretionary spending   562
economic policy   556
entitlements   548
excise taxes   562
formal agenda   542
implementation   543
impoundment   559
mandatory spending   562

means testing   551
national debt   563
Office of Management and
   Budget (OMB)   557
policy elites   542
policy entrepreneurs   542
policy evaluation   544
poverty level   548
progressive taxes   560
public agenda   542

public policies   538
regressive taxes   560
regulatory policy   538
social welfare policy   538
tariffs   560
tax expenditures   561
triggering mechanism   542
workfare   552

Suggested Readings

FRIEDMAN, MILTON, and WALTER HELLER. *Monetary versus Fiscal Policy.* New York: Norton, 1969. Classic presentation of the pros and cons of monetary and fiscal policy by a noninterventionist (Friedman) and an advocate of federal government intervention in the economy (Heller).

FUNIGELLO, PHILLIP J. *Health Care Security from FDR to George W. Bush.* Lawrence: University of Kansas Press, 2006. An excellent chronicle of the contentious political history behind the circumstances that have left 45 million Americans without adequate health insurance.

GREIDER, WILLIAM. *Secrets of the Temple: How the Federal Reserve Runs the Country.* New York: Simon & Schuster, 1987. A fascinating account of how the Federal Reserve Board actually conducts its business.

GRUBER, JONATHAN and DAVID A. WISE, eds. *Social Security Programs and Retirement Around the World.* National Bureau of Economic Research Conference Report. Chicago: University of Chicago Press, Spring 2004.

HARRINGTON, MICHAEL. *The Other America.* New York: Macmillan, 1994. The most widely read essay about poverty in the United States.

JENCKS, CHRISTOPHER. *Rethinking Social Policy: Race, Poverty, and the Underclass.* Cambridge, Mass.: Harvard University Press, 1992. A series of essays by a leading sociologist on social welfare policy and poverty.

MURRAY, CHARLES. *Losing Ground: American Social Policy, 1950–1980.* New York: Basic Books, 1984. A popular and controversial book that addresses the idea that social welfare programs for the poor have made things worse, not better.

ODELL, JOHN S. *Negotiating the World Economy.* Ithaca, N.Y.: Cornell University Press, 2000. An original analysis of strategies negotiators use to obtain maximum payoffs.

SAVAGE, JAMES. *Balanced Budgets and American Politics.* Ithaca, N.Y.: Cornell University Press, 1988. A scholarly historical account of ways the political environment affects budgeting in the United States.

SLEMROD, JOEL, and JON BAKIGA. *Taxing Ourselves.* 2d ed. Cambridge, Mass.: MIT Press, 2000. An excellent citizen's guide to the debate on taxation and reform.

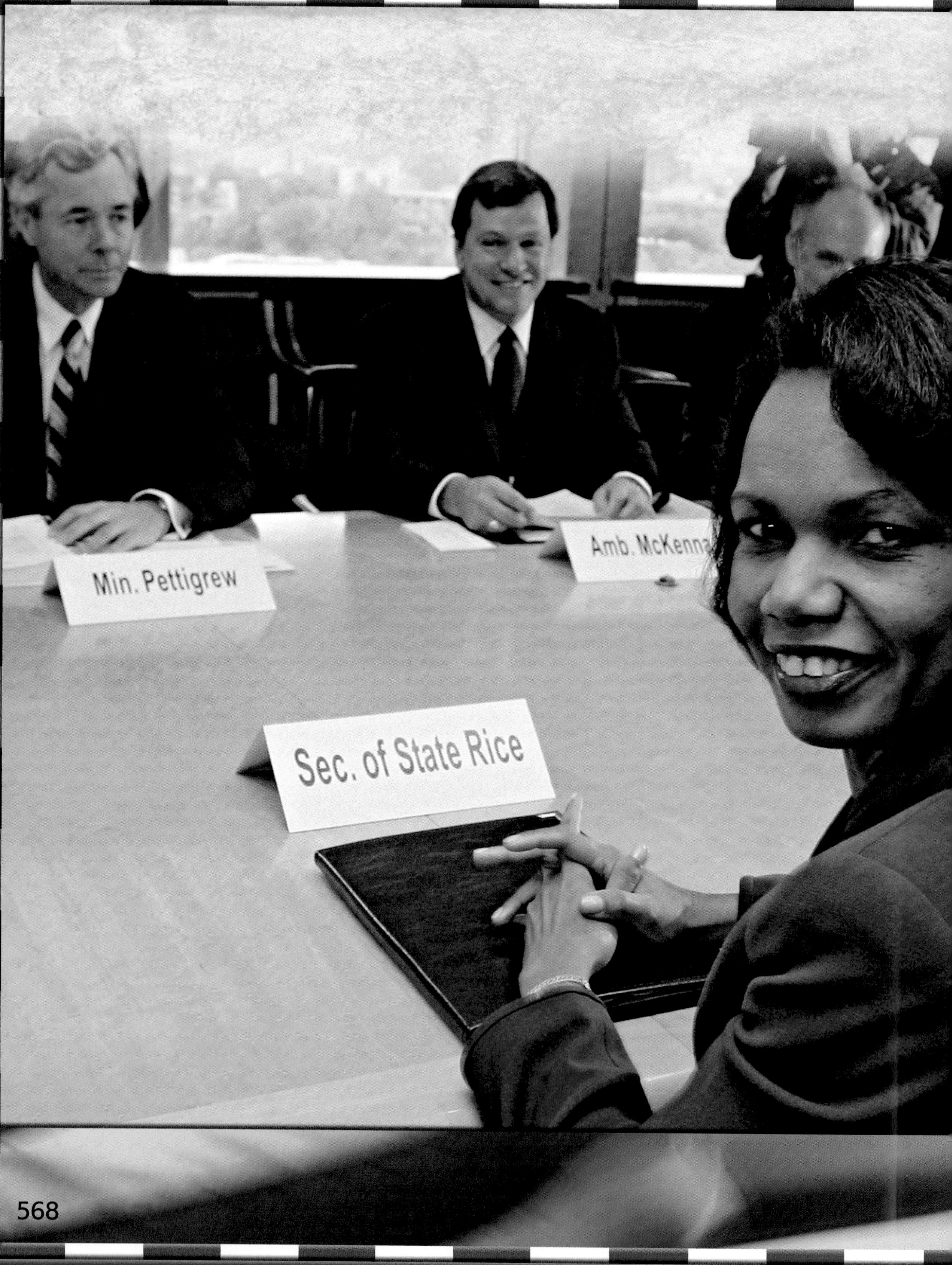
Min. Pettigrew
Amb. McKenna
Sec. of State Rice

★ CHAPTER 16 ★

FOREIGN POLICY

CHAPTER OUTLINE

Approaching Democracy

From Operation Enduring Freedom to Operation Iraqi Freedom

"The terrorists want to attack our country and harm our citizens. They believe that the world's democracies are weak, and that by killing innocent civilians they can break our will. They're mistaken. America will not retreat in the face of terrorists and murderers. And neither will the free world. As Prime Minister Blair said after the attacks in London, 'Our determination to defend our values and our way of life is greater than their determination to cause death and destruction to innocent people.' The attack in London was an attack on the civilized world. And the civilized world is united in its resolve: We will not yield. We will defend our freedom."

—PRESIDENT GEORGE W. BUSH
FBI Academy, Quantico, Virginia
July 11, 2005

In the wake of the September 11, 2001 attacks on the World Trade Center and the Pentagon, President George W. Bush undertook the leadership challenge of building an international coalition aimed at defeating international terrorism as well as its network of financial support. The Pentagon named its military campaign "Operation

★ In central Baghdad's Firdos Square, Iraqis cheered as a toppled statue of Saddam fell to the ground. The Iraqis broke the statue into pieces and dragged its head through the streets, while others—including children—pounded it with shoes, an act considered a supreme insult in the Arab world. "Saddam Hussein is now taking his rightful place alongside Hitler, Stalin, Lenin, Ceausescu in the pantheon of failed brutal dictators, and the Iraqi people are well on their way to freedom," said Secretary of Defense Rumsfeld.

Enduring Freedom," replacing an earlier name that was considered offensive to Muslims ("Operation Infinite Justice," because in the Islamic faith such finality is provided only by Allah).[1]

In the weeks following the attack, Great Britain and other sympathetic countries quickly supported U.S. resolve to bomb Taliban positions in Afghanistan, the stronghold of the al-Qaeda network. The international coalition showed signs of weakening during early 2002 when military strikes with mounting civilian deaths continued far longer than many allied nations expected. Afghanistan emerged from years of totalitarian Taliban rule a much-divided nation where warlords and tribal law held sway over international justice. The need to train a national army to provide security for the new Afghanistan tested the international coalition's resolve, but slowly the elements of stability and governmental forms emerged.

The situation was different in Iraq. The president told the 2002 graduating class at West Point, "we must take the

★ President Bush addresses the nation from aboard the USS Abraham Lincoln on May 1, 2003, with the banner "Mission Accomplished" in the background.

battle to the enemy, disrupt his plans and confront the worst threats before they emerge. The only path to safety is action. And this nation will act."[2] President Bush was in the process of redefining how America, the world's sole superpower, engaged the world. For the first time, he undertook the unilateral exercise of American military power through the doctrine of preemption and regime change. Operation Iraqi Freedom was the first time U.S. troops invaded an Arab country with the purpose of deposing its leader and changing the regime. In his June 1, 2002, West Point commencement address, the president explained that

> In defending the peace we face a threat with no precedent. Enemies in the past needed great armies and great industrial capabilities to endanger the American people and our nation. The attacks of September the 11th required a few hundred thousand dollars in the hands of a few dozen evil and deluded men. All of the chaos and suffering they caused came at much less than the cost of a single tank. . . . The gravest danger to freedom lies at the perilous crossroads of radicalism and technology. When the spread of chemical and biological and nuclear weapons, along with ballistic missile technology occurs, weak states and small groups could attain a catastrophic power to strike great nations. Our enemies have declared this very intention and have been caught seeking these terrible weapons. They want the capability to blackmail us or to harm our friends. And we will oppose them with all our power.[3]

On the evening of March 19, 2003 (the morning of March 20 in Baghdad), U.S. and United Kingdom military forces began an attempt to disarm Iraq of its weapons of mass destruction and to remove the Iraqi regime from power. On May 1, 2003, aboard the USS *Abraham Lincoln*, with a giant "Mission Accomplished" sign behind him, the president declared, "The battle of Iraq is one victory in a war on terror that began on September 11, 2001, and still goes on."[4]

Yet, many of the administration's justifications for going to war with Iraq have been undermined by information showing that Saddam Hussein no longer possessed weapons of mass destruction in 2003. The insurgency in Iraq has developed into a force much more difficult to contain than first anticipated; more than two thousand Americans have been killed in combat, along with an untold number of Iraqis. Although the Iraqi people voting in three elections provided an inspiring moment in Iraq's approach to democracy, we do not yet know whether or not the Iraqi constitution will provide legitimacy and stability, nor do we know when U.S. troops can return home. "More than two years after the fall of Saddam Hussein, Iraq remains a complex mix of tragedy and hope," observed Adriana Lins de Albuquerque and Michael E. O'Hanlon.[5] Amid increasing

★ American soldiers search Iraqi men looking for weapons. Some Iraqis have come to regard these as humiliating experiences. Dignified and proud, Iraqis don't like foreign soldiers searching their bodies and giving or denying them permission to move from one place to another inside their own country.

attacks on his policy, the president remained adamant: "An immediate withdrawal of our troops in Iraq, or the broader Middle East, as some have called for, would only embolden the terrorists and create a staging ground to launch more attacks against America and free nations. So long as I'm the president, we will stay, we will fight, and we will win the war on terror."[6]

QUESTION FOR REFLECTION

In what ways does the current conflict in Iraq resemble the war in Vietnam and what comparisons are inappropriate?

Introduction
FOREIGN POLICY AND DEMOCRACY

MakeItReal

Simulation: The Impact of Foreign Aid

Foreign policy refers to actions the U.S. government takes on behalf of its national interests abroad to ensure the security and well-being of Americans and the strength and competitiveness of the U.S. economy.[7] A secure citizenry requires protection of recognized national boundaries, a strong economy, and a stable, orderly society. Since the end of World War II, U.S. foreign policy has been a cautious balancing act between American democratic ideals and U.S. military and economic interests. Much of the history is rooted in the concept of so-called American exceptionalism. "We shall be as a City upon a Hill," proclaimed Puritan leader John Winthrop more than three centuries ago. Indeed, this core value comes closest to our theme of approaching democracy. "On every continent democracy is securing for more and more people the basic freedoms we Americans have come to take for granted," observed President Bill Clinton in his 1998 address to the Joint Chiefs of Staff and Pentagon staff about the situation in Iraq. President Bush has reiterated this theme many times during the American-led war in Iraq and Iraq's own attempt at constitution writing. In a late August 2005 weekly radio address, the president observed that "Iraqis are working together to build a free nation that contributes to peace and stability in the region, and we will help them succeed. . . . Like our own nation's founders more than two centuries ago, the Iraqis are grappling with difficult issues such as the role of the federal government. Better yet, they now address these issues through debate and discussion, not at the barrel of a gun."[8]

The end of the Cold War and the breakup of the Eastern bloc may have nearly eliminated the threat of a global nuclear war, but it also stimulated increasing hostility, violence, and warfare. The collapse of the Soviet Union set the stage for a violent showdown between Russian president Boris Yeltsin and his own parliament. The breakup of Yugoslavia triggered a genocidal war between various ethnic factions. The massive 1991 U.S. deployment in the Persian Gulf War with Iraq would have been almost unthinkable a decade earlier, when the Soviet Union was still a potential force to be reckoned with. Without the policy priority of anticommunism, the United States has had to weigh carefully both its own interests and its commitments to democracy and human rights before developing a foreign policy response.[9]

Moreover, following the collapse of the Soviet Union, the United States shifted its military focus to combat other international threats to American safety. Considered "rogue" for challenging the hegemony of American foreign policy, these nations command a minor amount of weapons capable of inflicting "massive destruction," like the nuclear weapons possessed by the United States.[10] Following the September 11 attacks of the Pentagon and World Trade Center, the idea of rogue nations striking the United States increasingly seemed an imminent possibility. President Bush named an "axis of evil" that included North Korea, Iraq, and Iran.

In this chapter we look at American foreign policy, its history, how it is made, and by whom. Perhaps the best way to start is by identifying the core goals of American foreign relations:[11]

MakeItReal

Visual Literacy: Foreign and Domestic Success and Failure

foreign policy Policy adopted and actions taken by the U.S. government on behalf of U.S. national interests abroad. The president is this country's chief foreign policy maker.

1. *Survival and independence:* A country's foreign relations are guided first and foremost by national security—the protection of those interests deemed necessary for the country's safety. Independence and survival are the United States' irreducible, fundamental security objectives.

2. *Territorial integrity and acquisition of new territory:* Preservation of territorial integrity is the mirror image of survival and always a national security priority.

3. *Military security:* Military security for any nation depends on a variety of factors, including weaponry, capabilities and intentions of other nations, advantages and disadvantages of geography, resources, and demographic trends.

4. *Economic security:* Two persistent themes of American foreign policy have been to keep the door open for trade wherever profit beckoned and be ready to employ costly economic measures to achieve goals. Economic advantage has long been an objective of U.S. foreign policy.

5. *Democratic values and ideals:* Promotion of democratic values and ideals worldwide has defined the national purpose of the United States' role in world affairs.

AN OVERVIEW OF AMERICAN FOREIGN POLICY

We can distinguish between two eras in U.S. foreign policy. The first, from the founding of the republic until approximately World War I, might be described as a period of isolationism from Europe, but with vigorous expansion in the Western Hemisphere. The second is characterized by an increasing globalization of American interests and commitments, including: two world wars, a cold war, and a post-cold war period of redefinition and refocusing of American national interests in foreign policy.

Isolationism and Regionalism

Once free of Britain's domination, the United States was not eager to reestablish binding relationships with European empires; however, the newly independent country was not about to commit economic suicide by cutting off lucrative ties with the great trading centers of Europe. A pattern of **isolationism** gradually developed in which the United States fostered economic relations with Europe without committing itself to strategic alliances that might draw the country into a European war. Initially, such a policy was easily pursued, since the United States had virtually no standing army and few military resources upon which European countries could call. The United States also enjoyed a favorable geographic isolation, situated as it was between two vast oceans in a time of slow and dangerous sea travel.

The **Monroe Doctrine**, enunciated by President James Monroe in his December 2, 1823, State of the Union Address, reinforced the country's isolationism by proclaiming the North and South American continents to be in the United States' *sphere of influence* and therefore out of bounds for European aspirations. In return, the United States agreed not to become involved in European affairs. The Monroe Doctrine also contributed to another crucial ideal of U.S. foreign policy: vigorous territorial expansion within its own continental land-mass that belied any absolute isolation of America. Under the banner of *Manifest Destiny*, U.S. foreign policy makers in the first half of the nineteenth century invoked divine guidance to take control of what is now the continental United States. Then, at the end of the century, the United States looked south to Central America, the Caribbean, and South America, turning from internal expansion to an enhanced role for America overseas.[12]

By this time, U.S. governmental and private agencies controlled vast oil fields in Mexico and plantations in the Dominican Republic and Cuba. American businesses and diplomats were also looking toward the reluctantly opening door to China. Yet U.S. foreign policy was still regional, with clear priority given to the resources and potential of the Western Hemisphere. In 1898, the United States went to war against Spain, and in the process seized the Philippines and Puerto Rico. In the same year, it annexed the Hawaiian Islands. In the first years of the twentieth century, under the leadership of President Theodore Roosevelt, the United States emerged as policeman of the Western Hemisphere. Roosevelt not only launched the Panama Canal project, but also mediated the Russo-Japanese War and accelerated the development of the United States Navy.

isolationism A pattern in which the United States fosters economic relations abroad without committing to strategic alliances that might draw the country into a war.

Monroe Doctrine A doctrine enunciated by President James Monroe in 1823 that proclaimed North and South America to be in the United States' sphere of influence, hence out of bounds for European aspirations. It reinforced growing isolationism by promising not to interfere in the internal concerns of European states.

Quick Review

The Lusitania

- Ocean liner *Lusitania* sunk by a German submarine in 1915.

- Death toll included American citizens.

- Act of aggression against the ship demonstrated Germany's policy of submarine warfare and the impossibility of containing the war within Europe.

- Germany resumed unrestricted submarine warfare in 1917 and the United States declared war.

National Security Act of 1947

- Created the Central Intelligence Agency (CIA) and the National Security Council (NSC).

- Signaled the readiness of the United States to move beyond regionalism to globalism.

- American "sphere of influence" included every corner of the globe where U.S. interests might be affected.

Enlargement

- Response to the new global economic environment.

- United States should support enlarging the sphere of market-oriented democracies.

- Additional open, democratic, and free-market societies will further the interests of the United States.

Question for Reflection

In what ways would the U.S.'s role in international affairs be different today if the Senate had approved joining the League of Nations?

World War I

With the start of World War I in Europe in 1914 and the collapse of the Russian monarchy three years later, the United States began to position itself as a global rather than regional player. Despite strong isolationist and pacifist movements at home and the country's policy of neutrality, the United States clearly favored Britain and the Allied Powers over Germany and the Central Powers. But as long as trans-Atlantic shipping lanes remained safe, the United States was reluctant to commit more than indirect support. Then, in 1915, a German submarine sank the ocean liner *Lusitania,* and the death toll included American citizens. Many historians argue that the *Lusitania* was not really a "neutral" vessel, since evidence suggests that she carried a large cache of munitions in her hold. For U.S. policy makers, though, this act of aggression exposed Germany's policy of unrestricted submarine warfare and the impossibility of containing the war within Europe. When Germany resumed unrestricted submarine warfare in 1917, the United States declared war, and the country's departure from its historic isolationism was rationalized as a commitment to "make the world safe for democracy" while fighting a "war to end all wars." U.S. forces, although undoubtedly turning the tide against Germany, suffered more than 120,000 casualties. Despite the rhetoric heralding the United States entry into the war, World War I vanquished neither antidemocratic nor warlike forces.

When hostilities ended in 1918, Americans were eager to put the horrors of war behind them. President Woodrow Wilson campaigned vigorously for an international organization of states to "outlaw" the sort of aggression that had triggered the war. Although his efforts ultimately led to the founding of the League of Nations, Wilson failed to persuade the U.S. Senate to approve the peace treaty and join the league. The prevailing mood favored a return to isolationism.

But the conditions that led to World War I and its consequences drew the United States into inevitable conflict with another European country: the newly founded Soviet Union. In the midst of wartime chaos, a small but determined Bolshevik party, led by Vladimir Ulyanov, better known as Lenin, had seized control of Russia. The future Union of Soviet Socialist Republics (USSR) was founded in 1917, the first large-scale attempt to form a modern socialist state and, designed as an alternative to liberal capitalism, an ideological adversary of the United States. With little public knowledge, Wilson dispatched approximately ten thousand Americans to aid other Allied troops in disrupting the revolutionary regime. This invasion set the stage for growing hostility between the United States and the USSR that would not be fully apparent until after another world war.

World War II

Tensions between the United States and the USSR were briefly tabled with the outbreak of World War II. Hitler invaded Poland in 1939, violating a nonaggression pact between Germany and the Soviet Union, but President Franklin D. Roosevelt refused to commit American military might to help stop the German advance. As in World War I, the United States was reluctant to encumber itself with strategic alliances, pursuing instead a policy of economic aid to the Allies. Only after Germany's Pacific ally, Japan, bombed the U.S. naval base at Pearl Harbor, Hawaii, on December 7, 1941, did the United States formally enter the war and send troops to Europe and the Pacific. This "Day of Infamy" galvanized Americans in an outrage that overcame the nation's traditionally isolationist orientation.

The wartime fates of the United States and the Soviet Union were strikingly different. For the United States, not yet recovered from the Great Depression, the expanded industrial production and employment demanded by wartime industrial mobilization actually helped jump-start an economic boom. Beyond the initial

◄ The December 7, 1941, Japanese bombing of Pearl Harbor galvanized the United States in outrage and subsequent willingness to enter World War II. Here, a motor launch rescues a survivor from the torpedo-damaged and sunken U.S.S. *West Virginia*.

destruction at Pearl Harbor, the country suffered no attacks on its home territory. In stark contrast, the Soviet Union was devastated. The Soviet Red Army stopped the eastward advance of Germany, but at tremendous cost; twenty million military personnel and civilians died, either from combat or through disease or starvation. As with most of battle-scarred Europe, the Soviet Union had the look of a defeated nation.

Given the striking differences between the United States and the Soviet Union at the end of World War II, it is surprising that the Soviet Union would emerge as the chief U.S. rival. So awesome would the dominance of the two countries become that they inspired a new concept—**superpower**. The term was intended to convey the disproportionate power—economic and military—that distinguished the United States and the Soviet Union from all other countries in the postwar era. The pervasive superpower rivalry caused American–Soviet relations to affect virtually every country in the world.

Globalism and the Cold War

The Second World War entirely changed the international arena. The United States emerged as the only major power with a completely intact infrastructure, booming industrial production, and a monopoly on the most revolutionary weaponry ever created—the atomic bomb. American planes dropped two atomic bombs on Japan at the end of World War II, not only to shock the Japanese into complete surrender but, some believe, to send a message to the Soviet Union that the United States not only possessed such military might but was prepared to use it.

U.S. foreign policy after 1946 followed the doctrine of **containment**, a concept delineated by George Kennan, then a State Department Soviet expert. Kennan observed that the USSR's expansionist foreign policy "moves along the prescribed path, like a persistent toy automobile wound up and headed in a given direction, stopping only when it meets some unanswerable force." According to Kennan, that

superpower The disproportionate power—economic and military—that distinguished the United States and the Soviet Union from all other countries in the postwar era.

containment A term coined in 1946 by George Kennan, who believed that Soviet aggression must be "contained by the adroit and vigilant application of counterforce by the United States."

Primary Source: United Nations
Charter (1945)

Primary Source: NATO Chronology,
1947–1999

globalism View in which the U.S.
sphere of influence has expanded beyond the western hemisphere to include
virtually every corner of the globe where
U.S. interests might be affected.

**North Atlantic Treaty
Organization (NATO)** Charter
signed by the United States, Canada,
Turkey, and eleven European nations in
1949 agreeing that an armed attack
against one or more of them in Europe
or North America would be interpreted
as an attack against all.

Cold War The bipolar power struggle
between the United States and the
Soviet Union that began in the 1950s
and ended in the 1990s.

bipolarity The fundamental division
of economic and military power between the poles of Western capitalism
and Eastern communism.

Warsaw Pact Treaty signed by the
Soviet Union and the Eastern bloc in
Europe agreeing to mutual defense, in
reaction to NATO.

"unanswerable force" must be the United States, and Soviet aggression must be "contained by the adroit and vigilant application of counterforce at a series of constantly shifting geographical and political points." Somewhat prophetically, Kennan argued that if the United States could contain the Soviet Union without weakening itself politically or economically, the result would be "either the break-up or the gradual mellowing of Soviet power."[13]

But the ultimate end of the Soviet Union remained decades away. Both the United States and the Soviet Union had joined the United Nations (UN) upon its creation in 1945, but the two countries remained adversaries. Soviet forces controlled all of Eastern Europe, installing virtual puppet regimes behind an "iron curtain" of military might and political resolve. The United States applied the counterforce of billions of dollars in economic aid to Western Europe under the Marshall Plan of postwar reconstruction as well as through numerous strategic treaties and agreements.

In a historic address to Congress on March 12, 1947, President Harry Truman invoked the doctrine of containment, pledging economic and military aid to Greece and Turkey to halt the spread of communism. This intention to help free and democratic nations beat back the threat of totalitarianism became known as the *Truman Doctrine*. At home, the National Security Act of 1947 created the Central Intelligence Agency (CIA) and the National Security Council (NSC), signaling U.S. readiness to move beyond regionalism to **globalism**. Now the American "sphere of influence" included virtually every corner of the globe where U.S. interests might be affected.

In 1949, the United States secured the commitment of eleven European nations to form the **North Atlantic Treaty Organization (NATO)**. The NATO charter also signaled the end of American isolationism and regionalism. Charter signatories agreed that an armed attack against one or more of them in Europe or North America would be interpreted as an attack against all. In the event of such an attack, the treaty bound all members of NATO to assist the attacked country, employing "forthwith, individually and in concert with the other Parties, such action as it deems necessary, including the use of armed forces;" but as we saw in the recent U.S. call to defeat international terrorism, some NATO members resisted placing their troops in the field.

Also in 1949, the U.S. monopoly of nuclear weapons ended when the Soviets detonated their first atomic bomb. In the same year, the American-backed regime in China collapsed and a communist state emerged under the direction of Mao Zedong. In April 1950, members of the NSC drafted a document that would become the "blueprint" for waging the **Cold War** during the next twenty years: National Security Council Paper 68 (NSC 68). NSC 68 outlined a sweeping mobilization of American economic and human resources in the effort to contain Soviet communism. It was the first major document to acknowledge the bipolar struggle between the American and Soviet superpowers.[14]

Bipolarity refers to the fundamental division of economic and military power between the poles of Western capitalism and Eastern communism. NSC 68 recommended against negotiation with the Kremlin and recommended a more powerful nuclear arsenal, rapid expansion of conventional military resources, and full mobilization of American society within a "government-created consensus" against the evils of communism. The document also called for a dramatic American commitment to international strategic and economic alliances against the Eastern bloc, indicating yet another push away from isolation and regionalism toward globalism. In 1955, the Soviet Union and its East European allies (called satellites) formed the **Warsaw Pact**, a military alliance to counter NATO.

In June 1950, just months after the drafting of NSC 68, war in Korea became a major test of the containment policy. Ironically, the challenger here was not the Soviet Union but the new communist regime in China. Ultimately, the Korean conflict proved a political and military stalemate. The decade closed with the declaration of a socialist revolution only ninety miles off the coast of Florida in Cuba and the ascension of Fidel Castro.

The Nuclear World   The nuclear age began with the U.S. bombing of Hiroshima and Nagasaki in August 1945. In September 1949, the Soviets exploded their atomic device and triggered a superpower arms race with frightening global implications. Over the next forty years, both the United States and the Soviet Union poured billions of dollars into developing ever more powerful nuclear weapons, just as they devoted increasing intellectual resources to creating foreign policies tailored to the new "nuclear world" that they had created.

The most dangerous nuclear confrontation of the Cold War occurred in 1962. Soviet Premier Nikita Khrushchev had begun constructing missile bases in Cuba, an act U.S. leaders saw as a direct provocation, despite the fact that the United States had installed similar missile bases in Turkey aimed at the Soviet Union. After several tense days of secret debates within the U.S. national security establishment, President John Kennedy took the unprecedented step of going before the American people and announcing a naval blockade of Cuba aimed at keeping out Soviet supply ships. In a televised speech, Kennedy demanded the immediate dismantling and removal of the bases. Ultimately, Khrushchev backed down and the bases were dismantled. Plans for a "hot line," providing a communications link between the two leaders, continued, and the Limited Test Ban Treaty was negotiated in 1963. But the threat of a nuclear exchange continued.

Mounting an Economic Offensive   Cold War policy makers did not restrict their activity to military planning. In line with the Truman doctrine, the United States continued to increase **foreign aid** as a hedge against Soviet advances into Third World countries. One such U.S. effort during the Kennedy administration was the **Peace Corps**. Volunteers went to all parts of the globe in programs ranging from improving literacy and building roads and schools to starting immunization and other health programs. The Peace Corps remains the country's foremost experiment in fusing the aims of foreign policy, government resources, and individual initiative and expertise.

MakeItReal

Civic Participation: The Peace Corps

A second program initiated at this time, focusing on Latin America, was the *Alliance for Progress*. The policy really began in the last year of the Eisenhower administration with the formation of the Inter-American Development Bank, but it was popularized in 1961 under President Kennedy. In exchange for a commitment of $20 billion over ten years, the United States asked participating Latin American countries to liberalize their tax, land distribution, and social policies, which major players such as Argentina, Brazil, and Mexico were reluctant to do. In the end, the alliance never lived up to its potential, either as a social and economic boon to Latin America or as a hedge against the blossoming of socialist and communist regimes in the region. By 1966, the alliance had all but vanished. The U.S. commitment to foreign aid for the developing world continued, but not at the level envisioned by the Kennedy administration.

Vietnam   At the height of the Cold War, the United States entered what would prove to be its most damaging military intervention thus far. In the southeastern Asian country of Vietnam, nationalist forces from the north, led by Ho Chi Minh, had defeated French colonial forces at Dien Bien Phu in 1954. In Geneva, where international talks on Korea were proceeding, Vietnam was partitioned into a communist north and a capitalist south, with the promise of elections in two years that could unify the country. The elections never materialized, as the struggle between the two Vietnams intensified. Determined to halt the spread of communism, the United States supported the corrupt but capitalist regime in the south.

foreign aid Small portion of the federal budget that goes to nonmilitary aid abroad, initially to mitigate against Soviet expansion.

Peace Corps Organization formed by President Kennedy to help with Third World development by having American volunteers live and work in needy communities.

MakeItReal

Primary Source: Tonkin Gulf
Resolution (1964)

Beginning early in the Kennedy administration, first hundreds and then thousands of U.S. military "advisers" were sent to South Vietnam. The American public saw little information about or discussion of U.S. policy in Southeast Asia, and policy makers were left to pursue their own course, which proved to be a mounting commitment of military personnel and equipment.[15]

Within a few weeks of each other in November 1963, both South Vietnamese Prime Minister Ngo Dinh Diem and President Kennedy were assassinated. Lyndon Johnson assumed the presidency with public declarations of no desire to "widen" the war in Vietnam. Yet he convinced Congress to support a massive military buildup in Southeast Asia. On August 2, 1964, the U.S. destroyer *Maddox* was returning from an electronic espionage mission when North Vietnamese torpedo boats fired on it. The attack was repulsed. Rather than withdrawing U.S. ships from this danger zone, Johnson ordered another destroyer, the *C. Turner Joy*, to join the *Maddox* in the Gulf of Tonkin. On August 4, both the *Maddox* and the *C. Turner Joy* reportedly came under attack by torpedo boats. Considerable doubt exists about this second attack, as weather conditions were so bad and tensions aboard ship so high that Johnson later quipped, "For all I know, our Navy was shooting at whales out there." But circumstantial evidence was all Johnson needed for ordering reprisals against North Vietnam. The **Gulf of Tonkin Resolution**, passed by Congress in August 1964, provided President Johnson with broad legal authority to combat North Vietnamese aggression.

In July 1965, Lyndon Johnson chose to Americanize the war by increasing U.S. combat strength in Vietnam from 75,000 to 125,000, with additional U.S. forces to be sent when requested by field commander General William Westmoreland. "Now," Johnson wrote in his memoirs, "we were committed to major combat in Vietnam. We had determined not to let that country fall under Communist rule as long as we could prevent it."[16] In December 2005, the National Security Agency (NSA) released hundreds of pages of previously classified top-secret documents that leave little doubt that intelligence was deliberately skewed in the 1964 Tonkin Gulf incident.[17]

By the early 1970s, the American military was mired in the Asian jungles, at a cost of billions of dollars and tens of thousands of lives. The U.S. national interest in the region was no longer clear, and the antiwar movement grew until the United States was hopelessly split on the issue. Finally, a treaty with the North Vietnamese government allowed the United States to withdraw in 1973. Ultimately, the war in Vietnam not only ravaged a nation and a people but cost more than fifty-eight thousand American lives, hundreds of thousands of Vietnamese, and undercut the credibility of much of the U.S. foreign policy apparatus.

Detente   In the wake of the withdrawal from Southeast Asia, the American people became profoundly anti-international and antimilitary. "No more Vietnams" became the rallying cry for those opposed to military intervention in Africa and Central America. Richard Nixon, ironically as anticommunist a president as ever existed, initiated a policy of **detente**, an attempt to relax tensions between the United States and the USSR. Each side began to discuss ways to reduce the nuclear threat. A series of strategic arms limitations talks culminated in the signing of the first **Strategic Arms Limitation Treaty (SALT)** in 1972. But conflict between the two superpowers heated up with the Soviet invasion of Afghanistan in December 1979. Both countries failed to ratify the SALT II agreements, and the arms race continued, now more sophisticated and involving weapons deployment in Europe.[18]

Some argue that the end of detente came in 1983, when President Ronald Reagan announced plans to devise a new satellite-based laser defense system, the Strategic Defense Initiative (SDI), popularly known as "Star Wars." The Soviets could not match the SDI either financially or technologically, but many critics insisted that it was a "pie-in-the-sky" scheme that even the Americans could not pull off. Beyond its

Gulf of Tonkin Resolution
Resolution passed by Congress that granted President Lyndon Johnson authority to pursue the war in Vietnam, supposedly based on a naval attack by North Vietnamese ships.

detente An attempt to relax tensions between the United States and the Soviet Union through limited cooperation.

Strategic Arms Limitation Treaty (SALT) Treaty signed by the United States (under President Nixon) and the Soviet Union to limit various classes of nuclear weapons.

◄ The World War II Normandy American Cemetery and Memorial is situated on a cliff overlooking Omaha Beach and the English Channel in Colleville-sur Mer, France. It contains the graves of 9,386 American military dead, most of whom gave their lives during the landings and ensuing operations of World War II. On the walls of the semicircular garden on the east side of the memorial are inscribed the names of 1,557 American missing who gave their lives in the service of their country, but whose remains were not located or identified. President Bush visited the cemetery on Memorial Day 2002 and delivered a somber yet moving speech.

technological challenges, both the United States and the Soviet Union had seriously undermined their own economies through decades of military buildup. By the end of the 1980s, the USSR had bankrupted itself, and the United States was more than a trillion dollars in debt.

In May 2002, President Bush and President Vladimir V. Putin signed an historic arms reduction treaty that committed both countries to reducing their arsenals from about 6,000 warheads each to no more than 2,200 by 2012. According to Article 1 of the treaty: "we are achieving a new strategic relationship. The era in which the United States and Russia saw each other as an enemy or strategic threat has ended. . . . We recognize that the security, prosperity and future hopes of our peoples rest on a benign security environment, the advancement of political and economic freedoms and international cooperation."[19] Table 16.1 shows the history of arms reduction pacts between the United States and Moscow.

Table 16.1 ▪ Limiting Nuclear Weapons

	SALT I	SALT II	START I	START II	START III	New Treaty
Warhead limit	No limit	No limit	**6,000**	**3,000–3,500**	**2,000–2,500**	**1,700–2,200**
Missile limit	U.S.: **1,710** USSR: **2,347**	**2,250**	**1,600**	No limit	No limit	No limit
Status	Expired	Never entered into force	In force	Never entered into force	Never negotiated	Signed, awaits ratification
Date signed	May 26, 1972	June 18, 1979	July 31, 1991	Jan. 3, 1993	Not applicable	May 24, 2002
Entered into force	Oct. 3, 1972	Not applicable	Dec. 5, 1994	Not applicable	Not applicable	Not applicable
Reduction deadline	Not applicable	Dec. 31, 1981	Dec. 5, 2001	Dec. 31, 2007	Dec. 31, 2007	Dec. 31, 2012
Expiration	Oct. 3, 1977	Dec. 31, 1985	Dec. 5, 2009	Dec. 5, 2009	Not applicable	Dec. 31, 2012

Source: Washington Post, July 7, 2002, p. A8. Copyright © 2002 *The Washington Post.* Reprinted by permission.

The Post–Cold War Era

The year 1989 saw a remarkable change in world politics. Eastern European communist regimes in power at the start of the year were gone by its end. Then, between August and December 1991, the Soviet Union—the Cold War focal point of U.S. foreign policy—ceased to exist. With its demise, the Soviet threat to the United States disappeared, the Cold War came to an end, and the basic premise that drove U.S. foreign policy for almost fifty years—containment—ceased to be relevant.[20]

The threat of cataclysmic nuclear war declined, despite a continuing threat of nuclear, biological, and chemical weapons proliferation as countries such as India and Pakistan developed atomic bombs (see Figure 16.1 for countries with high risks of

Figure 16.1   A More Peaceful World?

Source: CIDCM, Center for International Development and Conflict Management; http://www.cidcm.umd.edu originally published in *The Washington Post,* January 17, 2001, p. A13.

instability). The "predators of the twenty-first century" is how former President Clinton described rogue states that seek to build "arsenals of nuclear, chemical, and biological weapons and the missiles to deliver them."[21] In his 2002 State of the Union Address, President Bush identified an "axis of evil" that included North Korea, Iraq, and Iran. President Bush later shifted the rationale for American military strategy to preemptive action against hostile states and terrorist groups. This new Bush doctrine states that "while the United States will constantly strive to enlist the support of the international community, we will not hesitate to act alone, if necessary, to exercise our right of self-defense by acting preemptively against such terrorists."[22]

The New World Order The end of the Cold War brought with it a dizzying array of complicated foreign policy issues. Policy makers lost clear guideposts to determine the relative merits of issues and lacked a clear formula for addressing them. On August 2, 1990, Iraqi forces had invaded Kuwait. The invasion followed a summer of escalating tension between Iraq and Kuwait on economic disputes about oil production and pricing. Following the invasion, President George H. W. Bush sought and obtained international backing for United Nations Security Resolution 660 that posed economic sanctions and a naval blockade against Iraq. The Desert Shield military response began on August 7, involving a limited deployment of air and ground forces. Iraq was given until January 15, 1991, to withdraw its forces from Kuwait. On January 17, 1991, Operation Desert Storm began, and by February 26, 1991, the U.S.-led coalition restored sovereignty to Kuwait. Iraq withdrew its remaining troops on February 27. The United States led the charge to make sure Iraq went no further, and President George H. W. Bush heralded the beginning of a "New World Order."[23]

The outlines of this New World Order never came clearly into focus, and the concept means different things to different people. At a minimum, President George H. W. Bush seemed to have in mind the end of the bipolar order and the start of a new order involving the United Nations but actually led by the United States, the world's dominant military power. Just what the relationship between the United States and the UN should be—and even if a relationship should exist— continues to be debated, particularly in light of controversial military operations in Somalia, Bosnia, Haiti, and Iraq.

NATO NATO, the North Atlantic Treaty Organization, is undergoing what the Bush administration describes as "a robust enlargement." NATO is an alliance of

MakeItReal

ABC News Video: *Shoulder to Shoulder*

◀ The leaders who placed their signatures on the accord between the North Atlantic Treaty Organization and Russia in May 2002 celebrate the historic occasion. In the bottom row, second from the left, is President Vaclav Havel of the Czech Republic, a reminder of how our world approaches democracy.

Question for Reflection

The Cold War ended fifty years of U.S. foreign policy focused on containment, placing the international community on the road to a new world order. What changes to NATO might enhance progress on an international approach to democracy?

twenty-six North American and European countries committed to fulfilling the goals of the North Atlantic Treaty, signed April 4, 1949. NATO, intended to safeguard member countries' freedom and security by political and military means, is playing an increasingly important role in crisis management and peacekeeping. NATO ministers have approved a new body, the Russia-NATO Council, in which former enemies sit together in areas such as counter-terrorism, ballistic missile defense, peacekeeping, arms proliferation, and emergency planning.[24]

A Policy of Enlargement

One U.S. response to the new global economic environment has been to replace the policy of containment with a policy of *enlargement.* That is, the United States should support enlarging the sphere of market-oriented democracies on the assumption that additional open, democratic, and free-market societies will further U.S. interests. They are good for peace (based on the belief that democracies do not easily go to war with one another) and good for business (based on the belief that more market economies will expand the global market and global economic well-being).

By the 1990s, Asia had been the world's economic miracle for at least three decades. South Korea, Singapore, Hong Kong, Taiwan, Malaysia, Indonesia, and the Philippines achieved remarkable rates of economic success and growth. But by the middle of the decade these former "economic miracles" were struggling with collapsing currencies and plunging stock markets. The International Monetary Fund had to issue emergency loans to Thailand, Indonesia, and South Korea. How did it happen? The most straightforward explanation for the crisis was debt. Businesses had borrowed huge sums of money during the time of economic expansion. Most of the money was borrowed in U.S. dollars because our interest rates were much lower than their own currencies. The exchange rates were pegged against the dollar. All this was fine until 1995, when the dollar started to rise against most of the world's economies. Since Asian currencies were pegged to the dollar, their currencies rose with the dollar, and Asia's exports became more expensive and less competitive on world markets.

Foreign Aid and Economic Sanctions

These two traditional tools of foreign policy have also come under scrutiny and debate in the post–Cold War world. Since the end of World War II, foreign aid had been used to help support U.S. allies and interests abroad. Making up a tiny portion of the total federal budget, foreign aid programs—such as aid to Russia, Israel, Egypt, Africa, and Latin America—have come under fire during this period of tight budgets and are likely to be curtailed. Those who favor such programs argue that eliminating them would have severe negative consequences for U.S. interests around the world. In May 2002, the traveling odd couple—rock star Bono of U2 and Treasury Secretary Paul O'Neill—arrived in sub-Saharan Africa on a fact-finding mission that would determine how $50 billion in aid would be spent. In 2005, Bono explained that Africa's future is under threat:

> Africa is struggling under a triple crisis that keeps its people poor and its nations weak—the burden of unpayable DEBT that soaks up money that should go to health and education; the epidemic of AIDS that is taking the lives of an entire generation; and the unfair TRADE policies that keep Africans from being able to sell their products at world prices and earn their own way out of poverty. Sub-Saharan

▲ Rock star Bono of U2 and a fan at an AIDS benefit in South Africa.

Approaching Democracy Around the Globe

An Alliance with a Future: Vaclav Havel's Vision

A long time ago, when I was part of the opposition to Communist dictatorship, I thought that if the Iron Curtain ever fell, communism collapsed and the Warsaw Pact was dissolved, NATO would also lose its raison d'etre as a principal tool of the policy of "containment." But once the Iron Curtain did indeed begin to fall, and I entered practical politics, I soon realized how naive I had been and how important was NATO's continued existence.

In fact, I came to feel that NATO had just arrived at its great historic test: whether it would have the courage to embrace new European democracies and thus prove its genuine commitment to protecting the values it was called upon to defend at its founding. The alternative would be to show that it lacked that courage and was still rigidly entrenched in its Cold War ways—unwilling to be involved in creating a new world order.

But it seems that many of those who were, in the late 1980s and early 1990s, the most fervent advocates of NATO's continued existence now wonder whether it has outlived its purpose. Conversely, many who doubted that the Alliance would be meaningful in the future are now among its greatest defenders.

I am among those who sincerely believe the Alliance does have an irreplaceable role, now and likely in the future. And the deeper NATO goes in reflecting on its role, the more significant that role will be. Indeed, there are signs that we are coming to an era in which NATO must ponder its future thoroughly and then act quickly to translate its vision into a number of specific and audacious steps.

First and foremost, NATO will probably have to redefine itself and once again describe its position in today's world. NATO is known to have a cultural, historical, "value-based"—in more lofty terms, "civilizational"—identity alongside its geographic and strategic identity. Its membership is composed of democratic countries located in the Euro-Atlantic area, in what is referred to as "the West." Let me illustrate: No one would think of inviting New Zealand to join NATO, as close as its values and culture are to the NATO world, simply because New Zealand belongs to a different geographic space.

Conversely, it would make no sense to consider Russia for membership in NATO, even though its location and civilization are not far distant from the West. That is because, for various historical and geographic reasons, Russia is a world in itself. It is as large as all NATO members put together—a huge Eurasian empire with which we must enjoy the best possible partnership. And it is such a clearly independent part of today's world that its only relationship with NATO can and will be that of a separate entity.

If the future world order is really to defend peace and secure the survival of humankind, it will have to be based on equal and close cooperation among several regions. Such cooperation is possible only if these individual entities succeed in defining themselves—which requires, among other things, an understanding of where they begin and end. Many conflicts have been caused by insecure self-identification that leads to a blurred concept of one's "outer limits" and to diverging views of "spheres of interest."

In order to redefine itself, NATO will have to do two things: First, the Alliance must arrive at a new and unequivocal definition of its approach to other parts of the planet, infuse such an approach with the spirit of absolute equality, and begin to deepen it by institutional as well as practical cooperation. NATO is attempting to change the quality of its relations with Russia, which is certainly worthwhile; but, in doing so, it must not raise even a shadow of suspicion that the more affluent northern hemisphere is somehow ganging up on the other parts of the world and thus widening the gap that divides it from the southern part of the globe. It is for this reason—but certainly not only for this reason—that NATO must build its relations with China, India, Africa and other parts of the world.

Second, NATO must, in its own interest, open its doors to new European democracies, while at the same time setting a limit on its possible future enlargement. Otherwise, no future enlargement will make sense. (All the Balkan countries and all the "neutral European democracies" are undoubtedly considered possible candidates for future membership.) Saying that drawing such a borderline will create a new Iron Curtain means being mired in a Cold-War world, in which the only conceivable border is the one that separates us from our enemies and, therefore, has to be barb-wired.

In addition, NATO will have to significantly accelerate its internal transformation. September 11 has, one hopes, made everyone understand that the single powerful and clearly situated strategic enemy of the past, "the Evil Empire," has long since been replaced by what is perhaps an even more dangerous enemy: a dispersed evil that is sophisticated yet hard to grasp, whose empire, focal point or axis I would dare not identify (though some regimes certainly serve evil more than others).

Source: Vaclav Havel, *Washington Post,* May 19, 2002, p. B7. Copyright © 2002 *The Washington Post.* Reprinted by permission.

▶ Fidel Castro and Jimmy Carter prepare to toss out the first pitch in a baseball game in Havana. The former U.S. President became the first U.S. president—in or out of office—to visit the communist country since the 1959 revolution that put Fidel Castro in power. Carter said he was visiting "as friends of the people of Cuba and hope to know Cubans from different walks of life." In March 2006 Cuba was a finalist in the World Baseball Classic.

Africa, the part of the continent south of the Sahara Desert, is also the world's poorest place. Seventy percent of its people live on less than $2 a day. 200 million go hungry every day. This year at least a million Africans, most of them young children, will die of malaria and two million will die of AIDS. Africa is at a critical turning point, and could go either way—the crises could get far worse, or YOU can be part of helping Africa turn these crises around. Because Africans have shown they can turn back AIDS. Because debt relief and development assistance have shown they can be effective. Because more and more African leaders are committed to DEMOCRACY, ACCOUNTABILITY and TRANSPARENCY. Because whether and how we help Africa now is a test of our ability to prevent failing states that threaten our security, and even more important, a test of our humanity, and our willingness to respond to the moral crisis of our time.[25]

Economic sanctions have also been the subject of debate. A case in point involves Cuba and normalizing of relations by lifting the U.S. trade embargo that has been in place since the 1959 revolution. Here is how former President Jimmy Carter, who visited Cuba in 2002 and favors unrestricted trade, explained the political dilemma: "A newspaper cartoon published while I was in Cuba showed me alone in a small lifeboat in the Caribbean, surrounded by sharks. The caption was, 'I shouldn't have asked President Bush for a ride home.'"[26] In Carter's view, "one approach is to continue the four-decade effort to isolate and punish Cuba with restricted visits and an economic embargo. The other is for Americans to have maximum contact with Cubans, let them see clearly the advantages of a truly democratic society, and encourage them to bring about orderly changes in their society."[27]

In an economically interdependent world, the use of economic sanctions is often seen as a useful tool of foreign policy. But although sanctions logically seem appropriate to force policy change inside a targeted state, they are difficult to use. Sanctions may have helped force South Africa to eliminate its system of apartheid (strict racial segregation) and move in a more democratic direction, but sanctions against Iraq, Haiti, Bosnia, Serbia, and Cuba, for example, have not achieved their intended effect while clearly hurting ordinary citizens by depriving them of

economic sanctions The use of embargoes and boycotts rather than military force to compel compliance.

Table 16.2 ▪ Conflicting Views of America's Place in the World

	Total %	Bush Voters %	Kerry Voters %	Didn't Vote %
Military force is best way to defeat terrorism	39	66	17	33
Too much force creates hatred that leads to more terrorism	51	25	76	55
Neither/both/don't know (vol.)	10	9	7	12
	100	100	100	100
Take allies' interests into account	53	43	68	47
Follow own national interests	37	49	25	38
Neither/both/don't know (vol.)	10	8	7	15
	100	100	100	100
Best for country to be active in world affairs	44	57	37	34
We should concentrate on problems at home	49	37	57	59
Neither/both/don't know (vol.)	7	6	6	7
	100	100	100	100
Number of cases	2,000	808	706	358

Source: Pew Research Center for the People & the Press, December 2004.

goods or the opportunity to trade and earn a profit. The sanctions imposed on Iraq after its defeat in the 1991 Persian Gulf War clearly hurt his people, but Saddam Hussein continued to build more lavish palaces. Sanctions can fail unless targeted policy makers are moved by their people's suffering to alter their course, or unless they are overthrown. The United States and its allies struggle with questions about the propriety and effectiveness of economic sanctions in Iraq. Yet *coercive diplomacy*, the effort to compel policy change in a target state by means of economic sanctions and trade embargoes, will probably continue, especially against rogue states such as Iran and North Korea. Paradoxically, the end of the Cold War has left the United States more rather than less likely to use force. Cases in point include American military involvement in Panama, Bosnia, Somalia, Haiti, Iraq, Afghanistan, and Iraq again. Even while some talk of the new diplomacy based on economics, the old diplomacy based on the use of force is alive and well (see Table 16.2).

THE CONSTITUTION AND FOREIGN POLICY

As you learned in Chapter 2, the Constitution designates to the president and Congress certain formal powers especially significant for foreign policy. The president was given four types of broad authority in foreign policy:

1. As the commander in chief, the president has the power to commit troops to foreign lands.
2. The president has the power to negotiate treaties with other countries.
3. The president appoints U.S. ambassadors and the heads of all of the executive departments that make foreign policy.
4. The president decides whether or not to receive ambassadors—a decision that determines which nations the United States will formally recognize.

Congress has significant foreign policy powers, including the power to declare war, appropriate money, and make laws. Congress also has the power to raise and support the armed forces. Thus, it has the power to decide whether or not to back presidential initiatives abroad. Through the advise and consent powers, the Senate has the power to ratify treaties and confirm presidential appointments.

This division of powers reveals how the framers envisioned the roles of these two branches of government in the foreign policy arena. Remembering the problems of dealing with other countries under the Articles of Confederation, the framers gave the president power to conduct negotiations and use troops. Fearing the potential for tyranny, the framers gave Congress significant power to check and balance presidential decisions.

The President Versus Congress

If the executive is the driving force behind U.S. foreign policy, Congress acts as the brakes on the president's initiatives. Through its constitutional powers to control the nation's purse strings, to ratify treaties and approve certain officials, and to make war, Congress can counterbalance the considerable power of the president. This allows Congress to have considerable impact on the direction of U.S. foreign policy. Much of this influence, however, depends on the ever-changing willingness and ability of members of Congress to overcome partisanship and work together. Thus, Congress's influence in foreign policy has fluctuated greatly since World War II.

The very nature of Congress limits its influence on foreign policy. Congress is a domestically oriented institution whose members are primarily interested in issues that directly influence their constituents. This orientation dampens their interest in foreign policy and tends to warp policy to favor the narrow interests of individual districts. Furthermore, its size, procedures, and dispersed leadership limit Congress's ability to act with the speed often necessary for foreign policy decisions. Characteristically slow, deliberative procedures mean that, on issues of urgency, Congress cannot compete with a president who responds quickly and decisively to international events.

Finally, the president, as the head of the executive branch, enjoys access to the expertise of the executive bureaucracy, which coordinates and implements policy. Traditionally, Congress has felt inferior in this respect and has tended to defer to the executive on substantive foreign policy matters. However, Congress has increased its access to foreign policy information since the Vietnam War. The professional staff serving congressional committees has more than doubled since the early 1970s, now totaling about ten thousand. In addition to undertaking research, these staffers provide an important link between Congress and the foreign policy bureaucracy. As such ties between Congress and the bureaucracy have strengthened, the view that foreign policy is the exclusive domain of the president has diminished. Although Congress is not likely to act as the initiator of foreign policy, its oversight role of presidential actions provides a valuable check in our constitutional system.

Beyond Congress's constitutionally granted powers, Congress can influence foreign policy through **legislative oversight**. It can hold hearings, pass laws, and dictate the appropriation of money in an attempt to influence or rein in a president's foreign policy initiatives.

The War Powers Resolution Congress passed the **War Powers Resolution** of 1973 in an attempt to restore its balance of power with the executive branch and prevent military involvement without congressional approval. After passage of the legislation, a president could no longer commit troops for longer than sixty days

legislative oversight The legislature's review and evaluation of executive branch activities to ensure that programs are administered and implemented in a manner consistent with legislative intent.

War Powers Resolution A highly controversial measure passed over President Nixon's veto that stipulated that presidential commitments of U.S. military forces cannot extend beyond sixty days without specific congressional authorization.

U.S.A. Yesterday and Today

Vietnam–U.S. Relations

On September 2, 1945, before a crowd of 400,000 supporters, Ho Chi Minh, leader of the Vietnamese fight against colonialism, issued the historic Vietnamese proclamation of independence with Thomas Jefferson's stirring words, "We hold the truth that all men are created equal, that they are endowed by their Creator certain unalienable rights, that among these are life, liberty and the pursuit of happiness." Ho told his Viet Minh followers that "this immortal statement was made in the Declaration of Independence of the United States of America in 1776. In a broader sense it means: All peoples on earth are equal from birth, all peoples have a right to live, be happy and be free."

Ho had received the translation of the American Declaration of Independence from Archimedes Patti of the Office of Strategic Services (OSS). He had also helped rescue American pilots and furnished intelligence reports on Japanese operations, earning Ho the position OSS agent 19, code name Lucius. Viet Minh militia had joined with the OSS Deer team for training and exercises near the Chinese border. In certain ways, Ho and the United States had been cooperating against a common foe. Archival evidence shows that Ho saw the United States as more likely to be friend than enemy of the Viet Minh in defeating the Japanese and also in fostering fundamental rights. It was inconceivable in 1945 that the United States would eventually send more than 550,000 troops to fight a land war in Asia. But the United States did, and the war divided America.

During the past ten years, a new chapter has opened between the United States and Vietnam. The relationship began by building trust on issues left over from the war, such as the accounting for MIAs, reuniting families of refugees, and humanitarian programs. After normalization, both countries sought to widen the relationship with strengthened commercial and economic ties. In 1986, Vietnam embarked on a process of economic renovation, moving the country from a socialist-oriented centrally planned economy toward a socialist-oriented market economy. Economic reforms included market liberalization and decentralization policies that have already transformed the country. Paralleling these economic changes, Vietnam's foreign policy has thawed and opened in diplomatic relations as well as the process of normalization. The fruits of this approach to normalization in the economic relationship culminated in the Bilateral Trade Agreement (BTA), which took effect on December 10, 2001. The BTA is a key foundation and presents enormous opportunities for expanded cooperation. Progress has been made on a range of bilateral issues beyond commercial benefits. The deepening economic, commercial, military and assistance relationship with Vietnam promotes civil society, encourages reform, draws the country further into the rules-based international trading system, and promotes interests of American workers, consumers, farmers, and business people. Vietnam's implementation of a rules-based trading system based on WTO principles of transparency and its continued pursuit of structural economic reforms should accelerate development of the private sector, enhance the rule of law, and improve the atmosphere for progress in democracy and human rights. The two countries share geopolitical, security, and geoeconomic interests that have significance to peace, stability, and development in Southeast Asia as well as Asia and Pacific regions as a whole.

Sources: http://vietnam.usembassy.gov/; http://www.vietnamembassy-usa.org/.

without specific congressional authorization. An optional thirty-day extension was included for issues involving troop safety.

In one respect the War Powers Resolution sought to reverse the trend toward presidential domination of foreign affairs and fulfill the intent of the framers by ensuring "the collective judgment of the Congress and the President." But the act was also a response to the general expansion of presidential powers at the expense of legislative authority, an attempt to reassert congressional oversight over presidential actions and enhance the power of the legislature.

The "success" of the War Powers Resolution is difficult to gauge. Presidents have generally ignored its reporting requirement, seeing it as an unconstitutional infringement on the powers of the president as commander in chief. President Bush worked hard to gain a joint resolution authorizing the use of U.S. armed forces against Iraq.

▶ Exiled Tibetan spiritual leader the Dalai Lama met with President George W. Bush, wearing a scarf given to him by the Dalai Lama in November 2005. The two men discussed the political situation in Tibet and the war in Iraq, with the U.S. leader reaffirming his support for Tibet's separate cultural identity.

THE FOREIGN POLICY BUREAUCRACY

Assisting the president in foreign policy development and implementation are about thirty-eight separate government departments and agencies. We will look at four core national security areas and the organizations within each:

1. *Foreign affairs:* This is primarily the domain of the State Department, with other related agencies playing supporting roles. These other agencies include the Agency for International Development, the Arms Control and Disarmament Agency, and the United States Information Agency (which includes Radio Free Europe, Voice of America, and Radio Liberty).

2. *Defense:* National security issues related to defense are dominated by the Defense Department. In matters relating to nuclear energy, the Department of Energy is also involved.

3. *Intelligence:* Although dominated by the Central Intelligence Agency (CIA), the intelligence community also includes the State Department's Bureau of Intelligence and Research, the Defense Department's Defense Intelligence Agency, the National Reconnaissance Office, the intelligence components of the individual military services, the Federal Bureau of Investigation (FBI), the National Security Agency and the office of the Director of National Intelligence.

4. *Economic agencies:* Fierce global economic competition has increased the importance and influence of the departments and agencies responsible for developing and implementing U.S. trade policies, negotiating tariffs with other governments, and representing the United States in various trade forums. Involved are the Treasury Department, the Departments of Commerce and of Agriculture, and the Office of the United States Trade Representative.

MakeItReal

Civic Participation: The State Department

The State Department

The State Department is the oldest and preeminent department of the foreign policy bureaucracy. It manages day-to-day foreign affairs, including pursuing diplomatic relations with other countries and international organizations, protecting American citizens and their interests abroad, and gathering and analyzing information bearing on U.S. foreign policy. The department's embassies, foreign service officers, and representatives to international organizations make it the only department in the executive bureaucracy with a global view. Despite its important role, however, the State Department, with twenty-five thousand employees, is fairly small.

By presidential directive, President Bush has designated the State Department as the government leader in assisting countries engulfed by conflict. The intent is to plan for conflicts before they occur by monitoring weak states. According to a State Department spokesperson: "What is new is that it puts on paper a very clear mandate that says that the secretary of state has the responsibility to lead and coordinate an integrated U.S. government response and clearly lays out the specific functions that are expected of a secretary of state."[28]

The Defense Department

The secretary of defense is the president's principal military adviser, is responsible for general defense policy formulation, and oversees all matters of direct concern to the Defense Department. Under the direction of the president, the secretary oversees all American military activity.

The Defense Department is composed of four service branches (army, navy, air force, and marines) that often compete with each other for influence, authority, and resources. Each branch has a chief of staff. Heading all four branches is the chair of the Joint Chiefs of Staff, who acts as the voice of the military (as opposed to civilian) side of the Pentagon. The chair of the Joint Chiefs of Staff is one of the president's principal military advisers.

Each of the four service branches also reports to a civilian secretary. Civilian agencies within the Defense Department handle functions such as logistics and communications. This combination of military and civilian personnel often produces overlapping duties and role confusion.

In many areas where the State Department is weak, the Defense Department is exceptionally strong, making it a powerful force in foreign policy making. With nearly a million individuals employed by defense-related industries, the Defense Department has many people with a vested interest in its financial well-being. A cut in defense spending can mean the loss of a job for a welder in Lubbock, Texas, whereas a new air force base can turn a ghost town into a boom town. Thus, the Defense Department is an integral part of American social, political, and economic life. It has both domestic and international effects, which the State Department, with its exclusively global orientation, does not. The Defense Department is much larger than the State Department, with about three million military and civilian employees.

The Defense Department's strongest influence in foreign policy has historically been the result of the close ties between the Pentagon and the corporations that dominate the U.S. weapons industry. Even as early as 1961, President Dwight Eisenhower, in his farewell address, warned of the growing power and influence resulting from the "conjunction of an immense military establishment and a large arms industry." Eisenhower called this phenomenon the **military-industrial complex**. Its development meant that "the potential for the disastrous rise of misplaced power exists and will persist."[29]

The National Security Council

The National Security Council (NSC) was created in 1947 to advise the president on all domestic, foreign, and military policies relating to national security. Members of the NSC include the president (as chair); the president's national security adviser, who acts as the special assistant for national security; the vice president; and the secretaries of state and defense. The CIA director and the chair of the Joint Chiefs of Staff sit in as advisers. Various other cabinet and agency heads, such as the

military-industrial complex
What President Eisenhower in 1961 called the growing power and influence resulting from the "conjunction of an immense military establishment and a large arms industry."

 **MakeItReal**

Census 2000: Veterans: 2000

Question for Reflection

The military-industrial complex grew out of World War II and the Cold War; its existence helped pull the United States from the depths of the Depression. Yet, in 1961 President Eisenhower warned of its influence over policy. If the use of force as a diplomatic strategy were seriously curtailed, what impact would this have?

Quick Review

National Security Council

- Created in 1947 to provide the president with advice on policies relating to national security.
- National security adviser acts as the special assistant for national security.
- The vice president, secretaries of state and defense, director of the CIA, and chair of the Joint Chiefs of Staff sit in as advisers.
- Various other cabinet and agency heads participate as needed.

secretary of the treasury, the attorney general, and the U.S. ambassador to the United Nations, participate as needed.

Through the NSC, the president coordinates the different government agencies dealing with foreign or defense policy. The NSC became especially active under President Kennedy and his special assistant for national security, McGeorge Bundy. Under Bundy, the staff became the president's key personal foreign policy "team." What emerged was an informally structured organization for the formulation and implementation of foreign policy that has persisted to this day. Such an organization works both for and against the executive branch, however, affording a base for quick and secretive executive-level responses to national security problems but allowing a sometimes dangerous policy-making latitude to unelected and relatively unaccountable decision makers. For example, the controversial Iran-Contra "arms-for-hostages" operation was conceived in the NSC and run by Lieutenant Oliver North.

By decreasing the president's reliance on the bureaucracy for information and advice, the NSC adviser and staff can become a "screen" between the president and the rest of government, reducing the president's direct influence and personal leadership. This intervention has led to serious rivalries among the national security adviser, the secretaries of state and defense, the director of the CIA, and their staffs. The relative influence and access of each organization often depend on the personal relationship between each department head and the president.

The national security adviser's role has changed over the years, based on the personality of the appointee to the post. Presidents have shaped the position to fit their personal management styles. On the whole, however, the national security adviser remains an extremely influential, although often anonymous, policy maker.

The CIA and Intelligence Gathering

MakeItReal

Primary Source: *The World Fact Book*—Compiled by the CIA

The Central Intelligence Agency (CIA) is the dominant force in the intelligence community. It was established after World War II to be the president's nonpartisan resource for coordinated intelligence analysis. However, its mission quickly expanded to include covert operations such as espionage, psychological warfare, paramilitary maneuvers, and political and economic intervention.

The CIA's most important function is information gathering, although its failure to process intelligence information relating to the attacks on September 11, 2001, has raised serious charges of incompetence. It is responsible for collecting information about the state of leadership in other countries, as well as their political situation and stability, military capabilities, strengths and weaknesses, and possible intentions in political, economic, and military spheres. All of this information is analyzed and reported to policy makers so they can make better decisions on foreign policy issues.

In 2005, a special presidential commission (Silberman-Robb report), spurred by the September 11 attacks, found enormous flaws in U.S. intelligence efforts and made several important recommendations that would overhaul many spy agencies and assign broad authority to the office of director of national intelligence.[30] The Director of National Intelligence (DNI) serves as the head of the Intelligence Community (IC). The DNI also acts as the principal advisor to the President, the National Security Council, and the Homeland Security Council for intelligence matters related to the national security, and oversees and directs the implementation of the National Intelligence Program.

The Agencies Behind Economic Policy Making

In the 1960s, the United States' overwhelming economic superiority began to dwindle, in part because of economic dislocations triggered by financing the Vietnam War. But, more important, this period also witnessed the first stirrings of real economic strength from the European and Asian economies ravaged by World War II and rebuilt with considerable assistance from the United States. As the economies of Europe and Japan expanded, the corresponding American share of world markets decreased. In addition, U.S. foreign policy priorities changed with the end of the Cold War. Such global economic shifts and political changes led to similar shifts in the balance of influence among the government organizations involved in foreign policy. The foreign policy establishment, formerly dominated by the NSC, the State Department, and the Pentagon, now features such actors as the Department of Commerce and the Office of the Trade Representative in roles of unprecedented prominence. Economic power is the overriding issue for these agencies.

These departments and agencies play highly specialized roles in making foreign policy. The Department of Labor, for example, represented the United States in international negotiations on the General Agreement on Tariffs and Trade (GATT, now the World Trade Organization), the Organization for Economic Cooperation and Development (OECD), and the International Labor Organization (ILO). The Department of Agriculture has its own Foreign Agricultural Service, which formulates, administers, and coordinates the department's programs overseas. The Department of Energy conducts nuclear weapons research as well as development, production, and surveillance operations.

The Treasury and Commerce Departments, in particular, are central figures in making global economic policy. The Treasury Department is primarily concerned with financial policy development. It focuses on trade regulations, exchange rates, and the balance of payments. Unlike the State Department, which judges nations largely on the basis of their political systems, or the Defense Department, which looks at military strength, the Treasury Department addresses a foreign nation's economic system and how it affects the U.S. economy. For example, is a nation's exchange rate fair? Is its tariff structure conducive to U.S. exports? How do American exports to a particular nation compare with American imports from it?

Although the Treasury Department develops U.S. financial policy, the Commerce Department expands and protects U.S. commerce abroad through the Foreign Commercial Service. Similar to the State Department's Foreign Service, the Foreign Commercial Service works through U.S. embassies and consulates, advising foreign businesses on their U.S.-related business activities. The Commerce Department also maintains nearly fifty offices in the United States to encourage U.S. firms to export their products.

Much of the actual foreign policy making takes place within the nooks and crannies of the State Department, the Pentagon, and other agencies and departments, as career bureaucrats exercise their delegated and nondelegated discretionary decision-making power to develop policy. Because these bureaucrats have the expertise to analyze the immense volume of foreign policy information, a president needs the bureaucracy's support to be successful in foreign policy.

The bureaucracy also assists with policy implementation. This task is a far-flung process in terms of geography and the vast array of departments and agencies that must cooperate on a given issue. Officials in the field, for example, especially the State Department's Foreign Service officers, tend to believe that those in Washington, D.C., far removed from the problems of their post, do not understand the realities of their situation.

All but the lowest levels of the foreign policy bureaucracy are staffed by individuals who owe their jobs to the political process, political appointees who form a large and powerful contingent within the foreign policy bureaucracy: deputy secretaries, undersecretaries, assistant secretaries, and directors of the various departments and agencies. As a group, political appointees are ambitious people who want a hand in shaping U.S. foreign policy. Thus, they must play the bureaucratic game in a way that will keep them involved in the action for as long as possible; they perform a delicate dance to maintain and expand their spheres of influence. The end of the Cold War has brought about the need to reexamine the institutions of U.S. foreign policy and national security policy making. Under examination are the structure of the State Department and the future of the Arms Control and Disarmament Agency, the U.S. Information Agency, and the U.S. Agency for International Development. Special commissions have been put in place to examine the roles and missions of both the Defense Department and the intelligence community.

DEMOCRATIC CHECKS ON FOREIGN POLICY

In no other realm of government activity is the exercise of democratic control less apparent than in the making of foreign policy. Both the complex nature of global affairs and the crisis atmosphere that sometimes prevails can lead the national security establishment to ignore public opinion. Similarly, the increasing use of executive agreements and covert operations means that decisions often unfold out of public view and without any opportunity for public debate except after the fact.

Although the president is the primary initiator of foreign policy, important checks limit the president's power to make foreign policy. We have already looked at how Congress can check presidential foreign policy making using its oversight power to force open the decision-making process. The press and public opinion can also act as a check on foreign policy outcomes.

The Press

The press plays an important role in the surveillance, investigation, criticism, and advocacy of the government's foreign policy activities. The media provide American citizens with most of their knowledge of the rest of the world. Although the media are ostensibly neutral and objective, they typically mirror the opinions of the foreign policy establishment. However, the media sometimes offer competing perspectives on international affairs. On occasion, individual reporters have questioned or strongly opposed government policies, stimulating public opposition. Press criticism of the Johnson administration's direction of the Vietnam War, although not widespread, served to chip away at the "monopoly of information" enjoyed by the White House, challenging the government version of reality and stimulating public criticism of U.S. involvement in Southeast Asia.

More commonly, though, the press serves as a conduit for the opinions of various actors involved in the policy process. The leak, a calculated release of controversial information, is a tool used at all levels of the bureaucracy for a variety of purposes. The right words at the right time can stir up Congress, the public, and foreign governments and put an end to a controversial foreign policy initiative. Key players in the foreign policy process often release information to friendly reporters to test the waters of public response to policy options under consideration.

With few exceptions, the American press is reluctant to strongly oppose U.S. government actions, particularly where the deployment of American troops is involved. Throughout most of the Vietnam War, the press, like most of the general public, supported the U.S. presence in Southeast Asia, breaking with the official version of U.S. policy in Vietnam only when the inconsistencies and contradictions of that policy had become glaringly apparent. This supportive role was even more apparent during more recent actions, including the U.S. invasions of Grenada, Panama, and Iraq. In each case, most media analysts relied on government sources, accepted government explanations, and focused predominantly on tactical and technical, rather than ethical or moral, analysis.

The media can be credited with providing Americans with a wealth of information, thereby helping them to become better informed citizens. And the constitutional guarantees of a free press and free speech afford American citizens a small but sometimes persistent and influential voice in the otherwise elite-dominated foreign policy process.[31]

The Public

Often overlooked in analyses of foreign policy decision making is the role played by the public and public opinion. The voice of public opinion occasionally penetrates the carefully encrypted speech and muffled secrecy of foreign policy making to have an impact. Popular discontent with Vietnam is an example of the government abiding by public opinion to reverse a long-standing policy. The validity of this claim is open to argument, but the fact remains that typically the foreign policy-making process is among the least democratic in the American system. Historically, U.S. citizens have had little significant influence on the foreign policy created by their government. The public tends to rally around the president in times of national crisis, such as war or international confrontation.

Since 2002, the Pew Global Attitudes Project has been studying the relationship between the rest of the world and the world's remaining superpower. The surveys have explored attitudes on economic globalization, democracy and governance, security, terrorism and values. U.S. popularity waxes and wanes. Indeed, in the period immediately following the September 11 attacks, "we are all Americans" was a familiar refrain in Europe. Today, following the war in Iraq, the one theme that emerges is how negatively the rest of the world now views the United States.

Today, anti-Americanism is deeper and broader than at any time in modern history. According to the Pew analysis: "It is most acute in the Muslim world, but it spans the globe—from Europe to Asia, from South America to Africa. And although much of the animus is aimed directly at President Bush and his policies, especially the war in Iraq, this new global hardening of attitudes amounts to something larger than a thumbs down on the current occupant of the White House."[32] What is most interesting in the 2005 Pew study are the findings that the world both fears and resents the unrivaled power the United States has accumulated since the end of the Cold War. Many see the United States as a "worrisome colossus," whereas others believe the United States is "too quick to act unilaterally" and that it "doesn't do a good job of addressing the world's problems and it widens the gulf between rich and poor."[33] (See Table 16.3.)

Table 16.3 ■ Views of America: U.S. Favorability Ratings

	USIA* 1999/2000 %	Summer 2002 %	Mar. 2003 %	May 2003 %	Mar. 2004 %
Britain	83	75	48	70	58
France	62	63	31	43	37
Germany	78	61	25	45	38
Italy	76	70	34	60	–
Spain	50	–	14	38	–
Russia	37	61	28	36	47
Canada	71	72	–	63	–
Brazil	56	52	–	34	–
Japan	77	72	–	–	–
Indonesia	75	61	–	15	–
South Korea	58	53	–	46	–
Turkey	52	30	12	15	30
Nigeria	46	77	–	61	–
Pakistan	23	10	–	13	21
Jordan	–	25	–	1	5
Morocco	77	–	–	27	27

Source: Pew Global Attitudes, except as noted below.

*Countries where 1999/2000 survey data are available. Trends provided by the Office of Research, U.S. Department of State (Canada trend by Environics International, now Globescan).

Table 16.4 ▪ Global Perception Gap on American Unilateralism

	A Great Deal/ Fair Amount	U.S. Considers Others Not Much/Not At All	Don't Know/ Refused
U.S.	70	27	3
Great Britain	36	61	3
Morocco	34	57	8
Germany	29	69	2
Russia	20	73	2
Jordan	16	77	7
Pakistan	18	48	34
France	14	84	2

Source: Pew Global Attitudes, March 2004.

A single explanation for the decline in world opinion about America is the perception that the United States acts unilaterally on the international stage and does not take into account the interests of other nations. Nevertheless, the real story of America's role in the world and how it is perceived also reveals certain enduring strengths tied to our theme of approaching democracy. The Pew study found that "a majority of people around the world admire America's democratic values and much about its way of life. Although they feel deep misgivings about the U.S.-led war on terror, they feel more secure living in a world in which no other nation can challenge the United States militarily." Interestingly enough, the world seems to chafe and express suspicion about U.S. unilateralism but expresses relief that no other superpowers exist. World opinion admires the democratic ideals that have long been promoted around the world. See Table 16.4.

The United States faces an impressive array of foreign policy challenges. Policy makers and the public must cope with forces of change in politics, economics, technology, and demographics. The United States must assess not only its interests in world affairs but also its proper role. In this quickly changing world, questions about foreign policy abound. How will the United States lead in the post–Cold War era? What is the role of NATO, and how and at what pace should it expand? What is the proper relationship between the United States and the United Nations? What should be the future role of peacekeeping operations and foreign aid programs? How will the United States balance economic and political interests when they collide? How will it balance economic and political interests against humanitarian and environmental concerns?

As we have seen throughout this text, the United States must respond to such questions in the context of its ongoing experiment in self-government. Indeed, the United States faces two related foreign policy challenges today. First, the United States must try to determine its course in a complicated and changing international environment, one that involves an appropriate balance of commitments and resources. Second, it must do so within the democratic limits established in the Constitution. Ultimately, then, the paramount challenge is how to balance the interests of security and the requirements of democracy.

This also involves consideration of how others view United States military actions. Table 16.5 on Iraqi public opinion leaves us to consider approaches to the democratic ideal in both the United States and Iraq. Understanding the link between foreign policy and democracy requires that we first recognize the dramatically altered world environment in the wake of the Cold War and the new terrorist threat that faces all democratic nations, as well as those taking first steps in approaching democracy.

Table 16.5 ■ What Do the Iraqis Really Want?

On the eve of their election, a TIME-ABC News poll indicated that Iraqis were surprisingly upbeat—yet critical of the United States. December 19, 2005.

- Overall, how would you say things are going these days?
  in your life?   Very well _____ 22%   Quite well _____ 49%   Quite badly _____ 18%   Very badly _____ 11%
  in Iraq overall?   Very well _____ 14%   Quite well _____ 30%   Quite badly _____ 23%   Very badly _____ 30%

- What is your main priority for Iraq over the next 12 months?
  (Top five answers) Regaining public security _____ 57%   Getting U.S. forces out _____ 10%   Rebuilding infrastructure _____ 9%   Increasing oil production _____ 7%   Having a stable government _____ 5%

- How has the security situation changed since Iraq regained sovereignty in June 2004?
  Better: 41%   Worse: 31%   Same: 18%   Don't know: 10%

  Among those saying it's better: Who is responsible for the improvement?
  Iraqi police _____ 28%   Government _____ 22%   Iraqi army _____ 12%   Security forces _____ 10%

  Among those saying it's worse: Who is responsible for the deterioration?
  Americans _____ 34%   Government _____ 30%   Terrorists _____ 17%   Iraqi police _____ 5%

- Do you think security will improve or worsen in a year?
  Improve _____ 70%   Worsen _____ 12%

- Which of these systems would be best for Iraq _____ now?
  A democracy _____ 57%   A dictatorship _____ 26%   An Islamic state _____ 14%

- Which of these systems would be best for Iraq _____ in 5 years?
  A democracy _____ 64%   A dictatorship _____ 18%   An Islamic state _____ 12%

- How much confidence do you have that the elections planned for this month will create a stable Iraqi government?
  A great deal _____ 42%   Quite a lot _____ 34%   Not very much _____ 14%   None _____ 5%

- Percentage who think women should be able to _____
  99% _____ vote   99% _____ be a doctor   84% _____ drive a car   80% _____ run for national office   78% _____ instruct men at work   77% _____ run for local office   51% _____ be Governor   46% _____ be President

- Since the war, how do you feel about the way in which the U.S. and other coalition forces have carried out their responsibilities?
  Very good job _____ 10%   Quite a good job _____ 27%   Quite a bad job _____ 19%   Very bad job _____ 40%

- Do you support or oppose the presence of coalition forces in Iraq?
  Strongly support _____ 13%   Somewhat support _____ 19%   Somewhat oppose _____ 21%   Strongly oppose _____ 44%

- When should coalition forces leave Iraq?
  When security is restored _____ 31%   Now _____ 26%   After a new government is in place _____ 19%   When Iraqi security forces are ready _____ 16%

Source: Excerpted from a poll conducted for TIME, ABC News, the BBC, NHK, and *Der Spiegel* by Oxford Research International. Interviews were conducted in person from October 8 to November 13, in Arabic and Kurdish, among a random national sample of 1,711 Iraqis age 15 and older. Margin of error is +/− 2.5 percentage points.

Summary

1. Foreign policy refers to actions the government takes abroad to ensure the security and well-being of Americans and the strength and competitiveness of the U.S. economy. Foreign policy-making is often complex because of the need to balance democratic ideals against military and economic interests.

2. Before World War I, U.S. foreign policy was characterized by isolationism, in which the United States fostered trade with Europe without committing to strategic alliances. Despite its policy of neutrality, the United States clearly favored Britain and the Allies at the beginning of World War I and entered the war after Germany resumed unrestricted submarine warfare. Following the war, however, isolationism again prevailed.

3. The United States was initially reluctant to enter World War II but did so after Japan's surprise bombing of Pearl Harbor. After the war, its primary foreign policy goal was *containment* of communism, which placed it in direct opposition to the Soviet Union and led to the Cold War.

4. After 1949, both the United States and the Soviet Union poured vast amounts of money into developing and deploying nuclear weapons. During the same period, U.S. foreign aid commitments increased in an effort to prevent Soviet advances in less developed countries.

5. During the 1960s, the effort to contain communism gradually drew the United States into a full-scale war in Vietnam, a war that proved both a military and foreign policy disaster. After the war, the United States entered into a *detente* with the Soviet Union and began discussing ways to reduce the nuclear threat.

6. In 1991, the Soviet Union ceased to exist, thereby ending the Cold War and clearing the way for what President Bush hoped would be a New World Order.

7. U.S. foreign policy strategies are also changing. Foreign aid use has come under fire, as has the use of economic sanctions as a means of forcing a target nation to change its policies. The temptation to find military solutions to political problems remains strong.

8. The Constitution gives the president the authority to commit troops to foreign lands, negotiate treaties, appoint ambassadors, and decide whether or not to receive ambassadors, an action indicating formal recognition. Congress has the power to declare war, appropriate money, and make laws, thereby deciding which presidential initiatives abroad to support. The Senate also has the power to ratify treaties and confirm presidential appointments.

9. The president determines the general direction of foreign policy and the effectiveness of its implementation by the bureaucracy. The president's influence has increased as Congress has granted additional powers during emergencies. In addition, presidents have often entered into executive agreements with foreign governments instead of treaties, thereby avoiding the need for Senate ratification.

10. Congress tends to be oriented toward domestic policy and cannot respond quickly and decisively to international events. It has attempted to strengthen its foreign policy oversight through legislation. Congress can also restrict the executive branch's foreign policy efforts by limiting appropriations for foreign aid, military spending, and intelligence gathering.

11. Although the State Department has primary responsibility for developing and implementing foreign policy, the Defense Department also plays an important role through its large share of the federal budget and considerable political clout. For information and policy planning, however, the president depends on the National Security Council, consisting of the president, the national security adviser, the vice president, and the secretaries of state and defense.

12. The Central Intelligence Agency, along with several other agencies, gathers and analyzes intelligence about the activities of foreign governments. It also engages in covert operations such as espionage, psychological warfare, and paramilitary operations. Concern about the CIA's possible abuses of power has led to attempts to restructure the agency and bring it under greater congressional and executive control.

13. Most of the detailed analysis and development of foreign policy is done by career bureaucrats in the State Department. At the higher levels are political appointees such as deputy secretaries and undersecretaries.

Review Questions

1. In what ways has Congress given over foreign policy powers to the president?

2. When and how have they attempted to reassert Congressional power over foreign policy? Should the president have more control over foreign policy? Why or why not?

3. Compare American foreign policy in the nineteenth century with American foreign policy in the twentieth century.

4. How did the two World Wars affect America's foreign relations?

5. How did foreign relations evolve during the Cold War?

6. How will increasing globalism and the end of the Cold War affect America's international relationships?

Key Terms

bipolarity   576
Cold War   576
containment   575
detente   578
economic sanctions   584
foreign aid   577

foreign policy   572
globalism   576
Gulf of Tonkin Resolution   578
isolationism   573
legislative oversight   586
military-industrial complex   589

Monroe Doctrine   573
North Atlantic Treaty
   Organization (NATO)   576
Peace Corps   577
Strategic Arms Limitation Treaty
   (SALT)   578

superpower   575
War Powers Resolution   586
Warsaw Pact   576

Suggested Readings

CUSHMAN, THOMAS, ed. *A Matter of Principle: Humanitarian Arguments for the War in Iraq*. Berkeley: University of California Press, 2006. This book provides a collection of sobering essays, including entries by Adam Michnik and Robert Kagan, that challenge those opposed to intervention.

GERTZ, BILL. *Breakdown: How America's Intelligence Failures Led to September 11th*. New York: Regency, 2002. *New York Times* author shows how America's intelligence community completely broke down in the years prior to the attacks on the World Trade Center and Pentagon. He calls it the greatest intelligence failure since Pearl Harbor.

LEVITE, ARIEL E., BRUCE W. JENTLESON, and LARRY BERMAN, eds. *Foreign Military Intervention: The Dynamics of Protracted Conflict*. New York: Columbia University Press, 1992. Six case studies that examine the similarities and differences among nation-states that use military might to intervene in civil wars and otherwise reshape the domestic political order of weakened states.

KNIGHTS, MICHAEL, ed. *Operation Iraqi Freedom and the New Iraq*. Washington, D.C.: Washington Institute for Near East Policy, 2004. A compilation of the wartime insights of Iraqi experts from a wide variety of sources.

LIEBER, ROBERT. *The American Era: Power and Strategy for the 21st Century*. Cambridge, U.K.: Cambridge University Press, 2005.

LITWAK, ROBERT S. *Rogue States and U.S. Foreign Policy*. Washington, D.C.: Woodrow Wilson Center Press and The Johns Hopkins University Press, 2000. A seminal contribution to the discussion of so-called rogue states. President Clinton and other U.S. policy makers have warned that "rogue states" pose a major threat to international peace in the post–Cold War era. But what exactly is a "rogue state" and does the concept provide a useful approach to foreign policy?

NINCIC, MIROSLAV. *Renegade Regimes: Confronting Deviant Behavior in World Politics*. New York: Columbia University Press, 2005. A comprehensive and groundbreaking study of rogue states and the challenges to international regime security.

NYE, JOSEPH S., JR. *The Paradox of American Power: Why the World's Only Superpower Can't Go It Alone*. New York: Oxford University Press, 2002. An analysis of American foreign policy that pits America's preeminent position against the need to recognize and account for the interdependent global system.

REITER, DAN, and ALLAN C. STAM. *Democracies at War*. Princeton, N.J.: Princeton University Press, March 2002. A study of why 80 percent of the time democracies win the wars they fight.

ROSEN, GARY, ed. *The Right War? The Conservative Debate on Iraq*. Cambridge, U.K.: Cambridge University Press, 2006. The editor of *Commentary* is joined by a distinguished team of colleagues who evaluate all aspects of the Iraqi encounter.

ROTHKOPF, DAVID J. *Running the World: The Inside Story of the National Security Council and the Architects of American Power*. New York: Public Affairs Press, 2005. An insightful bureaucratic history of the National Security Council and the principal personalities.

WALT, STEPHEN M. *Taming American Power: The Global Response to U.S. Primacy*. New York: Norton, 2005. Walt rejects the Bush administration's interventionist approach and advocates a strategy of "offshore balancing," limiting direct American involvement as far as possible, focusing instead on regional stability and local alliances.

WALTER, BARBARA F. *Committing to Peace: The Successful Settlements of Civil Wars*. Princeton, N.J.: Princeton University Press, February 2002. An in-depth look at competing theories about why certain civil wars have ended with successfully implemented peace settlements and others have not.

Visualizing Democracy

Living on Alert Since 9/11

The U.S. Coast Guard patrols New York harbor after the Department of Homeland Security raised the nation's threat level to orange.

The creation of the Office of Homeland Security within the context of the September 11 attacks reveals the complex challenge our democracy faces. In the weeks following September 11, Tom Ridge helped to coordinate a remarkable infrastructure involving the FBI, FEMA, Department of Energy, Environmental Protection Agency, Coast Guard, Army National Guard, Departments of Justice, Transportation, and other agencies of the federal government. "I think one of the challenges that the Office of Homeland Security has is to make sure that it becomes a permanent part of how the federal government does business," said Ridge.

By June 6, 2002, we had learned just how permanent a structure was envisioned for homeland security when President Bush announced a proposal for the creation of a new cabinet department for

HOMELAND SECURITY ADVISORY SYSTEM

The color-coded terrorism warning system was created in the wake of 9/11 to indicate the risk level for threats against the U.S.

SEVERE
SEVERE RISK OF TERRORIST ATTACKS

HIGH
HIGH RISK OF TERRORIST ATTACKS

ELEVATED
SIGNIFICANT RISK OF TERRORIST ATTACKS

GUARDED
GENERAL RISK OF TERRORIST ATTACKS

LOW
LOW RISK OF TERRORIST ATTACKS

PROTECTING THE

'Homeland' became a household word and was institutionalized when President Bush created the cabinet level department of Office of Homeland Security.

domestic defense. In the President's words, "we have concluded that our government must be reorganized to deal more effectively with the threats of the twenty-first century. So tonight I ask the Congress to join me in creating a single permanent mission—securing the homeland and protecting the American people . . . . Tonight I propose a permanent cabinet-level Department of Homeland Security to unite essential agencies that must work more closely together . . . . What I am proposing tonight is the most extensive reorganization of the federal government since the 1940's."

In the aftermath of the Republican electoral victory in November 2002, the House and Senate passed legislation on establishing a new Department of Homeland Security. President Bush soon thereafter signed the bipartisan bill into law, thereby creating the Homeland Security Department—the most comprehensive reorganization of the Federal government in over fifty years. President Bush has nearly tripled homeland security discretionary funding and more than $18 billion has been awarded to state and local governments. ★

HOMELAND

Security checks and security personnel increased at airports across the U.S. after 9/11.

The heightened alert after 9/11 is very evident in Washington, D.C. where concrete visual monitoring of government buildings has become the norm.

APPENDICES

APPENDIX 1

INTRODUCING THE CONCEPT OF APPROACHING DEMOCRACY

EXCERPTS OF A SPEECH BY VACLAV HAVEL, PRESIDENT OF THE CZECH REPUBLIC TO A JOINT SESSION OF THE U.S. CONGRESS, WASHINGTON, D.C., FEBRUARY 21, 1990

Dear Mr. Speaker, dear Mr. President, dear senators and members of the House, ladies and gentlemen:

I've only been president for two months, and I haven't attended any schools for presidents. My only school was life itself. Therefore, I don't want to burden you any longer with my political thoughts, but instead I will move on to an area that is more familiar to me, to what I would call the philosophical aspect of those changes that still concern everyone, although they are taking place in our corner of the world.

As long as people are people, democracy in the full sense of the word will always be no more than an ideal; one may approach it as one would a horizon, in ways that may be better or worse, but it can never be fully attained. *In this sense you are also merely approaching democracy.* You have thousands of problems of all kinds, as other countries do. But you have one great advantage: You have been approaching democracy uninterruptedly for more than 200 years, and your journey toward that horizon has never been disrupted by a totalitarian system. Czechs and Slovaks, despite their humanistic traditions that go back to the first millennium, have approached democracy for a mere twenty years, between the two world wars, and now for three and a half months since the 17th of November of last year.

The advantage that you have over us is obvious at once.

The Communist type of totalitarian system has left both our nations, Czechs and Slovaks as it has all the nations of the Soviet Union, and the other countries the Soviet Union subjugated in its time a legacy of countless dead, an infinite spectrum of human suffering, profound economic decline, and above all enormous human humiliation. It has brought us horrors that fortunately you have not known.

At the same time, however unintentionally, of course it has given us something positive: a special capacity to look, from time to time, somewhat further than someone who has not undergone this bitter experience. A person who cannot move and live a normal life because he is pinned under a boulder has more time to think about his hopes than someone who is not trapped in this way.

What I am trying to say is this: We must all learn many things from you, from how to educate our offspring, how to elect our representatives, all the way to how to organize our economic life so that it will lead to prosperity and not poverty. But it doesn't have to be merely assistance from the well educated, the powerful, and the wealthy to someone who has nothing to offer in return.

We too can offer something to you: our experience and the knowledge that has come from it.

This is a subject for books, many of which have already been written and many of which have yet to be written. I shall therefore limit myself to a single idea.

The specific experience I'm talking about has given me one great certainty: Consciousness precedes Being, and not the other way around, as Marxists claim.

For this reason, the salvation of this human world lies nowhere else than in the human heart, in the human power to reflect, in human humbleness and in human responsibility.

Without a global revolution in the sphere of human consciousness, nothing will change for the better in the sphere of our Being as humans, and the catastrophe toward which this world is headed, whether it be ecological, social, demographic or a general breakdown of civilization, will be unavoidable. If we are no longer threatened by world war or by the danger that the absurd mountains of accumulated nuclear weapons might blow up the world, this does not mean that we have definitively won. We are in fact far from definite victory.

We are still a long way from that "family of man;" in fact, we seem to be receding from the ideal rather than drawing closer to it. Interests of all kinds: personal, selfish, state, national, group and, if you like, company interests still considerably outweigh genuinely common and global interests. We are still under the sway of the destructive and thoroughly vain belief that man is the pinnacle of creation, and not just a part of it, and that therefore everything is permitted. There are still many who say they are concerned not for themselves but for the cause, while they are demonstrably out for themselves and not for the cause at all. We are still destroying the planet that was entrusted to us, and its environment. We still close our eyes to the growing social, ethnic and cultural conflicts in the world. From time to time we say that the anonymous megamachinery we have created for ourselves no longer serves us but rather has enslaved us, yet we still fail to do anything about it.

In other words, we still don't know how to put morality ahead of politics, science and economics. We are still incapable of understanding that the only genuine backbone of all our actions if they are to be moral is responsibility. Responsibility to something higher than my family, my country, my firm, my success. Responsibility to the order of Being, where all our actions are indelibly recorded and where, and only where, they will be properly judged.

The interpreter or mediator between us and this higher authority is what is traditionally referred to as human conscience.

If I subordinate my political behaviour to this imperative, I can't go far wrong. If on the contrary I were not guided by this voice, not even ten presidential schools with 2,000 of the best political scientists in the world could help me.

This is why I ultimately decided after resisting for a long time to accept the burden of political responsibility.

I'm not the first nor will I be the last intellectual to do this. On the contrary, my feeling is that there will be more and more of them all the time. If the hope of the world lies in human consciousness, then it is obvious that intellectuals cannot go on forever avoiding their share of responsibility for the world and hiding their distastes for politics under an alleged need to be independent.

It is easy to have independence in your programme and then leave others to carry out that programme. If everyone thought that way, soon no one would be independent.

I think that Americans should understand this way of thinking. Wasn't it the best minds of your country, people you could call intellectuals, who wrote your famous Declaration of Independence, your Bill of Rights, and your Constitution, and who above all took upon themselves the practical responsibility for putting them into practice? The worker from Branik in Prague, whom your president referred to in his State of the Union message this year, is far from being the only person in Czechoslovakia, let alone in the world, to be inspired by those great documents. They inspire us all. They inspire us despite the fact that they are over 200 years old. They inspire us to be citizens.

When Thomas Jefferson wrote that "Governments are instituted among Men, deriving their just powers from the Consent of the Governed," it was a simple and important act of the human spirit.

What gave meaning to that act, however, was the fact that the author backed it up with his life. It was not just his words, it was his deeds as well.

I will end where I began. History has accelerated. I believe that once again, it will be the human spirit that will notice this acceleration, give it a name, and transform those words into deeds.

APPENDIX 2

				MAJORITY PARTY	
TERM	PRESIDENT AND VICE PRESIDENT	PARTY OF PRESIDENT	CONGRESS	HOUSE	SENATE
1789–97	**George Washington**	None	1st	N/A	N/A
	John Adams		2d	N/A	N/A
			3d	N/A	N/A
			4th	N/A	N/A
1797–1801	**John Adams**	Fed	5th	N/A	N/A
	Thomas Jefferson		6th	Fed	Fed
1801–09	**Thomas Jefferson**	Dem Rep	7th	Dem Rep	Dem Rep
	Aaron Burr (1801–5)		8th	Dem Rep	Dem Rep
	George Clinton (1805–9)		9th	Dem Rep	Dem Rep
			10th	Dem Rep	Dem Rep
1809–17	**James Madison**	Dem Rep	11th	Dem Rep	Dem Rep
	George Clinton (1809–12)[1]		12th	Dem Rep	Dem Rep
	Elbridge Gerry (1813–14)[1]		13th	Dem Rep	Dem Rep
			14th	Dem Rep	Dem Rep
1817–25	**James Monroe**	Dem Rep	15th	Dem Rep	Dem Rep
	Daniel D. Tompkins		16th	Dem Rep	Dem Rep
			17th	Dem Rep	Dem Rep
			18th	Dem Rep	Dem Rep
1825–29	**John Quincy Adams**	Nat'l Rep	19th	Nat'l Rep	Nat'l Rep
	John C. Calhoun		20th	Dem	Dem
1829–37	**Andrew Jackson**	Dem	21st	Dem	Dem
	John C. Calhoun (1829–32)[2]		22d	Dem	Dem
	Martin Van Buren (1833–37)		23d	Dem	Dem
			24th	Dem	Dem
1837–41	**Martin Van Buren**	Dem	25th	Dem	Dem
	Richard M. Johnson		26th	Dem	Dem
1841	**William H. Harrison**[1]	Whig			
	John Tyler (1841)				
1841–45	**John Tyler**	Whig	27th	Whig	Whig
	(VP vacant)		28th	Dem	Whig
1845–49	**James K. Polk**	Dem	29th	Dem	Dem
	George M. Dallas		30th	Whig	Dem
1849–50	**Zachary Taylor**[1]	Whig	31st	Dem	Dem
	Millard Fillmore				
1850–53	**Millard Fillmore**	Whig	32d	Dem	Dem
	(VP vacant)				
1853–57	**Franklin Pierce**	Dem	33d	Dem	Dem
	William R. D. King (1853)[1]		34th	Rep	Dem
1857–61	**James Buchanan**	Dem	35th	Dem	Dem
	John C. Breckinridge		36th	Rep	Dem
1861–65	**Abraham Lincoln**[1]	Rep	37th	Rep	Rep
	Hannibal Hamlin (1861–65)		38th	Rep	Rep
	Andrew Johnson (1865)		38th	Rep	Rep
1865–69	**Andrew Johnson**	Rep	39th	Union	Union
	(VP vacant)		40th	Rep	Rep
1869–77	**Ulysses S. Grant**	Rep	41st	Rep	Rep
	Schuyler Colfax (1869–73)		42d	Rep	Rep
	Henry Wilson (1873–75)[1]		43d	Rep	Rep
			44th	Dem	Rep
1877–81	**Rutherford B. Hayes**	Rep	45th	Dem	Rep
	William A. Wheeler		46th	Dem	Dem
1881	**James A. Garfield**[1]	Rep	47th	Rep	Rep
	Chester A. Arthur				
1881–85	**Chester A. Arthur**	Rep	48th	Dem	Rep
	(VP vacant)				
1885–89	**Grover Cleveland**	Dem	49th	Dem	Rep
	Thomas A. Hendricks (1885)[1]		50th	Dem	Rep

Presidents and Congresses, 1789–2006

TERM	PRESIDENT AND VICE PRESIDENT	PARTY OF PRESIDENT	CONGRESS	MAJORITY PARTY HOUSE	MAJORITY PARTY SENATE
1889–93	**Benjamin Harrison**	Rep	51st	Rep	Rep
	Levi P. Morton		52d	Dem	Rep
1893–97	**Grover Cleveland**	Dem	53d	Dem	Dem
	Adlai E. Stevenson		54th	Rep	Rep
1897–1901	**William McKinley**[1]	Rep	55th	Rep	Rep
	Garret A. Hobart (1897–99)[1]		56th	Rep	Rep
	Theodore Roosevelt (1901)				
1901–09	**Theodore Roosevelt**	Rep	57th	Rep	Rep
	(VP vacant, 1901–05)		58th	Rep	Rep
	Charles W. Fairbanks (1905–09)		59th	Rep	Rep
			60th	Rep	Rep
1909–13	**William Howard Taft**	Rep	61st	Rep	Rep
	James S. Sherman (1909–12)[1]		62d	Dem	Rep
1913–21	**Woodrow Wilson**	Dem	63d	Dem	Dem
	Thomas R. Marshall		64th	Dem	Dem
			65th	Dem	Dem
			66th	Rep	Rep
1921–23	**Warren G. Harding**[1]	Rep	67th	Rep	Rep
	Calvin Coolidge				
1923–29	**Calvin Coolidge**	Rep	68th	Rep	Rep
	(VP vacant, 1923–25)		69th	Rep	Rep
	Charles G. Dawes (1925–29)		70th	Rep	Rep
1929–33	**Herbert Hoover**	Rep	71st	Rep	Rep
	Charles Curtis		72d	Dem	Rep
1933–45	**Franklin D. Roosevelt**[1]	Dem	73d	Dem	Dem
	John N. Garner (1933–41)		74th	Dem	Dem
	Henry A. Wallace (1941–45)		75th	Dem	Dem
	Harry S. Truman (1945)		76th	Dem	Dem
			77th	Dem	Dem
			78th	Dem	Dem
1945–53	**Harry S Truman**	Dem	79th	Dem	Dem
	(VP vacant, 1945–49)		80th	Rep	Rep
	Alben W. Barkley (1949–53)		81st	Dem	Dem
			82d	Dem	Dem
1953–61	**Dwight D. Eisenhower**	Rep	83d	Rep	Rep
	Richard M. Nixon		84th	Dem	Dem
			85th	Dem	Dem
			86th	Dem	Dem
1961–63	**John F. Kennedy**[1]	Dem	87th	Dem	Dem
	Lyndon B. Johnson (1961–63)				
1963–69	**Lyndon B. Johnson**	Dem	88th	Dem	Dem
	(VP vacant, 1963–65)		89th	Dem	Dem
	Hubert H. Humphrey (1965–69)		90th	Dem	Dem
1969–74	**Richard M. Nixon**[3]	Rep	91st	Dem	Dem
	Spiro T. Agnew (1969–73)[2]		92d	Dem	Dem
	Gerald R. Ford (1973–74)[4]				
1974–77	**Gerald R. Ford**	Rep	93d	Dem	Dem
	Nelson A. Rockefeller[4]		94th	Dem	Dem
1977–81	**Jimmy Carter**	Dem	95th	Dem	Dem
	Walter Mondale		96th	Dem	Dem
1981–89	**Ronald Reagan**	Rep	97th	Dem	Rep
	George Bush		98th	Dem	Rep
			99th	Dem	Rep
			100th	Dem	Dem
1989–93	**George Bush**	Rep	101st	Dem	Dem
	J. Danforth Quayle		102d	Dem	Dem
1993–2001	**William J. Clinton**	Dem	103d	Dem	Dem
	Albert Gore, Jr.		104th	Rep	Rep
			105th	Rep	Rep
			106th	Rep	Rep
2001–2004, 2005–2006	**George W. Bush**	Rep	107th	Rep	Dem
	Richard Cheney		108th	Rep	Rep
			109th	Rep	Rep

[1]Died in office.
[2]Resigned from the vice presidency.
[3]Resigned from the presidency.
[4]Appointed vice president.

APPENDIX 3

Supreme Court Justices

Name[1]	Years on Court	Appointing President
JOHN JAY	1789–1795	Washington
James Wilson	1789–1798	Washington
John Rutledge	1790–1791	Washington
William Cushing	1790–1810	Washington
John Blair	1790–1796	Washington
James Iredell	1790–1799	Washington
Thomas Johnson	1792–1793	Washington
William Paterson	1793–1806	Washington
JOHN RUTLEDGE[2]	1795	Washington
Samuel Chase	1796–1811	Washington
OLIVER ELLSWORTH	1796–1800	Washington
Bushrod Washington	1799–1829	J. Adams
Alfred Moore	1800–1804	J. Adams
JOHN MARSHALL	1801–1835	J. Adams
William Johnson	1804–1834	Jefferson
Brockholst Livingston	1807–1823	Jefferson
Thomas Todd	1807–1826	Jefferson
Gabriel Duvall	1811–1835	Madison
Joseph Story	1812–1845	Madison
Smith Thompson	1823–1843	Monroe
Robert Trimble	1826–1828	J. Q. Adams
John McLean	1830–1861	Jackson
Henry Baldwin	1830–1844	Jackson
James M. Wayne	1835–1867	Jackson
ROGER B. TANEY	1836–1864	Jackson
Philip P. Barbour	1836–1841	Jackson
John Cartron	1837–1865	Van Buren
John McKinley	1838–1852	Van Buren
Peter V. Daniel	1842–1860	Van Buren
Samuel Nelson	1845–1872	Tyler
Levi Woodbury	1845–1851	Polk
Robert C. Grier	1846–1870	Polk
Benjamin R. Curtis	1851–1857	Fillmore
John A. Campbell	1853–1861	Pierce
Nathan Clifford	1858–1881	Buchanan
Noah H. Swayne	1862–1881	Lincoln
Samuel F. Miller	1862–1890	Lincoln
David Davis	1862–1877	Lincoln
Stephen J. Field	1863–1897	Lincoln
SALMON P. CHASE	1864–1873	Lincoln
William Strong	1870–1880	Grant
Joseph P. Bradley	1870–1892	Grant
Ward Hunt	1873–1882	Grant
MORRISON R. WAITE	1874–1888	Grant
John M. Harlan	1877–1911	Hayes
William B. Woods	1881–1887	Hayes
Stanley Matthews	1881–1889	Garfield
Horace Gray	1882–1902	Arthur
Samuel Blatchford	1882–1893	Arthur
Lucious Q. C. Lamar	1888–1893	Cleveland
MELVILLE W. FULLER	1888–1910	Cleveland
David J. Brewer	1890–1910	B. Harrison
Henry B. Brown	1891–1906	B. Harrison

Name[1]	Years on Court	Appointing President
George Shiras, Jr.	1892–1903	B. Harrison
Howel E. Jackson	1893–1895	B. Harrison
Edward D. White	1894–1910	Cleveland
Rufus W. Peckman	1896–1909	Cleveland
Joseph McKenna	1898–1925	McKinley
Oliver W. Holmes	1902–1932	T. Roosevelt
William R. Day	1903–1922	T. Roosevelt
William H. Moody	1906–1910	T. Roosevelt
Horace H. Lurton	1910–1914	Taft
Charles E. Hughes	1910–1916	Taft
EDWARD D. WHITE	1910–1921	Taft
Willis Van Devanter	1911–1937	Taft
Joseph R. Lamar	1911–1916	Taft
Mahlon Pitney	1912–1922	Taft
James C. McReynolds	1914–1941	Wilson
Louis D. Brandeis	1916–1939	Wilson
John H. Clarke	1916–1922	Wilson
WILLIAM H. TAFT	1921–1930	Harding
George Sutherland	1922–1938	Harding
Pierce Butler	1923–1939	Harding
Edward T. Sanford	1923–1930	Harding
Harlan F. Stone	1925–1941	Coolidge
CHARLES E. HUGHES	1930–1941	Hoover
Owen J. Roberts	1930–1945	Hoover
Benjamin N. Cardozo	1932–1938	Hoover
Hugo L. Black	1937–1971	F. Roosevelt
Stanley F. Reed	1938–1957	F. Roosevelt
Felix Frankfurter	1939–1962	F. Roosevelt
William O. Douglas	1939–1975	F. Roosevelt
Frank Murphy	1940–1949	F. Roosevelt
HARLAN F. STONE	1941–1946	F. Roosevelt
James F. Brynes	1941–1942	F. Roosevelt
Robert H. Jackson	1941–1954	F. Roosevelt
Wiley B. Rutledge	1943–1949	F. Roosevelt
Harold H. Burton	1945–1958	Truman
FREDERICK M. VINSON	1946–1953	Truman
Tom C. Clark	1949–1967	Truman
Sherman Minton	1949–1956	Truman
EARL WARREN	1953–1969	Eisenhower
John Marshall Harlan	1955–1971	Eisenhower
William J. Brennan, Jr.	1956–1990	Eisenhower
Charles E. Whittaker	1957–1962	Eisenhower
Potter Stewart	1958–1981	Eisenhower
Byron R. White	1962–1993	Kennedy
Arthur J. Goldberg	1962–1965	Kennedy
Abe Fortas	1965–1970	L. Johnson
Thurgood Marshall	1967–1991	L. Johnson
WARREN E. BURGER	1969–1986	Nixon
Harry A. Blackmun	1970–1994	Nixon
Lewis F. Powell, Jr.	1971–1987	Nixon
William H. Rehnquist	1971–1986	Nixon
John Paul Stevens	1975–	Ford
Sandra Day O'Connor	1981–2006	Reagan
WILLIAM H. REHNQUIST	1986–2005	Reagan
Antonin Scalia	1986–	Reagan
Anthony Kennedy	1988–	Reagan
David Souter	1990–	Bush
Clarence Thomas	1991–	Bush
Ruth Bader Ginsburg	1993–	Clinton
Stephen Brever	1994–	Clinton
JOHN G. ROBERTS, JR.	2005–	Bush
Samuel A. Alito, Jr.	2006–	Bush

[1]Capital letters designate Chief Justices
[2]Never confirmed by the Senate as Chief Justice

APPENDIX 4

THE DECLARATION OF INDEPENDENCE

IN CONGRESS, JULY 4, 1776
(The unanimous Declaration of the Thirteen United States of America)

Preamble

When, in the course of human events, it becomes necessary for one people to dissolve the political bands which have connected them with another, and to assume, among the powers of the earth, the separate and equal station to which the laws of nature and of nature's God entitle them, a decent respect to the opinions of mankind requires that they should declare the causes which impel them to the separation.

We hold these truths to be self-evident; that all men are created equal, that they are endowed by their Creator with certain unalienable rights, that among these are life, liberty, and the pursuit of happiness.

That, to secure these rights, governments are instituted among men, deriving their just powers from the consent of the governed.

That whenever any form of government becomes destructive of these ends, it is the right of the people to alter or to abolish it, and to institute new government, laying its foundation on such principles, and organizing its powers in such form, as to them shall seem most likely to effect their safety and happiness. Prudence, indeed will dictate that governments long established should not be changed for light and transient causes; and accordingly all experience hath shown that mankind are more disposed to suffer while evils are sufferable, than to right themselves by abolishing the forms to which they are accustomed. But when a long train of abuses and usurpations, pursuing invariably the same object, evinces a design to reduce them under absolute despotism, it is their right, it is their duty, to throw off such government, and to provide new guards for their future security.

Such has been the patient sufferance of these colonies; and such is now the necessity which constrains them to alter their former systems of government. The history of the present king of Great Britain is a history of repeated injuries and usurpations, all having in direct object the establishment of an absolute tyranny over these states. To prove this, let facts be submitted to a candid world.

He has refused his assent to laws, the most wholesome and necessary for the public good.

He has forbidden his governors to pass laws of immediate and pressing importance unless suspended in their operation till his assent should be obtained; and when so suspended, he has utterly neglected to attend to them.

He has refused to pass other laws for the accommodation of large districts of people, unless those people would relinquish the right of representation in the legislature, a right inestimable to them, and formidable to tyrants only.

He has called together legislative bodies at places unusual, uncomfortable, and distant for the depository of their public records, for the sole purpose of fatiguing them into compliance with his measures.

He has dissolved representative houses repeatedly, for opposing, with manly firmness, his invasions on the rights of people.

He has refused, for a long time after such dissolutions, to cause others to be elected; whereby the legislative powers incapable of annihilation, have returned to the people at large for their exercise; the state remaining, in the meantime, exposed to all the dangers of invasion from without and convulsions within.

He has endeavored to prevent the population of these states; for that purpose obstructing the laws of naturalization of foreigners, refusing to pass others to encourage their migration hither, and raising the conditions of new appropriations of lands.

He has obstructed the administration of justice, by refusing his assent to laws for establishing judiciary powers.

He has made judges dependent on his will alone for the tenure of their offices, and the amount and payment of their salaries.

He has erected a multitude of new offices, and sent hither swarms of officers to harass our people and eat out their substance.

He has kept among us, in times of peace, standing armies, without the consent of our legislature.

He has affected to render the military independent of, and superior to, the civil power.

He has combined with others to subject us to jurisdiction foreign to our constitution and unacknowledged by our laws, giving his assent to their acts of pretended legislation:

For quartering large bodies of armed troops among us;

For protecting them, by a mock trial, from punishment for any murders which they should commit on the inhabitants of these states;

For cutting off our trade with all parts of the world;

For imposing taxes on us without our consent;

For depriving us, in many cases, of the benefits of trial by jury;

For transporting us beyond seas, to be tried for pretended offenses;

For abolishing the free system of English laws in a neighboring province, establishing therein an arbitrary government, and enlarging its boundaries, so as to render it at once an example and fit instrument for introducing the same absolute rule into these colonies;

For taking away our charters, abolishing our most valuable laws, and altering, fundamentally, the forms of our governments;

For suspending our own legislatures, and declaring themselves invented with power to legislate for us in all cases whatsoever.

He has abdicated government here, by declaring us out of his protection and waging war against us.

He has plundered our seas, ravaged our coasts, burned our towns, and destroyed the lives of our people.

He is at this time transporting large armies of foreign mercenaries to complete the works of death, desolation, and tyranny already begun with circumstances of cruelty and perfidy scarcely paralleled in the most barbarous ages and totally unworthy of the head of a civilized nation.

He has constrained our fellow-citizens, taken captive on the high seas, to bear arms against their country, to become the executioners of their friends and brethren, or to fall themselves by their hands.

He has excited domestic insurrections among us, and has endeavored to bring on the inhabitants of our frontiers the merciless Indian savages, whose known rule of warfare is an undistinguished destruction of all ages, sexes, and conditions.

In every stage of these oppressions we have petitioned for redress in the most humble terms; our repeated petitions have been answered only by repeated injury. A prince whose character is thus marked by every act which may define a tyrant is unfit to be the ruler of a free people.

Nor have we been wanting in attention to our British brethren. We have warned them, from time to time, of attempts by their legislature to extend an unwarrantable jurisdiction over us. We have reminded them of the circumstances of our emigration and settlement here. We have appealed to their native justice and magnanimity; and we have conjured them, by the ties of our common kindred, to disavow these usurpations, which would inevitably interrupt our connections and correspondence. They, too, have been deaf to the voice of justice and of consanguinity. We must, therefore, acquiesce in the necessity which denounces our separation, and hold them, as we hold the rest of mankind, enemies in war, in peace, friends.

We, therefore, the representatives of the United States of America, in General Congress assembled, appealing to the Supreme Judge of the world for the rectitude of our intentions, do, in the name and by authority of the good people of these colonies, solemnly publish and declare, that these united colonies are, and of right ought to be, free and independent states; that they are absolved from all allegiance to the British crown, and that all political connection between them and the state of Great Britain is, and ought to be, totally dissolved; and that, as free and independent states, they have full power to levy war, conclude peace, contract alliances, establish commerce, and do all other acts and things which independent states may of a right do. And, for the support of this declaration, with a firm reliance on the protection of Divine Providence, we mutually pledge to each other our lives, our fortunes, and our sacred honor.

APPENDIX 5

THE FEDERALIST, NO. 10, JAMES MADISON

To the People of the State of New York: Among the numerous advantages promised by a well-constructed union, none deserves to be more accurately developed than its tendency to break and control the violence of faction. The friend of popular governments, never finds himself so much alarmed for their character and fate, as when he contemplates their propensity of this dangerous vice. He will not fail, therefore, to set a due value on any plan which, without violating the principles to which he is attached, provides a proper cure for it. The instability, injustice, and confusion introduced into the public councils, have, in truth, been the mortal diseases under which popular governments have everywhere perished; as they continue to be the favorite and fruitful topics from which the adversaries to liberty derive their most specious declamations. The valuable improvements made by the American constitutions on the popular models, both ancient and modern, cannot certainly be too much admired; but it would be an unwarrantable partiality, to contend that they have as effectually obviated the danger on this side, as was wished and expected. Complaints are everywhere heard from our most considerate and virtuous citizens, equally the friends of public and private faith, and of public and personal liberty, that our governments are too unstable; that the public good is disregarded in the conflicts of rival parties; and that measures are too often decided, not according to the rules of justice, and the rights of the minor party, but by the superior force of an interested and overbearing majority. However anxiously we may wish that these complaints had no foundation, the evidence of known facts will not permit us to deny that they are in some degree true. It will be found, indeed, on a candid review of our situation, that some of the distresses under which we labor have been erroneously charged on the operations of our governments; but it will be found, at the same time, that other causes will not alone account for many of our heaviest misfortunes; and, particularly, for that prevailing and increasing distrust of public engagements, and alarm for private rights, which are echoed from one end of the continent to the other. These must be chiefly, if not wholly, effects of the unsteadiness and injustice, with which a factious spirit has tainted our public administrations.

By a faction, I understand a number of citizens, whether amounting to a majority of the whole, who are united and actuated by some common impulse of passion, or of interest, adverse to the rights of other citizens, or to the permanent and aggregate interests of the community.

There are two methods of curing the mischiefs of faction: the one, by removing its causes; the other, by controlling its effects.

There are again two methods of removing the causes of faction: the one, by destroying the liberty which is essential to its existence; the other, by giving to every citizen the same opinions, the same passions, and the same interests.

It could never be more truly said, than of the first remedy, that it was worse than the disease. Liberty is to faction what air is to fire, an aliment without which it instantly expires. But it could not be a less folly to abolish liberty, which is essential to political life, because it nourishes faction, than it would be to wish the annihilation of air, which is essential to animal life, because it imparts to fire its destructive agency.

The second expedient is as impracticable, as the first would be unwise. As long as the reason of man continues fallible, and he is at liberty to exercise it, different opinions will be formed. As long as the connection subsists between his reason and his self-love, his opinions and his passions will have a reciprocal influence on each other; and the former will be objects to which the latter will attach themselves. The diversity in the faculties of men, from which the rights of property originate, is not less an insuperable obstacle to an uniformity of interests. The protection of these faculties is the first object of government. From the protection of different and unequal faculties of acquiring property, the possession of different degrees and kinds of property immediately results; and from the influence of these on the sentiments and views of the respective proprietors, ensues a division of the society into different interests and parties.

The latent causes of faction are thus sown in the nature of man; and we see them everywhere brought into different degrees of activity, according to the different circumstances of civil society. A zeal for different opinions concerning religion, concerning government, and many other points, as well of speculation as of practice; an attachment to different leaders ambitiously contending for preeminence and power; or to persons of other descriptions whose fortunes have been interesting to the human passions, have, in turn, divided mankind into parties, inflamed them with mutual animosity, and rendered them much more disposed to vex and oppress each other, than to cooperate for their common good. So strong is this propensity of mankind, to fall into mutual animosities, that where no substantial occasion presents itself, the most frivolous and fanciful distinctions have been sufficient to kindle their unfriendly passions and excite their most violent conflicts. But the most common and durable source of factions, has been the various and unequal distribution of property. Those who hold, and those who are without property, have ever formed distinct interests in society. Those who are creditors, and those who are debtors, fall under a like discrimination. A landed interest, a manufacturing interest, a mercantile interest, a moneyed interest, with many lesser interests, grow up of necessity in civilized nations, and divide them into different classes, actuated by different sentiments and views. The regulation of these various and interfering interests forms the principal task of modern legislation, and involves the spirit of the party and faction in the necessary and ordinary operations of the government.

No man is allowed to be a judge in his own cause; because his interest will certainly bias his judgment, and, not improbably, corrupt his integrity. With equal, nay, with greater reason, a body of men are unfit to be both judges and parties at the same time; yet what are many of the most important acts of legislation, but so many judicial determinations, not indeed concerning the right of single persons, but concerning the rights of large bodies of citizens? And what are the different classes of legislators, but advocates and parties to the causes which they determine? Is a law proposed concerning private debts? It is a question to which the creditors are parties on one side, and the debtors on the other. Justice ought to hold the balance between them. Yet the parties are, and must be, themselves the judges; and the most numerous party, or, in other words, the most powerful faction, must be expected to prevail. Shall domestic manufacturers be encouraged, and in what degree, by restrictions on foreign manufacturers? Are questions which would be differently decided by the landed and the manufacturing classes; and probably by neither with a sole regard to justice and the public good. The apportionment of taxes, on the various descriptions of property, is an act which seems to require the most exact impartiality; yet there is, perhaps, no legislative act, in which greater opportunity and temptation are given to a predominant party to trample on the rules of justice. Every shilling, with which they overburden the inferior number, is a shilling saved to their own pockets.

It is in vain to say, that enlightened statesmen will be able to adjust these clashing interests, and render them all subservient to the public good. Enlightened statesmen will not always be at the helm, nor, in many cases, can such an adjustment be made at all, without taking into view indirect and remote considerations, which will rarely prevail over the immediate interest which one party may find in disregarding the rights of another, or the good of the whole.

The inference to which we are brought is, that the causes of faction cannot be removed; and that relief is only to be sought in the means of controlling its *effects*.

If a faction consists of less than a majority, relief is supplied by the republican principle, which enables the majority to defeat its sinister views, by regular vote. It may clog the administration, it may convulse the society; but it will be unable to execute and mask its violence under the forms of the Constitution. When a majority is included in a faction, the form of popular government, on the other hand, enables it to sacrifice to its ruling passion or interest, both the public good and the rights of other citizens. To secure the public good, and private rights, against the danger of such a faction, and at the same time to preserve the spirit and the form of popular government, is then the great object to which our inquiries are directed. Let me add, that it is the great desideratum, by which alone this form of government can be rescued from the opprobrium under which it has so long laboured, and be recommended to the esteem and adoption of mankind.

By what means is this object attainable? Evidently by one of two only. Either the existence of the same passion or interest in a majority, at the same time, must be prevented; or the majority, having such coexistent passion or interest, must be rendered, by their number and local situation, unable to concert and carry into effect schemes of oppression. If the impulse and the opportunity be suffered to coincide, we well know that neither moral nor religious motives can be relied on as an adequate control. They are not found to be such on the injustice and violence of individuals, and lose their efficacy in proportion to the number combined together; that is, in proportion as their efficacy becomes needful.

From this view of the subject, it may be concluded, that a pure democracy, by which I mean a society consisting of a small number of citizens, who assemble and administer the government in person, can admit of no cure for the mischiefs of faction. A common passion or interest will, in almost every case, be felt by a majority of the whole; a communication and concert, results from the form of government itself; and there is nothing to check the inducements to sacrifice the weaker party, or an obnoxious individual. Hence, it is, that such democracies have ever been spectacles of turbulence and contention; have ever been found incompatible with personal security, or the rights of property; and have in general been as short in their lives, as they have been violent in their deaths. Theoretic politicians, who have patronized this species of government, have erroneously supposed, that by reducing mankind to a perfect equality in their political rights, they would, at the same time be perfectly equalized and assimilated in their possessions, their opinions, and their passions.

A republic, by which I mean a government in which the scheme of representation takes place, opens a different prospect, and promises the cure for which we are seeking. Let us examine the points in which it varies from pure democracy, and we shall comprehend both the nature of the cure and the efficacy which it must derive from the union.

The two great points of difference, between a democracy and a republic, are, first, the delegation of the government, in the latter, to a small number of citizens, elected by the rest; secondly, the greater number of citizens, and greater sphere of country, over which the latter may be extended.

The effect of the first difference is, on the one hand, to refine and enlarge the public views, by passing them through the medium of a chosen body of citizens, whose wisdom may best discern the true interest of their country, and whose patriotism and love of justice, will be least likely to sacrifice it to temporary or partial considerations. Under such a regulation, it may well happen, that the public voice, pronounced by the representatives of the people, will be more consonant to the public good, than if pronounced by the people themselves, convened for the purpose. On the other hand the effect may be inverted. Men of factious tempers, of local prejudices, or of sinister designs, may by intrigue, by corruption, or by other means, first obtain the suffrages, and then betray the interest of the people. The question resulting is, whether small or extensive republics are most favourable to the election of proper guardians of the public weal; and it is clearly decided in favour of the latter by two obvious considerations.

In the first place, it is to be remarked that, however small the republic may be, the representatives must be raised to a certain number, in order to guard against the cabals of a few; and that however large it may be, they must be limited to a certain number, in order to guard against the confusion of a multitude. Hence, the number of representatives in the two cases not being in proportion to that of the constituents, and being proportionally greatest in the small republic, it follows, that if the proportion of fit characters be not less in the large than in the small republic, the former will present a greater option, and consequently a greater probability of a fit choice.

In the next place, as each representative will be chosen by a greater number of citizens in the large than in the small republic, it will be more difficult for unworthy candidates to practice with success the vicious arts, by which elections are too often carried; and the suffrages of the people being more free, will be more likely to centre in men who possess the most attractive merit, and the most diffusive and established characters.

It must be confessed, that in this, as in most other cases, there is a mean, on both sides of which inconveniences will be found to lie. By enlarging too much the number of electors, you render the representatives too little acquainted with all their local circumstances and lesser interests; as by reducing it too much, you render him unduly attached to these, and too little fit to comprehend and pursue great and national objects. The federal constitution forms a happy combination in this respect; the great and aggregate interests being referred to the national, the local and particular to the state legislatures.

The other point of difference is, the greater number of citizens, and extent of territory, which may be brought within the compass of republican, than of democratic government; and it is this circumstance principally which renders factious combinations less to be dreaded in the former, than in the latter. The smaller the society, the fewer probably will be the distinct parties and interests composing it; the fewer the distinct parties and interests, the more frequently will a majority be found of the same party; and the smaller the number of individuals composing a majority, and the smaller the compass within which they are placed, the more easily will they concert and execute their plans of oppression. Extend the sphere, and you take in a greater variety of parties and interests; you make it less probable that a majority of the whole will have a common motive to invade the rights of other citizens; or if such a common motive exists, it will be more difficult for all who feel it to discover their own strength, and to act in unison with each other. Besides other impediments, it may be remarked, that where there is a consciousness of unjust or dishonourable purposes, communication is always checked by distrust, in proportion to the number whose concurrence is necessary.

Hence, it clearly appears, that the same advantage, which a republic has over a democracy, in controlling the effects of faction, is enjoyed by a large over a small republic—is enjoyed by the union over the states composing it. Does this advantage consist in the substitution of representatives, whose enlightened views and virtuous sentiments render them superior to local prejudices, and to schemes of injustice? It will not be denied that the representation of the union will be most likely to possess these requisite endowments. Does it consist in the greater security afforded by a greater variety of parties, against the event of any one party being able to outnumber and oppress the rest? In an equal degree does the increased variety of parties, comprised within the union, increase the security? Does it, in fine, consist in the greater obstacles opposed to the concert and accomplishment of the secret wishes of an unjust and interested majority? Here, again, the extent of the union gives it the most palpable advantage.

The influence of factious leaders may kindle a flame within their particular states, but will be unable to spread a general conflagration through the other states; a religious sect may degenerate into a political faction in a part of the confederacy; but the variety of sects dispersed over the entire face of it, must secure the national councils against any danger from that source: a rage for paper money, for an abolition of debts, for an equal division of property, or for any other improper or wicked project, will be less apt to pervade the whole body of the union than a particular member of it; in the same proportion as such a malady is more likely to taint a particular county or district, than an entire state.

In the extent and proper structure of the union, therefore, we behold a republican remedy for the diseases most incident to republican government. And according to the degree of pleasure and pride we feel in being republicans, ought to be our zeal in cherishing the spirit, and supporting the character of federalists.

APPENDIX 6

THE FEDERALIST, NO. 51, JAMES MADISON

To what expedient, then, shall we finally resort, for maintaining in practice the necessary partition of power among the several departments as laid down in the Constitution? The only answer that can be given is that as all these exterior provisions are found to be inadequate the defect must be supplied, by so contriving the interior structure of the government as that its several constituent parts may, by their mutual relations, be the means of keeping each other in their proper places. Without presuming to undertake a full development of this important idea I will hazard a few general observations which may perhaps place it in a clearer light, and enable us to form a more correct judgment of the principles and structure of the government planned by the convention.

In order to lay a due foundation for that separate and distinct exercise of the different powers of government, which to a certain extent is admitted on all hands to be essential to the preservation of liberty, it is evident that each department should have a will of its own; and consequently should be so constituted that the members of each should have as little agency as possible in the appointment of the members of the others. Were this principle rigorously adhered to, it would require that all the appointments for the supreme executive, legislative, and judiciary magistracies should be drawn from the same fountain of authority, the people, through channels having no communication whatever with one another. Perhaps such a plan of constructing the several departments would be less difficult in practice than it may in contemplation appear. Some difficulties, however, and some additional expense would attend the execution of it. Some deviations, therefore, from the principle must be admitted. In the constitution of the judiciary department in particular, it might be inexpedient to insist rigorously on the principle: first, because peculiar qualifications being essential in the members, the primary consideration ought to be to select that mode of choice which best secures these qualifications; second, because the permanent tenure by which the appointments are held in that department must soon destroy all sense of dependence on the authority conferring them.

It is equally evident that the members of each department should be as little dependent as possible on those of the others for the emoluments annexed to their offices. Were the executive magistrate, or the judges, not independent of the legislature in this particular, their independence in every other would be merely nominal.

But the great security against a gradual concentration of the several powers in the same department consists in giving to those who administer each department the necessary constitutional means and personal motives to resist encroachments of the others. The provision for defense must in this, as in all other cases, be made commensurate to the danger of attack. Ambition must be made to counteract ambition. The interest of the man must be connected with the constitutional rights of the place. It may be a reflection on human nature that such devices should be necessary to control the abuses of government. But what is government itself but the greatest of all reflections on human nature? If men were angels, no government would be necessary. If angels were to govern men, neither external nor internal controls on government would be necessary. In framing a government which is to be administered by men over men, the great difficulty lies in this: you must first enable the government to control the governed; and in the next place oblige it to control itself. A dependence on the people is, no doubt, the primary control on the government; but experience has taught mankind the necessity of auxiliary precautions.

This policy of supplying, by opposite and rival interests, the defect of better motives, might be traced through the whole system of human affairs, private as well as public. We see it particularly displayed in all the subordinate distributions of power, where the constant aim is to divide and arrange the several offices in such a manner as that each may be a check on the other—that the private interest of every individual may be a sentinel over the public rights. These inventions of prudence cannot be less requisite in the distribution of the supreme powers of the State.

But it is not possible to give to each department an equal power of self-defense. In republican government, the legislative authority necessarily predominates. The remedy for this inconveniency is to divide the legislature into different branches; and to render them, by modes of election and different principles of action, as little connected with each other as the nature of their common functions and their common dependence on the society will admit. It may even be necessary to guard against dangerous encroachments by still further precautions. As the weight of the legislative authority requires that it should be thus divided, the weakness of the executive may require, on the other hand, that it should be fortified. An absolute negative on the legislature appears, at first view, to be the natural defense with which the executive magistrate should be armed. But perhaps it would be neither altogether safe nor alone sufficient. On ordinary occasions it might not be exerted with the requisite firmness, and on extraordinary occasions it might be perfidiously abused. May not this defect of an absolute negative be supplied by some qualified connection between this weaker department and the weaker branch of the stronger department, by which the latter may be led to support the constitutional rights of the former, without being too much detached from the rights of its own department?

If the principles on which these observations are founded be just, as I persuade myself they are, and they be applied as a criterion to the several State constitutions, and to the federal Constitution, it will be found that if the latter does not perfectly correspond with them, the former are infinitely less able to bear such a test.

There are, moreover, two considerations particularly applicable to the federal system of America, which place that system in a very interesting point of view.

First. In a single republic, all the power surrendered by the people is submitted to the administration of a single government; and the usurpations are guarded against by a division of the government into distinct and separate departments. In the compound republic of America, the power surrendered by the people is first divided between two distinct governments, and then the portion allotted to each subdivided among distinct and separate departments. Hence a double security arises to the rights of the people. The different governments will control each other, at the same time that each will be controlled by itself.

Second. It is of great importance in a republic not only to guard the society against the oppression of its rulers, but to guard one part of the society against the injustice of the other part. Different interests necessarily exist in different classes of citizens. If a majority be united by a common interest, the rights of the minority will be insecure. There are but two methods of providing against this evil: the one by creating a will in the community independent of the majority—that is, of the society itself; the other, by comprehending in the society so many separate descriptions of citizens as will render an unjust combination of a majority of the whole very improbable, if not impracticable. The first method prevails in all governments possessing an hereditary or self-appointed authority. This, at best, is but a precarious security; because a power independent of the society may as well espouse the unjust views of the major as the rightful interests of the minor party, and may possibly be turned against both parties. The second method will be exemplified in the federal republic of the United States. Whilst all authority in it will be derived from and dependent on the society, the society itself will be broken into so many parts, interests and classes of citizens, that the rights of individuals, or of the minority, will be in little danger from interested combinations of the majority. In a free government the security for civil rights must be the same as that for religious rights. It consists in the one case in the multiplicity of interests, and in the other in the multiplicity of sects. The degree of security in both cases will depend on the number of interests and sects; and this may be presumed to depend on the extent of country and number of people comprehended under the same government. This view of the subject must particularly recommend a proper federal system to all the sincere and considerate friends of republican govern-ment, since it shows that in exact proportion as the territory of the Union may be formed into more circumscribed Confederacies, or States, oppressive combinations of a majority will be facilitated; the best security, under the republican forms, for the rights of every class of citizen, will be diminished; and consequently the stability and independence of some member of the government, the only other security, must be proportionally increased. Justice is the end of government. It is the end of civil society. It ever has been and ever will be pursued until it be obtained, or until liberty be lost in the pursuit. In a society under the forms of which the stronger faction can readily unite and oppress the weaker, anarchy may as truly be said to reign as in a state of nature, where the weaker individual is not secured against the violence of the stronger; and as, in the latter state, even the stronger individuals are prompted, by the uncertainty of their condition, to submit to a government which may protect the weak as well as themselves; so, in the former state, will the more powerful factions or parties be gradually induced, by a like motive, to wish for a government which will protect all parties, the weaker as well as the more powerful. It can be little doubted that if the State of Rhode Island was separated from the Confederacy and left to itself, the insecurity of rights under the popular form of government within such narrow limits would be displayed by such reiterated oppressions of factious majorities that some power altogether independent of the people would soon be called for by the voice of the very factions whose misrule had proved the necessity to it. In the extended republic of the United States, and among the great variety of interests, parties, and sects which it embraces, a coalition of a majority of the whole society could seldom take place on any other principles than those of justice and the general good; whilst there being thus less danger to a minor from the will of a major party, there must be less pretext, also, to provide for the security of the former, by introducing into the government a will not dependent on the latter, or, in other words, a will independent of the society itself. It is no less certain that it is important, notwithstanding the contrary opinions which have been entertained that the larger the society, provided it lie within a practicable sphere, the more duly capable it will be of self-government. And happily for the *republican cause,* the practicable sphere may be carried to a very great extent by a judicious modification and mixture of the *federal principle.*

GLOSSARY

actual groups Interest groups that have already been formed; they have headquarters, an organizational structure, paid employees, membership lists, and the like.

administration Performance of routine tasks associated with a specific policy goal.

administrative discretion The latitude that an agency, or even a single bureaucrat, has in interpreting and applying a law.

affirmative action Programs that attempt to improve the chances of minority applicants for jobs, housing, employment, or education by giving them a "boost" relative to white applicants with similar qualifications.

amicus curiae briefs Legal briefs that enable groups or individuals, including the national government, who are not parties to the litigation but have an interest in it, to attempt to influence the outcome of the case; literally, "friend of the court" briefs.

Antifederalists Strong states' rights advocates who organized in opposition to the ratification of the U.S. Constitution prior to its adoption.

appellate court The court that reviews an appeal of the trial court proceedings, often with a multijudge panel and without a jury; it considers only matters of law.

appellate jurisdiction The authority of a court to hear a case on appeal after it has been argued in and decided by a lower federal or state court.

appointment power The president's power to name agency officials. Of the current approximately three thousand about seven hundred are in policy-making positions, such as cabinet and subcabinet officials and bureau chiefs.

appropriations bill A separate bill that must be passed by Congress to fund spending measures.

Articles of Confederation The first constitutional framework of the new United States of America. Approved in 1777 by the Second Continental Congress, it was later replaced by the current Constitution.

authoritarian regime An oppressive system of government in which citizens are deprived of their basic freedom to speak, write, associate, and participate in political life without fear of punishment.

bicameral legislature A legislative system consisting of two houses or chambers.

Bill of Rights The first ten amendments to the Constitution, added in 1781.

bipolarity The fundamental division of economic and military power between the poles of Western capitalism and Eastern communism.

black codes Laws restricting the civil rights of African Americans.

block grant A federal grant that provides money to states for general program funding with few or even no strings attached.

Boston Massacre A 1770 incident in which British soldiers fired a volley of shots into a crowd of hecklers who had been throwing snowballs at the redcoats; five colonists were killed.

Boston Tea Party A 1773 act of civil disobedience in which colonists dressed as Native Americans dumped 342 chests of tea into Boston Harbor to protest increased taxes.

boycott Refusal to patronize any organization that practices policies perceived as politically, economically, or ideologically unfair.

briefs Written arguments to the court outlining not only the facts and legal and constitutional issues in a court case, but also answering all anticipated arguments of the opposing side.

bureaucracy A large and complex organizational system in which tasks, roles, and responsibilities are structured to achieve a goal.

bureaucrats People who work in a bureaucracy, not only the obscure, faceless clerks normally disparaged by critics of government but also "street-level bureaucrats" such as police officers, social workers, and schoolteachers.

cabinet Group of presidential advisers including secretaries of the major bureaucracy departments and any other officials the president designates.

cabinet departments Major administrative units whose heads are presidential advisers appointed by the president and confirmed by the Senate. They are responsible for conducting a broad range of government operations.

capital gains tax Tax on unearned income from rents, stocks, and interest.

casework Favors done as a service for constituents by those they have elected to Congress.

categorical grant The most common type of federal grant, given for specific purposes, usually with strict rules attached.

caucus Meeting of party adherents who gather to discuss, to deliberate, and finally to give their support to a candidate for president. They then select delegates who will represent their choices at higher-level party meetings; eventually, their votes are reflected at the national convention itself. Also means a conference of party members in Congress.

checks and balances Systems that ensure that every power in government has an equal and opposite power in a separate branch to restrain that force.

chief of staff The president's top aide.

civil cases Noncriminal cases in which courts resolve disputes among individuals and parties to the case over finances, property, or personal well-being.

civil disobedience Breaking the law in a nonviolent fashion and being willing to suffer the consequences, even to the point of going to jail, in order to publicly demonstrate that the law is unjust.

civil liberties The individual freedoms and rights guaranteed to every citizen in the Bill of Rights and the due process clause of the Fourteenth Amendment, including freedom of speech and religion.

civil rights The constitutionally guaranteed rights that the government may not arbitrarily remove. Among these rights are the right to vote and equal protection under the law.

civil service A system of hiring and promoting employees based on professional merit, not party loyalty.

class action suit A single civil case in which the plaintiff represents the whole class of individuals similarly situated, and the court's results apply to this entire class.

clear and present danger test A free speech test allowing states to regulate only speech that has an immediate connection to an action the states are permitted to regulate.

closed primary A system of conducting primary elections in which only citizens registered as members of a particular political party may participate in that party's primary.

cloture A procedure through which a vote of sixty senators can limit debate and stop a filibuster.

coattails effect "Riding the president's coattails into office" occurs in an election when voters also elect representatives or senators belonging to a successful presidential candidate's party.

Cold War The bipolar power struggle between the United States and the Soviet Union that began in the 1950s and ended in the 1990s.

collective action The political action of individuals who unite to influence policy.

Committees of Correspondence Formed in Boston in 1772, the first institutionalized mechanism for communication within and between the colonies and foreign countries.

Common Sense Thomas Paine's pamphlet of January 1776, which helped crystallize the idea of revolution for the colonists.

compact A type of agreement that legally binds two or more parties to enforceable rules.

concurrent powers Powers shared by both national and state levels of government.

concurring opinion A written opinion of a justice who agrees with the majority decision of the Court but differs on the reasoning.

conditions of aid National requirement that must be observed to receive benefits.

confederation A league of sovereign states that delegates powers on selected issues to a central government.

conference committees Committees that reconcile differences between versions of a bill passed by the House and the Senate.

congressional agenda A list of bills to be considered by Congress.

Congressional Budget Office (CBO) A government office created by Congress in 1974 to analyze budgetary figures and make recommendations to Congress and the president.

constitutional courts Courts mentioned in Article III of the Constitution whose judges have life tenure.

constructionist A view of presidential power espoused by William Howard Taft, who believed that the president could exercise no power unless it could be traced to or implied from an express grant in either the Constitution or an act of Congress.

containment A term coined in 1946 by George Kennan, who believed that Soviet aggression must be "contained by the adroit and vigilant application of counterforce by the United States."

contingency election An election held in the House if no candidate receives the required majority in the electoral college.

continuing resolution A bill passed by Congress and signed by the president that enables the federal government to keep operating under the previous year's appropriations.

cooperative federalism A cooperative system in which solutions for various state and local problems are directed and sometimes funded by both the national and state governments. The administration of programs is characterized by shared power and shared responsibility.

council of revision A combined body of judges and members of the executive branch having a limited veto over national legislation and an absolute veto over state legislation.

creative federalism An initiative that expanded the concept of the partnership between the national government and the states under President Lyndon Johnson in the 1960s.

criminal cases Cases in which decisions are made regarding whether or not to punish individuals accused of violating the state or federal criminal code.

culture theory A theory that individual preferences "emerge from social interaction in defending or opposing different ways of life."

de facto equality Equality of results, which measures real-world obstacles to equal treatment. For example: Do people actually live where they want? Do they work under similar conditions?

de jure equality Equality before the law. It disallows legally mandated obstacles to equal treatment, such as laws that prevent people from voting, living where they want to, or taking advantage of all the rights guaranteed to individuals by the laws of the federal, state, and local governments.

Declaration of Independence The formal proclamation declaring independence for the thirteen colonies of England in North America, approved and signed on July 4, 1776.

deficit A shortfall between the monies a government takes in and spends.

delegated powers Powers expressly granted or enumerated in the Constitution and limited in nature.

delegates Congress members who feel bound to follow the wishes of a majority of their constituents; they make frequent efforts to learn the opinions of voters in their state or district.

democracy A system of government in which the people rule, either directly or through elected representatives.

desegregation The elimination of laws and practices that mandate racial separation.

detente An attempt to relax tensions between the United States and the Soviet Union through limited cooperation.

deviating election Election in which the minority party captures the White House because of short-term intervening forces, and thus a deviation from the expectation that power will remain in the hands of the dominant party.

devolution Reducing the size and authority of the federal government by returning programs to the states.

devolution revolution A trend initiated in the Reagan administration and accelerated by then-Speaker of the House Newt Gingrich to send programs and power back to the states with less national government involvement.

direct democracy A type of government in which people govern themselves, vote on policies and laws, and live by majority rule.

discretionary spending The spending Congress actually controls; 33 percent of all spending.

dissenting opinion A written opinion of a justice who disagrees with the holding of the Court.

docket The Supreme Court's agenda of cases to consider.

double jeopardy Trying a defendant twice for the same crime; banned by the Fifth Amendment.

double standard The varying level of intensity by which the Supreme Court considers cases by which it protects civil liberties claims while also deferring to the legislation in cases with economic claims.

dual federalism A system in which each level of power remains supreme in its own jurisdiction, thus keeping the states separate and distinct from the national government.

economic policy Policy aimed at producing a vibrant, healthy, and growing economy.

economic sanctions The use of embargoes and boycotts rather than military force to compel compliance.

elections The central institution of democratic representative governments in which the authority of the government derives from the consent of the governed. The principal mechanism for translating that consent into governmental authority is the holding of free and fair elections.

electoral college The group of 538 electors who meet separately in each of their states and the District of Columbia on the first Monday following the second Wednesday in December after a national presidential election. Their majority decision officially elects the president and vice president of the United States.

electoral college system Votes in the national presidential elections are actually indirect votes for a slate of presidential electors pledged to each party's candidate. Each state has one elector for each of its representatives and senators. The winning slate of electors casts their votes in their state's capital after the public election. In the United States, election of the president and vice president is dependent upon receiving a majority (270) of the votes cast in the electoral college.

en banc Proceedings in which all of the appeals judges in a particular circuit serve as a tribunal.

enrolled act (or resolution) The final version of a bill, approved by both chambers of Congress.

entitlements Government-sponsored benefits and cash payments to those who meet eligibility requirements.

equal time rule A requirement that radio and television stations allow equal time to all candidates for office.

equality A state in which all participants have equal access to the decision-making process, equal opportunity to influence the decisions made, and equal responsibility for those decisions.

equality of opportunity The idea that "people should have equal rights and opportunities to develop their talents," that all people should begin at the same starting point in a race.

equality of result The idea that all forms of inequality, including economic disparities, should be completely eradicated; this may mean giving certain people a starting advantage so that everyone has fair chances to succeed.

excise taxes Charges on the sale or manufacture of products such as cigarettes, alcohol, and gasoline.

exclusionary rule Rule whereby evidence gathered by illegal means, and any other evidence gathered as a result, cannot be used in later trials.

executive agreement A government-to-government agreement with essentially the same legal force as a treaty. However, it may be concluded entirely without Senate knowledge and/or approval.

executive branch The branch of the government that executes laws.

Executive Office of the President (EOP) Created in 1939, this office contains all staff units that support the president in administrative duties.

executive privilege The president's implied or inherent power to withhold information on the ground that to release such information would affect either national security or the president's ability to discharge official duties.

exit polls Polls that question voters as they leave the voting booth to predict the outcome of an election.

factions According to James Madison in *The Federalist,* no. 10: "A number of citizens, whether amounting to a majority or a minority of the whole, who are united and actuated by some common impulse or passion or . . . interests."

fairness doctrine A policy, now abandoned, that radio and television stations provide time to all sides in programs of public interest.

faithless elector Member of the electoral college who casts his or her vote for someone other than the state's popular vote winner.

Federal Communications Commission (FCC) A government commission formed to allocate radio and television frequencies and regulate broadcasting procedures.

federal mandates A direct order from Congress that the states must fulfill.

federal matching funds System under which presidential candidates who raise a certain amount of money in the required way may apply for and receive matching federal funds.

federalism The relationship between the centralized national government and the individual state governments.

Federalists Those in favor of the Constitution, many of whom were nationalists at the Convention.

fighting words Certain expressions so volatile that they are deemed to incite injury and are therefore not protected under the First Amendment.

filibuster A technique in which a senator speaks against a bill or talks about nothing specific just to "hold the floor" and prevent the Senate from moving forward with a vote. He or she may yield to other like-minded senators, so that the marathon debate can continue for hours or even days.

First Continental Congress The meeting of fifty-six elected members (from provincial congresses or irregular conventions) held in Philadelphia's Carpenter's Hall in 1774. It resulted in a resolution to oppose acts of the British Parliament and a plan of association for the colonies.

foreign aid Small portion of the federal budget that goes to nonmilitary aid abroad, initially to mitigate against Soviet expansion.

foreign policy Policy adopted and actions taken by the U.S. government on behalf of U.S. national interests abroad. The president is this country's chief foreign policy maker.

formal agenda The policies actually scheduled for debate and potential adoption by Congress, the president, the Supreme Court, or executive departments and agencies.

formal rules In a bureaucracy, clearly defined procedures governing the execution of all tasks within the jurisdiction of a given agency.

formula grant A grant based on a prescribed legislative formula to determine how money will be distributed to eligible governmental units (states or major cities).

formula/project grant A grant in which competitive grants are awarded but also restricted by use of a formula.

franking privilege The free mailing of newsletters and political brochures to constituents by members of Congress.

free press Media characterized by the open reporting of information without government censorship.

free riders Members who invest no money or time in an interest group but still share in the collective benefits of group action.

freedom A value that suggests that no individual should be within the power or under the control of another.

freedom riders Civil rights activists who traveled throughout the American South on buses to test compliance with the Supreme Court's mandate to integrate bus terminals and public facilities accommodating interstate travelers.

frontloading The process by which most party primaries and caucuses are held early in the nomination schedule so that the majority of the delegate support is locked up early.

gender gap A difference in the political opinions of men and women.

general revenue sharing (GRS) A system of the New Federalism program in which money was given to the states with no restrictions on how it could be spent.

generational effect Socialization patterns in which a generation of adults who grew up during a certain decade or period appears to have its own outlook, differentiating itself from the previous age.

gerrymander Any attempt during state redistricting of congressional voting boundaries to create a safe seat for one party.

Gibbons v. Ogden The 1824 decision by Chief Justice John Marshall that gave Congress the power, under the "interstate and commerce" clause, to regulate anything that "affects" interstate commerce.

globalism View in which the U.S. sphere of influence has expanded beyond the western hemisphere to include virtually every corner of the globe where U.S. interests might be affected.

going public Actions presidents take to promote themselves and their policies to the American people.

good-character test A requirement that voting applicants wishing to vote produce two or more registered voters to vouch for their integrity.

government corporation A semi-independent government agency that administers a business enterprise and takes the form of a business corporation.

grant-in-aid Money paid to states and localities to induce them to implement policies in accordance with federally mandated guidelines.

grassroots activity The rallying of group members, as well as the public, behind a lobby's cause.

Great Compromise (also called the Connecticut Compromise) A plan presented at the Constitutional Convention that upheld the large-state position for the House, its membership based on proportional representation, balanced by the small-state posture of equal representation in the Senate, where each state would have two votes.

gridlock A condition in which major government initiatives are impossible because a closely balanced partisan division in the government structure, accompanied by an unwillingness to work together toward compromise, produces a stalemate.

group maintenance Activities by an interest group designed to affect policy. Includes enrolling new members and providing benefits for them.

Gulf of Tonkin Resolution Resolution passed by Congress that granted President Lyndon Johnson authority to pursue the war in Vietnam, supposedly based on a naval attack by North Vietnamese ships.

Hatch Act Approved by Congress in 1939 and named for its author, Senator Carl Hatch of New Mexico, a list of political dos and don'ts for federal employees; designed to prevent federal civil servants from using their power or position to engage in political activities to influence elections, thereby creating a nonpartisan, nonpolitical, professionalized bureaucracy.

hate speech Speech or symbolic actions intended to inflict emotional distress, to defame, or to intimidate people.

hearings Formal proceedings in which a range of people testify on a bill's pros and cons.

heightened scrutiny test A middle-level standard that would force the state to prove more than just the reasonableness of a law, though not its compelling nature, in order to justify it. For women's rights cases this means proving the important governmental objectives of the law's goals and linking it to the wording of the law.

hierarchy A clear chain of communication and command running from an executive director at the top down through all levels of workers.

hold A request by a senator not to bring a measure up for consideration by the full Senate.

House majority leader The person elected by the majority party caucus to serve as the party's chief strategist and floor spokesperson.

impeachment The process by which government actors can be removed from office for "treason, bribery, or other high crimes and misdemeanors." The House of Representatives votes on the charges and then the trial takes place in the Senate.

implementation The act of providing the organization and expertise required to put into action any policy that has become law; also refers to the actual execution of a policy.

implied powers Powers not specifically stated in the Constitution but inferred from the express powers.

impoundment The president's refusal to spend funds appropriated by Congress.

incorporation The process whereby the Supreme Court has found that Bill of Rights protections apply to the states.

incumbents Individuals who currently hold public office.

independent agencies Agencies established to regulate a sector of the nation's economy in the public interest.

independent expenditures Funds dispersed, as allowed by a loophole in campaign finance law, by a group or person not coordinated by a candidate, in the name of a cause.

independent judiciary A system in which judges are insulated from the political bodies and public opinion in order to preserve their ability to act as the final arbiter over those groups in interpreting the Constitution and the laws.

independent regulatory commissions Agencies established to regulate a sector of the nation's economy in the public interest.

indirect democracy A type of government in which voters designate a relatively small number of people to represent their interests; those people, or representatives, then meet in a legislative body and make decisions on behalf of the entire citizenry.

inherent powers Powers that do not appear in the Constitution but are assumed because of the nature of government. Also refers to a theory that the Constitution grants authority to the executive, through the injunction in Article II, Section 3, that the president "take care that the Laws be faithfully executed."

initiative A proposal submitted by the public and voted upon during elections.

integration Government efforts to balance the racial composition in schools and public places.

intensity In public opinion, a measure of the depth of feeling associated with a given opinion.

interest groups Formal organizations of people who share a common outlook or social circumstance and who band together in the hope of influencing government policy.

Intolerable Acts A series of punitive measures passed by the British Parliament in the spring of 1774 as a response to the Boston Tea Party.

investigative journalism The uncovering of corruption, scandal, conspiracy, and abuses of power in government and business; differs from standard press coverage in the depth of the coverage sought, the time spent researching the subject, and the shocking findings that often result from such reporting.

iron triangles Informal three-way relationships that develop among key legislative committees, the bureaucracy, and interest groups with a vested interest in the policies created by those committees and agencies.

isolationism A pattern in which the United States fosters economic relations abroad without committing to strategic alliances that might draw the country into a war.

issue advertisements Advertisements in a political campaign funded by an interest group advocating a position on an issue but technically not supporting a specific candidate.

issue advocacy The process of campaigning to persuade the public to take a position on an issue.

issue networks Networks composed of political actors in a particular policy area, usually including bureaucrats, congressional staffers, interest groups, think-tank researchers or academic experts, and media participants, all of whom interact regularly on an issue.

Jim Crow laws Laws passed by southern states that separated the races in public places such as railroads, streetcars, schools, and cemeteries.

joint committees Groups of members from both chambers who study broad areas that are of interest to Congress as a whole.

judicial activism An approach in which justices create new policy and decide issues, to the point, some critics charge, of writing their personal values into law.

judicial restraint An approach in which justices see themselves as appointed rather than elected officials, who should defer to the legislature and uphold a law or political action if at all possible.

judicial review The power of the Supreme Court established in *Marbury v. Madison* to overturn acts of the president, Congress, and the states if those acts violate the Constitution. This power makes the Supreme Court the final interpreter of the Constitution.

judiciary The branch of government that interprets laws.

"King Caucus" The process of selecting candidates for president in the early nineteenth century in which the members of each party's delegation in Congress did the nominating.

latency In public opinion, unspoken feelings, suggesting the potential for an attitude or behavior, but only when the right circumstances occur.

least restrictive means test A free-exercise-of-religion test in which the state was asked to find another way, perhaps through exemptions, to enforce its regulations while protecting all other religions.

legislative branch The branch of government that makes laws.

legislative courts Courts designed to provide technical expertise on specific subjects based on Article I of the Constitution.

legislative oversight The legislature's review and evaluation of executive branch activities to ensure that programs are administered and implemented in a manner consistent with legislative intent.

legislative veto A legislative action that allows the president or executive agencies to implement a law subject to the later approval or disapproval of one or both houses of Congress.

Lemon **test** A test from the 1971 Supreme Court case *Lemon v. Kurtzman* for determining the permissible level of state aid for church agencies by measuring its purpose on three counts: is it nonreligious in nature? does it either advance or inhibit religion? and/or does it produce excessive entanglement of church and state?

libel Published material that damages a person's reputation or good name in an untruthful and malicious way. Libelous material is not protected by the First Amendment.

limited government A type of government in which the powers of the government are clearly defined and bounded, so that governmental authority cannot intrude in the lives of private citizens.

line item veto The power given to the president to veto a specific provision of a bill involving taxing and spending. Previously the president had to veto an entire bill. Declared unconstitutional by the Supreme Court in 1998.

literacy test A requirement that voting applicants had to demonstrate an understanding of national and state constitutions. Primarily used to prevent African Americans from voting in the South.

lobbying The formal, organized attempt to influence legislation, usually through direct contact with legislators or their staff.

lobbyists People paid to pressure members of Congress to further the aims of an interest group.

local party organization The initial point of entry for those seeking involvement in politics as volunteers, organizers, or candidates.

logrolling A temporary political alliance between two policy actors who agree to support each other's policy goals.

machine politics An organizational style of local politics in which party bosses traded jobs, money, and favors for votes and campaign support.

maintaining election Election in which the majority party of the day wins both Congress and the White House, maintaining its control of government.

majority-minority district A congressional district drawn to include enough members of a minority group to greatly improve the chance of electing a minority candidate.

majority opinion A decision of the Supreme Court that represents the agreed-upon compromise judgment of all the justices in the majority.

majority rule A decision-making process in which, when more than half of the voters agree on an issue, the entire group accepts the decision, even those in the minority who voted against it.

mandatory spending Spending that must be allocated by law rather than by appropriations, for entitlements such as Social Security, Medicare, and Medicaid; 67 percent of the budget.

Marbury v. Madison The 1803 case in which Chief Justice John Marshall established the power of judicial review.

margin of error The measure of possible error in a survey, which means that the number for the entire population of voters will fall within a range of plus or minus several points of the number obtained from the small but representative sample of voters.

markup session A subcommittee meeting to revise a bill.

mass media The various media—newspapers, magazines, radio, television, and the Internet—through which information is transferred from its sources to large numbers of people.

McCulloch v. Maryland The 1819 decision by Chief Justice John Marshall that expanded the interpretation of the "necessary and proper" clause to give Congress broad powers to pass legislation and reaffirmed the national government's power over the states under the supremacy clause.

McGovern-Fraser Commission Democratic party commission that after the 1968 national convention opened up meetings and votes to a broad variety of party activists, made primaries rather than caucuses the common means of choosing convention delegates, weakened the power of party leaders, and set up rules to ensure that a wide range of party members could participate fully in all party operations.

means testing The changing of eligibility for entitlement benefits from everyone receiving benefits to only those with earnings and savings below a predetermined level, in an attempt to save money.

midterm elections Elections in which Americans elect members of Congress but not presidents; 2002, 2006, and 2010 are midterm election years.

military-industrial complex What President Eisenhower in 1961 called the growing power and influence resulting from the "conjunction of an immense military establishment and a large arms industry."

minor or third parties Parties in the American system other than the Democrats or Republicans.

minority leader The leader of the minority party in Congress.

minority rights Rights given to those in the minority; based on the idea that tyranny of the majority is a danger to human rights.

Miranda **warning** A warning that must be recited by police officers to a suspect before questioning: "You have the right to remain silent; anything you say can and will be used against you. You have the right to an attorney. If you cannot afford an attorney, one will be provided for you. Do you understand these rights and are you willing to speak with us?" Established in *Miranda v. Arizona*, 1966.

Monroe Doctrine A doctrine enunciated by President James Monroe in 1823 that proclaimed North and South America to be in the United States' sphere of influence, hence out of bounds for European aspirations. It reinforced growing isolationism by promising not to interfere in the internal concerns of European states.

muckraking A word used to describe a style of investigative reporting that uncovered many scandals and abuses.

multiparty system A political system in which five to ten or more parties regularly compete in elections, win seats, and have some chance of gaining power. Promoted by systems with proportional representation and characteristic of most democratic nations.

national debt The cumulative total of all budget deficits.

national party convention The national meeting of the party every four years to choose the ticket for the presidential election and write the party platform.

national party organization Party organization at the national level whose primary tasks include fund raising, distribution of information, and recruitment.

necessary and proper clause A clause in Article I, Section 8, Clause 18, of the Constitution stating that Congress can "make all Laws which shall be necessary and proper for carrying into Execution the foregoing Powers."

netizens Groups of people joined in a cyber-society for political purposes.

New Deal coalition Brought together by Franklin Roosevelt in 1932, a broad electorate made up of the urban working class, most members of the newer ethnic groups, the bulk of American Catholics and Jews, the poor, the South, and liberal intellectuals.

"New Democrat" A conservative Democrat who supports states' rights and a less activist national government.

New Federalism A program under President Nixon that decentralized power as a response to New Deal centralization.

New Jersey Plan A plan presented to the Constitutional Convention of 1787 designed to create a unicameral legislature with equal representation for all states. Its goal was to protect the interests of the smaller, less populous states.

no incorporation An approach in which the states would be bound only by the dictates of due process contained in the Fourteenth Amendment.

nomination A candidate's "sponsorship" by a political party.

North Atlantic Treaty Organization (NATO) Charter signed by the United States, Canada, Turkey, and eleven European nations in 1949 agreeing that an armed attack against one or more of them in Europe or North America would be interpreted as an attack against all.

nullification A nineteenth-century theory that upholds that states faced with unacceptable national legislation can declare such laws null and void and refuse to observe them.

Office of Management and Budget (OMB) The unit in the Executive Office of the President whose main responsibilities are to prepare and administer the president's annual budget. A president and the OMB can shape policy through the budget process; the process determines which departments and agencies grow, are cut, or remain the same as the year before.

omnibus legislation A large bill that combines a number of smaller pieces of legislation.

open primary A system of conducting primary elections in which citizens vote in whichever party's primary they choose.

opinion A written version of the decision of a court.

order A condition in which the structures of a given society and the relationships thereby defined among individuals and classes comprising it are maintained and preserved by the rule of law and police power of the state.

original jurisdiction The authority of a court to be the first to hear a case.

override The two-thirds vote of both houses of Congress required to pass a law over the veto of the president.

oversight Congressional function that involves monitoring the effectiveness of laws by examining the workings of the executive branch.

participation Mass political involvement through voting, campaign work, political protests, civil disobedience, among many others.

party caucus A conference of party members in Congress.

party identification A psychological orientation, or long-term propensity to think positively of and vote regularly for, a particular political party.

party platform The statement of principles and policies; the goals that a party pledges to carry out if voters give it control of the government.

Peace Corps Organization formed by President Kennedy to help with Third World development by having American volunteers live and work in needy communities.

peonage A system in which employers advance wages and then require workers to remain on their jobs, in effect enslaving them, until the debt is satisfied.

plea bargains Agreements in which the state presses for either a reduced set of charges or a reduced sentence in return for a guilty plea.

pluralism A system that occurs when those in the minority form groups based on particular interests and seek to influence policy by allying with other groups.

plurality opinion Less than a majority vote on an opinion of the Court; does not have the binding legal force of a majority opinion.

pocket veto Presidential refusal to sign or veto a bill that Congress passes in the last ten days of its session; by not being signed, it automatically dies when Congress adjourns.

police powers The powers to regulate health, morals, public safety, and welfare, which are reserved to the states.

policy elites Members of Congress, the president, Supreme Court justices, cabinet officers, heads of key agencies and departments, leading editorial writers, and influential columnists and commentators.

policy entrepreneurs Leaders who invest in, and who create the conditions for, a potential group to become an actual interest group. Ralph Nader stands as a classic example of a policy entrepreneur.

policy evaluation The required period of monitoring and analysis of federal policies following their implementation.

policy networks Networks characterized by a wide-ranging discussion of options as issues are resolved, conveying a more inclusive and less conspiratorial image of the policy process than iron triangles do.

political action committees (PACs) Committees formed as the fund-raising and financial distribution arm of specific interest groups.

political culture A political perspective based on core values, political ideology, culture, and lifestyle.

political ideology A coherent way of viewing politics and government; ideological perspectives include beliefs about the military, the role of government, the proper relation between government and the economy, the value of social welfare programs, and the relative importance for society of liberty and order.

political parties Organizations that exist to allow like-minded members of the population to group together and magnify their individual voices into a focus promoting individual candidates and government action.

political socialization The process by which we learn about the world of politics and develop our political beliefs.

political violence Violent action motivated primarily by political aims and intended to have a political impact.

politics Greek *politika;* the art of science of government; the art or science concerned with guiding or influencing government; the art or science concerned with winning and holding control over a governmental policy.

poll tax A fee that had to be paid before one could vote; used to prevent African Americans from voting; now unconstitutional.

pork-barrel legislation Policies and programs designed to create special benefits for a member's district, such as bridges, highways, dams, and military installations, all of which translate into jobs and money for the local economy and improve reelection chances for the incumbent.

potential groups Interest groups that could form under the right circumstances; as yet, they have no substantive form and may never have one, but they cannot be discounted by political participants.

poverty level The federally determined income below which a family of four is considered poor.

precedents Previously decided court cases on an issue similar to the one being considered.

president of the Senate The vice president of the United States.

president pro tempore The majority party member with the longest continuous service in the Senate; serves as the chief presiding officer in the absence of the vice president.

primary election A pre-election that allows all members of a party, not just its leadership, to select the party's candidate for the general election in the fall.

primary system The system of nominating candidates in which voters in the state make the choice by casting ballots.

prior restraint An action in which the government seeks to ban the publication of controversial material by the press before it is published; censorship.

privatization The turning over of public responsibilities to privately owned and operated enterprises for regulation and for providing goods and services.

probable cause A reasonable belief that a crime has been, is being, or is about to be committed. Searches also require a belief that evidence of that crime may be located in a particular place. Police must establish this to a judge to secure a search warrant or retroactively justify a search that has already taken place.

progressive taxes System of taxation in which those who make more money are taxed at a higher rate. An example is the income tax.

project grant A grant not based on a formula, but distributed for specific purposes after a fairly competitive application and approval process.

proportional representation A system of representation popular in Europe whereby the number of seats in the legislature is based on the proportion of the vote received in the election.

proposal The first stage of the constitutional amendment process, in which a change is proposed.

protest Expression of dissatisfaction; may take the form of demonstrations, letters to newspapers or public officials, or simple "opting out" of the system by failing to vote or participate in any other way.

protest march March in which people walk down a main street carrying signs, singing freedom songs, and chanting slogans.

public agenda The set of topics that concern policy elites, the general public, or both.

public interest groups Groups that focus not on the immediate economic livelihood of their members, but on achieving a broad set of goals that represent their members' vision of the collective good. Examples include the National Taxpayers Union, the League of Women Voters, and Common Cause.

public opinion The collective expression of attitudes about the prominent issues and actors of the day.

public policies The decisions, actions, and commitments of government.

quota programs Programs that guarantee a certain percentage of admissions, new hires, or promotions to members of minority groups.

random sample A strategy required for a valid poll whereby every member of the population has an equal chance of appearing in the sample.

ratify An act of approval of proposed constitutional amendments by the states; the second step of the amendment process.

realigning election Election characterized by massive shifts in partisan identification, as in 1932 with the New Deal coalition.

realignment A shift in fundamental party identification and loyalty caused by significant historical events or national crises.

reapportionment A process of redrawing voting district lines from time to time and adjusting the number of representatives allotted each state.

recruitment The process through which parties look for effective, popular candidates to help them win votes and offices.

red tape The excessive number of rules and regulations that government employees must follow.

redistricting The redrawing of boundary lines of voting districts in accordance with census data or sometimes by order of the courts.

referenda Proposed policy measures submitted for direct popular vote.

referendum A proposal submitted by a state legislature to the public for a popular vote, often focusing on whether a state should spend money in a certain way.

regressive taxes System of taxation in which taxes take a higher fraction of the income of lower income taxpayers; examples are taxes on gasoline, cigarettes, and alcohol.

regulation A rule-making administrative body must clarify and interpret legislation, its enforcement, and the adjudication of disputes about it.

regulatory policy Policy that involves the use of police powers by the federal government to supervise the conduct of individuals, businesses, and other governmental agencies.

reorganization Having the power to move programs around within specific agencies.

representative democracy A system of government in which the voters select representatives to make decisions for them.

representative sample A sample that includes all the significant characteristics of the total population.

republic A system of government that allows indirect representation of the popular will.

reserved powers Powers not assigned by the Constitution to the national government but left to the states or to the people, according to the Tenth Amendment.

retrospective voting A particularly powerful form of issue voting in which voters look back over the past term or two to judge how well an incumbent or the "in party" has performed in office.

Revolution of 1800 The first election in world history in which one party (the Federalist party of John Adams) willingly gave up power because of a lost election to another party (the Republican party of Thomas Jefferson) without bloodshed.

rider An amendment to a bill in the Senate totally unrelated to the bill subject but attached to a popular measure in the hopes that it too will pass.

right of rebuttal The right to refute the allegations presented on a radio or television station, free of charge, within a reasonable time.

right to privacy The right to have the government stay out of the personal lives of its citizens.

rule of four A means of determining which cases the Supreme Court will hear; at least four justices must vote to hear a case and grant the petition for a *writ of certiorari* for the case to be put on the Court's docket.

rules The decisions made by the House Rules Committee and voted on by the full House to determine the flow of legislation—when a bill will be discussed, for how long, and if amendments can be offered.

salience In public opinion, the extent to which people see an issue as having a clear impact on their own lives.

sampling bias A bias in a survey whereby a particular set of people in the population at large is more or less likely to appear in the final sample than other sets of people.

schemas Intellectual frameworks for evaluating the world.

Second Continental Congress A meeting convened on May 10, 1775, with all thirteen colonies represented. The Congress met to decide whether or not to sever bonds with England and declare independence.

secular regulation rule Rule denying any constitutional right to exemption on free exercise grounds from laws dealing with nonreligious matters.

select committees (or special committees) Temporary congressional committees that conduct investigations or study specific problems or crises.

selective incorporation An incorporation standard in which some portions of the Bill of Rights, but not all, were made part of the Fourteenth Amendment's due process clause, and thus guaranteed against invasion by the states.

Senate majority leader A senator selected by the majority party whose functions are similar to those of the speaker of the House.

senatorial courtesy A procedure in which a president submits the names of judicial nominees to senators from the same political party who are also from the nominee's home state for their approval prior to formal nomination.

seniority An informal, unwritten rule of Congress that more senior members (those who have served longer than others) are appointed to committees and as chairpersons of committees. This "rule" is being diluted in the House as other systems are developed for committee appointments.

separation of powers State in which the powers of the government are divided among the three branches: executive, legislative, and judicial.

sexism Prejudice against the female gender.

single-member districts Districts in which a seat goes to the candidate with the most votes. In this system, a small party, say, one that wins 10 percent in every district across the nation, would fail to secure a single seat in the legislature.

sit-in A protest technique in which protesters refuse to leave an area.

slander Speech that is untruthful, malicious, or damaging to a person's reputation or good name and thus not protected by the free speech clause of the First Amendment.

social contract theorists A group of European philosophers who reasoned that the most effective way to create the best government was to understand human nature in a state prior to government.

social welfare policy Policy that uses positive incentives (cash assistance, stipends, entitlements, grants, etc.) to promote or encourage basic social and economic fairness.

socialization The process by which people learn to conform to their society's norms and values.

soft money Campaign contributions directed to advancing the interests of a political party or an issue in general, rather than a specific candidate.

solicitor general The third-ranking official in the Justice Department, appointed by the president and charged with representing the U.S. government before the Supreme Court.

sovereignty The independence and self-government of a political entity.

Speaker of the House The only presiding officer of the House mentioned in the Constitution. The leader of the majority party in Congress and third in line for the presidency.

special revenue sharing A system of the New Federalism program in which groups of categorical grants-in-aid in related policy areas, such as crime control or health care, are consolidated into a single block grant.

specialization A principle that, in a bureaucracy, specific tasks should be delegated to individuals whose training and experience give them the expertise to execute them. Also refers to a norm used to push legislation through Congress in which members who lack expertise in a particular policy area defer to policy specialists with more knowledge.

split-ticket ballots Ballots on which people vote for candidates from more than one party.

spoils system A system in which government jobs and contracts are awarded on the basis of party loyalty rather than social or economic status or relevant experience.

stability The degree to which an entity is resistant to sudden change or overthrow.

Stamp Act A British act of 1765 that required that revenue stamps be placed on all printed matter and legal documents, making it felt in every aspect of commercial life in the colonies.

standing committees Permanent congressional committees that determine whether proposed legislation should be sent to the entire chamber for consideration.

stare decisis A doctrine meaning "let the decision stand," or that judges deciding a case should adhere if at all possible to previously decided cases similar to the one under consideration.

state action Action taken by state officials or sanctioned by state law.

state party organizations Party organizations at the state level; they organize elections and provide the electoral college votes needed to win the presidency; they also supervise the various functions vital to state parties, such as fund raising, identifying potential candidates, providing election services, offering advice on reapportionment matters, and developing campaign strategies.

states' rights Rights the U.S. Constitution neither grants to the national government nor forbids to the states.

statutory construction The power of the Supreme Court to interpret or reinterpret a federal or state law.

stewardship An approach to presidential power articulated by Theodore Roosevelt and based on the presidencies of Lincoln and Jackson, who believed that the president had a moral duty to serve popular interests and did not need specific constitutional or legal authorization to take action.

straight-party ticket Ballots on which people vote for only one party.

Strategic Arms Limitation Treaty (SALT) Treaty signed by the United States (under President Nixon) and the Soviet Union to limit various classes of nuclear weapons.

straw poll A nonscientific method of measuring public opinion.

strict scrutiny test Test of laws that discriminate on the basis of a characteristic "immutable (or unchangeable) by birth," such as race or nationality; in such cases, the burden shifts from the plaintiff to the state, forcing the government to show the compelling reasons for the law.

subcommittees The subgroups of congressional committees charged with initially dealing with legislation before the entire committee considers it.

subsequent punishment Laws that would punish someone for an action after it has taken place. For example, laws such as those banning libel and obscenity because they are harmful to reputations or public sensibilities punish writers, editors, and publishers after an item appears in print.

suffrage The right to vote.

Sugar Act A British act of 1764 that levied a three-penny-per-gallon tax on molasses and other goods imported into the colonies.

superdelegates Delegates to the Democratic National Convention not bound to vote for any particular candidate; usually prominent members of the party or elected officials.

supermajority A majority vote required for constitutional amendments; consists of more than a simple majority of 50 percent plus one.

superpower The disproportionate power—economic and military—that distinguished the United States and the Soviet Union from all other countries in the postwar era.

supremacy clause A clause in Article IV of the Constitution holding that in any conflict between federal laws and treaties and state laws, the will of the national government always prevails.

symbolic speech Some actions, such as burning the American flag, that take the place of speech because they communicate a message.

tariffs The imposition of import taxes on foreign goods in an attempt to protect a nation's industry and/or labor.

task force An informal procedure used by Congress to assemble groups of legislators to draft legislation and negotiate strategy for passing a bill.

tax expenditures Deductible expenses that reduce the amount of income subject to taxes; for example, home mortgages, business equipment, or business-related entertainment.

term limits A legislated limit on the amount of time a political figure can serve in office.

test of reasonableness Test in court cases of what reasonable people would agree to be constitutional because the law has a rational basis for its existence.

three-fifths compromise A compromise that stated that the apportionment of representatives by state should be determined "by adding to the whole number of free persons . . . three-fifths of all other persons" (Article I, Section 2), meaning that it would take five slaves to equal three free people when counting the population for representation and taxation purposes.

total incorporation An approach arguing that the protections in the Bill of Rights were so fundamental that all of them should be applied to the states by absorbing them into the due process clause of the Fourteenth Amendment.

town meeting A form of governance dating back to the 1700s in which town business is transacted by the consent of a majority of eligible citizens, all of whom have an equal opportunity to express their views and cast their votes at an annual meeting.

Townshend Revenue Acts A series of taxes imposed by the British Parliament in 1767 on glass, lead, tea, and paper imported into the colonies.

tracking polls Polls used by the media to track the support levels for candidates over time.

treaties Formal international agreements between sovereign states.

triad of powers Three constitutional provisions—the interstate commerce clause, the general welfare clause, and the Tenth Amendment—that help to continually shift the balance of power between the national and state governments.

trial court The point of original entry in the legal system, with a single judge and at times a jury deciding matters of both fact and law in a case.

triggering mechanism A critical development that converts a routine problem into a widely shared, negative public response.

trustees Congress members who feel authorized to use their best judgment in considering legislation.

Two Congresses A term denoting the differing views the public has toward Congress as a whole and their representative individual, noting that the opinions are more positive for the individual representative than for the body as a whole.

unanimous consent agreement The process by which the normal rules of Congress are waived unless a single member disagrees.

unfair discrimination Unequal treatment based on race, ethnicity, gender, and other distinctions.

unicameral legislature A legislative system consisting of one chamber.

U.S. courts of appeals The middle appeals level of judicial review beyond the district courts; in 1999, consisted of 167 judges in 13 courts, 12 of which are geographically based.

U.S. district courts The trial courts serving as the original point of entry for almost all federal cases.

universal suffrage The requirement that everyone must have the right to vote.

veto Presidential power to forbid or prevent an action of Congress.

vice president The second-highest elected official in the United States.

Virginia Plan A plan presented to the Constitutional Convention; favored by the delegates from the bigger states.

voter turnout The percentage of eligible voters who actually show up and vote on election day.

War Powers Resolution A highly controversial measure passed over President Nixon's veto that stipulated that presidential commitments of U.S. military forces cannot extend beyond sixty days without specific congressional authorization.

Warsaw Pact Treaty signed by the Soviet Union and the Eastern bloc in Europe agreeing to mutual defense, in reaction to NATO.

welfare state A social system whereby the government assumes primary responsibility for the welfare of citizens.

whips Congress members charged with counting prospective votes on various issues and making certain that members have the information they need for floor action.

Whistleblower Protection Act This act encourages civil servants to report instances of bureaucratic mismanagement, financial impropriety, corruption, and inefficiency. It also protects civil servants from retaliation, such as being fired, demoted, or relocated.

winner-take-all system A system in which the winner of the primary or electoral college vote receives all of the state's convention or electoral college delegates.

workfare The requirement that recipients of welfare programs such as AFDC work on public works unless they find employment elsewhere.

writ of certiorari A Latin term meaning "to be made more certain"; this writ enables the Court to accept cases for review only if there are "special and important reasons therefore."

writ of habeas corpus A Latin term meaning literally "to produce the body" this is a judicial order enabling jailed prisoners to come into the court, or return to the court after being convicted and sentenced, in order to determine the legality of their detention. By Constitutional rules it can only be suspended in times of crisis by Congress.

writs of assistance A general search warrant issued for British customs officials to search colonists' houses to enforce the taxes on goods that enabled them as well to search every part of a house for evidence of a crime, whether real or perceived.

yellow journalism Brash, colorful, generously illustrated, often lurid and sensationalized organs of half-truth, innuendo, and sometimes outright lies, usually associated with the big-city daily newspapers of Joseph Pulitzer and William Randolph Hearst.

NOTES

CHAPTER 1

1. The case study is based on Rene Sanchez, "Honoring Chavez and Hispanic Clout," *Washington Post*, April 24, 2000, p. A3, http://ufw.org. See also "The Fight in the Fields: Cesar Chavez and the Farmworkers' Struggle." WETA/PBS at http://www.pbs.org/itvs/fightfields/, especially "Cesar Chavez and the UFW."

2. See www.farmworkermovement.org, the Farmworker Movement Documentation Project: Cesar Chavez: The Farmworker Movement 1962–1993: Primary Source Accounts by the Volunteers Who Built the Movement.

3. "Inside America's Largest Majority," *Time*, August 22, 2005, p. 56; Eric Schmitt, "Census Shows Bid Gain for Mexican-American," *New York Times*, May 10, 2001, p. A22; Pauline Jelinek, "Hispanics Are Fastest Growing Minority," AP, June 9, 2005, http://www.census.gov/population/www/socdemo/hispanic.html.

4. Arian Campo Flores and Howard Fineman, "A Latin Power Surge," *Newsweek*, May 30, 2005, http://www.msnbc.msn.com/id/7937184/site/newsweek; Michael Finnegan and Mark Z. Barabak, "Villaraigosa Landslide," *Los Angeles Times*, May 18, 2005; Raphael J. Sonenshein and Susan H. Pinkus, "Latino Incorporation Reaches the Urban Summit: How Antonio Villaraigosa Won the 2005 Los Angeles Mayor's Race," *PS*, October 2005, pp. 713–21.

5. Congressional Record-House, February 21, 1990, p. H392–95.

6. Carlotta Gall, "Afghan Legislators Get a Crash Course in Ways of Democracy," *New York Times*, December 19, 2005, p. A14; "Parliament Convenes in Afghanistan." *The Davis Enterprise*, December 19, 2005, p. A4.

7. Edward Wong, "Turnout in the Iraqi Election Is Reported at 70 Percent," *New York Times*, December 22, 2005, p. A10; Dexter Filkins, "Iraqis, Including Sunnis, Vote In Large Numbers on a Calm Day," *New York Times*, December 16, 2005, p. A1; David Sanger and Steven R. Weisman, "Vote Over, Iraq Faces Task of Forming a Government," *New York Times*, February 1, 2005, p. A1; "A Guide to Iraq's Elections," *Washington Post*, p. A17.

8. See http://www.whitehouse.gov/ for the text of President Bush's speech.

9. *Global Survey 2006: Middle East Progress Amid Global Gains in Freedom*, at http://www.freedomhouse.org/template.cfm?page=70&release=317.

10. Alexis de Tocqueville, *Democracy in America* (first published 1835–40). Available in many editions. See also "The 2500 Anniversary of Democracy: Lessons of Athenian Democracy," *PS* (September 1993): 475–93.

11. From a letter from John Adams to John Taylor of Caroline, 1814, cited in Richard Hofstadter, *The American Political Tradition and the Men Who Made It* (New York: Vintage Books, 1948), p. 13.

12. Sheldon Wolin, "Democracy: Electoral and Athenian," *PS* (September 1993): p. 475–7.

13. Quoted in J. Roland Pennock, *Democratic Political Theory* (Princeton, N.J.: Princeton University Press, 1979), p. 20.

14. Isaiah Berlin, *Two Concepts of Liberty* (Oxford: Clarendon Press, 1958).

15. Sidney Verba and Gary R. Orren, *Equality in America: The View from the Top* (Cambridge, Mass.: Harvard University Press, 1985), p. 5; Robert Dahl, *Democracy and Its Critics* (New Haven, Conn.: Yale University Press, 1989). Friedrich A. Hayek, *The Constitution of Liberty* (Chicago: University of Chicago Press, 1960), pp. 103–17; Carole Pateman, *Participation and Democratic Theory* (Cambridge, Mass.: Cambridge University Press, 1970).

16. E. E. Schattschneider, *Two Hundred Million Americans in Search of a Government* (Hillsdale, Ill.: Dryden Press, 1969), p. 27.

17. Quoted in J. D. Richardson, ed., *Messages and Papers of the Presidents, 1789–1902*, 20 vols. (Washington, D.C., 1917), 1:309–12; Joshua Cohen and Joel Rogers, *On Democracy* (Harmondsworth, Middlesex, U.K.: Penguin, 1983), pp. 48–73.

18. See Adam Michnik, "After the Revolution," *New Republic*, July 2, 1990, p. 28.

CHAPTER 2

1. Carl Hulse, "Bipartisan Group in Senate Averts Judge Showdown," *New York Times*, May 24, 2005; Sheryl Gay Stolberg, "Efforts of 2 Respected Elders Bring Senate Back from Brink," *New York Times*, May 24, 2005; David Ignatius, "A New Beginning?" *Washington Post*, May 25, 2005.

2. See Gordon S. Wood, "The Origins of the Constitution," *This Constitution* 15 (Summer 1987): 4; Gordon S. Wood, "The Intellectual Origins of the American Constitution," *National Forum* 4 (Fall 1984): 5–8.

3. See George Brown Tindall, *America: A Narrative History* (New York: Norton, 1988), pp. 58–62; Alfred H. Kelly and Winfred A. Harbison, *The American Constitution: Its Origin and Development* (New York: Norton, 1976), pp. 7–16.

4. Quoted in Tindall, *America*, p. 168; Ronald W. Clark, *Benjamin Franklin: A Biography* (New York: Random House, 1983), pp. 107–8.

5. Quoted in Kelly and Harbison, *American Constitution*, p. 69; Tindall, *America*, pp. 194–95. See also Philip B. Kurland and Ralph Lerner, *The Founders Constitution* (Chicago: University of Chicago Press, 1987).

6. Brinkley, *Unfinished Nation*, p. 108.

7. James MacGregor Burns, *The Vineyard of Liberty* (New York: Vintage Books, 1983), p. 83.

8. Quoted in Tindall, *America*, pp. 206–7.

9. Ibid., pp. 207–8.

10. Brinkley, *Unfinished Nation*, p. 133.

11. Diane Ravitch, *The Democracy Reader* (New York: HarperCollins, 1972), pp. 103–104.

12. James Madison, *Notes of the Debates in the Federal Convention of 1787*, James Madison speaking, July 17, 1787, found at http: www.constitution.org/dfc/dfc-0717.htm.

13. Christopher Collier and James Lincoln Collier, *Decision in Philadelphia* (New York: Random House, 1986), p. 11; Robert A. Feer, *Shay's Rebellion* (New York: Garland, 1988), pp. 504–29; and David Szatmary, *Shay's Rebellion* (Amherst: University of Massachuestts Press, 1980), pp. 120–34.

14. For more on the motivations of the framers, see Richard B. Bernstein, with Kym S. Rice, Are We to Be a Nation? *The Making of the Constitution* (Cambridge, Mass.: Harvard University Press, 1987), passim.

15. Quoted in Bowen, *Miracle at Philadelphia*, p. 12.

16. The number of slaves at the time is taken from the notes of Convention delegate Charles Cotesworth Pinckney, July 10, 1787, found in Supplement to *Max Farrand's "The Records of the Federal Convention of 1787,"* ed. James H. Hutson (New Haven, Conn.: Yale University Press, 1987), p. 160.

17. Christopher Collier and James Lincoln Collier, *Decision in Philadelphia: The Constitutional Convention of 1787* (New York: Random House, 1986), p. 16.

18. Ibid., p. 94.

19. For more on this possible motivation, see John E. O'Connor, *William Paterson, Lawyer and Statesman, 1745–1806* (New Brunswick, N.J.: Rutgers University Press, 1979).

20. Quoted in Supplement to Farrand's "Records," Hutson, ed., p. 305.

21. Robert A. Goldwin, "Why Blacks, Women and Jews Are Not Mentioned in the Constitution," *Commentary*, May 1987, p. 29.

22. Bowen, Miracle at Philadelphia, pp. 55–56; see also Collier and Collier, *Decision in Philadelphia*, chaps. 18, 19.

23. Quoted in Bowen, *Miracle at Philadelphia*, p. 263.

24. George Washington, September 17, 1787, in Supplement to Farrand's "Records," ed. Hutson, p. 276.

25. Collier and Collier, *Decision in Philadelphia*, pp. 255–56.

26. Alexander Hamilton, James Madison, and John Jay, *The Federalist Papers* (New York: New American Library, 1961), no. 51, p. 322.

27. David Stout, "Appeals Court Backs Cheney," *New York Times*, May 11, 2005, p. 1.

28. *Youngstown Sheet and Tube* v. *Sawyer*, 343 U.S. 579, p. 635 (1952).

29. Richard E. Neustadt, *Presidential Power: The Politics of Leadership from FDR to Carter* (New York: Wiley, 1980), p. 26.

30. "Relief of the Parents of Theresa Marie Schiavo," March 20, 2005, found at www.findlaw.com/hdocs/docs/schiavo/bill31905.html last accessed on June 17, 2005.

31. Anna Badkhen, "In Massachusetts, Gay Weddings are Now Routine," *San Francisco Chronicle*, May 17, 2005. Hawaii later abandoned this law in favor of a domestic partnership law providing same-sex couples with lesser rights.

32. Hamilton, Madison, and Jay, *Federalist Papers*, no. 10, p. 78.

33. Quoted in Charles L. Mee Jr., *The Genius of the People* (New York: Harper & Row, 1987), p. 300.

34. Ibid., p. 299.

35. Quoted in Bowen, *Miracle at Philadelphia*, p. 310.

36. Herbert Mitgang, "Handwritten Draft of a Bill of Rights Found," *New York Times*, July 29, 1987, p. 1.

37. *Dillon* v. *Gloss*, 256 U.S. 368 (1921). The Court refused to rule in 1939 in a case involving time limits contained in a child labor amendment, saying that it was a "political question," or a matter for the political bodies to decide. *Coleman* v. *Miller*, 307 U.S. 433 (1939). Since 1939 the Supreme Court has refused to rule on such time limits.

38. *Immigration and Naturalization Service* v. *Chadha*, 462 U.S. 919 (1982), p. 978.

39. Garry Wills, *Lincoln at Gettysburg: The Words that Remade America* (New York: Simon and Schuster, 1992), p. 120.

CHAPTER 3

1. *Gonzales* v. *Raich*, 125 S.Ct. 2195 (2004); *Gonzales* v. *Oregon*, 126 S.Ct. 904, (2006); George Will, "Supreme Court Justices Defy Labels in Marijuana Ruling," *Chicago Sun Times*, June 9, 2005, p. 43; Charles Lane, "A Defeat for Users of Medical Marijuana," *Washington Post*, June 7, 2005, p. A1; Linda Greenhouse, "Justices Accept Case Weighing Assisted Suicide," *New York Times*, February 23, 2005, p. 1.

2. My thanks to John Kincaid for helping me to shape this definition of federalism. See John Kincaid, "Federalism," in Charles N. Quigley and Charles F. Bahmueller, *Civitas: A Framework for Civic Education*, (Calabasas, Calif.: Center for Civic Education), 1991, pp. 391–92; John Kincaid, "Federalism: It's Time has Come," 8/29/05, unpublished draft in the possession of the author; *Black's Law Dictionary*, 5th ed. St. Paul, Minn.: West, 1979, p. 549–50; Jay. M. Safritz, *The Harpercollins Dictionary of American Government and Politics* (New York: Harper Collins), 1992, p. 226.

3. Alexander Hamilton, James Madison, and John Jay, *The Federalist Papers* (New York: New American Library, 1961), no. 10, p. 83. *The Federalist*, no. 10, is reprinted in the Appendix.

4. Richard A. Knox, "Health Reform Fizzling in States," *Boston Globe*, July 17, 1994, pp. 1, 16.

5. Robert Pear, "States Proposing Sweeping Change to Trim Medicaid," *New York Times*, May 9, 2005, p. 1.

6. *New State Ice Co.* v. *Liebmann*, 285 U.S. 262 (1932), p. 311.

7. Melanie Markley and Karen Masterson, "Education Act Modeled after Texas Reforms," *Houston Chronicle*, December 19, 2001.

8. Michael Cottman, "Atlanta Crowd Demands Voting Rights Act Renewal," August 15, 2005, *NCM*, at http://news.ncmonline.com/news/view.

9. *Heart of Atlanta Motel* v. *United States*, 379 U.S. 241 (1964); *Katzenbach* v. *McClung*, 379 U.S. 294 (1964).

10. In June 1987 the Supreme Court upheld the law, with Chief Justice William H. Rehnquist ruling that Congress has the power to act "indirectly under its spending power to encourage uniformity in the States' drinking ages." *South Dakota* v. *Dole*, 483 U.S. 203 (1987).

11. *United States* v. *E. C. Knight*, 156 U.S. 1 (1895); *Hammer* v. *Dagenhart*, 247 U.S. 251 (1918); *Carter* v. *Carter Coal*, 298 U.S. 238 (1936).

12. *United States* v. *Darby Lumber Co.*, 312 U.S. 100 (1941).

13. *Printz* v. *United States* and *Mack* v. *United States*, 117 S. Ct. 2635 (1997); "Symposium: American Federalism Today," in *Rockefeller Institute Bulletin* (1996): 1–23.

14. See *Pennsylvania* v. *Nelson*, 350 U.S. 497 (1956).

15. Tom Gorman, "Nev. Governor Faces Long Odds to Block Yucca Nuclear Dump," *Los Angeles Times*, April 19, 2002; Wayne Parry, "Detainees' Names to Remain Secret," *Philadelphia Inquirer*, April 19, 2002, p. A15.

16. Brad Knickerbocker, "Assisted Suicide Movement Gets a Boost," *Christian Science Monitor*, April 19, 2002.

17. *McCulloch* v. *Maryland*, 4 Wheaton 316 (1819).

18. *Gibbons* v. *Ogden*, 9 Wheaton 1 (1824), p. 195.

19. "New Hampshire State Legislature Hearings: Reject USA Patriot Act," March 14, 2005, at http://www.infowars.com/articles/us/patriot_act_nh_leg_reject.htm.

20. Donald Lambro, "Alabama Limits Eminent Domain," *Washington Times*, August 4, 2005; the case is *Kelo* v. *City of New London*, 125 S. Ct. 2655, 2005.

21. *United States* v. *E. C. Knight Co.*, 156 U.S. 1 (1895).

22. *Hammer* v. *Dagenhart*, 247 U.S. 251 (1919), p. 274.

23. *Schechter Poultry Corp.* v. *United States*, 295 U.S. 495 (1935); *Carter* v. *Carter Coal Co.*, 298 U.S. 238 (1936); *United States* v. *Butler*, 297 U.S. 1 (1936).

24. *National Labor Relations Board* v. *Jones and Laughlin Steel Corp.*, 301 U.S. 1 (1937); and see *N.L.R.B.* v. *Fruehauf Trailer Co.*, 801 U.S. 1 (1937) and *N.L.R.B.* v. *Friedman-Harry Marks Clothing Co.*, 301 U.S. 58 (1937).

25. *United States* v. *Darby Lumber Co.*, 312 U.S. 100 (1941), p. 124.

26. For the constitutional theory here, see Marshall E. Dimock, *Modern Politics and Administration: A Study of the Creative State* (New York: American Book, 1937), pp. 54–55.

27. *National League of Cities* v. *Usery*, 426 U.S. 833 (1976); *Garcia* v. *San Antonio Metropolitan Transit Authority*, 469 U.S. 528 (1985); *South Carolina* v. *Baker*, 485 U.S. 505 (1988).

28. *Powell* v. *Alabama*, 287 U.S. 45 (1932).

29. *Brown* v. *Board of Education of Topeka*, 347 U.S. 483 (1954).

30. *Reynolds* v. *Sims*, 377 U.S. 533 (1964).

31. See *United States* v. *Butler*, 297 U.S. 1 (1936); *Steward Machine Co.* v. *Davis*, 301 U.S. 548 (1937); *Wickard* v. *Filburn*, 317 U.S. 111 (1941).

32. "Rolling Out the New 0.08% Limit," *Minnesota Star Tribune*, August 2, 2005.

33. Advisory Commission on Intergovernmental Relations (ACIR), *Characteristics of Federal Grant-in-Aid Programs to State and Local Governments: Grants Funded FY 1995* (Washington, D.C.: ACIR, 1996), pp. 1–2.

34. John Kincaid, "State-Federal Relations: Defense, Demography, Debt, and Deconstruction as Destiny," *Book of the States*, vol. 37, 2005, p. 26.

35. Ibid., p. 2.

36. Eric Lipton, "New Rules Set for Giving Out Anti-Terror Aid," *New York Times*, January 3, 2006, p. 1; Lawrence Mishel, "Changes in Federal Aid to State and Local Governments, as Proposed in the Bush Administration FY2002 Budget," *Economic Policy Institute Briefing Paper*, May 2001; and "$20 Billion Anti-Terror Package Is on Bush's Desk," *St. Louis Post Dispatch*, December 21, 2001.

37. See http://www.cfda.gov/public/browse_by_typast.asp, last consulted May 3, 2002; see also *Advisory Commission on Intergovernmental Relations (ACIR)*, *Characteristics of Federal Grant-in-Aid Programs to State and Local Governments: Grants Funded FY 1995* (Washington, D.C.: ACIR, 1996), p. 2.

38. Ibid., pp. 22–42.

39. Calculations from http://www.cfda.gov/public/browse by typast.asp and ibid., p. 14.

40. John Kincaid, "State-Federal Relations: Defense, Demography, Debt, and Deconstruction as Destiny," *Book of the States*, vol. 37, 2005, pp. 25–30; John Kincaid, "Trends in Federalism: Continuity, Change and Polarization," *Book of the States* 2004, vol. 36, pp. 21–27.

41. Kincaid, Book of the States, 2005, pp. 26–7.

42. "Federal Spending on the Elderly and Children," May 3, 2002; see http://www.cbo.gov.

43. John Kincaid, "De Facto Devolution and Urban Defunding: The Priority of Persons Over Places," *Journal of Urban Affairs* 21, no. 2 (1999) pp. 135–167, at p. 163.

44. ABC Nightly News, "American Agenda," October 27, 1993.

45. Richard P. Nathan, "The 'Devolution Revolution': An Overview," in ibid., p. 12.

46. ACIR, "Reconsidering Old Mandates," in ibid., pp. 43–44.

47. Andrew Garber, "REAL IDs Cost Angers State Leaders," *Seattle Times*, August 17, 2005, p. B1.

48. "Can States Afford Bush's Flu Plan?" CNN.com, November 3, 2005.

49. National Conference of State Legislatures (NCSL) at http://www.ncsl.org/.

50. Discussion is based on "The States: Policy Innovation Amid Fiscal Constraint, Trends 2005," *Politics and Policy News State by State*, at www.stateline.org.

51. Iris J. Lav, "Deep Cuts in Federal Grants in FY 2006 Budget Will Squeeze States and Localities," February 9, 2005, Center on Budget and Policy Priorities, at www.cbpp.org.

52. Iris J. Lav, "Deep Cuts in Federal Grants in FY 2006 Budget Will Squeeze States and Localities," February 9, 2005, Center on Budget and Policy Priorities, www.cbpp.org; Pamela M. Prah, "Medicaid—Cost and Complexity Tax Reform Efforts," May 6, 2005, www.stateline.org; Robert Pear, "Most States Cutting Back on Medicaid, Survey Finds," *New York Times*, January 14, 2003, p. A24.

53. David B. Walker, *Toward a Functioning Federalism* (Cambridge, Mass.: Winthrop, 1981), pp. 68, 79.

54. John E. Schwarz, *America's Hidden Success: A Reassessment of Public Policy from Kennedy to Reagan* (New York: Norton, 1988), pp. 17–71.

55. Jeffrey Pressman and Aaron Wildavsky, *Implementation* (Berkeley: University of California Press, 1973).

56. See Schwarz, *America's Hidden Success*; Allen Matusow, *The Unraveling of America: A History of Liberalism in the 1960s* (New York: Harper & Row, 1984).

57. Nathan, "'Devolution Revolution,'" pp. 8–9.

58. Ronald Reagan, Inaugural Address, January 20, 1981, in *A Documentary History of the United States*,

ed. Richard D. Heffner (New York: Mentor Books, 1991), pp. 398–401.

59. Ronald Reagan, speech to Congress, February 18, 1981, reprinted in *Congressional Quarterly,* February 21, 1981, pp. 15ff, p. 16.

60. Marshall Kaplan and Sue O'Brien, *The Governors and the New Federalism* (Boulder, Colo.: Westview Press, 1991), p. 2.

61. Michael de Courcy Hinds, "80's Leave States and Cities in Need," *New York Times,* December 30, 1990, pp. 1, 16.

62. ACIR, *Federal Grant-in-Aid Programs,* p. 14.

63. Walker, *Toward a Functioning Federalism,* p. 114.

64. Peter Edelman, "The Worst Thing Bill Clinton Has Done," *Atlantic Monthly,* March 1997, p. 43; Richard P. Nathan, "'Devolution Revolution,'" p. 12.

65. Peter Grier, "The Rising Economic Cost of the Iraq War," *Christian Science Monitor,* May 19, 2005, p. 1.

66. John Kincaid, "State-Federal Relations," *Book of the States,* 2005, p. 27.

67. Alison Mitchell, "Wellstone Death Brings New Focus to Senate Battles," *New York Times,* October 27, 1997, p. 1; Ron Eckstein, "Federalism Bills Unify Usual Foes," *Legal Times,* October 18, 1999.

68. *New York* v. *United States,* 112 S. Ct. 2408, 2435 (1992). This entire discussion of the Court's recent stance on federalism benefited from Tinsley Yarbrough, "The Rehnquist Court and the 'Double Standard,'" paper presented at the annual meeting of the Southern Political Science Association, Norfolk, Va., November 6–8, 1997.

69. *United States* v. *Lopez,* 131 L. Ed. 2d 626 (1995).

70. *U.S. Term Limits* v. *Thornton,* 115 S. Ct. 1842 (1995).

71. *Seminole Tribe* v. *Florida,* 134 L. Ed. 2d 252 (1996).

72. *Printz* v. *United States,* 117 S. Ct. 2635 (1997), p. 2638.

73. *Reno* v. *Condon,* 528 U.S. 141 (2000).

74. *United States* v. *Morrison,* 529 U.S. 598, 2000.

75. See *Nevada Department of Human Resources* v. *Hibbs,* 123 S. Ct. 1972 (2003); *Ashcroft* v. *A.C.L.U.* 542 U.S. 656, (2004); Child Online Protection Act case, *Tennessee* v. *Lane* 124 S. Ct. 1978 (2004).

76. Both quoted in Adam Clymer, "Switching Sides on States' Rights," *New York Times,* June 1, 1997, pp. E1, E6.

CHAPTER 4

1. Based on Diane Dwyre and Victoria A. Farrar-Myers, *Legislative Labyrinth: Congress and Campaign Finance Reform* (Washington, D.C.: Congressional Quarterly, 2001); Alison Mitchell, "Sponsors Thwart Moves to Scuttle Soft-Money Bill," *New York Times,* February 14, 2002, p. 1; Alison Mitchell, "Campaign Finance Bill Wins Final Approval in Congress and Bush Says He'll Sign It," *New York Times,* March 21, 2002, p. 1. Also see *McConnell* v. *Federal Election Commission,* 540 U.S. 93, (2003).

2. See Morris P. Fiorina, *Congress: Keystone of the Washington Establishment* (New Haven, Conn.: Yale University Press, 1977).

3. On comparisons between the House and the Senate, see Ross K. Baker, *House and Senate,* 2d ed. (New York: Norton, 1995).

4. See *How Congress Works* (Washington, D.C.: Congressional Quarterly Press, 1994).

5. See *The Federalist,* nos. 17, 39, and 45, in Alexander Hamilton, James Madison, and John Jay, *The Federalist Papers* (New York: New American Library, 1961).

6. *Reno* v. *American Civil Liberties Union,* 117 S.Ct. 2329 (1997).

7. *Clinton* v. *New York,* 66 U.S. L. W. 4543 (1998).

8. *Dickerson* v. *United States,* 530 U.S. 428 (2000).

9. See Glenn R. Simpson, "Of the Rich, by the Rich, for the Rich: Will the Millionaires Turn Congress into a Plutocracy?" *Washington Post,* April 17, 1994, p. C4. Compare with Allan Freedman, "Lawyers Take a Back Seat in the 105th Congress," *Congressional Quarterly Weekly Report,* January 4, 1997, p. 29.

10. See Hannah Fenichel Pitkin, *The Concept of Representation* (Berkeley: University of California Press, 1967).

11. Donna Cassata, "Freshman Class Boasts Résumés to Back Up 'Outsider' Image," *Congressional Quarterly,* November 12, 1994, pp. 9–12. Also see Mildred L Amer, "Membership of the 109th Congress: A Profile," *CRS Report for Congress,* May 30, 2005.

12. Gary C. Jacobson, *The Politics of Congressional Elections* (New York: HarperCollins, 1992), p. 13; "Rethinking Texas' Redistricting," *New York Times,* October 22, 2004, p. 22; Ralph Blumenthal, "Texas Democrats Look at New Map and Point Out Victims," *New York Times,* October 14, 2003, p. A14; David Barboza and Carl Hulse, "Hiding Out in Oklahoma Texas Democrats Protest," *New York Times,* May 14, 2003, p. A17; and Ralph Blumenthal, "After Bitter Fight, Texas Senate Redraws Congressional Districts," *New York Times,* October 13, 2004, p. 1; *Vieth* v. *Jubelirer,* 541 U.S. 267 (2004).

13. Gregory L. Giroux, "A Line in the Suburban Sand," *CQ Weekly,* June 27, 2005, pp. 1714–15.

14. Elaine R. Jones, "In Peril: Black Lawmakers," *New York Times,* September 11, 1994, p. E19; Ronald Smothers, "Fair Play or Racial Gerrymandering? Justices Study a 'Serpentine' District," *New York Times,* April 16, 1993, p. B12.

15. *Shaw* v. *Reno,* 509 U.S. 630 (1993), p. 637.

16. *Miller* v. *Johnson,* 132 L.Ed. 2d 762 (1995).

17. *Abrams* v. *Johnson,* 117 S. Ct. (1997).

18. "Race and Redistricting," *Washington Post,* June 23, 1997, p. A18; Roger H. Davidson and Walter J. Oleszek, *Congress and Its Members,* 8th ed. (Washington, D.C.: Congressional Quarterly Press, 2002), p. 55.

19. *Hunt* v. *Cromartie,* 143 L.Ed. 2d 791 (1999).

20. Edward Walsh, "Supreme Court Upholds Mississippi Redistricting Plan," *Washington Post,* April 1, 2003; David E. Rosenbaum, "Fight Over Political Map Centers on Race," *New York Times,* Feb. 21, 2004, p. A18.

21. Charles Clapp, *The Congressman: His Job as He Sees It* (Washington, D.C.: Brookings Institution, 1963); Roger H. Davidson, *The Role of the Congressman* (Indianapolis, Ind.: Bobbs-Merrill, 1969).

22. John F. Kennedy, *Profiles in Courage* (New York: Harper & Row, 1956).

23. Davidson and Oleszek, *Congress and Its Members,* p. 62; Cassata, "Freshman Class," p. 3237.

24. Alan Abramowitz, "The 2004 Congressional Elections," APSA Network, at www.apsanet.org/content_5179.cfm.

25. See David Mayhew, *Congress: The Electoral Connection* (New Haven, Conn.: Yale University Press, 1974).

26. For more on casework and Congress, see John R. Johannes, *To Serve the People: Congress and Constituency Review* (Lincoln: University of Nebraska Press, 1984); Morris P. Fiorina, *Congress: Keystone of the Washington Establishment,* 2d ed. (New Haven, Conn.: Yale University Press, 1989).

27. Davidson and Oleszek, *Congress and Its Members,* pp. 128–29.

28. Davidson and Oleszek, *Congress and Its Members,* p. 76.

29. Joseph E. Cantor, "Campaign Financing," October 28, 2004, Congressional Research Service Report, at http://fpc.state.gov/documents/organization/37875.pdf.

30. David B. Magleby and Candice J. Nelson, *The Money Chase* (Washington, D.C.: Brookings Institution, 1990), p. 71.

31. *U.S. Term Limits* v. *Thornton,* 115 S. Ct. 1842 (1995).

32. *Arkansas Term Limits* v. *Donovan,* 138 L. Ed. 2d 874 (1997).

33. B. Drummond Ayres Jr., "Term Limit Laws Are Transforming More Legislatures," *New York Times,* April 28, 1997, p. 1.

34. See "California Voters Soundly Reject Attempt to Kill Term Limits," *No Uncertain Terms,* April 4, 2002, vol. 10, no. 4, www.termlimits.org/Press/No_Uncertain_Terms/2002/0204nut.pdf.

35. "Term Limits Extensions Crushed by Voters in Arkansas, Montana," U.S. Term Limits Web site at www.termlimits.org/pr11304.html.

36. Mildred L Amer, "Membership of the 109th Congress: A Profile," *CRS Report for Congress,* May 30, 2005.

37. ABC News/Washington Post poll, June 2–5, 2005, at www.pollingreport.com.

38. See Davidson and Oleszek, *Congress and Its Members,* p. 407; Glenn R. Parker and Roger H. Davidson, "Why Do Americans Love Their Congressmen So Much More Than Their Congress?" *Legislative Studies Quarterly* 4 (February 1979): 53–61.

39. For the Democratic party, the names of these bodies are different: the Steering and Policy Committee is chosen by the caucus.

40. Barbara Sinclair, *Majority Leadership in the U.S. House* (Baltimore: Johns Hopkins University Press, 1983).

41. Ward Sinclair, "High Theater Starring Tip and Cast of 434," *Washington Post,* August 20, 1982, p. 1.

42. For more on minority leaders, see Charles O. Jones, *Minority Party in Congress* (Boston: Little, Brown, 1970).

43. See Barbara Sinclair, *The Transformation of the U.S. Senate* (Baltimore: Johns Hopkins University Press, 1989).

44. Rowland Evans and Robert Novak, *Lyndon B. Johnson: The Exercise of Power* (New York: New American Library, 1966); Merle Miller, *Lyndon: An Oral Biography* (New York: Ballantine Books, 1980), chap. 2.

45. Harry McPherson, oral history, Lyndon Johnson Library, Austin, Tex., pp. 78–88; see also Robert A. Caro, *Master of the Senate,* (New York: Alfred A. Knopf, 2002).

46. *Washington Post,* June 12, 1985, p. 5.

47. Trent Lott, *Herding Cats: A Life in Politics,* New York: Regan Books, 2005.

48. Woodrow Wilson, *Congressional Government* (New York: Meridian, 1967), p. 28.

49. Davidson and Oleszek, *Congress and Its Members,* p. 349.

50. Lawrence D. Longley and Walter J. Oleszek, *Bicameral Politics: Conference Committees in Congress* (New Haven, Conn.: Yale University Press, 1995).

51. Richard F. Fenno Jr., *Congressmen in Committees* (Boston: Little, Brown, 1973), p. 280.

52. The classic source on committees and the roles of members of Congress is Richard F. Fenno Jr., *Congressmen in Committees* (Boston: Little, Brown, 1973). See also Steven Smith and Christopher Deering, *Committees in Congress*, 2d ed. (Washington, D.C.: Congressional Quarterly Press, 1990).

53. Allan Freedman, "Returning Power to Chairmen," *Congressional Quarterly Weekly Report*, November 23, 1996, p. 3300.

54. Quoted in James T. Murphy, "Political Parties and the Porkbarrel: Party Conflict and Cooperation in House Public Works Committee Decision Making," in *Studies in Congress*, ed. Glen Parker (Washington, D.C.: Congressional Quarterly Press, 1985), pp. 237–38.

55. Davidson and Oleszek, *Congress and Its Members*, pp. 206.

56. See Leroy N. Rieselbach, *Legislative Reform: The Policy Impact* (Lexington, Mass.: Lexington Books, 1978).

57. Jill Abramson, "Tobacco Industry Steps Up Flow of Campaign Money," *New York Times*, March 8, 1998, p. 1.

58. Thomas E. Mann and Norman J. Ornstein, eds., *Renewing Congress: A Second Report* (Washington, D.C.: American Enterprise Institute and the Brookings Institution, 1993).

59. Tom Brune, "Specter Seeks to Bargain," *Newsday*, February 25, 2005, p. 38; and Richard E. Cohen, "Crackup of the Committees," *National Journal*, July 31, 1999, pp. 2210–17.

60. Walter J. Oleszek, *Congressional Procedures and the Policy Process* (Washington, D.C.: Congressional Quarterly Press, 1989).

61. Stanley Bach and Steven Smith, *Managing Uncertainty in the House of Representatives: Adaptation and Innovation in Special Rules* (Washington, D.C.: Brookings Institution, 1988).

62. D. B. Hardeman and Donald C. Bacon, *Rayburn: A Biography* (Lanham, Md.: Madison Books, 1987).

63. Quoted in David E. Rosenbaum, "Tax Bill Faces Fight, but First the Rules," *New York Times*, April 2, 1995, p. 20.

64. See Steven S. Smith, *Call to Order: Floor Politics in the House and Senate* (Washington, D.C.: Brookings Institution, 1989).

65. Helen Dewar, "As Senate Crunch Nears, Holdups Threaten," *Washington Post*, November 15, 1999, p. 21.

66. Quoted in Alison Mitchell, "Rule No. 1: My Way or No Way," *New York Times*, November 2, 1997, p. WK6.

67. Quoted in Sarah A. Binder and Steven S. Smith, "The Politics and Principles of the Senate Filibuster," *Extensions* (Fall 1997); see also Sarah A. Binder and Steven S. Smith, *Politics or Principles? Filibustering in the U.S. Senate* (Washington, D.C.: Brookings Institution, 1997), p. 69.

68. See Fred R. Harris, *Deadlock on Decision: The U.S. Senate and the Rise of National Politics* (New York: Oxford University Press, 1993).

69. Donald Matthews, *U.S. Senators and Their World* (Chapel Hill: University of North Carolina Press, 1960), p. 54; see also Ross K. Baker, *House and Senate*, 2d ed. (New York: Norton, 1995), chap. 2.

70. John E. Yang, "Notion of House Civility Gets a Push Backward," *Washington Post*, April 10, 1997, p. A23.

71. Frank Ahrens, "Putting 'Polite' into Politics," *Washington Post*, March 6, 1997, p. B1.

72. Sheryl Gay Stolberg, "The High Costs of Rising Incivility on Capitol Hill," *New York Times*, November 30, 2003, p. 10.

73. Burdett Loomis, "Civility and Deliberation: A Linked Pair?" in Burdett Loomis, ed. *Esteemed Colleagues: Civility and Deliberation in the U.S. Senate* (Washington, D.C.: Brookings Institution Press, 2000), p. 1.

74. For more on the importance of seniority, apprenticeship, and political loyalty in Congress, see John R. Hibbing, *Congressional Careers: Contours of Life in the U.S. House of Representatives* (Chapel Hill: University of North Carolina Press, 1991), pp. 113–28; Donald Matthews, *U.S. Senators and Their World* (Chapel Hill: University of North Carolina Press, 1960), chap. 5.

75. John Ferejohn, "Logrolling in an Institutional Context: A Case of Food Stamp Legislation," in *Congress and Policy Change*, ed. Gerald C. Wright Jr., Leroy Rieselbach, and Lawrence C. Dodd (New York: Agathon Press, 1986).

76. Davidson and Oleszek, *Congress and Its Members*, p. 271.

77. Anick Jesdanun, "Specter Gets 'Oinker' Award from Critical Citizens' Group," *Centre Daily Times*, March 11, 1998, p. 3A.

78. Quoted in Elsa C. Arnett, "Citizens, Interest Groups Fear New Round of Spending," *Centre Daily Times*, March 11, 1998, p. 3A.

79. Quoted in Donald G. Tacheron and Morris K. Udall, *The Job of the Congressman*, 2d ed. (Indianapolis, Ind.: Bobbs-Merrill, 1970), p. 18.

80. Douglas Arnold, *The Logic of Congressional Action* (New Haven, Conn.: Yale University Press, 1990), pp. 64–84; V. O. Key Jr., *Public Opinion and American Democracy* (New York: Knopf, 1961), pp. 265–85.

81. Davidson and Oleszek, *Congress and Its Members*, 9th ed., p. 273; William R. Shaffer, *Party and Ideology in the United States Congress* (Lanham, Md.: University Press of America, 1980); Norman Ornstein, Thomas E. Mann, and Michael Malbin, *Vital Statistics on Congress: 1993–94* (Washington, D.C.: Congressional Quarterly Press, 1994), p. 200.

82. Statistics taken from "President Support and Opposition: Senate," *Congressional Quarterly*, for the years 1992, p. 3897; 1991, p. 3785; 1990, p. 4209; 1989, p. 3566; 1988, p. 3348; 1987, p. 3213; 1986, p. 2688; 1985, pp. 741–46; 1984, pp. 2802–2808; 1983, p. 2781; and 1982, p. 2796.

83. David Rohde, *Parties and Leaders in the Post-Reform House* (Chicago: University of Chicago Press, 1991); Robert L. Peabody, *Leadership in Congress* (Boston: Little, Brown, 1976).

84. Stephen Wayne and George Edwards III, *Presidential Influence in Congress* (San Francisco: Freeman, 1980); Stephen Wayne, *The Legislative Presidency* (New York: Harper & Row, 1978).

85. R. W. Apple, "In Pennsylvania, Feeling the Consequences of One Vote," *New York Times*, September 27, 1994, p. A22.

86. See Jeffrey Birnbaum, *The Lobbyists* (New York: Times Books, 1992); Jeffrey Birnbaum and Alan S. Murray, *Showdown at Gucci Gulch* (New York: Vintage Books, 1987).

87. See Harrison W. Fox Jr., and Susan Webb Hammond, *Congressional Staffs: The Invisible Force in American Lawmaking* (New York: Free Press, 1977).

88. Richard Fenno, *Home Style: House Members in Their Districts* (New York: HarperCollins, 1987).

89. Donald R. Matthews and James A. Stimson, *Yeas and Nays* (New York: Wiley, 1975); David M. Kovenock, "Influence in the U.S. House of Representatives: A Statistical Study of Communications," *American Politics Quarterly* 1 (October 1973): 456ff.

90. John W. Kingdon, *Congressional Voting Decisions*, 3d ed. (Ann Arbor: University of Michigan Press, 1989); Aage R. Clausen, *How Congressmen Decide* (New York: St. Martin's Press, 1973).

91. Roughly ten thousand bills are introduced in each two-year session of Congress, and about six hundred laws are passed from that group. See Barry, "Bills Introduced and Laws Enacted," p. 2.

92. John W. Kingdon, *Agendas, Alternatives, and Public Policies* (Boston: Little, Brown, 1984).

93. See Paul Light, *Forging Legislation* (New York: Norton, 1992).

94. Longley and Oleszek, *Bicameral Politics*, passim.

95. Davidson and Oleszek, *Congress and Its Members*, p. 247.

96. Josh Burek, "Bush Makes History—A Five Year Streak Without Saying No," *Christian Science Monitor*, August 16, 2005.

97. Marc Sandalow, "Frist's Shift May Lead to Bush's First Veto," *San Francisco Chronicle*, July 30, 2005, p. A16.

98. Helen Dewar, "Campaign Finance Bill Dies in Senate," *Washington Post*, February 27, 1998, p. 1.

99. For more on how changes in House operation rules by Newt Gingrich and the Republican Congress may influence the theory of legislating in Congress, see John H. Aldrich and David W. Rohde, "The Transition to Republican Rule in the House: Implications for Theories of Congressional Politics," *Political Science Quarterly* 112, no. 4 (1997–98): 541–67.

100. Davidson and Oleszek, *Congress and Its Members*, p. 226.

101. Ibid., p. 363.

102. Sinclair, *Transformation of the U.S. Senate*, passim.

103. Joel D. Aberbach, *Keeping a Watchful Eye: The Politics of Congressional Oversight* (Washington, D.C.: Brookings Institution, 1990); James Q. Wilson, *Bureaucracy: What Government Agencies Do and Why They Do It* (New York: Basic Books, 1991).

104. *Immigration and Naturalization Service* v. *Chadha*, 462 U.S. 919 (1983).

105. Aaron Wildavsky, *The New Politics of the Budgetary Process* (Glenview, Ill.: Scott, Foresman/Little, Brown, 1988); Allen Schick, *The Capacity to Budget* (Washington, D.C.: Urban Institute, 1990).

106. Ross Baker, quoted in Robin Toner, "Capitol Dynamic to Do the Framers Proud," *New York Times*, February 26, 1995, p. 1.

107. Jill Barshay, "A Year of Power Struggles and Common Purpose," *CQ Weekly*, December 22, 2001, p. 3018.

108. David Firestone, "G.O.P. Moderates Show Signs of Strength," *New York Times*, March 31, 2003, p. A11.

109. Andrea Stone, "Parts of the Republican Revolution Fade with Age," *USA Today*, January 20, 2003, p. 5A.

110. Bob Beneson and Gregory L. Giroux, "Shades of '94—But Cloudier," *CQ Weekly*, August 15, 2005, pp. 2230ff.

CHAPTER 5

1. Ron Fournier, "From 'Accidental President' to Commander in Chief," *Allentown Morning Call,* January 22, 2002; Dana Milbank, "In War, It's Power to the President," *Washington Post,* November 20, 2001; Ramesh Ponnuru, "Rising Freshman," *National Review,* January 28, 2002. See Elisabeth Bumiller, "At First Year's End, Bush Cites Both Victories and Challenges," *New York Times,* December 30, 2001, p. B3. See also online *News Hour,* Shields and Books, "A President Expanded in Scope." www.pbs.org/ newshour; "Assessment of Bush's First Year and Future," Brookings Institution National Issues Forum, January 30, 2002, www.brooking.edu/ comm/transcripts/20020130nif.htm. "There Is No Doubt in My Mind. Not One Doubt." Interviews with President Bush on December 20, 2001. *Washington Post,* p. A14.

2. See Richard W. Stevenson, "For This President, Power Is There for the Taking," *New York Times,* May 15, 2005. BW WK, p. 3; Also, David E. Rosenbaum, "When Government Doesn't Tell," *New York Times,* February 3, 2002, Section 4, p. 1; Elisabeth Bumiller with David Sanger, "Taking Command in Crisis, Bush Wields New Power," *New York Times,* January 1, 2002, p. A1; David E. Sanger, "In Address, Bush Says He Ordered Domestic Spying," *New York Times,* December 18, 2005, p. A1. For information on Professor Berman's lawsuit against the CIA see http://www.gwu.edu/~nsarchiv/pdbnews/.

3. See Kitty Kelley, "Bush's Veil Over History," *New York Times,* October 10, 2005, p. A23.

4. David E. Sanger, "Bush Wants to Consider Broadening of Military's Powers During Natural Disasters," *New York Times,* September 27, 2005, p. A18; See "Government Secrecy: Is Too Much Information Kept from the Public?" *CQ Researcher,* vol. 15, no. 42 (Dec. 2, 2005): 1005–1028.

5. Carl M. Cannon, "The Uncompromising Mr. Bush," *Washington Post,* May 29, 2005, p. B1.

6. See http://people-press.org/reports/ print.php3?ReportID=233.

7. "Plurality Now Sees Bush Presidency as Unsuccessful: Discontent with Bush and State of the Nation Ever Higher," http://people-press .org/reports/display.php3?ReportID=259. Todd S. Purdum and Majorie Connelly, "Support for Bush Continues to Drop as More Question His Leadership Skill, Poll Finds." *New York Times,* September 15, 2005, p. A14.

8. Richard W. Stevenson, "Amid the Ruins, a President Tries to Reconstruct His Image, Too." *New York Times,* September 16, 2005, p. A19; Elisabeth Bumiller, "Far Away from Home, No Rest for a Weary President," *New York Times,* November 7, 2005, p. A6; David E. Sanger, "President Uses Vacation to Prepare Agenda for 2006," *New York Times,* January 1, 2006, p. A13.

9. Todd S. Purdum and Majorie Connelly, "Support for Bush Continues to Drop as More Question His Leadership Skill, Poll Finds." *New York Times,* September 15, 2005, p. A14; Elisabeth Bumiller and Marjorie Connelly, "Ports Argument and Iraq Hurt Bush in a New Survey," *New York Times,* February 28, 2006, A15.

10. See Sidney M. Milkis and Michael Nelson, *The American Presidency: Origins and Development, 1776–1990* (Washington, D.C.: CQ Press, 1990); Thomas E. Cronin, ed., *Inventing the Presidency* (Albany: State University of New York Press, 1988), p. 20.

11. See Robert J. Spitzer, *The Presidential Veto: Touchstone of the American Presidency* (Albany: State University of New York Press, 1988), p. 20.

12. "Bush Holds Fast to Stem-Cell Veto Threat," AP Online, July 29, 2005; "Bush Renews Veto Threat for Highway Bill," AP Online, June 9, 2005.

13. "A Look at Presidential Recess Appointments," Associated Press, August 1, 2005; Elisabeth Bumiller and Sheryl Gay Stolberg, "President Sends Bolton to U.N.; Bypasses Senate," *New York Times,* August 2, 2005, p. 1; "In Recess Appointment Bush Names Transport Security Chief," *New York Times,* January 8, 2002, p. A16; "Bush Bypasses Senate on 2 More Nominees," *New York Times,* January 12, 2002, p. A10.

14. See especially, "Woodrow Wilson and Colonel House: A Personality Study" by Alexander L. George and Juliette L. George.

15. See "Clinton, Congress and Trade," *Legislate News Service,* November 10, 1997, p. 1; see Lael Brainard and Hal Shapiro, "Fast-Track Trade Promotion Authority," Policy Brief #91, December 2001. Published on Brookings Web site, November 30, 2001, www.brook.edu.

16. Gerald R. Ford, "Ford: I Had 'Fast-Track,' Clinton Deserves It, Too," *USA Today,* October 22, 1997, p. 15A.

17. See U.S. Department of State, Fact Sheet, *Trade Promotion Authority,* August 23, 2002.

18. Deb Reichman, "Presidents Assert Executive Privilege," *WashingtonPost.com,* January 29, 2002; see Ellen Nakashima, "Bush Invokes Executive Privilege on Hill," *Washington Post,* December 14, 2001, p. A43; "Symposium on Executive Privilege and the Clinton Presidency," *William & Mary Bill of Rights Journal,* April 2000, vol. 8, issue 3, pp. 583–629.

19. See Mike Allen, "GAO to Sue Cheney within 2 or 3 Weeks," *Washington Post,* January 31, 2002, p. A4; Dana Milbank, "Cheney Refuses Records Release," *Washington Post,* January 28, 2002, p. A01.

20. Richard W. Stevenson, "President, Citing Executive Privilege, Indicates He'll Reject Requests for Counsel's Documents." *New York Times,* October 5, 2005, p. A17.

21. "Your Right To Know: How Private Are Records of Ex-Presidents? Reagan-Era Memos at Heart of Legal Battle over Bush Order on Withholding Documents." *Atlanta Journal and Constitution,* March 18, 2005.

22. See "Law and the War on Terrorism." *Harvard Journal of Law and Public Policy,* 25th anniversary issue, Spring 2002, vol. 25, no. 2; See John Mueller, *Wars, Presidents and Public Opinion,* (New York: Wiley, 1970); Mueller, *Policy, Opinion and the Gulf War,* (Chicago: University of Chicago Press, 1994), p. 645; *United States* v. *Nixon,* 418 U.S. 683 (1974); See *Washington Post* series, "America's Chaotic Road to War," January 27, 2002–February 3, 2002.

23. Quoted in Richard Neustadt, "Presidency and Legislation: Planning the President's Program," *American Political Science Review* 49 (December 1955): 980–1021; Neustadt, "Presidency and Legislation: The Growth of Central Clearance," *American Political Science Review* 48 (September 1954): 641–71.

24. Clinton Rossiter, *The American Presidency,* rev. ed. (Baltimore: Johns Hopkins University Press, 1987), p. 52.

25. See James Carville. *We're Right, They're Wrong* (New York: Random House), 1996.

26. Quoted in George Wolfskill, *Happy Days Are Here Again!* (Hinsdale, Ill.: Dryden, 1974), p. 189; See also James MacGregor Burns, *Roosevelt: The Lion and the Fox* (New York: Harcourt Brace Jovanovich, 1956); Burns, *Roosevelt: The Soldier of Freedom, 1940–1945* (New York: Harcourt Brace

Jovanovich, 1970); Frank Freidel, *Franklin D. Roosevelt,* 4 vols. (Boston: Little, Brown, 1952–53); Arthur Schlesinger, Jr., *The Age of Roosevelt,* 3 vols. (Boston: Houghton Mifflin, 1957–60).

27. Theodore Roosevelt, "The Stewardship Doctrine," in *Classics of the American Presidency,* ed. Harry Bailey (Oak Park, Ill.: Moore, 1980), pp. 35–36. See also *The Autobiography of Theodore Roosevelt* (New York: Scribner's, 1913), pp. 197–200.

28. John Morton Blum, *The Republican Roosevelt* (New York: Atheneum, 1962), pp. 129–30.

29. See Larry Berman, *The New American Presidency* (Little, Brown, 1986), pp. 54–56. See William Howard Taft, *Our Chief Magistrate and His Powers,* (New York: Columbia University Press, 1916), pp. 138–45.

30. Richard W. Stevenson and Adam Liptak, "Cheney Defends Eavesdropping Without Warrant," *New York Times,* December 21, 2005, p. A22; See also www.fas.org/irp/agency/doj/fisa/ doj122205.pdf.

31. *United States* v. *Curtiss-Wright,* 299 U.S. 304 (1936).

32. For detailed accounts of Johnson's views from White House tapes, see Michael Beschloss, *Reaching for Glory,* (New York: Simon & Schuster 2000).

33. *Youngstown Sheet and Tube Co.* v. *Sawyer,* 343 U.S. 579 (1952); See Maeva Marcus, *Truman and the Steel Seizure Case* (New York: Columbia University Press, 1977); Alan Weston, *The Anatomy of a Constitutional Law Case* (New York: Macmillan, 1958); and Arthur M. Schlesinger Jr., *The Imperial Presidency* (Boston: Houghton Mifflin, 1973).

34. See U.S. Congress, Senate, *Congressional Record,* 93rd Cong., 1st sess., 1973, p. 119; See also U.S. Congress, Subcommittee on International Security and Scientific Affairs, *The War Powers Resolution: Relevant Documents, Correspondence, Reports,* 93rd Cong., 3rd sess., June 1981.

35. See Louis Fisher and David Gray Adler, "The War Powers Resolution: Time to Say Goodbye," *Political Science Quarterly* 113, no. 1, 1998: 1–20; See David P. Auerswald and Peter F. Cowhey, "Ballotbox Diplomacy: The War Powers Resolution and the Use of Force," *International Studies Quarterly* 41 (1987): 505–28.

36. W. Taylor Reveley III, "Presidential War Making: Constitutional Prerogative or Usurpation?" *Virginia Law Review* 55 (November 1969): 1243–1305; and Reveley, *"Resolved: That the Powers of the Presidency Should Be Curtailed," A Collection of Excerpts and Bibliography Relating to the Intercollegiate Debate Topic, 1974–75* (Washington, D.C.: U.S. Government Printing Office, 1974), pp. 91–133; U.S. Congress, Senate, Committee on Foreign Relations, *Powers of the President to Send Armed Forces Outside the United States,* 82d Cong., 1st sess., 1951; See Elisabeth Palmer, "Executive Powers in Crises Are Shaped by Precedent, Personality, Public Opinion," *CQ Weekly* (September 15, 2001): 2122–3.

37. See www.washingtonpost.com/wp-dyn/articles/ A38075-2002Oct29.html; www.washingtonpost .com/ac2/wp-2002Sep19; www.whitehouse.gov/ infocus/iraq/index.html; www. washingtonpost.com/ac2/wp-dyn/A33534-2002Oct16.

38. Samuel Kernell, *Going Public: New Strategies of Presidential Leadership* (Washington, D.C.: CQ Press, 1993); rev. ed. 1997 Jeffrey K. Tulis, *The Rhetorical Presidency* (Princeton, N.J.: Princeton University Press, 1977), pp. 61–87.

39. John Hart, *The Presidential Branch* (Chatham, N.J.: Chatham House, 1995), pp. 37–38; Peri Arnold, *Making the Managerial Presidency* (Princeton, N.J.: Princeton University Press, 1986).

40. See Louis Brownlow, *The President and the Presidency* (Chicago: Public Administration Service, 1949).

41. Jack Valenti, "Life's Never the Same after the White House Power Trip," *Washington Post National Weekly Edition,* (March 19, 1984), p. 21.

42. Thomas Cronin, "Everybody Believes in Democracy Until He Gets to the White House: An Examination of White House-Departmental Relations," *Law and Contemporary Problems* 35 (Summer 1970): 573–625.

43. Fred I. Greenstein, *The Hidden-Hand Presidency: Eisenhower as Leader* (New York: Basic Books, 1982), p. 55.

44. Elisabeth Bumiller, "Talk of Changes in White House Staff Turns to Its Chief." *New York Times,* December 5, 2005, p. A16.

45. Larry Berman, *The Office of Management and Budget and the Presidency, 1921–1977* (Princeton, N.J.: Princeton University Press), 1977.

46. Quoted in Alexander Groth, *Lincoln: Authoritarian Savior* (Lanham, Md.: University Press of America, 1996), pp. 130–131.

47. See Lizett Alverez and Eric Schmitt, "Cheney Ever More Powerful as Crucial Link to Congress," *New York Times,* May 13, 2001, p. A1; Alvin Felzenberg, "The Vice Presidency Grows Up," *Policy Review* (January 31, 2002). See www.heritage.org; Susan Page, "Cheney Takes 'Backseat' in a Strong Way," *USA Today,* November 16, 2001, p. 13A; Mike Allen, "The Long, hard Autumn of Dick Cheney," *Time,* November 21, 2005. p. 40; "Mr. Cheney's Imperial Presidency," *New York Times,* December 23, 2005, p. A26.

CHAPTER 6

1. James S. Todd, "Overturning Acts of Congress on the Rehnquist Court: Will the Real Judicial Activist Please Stand Up?" American Political Science Association Convention, September 2004, p. 1; Dan Balz, "Nomination Could be Defining Moment for Bush," *Washington Post,* July 2, 2005, p. 1; Charles Lane, "In Other News from the Middle, Some Shifts by Justice Kennedy," *Washington Post,* July 4, 2005, p. 15; Linda Greenhouse, "O'Connor Held Balance of Power," *New York Times,* July 2, 2005.

2. Alexander Hamilton, James Madison, and John Jay. *The Federalist Papers,* no. 78. (New York: New York American Library, 1961), p. 465.

3. *Marbury* v. *Madison,* 5 U.S. 137 (1803). The U.S. court of appeals was not established by congressional act until 1891. Before this time, the appellate courts were staffed by a panel of two district court judges and one circuit-riding Supreme Court justice.

4. Edward S. Corwin, review of Benjamin F. Wright's *Growth of American Constitutional Law, Harvard Law Review* 56 (1942): 487.

5. Henry J. Abraham, *The Judicial Process,* 6th ed. (New York: Oxford University Press, 1993), p. 272; See also David O'Brien. *Constitutional Law and Politics,* vol. 1, *Struggles for Power and Governmental Accountability,* (New York: Norton, 1991), p. 38.

6. Justice Antonin Scalia speech, "The Legacy of the Rehnquist Court," Federalist Society, Milwaukee, Wisconsin, February 22, 2006, quoted in Gina Barton, "Rehnquist Court Made Clearer, Scalia Says," *JSOnline* (Milwaukee Journal Sentinel), www.jsonline.com. James S. Todd, "Overturning Acts of Congress on the Rehnquist Court: Will the Real Judicial Activist Please Stand Up?" American Political Science Association Convention, September 2004, p. 1.

7. Linda Greenhouse, "Justices Limit Gun Law that Bars Possession by Felons," *New York Times,* April 27, 2005.

8. Ann McFeatters, "Reporter Sent to Jail Writer Refuses to Reveal Sources," *Pittsburgh Post-Gazette,* July 7, 2005.

9. For more here, see William H. Rehnquist, *Grand Inquests: The Historic Impeachments of Justice Samuel Chase and President Andrew Johnson* (New York: Morrow, 1992).

10. See John Aloysius Farrell, "Republicans Take Aim at the Federal Judiciary," *Boston Globe.* September 24, 1997, p. 1; David Kairys, "Clinton's Judicial Retreat," *New York Times,* September 7, 1997, p. C1.

11. Richard Davis, *Electing Justice: Fixing the Supreme Court Nomination Process* (New York: Oxford University Press, 2005).

12. David Garrow, "Mental Decrepitude on the U.S. Supreme Court: The Historical Case for a 28th Amendment," *University of Chicago Law Review,* vol. 67, Fall 2000, pp. 995ff; Artemis Ward,. (SUNY Press, 2003); and David N. Atkinson, *Leaving the Bench: Supreme Court Justices at the End.* (University of Kansas Press, 1999).

13. Bruce Allen Murphy, *Wild Bill: The Legend and Life of William O. Douglas* (New York: Random House, 2003).

14. Judith Resnick and Theodore Ruger, "One Robe, Two Hats," *New York Times,* July 17, 2005.

15. See Milton Heumann, *Plea Bargaining: The Experiences of Prosecutors, Judges and Defense Attorneys* (Chicago: University of Chicago Press, 1977); John H. Langbein, "Torture and Plea Bargaining," *Public Interest,* vol. 21 (Winter 1980): 24–26.

16. Tom Fowler, "The Fall of Enron," *Houston Chronicle,* July 12, 2005.

17. Jennifer Lin, "First Class-Action Lawsuit Filed Against Terrorists," *Pittsburgh Post-Gazette,* February 20, 2002.

18. Adam Nagourney and Richard W. Stevenson, "Democrats See Wide Bush Stamp on Court System," *New York Times,* January 15, 2006, www.nyt.com; Warren Richey, "Conservatives Near Lock on US Courts, *Christian Science Monitor,* April 14, 2005; Carrie Johnson, "Testing the Limits," *Legal Times,* October 4, 1999, p. 1; Neil Lewis, "A Court Becomes a Model of Conservative Pursuits," *New York Times,* May 24, 1999, p. 1.

19. Abraham, *Judicial Process,* p. 163.

20. J. Woodford Howard, Jr., *Courts of Appeals in the Federal Judicial System* (Princeton, N.J.: Princeton University Press, 1981), p. 58.

21. William Glaberson, "Caseload Forcing Two-Level System for U.S. Appeals," *New York Times,* March 14, 1999, p. 1.

22. Judith Resnick and Theodore Ruger, "One Robe, Two Hats," *New York Times,* July 17, 2005.

23. See Laurence H. Tribe, *God Save This Honorable Court* (New York: Random House, 1985), pp. 50–77; William H. Rehnquist, *The Supreme Court: How It Was, How It Is* (New York: Morrow, 1987), pp. 235–53. And see John B. Gates and Jeffrey E. Cohen, "Presidents, Supreme Court Justices and Racial Equality Cases: 1954–1984," *Political Behavior* 10, no. 1 (1994): 22–36.

24. Henry J. Abraham, *Justices and Presidents: A Political History of Appointments to the Supreme Court* (New York: Oxford University Press, 1992), p. 266.

25. Abraham, *Justices and Presidents,* p. 238.

26. See Barbara Perry, A *"Representative" Supreme Court? The Impact of Race, Religion, and Gender on Appointments* (New York: Greenwood Press, 1991).

27. Until the Bush administration the ratings included "exceptionally well qualified," as well.

28. For more on the role of the ABA in the appointment process, see Joel Grossman, *Lawyers and Judges: The ABA and the Politics of Judicial Selection* (New York: Wiley, 1965).

29. Quoted in Henry J. Abraham, *Justices and Presidents: A Political History of Appointments to the Supreme Court,* 3d ed. (New York: Oxford University Press, 1992), pp. 16–17.

30. For more on the Bork battle, see Ethan Bronner, *Battle for Justice: How the Bork Nomination Shook America* (New York: Norton, 1989).

31. For more on the Thomas confirmation battle, see Timothy M. Phelps and Helen Winternitz, *Capitol Games* (New York: Hyperion Books, 1991); Jane Mayer and Jill Abramson, *Strange Justice: The Selling of Clarence Thomas* (Boston: Houghton Mifflin, 1994); John C. Danforth, *Resurrection: The Confirmation of Clarence Thomas* (New York: Viking Press, 1994).

32. For more on the Fortas nomination, see Bruce Allen Murphy, *Fortas: The Rise and Ruin of a Supreme Court Justice* (New York: Morrow, 1988); for more on the confirmation process in general, see John Massaro, *Supremely Political: The Role of Ideology and Presidential Management in Unsuccessful Supreme Court Nominations* (Albany: State University of New York Press, 1990).

33. Henry J. Reske, "The Safe Debate," *ABA Journal,* vol. 48 (July 1994): 20.

34. Sheldon Goldman, "Bush's Judicial Legacy: The Final Imprint, *Judicature* 76, no. 6 (April/May 1993): 295.

35. For more on the appointment process for district court judges, see Neil McFeeley. *Appointment of Judges: The Johnson Presidency* (Austin: University of Texas Press, 1987); Harold Chase, *Federal Judges: The Appointing Process* (Minneapolis: University of Minnesota Press, 1972).

36. Warren Richey, "Conservatives Near Lock on US Courts," *Christian Science Monitor,* April 14, 2005.

37. This information comes from Sheldon Goldman and Matthew D. Saronson, "Clinton's Nontraditional Judges: Creating a More Representative Bench," *Judicature* 78, no. 2 (September/October 1994): 73; See also Goldman, "Bush's Judicial Legacy": Goldman, "The Bush Imprint on the Judiciary: Carrying on a Tradition," *Judicature* 74, no. 6 (April/May 1991): 294–306.

38. Sheldon Goldman, "Reagan's Second Term Judicial Appointments: The Battle at Midway," *Judicature* 70, no. 4 (April/May 1987): 328–31.

39. Sheldon Goldman, Elliot Slotnick, Gerard Gryski, and Sara Schiavoni, "W. Bush's Judiciary: The First Term Record," *Judicature* 88, no. 6 (May/June 2005): 269.

40. Sheldon Goldman and Elliot Slotnik, "Clinton's First-Term Judiciary: Many Bridges to Cross," *Judicature* 80, no. 6 (May/June 1997): 270.

41. Goldman and Saronson, "Clinton's Nontraditional Judges," p. 69.

42. Sheldon Goldman, Elliot Slotnick, Gerard Gryski, and Sara Schiavoni, "W. Bush's Judiciary: The First Term Record," *Judicature* 88, no. 6 (May/June 2005): 269.

43. Sheldon Goldman and Elliot Slotnick, "Picking Judges under Fire," *Judicature* 86, no. 6 (May/June 1999): 265–78.

44. David O'Brien, *Storm Center: The Supreme Court in American Politics,* 4th ed. (New York: Norton, 1996), pp. 165–66.

45. Rehnquist, *Supreme Court*, p. 265; See also H. W. Perry, Jr., *Deciding to Decide: Agenda Setting in the United States Supreme Court* (Cambridge, Mass.: Harvard University Press, 1991); Gregory A. Caldeira and John R. Wright, "The Discuss List: Agenda Setting in the Supreme Court," *Law and Society Review* 24 (1990): 809–13.

46. Tony Mauro, "Justices Give Pivotal Role to Novice Lawyers," *USA Today*, March 13–15, 1998, pp. 1–2.

47. *Escobedo* v. *Illinois*, 378 U.S. 478 (1964).

48. *Miranda* v. *Arizona*, 384 U.S. 436 (1966). Besides the lead case, *Miranda*, the other appeals accepted were *Vignera* v. *New York*, *Westover* v. *United States*, and *California* v. *Stewart*. Regarding the rest of the cases, the Court had also decided there would be no "retroactivity;" that is, the broad protections would not be extended back to previously decided cases; See *Linkletter* v. *Walker*. 381 U.S. 618 (1965).

49. Liva Baker. *Miranda, Crime, Law, and Politics* (New York: Atheneum Press, 1983), p. 88.

50. Cass R. Sunstein, "Supreme Caution," *Washington Post*, July 6, 1997, pp. C1, C5; and Linda Greenhouse, "Benchmarks of Justice." *New York Times*, July 1, 1997, pp. A1, A18.

51. David M. O'Brien, "The Rehnquist Court's Shrinking Plenary Docket," *Judicature* 81, no. 2 (September–October, 1997): pp. 58–65.

52. Tony Mauro, "Justices Give Pivotal Role to Novice Lawyers," *USA Today*, March 13–15, 1998, pp. 1–2.

53. Lincoln Caplan, "Uneasy Days in Court," *Newsweek*, October 10, 1994, pp. 62–64; Linda Greenhouse, "Which Counts, Congress's Intent or Its Words," *New York Times*, October 6, 1994, p. A18.

54. Joan Biskupic, "10th Justice States His Case," *Washington Post*, March 2, 1998, p. A15.

55. Tim Russert, *Constitutional Conversation with Justices Sandra Day O'Connor, Antonin Scalia, and Stephen Breyer*, National Archives and the Aspen Institute, April 22, 2005.

56. *Brown* v. *Board of Education*, 347 U.S. 483 (1954).

57. Richard Kluger, *Simple Justice* (New York: Knopf, 1975).

58. Joan Biskupic, "Nothing Subtle About Scalia, The Combative Conservative," *Washington Post*, February 18, 1997, p. A4.

59. Joan Biskupic, "Lawyers Emerge as Supreme Court Specialists," *USA Today*, May 16, 2003, p. 6A; Joan Biskupic, "Women Are Still Not Well Represented Among Lawyers Facing Supreme Test," *Washington Post*, May 27, 1997, p. A3; and Joan Biskupic, "Justices Growing Impatient with Imprecision," *Washington Post*, May 5, 1997, p. A7.

60. See letters from Robert Bradley, Chief Justice Rehnquist, and Henry J. Abraham in American Political Science Association, *Law, Courts and Judicial Process Section Newsletters* 6, no. 4 (Summer 1989): 2–3, and 7; and no. 1 (Fall 1989): 3; See also Abraham, *Judicial Process*, p. 196.

61. Linda Greenhouse, "Ruling Fixed Opinions," *New York Times*, February 22, 1988, p. A16.

62. Joan Biskupic, "Justices in Conference: A Tradition Wanes," *Washington Post*, February 2, 2000.

63. Phillip Cooper and Howard Ball, *The United States Supreme Court: From the Inside Out* (Upper Saddle River, N.J.: Prentice Hall, 1996), p. 218.

64. *Roe* v. *Wade*, 410 U.S. 113 (1973).

65. *Planned Parenthood of Southeastern Pennsylvania* v. *Casey*, 112 S. Ct. 931 (1992).

66. David J. Garrow, "Justice Souter Emerges," *New York Times Magazine*, September 25, 1994, pp. 36–42.

67. Quoted in Nat Hentoff, "The Constitutionalist," *New Yorker*, March 12, 1990, p. 60.

68. Harold Spaeth, *Studies in U.S. Supreme Court Behavior* (New York: Garland Press, 1990); Saul Brenner and Harold Spaeth, "Ideological Positions as a Variable in the Authoring of Dissenting Opinion," *American Politics Quarterly* 16 (July 1988): 17–28.

69. See *Webster* v. *Reproductive Health Services*, 492 U.S. 490 (1989), pp. 533–35. For the behind-the-scenes account of the battle, see David Savage, *Turning Right: The Making of the Rehnquist Supreme Court* (New York: Wiley, 1992), pp. 209–14, 255–72, 288–98, esp. pp. 292–93.

70. *Lamb's Chapel* v. *Center Moriches Union Free School District*, 124 L. Ed. 2d. 352 (1993), p. 365.

71. *New York Times Co.* v. *United States*, 403 U.S. 713 (1971).

72. Tony Mauro, "Justices Give Pivotal Role to Novice Lawyers," and "Corps of Clerks Lacking in Diversity," *USA Today*, March 13, 1998, pp. 1A, 12–13A.

73. Ed Lazarus, *Closed Chambers* (New York: Times Books, 1998), p. 271.

74. Joyce Murdoch and Deb Price, *Courting Justice* (New York: Basic Books, 2001), chaps. 11–12.

75. David J. Garrow, "The Brains Behind Blackmun," *Legal Affairs* (May-June 2005), pp. 27–34.

76. David Margolick, "The Path to Florida," *Vanity Fair*, October 2004, pp. 310–22.

77. Bernard Schwartz, *The Ascent of Pragmatism* (Reading, Mass.: Addison-Wesley, 1990); Bob Woodward and Scott Armstrong, *The Brethren: Inside the Supreme Court* (New York: Avon Books, 1979).

78. *Stanley* v. *Georgia*, 394 U.S. 557 (1969).

79. *Payne* v. *Tennessee*, 59 *Law Week*, 4823 (1991).

80. Abraham, *Judicial Process*, p. 325.

81. James F. Spriggs II and Thomas Hansford, "Explaining the Overruling of U.S. Supreme Court Precedent," Midwest Political Science Association, April, 1998.

82. See Herbert Wechsler, *Principles, Politics, and Fundamental Law* (Cambridge, Mass.: Harvard University Press, 1961); See also Alexander M. Bickel, *The Least Dangerous Branch* (Indianapolis, Ind.: Bobbs-Merrill, 1962); Raoul Berger, *Government by Judiciary: The Transformation of the Fourteenth Amendment* (Cambridge, Mass.: Harvard University Press, 1977); Jesse H. Choper, *Judicial Review and the National Political Process* (Chicago: University of Chicago Press, 1980); John Hart Ely, *Democracy and Distrust: A Theory of Judicial Review* (Cambridge, Mass.: Harvard University Press, 1980).

83. Jeffrey Segal and Albert Cover, "Ideological Values and the Votes of U.S. Supreme Court Justices," *American Political Science Review* 83 (1989): 557–65.

84. *West Virginia Board of Education* v. *Barnette*, 319 U.S. 624 (1943), pp. 646–47.

85. *Griswold* v. *Connecticut*, 381 U.S. 479 (1965).

86. *Sierra Club* v. *Morton*, 405 U.S. 727 (1972), pp. 742–43.

87. For a fine example of this argument detailing the problems of the Court as a "superlegislature," see Robert Bork, *The Tempting of America: The Political Seduction of the Law* (New York: Macmillan, 1990).

88. Hugo Black, *A Constitutional Faith* (New York: Knopf, 1968), p. 21. For more on Black's judicial philosophy, see Roger K. Newman, *Hugo Black: A Biography* (New York: Pantheon Books, 1994), p. 512.

89. Quoted in *New York Times Magazine*, October 5, 1986, p. 74.

90. David J. Danelski, "The Influence of the Chief Justice in the Decisional Process of the Supreme Court," in *Courts, Judges and Politics*, ed. Walter Murphy and Charles Herman Pritchett (New York: Random House, 1986), p. 568.

91. Joan Biskupic, "Centrist Justice Sought 'Social Stability,'" *Washington Post*, July 5, 2005.

92. Paul Muschick, "County to Keep the Commandments," *Allentown Morning Call*, July 13, 2005, p. 1.

93. Eisenhower was backing the decision by the Supreme Court to desegregate Central High School in Little Rock, Arkansas—*Cooper* v. *Aaron*, 358 U.S. 1 (1958).

94. The decision banning school prayer is *Engel* v. *Vitale*, 370 U.S. 421 (1962).

95. *Worcester* v. *Georgia*, 31 U.S. 515 (1832). See Albert Beveridge, *Life of John Marshall*, vol. 4 (Boston: Houghton Mifflin, 1919), p. 551. Presidential opposition is not unusual.

96. *Employment Division, Department of Human Resources of Oregon* v. *Smith*, 110 S. Ct. 1595 (1990).

97. David E. Anderson, "Signing of Religious Freedom Act Culminates Three-Year Push," *Washington Post*, November 20, 1993, p. C6.

98. *City of Boerne* v. *Flores*, 138 L. Ed. 2d 624 (1997), p. 633.

99. Thomas Marshall, *Public Opinion and the Supreme Court* (Boston: Unwin Hyman, 1989).

100. "Supreme Court's Image Declines as Nomination Battle Looms," June 15, 2005, Pew Research Center for the People and the Press, Washington, D.C.

101. Woodrow Wilson, *Constitutional Government in the United States* (New York: Columbia University Press, 1907), p. 142.

CHAPTER 7

1. "Parade," *Sacramento Bee*, January 27, 2002, pp. 4–6; "The Office of Homeland Security," www.whitehouse.gov/homeland; "Does Ridge Have the Clout to Carry It Off?" *Congressional Quarterly Weekly*, November 3, 2001, pp. 2586–87; Eric Pianin and Bradley Graham, "Ridge: Goal Isn't to Create Bureaucracy," *Washington Post*, October 4, 2001, p. A24; Alison Mitchell, "Disputes Erupt on Ridge's Needs for His Job," *New York Times*, November 4, 2001; Mark Benjamin, "Ridge: Government Might Need Reorganizing," *United Press International*, February 7, 2002; Bill Miller, "$37.7 Billion for Homeland Defense Is a Start, Bush Says," *Washington Post*, January 25, 2002, p. A15; Bill Miller, "Ridge Lacks Power to Do His Job, Says Panetta at Hearing, Cabinet Rank, Budget Clout Urged," *Washington Post*, April 18, 2002, p. A19; Joel Brinkley and Philip Shenon, "Ridge Meeting Opposition from Agencies," *New York Times*, February 7, 2002, A12; Elizabeth Becker, "Ridge Briefs Home Panel, but Discord Is Not Resolved," *New York Times*, April 1, 2002, p. A17; Bill Miller, "Ridge Will Meet Informally with 2 House Committees," *Washington Post*, April 4, 2002, p. A15.

2. President George W. Bush, transcript of a speech reprinted as "The Plan: We Have Concluded that Our Government Must Be Reorganized," *New York Times*, June 6, 2002, p. A18. See also Department of Homeland Security, President George W. Bush, June 2002, www.whitehouse.gov/homeland/.

3. Eric Lipton and Scott Shane, "Leader of Federal Effort Feels the Heat," *New York Times*, September 3, 2005, p. A11.

4. Neal Conan, "Analysis: Rethinking Homeland Security after Katrina," *Talk of the Nation* (NPR); 09/08/2005.

5. David E. Rosenbaum, "Study Ranks Homeland Security Department Lowest in Morale." *New York Times*, October 16, 2005, A1.

6. Barry Bozeman, *Bureaucracy and Red Tape* (Upper Saddle River, N.J.: Prentice Hall, 2000), p. 1.

7. See Max Weber, *Essays in Sociology*, trans. and ed. H. H. Garth and C. Wright Mills (New York: Oxford University Press, 1958), p. 232.

8. Anthony Downs, *Inside Bureaucracy* (Boston: Little, Brown, 1967), pp. 24–25.

9. David Frum, *Dead Right* (New York: Basic Books, 1994), pp. 42–43; "Kingsize Tribute," *Sacramento Bee*, July 18, 1997, p. A16.

10. William L. Riordon, *Plunkitt of Tammany Hall* (New York: Dutton, 1963), chapter 9.

11. "Changes in Federal Civilian Employment: An Update," June 1999, TRAC Data Services, http://trac.syr.edu/aboutOrder/index.html. See Ellen Nakashima, "The Shifting Federal Workforce," *Washington Post*, September 21, 2001, p. A2. Also, www.cbo.gov.

12. See Wilson, *Bureaucracy*, chapter 7. See also Guy Benveniste, *Bureaucracy* (San Francisco: Boyd and Frasier, 1977).

13. Larry Hill, ed., *The State of Public Bureaucracy* (New York: M. E. Sharpe, 1992).

14. Quoted in Richard Neustadt, *Presidential Power* (New York: Mentor, 1960), p. 22.

15. See David Stockman, *The Triumph of Politics: The Inside Story of the Reagan Revolution* (New York: Avon, 1987).

16. See Richard Nathan, *The Plot that Failed* (New York: Wiley, March 1975).

17. Herbert Kaufman, *Red Tape: Its Uses and Abuses* (Washington, D.C.: Brookings Institution, 1997).

18. David Bullier and Joan Claybrook, "Regulations That Work," *Washington Monthly*, April 1986, pp. 47–54.

19. Bill Miller, "More Help Sought for Those Who Blow Whistle," *Washington Post*, February 28, 2002, p. A21; see also "F.B.I. to Pay Whistle Blower $1.1 Million in a Settlement," *New York Times*, February 27, 1998, p. 15; Greg Schneider, "No Whistle Blowing Protection for Airport Baggage Screeners," *Washington Post*, February 8, 2002, p. A29.

CHAPTER 8

1. Quoted in Michael Wheeler, *Lies, Damn Lies, and Statistics: The Manipulation of Public Opinion in America* (New York: Dell, 1976), p. 82; See also Albert Hadley Cantril with Mildred Strunk, *Public Opinion, 1935–1946* (Princeton, N.J.: Princeton University Press, 1951), pp. 151–55; See George Gallup, "Professor Gallup Describes a New Way of Measuring Public Opinion," *Independent Journal*, November 15, 1935; See also Gallup, "The Quintamensional Plan of Question Design," *Public Opinion Quarterly* 11, no. 3 (Fall 1947): 385–93; Gallup, "Polls and the Political Process: Past, Present and Future," *Public Opinion Quarterly* 29, no. 4 (Winter 1965–66): 544–49.

2. See Walter Lippmann, *The Phantom Public* (New York: Macmillan, 1927), pp. 13–14.

3. Alexander Hamilton, James Madison, and John Jay, *The Federalist Papers* (New York: New American Library, 1961), no. 10, p. 119. *The Federalist*, no. 10, appears in the appendices.

4. William Flanagan and Nancy H. Zingale, *Political Behavior of the American Electorate* (Washington, D.C.: *Congressional Quarterly Press*, 1998), p. 179; Herbert Asher, *Polling and the Public: What Every Citizen Should Know*, 4th ed. (Washington, D.C.: *Congressional Quarterly Press*,) 1988.

5. Quoted in Gary Langer, "Responsible Polling in the Wake of 9/11," *Public Perspective*, March/April 2002, pp. 14–16.

6. See the discussion in Robert S. Erikson and Kent L. Tedin, *American Public Opinion: Its Origins, Content, and Impact*, 5th ed. (Boston: Allyn and Bacon, 1995), pp. 128–30.

7. See "National Election Pool," frequently asked questions at www.exit-poll.net/faq.html.

8. See Richard Morin, "Surveying the Damage: Exit Polls Can't Predict Winners, So Don't Expect Them To," *Washington Post Outlook*, Nov. 21, 2004, p. B1.

9. Ibid; also Andrew Kohut, "Polls Apart," *New York Times*, October 21, 2004, p. A29.

10. See Fred Greenstein, *Children and Politics* (New Haven, Conn.: Yale University Press, 1965), p. 119.

11. Urie Bronfenbrenner, *Two Worlds of Childhood: U.S. and USSR*, (New York: Simon and Schuster, 1970).

12. Robert D. Putnam, "Bowling Alone: America's Declining Social Capital," *Journal of Democracy* 6 (1995): 65–78; See also Robert D. Putman, Bowling Alone: The Collapse and Revival of American Community. New York: Simon & Schuster, 2000.

13. Todd Gitlin, *The Whole World Is Watching: Mass Media in the Making and Unmaking of the New Left* (Berkeley: University of California Press, 1980), p. 201; See also Gitlin, *Watching Television: A Pantheon Guide to Popular Culture* (New York: Pantheon Books, 1986).

14. Janny Scott and David Leonhardt, "Class in America: Shadowy Lines That Still Divide," *New York Times*, May 15, 2005, p. A1.

15. Benamin I. Page and Robert Y. Shapiro, *The Rational Public* (Chicago: University of Chicago Press, 1992), p. 201; See also William Flanagan and Nancy Zingale, *Political Behavior of the American Electorate* (Washington, D.C.: Congressional Quarterly Press, 2005), p. 174; William H. Flanagan, *Political Behavior of the American Electorate*, (Washington, D.C.: Congressional Quarterly Press, 1998) p. 174.

16. See "The American Public: Opinions and Values in a 51%–48% Nation," Pew Research Center, 2005.

17. See www.cawp.rutgers.edu/Facts5.html.

18. "The 2005 Political Typology," Pew Research Center for the People and the Press, May 10, 2005, http://people-press.org/reports/pdf/242.pdf#search='2005%20political%20typology%20pew%20center'.

19. Ibid.

20. James Gibson, "The Political Consequences of Intolerance: Cultural Conformity and Political Freedom," *American Political Science Review* 86 (June 1992): 338–56.

21. Ibid., p. 341.

22. Elizabeth Noelle-Neumann, *The Spiral of Silence* (Chicago: University of Chicago Press, 1984).

23. Norman R. Luttbeg and Michael M. Gant, *American Electoral Behavior, 1952–1992*, 2d ed.

(Itasca, Ill.: Peacock, 1995), esp. pp. 91–164; See also Aaron Wildavsky, "Choosing Preferences by Constructing Institutions: A Cultural Theory of Preference Formation," *American Political Science Review* 81 (March 1987): 3–23.

24. Walter Lippmann, *The Phantom Public*. (New York: Macmillan, 1927), pp. 13–14.

25. Joseph Schumpeter, *Capitalism, Socialism and Democracy* (New York: Harper & Bros., 1950), p. 262; Luttbeg and Gant, *American Electoral Behavior*, esp. chaps. 3–4, p. 67; See also Philip E. Converse, "Information Flow and the Stability of Partisan Attitudes," *Public Opinion Quarterly* 26, no. 4 (Winter 1962): 578–99.

26. Benjamin Page and Robert Shapiro, *The Rational Public: Fifty Years of Trends in Americans' Policy Preference* (Chicago: University of Chicago Press, 1992); See also Paul Brace and Barbara Hinckley, *Follow the Leader: Opinion Polls and Modern Presidents* (New York: Basic Books, 1992), pp. 97–115.

27. See Angus Campbell, Philip Converse, Warren Miller, and Donald Stokes, *The American Voter* (New York: Wiley, 1960).

28. Benjamin Page, *Choices and Echoes in Elections: Rational Man and Electoral Democracy* (Chicago: University of Chicago Press, 1978), chap. 8; See also Sidney Verba and Norman H. Nie, *Participation in America: Political Democracy and Social Equality* (New York: Harper & Row, 1972), pp. 25–26.

CHAPTER 9

1. Joe Hallett, "Churches Flexing Political Muscle," *Columbus Dispatch*, April 11, 2005, p. 01A; Alan Cooperman and Thomas B. Edsall, "Evangelicals Say they Led Charge for the GOP," *Washington Post*, November 8, 2004, p. A 01; John Cochran, "Religious Right Lays Claim to Big Role in GOP Agenda," *Congressional Quarterly Weekly*, November 13, 2004, pp. 2684–89; David Nather, "Social Conservatives Propel Bush, Republicans to Victory," *Congressional Quarterly Weekly*, November 6, 2004, pp. 2586–91; and based on Brian Kim's excellent independent study paper, "The Evangelical Movement in America," (Easton, Penn.: Lafayette College, May 2005).

2. See E. E. Schattschneider, *The Semisovereign People* (New York: Holt, 1960); V. O. Key, Jr., *Politics, Parties, and Pressure Groups* (New York: Crowell, 1964).

3. Quoted in *National Party Conventions, 1831–1988* (Washington, D.C.: Congressional Quarterly Press, 1991), p. 2; See also Michael Nelson, ed., *Guide to the Presidency* (Washington, D.C.: Congressional Quarterly Press, 1989), pp. 268–69.

4. Quoted in Noble E. Cunningham, *The Making of the American Party System, 1789 to 1809* (Upper Saddle River, N.J.: Prentice Hall, 1965); See also Cunningham, *The Jeffersonian Republicans* (Chapel Hill: University of North Carolina Press, 1957).

5. See Warren E. Miller, "Party Identification, Realignment, and Party Voting: Back to the Basics," *American Political Science Review* 85 (1991): 557.

6. See Ralph Ketcham, *Presidents Above Party* (Chapel Hill: University of North Carolina Press, 1984).

7. See Frank Freidel, *Franklin D. Roosevelt: The Triumph* (Boston: Little, Brown, 1956), pp. 248–49.

8. James David Barber, *The Pulse of Politics* (New York: Norton, 1980), pp. 238–63.

9. See William Leuchtenburg, *In the Shadow of FDR* (Ithaca, N.Y.: Cornell University Press, 1983).

10. "Democrats Gain Edge in Party Identification," Pew Research Center for the People and the Press, July 26, 2004.

11. Charles Babington, "Divided Outcome Extends to State Legislatures Too," *Washington Post,* November 9, 2000, supplemented by author's calculations of the party balance in the Washington State and Oregon legislatures from the Web sites of those states' legislatures.

12. Alfred J. Tuchfarber, "The Republican Tidal Wave of 1994: testing hypotheses about realignment, restructuring, and rebellion," APSA paper, 1995.

13. Kirk Victor, "Road to Realignment?" *National Journal,* June 19, 2004; pp. 1920–26; supplemented by survey of information on www.nationaljournal.com.

14. "National Security More Linked with Partisan Affiliation," Pew Research Center for the People and the Press, January 24, 2005.

15. Ibid.

16. "Beyond Red vs. Blue," Pew Research Center for the People and the Press, May 10, 2005.

17. See Austin Ranney, *The Doctrine of Responsible Party Government: Its Origins and Present State* (Urbana: University of Illinois Press, 1962); Samuel J. Eldersvald, *Political Parties in American Society* (New York: Basic Books, 1982).

18. See L. Sandy Maisel, *Parties and Elections in America* (New York: McGraw Hill, 1992).

19. See John Aldrich, *Before the Convention: Strategies and Choices in Presidential Nomination Campaigns* (Chicago: University of Chicago Press, 1980).

20. See American Political Science Association, Committee on Political Parties, "Toward a More Responsible Two-Party System," *American Political Science Review* 64 (1950).

21. Edmond Constantini and Linda Ol Valenty, "The Motives-Ideology Connection Among Political Party Activists;" Peter B. Clark and James Q. Wilson, "Incentive Systems: A Theory of Organization," *Administrative Science Quarterly* 6 (1961): 129–66.

22. Byron York, "America Coming Together Comes Apart," August 3, 2005, at www.nationalreview.com/york/york200508030928.asp.

23. See William L. Riordan, *Plunkitt of Tammany Hall* (New York: Knopf, 1963); Harold Gosnell, *Machine Politics* (Chicago: University of Chicago Press, 1939).

24. See Xandra Kayden and Eddie Mahe, Jr., *The Party Goes On: The Persistence of the Two-Party System in the United States* (New York: Basic Books, 1985).

25. See Howard Reiter, *Parties and Elections in Corporate America* (New York: Longman, 1973).

26. Sandra Sobieraj, "President Pushes 2002 Fund-Raising Tally for Himself, Cheney Over $100 Million Mark," *Allentown Morning Call,* June 22, 2002, p. A 23.

27. See www.opensecrets.org/presidential/index.asp.

28. See Byron E. Shafer, *Quiet Revolution: The Struggle for the Democratic Party and the Shaping of Post-Reform Politics* (New York: Russell Sage Foundation, 1983).

29. Paul West, "An Early Start for Democrats," *Baltimore Sun,* February 4, 2002; Richard L. Berke, "Nominees May Be Chosen Quickly in Rare Competitive Primary Season," *New York Times,* January 2, 2000, p. 22.

30. Dean E. Murphy, "California Moves to Reschedule Its Primary from March to June," *New York Times,* August 30, 2004, p. 9.

31. See Theodore H. White, *The Making of the President, 1968* (New York: Atheneum, 1969).

32. See David E. Price, *Bringing Back the Parties* (Washington, D.C.: Congressional Quarterly Press, 1983).

33. Thomas B. Edsall, "GOP Gains Advantage on Key Issues, Poll Says," *Washington Post,* January 27, 2002, p. A4; Juliet Eilperin, "After McCain-Feingold, A Bigger Role for PACs," *Washington Post,* June 1, 2002, pp. 1, 7.

34. Derek Willis, "527 Fundraising Nets a Record Haul," August 16, 2005, www.publicintegrity.org/527/report.aspx?aid=403.

35. See Samuel Patterson, "The Etiology of Party Competition," *American Political Science Review* 78 (1984): 691.

36. The tendency of single-member district systems to be found in conjunction with two parties, while multimember districts correlate with a multiparty system, is often known as Duverger's Law. It is named for a well-known French political scientist, Maurice Duverger, who first enunciated this theory in his book *Political Parties* (London: Methuen, 1954).

37. See Everett Carl Ladd, *American Political Parties: Social Change and Political Response* (New York: Norton, 1970); James L. Sundquist, *Dynamics of the Party System* (Washington, D.C.: Brookings Institution, 1973).

38. See Warren E. Miller, "Party Identification," in *Political Parties and Elections in the United States: An Encyclopedia,* ed. L. Sandy Maisel (New York: Garland, 1991).

39. See Frank Smallwood, *The Other Candidates: Third Parties in Presidential Elections* (Hanover, N.H.: University Press of New England, 1983); Steven J. Rosenstone, Roy L. Behr, and Edward H. Lazarus, *Third Parties in America: Citizen Response to Major Party Failure* (Princeton, N.J.: Princeton University Press, 1984).

40. See www.feinstein.org/greenparty/elections.html.

41. See Byron Shafer, ed., *Beyond Realignment? Interpreting American Electorial Eras* (Madison: University of Wisconsin Press, 1991).

42. Roger H. Davidson and Walter J. Oleszek, *Congress and Its Members,* (Washington D.C.: CQ Press, 2004), p. 273; William R. Shafer, *Party and Ideology in the United States Congress* (Lanham, Md.: University Press of America, 1980); Norman Ornstein, Thomas E. Mann, and Michael Malbin, *Vital Statistics on Congress, 1993–94* (Washington, D.C.: Congressional Quarterly Press, 1994), p. 200.

43. David Broder, *The Party's Over* (New York: Harper & Row, 1971).

44. "Battleground 2002 (XXI)," Study #8794, The Tarrance Group, found at www.azwins.org/Battleground%202002.pdf, and Thomas B. Edsall, "GOP Gains Advantage on Key Issues, Polls Say," *Washington Post,* January 27, 2002, p. A4.

CHAPTER 10

1. See Peter Baker, "Motor Voter Apparently Didn't Drive Up Turnout," *Washington Post,* November 6, 1996, p. B7; Also see B. Drummond Ayres Jr., "Law to Ease Voter Registration Has Added 5 Million to the Polls," *New York Times,* September 3, 1995, p. A1; "'Motor Voter' Bill Enacted after 5 Years," *CQ Almanac* 49 (1993): 199–201; See Executive Summary, Federal Election Commission's Report to the Congress, "The Impact of the National Voter Registration Act of 1993 on Federal Elections, 1999–2000," www.fee.gov./pages/nvrareport2000/nvrareport2000.htm; Raymond Wolfinger and Jonathan Hoffman, "Requesting and Voting with Motor Voter," *PS*

(March 2001): 85–92; Benjamin Highton, "Voter Registration and Turnout in the United States." *Perspectives on Politics* 2, no. 3 (September 2004): 507–15.

2. See U.S. Census Bureau News, United States Department of Commerce, www.census.gov, May 26, 2005; "U.S. Voter Turnout Up in 2004," Census Bureau Reports; Brian Faler, "Election Turnout in 2004 Was Highest Since 1968," *Washington Post,* January 15, 2005, p. A5.

3. "National Commission on Federal Election Reform," *Summary of Principal Recommendations,* The Century Foundation, at www.tcf.org/Press Releases/ElectionReform.html 1/30/02.

4. *Building Confidence in U.S. Elections,* Report of the Commission on Federal Election Reform, September 2005, www.american.edu/ia/cfer/report/report.html; See "New Standards for Elections," *New York Times,* editorial, November 7, 2005, p. A10; "Fixing Democracy," *New York Times,* editorial, January 18, 2004, p. A10.

5. Sidney Verba and Norman H. Nie, *Participation in America: Political Democracy and Social Equality* (New York: Harper & Row, 1972); See Karen M. Arlington and William L. Taylor, eds., *Voting Rights in America: Continuing the Quest for Full Participation* (Lanham, Md.: University Press of America, 1992); See Francis Fox Piven and Richard A. Cloward, *Why Americans Don't Vote* (New York: Pantheon, 1988); Raymond E. Wolfinger and Steven J. Rosenstone, *Who Votes* (New Haven, Conn.: Yale University Press, 1980).

6. See Dan Keating and John Mintz, "Florida Black Ballots Affected Most in 2000," *Washington Post,* November 13, 2001, p. A3; Ford Fessenden, "Ballots Cast by Blacks and Older Voters Were Tossed in Far Greater Numbers," *New York Times,* November 12, 2001, p. A47.

7. See Caltech-MIT/Voting Technology Project, www.vote.caltech.edu/.

8. "California Voter Foundation Releases Comprehensive Results of Survey on Voting Incentives and Barriers," April 7, 2005. California Voter Foundation, at www.calvoter.org.

9. See CalTech/MIT Voting Technology Project, February 2005.

10. See www.idea.int/vt/index.cfm, the home page for International Voter Turnout.

11. Steven J. Rosenstone and Raymond E. Wolfinger, "The Effect of Registration Laws on Voter Turnout," *American Political Science Review* 72 (March 1998): 25–30.

12. Richard Morin, "The Dog Ate My Forms, and, Well, I Couldn't Find a Pen," *Washington Post National Weekly Edition,* November 5–11, 1990, p. 38; George Will, "In Defense of Nonvoting," *Newsweek,* October 10, 1983, p. 96.

13. *Building Confidence in U.S. Elections: Report of the Commission on Federal Election Reform,* September 2005, Electionline.org/The Pew Charitable Trusts, www.american.edu/ia/cfer/report/report.html.

14. See Michael Kagay, "The Mystery of Nonvoters and Whether They Matter," *New York Times,* August 27, 2000, Section 4, p. 1; See Michael M. Grant and William Lyons, "Democratic Theory, Nonvoting, and Public Policy: The 1972–1988 Presidential Elections," *American Politics Quarterly* 21 (April 1993): 185–204; Priscilla L. Southwell, "Alienation and Nonvoting in the United States: A Refined Operationalization," *Western Political Quarterly* 38 (December 1985): 663–75; Richard Berke, "Nonvoters Are No More Alienated Than Voters, Survey Shows," *New York Times,* May 30, 1996. For the complete survey and analysis, visit the League of Women Voters

home page at www.lwv.org; Angus Campbell, Philip E. Converse, Warren E. Miller, and Donald Stokes, et al., *The American Voter* (New York: Wiley, 1960).

15. "California Voter Foundation Releases Comprehensive Results of Survey on Voting Incentives and Barriers," April 7, 2005, California Voter Foundation, at www.calvoter.org.

16. Ibid.

17. The data and analysis come from several sources: See "Votes for Women 2004" Gender Gap Updates at www.votesforwomen2004.org/gender.htm; Also see Gebe Martinez and Mary Agnes Carey, "Erasing the Gender Gap Tops Republican Playbook," *CQ Weekly*, March 6, 2004.

18. See National Initiative News, The Democracy Foundation, http://p2dd.org/nationalinitiative/newsletter/; Also see "The Experiences of Other States: A Comparison of the Initiative and Referendum." National Council of State Legislatures at www.ncsl.org.

19. Ibid.

20. Ibid. Initiative and Referendum Institute (IRI), www.iandrinstitute.org/home.asp. This Web site and www.ballot.org were created to provide in-depth nonpartisan and nonpolitical information about the initiative and referendum process at the local, state, and national levels as well as to provide a glimpse of what is happening with initiative and referendum around the world.

21. See Stanley Kelley Jr., *Interpreting Elections* (Princeton, N.J.: Princeton University Press, 1983).

22. Morris P. Fiorina, *Retrospective Voting in American National Elections* (New Haven. Conn.: Yale University Press, 1979); See Nelson Polsby and Aaron Wildavsky, *Presidential Elections*, 9th ed. (New York: Free Press, 1995).

23. See M. Margaret Conway, *Political Participation in the United States* (Washington, D.C.: Congressional Quarterly Press, 1991), p. 8, Table 1–2.

24. Martin Diamond, *The Electoral College and the American Idea of Democracy* (Washington, D.C.: American Enterprise Institute, 1977).

25. See Michael Glennon, *When No Majority Rules: The Electoral College and Presidential Succession*, (Washington DC: CQ Press, 2000, 2002); Verba and Nie, *Participation in America*, pp. 25–40.

26. See www.fee.gov/, "Campaign Finance," a report and study by the League of Women Voters at www.lwv.org; Also see Common Cause Web site, www.commoncause.org.

27. *Buckley* v. *Valeo*, 424 U.S. 1 (1976); *Federal Election Commission* v. *National Conservative Political Action Committee*, et al., 450 U.S. 480 (1985); See also Larry Sabato, *The Party's Just Begun* (Glenview, Ill.: Scott, Foresman/Little, Brown, 1988), p. 125; See "Charting the Health of American Democracy," a report by the League of Women Voters, June 1997, www.lwv.org.

28. See "The McCain-Feingold-Cochran Campaign Reform Bill" at www.campaignfinancesite.org/legislation/mccain.html.

29. For 527s see Public Citizen at www.citizen.org/congress/campaign/issues/nonprofit; Also see The League of Woman Voters: Campaign Finance Reform, S. 271; See http://interactive.lwv.org/News/News.cfm?ID=1401&c=7; Also see the Common Cause Web site at www.commoncause.org.

30. See Thomas Edsall, "Panel Backs Bill to Rein in '527' Advocacy Groups," *Washington Post*, April 28, 2005, p. A21.

CHAPTER 11

1. Elisabeth Bumiller, "Armies Ready for Court Battle but Are Unable to Find a Fight," *New York Times*, July 24, 2005; Howard Fineman and Debra Rosenberg, "Threading the Needle," *Newsweek*, August 1, 2005, pp. 30–33; Karen Tumulty, "Why Washington Canceled a Showdown," *Time Magazine*, August 1, 2005, pp. 26–27.

2. See Jeffrey M. Berry, *The Interest Group Society*, 3d ed. (New York: Longman Press, 1997); Allan J. Cigler and Burdett A. Loomis, eds., *Interest Group Politics*, 4th ed. (Washington, D.C.: Congressional Quarterly Press, 1995).

3. Alexis de Tocqueville, *Democracy in America* (New York: Knopf, 1991), p. 485.

4. James Madison, *The Federalist*, no. 10, is reprinted in Appendix 5.

5. See Arthur F. Bentley, *The Process of Government* (Chicago: University of Chicago Press, 1906); David Truman, *The Governmental Process* (New York: Knopf, 1951); E. E. Schattschneider, *The Semi-Sovereign People* (New York: Holt, 1960).

6. Tocqueville, *Democracy in America*, p. 487.

7. See Burdett A. Loomis and Allan J. Cigler, "The Changing Nature of Interest Group Politics," in *Interest Group Politics*, ed. Loomis and Cigler, pp. 1–31; Jack Walker, *Mobilizing Interest Groups in America* (Ann Arbor: University of Michigan Press, 1991).

8. Matt Bai, "Fight Club," *New York Times Sunday Magazine*, August 10, 2003, pp. 24–27.

9. Jason DeParle, "Nomination Stirs a Debate on Federalists' Sway," *New York Times*, August 1, 2005; and see "Attention: Media Interested in Finding Experts on the Rehnquist Court and the Role of the Courts," at www.fed-soc.org/, August 1, 2005.

10. See Mancur Olson Jr., *The Logic of Collective Action* (Cambridge, Mass.: Harvard University Press, 1965), pp. 5–52; Dennis Chong, *Collective Action and the Civil Rights Movement* (Chicago: University of Chicago Press, 1991).

11. See www.nags.org/ and www.securityfocus.com/news/10251.

12. Elizabeth Mehren, "Political Lightning Rod Planted on New Hampshire Farmhouse" *Los Angeles Times*, August 1, 2005; *Kelo* v. *New London*. See also www.freestarmedia.com, www.castlecoalition.org/ and www.ij.org/privateproperty/connecticut/.

13. See David Vogel, *Fluctuating Fortunes: The Political Power of Business in America* (New York: Basic Books, 1989); William Greider, *Who Will Tell the People? The Betrayal of American Democracy* (New York: Simon & Schuster, 1992).

14. See Jeffrey H. Birnbaum and Alan S. Murray, *Showdown at Gucci Gulch* (New York: Vintage Books, 1988); Kay Lehman Schlozman and John T. Tierney, *Organized Interests and American Democracy* (New York: Harper & Row, 1986).

15. See the argument in John Kenneth Galbraith, *American Capitalism: The Concept of Countervailing Power* (Boston: Houghton Mifflin, 1952).

16. Joel Dresang, "Split at the Top Seen As Challenge to Unions' Effectiveness, Survival," *Milwaukee Journal Sentinel*, July 31, 2005.

17. Shaila K. Dewan, "Black Farmers' Refrain: Where's All Our Money?" *New York Times*, August 1, 2004, www.nyt.com.

18. See Lawrence S. Rothenberg, *Linking Citizens to Government: Interest Group Politics at Common Cause* (New York: Cambridge University Press, 1992); Andrew S. McFarland, *Common Cause:*

Lobbying in the Public Interest (Chatham, N.J.: Chatham House, 1984).

19. *Garcia* v. *San Antonio Metropolitan Transit Authority*, 469 U.S. 528 (1985).

20. See Karen O'Connor, *Women's Organizations' Use of the Courts* (Lexington, Mass.: Lexington Books, 1980); Mark P. Petracca, ed., *The Politics of Interests* (Boulder, Colo.: Westview Press, 1992).

21. Olson, *Logic of Collective Action*. See also Robert H. Salisbury, "An Exchange Theory of Interest Groups," *Midwest Journal of Political Science* 13 (1969): 1–32.

22. For an extended discussion of the reasons why people decide to participate in full-time political activity, including work within interest groups, see James L. Payne et al., *The Motivation of Politicians* (Chicago: Nelson-Hall, 1984).

23. See Jeffrey M. Berry, *Lobbying for the People* (Princeton, N.J.: Princeton University Press, 1977).

24. See Ronald J. Hrebenar and Clive S. Thomas, "The Japanese Lobby in Washington: How Different Is It?" in *Interest Group Politics*, ed. Cigler and Loomis, pp. 349–68; Pat Choate, *Agents of Influence: How Japan's Lobbyists in the United States Manipulate America's Political and Economic System* (New York: Knopf, 1990).

25. Jeffrey H. Birnbaum, "The Road to Riches Is Called K Street" *Washington Post*, June 22, 2005, p. A1.

26. See Laura Woliver, *From Outrage to Action* (Urbana: University of Illinois Press, 1993).

27. James L. Guth et al., "Onward Christian Soldiers: Religious Activist Groups in American Politics," in *Interest Group Politics*, ed. Cigler and Loomis, pp. 42–75.

28. See Frank J. Sorauf, "Adaptation and Innovation in Political Action Committees," in *Interest Group Politics*, ed. Cigler and Loomis, pp. 175–92; Dan Clawson, Alan Neustadt, and Denise Scott, *Money Talks: Corporate PACs and Political Influence* (New York: Basic Books, 1992), p. 29; See www.opensecrets.org.

29. *United States* v. *Harris*, 347 U.S. 612 (1954).

30. Jonathan D. Salant, "Highlights of the Lobby Bill," *Congressional Quarterly Weekly Report*, December 2, 1995, p. 3632.

31. Jonathan Rauch, *Demosclerosis: The Silent Killer of American Government* (New York: Random House, 1994).

32. Arthur Bentley, *The Process of Government, A Study of Social Pressures* (Chicago: University of Chicago Press, 1908).

33. David B. Truman, *The Governmental Process* (New York: Knopf, 1951).

34. Theodore Lowi, *The End of Liberalism* (New York: Norton, 1979). See also Robert Dahl, *Preface to Democratic Theory* (Chicago: University of Chicago Press, 1956).

35. Hugh Heclo, "Issue Networks and the Executive Establishment," in *The New American Political System*, ed. Anthony King (Washington, D.C.: American Enterprise Institute, 1978), pp. 55–82.

36. John P. Heinz, Edward O. Lauman, Robert L. Nelson, and Robert H. Salisbury, *The Hollow Core* (Cambridge, Mass.: Harvard University Press, 1993).

37. Based on Brian Kim's excellent independent study paper, "The Evangelical Movement in America," Lafayette College, May 2005.

38. Congress Watch Division of Public Citizen, study, July 27, 2005: Jeffrey H. Birnbaum, "Hill a

Steppingstone to K Street for Some," *Washington Post,* July 27, 2005, p. A19.40; Sheryl Gay Stolberg, "Lobbyist's Downfall Leads to Charities' Windfall," *New York Times,* January 6, 2006, www.nyt.com; Anne E. Kornblut and Abby Goodnough, "Bush and Others Shed Donations Tied to Lobbyist," *New York Times,* January 5, 2006, www.nyt.com; Susan Schmidt, "Ex-Lobbyist is Focus of Widening Investigations," *Washington Post,* July 16, 2004, p. A19.

39. Carl Hulse, "Ohio Congressman Linked to Scandal Gives Up Post," *New York Times,* January 16, 2006, www.nyt.com.

40. Frank Rich, "Is Abramoff the New Monica?" *New York Times,* January 15, 2006; ———, "Ethics Complaint on Ralph Reed," *New York Times,* December 2, 2005; David Kirkpatrick and Philip Shenon, "Ralph Reed's Zeal for Lobbying is Shaking His Political Faithful," *New York Times,* April 18, 2005.

41. *Colorado Republican Federal Campaign Committee* v. *Federal Election Commission,* 135 L. Ed. 2d 795 (1996), p. 803.

42. Quoted in Richard L. Berke, "Interest Groups Prepare to Spend on Campaign Spin," *New York Times,* January 11, 1998, p. 1.

43. Adam Clymer, "The Supreme Court: Campaign Money," *New York Times,* June 26, 2001. Article discusses *Federal Election Commission* v. *Colorado Republican Federal Campaign Committee* 533 U.S. 431 (2001).

44. Glen Justice, "Even with Campaign Finance Law, Money Talks Louder than Ever," *New York Times,* November 8, 2004, p. A16; and Open Secrets Web site, http://www.opensecrets.org/527s/527cmtes.asp?level=C&cycle=2004 and Political Money Line's site at www.politicalmoneyline.com/.

45. Leslie Wayne, "G.O.P. Supports Conservative Races" *New York Times,* April 11, 2004, p. 25.

46. Glen Justice, "Concern Grows About Role of Interest Groups in Elections," *New York Times,* March 9, 2005, p. A20; See also financial figures on www.fec.gov/finance/disclosure/ecname01.shtml; And see "Ad Watch: Citizens for a Strong Senate", October 20, 2004, at www.newsok.com/electok/article/1342812/.

47. Carl Hulse, "Democrats Claim a Better Idea on Controlling Lobbying," *New York Times,* January 19, 2006, www.nyt.com.

CHAPTER 12

1. Daniel W. Drezner and Henry Farrell, "Web of Influence," *Foreign Policy,* www.foreignpolicy.com, November/December 2004; Also see their paper "The Power and Politics of Blogs," July 2004, paper presented at the 2004 American Political Science Association Meeting; Michael Cornfield, Jonathan Carson, Alison Kalis, and Emily Simon, "Buzz, Blogs, and Beyond: The Internet and the National Discourse in the Fall of 2004," www.buzzmetrics.com BuzzMetrics.

2. "The State of Blogging," January 2, 2005, at www.pewinternet.org/PPF/r/144/report_display.asp.

3. Tom Zeller, "Are Bloggers Setting the Agenda? It Depends on the Scandal," *New York Times,* May 23, 2005.

4. See the Intelliseek Web site at www.intelliseek.com; Also see www.blogpulse.com; Also see www.prnewswire.com.

5. Ibid.

6. Ibid.

7. Quoted in Harold W. Chase and Allen H. Lerman, *Kennedy and the Press* (New York: Crowell, 1965), p. 26.

8. Robert M. Entman, *Democracy Without Citizens: Media and the Decay of American Politics* (New York: Oxford University Press, 1989), p. 8; Shanto Iyengar, *Is Anyone Responsible? How Television Frames Political Issues* (Chicago: University of Chicago Press, 1991); W. Russell Newman, *The Paradox of Mass Politics* (Cambridge, Mass.: Harvard University Press, 1986).

9. Joe Strupp, "New Survey Finds Huge Gap Between Press and Public on Many Issues," *Editor & Publisher.com,* May 15, 2005, http://editorandpublisher.com/eandp/news/article_display.jsp?vnu_content_id=1000920962.

10. "Gallup: Public Confidence in Newspapers, TV News Falls to All-Time Low," June 10, 2005, http://editorandpublisher.com/eandp/news/article_display.jsp?vnu_content_id=1000954852.

11. Thomas Jefferson, quoted in Samuel Kernell, *Going Public* (Washington, D.C.: Congressional Quarterly Press, 1993), p. 94; George Washington, quoted in Jeffrey K. Tulis, *The Rhetorical Presidency* (Princeton, N.J.: Princeton University Press, 1987), p. 131.

12. Ronald Berkman and Laura W. Kitch, *Politics in the Media* (New York: McGraw-Hill, 1986); Deane E. Alger, *The Media and Politics* (Upper Saddle River, N.J.: Prentice Hall, 1989); See W. Russell Neuman, Marion R. Just, and Ann N. Crigler, *Common Knowledge: News and the Construction of Political Meaning* (Chicago: University of Chicago Press, 1992); Stephen Ansolabehere, Roy Behr, and Shanto Iyengar, *The Media Game: American Politics in the Television Age* (New York: Macmillan, 1993).

13. David Halberstam, *The Powers That Be* (New York: Dell, 1979), p. 72.

14. Richard E. Neustadt, *Presidential Power and the Modern Presidents: The Politics of Leadership from Roosevelt to Reagan* (New York: Free Press, 1990), p. 260; See also Todd Gitlin, ed., *Watching Television* (New York: Pantheon, 1986).

15. See Alessandra Stanley, "Bringing Out the Absurdity of the News," *New York Times,* October 25, 2005, p. B1.

16. See Todd Gitlin, ed., *Watching Television* (New York: Pantheon, 1986). See Thomas E. Patterson, *Out of Order* (New York: Knopf, 1993); Patterson, *The Mass Media Election: How Americans Choose Their President* (New York: Praeger, 1980); *1-800-President: The Report of the Twentieth-Century Fund Task Force on Television and the Campaign of 1992* (New York: Twentieth-Century Fund Press, 1993); Sig Mickelson, *The Electric Mirror* (New York: Dodd, Mead, 1972), p. 154; See also Larry Speakes, *Speaking Out: The Reagan Presidency from Inside the White House* (New York: Scribner's, 1988), p. 111.

17. Austin Ranney, *Channels of Power: The Impact of Television on American Politics* (New York: Basic Books, 1983), p. 144.

18. See Lawrence Grossman, *The Electronic Republic* (New York: Viking, 1995), p. 60.

19. "Cable and Internet Loom Large in Fragmented Political News Universe—Perceptions of Partisan Bias Seen as Growing, Especially by Democrats," January 11, 2004, http://people-press.org/reports/display.php3?ReportID=200.

20. Doris Graber, *Mass Media and American Politics* (Washington, D.C.: Congressional Quarterly Press, 1989), p. 12.

21. Graber, *Mass Media and American Politics,* p. 20.

22. David Broder, *Behind the Front Page: A Candid Look at How News Is Made* (New York: Simon &

Schuster, 1987), p. 114; See also Jay Rosen and Paul Taylor, *The New News v. the Old News: The Press and Politics in the 1990s* (New York: Twentieth-Century Fund, 1992).

23. Marshall McLuhan, *Understanding Media: The Extensions of Man* (New York: McGraw-Hill, 1965); See Thomas Dye, Harmon Zeigler, and S. Robert Lichter, *American Politics in the Media Age* (Pacific Grove, Calif.: Brooks/Cole, 1992), p. 5.

24. Iyengar, *Is Anyone Responsible?* See also Douglas Kellner, *Television and the Crisis of Democracy* (Boulder, Colo.: Westview Press, 1990); See also Eric Barnouw, *Tube of Plenty: The Evolution of American Television* (New York: Oxford University Press, 1982), p. 415.

25. Ben Bagdikian, *The Media Monopoly,* 4th ed. (Boston: Beacon Press, 1994).

26. *Red Lion Broadcasting* v. *FCC,* 395 U.S. 367 (1969).

27. *New York Times Co.* v. *United States,* 403 U.S. 714 (1971), p. 717.

28. Mark Cook and Jeff Cohen, "The Media Go to War: How Television Sold the Panama Invasion," *FAIR,* no. 2 (January/February 1991): pp. 22–25; *Miami Herald Publishing Co.* v. *Tornillo,* 418 U.S. 241 (1974).

29. Robert Lichter, Stanley Rothman, and Linda Litcher, *The Media Elite* (Bethesda, Md.: Alder and Alder, 1986).

30. Bernard Goldberg, *Bias* (New York: Regency, 2001); See Andrew Kohut, "Listen Up, Bias Mongers! The Audience Doesn't Agree," *Columbia Journalism Review On-line,* www.cjr.org/year/02/2/kohut.asp.

31. See Jeff Cohen, "Maybe the Public—Not the Press—Has a Leftist Bias," www.fair.org/articles/liberal-media.html.

32. See http://www.csra.uconn.edu.

33. William Greider, *Who Will Tell the People? The Betrayal of American Democracy* (New York: Simon & Schuster, 1992).

34. Bagdikian, *Media Monopoly.*

35. See Christopher Stern, "Limits on Media Ownership Voided," *Washington Post,* February 20, 2002, pp. E1, E3; See also "Protecting Media Diversity," *New York Times,* February 23, 2002, p. A30.

36. Daniel Hallin, "Sound Bite News: Television Coverage of Elections, 1968–1988," Media Studies Project Occasional Paper (Washington, D.C.: Woodrow Wilson International Center for Scholars, 1990); Mickey Kaus, "Sound-Bitten," *New Republic,* October 26, 1992, pp. 16–18; Kiku Adatto, "The Incredible Shrinking Sound Bite," *New Republic,* May 28, 1990, pp. 20–21.

37. Edwin Diamond and Stephen Bates, *The Spot: The Rise of Political Advertising on Television* (Cambridge, Mass.: MIT Press, 1992), p. 38.

38. The report was released in advance of World Press Freedom Day, May 3. See www.freedomhouse.org.

CHAPTER 13

1. Nedra Pickler, "Bush Signs Renewal of Patriot Act," *Washington Post,* March 10, 2006; Sheryl Gay Stolberg, "Senate Passes Legislation to Renew Patriot Act," *New York Times,* March 3, 2006; Judy Keen, "Bush Defends Patriot Act as 'Making Americans Safer,'" *USA Today,* April 20, 2004; Dan Eggen, "Secret Court Poses Challenges," *Washington Post,* August 30, 2004; "UK's Public Opinion on Patriot Act and Threats to Civil Liberties," Feb. 2004, www.bordc.org/resources/public/php; Mary Curtius, "House OKs Renewal of Key Patriot

Act Powers," *Los Angeles Times*, July 22, 2005, p. 19; and Dan Eggen, "Senate Approves Partial Renewal of Patriot Act," *Washington Post*, July 30, 2005.

2. For more on this argument, see Henry J. Abraham and Barbara A. Perry, *Freedom and the Court: Civil Rights and Liberties in the United States*, 7th ed. (New York: Oxford University Press, 1998), pp. 3–9.

3. Paul Gewirtz and Chad Golder, "So Who Are the Activists?" *New York Times*, July 6, 2005.

4. *United States* v. *Carolene Products Co.*, 304 U.S. 144; 58 S. Ct. 778 (1938); For more on the genesis of this footnote, and its meaning, see Louis Lusky, *By What Right* (Charlottesville, Va.: Michie, 1974).

5. *Barron* v. *Baltimore*, 32 U.S. 243 (1833).

6. *Slaughterhouse Cases*, 83 U.S. 36 (1873).

7. For more on this process, see *Palko* v. *Connecticut*, 302 U.S. 319 (1937); *Adamson* v. *California*, 332 U.S. 46 (1947).

8. *Hurtado* v. *California*, 110 U.S. 516 (1884).

9. *Twining* v. *New Jersey*, 211 U.S. 78 (1908).

10. *Chicago, Burlington and Quincy Railway Co.* v. *Chicago*, 166 U.S. 226 (1897).

11. *Schenck* v. *United States*, 249 U.S. 47 (1919).

12. *Frohwerk* v. *United States*, 249 U.S. 204 (1919).

13. *Debs* v. *United States*, 249 U.S. 211 (1919).

14. *Abrams* v. *United States*, 250 U.S. 616 (1919).

15. *Gitlow* v. *New York*, 268 U.S. 652 (1925).

16. *Near* v. *Minnesota*, 283 U.S. 697 (1931).

17. *Powell* v. *Alabama*, 287 U.S. 45 (1932).

18. *Hamilton* v. *Regents of the University of California*, 293 U.S. 245 (1934).

19. *Palko* v. *Connecticut*, 302 U.S. 319 (1937).

20. See *Williams* v. *Florida*, 399 U.S. 78 (1970); *Apodaca* v. *Oregon*, 406 U.S. 404 (1972); *Johnson* v. *Louisiana*, 406 U.S. 356 (1972).

21. For more, see Anson Phelps Stokes and Leo Pfeffer, *Church and State in the United States* (New York: Harper & Row, 1964).

22. *Walz* v. *Tax Commission*, 397 U.S. 664 (1970).

23. Abraham and Perry, *Freedom and the Court*, pp. 220–320.

24. *Everson* v. *Board of Education of Ewing Township*, 330 U.S. 1 (1947).

25. *Engel* v. *Vitale*, 370 U.S. 24 (1962).

26. *Abington School District* v. *Schempp*, 374 U.S. 203 (1963).

27. *Lemon* v. *Kurtzman*, 403 U.S. 602 (1971).

28. *Wolman* v. *Walter*, 433 U.S. 229 (1977).

29. *Roemer* v. *Board of Public Works of Maryland*, 426 U.S. 736 (1976).

30. *Committee for Public Education* v. *Nyquist*, 413 U.S. 756 (1973).

31. *Levitt* v. *Committee for Public Education and Religious Liberty*, 413 U.S. 472 (1973).

32. *Meek* v. *Pittenger*, 421 U.S. 349 (1975).

33. *Mueller* v. *Allen*, 463 U.S. 388 (1983).

34. *Marsh* v. *Chambers*, 463 U.S. 783 (1983).

35. *Lynch* v. *Donnelly*, 465 U.S. 668 (1984).

36. *Stone* v. *Graham*, 449 U.S. 39 (1980).

37. *Wallace* v. *Jaffree*, 472 U.S. 38 (1985).

38. *Grand Rapids School District* v. *Ball*, 473 U.S. 373 (1985).

39. *Edwards* v. *Aguillard*, 482 U.S. 578 (1987).

40. Patty Reinert, "Commandment Case Rejected," *Houston Chronicle*, February 26, 2002.

41. *McCreary County* v. *A.C.L.U.*, 125 S. Ct. 2722 (2005); and *Van Orden* v. *Perry* 125 S. Ct. 2854 (2005).

42. *County of Allegheny* v. *Greater Pittsburgh ACLU*, 497 U.S. 573 (1989).

43. *Lee* v. *Weisman*, 112 S. Ct. 2649 (1992).

44. *Zelman* v. *Simmons-Harris*, 153 L. Ed. 2d 604 (2002); David Savage, "School Vouchers Win Backing of High Court," *Los Angeles Times*, June 28, 2002, p. 1.

45. Lisa Snell, "Questioning State Aid for Students at Private Colleges," *San Diego Union-Tribune*, June 3, 2005.

46. Claudia Wallis, "The Evolution Wars," *Time*, August 15, 2005, pp. 27–35; *Edwards* v. *Aguillard*, 482 U.S. 581 (1987).

47. David Von Drehle, "Judge Blocks Decision During Appeals," *Washington Post*, June 28, 2002.

48. *Reynolds* v. *United States*, 98 U.S. 145 (1879).

49. See *Braunfeld* v. *Brown*, 366 U.S. 599 (1961); *McGowan* v. *Maryland*, 366 U.S. 420 (1961); *Sherbert* v. *Verner*, 374 U.S. 398 (1963).

50. *Oregon Department of Human Resources* v. *Smith*, 294 U.S. 872 (1990).

51. *Church of Lukumi Babalu Aya* v. *Hialeah*, 508 U.S. 520 (1993).

52. Bob Cohn and David A. Kaplan, "A Chicken on Every Altar?" *Newsweek*, November 9, 1992, p. 79.

53. *City of Boerne* v. *Flores*, 117 S. Ct. 2157 (1997). Ibid., p. 2162.

54. *Good News Club* v. *Milford Central School*, 533 U.S. 98 (2001).

55. *Watchtower Bible and Tract Society of New York* v. *Village of Stratton, Ohio*, 153 L. Ed. 2d 205 (2002); see Tony Mauro, "In God's Hands," *Legal Times*, February 25, 2002, p. 1.

56. See Alexander Meiklejohn, *Free Speech and Its Relation to Self-Government* (New York: Harper, 1948).

57. *Abrams* v. *United States*, 250 U.S. 187 (1919).

58. *Dennis* v. *United States*, 339 U.S. 494 (1951).

59. *Yates* v. *United States*, 354 U.S. 298 (1957).

60. See *Scales* v. *United States*, 367 U.S. 203 (1961); *United States* v. *Robel*, 389 U.S. 258 (1967).

61. *Brandenburg* v. *Ohio*, 385 U.S. 444 (1969).

62. *Nixon* v. *Shrink Missouri Gov't PAC*, 528 U.S. 377 (2000). Discussed in Warren Richey, "Court Affirms Campaign Finance Laws," *Christian Science Monitor*, January 25, 2000, p. 1; See also, *Buckley* v. *Valeo*, 424 U.S. 1 (1976).

63. *Federal Election Commission* v. *Colorado Republican Federal Campaign Committee*, 533 U.S. 431 (2001).

64. See *Edwards* v. *South Carolina*, 372 U.S. 229 (1963); *Brown* v. *Louisiana*, 383 U.S. 131 (1966); *Chaplinsky* v. *New Hampshire*, 315 U.S. 568 (1942).

65. *Terminiello* v. *Chicago*, 337 U.S. 1 (1949).

66. *RAV* v. *City of St. Paul*, 505 U.S. 377 (1992); *Wisconsin* v. *Mitchell*, 508 U.S. 476 (1993).

67. *Adderly* v. *Florida*, 385 U.S. 39 (1967).

68. *Cox* v. *Louisiana*, 379 U.S. 569 (1965).

69. *Cohen* v. *California*, 403 U.S. 15 (1971) and *Texas* v. *Johnson* 491 U.S. 397 (1989).

70. *RAV* v. *City of St. Paul, Minnesota*, 505 U.S. 377 (1992).

71. *Wisconsin* v. *Mitchell*, 508 U.S. 476 (1993).

72. *Madsen* v. *Women's Health Center*, 115 S. Ct. 2338 (1995).

73. *Schenck* v. *Pro-Choice Network of Western New York*, 117 S. Ct. 855 (1997).

74. Bill McAllister, "Two Victories for Abortion Rights," *Denver Post*, June 29, 2000, p. 1.

75. *New York Times Co.* v. *United States*, 403 U.S. 713 (1971).

76. *Nebraska Press Assn.* v. *Stuart*, 427 U.S. 539 (1976).

77. *Richmond Newspapers Inc.* v. *Virginia*, 448 U.S. 555 (1980).

78. See *New York Times* v. *Sullivan*, 376 U.S. 254 (1964); *Curtis Publishing Co.* v. *Butts*, 388 U.S. 130 (1967).

79. *Gertz* v. *Robert Welch Inc.*, 418 U.S. 323 (1974); *Rosenbloom* v. *Metromedia*, 403 U.S. 29 (1971).

80. *Herbert* v. *Lando*, 441 U.S. 153 (1979).

81. "First Amendment Decision: The Press Wins," *New York Times*, October 23, 1999, p. 1.

82. *Roth* v. *United States*, 354 U.S. 476 (1957).

83. *Memoirs* v. *Massachusetts*, 383 U.S. 413 (1966).

84. *Ginzburg* v. *United States*, 383 U.S. 463 (1966); *Ginsberg* v. *New York*, 390 U.S. 629 (1968); *Mishkin* v. *New York*, 383 U.S. 502 (1966); *Redrup* v. *New York*, 386 U.S. 767 (1967).

85. *Miller* v. *California*, 413 U.S. 15 (1973).

86. *Jenkins* v. *Georgia*, 418 U.S. 153 (1974).

87. *Knox* v. *United States*, 114 S. Ct. 375 (1993).

88. *Reno* v. *American Civil Liberties Union*, 117 S. Ct. 2329 (1997); See also Greg Miller, "Law to Control Online Porn Creates Strange Bedfellows," *Los Angeles Times*, February 15, 1999, p. 1; and Greg Miller, "Court Rejects Child Online Protection Act," *Los Angeles Times*, June 23, 2000, p. 1.

89. *Ashcroft* v. *Free Speech Coalition*, 152 L. Ed. 2d 403 (2002).

90. *Ashcroft* v. *American Civil Liberties Union* 535 U.S. 564 (2002).

91. Lyle Denniston, "Justices to Weigh Library Web Access," November 13, 2002; Robert O' Harrow Jr. "U.S. Court Overturns Internet Smut Law Ruling in Library Case is 3rd Loss for Congress," *Boston Globe*, June 1, 2002; And see Michael S. Romano, "Putting Up a Filter for the Kids," *New York Times*, April 4, 2002.

92. *Branzburg* v. *Hayes*, 408 U.S. 665 (1972).

93. Katherine Q. Seelye, "Journalists Testify in Favor of Shield Law" *New York Times*, October 19, 2005, p. 1; David Johnston and Richard W. Stevenson, "Cheney Aide Charged With Lying in Leak Case," *New York Times*, October 29, 2005, p. 1; and Don Van Natta Jr., Adam Liptak, and Clifford J. Levy, "The Miller Case: A Notebook, A Cause, a Jail Cell and a Deal," October 16, 2005, p. 1.

94. *People of New York* v. *Defore*, 242 N.Y. 13, pp. 19–25 (1927).

95. *Weeks* v. *United States*, 232 U.S. 383 (1914).

96. For more, see David Fellman, *The Defendant's Rights Today* (Madison: University of Wisconsin Press, 1976), pp. 292–97.

97. *Wolf* v. *Colorado*, 338 U.S. 25 (1949); *Rochin* v. *California*, 342 U.S. 165 (1952).

98. *Breithaupt* v. *Abram*, 352 U.S. 432 (1957).

99. *Mapp* v. *Ohio*, 367 U.S. 643 (1961).

100. Dissent by Warren Burger, *Bivens* v. *Six Unknown Named Agents of Federal Bureau of Narcotics*, 403 U.S. 388 (1971).

101. *United States* v. *Calandra*, 414 U.S. 338 (1974).

102. *Stone* v. *Powell*, 428 U.S. 465 (1976).

103. *United States* v. *Leon*, 468 U.S. 902 (1984).

104. *Illinois* v. *Rodriguez*, 110 S. Ct. 2793 (1990).

105. *Arizona* v. *Evans*, 514 U.S. 1 (1995).

106. See *Carroll* v. *United States*, 267 U.S. 132 (1925); *United States* v. *Chadwick*, 433 U.S. 1 (1977); *Cady* v. *Dombroski*, 413 U.S. 433 (1973).

107. *Katz* v. *United States*, 389 U.S. 347 (1967), p. 351.

108. See *Chimel* v. *California*, 395 U.S. 752 (1969); *Coolidge* v. *New Hampshire*, 403 U.S. 443 (1971); *Schneckloth* v. *Bustamonte*, 412 U.S. 218 (1973); *United States* v. *Cortez*, 449 U.S. 411 (1981).

109. *Terry* v. *Ohio*, 391 U.S. 1 (1968).

110. *New Jersey* v. *T.L.O.* 469 U.S. 325 (1995).

111. *California* v. *Hodari D.*, 111 S. Ct. 1547 (1991).

112. *Florida* v. *Bostick*, 111 S. Ct. 2382 (1991).

113. *Vernonia School District 47J* v. *Acton*, 515 U.S. 646 (1995).

114. Tamar Lewin, "Schools Across U.S. Await Ruling on Drug Tests," *New York Times*, March 20, 2002.

115. *Board of Education* v. *Earls*, 153 L. Ed. 2d 735 (2002).

116. *Katz* v. *United States*, 389 U.S. 347 (1967), p. 361.

117. *Illinois* v. *Wardlow*, 528 U.S. 119 (2000).

118. *United States* v. *Drayton* 153 L. Ed. 2d 242 (2002).

119. *Hiibel* v. *Sixth Judicial District of Nevada*, 542 U.S. 177 (2004).

120. *Kyllo* v. *United States*, 533 U.S. 27 (2001).

121. Dan Eggen, "FBI Misused Secret Wiretaps, According to Memo," *Washington Post*, October 10, 2002, p. A14; Dan Eggen, "Broad U.S. Wiretap Powers Upheld," *Washington Post*, November 19, 2002, P. A01; "Threats and Responses," *New York Times*, November 19, 2002, p. 19; John Mintz, "Trial to Reveal Reach of U.S. Surveillance," *Washington Post*, June 5, 2005, p. A03.

122. *Brown* v. *Mississippi*, 297 U.S. 278 (1936).

123. *Haynes* v. *Washington*, 373 U.S. 503 (1963).

124. *Escobedo* v. *Illinois*, 378 U.S. 478 (1964).

125. *Miranda* v. *Arizona*, 384 U.S. 436 (1966).

126. *Harris* v. *New York*, 401 U.S. 222 (1971).

127. *Rhode Island* v. *Innis*, 446 U.S. 291 (1980); See also *Michigan* v. *Tucker*, 417 U.S. 433 (1974).

128. *New York* v. *Quarles*, 467 U.S. 669 (1984).

129. *Oregon* v. *Elstad*, 470 U.S. 298 (1985).

130. *Arizona* v. *Fulminante*, 111 S. Ct. 1246 (1991).

131. *United States* v. *Dickerson*, 530 U.S. 428 (2000).

132. Jan Hoffman, "Police Tactics Chipping Away at Suspects' Rights," *New York Times*, March 29, 1998, p. 1; and Jan Hoffman, "As Miranda Rights Erode, Police Get Confessions from Innocent People," *New York Times*, March 30, 1998, p. 32.

133. David Rosenzweig, "U.S. Judge Voids Portion of Patriot Act as Illegally Vague," *Los Angeles Times*, July 30, 2005, p. 19; and Eric Lichtblau, "Citing Free Speech, Judge Voids Part of Antiterror Act," *New York Times*, January 27, 2004, p. 16.

134. For an update on the death penalty issue, see the Death Penalty Information Center. For more on recent changes in the death penalty issue, see Jodi Wilgoren, "Three Cleared by

DNA Tests Enjoy Liberty After 15 Years," *New York Times*, December 6, 2001, p. A20; Henry Weinstein, "Death Penalty Study Suggests Errors," *Los Angeles Times*, February 11, 2002; David G. Savage, "'92 Execution Haunts Death Penalty Foes," *Los Angeles Times*, July 22, 2001; Jonathan Alter, "The Death Penalty on Trial," *Newsweek*, June 12, 2000, pp. 24–35; Raymond Bonner and Marc Lacey, "U.S. Plans Delay in First Execution in Four Decades," *New York Times*, July 7, 2000, p. 1; and Fox Butterfield, "Death Sentences Being Overturned in 2 of 3 Appeals," *New York Times*, June 12, 2000, p. 1.

135. *Atkins* v. *Virginia*, 536 U.S. 304, (2002).

136. *Roper* v. *Simmons*, 125 S. Ct. 1183 (2005).

137. *Griswold* v. *Connecticut*, 381 U.S. 479 (1965). For more on this case and the issues surrounding it, also see David J. Garrow, *Liberty and Sexuality: The Right to Privacy and the Making of Roe v. Wade* (New York: Macmillan, 1994), pp. 16–195. For more on opponents of the *Griswold* decision, see Robert Bork, *The Tempting of America* (New York: Free Press, 1989); Ethan Bronner, *Battle for Justice: How the Bork Nomination Shook America* (New York: Norton, 1989).

138. *Eisenstadt* v. *Baird*, 405 U.S. 438 (1972); *Doe* v. *Bolton*, 410 U.S. 179 (1973).

139. *Bowers* v. *Hardwick* 478 U.S. 176 (1987). Joyce Murdoch and Deb Price, *Court Justice: Gay Men and Lesbians v. the Supreme Court* (New York: Basic Books, 2001); Art Harris "The Unintended Battle of Michael Hardwick," *Washington Post*, August 21, 1986, pp. 1, 4.

140. Quoted in John C. Jeffries Jr., *Justice Lewis E. Powell, Jr: A Biography* (New York: Charles Scribner's Sons, 1994), p. 530.

141. *Romer* v. *Evans*, 517 U.S. 620 (1995). For more on Justice Kennedy's work in this case and the reasons behind his decision making, see Jeffrey Toobin, "Supreme Sacrifice," *New Yorker*, July 8, 1996, pp. 43–47; and Jeffrey Rosen, "The Agonizer," *New Yorker*, November 11, 1996, pp. 82–90.

142. *Boy Scouts of America* v. *Dale*, 530 U.S. 640 (2000); See also Linda Greenhouse, "Supreme Court Backs Boy Scouts," *New York Times*, June 29, 2000, p. 1.

143. Carlos Frias, "Ga. Court Rejects Same-Sex Bond," *Atlanta Constitution*, January 26, 2002; Pamela Ferdinand, "With Vermont in the Lead: Controversy Progresses: Battle Over Same-Sex Unions Moves to Other States," *Washington Post*, September 4, 2001; Pamela Ferdinand, "Vermont Legislature Clears Bill Allowing Civil Unions," *Washington Post*, April 26, 2000, p. A3; and Fred Bayles, "Vermont Gay Union Bill Leaves Questions Unanswered," *USA Today*, April 17, 2000, p. 7.

144. *Lawrence* v. *Texas*, 539 U.S. 558 (2003).

145. Chris Cilliza, "Corzine Defeats Forrester To Become N.J. Governor; Bloomberg Wins Easily" *Washington Post*, November 9, 2005, p. 1.

146. Raphael Lewis, "Petition vs. Gay Marriage Advances," *Boston Globe*, December 22, 2005, p. B1; and Raphael Lewis, "Suit Seeks to Bar Ballot Query," *Boston Globe*, January 4, 2006, p. B5.

147. *Roe* v. *Wade*, 410 U.S. 113 (1973).

148. *Harris* v. *McRae*, 448 U.S. 297 (1980).

149. *Planned Parenthood of Central Missouri* v. *Danforth*, 428 U.S. 52 (1976).

150. *Akron* v. *Akron Center for Reproductive Health*, 462 U.S. 416 (1983).

151. *Webster* v. *Reproductive Health Services*, 492 U.S. 490 (1989).

152. *Planned Parenthood of Southeastern Pennsylvania* v. *Casey*, 112 S. Ct. 2791 (1992).

153. Linda Greenhouse, "U.S. Court Voids Ohio Ban on Late-Term Abortion," *New York Times*, November 19, 1997.

154. *Stenberg* v. *Carhart*, 530 U.S. 914 (2000).

155. Julia Preston, "Appeals Court Voids Ban on 'Partial Birth' Abortions," *New York Times*, July 9, 2005.

156. *Cruzan by Cruzan* v. *Director, Missouri Department of Health*, 110 S. Ct. 2841 (1990).

157. *Washington* v. *Glucksberg*, 117 S. Ct. 2258 (1997); and *Vacco* v. *Quill*, 117 S. Ct. 2293 (1997).

158. Daniel Eisenberg, "Lessons of the Schiavo Battle," *Time*, April 4, 2005, pp. 22–30.

159. *Gonzales* v. *Oregon*, 2006 U.S. Lexis 767 (2006), also can be found at www.supremecourtus.gov/.

160. Gina Holland, "Supreme Court Upholds Oregon Suicide Law," www.washingtonpost.com, January 17, 2006.

CHAPTER 14

1. The case study is based on David J. Garrow, "How Much Weight Can Race Carry?" *New York Times*, May 19, 2002, p. 4wk; Gary Haber, "Minority Enrollment Shrinks at USF but Grows Statewide," *Tampa Tribune*, September 16, 2004; Mark Clayton, "Michigan Affirmative Action Case Will Reverberate Widely," *Christian Science Monitor*, October 23, 2001; Ben Feller, "One Florida Sustains Universities' Diversity," *Tampa Tribune*, September 6, 2001; Barry Klein, "UF Ends Race-Based Scholarship Program," *St. Petersburg Times*, August 31, 2001; Travis Gosselin, "Divided We Stand: Affirmative Action: Why It Should Remain," *St. Louis Post Dispatch*, April 11, 2001; David J. Garrow, "The Path to Diversity? Different Differences, *New York Times*, September 2, 2001, p. 4; Peter Kilborn, "Jeb Bush Roils Florida on Affirmative Action," *New York Times*, February 4, 2000.

2. 347 U.S. 483 (1954).

3. Donald G. Nieman, *Promises to Keep: African Americans and the Constitutional Order, 1776 to the Present* (New York: Oxford University Press, 1991), pp. 3–5.

4. *Dred Scott* v. *Sandford*, 19 Howard 393 (1857).

5. *United States* v. *Cruikshank*, 92 U.S. 214 (1876).

6. *Civil Rights Cases*, 109 U.S. 3 (1883).

7. *Plessy* v. *Ferguson*, 163 U.S. 537 (1896).

8. *Cumming* v. *County Board of Education*, 175 U.S. 528 (1899).

9. C. Vann Woodward, *Origins of the New South: 1877–1913*, 2d ed. (Baton Rouge: Louisiana University Press, 1987), pp. 331–38, 372–75.

10. *Bailey* v. *Alabama*, 219 U.S. 219 (1911).

11. *Guinn* v. *United States*, 238 U.S. 347 (1915); See also Nieman, *Promises to Keep*, pp. 123–27.

12. *Nixon* v. *Herndon*, 273 U.S. 536 (1927).

13. Richard Kluger, *Simple Justice* (New York: Knopf, 1976), p. 250.

14. *Missouri ex rel. Gaines* v. *Canada*, 305 U.S. 337 (1938).

15. *Sweatt* v. *Painter*, 339 U.S. 629 (1950).

16. *McLaurin* v. *Oklahoma State of Regents*, 339 U.S. 637 (1950).

17. *Brown* v. *Board of Education of Topeka, Kansas*, 347 U.S. 483 (1954).

18. *Bolling* v. *Sharpe*, 347 U.S. 497 (1954).

19. *Brown* v. *Board of Education of Topeka, Kansas*, 349 U.S. 294 (1955).

20. Alfred H. Kelly and Winfred A. Harbison, *The American Constitution: Origins and Development,* 4th ed. (New York: Norton, 1970), p. 940.

21. Jack W. Peltason, *Fifty-Eight Lonely Men* (New York: Harcourt Brace Jovanovich, 1961).

22. Nieman, *Promises to Keep*, pp. 166–76.

23. *Heart of Atlanta Motel* v. *United States,* 379 U.S. 241 (1964).

24. *Katzenbach* v. *McClung,* 379 U.S. 294 (1964).

25. *Harper* v. *Virginia Board of Elections,* 383 U.S. 663 (1966).

26. Nieman, *Promises to Keep,* p. 180.

27. *Jones* v. *Alfred H. Mayer,* 329 U.S. 409 (1968).

28. *Alexander* v. *Holmes County Board of Education,* 396 U.S. 19 (1969).

29. Nieman, *Promises to Keep,* p. 179.

30. *Swann* v. *Charlotte-Mecklenburg Board of Education,* 402 U.S. 1 (1971).

31. *Keyes* v. *School District #1, Denver, Colorado,* 413 U.S. 189 (1973).

32. *Milliken* v. *Bradley,* 418 U.S. 717 (1974).

33. Leslie Goldstein, "Affirmative Action Toward the 21st Century," address to the graduate seminar "The Constitution and Bill of Rights in the New Millennium," August 1, 1997, Freedom's Foundation, Valley Forge, Pa.

34. Sidney Verba and Gary R. Orren, *Equality in America: The View from the Top* (Cambridge, Mass.: Harvard University Press, 1985), p. 5.

35. *DeFunis* v. *Odegaard,* 416 U.S. 312 (1974).

36. *Regents of the University of California* v. *Bakke,* 438 U.S. 265 (1978).

37. *United Steelworkers* v. *Weber,* 443 U.S. 193 (1979).

38. *Fullilove* v. *Klutznick,* 448 U.S. 448 (1980).

39. Steven L. Carter, *Reflections of an Affirmative Action Baby* (New York: Basic Books, 1991), p. 69.

40. *Firefighters Local Union No. 1784* v. *Stotts,* 467 U.S. 561 (1984).

41. *Wygant* v. *Jackson Board of Education,* 476 U.S. 267 (1986).

42. *Local Number 93, International Association of Firefighters* v. *City of Cleveland,* 478 U.S. 501 (1986).

43. *Local 28 of the Sheet Metal Workers' International Association* v. *EEOC,* 478 U.S. 421 (1986).

44. *U.S.* v. *Paradise,* 480 U.S. 149 (1987).

45. *Martin* v. *Wilks,* 109 S. Ct. 2180 (1989).

46. *City of Richmond* v. *Croson,* 488 U.S. 469 (1989).

47. *Patterson* v. *McLean Credit Union,* 109 S. Ct. 2363 (1989).

48. *Lorance* v. *AT&T Technologies,* 490 U.S. 900 (1989).

49. *Independent Federation of Flight Attendants* v. *Zipes,* 491 U.S. 754 (1989).

50. *Wards Cove Packing Co.* v. *Antonio,* 109 S. Ct. 2115 (1989).

51. Ronald Smothers, "Mississippi Mellows on Issue of Bias in State Universities," *New York Times,* March 13, 1995, p. A14.

52. *Adarand Constructors* v. *Pena,* 115 S. Ct. 2097 (1995).

53. Rene Sanchez and Sue Anne Pressley, "Universities Admit Fewer Minorities," *Washington Post,* May 19, 1997, p. A1.

54. Scott Jaschik, "A Year After the Supreme Court Upheld Affirmative Action at the University of Michigan, Why Has Minority Enrollment Gone Down?" *Boston Globe,* June 13, 2004.

55. Quoted in Nancy E. McGlen and Karen O'Connor, *Women's Rights: The Struggle for Equality in the Nineteenth and Twentieth Centuries* (New York: Praeger, 1983), pp. 389–91.

56. Ibid., pp. 272–74.

57. *Bradwell* v. *State of Illinois,* 83 U.S. 130 (1873).

58. *Minor* v. *Happersett,* 88 U.S. 162 (1875).

59. *Goesaert* v. *Cleary,* 335 U.S. 464 (1948).

60. *Hoyt* v. *Florida,* 368 U.S. 57 (1961).

61. *Reed* v. *Reed,* 404 U.S. 71 (1971).

62. *Frontiero* v. *Richardson,* 411 U.S. 677 (1973).

63. *Kahn* v. *Shevin,* 416 U.S. 351 (1974).

64. *Craig* v. *Boren,* 429 U.S. 190 (1976).

65. *United States* v. *Virginia,* 116 S. Ct. 2264 (1996).

66. Donald P. Baker and Tod Robberson, "Admit Women, Keep 'Rat Line,' VMI Alumni Say," *Washington Post,* July 2, 1996, p. B1; Michael Janofsky, "Citadel, Bowing to Court, Says It Will Admit Women," *New York Times,* June 29, 1996, p. 6; Donald P. Baker, "By One Vote, VMI Decides to Go Coed," *Washington Post,* September 22, 1996, p. 1.

67. *Farragher* v. *Boca Raton,* 66 U.S.L.W. 4643 (1998); *Burlington Industries* v. *Ellerth,* 66 U.S.L.W. 4643 (1998); and Joan Biskupic, "Court Draws Line on Harassment," *Washington Post,* June 27, 1998, pp. 1, 11. See also *Meritor Savings Bank* v. *Vinson,* 477, U.S. 57 (1986); *Harris* v. *Forklift Systems,* 510, U.S. 510 (1993); *Oncale* v. *Sundowner Offshore Services,* 66 U.S.L.W. 4172 (1998); and *Gebser* v. *Lago Vista Independent School District,* 66 U.S.L.W. 4501 (1998).

68. *U.S.* v. *Morrison,* explained in Stuart Taylor Jr., "The Tipping Point," *National Journal,* June 10, 2000, pp. 1810–19.

69. *Katzenbach* v. *Morgan,* 384 U.S. 641 (1966).

70. *San Antonio Independent School District* v. *Rodriguez,* 411 U.S. 1 (1973).

71. *Plyler* v. *Doe,* 457 U.S. 202 (1982).

72. Updated figures found at www.infoplease.com/ipa/A0762156.html, November 17, 2005. The U.S. Census figures based on the 2000 census can be accessed at www.census.gov.

73. Michael A. Fletcher and Dan Balz, "Bush Faces Pressure to Diversify Supreme Court," *Washington Post,* September 25, 2005, p. 04; Susan Page, "What Americans Want in O'Connor Court Vacancy," *USA Today,* July 14, 2005, p. 1.

74. *Elk* v. *Wilkins,* 112 U.S. 94 (1884).

75. Dee Brown, *Bury My Heart at Wounded Knee: An Indian History of the American West* (New York: Holt, Rinehart & Winston, 1971).

76. Jay Mathews, "Landmark Law Failing to Achieve Workplace Goals," *Washington Post,* April 16, 1995, p. 1.

77. Marcia Coyle, "ADA: Clarified or Ruined?" *National Law Journal,* July 5, 1999, pp. 1, 10.

78. *Board of Trustees of the University of Alabama* v. *Garrett,* 531 U.S. 356 (2001).

79. *Tennessee* v. *Lane,* 541 U.S. 509 (2004).

80. *Kimel* v. *Florida Board of Regents,* 528 U.S. 62 (2000).

81. Michael A. Fletcher, "Diversity's Future?" *Washington Post,* March 18, 2002, p. 1.

82. *Center for National Security Studies* v. *United States Department of Justice,* 2002 U.S. Dist. LEXIS 14168, Civ. 01-2500 (D.D.C. August 2, 2002; Kessler, J.).

83. *Detroit Free Press* v. *John Ashcroft,* 303 F. 3d 681 (2002).

CHAPTER 15

1. David E. Sanger, "President's Signature Turns Broad Tax Cut, and a Campaign Promise, Into Law," *New York Times,* June 8, 2001, p. A18.

2. See www.whitehouse.gov/news/usbudget/blueprint/bud02.html.

3. Stephen Moore, "Bush Tax Cut: A Good First Step." *Human Events Online,* www.humaneventsonline.com/articles/06-11-01/moore.html; See Gary Klott, "Congress Approves $1.35 Trillion Tax-Cut Plan," Tax Planet.com at www.taxplanet.com/taxnews/final52601/final52601.html.

4. David E. Sanger, "President's Signature Turns Broad Tax Cut, and a Campaign Promise, Into Law," *New York Times,* June 8, 2001, p. A18; See also www.whitehouse.gov/news/usbudget/blueprint/bud02.html; See Jackie Koszczuk, "GOP-Led House Votes to Make Bush Tax Cuts Permanent," *Washington Post,* June 7, 2002, p. A5; Carl Hulse, "Senate Leader, in Surprise Move, Opens Debate on Estate Tax Repeal," *New York Times,* June 12, 2002, p. A16; Helen Dewar and Juliet Eilperin, "Senate Votes Down Permanent Repeal of the Inheritance Tax," *Washington Post,* June 13, 2002, p. A5.

5. See Scott Lindlaw, Associated Press, "Bush Renews Push for Extensions of His Tax Reductions," *Record* (Bergen County, N.J.), February 17, 2004; See also, "The President's Agenda for Tax Relief," www.whitehouse.gov/news/reports/taxplan.html.

6. Larry Gerston, *Making Public Policy: From Conflict to Resolution* (Boston: Little, Brown, 1983), p. 6; See Bruce Ingersoll, "U.S. Regulators to Raise a Stink about Cigars," *Wall Street Journal,* February 9, 1998, p. B1.

7. Leading process models of policy making include Randall Ripley and Grace Franklin, *Congress, the Bureaucracy, and Public Policy,* 5th ed. (Pacific Grove, Calif.: Brooks-Cole, 1991); Ripley and Franklin, *Policy Implementation in the United States,* 2d ed. (Homewood, Ill.: Dorsey Press, 1986); James E. Anderson, *Public Policymaking* (Boston: Houghton Mifflin, 1990); Leading policy typologies include Theodore Lowi, "Four Systems of Policy, Politics, and Choice," *Public Administration Review* 32, (July/August 1972): 298–310; Paul Peterson, *City Limits* (Chicago: University of Chicago Press, 1981); John W. Kingdon, *Agendas, Alternatives, and Public Policies* (Boston: Little, Brown, 1984); Leading scholars in the agenda-setting approach to understanding public policy include Roger Cobb and Charles Elder, *Participation in American Politics: The Dynamics of Agenda-Building,* 2d ed. (Baltimore: Johns Hopkins University Press, 1983); Bryan Jones, *Governing Urban America: A Policy Focus* (Boston: Little, Brown, 1982); Barbara Nelson, *Making an Issue of Child Abuse* (Chicago: University of Chicago Press, 1984); and Robert Waste, *The Ecology of City Policymaking* (New York: Oxford University Press, 1989).

8. Christopher Bosso, *Pesticides and Politics: The Life Cycle of a Public Issue* (Pittsburgh: University of Pittsburgh Press, 1987). The examples are based on the excellent account in Randy Shilts, *And the Band Played On: Politics, People, and the Epidemic* (New York: St. Martin's Press, 1987), p. 20; See also John Kinsella, *Covering the Plague: AIDS and the American Press* (New Brunswick, N.J.: Rutgers University Press, 1989); "Clinton to Seek More Money for AIDS Drugs," *New York Times,* December 30, 1997, p. A16; "Funding for AIDS Programs in Final Stretch," www.thebody.com/aac/sep1897.html.

9. For a discussion of policy entrepreneurs, see Eugene Lewis, *Public Entrepreneurship: Toward a Theory of Bureaucratic Political Powers* (Bloomington:

Indiana University Press, 1980). See also the discussion of policy entrepreneurs and "policy windows" in John Kingdon, *Policies, Politics, and Agendas*, 2d ed. (Chatham, N.J.: Chatham House, 1992). For an interesting account of policy entrepreneurs—some successful and some not—in the Great Depression, see Alan Brinkley, *Voices of Protest: Huey Long, Father Coughlin, and the Great Depression* (New York: Knopf, 1982).

10. See Henry J. Abraham, *Freedom and the Court* (New York: Oxford University Press, 1988); Richard Klugar, *Simple Justice* (New York: Knopf, 1976); Gerald Rosenberg, *The Hollow Hope: Can Courts Bring About Social Change?* (Chicago: University of Chicago Press, 1992).

11. *Roe* v. *Wade*, 413 U.S. 113 (1973); *Webster* v. *Reproductive Health Services*, 424 U.S. 490 (1989).

12. Lizette Alvarez, "Senate, 54–41, Rejects Republican Bill to Ban Cloning," *New York Times*, February 12, 1998, p. A18; see also William Powers, "A Slant on Cloning," *National Journal*, January 10, 1998, p. 58; "FDA Is Prepared to Block Unapproved Cloning Efforts," *New York Times*, January 20, 1998, p. A13; "Cloning Foes Consider Moratorium," *Washington Post*, June 12, 2002, p. A7; Helen Dewer, "Anti-Cloning Bills in Senate, Vote Unlikely Soon," *Washington Post*, June 14, 2002, p. A4; Rick Weiss, "Debate over Cloning Puts the Political in Science," *Washington Post*, June 10, 2002, p. A9.

13. *Brown* v. *Board of Education of Topeka*, 347 U.S. 483 (1954); *Brown* v. *Board of Education of Topeka*, 349 U.S. 294 (1955).

14. Jonathan Kozol, *Savage Inequalities: Children in America's Schools* (New York: Crown, 1991); See also Alex Kotlowitz, *There Are No Children Here* (New York: Doubleday, 1991); Tracy Kidder, *Among Schoolchildren* (New York: Avon, 1989).

15. Eric Planin, "EPA Proposes to Ease Rules on Clean Air," *Washington Post*, June 14, 2002, p. A1, A8.

16. For a case in point that agencies, programs, and policies are extremely difficult to terminate, see Fred Bergerson, *The Army Gets an Air Force: The Tactics of Bureaucratic Insurgency* (Baltimore: Johns Hopkins Press, 1976). The discussion of the demise of public policies draws heavily on the similar discussion of reasons for the demise of public agencies in Anthony Downs, *Inside Bureaucracy* (Boston: Little, Brown, 1959).

17. Kenneth J. Meier, *Regulation: Politics, Bureaucracy, and Economics* (New York: St. Martin's Press, 1985), p. 1; See also Michael D. Reagan, *The Politics of Policy* (Boston: Little, Brown, 1987). This discussion of the types of federal government regulatory activity draws heavily upon the discussion of regulatory activity in Meier, *Regulation*, pp. 1–2.

18. Rachel Carson, *Silent Spring* (Boston: Houghton Mifflin, 1962); See also Kent E. Portney, *Controversial Issues in Environmental Policy* (Newbury Park, Calif.: Sage, 1992). The best single account of environmental policy making in this period is the agenda-setting study by Bosso, "Pesticides and Politics." See also Thomas Dunlap, *DDT: Scientists, Citizens, and Public Policy* (Princeton, N.J.: Princeton University Press, 1981); Charles O. Jones, *Clean Air: The Policies and Politics of Pollution Control* (Pittsburgh: University of Pittsburgh Press, 1975).

19. William Stevens, "In Kyoto, the Subject Is Climate; the Forecast Is for Storms," *New York Times*, December 1, 1997, p. D1; See also "The Kyoto Protocol on Climate Change," www.epa.gov/globalwarming.

20. See http://en.wikipedia.org/wiki/Kyoto_Protocol.

21. Andrew C. Revkin, "U.S. Under Fire, Refuses to Shift in Climate Talks," *New York Times*, December 10, 2005, p. A1; "America's Shame in Montreal," *New York Times*, December 13, 2005, p. A34; "White House Warns on Climate Change," *New York Times Online*, June 3, 2002, www.nytimes.com/aponline/n.../AP-Climate-change.html?pagewanted=print&position=to, 6/4/02; See also, George Archibald, "White House Defends U-Turn on Global Warming," *Washington Times*, June 4, 2002. See www.washingtontimes.com/national/20020604-15929206.htm. Quoted in Marc Lacey, "Clinton Targets Polluted Runoff to Clean Up Water," *Sacramento Bee*, February 20, 1998, p. A10.

22. Lincoln Steffens, *The Shame of the Cities* (New York: McClure, 1904); Robert Hunter, *Poverty* (New York: Macmillan, 1904); See also William Julius Wilson, *The Truly Disadvantaged* (Chicago: University of Chicago Press, 1987). For documentation that public opinion strongly favors supporting programs that aid the needy, see Theodore R. Marmor, Jerry L. Mashaw, and Philip L. Harvey, *America's Misunderstood Welfare State* (New York: Basic Books, 1990).

23. See Constantijin Panis et al., *The Effects of Changing Social Security Administration's Early Entitlement Age and the Normal Retirement Age*, (Santa Monica: Rand, 2002); Robin Toner, "Republicans Weigh Voter Response to Retirement Plan," *New York Times*, March 10, 2005, p. A21.

24. Christine Himes, "The Future of Social Security," Washington, DC: Population Reference Bureau, 2005, at www.prb.org/; David, John, "Social Security: The Crisis Is Real," *The Heritage Foundation Online*, April 26, 2002, www.heritage.org/press/commentary/ed042602.cfm. The CNN/Gallup USA Poll can be found at www.socialsecurity.org/.

25. Daniel Patrick Moynihan, *Maximum Feasible Misunderstanding: Community Action and the War on Poverty* (New York: Free Press, 1969).

26. Two dated but still excellent accounts of policy-making battles surrounding the enactment of Medicare are Robert Alford, *Health Care Politics* (Chicago: University of Chicago Press, 1975); Theodore Marmor, *The Politics of Medicare* (Chicago: Aldine, 1973).

27. See Mary Jo Bane, "Welfare as We Know It," *American Prospect*, no. 30 (January/February, 1997): 47–53, www.epn.org/prospect/30/30bane.html; "Welfare Reform," at www.libertynet.org/~edeivic/welfref.html; See Pamela Winston, *Welfare Policy in the States* (Georgetown University Press, 2002); Robert Pear, "Federal Welfare Rolls Shrink, But Drop Is Smallest Since '94," *New York Times*, May 21, 2002, p. A12.

28. "Welfare Rolls Continue to Fall," *HHS News*, February 9, 2005, at www.acf.hhs.gov/news/press/2005/TANFdeclinceJune04.htm.

29. Ibid.

30. See *The 2005 HHS Poverty Guidelines*, at http://aspe.hhs.gov/poverty/05poverty.shtml.

31. James L. Gosling, *Budgetary Politics in American Governments* (New York: Longman, 1992), pp. 73–74; Howard E. Shuman, *Politics and the Budget: The Struggle between the President and the Congress* (Upper Saddle River, N.J.: Prentice Hall, 1988), p. 220.

32. James Pfiffner, ed., *The President and Economic Policy* (Philadelphia: Institute for Human Issues, 1986).

33. Denise E. Markovich and Ronald E. Pynn, *American Political Economy: Using Economics with Politics* (Monterey, Calif.: Brooks-Cole, 1988), p. 214; John T. Woolley, *Monetary Politics: The Federal Reserve and the Politics of Monetary Policy* (London: Cambridge University Press, 1984); Kevin Phillips, *The Politics of Rich and Poor: Wealth and the American Electorate in the Reagan Aftermath* (New York: Random House, 1990); Donald F.

Kettl, *Deficit Politics* (New York: Macmillan, 1992); Robert Heilbronce and Peter Bernstein, *The Debt and Deficit* (New York: Norton, 1989).

34. Benjamin Friedman, *Day of Reckoning: The Consequences of American Economic Policy under Reagan and After* (New York: Random House, 1988); David S. Stockman, *The Triumph of Politics: Why the Reagan Revolution Failed* (New York: Harper, 1986); Kevin Phillips, *Boiling Point: Democrats, Republicans, and the Decline of Middle Class Prosperity* (New York: Random House, 1993); Herbert Stein, *Presidential Economics: The Making of Economic Policy from Roosevelt to Reagan and Beyond*, 2d ed. (Washington, D.C.: American Enterprise Institute, 1988).

35. Larry Rohter and Elisabeth Bumiller, "Hemisphere Meeting Ends Without Trade Consensus," *New York Times*, November 6, 2005, p. A8.

CHAPTER 16

1. Reuters News, "Saudis Praise Bush, Urge Speedy Action on Middle East, *New York Times*, April 28, 2002; Also see "Pentagon Now Calls It 'Enduring Freedom'," www.washingtonpost.com, p. A7.

2. UPI, "Do-Little 'Allies' Anger U.S.," www.NewsMax.com, Wires, March 29, 2002.

3. See Mike Allen and Karen DeYoung, "Bush: U.S. Will Strike First at Enemies," *Washington Post*, June 2, 2002, p. A1, A8; The complete text of the president's West Point commencement speech can be found at www.whitehouse.gov, June 1, 2002; See also "Text of Bush's Speech at West Point," *New York Times*, June 1, 2002; www.nytimes.com, June 1, 2002.

4. See Dana Bash, "White House Pressed on 'Mission Accomplished' Sign," www.cnn.com/insidepolitics.com, October 29, 2003.

5. Adriana Lins de Albuquerque and Michael E. O'Hanlon, "The State of Iraq: An Update," www.brookings.edu/views/op-ed/20050603.htm.

6. Sam Coates and Mike Allen, "We Will Stay, We Will Fight." *Washington Post*, August 25, 2005, p. A1; Mike Allen and Sam Coates, "Bush Says U.S. Will Stay and Finish Task," *Washington Post*, August 23, 2005, p. A10.

7. See Hans Morgenthau, *Politics Among Nations: The Struggle for Power and Peace*. (New York: Knopf, 1973); Robert C. Johansen, *The National Interest and the Human Interest: An Analysis of U.S. Foreign Policy* (Princeton, N.J.: Princeton University Press, 1980).

8. The president's radio addresses are available at www.whitehouse.gov/.

9. See Bruce W. Jentleson and Thomas G. Paterson, *Encyclopedia of U.S. Foreign Relations* (New York: Oxford University Press, 1997), vol. 1; See Thomas G. Paterson and J. Garry Clifford, *America Ascendant: U.S. Foreign Relations since 1939* (Lexington, Mass.: D.C. Heath, 1995).

10. See Miroslav Nincic, *Renegade Regimes: Confronting Deviant Behavior in World Politics* (New York: Columbia University Press, 2005).

11. Bruce W. Jentleson and Thomas G. Paterson, *Encyclopedia of U.S. Foreign Relations* (New York: Oxford University Press, 1997), vol. 1.

12. See Ernest K. King, *The Making of the Monroe Doctrine* (Cambridge, Mass.: Harvard University Press, 1975); David F. Ronfeldt, "Rethinking the Monroe Doctrine," *Orbis* 28 (Winter 1985): 38–41; Barton J. Bernstein, "Roosevelt, Truman, and the Atomic Bomb, 1941–1945," *Political Science Quarterly* 40 (Spring 1975): 61.

13. George F. Kennan, "The Sources of Soviet Conduct," *Foreign Affairs* 25 (July 1947): 566–82.

14. Walter LaFeber, *America, Russia, and the Cold War, 1945–1990*, 6th ed. (New York: McGraw-Hill, 1991).

15. See Ernest R. May and Philip D. Zelikow, eds., *The Kennedy Tapes: Inside the White House* (Boston: Harvard University Press, 1997); Graham Allison, *Essence of Decision: Explaining the Cuban Missile Crisis* (Boston: Little, Brown, 1971); Robert Kennedy, *Thirteen Days* (New York: Signet Books, 1969), pp. 38–39; James G. Blight, Joseph S. Nye Jr., and David A. Welch, "The Cuban Missile Crisis Revisited," *Foreign Affairs* 66 (Fall 1987): 170–88.

16. See Larry Berman, *Planning a Tragedy: The Americanization of the War in Vietnam* (New York: Norton, 1982); Larry Berman, *Lyndon Johnson's War: The Road to Stalemate in Vietnam* (New York: Norton, 1989); See Larry Berman, "No Peace, No Honor: Nixon, Kissinger and Betrayal in Vietnam," *Free Press*, 2001; Also see Arnold Issacs, *Without Honor: Defeat in Vietnam and Cambodia* (Baltimore: Johns Hopkins University Press, 1984); Townsend Hoopes, *The Limits of Intervention* (New York: Norton, 1987).

17. Scott Shane, "Vietnam War Intelligence 'Deliberately Skewed,' Secret Study Says," *New York Times*, December 2, 2005, p. A11.

18. Raymond L. Garthoff, *Détente and Confrontation: American–Soviet Relations from Nixon to Reagan* (Washington, D.C.: Brookings Institution, 1985); Beth A. Fischer, "Toeing the Hardline? The Reagan Administration and the Ending of the Cold War," *Political Science Quarterly* 112, no. 3 (1997): 477–96.

19. McGeorge Bundy, George F. Kennan, Robert S. McNamara, and Gerard Smith, "The President's Choice: Star Wars or Arms Control," *Foreign Affairs* Winter 1984–85; Also see "A Treaty to 'Reduce and Limit' Warheads and a Declaration of a New Relationship," *New York Times*, May 25, 2002, p. A7.

20. See Larry Berman and Bruce W. Jentleson, "Bush and the Post–Cold War World: New Challenges for American Leadership," in *The Bush Presidency: First Appraisals*, ed. Colin Campbell and Bert Rockman (Chatham, N.J.: Chatham House, 1991), pp. 93–94.

21. "In Clinton's Words: Containing the Predators of the 21st Century," *New York Times*, February 18, 1998, p. A12.

22. See Robert Litwak, *Rogue States and U.S. Foreign Policy: Containment After the Cold War* (Woodrow Wilson Center Press, 2000); "'Rogue' Nations Policy Builds on Clinton's Lead, *Washington Post*, March 12, 2002, p. A4; David E. Sanger, "Bush to Outline Doctrine of Striking Foes First," *New York Times*, September 20, 2002, p. A2.

23. Bruce W. Jentleson, *With Friends Like These* (New York: Norton, 1994).

24. David Sanger, "NATO Formally Welcomes Russia as a Partner," *New York Times*, May 29, 2002, p. A1, A7; Tom Roam, "NATO Embraces Russia as Partner," *Chicago Tribune*, May 28, 2002, www.chicagotribune.com.; Steven Erhanger, "For NATO, Little Is Sure Now But Growth," May 19, 2002, p. A8; Vernon Loeb, "U.S. Looks Eastward in New NATO," *Washington Post*, May 28, 2002, p. A10.

25. James Taub, The Statesman: Why, and How, Bono Matters" *New York Times Magazine*, September 18, 2005, p. 81; See www.u2.com/ and www.one.org/.

26. Jimmy Carter, "Opening to Cuba," *Washington Post*, May 14, 2002, p. A35.

27. Kevin Sullivan, "Carter Begins Historic Trip," *Washington Post*, May 13, 2002, p. A7.

28. Steven R. Weisman, "Bush Gives State Dept. Priority IN Helping Nations to Rebuild," *New York Times*, December 15, 2005, p. A18.

29. Barry Rubin, *Secrets of State: The State Department and the Struggle over U.S. Foreign Policy* (New York: Oxford University Press, 1985); James Fallows, *National Defense* (New York: Random House, 1981); Donald Bletz, *The Role of the Military Professional in U.S. Foreign Policy* (New York: Praeger, 1972); Asa A. Clark IV, Peter W. Chiarelli, Jeffery S. McKitrick, and James W. Reed, *The Defense Reform Debate* (Baltimore: Johns Hopkins University Press, 1984); James Clotfelter, *The Military in American Politics* (New York: Harper & Row, 1973); Adam Yarmolinsky, *The Military Establishment* (New York: Harper & Row, 1971). Quoted in Robert J. Art, "Restructuring the Military-Industrial Complex: Arms Control in Institutional Perspective," *Public Policy* 22 (Fall 1974).

30. See Rhodri Jeffreys-Jones, *The CIA and American Democracy* (New Haven, Conn.: Yale University Press, 1989); Loch K. Johnson, *America's Secret Power: The CIA in a Democratic Society* (New York: Oxford University Press, 1989); John Prados, *President's Secret Wars: CIA and Pentagon Covert Operations Since World War II* (New York: Morrow, 1986). Quoted in Kegley and Wittkopf, eds., *Perspectives on American Foreign Policy*, p. 383.

31. Daniel C. Hallin, *The Uncensored War: The Media and Vietnam* (New York: Oxford University Press, 1986); Philip M. Taylor, *War and the Media* (New York: Manchester University Press, 1992); John Mueller, *Policy and Opinion in the Gulf War* (Chicago: University of Chicago Press, 1994); Miroslov Nincic, "Domestic Costs, the U.S. Public, and the Isolationist Calculus," *International Studies Quarterly* 41 (1997): 593–610.

32. Pew Center Survey http://people-press.org/ "U.S. Image Up Slightly, But Still Negative American Character Gets Mixed Reviews"; See also http://pewglobal.org/reports/display.php?ReportID=247.

33. Ibid.

PHOTO CREDITS

Inc.–Agence France Presse; page 440: Stephen Crowley/*New York Times* Agency; page 446: AP/Wide World Photos; page 446: Susan Steinkamp/Corbis–NY; page 446: Donna Binder/Donna Binder; page 446: Gary Tramontina/Getty Images; page 447: AP/Wide World Photos; page 447: Carola Barria/Corbis/Reuters America LLC; page 447: WIN MCNAMEE/Corbis/Reuters America LLC.

CHAPTER 13 Page 448: Luke Frazza/Getty Images; page 450: AP/Wide World Photos; page 451: AP/Wide World Photos; page 454: AP/Wide World Photos; page 460: AP/Wide World Photos; page 463: Corbis/Bettmann; page 474: Frank Fisher/Getty Images, Inc–Liaison; page 480: Cynthia Howe/*New York Times* Agency; page 481: HO/AFP/*Washington Post*/Getty Images, Inc.–Agence France Presse; page 484: Robert Spencer/Robert Spencer; page 488: Mike Keefe/*The Denver Post* 2005/Cagle Cartoons Inc.; page 490: Carlos Barria/Reuters/Corbis–NY.

CHAPTER 14 Page 494: Mike Simons; page 496: AP/Wide World Photos; page 497: AP/Wide World Photos; page 499: Elliott Erwitt/Magnum Photos, Inc.; page 504: AP/Wide World Photos; page 505: Carl Iwasaki/Getty Images/Time Life Pictures; page 506: AP/Wide World Photos; page 506: UPI/Corbis/Bettmann; page 507: Corbis/Bettmann; page 509: Stanley J. Forman/Stanley Forman; page 515: Sarony/The Schlesinger Library; page 518: Bill Frakes/*Time* Inc. Magazines/*Sports Illustrated*; page 520: Nancy Andrews/*Washington Post* Writers Group; page 524: AP/Wide World Photos; page 524: Michael Springer/Getty

Images, Inc–Liaison; page 525: Richard Lee; page 532: AP/Wide World Photos; page 532: Library of Congress; page 532: Laima Druskis/Pearson Education/PH College; page 532: The Granger Collection; page 533: Teru Iwasaki/AP/Wide World Photos; page 533: Corbis/Bettmann; page 533: Paul Conklin/PhotoEdit Inc.; page 533: Lawrence K. Ho/Tribune Media Services TMS Reprints.

CHAPTER 15 Page 535: Monica Almeida/*New York Times* Agency; page 536: *New York Times* Agency; page 537: AP/Wide World Photos; page 537: AP/Wide World Photos; page 539: AP/Wide World Photos; page 545: U.S. Department of Transportation; page 548: Eric Draper/AP/Wide World Photos; page 551: Yoichi R. Okamoto/Lyndon Baines Johnson Library Collection; page 562: The Cartoon Bank; page 564: Doug Mills/*New York Times* Agency.

CHAPTER 16 Page 568: AP/Wide World Photos; page 570: Stephen Jaffe/AFP/Getty Images, Inc.–Agence France Presse; page 571: AP/Wide World Photos; page 571: AP/Wide World Photos; page 575: National Archives and Records Administration; page 579: Stephen Crowley/*New York Times* Agency; page 581: AP/Wide World Photos; page 582: Mike Hitchings/Reuters/Landov LLC; page 584: Rafael Perez/Corbis/Bettmann; page 588: AP/Wide World Photos; page 598: Ron Edmonds/AP/Wide World Photos; page 598: U.S. Government/HO/AP/Wide World Photos; page 598: Mark Wilson/Getty Images, Inc–Liaison; page 599: AP/Wide World Photos; page 599: PA3 Mike Lutz/SIPA Press/SIPA Press.

STUDENT GUIDE

ABC NEWS™/PRENTICE HALL

VIDEOS IN AMERICAN GOVERNMENT

DVD 1

FEDERALISM

MOMENT OF CRISIS—SYSTEM FAILURE
Primetime
Originally Aired: 9/15/05

Katrina ranks as the country's most expensive natural disaster and one of the deadliest in U.S. history. It has killed more than 700 people, uprooted tens of thousands of families, destroyed countless homes, and forced the evacuation of a major American city. Two and a half weeks after the hurricane roared ashore, just east of New Orleans, the country is trying to make sense of the resulting failures of local, state, and federal government. On this program, ABC News will piece together what we know and where the breakdowns occurred.

Born as a garden-variety tropical depression, Katrina grew into a tropical storm and officially earned hurricane status on August 24, 2005. It initially made landfall north of Miami, causing serious flooding and eleven deaths. But only when it marched across the Florida peninsula and hit the warm waters of the Gulf of Mexico did Katrina rapidly intensify and unleash its full fury. And as it evolved into a monster storm, the National Hurricane Center issued pointed warnings to the target communities along the Gulf Coast. The director made phone calls to key officials, including the mayor of New Orleans, saying Katrina could be "the big one" officials had long feared. Simultaneously, weather service bulletins were issued with unusually apocalyptic language. One predicted a storm of "unprecedented strength," "the area will be uninhabitable for weeks," and went on to predict human suffering "incredible by modern standards."

Given the dire warnings, should the deaths and suffering throughout the Gulf region have been as great? Were the recommendations issued by the 9/11 Commission put into practice?

Ted Koppel hosts a *Primetime* special edition, "Moment of Crisis: System Failure," a moment-by-moment chronology of what went so terribly wrong in the horrific days following Katrina's strike on the Gulf Coast. This was America's first major test of emergency response since 9/11, a test that has received failing grades.

Questions for Review

1. Throughout "Moment of Crisis: System Failure," state and local officials accuse federal officials of responding far too slowly to the deadly hurricane and of failing to grasp the magnitude of the disaster when there might still have been time to lessen

its impact on New Orleans residents. Federal officials argue that they were ready to respond but that state and local officials failed to articulate clearly what they needed from the federal government, and this lack of communication is to blame for the grossly inadequate response to the catastrophe. What are the federal government's responsibilities, particularly agencies such as FEMA and the Department of Homeland Security, in regard to both natural and manmade disasters? What responsibilities do state and local governments have?

2. How much of a role did poverty play in the tragic aftermath of Hurricane Katrina? After viewing the program, do you believe that race had any impact on the way the federal government responded to the crisis?

3. Could this disaster have been averted? Do you think that officials at all levels of government knew for years that a hurricane of this magnitude could strike New Orleans and that the levee system in place to protect the city should have been reinforced, despite the cost, to prevent something like this from happening? Does the federal government have an obligation to maintain and update the infrastructure in places such as New Orleans, or is this the responsibility of state and local governments?

4. Does the Constitution provide any guidance on whether the response to disasters such as Hurricane Katrina should be orchestrated at the federal level or at the state and local levels?

5. In light of the response to Hurricane Katrina, what can be said about American federalism both in theory and in practice? Would a stronger federal government have been better equipped to deal with the crisis or was the inadequate response an isolated case of mismanagement that inaccurately reflects the basic structure of the U.S. government?

REPORT CARD
Nightline
Originally Aired: 10/8/03

Public education is one of the great promises of this country. But is America keeping that promise? This ABC News program offers a timely report card on the nation's public education system. Hard hit by state budget cuts in recent years, the system is also under immense pressure from the No Child Left Behind initiative—legislation that demands much of schools but, say critics, provides little funding to help them meet the mandated goals. Visits to a school in Arlington, Massachusetts, and The University of Texas at Austin amply illustrate the hard realities of faculties being slashed and class sizes swelling . . . and the promise of public education steadily fading.

Questions for Review

1. What is an unfunded mandate? Give examples of unfunded mandates in the No Child Left Behind Act discussed in "Report Card."

2. In "Report Card," author Jonathan Kozol says the "way we finance education in the United States is archaic, chaotic, and utterly undemocratic." What about our education financing led him to say this?

3. States have raised objections to federal education standards. Briefly discuss two objections that states might have.

INTEREST GROUPS

GOD AND COUNTRY
Nightline
Originally Aired: 11/26/02

Over the last couple of years, what has come to be called the Christian Right has become more and more active in supporting the Sharon government in its war with the Palestinians. And their political clout with the Bush administration is considerable. They are opposed to giving the Palestinians any land, taking a much harder line than many Americans. The reason? Prophecy. Many believe that what is playing out now in the Middle East is all part of the process leading toward the Second Coming. The existence of the state of Israel is crucial to that process and many believe that Israel must cover all of the land, including the occupied territories, in order for this process to move forward. So they send money, take trips to Israel, meet regularly with Israeli officials, including Sharon, and at the same time, seem to be breaking what was a strong alliance between American Jews and the Democratic party. That would certainly change the political landscape in this country as well. Israel needs friends now, facing serious criticism from much of the world over its tactics in the current conflict.

And so both sides are sort of glossing over a theological issue. According to the prophecies that many Christians believe, as part of the Second Coming, Jews will have the opportunity to either convert to Christianity, or perish. In other words, they will disappear as a people, or religion, one way or the other. You might think that this would be a point of contention between the two religions but it doesn't appear to be. Ted Koppel interviews Pat Robertson, founder and chairman of the Christian Broadcasting Network. He is a former presidential candidate and arguably one of the most recognized leaders of the evangelical Christian community.

Questions for Review

1. In "God and Country," conservative Christians explain their strong support for Israel, especially their support of Jewish occupation of the West Bank. Briefly discuss the reasons they give for this support.

2. Not all Jews welcome the support of conservative American Christians. What implications of that support concern them?

3. As a general rule, interest groups rarely have a decisive role in formulating foreign policy. How might conservative Christian support for Israel be an exception to that rule?

PUBLIC OPINION, PARTICIPATION, AND VOTING

AIR WARS
Nightline
Originally Aired: 8/25/04

The group known as the "Swift Boat Veterans for Truth" continues to stir the 2004 presidential election. One of President Bush's election lawyers, Benjamin Ginsberg, stepped down from his role in the Bush campaign after admitting ties with the group that has been attacking John Kerry's war record. Mr. Ginsberg resigned after voluntarily disclosing his role as an advisor to both the Bush campaign and the "Swift Boat Veterans for Truth." Is this dual role a violation of federal election laws? Technically it isn't, but the appearance of a "connection" could still have political consequences. Ginsberg's admission of ties with the so-called "527 group" comes after the president has categorically denied that a connection exists between his campaign and the television ads in question. Chris Bury talks to Benjamin Ginsberg about his connection with the "Swift Boat Veterans for Truth," his decision to resign from his position as National Counsel to the Bush campaign, and what this means for the Republicans.

Both sides of the political spectrum have 527 groups—for example, you may have heard of the liberal Moveon.org or conservative Club for Growth. What's important to note is that a significant amount more—$136 million more—has been raised by Democratic-tied groups over the Republican-tied groups.

On this program, ABC's Jake Tapper will help us understand these groups and their impact on the 2004 election. He'll also explain the political connections on both sides to these groups.

Questions for Review

1. The Bipartisan Campaign Reform Act (BCRA) bans most forms of soft money. According to "Air Wars," a loophole in BCRA has allowed outside groups to raise and spend unlimited amounts of money supporting or attacking candidates as long as the candidate's campaign doesn't "coordinate the messages." What does this mean? Use examples from the video.

2. What is a 527 group? What are 527 groups allowed to do? What aren't they allowed to do?

3. In "Air Wars," political scientist Ken Goldstein gives reasons why negative ads are so successful. Briefly discuss at least three of these reasons.

4. What important campaign finance-related issues does BCRA not address? Briefly discuss one or two of these issues and any efforts to address them independently of BCRA.

MASS MEDIA

Q&A
Nightline
Originally Aired: 4/28/05

Every year, at more or less the same time, the president gets to address the nation—and the world—on his vision for the coming term. Where we are and where we're going. What he intends to do. How does he take all the issues—from social security to gay marriage, from Iraq to Iran, from the nuclear threat to terrorism—and figure out what gets priority? On this program, we talk to some people who have worked closely with presidents and who have actually written many of the State of the Union speeches. We'll see what goes into the address and what the president is actually trying to say. One of our panelists is a consultant on the popular TV show "West Wing." Over the years, they've tried to give the audience a behind-the-scenes look at the frenzied jockeying and preparation that goes into this yearly address. We hope our panel will tell us whether the television show comes close.

A veteran of hard-nosed politics, Mary Matalin has most recently served as an assistant to President Bush and as counselor to Vice President Cheney. Michael Waldman was President Bill Clinton's chief speechwriter from 1995 to 1999. He cranked out 2,000 speeches for the president, including many of the State of the Union Addresses. Ken Duberstein was President Ronald Reagan's chief of staff from 1988 to 1989. He's also a consultant to "West Wing." Ted Koppel joins this panel prior to the 2005 State of the Union address to try to pick apart what the president does. They'll view a few scenes from previous "West Wing" episodes to see how close their storylines come to reality. Who does he hear from? What are the issues that get into the speech? How important is every adjective and every adverb? There are fights, literally, over every single word and issue that goes into the speech. It's a statement of intent for the year. And this one is particularly important during a volatile period in this country's history. It will be interesting to see what President Bush sets out to do on the heels of his victory in November.

After we record the first part of the conversation, we'll review to the speech, and then come back to our panelists to see how President Bush did. What were the surprises? How was the tone? What did he focus on? Was it a wide-ranging and all-encompassing speech or a narrowly focused one?

Questions for Review

1. Briefly compare press conferences with the U.S. president and press conferences with the British prime minister.

2. Why do the reporters in "Q&A" believe U.S. presidents are questioned less aggressively than are leaders of other countries?

3. Although the number of presidential addresses and appearances has grown dramatically in the past fifty years, the number of presidential press conferences has dropped just as dramatically. Why might this be so?

AMERICA IN BLACK & WHITE
Nightline
Originally Aired: 9/24/96

Discusses racial issues concerning local television news reporting.

Questions for Review

1. After studying local television stations in Philadelphia, what conclusions did an Annenberg study draw about coverage based on race?

2. What guidelines did an Austin television station put into place to avoid negative racial stereotypes in its reporting?

3. While most experts agree the media have the power to shape public opinion, certain factors do limit media influence. Briefly discuss a few of these factors that might apply to local television coverage of race.

CONGRESS

PRICE OF VICTORY
Nightline
Originally Aired: 3/25/04

It was meant to be a victory that could be savored all the way through the 2004 election. When the president signed the Medicare bill into law last December, it was a landmark event. This bill had managed to achieve what seniors had been demanding for years—prescription drug coverage. That's definitely something to celebrate. Well, a funny thing happened on the way to the bill becoming law: accusations of bribery, lying, intimidation, political shenanigans—it has become quite a Washington drama. A bureaucrat whom you probably wouldn't normally hear about testified on Capitol Hill. Richard Foster is the chief actuary of the Medicare program and he says that his boss threatened to fire him if he publicized his estimates of how much the Medicare bill would actually cost. His boss happens to be a political appointee. The bill that passed had a cost estimate of around $400 billion. Foster's estimate—$534 billion—became public a month after the signing of the bill. Needless to say, people are furious, including Republicans who now say if they knew then what they know now, they would not have voted for the bill.

Then there is that story of the endless vote in the House—a fifteen-minute roll call that stayed open for three hours. A lot of arm-twisting occurred that night, including allegations that retiring Congressman Nick Smith (R.-MI) was told that if he voted for the bill his son would get $100,000 worth of help for his upcoming congressional race. Smith voted against the bill, but there is another investigation of this allegation.

There are some people who roll their eyes at the very thought of the congressional process. But this is a dramatic one. People are really emotional about it, as you will see in this program.

Questions for Review

1. In "Price of Victory," Medicare actuary Richard Foster accuses the administration of what?

2. In the process of passing the 2003 Medicare bill, what was unusual in regard to the timing of the vote?

3. In "Price of Victory," of what does Representative Nick Smith accuse the House leadership?

4. Your text describes the process by which bills become laws. How does the process in the text differ from the process in the video?

DVD 2
CIVIL LIBERTIES

LIFE OR DEATH DECISION, PART 2
Nightline
Originally Aired: 3/22/05

The Terri Schiavo case is the ultimate "on the one hand, on the other hand" debate. Each aspect of this debate—legal, medical, political, even the moral and ethical—has a deep rift of opinions. And all sides were watching the Eleventh Circuit Court of Appeals in Atlanta for the next step in this case.

A federal judge denied a request for an emergency order to restore Terri Schiavo's feeding tube. The judge took the position that the lawyers representing her parents were unlikely to succeed in a resulting federal trial. Her parents immediately appealed the case to the Eleventh Circuit. If the Schindlers, Schiavo's parents, lose there, it will almost certainly be taken quickly to the U.S. Supreme Court, which has already declined to hear the case three times.

But in the meantime, Terri Schiavo is in her fourth day without nutrition. Doctors say she could live another week or more without food or water.

And so the debate rages on, with all sides staking out firm positions. In the medical debate, there are those that point to the evidence that her brain function is irreversibly damaged. But on the other hand, there is the loving care that her parents have shown for their profoundly disabled daughter.

The intervention of Congress turned this into a major political battle. On the one hand, there are right-to-life advocates who see this as another test of the sanctity of life. On the other hand, there are those who are offended at Congress for inserting itself into a family tragedy.

And finally, there are the ethical issues that are at the heart of so many of these factors—the medical, the legal, and the political. If you believe it is wrong, simply wrong, to remove a feeding tube in order to expedite death, how can you ever accept any of the other arguments? And on the other side, if you believe Michael Schiavo is holding strong for his wife's stated intentions, how can you ever accept any of the other arguments?

On this program, George Stephanopoulos discusses all of these matters—medical, legal, political, and ethical—with a panel of guests.

Questions for Review

1. Given that the Terry Schiavo case had spent years in state court, on what grounds was the case sent to federal court?

2. The experts in "Life or Death Decision, Part 2" differentiate between the right to die and the right to refuse unwanted medical intervention. Describe the differences between these two concepts.

3. Those who supported keeping Terri Schiavo alive often referred to her right to due process under the Fourteenth Amendment. To what do you think they were referring? Would procedural due process apply to this case? Would substantive due process apply to this case?

CRIME & PUNISHMENT
Nightline
Originally Aired: 12/1/04

Voting to have a man or woman put to death has to be one of the hardest decisions facing any American juror. How do we ever know for sure if the person convicted of the crime actually committed it? One death row prisoner in Texas, Ernest Willis, served seventeen years for a crime he didn't commit and his case was built entirely on circumstantial evidence. At one point, he was days away from being executed, but now he is a free man.

Ernest Willis, who on four different dates was scheduled for execution, learned in October 2004 that he would be exonerated and released from prison. After years of appeals, litigation, and the drive of a young lawyer in a large law firm, Willis was completely exonerated of the murder charges that put him on death row. ABC correspondent Mike von Fremd was at the prison when he was released after seventeen years. They sat down for a conversation about how he ended up on death row, his feelings on facing execution, his surprising release, and what it was like to finally meet the woman he had married while he was in prison.

Questions for Review

1. Appeals courts that overturn a death sentence often do so because of the defendant's attorney incompetence. As an example of this, describe the problems with Ernest Willis' attorney in "Crime & Punishment."

2. In "Crime & Punishment," Ori White, the Pecos County, Texas, district attorney, says prosecutors often believe that "the ends justify the means." What do you think he meant by this?

3. More than two-thirds of all death sentences are overturned on appeal. On what grounds are they overturned?

ILLEGAL IMMIGRANT WORKERS

Nightline
Originally Aired: 12/14/04

When Bernard Kerik, President Bush's first choice to run the Department of Homeland Security, withdrew his nomination because of a nanny who was an undocumented worker that he hired and failed to pay taxes on, it was a story that probably sounded familiar. Cabinet nominees have been tripped up on this issue before in both the Clinton and Bush administrations. So the question is, why does this keep happening?

One of the reasons it keeps happening is that it is pretty easy to get by hiring undocumented workers. It seems that the only way to get tripped up is if you undergo a background check for an important government post. You would be hard pressed to find any aspect of the nation's economy where undocumented workers are not making a contribution. It could be in the service industry or the construction business. You will eat something today that has been brought to you as a result of the labor of illegal immigrants working here. A conservative estimate is that at least 50 percent of agricultural laborers are undocumented workers. So is this a result of American employers being cheap or is it a result of the efficiency of market forces? Many employers say it is not easy to find Americans willing to do a lot of the low-paying, menial, and tedious tasks that immigrants are willing to do. Labor advocates say that illegal immigrants depress the wage market so Americans are shut out of these jobs. Everyone can find statistics to back their argument.

So what is the solution? When the president announced a proposal earlier this year to grant legal status to millions of undocumented workers in the United Stated, it wasn't greeted with unanimous enthusiasm. "Out of common sense and fairness, our laws should allow willing workers to enter our country and fill jobs that Americans are not filling" the president said. He wasn't calling for amnesty but a temporary guest worker program. But will that satisfy both sides? Michel Martin examines the arguments advanced on something that has always been a hot-button issue. We also speak with Senator John McCain of Arizona. His state has addressed the illegal immigration issue by voting for a sweeping proposition that bans all government services to illegal immigrants. He says that this is an issue that the nation has to wake up to and start dealing with as a high priority.

Questions for Review

1. Why aren't immigration laws more strictly enforced?

2. Explain the "geographic" component to immigration law enforcement.

3. The inability to bar illegal aliens from entering the country is not a question of power. Rather, the problems are political and practical. Briefly explain what this means.

CHURCH & STATE, AND PLEDGE OF ALLEGIANCE
Nightline
Originally Aired: 7/8/02

Where does religion fit into American politics? In light of the furor over the decision by a federal appeals court on the 'Pledge of Allegiance,' what about 'In God We Trust'? Does this country treat religion differently than other countries? *Nightline* looks at the connection between church and state.

Questions for Review

1. Why are voters so interested in a candidate's religion, according to "Church & State, and Pledge of Allegiance"?
2. Under what circumstances was the phrase "under God" made part of the Pledge of Allegiance?
3. Justice Sandra Day O'Connor's "endorsement test" has been the basis of several Supreme Court decisions. What is it, and how might it apply to the Pledge of Allegiance?

VOICES OF DISSENT
Nightline
Originally Aired: 11/2/01

Disagreement is an essential component of one of America's most cherished freedoms: the right to free speech. On this program, *Nightline* makes room for voices representing opinions that are likely to be less popular or less mainstream than what is normally heard in the media.

Questions for Review

1. In "Voices of Dissent," author Arundhati Roy says, "Operation Enduring Freedom is ostensibly being fought to uphold the American way of life. It'll probably end up undermining it entirely." What does she mean by this?
2. In "Voices of Dissent," cartoonist Aaron McGroder says that "in the six days after the bombing, America became the most intensely stupid place on the planet." Why does McGroder believe this to be true?
3. Although Americans overwhelmingly support the principle of free speech, many do not support the freedom to say things with which they disagree. Why might it be even more important to protect free speech in times of crisis than in normal times?

MUSLIMS IN AMERICA
Nightline
Originally Aired: 5/4/95

Nightline looks at one of the fastest-growing groups in America: Muslims. Members of the oldest Muslim community in Cedar Rapids, Iowa, speak to Ted Koppel about their beliefs and customs.

Questions for Review

1. Differentiate between Arabs and Muslims.
2. The video "Muslims in America" gives several possible explanations why, even before the September 11, 2001, attacks, Americans were quick to blame Muslims for every terrorist act. Briefly discuss two explanations.
3. If the equal protection clause applies only to government actions, how may we limit the discriminatory actions of private individuals?

SOCIAL POLICY

ON THE EDGE
Nightline
Originally Aired: 4/15/04

When we say "poor" or "poverty-stricken Americans," what image comes to mind? The homeless man sleeping on the grate? The unemployed person standing in line at the unemployment or welfare office? What about someone who has a full-time job making $9 an hour? That sounds like a decent wage, right? Well, that actually comes out to just above $18,000 a year, and for a family with one adult and three children, that means poverty. We've decided to launch a new, occasional series that looks at the working poor: the millions of Americans who live on the edge of poverty.

The genesis of tonight's show was a new book by former *New York Times* reporter and Pulitzer Prize-winner, David Shipler. "The Working Poor" takes a comprehensive look at the lives of people set to plunge into the abyss of financial ruin if just one payment isn't met, if their car breaks down, or if they call in sick at work. Such seemingly minor events can have catastrophic effects on this segment of the population, and Mr. Shipler has documented many of their lives, weaving economic analysis into the story of what these people face trying to survive from day to day. Ted Koppel sat down with Mr. Shipler for an extensive interview on his findings.

Questions for Review

1. How does author David Shipler define "working poor"?

2. How does the video's title, "On the Edge," apply to the working poor?

3. The underlying problem of the working poor seems to be their vulnerability in every area of life. Explain how the working poor are vulnerable in ways not experienced by other economic groups.

4. Author David Shipler disagrees with the concept of a "culture of poverty." Instead, he speaks of an "ecological system of interactions." What does he mean?

5. What is the difference between an entitlement and a means-tested entitlement?

INDEX

ABC News/Prentice Hall Video Library

American Government

STUDENT LIBRARY

ABC NEWS

DVD 2 SET

See how the issues that you discuss in your American Government class affect your everyday life!

Few will dispute the power of video to enhance a classroom presentation. Prentice Hall and ABC News™ have assembled this unparalleled 2-DVD set, combining fourteen clips into over three hours of quality ABC News™ programming. Through award-winning ABC News™ programs, such as *Nightline*, ABC News™ offers a resource for feature- and documentary-style videos related to the topics typically covered in your American Government course.

Included in this textbook is a listing that provides a brief summary of each video as well as discussion questions to help you focus on how the topics covered in the videos tie in with the topics discussed in your American Government course.

ABC NEWS/Prentice Hall Video Library: American Government 2-DVD Set—Contents